# NEW JERSEY    PENNSYLVANIA

# ®TourBook

## An annual catalog of selected travel information

American Automobile Association
1000 AAA Drive
Heathrow, FL 32746-5063

Valid through April 1996

Printed in the USA by Quebecor Printing Buffalo, Inc., Buffalo, NY

# Head out on your own Great Days Inn Road Trip.

Staying at Days Inn can mean big savings on the road. Especially if you're a AAA member. You'll receive our low rates at over 1500 Days Inn locations worldwide. Not to mention plenty of Flintstones fun the whole family will enjoy. For more information or to make reservations, contact your travel agent or call **1-800-AAA-DAYS.**

**DAYS INN**®

**The Best Value Under The Sun.**℠

# CONTENTS

## INTRODUCTION: USING YOUR TOURBOOK

## TIPS FOR THE TOURBOOK TRAVELER

## ATTRACTIONS

# LODGINGS & RESTAURANTS

# MAPS

# FOR YOUR INFORMATION

# INDEXES

# 🅐 SUPERNUMBER 1-800-AAA-HELP

Call for 24-hour road service when away from home and unable to find AAA or CAA in the phone book. 1-800-955-4TDD for hearing impaired. ..................................................... 17

# COMMENTS

Write: AAA Member Comments
Box 61, 1000 AAA Dr.
Heathrow, FL 32746-5063

# ADVERTISING (407) 444-8280

published by **American Automobile Association**®    1000 AAA Drive, Heathrow, FL 32746-5063

Cover: *Elfreth's Alley, Philadelphia, Pa.* / Gala/SuperStock

    4617

# USING YOUR TOURBOOK

This TourBook has one purpose: to make your trip as enjoyable as possible by providing reliable, detailed information about attractions, lodgings and restaurants in the area through which you are traveling.

Attractions and AAA rated lodgings and restaurants are listed in this book under the name of the city in which they physically are located. If the establishment is located in an unincorporated area, it is listed under the nearest recognized city. This policy—called geographical listing—ensures AAA books are consistent, specific and accurate. Use AAA maps in conjunction with this book when planning your trip.

No attraction, lodging or restaurant pays for a listing. Each is listed on the basis of merit alone after a AAA field inspector or a designated AAA representative has carefully evaluated it. AAA's unique network of local club travel specialists checks information dealing with attractions and touring areas annually. Road reporters and cartographic researchers keep maps current.

There are three components that comprise the book's information:

- Attractions
- Maps
- Lodgings & Restaurants

Knowing *about* these components—discussed here in the order in which you will discover them in the book—is your key to unlocking this TourBook, which AAA publishes to provide its members with the most accurate travel information available.

# ABOUT ATTRACTIONS

The Attractions section of your TourBook serves as a guide to selected places rather than as a commercial, geographic or promotional encyclopedia. Communities or areas included offer something for you to do or see that sets them apart from others in the area or nation. We call these "points of interest."

Each state begins by introducing you to historical, geographic, economic and other factors that contribute to the state's character. The Recreation Areas chart lists facilities available in national and state parks and other areas; unusual or special features of a park are also mentioned.

## SCHEDULES AND PRICES

All information was reviewed before publication for accuracy at press time. However, changes often occur between annual editions. We regret any inconvenience resulting from such instances, but they are beyond our control. Please use the phone numbers in the attraction write-ups if you wish to confirm prices.

## READING THE LISTINGS

Any attraction with a separate heading has been approved by a AAA field inspector or designated AAA representative. An attraction's quality is reflected in the length and scope of its general description. We have placed a star (★) before attractions of exceptional interest and quality. An index to starred attractions appears with the orientation map. *(See ABOUT MAPS, page 6.)*

Attractions are listed alphabetically under the name of the nearest community; in most cases the distances given are computed from the center of town, unless otherwise specified, using the following highway designations: I (interstate highway), US (federal highway), SR (state route), CR (county road), FM (farm to market road), FR (forest road) and MM (mile marker).

Descriptive information about the attraction follows the location description. Next come the days, hours and seasons the attraction is *open*. These may be preceded by a suggested minimum visiting time. Following are admission prices quoted *without* sales tax; children under the lowest age specified are admitted free when accompanied by an adult. Days, months and age groups written with a hyphen are *inclusive*.

Credit cards accepted for admissions or fares may be indicated at the end of the listing as follows: AE, American Express; CB, Carte Blanche; DI, Diners Club; DS, Discover; ER, EnRoute; JCB; MC, MasterCard; VI, VISA. Minimum amounts that may be charged appear in parentheses when applicable.

## ADMISSION DISCOUNTS

Your AAA membership card is the key to reduced prices at many attractions because they value your patronage and respect the AAA name. Whether or not a listing shows a discount, present your valid AAA or CAA card when purchasing tickets; some attractions not formally enrolled in the program may still give members a discount. A full list of participating attractions appears in the Indexes section of this book. Discounts are offered for the validity period noted on the title page of this book.

Participating attractions individually determine the terms of the discount they offer. The discount may not apply if any other price reduction is offered or if tickets are purchased through an outlet other than the attraction's ticket office.

# ABOUT MAPS

Maps created specifically for this book have precise purposes and should be used in *conjunction* with the more complete sheet maps and Triptik maps provided by your AAA travel counselor. To ensure your complete satisfaction, use book maps as *supplementary* guides only. Not every book will contain every map type listed below.

**State and province orientation maps** appear before the Points of Interest listings in the Attractions section. **Regional orientation maps** appear with the description of the points of interest. Their purpose is to illustrate the relative positions of towns, recreation facilities and starred points of interest listed in the TourBooks. Only major road networks are portrayed on these maps.

Coordinates (for example: A-3) following the place or city names in the Points of Interest listings refer to this map; stars next to town names on the maps indicate the presence of highly recommended attractions. An index to starred attractions appears with or adjacent to each orientation map.

**Accommodations orientation maps** are used for large geographical areas that are attractions in themselves (for example: the Finger Lakes region in New York and Michigan's Upper Peninsula). These maps are located in the Lodgings & Restaurants section of your book. Because the maps are on such a small scale, lodgings and restaurants are not shown, but the towns that have these types of facilities are printed in magenta type so you can plan your trip accordingly.

**Spotting maps** assist you in locating the facilities listed in the Lodgings & Restaurants section of your book. These maps locate, or "spot," lodgings with a black-background numeral ( **20**, for example); restaurants are spotted with a white-background numeral ( **20**, for example). Indexes found near the map match the number symbol to the property.

**Downtown spotting maps** are provided when spotted facilities are more concentrated. Starred points of interest also appear on these maps.

**City/Area spotting maps** show the main roads required to find a dining or lodging facility, as well as the major landmarks that are near the lodgings and restaurants. Airports are also shown on city/area spotting maps. The names of cities that have AAA-rated properties are shown in magenta type.

**City maps** show metropolitan areas where numerous attractions are concentrated. While reading an attraction description, refer to this map to see where it is located in relation to major roads, parks, airports, etc.

**Walking or Self-Guiding tour maps** provide an exceptional level of detail, showing specific routes corresponding to text in the TourBooks. Well-known buildings are often outlined for easier identification. Routes are well-marked with beginning and ending points as well as directional arrows.

**National park maps** familiarize drivers with the area in and around the park. The main features depicted are mountains, streams, hiking trails, canyons, ice fields, etc. Some of the campground sites and lodges spotted on the maps do not meet AAA criteria, but have been listed as a service to members who wish to stay at these facilities.

**Driving distance maps** located in the For Your Information section of the book are intended to be used only for trip-distance and driving-time planning. Refer to more detailed AAA maps available from your club for actual route numbers.

# ABOUT LODGINGS & RESTAURANTS

Lodging and restaurant listings appear after the attraction listings and are introduced by a title page. Both types of properties are listed alphabetically under the nearest town or city, with lodgings listed first. To help you plan your trips, these towns and cities are printed in red on AAA regional, state, provincial and Triptik maps. The TourBook includes special accommodation "spotting" maps to help you find lodgings and restaurants. *(See ABOUT MAPS.)*

AAA inspectors carefully evaluate every lodging establishment and restaurant listed in this publication at least once every year. Their rigorous inspection helps ensure that all properties meet AAA's exacting standards for quality.

AAA monitors member satisfaction through your comments and surveys. AAA rating criteria reflect your needs and expectations and the design and service standards determined by the lodging industry.

Additionally, we maintain an open dialogue with individual establishment operators, the American Hotel and Motel Association and most major lodging chains.

## USING LODGING LISTINGS

To use this book most effectively, read the sample lodging listing along with the explanation of the terms appearing on page 9. The location is given from the center of town unless noted otherwise. Baths are not mentioned if all rooms have private baths. All showers are tub showers unless otherwise noted.

If parking is provided on the premises at no charge, it is not mentioned in the listing. Other parking conditions such as no parking available, off-site parking, street parking only or off-site valet parking, and any charges, are specifically noted in the listing. **Check-in** times are shown only if they are after 3 p.m.; **check-out** times are shown only if they are before 10 a.m. Service charges are not shown unless they are $1 or more, or at least 5 percent of the room rate.

## GUEST SAFETY

AAA/CAA requires that all lodgings listed in the 1995 TourBooks for the United States and Canada must comply with AAA's revised guest room security requirements. In response to AAA/CAA members' concern about their safety at accommodations, AAA/CAA rated properties must have deadbolt locks on all guest room entry doors and connecting room doors. If the area outside the guest room door is not visible from inside the room through a window or door panel, viewports must be installed on all guest room entry doors. Bed and breakfast properties and country inns are not required to have viewports. Ground floor and easily accessible sliding doors must be equipped with secondary locks.

Verification that the required hardware was in place at each AAA/CAA rated property listed in the 1995 TourBooks was obtained by one of the following methods. Either the field inspector, on a random selection of inspected rooms, observed the correct hardware; or, AAA received a signed, notarized affidavit from the property, attesting that the appropriate locks were installed by a specified deadline. AAA field inspectors view a percentage of rooms at each property. Because it is not feasible for the inspectors to evaluate every room in every lodging establishment, AAA cannot guarantee that there are working locks on all doors and windows in all guest rooms.

Guest security is a significant concern for AAA/CAA members and all travelers. Research shows that 99% of members expect deadbolts on guest room doors. While safety can never be guaranteed, our revised security guidelines address this major issue.

## THE LODGING DIAMONDS

Before a property may be listed in this book, it must satisfy a set of minimum standards that reflect the basic lodging needs AAA members have identified. If a property meets those requirements, it is assigned a diamond rating reflecting the overall quality of the establishment. The ratings range from one to five diamonds and reflect the physical and service standards typically found at each diamond level.

Ratings are assigned according to the property's classification, which appears beneath the diamond rating in the lodging listing. The classification represents the physical design and level of services provided by the property. For ex-

ample, a motel offers limited services and recreational facilities. A resort hotel offers extensive guest services and recreational facilities. Comparing a motel to a resort hotel would be like comparing an apple to an orange. By assigning ratings according to classification AAA compares apples to apples. A description of classifications is on pages 10 & 11.

Although one diamond is AAA's minimum rating, a one diamond property still is better than one-third of the lodgings in operation, since the majority of unlisted properties do not meet AAA's minimum standards.

Lodgings AAA rated ◆ provide good but modest accommodations. Establishments are functional, emphasizing clean and comfortable rooms. They must meet the basic needs of privacy and cleanliness. Rates are generally economical.

The ◆◆ lodging maintains the attributes offered at the one diamond level, while showing noticeable enhancements in decor and/or quality of furnishings. They may be recently constructed or older properties, both targeting the needs of a budget-oriented traveler.

Establishments rated ◆◆◆ offer a degree of sophistication. Additional amenities, services and facilities may be offered. There is a marked upgrade in services and comfort.

Excellent properties displaying a high level of service and hospitality are AAA rated ◆◆◆◆. Properties offer a wide variety of amenities and upscale facilities, both inside the room, on the grounds and in the public areas.

Lodgings awarded ◆◆◆◆◆ are renowned. They exhibit an exceptionally high degree of service; striking, luxurious facilities; and many extra amenities. Guest services are executed and presented in a flawless manner. The guest will be pampered by a very professional, attentive staff. The property's facilities and operation help set the standards in hospitality and service.

A few properties are listed without a rating. They were either under construction or undergoing such a substantial renovation at press time that it was impossible to assign an accurate rating.

## RATE OPTIONS AND DISCOUNTS

Annually, lodging operators are asked to update rates, discounts and rate options for Tour-Book publication. Properties are not required to offer a discount to be listed in the book. But they commit to one of three rate options to offer AAA members. That option appears in the listing.

---

### Lodging Evaluation Criteria

Regardless of the diamond rating, properties listed by AAA are required to provide:

- Clean and well-maintained facilities throughout
- Hospitable staff
- A well-kept appearance

Regardless of the rating, each guest room is required to have:

- Comfortable beds and good quality bedding
- Locks on all doors and windows
- Comfortable furnishings and pleasant decor
- Smoke detectors
- Adequate towels and supplies
- At least one chair
- Adequate illumination at each task area

**(1) Special Value Rates**—The establishment not only guarantees rates will not exceed the maximum rates printed in the TourBook, they also offer a minimum discount of 10 percent off printed rates. This is the only rate option that contains a discount. Since these rates are discounted only for AAA members, you *must* identify yourself as a AAA member and request the **AAA Special Value Rate** when making reservations. Show your membership card at registration and verify the AAA Special Value Rate. *Note:* Members may take either the **Special Value Rate** or the **Senior Discount**, but not both.

**(2) Guaranteed Rates**—The establishment guarantees AAA members will not be charged more than the maximum rates printed in the Tour-Book. To receive these rates you *must* identify yourself as a AAA member and request the AAA guaranteed rate when making reservations. Show your AAA card at registration and verify the rate.

**(3) Rates Subject To Change**—The printed rates are the establishment's estimated charges for the periods noted. The actual rates charged may be reasonably higher or lower than those printed in the TourBook.

**Exceptions:** Lodgings may temporarily increase their room rates or modify their policies during a special event or for those traveling as part of a group or convention. Examples of such events range from Mardi Gras and the Kentucky Derby to college football homecoming games, holidays and state fairs. At these times the **Special Value** and **Guaranteed** rate options do not apply.

**Senior Discount**: Some establishments offer the senior discount with either the **Rates Guaranteed** option or the **Rates Subject to Change** option. Where the words "Senior Discount" are included in a listing, a minimum discount of 10 percent off the prevailing or guaranteed rate is available to AAA members who are 60 years of age or older. This discount is in effect whenever the establishment is open. You *must* identify yourself as a AAA member *and* request the Senior Discount when making reservations. Show your AAA card at registration and verify the rate and discount. Members may take this discount or the AAA Special Value Rate, but not both. Senior discounts might not apply during special events.

**Rate lines:** Rates are for typical rooms, not special units. Rates do not include taxes. Multiple rate lines are used to indicate a seasonal rate difference.

## USING RESTAURANT LISTINGS

We strive to approve consistently good dining establishments. In metropolitan areas, where many are above average, we select some of those known for the superiority of their food, service and atmosphere and also those offering a selection of quality food at moderate prices (including some cafeterias and family restaurants). In small communities the restaurants considered to be the best in the area may be listed.

Restaurants are classified by major cuisine type (Italian, French, etc.). Some listings indicate the availability of a senior discount for members 60 years or older; some also indicate the availability of "earlybird specials" if they are offered at least 5 days a week. Phone ahead for details on discounts and specially priced meals.

The range of prices is approximate and reflects dinner (salad or appetizer, a main course, and a non-alcoholic beverage) for one person. Taxes and tips are not included.

Cafeterias, buffets and other self-service operations are rated only as compared to similar establishments. Listings in this category are suited to family dining.

## THE RESTAURANT DIAMONDS

Restaurants rated ◆ provide good but unpretentious dishes. Table settings are usually simple and may include paper placemats and napkins. If alcoholic beverages are offered, wine and beer selections may be limited. The restaurants are usually informal, with an atmosphere conducive to family dining.

The AAA rated ◆ ◆ restaurant will usually have more extensive menus that represent more complex food preparation. A wider variety of alcoholic beverages will usually be available. The atmosphere is appealing and suitable for family or adult dining. Although service may be casual, host or hostess seating can be expected. Table settings may include tablecloths and cloth napkins.

Most ◆ ◆ ◆ restaurants have extensive or specialized menus and a more complex cuisine preparation that requires a professional chef. Cloth table linens, above-average quality table settings, a skilled service staff and an inviting decor should all be provided. Generally, the wine list will include representatives of the best domestic and foreign wine-producing regions. Restaurants in this category can offer a formal dining experience or a special family occasion.

AAA rated ◆ ◆ ◆ ◆ restaurants have appealing ambience, often enhanced by fresh flowers and fine furnishings. The overall sophistication and formal atmosphere create a dining experience more for adults than for families. A wine steward presents an extensive list of the best wines. A smartly attired, highly skilled staff will be capable of describing how any dish is prepared. Elegant silverware, china and correct glassware are typical. The menu will include creative dishes prepared from fresh ingredients by a chef who frequently has international training. Eye-appealing desserts will be offered at tableside.

The few restaurants that are awarded ◆ ◆ ◆ ◆ ◆ are world-class operations. They have the attributes of a four diamond restaurant with even more luxury and sophistication and feature exceptional, innovative cuisine. A proportionally large staff, expert in preparing tableside delicacies, will provide flawless service, with impeccable linens, silver and crystal glassware.

**MARINA'S COVE**  AAA Special Value Rates  Phone: 808/931-231 ⑩
Ⓐ  All Year [AP]  1P: $265- 430  2P/1B: $265- 430  2P/2B: $265- 430  XP: $45  F-17
Hotel  **Location:** Oceanfront; 5 blks s of Kalakaua Ave via Kanekapolei St. 2199 Kapahulu Rd 96815
FAX 808/931-8004. **Terms:** Reserv deposit, 3 day notice; 4 night min stay, 12/28-1/1; no pets. **Facility:** 456 rooms. Distinctive hotel with refined atmosphere. Exceptional service. Spacious guest rooms & suites with simplistic elegance. Diamond Head & ocean backdrop from large lanai. 44 suites, $580-$3500; 6-22 stories; interior corridors; conference facilities; beach, pool; exercise room. **Dining & Entertainment:** 2 dining rooms; 7 am-10 pm; $20-$38; cocktails/lounge; 24-hour room service; afternoon tea; also, La Mer, see separate listing; entertainment. **Services:** secretarial services; valet laundry. childcare; massage, airport transportation; valet parking. **Recreation:** children's program 6/1-8/31; swimming. **All Rooms:** honor bars, refrigerators, safes, cable TV. **Some Rooms:** CP's. **Cards:** AE, CB, DI, JCB, MC, VI. A Preferred Hotel.  Roll in showers. 🖳 🖩 Ⓓ Ⓢ ⊗

① This section of the listing shows: whether the lodging is a AAA Official Appointment (see What The Ⓐ Means pg. 13), what the lodging's diamond rating is (see pg. 7), and under what classification the lodging was rated (see pgs. 10-11).

② This is the Rate Option the lodging has chosen to offer AAA members (see Rate Options and Discounts pg. 7).

③ This section of the listing is comprised of the rate lines, which show from left to right: dates the rates in that line are effective, any meal plan included in the rate (CP=Continental Plan of pastry, juice and another beverage; BP=Breakfast Plan of full breakfast; AP=American Plan of three meals daily; MAP=Modified American Plan of two meals daily), number of Persons/Beds allowed/provided for the rates shown, the rates charged, the extra person (XP) charge and, if applicable, the family plan indicator (F17=children 17 and under stay free; D17=discount for children 17 and under; F=children stay free; D=discounts for children). The establishment may limit the number of children to whom the family plan applies.

④ If present, this number locates the lodging on accommodations spotting maps provided for some communities (see About Maps pg. 6).

⑤ The Facility section lists all the key elements of the lodging's common areas, the physical attributes of the property all guests may experience—including pools and other recreation facilities. The list of facility elements for which there are charges is preceded by "Fee:".

⑥ The Dining section describes food and beverage services, including the hours of operation and price range for dinner.

⑦ The Services section iterates additional non-recreation types of assistance, equipment or benefits available from the lodging. The list of services for which there are charges is preceded by "Fee:".

⑧ The Recreation section inventories leisure opportunities and activities. The list of recreation options for which there are charges is preceded by "Fee:". Equipment available at a cost is preceded by "Rental:".

⑨ The All Rooms section shows the amenities offered within the guest rooms. Amenities with limited availability are listed after the words "Some Rooms:". Amenities available for a charge follow the word "Fee:".

⑩ Up to five symbols may appear in the lodging listing. As shown here they mean, from left to right: 🖳 wheelchair and 🖩 hearing impaired accessibility (see Access for the Disabled pg. 13), Ⓓ all rooms have smoke detectors, Ⓢ all rooms have fire protection sprinklers, and ⊗ non-smoking rooms are available. The words "Roll in showers" will appear before the symbols if such a facility is available for the disabled guest.

# LODGING CLASSIFICATIONS

Lodgings are classified according to the physical design and services offered. The classification appears beneath the diamond rating in each lodging listing.

**BED AND BREAKFAST** (limited service)—Usually a smaller establishment emphasizing personal attention. Guest rooms are individually decorated with an **at home** feeling and may lack some modern amenities such as TVs, phones, etc. Usually owner-operated with a common room or parlor where guests and owners can interact during evening and breakfast hours. May have shared bathrooms. A Continental or full hot breakfast is served and is included in the room rate. Parking may be limited or on the street.

**COMPLEX** (service varies depending on type of lodgings)—A combination of two or more kinds of lodging classifications.

**COTTAGE** (limited service)—Individual bungalow, cabin or villa, usually containing one rental unit equipped for housekeeping. May have a separate living room and bedroom(s). Parking is usually available at each unit. Although basic cleaning supplies must be provided, cottages are not required to offer daily housekeeping service.

**COUNTRY INN** (moderate service)—Although similar in definition to a bed and breakfast, country inns are usually larger in size. Specialized decor may include antiques. Offers a dining room reflecting the ambiance of the inn. At a minimum, breakfast and dinner are served. Parking may be limited. Note: The Country Inns Index also lists establishments that are primarily restaurants and may not have lodging facilities.

**HOTEL** (full service)—A multistory building usually including a coffee shop, dining room, lounge, a pool and exercise equipment, room service, convenience shops, valet, laundry and full banquet and meeting facilities. Parking may be limited.

**LODGE** (moderate service)—Typically two or more stories with all facilities in one building. Located in vacation, ski, fishing areas, etc. Usually has food and beverage service.

**MOTEL** (limited service)—Usually one or two stories. Food service, if any, consists of a limited facility or snack bar. Often has a pool or playground. Ample parking, usually at the guest room door.

**MOTOR INN** (moderate service)—Usually two or three stories, but may be a high-rise. Generally has recreational facilities and food service. May have limited banquet and meeting facilities. Ample parking.

**RANCH** (moderate service)—may be any classification featuring outdoor, Western-style recreation. Accommodations and facilities may vary in size.

# SUBCLASSIFICATIONS

The following are subclassifications that may appear along with the classifications on page 10 to provide more description about the lodging:

**APARTMENT**—Usually four or more stories with at least half the units equipped for housekeeping. Units typically provide a full kitchen, living room and one or more bedrooms, but may be studio-type rooms with kitchen equipment in an alcove. May require minimum stay and/or offer discounts for longer stays. Although basic housekeeping supplies must be available, apartments are not required to offer daily housekeeping service. This classification may also modify any of the other lodging types.

**CONDOMINIUM**—A destination property located in a resort area; may apply to any classification. Guest units consist of a bedroom, living room and kitchen. Kitchens are separate from bedrooms and are equipped with a stove, oven or microwave, refrigerator, cooking utensils and table settings for the maximum number of people occupying the unit. Although basic housekeeping supplies must be available, condominiums are not required to offer daily housekeeping service.

**HISTORIC**—May apply to any type of lodging. Accommodations in restored structures more than 50 years old, reflecting the ambience of yesteryear and the surrounding area. Antique furnishings complement the overall decor of the property. Rooms may lack some modern amenities and have shared baths. Usually owner-operated and food service is often available. Note: The Historical Lodgings and Restaurants Index also lists establishments that are primarily restaurants and may not have lodging facilities.

**RESORT**—May apply to any other type of lodging. Has a vacation atmosphere offering extensive recreational facilities for such specific interests as golf, tennis, fishing, etc. Rates may include meals under American or Modified American plans.

**SUITE**—One or more bedrooms and a living room, which may or may not be closed off from the bedrooms.

## REMEMBER:

AAA inspectors assign diamond ratings by evaluating lodging establishments based on their classification. Thus, "Hotels" are rated in comparison with other "Hotels," and so on with all classifications.

# TIPS FOR THE TOURBOOK TRAVELER

## OUR CUSTOMERS ALWAYS WRITE

We encourage your communication to tell us what we need to improve and what we have done well. We respond through our products and services, and we reply to thousands of letters from members every year.

We encourage you to report both pleasant and unpleasant experiences by visiting your local AAA club for assistance in completing a form prepared for this purpose. Or, if you prefer, write directly to AAA Member Comments, 1000 AAA Dr., Box 61, Heathrow, FL 32746-5063.

## PROTECT YOURSELF AND YOUR PROPERTY

Travelers are faced with the dual task of protecting their homes while away and protecting themselves while in a strange environment. There is no way to guarantee absolute insulation from crime. But the experts—law enforcement officials—advise travelers to take a pro-active approach to securing their property and ensuring their safety.

### BEFORE YOU LEAVE:

- Many law enforcement departments offer free home security checks. Take advantage of them.
- Know your neighbors and ask them to take in your mail and newspapers. Do NOT stop delivery. Also, make sure neighbors know who should and who should not have access to your home.
- Fix any doors and windows that do not operate properly, making sure the locks are sturdy.
- Make arrangements to have your lawn mowed.
- Put lights and a television or radio on timers, or ask a neighbor to turn them on and off.
- Ask police to patrol past your home on a regular basis. Many departments offer free "home-watch" programs, but prior arrangements must be made.
- Use steel bars in the tracks of all sliding-glass doors and windows.
- Do not leave ladders or other objects outside your home that a burglar could use to gain access to a second floor.

Once you've secured your home and property, consider actions that will help prevent being victimized while on the road. Above all, do not leave your common sense at home. You are more vulnerable when in unfamiliar surroundings; do not be complacent. Your safety begins with you.

### ON THE ROAD:

- Be aware of your surroundings. Watch who is watching you.
- If your car is bumped from behind or if someone says there is something wrong with your car don't stop. Go to a service station or a well lit area and call for help.
- Don't pull over for flashing headlights; police have red or blue lights.
- Make sure the hotel desk clerk does not announce your room number; if so, quietly request a new room assignment.
- Never count money or display expensive jewelry in public. Use credit cards and/or traveler's checks as much as possible. Leave unneeded credit cards (department store, gas, etc.) at home.
- Use room safes or safety deposit boxes provided by the hotel. Store all valuables out of sight, even when you are in the room.
- Use deadbolt and other locks provided by the hotel. Make sure adjoining room doors are securely locked and all sliding-glass doors and windows have steel bars in the tracks.
- Never leave room keys unattended or needlessly display your keys. If you plan to be at the pool, check your key at the front desk.
- Ask front desk personnel which areas of town to avoid and what, if any, special precautions should be taken when driving a rental car (some criminals target tourists driving rental cars).
- Never open the door to a stranger; use the peephole and request identification. If you are still unsure, call the front desk to verify the identity of the person and the purpose of his/her visit.
- Never leave video cameras, car phones or other expensive equipment visible in your car; lock them in the trunk.
- Carry money separately from credit cards or use a "fanny pack." Carry your purse close to your body and your wallet in an inside coat or front trouser pocket. Never leave luggage unattended, and use your business address, if possible, on luggage tags.
- Beware of distractions staged by would-be scam artists, especially groups of children that surround you or a stranger who accidently spills something on you. They may be lifting your wallet.
- Travel in groups when possible. Walk only in well-lit areas and fill the gas tank before dark.

- If using an automatic teller machine (ATM), choose one in a well-lit area with plenty of foot traffic, such as one at a grocery store. Machines inside establishments are the safest to use.

- Walk with a purpose, as if you know where you are and where you are going.

- Have your car keys in hand before walking to the car and check the back seat before entering it. Lock the doors as soon as you get in the car.

- Report suspicious persons or situations to police or the hotel front desk. If a situation "doesn't feel right," it probably isn't. Remove yourself from the area immediately.

- Avoid poorly lit parking lots, dark doorways and shrubbery.

- Law enforcement agencies consider card-key (electronic) door locks the most secure.

- Uniformed security personnel in and around the hotel often indicates that management is aware of the potential for crime and is taking positive steps to ensure guest safety.

## ADVERTISING

All attractions, lodgings and restaurants are inspected and approved for listing for their inherent value to members. An establishment's decision to advertise has no bearing on its inspection, evaluation or rating. Advertising for services or products does not imply AAA endorsement.

## WHAT THE ⊛ MEANS

Lodgings and restaurants approved by AAA are eligible for our Official Appointment Program, which permits the display and advertising of the ⊛ emblem. The ⊛ preceding a listing printed in bold type identifies that property as an Official Appointment establishment with a special interest in serving AAA members. The ⊛ sign helps traveling members—like you—find accommodations on which they can depend. These properties want AAA business.

## ACCESS FOR THE DISABLED

Many lodging establishments and restaurants listed in this publication have symbols indicating that they are accessible to individuals with disabilities.

For lodging establishments, the 🔲 ensures there is at least one fully accessible guest room and that an individual with mobility impairments will be able to park their vehicles, check-in, and use at least one food and beverage outlet. For restaurants, the symbol indicates that parking, dining rooms and restrooms are accessible.

The 🔲 indicates that a lodging establishment provides closed caption decoders, text telephones, visual notification for fire alarms, incoming phone calls and door knocks, and phone amplification devices.

AAA does not evaluate recreational facilities, banquet rooms or convention and meeting facili-

ties for accessibility. You should call a property directly to inquire about your needs for these areas.

The criteria used by AAA are consistent with, but do not represent the full scope of, the Americans with Disabilities Act of 1990. AAA urges members with disabilities to always phone ahead to fully understand accommodations offerings.

## MAKING RESERVATIONS

Always make lodging reservations before leaving home. Your local club can make reservations for you and will provide written confirmation if you request it. Remember that a room is most likely to be held if a deposit accompanies your request. Establishments don't always allow you to guarantee reservations with a credit card, although the card may be used for final payment. The establishment might require you to submit a check to guarantee your reservations absolutely. As a rule, a room reserved without a deposit will be released if it is not claimed by a specified time (usually 4 p.m.-6 p.m.), unless the establishment agrees in advance to a late arrival time. Resorts invariably require a deposit.

When making reservations, you must identify yourself as a AAA member. Give all pertinent information about your planned stay. Request written confirmation to guarantee: type of room, rate, dates of stay, and cancellation and refund policies.

Most establishments give full deposit refunds if they have been notified at least 48 hours before the normal check-in time. However, when making reservations, confirm the property's deposit, cancellation and refund policies. Some properties may charge a cancellation or handling fee. When this applies, "cancellation fee imposed" will appear in the listing. If you cancel too late, you have little recourse if a refund is denied. When an establishment requires a full or partial payment in advance, and your trip is cut short, a refund may not be given.

When canceling reservations, call the lodging immediately. Make a note of the date and time you called, the cancellation number if there is one, and the name of the person who handled the cancellation. If your AAA club made your reservation, allow them to make the cancellation for you as well so you will have proof of cancellation.

When you are charged more than the rate listed in the TourBook, under the headings **Rates Guaranteed** or **AAA Special Value Rates**, or you qualify for the **Senior Discount** and did not receive it, question the additional charge. If management refuses to adhere to the published rate, pay for the room and submit your receipt and membership number to AAA *within 30 days (see address page 12)*. Include all pertinent information: dates of stay, rate paid, itemized paid receipts, number of persons in your party, the room number you occupied, and list any extra room equipment used. A refund of the amount paid in excess of the stated maximum will be made when our investigation indicates that unjustified charging has occurred.

When you find your room is not as specified, and you have written confirmation of reservations for a certain type of accommodation, you should be given the option of choosing a different room or finding one elsewhere. Should you choose to go elsewhere and a refund is refused or resisted, submit the matter to AAA *within 30 days* along with complete documentation, including your reasons for refusing the room and copies of your written confirmation and any receipts or canceled checks associated with this problem.

## GOLDEN PASSPORTS

U.S. residents 62 and older can obtain Golden Age passports for a one-time $10 fee. Golden Access passports are free to the medically blind and permanently disabled. Both cover entrance fees for the holder and accompanying private party to all national parks and historic sites, monuments and battlefields within the national park system, plus half off camping and other fees. Apply in person at most federally operated areas.

The Golden Eagle Passport costs $25 annually and covers entrance fees for the holder and accompanying private party to all federally operated areas. Obtain the pass in person at any national park or regional office of the U.S. Park Service or Forest Service.

## HOTEL/MOTEL FIRE SAFETY

The AAA inspection program is designed to provide you with the most useful information for selecting the lodgings best suited to your needs. Because of the highly specialized skills needed to conduct professional fire safety inspections, however, AAA inspectors cannot assess fire safety.

All listed establishments provide smoke detectors and/or automatic sprinkler systems in guest rooms. Lodgings that provide this added protection are identified with symbols (see the Sample Listing). At each establishment whose listing shows these symbols, a AAA inspector has evaluated a sampling of the rooms and verified that this equipment is in place.

For additional fire safety information read the page posted on the back of your lodging room door, or write the National Fire Protection Association at 1 Batterymarch Park, P.O. Box 9101, Quincy, MA 02269-9101.

## AUTOMOBILE MAINTENANCE

A broken radiator hose or dead battery can put a damper on even the best planned vacation. In order to ensure a safe, hassle-free road trip, there are a few things you should do before setting out on the open road. AAA Automotive Engineering and Road Service offers the following suggestions for a pre-trip checkup and on the road maintenance.

- If your vehicle is due for a tune-up, have it done before you go; consult your car owner's manual for manufacturer's recommendations for maintenance.

- Normally, the oil level should be checked with every fill up, and the oil and oil filter should be changed every 3,000 miles or every 3 months.

- Make sure that your tires are properly inflated before you begin your trip. Also check for cuts, bulges and uneven or excessive tread wear. Tire pressure should be checked while the tires are cool. To achieve better fuel economy and tire life, 2 to 3 more pounds per square inch (psi) of pressure over the car manufacturer's recommendation can be safely added if the new pressure does not exceed the maximum indicated on the tire sidewall. Remember to also check the spare.

- Check the cooling system. Look for leaks in the radiator. Check both the coolant level and the antifreeze-water mixture in the radiator. The coolant level should be checked when the engine is cool. If your car has a coolant recovery tank, maintain the level indicated. Otherwise the coolant level should be 1 to 2 inches below the filler neck of the radiator. A 50/50 mixture of antifreeze and water is recommended.

- Also check the radiator and heater hoses for soft, spongy or swollen spots. A worn hose can burst at any time, especially during hot-weather driving.

- Loose belts reduce the efficiency of the devices that they operate. Worn belts can snap unexpectedly, so it is important to check the belts that drive the alternator, air conditioner, water pump, air pump and power steering. Make sure that the engine is turned off before inspecting any belts. Roll each belt between your thumb and forefinger, checking the sides and the bottom for cracks, splits, or contamination from grease or oil. A correctly tensioned belt has about half an inch of give or pull.

- It is important to check the brake pad linings, brake shoes and brake fluid levels before setting out. Also look for leaks.

- Do not forget to check the transmission and power steering fluid.

- Check all of the lights, including brake lights, turn signals, headlights and hazard lights, to ensure they are in proper working order.

- Finally, it is imperative that you be able to see clearly, so clean the windshield and top off the washer fluid with each fill-up.

Your local AAA club can assist in planning your trip and provide you with further information about auto maintenance.

## HEALTH ON THE ROAD

Most travelers expect to have a carefree trip, leaving their worries and troubles behind. However, a minor illness or accident can turn a great vacation into one that you would rather forget. A few simple precautions can save a vacation.

**BEFORE YOU LEAVE:**

• If you are going on a long trip or traveling a far distance you might want to get a medical and dental check-up to ensure a clean bill of health.

• Read your medical insurance policies very carefully. Does your policy provide complete coverage during your travels?

• Take advantage of a CPR or first-aid course. Your local American Red Cross provides frequent courses for a minimal fee.

• Get ready to walk! Taking daily walks a few weeks before your trip can help eliminate fatigue and leg cramps.

• Bring a medical identification card that includes a list of persons to contact in the event of an emergency, specific medical needs, allergies, blood type, and your doctor's name, address and phone number.

• Update your prescription medicine and bring the instructions and dosage amounts. Be aware: You should never combine various medications into the same bottle.

**WHAT TO BRING:**

• Bring your medical insurance card and a claims form in case of an illness or injury.

• Pack comfortable clothing and shoes. Pack several pair of shoes that have already been broken in to avoid painful and blistered feet.

• Bring an extra pair of glasses or contact lenses and a copy of your prescription.

• A first-aid kit is essential. The American Red Cross advises that a basic kit include a pair of scissors, waterproof tape, antiseptic, cleansing wipes, a pair of latex gloves, a variety of bandages and a blanket. Customize your first-aid kit to fit your needs.

**CLIMATE AND ALTITUDE:**

• Protect yourself from the sun. If you are traveling in a hot or dry climate pack plenty of sunscreen. Try to avoid the midday sun, wear light and loose-fitting clothes, and drink a lot of liquids. Heat strokes and heat exhaustion can be very dangerous.

• If you are visiting a wet and humid climate, an insect repellent will prove to be invaluable. This type of climate tends to be the perfect breeding ground for mosquitos.

• Frostbite can occur in a matter of seconds if the temperature falls below 32 F and the wind is blowing (strongly). Wear layers of clothing—wool over cotton tends to provide the best insulation. Wear a hat.

• Traveling to a higher altitude can sometimes cause high altitude sickness or mountain sickness. Because of the change in oxygen intake you might experience some dizziness, shortness of breath, headaches and nausea. The symptoms usually strike at around 8,000 feet in altitude.

**ON THE ROAD:**

• Avoid alcohol, sedatives and tranquilizers.

• Rotate drivers to prevent drowsiness.

• Always wear your seatbelt.

• Take a break. AAA Traffic Safety suggests that a traveler stop every 3 hours to stretch and exercise. This will aid in preventing fatigue and loss of concentration.

• If you tend to get motion sickness, drive or sit in the front passenger seat and open a window for some fresh air. Don't read while the car is moving. If symptoms persist, consider taking a motion sickness medication.

Remember to think before you travel. Leave your worries behind but don't forget to pack your common sense. A little time and effort before your trip can go a long way—especially when you are far from home.

# PLAN YOUR PET'S VACATION

The first decision to be made is whether to leave your furry friend behind or take him along. The American Society for the Prevention of Cruelty to Animals (ASPCA) maintains that pets are most comfortable in familiar surroundings and it is better, therefore, to leave them behind.

If you feel you must take your pet along due to the duration of the trip, or because you can't live without him, you should plan every detail of your pet's travel with his safety and comfort in mind.

A trip to the veterinarian, preferably one who has cared for him on a regular basis, is the first order of business. All vaccinations should be up-to-date and certificates obtained: Requirements differ among states, so it is best to contact the appropriate state or county department before beginning your trip.

**PETS ON THE ROAD:**

• Pets feel a sense of security when they are in a confined area; an animal crate or cat carrier is a wise investment. For information on appropriate carrier sizes, consult your veterinarian or the ASPCA, 441 E. 92nd St., New York, NY 10128; phone (212) 876-7700.

• Ask your vet for advice regarding your specific pet.

• Use motion sickness medication or a tranquilizer only if necessary.

• Make sure your pet is properly licensed and has collar tags or a permanent ID tattoo.

• Stop often for exercise and bathroom breaks, allowing your pet time to stretch. Always keep him on a leash.

• If you plan to stay in a hotel or motel, make arrangements in advance. AAA TourBook lodging listings specify whether pets are allowed and whether there are fees or other restrictions attached. Phone all establishments prior to departure to verify the information and make reservations.

- Bring your pet's food and water dishes, as well as his bedding and a favorite toy.

- Bring a small amount of food and a jug of drinking water from home to help your pet become acclimated to new sources of food and water. Keep extra drinking water in the car.

## TAKING CHILDREN ALONG

Taking children on a vacation can be rewarding and educational for the whole family, but it requires advance planning, flexibility and a positive attitude. Pediatricians, child psychologists and experienced parents offer the following helpful hints for a smooth vacation.

**Involve children in the planning.**

- Let them suggest where they would like to go on vacation.

- Point out the route and destination on a map. Let the kids have their own map and help them trace your route using bright markers.

- Read about what will be seen on the way to and at your destination. Make this a family affair and let each member plan a daily activity.

- Pack a change of clothes for everyone in a separate bag for the first overnight stop.

- For short trips take just what is needed, but be sure to include swimwear.

- Bring a first-aid kit—it's better to be safe than sorry.

**Car rules must be obeyed.**

- All passengers must utilize car seats or seat belts at all times.

- Feet, hands and head should always stay inside the vehicle, and do not distract the driver.

- Never play with the door locks and handles.

**Travel on a schedule, but leave enough extra time for unexpected situations.**

- Be aware of detours or construction along your route, and don't travel at rush hour.

- Keep the child's regular nap, meal and bedtimes as much as possible.

**Keep kids occupied on the road.**

- Practice alphabet skills with road signs or collect state names from license plates. Memory and counting games are other good activities.

- A tape recorder (with earphones), favorite tapes and blank tapes for recording themselves can be real lifesavers.

- Activity books and colored pencils—no crayons, they melt—or washable felt-tip pens can keep children occupied for hours. Don't forget a small pencil sharpener. Get a copy of the AAA Children's Travel Activity Book from your club.

- Let children be responsible for their own tote bag with books, toys, travel games and note pads. The bags can be hung around front seat headrests for easy accessibility.

- Take healthy snacks rather than junk food.

- Keep plenty of water available.

- Remember to take napkins, pre-moistened wipes and a bag for garbage.

- Try to stop when you sense the kids are getting irritable, before a real problem develops. Give them some time to stretch.

**Provide reassurance on the road.**

- When stopping at an unfamiliar place to sleep, make sure youngsters have something from home, such as their own pillow or special blanket, to comfort them.

Show appreciation for how well the children behave while traveling. Stop for an ice cream cone or other favorite treat. And remember that just being together is the most important part of your vacation.

## TIPPING

Tipping is an accepted practice and many service industry personnel depend upon tips for a large part of their incomes. At airports 50¢ to $1 per bag is appropriate for skycaps if the service is to the curb, more if the bag handling is farther. Taxi drivers expect 15 percent. In hotels it is appropriate to tip the bellperson or porter no less than $1, and often $1 per bag; the maid is left $2 per day; the doorman receives $1 to $5 depending upon the difficulty of the service he performs; the garage attendant is given $1 to $2; bathroom attendants receive 50¢ to $1.

Since the job of the concierge is to help guests, he or she usually should not be tipped unless an unusual or very difficult task is performed; then a minimum of $5 is appropriate.

Tipping in restaurants depends upon the luxuriousness and sophistication of the establishment and, of course, upon the quality of the service. The standard for waiters and waitresses is 15 percent of the bill. If some person other than your server helps serve your meal, a 5 percent tip is appropriate. If you are paying by credit card it is acceptable and less awkward to put a 20 percent tip on the form and allow these personnel to sort out their portions.

# When traveling away from home . . .

**SUPERNUMBER®**
1-800-AAA-HELP
1-800-955-4TDD (Hearing Impaired)

## a 24-hour toll-free Emergency Road Service information system.

It's easy to use Triple A's *SUPERNUMBER*® when traveling outside your local club area.

1. Look in the white pages of the telephone book for a listing under "AAA" in the United States or "CAA" in Canada, since road service is dispatched by the local club in many communities.

2. If there is no listing, have your membership card handy and call *SUPERNUMBER*® 1-800-AAA-HELP for the nearest road service facility. *Hearing impaired call 1-800-955-4TDD.*

*SUPERNUMBER*® available 24 hours a day, is only for Emergency Road Service . . . and only when traveling outside the area served by your home club. Questions regarding other club services should be directed to the nearest club office.

# Four Names Everyone Says Yes To

**Ours** ▼

**Theirs** ◄▲

▲ **Yours**

AAA is the most trusted name in travel. And, VISA and MASTERCARD are the most accepted names in credit cards. Put AAA on each credit card and there's only one name missing—*yours.* Increase the advantages of your AAA membership by using the new, exclusive AAA/VISA or AAA/MASTERCARD credit card for all your purchases. Ask your AAA club about the many benefits. They're two cards everyone says "yes" to. Why don't you? Call your local AAA office now to apply.

The AAA/VISA and AAA/MASTERCARD credit cards are owned and issued by sponsoring VISA and MASTERCARD issuers and are available only to members of participating AAA clubs. Both cards are accepted in over 160 countries worldwide in over 10 million locations.

©1989 American Automobile Association.

**The Most Trusted Name in Travel.**

# ATTRACTIONS

Whether your interests
are amusement parks
or historical monuments,
the attraction listings offer
a quick, concise overview
of descriptive information
on sightseeing destinations
throughout the United States
and Canada.

# AAA Members

When you're planning your next trip, whether it's a day, weekend or week,

Hertz has your wheels. Hertz offers AAA members special discounts and benefits all year long.

For more information call your AAA office or Hertz at 1-800-654-3080.

**The Hertz/AAA partnership saves you money!**

Hertz rents Fords and other fine cars.
®REG. U.S. PAT. OFF. ©HERTZ SYSTEM INC. 1994/418-94

Show Your Card & Save

*Hertz*

# NEW JERSEY

## An introduction to the state's history, geography, economy and recreation

NEW JERSEY IS a study in contrasts. Only four states are smaller in land area; fewer than 10 have a larger population. A transportation system that is among the nation's busiest snakes through stretches of pine forest and the rolling green hills of horse country. Known as the Garden State, New Jersey also is one of the country's most urbanized areas. While bedroom communities and historic towns form interlocking webs of business and commerce, Atlantic City offers a glittering getaway.

### HISTORY

In 1524 only the shorebirds and the Lenni Lenape Indians knew the New Jersey coast, and Giovanni de Verrazano's brief appearance in that year did not interfere with their dominion. In 1609 Henry Hudson claimed the area for the Dutch. By 1623 the land was called New Netherland, and busy trading settlements had sprung up along the Hudson and Delaware rivers. New Sweden was established along the Delaware River for several decades in the mid-1600s before the Dutch captured the rival colony.

When England assumed control of New Netherland in 1664, New Jersey was part of the area deeded by King Charles II to his brother James, Duke of York. The duke granted the region between the two rivers to John Berkeley, Baron of Stratton, and to Sir George Carteret. Carteret, former governor and defender of the Isle of Jersey, named the colony.

In 1676 Berkeley sold his portion of the land to English Quakers who formed a business called the Board of Proprietors of West Jersey. Carteret was bought out by the East Jersey Board of Proprietors in 1682. In 1702 the boards relinquished the right to govern the colony to the Crown, which was then responsible for appointing a royal governor.

Anti-British sentiment grew, fueled by commercial limitations imposed by England and the constant conflict among the proprietors, the popular assemblies and the royal governors.

The first provincial congress met in New Brunswick in 1774 to appoint delegates to the proposed Continental Congress at Philadelphia. By mid-1776 the last royal governor was deposed; on July 2 the provincial congress adopted a combined state constitution and declaration of independence.

Four times during the Revolutionary War the Continental Army crossed the state; Washington headquartered at Morristown during two harsh winters and at Camp Middlebrook near Somerville during the mild winter of 1778-79. Among the more than 100 battles fought on New Jersey soil were the engagements of Trenton, Princeton and Monmouth. Twice New Jersey claimed the nation's capital: Congress met at Princeton in 1783 and at Trenton in 1784.

On Dec. 18, 1787, New Jersey ratified the Constitution. The state had earlier left its mark on that document by advocating equal state representation in the Senate. Trenton was designated the state capital in 1790.

Diversified industrial development began early, aided by ample water power, excellent harbors and the construction of canals and railroads. The machinery for the *Savannah,* the first steamship to cross the Atlantic, was built near Morristown. The first industrial city—later called Paterson—grew up around a textile-printing establishment on the Passaic River.

New Jersey, though suffering the same internal dissension as the other states, fought fiercely for the Union during the Civil War. Growing distrust of the corporate giants resulted in the antitrust laws of 1913, popularized by Gov. Woodrow Wilson. In response to the needs of World Wars I and II, the mammoth industrial concerns produced avalanches of goods for the war efforts.

## GEOGRAPHY

Far from its stereotype of an undistinguished flatland overrun by pavement, New Jersey displays a billion years of geologic evolution in its varied terrain. From mountain building through flood and uplift, glaciation and subsequent erosion, the history of the land can be read in its terrace-like descent from the Kittatinny Ridge of the Appalachians to the broad outwash of the coastal plain.

Rocky and wooded, the folded roots of the Appalachian Mountains form the northwestern part of the state. These drop to a narrow highland belt, which gives way to the rolling Piedmont. Throughout this area ribs of traprock are interspersed with countless lakes; both are the legacy of the last ice age.

Scraping southward, the glaciers plowed the softer rock from between the hard ridges and dumped it, pulverized, in a line of moraines that straggles southwest from Staten Island into Pennsylvania. The three-fifths of the state south of this zone is the level coastal plain, marked by sandy soil and the extensive Pine Barrens.

The Pine Barrens are truly unique. Once encompassing nearly one-fourth of the state, the "Pines" are now 1,000 square miles of virtually uninhabited marsh and woods centering around Chatsworth. Hardly less fragile than the ecosystem of the area is the timeless lifestyle of the "Pineys," those few individualistic residents who live on the seasonal gifts of their forest and wouldn't live anywhere else.

Except for the 48-mile boundary with New York, New Jersey is surrounded by water. The Delaware River forms the western boundary of the state, separating it from Pennsylvania and Delaware; on the east the Hudson River and New York Bay divide it from New York. Between the Atlantic and the deeply serrated mainland coast lies a strip of long, narrow barrier beaches that is a major vacation area.

## ECONOMY

Although New Jersey is one of the most industrialized states in the nation, tourism and farming also are important to the economy. New Jersey manufactures a greater variety of commodities than any other state. Pharmaceuticals, chemicals, textiles and clothing, foodstuffs, machinery, transportation equipment, primary and fabricated metal goods, rubber products, leather and refined oil are produced in staggering quantities.

The greatest industrial concentration adjoins New York City: It extends from Paterson and Hackensack through Hoboken, Jersey City, Newark, Bayonne and Elizabeth to Perth Amboy and

---

## FOR YOUR INFORMATION

### FURTHER INFORMATION FOR VISITORS:

New Jersey Department of Commerce
and Economic Development
Division of Travel and Tourism
CN 826
Trenton, NJ 08625
(800) JERSEY-7

### RECREATION INFORMATION:

Division of Parks and Forestry
State Park Service
501 E. State St., CN 404
Trenton, NJ 08625
(609) 292-2797
(800) 843-6420

### FISHING AND HUNTING REGULATIONS:

Department of Environmental
Protection
Division of Fish, Game and Wildlife
501 E. State St., CN 400
Trenton, NJ 08625
(609) 292-2965

**SPECIAL REGULATIONS:** Motorists are not permitted to pump their own gas at service stations in New Jersey.

New Brunswick. A second complex, focusing on the Philadelphia marketing center, includes Trenton and Camden. High-tech and service industries, however, began replacing the traditional "smokestack" industries in the 1970s.

In Mauricetown high-grade silica sand is prepared for shipment to glass manufacturers and steel foundries throughout the country. The glassmaking industry is important in Flemington and in such southern cities as Bridgeton and Millville. Illuminite, used in the manufacture of paints, is mined in the southern part of the state.

As diversified as the industrial products are the crops of central and southern New Jersey. Cranberries, blueberries, peaches, tomatoes, asparagus, sweet corn, lettuce, cucumbers, bell peppers and spinach are primary; beets, beans, potatoes, onions, eggplants, apples and grapes also are grown. Nursery and greenhouse products are the state's leading cash crops.

In the livestock category, dairying is the leader in the nine northern counties, followed by egg production: More than 500 million eggs are sent to market each year. New Jersey is one of the leading commercial fishing states in the nation. Commercial fishing centers profit from the shellfish taken from the Atlantic coast and Delaware Bay; Atlantic mackerel, cod, sea bass, croaker, flounder and bluefish also are caught. Most of the harvest is processed locally.

## RECREATION

New Jersey's beaches protect the interconnected bays and channels behind them, providing excellent **boating**. Water transportation is as common in the seaside towns as the automobile. Float trips range from **canoeing** along the state's inland waterways to **white-water rafting** within the Delaware Water Gap National Recreation Area.

**Saltwater fishing** along the coast yields marlin, tuna and sea bass; Atlantic City, Belmar, Cape May and the Wildwoods in particular have numerous boat charters for **deep-sea fishing**. Many good fishing spots exist among the islands south of Great Bay near Pleasantville. The state's inland lakes, rivers and streams offer good fishing for trout, shad, bass, perch, bluegill, northern pike and pickerel. A license is required for **freshwater fishing**.

**Hunting** in the Pine Barrens of the southern part of the state and in the mountains of the northwest yields deer, squirrels, rabbits and raccoons. Migratory waterfowls flock to the marshy bays; Brigantine National Wildlife Refuge offers selective hunting during specified seasons. State forests, some parks and the state fish and game management areas also permit hunting. A license is required for hunting.

In the winter, sports traffic turns inland. Vernon Valley/Great Gorge on Hamburg Mountain in Vernon offers **downhill skiing** early December through mid-April, depending on conditions, on more than 50 slopes. Other ski areas in northern New Jersey are Hidden Valley in Vernon, Craigmeur in Newfoundland and Campgaw in Mahwah.

**Cross-country skiing, tobogganing, snowmobiling, ice skating** and **snowshoeing** are possible in many of the state parks and forests.

The beaches and the state parks and forests are New Jersey's largest recreation centers. More than 305,000 acres are state park and forest land; the largest is the 109,328-acre Wharton State Forest in southern New Jersey. The state parks and forests provide many recreational opportunities such as **hiking, swimming, picnicking, nature study** and **camping**.

The Appalachian Trail runs through High Point and Wawayanda state parks, Abram Hewitt, Stokes and Worthington state forests and the Delaware Water Gap National Recreation Area. Several offshoots of this trail tour the Kittatinny Mountains and the New Jersey Highlands. The Batona Trail, which runs through Lebanon, Wharton and Bass River state forests, explores the Pine Barrens.

Many parks and forests charge entrance or parking fees daily from Memorial Day through Labor Day. Fees also are levied on such facilities as cabins and campsites. Reservations must be made through the individual park office at least 5 days in advance; contact the New Jersey Division of Parks and Forestry *(see For Your Information box)* for addresses. For complete information on camping *see the AAA Mideastern CampBook.*

---

## PLAN AHEAD FOR ECONOMY.

- Select the optimum route in terms of distance and type of highway. A AAA Travel Counselor can assist you.
- Travel light and avoid using a car-top rack. The less weight and wind resistance, the better the mileage.
- Combine short trips, such as visits, errands and shopping.

## RECREATION AREAS

| RECREATION AREAS | MAP LOCATION | CAMPING | PICNICKING | HIKING TRAILS | BOATING | BOAT RAMP | BOAT RENTAL | FISHING | SWIMMING | PETS ON LEASH | BICYCLE TRAILS | WINTER SPORTS | VISITOR CENTER | LODGE/CABINS | FOOD SERVICE |
|---|---|---|---|---|---|---|---|---|---|---|---|---|---|---|---|
| **NATIONAL RECREATION AREAS** *(See place listings)* | | | | | | | | | | | | | | | |
| **Delaware Water Gap (A-2)** 70,000 acres. Hunting. | | • | • | • | • | • | | • | • | • | | • | • | | • |
| **Gateway (I-6)** Sandy Hook Unit; 1,600 acres. | | | • | • | | • | | • | • | | | | • | | • |
| **STATE** | | | | | | | | | | | | | | | |
| **Allaire (C-6)** 3,040 acres just off I-195 exit 31B. Historic. Cross-country skiing; bridle trails, horse rental, nature trails. *(See Farmingdale)* | 1 | • | • | • | | | | • | | • | | | • | | • |
| **Allamuchy Mountain (Stephen's Park) (B-3)** 7,276 acres 2 mi. n. of Hackettstown on CR 517. | 2 | • | • | • | | | | • | | • | | | • | | |
| **Bass River Forest (F-3)** 23,585 acres 3 mi. w. of Tuckerton on CR 592. Hunting; horse rental, nature programs. | 4 | • | • | • | • | • | • | • | • | • | | | | • | • |
| **Belleplain Forest (G-2)** 11,780 acres on CR 550 at Belleplain. Hunting; horse rental. | 5 | • | • | • | • | • | • | • | • | • | | | | | • |
| **Cape May Point (H-2)** 190 acres 2 mi. w. of Cape May on CR 606. Historic. Nature trails. *(See Cape May)* | 6 | | • | • | | | | • | | • | | | • | | |
| **Cheesequake (I-5)** 1,284 acres 3 mi. w. of Matawan on SR 34. Cross-country skiing; nature trails. | 7 | • | • | • | | | | • | • | • | | | | | • |
| **Corson's Inlet (G-3)** 341 acres just n. of Strathmere on Ocean Dr. | 8 | | | • | • | • | • | • | | • | | | | | |
| **Delaware and Raritan Canal (I-4)** 3,723 acres 7 mi. w. of New Brunswick on CR 514. | 9 | | • | • | • | • | • | • | | • | • | • | | | |
| **Bull's Island Section (C-2)** 79 acres 3 mi. n. of Stockton on SR 29. | 10 | • | • | • | • | • | • | • | | • | | | | | |
| **Hacklebarney (B-5)** 892 acres 3 mi. s.w. of Chester via US 206. | 12 | | • | • | | | | • | | • | | | | | |
| **High Point (A-3)** 14,193 acres 8 mi. n.w. of Sussex on SR 23. Scenic. Cross-country skiing, ice fishing, snowmobiling; nature trails. | 13 | • | • | • | • | • | | • | • | • | | • | • | | • |
| **Hopatcong (B-3)** 113 acres 2 mi. n. of Landing off I-80. Ice fishing, ice skating, snowmobiling. | 14 | | • | | • | • | • | • | | • | | • | | | |
| **Island Beach (E-4)** 3,002 acres 3 mi. s. of Seaside Park on SR 35. A 10-mile strip from Seaside Park to Barnegat Inlet. Nature trails. | 15 | | • | • | | | | • | • | • | | | | | • |
| **Jenny Jump Forest (B-2)** 1,387 acres 3 mi. e. of Hope off CR 519. | 16 | • | • | • | | | | | | • | | • | | | |
| **Lebanon Forest (E-3)** 31,879 acres s. of Fort Dix off SRs 70 and 72. Hunting. | 17 | • | • | • | | | | • | | • | | | | | • |
| **Liberty (H-6)** 1,114 acres off the N.J. Tpke. Ext. *(See Jersey City)* | 18 | | • | | | | | | | | | | • | • | | • |
| **Parvin (F-2)** 1,125 acres 6 mi. w. of Vineland on CR 540. Nature trails. | 19 | • | • | • | • | • | • | • | • | • | | | | | • |
| **Penn Forest (E-3)** 3,366 acres 5 mi. s.e. of Chatsworth off CR 563. Hunting; bridle trails, horse rental. | 20 | | • | • | | | | • | | • | | | | | |
| **Ringwood (B-4)** 6,199 acres 8 mi. s.w. of Sloatsburg, N.Y. on Sloatsburg Rd. *(See Ringwood)* | 22 | | • | • | | | | • | • | • | | | | • | |
| **Ringwood Manor** 895 acres. Historic. | | | • | • | | | | • | | • | | | | • | |
| **Shepherd Lake** 1,220 acres. Ice fishing, ice skating. | | | • | • | • | | | • | • | • | | • | | • | |
| **Skyland Section** 4,084 acres. Snowmobiling. | | | • | | | | | | | • | | • | | | |
| **Round Valley (C-4)** 3,639 acres 2 mi. s. of Lebanon off US 22. Cross-country skiing, hunting, ice fishing, ice skating, wilderness camping. | 23 | • | • | • | • | • | | • | • | • | | • | | | |
| **Spruce Run (C-2)** 1,961 acres 3 mi. n. of Clinton on SR 31. | 24 | • | • | • | • | • | • | • | • | • | | | | | • |
| **Stokes Forest (A-3)** 15,482 acres 3 mi. n. of Branchville on US 206. Cross-country skiing, hunting, ice skating, snowmobiling; bridle trails, horse rental, nature trails. | 25 | • | • | • | | | | • | • | • | | • | • | • | • |
| **Swartswood (B-3)** 1,718 acres 5 mi. w. of Newton on CRs 622 and 619. Ice fishing, ice skating, snowmobiling. | 26 | • | • | • | • | • | • | • | • | • | | | | | • |
| **Voorhees Park (B-4)** 613 acres 2 mi. n. of High Bridge on CR 513. | 27 | • | • | • | | | | | • | | | | • | | |
| **Washington Crossing (C-4)** 841 acres 7 mi. n. of Trenton on SR 29. Historic. Nature programs. *(See Trenton)* | 28 | | • | • | | | | | | • | | | • | • | | |
| **Wawayanda (A-4)** 11,332 acres 3 mi. e. of Vernon on CR 94. Cross-country skiing, ice fishing, ice skating, snowmobiling. | 29 | • | • | • | • | • | • | • | • | • | | • | | | |

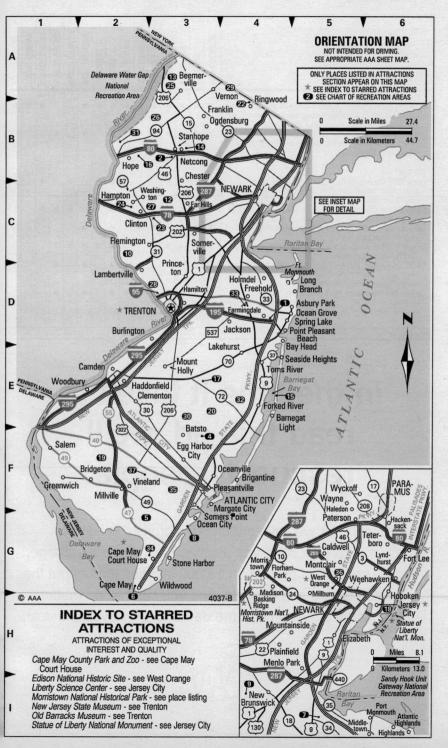

## ORIENTATION MAP
NOT INTENDED FOR DRIVING.
SEE APPROPRIATE AAA SHEET MAP.

ONLY PLACES LISTED IN ATTRACTIONS
SECTION APPEAR ON THIS MAP
★ SEE INDEX TO STARRED ATTRACTIONS
❷ SEE CHART OF RECREATION AREAS

Scale in Miles    27.4
Scale in Kilometers    44.7

SEE INSET MAP
FOR DETAIL

© AAA    4037-B

## INDEX TO STARRED ATTRACTIONS
ATTRACTIONS OF EXCEPTIONAL
INTEREST AND QUALITY

Cape May County Park and Zoo - see Cape May Court House
Edison National Historic Site - see West Orange
Liberty Science Center - see Jersey City
Morristown National Historical Park - see place listing
New Jersey State Museum - see Trenton
Old Barracks Museum - see Trenton
Statue of Liberty National Monument - see Jersey City

| RECREATION AREAS | MAP LOCATION | CAMPING | PICNICKING | HIKING TRAILS | BOATING | BOAT RAMP | BOAT RENTAL | FISHING | SWIMMING | PETS ON LEASH | BICYCLE TRAILS | WINTER SPORTS | VISITOR CENTER | LODGE/CABINS | FOOD SERVICE |
|---|---|---|---|---|---|---|---|---|---|---|---|---|---|---|---|
| **Wharton Forest (E-3)**   109,328 acres 35 mi. s. of Trenton off US 206. Canoeing, hunting, ice fishing, ice skating; bridle trails, nature programs. *(See Batsto)* | 30 | ● | ● | ● | ● | ● | ● | ● | ● | ● |  | ● |  | ● | ● |
| **Worthington Forest (B-2)**   5,770 acres 16 mi. n.e. of Blairstown on Millbrook Rd. Cross-country skiing, hunting, snowmobiling. | 31 | ● | ● | ● | ● | ● |  | ● |  | ● |  | ● |  |  |  |
| **OTHER** | | | | | | | | | | | | | | | |
| **Cape May County (G-3)**   120 acres 2 mi. n. of Cape May Court House on SR 9. Nature trails. *(See Cape May Court House)* | 34 |  | ● | ● |  |  |  |  |  | ● |  | ● | ● |  | ● |
| **Estell Manor County Park (F-3)**   1,672 acres 3 mi. s. of Mays Landing on SR 50. | 35 |  | ● | ● |  |  |  |  |  | ● | ● | ● | ● |  |  |
| **Lake Lenape Park (F-2)**   1,800 acres on Old Harding Hwy. in Mays Landing. | 37 | ● | ● | ● | ● | ● |  |  |  | ● |  | ● |  |  |  |
| **Ocean County (E-4)**   325 acres in Lakewood on SR 88. Golf, tennis; nature trails. | 32 |  | ● | ● |  |  |  | ● | ● | ● | ● | ● |  |  |  |
| **South Mountain Reservation (G-5)**   2,047 acres off I-280 exit 7, then 2 mi. s. on Pleasant Valley Way in West Orange. Indoor ice skating; bridle trails. | 36 |  | ● | ● |  |  |  |  |  | ● |  | ● |  | ● |  |
| **Turkey Swamp County Park (C-5)**   498 acres 4½ mi. s. of Freehold via US 9, CR 524 and Georgia Rd. Ice skating; archery range, nature trails. | 33 | ● | ● | ● | ● |  |  | ● | ● | ● |  | ● |  |  |  |

# POINTS OF INTEREST

**ASBURY PARK (C-6) pop. 16,800, elev. 23′**

Established in 1871 as a summering spot for temperance advocates so that the nearby camp meeting center of Ocean Grove *(see place listing)* would have no unseemly neighbors, Asbury Park subsequently became one of New Jersey's leading seaside resorts. During the late 1930s and 1940s Asbury Park's mile-long Boardwalk and its centerpiece, Convention Hall, made the city one of the premier shore resorts.

The city declined during the 1960s as newly constructed shopping centers drew people away. It gained new life, however, as a music center. At one time Convention Hall was the only North Jersey shore auditorium that permitted rock music concerts. Local blue-collar bars began nurturing their own brand of home-grown rock 'n' roll, which soon was made internationally famous by such performers as Bruce Springsteen and Southside Johnny.

Additional area information can be obtained from the Greater Asbury Park Chamber of Commerce, 100 Lake Ave., P.O. Box 649, Asbury Park, NJ 07712; phone (908) 775-7676.

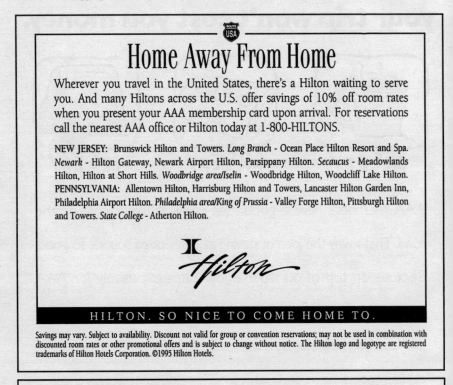
# TAKE A BREAK!

Each 2 hours of driving deserves a 10-minute stop to stretch, walk or sip a refreshing drink.

**STAY ALERT TO AVOID ACCIDENTS!**

# Atlantic City

Casino gambling has stimulated development in a city whose halcyon days were further back than most citizens cared to remember. Since 1978 nearly a dozen casino-hotels have opened, primarily situated along the Boardwalk area. The marina area, which opens onto the Absecon Inlet northwest of the Boardwalk and casino-hotel strip, also has felt the effects of the city's revitalization.

What was to become one of the leading East Coast resorts during the late 1800s began as a fishing village at the north end of Absecon Island, a swath of sand separated from the mainland by a maze of bays, inlets and salt marshes. It probably would have remained so had not someone noted that the configuration of the coast spared the island some heavy storms, and that the nearness of the Gulf Stream tempered its climate.

The Camden & Atlantic Railroad simultaneously began to lay track and promote the area. When the first train arrived in 1854, Atlantic City was incorporated, the railroad's land company was selling lots and there was a hotel. By the 1880s two rail lines were carrying streams of passengers to the many hotels of a town that had assumed the shape and character it was to exhibit until the casino law was passed.

Since the first 8-foot-wide lane of planks was laid directly on the sand in 1870 to keep hotel lobbies and railroad cars free from sand, the Boardwalk has been the city's best-known attraction. Four-and-one-eighth miles long (6 if you include the adjacent towns' footage) and 60 feet wide, the current steel and concrete structure is surfaced with planks arranged in a diagonal pattern. It is a foundation for stores, amusements, concessions and thousands of adventure-seeking visitors.

The Boardwalk's success spawned such now familiar forms of entertainment and promotion as the rolling chair, which is still a popular mode of transportation, and the picture postcard. Probably the best known innovation, however, was the amusement pier, the first of which was built in 1882.

Applying the same principle as the skyscraper but in a horizontal direction, each pier occupied as little space on the Boardwalk as possible, yet packed as much entertainment as would fit behind its entrance. Jutting into the ocean, Million

## THE INFORMED TRAVELER

### POPULATION: 38,000; metro 309,200      ELEVATION: 21 ft.

### Whom to Call

**Emergency:** 911

**Police (non-emergency):** (609) 347-5780

**Time:** (609) 976-1616

**Temperature:** (609) 646-6400

**Hospitals:** Atlantic City Medical Center, (609) 344-4081.

### Where to Look

**Newspapers**

*The Press* is published daily. Check the events section for listings of current entertainment offerings.

**Radio and TV**

Atlantic City radio station WOND (1400 AM) is an all-news/weather station; WHYY (90.1 FM) is a member of National Public Radio.

The major TV channels are 3 and 40 (NBC), 6 (ABC), 10 (CBS), 12 and 23 (PBS) and 29

(FOX). For a complete list of radio and television programs, consult the daily newspaper.

**Visitor Information**

The Greater Atlantic City Convention & Visitors Bureau, 2314 Pacific Ave., Atlantic City, NJ 08401, provides information about entertainment, transportation and city tours; phone (609) 348-7100. The free weekly papers *Whoot* and *At The Shore* provide information about cultural activities.

### What to Wear

The ocean and its breezes have a moderating effect on Atlantic City's weather, delaying the onset of the warmest weather by a few weeks and maintaining mild temperatures into late autumn. High temperatures average in the mid-80s in July and August and in the low 40s

in January and February. Average low temperatures range from the mid- to upper 60s in summer to the mid-20s in winter. The annual precipitation of 45 inches is fairly evenly distributed throughout the year. Snowfall averages 16 inches annually.

Dollar Pier, Steeplechase Pier, Central Pier, Steel Pier and others became the glittering jewels in the crown of the "Queen of Resorts."

Atlantic City's reign declined as the automobile's increasing popularity and the introduction of air transportation freed people to travel farther from home. Age and neglect took their toll on the city until the arrival of the casinos, which became the successors to the entertainment piers. The casinos have built on—and in some ways surpassed—their predecessors' tradition of opulent entertainment.

While some of the Boardwalk's new palaces reflect the gracious past, others, such as the $1 billion Trump Taj Mahal, have razed several city blocks and erected dramatically modern commercial castles. Saltwater taffy, palm readers and rolling chairs are a few of the threads of continuity that have remained during this transition from frayed resort to glossy playground.

## Approaches
### By Car

The city's principal gateway is the Atlantic City Expressway, a superhighway that connects with nearly all major mid-Atlantic highways. In the Philadelphia-Camden metropolitan area the expressway collects I-76 traffic from central Pennsylvania; I-95 from the Washington, D.C.-Baltimore-Wilmington corridor to the southwest and Newark-New York City to the northeast; I-295 between Wilmington and Trenton; and the New Jersey Turnpike.

A few miles west of Atlantic City the expressway intersects with the Garden State Parkway, a major coastal route linking Newark to the north and, via the Cape May-Lewes ferry, Delaware and southern Maryland to the south. US 30 and US 40/322 also enter Atlantic City, arriving via Absecon Boulevard and Albany Avenue respectively. The Atlantic City Expressway is the preferred route.

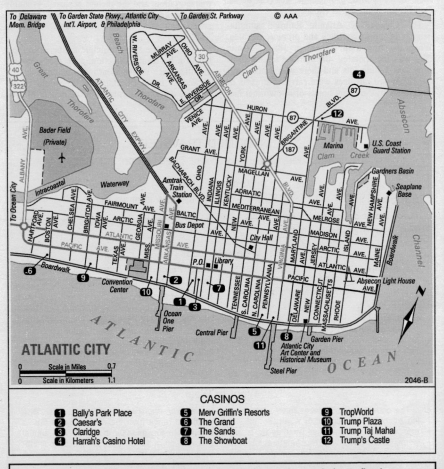

ATLANTIC CITY

| Scale in Miles | 0 | 0.7 |
| Scale in Kilometers | 0 | 1.1 |

2046-B

### CASINOS

| | | | |
|---|---|---|---|
| 1 Bally's Park Place | 5 Merv Griffin's Resorts | 9 TropWorld |
| 2 Caesar's | 6 The Grand | 10 Trump Plaza |
| 3 Claridge | 7 The Sands | 11 Trump Taj Mahal |
| 4 Harrah's Casino Hotel | 8 The Showboat | 12 Trump's Castle |

Going somewhere? AAA's already been there. Ask us first!

### By Plane, Train and Bus

The International Airport in Pomona is a 15-minute trip via the Atlantic City Expressway. Airlines serving International Airport include Northwest Airlink, (800) 225-2525, with a connection through Newark; USAir, (800) 428-4322, with a connection through Pittsburgh; and USAir Express, (800) 428-4322, with connections through Washington, New York, Philadelphia and Baltimore.

Limousine, taxi and bus service are available between the airport and downtown. Limousines are available from Custom Limousine Service, (800) 624-2374 in New Jersey, and Limo One, (800) 624-1751 in New Jersey.

Amtrak, (800) 872-7245, offers daily rail service from its station at 1 Atlantic City Expwy. to New York, Philadelphia, Pittsburgh, Baltimore and Washington, D.C., with connecting service from all over the Northeast. New Jersey Transit, 800-AC-TRAIN in southern New Jersey, also offers local rail service from the Atlantic City Rail Terminal to Absecon, Egg Harbor, Hammonton, Atco, Lindenwold, Cherry Hill and Philadelphia's 30th Street Station.

The bus terminal at Arctic and Arkansas avenues serves Greyhound Lines Inc., (800) 582-5946 in southern New Jersey, and New Jersey Transit, (609) 343-7876, which offers express service to New York and Philadelphia.

### Getting Around
#### Street System

As neatly gridlike as the Monopoly board on which some of its street names are perpetuated, Atlantic City's basic street plan is easy to comprehend. Avenues parallel to the ocean are named for oceans or seas: Arctic, Mediterranean and Baltic. Some of these change names near the inlet or "downbeach"; for example, Baltic becomes Madison at its north end and Winchester at its south.

With a few exceptions, streets perpendicular to the ocean bear the names of states in an order roughly approximating the state's geographic position. New Hampshire and Vermont are at the northeast end of the island; Indiana and Illinois are about in the middle. Why Iowa Avenue is farther south than Texas and California avenues remains a mystery.

Numbers are in blocks of 100, increasing as they progress southward from Maine Avenue and inland from the Boardwalk. The few diagonal streets are mostly extensions of the roads that lead into the city.

### Parking

Most businesses provide parking space near their premises, and casino-hotels charge a state-mandated $2 fee for parking. That fee is valid at all Atlantic City casino-hotels for one day, with the proceeds earmarked for the revitalization of Atlantic City.

Public parking lots are many and scattered throughout the city, and the Atlantic City Convention Hall at Mississippi Avenue and Boardwalk offers indoor parking. Daily rates—sometimes applied to any part of a 12-hour period—at privately owned lots range from $3 to $5 on weekdays and from $4 to $12 on weekends.

### Rental Cars

Hertz, 590 W. Delilah Rd. in Pleasantville, offers discounts to AAA members; phone (609) 646-1212 or (800) 654-3080. For listings of other agencies check the telephone directory.

### Public Transportation

The buses of New Jersey Transit operate along Atlantic and Ventnor avenues as far south as Longport. Buses can be boarded at any corner along Atlantic Avenue; minimum fare is $1.25. New Jersey Transit also has service to Brigantine, Ocean City and other New Jersey cities. Minibuses (jitneys) offer transportation 24 hours a day up and down Pacific Avenue, the length of Atlantic City.

Jitneys displaying a pink sign stay on Pacific and Ventnor avenues only, and those displaying a blue sign travel from Jackson Avenue to Pennsylvania Avenue, then across town to Harrah's Marina and Trump's Castle. Those with green signs travel from Caspian to Arkansas avenues, with stops at the bus terminal and within two blocks of the Amtrak terminal, then across town to the marina casinos. The fare for the jitneys is $1.25.

### Taxis

The major cab companies are City, (609) 345-3244; Radio, (609) 345-1105; and Yellow, (609) 344-1221. The base fare is $1.45, and the rate is 30c for each one-tenth mile. The base fare increases 30c for each additional passenger.

### What To See

**ATLANTIC CITY ART CENTER AND HISTORICAL MUSEUM,** on the boardwalk at New Jersey Ave., consists of two facilities. The museum contains exhibits depicting Atlantic City's reign as a vacation playground, Miss America memorabilia and a display saluting the Steel Pier's celebrated diving horse. The art center has rotating displays of works by local artists. Allow 1 hour minimum. Daily 10-4; closed Dec. 25. Free. Parking is available at the adjacent Showboat Casino. Phone (609) 347-5837.

**ATLANTIC CITY CONVENTION CENTER** is on the Boardwalk from Mississippi to Florida aves. The main auditorium seats 22,000 and has one of the world's largest stages; meeting rooms accommodate 150 to 5,000 people. Other attractions are a ballroom and facilities for boxing, football, baseball and exhibits.

**EDWIN B. FORSYTHE NATIONAL WILDLIFE REFUGE**—see Oceanville.

**HISTORIC RENAULT WINERY**—see Egg Harbor City.

**LUCY THE MARGATE ELEPHANT**—see Margate City.

**STORYBOOK LAND**—see Pleasantville.

**TIVOLI PIER,** in the TropWorld Casino and Entertainment Resort at Brighton Ave. and the Boardwalk, is a 2½-acre indoor theme park. Attractions include a Ferris wheel, a roller coaster and strolling entertainers. Allow 1 hour minimum. Mon.-Fri. 4-10, Sat.-Sun. 4-midnight, July-Aug.; Sat.-Sun. noon-8, Sept. 1-Jan. 1 and Feb. 13-June 30. All-inclusive admission $9.95. Show ticket $5. Phone (609) 340-4444.

## What To Do
### Gambling

Gambling in Atlantic City is confined to the casino-hotels. To qualify for a casino operation, a hotel must have a minimum of 500 rooms and meet architectural requirements, not the least of which is approval of the design by the Atlantic City Planning Board and the New Jersey Casino Control Commission. Casinos are open daily 24 hours. The minimum age for participation is 21.

Baccarat, minibaccarat, big six wheel, blackjack, craps, poker, red dog, pai gow, sic bo, roulette, slots and keno are available, making the visitor who resists the temptation to gamble even a little a rarity. It is recommended that those who accept the challenge to gamble first pick up one of the readily obtainable "how-to" books on gambling. While knowing something about the game won't alter the odds, which ultimately favor the house, it will increase the chances of breaking even or provide some understanding of why the bet was lost.

Some casinos will provide literature on the games; some even give classes for novice patrons. For first-time visitors, credit will be tight or non-existent. With further visits, once credit has been established, it will be as easy to obtain $1,000 as $10.

### Sightseeing
#### Boardwalk Tours

Atlantic City's highlight is its Boardwalk, which can be explored on foot or by bicycle. Another way of seeing the Boardwalk is in the legendary rolling chair, which resembles a huge wicker chair on wheels. Pushed by an attendant, the chairs seat up to three people. The chairs operate Sun.-Thurs. 10 a.m.-2 a.m., Fri.-Sat. 10 a.m.-5 a.m., Memorial Day to mid-Sept.; Sun.-Thurs. 10-10, Fri.-Sat. 10 a.m.-2 a.m., Feb. 1-day before Memorial Day and mid-Sept. to mid-Dec.; Sun.-Thurs. 10-10, Fri.-Sat. 10 a.m.-midnight, rest of year (10 a.m.-6 a.m. on Dec. 31).

The fare is $5 for five blocks and under, and $10 for six to 15 blocks, or $15 per half-hour and $25 per hour for two people. Phone (609) 347-7148.

### Sports and Recreation

Before gambling came to this resort, it was the sun, the ocean breezes and the breakers washing the wide sand beach that made Atlantic City a leading playground. Popular as early as the 19th century, the beach is still a major attraction. Because there is less undertow than at other beach areas, **swimming** is particularly good. **Surfing** is permitted Mon.-Fri. 6:30 a.m. to 8:30 p.m. Lifeguards are on duty from about Memorial Day to mid-September.

**Fishing** is as close as the ocean or inlet. Surf or pier fishing brings in striped bass, flounder, tautog, kingfish and snapper blues; the inlet also yields croakers and crabs. Farther out, such fighters as marlin, tuna and bonito can be caught. In general, the summer months see the heaviest runs of most species.

**Boating** can be for fun as well as for fish; the Thorofares—the network of waterways that separates Absecon and other islets from the mainland—provide a different perspective from which to view the city. Rental crafts ranging from one-person day sailers to six-person powerboats are available.

**Bicycling** is a popular pastime, particularly along the Boardwalk. Bicycle rentals, available about 6 a.m. to 10 p.m., are conveniently located along the length of the Great Wood Way.

Some large hotels provide facilities for **racquetball, squash** or **tennis;** some also have an arrangement with the club in Brigantine, (609) 266-1388, for **golf** privileges for their guests. The Showboat Hotel has an ultramodern 60-lane **bowling** center equipped with electronic scoring. Public tennis courts are on Albany Avenue at Bader Field; at N. Huntington and Fremont avenues in Margate; and at S. Suffolk and Atlantic avenues in Ventnor.

**Horse racing** takes place at the Atlantic City Race Course, 14 miles west at the junction of US 40/322. Post time is Tues.-Sat. at 7:25 p.m., early June-early September; phone (609) 641-2190.

**Note:** Policies concerning admittance of children to pari-mutuel betting facilities vary. Phone for information.

### Where To Shop

The casinos have made the Boardwalk the heart of Atlantic City and have helped to revitalize shopping along the beach. The centerpiece of this revival is Ocean One, a mall at Arkansas Avenue and the Boardwalk built on the site of the legendary Million Dollar Pier. This emporium houses restaurants and 150 shops featuring everything from designer clothes to T-shirts. More high-fashion boutiques can be found in the casinos.

The glitter of the casinos has not diminished the Boardwalk's older charms: A wide range of stores offers everything from plastic souvenirs to fine jewelry. Between these extremes you can find nearly anything you might want or need: Toys, fudge and saltwater taffy, T-shirts emblazoned while you wait, swimwear and other beach supplies are a sampling of available merchandise.

In addition to the Boardwalk and Atlantic Avenue, Pennsylvania Avenue to Albany Avenue is considered the main downtown shopping section. A downtown highlight in the 1000 block of Atlantic Avenue is Gordon's Alley—New Jersey's first shopping mall—containing more than 30 shops and restaurants.

Beyond the beach and Atlantic City are several other popular shopping areas, including the Central Square Shopping Center on US 9 in Linwood, with more than 70 specialty stores; Hamilton Mall in Mays Landing next to the Atlantic City Race Course; the New Shore Mall on the Black Horse Pike in Pleasantville; and the Towne of Historic Smithville, offering Colonial-style crafts.

## Where To Dine

Casinos dominate the restaurant scene; each of them has at least six restaurants offering a sampling of the world's cuisines. Among the culinary choices available, Caesar's and The Sands each have a Chinese restaurant; Caesar's offers Japanese fare; The Showboat and Harrah's Casino Hotel serve French dishes; TropWorld and Trump's Castle offer Italian fare; and Merv Griffin's Resorts and The Showboat offer seafood eateries.

Traditional boardwalk fare—hot dogs, pizza, fries, shaved ice—is available from the many shops found along this wooden thoroughfare. The pleasures of fast food are enhanced by a splendid view from the outdoor areas on the second and third levels of Ocean One, which has a host of restaurants.

An Atlantic City tradition is local seafood. Among the well-known purveyors of marine delicacies are Abe's Oyster House, 2031 Atlantic Ave., and Dock's Oyster House, 2405 Atlantic Ave. The White House Sub Shop, 2301 Arctic Ave., also is a local favorite.

While fare from the sea and stockyard share the menu at many restaurants, they do so in few places more widely acclaimed than the Knife and Fork Inn at Atlantic and Albany avenues. Caruso's, in The Grand, offers regional Italian cuisine in elegant surroundings.

Several notable dining spots in Atlantic City don't accept reservations, but you can phone ahead to determine the least crowded hours. A number of Atlantic City's favorite dining spots operate only during the summer and major convention periods.

## Nightlife

Although nightlife is not limited to the casino-hotels, it is in these plush, glittering establishments that the biggest names and most elaborate productions are found. Because Lady Luck smiles most kindly upon the house, the house thanks its patrons by providing some of the world's finest entertainment at quite reasonable prices.

There are two general categories of entertainment: big room and lounge. The big rooms, seating up to 1,700, present top stars in a dinner or cocktail show format; revues or production shows also are presented. Early shows begin between 6 and 8 p.m.; late shows, during which only drinks are usually available, start between 11:30 p.m. and 12:30 a.m. Some big rooms also schedule a third show after 2 a.m. on weekends.

Prices vary with the entertainment. Revues usually range from $10 to $20 per person, and celebrity headliners from $20 to $45 per person; there is sometimes a cover charge or a drink minimum. Big rooms usually require reservations, which should be made 24 to 48 hours in advance for the most popular shows. Check with the establishment regarding show times, minimums and reservation policies.

Somewhat smaller and more intimate in atmosphere are the lounges. Their offerings run the gamut from live music and dancing to jazz to moderately well-known performers with supporting acts. Cover charges or drink minimums often are in effect in the lounges; check with the establishment. Some lounges overlook the casino, adding people-watching to the entertainment list. For information about current entertainment consult the daily newspaper or the local weeklies *Whoot* and *At The Shore*.

**Note:** The mention of any area or establishment in the preceding sections is for information only and does **not** imply endorsement by AAA.

## Especially for Children

Although its glossy amusements are strictly for adults, the essential Atlantic City—sea, sun and Boardwalk—remains as much a child's province as ever. A youngster tired of walking might enjoy a ride on one of the modernized versions of the original Atlantic City rolling chair.

For more thrills, the roller coaster and Ferris wheel in TropWorld's Tivoli Pier or the rides on Central Pier are only part of the fun awaiting young and old alike. Young bowlers can pursue their sport at the bowling center at the Showboat Hotel. Not the least of attractions for a child of any age is another local specialty, saltwater taffy.

The significance of its architecture might elude children, but the idea that they can enter an elephant and emerge alive could make a visit to Lucy the Margate Elephant *(see Margate City)* an interesting diversion. Storybook Land in nearby Pleasantville *(see place listing)* features buildings, displays and rides depicting storybook characters in fanciful settings.

While children are welcome in the hotels, remember that they are not permitted in the casinos and that some of the late shows may be intended for adult audiences. Most large hotels provide entertainment centers for youngsters.

## Special Events

Shortly after Labor Day the Miss America Pageant commences with Pageant Week, during which preliminary competitions and a parade take place. The selection of a new queen from the annual parade of contenders remains the hub around which the local calendar revolves. The pageant has been considered synonymous with the community since the first competition in 1921.

In addition to the Miss America Pagaent, many other shows and events take place in the Convention Hall. Shows include the Antique and Classic Car Auction and Flea Market in mid-February and the Atlantic City Boat Show and the Antiques and Collectibles Exposition, both in mid-March. The Archery Classic is held in late April. Three arts and crafts shows are held in Brighton Park: one in mid-May, one in early July and one in early September.

Other special events in Atlantic City include the New Jersey Fresh Seafood Festival, which takes place at Gardner's Basin Maritime Park the third weekend after Memorial Day, and the National Boardwalk Professional Art Show held in mid-June.

Harborfest, which includes the World Championship Ocean Marathon Swim around Absecon Island, occurs in August. The Labor Day Weekend Festival features arts, crafts, antiques and collectibles in Brighton Park. The Indian Summer Art Show is held on the Boardwalk in September, and the Atlantic City Christmas Parade takes place in December.

## ATLANTIC HIGHLANDS (I-6) pop. 4,600, elev. 26'

SANDY HOOK LADY, an authentic 85-foot paddle-wheeler, sails along the Shrewsbury and Navesink rivers from the public pier ½ mi. e. on 1st Ave., following signs. Lunch, dinner and Sunday brunch cruises are available. Sightseeing, special theme and holiday cruises also are offered. Three-hour dinner cruises depart Wed., Fri. and Sat. at 7, Sun. at 6:30, May-Oct. Dinner cruise $35 Wed., Fri. and Sun., $45 Sat. Fares for other cruises vary. MC, VI. Reservations are recommended. Phone (908) 291-4354.

## BARNEGAT LIGHT (E-4) pop. 700

Barnegat Light, the northernmost community on Long Beach Island, was settled by Scandinavian fishermen. Fishing, particularly for tuna, and summertime diversions sustain this town and others on the island. Whalers first came to the isle in the early 18th century. Fishermen, sea captains and pilots followed, establishing such other towns as Ship Bottom and Harvey Cedars.

Because the area around Loveladies Harbor has a scenic appeal likened to that of Cape Cod, the town, named for an 18th-century landowner, has become a well-known art colony. The Beach Havens are popular resort communities at the southern end of the island.

Long Beach Island is an 18-mile-long segment of the barrier isles that outline the New Jersey coast. Its width ranges from about three blocks to 1 mile. A long causeway carries SR 72 across Manahawkin Bay to Ship Bottom.

BARNEGAT LIGHTHOUSE STATE PARK, on the n. tip of Long Beach Island, is 31 acres of parkland surrounding historic Barnegat Lighthouse. Picnic facilities are available, but fires are not permitted. Daily dawn-dusk. Free. Phone (609) 494-2016. See Recreation Chart.

Barnegat Lighthouse, known as the "Grand Old Champion of the Tides," was built 1857-58 by Gen. George G. Meade after the original structure, built in 1834, toppled into the water. The lighthouse, which rises 172 feet above the tides, marks Barnegat Shoals, the scene of more than 200 shipwrecks. A fine view is available from the top of the lighthouse, 217 steps above the base.

Daily 10-4:30, Memorial Day-Labor Day; Sat.-Sun. 10-4:30, May 1-day before Memorial Day and day after Labor Day-Oct. 31. Admission $1, under 12 free.

## BASKING RIDGE (H-4) elev. 357'

Animals coming from the surrounding swampland to sun themselves on a hillside inspired the name Basking Ridge. More than 10,000 years ago most of the area to the east was part of Lake Passaic, created when the terminal accumulation of earth and stone carried by the Wisconsin Glacier blocked the Passaic River. The remaining portion of the former lake—now a wetland containing many plant and animal habitats—is known as the "Great Swamp" of New Jersey.

GREAT SWAMP NATIONAL WILDLIFE REFUGE is e. from N. Maple Ave. on Madisonville Rd. to Long Hill Rd. The 7,355-acre refuge, rescued by residents from being turned into an airport, preserves the marsh and swamp woodland habitat of muskrats, foxes, fish, wildfowls and 223 bird species. A wildlife observation center features a boardwalk trail into the swampy area; interpretive displays and blinds for observing wildlife also are available.

The swamp's habitats contain more than 8 miles of hiking trails. Center open Mon.-Fri. 8-4:30. Trails open daily dawn-dusk. Free. Phone (201) 425-1222.

SOMERSET COUNTY PARK COMMISSION'S ENVIRONMENTAL EDUCATION CENTER is in Lord Stirling Park, 3 mi. s. from I-287 on S. Maple Ave., then 1 mi. e. to 190 Lord Stirling Rd. The center is on a 427-acre tract that is part of the Great Swamp Basin. The interpretive building, said to be the country's first solar-heated and cooled public building, offers an environmental library, exhibit areas and natural science programs.

River, pond, marsh, swamp, field and woodland habitats support native wildlife, which can be seen from 8½ miles of nature trails and boardwalks. Observation towers, blinds and a special-use trail also are available. Allow 1 hour, 30 minutes minimum. Center open daily 9-5; closed holidays. Trails open daily dawn-dusk. Free. Phone (908) 766-2489.

## BATSTO (F-3)

**BATSTO HISTORIC VILLAGE,** on CR 542, is part of the Wharton State Forest's *(see Recreation Chart)* 109,328 acres in the Pine Barrens. Established in 1766, Batsto became a prominent iron foundry and was of great military importance to the Patriots' cause during the Revolution. The village's prosperity grew after the war; its ironworks, brickyard, gristmill, sawmill and glassworks provided livelihoods for nearly 1,000 people.

Batsto's fortunes dwindled as competition from cheap Pennsylvania coal forced the town's more expensive charcoal-fired furnaces to close in 1848. The town became a virtual ghost town and almost disappeared when fire consumed half its buildings in 1874. Two years later Joseph Wharton, the wealthy Philadelphia financier, bought Batsto and the surrounding 100,000 acres.

Wharton planned to buy all of the Pine Barrens in a scheme to divert all the area's water into a reservoir for use by Philadelphia, which desperately needed clean water. The state legislature foiled this scheme, and Wharton contented himself with renovating some of the village's remaining buildings. After his death in 1909 the area languished until concerned citizens urged the state to establish a state forest in 1954.

Batsto Village includes the restored ironmaster's mansion, sawmill, gristmill and furnace site. Guided tours of the mansion are available. Stagecoach tours are given Memorial Day-Labor Day; inquire at the visitor center for times.

Allow a full day. Grounds open daily dawn-dusk. Buildings open daily 10-4, Memorial Day-Labor Day; otherwise varies. Guided tours are

## The Pine Barrens

If most people don't know about New Jersey's Pine Barrens, it could be because the 450,000 year-round residents of this national reserve that overlies more than a million acres of the state's bottom half, prefer to keep a good thing to themselves. Wedged between the roar of traffic along the New Jersey Turnpike and the Garden State Parkway, this quiet wilderness shows little evidence of the human settlement and enterprise that have occurred. Yet the Pines are far from barren.

The area's heart is a tapestry of impenetrable scrub and pitch pine, rivers, swamps and bogs where rebelling Colonials mined iron to make cannonballs. Villages, foundries and glassworks churned out the region's products until the late 1800s, after which the forest resumed full reign. Local residents, affectionately called the "Pineys," learned to "work the woods" by selling its seasonal gifts and tending its cranberry and blueberry crops. Cranberries have been commercially raised in the Pine Barrens since about 1835, while the first commercial blueberry planting was made in 1916. The Pine Barrens account for approximately 25 percent of the state's agricultural income.

Many recreational opportunities exist in the Pine Barrens. Boating, canoeing, swimming, fishing and hunting are popular activities. Hikers can enjoy the Batona Trail, a marked wilderness trail that traverses the Pine Barrens, or explore old abandoned towns and the restored Batsto Village. More than 1,000 known sites in the vicinity show that man lived in this area as early as 10,000 B.C.

Left undisturbed are the woodland's wonders: a confusing tangle of sand roads cut during Colonial times, 12,000 acres of stunted pygmy pines in an area called the Plains, insectivorous plants, exotic orchids, ventriloquist tree frogs found almost nowhere else and a legendary winged creature known as the "Jersey Devil."

The muck soil in the Pine Barrens produces monobactum, a microorganism expected to revolutionize the antibiotics industry. An aquifer inside the Pine's deep sand beds holds 17 trillion gallons of water with the purity of glacial ice. The water in this shallow aquifer usually is at or near the surface, producing bogs, marshes and swamps. A maze of serpentine streams fed by the aquifer, stained the color of tea by cedar sap, rises within the low dome of land on which the Pines exist. With development encroaching on all sides, the Pines' uniqueness becomes more apparent each year—except to local residents, who have always known it.

offered daily 10-3:30. Guided tours $3; ages 6-11, $1. Stagecoach rides $1. Parking $5 Sat.-Sun. and holidays, Memorial Day-Labor Day. Phone (609) 561-3262.

## BAY HEAD (E-5) pop. 1,200

The earliest inhabitants of this Barnegat Beach Island community were Lenni Lenape Indians who took refuge here during the stormy winter months. The area remained basically rural and remote until the 1870s when David Mount, a Princeton banker, and two fellow bankers formed the Bay Head Land Co. Soon after, the area's farms, woods and cranberry bogs were developed into a beachside community.

With the advent of rail transportation and then automobiles, the town became a popular summer resort, cultivating a refined atmosphere that still remains. Art is honored in Bay Head during spring and summer. The first weekend in April the town celebrates Art Appreciation Weekend, as shops, inns and restaurants turn into art galleries. In mid-June "Art in the Park" is held in Centennial Park.

## BEEMERVILLE (A-3) elev. 760'

SPACE FARMS ZOO AND MUSEUM is just n. on CR 519, w. of Sussex. The 100-acre preserve is home to bears, bobcats, otters and many other species of North American wildlife; exotic animals, birds and reptiles also can be seen. The museum displays such Americana as antique automobiles and horse-drawn vehicles. Picnic facilities are available. Daily 9-5, May-Oct. Admission $8; ages 3-12, $3.50. Phone (201) 875-5800.

## BRIDGETON (F-2) pop. 18,900, elev. 60'

Bridgeton mingles its New England atmosphere and the architecture of past centuries with the advancements and automation of the present. Quakers settled this area in the late 1600s and within 50 years constructed the bridge across Cohansey Creek that would lend the town its name.

The 19th century saw the growth of Bridgeton, by then the seat of Cumberland County, and the establishment of a woolen mill, a nail factory and an ironworks. As the residents prospered, they constructed the many Colonial, Federal and Victorian buildings that remain. Reminders of early Bridgeton still crowd its historic district, which has more than 2,200 period homes and commercial buildings.

Bridgeton hosts a number of annual events, including a Folk Festival in June and a Seafood Festival the last Sunday in July. The Bridgeton Invitational Semi-Pro Baseball Tournament is a 2-week event held in early August. Labor Day is celebrated with a Victorian Fair, and a Holiday Open House Tour takes place the Sunday prior to Thanksgiving. For additional information contact the Bridgeton Chamber of Commerce, P.O. Box 100, Commerce & Laurel Streets, Bridgeton, NJ 08302; phone (609) 455-1312.

**Self-guiding tours:** Brochures outlining self-guiding tours past period homes on Bridgeton's historic east and west sides are available at the Bridgeton/Cumberland Tourist Center, 50 E. Broad St., Bridgeton, NJ 08302; phone (609) 451-4802. Audiocassettes that complement the brochures are available for a small fee.

**Shopping areas:** Cohansey Crossing on West Commerce Street is a row of restored Victorian buildings containing a variety of shops. Dutch Neck Village, an enclave of antique and craft shops 1 mile southwest of town, also evokes the past.

BRIDGETON CITY PARK, W. Commerce St. and Mayor Aitken Dr., encompasses 1,100 acres and has facilities for boating, fishing and swimming as well as a zoo and a recreation center. Also on the grounds are the Nail Mill Museum, a diverse collection of memorabilia and items related to local history, and the New Sweden Farmstead Museum, a reproduction of 17th-century buildings typical of the area's early Swedish settlement.

Park open daily dawn-dusk. Nail Mill Museum open Tues.-Fri. 10:30-3:30, Sat.-Sun. 11-4, Apr.-Dec. New Sweden Farmstead Museum open weekends in summer. Free. Phone (609) 455-3230.

Cohanzick Zoo focuses on wildlife native to New Jersey and also contains primate and feline groups. Daily dawn-dusk. Free. Parking $1. Phone (609) 455-3230.

WOODRUFF INDIAN MUSEUM, in the Bridgeton City Library at 150 E. Commerce St., includes 20,000 American Indian relics collected within a 30-mile radius of Bridgeton. Many of the stone and organic implements, though found locally, were brought into the area during tribal meetings, migrations or warfare.

Arrowheads, gravers and knives date from 10,000 to 8000 B.C.; more recent artifacts such as the ceramic pipes of the Lenni Lenape Indians date from A.D. 700 to 1800. Big game hunting as well as the archaic and woodland periods are represented. Mon.-Sat. 1-4, Sept.-May; Mon.-Fri. 1-4, Sat. 10-3, rest of year. Free. Phone (609) 451-2620.

## BRIGANTINE (F-4) pop. 11,400

MARINE MAMMAL STRANDING CENTER, just s. of the lighthouse at 3625 Brigantine Blvd., is devoted to the rescue and rehabilitation of stranded or distressed marine mammals that come ashore along the New Jersey coast. Whales, dolphins, seals and sea turtles are among the mammals the center has assisted. Displays are offered at the Sea Life Educational Center, and rescued sea animals may be observed in observation tanks.

Allow 30 minutes minimum. Daily 11-5, Memorial Day-Labor Day; Sat.-Sun. noon-4, rest of year. Donations. Phone (609) 266-0538.

## BURLINGTON (D-4) pop. 9,800, elev. 13'

One of the first permanent settlements in the western part of the colony, Burlington was established by members of the Society of Friends in 1677. It became the capital of West Jersey and shared that status with Perth Amboy after East and West Jersey united. Its location on the Delaware River between Trenton and Camden made the flourishing port so prosperous that its inhabitants—mainly Quaker settlers and pacifists—were relatively uninvolved with the Revolution.

Still a busy manufacturing and distribution community, Burlington retains much evidence of its past. Though there has been some modernizing of facades, many buildings stand out as having been built in Colonial times.

Among those that are open by appointment are the 1703 Old St. Mary's Church, Broad and Wood streets; the 1685 Revell House, 200 block of Wood Street; the 1784 Friends Meeting House, High Street near Broad Street; the John Hoskins House, 202 High St.; and the 1792 Friend's School, York and Penn streets.

For additional area information contact the Greater Burlington Chamber of Commerce, P.O. Box 67, Burlington, NJ 08016; phone (609) 387-0963.

**CAPT. JAMES LAWRENCE HOUSE,** 459 High St., is the birthplace of the American naval hero of the War of 1812. As commander of the USS *Chesapeake* when it suffered a beating from the HMS *Shannon,* the mortally wounded Lawrence issued his famous last command, "Don't give up the ship." The house, refurbished to the period during which Lawrence lived, also contains costumes and toys. Guided tours are available. Mon.-Thurs. 1-4, Sun. 2-4; closed holidays. Donations. Phone (609) 386-4773.

**JAMES FENIMORE COOPER HOUSE,** 457 High St., is the birthplace of the author of the "Leatherstocking Tales," novels about American frontiersmen and American Indians. "The Last of the Mohicans" and "The Deerslayer" are among the best known of this series, written 1826-41. The 1780 Cooper House has four museum rooms and also serves as the headquarters of the Burlington County Historical Society.

Among the displays are bedroom furnishings that belonged to Joseph Bonaparte, successively king of Naples and of Spain, who settled nearby after his brother's defeat at Waterloo. Also in the complex are the historical society's museum and the Corson Poley Center, which houses the society's meeting room as well as the Delia Biddle Pugh Library. The library contains materials on genealogy and local history. Guided tours are available.

Complex open Mon.-Thurs. 1-4, Sun. 2-4; closed holidays. Donations. Phone (609) 386-4773.

**BARD-HOW HOUSE,** 453 High St., was built in 1740. Period furnishings, clocks and other accessories decorate the restored house. Guided tours are conducted. Open Mon.-Thurs. 1-4, Sun. 2-4; closed holidays. Donations. Phone (609) 386-4773.

## CALDWELL (G-5) pop. 7,500, elev. 411'

**GROVER CLEVELAND BIRTHPLACE STATE HISTORIC SITE,** 207 Bloomfield Ave., is the house in which the 22nd and 24th president of the United States was born in 1837. He lived in the house until 1841. Restored by the state, it contains many of his possessions. Allow 2 hours minimum. Wed.-Sat. 9-noon and 1-5, Sun. 1-5; closed holidays and periodically without notice. Free. Phone (201) 226-1810.

## CAMDEN (E-2) pop. 87,500, elev. 25'

The industrial and transportation center of southern New Jersey, Camden began in the 1680s as the site of William Cooper's ferryboat operation on the Delaware River. Becoming the terminus for the Camden & Amboy Railroad in 1834 marked the beginning of the city's real growth. Part of the industrial growth was based on Camden's farm produce.

The deep, broad Delaware provides an excellent port. Shipbuilding boomed during World Wars I and II. The first nuclear-powered merchant ship, the *Savannah,* was built in Camden. Electronic communications, printing and publishing are other major area industries.

Poet Walt Whitman, whose unfettered, subjective style had revolutionized poetic expression in the mid-19th century, lived his last years in Camden. The tomb of the "good gray poet" is in Harleigh Cemetery on Haddon Avenue.

**CAMDEN COUNTY HISTORICAL SOCIETY** is on Park Blvd. at Euclid Ave.; from US 130 take Haddon Ave. w. to Euclid Ave. The society's museum contains period furniture, antique glass, toys, fire-fighting equipment, 18th- and 19th-century newspapers and an original Victor Talking Machine.

The brick Georgian home, Pomona Hall, built in 1726 and extensively enlarged in 1788 by descendants of William Cooper, is on the grounds and is furnished in period. The society's library has maps and other historical and genealogical data. Mon.-Thurs. 12:30-4:30, Sat. 1-4, Sun. 2-4, Sept.-July; closed holidays. Admission $2, under 16 free. Library $1. Phone (609) 964-3333.

**CAMPBELL MUSEUM** is at the Campbell Soup Co. on Campbell Pl., just off US 30. The museum presents more than 250 soup tureens, bowls, ladles and related utensils from 24 countries. Pieces date from 500 B.C., with most coming from 18th- and 19th-century European royal households. The tureens exhibit a wide range of designs and imaginative uses of different materials; a film is shown by appointment. Allow 1 hour minimum. Mon.-Fri. 9-4:30; closed holidays. Free. Phone (609) 342-6440.

**THOMAS H. KEAN NEW JERSEY STATE AQUARIUM AT CAMDEN** is on the banks of the Delaware River, 1¼ mi. w. of I-676 exit 5A to Riverside Dr. via Mickle Blvd. The aquarium features a 760,000-gallon tank containing a submerged shipwreck and more than 400 fish representing 40 species. The facility includes a dome that changes color with the weather, an outdoor trout stream, a seal tank, an aquatic nursery and interactive exhibits designed to educate and entertain. Food is available.

Allow 2 hours minimum. Daily 9:30-5:30, Mar. 16-Sept. 14 (also Sun. 5:30-8:30, Apr. 1-Labor Day); Wed.-Sun. 10-5, rest of year. Closed Jan. 1, Thanksgiving and Dec. 25. Admission $9.95; over 64 and students with ID $8.45; ages 2-12, $6.95. AE, DS, MC, VI ($14). Parking $5-$8, depending on facility. **Discount.** Phone (609) 365-3300, or (800) 922-NJSA for ticket reservations.

**CAPE MAY (G-2)** pop. 4,700, elev. 16′

Explorer Cornelius Jacobsen Mey, sent by the Dutch East India Company to explore the coast, found the climate "charming" and lent his name to the shore area. The gingerbread of Victorian architecture is a recurrent theme in Cape May; the prevalence of well-preserved late 19th-century structures resulted in the community being designated a national historic landmark.

Representative of this architectural style is the Emlen Physick Estate, 1048 Washington St., designed in 1879 by noted architect Frank Furness (**discount**). The Pink House on Perry Street also typifies the ornate "wedding cake" style.

At the southeasternmost tip of the state, Cape May is one of the oldest seashore resorts on the Atlantic Coast. During the first half of the 19th century it rivaled Newport as a favored summer retreat for Philadelphia and New York socialites. Presidents Buchanan, Grant, Harrison and Pierce were among the luminaries who vacationed at the resort. An earlier, less extolled visitor was pirate Captain Kidd, who filled his water casks near Lily Pond.

In addition to the pleasures of the beach and the amusements of the promenade, Cape May offers good boating and fishing. Various craft can be rented for fishing in the ocean or in Delaware Bay. Rockhounds pursue their interest also, for the tide-worn quartz pebbles known as "Cape May Diamonds" can be found on the beach at nearby Cape May Point and along the lower Delaware Bay.

During the Tulip Festival held in late April, Cape May celebrates its Dutch heritage with dancing, banjo music and crafts. The city hosts the Cape May Music Festival from May 14 through June 15 and the Cape May Summer Theater Festival from June through September. Period homes provide the perfect backdrop for the Victorian Week festival beginning Columbus Day weekend; for 10 days Cape May's Victorian architecture, heritage and customs are celebrated. For information on special events and concerts contact the Cape May Department of Civic Affairs; phone (609) 884-9565.

At Cape May Point State Park *(see Recreation Chart)*, a mile southwest of Sunset Boulevard, is the historic Cape May Point Lighthouse, erected in 1859. Visitors can climb the spiral staircase to the watchroom for a panoramic view of the ocean and bay. The state park is one of three places adjacent to Cape May Bird Observatory in nearby Cape May Point that offers prime bird watching areas. Higbee's Beach Wildlife Management Area and Cape May Migratory Bird Refuge also provide observation points.

Cape May can be explored on several tours offered daily spring through fall and on a reduced schedule the rest of the year. Trolley tours of the historic district depart from the Washington Street Mall information booth; for schedule phone (609) 884-5404.

Carriage tours and guided walking tours also start at the Washington Street Mall information booth. Tickets for special evening house tours can be purchased at the Physick Estate; the Cape May County Art League is on the estate and offers exhibits, classes and workshops. Christmas in Cape May is filled with tours and special holiday events.

For details on these and other tours contact the Mid-Atlantic Center for the Arts, P.O. Box 340, 1048 Washington St., Cape May, NJ 08204; phone (609) 884-5404 or (800) 275-4278. The Cape May Welcome Center, 405 Lafayette St., Cape May, NJ 08225, also dispenses information daily 9-5; phone (609) 884-9562.

The Cape May-Lewes ferry runs between Cape May and Lewes, Del. Its terminal is on US 9, 3 miles west of the southern terminus of the

Garden State Parkway. For schedule information write P.O. Box 827, North Cape May, NJ 08204. Phone (609) 886-2718 or (800) 64-FERRY *(see ad)*.

**Self-guiding tours:** The Washington Street Mall information booth provides brochures outlining a walking tour of Cape May's historic sites.

**CAPE MAY SUNSET DINNER & DOLPHIN CRUISE,** departing from the dock at the foot of Washington St., offers dinner cruises of the inner harbor and intracoastal waterway. Passengers can enjoy a seafood buffet as they watch the setting sun. Dolphins frolicking around the boat may also be seen. Allow 3 hours minimum. Cruise departs daily at 6 p.m., Apr.-Nov. Fare $27.95; ages 3-11, $19.50. DS, MC, VI. Reservations are required. Phone (609) 898-0999 or (800) WHALES-3.

**HISTORIC COLD SPRING VILLAGE,** 3 mi. n. off Garden State Pkwy. exit 4A at 720 US 9, represents a 19th-century southern New Jersey farm village. The complex's 20 restored buildings include working craftsmen offering demonstrations, a country store and farm animals. Narrated horse and buggy tours of the grounds are available for $3. Free twilight concerts are available on Saturday night between July 4 and Labor Day.

Allow 3 hours minimum. Daily 10-4:30, mid-June through Labor Day; Sat.-Sun. 10-4:30, Memorial Day to mid-June and day after Labor Day-Columbus Day. Admission $3.50; over 62, $3; ages 5-14, $1. Phone (609) 898-2300.

**THE SCHOONER** *YANKEE,* 1 mi. e. on CR 621 (Ocean Dr.) from s. terminus of Garden State Pkwy. to Ocean Hwy. Dock, offers 2-, 2½- and 3-hour harbor, Intracoastal Waterway and ocean cruises aboard an 80-foot schooner. The 3-hour afternoon cruise allows visitors to assist in setting sails and manning the helm or to simply relax and enjoy the ocean breezes. Sightings of dolphins or whales are possible on this cruise. Refreshments are included on afternoon cruises.

Cruises depart daily at 10, 2 and 6, Memorial Day-Sept. 30. Fare for a.m. cruise $20; under 13, $10. Fare for p.m. cruises $25; under 13, $18. MC, VI. **Discount.** Reservations are recommended. Phone (609) 884-1919 or 886-9003.

**CAPE MAY COURT HOUSE (G-2)**
**pop. 3,600, elev. 18'**

The county seat, Cape May Court House is a good place to begin a tour of the Victorian and historic homes throughout Cape May County. An information center at Crest Haven Road and the Garden State Parkway offers orientation material daily 9-5, Memorial Day to mid-Oct.; Mon.-Fri. 9-4:30, rest of year. Phone (609) 465-7181.

★**CAPE MAY COUNTY PARK AND ZOO,** 707 SR 9N, houses nearly 250 species of animals including bobcats, leopards, tigers, monkeys, foxes, prairie dogs, lions, giraffes, zebras, black bucks, oryxes, deer, reptiles and exotic birds. Many of the creatures on display, such as the golden lion tamarin from Brazil, are members of rare or endangered species. In addition to the zoo the park encompasses grassy sport fields, tennis and basketball courts, a nature trail, a gazebo and a small lake with a fountain. Picnicking is permitted. Food is available.

Park open daily 9-dusk. Zoo daily 9-5. Closed Dec. 25. Donations. Phone (609) 465-5271. *See Recreation Chart.*

**HISTORICAL MUSEUM,** ¾ mi. n. on US 9, is in the John Holmes House. Its collections of local American Indian artifacts, whaling implements, glass, costumes, ship models and other antiquities, as well as genealogical material, provide a survey of life in early Cape May County.

Allow 1 hour, 30 minutes minimum. Mon.-Sat. 10-4, mid-June to mid-Sept.; Tues.-Sat. 10-4, Apr. 1 to mid-June and mid-Sept. through Dec. 31. Last tour begins 1 hour before closing. Closed holidays. Admission $2; under 12, 50c. Phone (609) 465-3535.

**LEAMING'S RUN GARDENS AND COLONIAL FARM,** ½ mi. w. of Garden State Pkwy. exit 13, then 1 mi. n. on US 9, offers 25 gardens, each with its own theme, as well as a reconstructed Colonial farm. A winding path leads visitors through 30 acres of seasonal gardens. The farm's one-room log cabin depicts 17th-century life and the animals and crops it supported. Allow 2 hours minimum. Daily 9:30-5, May 15-Oct. 20. Admission $5; ages 6-12, $1. Phone (609) 465-5871.

**CHESTER (B-3) pop. 1,200, elev. 860'**

**COOPER MILL** is on SR 24 in Black River Park, 1 mi. w. of jct. US 206. The mill, used for grinding flour in the 1760s, served as a gristmill until closing in 1913; the present building dates to 1826. The restored Cooper Mill represents a typical gristmill of the 1880s. Four sets of grinding

stones once produced 1,600 pounds of whole wheat flour and corn meal per hour. Two sets of millstones continue to operate. Tours are conducted on a continuous basis.

Allow 30 minutes minimum. Fri.-Tues. 10-5, July-Aug.; Sat.-Sun. 10-5, May-June and Sept.-Oct. Last tour begins 1 hour before closing. Closed holidays except Memorial Day. Donations. Phone (908) 879-5463.

## CLEMENTON (E-3) pop. 5,600, elev. 96'

**CLEMENTON AMUSEMENT PARK & SPLASH WORLD WATER PARK,** ¾ mi. w. of US 30 on White Horse Ave., is set on the shore of a small lake. The amusement park has rides, carnival games and a children's section with a petting zoo. Three water slides are the attraction at the water park. Bathing suits must be worn at the water park; lockers and changing facilities are available. Picnicking is permitted. Food is available.

Daily noon-10, June 24-Labor Day; Thurs.-Sun. noon-10, May 6-June 23. Water park closes at 8 p.m. Admission to either park $11.50; over 64, $10.35. After 5, $8.50; over 64, $7.65. Under 2 free. Combination ticket $16.50; over 64, $14.85. After 5, $13.50; over 64, $12.15. DS, MC, VI. Phone (609) 783-0263.

## CLINTON (C-4) pop. 2,100, elev. 184'

Clinton, a prominent milling town and stagecoach stop in the mid-1800s, presents a pleasing picture with its dam, waterfall and mill structures. Nearby Spruce Run and Round Valley state parks *(see Recreation Chart)* offer recreation.

**CLINTON HISTORICAL MUSEUM** is ½ mi. n.w. of the Clinton-Pittstown exit off I-78 at 56 Main St. The 10-acre park is highlighted by the Old Red Mill, built in 1810. Its three floors of displays depict early regional life, agriculture and industries. Other buildings include a blacksmith shop, general store, log cabin and schoolhouse.

Recalling the area's former limestone quarrying industry which converted limestone from the surrounding cliffs into fertilizer are a stone crusher/sorter, old lime kilns and machinery sheds. Outdoor concerts are presented Saturday in the summer. Allow 1 hour minimum. Tues.-Sun. 10-4, Apr.-Oct. Admission $3; over 65, $1.50; ages 6-16, $1. Phone (908) 735-4101.

**HUNTERDON ART CENTER** is in the center of town on the south branch of the Raritan River at 7 Lower Center St. Housed in a restored grain mill, the center displays works by contemporary New Jersey artists. Also offered are educational programs and musical performances. A Children's Art Festival in late September features do-it-yourself art for young hands.

Allow 1 hour, 30 minutes minimum. Wed.-Sun. 11-5; closed major holidays. Admission $2.50; over 65, $1.50; ages 6-16, $1; family rate $6. Phone (908) 735-8415.

## DELAWARE WATER GAP NATIONAL RECREATION AREA (A-2)

Popular with artists and wealthy vacationers during the late 1800s, the Delaware Water Gap is a picturesque break in the Kittatinny Ridge of the Appalachian Mountains. The gap is threaded by the Delaware River, which runs the entire length of the recreation area. The wooded Tammany and Minsi mountains rise abruptly about 1,200 feet above the river, which is about 60 feet deep at the gap.

The park encompasses 70,000 acres in both New Jersey and Pennsylvania along a 35-mile stretch of the Delaware River. Over 200 miles of scenic roads meander through the valleys and ridges of the park. Trails, wildlife and waterfalls can be viewed along the way. A 25-mile portion of the Appalachian Trail winds its way along the Kittatinny Ridge in New Jersey. Camping, swimming, boating and winter activities such as snowmobiling, cross-country skiing and ice skating are popular pastimes.

During the summer, park naturalists conduct several recreational and interpretive programs on both the New Jersey and Pennsylvania sides of the recreation area. Free guided canoe trips are available by reservation—visitors must provide their own canoes; phone (717) 828-7802.

Millbrook Village, 12 miles north of the Kittatinny Point Visitor Center along Old Mine Road, is a re-created rural community featuring shops, residences and other buildings of the late 19th century. Interpreters in period dress demonstrate rural lifestyles. Millbrook Days, an annual folk festival, is held the first weekend in October. The village is open daily 9-5, mid-June to mid-Oct.; Sat.-Sun. 9-5, May 1 to mid-June. Phone (908) 841-9520.

Peters Valley, 8 miles northwest of Branchville via US 521, then south on CR 615, has several historic buildings that have been converted into studios for artisans. Craftsworkers can be observed in their studios Fri.-Sun. 2-5, June-Aug.; phone (201) 948-5200.

In Pennsylvania at Slateford Farm, 3 miles south of I-80 via US 611, following signs, is one of the state's early slate quarries. The farmhouse is open Sat.-Sun. noon-5, mid-June through Labor Day.

Trails of various lengths meander through the park. Camping by hikers is permitted only along the Appalachian Trail in areas more than a half-mile from road accesses. Open fires are prohibited.

The Kittatinny Point Visitor Center, on I-80 near the toll bridge that crosses the Delaware River into Pennsylvania, has exhibits, audio-visual programs and literature about the recreation area. It is open daily 9-5, May 1-Nov. 1; Sat.-Sun. 9-4:30, rest of year. Phone (908) 496-4458.

Dingmans Falls Visitor Center, 1 mile west of US 209 near Dingmans Ferry, Pa., offers an audiovisual program, nature exhibits and nature walks and is open daily 9-5, May 1-Nov. 1; phone (717) 828-7802. In the summer lifeguards are on duty at Smithfield Beach and Milford Beach, Pa.

The park headquarters, 1 mile east of US 209 near Bushkill, Pa., on River Road, is open Mon.-Fri. 8-4:30; closed holidays. Phone (717) 588-2435. *See Recreation Chart.*

## EGG HARBOR CITY (F-3) pop. 4,600

The hallmark of Egg Harbor City is neither eggs nor a harbor, but acres of vineyards. The 1858 discovery that the soil was conducive to growing wine grapes brought German vintners to the area, and the town prospered. A second boom ensued as Italian growers arrived after the Civil War. Some of the vineyards are operated by the original families. For additional area information contact the Egg Harbor City Chamber of Commerce, P.O. Box 129, Egg Harbor City, NJ 08215; phone (609) 965-1091.

**HISTORIC RENAULT WINERY,** n. of US 30 on Breman Ave., was established in 1864. Tours and wine tastings are offered. Food is available. Mon.-Sat. 10-5, Sun. noon-5; closed Jan. 1 and Dec. 25. Tours $1, under 18 free. Phone (609) 965-2111.

## ELIZABETH (H-5) pop. 110,000, elev. 29'

As part of the great industrial, densely populated urban area associated with New York City, Elizabeth and the adjoining sections of Union County are home to more than 1,500 manufacturing concerns. The city's marine terminal is one of the largest container ports in the world. It was here that John Philip Holland assembled the first successful submarine, later purchased by the U.S. Navy. The school that ultimately would become Princeton University was founded in this city by Jonathan Dickinson in 1746 as the College of New Jersey.

Elizabeth was the home of Alexander Hamilton and Aaron Burr, both of whom attended the old academy on the site now occupied by the First Presbyterian Church parish house. Other historic figures from Elizabeth include James Caldwell, the fiery "Fighting Parson" of the Revolution; William Livingston, who as governor of New Jersey 1776-90, lived at Liberty Hall, now known as Ursino; and Gen. Winfield Scott, the 1852 Whig presidential candidate.

Although the city suffered many attacks and skirmishes during the Revolution, nearly two dozen pre-Revolutionary buildings remain. Identified by plaques, several of these are in the 1000 and 1100 blocks of East Jersey Street; the Bonnell House, at 1045, dates from about 1682 and is one of the oldest structures in Elizabeth.

Several parks offer respite from business, commerce and history. One of the largest is

Warinanco Park at the west edge of town on Rahway Avenue. In addition to recreation, it offers a stadium and the Chatfield Memorial Garden, adorned by flowering trees, shrubs and other seasonal displays.

For additional information contact the Union County Chamber of Commerce, 135 Jefferson Ave., P.O. Box 300, Elizabeth, NJ 07207-0300; phone (908) 352-0900.

**BOXWOOD HALL STATE HISTORIC SITE** is at 1073 E. Jersey St. A noted resident was Elias Boudinot, a president of the Continental Congress and signer of the Treaty of Peace with Great Britain. The house, also known as Boudinot Mansion, was built in the 1750s. George Washington was entertained in the mansion on April 23, 1789, en route to his presidential inauguration in New York City. Wed.-Sat. 10-noon and 1-6, Sun. 1-6; closed major holidays. Free. Phone (201) 648-4540.

## FAR HILLS (C-5) pop. 700, elev. 166'

On the western fringe of the northeastern New Jersey metropolitan complex, Far Hills developed as the center of a rolling region of grand estates where the wealthy engaged in farming and fox hunting. Recent years have seen a number of these estates converted into institutions and corporate headquarters.

**GOLF HOUSE—U.S. GOLF ASSOCIATION,** 2 mi. e. of US 202 on CR 512, has a library and museum with paintings, memorabilia and exhibits tracing the history of golf. The house is a three-story Georgian mansion that was the heart of the 60-acre W.J. Sloane estate. Allow 1 hour minimum. Mon.-Fri. 9-5, Sat.-Sun. 10-4; closed Jan. 1, Easter, Thanksgiving and Dec. 25. Free. Phone (908) 234-2300.

**LEONARD J. BUCK GARDEN** is on Layton Rd., 1 mi. s.e. of US 202 via Liberty Corner Rd. This 33-acre garden contains a network of wooded trails connecting a series of naturalistic gardens blended with natural rock outcroppings. Each area presents selections of alpine and woodland plants. Highlights include extensive collections of ferns and wildflowers; the peak blooming season is April through May. Picnicking is not permitted.

Allow 1 hour minimum. Mon.-Sat. 10-4, Sun. noon-5, Mar.-Nov.; closed federal holidays. Admission $1. Phone (908) 234-2677.

## FARMINGDALE (C-5) pop. 1,500, elev. 72'

**ALLAIRE STATE PARK** is 1½ mi. w. of Garden State Pkwy. exit 98. Within the 3,040-acre park is the historic Howell Works, the site of a bog ore furnace and forge where iron was smelted in the late 1800s. The smelter was constructed and operated by industrialist and inventor James P. Allaire.

Allaire Village was built in 1822 as a company town for employees of the ironworks.

Among the many buildings in the village are blacksmith and carpenter shops, houses, an enameling furnace, a community church, bakery, carriage house and general store. A visitor center provides brochures with maps of the village.

The narrow-gauge Pine Creek Railroad displays six antique trains, two of which offer continuous 10-minute rides.

Allow a full day. Park open daily 8-dusk. Visitor center open Wed.-Sun. 10-5, Memorial Day-Labor Day; Sat.-Sun. 10-4, day after Labor Day-Oct. 31. Buildings open Wed.-Sun. 10-4, Memorial Day-Labor Day; Sat.-Sun. 10-4, day after Labor Day-Oct. 31. Train rides daily noon-4:30, July-Aug.; Sat.-Sun. noon-4:30, May-June and Sept.-Oct. Building tours $1.50. Train $1.50. Parking $3 Sat.-Sun. and holidays, Memorial Day-Labor Day. Phone (908) 938-2371. *See Recreation Chart.*

## FLEMINGTON (C-4) pop. 4,000, elev. 183'

Already a prosperous distribution point for the region's agricultural products, Flemington became widely known in the early 20th century for the manufacture of pottery and cut glass; one glass company continues to operate. A different kind of notoriety came to town in 1935 when the much-publicized Lindbergh kidnapping trial was held in the county courthouse.

One of the area's highlights is the seven-story Volendam Windmill, about 21 miles northwest via SR 12 and CR 519 to Adamic Hill Road in Milford. With sail arms spanning 68 feet from tip to tip, this operating Holland-style windmill is an unusual sight. The first three floors of the windmill can be toured May through October.

Flemington hosts the New Jersey State Agricultural Fair each year from late August to early September.

**Shopping areas:** Liberty Village features specialty shops and outlet stores housed in Colonial-style buildings on the site of an old railroad turntable.

THE BLACK RIVER & WESTERN RAILROAD offers 11-mile round trips between Ringoes and Flemington. The steam-engine-drawn train departs Flemington every 1½ hours Sat.-Sun. and holidays 11:30-4, Easter to mid-Dec. (also Mon.-Fri. 11:30-2:30, July-Aug.). Fare $6; ages 4-12, $3. Phone (908) 782-9600.

## FLORHAM PARK (G-4) pop. 8,500

The name Florham Park was derived from the first names of millionaire Hamilton Twombly and his wife, Florence; the "Park" was added in honor of Dr. Leslie D. Ward's estate, Brooklake Park.

The College of St. Elizabeth, a Catholic liberal arts college for women founded in 1899, is said to be the oldest women's college in the state. The 420-acre campus is partially in the town of Convent Station. Shared by the town of Madison, the Florham-Madison campus of Fairleigh Dickinson University occupies 187 acres on the site of the former Twombly estate. Tours of the campus are available by appointment through the Admissions Office; phone (201) 593-8900.

The Little Red Schoolhouse, Ridgedale Avenue and Columbia Turnpike, was built in 1866 and used as a school until 1914. Now a museum operated by the Florham Park Historical Society, the schoolhouse is open Sun. 2-4, Sept.-June. The Twombly Mansion, begun in 1893 and completed in 1896, serves as an administration building at Fairleigh Dickinson University. The 100-room manor house is a replica of one wing of Hampton Court in England.

Florham Park provides the summer training grounds for the New York Giants professional football team. The practice sessions, which are held at Fairleigh Dickinson University, are open to the public; parking is available at the Park Avenue lot. The Hamilton Park Conference Center, 175 Park Ave., is the home of the New Jersey Stars, a professional tennis team; phone (201) 377-2424.

## FORKED RIVER (E-4) pop. 4,200, elev. 13'

JERSEY CENTRAL POWER & LIGHT ENERGY SPECTRUM, on US 9 1 mi. s. of Lacey Rd. at Gate 2 of the Oyster Creek Power Plant, features participatory displays, exhibits and computer games related to energy resources. Visitors can generate their own power; learn how heating and cooling systems work; meet Lacey, the talking light bulb; and see what types of power the future will bring. Allow 1 hour minimum. Tues.-Fri. 10-3:30, Sat. 10-5; closed major holidays. Free. Phone (609) 971-2100.

POPCORN PARK ZOO, on Lacey Rd. 7 mi. w. of Garden State Pkwy. exit 74, provides a haven for more than 200 wild, domestic and exotic animals no longer able to exist in their natural habitats. Visitors are greeted by friendly geese, goats and deer who often serve as escorts through the zoo. A Bengal tiger, lions, black bears, foxes, bulls and a macaw live in comfortable compounds. Many animals roam freely, and petting and feeding are encouraged. Picnicking is permitted.

Allow 1 hour, 30 minutes minimum. Daily 11-5, May-Sept.; 1-5, rest of year. Admission $3; over 65 and ages 1-11, $2. Phone (609) 693-1900.

## FORT LEE (G-6) pop. 32,000, elev. 141'

In one of her endless succession of perils, Pauline clings to the sheer cliff above the river; the Sheik perpetrates an incendiary love scene in a silken tent. These great moments on the silver screen were filmed not in Hollywood but in Fort Lee, movie capital from 1907 until the mid-1920s. At the peak of activity before World War I, seven studios and 21 companies produced the silent films that revolutionized entertainment around the world.

The convenient and dramatic location on the Hudson River palisades that made Fort Lee the first movie capital had some 130 years earlier made it a critical point in Gen. George Washington's unsuccessful attempt to stem the tide of British forces.

Fort Lee has matured into a residential suburb of New York City, to which it is connected by the George Washington Bridge. The bridge also serves as the southern terminus of the Palisades Interstate Parkway, a scenic section of highway that skirts the Hudson River and continues north into New York. For additional area information contact the Greater Fort Lee Chamber of Commerce, 2357 Lemoine Ave., Fort Lee, NJ 07024; phone (201) 944-7575.

**FORT LEE HISTORIC PARK,** on Hudson Terr. s. of the George Washington Bridge, is in Palisades Interstate Park. Fort Lee was built in 1776 by Washington's troops as a major link in fortifications defending New York and the Hudson River against British warships.

However, Gen. Charles Cornwallis and more than 5,000 seasoned soldiers crossed the river 5 miles north of the fort. To avoid entrapment and capture, Washington led his demoralized army on a hasty retreat across the Delaware River during the winter of 1776-77. These were the days later described by Thomas Paine as the "times that try men's souls."

Reconstructed cannon batteries, a rifle parapet and a firing step overlook the river and the Manhattan skyline beyond. A visitor center offers a 12-minute film hourly; lighted displays depict the campaign. Exhibits include models, miniature scenes and pictures accompanied by descriptive text. Wed.-Sun. 10-5, Mar.-Dec. Free. Parking $3, Apr.-Oct. Phone (201) 461-1776.

## FORT MONMOUTH (C-6)

Fort Monmouth began in 1917 as the Signal Corps Camp—a cluster of tents on a small portion of the present installation. The camp has evolved into the home of the U.S. Army Communications and Electronics Command headquarters, one of the largest military and technological centers devoted to developing, supplying and overseeing the communications and automatic data processing systems used by U.S. troops worldwide.

**U.S. ARMY COMMUNICATIONS-ELECTRONICS MUSEUM,** in Kaplan Hall on the Avenue of Memories, displays systems used by the U.S. Army for communication, from its earliest developments to current technology. Included are exhibits on the Army Pigeon Service from World War I, radios developed by early radio pioneer Edwin Armstrong and radar and satellite dishes. Mon.-Fri. noon-4. Free. Phone (908) 532-4390.

**FRANKLIN (B-3) pop. 5,000, elev. 554'**

Rockhounds swarming over the old mine dumps at Franklin are often amply rewarded, for nearly 300 different minerals are found in the town. Zinc, however, was the reason for Franklin's development. For nearly a century, until the ore body was depleted in the 1950s, the New Jersey Zinc Co. mined 500,000 tons of ore annually.

**FRANKLIN MINERAL MUSEUM,** on Evans St. ½ mi. n.w. of jct. SR 23 and SR 94 spur, has samples of the minerals mined from the area. In the Fluorescent Room ores and minerals are displayed under ultraviolet light, producing brilliant, fluorescent colors; an adjacent mine replica demonstrates zinc mining. Dinosaur footprints and fossils from around the world also are on display. Visitors can prospect at a nearby site which operates during museum hours.

Allow 1 hour minimum. Mon.-Sat. 10-4, Sun. 12:30-4:30, Mar. 1-Dec. 1; closed Easter and Thanksgiving. Museum $4, students $2. Prospecting $4, students $2. Combination rate for museum and prospecting $7, students $3. MC, VI. Phone (201) 827-3481.

**FREEHOLD (C-6) pop. 10,700, elev. 180'**

The Battle of Monmouth occurred in Freehold on June 28, 1778, when Gen. George Washington's army overtook Sir Henry Clinton's army as it retreated from Philadelphia. During this battle Molly Pitcher—so called because she brought water to the battlefield for the soldiers—helped to keep her husband's cannon in action when he was overcome by the 100-degree heat.

Just before the battle Clinton used the home of farmer William Covenhoven as his headquarters; the house at 150 W. Main St. dates from the early 1750s and contains period furnishings. In addition to maintaining its Revolutionary period associations, modern Freehold is a glass and food products manufacturing center.

Entertainment includes harness racing at the Freehold Raceway, US 9 and SR 33, during most of the year. Outdoor recreation is available at nearby Turkey Swamp County Park (see Recreation Chart). For additional area information contact the Western Monmouth Chamber of Commerce, 49 E. Main St., Freehold, NJ 07728; phone (908) 462-3030.

**MONMOUTH BATTLEFIELD STATE PARK,** 3 mi. w. on SR 33, was the scene of one of the largest and longest Revolutionary battles, fought on June 28, 1778.

British troops under Sir Henry Clinton stopped at Freehold before proceeding to Sandy Hook, where ships were waiting to carry them to New York. Before they could leave, Gen. George Washington led his troops from Valley Forge into a head-on collision with the British. The American troops, trained by Maj. Gen. Friedrich Von Steuben, matched British regulars in pitched battles for the first time.

The park visitor center features interpretive displays that trace the troops' movements during the battle. On the park grounds is the Craig House, built in 1710 and restored to its 18th-century appearance. The British used the house as a field hospital during the battle. Owl Haven, on CR 522 in the park, is a nature center with live animals.

Park open daily 8-dusk. Visitor center open daily 9-5, Memorial Day-Labor Day; 9-4, rest of year. Owl Haven open Tues.-Sun. 1:30-4:30. Craig House open Wed. and Sun. 12:30-4:30, Apr. 23-Nov. 20. Free. Phone (908) 462-9616.

**MONMOUTH COUNTY HISTORICAL ASSOCIATION MUSEUM AND LIBRARY** is at 70 Court St. Collections of furniture, paintings and decorative arts, most of which were owned or made in New Jersey, occupy two floors. Highlights include English and Chinese ceramics, folk art, toys and items pertaining to local history.

The research library contains collections on genealogy and regional history, including books and other printed materials, photographs, glass plate negatives, personal manuscripts as well as church and business records and early Monmouth County newspapers.

Museum open Tues.-Sat. 10-4, Sun. 1-4. Library open Wed.-Sat. 10-4. Both closed Jan. 1, July 4, Thanksgiving and Dec. 24-25. Admission $2; senior citizens $1.50; ages 6-18, $1. Phone (908) 462-1466.

## GATEWAY NATIONAL RECREATION AREA (I-6)

Gateway National Recreation Area, so named because it is at the entrance to the great New York-New Jersey estuary, consists of the Breezy Point, Jamaica Bay and Staten Island units in New York and the Sandy Hook Unit in New Jersey. The recreation area was created by Congress in 1972 to reclaim the parkland's ocean beaches, dunes, wooded uplands and bays from the effects of urbanization, which had decimated the region's bird, fish and animal populations.

Among the numbers of replenished wildlife are more than 300 species of birds that frequent the Jamaica Bay Wildlife Refuge and Sandy Hook Unit along the Atlantic flyway.

**SANDY HOOK UNIT,** entered by bridge from SR 36 at Highlands, is a barrier beach peninsula extending into the mouth of New York Harbor. First sighted by the crew of Henry Hudson's *Half Moon* in 1609, the hook was a favorite fishing and clamming ground of the Lenni Lenape Indians. It was later the estate of Richard Hartshorne, an English Quaker. During the Revolution the site was occupied by British troops as part of their defense of New York City.

Fort Hancock, built 1896-99, is still largely intact, as are the gun emplacements that defended the entrance to New York Harbor during the Spanish-American War and World Wars I and II. Also present are the remains of the Sandy Hook Proving Ground, where new U.S. Army ammunition and weapons were tested 1874-1919.

The Sandy Hook Lighthouse, one of the oldest in the nation, has operated since 1764. Because many shipwrecks occurred despite New Jersey's lighthouses, the first station of the U.S. Life Saving Service was established at Sandy Hook in 1849.

Sandy Hook presents a variety of natural environments unusual in so compact an area. A forest of large holly trees, a dune area supporting some of the beach plums sought by the American Indians, a salt marsh, mudflats and the seashore—each with its individual ecosystem—are available for exploration.

The peninsula's ocean beaches provide opportunities for swimming and surf fishing. A visitor center at Spermaceti Cove is open daily 10-5. The Sandy Hook ranger station is staffed 24 hours a day. The Sandy Hook Unit charges a $4 parking fee Mon.-Fri., $5 Sat.-Sun. and holidays, Memorial Day weekend-Labor Day. *See Recreation Chart.*

**Sandy Hook Museum** is housed in an 1899 building that served as the post guardhouse, or jail. The museum features the original jail cells, photographs that depict the history of Fort Hancock and dioramas of the fort's buildings. Daily 1-5, July-Aug.; Sat.-Sun. 1-5, rest of year. Free. Phone (908) 872-0115.

## GREENWICH (F-1) pop. 900

**GIBBON HOUSE,** on Ye Greate St., was built in 1730 by wealthy merchant Nicholas Gibbon and is patterned after a London townhouse. The house is furnished with 18th- and 19th-century items, including locally made rush-seated "Ware" chairs. Events held on the grounds include a craft show the first week in October, an antique show in November and an open house tour the first week in December. Open Tues.-Sat. noon-4, Sun. 2-5, Apr.-Nov. Donations. Phone (609) 455-4055.

## HACKENSACK (G-6) pop. 37,000, elev. 11'

Remembering where their journeys had begun, the Manhattan Dutchmen who crossed the Hudson to establish a trading post on a lesser river about 4 miles west called their site New Barbados. For 274 years the name, as well as the architecture of some buildings and institutions, retained the Dutch stamp. Not until 1921, in an act that traded euphony for a city charter, did New Barbados become Hackensack, an American Indian term meaning "place of sharp ground."

Because the village was on the road that linked Manhattan and its bastion at Fort Lee *(see place listing)* with the Passaic River, it was a strategic point during the Revolution. Gen. George Washington and his troops stopped in the village after evacuating Fort Lee. Throughout the war intrigue and skirmishes were common. In 1780 a plundering party of Hessians and Britons burned the New Barbados courthouse.

The Green at the south end of Main Street was the core of New Barbados. It contained in one small area the courthouse for government and justice, the pillories for punishment and the Church on the Green for absolution. Built at the Green's northeast corner in 1696 and reconstructed several times since, the church is one of the oldest in the state. Its Dutch Colonial architecture served as a prototype for several churches in the area.

A major 20th-century project in the vicinity was the draining of the tidal marshes known as the Meadowlands south of Hackensack in nearby East Rutherford.

The resulting Meadowlands Sports Complex includes Giants Stadium, home of both the Giants and Jets of the National Football League; Brendan Byrne Arena, home court of the National Basketball Association's New Jersey Nets; and Meadowlands Racetrack, which features both thoroughbred and harness racing. With a combined seating capacity of 135,000, the complex is located at the intersection of exit 16W of the New Jersey Turnpike and SR 3.

To obtain additional area information contact the Hackensack Chamber of Commerce, 140 Main St., Hackensack, NJ 07601; phone (201) 489-3700.

**STEUBEN HOUSE STATE HISTORIC SITE** (Ackerman-Zabriskie-Steuben House) is at 1209 Main St., n. of SR 4 on the Hackensack River in River Edge. The 1713 house was Gen. George Washington's headquarters in 1780.

Presented to Maj. Gen. Friedrich von Steuben by the state in gratitude for his services to the Continental Army, the house now displays the museum collection of the Bergen County Historical Society as well as 1650-1850 Jersey Dutch furnishings. Wed.-Sat. 10-noon and 1-5, Sun. 2-5; closed Jan. 1, Thanksgiving and Dec. 25. Free. Phone (201) 487-1739.

**SUBMARINE USS *LING* NEW JERSEY NAVAL MUSEUM,** 150 River St. at Court St., is a memorial to those who served aboard U.S. submarines during World War II. The museum includes a pictorial history of the development of the submarine from 1900 to the nuclear age, uniforms, medals, a two-man periscope and models of Navy vessels and aircraft. Allow 1 hour minimum. Tours Wed.-Sun. 10:15-4. Admission $3; ages 3-11, $2. **Discount.** Phone (201) 342-3268.

## HADDONFIELD (E-2) pop. 11,600, elev. 74'

Elizabeth Haddon was sent from England by her sonless father in 1701 to develop 550 acres southeast of Camden. In less than a year the Quaker girl had built a house, begun the colony

and proposed marriage to Quaker missionary John Estaugh—he accepted. The romance is the theme of "The Theologian's Tale" in Henry Wadsworth Longfellow's "Tales of a Wayside Inn."

**INDIAN KING TAVERN HOUSE MUSEUM,** 1½ blks. n. of Haddon Ave. at 233 Kings Hwy., was built about 1750 and was for many years an important social, political and military center along the historic Kings Highway. The three-story structure is furnished in period and contains historical relics, including items once owned by former first lady Dolly Madison. Allow 30 minutes minimum. Wed.-Sat. 9-noon and 1-4, Sun. 1-4; closed Jan. 1, Thanksgiving and Dec. 25. Free. Phone (609) 429-6792.

## HALEDON (F-5) pop. 7,000

During the 1913 Paterson Silk strike, Haledon achieved a certain notoriety when its socialist mayor allowed strikers to meet in co-worker Pietro Botto's home. Thousands gathered, unmolested by the Paterson authorities, to hear labor organizer William "Big Bill" Haywood and writers John Reed and Upton Sinclair. Although the workers' demands were not immediately met, the Paterson Silk strike was a major turning point in the history of unionized labor.

**AMERICAN LABOR MUSEUM/BOTTO HOUSE NATIONAL LANDMARK,** 83 Norwood St., occupies the 1908 Botto House, which was the home of an Italian immigrant weaver. The first floor contains period rooms, while the second floor houses changing exhibits that illustrate the history of the labor movement in the United States and the lifestyle of immigrant workers and their families. An exhibit on the Paterson Silk strike in 1913 is in the library.

Allow 1 hour, 30 minutes minimum. Wed.-Sat. 1-4; closed holidays except Labor Day. Admission $1.50, under 12 free. Phone (201) 595-7953.

## HAMILTON (C-5) pop. 86,600, elev. 191'

Hamilton, in the southern part of Mercer County, is next to the Trenton metropolitan area. Dedicated to area residents who served in the U.S. Armed Forces, 320-acre Veterans' Park contains almost 7 miles of bicycle and walking trails, a measured jogging course and a boardwalk as well as lighted ballfields and game courts, tennis courts and playground and picnic areas.

Camp Olden, a Civil War re-enactment, is held in the park the first week in August; for further information phone (609) 581-4129. In early September, Hamilton hosts Septemberfest in the Park. Contact the Hamilton Township Recreation Department for further information; phone (609) 890-3684.

**KUSER FARM MANSION AND PARK,** 390 Newkirk Ave., is the restored 22-acre estate of prominent businessman Fred Kuser. The Kuser family was instrumental in forming the Fox Film Corp., later to become 20th Century Fox. A private projection and viewing room are among the 22 rooms open in the mansion, which was built in 1892 by German craftsmen. The house is furnished with original and period pieces.

The family also manufactured the Mercer Motor Car in Hamilton; Mercer-related items are on display in the mansion. A self-guiding walking tour visits the formal garden, tennis house, windmill, gazebo and other outbuildings. Free concerts are held in summer. Picnic and playground facilities are available. A Victorian Christmas open house is a yearly feature.

Allow 1 hour minimum. Thurs.-Sun. 11-3, May-Nov.; Sat.-Sun. 11-3, Feb.-Apr. Last tour begins at 2:30. Free. Phone (609) 890-3630.

## HAMPTON (C-2) pop. 1,500

**TOWNSHIP OF LEBANON MUSEUM** is 7 mi. n. of I-78 off SR 31 at 57 Musconetcong River Rd. This Greek Revival structure was built in 1823 as a one-room schoolhouse; a second story was added in the 1870s. The first floor is a re-created schoolroom with period furnishings. The second floor displays changing exhibits. Tues. and Thurs. 9:30-5, Sat. 1-5; closed holidays. Free. Phone (908) 537-6464.

## HIGHLANDS (I-6) pop. 4,800

Summer vacationers and anglers are the backbone of the economy of Highlands, connected by bridge to the Sandy Hook Unit of the Gateway National Recreation Area (see place listing). With neighboring Highlands Beach and Atlantic Highlands, the town takes its name from the hills that rise abruptly from the shore.

Nearby 266-foot Mount Mitchill is one of the first points of land sighted by ships bound for New York Harbor. Ocean Boulevard, a scenic drive off SR 36, connects Highlands to Atlantic Highlands. The Highlands hills provided the setting for James Fenimore Cooper's 1831 book "The Water Witch." The title of the novel referred to the hero's vessel, which hid among the coves of Sandy Hook.

**TWIN LIGHTS STATE HISTORIC SITE,** Lighthouse Rd. off Highland Ave., is a twin-towered 1862 lighthouse that replaced a structure built in 1828. The museum contains exhibits about the lighthouse and the development of the U.S. Life Saving Service. Visitors can climb the north tower. Allow 2 hours minimum. Grounds open daily 9-dusk. North tower and museum open Wed.-Sun. 10-5. Closed Jan. 1, Thanksgiving and Dec. 25. Free. Phone (908) 872-1814.

## HOBOKEN (H-6) pop. 33,400, elev. 7'

Squeezed into little more than a square mile of land between the Hudson River and North Bergen, Hoboken is a major railroad terminal and seaport

across the river from New York City. West of the Hudson River is the Stevens Institute of Technology, founded in 1870 as an engineering academy. The college has expanded from its original location at Castle Point to include centers for science, research, management and engineering.

Pleasure and art, rather than business, were the foundation of Hoboken's early reputation. While beer gardens, fireworks and assorted cheery charlatans attracted throngs to the city's River Walk, the pretty countryside drew such literary, artistic and society figures as John Jacob Astor, Washington Irving and William Cullen Bryant. A prominent Hoboken native was John Stevens, who built the country's first steam locomotive in 1824.

## HOLMDEL (C-5) pop. 11,500, elev. 101'

The tree-shaded village of Holmdel is one of the oldest communities in Monmouth County, having been settled by the Holmes family in the mid-1600s. The Holmes-Henrickson House, built by William Holmes about 1754, still stands at Longstreet and Roberts roads and is a fine example of local Dutch building traditions. Visitors can see the house from May through October; phone (908) 462-1466.

**GARDEN STATE ARTS CENTER,** off the Garden State Pkwy. exit 116 at Telegraph Hill Park, contains a 5,300-seat amphitheater in a landscaped setting and a park with picnic sites and nature trails. An additional 4,500 can be seated on the lawn area. Popular and classical musical performances are offered May through September, and ethnic heritage festivals are held in the spring and fall. Phone (908) 442-9200.

## HOPE (B-2) pop. 1,700, elev. 415'

"Jenny, jump!" Apparently the little girl did, foiling the Indians whom her father had spotted sneaking up on her. No one knows the true story, but the warning cry is commemorated in the name of the mountain that rises above Hope. The village was founded in 1774 by Moravians from Bethlehem, Pa. They built a sturdy, self-sustaining community, with homes, a church, a public inn, mills, a brewery and a distillery.

Several of the structures remain, their stone walls contrasting with newer concrete buildings. The Moravians' position as conscientious objectors during the Revolution did not endear them to the Patriot forces, but they won respect by their care for sick or wounded soldiers. The colony—or the few who had survived a smallpox epidemic—returned to Pennsylvania in 1808.

**Self-guiding tours:** Brochures outlining a walking tour past Hope's Moravian architecture can be obtained at stores and banks throughout town and at the Municipal Building Clerk's Office on Great Meadows Road (CR 611), Mon.-Fri. 9-1; phone (908) 459-5011.

**LAND OF MAKE BELIEVE,** ¾ mi. s. on CR 611 off I-80 exit 12, is an amusement and water park oriented to children under 13 that offers rides, shows and attractions in addition to play areas and water activities. Features include Pirates Cove, a life-size pirate ship with slides; an enchanted Christmas Village; an 1862 train; a World War II airplane cockpit; hayrides; a roller coaster; and "Old McDonald's Farm." Picnicking is available.

Daily 10-5, mid-June through Labor Day; Sat.-Sun. 10-6, Memorial Day weekend to mid-June; Sun. 10-6, day after Labor Day-Sept. 30. Ages 2-12, $11.50; over 12 and ages 18 months-2 years, $9.50; over 61, $8.50. Phone (908) 459-5100. *See ad.*

### JACKSON (D-5) pop. 33,200

A township at the northern fringes of the Pine Barrens, Jackson is sustained by dairying, small farming and cranberry growing. The Jackson Forest Nursery is off CR 527-528. Prospertown Lake, a wildlife management area west on CR 537, offers hunting and fishing.

SIX FLAGS GREAT ADVENTURE is about 1 mi. s. of I-195 off CR 537. It features a 350-acre drive-through safari containing 1,500 animals from six continents and a theme park with approximately 100 rides, shows and attractions in areas such as Fantasy Forest, Boardwalk, Frontier Adventures and Movietown. Other highlights include a water ride section and a children's area that offers rides and activities for youngsters under 54 inches tall.

Allow a full day. Theme park opens daily at 10, mid-May through Labor Day; otherwise varies. Closing times vary between 6 and 11 p.m. Safari open daily 9-4, mid-May through Labor Day; otherwise varies. Safari and theme park $32, under 54 inches tall $20, under age 3 free. Safari only, $11. AE, DS, MC, VI. Parking $5. **Discount.** Phone (908) 928-1821.

### JERSEY CITY (H-6) pop. 228,500, elev. 180'

Jersey City is a major manufacturing and transportation center on a peninsula in the Hudson River west of Manhattan Island. Each year more than $1.3 billion in steel, chemicals, soaps, perfumes, elevators and a myriad of other products pour from approximately 600 industrial plants. Completion of the Hudson River railroad tunnels in 1910 cemented the city's position as the transportation and distribution heart of the New York-New Jersey megalopolis.

The peninsula, Paulus Hook, was first settled by the Dutch about 1630, but less-than-friendly relations with the American Indians postponed the establishment of the first permanent settlement at Bergen until 1660. Gradually the Hook became a strategic link between New York and cities to the west and south. As such it played an important role in the American Revolution; it was the 1779 site of the Battle of Paulus Hook.

Urban revitalization has rescued such architectural treasures as the brownstone houses in which the city's rich and powerful lived during the late 19th and early 20th centuries. The Hamilton Park area boasts a number of these restored homes. For additional area information contact the Hudson County Chamber of Commerce, 574 Summit Ave. #404, Jersey City, NJ 07306; phone (201) 653-7400.

COLGATE CLOCK, 105 Hudson St., faces the bay. The dial is 50 feet in diameter; the minute hand weighs 2,200 pounds and moves 23 inches every minute.

★LIBERTY SCIENCE CENTER, 251 Phillip St. in Liberty State Park, presents more than 250 interactive exhibits, theater shows and displays on four levels. An 11-ton geodesic dome houses an OMNIMAX® theater, and a tower capped with a glass observation deck provides views of the Manhattan skyline. Exhibits are divided into three categories—Environment, Health and Invention—each with its own floor.

The Environment floor features salt marsh displays, a Bug Zoo and an interactive theater where audiences decide the environmental outcome. On the Health level, visitors can navigate a darkened Touch Tunnel using their tactile sense, enter a 3-D theater and view a hologram display. The Invention floor provides opportunities to create your own animation or build structures with the aid of a 10-foot-tall electromagnetic crane. Scientific demonstrations are presented throughout the day. Under 12 must be with an adult. Food is available.

Allow 6 hours minimum. Sun.-Wed. 9:30-6, Thurs.-Sat. 9:30-8:30, June 24-Labor Day; Fri.-Sun. and Mon. holidays 9:30-6:30, Tues.-Thurs. 9:30-5:30, day after Labor Day-day before Memorial Day; Mon.-Thurs. 9:30-5:30, Fri.-Sun. 9:30-6:30, rest of year. Closed Jan. 1, Jan. 3-6, Thanksgiving and Dec. 25. OMNIMAX® shows begin on the hour.

Exhibit admission $9; over 62 and ages 13-17, $8; ages 2-12, $6. OMNIMAX® admission $7;

over 62 and ages 13-17, $6; under 12, $5. Combination ticket $13; over 62 and ages 13-17, $11; ages 2-12, $9. AE, DS, MC, VI. Parking $4. Tickets should be reserved at least 2 days prior to visiting. For reservations and information phone (201) 200-1000.

**LIBERTY STATE PARK,** off exit 14B of the New Jersey Tpke. extension, is a 1,114-acre urban-based park facing Liberty Island, site of the Statue of Liberty, and Ellis Island, the nation's immigration center for several decades. The park, which has a view of the New York City skyline, has a picnic area, playground and free summer concerts. The historic Central Railroad Terminal, from which early settlers departed, also is in the park.

The toll ferry *Miss Freedom* makes daily trips to the Statue of Liberty and Ellis Island. Park open daily 6 a.m.-10 p.m., Apr.-Oct.; 8-8, rest of year. Ferry operates daily 9-5, Memorial Day-Labor Day; 9:30-3:30, rest of year. Closed Dec. 25. Park free. Ferry $6; senior citizens $5; ages 3-17, $3. Parking $3. Phone (201) 915-3400 or 915-3401. *See Recreation Chart.*

★**STATUE OF LIBERTY NATIONAL MONUMENT,** Upper New York Bay, on Liberty Island, is reached by boats operating from Liberty State Park and the Battery, New York City. The statue was presented to the United States by France in 1884 in commemoration of the two countries' alliance during the American Revolution.

Measuring 151 feet high and standing on a pedestal 156 feet high, it is the tallest statue of modern times. The American Museum of Immigration, in the base, traces the history of immigration to the United States. Monument and museum open daily. Free. Phone (212) 363-3200, (201) 915-3400 or 915-3401.

## LAKEHURST (E-4) pop. 3,100, elev. 72′

Surrounded by fish and wildlife management areas, Lakehurst is best known for its role in aviation history. The community served as the American terminal for the huge, transatlantic lighter-than-air craft during the 1920s and 1930s. The naval air station at Lakehurst was home to the German dirigibles Graf Zeppelin and Hindenburg. In 1937 the Hindenburg burned in the air while landing, resulting in the loss of 36 lives. Hangar #1 is a reminder of that era.

The event is commemorated by a small monument on the Naval Air Engineering Station grounds. An area is outlined that approximates the size of the gondola of the airship. Self-guiding tours of the area outside the hangar are available; for information phone (908) 323-2620.

## LAMBERTVILLE (C-4) pop. 3,900

**HOWELL LIVING HISTORY FARM,** 2 mi. s. via SR 29 and 2 mi. e. on Valley Rd., is a restoration of an early 1900s farm. This 126-acre homestead presents a portrait of the period, with farmworkers tilling the fields and tending livestock just as their ancestors did.

A self-guiding tour brochure is available at the visitor center. Saturday events ranging from ice cream socials and hayrides to ice harvests and corn planting are presented throughout the year. Tues.-Sat. 10-4, Sun. noon-4, Feb.-Nov. Free. Phone (609) 737-3299.

## LONG BRANCH (C-6) pop. 28,700, elev. 28′

One of America's first seashore resorts, Long Branch rivaled Saratoga, N.Y., in popularity during its heyday. Founded upon stiff Philadelphia moral codes in the late 18th century, the resort required that a female beachgoer be escorted to the water by a male companion. Preferring to choose their own partners, the wealthy socialites fostered a lucrative business for available young men, an enterprise that lasted until the Gay '90s.

Having relaxed its mores, Long Branch boomed, with coed beaches, gambling and other adult amusements introduced and perpetuated by the rich and famous. Such colorful personalities as Diamond Jim Brady and Lily Langtry frequented the town. Long Branch also was the preferred summer home of Presidents Ulysses S. Grant, Rutherford B. Hayes, James A. Garfield, Chester A. Arthur, Benjamin Harrison, William McKinley and Woodrow Wilson.

Long Branch offers a 2-mile boardwalk and 5 miles of oceanfront with good swimming, sunbathing and surf fishing. Seven Presidents Park, (908) 229-0924, has 33 acres along the oceanfront. Monmouth Park, just inland in Oceanport,

offers horse racing early June through early September. For additional area information contact the Greater Long Branch Chamber of Commerce, 540 Broadway, Long Branch, NJ 07740; phone (908) 222-0400.

## LYNDHURST (G-6) pop. 18,300, elev. 39′

**MEDIEVAL TIMES DINNER AND TOURNAMENT** is off New Jersey Tpke. exit 16W, w. on SR 3, then s. on SR 17 to 149 Polito Ave. In a building resembling an old European castle, visitors are treated as guests of a royal family. Serfs and wenches serve dinner during an arena performance of knights on horseback catching flags, piercing rings, throwing javelins and fighting with swords.

Allow 3 hours minimum. Wed.-Thurs. at 7:30 p.m., Fri.-Sat. at 8 p.m., Sun. at 4:30. Admission Fri.-Sat. $35.95, Sun. and Wed.-Thurs. $32.95; under 12, Fri.-Sat. $26.95, Sun. and Wed.-Thurs. $24.95. AE, DS, MC, VI.**Discount.** Reservations are suggested. Phone (201) 933-2220 or (800) 828-2945. *See ad.*

## MADISON (G-4) pop. 15,900, elev. 248′

Madison, settled about 1685, was known as Bottle Hill after a local tavern that existed in Colonial days. It was renamed for President James Madison in 1834. Tours of the Drew University and Fairleigh Dickinson University campuses can be arranged through their admissions offices; phone (201) 408-3739 for Drew University or (201) 593-8900 for Fairleigh Dickinson University.

The New Jersey Shakespeare Festival, in residence at Drew University, presents Shakespearean works as well as classical and modern plays from late June to late December. For additional information contact the Madison Chamber of Commerce, P.O. Box 152, Madison, NJ 07940; phone (201) 377-7830.

**MUSEUM OF EARLY TRADES AND CRAFTS,** Main St. and Green Village Rd., explains the tools and techniques of trades and crafts from the late 1600s to 1850. The museum displays implements used by cobblers, coopers, tinsmiths, wheelwrights, leather workers and others whose trades have either disappeared or been mechanized. Changing exhibits also are presented throughout the year.

Arranged in such settings as a schoolroom, Colonial kitchen and workshop, many of these tools and other items evoke the lifestyles of early New Jersey settlers. Tues.-Sat. 10-4, Sun. 2-5; closed Jan. 1, July 4, Labor Day, Thanksgiving and Dec. 25. Admission $2; under 13, $1. Phone (201) 377-2982.

## MARGATE CITY (G-4) pop. 8,400

**LUCY THE MARGATE ELEPHANT,** 9200 Atlantic Ave., is a building in the shape of an elephant, complete with a canopied seat—called a howdah. Six stories high and built of wood and tin, it was constructed in 1881 by real estate developer James V. Lafferty to draw prospective buyers to his holdings. It has served as a real estate office, a residence and a tavern.

Lucy can be toured daily 10-8, June 15-Labor Day; Sat.-Sun. 10-4:30, Apr. 1-June 14 and day after Labor Day-Oct. 31. Admission $2; under 12, $1. Phone (609) 823-6473.

## MENLO PARK (H-4) elev. 78′

A suburb at the fringe of the industrial metropolis, Menlo Park was less congested when Thomas Alva Edison moved to the area in 1876. For the next decade the "Wizard of Menlo Park" astonished his neighbors by conducting field experiments on an electric railway and by creating the first Christmas holiday light display in the area; he amazed the world with such innovations as the dynamo, phonograph, automatic telegraph and incandescent light bulb (*see West Orange, Edison National Historic Site*).

**THOMAS A. EDISON MEMORIAL TOWER AND MUSEUM** is ⅔ mi. w. of Garden State Pkwy. exit 131 to Christie St. On the site of Edison's laboratory is the Edison Memorial Tower, designed to incorporate the devices pioneered by the inventor. A 13-foot replica of the first incandescent

bulb tops the edifice. The museum contains some of Edison's early inventions and other memorabilia.

Allow 1 hour minimum. Tues.-Fri. 12:30-4, Sat.-Sun. 12:30-4:30, Memorial Day-Labor Day; Wed.-Fri. 12:30-4, Sat.-Sun. 12:30-4:30, rest of year. Donations. Phone (908) 549-3299.

## MIDDLETOWN (I-5) pop. 68,200, elev. 111'

A Colonial atmosphere prevails along some of Middletown's residential streets, where ancient shade trees tower over large old homes. Some 17th-century structures remain. For additional information contact the Middletown Area Chamber of Commerce, 24 Leonardville Rd., Middletown, NJ 07748-0338; phone (908) 671-3360.

**MARLPIT HALL** is at 137 Kings Hwy. Built in 1685 as a one-room Dutch cottage, the home was greatly enlarged in the English style about 1740 by John Taylor, a Tory merchant in whose family the hall remained until 1936. The restored house and collection of early furnishings reflect life in Middletown over several generations. Tues., Thurs. and Sun. 1-4, Sat. 10-4, May-Oct. Admission $2; over 64, $1.50; ages 6-18, $1. Phone (908) 462-1466.

## MILLBURN (G-5) pop. 18,600

Millburn, settled in the 1720s, evolved from a 1664 land grant by Charles II. Having acquired more than 1,500 acres in Millburn in 1877, Stewart Hartshorn, inventor of the window shade, designed a village called Short Hills. Although it probably cut into sales of his invention, Hartshorn's meandering street plan called for the preservation of as many trees as possible.

The success of Millburn's many lumber, paper, fulling, cloth and hat mills became assured with the arrival of the Morris and Essex Railroad, later the Erie-Lackawanna Railroad, which linked the town with Newark and New York City and the coal industry to the northwest.

One of the town's former mills is now the home of the Paper Mill Playhouse, New Jersey's designated state theater. This facility on Brookside Drive presents plays, musicals and children's theater Wednesday through Sunday; phone (201) 376-4343.

For additional area information contact the Millburn-Short Hills Chamber of Commerce, 56 Main St., P.O. Box 651, Millburn, NJ 07041; phone (908(201) 379-1198.

## MILLVILLE (F-2) pop. 26,000, elev. 35'

At the head of tidewater on the Maurice (MOR-ris) River, Millville began as a river port, but with the discovery of silica sand the town soon became a glass-making center. By the end of the 19th century the only American city to produce more glassware than Millville was Pittsburgh. Glass remains among the city's diversifed industries.

The region also is noted for having been the home of hunter and woodsman "Stretch" Garrison, whose alleged feats included riding sharks and porpoises up the Maurice River and raising a rooster so tall that it ate from the porch roof. Although it is suspected that his nickname resulted from what he might have done to the truth, "Stretch" remains a local folk hero.

For additional area information contact the Millville Chamber of Commerce, 13 S. High St., P.O. Box 831, Millville, NJ 08332; phone (609) 825-7000, ext. 396.

**WHEATON VILLAGE,** off Wade Blvd. following signs to 1501 Glasstown Rd., is an 88-acre recreation of a glassmaking community. Glassmaking demonstrations are given daily in the working 1888 glass factory; crafts typical of the era are demonstrated in a crafts arcade. Other features include an 1876 one-room schoolhouse, the 1880 Palermo train station, a general store, period-style shops, a children's play area, a train ride and picnic facilities.

Daily 10-5, Apr.-Dec.; Wed.-Sun. 10-5, rest of year. Closed Easter, Thanksgiving and Dec. 25. Admission $6; over 62, $5.50; ages 6-18, $3.50; family rate $12. **Discount.** Phone (609) 825-6800.

**Museum of American Glass** is the highlight of the village. Displays include more than 7,000 objects, from paperweights and Mason jars to Tiffany art glass and one of the largest bottles in the world.

## MONTCLAIR (G-5) pop. 37,700, elev. 241'

Because West Bloomfield wanted a rail link to New York City and Bloomfield did not, the former separated from the latter in 1868, renamed itself Montclair and built the railroad. The result is a prosperous suburban business center, of which very little could be purchased with the original price paid the Indians for the region— "two guns, three coats and 13 cans of rum."

For a backdrop Montclair has First Mountain, from which the British were prevented from entering the upper Passaic River Valley during the Revolution. Mountainside Park on Upper Mountain Avenue in neighboring Upper Montclair includes the Presby Iris Gardens, which usually bloom in May. For additional area information contact the Montclair Chamber of Commerce, 50 Church St., Montclair, NJ 07042; phone (201) 744-7660.

**MONTCLAIR ART MUSEUM,** Bloomfield and S. Mountain aves., houses permanent collections of American and American Indian paintings. Gallery talks, recitals and special programs also are offered. Allow 1 hour minimum. Tues.-Wed. and Fri.-Sat. 11-5, Thurs. and Sun. 1-5, Sept.-May; schedule varies, rest of year. Closed major holidays. Museum $4, senior citizens and college students with ID $3, under 12 free. Phone (201) 746-5555.

**MORRISTOWN (G-4)** pop. 16,200, elev. 404'

The Revolutionary War demanded iron, and iron it got, processed at the furnaces and forges of Morristown. Much of the powder used by the Continental Army was made at Jacob Ford's powder mill. These operations were attractive targets for the British, who made several attempts to take the town.

It was this defensibility that led Gen. George Washington to select Morristown for his army's winter quarters in 1777 and again 1779-80 *(see Morristown National Historical Park)*. The annual Winter Encampment of Washington's Army Re-enactment is held in mid-March. Elaborate Victorian homes remain in some of the oldest neighborhoods.

Those dogs wandering along Morristown's streets are not average canines, but highly trained students of the Seeing Eye Headquarters on Washington Valley Road. Started in 1929 in Nashville, the school was moved to Morristown in 1965. Tours are offered by appointment; phone (201) 539-4425.

For additional area informatioan contact the Morris County Chamber of Commerce, 10 Part Ave. at Columbia Tpke., Morristown, NJ 07960; phone (201) 539-3882.

**FOSTERFIELDS LIVING HISTORICAL FARM** is off I-287 exit 35, then w. on SR 24 (Madison Ave.) to Kahdena Rd. The farm, which represents the years 1880-1910, was purchased in 1852 by the grandson of Paul Revere. Joseph Warren Revere built The Willows, a 19th-century Gothic Revival house with a two-story veranda, steeply pitched roofs and decorative arched pillars.

The farm was named by Charles Foster, a wealthy businessman who moved to Morristown in the 1880s to farm. Visitors can explore the farm on a self-guiding tour, view exhibits, watch an introductory film and see demonstrations of late 19th-century farming practices.

Allow 1 hour, 30 minutes minimum. Grounds open Wed.-Sat. 10-5, Sun. 1-5, Apr.-Oct. House open Thurs.-Sun. 1-4, Apr.-Oct. Grounds $3 Sat.-Sun.; over 64 and ages 6-16, $2; free to all Wed.-Fri. House $4 Sat.-Sun. (includes grounds admission), $3 Thurs.-Fri.; over 64 and ages 6-16, $3 Sat.-Sun. (includes grounds admission), $2 Thurs.-Fri. Phone (201) 326-7645.

**FRELINGHUYSEN ARBORETUM** is 3 mi. e. on Morris Ave., then n. on Ridgedale Ave. and e. to 53 E. Hanover Ave., opposite the Morris County Library. Contrasts between field and woodland, naturalized plantings and formal gardens characterize the 127-acre preserve, which surrounds a historic Colonial Revival mansion that is the headquarters for the Morris County Park Commission.

Trees and shrubs are labeled. Two self-guiding trails and a braille nature trail are available; a guide book is available for $2. An education center features exhibits for all ages. Wear comfortable footwear. Pets are not permitted. Allow 1 hour, 30 minutes minimum. Visitor center Mon.-Sat. 9-4:30, Sun. noon-4:30. Grounds daily 8-dusk. Mansion closed major holidays. Donations. Phone (201) 326-7600.

**HISTORIC SPEEDWELL,** 333 Speedwell Ave., preserves part of the Speedwell Iron Works built by Stephen Vail in the early 1800s. It contains the home and factory of Vail, who in 1818 made the engine for the *Savannah,* the first steamship to cross the Atlantic. In 1837 Samuel F.B. Morse and Stephen's son Alfred conducted the first successful public demonstration of the telegraph at this location.

There are patterns for early engine parts and other items relating to the ironworks. A collection of early communications equipment traces the history of the electromagnetic telegraph. Five farm buildings and three historic homes are on the grounds. Thurs.-Fri. noon-4, Sat.-Sun. 1-5, May-Sept.; Sat.-Sun. 1-5, in Oct. Last admission 1 hour before closing. Admission $3; senior citizens $2; ages 6-16, $1. **Discount.** Phone (201) 540-0211.

**THE MORRIS MUSEUM,** 2½ mi. e. on CR 510 at Normandy Heights and Columbia rds., is one of the largest museums in the state. The galleries on natural and earth sciences include minerals, fossils and mounted and live small animals.

The museum also has exhibits on the Indians of North America, Colonial life and decorative and fine arts, as well as a 5,000-square-foot gallery that houses changing national and international exhibits. The Five Senses Gallery is designed for those under age 6. Special events are scheduled throughout the year; phone for schedule and rates.

Allow 2 hours minimum. Mon.-Sat. 10-5, Sun. 1-5; closed major holidays. Admission $4; over 60 and under 3, $2. Phone (201) 538-0454.

**★MORRISTOWN NATIONAL HISTORICAL PARK (H-4)**

Morristown National Historical Park consists of three units: Washington's Headquarters and the Historical Museum and Library, Fort Nonsense and Jockey Hollow. The first two units are in Morristown, and the last is about 5 miles southwest. Gen. George Washington selected this easily defensible site for his military headquarters and the main encampment of his Continental Army in the winter and spring of 1777 and again during the bitter winter of 1779-80.

Despite starvation, disease and mutiny, he reorganized his weary and depleted forces almost within sight of strong British lines in New York. For a time this village was the U.S. military capital. Most park buildings are open daily 9-5; closed Jan. 1, Thanksgiving and Dec. 25. Admission, paid at the Historical Museum and Library, is $2, over 61 and under 17 free. Phone (201) 539-2085.

**FORT NONSENSE**, accessible from Washington St., is the site of an earthen fort built at Washington's order in 1777 as a defense for supplies stored in the village. Built on a hill adjoining Morristown, the fort's cannons protected the town below and the main roads leading north and south. Legend has it that the fort's name derives from the intent of Washington to keep his troops busy, thus preventing idleness and desertion. Allow 1 hour minimum. Daily 9-6. Free.

**HISTORICAL MUSEUM AND LIBRARY** are at the rear of Washington's Headquarters. The museum displays material relating to the 1779-80 encampment, historical objects, documents and a collection of military weapons. The library houses some 40,000 manuscripts and more than 20,000 printed works dealing with both the Colonial and Revolutionary eras. A 20-minute film is shown every half-hour. Park headquarters are on the premises.

Allow 2 hours minimum. Museum open daily 9-5. Guided tours are given daily on the hour 10-4. Library open by appointment. Phone (201) 539-2016.

**JOCKEY HOLLOW**, 5 mi. s.w. of Morristown, contains most of the sites occupied by the Continental Army 1779-80. That "Hard Winter" proved to be one of the harshest of the 18th century. The army used the abundant timber in the area to construct log huts and provide the firewood necessary to withstand the winter. Five reconstructed soldiers' huts can be seen. The area is a wildlife sanctuary with wooded hills, streams and a variety of flowers. Several hiking trails wind through this section. A visitor center offers displays and a short film.

Allow 1 hour minimum. Grounds open daily 8-5. Visitor center and Wick House open daily 9-5, Apr.-Nov.; Wed.-Sun. 9-5, rest of year. Call to verify winter hours. Free. Phone (201) 539-2085.

**Soldier Huts** are reconstructions of lodgings on the site occupied by Continental Army troops during the 1779-80 encampment.

**Wick House** is a restored 18th-century farmhouse that was occupied by Maj. Gen. Arthur St. Clair 1779-80. The house, with its garden and buildings, reflects the life of a relatively prosperous farmer during the Revolutionary period.

**WASHINGTON'S HEADQUARTERS** (Ford Mansion), Washington Pl., was built 1772-74 for Col. Jacob Ford Jr. A Colonial house furnished in period, it has many original 18th-century pieces. During the winter of 1779-80 it was the home of Gen. and Mrs. George Washington. Allow 1 hour, 30 minutes minimum. Admittance is by guided tour leaving from the historical museum daily on the hour 10-4. Free.

## MOUNTAINSIDE (H-4) pop. 6,700

On the weekends of Memorial Day and Halloween, Mountainside plays host to the Watchung Troop Spring and Fall Horse Show held at Watchung Stables on Summit Lane in the Watchung Reservation. More than 500 competitors test their skills in jumping, formation riding and other equestrian events.

**TRAILSIDE NATURE AND SCIENCE CENTER** is n. off US 22 New Providence Rd. exit, n. on Ackerman Ave., then n. on Coles Ave. in the Watchung Reservation. The 2,000-acre preserve has a visitor center with changing exhibits on human and natural history as well as a collection of live reptiles. A museum contains taxidermy displays, fossils and a hands-on discovery room for preschoolers. The planetarium has a Nova star projector and offers shows Sunday at 2 and 3:30. Under 6 are not admitted to planetarium shows.

Park open daily dawn-dusk. Visitor center open daily 1-5. Museum open daily 1-5, Apr.-Nov.; Sat.-Sun. 1-5, rest of year. Visitor center and museum closed Jan. 1, Easter, July 4, Thanksgiving, day after Thanksgiving and Dec. 25. Donations. Planetarium shows $2.50, senior citizens $2.10. Phone (908) 789-3670.

## MOUNT HOLLY (E-3) pop. 10,600, elev. 45'

Named after a nearby 183-foot "mountain," Mount Holly is a Quaker town dating from 1676. It served as the capital of the state for 2 months in 1779. John Woolman, the Quaker abolitionist known for his 1774 "Journal," taught at the Old School House. Other historic county buildings include the 18th- and 19th-century county buildings on High Street between Garden and Union streets.

Smithville Mansion, 2 miles east in nearby Eastampton, is the Victorian home of Hezekiah B. Smith, former owner of a local foundry (**discount**). The estate also includes a building devoted to Smith's bicycles and an art gallery. Christmas and Candlelight tours are offered in December; phone (609) 265-5068.

## NETCONG (B-3) pop. 3,300, elev. 882'

**WILD WEST CITY**, ½ mi. e. of jct. US 206 and CR 607 (Lackawanna Rd.), re-creates the Old West. Visitors can experience a stagecoach ride complete with a hold-up by masked bandits; see Pony Express riders race into town; witness gunslingers in action; and view a re-enactment of the Gunfight at the O.K. Corral. Train and pony rides, a petting zoo, live entertainment and panning for gold also are available. Picnicking is permitted. Food is available.

Allow 3 hours minimum. Daily 10:30-6, mid-June through Labor Day; Sat.-Sun. and holidays 10:30-6, May 1 to mid-June and day after Labor Day through Columbus Day. Admission $6.40; ages 3-11, $5.90. AE, MC, VI. Stagecoach, pony and train rides are additional. **Discount.** Phone (201) 347-8900.

## NEWARK (H-5) pop. 275,200, elev. 225'

From two streets laid out by Puritans from Connecticut in 1666, Newark has become New Jersey's largest city and a major land, sea and air transportation center. Although manufacturing is important, Newark is increasingly concerned with commerce, government and education. Newark is headquarters for several leading insurance, banking, retail and commercial businesses as well as many federal and state agencies.

The city's midtown college complex is the home of five institutions: Rutgers University at Newark, Seton Hall Law School, the University of Medicine and Dentistry of New Jersey, the New Jersey Institute of Technology and Essex County College. The Rutgers Institute of Jazz Studies maintains an extensive collection of jazz recordings. A gallery in Rutgers' Paul Robeson Center displays changing art exhibits.

Statuary in Military Park includes the monumental "Wars of America" by Mount Rushmore sculptor Gutzon Borglum and a bust of President John F. Kennedy by Jacques Lipchitz. Eight hundred acres of county and municipal parks include Branch Brook Park, where the Newark Cherry Blossom Festival is celebrated each April amid more than 3,000 flowering trees.

Symphony Hall, 1020 Broad St., is home of the New Jersey Symphony, (800) 255-3476, and the New Jersey State Opera, (201) 623-5757. The Newark City Hall, 920 Broad St., is a fine example of Beaux Arts architecture. Dedicated in 1906, the building features a grand central staircase and a skylight. Also of interest is the section known as James Street Commons. Next to the business section and Washington Park, this 20-block area has a number of well-preserved Victorian rowhouses.

To obtain additional area information contact the Metro Newark Chamber of Commerce, One Newark Center, 22nd Floor, Newark, NJ 07102-5265; phone (201) 242-6237.

**CATHOLIC CATHEDRAL OF THE SACRED HEART** is at Clifton and Park aves. The French Gothic cathedral, comparable in size to Westminster Abbey, resembles the basilica at Rheims. Among its features are hand-carved reredos, more than 200 stained-glass windows, bronze doors and 14 bells cast in Italy. The towers are 232 feet high. Mon.-Sat. 9-9, Sun. 1-5. Donations. Phone (201) 484-4600.

**NEWARK MUSEUM**, 49 Washington St., is a four-building structure with 60,000 square feet of exhibit space. The museum has American paintings and sculpture; decorative arts including glass and ceramics from the Renaissance to the present; American Indian and African articles; one of the main collections of ancient glass in the United States; a sculpture garden; a miniature zoo; and a planetarium.

An Asian collection includes one of the largest displays of Tibetan art and objects in the Western Hemisphere. The museum garden contains a firehouse and schoolhouse. Allow 1 hour, 30 minutes minimum. Wed.-Sun. noon-5; closed Jan. 1, July 4, Thanksgiving and Dec. 25. Free. Phone (201) 596-6550.

**Ballantine House** was the mansion of brewer John H. Ballantine. The restored 1885 Victorian house contains paintings and other objects from the museum's collections and many original furnishings.

**NEWARK PUBLIC LIBRARY**, 5 Washington St. opposite Washington Park, is one of the largest public libraries in the state and a major resource center. It has large collections on the history of the city and state, fine arts, business and current affairs. Also housed in the 1901 library are more than 1 million books, pictures and periodicals. Changing exhibits are presented.

Allow 1 hour minimum. Mon.-Sat. 9-5:30 (also Tue.-Thurs. 5:30-8:30); closed state and federal holidays. Free. Phone (201) 733-7800 or 733-7784.

**NEW JERSEY HISTORICAL SOCIETY**, 230 Broadway at Taylor St., was established in 1845. The Georgian-style building houses historical collections, which include original land grants, prints and decorative arts, furniture and changing exhibits relating to New Jersey themes. Permanent exhibits include KIDS, an educational center for children that encourages interaction, and Life in Early New Jersey.

The reference and research library contains historic manuscripts, maps, documents and publications that feature scholarly and popular works. Allow 1 hour minimum. Wed.-Fri. and first and third Sat. of the month 10-4. Museum and library $3, senior citizens $2. Library $1. Phone (201) 483-3939.

## NEW BRUNSWICK (I-4) pop. 41,700, elev. 47'

Diversified industry and higher education support the busy city of New Brunswick, which originated in 1686 as a ferry crossing in a settled area known as Prigmore's Swamp. The good port and water power afforded by the Raritan River made the city one of New Jersey's major shipping and milling depots by the 1750s.

A 1770 charter resulted in the opening of Queen's College the following year in a tavern. After years of shifting locations and monetary struggles, the college took form in 1809 and was renamed Rutgers in 1825. It now occupies several campuses in the city.

Buccleuch Park, a 78-acre park at the north end of College Avenue, overlooks the Raritan River. In addition to recreational facilities, it contains a house built in 1729 by a British officer. The birthplace of Alfred Joyce Kilmer, best known for his poem "Trees," is at 17 Joyce Kilmer Ave.

**NEW JERSEY MUSEUM OF AGRICULTURE** is off US 1 on College Farm Rd., on the Cook College campus at Rutgers. The museum depicts agricultural science from the American Indian period to the present. Highlights include exhibits on everyday life in Colonial New Jersey, agricultural science, industrialization, household technology and the hall of machines. There also is a collection of 19th- and 20th-century photographs. Allow 1 hour minimum. Wed.-Sat. 10-5, Sun. noon-5; closed holidays. Admission $3; ages 5-11, $1. Phone (908) 249-2077.

**RUTGERS UNIVERSITY,** in addition to its Colonial background, claims origins as a land grant college and the status of a state university. The first formal collegiate football game was held in 1869, with Rutgers beating Princeton six goals to four. Old Queens, a three-story 1809 brownstone building, originally held all the facilities; it now serves as the administrative center of the university. Phone (908) 932-1766.

**Geology Museum,** College Ave. and Somerset St. on the College Avenue Campus, displays minerals, vertebrate fossils, American Indian artifacts and an Egyptian mummy. Mon. 1-4, Tues.-Fri. 9-noon; closed holidays and Dec. 25-Jan. 2. Free. Phone (908) 932-7243.

**The Jane Voorhees Zimmerli Art Museum,** at George and Hamilton sts. on the College Avenue Campus, contains a permanent collection of Western art, including 19th- and 20th-century paintings, drawings and sculptures. Of particular note is the display devoted to printmaking. Changing exhibits also are featured. Tues.-Fri. 10-4:30, Sat.-Sun. noon-5; closed holidays and Dec. 25-Jan. 2. Free. Phone (908) 932-7237.

**Rutgers Display Gardens and Helyar Woods** are entered via Ryders Ln. just e. of US 1 and s. of SR 18. The 20-acre garden displays plants suitable for New Jersey landscaping. The peak season for annuals is mid-June through September; flowering shrubs bloom from late April to early May and are in fall color from early to mid-October. Helyar Woods is a 41-acre forest. Daily 8:30-dusk, May-Sept.; 8:30-4:30, rest of year. Donations. Phone (908) 932-9271.

**William L. Hutcheson Memorial Forest,** a 65-acre tract of uncut hardwood forest that lies w. of New Brunswick near East Millstone, is a small remnant of the primeval forest that blanketed the New World. Continuous ownership by one family 1701-1955 accounts for the preservation of the tract. It is now maintained as a living forest laboratory.

Tours are offered at 2:30 on selected Sundays; for a schedule write to the director, Hutcheson Memorial Forest, Department of Biological Sciences, Rutgers University, P.O. Box 1059, Piscataway, NJ 08854. Phone (908) 932-2075.

**NORTH WILDWOOD**—see *Wildwood.*

## OCEAN CITY (G-3) pop. 15,500, elev. 10'

When the Lake brothers, ministers all, established Ocean City as a proper Christian summer resort in 1879, they decreed that no liquor would be sold. Still in effect, this injunction might account in part for the town's long-standing popularity with families. The other reasons are obvious: the 8-mile-long beach, the equable climate, excellent sport fishing and all the standard pleasures of a well-mannered seashore vacation community.

At the north end of an island between the Atlantic Ocean and Great Egg Harbor, Ocean City offers easy access to the ocean and inland waterways, making it a favorite summer port with yachtsmen. Its many recreational facilities include a golf course, tennis courts and the boardwalk, with shops and amusements. Marinas house visiting craft as well as charter boats for sightseeing and fishing.

The Music Pier is the primary entertainment center in summer when band concerts regularly take place. Wonderland Pier and Playland have amusement parks, which operate during the summer. Ocean City Arts Center presents monthly art exhibits.

A colorful pageant on the bay in July, the Night in Venice Boat Parade features a procession of elaborately decorated boats. Bayfront homes are festively adorned for the occasion; spectators watch from the shore as boaters compete for prizes.

Each year in August local decapods compete in the Miss Crustacean Hermit Crab Beauty Pageant. This stirring event is followed by the World's Championship Hermit Tree Crab Race, run by entrants wearing colorful shells and costumes. A sand sculpting contest also takes place. The Baby Parade is on the second Thursday in August. Ocean City's big fall event is its Indian Summer Weekend, held on Columbus Day weekend. First Night Ocean City celebrates New Year's Eve with a family-centered performing arts festival that includes music, poetry, dancers and fireworks.

An information center/chamber of commerce just northwest of town on SR 52 is open daily 9-6, Memorial Day-Labor Day; Mon.-Sat. 10-5, rest of year. Closed Jan. 1 and Dec. 25. Phone (609) 399-6344 or (800) BEACH NJ.

**OCEAN CITY HISTORICAL MUSEUM,** 17th and Simpson Ave., depicts life in the region during the late 19th century. Exhibits include period room settings, fashions, dolls and a maritime room dedicated to the *Sindia,* which ran aground on the island in a gale in 1901. Mon.-Fri. 10-4, Sat. 1-4, Memorial Day-Dec. 31; otherwise varies. Closed holidays. Free. Phone (609) 399-1801.

## OCEAN GROVE (C-2) elev. 20'

Ocean Grove, a family-oriented seaside resort, has been under the leadership of the Camp Meeting Association since 1869. Musical performances featuring well-known pop and symphony concert artists, as well as entertainers, cultural events and religious services and programs, are held throughout the summer at the 6,500-seat Great Auditorium. Organ concerts are given Wednesday and Saturday on the auditorium's 1908 Hope-Jones pipe organ.

Of historical interest is the Victorian architecture so typical of many of the community's homes. Centennial Cottage, a restored 1874 vacation home at Central Avenue and McClintock Street, is open to visitors. Also of interest is the tent colony surrounding the auditorium. A tabernacle, chapel, pavilions, parks, the boardwalk and the beach complete Ocean Grove's chautauqua setting.

For additional information on the area, contact Ocean Grove Camp Meeting Association, Box 126, 54 Pitman Ave., Ocean Grove, NJ 07756; phone (908) 775-0035.

## OCEANVILLE (F-4)

**EDWIN B. FORSYTHE NATIONAL WILDLIFE REFUGE,** Brigantine Division, covers more than 24,000 acres on the Atlantic coast; its headquarters is 1 mi. e. of US 9 on Great Creek Rd. More than 275 species of waterfowl and other birds have been sighted at the refuge's bays, channels and tidal marshes. The best times for wildlife observation are spring and fall. There is an 8-mile drive through wetland and upland areas as well as two short nature trails. Daily dawn-dusk. Admission $4 per private vehicle. Phone (609) 652-1665.

**THE NOYES MUSEUM,** off SR 9 on Lily Lake Rd., exhibits permanent collections of paintings, mid-Atlantic folk art, sculpture and works on paper by contemporary American artists. The museum also features a gallery of bird and animal decoys. Rotating fine arts and crafts exhibits are displayed. Allow 30 minutes minimum. Wed.-Sun. 11-4; closed major holidays. Admission $3; over 65, $1.50; ages 5-18, 50c. **Discount.** Phone (609) 652-8848.

## OGDENSBURG (B-4) pop. 2,700, elev. 629'

**STERLING HILL MINE & MUSEUM** is ½ mi. s. on CR 517, 1 mi. w. on Brooks Flat Rd., then 1 mi. n. to 30 Plant St., following signs. Visitors can learn about the mining process during a guided 1½-hour walking tour through the underground tunnels of what was the last operating zinc mine in the state. A museum displays minerals and mining relics. Tour is not recommended for preschoolers.

Allow 1 hour, 30 minutes minimum. Daily 10-5, Mar.-Nov. Last tour begins 2 hours before closing. Admission $7.50; over 64, $6.50; under 17, $5. **Discount.** Phone (201) 209-7212.

## PARAMUS (F-6) pop. 25,100

**BERGEN MUSEUM OF ART AND SCIENCE,** Ridgewood and Farview aves., features the Hackensack mastodon skeleton as the centerpiece of its science and art collections. The museum also offers a variety of changing exhibits, workshops and events throughout the year. Tues.-Sat. 9:30-4:30, Sun. 1-5. Donations. Phone (201) 265-1248.

**NEW JERSEY CHILDREN'S MUSEUM,** 599 Industrial Ave., is an interactive learning and play center designed for children 8 and under. Each of the museum's 30 rooms has its own theme. In Aviation youngsters can climb inside a real helicopter and use an authentic flight simulator. They can operate cash registers in the Grocery and Pizzeria and watch themselves on television in the T.V. Studio.

Allow 2 hours, 30 minutes minimum. Daily 9-5; closed Thanksgiving and Dec. 25. Admission $6 Mon.-Fri., $7 Sat.-Sun., under 1 free. MC, VI. Phone (201) 262-5151.

## PATERSON (G-5) pop. 140,900, elev. 118'

The potential power of the Great Falls of the Passaic River, which can be viewed at McBride Avenue and Spruce Street, inspired Alexander Hamilton to organize the Society for Establishing Useful Manufactures (S.U.M.) and to plan Paterson as America's first industrial city. Pierre L'Enfant, planner of Washington, D.C., designed the three-tiered raceway that harnessed the falls and supplied water power to the industrial mills.

The restored upper raceway parallels a section of Spruce Street, the site of such early mill complexes as the Rogers Locomotive Erecting Shop, which produced the "General" and other historic engines. In the Old Gun Mill, Van Houten and Mill streets, Samuel Colt made the first successful repeating revolvers, and John Ryle launched the silk industry for which the city was to become well-known.

Paterson, still an important center of diversified manufacturing, is striving to infuse new life into parts of the old industrial area while preserving it as the Great Falls/S.U.M. Historic District. Restorations on Mill and Van Houten streets are forerunners of the program of adaptive re-use of the old mills. For additional area information contact the Greater Paterson Chamber of Commerce, 100 Hamilton Plaza, Paterson, NJ 07505; phone (201) 881-7300.

**Self-guiding tours:** A brochure outlining a self-guiding walking and/or driving tour, as well as information and appointments for guided walking tours, can be obtained Mon.-Fri. 10-4:30 at the Great Falls Visitor Center, 65 McBride Ave., Paterson, NJ 07501; phone (201) 279-9587.

**LAMBERT CASTLE,** in the Garret Mountain Reservation overlooking the city, was built in 1892 by Catholina Lambert, a wealthy silk manufacturer. The elaborate stone building houses the

Passaic County Historical Society Museum, with period rooms and changing historical exhibits on decorative and folk art, textiles and costumes. Allow 1 hour minimum. Wed.-Sun. 1-4; closed Jan. 1, Easter, July 4, Thanksgiving and Dec. 25. Admission $1.50, senior citizens $1, under 15 free. Phone (201) 881-2761.

ROGERS MILL (PATERSON MUSEUM), 2 Market St., has American Indian artifacts; mineralogy collections; archeological, geological and historical exhibits; and an exhibit on the silk industry. Of note are the hulls of the first two submarines, invented and constructed by J.P. Holland of Paterson. Tues.-Fri. 10-4, Sat.-Sun. 12:30-4:30; closed holidays. Admission $1, under 18 free. Phone (201) 881-3874.

## PLAINFIELD (H-4) pop. 46,600, elev. 102'

At the south end of the Watchung Mountains, Plainfield has become one of the many suburbs that radiate from the Elizabeth and Newark metropolitan areas (see place listings). A few reminders of the Revolutionary period remain.

While planning the Battle for the Watchungs, Gen. George Washington often stayed at the Plainfield home of a friend, the Rev. Nathaniel Drake. The 1746 house is headquarters for the local historical society. Another 18th-century building still in use is the 1788 Friends Meeting House.

For additional area information contact the Central Jersey Chamber of Commerce, 120 W. 7th St. #217, Plainfield, NJ 07060; phone (908) 754-7250.

## PLEASANTVILLE (F-4) pop. 16,000, elev. 20'

STORYBOOK LAND, 2 mi. w. of the Garden State Pkwy. on US 40/322, features rides, live animals and more than 50 buildings and displays depicting storybook characters and scenes. The park is decorated with special holiday lighting mid-November through December.

Daily 10-5:30, mid-June to mid-Sept.; Mon.-Fri. 10-3, Sat.-Sun. 11-5, May 1 to mid-June; Thurs.-Fri. 10-3, Sat.-Sun. 11-5, mid-Sept. through Oct. 31; Sat.-Sun. 11-5, mid-Mar. through Apr. 30. Closed Dec. 24-25. Admission $9.95; over 65, $7.50; under 1 free. **Discount.** Phone (609) 641-7847.

## POINT PLEASANT BEACH (C-2) pop. 5,100

The Unami Indians spent spring and summer collecting shells and fish along the coast of what is now Point Pleasant Beach. This ritual ended in the 1700s with the arrival of the first European settlers. Farming and boat building were common occupations until the mid-1800s, when the area began developing as a seaside community. Rail service and the completion of the Garden State Parkway turned Point Pleasant Beach into one of New Jersey's leading summer resorts.

A mile-long boardwalk offers family-style amusements. Point Pleasant Beach borders Manasquan Inlet, providing access to the ocean and opportunities for boat watching. Nightly entertainment includes laser shows, fireworks and concerts on the beach featuring classical and popular music. September brings the Ocean Inner Tube Race as well as the Festival of the Sea, a street fair featuring arts and crafts vendors and a variety of food, including fresh seafood.

For additional information contact the Greater Point Pleasant Area Chamber of Commerce, 517A Arnold Ave., Point Pleasant Beach, NJ 08742; phone (908) 899-2424.

## PORT MONMOUTH (I-6) elev. 12'

Port Monmouth overlooks Sandy Hook Bay, the scene of fierce whaleboat warfare during the Revolution. Commercial fishing continues to be the mainstay of the community.

The Spy House Museum, a hands-on learning center, is at 119 Port Monmouth Rd. Over a 250-year period this 1663 structure evolved from a one-room cabin to an expansive house. During the Revolution the house served as an inn and was the headquarters for raids against the British fleet anchored in New York Harbor. The building also was a haunt for pirates. The museum, open weekends, illustrates the lifestyle of the area's early settlers and American Indians, the waterman trades and the heritage of the bayshore; phone (908) 787-1807.

## PRINCETON (C-5) pop. 12,000, elev. 213'

The key to Princeton's future was turned in 1756 when the College of New Jersey, founded in Elizabeth by royal charter in 1746, was moved to the town; it was not officially renamed Princeton University until 1896. In its Nassau Hall occurred another pivotal event: the 1776 meeting of the first New Jersey State Legislature, which inaugurated William Livingston as governor.

Shortly thereafter, Gen. Charles Cornwallis' troops occupied Nassau Hall as they pushed Gen. George Washington's army westward. Early the next year Washington followed up his victory at Trenton by surprising and defeating the British in the Battle of Princeton. A monument at Mercer, Nassau and Stockton streets commemorates the battle.

In 1783 the Continental Congress met in Nassau Hall when mutinous American soldiers drove its members from Philadelphia. During this time the members received the news of the treaty of peace with Great Britain.

The life of the community has melded increasingly with that of the university and the other institutions of higher education. Albert Einstein spent his last years at the Institute for Advanced Study.

The Historical Society of Princeton offers a 2-hour guided walking tour of historic Princeton every Sunday at 2 for $5. For additional information contact the Chamber of Commerce of the Princeton Area, Princeton Forrestal Village, 100-300 Village Blvd., P.O. Box 431, Princeton, NJ 08540; phone (609) 520-1776 or 921-7676.

**Self-guiding tours:** The Historical Society of Princeton has brochures outlining walking tours with such topics as 18th-century houses and architecture. These brochures can be obtained at the society's museum shop in the Bainbridge House *(see attraction listing).*

**BAINBRIDGE HOUSE,** 158 Nassau St., was the birthplace of William Bainbridge, commander of the USS *Constitution* during the War of 1812. The restored 1766 residence serves as a museum with changing exhibitions, a library, photo archives and a museum shop; the house also is the headquarters of the Historical Society of Princeton. Tues.-Sun. noon-4. Free. Phone (609) 921-6748.

**PRINCETON UNIVERSITY** encompasses more than 1,660 acres with many fine buildings representing a wide variety of architecture. The campus's original 1756 building, Nassau Hall, served as a barracks and hospital during the Revolutionary War and was the temporary home of the Continental Congress. Sculptures from the John B. Putnam Jr. Memorial Collection, including works by Alexander Calder, Jacques Lipchitz, Henry Moore, Louise Nevelson and Pablo Picasso, are displayed on the campus.

Free tours of the campus, including Nassau Hall and the University Chapel, are available Mon.-Sat. at 10, 11, 1:30 and 3:30, Sun. at 1:30 and 3:30; closed holidays and mid-Dec. to early Jan. Visitors should contact the Maclean House, 73 Nassau St., Princeton, NJ 08540; phone (609) 258-3603.

**The Art Museum** contains outstanding paintings and sculpture spanning ancient and modern times. Noteworthy are Chinese paintings and bronzes and examples of pre-Columbian and African art. Tues.-Sat. 10-5, Sun. 1-5. Free. Phone (609) 258-3787.

**The James Forrestal Campus,** a 440-acre tract 3 mi. from the main campus, is part of the university's advanced training and research in the basic and engineering sciences. The largest research facility at Forrestal is the Plasma Physics Laboratory, which is attempting to develop magnetic fusion energy for use in generating electricity. Free tours are offered by appointment. Phone (609) 243-2750.

**Natural History Museum,** in Guyot Hall, is dedicated to evolution and geology. Displays pertain to marine and land inhabitants ranging from prehistoric to modern species. A nearby geology library also is open. Museum open Mon.-Fri. 9-5. Free. Phone (609) 258-4102.

**The University Chapel,** near Firestone Library, is one of the world's largest university chapels. The pulpit and lectern, which date from the mid-16th century, were brought from France. Of interest are the chapel's stained-glass windows and pews. Sun.-Fri. 8 a.m.-11 p.m., Sat. 8-6:30, third Sun. in Sept.-second Sun. in June; daily 8-4:30, rest of year. Free. Phone (609) 258-3050.

**ROCKINGHAM STATE HISTORIC SITE,** 5 mi. n. on CR 518 at Rocky Hill, was Washington's headquarters in 1783 while the Continental Congress was in session in Princeton. He wrote his "Farewell Orders to the Armies" at this site. The restored house contains period furnishings. Wed.-Sat. 10-noon and 1-4, Sun. 1-4; closed Jan. 1, Thanksgiving and Dec. 25. Free. Phone (609) 921-8835.

**THE THOMAS CLARKE HOUSE,** 1½ mi. s.w. on Mercer St., is in Princeton Battlefield State Park, where Gen. George Washington led his forces to victory in 1777. Gen. Hugh Mercer, an American, died in the house from wounds suffered in the battle. Thomas Clarke, a Quaker farmer, built the Georgian-style home about 1770 and lived in it until his death in 1802.

The house, furnished in the Revolutionary style, is being developed as a working Colonial farm. Weapons, paintings and maps highlighting the battle are some of the items exhibited. Guided tours Wed.-Sat. 10-noon and 1-4, Sun. 1-4. Closed Jan. 1, Thanksgiving and Dec. 25. Free. Phone (609) 921-0074.

## RINGWOOD (B-4) pop. 12,600, elev. 339'

Claiming a colorful past as an iron-mining and forging center, Ringwood has been described as "more a company than a town, and more a tradition than a company." The iron-rich Ramapo Mountains first gained attention in the early 1700s; the first forge was built in 1739. By 1771 the forge had been sold twice and had become the lucrative London-based American Iron Co. Vast tracts of land became the homes of wealthy mine and forge owners.

When the Revolutionary War erupted, ironmaster Robert Erskine sided with the Colonies and became the surveyor general for the Continental Armies. Meanwhile his forges worked overtime turning out munitions, cannons and most of the huge chain that was stretched across the Hudson to prevent British ships from reaching West Point. The Ringwood iron mine produced steadily until 1931, when it succumbed to competition from Western iron ranges.

To obtain additional information contact the Ringwood Chamber of Commerce, P.O. Box 62, Ringwood, NJ 07456; phone (201) 962-7916.

**RINGWOOD STATE PARK,** 2½ mi. n. via Skyland Dr., CR 511 and Sloatsburg Rd., consists of three units totaling 6,199 acres. The Shepherd Lake section, which offers water sports, is 14 miles north of Pompton Lakes. The Ringwood Manor and Skylands sections boast mansions and gardens. Phone (201) 962-7031. *See Recreation Chart.*

**New Jersey State Botanical Gardens** surround the 44-room Tudor Skyland Manor; the 1924 mansion is closed. The 300 acres of gardens contain flowering trees from around the world; annuals and perennials bloom from spring through the first frost. Marked trails traverse the gardens. Guided tours are available on Sunday at 2 from May through October. Gardens open daily dawn-dusk. Admission $3 Sat.-Sun., Memorial Day-Labor Day; otherwise free, rest of year.

**Ringwood Manor** is the grand former home of Gen. Robert Erskine; Peter Cooper, founder of the Cooper Union in New York; and Abraham S. Hewitt, a leading ironmaster of the 19th century. Twenty-one of the mansion's 78 rooms have been restored; the third floor contains exhibits depicting the history of the iron industry from 1740 to the 1920s. Woodlands and formal gardens are on the grounds. Picnicking is permitted. Tues.-Sun. 10-4, May-Oct.

### SALEM (F-1) pop. 6,900, elev. 14'

Settled in 1675 by Quakers, Salem is one of the oldest English settlements on the Delaware River. Its early importance as a port—the Salem River provides good harborage—made it a prize during the Revolutionary War; the city was occupied by the British. After the war Camden *(see place listing)* surpassed Salem as a shipping center, and attention was turned to commerce based on the surrounding agricultural area.

In addition to supporting some light industry, Salem serves visitors who come to view its 18th-century architecture as well as sportsmen who hunt and fish in the nearby wetlands.

The restored 1721 Alexander Grant House at 78 Market St. displays articles from the Colonial and Federal periods. The 1734 Hancock House was the scene of a massacre during the Revolution. In retaliation against the Quaker community for supplying cattle to Gen. George Washington's starving troops at Valley Forge, 300 men under Maj. John Simcoe surprised and killed 30 local men asleep in the house, used as a barracks at the time.

One original resident still lives: the carefully nurtured oak, estimated to be more than 5 centuries old, that guards the entrance to the Friends Burying Ground on West Broadway. Beneath its branches John Fenwick bargained with the Lenni Lenape Indians for the land on which he would establish Salem.

For additional information on the area contact the Greater Salem Chamber of Commerce, 104 Market St., Salem, NJ 08079; phone (609) 935-1415.

**FORT MOTT STATE PARK,** 104 acres 6 mi. n.w., fronts on the Delaware River. Next to the park is the Finns Point National Cemetery, the burial ground of 2,436 Confederate prisoners of war and 300 Union soldiers. Old fortifications and defense structures are in the park. Daily 8-7:30, Memorial Day-Labor Day; 8-4, rest of year. Free. Phone (609) 935-3218.

### SEASIDE HEIGHTS (E-5) pop. 2,400

Established in 1913, Seaside Heights lies between the Atlantic Ocean and Barnegat Bay. The town features a mile of boardwalk that has two amusement piers, an antique Dentzel/Looff carrousel, games of chance, fishing, arcades, nightclubs and Wednesday night fireworks. The beaches as well as most establishments are open daily Memorial Day through Labor Day. The boardwalk is open year-round, with bicycling permitted in the early morning hours.

Events in Seaside Heights include the Palm Sunday Egg Hunt, which brings thousands of youngsters to the beach, as well as the Easter Promenade, held on the boardwalk in mid-April. During mid-September, Mardi Gras features fireworks, a parade, arts and crafts, live entertainment and a tavern night. Clownfest, which occurs in late September, includes performances on the boardwalk by more than 400 professional clowns, a parade and fireworks.

**CASINO PIER AND WATER WORKS,** 800 Ocean Terr., is an amusement park with a variety of rides. The highlight is the water park, with slides, river rides and an activity pool. Complex open daily, Memorial Day-Labor Day; amusement park also open Sat.-Sun., Easter-day before Memorial Day. Hours vary; phone for schedule. Water park $10 for 2 hours. Amusement park free; rides priced individually. Phone (908) 793-6488.

### SOMERS POINT (G-4) pop. 11,200

**ATLANTIC COUNTY HISTORICAL SOCIETY LIBRARY AND MUSEUM,** just n. of the traffic circle at 907 Shore Rd. (CR 585), has a 20,000-item collection of historical artifacts ranging from a continental dollar to an 1870 bed. Shipbuilding, one of the county's major 19th-century industries, is represented by boat models, paintings and tools. Other items displayed include American Indian stone implements, weapons, antique furniture and turn-of-the-20th-century clothing.

The historical society's library is open to the public for genealogical research. Guided tours of the museum are available. Allow 30 minutes minimum. Wed.-Sat. 10-3:30; closed holidays. Museum free; $5 fee for library research. Phone (609) 927-5218.

**SOMERS MANSION,** adjacent to the traffic circle at 1000 Shore Rd. (CR 585), was built around 1725 by Richard Somers, son of an early area settler. The three-story brick dwelling, the oldest house in Atlantic County, is furnished with 18th-century antiques. An interesting architectural detail is the interior woodwork decorated with heart-shaped perforations. A textile collection includes locally fashioned quilts, coverlets and samplers.

Allow 30 minutes minimum. Wed.-Sat. 10-noon and 1-5, Sun. 1-4; closed winter holidays. Free. Phone (609) 927-2212.

## SOMERVILLE (C-5) pop. 11,600, elev. 91'

Somerville's occupation with commerce, county government and industry exemplifies its position in the transitional zone between city and country. The area was first settled by American Indians who later negotiated with European settlers for a peaceful withdrawal. Later, soldiers of the Continental Army frequented the area, then called Raritan, while Gen. George Washington stayed at the Wallace House. Somerville began to take shape with the construction of a courthouse in 1784.

For additional area information contact the Somerset County Chamber of Commerce, 64 W. End Ave., P.O. Box 833, Somerville, NJ 08876; phone (908) 725-1552.

**DUKE GARDENS,** 1¼ mi. s. of Somerville Cir. on US 206S, has 11 glass-enclosed gardens, each representing a country. Guided tours daily noon-4, Oct.-May; closed Jan. 1, Thanksgiving and Dec. 25. Admission $5; senior citizens and ages 6-12, $2.50. Reservations are required. Phone (908) 722-3700 Mon.-Fri. 10-3.

**OLD DUTCH PARSONAGE STATE HISTORIC SITE,** 65 Washington Pl., was built in 1751 and was the 1758-81 home of Rev. Jacob Hardenbergh, founder of Queens College in New Brunswick. The college later became Rutgers University. The site contains exhibits pertaining to local history and early American crafts and lifestyles. Wed.-Sat. 10-noon and 1-4, Sun. 1-4; closed holidays. Donations. Phone (908) 725-1015.

**WALLACE HOUSE STATE HISTORIC SITE,** 38 Washington Pl., was occupied by Gen. George Washington during the winter of 1778-79 while his Continental Army stayed at Camp Middlebrook. The house contains period furnishings. Wed.-Sat. 10-noon and 1-4, Sun. 1-4; closed holidays. Donations. Phone (908) 725-1015.

## SPRING LAKE (C-2) pop. 3,500

Spring Lake's name is derived from the crystal clear water which flows from many underground springs. The seaside town, approximately 60 miles from both New York City and Philadelphia, has been transformed from an affluent, turn-of-the-20th-century Victorian resort into a

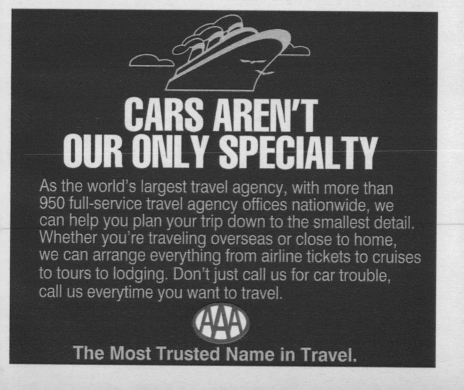

year-round beach and residential community. The area boasts one of the longest non-commercial boardwalks in the state.

**VITALE & VITALE,** 315 Morris Ave., houses one of the finest and most extensive collections of timepieces in the world. The gallery and museum showcase the intricate art of clockmaking with examples of rare and decorative antique clocks from the 17th, 18th and 19th centuries. Functioning, handcrafted designs from longcase to table clock size are displayed in an impressive neoclassical gallery. Allow 1 hour minimum. Fri.-Mon. 10-5:30. Free. Phone (908) 449-3000.

## STANHOPE (B-3) pop. 3,400, elev. 873′

Stanhope serves the needs of local farmers as well as visitors to Hopatcong State Park *(see Recreation Chart),* on nearby Lake Hopatcong. The town dates from Revolutionary times when the Sussex Iron Works was a major industry; a few ironworkers' cottages, resembling French peasant bungalows, remain. The nation's first anthracite furnace was built in town about 1821.

Stanhope is the eastern terminus for a scenic stretch of I-80 that runs 28 miles to the Delaware Water Gap and continues into Pennsylvania.

**WATERLOO VILLAGE** is off I-80 exit 25. The village's beginnings in the 1740s revolved around the forge established to make use of the area's vast water and timber resources. Andover Forge was a major supplier of armaments for the Continental Army. Renamed Waterloo after Napoleon Bonaparte's 1815 defeat there, the village declined briefly when the forests that fed the ironworks' furnaces were depleted, but revived with the 1831 opening of the Morris Canal.

Waterloo flourished as a cargo and transshipment station until the railroad, which supplanted the canal as the primary carrier, built a bypass around it in 1881. By 1927, when the canal was dismantled, the village was a dozing residential hamlet.

The restoration of Waterloo has resulted in the preservation of the village as a living-history museum covering 200 years of America. Costumed guides and artisans explain 18th- and 19th-century life in more than 28 Colonial and Victorian buildings, including an inn, church, gristmill, blacksmith shop and carriage house. The Lenape/Delaware way of life is depicted at Winakung, a life-size reconstruction of a Minisink Indian village.

Special events are scheduled throughout the summer and fall. The Waterloo Festival of the Arts, held May through October, features concerts devoted to such varied offerings as opera, classical, jazz and rock music, antique and craft shows and dance events. Picnicking is permitted. Food is available.

Wed.-Sun. 10-6, mid-Apr. through Sept. 30; Tues.-Sun. 10-5, Oct.-Dec. Closed Easter, Thanksgiving and Dec. 25. Schedule may vary; phone ahead. Admission $8; over 62, $7; ages 6-15, $6. Additional fees may be charged during concerts or special events. **Discount.** Phone (201) 347-0900, or 347-2530 for concert or special event information.

## STONE HARBOR (G-3) pop. 1,000, elev. 7′

While Stone Harbor caters to the many boaters along the Intracoastal Waterway and vacationers enjoying the beach, its non-human visitors attract the greatest attention. Stone Harbor is a noted nesting place for herons; the Stone Harbor Bird Sanctuary, on 3rd Avenue between 111th and 116th streets, is the nation's only heronry sponsored by and within a town.

Although visitors may not enter the sanctuary, the herons and egrets can be seen flying into and out of the area during their residency March through October. The best viewing times are just before dawn and just before sunset. A parking lot and an information station are available on Ocean Drive.

**THE WETLANDS INSTITUTE,** 3 mi. s.e. of Garden State Pkwy. exit 10 on CR 657, is dedicated to providing education and research on coastal ecosystems. The education center houses saltwater aquariums, exhibits depicting life in the local saltwater marshes, a touch tank, a children's discovery room and an observation deck. A self-guiding salt marsh trail, observation tower and marsh boardwalk also are featured.

Allow 1 hour minimum. Mon.-Sat. 9:30-4:30, Sun. 10-4, May 15-Oct. 15; Tues.-Sat. 9:30-4:30, rest of year. Admission $4; ages 4-13, $2. Phone (609) 368-1211.

## TETERBORO (G-6)

**AVIATION HALL OF FAME & MUSEUM OF NEW JERSEY,** off SR 17, following signs, is in two locations at Teterboro Airport—the old control tower and an educational center on the east side of the airport. The museum contains aviation memorabilia and historic aircraft equipment as well as depicting the roles played in aviation history by New Jerseyans. Visitors can hear radio transmissions between air-traffic controllers in the tower and pilots.

Tues.-Sun. 10-4; closed Jan. 1, Easter, July 4, Thanksgiving and Dec. 25. Admission $3; over 65 and under 12, $2. **Discount.** Phone (201) 288-6344.

## TOMS RIVER (E-4) pop. 7,500, elev. 33′

Founded in the early 18th century, Toms River was a haven from which privateers wreaked havoc on British shipping early in the Revolutionary War. It rose to brief post-Revolutionary prominence in 1782 when Tories tried to seize the highly prized local saltworks and warehouses by burning the blockhouse, killing its defenders and hanging its commander, Capt. Joshua Huddy.

Huddy Park and a replica of the original block-house, both near the waterfront in downtown Toms River, commemorate this event.

Linked to the sea and bay, the town primarily relied on the whaling, shipping and seafood in-dustries. The first tourists, adventurous harbin-gers of a thriving modern industry, reputedly arrived aboard seafood carts that were empty af-ter the morning's deliveries to Philadelphia.

Winding River Park, north on Main Street to SR 37, then 1 mile west, straddles the Toms River, which offers a 6-mile run for canoe enthu-siasts. Nature, hiking, bicycle and bridle trails weave through its 40 developed acres. The park's northern section, west on CR 571 off US 9, con-tains the park headquarters and an ice/roller skat-ing rink.

For additional information contact the Toms River-Ocean County Chamber of Commerce, 1200 Hooper Ave., Toms River, NJ 08753; phone (908) 349-0220.

**CATTUS ISLAND COUNTY PARK,** 1170 Cattus Island Blvd., is really a peninsula jutting into Barnegat Bay. The 500-acre park is the quintes-sential transition zone between land and sea, with salt marsh blending into pine-oak uplands. The Cooper Environmental Center presents ex-hibits that relate to the area. Trails wind through the preserve, and boat and van tours are offered in July and August. Daily 10-4. Free. Phone (908) 270-6960.

*RIVER LADY* **CRUISE AND DINNER BOAT,** ½ mi. e. of Garden State Pkwy. exit 81, just e. of SR 166 (Main St.) overlooking the Toms River, offers dinner, dance, lunch, theme and sightsee-ing cruises along Barnegat Bay and the Toms River aboard a reproduction of a paddle-wheel riverboat. The 2-hour historical sightseeing cruise provides narration about area history. Other cruises vary in length from 2-6½ hours.

Sightseeing cruises depart Tues. and Thurs. at 11 and 2, Sat. at 2, June-Sept. Fare $9.50; senior citizens $9; under 12, $5.50. MC, VI. Reserva-tions are required. Phone (908) 349-8664.

**ROBERT J. NOVINS PLANETARIUM,** on College Dr. off Hooper Ave. on the campus of Ocean County Community College, presents a variety of star shows. Tues.-Wed. at 2, Thurs. at 2 and 8, Fri. at 1, 2 and 8, July-Aug.; Fri. at 8, Sat. at 1, 2, 3:15 and 8, Sun. at 2 and 3:15, Sept.-May. Show at 1 is for ages 3-6. Admission $4.50; un-der 13, $3. **Discount.** Phone (908) 255-0342.

**TRENTON (C-4) pop. 88,700, elev. 42′**

Capital of the state, Trenton was settled about 1680 with the building of a mill at the falls of the Delaware River. The site's potential for in-dustry, trade and shipping was recognized by Philadelphia merchant William Trent, who pur-chased the original mill in 1714. By 1719, with Trent's vision and financial support, the village

had developed to such an extent that its name was changed from The Falls to Trenton.

In 1776 the Hessians occupied the city while pursuing Gen. George Washington and his troops across New Jersey and into Pennsylvania. On Dec. 26, 1776, after crossing the Delaware 8 miles upstream, Washington surprised the Hes-sian garrison, taking about 1,000 prisoners. The troops sent by Gen. Charles Cornwallis to bolster the Trenton garrison arrived on Jan. 2, 1777, and met Washington's troops the next day in the Sec-ond Battle of Trenton. These American victories were a turning point in the Revolutionary War.

Trenton became the state capital in 1790. The world's first fully operative steamboat, perfected by a Trentonian named John Fitch, plied the Delaware River daily between Philadelphia and Trenton. In-dustry expanded, and the city's name traveled around the world on rubber products, steel cable and pottery. Porcelain from Boehm and Cybis are now among Trenton's major products.

Trenton's historic districts preserve many key Colonial buildings and sites. The Mill Hill His-toric District between Mercer and Jackson streets has brick sidewalks, gaslights and restored Victo-rian homes. The State House Historic District, W. State Street between Willow and Calhoun streets, is an architecturally eclectic residential area where Trenton's prominent families lived during the late 19th century.

To obtain additional information contact the Mercer County Chamber of Commerce, 214 W. State St., Trenton, NJ 08607; phone (609) 393-4143.

**CADWALADER PARK,** W. State St. and Parkside Ave., honors Dr. Thomas Cadwalader, the com-munity's first chief burgess and a pioneer in the use of preventive inoculation. He vaccinated the populace of Trenton for smallpox in the late 1740s. Laid out in 1891 by Frederick Law Olm-stead, one of America's foremost landscape de-signers, the park includes a deer paddock, stream, small lake, hundreds of trees and an arm of the historic Delaware-Raritan Canal. Daily dawn-dusk. Free.

**Ellarslie—The Trenton City Museum** contains art galleries with changing displays as well as Trenton exhibits and period rooms. Allow 30 minutes minimum. Tues.-Sat. 11-3, Sun. 2-4. Do-nations. Phone (609) 989-3632.

★**NEW JERSEY STATE MUSEUM,** 205 W. State St., is in the State House Historic District. Allow 1 hour minimum. Tues.-Sat. 9-4:45, Sun. noon-5; closed state holidays. Free. Phone (609) 292-6464 or 292-6308.

**The Main Museum** has three floors of exhibits dealing with archeology, fine arts, cultural his-tory and natural science. Highlights include American Indian artifacts, mastodon skeletons, a full-size model of a dinosaur and a mine replica with fluorescent minerals. Changing art exhibits also are presented. The auditorium offers films, concerts and lectures. Museum free. Fees are charged for special exhibits and programs.

**The Planetarium** offers changing programs emphasizing the solar system and the night sky. Laser concerts also are presented. Under 5 are not admitted. Programs Sat.-Sun. at noon, 1, 2 and 3. Admission $1. Phone (609) 292-6333.

★**OLD BARRACKS MUSEUM**, Barrack St., is the only surviving British colonial barracks in the United States. Constructed in 1758, it was occupied at various times by British, Hessian and Continental troops and by Tory refugees. Gen. George Washington and his troops crossed the Delaware to reach the barracks in the Battle of Trenton.

A cultural history museum includes a restored officers' quarters with 18th-century furnishings and permanent and changing exhibits. Costumed guides portray New Jerseyans of the Revolutionary era. The officers' quarters is temporarily closed for restorations. Tues.-Sat. 11-5, Sun. 1-5, Mon. by appointment; closed Jan. 1, Easter, Thanksgiving and Dec. 24-25. Admission $2; senior citizens and students with ID $1; under 13, 50c. Phone (609) 396-1776.

**STATE HOUSE**, W. State St., has collections of art as well as period rooms. A gold dome crowns the 1792 building, which has undergone many changes since its construction. Guided tours are offered Tues.-Wed. and Fri. 9-4, unless the Legislature is in special session. Free. Reservations are required. Phone (609) 292-4661.

**TRENT HOUSE**, 15 Market St., is said to be Trenton's oldest house. Built in 1719 by William Trent, it was subsequently the home of a number of prominent men, including the first Colonial governor of New Jersey, Lewis Morris. Notable among the period furnishings are the curtains and copies of old fabrics. Allow 1 hour minimum. Daily 10-2; closed Jan. 1, Good Friday, Thanksgiving and Dec. 25. Admission $1.50; under 12, 50c. Phone (609) 989-3027.

**WASHINGTON CROSSING STATE PARK** is 8 mi. n.w. on SR 29, then n.e. on CR 546 to the entrance. The park is the site of the historic crossing of the Delaware River by Gen. George Washington and the Continental Army before the Battle of Trenton.

Continental Lane, over which the Colonial troops marched on Christmas night in 1776, extends nearly the length of the park and is marked with memorials. This route is the staging area for the annual Re-enactment of Washington Crossing the Delaware, which begins on the Pennsylvania side at 2 on December 25.

A visitor center has exhibits on the 1776 period and is open Wed.-Sun. 9-4:30. Historical tours can be arranged through the visitor center; phone (609) 737-9304. Nature tours, offered by

appointment, depart from the nature center, which has a small museum and is open Wed.-Sun. 9-4, Sun. 1-4; phone (609) 737-0609.

The Nelson House, across SR 29 near the river bank, is a small museum that has historical exhibits and Colonial crafts; phone for schedule. The George Washington Memorial Arboretum has an assortment of native trees and shrubs.

The park is open daily 8-8, Memorial Day weekend-Labor Day; 8-4:30, rest of year. Parking $3 Sat.-Sun. and holidays, Memorial Day-Labor Day. Phone (609) 737-0623. *See Recreation Chart.*

**The Ferry House**, at the s. end of Continental Ln., has been restored as a Dutch farmhouse; a taproom, kitchen and bedroom contain period furnishings. Wed.-Sun. 9-4:30. Free. Phone (609) 737-2515.

**Open Air Theatre** is the site of the Summer Festival of Performing Arts. Performances are given Thurs.-Sat. and every other Wed. at 8:30 p.m., June 15-Labor Day. Tickets Fri.-Sat. $7.50; under 12, $3.75. Wed.-Thurs. $6.50; under 12, $3.25. The box office opens at 6:30 p.m. on performance dates only. Phone (609) 737-1826.

## VERNON (A-4) pop. 2,200

**ACTION PARK/VERNON VALLEY GREAT GORGE**, 5¼ mi. n. of SR 23 on SR 94, is a summer theme park and a winter ski resort on 1,200 acres of hills and wooded slopes. The theme park has more than 75 attractions, including more than 40 water rides (water slides along with white water tube and raft rides), speed boats, bungee jumping and six alpine slides. The park also features daily live shows; weekend festivals and concerts are held in the park's 5,000-seat festival tent. Changing rooms, lockers and food are available.

In winter the park converts into the Vernon Valley/Great Gorge ski resort, featuring 17 lifts and more than 50 slopes and trails spread over three mountains. Night skiing, snowboarding, ski lessons, rentals and children's programs are available.

Allow a full day. Action Park open daily 10-8, June 12-Labor Day; daily 10-6, Memorial Day-June 11. Ski resort season early Dec. to mid-April, depending on conditions. Action Park all-inclusive admission $27, under 48 inches tall $18. Full-day Great Gorge lift ticket $38; under 13, $27. AE, CB, DI, DS, MC, VI. Parking $3 in summer. **Discount.** Phone (201) 827-2000 for information and snow conditions.

## VINELAND (F-2) pop. 54,800, elev. 115'

Business with plenty of room to grow is the hallmark of 69-square-mile Vineland, geographically the largest city in the state. One of the largest poultry centers in the country and the primary marketing and distributing point in southern New Jersey, Vineland also is an industrial city. The city has many specialty glass, food-processing and clothing factories as well as numerous transportation concerns and retail and factory outlets.

As its name implies, Vineland was intended to be the focus of a wine-producing region. In 1861 promoter Charles K. Landis attracted to the area farmers from the mid-Atlantic states and Italian immigrants familiar with vineyards. For the town, Landis platted a 1-square-mile grid with equally spaced streets, houses and trees. While this plan remains evident as the nucleus of present-day Vineland, the vineyards did not last.

After a quarter-century of growth, disease struck the vines, and most of the wine-grape industry was abandoned. All was not lost, however: An enterprising dentist developed a nonfermentative method of preserving grape juice, one that permanently associated the product with his name—Thomas Welch.

In 1868 the women of Vineland staged one of the earliest women's suffrage demonstrations in the country. Unwilling to allow their opinions to go unheard during that presidential election, 172 women defiantly cast their token votes, a number of which supported Elizabeth Cady Stanton for president.

Recreational facilities are provided in Landis, Magnolia, Gittone and Giampetro parks. Six miles west of town via CR 540 is Parvin State Park (see Recreation Chart and the AAA Mideastern Campbook). For additional area information contact the Greater Vineland Chamber of Commerce, City Hall #106, 7th & Wood Sts., P.O. Box 489, Vineland, NJ 08360-0489; phone (609) 691-7400.

**VINELAND HISTORICAL AND ANTIQUARIAN SOCIETY,** 108 S. 7th St., has material relating to Vineland and its surroundings, including items belonging to town founder Charles K. Landis and his family; locally crafted glassware; military memorabilia; a music room; old firefighting equipment; American Indian relics; and period furniture and clothing. Archives are available for genealogical research. Free museum tours are given on Saturday.

Tues.-Wed. and Fri.-Sat. 1-4, Aug.-June; closed major holidays. Free. Genealogical research fee $12. Phone (609) 691-1111.

## WASHINGTON (B-4) pop. 5,400, elev. 490'

**MINIATURE KINGDOM,** 1 mi. s. on SR 31, offers self-guiding tours through a scale-model European community with castles, cathedrals, monuments, trains and ships. The scale is ½-inch-to-1-foot.

Allow 1 hour minimum. Daily 10-5, Memorial Day-Labor Day; Tues.-Sun. 10-5, Apr. 1-day before Memorial Day and day after Labor Day-Nov. 30. Closed Easter and Thanksgiving. Admission $4.50; over 65, $4; ages 5-18, $3.50;

ages 2-4, $1.50. **Discount.** Phone (908) 689-6866.

**SHRINE OF THE IMMACULATE HEART OF MARY,** off SR 31, 1 mi. w. on CR 632, 1 mi. n. on Cemetery Hill Rd., then ¼ mi. w. on Mountain View Rd., following "Blue Army Shrine" signs, includes the shrine; Capelinha, U.S.A., an exact replica of the chapel at Fatima; the Rosary Garden; outdoor Stations of the Cross; and Holy House, U.S.A., a replica of the Holy House of Loreto, Italy. Modest dress is required. Daily 11-4, May-Oct. Mass is celebrated daily at 11:30. Free. Phone (908) 689-1700.

## WAYNE (F-5) pop. 47,000

The Wayne area is familiar to dog fanciers as the setting for Albert Payson Terhune's "Lad, A Dog" and other books about the collies he raised until his death in 1942. Sunnybank, Terhune's estate, is 4 miles north of Wayne on US 202; it is now Terhune Memorial Park, featuring gardens and a picnic ground. For additional information contact the Greater Wayne Area Chamber of Commerce, 2055 Hamburg Tpke., Wayne, NJ 07470; phone (201) 831-7788.

**Shopping areas:** Wayne Town Center, at the junction of SRs 46E and 23S, has a JCPenney. Across the street is Willow Brook, which offers Macy's, Sears, Steinbeck and Sterns among its stores.

**DEY MANSION,** 199 Totowa Rd. in Preakness Valley Park, is a brick and brownstone Georgian house built in the 1740s by Dirck Dey, the father of the commander of the Bergen County militia, Col. Theunis Dey. At Dey's invitation, Gen. George Washington used it for his headquarters in July, October and November 1780. That fall the home was supposedly offered to Washington as a haven after a British plot to kidnap him was discovered.

The detached kitchen and the main house display antiques and items from the 18th century. Guided tours and picnic facilities are available. Wed.-Fri. 1-4, Sat.-Sun. 10-noon and 1-4. Last tour begins 30 minutes before closing. Closed Jan. 1, Easter, Thanksgiving and Dec. 25. Admission $1. Phone (201) 696-1776.

## WEEHAWKEN (G-6) pop. 12,400, elev. 189'

*SPIRIT OF NEW JERSEY,* 2 blks. e. of Lincoln Tunnel entrance at Lincoln Harbor Marina, offers sightseeing cruises of the New York City harbor. The Statue of Liberty, Empire State Building, World Trade Center, Ellis Island and Brooklyn Bridge are landmarks that can be seen on the 2-, 2½- and 3-hour lunch, brunch and dinner cruises. Weekend moonlight cruises also are available. Music and entertainment are provided. Boarding is 30 minutes prior to departure.

Lunch cruises depart Mon.-Fri. at noon; brunch cruises depart Sat.-Sun. at noon; dinner cruises depart daily at 7. Lunch cruise $25.95; under 12,

$13.80. Brunch cruise $34.95; under 12, $17.50. Dinner cruise Sun.-Thurs. $49.25, Fri. $55.50, Sat. $61.45. AE, CB, DS, MC, VI. Reservations are required. Phone (201) 867-5518.

## WEST ORANGE (G-5) pop. 39,100

With its sister municipalities—Orange, South Orange, East Orange and Maplewood—the city of West Orange is a primarily residential section of the Newark suburbs. An overlook in Eagle Rock Reservation, west on Eagle Rock Avenue, affords a view of much of the densely populated metropolitan area. West Orange is probably best known for its association with Thomas Edison.

★EDISON NATIONAL HISTORIC SITE, Main St. and Lakeside Ave., consists of the preserved laboratory complex and Glenmont, the home of inventor Thomas Alva Edison and his wife, Mina Miller Edison. The visitor center features exhibits and films; access beyond the visitor center is by guided tour only. Passes must be obtained at the visitor center.

Allow 2 hours, 30 minutes minimum. Visitor center open daily 9-5. Glenmont tours depart on the hour Wed.-Sun. 11-4. Laboratory complex tours depart from the visitor center on the half hour daily 10:30-3:30. Video cameras are not allowed on the tours. Closed Jan. 1, Thanksgiving and Dec. 25. Admission (includes both sites) $2, over 61 and under 17 free. Phone (201) 736-5050 or 736-0550.

**Glenmont,** Edison's home from 1886 until his death in 1931, is on a 15½-acre estate in Llewellyn Park, about a mile from the laboratory. The 23-room Queen Anne-style mansion contains its original furnishings. Of special interest is the living room on the second floor, where, seated at his "thought bench," Edison conceived many of his inventions. The graves of Mr. and Mrs. Edison are behind the house.

**Laboratory Complex,** built in 1887, includes chemical, physics and metallurgical laboratories, a machine shop, stock room and Edison's library/office. Many original inventions are on display. A full-size reproduction of the Black Maria, the world's first motion picture studio, is in the complex. Baby strollers and videotape cameras are not permitted.

**TURTLE BACK ZOO,** in South Mountain Reservation at 260 Northfield Ave. (CR 508) between Cherry Ln. and Prospect Ave., houses a variety of animals in paddock enclosures and an animal nursery. An 1850 miniature train offers a free, scenic 1-mile ride around the grounds. All zoo exhibits are outdoors. Picnicking is permitted. Food is available.

Allow 2 hours minimum. Mon.-Sat. 10-5, Sun. and major holidays 10:30-6, Apr.-Oct.; daily and holidays 10-4:30, rest of year. Closed Jan. 1, Thanksgiving and Dec. 24-25 and 31. Admission Apr.-Oct, $6; over 61 and ages 2-12, $2.50. Admission rest of year, $5; over 61 and ages 2-12, $2. Phone (201) 731-5800.

## WILDWOOD (G-3) pop. 4,500, elev. 8′

Rarely are the three communities that constitute this popular shore resort referred to in other than the plural. Although the Wildwoods—Wildwood, Wildwood Crest and North Wildwood—are separate entities, their boundaries are indistinguishable. Together they occupy the southernmost isle just north of Cape May.

Because the surf line lies as far as 1,000 feet from shore, the Wildwoods' beach is one of the safest in the state. The 2½-mile-long boardwalk includes seven amusement piers and a variety of shops. North Wildwood's 1873 lighthouse at First and Central avenues is open in the summer. There are opportunities for bicycling, swimming, fishing, boating and golfing; charter fishing boats and sightseeing cruises also are available.

Downtown on Pacific Avenue, Holly Beach Station is an open-air mall with shops, restaurants and nightclubs. The Spring Car Show, which features a display on the boardwalk, is held Mother's Day weekend. Wildwood hosts the East Coast Stunt Kite Championships in late May and the National Marbles Tournament on the beach at Wildwood Avenue in late June. A Fall Auto Show is in late September.

For additional area information contact the Greater Wildwood Chamber of Commerce, Schellenger on the Boardwalk, P.O. Box 823, Wildwood, NJ 08260; phone (609) 729-4000.

**CAPTAIN SCHUMANN'S BOAT RIDES,** 2¾ mi. s.e. on SR 47 from Garden State Pkwy. exit 4B to Park Blvd., then 3½ blks. n. to 4500 Park Blvd., are aboard *Big Blue,* a converted World War II PT boat. Schumann shares his knowledge of wildlife, ecology and the local fishing industry during 2½-hour cruises along the Wildwood and Cape May coasts. Morning, afternoon and sunset cruises are available, with the afternoon cruise the most likely for spotting dolphins. Food is available.

Cruises depart daily at 10:30, 2 and 7, July 1-Labor Day. Fare $8, under 6 free. Phone (609) 522-2919.

**CAPTAIN SINN'S SIGHTSEEING CENTER,** 6006 Park Blvd. in Wildwood Crest, is the departure point for sightseeing and whale and dolphin watching cruises. The sightseeing cruise sails in the inner harbor and along the coasts of Wildwood and Cape May.

Allow 3 hours minimum. Sightseeing cruise departs daily at 10:30 and 7 p.m., May-Sept.; Sat.-Sun. at 10:30, in Apr. and Oct. Whale and dolphin watching cruises depart daily at 1, May-Sept.; Sat.-Sun. at 1, in Apr. and Nov. Fare for sightseeing cruise $10; ages 6-11, $5. Whale and dolphin watching cruise $12. Under 6 free with adult. Phone (609) 522-3934.

*DELTA LADY* **SIGHTSEEING CRUISES,** aboard an 1850s replica stern-wheeler, sail from the Wildwood Marina at the foot of the bridge at Rio Grande and Susquehanna aves. Passengers are introduced to local wildlife, the U.S. Coast Guard Base, commercial fishing fleets and other sights on a 2-hour narrated cruise on the Intracoastal Waterway. A banjo player and sing-alongs are featured on the 10 p.m. cruise.

Cruises depart daily at 10:30, 2, 7 and 10 p.m., July-Aug.; otherwise varies, May-June and Sept. 1 to mid-Oct. Fare $7.95; ages 6-11, $4.95; under 6 free with adult. Banjo cruise $9.95. AE, MC, VI. **Discount.** Phone (609) 522-1919.

**GEORGE F. BOYER HISTORICAL MUSEUM,** Garden State Pkwy. exit 4, 3 mi. s. on SR 47, then ½ mi. n. to 3907 Pacific Ave., contains local antiques, photographs and memorabilia from the late 1800s and early 1900s. A postcard collection and displays about the beach patrol and fire and police departments offer glimpses into the past of a beachside town.

Allow 1 hour minimum. Mon.-Fri. 9:30-2:30 (also Fri. 6:30-8:30 p.m.), Sat.-Sun. 10:30-2:30, May 1-Oct. 1; Thurs.-Sun. 10:30-2:30, rest of year. Donations. Phone (609) 523-0277.

**HEREFORD INLET LIGHTHOUSE,** First and Central aves. in North Wildwood, began operation in 1874 when the area was known as the fishing village of Anglesea. The restored Victorian lighthouse is notable for its five chimneys and T-shaped design. It is surrounded by flower and herb gardens and a gazebo; paths lead to the nearby shore. Allow 30 minutes minimum. Mon.-Sat. 9-4, Sun. and holidays noon-4. Donations. Phone (609) 522-4520 or 522-2030.

**MARINER'S LANDING AND RAGING WATERS WATER THEME PARK** is e. on SR 47, n. on Susquehanna Ave., then e. on Schellenger Ave. to the boardwalk. Overlooking the Jersey shore, the amusement center has several rides, including a carrousel, roller coaster and Ferris wheel. Food is available.

Park open April 15-Labor Day weekend. Hours vary; phone ahead. Unlimited ride pass $18. Phone (609) 522-3900.

**Raging Waters** is a water recreation park with raft rides, slides, a 900-foot river, an activity pool and an adult spa. Food and locker facilities are available. Daily 9-7:30, Memorial Day-Labor Day. Admission $16.95 all day, $14.95 for 3 hours, $12 for 2 hours; under 48 inches tall $12.95 all day, $10.95 for 3 hours, $8 for 2 hours. MC, VI.

**WILDWOOD CREST**—*see Wildwood.*

**WOODBURY (E-1) pop. 10,900, elev. 34′**

Of considerable importance during the Revolution, Woodbury was occupied by British troops in November 1777. Gen. Charles Cornwallis chose as his headquarters the home of John Cooper, a Continental Congress member denounced for his patriotism by his pacifist Quaker friends. A number of other 18th-century buildings distinguish Woodbury as a Revolutionary-period community.

"Light Horse" Harry Lee, father of Robert E. Lee, used Woodbury as his headquarters during his campaigns in South Jersey in 1779. Other personages associated with Woodbury are Commodore Stephen Decatur and Capt. James Lawrence, both educated at Woodbury Academy. The Hunter-Lawrence House, 58 N. Broad St., was the boyhood home of Lawrence, known for his dying command, "Don't give up the ship," given during the War of 1812. His home is open to visitors.

To obtain additional area information contact the Greater Woodbury Chamber of Commerce, Kings Hwy., P.O. Box 363, Woodbury, NJ 08096; phone (609) 845-4056.

**RED BANK BATTLEFIELD PARK** (Fort Mercer) is 2 mi. w. of US 130 at Riverfront. During the Revolutionary War an earthen redoubt—Fort Mercer—was hastily built at this site to help protect the channels of the Delaware River and the port of Philadelphia from the British forces. In 1777, 400 Patriots under Gen. Nathanael Greene vanquished 1,200 Hessians led by Count Van Dorop by holding their fire until the Hessians were nearly upon them.

Van Dorop, mortally wounded, was taken prisoner. This victory was instrumental in helping France decide to join the American forces. The house of Ann Whitall, who supposedly continued to spin her wool while the battle raged around her home, has been restored. Park open daily dawn-dusk. House open Wed.-Fri. 9-4, Sat.-Sun. 1-4, Apr.-Sept. Free. Phone (609) 853-5120.

**WYCKOFF (F-5) pop. 15,400**

**JAMES A. McFAUL WILDLIFE CENTER OF BERGEN COUNTY,** on Crescent Ave., is an 81-acre wildlife sanctuary. A nature trail, waterfowl pond, native birds and mammals, an herb garden and flowering displays are on the grounds. An indoor exhibit hall contains natural history displays, live animals and monthly art exhibits. Free public programs are offered on Tuesdays and weekends; phone for schedule. Picnic facilities are available.

Sanctuary grounds open daily 8-dusk. Exhibit hall open Mon.-Fri. 8:30-4:45, Sat.-Sun. noon-4:45. Donations. Phone (201) 891-5571.

```
- TRAVEL TIP -
On the road, be dependable
and predictable.
Signal your intentions.
```

# PENNSYLVANIA

## An introduction to the state's history, geography, economy and recreation

IN THE KEYSTONE POSITION among the 13 Colonies, Pennsylvania also has been the keystone in the development of the nation. Democracy was born of William Penn's "Great Law," and his Philadelphia became its cradle. The nation found its strength at Valley Forge, chose its course at Gettysburg, and defended its freedom from the steel mills of Pittsburgh and the shipyards of Philadelphia. If America is the flag, then Pennsylvania is the pole.

### HISTORY

Pennsylvania was occupied by some 15,000 Delaware, Shawnee, Susquehanna and Iroquois Indians before the first Europeans arrived. In 1609 English explorer Henry Hudson charted the coasts along the Delaware River, and in 1643 New Sweden governor Johan Printz established a colony north of the Wilmington, Del., area on Tinicum Island near Chester. The settlement fell into Dutch hands in 1655 and was claimed by the English in 1664.

In 1681 King Charles II availed himself of the opportunity to be rid of a troublesome young Quaker named William Penn while also making good on a £16,000 debt owed Penn's father. He granted Penn a huge tract of land—between 40 and 43 degrees longitude and up to 5 degrees west of the Delaware River—to be called Penn's Woodlands, or Pennsylvania. The 37-year-old Penn immediately set out to establish his "city of brotherly love" at the confluence of the Delaware and Schuylkill rivers.

Religious freedom became the purpose to which the new colony would be dedicated. Penn's "Holy Experiment"—an exercise in social idealism—was soon delineated in his "Great Law of Pennsylvania," guaranteeing freedom of conscience, judicial restraint, voting rights, fair taxation, education and gainful employment. Penn's tenets gradually evolved into his Charter of Privileges of 1701, which made Pennsylvania's government the soundest in the land.

## FAST FACTS

**POPULATION:** 11,881,600.

**AREA:** 45,308 square miles; ranks 33rd.

**CAPITAL:** Harrisburg.

**HIGHEST POINT:** 3,213 ft., Mount Davis.

**LOWEST POINT:** Sea level, Delaware River.

**TIME ZONE:** Eastern. DST.

**MINIMUM AGE FOR DRIVERS:** 16.

**SEAT BELT/CHILD RESTRAINT LAWS:** Seat belts required for driver and front-seat passengers; child restraints required for under 4.

**HELMETS FOR MOTORCYCLISTS:** Required for driver.

**RADAR DETECTORS:** Permitted.

**FIREARMS LAWS:** Vary by state and/or county. Contact Pennsylvania State Police Headquarters, 1800 Elmerton Ave., Harrisburg, PA 17110; phone (717) 783-5504.

**HOLIDAYS:** Jan. 1; Martin Luther King Jr.'s Birthday, Jan. (3rd Mon.); Presidents Day, Feb. (3rd Mon.); Memorial Day, May (last Mon.); July 4; Labor Day, Sept. (1st Mon.); Columbus Day, Oct. (2nd Mon.); Veterans Day, Nov. 11; Thanksgiving; Dec. 25.

**TAXES:** Pennsylvania's statewide sales tax is 6 percent. Pittsburgh levies a 10-percent amusements tax. Local options allow certain lodgings taxes of up to 6 percent.

**STATE WELCOME CENTERS:** Three centers are on the Pennsylvania Turnpike: one near Sideling Hill, one eastbound between exits 2 and 3 and one westbound between exits 28 and 29. Others are on I-79S at Edinboro; I-80E at the Ohio line; I-70W at the Maryland line; I-83N at the Maryland line; I-81N near Newville; I-95N at the Delaware line; I-78W at the New Jersey line; and I-81S south of Lenox. Centers are open daily 8-6, May-Sept.; 8-5, rest of year. Centers are closed Jan. 1, Martin Luther King Jr.'s Birthday, Presidents Day, Easter, Thanksgiving and Dec. 25.

Pennsylvania attracted increasing numbers of European immigrants in the 1700s. Joining the English, Welsh and Dutch Quakers were Rhineland Germans representing several religious sects. These Amish, Dunkers, Mennonites, Moravians and Schwenkfelders—who gained the collective misnomer Pennsylvania Dutch—settled in the fertile farming region northwest of Philadelphia. A third major group braved the frontier; the trail for the hardy Scotch-Irish led past the English and German settlements into western Pennsylvania.

Penn's scrupulous dealings with the Indians helped to forestall the conflict, but by 1750 the natives had grown weary of increasing encroachment into their lands. The French, too, were concerned; their claim to the Ohio Valley, an essential trade route, was at stake. The French-Indian alliance was established, and the British were intent on gaining the frontier for themselves.

In December 1753, George Washington, a 21-year-old major in the Virginia Militia, led an expedition to French Fort LeBoeuf south of Lake Erie. He was politely but firmly rebuffed and soon retreated home. Washington's return the following spring was both historic and inauspicious. After defeating a French detachment east of present-day Uniontown, he was soon besieged by a large French force at hastily constructed Fort Necessity. The first real battle of the French and Indian War began and ended there on July 3, 1754.

The tide began to turn for the British in 1758 with a series of important victories, among them the capture of Fort Duquesne by British general John Forbes. Rebuilt and renamed Fort Pitt, the outpost not only hastened the departure of the French, but also opened the region to new settlement. France relinquished all claims to North America in 1763, but the British toll was high. War debts and unwieldy new growth so weakened the empire that within a decade they were vulnerable to a new threat—by the colonists.

By 1774 Pennsylvania had become the military, economic and political center of the colonies. The First Continental Congress convened in Philadelphia in 1774 and the Second Continental Congress 1775-76, where the Declaration of Independence was drafted and approved on July 4, 1776. When the Articles of Confederation were endorsed in York in 1777, the 13 Colonies effectively became one nation. On Dec. 12, 1787, Pennsylvania became the second colony to ratify the U.S. Constitution—drafted at the Pennsylvania State House in Philadelphia—thus becoming the nation's second state. Philadelphia was the national capital 1790-1800.

Pennsylvania also was a major battleground during the American Revolution. George Washington, now a general and commander in chief of the American forces, earned a pivotal early victory at Trenton, N.J., after leading his troops across the Delaware River on Christmas night

1776. After suffering a serious setback at Brandywine Creek in September 1777, Washington's forces regained some success at Germantown before quartering for that legendary winter at Valley Forge.

The 19th century brought tremendous growth and development to Pennsylvania. An intricate network of roads, bridges and canals hastened an already rapid westward expansion; between 1794 and 1832, the original Philadelphia-Lancaster Turnpike had grown to include some 3,000 miles of roadway. With the arrival of the railroad in the mid-1800s came the ability to fully exploit Pennsylvania's extensive coal, oil, iron and lumber resources, making the state among the nation's richest.

Pennsylvania was staunchly pro-Union during the Civil War. The state had guaranteed the end of slavery with the Pennsylvania Emancipation Act of 1781, and the Mason-Dixon Line, established as the state's southern boundary in 1769, became the official dividing line between North and South. Pennsylvania lent nearly 340,000 soldiers and all its industrial might to the Union cause. So critical were Pennsylvania's supply routes that in the summer of 1863 they brought Confederate general Robert E. Lee and some 70,000 seasoned troops into the Cumberland Valley.

The 3-day battle at Gettysburg resulted in more than 51,000 casualties—nearly equal to America's toll in all of the Vietnam War—and

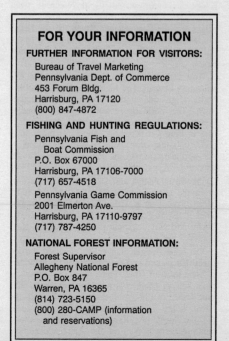

## FOR YOUR INFORMATION

**FURTHER INFORMATION FOR VISITORS:**

Bureau of Travel Marketing
Pennsylvania Dept. of Commerce
453 Forum Bldg.
Harrisburg, PA 17120
(800) 847-4872

**FISHING AND HUNTING REGULATIONS:**

Pennsylvania Fish and
 Boat Commission
P.O. Box 67000
Harrisburg, PA 17106-7000
(717) 657-4518

Pennsylvania Game Commission
2001 Elmerton Ave.
Harrisburg, PA 17110-9797
(717) 787-4250

**NATIONAL FOREST INFORMATION:**

Forest Supervisor
Allegheny National Forest
P.O. Box 847
Warren, PA 16365
(814) 723-5150
(800) 280-CAMP (information
 and reservations)

marked the beginning of the end for the Confederacy. President Abraham Lincoln's dedication of the national cemetery there on Nov. 19, 1863, was the occasion of his simple but brilliant summation of America's purpose known as the Gettysburg Address.

At the end of the war, Pennsylvania found itself at the forefront of the Industrial Revolution. It was home to the three largest steel mills in the country, and by 1870 Pittsburgh's mills alone were producing two-thirds of the national total. Such industrial magnates as Andrew Carnegie, Henry Clay Frick and J. P. Morgan forever changed the face of American business and commerce, and Ohioan John D. Rockefeller built his refining empire on Pennsylvania crude. Also from Pennsylvania's industrial boom came the labor movement, whose influence is still felt today.

A series of extensive public works programs kept Pennsylvanians busy during the Great Depression, and they regained their industrial and military prominence with the onset of World War II. Though some undesirable effects of the waning industrial age remain in Pennsylvania, the sort of modern pioneering that brought the nation the first commercial radio station and the first digital computer today makes the state a leader in the fields of science, medicine and technology.

## GEOGRAPHY

The most prominent feature of this rectangular state is the arc of rocky, nearly unbroken parallel ridges and narrow valleys that curves from southwest to northeast. East of the Appalachian ridges and the Susquehanna River, the southeastern lowlands roll gradually down to a strip of the Atlantic Coastal Plain along the lower Delaware River.

West and north of the mountains lies the Appalachian Plateau. The highest section, called the Laurel Highlands, abuts Maryland east of Uniontown. The northern section of the plateau is Pennsylvania's wooded wilderness; its main feature is Pine Creek Gorge, about 50 miles long and 1,000 feet deep. The Pocono Mountains in the northeastern part of Pennsylvania also are part of the Appalachian Plateau.

The Susquehanna and Delaware river systems drain the central and eastern part of the state. Most of the west is within the Ohio River watershed, to which Pennsylvania contributes the Allegheny and Monongahela rivers. A narrow plain borders Lake Erie.

The hard Appalachian ridges diverted the ice sheet that planed and enriched northern New Jersey and most of Ohio. Thus, much of Pennsylvania's soil is shallow sandstone and shale. The limestones of the southeast lowlands and the Great Valley, as well as some riverbottom soils, are the most productive. Short summers and harsh winters prevail in the Appalachians and northern Allegheny Plateau; the rest of the state has the hot, humid summers and fairly mild winters associated with the mid-Atlantic region.

## ECONOMY

Pennsylvania was at the forefront of America's Industrial Revolution. The world's first oil well was drilled in Titusville in 1859, marking the birth of the petroleum industry, and it was in Pennsylvania that Andrew Carnegie established the forerunner of the U.S. Steel Corp. By the start of the 20th century, Pennsylvania had emerged as an industrial giant, out-producing not only the rest of the country but the world.

In recent years, Pennsylvania diversified its economy so that it was no longer dependent on heavy manufacturing. The state blended its manufacturing and industrial strengths with its high-technology. New market opportunities have emerged to complement the state's traditional industries, particularly in the specialized manufacturing and high-growth area of biotechnology.

Tourism is Pennsylvania's second largest industry, surpassed only by agriculture. Popular destinations for vacationers include the Pocono Mountains, Gettysburg, Lancaster and the Pennsylvania Dutch Country, the Laurel Highlands, Philadelphia and Pittsburgh. Still others find themselves drawn to Hershey—Chocolate Town U.S.A.—and Reading, which calls itself the "Outlet Capital of the World."[®]

From trim farms come corn, buckwheat, potatoes, tobacco and oats and other grains. The mountain valleys of the southcentral counties and the far northwest grow apples, peaches, cherries, berries and grapes. Pennsylvania is the leading producer of mushrooms in the nation; mushroom farms lend their fusty scent to the countryside surrounding Kennett Square near Longwood.

Through extensive reforestation, a significant lumber industry has emerged in Pennsylvania; the state has the nation's largest supply of hardwood resources. Also significant is the production of Christmas trees—the town of Indiana is reputedly the "Christmas Tree Capital of the World."

Basic to Pennsylvania is coal, and due largely to a coal mining industry that produces more than 87 million tons annually, Pennsylvania is the nation's second leading producer of electricity. The only anthracite deposit in the eastern United States underlies the northeast section of the state. In the west the reserves of bituminous coal are at the northern end of the vast Appalachian coalfields.

## RECREATION

Wooded mountains provide the setting for most outdoor recreation. The main vacation areas are the Poconos, Allegheny National Forest and the Laurel Highlands. Resorts with complete social and recreational programs dot the Poconos, which encompass the picturesque Delaware Gap and numerous waterfalls. The Allegheny National

Forest remains mostly natural, with miles of fishing streams and forested hills for hiking.

Water sports are popular at the Allegheny Reservoir east of Warren, in the Laurel Highlands at Somerset and Ligonier, at Lake Wallenpaupack in the Poconos, at Pine Creek Gorge and at Conneaut Lake and Pymatuning Reservoir in western Pennsylvania. **White-water rafting** is popular on several of the state's rivers, most notably the Youghiogheny River at Ohiopyle State Park and the Lehigh River in Lehigh Gorge State Park.

**Fishing** is a rewarding sport throughout Pennsylvania. Anglers find the lakes and streams stocked with bass, bluegill, crappie, muskellunge, perch and trout. **Hunting** is most profitable in the forested regions of the state. Hunters find bear, deer, grouse, pheasant, quail, rabbit, squirrel, wild turkey and woodcock in the Allegheny National Forest and in several Appalachian areas.

**Horseback riding** also is popular throughout Pennsylvania. One trail, the Horse-Shoe Trail, extends some 130 miles west from Valley Forge where it joins the Appalachian Trail. A detailed guidebook is available for $6. For more information contact the Horse-Shoe Trail Club, Warwick County Park, RD 2, Pottstown, PA 19464; phone (215) 469-9461.

Winter sports flourish in this mountainous state. **Snowmobiling, downhill skiing** and **cross-country skiing** are possible at numerous state parks. Resort areas in the Poconos and the Laurel Highlands have facilities that cater to both the beginner and to the more advanced skier. Other areas popular for snow sports are near Gettysburg, Scranton and York.

**Camping** season usually runs mid-April to mid-October, though some parks offer extended seasons. **Hiking** and **backpacking** trails are in most state parks. The parks are open daily 8 a.m.-dusk, all year. Although no entrance fees are charged, user fees are charged for some facilities. Pets are not permitted in camping or swimming areas. For more information about Pennsylvania's state parks phone the Bureau of State Parks at (800) 63-PARKS. For information about camping in Pennsylvania *see the AAA Mideastern CampBook.*

| RECREATION AREAS | MAP LOCATION | CAMPING | PICNICKING | HIKING TRAILS | BOATING | BOAT RAMP | BOAT RENTAL | FISHING | SWIMMING | PETS ON LEASH | BICYCLE TRAILS | WINTER SPORTS | VISITOR CENTER | LODGE/CABINS | FOOD SERVICE |
|---|---|---|---|---|---|---|---|---|---|---|---|---|---|---|---|
| **NATIONAL FOREST** *(See place listing)* **Allegheny** 513,000 acres. Northwestern Pennsylvania. | | ● | ● | ● | ● | ● | ● | ● | ● | ● | ● | ● | ● | | ● |
| **ARMY CORPS OF ENGINEERS** | | | | | | | | | | | | | | | |
| **Cowanesque Lake (C-7)** 3,200 acres 3 mi. w. of Lawrenceville off SR 15. Hunting, water skiing. | 87 | ● | ● | ● | ● | ● | | ● | ● | ● | | ● | | | ● |
| **Raystown Lake (G-6)** 29,300 acres s.w. of Huntingdon off SR 26. Water skiing. | 84 | ● | ● | ● | ● | ● | ● | ● | ● | ● | | | | ● | ● |
| **Tioga-Hammond Lakes (D-7)** 6,700 acres 12 mi. n. of Mansfield on US 15. Hunting, water skiing. | 89 | ● | ● | ● | ● | ● | | ● | ● | ● | | | ● | | ● |
| **STATE** | | | | | | | | | | | | | | | |
| **Bald Eagle (F-7)** 5,900 acres off SR 26 at Howard. Tobogganing. | 1 | ● | ● | ● | ● | ● | ● | ● | ● | | | ● | | | ● |
| **Beltzville (F-10)** 2,972 acres 6 mi. e. of Lehighton off US 209. Cross-country skiing, tobogganing. | 2 | | ● | ● | ● | ● | ● | ● | ● | ● | | ● | | | ● |
| **Bendigo (E-5)** 100 acres 3 mi. n.e. of Johnsonburg off US 219. Tobogganing. | 3 | | ● | | | | | ● | ● | ● | | | | | ● |
| **Big Pocono (F-11)** 1,306 acres 13 mi. w. of Tannersville off I-80. | 4 | | ● | ● | | | | | | | | ● | | | ● |
| **Big Spring (H-7)** 45 acres 4 mi. w. of New Germantown on SR 272. Cross-country skiing, snowmobiling. | 90 | | ● | ● | | | | ● | | | | | | | |
| **Black Moshannon (F-6)** 3,481 acres 9 mi. e. of Philipsburg on SR 504. Cross-country skiing. | 5 | ● | ● | ● | ● | ● | ● | ● | ● | ● | | ● | | ● | ● |
| **Blue Knob (H-5)** 5,600 acres 5 mi. n.w. of Pavia off SR 869. Cross-country and downhill skiing, snowmobiling. | 6 | ● | ● | ● | | | | | ● | ● | | ● | | ● | ● |
| **Caledonia (I-7)** 1,130 acres 4 mi. e. of Fayetteville on US 30. Historic. Cross-country skiing. | 7 | ● | ● | ● | | | | ● | ● | ● | | ● | ● | ● | ● |
| **Canoe Creek (G-5)** 959 acres 7 mi. e. of Hollidaysburg off US 22. Cross-country skiing, tobogganing; horse rental. | 8 | ● | ● | ● | ● | ● | ● | ● | ● | ● | | ● | | ● | ● |
| **Chapman (D-4)** 805 acres 5 mi. w. of Clarendon off US 6. Cross-country skiing, snowmobiling, tobogganing. | 9 | ● | ● | ● | ● | ● | | ● | ● | ● | | ● | | | ● |

# INDEX TO STARRED ATTRACTIONS

ATTRACTIONS OF EXCEPTIONAL
INTEREST AND QUALITY

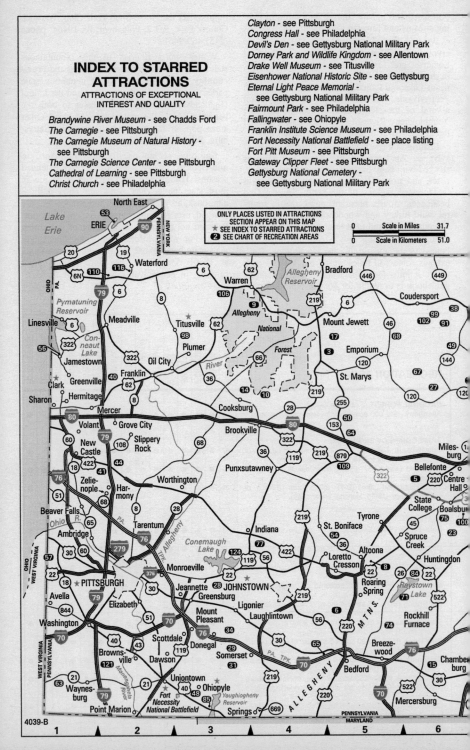

4039-B

© AAA

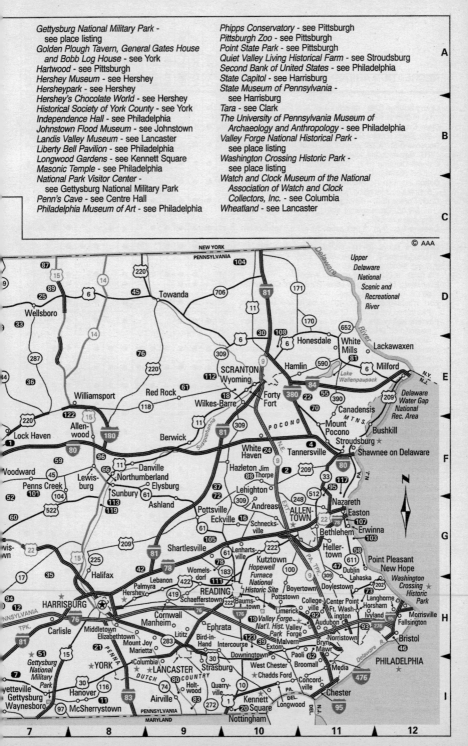

| RECREATION AREAS | MAP LOCATION | CAMPING | PICNICKING | HIKING TRAILS | BOATING | BOAT RAMP | BOAT RENTAL | FISHING | SWIMMING | PETS ON LEASH | BICYCLE TRAILS | WINTER SPORTS | VISITOR CENTER | LODGE/CABINS | FOOD SERVICE |
|---|---|---|---|---|---|---|---|---|---|---|---|---|---|---|---|
| **Cherry Springs (D-6)** 48 acres 4 mi. e. of Coudersport on US 6, then 11 mi. s.e. on SR 44. Hunting, snowmobiling. | 91 | • | • | • | | | | | | | | • | | | |
| **Clear Creek (E-4)** 1,209 acres 4 mi. n. of Sigel off SR 949. Cross-country skiing. | 10 | • | • | • | • | | | • | • | • | • | | • | • | • |
| **Codorus (I-8)** 3,320 acres 2 mi. e. of Hanover off SR 216. Snowmobiling, tobogganing. | 11 | • | • | • | • | • | • | • | • | • | • | • | • | | • |
| **Colonel Denning (H-7)** 273 acres 9 mi. n. of Newville off SR 233. Cross-country skiing, tobogganing. | 12 | • | • | • | | | | • | • | • | | | • | • | • |
| **Colton Point (D-7)** 368 acres 5 mi. s. of Ansonia off US 6. Cross-country skiing, snowmobiling. *(See Wellsboro)* | 13 | • | • | • | | | | | • | | | | • | | |
| **Cook Forest (E-3)** 6,422 acres 1 mi. n. of Cooksburg off SR 36. Cross-country skiing, sledding, snowmobiling; horse rental. | 14 | • | • | • | | | • | • | • | • | • | • | • | • | • |
| **Cowans Gap (I-6)** 1,085 acres 10 mi. n.e. of McConnellsburg off US 30. Cross-country skiing. | 15 | • | • | • | • | • | • | • | • | • | • | | • | • | |
| **Delaware Canal (G-11)** 60-mile area along SR 32; headquarters is in Upper Black Eddy. Cross-country skiing, sledding. | 103 | | • | • | • | | • | • | | | • | • | • | | |
| **Elk (D-5)** 3,192 acres 9 mi. e. of Wilcox. | 17 | | • | • | • | • | | • | | • | | • | | • | |
| **Evansburg (H-11)** 3,349 acres 2 mi. e. of Collegeville on US 422. Golf (18 holes). | 92 | | • | • | | | | • | • | • | | • | | • | |
| **Fort Washington (H-11)** 493 acres at 500 Bethlehem Pike in Fort Washington. Cross-country skiing, sledding. | 93 | | • | • | | | | | | • | | • | | | |
| **Fowlers Hollow (H-7)** 104 acres 4 mi. s. of New Germantown off SR 274 on Upper Buck Ridge Rd. Cross-country skiing, snowmobiling. | 94 | • | • | • | | | | • | | • | | • | | | |
| **Frances Slocum (E-10)** 1,035 acres 4 mi. e. of Dallas off SR 309. Cross-country skiing, sledding. | 18 | • | • | • | • | • | • | • | • | • | • | • | • | | • |
| **French Creek (H-10)** 7,339 acres 6 mi. n.e. of Pennsylvania Tpke. exit 22 on SR 345. | 19 | • | • | • | • | | • | • | • | • | • | | | • | • |
| **Gifford Pinchot (H-8)** 2,338 acres 2 mi. e. of Rossville off SR 74. Cross-country skiing. | 21 | • | • | • | • | • | • | • | • | • | • | • | • | | |
| **Gouldsboro (E-11)** 3,050 acres s. of Gouldsboro. | 22 | | • | • | • | • | | • | • | • | | • | • | | |
| **Greenwood Furnace (G-6)** 406 acres 5 mi. n.w. of Belleville on SR 305. Snowmobiling. | 23 | • | • | • | | | | • | • | • | • | • | | • | |
| **Hickory Run (F-10)** 15,500 acres 5 mi. s.e. of White Haven on SR 534. Cross-country skiing, snowmobiling. | 24 | • | • | • | | | | • | • | • | | • | | • | |
| **Hills Creek (D-7)** 407 acres 7 mi. n.e. of Wellsboro off SR 6. Tobogganing. | 25 | • | • | • | • | • | • | • | • | • | | • | | • | |
| **Hyner Run (E-6)** 180 acres 7 mi. e. of Renovo off SR 120. Snowmobiling. | 26 | • | • | • | | | | • | • | | | • | | • | • |
| **Jacobsburg (F-11)** 1,167 acres 6 mi. n. of Easton off SR 33 (Belfast exit). Cross-country skiing, sledding, snowmobiling; horse rental. | 95 | | • | • | | | | • | | • | • | • | • | | |
| **Kettle Creek (E-6)** 1,626 acres 8 mi. n.w. of Westport off SR 120. Sledding, snowmobiling; horse rental. | 27 | • | • | • | • | • | • | • | • | • | | • | | • | • |
| **Keystone (H-3)** 1,190 acres 3 mi. s.e. of New Alexandria on SR 981. Snowmobiling; horse rental. | 28 | • | • | • | • | • | • | • | • | • | | • | | • | |
| **Kooser (H-3)** 170 acres 10 mi. w. of Somerset on SR 31. Cross-country skiing. | 29 | • | • | • | | | | • | • | • | • | • | | • | • |
| **Lackawanna (D-10)** 1,373 acres 3 mi. n. of Waverly on SR 407. Tobogganing. | 30 | • | • | • | • | • | • | • | • | • | • | • | • | • | • |
| **Laurel Hill (I-3)** 3,935 acres 10 mi. w. of Somerset off SR 31 near Trent. Snowmobiling. | 31 | • | • | • | • | • | • | • | • | • | | • | | • | • |
| **Leonard Harrison (D-7)** 585 acres 10 mi. s.w. of Wellsboro off SR 660. *(See Wellsboro)* | 33 | • | • | • | | | | • | | | | • | | | |
| **Linn Run (H-3)** 565 acres 10 mi. s.e. of Ligonier off SR 711. Snowmobiling. | 34 | | • | • | | | | • | | | | • | | • | |
| **Little Buffalo (G-7)** 830 acres 4 mi. s.w. of Newport off SR 34. Cross-country skiing, tobogganing. | 35 | | • | • | • | • | • | • | • | • | | • | | | • |
| **Little Pine (E-7)** 2,158 acres 3 mi. n. of Waterville off SR 44. Cross-country skiing, ice fishing, ice skating, sledding, snowmobiling. | 36 | • | • | • | • | • | • | • | • | • | | • | • | • | |
| **Locust Lake (F-9)** 1,144 acres 3 mi. s. of Mahanoy City, exit 37 off I-81. | 37 | • | | • | • | • | • | • | • | • | | • | • | | |
| **Lyman Run (D-6)** 595 acres 8 mi. s.w. of Galeton off US 6. Snowmobiling. | 38 | • | • | • | • | • | • | • | • | • | | | | | • |

## RECREATION AREAS

| RECREATION AREAS | MAP LOCATION | CAMPING | PICNICKING | HIKING TRAILS | BOATING | BOAT RAMP | BOAT RENTAL | FISHING | SWIMMING | PETS ON LEASH | BICYCLE TRAILS | WINTER SPORTS | VISITOR CENTER | LODGE/CABINS | FOOD SERVICE |
|---|---|---|---|---|---|---|---|---|---|---|---|---|---|---|---|
| **Marsh Creek (H-10)** 1,705 acres 5 mi. n.w. of Downingtown off SR 282. Iceboating, ice fishing, ice skating, sledding; horse rental. | 39 | ● | ● | ● | ● | ● | ● | ● | ● | ● | | ● | | | ● |
| **Maurice K. Goddard (E-2)** 1,417 acres 14 mi. w. of Franklin on US 62. | 40 | ● | ● | ● | ● | ● | ● | ● | ● | ● | | ● | | | |
| **McConnells Mill (F-2)** 2,534 acres 8 mi. s.e. of New Castle off US 422. Tobogganing. | 41 | ● | ● | ● | | | | ● | | ● | | ● | | | |
| **Memorial Lake (G-8)** 230 acres 5 mi. n.e. of Grantville off US 22 and I-81. Cross-country skiing. | 42 | ● | ● | ● | ● | ● | ● | ● | | ● | | ● | | | |
| **Milton (F-8)** 77 acres on the island between Milton and West Milton. | 96 | ● | ● | ● | ● | ● | | ● | | | | | | | |
| **Mont Alto (I-7)** 24 acres 1 mi. n. of SR 233. Snowmobiling; playground. | 97 | ● | | | | | | ● | | ● | | ● | | | |
| **Moraine (F-2)** 15,838 acres 8 mi. n.w. of Butler off US 422. Cross-country skiing, hunting, iceboating, ice fishing, snowmobiling, tobogganing. | 44 | ● | ● | ● | ● | ● | ● | ● | ● | ● | ● | ● | ● | | ● |
| **Mount Pisgah (D-8)** 1,302 acres 10 mi. n.w. of Troy off US 6. Cross-country skiing, ice fishing, ice skating, sledding, snowmobiling. | 45 | ● | ● | ● | ● | ● | ● | ● | | ● | | ● | | | |
| **Neshaminy (H-12)** 330 acres near Croydon off SR 132. | 46 | ● | ● | | | | | | ● | ● | | ● | | | ● |
| **Nockamixon (G-11)** 5,283 acres 5 mi. e. of Quakertown off CRs 513 and 563. Tobogganing; horse rental. | 47 | ● | ● | ● | ● | ● | ● | ● | | ● | | | | ● | ● |
| **Ohiopyle (I-3)** 18,719 acres 14 mi. e. of Uniontown on SR 381. Cross-country skiing, snowmobiling. | 48 | ● | ● | ● | | | | ● | | ● | | ● | ● | | ● |
| **Oil Creek (E-3)** 7,007 acres 4 mi. n. of Oil City on SR 8 via signs. Cross-country skiing. | 98 | ● | ● | ● | | | | ● | | | | ● | | | |
| **Ole Bull (E-6)** 117 acres 3 mi. s.w. of Oleona off SR 144. | 49 | ● | ● | ● | | | | ● | ● | | | | | | |
| **Parker Dam (F-5)** 968 acres 4 mi. e. of Penfield off SR 153. Cross-country skiing, snowmobiling. | 50 | ● | ● | ● | ● | ● | ● | ● | ● | | | ● | | ● | |
| **Patterson (D-6)** 10 acres off SR 44 between Cherry Springs and Sweden Valley. | 99 | ● | ● | ● | | | | | | | | | | | |
| **Penn Roosevelt (G-6)** 41 acres 10 mi. w. of Milroy off US 322. Snowmobiling. | 100 | ● | ● | ● | | | | ● | | | | ● | | | |
| **Pine Grove Furnace (H-7)** 696 acres at Pine Grove Furnace on SR 233. Cross-country skiing. | 51 | ● | ● | ● | ● | ● | | ● | ● | ● | | ● | | | |
| **Poe Paddy (F-7)** 10 acres n.e. of Milroy off US 322. | 101 | ● | ● | ● | ● | ● | | ● | | | | | | | |
| **Poe Valley (F-7)** 620 acres 10 mi. n.e. of Milroy off US 322. Snowmobiling. | 52 | ● | ● | ● | ● | ● | ● | ● | ● | | | ● | | | |
| **Presque Isle (C-2)** 3,200 acres 5 mi. n. on Peninsula Dr. (SR 832). Historic. *(See Erie)* | 53 | | ● | ● | ● | ● | ● | ● | ● | ● | ● | ● | ● | ● | ● |
| **Prince Gallitzin (G-5)** 6,249 acres 16 mi. n.w. of Altoona off SR 53. Cross-country skiing, tobogganing; horse rental. | 54 | ● | ● | ● | ● | ● | ● | ● | ● | ● | | ● | ● | ● | ● |
| **Promised Land (E-11)** 2,971 acres 10 mi. n. of Canadensis on SR 390. Cross-country skiing, snowmobiling. | 55 | ● | ● | ● | ● | ● | ● | ● | ● | ● | | ● | ● | ● | ● |
| **Prouty Place (D-6)** 5 acres 8 mi. s. on unmarked route off SR 44 between Cherry Springs and Sweden Valley. | 102 | ● | ● | ● | | | | | ● | | | | | | |
| **Pymatuning (E-1)** 21,122 acres 4 mi. n. of Jamestown off US 322. Cross-country skiing, iceboating, ice fishing, ice skating, snowmobiling. | 56 | ● | ● | ● | ● | ● | ● | ● | ● | | | | ● | ● | ● |
| **Raccoon Creek (G-1)** 7,323 acres 2 mi. n. of Frankfort Springs on SR 18. Cross-country skiing. | 57 | ● | ● | ● | ● | ● | ● | ● | ● | | | ● | | | |
| **Ralph Stover (G-11)** 45 acres 9 mi. n.w. of New Hope on SR 32. Tobogganing. | 58 | ● | ● | | | | | ● | | | | ● | | ● | ● |
| **Raymond B. Winter (F-7)** 695 acres 20 mi. w. of Lewisburg on SR 192. | 59 | ● | ● | ● | | | | | ● | ● | | ● | | | |
| **Reeds Gap (G-7)** 220 acres 13 mi. n.e. of Lewistown off US 322. Tobogganing. | 60 | ● | ● | ● | | | | | ● | ● | | ● | | | |
| **Ricketts Glen (E-9)** 13,050 acres 12 mi. n. of Benton on SR 487. Cross-country skiing, snowmobiling. *(See Red Rock)* | 61 | ● | ● | ● | ● | ● | ● | ● | ● | | | ● | | ● | |
| **Ridley Creek (H-11)** 2,600 acres 7 mi. e. of West Chester via SRs 3 or 352. | 62 | ● | ● | | | | | ● | | | ● | ● | ● | | ● |
| **Ryerson Station (I-1)** 1,164 acres 1 mi. s. of Wind Ridge off SR 21. Tobogganing. | 63 | ● | ● | ● | ● | | | ● | ● | | | ● | | | |
| **Salt Springs (D-10)** 400 acres 1 mi. w. of Franklin Forks off SR 29. Primitive. | 104 | | ● | ● | | | | ● | | ● | | | | | |

| RECREATION AREAS | MAP LOCATION | CAMPING | PICNICKING | HIKING TRAILS | BOATING | BOAT RAMP | BOAT RENTAL | FISHING | SWIMMING | PETS ON LEASH | BICYCLE TRAILS | WINTER SPORTS | VISITOR CENTER | LODGE/CABINS | FOOD SERVICE |
|---|---|---|---|---|---|---|---|---|---|---|---|---|---|---|---|
| **S.B. Elliott (F-5)** 318 acres 9 mi. w. of Clearfield on SR 153. Snowmobiling. | 64 | ● | ● | ● | | | | | | | | ● | | ● | |
| **Shawnee (H-4)** 3,983 acres 9 mi. w. of Bedford off US 30. Cross-country skiing, snowmobiling. | 65 | ● | ● | ● | ● | ● | ● | ● | ● | ● | ● | ● | ● | ● | ● |
| **Shikellamy (F-8)** 125 acres 1 mi. n. of Shamokin Dam off SR 11. | 66 | | ● | ● | ● | ● | ● | ● | | | ● | ● | ● | | ● |
| **Sinnemahoning (E-6)** 1,910 acres 10 mi. n. of Sinnemahoning on SR 872. Snowmobiling. | 67 | ● | ● | ● | ● | ● | ● | ● | ● | ● | ● | ● | ● | ● | ● |
| **Sizerville (E-5)** 386 acres at Sizerville off SR 155. Cross-country skiing, snowmobiling. | 68 | ● | ● | ● | | | | | ● | ● | ● | ● | ● | | ● |
| **Tobyhanna (E-11)** 5,440 acres 2 mi. e. of Tobyhanna on SR 423. Snowmobiling. | 70 | ● | ● | ● | ● | ● | ● | ● | ● | ● | | ● | ● | ● | |
| **Trough Creek (H-6)** 541 acres 3 mi. n. of Entriken off SR 994. Snowmobiling. | 71 | ● | ● | ● | | | | ● | | ● | | ● | | ● | |
| **Tuscarora (F-9)** 1,716 acres 5 mi. n.w. of Tamaqua off SR 309. Tobogganing. | 72 | | ● | | ● | ● | ● | ● | ● | ● | | ● | | | ● |
| **Tyler (H-11)** 1,711 acres 1½ mi. w. of Newtown off SR 413. Cross-country skiing, sledding; horse trails. | 73 | | ● | ● | | | | ● | ● | ● | | ● | | ● | |
| **Warriors Path (H-5)** 334 acres 1 mi. s. of Saxton on SR 26. | 74 | ● | ● | | | | | | ● | | | ● | | ● | |
| **Whipple Dam (G-6)** 256 acres 12 mi. s. of State College off SR 26. Snowmobiling. | 75 | ● | ● | ● | ● | | | ● | ● | ● | | ● | | | ● |
| **Worlds End (E-8)** 780 acres 7 mi. n.w. of Laporte on SR 154. Snowmobiling. | 76 | ● | ● | ● | | | | ● | ● | ● | | ● | ● | ● | |
| **Yellow Creek (G-4)** 2,981 acres 18 mi. n.w. of Ebensburg on US 422. Cross-country skiing, sledding, snowmobiling. | 77 | | ● | ● | ● | ● | ● | ● | ● | ● | | ● | | ● | |

**OTHER**

| RECREATION AREAS | MAP LOCATION | CAMPING | PICNICKING | HIKING TRAILS | BOATING | BOAT RAMP | BOAT RENTAL | FISHING | SWIMMING | PETS ON LEASH | BICYCLE TRAILS | WINTER SPORTS | VISITOR CENTER | LODGE/CABINS | FOOD SERVICE |
|---|---|---|---|---|---|---|---|---|---|---|---|---|---|---|---|
| **Auburn Dam (G-9)** 187 acres 1 mi. from Landingville on LR 53075. | 105 | ● | | ● | ● | | ● | | ● | | | | | | |
| **Blue Marsh Lake (G-9)** 6,276 acres 8 mi. n. of Reading on SR 183. Ice fishing, ice skating, sledding, water skiing. | 78 | | ● | ● | ● | ● | ● | | ● | ● | | ● | | | |
| **Buckaloons Access Area (D-3)** 5 mi. w. of Warren at jct. US 6 and US 62. | 106 | ● | ● | ● | ● | ● | | | | ● | ● | ● | ● | | |
| **Chapman Lake (D-10)** 98 acres near Montdale. | 108 | ● | ● | | | | | ● | | | | | | | ● |
| **Conemaugh River Lake (G-3)** 7,609 acres 8 mi. n. of New Alexandria off SR 981. | 124 | ● | ● | ● | | | | ● | | ● | | | ● | ● | ● |
| **Curwensville Lake (F-5)** 362 acres 3 mi. s. of Curwensville on SR 453. Cross-country skiing. | 109 | ● | ● | ● | ● | ● | | | ● | ● | | ● | | | ● |
| **Edinboro Lake (D-1)** 240 acres on SR 99 in Edinboro. | 110 | | ● | | ● | ● | ● | ● | ● | ● | | | ● | ● | ● |
| **Felix Dam (H-9)** 3½-mile area n. of Reading at Tuckerton, via Tuckerton Rd. to Stoudts Ferry Bridge Rd. Water skiing. | 111 | | ● | | ● | ● | | ● | | | | | | | |
| **Harveys Lake (E-9)** 658 acres near Harveys Lake. | 112 | ● | ● | | ● | ● | | ● | | ● | | | | | ● |
| **Hibernia Park (H-10)** 800 acres 6 mi. n. of Coatesville on SR 82, then w. on Cedar Knoll Rd. | 123 | ● | ● | ● | | | | ● | | ● | ● | ● | | | |
| **Hugh Moore Park (G-11)** 260 acres on SR 611 in Easton. | 107 | | ● | ● | ● | | ● | | | ● | ● | | ● | ● | |
| **Lake Aldred (I-9)** 5,000 acres 25 mi. s.e. of York on SR 425. | 80 | ● | ● | ● | ● | ● | ● | ● | ● | ● | | ● | | | |
| **Lake Augusta (G-8)** 3,000 acres near Sunbury. | 113 | ● | ● | | ● | ● | ● | ● | | ● | | | | | |
| **Lake Leboeuf (D-2)** 70 acres 2 blks. s. on Hazel St. in Waterford. | 116 | ● | ● | | ● | ● | ● | ● | ● | ● | | | | | |
| **Lake Wallenpaupack (E-11)** 5,700 acres 10 mi. e. of Hamlin off SR 590. Horse rental. | 81 | ● | ● | | ● | ● | ● | ● | | ● | | | ● | ● | ● |
| **Leaser Lake (G-10)** 396 acres on SR 143 in Jacksonville. Bridle trails. | 16 | | ● | ● | ● | ● | | ● | | ● | | | ● | | |
| **Martins Creek (G-11)** 225 acres 3 mi. n. of Martins Creek via SR 611N to LR 48025. | 117 | | ● | ● | ● | ● | | ● | | ● | ● | | | | |
| **Mauch Chunk Lake (F-10)** 2,445 acres 4 mi. w. of Jim Thorpe. Cross-country skiing. | 88 | ● | ● | ● | ● | ● | ● | ● | ● | | | ● | ● | ● | ● |
| **Muddy Run (I-9)** 700 acres 4 mi. w. of Buck on SR 372. | 83 | ● | ● | ● | ● | ● | ● | ● | | ● | ● | ● | | ● | ● |
| **Nottingham (I-10)** 651 acres ¼ mi. s. of Nottingham at 150 Park Rd. Birdwatching, cross-country skiing. | 20 | ● | ● | ● | | | | ● | | ● | | ● | ● | | |
| **Susquehanna Access Area (G-8)** 10-mile area near Selinsgrove. | 119 | | ● | | ● | ● | | | | | | | | | |

| RECREATION AREAS | MAP LOCATION | CAMPING | PICNICKING | HIKING TRAILS | BOATING | BOAT RAMP | BOAT RENTAL | FISHING | SWIMMING | PETS ON LEASH | BICYCLE TRAILS | WINTER SPORTS | VISITOR CENTER | LODGE/CABINS | FOOD SERVICE |
|---|---|---|---|---|---|---|---|---|---|---|---|---|---|---|---|
| **Susquehanna Park (E-7)**  20 acres on Susquehanna River in Williamsport. | 122 | • | • | • | | | | • | | • | | | | | |
| **Ten Mile Creek Access Area (I-2)**  two sites: 3-mile area at Prosperity and an 11-mile area at Marianna. | 121 | • | • | • | | | | • | | | | | | | |
| **Youghiogheny Reservoir (I-3)**  4,034 acres 20 mi. s.e. of Uniontown on US 40. | 85 | • | • | | • | • | • | • | • | • | | | • | | |

# POINTS OF INTEREST

## AIRVILLE (I-9)

On the grounds of the Indian Steps Museum is a giant holly tree that is more than 350 years old. Each year a small branch of the tree is broken off and presented to the Pennsylvania Power and Light Co. as payment of rent for the land occupied by the nature trail behind the museum.

**INDIAN STEPS MUSEUM,** 4½ mi. n.e. on SR 425, then ¾ mi. s.e. on Indian Steps Rd., houses Indian relics. Animal and Indian patterns from 1500 B.C. through the Colonial period are imbedded in the walls. Behind the museum, a nature trail winds through 26 acres of wooded hillsides; there also is an arboretum containing 60 identified tree species. A separate building houses a nature center.

Allow 30 minutes minimum. Thurs.-Fri. 10-4, Sat.-Sun. and holidays 11-6, Apr. 15-Oct. 15. Donations. Phone (717) 862-3948.

## ALLEGHENY NATIONAL FOREST

> *Elevations in the forest range from 2,044 ft. at Jakes Rocks to 1,071 ft. at Baker Island near Tionesta. Refer to AAA maps for additional elevation information.*

Allegheny National Forest, the only national forest in Pennsylvania, extends 40 miles south from the New York-Pennsylvania border through the counties of Warren, Forest, Elk and McKean. Its 513,000 acres include 500 miles of fishing streams, 226 miles of hiking and cross-country ski trails, 297 miles of snowmobile trails and 106 miles of trailbike and ATV routes.

Six boat launches and a full-service marina provide access to the 12,000-acre Allegheny Reservoir, impounded by the Kinzua Dam. Water skiing is popular, and 10 of the forest's 16 campgrounds are on or near the shore. Five of these can be reached only by boat or on foot. Rimrock and Jake's Rocks overlooks offer picnicking and views of the dam and reservoir, as well as spectacular displays of Pennsylvania's state flower, the mountain laurel, in June. Seven other picnic areas are available throughout the forest—four with unsupervised swimming facilities.

Other recreational activities include fishing; hunting for dear, bear, grouse and small game; ATV riding; and cross-country skiing. Canoeing is popular on the Allegheny Wild and Scenic River, the Clarion River and, in the early spring, Tionesta Creek. Heart's Content, a 122-acre primeval tract of 300- to 400-year-old hemlock and beech trees, is 15 miles south of Warren.

The 8,570-acre Hickory Creek Wilderness provides opportunities for primitive camping, hiking, hunting, fishing and wildlife watching. Allegheny Islands Wilderness, comprised of seven islands totalling 368 acres in the Allegheny River, holds the distinction of being the smallest federally designated wilderness in the United States.

For more information contact the Forest Headquarters, Allegheny National Forest, P.O. Box 847, Warren, PA 16365. Phone (814) 723-5150, or 726-2710 for TDD. *See Recreation Chart and the AAA Mideastern CampBook.*

## ALLENTOWN (G-11) pop. 105,100, elev. 304'

The business hub for a rich agricultural area, Allentown was originally incorporated as Northamptontown. The city later adopted the name of its founder, Pennsylvania Chief Justice William Allen. German settlers played a key role in the development of the fledgling community.

Allentown contributed to several aspects of early American history. After the Battle of Brandywine in 1777, George Washington had no hope

of saving Philadelphia from the British. The Liberty Bell and the bells of Christ Church were secretly removed by wagon to Allentown and hidden in Zion's Church for safekeeping.

June through September weekends, several of the area's historic homes are open, including the Troxell-Steckel House, 4229 Reliance St. in Egypt; the George Taylor House, Lehigh and Poplar streets in Catasauqua; and the Frank Buchman House, 117 N. 11th St. in Allentown.

Haines Mill Museum, 3600 Dorney Park Rd., is an operating gristmill built in 1760 and restored in 1909. The Lock Ridge Furnace Museum on Franklin Street in Alburtis chronicles the growth of the iron industry in the 19th century. Both are open on weekends, May through September.

The Old-Fashioned Rose Garden, Parkway Boulevard and 27th Street, contains more than 100 varieties of roses, as well as water plants in lagoons and many other flowers. The peak bloom seasons are in the spring and fall. The Old Courthouse County Museum, at Hamilton and 5th streets, was built 1814-17 and houses local history exhibits.

Nearby Trexlertown boasts the Lehigh County Velodrome, one of only about a dozen outdoor bicycle tracks in the country. National and international cycling events are held at the track every Friday night, June through August. The track also is open to the public for leisure riding when races are not taking place; phone (610) 967-7587.

**Self-guiding tours:** A brochure describing a self-guiding driving tour of the area's covered bridges is available at the Lehigh Valley Convention and Visitors Bureau at 2200 Avenue A, Bethlehem, PA 18017; phone (610) 882-9200 or (800) 747-0561 *(see ad)*. A brochure for a self-guiding walking tour of downtown Allentown is available from the Allentown Downtown Improvement District Authority, 805 Hamilton Mall, Allentown, PA 18101; phone (610) 776-7117.

**Shopping areas:** Three malls form a local shopping center cluster. Lehigh Valley Mall, N. MacArthur Road and US 22, includes JCPenney, Macy's and Wanamakers. Whitehall Mall, MacArthur Road and Grape Street, contains Clover, Leh's and Sears. Whitehall Square Mall, also on MacArthur Road, features Bradlees. Hess's, Hamilton Mall at 9th Street, also is popular.

**ALLENTOWN ART MUSEUM,** 5th and Court sts., displays 14th- through 20th-century European and American artwork. The collection of paintings, sculpture and decorative arts includes the work of Albert Bierstadt, George Bellows, Frans Hals, Charles Peale, Rembrandt, Gilbert Stuart and Frank Lloyd Wright. Rotating exhibits also are featured.

Allow 1 hour minimum. Wed.-Fri. 11-3 (also Thurs. 3-7:30), Sat. 10-3, Sun. noon-3:30; closed major holidays. Admission $3.50; over 61, $3; students with ID $2; under 13 free; free to all on Sun. noon-1. MC, VI ($10). Phone (610) 432-4333.

**CLOVER HILL VINEYARDS & WINERY,** 2.7 mi. w. of SR 100 via Schantz Rd., then e. on Newtown Rd., offers self-guiding tours and tastings. Guided tours are available by appointment. Picnicking is permitted. Allow 30 minutes minimum. Mon.-Sat. 11-5, Sun. noon-5; closed major holidays. Free. Phone (610) 395-2468.

★**DORNEY PARK AND WILDWATER KINGDOM,** I-78 w. to exit 16B, then e. on Hamilton Blvd., or e. on SR 22 and s. on Cedar Crest Blvd., following signs, is a 200-acre entertainment complex that includes Hercules, one of the country's tallest wooden roller coasters, as well as more than 100 rides and attractions. Dorney Park features three rollercoasters, kiddie rides, a carrousel, sky rides, race cars, miniature golf and Berenstain Bear Country, which features many shows and activities for children.

Wildwater Kingdom offers a wave pool, the White Water Landing "waterfall plunge"—considered the world's tallest, rides on Runaway River and Riptide Run, whitewater rafting at Thunder Canyon, bumper boats and waterslides, including the Aquablast—purportedly the world's longest. The Cedar Creek Cannonball train ride connects the two parks. Live entertainment is provided. Food is available. Picnic facilities are provided outside of the park.

Allow a full day. Dorney Park open daily at 10, May 26-Labor Day; Fri.-Sun. at 10, May 6-25; Sat.-Sun. at 10, day after Labor Day-Oct. 1. Wildwater Kingdom open daily at 10, Memorial Day weekend-Labor Day; Sat.-Sun. at noon, Sept. 9-10. Closing times vary.

Admission (including rides) $24.95, over 59 and under 48 inches tall $4.95, under age 3 free; after 5 p.m. $10.50. Two-day pass $32.95, over 59 and under 48 inches tall $9.90. Admission to Dorney Park $19.95, May 6-26 ($16.50, Sept. 16-17, 23-24, 30 and Oct. 1). Parking $3. DS, MC, VI. Phone (610) 395-3724, or (800) 253-8636 in Pa., or (800) 551-5656 in N.J., N.Y., Del., Md., Va. and Conn. *See ad p. 76.*

**LEHIGH COUNTY HISTORICAL MUSEUM,** 5th and Hamilton sts., is in the old courthouse. Displays depict Pennsylvania German heritage and the development of the area's iron, coal, trucking and silk industries. Indian artifacts also are featured. Mon.-Sat. 10-4, Sun. 1-4. Free. Phone (610) 435-4664.

**LIBERTY BELL SHRINE,** in Zion's Reformed Church, Hamilton Mall at Church St., houses a replica of the Liberty Bell on the spot where the original was hidden during the Revolutionary War. A mural incorporates sound and light to describe the Liberty Bell. Mon.-Sat. noon-4; closed Jan. 1, Thanksgiving and Dec. 25. Free. Phone (610) 435-4232.

**LIL'LE'HI TROUT NURSERY,** off the Little Lehigh Pkwy. on Fish Hatchery Rd., contains 65,000 brook, brown and rainbow trout. Fish food can be purchased; exact change is required in winter. Daily 9-dusk. Free. Phone (610) 437-7656.

**TROUT HALL,** 4th and Walnut sts., was built in 1770 by James Allen, son of William Allen, city founder and Pennsylvania chief justice. The building contains period furniture and a museum. Tues.-Sat. noon-3, Sun. 1-4, Apr.-Nov.; closed holidays. Free. Phone (610) 435-4664 or 820-4043.

### ALLENWOOD (F-8) elev. 481'

**CLYDE PEELING'S REPTILAND,** 6 mi. n. of I-80 exit 30B on US 15, provides close-up views of turtles, tortoises, lizards, alligators, crocodiles, birds and exotic and native snakes. The animals are displayed in tropical-like garden settings with pools and ornamental grasses. Live demonstrations are held daily at noon, 1:30 and 4:30. Visitors are allowed to touch a tame boa. Tortoises are not displayed during cold weather. Picnic facilities are available.

Allow 1 hour, 30 minutes minimum. Daily 9-7, May-Sept.; 10-5, rest of year. Closed Jan. 1, Thanksgiving and Dec. 25. Admission $6.50; ages 4-11, $4.50. Phone (717) 538-1869.

### ALTOONA (G-5) pop. 52,000, elev. 1,171'

The Pennsylvania Railroad, now Conrail, founded Altoona in 1849 during construction of the first railroad over the Alleghenies. For years the town's economy depended on railroad building and repair shops; other industries have since developed.

Popular events in Altoona include the the the Keystone Country Festival in early September.

For more information contact the Altoona-Blair County Chamber of Commerce, 1212 Twelfth Ave., Altoona, PA 16601; phone (814) 943-8151.

**Shopping areas:** The major local shopping center is Logan Valley Mall, US 220 and Goods Lane. It features JCPenney, Kaufman's and Sears.

**ALTOONA RAILROADERS MEMORIAL MUSEUM,** 1300 9th Ave. in Station Mall Complex, traces the development of the Pennsylvania Railroad and its impact on local and national history. On exhibit are the "Loretto," the private railroad car of steel baron Charles M. Schwab; and "Nancy," a locomotive built in 1918.

Allow 1 hour, 30 minutes minimum. Daily 10-6, Apr. 3-Oct. 29; Tues.-Sun. 10-5, rest of year. Closed holidays. Admission $2.50; over 62, $2; ages 3-12, $1.50; family rate $7. Phone (814) 946-0834.

**BAKER MANSION,** 1 mi. w. of US 220 via Logan Blvd., was the Greek Revival home of ironmaster Elias Baker. The 1844 mansion has carved oak pieces he imported from Belgium, as well as Indian and railroad artifacts and material about Abraham Lincoln. Guided tours are available. Christmas tours are given the first 2 weekends in December.

Allow 1 hour minimum. Tues.-Sun. 1-4:30, Memorial Day weekend-Labor Day; Sat.-Sun. 1-4:30, mid-Apr. through day before Memorial Day weekend and day after Labor Day-Oct. 31. Last tour departs 1 hour before closing. Closed major holidays. Admission $3; over 65 and ages 13-18, $2.50; ages 5-12, $1. **Discount.** Phone (814) 942-3916.

**BENZEL'S PRETZEL FACTORY,** 5200 Sixth Ave., offers self-guiding tours that illustrate the pretzel making process. Visitors can view workers through windows and monitors. A 7-minute videotape presentation also is featured. Freshly baked pretzels are provided at the end of the tour. Allow 30 minutes minimum. Mon.-Fri. 9-5 (also Fri. 5-6), Sat. 9-1; closed major holidays. Free. Phone (814) 942-5062 or (800) 344-4438.

**FORT ROBERDEAU,** in Sinking Valley, 9 mi. n.e. via US 220 to Kettle St., is a reconstructed log fort on the original site of a Revolutionary War fort established to mine lead for the army. The enlisted men's barracks, officers' quarters and kitchen reflect the accommodations of 18th-century militiamen. Other facilities include a blacksmith shop and lead smelters. An adjacent nature area has marked trails and a rock and mineral museum; picnic facilities are available. Special events include a military re-enactment in late July. Allow 1 hour minimum. Tues.-Sat. 11-5, Sun. 1-5, mid-May to early Oct.; closed holidays. Admission $3; senior citizens $2.50; under 13, $1. Phone (814) 946-0048.

**HORSESHOE CURVE NATIONAL HISTORIC LANDMARK,** 6 mi. w., showcases the Horseshoe Curve, which opened in 1854 and revolutionized rail travel. The two sides of the arc are almost parallel, an engineering masterpiece in conquering the Alleghenies. The entire curve is visible from the trackside observation area which is reached by a short funicular ride or by climbing 194 stairs. A visitor center features the Altoona Railroaders Memorial Museum (see attraction listing). Food is available. Visitor center open daily 9:30-7, Apr. 3-Oct. 29; Tues.-Sun. 10-4:30, rest of year. Funicular closed first Tues. of the month in summer. Funicular $1.50 round trip. Phone (814) 946-0834.

**LAKEMONT PARK,** 700 Park Ave., is an amusement park with more than 30 rides and attractions. Food is available. Mon.-Fri. noon-9:30, Sat.-Sun. and holidays noon-10, Memorial Day-Labor Day. Free. All-day ride pass $5.95. Phone (814) 949-7275.

**WOPSONONOCK TABLELAND,** 6 mi. n.w., rises to an elevation of 2,580 feet and affords a panoramic view of the city and six surrounding counties.

## AMBRIDGE (G-1) pop. 8,100, elev. 700′

Ambridge celebrates its roots with Nationality Days, a mid-May festival featuring ethnic cultural displays, foods, music and dancing. For more event information contact the Ambridge Area Chamber of Commerce, 719 Merchant St., 2nd floor, Ambridge, PA 15003; phone (412) 266-3040.

**OLD ECONOMY VILLAGE** derives its title from the original town of Economy, built 1824-30 by the Harmony Society (see Harmony). Founded in 1804 by German immigrants, the society thrived on highly skilled craftsmanship and farming; the rule of celibacy led to its dissolution in 1905. Embracing two blocks, the village contains 18 original structures.

Visitors may tour the restored buildings, which include the Feast Hall; a community kitchen; tailor, shoe and cabinet shops; a general store; and a wine cellar. The George Rapp House and Frederick Rapp House have 17 rooms open to the public. Formal gardens are on the grounds.

Special events include Charter Day in March and 19th-century Christmas programs. Guided tours are available. Allow 1 hour, 30 minutes

minimum. Open Tues.-Sat. 9-4, Sun. noon-4. Last admission 1 hour before closing. Closed Jan. 1, Thanksgiving and Dec. 25. Admission $5; over 60, $4; ages 6-17, $3. Phone (412) 266-4500.

## ANDREAS (G-10) elev. 587′

**JEM CLASSIC CAR MUSEUM,** 5 mi. e. of SR 309 on SR 443, displays about 40 vintage automobiles, including a 1902 Curved Dash Oldsmobile, a 1929 Stutz Blackhawk and a 1931 Cadillac Cabriolet. The 1929 Graham-Paige is thought to be one of only two remaining in the country. Allow 30 minutes minimum. Mon.-Fri. 10-4, Sat.-Sun. and holidays noon-4, Memorial Day weekend-Oct. 31. Admission $4; over 60, $3.50; ages 5-12, $2.50. **Discount.** Phone (717) 386-3554.

## ASHLAND (G-9) pop. 3,900, elev. 885′

**MUSEUM OF ANTHRACITE MINING** is ¼ mi. off SR 61 at 17th and Pine sts., next to the Pioneer Tunnel Coal Mine. Tools, machinery, models, photographs and graphic displays explain the mining and processing of anthracite. Allow 30 minutes minimum. Mon.-Sat. 10-6, Sun. noon-6, May-Oct.; Tues.-Sat. 9-5, Sun. noon-5, rest of year. Closed Jan. 1, Easter, Thanksgiving and Dec. 25. Admission $3.50; over 60, $2.50; ages 6-17, $1.50. Admission $2.50 with ticket stub from Pioneer Tunnel or steam train ride. Phone (717) 875-4708.

**PIONEER TUNNEL COAL MINE AND STEAM TRAIN RIDE,** 4 blks. off SR 61, following signs, offers a tour through a coal mine on battery-powered mine cars. Experienced miners act as guides and explain the operation. Mine temperatures range from 48 to 52 degrees Fahrenheit; a sweater or light jacket is advised. On another tour, a 1920s steam train powers mine cars three-fourths of a mile around a mountainside to an abandoned strip mine and bootleg coal hole. Picnicking is permitted.

Allow 1 hour, 30 minutes minimum. Mine tours and train rides daily 10-6, Memorial Day-Labor Day; otherwise varies. Mine tour $5; under 12, $3. Train ride $2.50; under 12, $1.50. **Discount.** Phone (717) 875-3850 or 875-3301.

## AUDUBON (H-11)

In the early 1900s some of the country's first feature-length motion pictures were produced a few miles east of Audubon in Betzwood, site of a studio set up by Sigmund Lubin, a noted Philadelphia optician and movie producer. The lot, which accommodated 40 cowboys, 25 Indians and 100 horses, was used to film the "Battle of Shiloh," one of the first epic spectacles filmed.

**AUDUBON WILDLIFE SANCTUARY** is ½ mi. s.w. On the 175-acre nature preserve is Mill Grove, home in the early 1800s of John James

Audubon, noted artist, author and naturalist. Now a museum, the house contains displays of Audubon's paintings, drawings and taxidermy specimens. Numerous trails wind through the grounds, which serve as a bird sanctuary. Allow 30 minutes minimum. Tues.-Sat. 10-4, Sun. 1-4; closed Jan. 1, Thanksgiving and Dec. 25. Grounds open Tues.-Sun. dawn-dusk. Free. Phone (610) 666-5593.

## AVELLA (H-1)

**MEADOWCROFT MUSEUM OF RURAL LIFE,** 3 mi. w. on SR 50, following signs, is a 19th-century rural community; buildings from other locations have been rebuilt on the site. Allow 2 hours minimum. Wed.-Sat. 10-5, Sun. 1-6, May-Oct. Admission $6; over 60, $5; ages 6-16, $3. **Discount.** To verify prices phone (412) 587-3412.

## BAUMSTOWN (H-10)

**DANIEL BOONE HOMESTEAD,** 9 mi. e. of Reading on US 422, then 1 mi. n. on Daniel Boone Rd., was the birthplace of the famous frontiersman. The 579-acre restored Boone Homestead incorporates the original 10-room stone house built 1730-79 by the Boones. The home is furnished with mid-18th-century Pennsylvania furniture.

Included on the site are a restored blacksmith shop, sawmill and barn, the 1730 Bertolet log house, picnicking and hiking areas and a visitor center. Allow 1 hour minimum. Tues.-Sat. 9-5, Sun. noon-5; closed holidays. Admission $4; over 59, $3; ages 6-17, $2. Phone (610) 582-4900.

## BEAVER FALLS (G-1) pop. 10,700, elev. 787'

**AIR HERITAGE MUSEUM AND AIRCRAFT RESTORATION FACILITY,** at the Beaver County Airport, 2 mi. n. on SR 51, houses memorabilia from World Wars I and II, including uniforms, flight suits and airplane models. In an adjacent hangar visitors can observe vintage aircraft being restored. Allow 30 minutes minimum. Daily noon-5. Donations. Phone (412) 843-2820.

## BEDFORD (I-5) pop. 3,100, elev. 1,060'

The Allegheny mountain area of Bedford was first settled in 1751 by Robert Ray, after whom Fort Raystown was named when it was built in 1758. Eventually, the community was renamed in honor of the Duke of Bedford. Several historic buildings have been preserved in downtown Bedford, including the Espy House, which served as President Washington's headquarters in 1794 when he led Federal troops into western Pennsylvania to quell the Whiskey Rebellion. Also, the Anderson House, 137 E. Pitt St., was built 1814-15 and housed what is believed to be the first bank west of the Allegheny Mountains. The original bank vault can still be seen.

During the French and Indian War historic Forbes Road (US 30) was used by Gen. John Forbes on his way to capture Fort Duquesne, which is now known as the city of Pittsburgh. The road winds through the farmlands and valleys of Bedford County and over more than 14 covered bridges. Schellsburg Church, built in 1806, also is along Forbes Road.

The Great Bedford County Fair is held in August, and the Fall Foliage Festival in early October features an antique car parade.

**Self-guiding tours:** Brochures for self-guiding walking and driving tours are available at the Bedford County Tourist Information Center, 137 E. Pitt St., P.O. Box 1771, Bedford, PA 15522; phone (814) 623-1771 or (800) 765-3331.

**FORT BEDFORD MUSEUM,** N. Juliana St., is housed in a reproduction of an early blockhouse. The museum displays a scale model of the original fort. Daily 10-5, Memorial Day weekend-Labor Day; Wed.-Mon. 10-5, May 1-day before Memorial Day weekend and day after Labor Day-Oct. 31. Admission $2.50; over 60, $2; ages 6-18, $1.50. **Discount.** Phone (814) 623-8891.

**OLD BEDFORD VILLAGE,** 1 mi. n. on US 220, ¾ mi. s. of Pennsylvania Tpke. exit 11, is a 40-building reproduction of a village from the 1750-1850 period. Many of the log cabins, one-room schoolhouses and other buildings were brought from their original locations and reassembled. Among the crafts demonstrated are gunmaking, tinsmithing, broom making, leather making, quilting, spinning, weaving and woodworking.

Special events include the Old Bedford Village Crafts Festival, June 18-19; Settler Days, July 9-10; Old Bedford Village Bluegrass Festival, July 23-24; Gospel Music Festival, Aug. 13-14; Pioneer Days Celebration, Labor Day weekend; Civil War Re-enactment, Sept. 10-11; Senior Citizen Days, Sept. 17-18; Mystery Village Evenings, Oct. 1, 8 and 15; The Great Pumpkin Festival, Oct. 22-23; and The Fashioned Christmas Celebration from early to mid-December. Theater performances are given Fri.-Sat. at 8 p.m., mid-May to mid-Sept.

Allow 1 hour, 30 minutes minimum. Daily 9-5, early May-late Oct. Admission $6.95; over 60, $5.95; ages 6-12, $4.45. MC, VI. **Discount.** Phone (814) 623-1156 or (800) 238-4347.

**REYNOLDSDALE FISH CULTURAL STATION,** 12 mi. n.w. on SR 56, is a modern plant operated by the Pennsylvania Fish and Boat Commission for the propagation of mountain trout. Daily 8-3:45. Free. Phone (814) 839-2211.

## BELLEFONTE (F-6) pop. 6,300, elev. 747'

Built on several hills at the base of Bald Eagle Mountain, Bellefonte was named for its "beautiful fountain," the spring that furnishes the town's water supply. Many of Bellefonte's homes are fine examples of early Georgian architecture.

Known as the "Home of Governors," seven of the town's residents have become governors of Pennsylvania and other states.

**Self-guiding tours:** A walking-tour brochure can be obtained Monday through Friday from the Bellefonte Area Chamber of Commerce, Train Station, 320 W. High St., Bellefonte, PA 16823; phone (814) 355-2917.

**BIG SPRING,** on SR 150, maintains a temperature of 50 degrees Fahrenheit all year. It flows at the rate of 11,500,000 gallons daily; its overflow forms part of Spring Creek. Free.

**FISHERMAN'S PARADISE,** 3 mi. s.w. on Spring Creek, offers supervised fly fishing along 1 mile of the stream. A state fishing license is required, and fish must be released. A fish hatchery also is featured. Picnicking is permitted. Fly fishing daily dawn-dusk; hatchery 8-3. Free. Phone (814) 355-4159.

## BERNVILLE (G-9) pop. 800, elev. 317'

**KOZIAR'S CHRISTMAS VILLAGE** is 1 mi. s.w. via SR 183; follow signs to Christmas Village Rd. One of the largest Christmas displays in the country, the village uses half a million colored lights, tinsel and replicas of storybook characters to portray various Christmas themes. The village is a converted farm; a dozen buildings house displays that depict different facets of Christmas, including a miniature train display. Children can visit with Santa Claus.

Allow 1 hour minimum. Mon.-Fri. 6-9 p.m., Sat.-Sun. 5-9:30 p.m., Thanksgiving-Jan. 1; Fri.-Sun. 5:30-9:30 p.m., Nov. 1-day before Thanksgiving; Sat.-Sun. 7:30-9:30 p.m., in Oct. Admission $5; over 65 and ages 6-12, $4. Phone (610) 488-1110.

## BERWICK (F-9) pop. 11,000, elev. 505'

Berwick was founded as a religious refuge in 1786 by the Quaker Evan Owen, who named his community after Berwick-upon-Tweed, an English town on the Scottish border. Berwick is an industrial community that produces clothing, boxes, decorative ribbons, containers, snack foods and metal parts. For more area information contact the chamber of commerce, 120 E. Third St., Berwick, PA 18603; phone (717) 752-3601.

**SUSQUEHANNA ENERGY INFORMATION CENTER AND RIVERLANDS** is 5 mi. n. on US 11, or 12½ mi. n. of I-80 exit 36N. The Energy Information Center has energy-related computer games and displays explaining nuclear energy, as well as a nature center exhibit. Films are shown on request. Free 45-minute perimeter bus tours of the Susquehanna Steam Electric Station and a 2½-hour plant tour are available by advance arrangement.

Next to the center is Riverlands, a 1,400-acre recreation and nature area that offers picnicking, fishing, canoeing, boating (electric motors only),

cross-country skiing and nature trails. The Energy Information Center is open Mon.-Sat. and holidays 8-5, Sun. noon-5, Apr.-Oct.; Mon.-Fri. and holidays 8-5, Sat. 11-4, Sun. noon-4, rest of year. Riverlands is open daily 8 a.m.-dusk. Both closed Jan. 1, Easter, Thanksgiving and Dec. 25. Free. Phone (717) 542-2131 or 759-4905.

## BETHLEHEM (G-11) pop. 71,400, elev. 236'

In 1741, a group of Moravian missionaries from Europe arrived in what is now Bethlehem and established a communal church-village. They christened their settlement during their traditional Vigils on Christmas Eve with their patron, Count von Zinzendorf, who was visiting from Europe. Many of the large stone buildings constructed by the Moravians are still in use; the structures are considered among the finest examples of pre-Revolutionary German architecture in the country.

The Bach Festival is a development of the Moravian's love of music. Orchestras accompany the choir of local singers and guest soloists in this nationally known event held in May.

The town's Yuletide observance includes a large lighted Star of Bethlehem on the south mountain, hundreds of lighted trees and other decorations and a Moravian Christmas manger. Additional highlights include a live Christmas pageant, nightly bus tours with costumed guides, vigils and lovefeasts in the Moravian Church.

Bethlehem Steel Corp., among the largest steelmakers in North America, is an important addition to the town. Bethlehem also is the home of three institutions of higher education: Lehigh University, Moravian College and Northampton Community College. Moravian, established in 1742, is one of American's oldest colleges, and Lehigh is a major research university with facilities that include the Iacocca Institute, spearheaded by alumnus Lee Iacocca.

**Self-guiding tours:** Brochures detailing self-guiding walking tours of the town's historic district are available from the Bethlehem Visitors Center, 52 W. Broad St., Bethlehem, PA 18018; phone (610) 868-1513 or (800) 360-8687. Guided tours also can be arranged.

**EIGHTEENTH-CENTURY INDUSTRIAL QUARTER,** along Monocacy Creek at 459 Old York Rd. (access via Union Blvd.), features a restored 1761 tannery, the 1764 Springhouse, 1869 Luckenbach Mill and the 1762 waterworks—the first municipal pumping system in the Colonies. Interpreters in Moravian dress assist visitors. Artisans demonstrate Colonial trades. Guided tours begin at the Bethlehem Visitors Center, 52 W. Broad St., daily at 11 and 2; closed major holidays. Admission $6; under 12, $3. Phone (610) 868-1513 or (800) 360-8687.

**John Sebastian Goundie House,** 501 Main St., was built in 1810 and is considered to be the first Federal-style brick residence in Bethlehem. The north rooms are furnished in period. A tour is included with the Eighteenth-Century Industrial Quarter tour.

**THE KEMERER MUSEUM OF DECORATIVE ARTS,** 427 N. New St., is housed in two early 19th-century brick homes that are now joined together. Displays include glass, china, antique furniture, toys and grandfather clocks. Rotating exhibits and local artwork are featured in two art galleries. Guided tours are available. Allow 1 hour minimum. Tues.-Sun. noon-5; closed major holidays. Admission $3; over 55, $2; under 18, $1; family rate $7. **Discount.** Phone (610) 868-6868.

**MORAVIAN MUSEUM OF BETHLEHEM,** 66 W. Church St., is in the 1741 Gemein Haus (community house), the oldest building in Bethlehem. The museum displays silver, musical instruments, seminary art, needlework, Moravian furniture and clocks. Tues.-Sat. 1-4, Feb.-Dec. Admission $5, students $3. Phone (610) 867-0173.

**SUN INN,** 564 Main St., was established in 1758 as a way-station for such Colonial statesmen as George Washington, the Marquis de Lafayette and John Adams. It is fully restored and furnished in period. Food is available. Allow 1 hour minimum. Guided tours Tues.-Thurs. 12:30-4, Fri. 12:30-9, Sat. 10-9; other times by appointment. Admission $2; over 60 and ages 6-12, $1. Phone (215) 866-1758.

## BIRD-IN-HAND (H-9) elev. 360'

As did many early Lancaster County settlements, Bird-in-Hand took its name from a tavern sign, which pictured a bird resting in a hand. Taverns of the period chose pictures over words because it was immediately recognizable to travelers, many of whom could not read. Four hotels have since stood on the site of the original Bird-in-Hand, which was built to serve travelers on the Philadelphia Turnpike. *Also see Pennsylvania Dutch Country.*

**OLD VILLAGE STORE,** on SR 340, remains much as it was in 1890, with checkerboards and a potbellied stove. It is one of the older hardware stores in the country. Allow 30 minutes minimum. Mon.-Sat. 9-5:30, May-Oct.; 9-5, rest of year. Free. Phone (717) 397-1291.

**PLAIN AND FANCY FARM,** 1 mi. e. on SR 340, is a shopping village featuring buggy rides and craft and gift shops. Phone (717) 768-8281.

**Old Order Amish House** is furnished to reflect the Amish way of life. Guided tours are available. Allow 30 minutes minimum. Mon.-Sat. 10-5, Mar.-Dec.; closed Dec. 25. Admission $3; ages 6-10, $1.50.

**WEAVERTOWN ONE-ROOM SCHOOLHOUSE** is ¾ mi. e. on SR 340. A 30-minute program using animated wax figures depicts a typical day in a Pennsylvania Dutch school. The bell, desks and blackboards are original. The school held classes for almost a century, until 1969. Daily 9-5, Memorial Day-Labor Day; 10-5, Apr. 8-day before Memorial Day and day after Labor Day-Nov. 26. Admission $2; senior citizens $1.75; ages 5-11, $1.50. Phone (717) 768-3976 or 291-1888.

## BOALSBURG (G-6)

An early stagecoach stop founded in 1808, Boalsburg has retained much of its original architecture and street layout. The nation's first Memorial Day was celebrated in the village cemetery in 1864, a tradition Boalsburg continues with an annual Memorial Day Festival drawing more than 25,000 people.

**Shopping areas:** The Village of Boalsburg offers taverns and quaint shops filled with antiques, art, flowers, crafts, gifts and collectibles. Many of the shops are housed in historic homes.

**COLUMBUS CHAPEL AND BOAL MANSION MUSEUM** are on US 322 Business Route. The Columbus Chapel, a centuries-old Spanish chapel once belonging to the Christopher Columbus family, was inherited by Columbus' descendants in the Boal family and brought to the estate in 1909. The chapel features an Admiral's desk once owned by Columbus, family heirlooms dating to the 1400s, Renaissance and baroque art and religious relics.

The Boal Mansion, home to nine generations of the Boal family, contains the original furnishings. The grounds include a 1789 stone frontier cabin, a 1798 farmhouse addition and an 1898 ballroom and servants' quarters.

In addition, two exhibit buildings display a variety of family items, including carriages, weapons and farm implements. Allow 1 hour minimum. Wed.-Mon. 10-5, mid-June through Labor Day; 1:30-5, May 1 to mid-June and day after Labor Day-Oct. 31. Admission $5; ages 7-11, $2. Phone (814) 466-6210.

**PENNSYLVANIA MILITARY MUSEUM,** on US 322, honors Pennsylvania's soldiers from Benjamin Franklin's first volunteer unit in the Revolutionary War through Vietnam and Operation Desert Storm. Displays include a full-scale World War I trench scene, cannon, infantry weapons, uniforms, memorabilia, military equipment and vehicles. The 66-acre park also features monuments and memorials commemorating the sacrifices of generations of Pennsylvania patriots.

Allow 1 hour minimum. Tues.-Sat. 9-5, Sun. noon-5; closed Jan. 1, Thanksgiving and Dec. 25. Admission $3.50; over 59, $2.50; ages 6-17, $1.50. Phone (814) 466-6263.

## BOYERTOWN (H-11) pop. 3,800, elev. 386'

**BOYERTOWN MUSEUM OF HISTORIC VEHICLES,** w. from SR 100 to jct. SRs 73 and 562, then 2 blks. s. to 28 Warwick St., displays southeastern Pennsylvania vehicles from the 18th,

19th and 20th centuries. Sleighs, carriages, wagons and bicycles are exhibited, as well as electric-, steam- and gas-powered vehicles and the tools used to assemble them. Prototype electric vehicles also are displayed.

Allow 1 hour minimum. Tues.-Fri. 9-4, Sat.-Sun. 10-4; closed Dec. 25. Admission $4; over 60, $3.50; ages 6-18, $2. **Discount.** Phone (610) 367-2090.

### BRADFORD (D-5) pop. 2,500, elev. 1,437'

Bradford began as a sparse community on the Tunungwant Creek in 1843. In 1875, oil was discovered and the price of land soared from 6¼ cents to $1,000 an acre. The city boomed as residents sank wells everywhere. Bradford also has become a leader in manufacturing: Lumber products, cutlery, electronic parts and boxes are produced locally.

The Penn-Brad Oil Museum, 1 mi. s. on SR 219, features a 72-foot-tall wooden drilling rig and displays local artifacts from the town's oil-producing days.

One mile north of Bolivar Drive on the Seaward Avenue extension is Crook Farm, a collection of restored buildings that includes a farmhouse, barn, carpenter shop, one-room schoolhouse and nature trails. For more area information contact the chamber of commerce, 10 Main St., Bradford, PA 16701; phone (814) 368-7115.

### BRISTOL (H-12) pop. 10,400, elev. 21'

GRUNDY MUSEUM, 610 Radcliffe St., was built in the early 19th century. In later years, when it served as the family home of Sen. Joseph R. Grundy, it was remodeled and furnished in the Victorian style. Allow 30 minutes minimum. Mon.-Fri. 1-4, Sat. 1-3, Sept.-June; Mon.-Fri. 1-4, rest of year. Free. Phone (215) 788-9432.

### BROOKVILLE (F-3) pop. 4,200, elev. 1230'

Brookville was settled in 1796 at the confluence of Sandy Lick and Mill creeks by Samuel Scott and Joseph and Andrew Barnett. Growth was slow, but in 1830 the town was named the county seat and settlement began in earnest. By the early 19th century, Brookville had a thriving lumber industry and supplied all the lumber markets in Pittsburgh. The arrival of the railroad in 1873 augmented industrial and commercial development.

A 90-acre historic district features more than 300 buildings dating from the 19th century. The Jefferson County Courthouse, Main and Pickering streets, is a three-story Italianate structure built in 1867. The Marlin Opera House is a 900-seat hall built in 1883 by Civil War veteran Col. Silas Marlin.

The Western Pennsylvania Laurel Festival, held the third week in June, features a carnival, art exhibits, golf tournaments, entertainment, a craft show and sports contests. During the first weekend in December, citizens dress in period costumes for the Victorian Christmas Celebration, which features Christmas caroling, puppet shows and a children's story hour.

**Self-guiding tours:** Free maps detailing a self-guiding walking tour of the town's historic district are available at the Brookville Chamber of Commerce, 233 Main St., Brookville, PA 15825; phone (814) 849-8448.

JEFFERSON COUNTY HISTORICAL AND GENEALOGICAL SOCIETY, 232 Jefferson St., is in the Brady Craig House. The home, built in the late 1830s or early '40s, displays Victorian furniture, maps, diaries and photographs. A genealogical library offers a newspaper collection and periodical references. Allow 1 hour minimum. Tues.-Sun. 2-5; closed major holidays. Free. Phone (814) 849-0077.

### BROOMALL (I-11)

THOMAS MASSEY HOUSE, 1 mi. s. from SR 3 on Lawrence Rd. at Springhouse Rd., was built in 1696 and is one of the older English Quaker homes in Pennsylvania. Restored to its original condition, it contains period furnishings and implements. The grounds include small kitchen gardens and a carriage/woodshed with a blacksmith forge.

Special events include Colonial Craft Days in June, Colonial Harvest Days in October and Colonial Christmas in December. Candlelight tours and public dinners are held throughout the winter months. A junior guide program in the summer allows children to learn Colonial crafts and experience Colonial living. Allow 1 hour minimum. Mon.-Fri. 10-4, Sun. 2-4:30. Admission $2; over 65 and ages 6-18, $1. Phone (610) 353-3644.

### BROWNSVILLE (H-2) pop. 3,200, elev. 380'

NEMACOLIN CASTLE, Brashear and Front sts., was built in 1789. The stately brick home features 22 rooms furnished in various manners. A frontier trading post is represented as well as a formal Victorian style. Allow 1 hour minimum.

Tues.-Fri. 11-4:30, Sat.-Sun. 10-4:30, June 1-Labor Day; Sat.-Sun. 10-4:30, Easter-May 31 and day after Labor Day to mid-Oct. Candlelight tours daily 4-9, late Nov.-early Dec. Admission $5; senior citizens $4; under 12, $2. **Discount.** Phone (412) 785-6882.

### BRYN MAWR (H-11) elev. 412'

**HARRITON HOUSE** is 1¼ mi. n. of US 30 on Morris Ave., then ½ mi. w. on Old Gulph Rd., then n. on Harriton Rd. to entrance. Built in 1704, the two-story stone house was the home of Charles Thomson, secretary of the Continental Congress. The house has some original furnishings and has been restored to its original appearance. The grounds cover 16½ acres; picnicking is permitted. Guided tours are available by prior arrangement.

Wed.-Sat. 10-4; other times by appointment. Closed holidays. Admission $2, students with ID free. Phone (610) 525-0201.

### BUCKS COUNTY

One of the larger and more historic counties of the commonwealth, Bucks County stretches into the countryside surrounding northern Philadelphia. This quiet, wooded region bordering the Delaware River is replete with rolling hills, old stone houses and covered bridges. William Penn named the county for its resemblance to Buckinghamshire in England. An interesting driving tour covering much of Bucks County follows the Delaware River along SR 32.

The narrow, winding streets of Doylestown, once an overnight stagecoach stop between Philadelphia and Easton, capture Bucks County's historic charm, as do Fallsington and Washington Crossing Historic Park.

The Delaware Canal, built in 1831, flows through New Hope, an artists' and writers' colony settled along the river. New Hope is known for its natural settings, book and antique shops, art galleries and cafes on the banks of both the river and the canal. The town also is home to one of the nation's older and most famous summer theaters, the Bucks County Playhouse.

For more information contact the Bucks County Tourist Commission, 152 Swamp Rd., Doylestown, PA 18901; phone (215) 345-4552. The offices are open Mon.-Fri. 8:30-5:30, Sat. 10-4.

Places and towns in Bucks County listed individually are Bristol, Doylestown, Dublin, Fallsington, Lahaska, Langhorne, Morrisville, New Hope, Point Pleasant and Washington Crossing Historic Park.

### BUSHKILL (F-12)

**BUSHKILL FALLS** is 2 mi. n.w. off US 209. Rustic bridges and a 1½-mile nature trail lead through virgin forests and a scenic gorge to the 300-foot series of eight waterfalls. Bushkill Falls, the largest, drops 100 feet. A wildlife exhibit features mounted native birds and animals. Comfortable walking shoes are required. Picnicking, paddleboating and fishing are permitted; food is available.

Allow 3 hours minimum. Daily 9-dusk, Apr.-Nov. Last admission approximately 1 hour, 30 minutes before closing. Admission $6; over 62, $5.25; ages 6-12, $1. For further schedule information phone (717) 588-6682. *See ad.*

**POCONO INDIAN MUSEUM,** 8 mi. n. on US 209 from I-80, depicts the lifestyle of the Delaware Indians and displays examples of their bark houses, pottery, food and weapons. Many of the items on display were unearthed in the Delaware Water Gap area. Allow 30 minutes minimum. Daily 9:30-5:30. Admission $3.50; over 62, $2.50; ages 6-16, $2. AE, MC, VI. **Discount.** Phone (717) 588-9338.

### CANADENSIS (E-11)

Canadensis shares its name with the giant hemlocks, or *Tsuga canadensis,* of the surrounding Poconos *(see place listing).* In the 19th century, the trees were the prize of tanneries, which used the tannic acid in the tree's bark to tan leather.

**COLONY VILLAGE,** 3½ mi. s. on SR 447, is a complex that contains a mine replica and mineral museum, the 1867 McComas Chapel, a petrified wood garden, antique carriages and craft and gift shops. Miniature golf and food also are available. Allow 2 hours minimum. Fri.-Mon. 10-5. Free. Phone (717) 595-2568 or 421-6464.

### CARLISLE (H-7) pop. 18,400, elev. 469'

Founded in 1751, Carlisle was the home of James Wilson and George Ross, two of the signers of the Declaration of Independence. The First Presbyterian Church, facing the main square of town, was built in 1757. In this church the citizens of Carlisle chose Wilson and Ross to represent them at the Continental Congress. Mary L. Hays, the famous Molly Pitcher of the Battle of

Monmouth *(see Freehold, N.J.)*, also lived in Carlisle. A life-size memorial in a cemetery on E. South Street marks her grave.

During the Confederate invasion in 1863, Gen. A.G. Jenkins and about 500 cavalry fresh from victory at Chambersburg took Carlisle without resistance. They were followed by Gen. Richard S. Ewell's corps, some of whom camped on the grounds of Dickinson College. The occupation lasted 3 days. After their departure, Union troops occupied Carlisle. The retreating Confederates then shelled the town.

Carlisle Indian School, the first non-reservation school for Indians, was established in 1879 at Carlisle Barracks, which is now the site of the U.S. Army War College. During its 39 years of existence, the Indian school attained an enrollment of 6,000 students representing all tribes in the United States. Jim Thorpe, winner of the pentathlon and the decathlon in the 1912 Olympic Games, attended the school. Monuments at the courthouse square, High and Hanover streets, honor Thorpe and Cumberland County's Civil War dead.

For additional area information contact the Greater Carlisle Chamber of Commerce, 212 N. Hanover St., P.O. Box 572, Carlisle, PA 17013; phone (717) 243-4515.

**CARLISLE BARRACKS** is 1 mi. n. on US 11. One of the older Army posts in the United States, it was the site of a Revolutionary War forge. The Hessian Powder Magazine Museum, in a magazine built by Hessian soldiers in 1777, is open Sat.-Sun. 1-4, late May-early Sept. Also on the grounds is the Omar N. Bradley Museum, which displays personal items and military memorabilia of the five-star general who was chairman of the joint chiefs of staff 1949-53. Allow 30 minutes minimum for each museum. Mon.-Fri. 8-4; closed federal holidays. Free. Phone (717) 245-3152.

**CUMBERLAND COUNTY HISTORICAL SOCIETY LIBRARY AND MUSEUM,** 21 N. Pitt St., exhibits one of the older American printing presses, a fine collection of Schimmel and Mountz woodcarvings, collections of early mechanical banks and 18th-century iron-furnace products, memorabilia of the Carlisle Indian School and products made by Cumberland County artisans and manufacturers.

The library contains extensive collections of books, monographs, newspapers, manuscripts and other materials relating to local history. Mon. 7-9 p.m., Tues.-Wed. 1-4, Thurs.-Fri. 10-4, Sat. 10-1. Library $2. Museum donations. Phone (717) 249-7610.

**TROUT ART GALLERY,** on High St., is in the Emil R. Weiss Center for the Arts on the Dickinson College campus. The gallery's upper level houses changing exhibits, while the lower level displays the college's permanent pieces, which

compose one of the nation's oldest collegiate collections. Begun in 1836, it boasts works dating from classical Greece through the 20th century and includes African and Oriental art.

Special medieval and Renaissance pieces are on loan from the Metropolitan Museum of Art. Guided tours are available by prior arrangement. Allow 30 minutes minimum. Tues.-Sat. 10-4, mid-Jan. to late June and early Sept. to mid-Dec. Free. Phone (717) 245-1711.

## CENTER POINT (H-11)

About 3 miles west on SR 73 in Skippack, Skippack Village contains more than 50 specialty shops and restaurants housed in restored turn-of-the-20th-century homes and buildings.

**PETER WENTZ FARMSTEAD,** ³⁄₁₀ mi. s.e. of jct. SRs 73 and 363, is an 18th-century working farm of more than 90 acres, with an 18th-century Georgian-style mansion furnished in period. The house was twice used by George Washington as headquarters during the Revolutionary War.

On the grounds are livestock, a German kitchen garden and orchards of apples, peaches and pears. Period craft and farming demonstrations are given on some Saturday afternoons; costumed guides conduct tours. A slide presentation also is available.

Allow 1 hour minimum. Tues.-Sat. 10-4, Sun. 1-4; closed Jan. 1, second week in Sept., Thanksgiving and Dec. 25. Last tour 30 minutes before closing. Free. Phone (610) 584-5104.

## CENTRE HALL (F-6) pop. 1,200, elev. 1,187'

★**PENN'S CAVE,** 5 mi. e. on SR 192, is America's only all-water cavern. It presents unusual, highly colored limestone formations, including the "Statue of Liberty" and "Niagara Falls." A 1-hour tour includes a motorboat trip in the cavern and a ride on Lake Nitanee. A 90-minute tour of Penn's Cave Farms and Wildlife Sanctuary, where white-tailed deer, elk, mountain lions and wolves can be seen, is available by reservation; fee $8.

Cavern tours depart on the half-hour daily 9-7, June-Aug.; on the hour 9-5, mid-Feb. through May 31 and Sept.-Nov.; on the hour Sat.-Sun. 11-4, in Dec. Closed Thanksgiving and Dec. 25. Admission $8.50; over 65, $7.50; ages 3-12, $4.

A 15-minute plane ride offers a view of nearby Amish farms and Pennsylvania's scenic ridge and valley area, weather permitting. Fare $15, under 2 free. Combined cavern admission and flight $19.50; ages 3-12, $15; age 2, $11. MC, VI. Phone (814) 364-1664.

## CHADDS FORD (I-10) elev. 129'

Chadds Ford is in the Brandywine Valley, where several major Revolutionary War skirmishes occurred, including the Battle of Brandywine. Celebrating the town's Colonial history is

Chadds Ford Days on the second weekend in September. Featured are Colonial arts and crafts, country rides and live music. Visitors can sample fruits of the apple harvest during Apple Weekend, held mid-October at the Barns-Brinton House. The Great Pumpkin Weekend, featuring foods made from pumpkins, is held the last weekend in October at the John Chads House. A Candlelight Christmas is held the first Saturday in December and includes a tour of historic homes and sites.

For further information contact the Chadds Ford Historical Society, Box 27, Chadds Ford, PA 19317; phone (610) 388-7376.

**BRANDYWINE BATTLEFIELD PARK** embraces 50 acres along the n. side of US 1, ¾ mi. e. of SR 100. The Battle of Brandywine was fought nearby on Sept. 11, 1777. This defeat of the American forces under George Washington left Philadelphia open to advancing British troops. The visitor center contains audiovisual programs and exhibits about the battle. Restored farmhouses used by Washington and the Marquis de Lafayette also are on the grounds.

Special events include a re-enactment of the Battle of Brandywine in September and a Candlelight Christmas in December.

Allow 1 hour minimum. Grounds open daily 9-8, in summer; Tues.-Sat. 9-5, Sun. noon-5, rest of year. Visitor center and historic buildings open Tues.-Sat. 9-5, Sun. noon-5; closed holidays. Admission to historic buildings $3.50; over 64, $2.50; ages 6-17, $1.50; battlefield free. Phone (610) 459-3342.

★**BRANDYWINE RIVER MUSEUM**, 1 blk. s.w. of SR 100 on US 1, is housed in a restored 19th-century gristmill on the Brandywine River. The museum features works by the Wyeth family, with one gallery devoted to the paintings of Andrew Wyeth. Works of American illustrators, Brandywine Valley landscapes and still lifes are represented. The galleries in the restored mill have hand-hewn beams, pine floors and white plaster walls.

The grounds of the museum are landscaped with wildflowers and native plants. A 1-mile river trail connects the museum with the John Chad House, an 18th-century dwelling built by a local innkeeper and ferry operator. The house is open for tours Sat.-Sun. noon-6, May-Sept.

Guided tours are available Monday through Friday by prior arrangement. Some galleries are closed for exhibit installation during the week preceding Memorial Day and Thanksgiving. Food is available. Allow 1 hour, 30 minutes minimum. Daily 9:30-4:30; closed Dec. 25. Admission $5; over 65, students with ID and ages 6-12, $2.50. John Chad House tour $2; under 12, 50c. MC, VI ($15). **Discount.** Phone (610) 388-2700.

**CHAMBERSBURG (I-6)** pop. 16,600, elev. 613'

Nestled in the historic Cumberland Valley, Chambersburg was occupied by Confederate forces three times during the Civil War. The last time ended in 1864 with the burning of the city upon its refusal to pay an indemnity. Chambersburg also served as a base of operations for John Brown prior to his raid on Harper's Ferry, W. Va.

Residents commemorate Chambersburg's part in the Civil War with Chamberfest, a week-long festival in late July. The Franklin County Fair is held the third week in August at the Chambersburg Rod and Gun Club. Highlights include arts, crafts, tractor pulls and a horse show.

The Cumberland Valley Visitor Station, 1235 Lincoln Way East (I-81 exit 6), offers self-guiding walking and driving tour brochures for Chambersburg and other communities in the Cumberland Valley. This full-service center also has a nature walk and picnic area; phone (717) 261-1200.

**Self-guiding tours:** Free brochures detailing walking tours of downtown Chambersburg are available at the Greater Chambersburg Chamber of Commerce, 75 S. Second St., Chambersburg, PA 17201; phone (717) 264-7101.

**CHAMBERSBURG VOLUNTEER FIREMAN'S MUSEUM,** 441 Broad St., houses 19th-century trucks, hose carriages, pumpers, a steamer and other fire equipment as well as memorabilia dating from the 1900s. The museum is within an original firehouse. Sat. 1-9, Sun. 1-5, in summer; by appointment, rest of year. Donations. Phone (717) 263-1049.

**THE OLD JAIL,** 175 E. King St., was built in 1818 and was one of the few buildings that survived the burning of Chambersburg by Confederate forces in 1864. The building houses the Kittochtinny Historical Society, which features an early drugstore, a pioneer kitchen, gun collection and genealogical library. Thurs.-Sat. 9:30-4, Apr.-Dec.; closed holidays. Donations. Phone (717) 264-1667.

**CHESTER (I-11)** pop. 41,900, elev. 23'

Settled by Swedes and Finns in 1644, Chester is one of the oldest settlements in Pennsylvania. Until its power waned in 1683, it was the most important town in the colony and the seat of its courts. The first meeting of the Pennsylvania Assembly was held in Chester in 1682, the year William Penn arrived.

The Caleb Pusey House, 2 miles west at 15 Race St. on Landingford Plantation in Upland, is a restored cottage built in 1683 of handmade bricks.

**CLARK (E-1)** pop. 600, elev. 774'

★**TARA,** I-80 exit 1N, then 7 mi. n. on SR 18 to SR 258, is a country inn recalling "Gone With the Wind." Spacious lawns dotted with blossoming flowers in the summer and a long veranda with white wicker furntiure help enhance the Southern atmosphere of the Greek Revival mansion, built in 1854. Each room is named after a character from "Gone With the Wind" and is decorated accordingly with antiques, period furnishings and original works of art.

Opulent chandeliers, luxurious Oriental rugs and a very large collection of art and antiques create an atmosphere of Southern elegance. Tours are conducted by guides in Civil War era costumes. Food is available. Allow 1 hour minimum. Mon.-Sat. 10-3, Sun. noon-3. Admission $5. Phone (412) 962-3535 or (800) 782-2803.

## COLLEGEVILLE (H-11) pop. 4,200, elev. 155'

BERMAN MUSEUM OF ART, ½ mi. w. on Main St. to the Ursinus College campus, features paintings, sculpture, prints, drawings and historical artifacts. Works of regional artists and turn-of-the-20th-century Pennsylvania artists are highlighted. Allow 1 hour minimum. Tues.-Fri. 10-4, Sat.-Sun. noon-4:30; closed major holidays and Dec. 24-31. Free. Phone (610) 489-4111.

## COLUMBIA (I-9) pop. 10,700, elev. 252'

Founded in the early 1700s, Columbia is in the Susquehanna River Valley, a location that encouraged the development of the town's livelihood as a transportation and commercial center. For more area information contact the chamber of commerce at 5th and Linden sts., P.O. Box 510, Columbia, PA 17512; phone (717) 684-5249.

★WATCH AND CLOCK MUSEUM OF THE NATIONAL ASSOCIATION OF WATCH AND CLOCK COLLECTORS INC., off US 30 and SR 441 at 5th and Poplar sts., contains more than 8,000 horological items from around the world, including clocks, watches, movements, tools and machinery. Changing exhibits trace the history of timekeeping from the 1600s through the present. There are examples of various styles and technological developments, from the earliest mechanical to the futuristic "atomic clock."

The museum displays Stephen D. Engle's "Monumental Clock," an 1877 timepiece with 48 moving figures and two organ movements. A reference library is available. Allow 1 hour minimum. Tues.-Sat. 9-4, Sun. noon-4, May-Sept.; Tues.-Sat. 9-4, rest of year. Admission $3; over 59, $2.50; ages 6-17, $1. Discount. Phone (717) 684-8261. See ad p. A152.

WRIGHT'S FERRY MANSION, 2nd and Cherry sts., was the Colonial home of Susanna Wright, a literary Quaker. The restored 1738 English-style stone house contains a collection of early 18th-century Philadelphia furniture and reflects life in a Pennsylvania Quaker household prior to 1750. Allow 1 hour minimum. Guided tours are offered

Tues.-Wed. and Fri.-Sat. 10-3, May-Oct.; closed July 4. The last tour begins at 3. Admission $5; ages 6-18, $2.50. Phone (717) 684-4325.

## CONCORDVILLE (I-11)

NEWLIN MILL PARK consists of 150 acres 1½ mi. e. on US 1. The restored gristmill, with a 16-foot wheel, dates from 1704. The miller's house, built in 1739, is furnished in period. A blacksmith shop, springhouse and log cabin also are in the park. Guided tours are available. There are 3 miles of nature trails along the millrace and the stream. Picnicking and trout fishing are permitted, and there are tennis courts on the grounds.

Allow 1 hour minimum. Daily 9-dusk, Mar.-Sept.; 8-5, rest of year. Combined admission to all three buildings $1.50; ages 2-12, 75c. Phone (610) 459-2359

## CONNEAUT LAKE (E-1) pop. 700

The largest natural lake wholly within the state, Conneaut Lake is 3 miles long and 1½ miles across at its widest point. Conneaut Cellars Winery makes more than a dozen kinds of wine in its old-fashioned vertical press. Free tours and tastings are available throughout the year. The annual Jazz Festival takes place in August at Conneaut Lake Park.

CONNEAUT LAKE CRUISES, 2 mi. n. of US 6 on SR 618, offers 45-minute sightseeing tours on the Barbara J., an authentic, 80-passenger, double-decker stern-wheeler. Trips include narration about the lake and other sights. Tours leave on the hour daily noon-8, Memorial Day-Labor Day; schedule varies, May 1-day before Memorial Day and day after Labor Day-Sept. 30. Fare $6; over 60, $5; ages 2-11, $3. DS, MC, VI. Discount. Phone (814) 382-7472 or (800) 626-2621.

CONNEAUT LAKE PARK, 2 mi. n. of US 6 on SR 618, is an early 20th-century-era amusement park with rides, water attractions and a beach. Special events and festivals are held throughout the season.

Allow 2 hours minimum. Open daily at noon, Memorial Day weekend-Labor Day; closing times vary. Schedule varies May 1-day before Memorial Day weekend and day after Labor Day-Sept. 30. Numerous admission options are available. DS, MC, VI. Phone (814) 382-5115 for general information or (800) 828-9619 for schedule, pricing and event information.

## COOKSBURG (E-3)

Cook Forest State Park is 1 mile north of Cooksburg off SR 36. The park comprises nearly 6,500 acres of scenic drives and hiking trails set against the backdrop of the winding Clarion River. The area is noteworthy for its abundance of deer. River activities—canoeing, tubing, and watersliding—are popular. The Green Acres Stable offers 1-hour horseback rides along a well-marked forest trail. Mountain streams and reservoirs in the vicinity offer good trout fishing. *See Recreation Chart and the AAA Mideastern CampBook.*

## CORNWALL (H-9) pop. 3,200

The Cornwall Ore Banks, on the knobs of South Mountain, Grassy Hill, Middle Hill and Big Hill, contain one of the more valuable deposits of iron ore in the East. The mines operated from 1735 to 1972.

CORNWALL IRON FURNACE is off US 322, following markers, 4 mi. n. of I-76 off SR 72 on SR 419. The furnace, built by Peter Grubb in 1742, operated until 1883. In the early days it produced stoves, kitchenware and farm tools. During the Revolution it cast cannon and ammunition for the Continental Army.

Structures on the grounds include the original furnace stack; the blast machinery, with an early 19th-century steam engine; blowing tubs; the Great Wheel, measuring 24 inches in diameter; wagon and blacksmith shops; the open-pit mine; the ironmaster's mansion; and the Charcoal House, which is now a visitor center with displays depicting mining operations, charcoal making and iron making. Guided tours are available.

Special events include Charter Day the second Sunday in March and William Penn Heritage Day the third Sunday in October. Allow 1 hour minimum. Tues.-Sat. 9-5 (also Memorial Day and Labor Day), Sun. noon-5. Last tour 1 hour before closing. Closed Jan. 1, Thanksgiving and Dec. 25. Admission $3.50; over 59, $2.50; ages 6-17, $1.50. **Discount.** Phone (717) 272-9711.

## COUDERSPORT (D-6) pop. 2,800, elev. 1,650'

Coudersport was founded by John Keating, an Irish mercenary who managed the Ceres Land Co., which owned most of the county. Keating gave 50 acres to each of the first 50 settlers and named the community after Jean Samuel Couderc, a Dutch banker.

Coudersport is a light manufacturing community on the banks of the Allegheny River. A monument to David Zeisberger, a Moravian missionary who camped nearby in October 1767, is in the county courthouse square at Second and Main streets. For more area information contact the chamber of commerce, P.O. Box 261, Coudersport, PA 16915; phone (814) 274-8165.

PENNSYLVANIA LUMBER MUSEUM, 10 mi. e. on US 6, preserves the colorful heritage of the state's prosperous lumber era—more than a century ago when white pine and hemlock were the wealth of the nation. More than 3,000 objects, from everyday tools to a logging locomotive, are displayed. A tour of the museum includes a walk among the weathered wooden buildings of a logging camp and sawmill.

The Bark Peelers' Convention is held in early July and features entertainment, logging demonstrations and contests. Allow 1 hour, 30 minutes minimum. Mon.-Sat. 9-4:30, Sun. 10-4:30; closed holidays. Admission $3.50; over 59, $2.50; ages 6-17, $1.50. Phone (814) 435-2652.

## CRESSON (H-4) pop. 1,800, elev. 2,022'

ALLEGHENY PORTAGE RAILROAD NATIONAL HISTORIC SITE, 3 mi. e. on US 22, preserves traces of the first railroad crossing of the Allegheny Mountains. Built in the early 1830s, this railroad contained 11 levels to connect the eastern and western divisions of the Pennsylvania Mainline Canal. Carrying passengers, freight and sectional canal boats, the railroad provided a critical link for travel and trade between Pittsburgh and Philadelphia. It was eventually abandoned in 1857 upon completion of the Pennsylvania Railroad.

Remnants of the Allegheny Portage Railroad, including the Skew Arch Bridge, stone railroad ties, and stone quarry can be seen. The visitor center has a 20-minute slide and film presentation, models, exhibits and artifacts that depict the history of the railroad and the canal. The Engine House 6 Interpretive Shelter offers exhibits about stationary steam engines.

A picnic area and hiking trails are available. Ranger-conducted programs and stone-cutting demonstrations are held during the summer. Allow 1 hour minimum. Daily 9-6, Memorial Day-Labor Day; 9-5, rest of year. Closed Dec. 25. Free. Phone (814) 886-6150.

## DANVILLE (F-9) pop. 5,200, elev. 456'

MONTOUR PRESERVE, 5 mi. w. of I-80 exit 33 on SR 54, then 4½ mi. n.e., following signs, is a nature preserve and recreation area centering on 165-acre Lake Chillisquaque. Visitors enjoy boating, hiking, picnicking and fishing in summer and cross-country skiing and ice fishing in winter. There are four marked nature trails and a visitor center displaying nature, wildlife and history exhibits.

Allow 1 hour minimum. Visitor center open Mon.-Fri. 9-4, Sat.-Sun. noon-4; closed major holidays. Trails open daily dawn-dusk. Free. Phone (717) 437-3131.

## DAWSON (I-2) pop. 500, elev. 850'

The Linden Hall Mansion, on SR 819, is a 35-room English Tudor mansion built in 1913. Open weekends March through October; phone (412) 529-7543 or 461-2424.

## DELAWARE WATER GAP NATIONAL RECREATION AREA—*see New Jersey.*

## DONEGAL (H-3) pop. 200

Just off I-76 west of Somerset, the small community of Donegal is surrounded by the Laurel

Mountains and is convenient for such outdoor recreation as hiking on the Laurel Highlands Trail, which traverses several nearby state parks. One of the area's historical landmarks is a restored 1850s farmhouse on Mountain View Road, once part of an 18th-century land grant witnessed by Benjamin Franklin. It is now the Mountain View Bed and Breakfast; visitors can tour the house and see its period furnishings and antiques.

## DOWNINGTOWN (H-10) pop. 7,700, elev. 264'

**SPRINGTON MANOR FARM,** 5 mi. w. off US 322 on Springton Rd., is a 300-acre demonstration farm. Features include the giant Great Barn, a pig barn, poultry house and petting area. A nature trail and wildlife pond are on the grounds. Picnicking is permitted. Allow 1 hour minimum. Daily 10-4. Free. Phone (610) 942-2450.

## DOYLESTOWN (H-11) pop. 8,600, elev. 351'

Settled in 1735, Doylestown is in Bucks County *(see place listing)*, one of Pennsylvania's finest farming areas. Among the town's special events are the Polish-American Festival held in early September and the Bucks County Wine and Food Festival held in early November. For more event details contact the Central Bucks Chamber of Commerce, 115 W. Court St. Doylestown, PA 18901; phone (215) 348-3913.

**FONTHILL MUSEUM,** E. Court St., is the castle-like dream house of Dr. Henry Chapman Mercer. Works in tile, prints, engravings and other memorabilia of Mercer's life are featured. Allow 1 hour minimum. Mon.-Sat. 10-5, Sun. noon-5; closed Jan. 1, Thanksgiving and Dec. 25. Admission $4.50; over 65, $4; students with ID $1; under 6 free. Reservations are suggested. Phone (215) 348-9461.

**JAMES A. MICHENER ART MUSEUM,** 138 S. Pine St., is in the renovated 1884 Bucks County prison. The galleries promote the arts through their collection of 20th-century American art with a special focus on Bucks County, sculpture and changing exhibits. A permanent exhibit on Michener includes his desk, typewriter and a manuscript from one of his novels. The Nakashima Reading Room overlooks the courtyard. A tea room also is on the grounds.

Allow 1 hour, 30 minutes minimum. Tues.-Fri. 10-4:30, Sat.-Sun. 10-5; closed holidays. Admission $5; over age 60, $4.50; students with ID and ages 12-18, $1.50. MC, VI. Phone (215) 340-9800.

**MERCER MUSEUM,** Pine and Ashland sts., occupies a huge Gothic-style building. Exhibits trace the pre-industrial history of the nation from colonization to the Civil War. Artifacts and implements from the 18th and 19th centuries represent more than 60 crafts and trades. There also are folk art displays and changing exhibits. The Spruance Library has a research collection about Bucks County history, genealogy and the history of trade, crafts and early industry.

The Folk Fest, held the second full weekend in May, features local crafts, music, dancing and food. Allow 2 hours minimum. Museum open Mon.-Sat. 10-5, Sun. noon-5. Library open Wed.-Sat. 10-5, Tues. 1-9. Museum and library closed Jan. 1, Thanksgiving and Dec. 25. Admission $5; over 65, $4.50; students with ID $1.50; under 6 free. Phone (215) 345-0210.

**MORAVIAN POTTERY AND TILE WORKS,** E. Court St. and Swamp Rd., is the restored building used by Dr. Henry Chapman Mercer for the production of pottery and tile. Self-guiding tours illustrate the tile-making process. Daily 10-4:45; closed holidays. Last tour 45 minutes before closing. Admission $2.50; over 60, $2; ages 7-17, $1. Phone (215) 345-6722.

**NATIONAL SHRINE OF OUR LADY OF CZESTO-CHOWA** (chen-sto-HO-va) is 1½ mi. n. on SR 611, then 1½ mi. n.w. on SR 313 and 2 mi. w. on Ferry Rd. On a picturesque tract of 250 acres, the shrine includes a monastery. The upper church's striking stained-glass windows depict 1,000 years of Polish Christianity. "The Holy Trinity," a sculpture above the altar area, is a copy of the painting "Our Lady of Czestochowa." Daily 9-5. Free. Phone (215) 345-0600.

## DUBLIN (G-11) pop. 2,000

**THE PEARL S. BUCK HOUSE,** 1 mi. s. of SR 313 at 520 Dublin Rd. on Green Hills Farm, was the home of author and humanitarian Pearl S. Buck. The 1835 stone farmhouse displays her Nobel and Pulitzer prizes and many personal mementos collected in China. Picnicking is permitted. Guided tours are offered Tues.-Sat. at 10:30, 1:30 and 2:30, Sun. at 1:30 and 2:30, Mar.-Dec.; closed major holidays. Fee $5; over 62 and students with ID $4; under 6 free. Phone (215) 249-0100.

## EASTON (G-11) pop. 26,300, elev. 280'

Rich in history, Easton served as a focal point of the Revolutionary War. The first public reading of the Declaration of Independence in the Colonies occurred on the steps of Northampton County Courthouse when it was located in Centre Square. Easton was also the home of George Taylor, a signer of the Declaration of Independence. The Parson-Taylor House, a stone house built in 1757, still stands on S. 4th Street.

During the 19th century, Easton became one of America's earliest industrial centers due to its strategic location at the confluence of the Delaware and Lehigh rivers, the Morris Canal and five major railroads. It was during the height of the canal era that many of Easton's fine examples of American architecture were built.

Easton's industrial prosperity was reflected in the founding of Lafayette College in 1832. Daniel Chester French's heroic bronze statue of Lafayette, the French aristocrat who fought with the American Colonists against the British, stands above the city on the Lafayette College campus.

The State Theater, 453 Northhampton St., is a restored 1926 vaudeville theater. The adjacent art gallery exhibits art by local and regional artists.

**Self-guiding tours:** A self-guiding walking tour of the Easton Historic District is available through Easton Heritage Alliance, P.O. Box 994, Easton, PA 18044-0994; phone (610) 258-1612. Additional information is available at the Two Rivers Area Chamber of Commerce, 157 S. Fourth St., P.O. Box 637, Easton, PA 18044; phone (610) 253-4211.

**Shopping areas:** Palmer Park Mall, SR 248 and Park Avenue, is a major local shopping center.

**CANAL BOAT RIDES** are offered in Hugh Moore Park, 2½ mi. from I-78 or 2 mi. s. off US 22, 25th St. exit, following signs. The mule-drawn canal boat operates on a section of the Lehigh Canal. An 1890s locktender's house, now a museum, is nearby. Bicycle and boat rentals are available; picnicking is permitted

Allow 1 hour minimum. Trips depart Wed.-Sat. at 11, 1, 2:30 and 4, Sun. at 1, 2:30 and 4, Memorial Day weekend-Labor Day; Sat.-Sun. at 1, 2:30 and 4, May 1-day before Memorial Day and day after Labor Day-Sept. 30. Fare $4.50; over 62, $4.05; ages 5-12, $2.50; includes locktender's house. Phone (610) 250-6700.

**CANAL MUSEUM,** ½ mi. n. of I-78 or 1 mi. s. of US 22 on SR 611, contains exhibits about the history and technology of America's 19th-century canals. Allow 30 minutes minimum. Mon.-Sat. 10-4, Sun. 1-5; closed Jan. 1, Thanksgiving and Dec. 25. Admission $1.50; over 62, $1.35; ages 5-12, 75c. MC, VI. **Discount.** Phone (610) 250-6700.

**SOLDIERS AND SAILORS MONUMENT** is on the square in the business district. On this site stood Northampton County's first courthouse, built in 1765 on a tract presented by the Penn family at an annual rent of one red rose.

**WELLER CENTER FOR HEALTH EDUCATION,** 2009 Lehigh St., presents lectures, exhibits and audiovisual programs designed to promote healthful living. Though especially designed for school group tours, the center is open for others on a walk-in basis. Allow 30 minutes minimum. Mon.-Fri. 9-4, Labor Day to mid-June. Admission $4; ages 3-18, $2.25. **Discount.** Phone (610) 258-8500.

## ECKVILLE (G-10)

**HAWK MOUNTAIN SANCTUARY,** 2 mi. e. on Hawk Mountain Rd., is one of the few sanctuaries in the world set aside primarily for migrating birds of prey. The area covers about 2,400 acres of forested Appalachian mountaintop with bold rock promontories. The visitor center contains birds of prey exhibits and a museum. A path leads from the visitor center to various scenic overlooks.

The chief attraction is the hawk and eagle migration from late August to late November. Shoes appropriate for hiking are recommended. Pets are not permitted. Allow 2 hours minimum. Daily 8-5, day after Labor Day-Thanksgiving; 9-5, rest of year. Admission $4; senior citizens $3; ages 6-12, $2. Phone (610) 756-6961.

## ELIZABETH (H-2) pop. 1,600. elev. 752'

**ROUND HILL EXHIBIT FARM,** ½ mi. e. of SR 51 on SR 48, then s. on Round Hill Rd., is a complete small-scale working farm, started in 1790. Highlights include a brick farmhouse built in 1838 and livestock, including dairy and beef cattle, sheep, pigs, chickens and horses. There also are an adjoining park, a picnic area and duck pond. Dairy cows are milked at 4. Allow 30 minutes minimum. Farm daily; 8-dusk office Mon.-Fri. 8-4. Free. Phone (412) 384-8555 or 384-4701.

## ELIZABETHTOWN (H-8) pop. 10,000, elev. 462'

**THE MASONIC HOMES** of the Grand Lodge of Free and Accepted Masons of Pennsylvania are on 1,730 acres on the s.w. edge of town on SR 241. The Masonic Homes serve as a retirement residence and Masonic health care facility for Masons and their relatives. A 6½-acre garden is on the grounds. Guided tours are available. Daily 8-noon and 12:30-4. Free. Phone (717) 367-1121.

## ELYSBURG (F-9)

**KNOEBELS AMUSEMENT RESORT,** 2 mi. n. on SR 487, has more than 35 rides and games, free entertainment, miniature golf, two 400-foot waterslides, speed slides, a swimming pool and an electronically animated musical bear show. Picnicking is permitted. Allow 6 hours minimum. Daily 11-10, Memorial Day weekend-Labor Day; Sat.-Sun. noon-8, May 1-day before Memorial Day weekend and in early Sept. Park admission free. Rides 40c-$1.50, children's rides 30c-$1.20. All-day ride pass available Mon.-Fri. after mid-June. Phone (717) 672-2572 or (800) ITS-4FUN.

## EMPORIUM (E-5) pop. 2,500, elev. 1,040'

**BUCKTAIL STATE PARK,** 23,013 acres on SR 120 between Emporium and Lock Haven, commemorates the Civil War regiment of area woodsmen known as the Bucktail Regiment because of their bucktail insignia. Daily dawn-dusk. Free. Phone (814) 486-3365.

## EPHRATA (H-9) pop. 12,100, elev. 381'

The Ephrata-Denver area has a number of factories that maintain retail outlets. The Green

Dragon Auction Market offers almost everything from live animals to hardware at its indoor and outdoor stands. For more information contact the chamber of commerce, 23 Washington Ave., Ephrata, PA 17522; phone (717) 738-9010. *Also see Pennsylvania Dutch Country.*

**EPHRATA CLOISTER,** 632 W. Main St., was one of America's earliest communal societies. Occupying a distinctive group of medieval-style buildings, this community of religious celibates practiced an austere lifestyle, emphasizing spiritual goals rather than material ones. Known for its original music and fraktur, a style of lettering used in German printing, the Ephrata Cloister also was an early center for publishing and printing in Pennsylvania.

Ten of the original buildings have been restored and furnished to re-create the atmosphere of the 18th-century communal village. Allow 1 hour minimum. Mon.-Sat. 9-5, Sun. noon-5; closed holidays. Last tour begins 1 hour before closing. Admission $5; over 60, $4; ages 6-17, $3. Phone (717) 733-6600.

**ERIE (C-2) pop. 108,700, elev. 710'**

Pennsylvania's only port on the Great Lakes, Erie is a city of widely diversified industry and commerce and has complete facilities for overseas shipping.

Erie's first known inhabitants were the Eriez Indians, for whom the lake and city were named. In 1753 a French military expedition built Fort Presque Isle on the site of Erie and Fort LeBoeuf on the site of Waterford *(see place listing)*. A small village of French and Indians grew up around Fort Presque Isle. The French abandoned their forts in 1759, and the next year the English took possession and rebuilt them.

Three years later the English were driven out by Indians led by Chief Pontiac, who destroyed both forts. The region remained deserted by white men until 1795, when a permanent settlement was laid out. During the War of 1812, ships built at Erie under the command of Commodore Oliver Hazard Perry were instrumental in eliminating British naval control of Lake Erie.

One-hour sightseeing boat trips depart from the East Public Dock at the foot of State Street, Memorial Day through Labor Day; charter service specializing in coho salmon fishing is available May through October.

For more area information contact the chamber of commerce, 1006 State St., Erie, PA 16501; phone (814) 454-7191.

**Shopping areas:** The major shopping center in Erie is Millcreek Mall, I-19 and Interchange Road, featuring Dahlkemper's, JCPenney, Kaufmann's, Lazarus and Sears. Blair Warehouse, outside of the Millcreek Mall, is a major warehouse clothing outlet, and Summit Town Center, 7200 Peach St., includes a Kmart.

**ERIE ART MUSEUM,** 411 State St., is in a Greek Revival-style brick and marble building built in 1839. The galleries display changing exhibits of paintings, drawings, photography, sculpture, ceramics and other media. Allow 30 minutes minimum. Tues.-Sat. 11-5, Sun. 1-5; closed holidays. Admission $1.50; senior citizens and students with ID 75c; under 12, 50c; free to all Wed. Phone (814) 459-5477.

**ERIE HISTORY CENTER,** 417 State St., is in an 1840 building. Exhibits highlight local industry and architecture. The complex includes the 1839 Cashiers House, the Greek Revival residence of the chief officer of the United States Bank, located next door. Walking and driving tours also are available. Allow 30 minutes minimum. Center open Tues.-Sat. 9-5. Cashiers House open Tues.-Sat. 1-4. Donations. Phone (814) 454-1813.

**ERIE ZOO** is 3 mi. n. of I-90 via exit 7. The main zoo contains more than 300 animals on 15 acres. Food is available. Allow 1 hour minimum. Open daily 10-5; closed Jan. 1 and Dec. 25. Children's zoo open May 1-Labor Day. The park is open daily all year. An ice arena next to the zoo is open Oct.-Mar.; phone (814) 868-3651. Admission, including park and main zoo, $4.50; over 62, $4.25; ages 3-11, $2.50. Train ride $1. Ice arena $3.50; over 62 and ages 3-11, $3. Phone (814) 864-4091.

**GANNON UNIVERSITY HISTORICAL MUSEUM,** 356 W. 6th St., is in a 24-room mansion. The museum highlights local history and contains art and changing exhibits. Allow 1 hour minimum. Tues.-Sun. 1-5, Sept.-May; Tues.-Fri. 10-5, rest of year. Closed holidays. Admission $2; ages 3-12, $1. Phone (814) 871-5790.

**Erie Planetarium** creates images of the sun, moon, planets and stars and their movements. Allow 1 hour minimum. Shows Thurs.-Sat. at 2, Sun. at 2 and 3, mid-July through Aug. 31; Sat. at 2, Sun. at 2 and 3, rest of year. Closed holidays. Admission $2; ages 3-12, $1. Phone (814) 871-5794.

**PRESQUE ISLE STATE PARK,** 3,200 acres, is 7 mi. n. on Peninsula Dr. (SR 832). It was in Presque Isle that Commodore Oliver Hazard Perry took command of a small fleet and defeated the British in the Battle of Lake Erie in 1813. A monument erected in his honor stands near the center of the grounds. The park is a wildlife refuge and conservation area with miles of beaches. Nature trails, swimming, boating, fishing, birdwatching and picnicking are available. A visitor center contains ecological and nature exhibits. Daily 5 a.m.-dusk; beaches are open Memorial Day weekend-Labor Day. Phone (814) 871-4251. *See Recreation Chart.*

**US BRIG** *NIAGARA,* 164 E. Front St., was the flagship of the fleet that Commodore Oliver Hazard Perry used against the British to win the Battle of Lake Erie in 1813. Nautical equipment, including a bilge pump, rigging and a movable block and tackle are on display.

Phone to verify that the ship is in port. Allow 1 hour minimum. Mon.-Sat. 9-5, Sun. noon-5, Memorial Day weekend-Labor Day; Sat. 9-5, Sun. noon-5, Apr. 1-day before Memorial Day weekend and day after Labor Day-Oct. 31. Admission $4; over 60, $3; ages 6-17, $2. Phone (814) 452-2744.

**WALDAMEER PARK & WATER WORLD,** 5 mi. n. on Peninsula Dr. (SR 832) at the entrance to Presque Isle State Park, is an amusement and water park complex. The amusement park contains rides, puppet shows, midway games and a video arcade. The water park features 16 slides, a lazy river ride and children's play areas. Food is available. Picnicking is permitted.

Waldameer Park open Tues.-Sun. and Mon. holidays 1-10 (weather permitting), Memorial Day-Labor Day. Water World open Tues.-Sun. and Mon. holidays 11-7:30 (weather permitting), Memorial Day-Labor Day. Waldameer Park free. Individual ride tickets 65c. Unlimited ride pass $10.50, under 42 inches tall $7.25. Water World $9.25. Unlimited ride pass $9.25, under 42 inches tall $7.25. Combination unlimited Waldameer Park and Water World ride pass $12.95, under 42 inches tall $9.25. Rates are $1 less in the evening. Phone (814) 838-3591.

## ERWINNA (G-11) pop. 100

**SAND CASTLE WINERY,** ½ mi. s. on SR 32, overlooks the Delaware River Valley from a hilly vantage point on the banks of the Delaware River. Tours of the underground wine cellar afford an opportunity to view winemaking equipment, storage tanks and wine casks. Tastings of the vinifera wines are given and staff members are available to answer questions about the wines and viticulture. Allow 1 hour minimum. Mon.-Sat. 10-6, Sun. 11-6. Admission $2, children free. AE, MC, VI. Phone (610) 294-9181 or (800) 722-9463.

## EXTON (H-10) elev. 321'

Exton is the site of the Thomas Newcomen Library and Museum, reached via Ship and Newcomen roads. The library features some 3,000 volumes about the history of steam power and its pioneers. The museum traces the development of steam power in the 18th and 19th centuries through actual and working model steam engines and model railroad engines and steamboats. Phone (610) 363-6600.

## FALLSINGTON (H-12)

**HISTORIC FALLSINGTON** is just off Tyburn Rd. between US 1 and US 13. This well-preserved village has pre-Revolutionary, Federal and Victorian buildings, including three Friends meetinghouses around a picturesque square. Also included are restored buildings with period furnishings and a 15-minute audiovisual presentation. Walking tour maps are available.

Allow 1 hour minimum. Guided tours are available on the hour Mon.-Sat. 10-4, Sun. 1-4, May-Oct.; closed major holidays. Admission $3.50; over 65, $2.50; ages 6-18, $1.Reservations are recommended. **Discount.** Phone (215) 295-6567.

## FAYETTEVILLE (I-7) elev. 792'

Totem Pole Playhouse in Caledonia State Park (see Recreation Chart and the AAA Mideastern CampBook) is a 450-seat theater that presents summer stock productions featuring nationally known actors, directors and designers. Performances are held early June to early September. The box office opens March 1. For more information phone (717) 352-2164.

Also of interest in the park are artifacts and displays in the reconstructed Thaddeus Stevens' Blacksmith Shop. Recreational facilities include an Olympic-size swimming pool, 18-hole golf course, nature trails and cross-country ski trails.

## ★FORT NECESSITY NATIONAL BATTLEFIELD (I-2)

Fort Necessity National Battlefield, 11 miles east of Uniontown on US 40, surrounds a reconstruction of the fort built by George Washington in 1754. The Battle of Fort Necessity, in which Washington led Virginia militiamen and South Carolina regulars against a strong force of French and Indians, occurred at the site on July 3, 1754. This was Washington's first campaign and the marked beginning of the French and Indian War.

Reconstructions of the fort, entrenchments and earthworks have been erected on their original sites. Picnic facilities are available. Allow 30 minutes minimum. A visitor center features exhibits and a 10-minute audiovisual presentation daily 8:30-5. Battlefield open daily dawn-dusk; closed Dec. 25.

Mount Washington Tavern, on US 40 near the fort, is a restored 19th-century stagecoach inn. Refurnished period rooms include the barroom, parlor, kitchen and bedrooms. The dining room has exhibits pertaining to the National Road. Allow 30 minutes minimum. Daily 8:30-5; closed Dec. 25.

A mile west on US 40 is the grave of Gen. Edward Braddock. During the Battle of the Monongahela, Braddock was fatally wounded; his aide-de-camp, George Washington, had two horses shot out from under him. The troops carried Braddock back as far as the site of the Old Orchard Camp, where he died. He was buried in the road, and wagons were driven over his grave to prevent the Indians from finding the body and desecrating it. In 1804 remains said to be those of Braddock were moved to the present gravesite, which is marked by a monument.

Jumonville Glen, 7½ miles from Fort Necessity, is reached via Jumonville Road (LR 26115), 2½ miles north of US 40 at Mount Summit. It was the site of a 15-minute skirmish between French and British forces that led to the battle of Fort Necessity, which also is said to have been the spark that ignited the French and Indian War. Allow 30 minutes minimum. Daily 10-5, midspring to late fall.

The general entrance fee, which covers the fort, tavern, visitor center, Jumonville Glen, Braddock's grave and the park grounds, is payable at the visitor center. Admission $2, over 62 and under 17 free; family rate $4. For more information write the Superintendent, Fort Necessity National Battlefield, R.D. 2, Box 528, Farmington, PA 15437; phone (412) 329-5512.

## FORT WASHINGTON (H-11) elev. 174′

HOPE LODGE is reached via Pennsylvania Tpke. exit 26 S., to Pennsylvania Ave., then 3 blks. to Bethlehem Pike, following signs. Built in 1743 by prosperous Quaker gristmill operator Samuel Morris, the lodge is now filled with antique art and furnishings from the 18th, 19th and 20th centuries. Allow 1 hour minimum. Tues.-Sat. 9-4, Sun. noon-4; closed holidays. Admission $3.50; over 60, $2.50; ages 6-17, $1.50; free to all the first Wednesday of each month. Phone (215) 646-1595.

## FORTY FORT (E-10) pop. 5,000, elev. 554′

The Nathan Denison House, 1 mile north of town via Wyoming Avenue at 35 Denison St., was built in 1790 by a Revolutionary War colonel in the style typical of early New England. It is considered the oldest frame dwelling in the Wyoming Valley. The restored home is furnished with antiques and period pieces. Costumed interpreters are available Sunday afternoons, May through August and by appointment. Candlelight tours are offered on weekends in early December; phone (717) 288-5531 or 287-7055.

## FRANKLIN (E-2) pop. 4,100, elev. 1,017′

Franklin's history dates back to the French Fort Machault, built in 1753 near the confluence of French Creek and the Allegheny River. In 1760, the British built Fort Venango, which fell to the Indians during Pontiac's War in 1763. According to local legend, the Indians often played ball near the fort, and the British would allow them entry if the ball went over the fort's wall.

On the day of the raid many more Indians than usual were playing. The ball went into the fort, and the British opened the gate to disaster.

In 1859 a resident struck oil, and the oil industry soon supported the town's economy. Manufacturers today produce mining machinery, small tools and other products.

Of interest downtown at South Park and Elk streets is the Hoge-Osmer House, a circa-1865 building with displays about local history. The Venango County Courthouse at 12th and Liberty streets has an interesting architectural design, and the Pioneer Cemetery at Otter and 15th streets dates from 1795. A farmers' market is held on 12th Street on Wednesday and Saturday.

**Self-guiding tours:** Brochures outlining a walking tour of historic Franklin can be obtained at the Franklin Area Chamber of Commerce, 1256 Liberty St., Franklin, PA 16323; phone (814) 432-5823.

DεBENCE'S ANTIQUE MUSIC WORLD is off I-80, 16 mi. n.e. via SR 8 at 1261-1263 Liberty St. A collection of more than 100 working music boxes ranges from small boxes to such large carnival organs as the nickelodeon, calliope and orchestrion. Guides provide historical facts and demonstrations of each machine. A potpourri of other antiques also is on view. Allow 1 hour minimum. Tues.-Sat. 10-5, Sun. noon-5. Hours may vary; phone ahead. Admission $6; senior citizens $5; ages 15-18, $4; ages 8-14, $3. Phone (814) 432-5668.

## GETTYSBURG (I-7) pop. 7,000, elev. 520′

Marsh Creek Settlement was founded between two low ridges just north of the Mason-Dixon Line in the 1780s. Renamed Gettysburg in honor of Gen. James Gettys, the town grew quickly after being incorporated in 1806. Its square, at the crossroads of four major highways and several secondary roads, was a stopping point for travelers. This strategic location led to the town's involvement in one of the bloodiest battles of the Civil War (see Gettysburg National Military Park).

Major events in Gettysburg include the Apple Blossom Festival the first weekend in May, Civil War Heritage Days from late June to early July, and the Apple Harvest Festival held the first and second weekends in October.

**Self-guiding tours:** Area sightseeing excursions include a 14-block walking tour past 90 restored buildings in downtown Gettysburg and a

36-mile driving tour of the surrounding valley. A 40-mile driving tour includes East Cavalry Field, Victorian New Oxford and Early American East Berlin. Free brochures describing these tours are available from the Gettysburg Travel Council, 35 Carlisle St., Gettysburg, PA 17325; phone (717) 334-6274. The council is open daily 9-5; closed Jan. 1 and Dec. 25.

CONFEDERATE STATES ARMORY AND MUSEUM, 529 Baltimore St., displays a variety of Confederate and Union Civil War memorabilia including small arms and swords. Guided tours are available. Allow 30 minutes minimum. Wed.-Mon. noon-8, Apr.-Oct. Hours may vary; phone ahead. Admission $3; over 60, ages 6-11 and family rate $2. Discount. Phone (717) 337-2340.

"THE CONFLICT," ¾ mi. s. on US 15, features "Three Days at Gettysburg," a definitive study of the famous battle; "Adventure at Gettysburg," which explains the battle to ages 8-14; "The War Within," which chronicles the entire Civil War; and a four-program documentary that offers a more complete account of the war and its battles (summer only). Allow 1 hour minimum per program.

Daily 9-9, Memorial Day-Labor Day; Mon.-Sat. 10-7, Apr. 1-day before Memorial Day and day after Labor Day-Nov. 30; Mon.-Tues. and Thurs.-Sat. noon-5, Sun. 1-5, rest of year. Individual programs $5, students with ID $4. Two programs $9, students with ID $7. AE, DS, MC, VI. Phone (717) 334-8003.

"Mr. Lincoln Returns to Gettysburg," at "The Conflict," is a live one-man performance that traces Abraham Lincoln's life from his boyhood in Kentucky to the nation's capital, giving special emphasis to Gettysburg. Allow 1 hour minimum. Mon.-Fri. at 8 p.m., June 12-Labor Day; phone for weekend schedule. Admission $6; ages 6-12, $5. Reservations are suggested. Phone (717) 334-6049.

★EISENHOWER NATIONAL HISTORIC SITE is accessible by a shuttle bus that departs from the National Park Visitor Center on SR 134. The 231-acre Eisenhower farm was the only home ever owned by President Dwight D. Eisenhower and his wife, Mamie. The house, grounds and buildings are carefully preserved. On display are the Eisenhower's formal living room, sun porch, original furniture and photographs, as well as many of the president's paintings, gifts and other items.

Among the dignitaries who visited the estate were Nikita Khrushchev, Charles DeGaulle and Winston Churchill. Only 1,100 visitors are allowed per day; no individual reservations are accepted. Allow 1 hour minimum. Tour center open 8:30-4. Shuttle departs at regular intervals 9-4. Hours and days of operation may vary; phone before visiting. Admission $3.60; over 61 and ages 13-16, $1.60; ages 6-12, $1.05. Phone (717) 334-1124.

LAND OF LITTLE HORSES, 3 mi. w. on US 30, then 2 mi. s. on Knoxlyn Rd., is a 100-acre miniature horse farm featuring a herd of Falabella miniature performing horses, which reach a height of no more than 3 feet at maturity. Daily 10-6, June 15-Labor Day; 10-4, Apr. 1-June 14 and day after Labor Day-Oct. 31. Admission $6.50; senior citizens $5.50; ages 2-12, $3.50. MC, VI. Phone (717) 334-7259.

LEE'S HEADQUARTERS AND MUSEUM is ¾ mi. w. on US 30. On July 1, 1863, Gen. Robert E. Lee established his personal headquarters in this old stone house, which dates from the 1700s. Displays include Union and Confederate military equipment and Civil War photographs and documents. Allow 1 hour minimum. Daily 9-9, mid-Apr. to mid-Oct.; 9-5, mid-Mar. to mid-Apr. and mid-Oct. through Nov. 30. Admission $1. Phone (717) 334-3141.

LINCOLN ROOM MUSEUM, in the Wills House on the square at US 15 Business Route and US 30, is where Abraham Lincoln stayed in 1863 and completed his Gettysburg Address. The furnishings are original. Lincoln's famous speech is presented in stereo. Visitors can have their photograph taken with a life-size bronze sculpture of Lincoln created by J. Seward Johnson. Allow 30 minutes minimum. Daily 9-7, Memorial Day weekend-Labor Day; otherwise varies. Admission $4; over 62, $3.75; ages 9-18, $2.50. MC, VI. Discount. Phone (717) 334-8188.

MAGIC TOWN OF GETTYSBURG, 49 Steinwehr Ave., is a miniature American neighborhood created by artist Michael Garman. Holograms, mirrors, lights, sound effects and grand illusions make the city come alive. Allow 30 minutes minimum. Daily 10-9 (also Fri.-Sat. 9-11 p.m.), June-Aug.; daily noon-8, Mar.-May and Sept.-Dec.; Fri.-Sun. noon-8, rest of year. Closed Jan 1 and Dec. 25. Admission $2.75. Discount. Phone (717) 337-0442 or (800) 878-4276.

NATIONAL CIVIL WAR WAX MUSEUM, 1 mi. s. on US 15 Business Route at 297 Steinwehr Ave., presents an audiovisual account of the Civil War. Tableaux comprising more than 200 life-size wax figures delineate the causes and effects of the conflict. A scene re-creating the climactic Battle of Gettysburg is in the Battle room. Allow 1 hour minimum.

Daily 9-9, mid-June through Labor Day; daily 9-7, mid-Apr. to mid-June; daily 9-5, day after Labor Day-Nov. 30 and Mar. 1 to mid-Apr.; Sat.-Sun. 9-5, rest of year. Admission $4.50; over 62, $3.50; ages 13-17, $2.50; ages 6-12, $1.75. Discount. Phone (717) 334-6245.

NATIONAL TOWER, ½ mi. s. on US 97 or SR 134, across from the National Park Visitor Center, is a 307-foot observation tower offering views from enclosed and open decks. A 12-minute audio program describing the battle is presented. Allow 1 hour minimum. Daily 9-6:30, June-Aug.; 9-5, Apr.-May and Sept.-Oct.; Fri.-Sun. 10-4, in Nov. Admission $4.35; over 62, $3.85; ages 6-14, $2.25. Phone (717) 334-6754.

**SAMUEL COLT HERITAGE MUSEUM,** 241 Steinwehr Ave., exhibits firearms dating from the early 1700s to the present. A tribute to gun manufacturer Samuel Colt, the museum contains rare and historic guns including the Flintlock, cap and ball, the Gatling, automatics and machine guns. Many guns are fully engraved and inlaid. Allow 45 minutes minimum. Daily 9-8, May-Aug.; 10-6, Mar.-Apr. and Sept.-Oct.; closed Thanksgiving. Admission $4; ages 6-16, $2.50. AE, DS, MC, VI. **Discount.** Phone (717) 334-6852.

## ★GETTYSBURG NATIONAL MILITARY PARK (I-7)

Gettysburg National Military Park virtually surrounds the city of Gettysburg; the main entrance is at the National Park Visitor Center on SR 134. The park comprises the Gettysburg battlefield, where one of the most important and hotly contested battles of the Civil War was waged on July 1, 2 and 3, 1863. Resulting in 51,000 casualties, it also was the bloodiest battle of the war.

The Federal Army of the Potomac, with some 92,000 men under Gen. George Meade, met the Confederate Army of Northern Virginia, with about 70,000 men under Gen. Robert E. Lee. The battlefield covers 25 square miles. About 5,900 acres are in Gettysburg National Military Park, and 21 acres are in Gettysburg National Cemetery.

After his victory at Chancellorsville, Va., Lee invaded Pennsylvania, hoping to destroy the Union Army on its own soil. On the morning of July 1, a Confederate division attacked Gen. John Buford's cavalry. Fierce fighting followed, and the Union forces were driven to the heights south of town, known as Cemetery Hill, Cemetery Ridge and Culp's Hill. That night the armies moved into battle position. Confederate assaults on both Union flanks gained some ground late the next day.

On the third day, after a heavy 2-hour artillery barrage, a Confederate force advanced on the center of the Union line in the face of deadly fire that shattered their ranks and spelled disaster. They retreated on the evening of July 4, ending the last major offensive of Lee's army and presaging the war's outcome.

On Nov. 19, 1863, President Lincoln dedicated Gettysburg National Cemetery on the battlefield, delivering his most famous speech, the Gettysburg Address.

There are now more than 1,300 monuments, statues and markers, three observation towers and 31 miles of marked avenues. The park roads are open daily 6 a.m.-10 p.m.

Monuments and historical points are scattered throughout the park. On Cemetery Ridge, Meade, commander of the Union forces, is depicted on his horse. His headquarters on Taneytown Road is preserved. In the summer there are interpretive walks to the High Water Mark, where there is a monument to the bravery of both armies, and to the National Cemetery.

Many states have erected monuments in the park. The Virginia memorial is surmounted by a statue of Lee, and the North Carolina memorial was designed and carved by Gutzon Borglum, sculptor of Mount Rushmore.

**CCINC. AUTO TAPE TOURS** describe historical points of interest in the park. The Civil War battle is presented with voice, music and sound effects and is explained with reference to the specific battle sites. The tapes can be purchased for $12.95 at the National Civil War Wax Museum *(see attraction listing in Gettysburg),* or the tape can be purchased in advance by sending $14.95 (includes postage) to CCInc., P.O. Box 227, Allendale, NJ 07401; phone (201) 236-1666..

★**DEVIL'S DEN** is a group of huge boulders from which Union troops were driven in Gen. James Longstreet's attack of July 2, 1863. A barricade used by Confederate sharpshooters who fired on Little Round Top can still be seen.

★**EISENHOWER NATIONAL HISTORIC SITE—** *see Gettysburg.*

★**ETERNAL LIGHT PEACE MEMORIAL** is on Oak Hill, scene of some of the first day's fighting in the Battle of Gettysburg. It was dedicated by President Franklin D. Roosevelt on the 75th anniversary of the battle. A perpetual flame lights the top of the monument, and an inscription reads, "Peace Eternal in a Nation United."

★**GETTYSBURG NATIONAL CEMETERY,** 21 acres, contains the graves of 3,706 Civil War dead, 1,664 of them unknown. The Soldiers' National Monument stands near the spot where

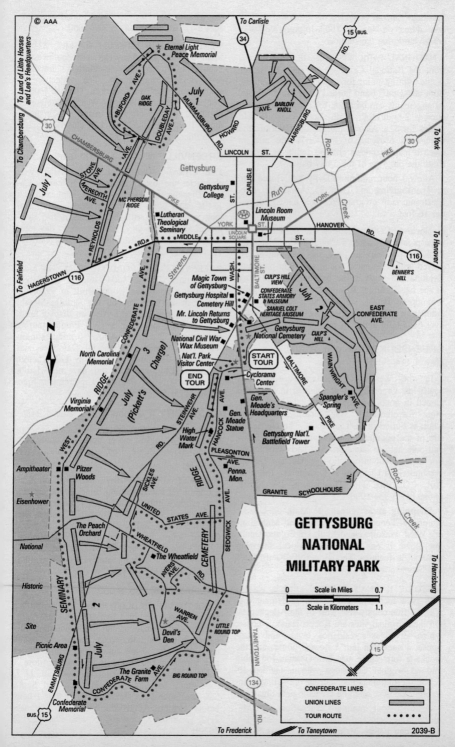

© AAA

To Land of Little Horses
and Lee's Headquarters

To Chambersburg

To Fairfield

To Carlisle

**34**

**15** BUS.

**30**

To York

**30**

To Hanover

**116**

Eternal Light
Peace Memorial

**July 1**

BUFORD AVE.

OAK RIDGE

DOUBLEDAY AVE.

MUMMASBURG RD.

HOWARD

AVE.

BARLOW KNOLL

HARRISBURG

Rock

CHAMBERSBURG

PIKE

LINCOLN ST.

STONE AVE.

MEREDITH AVE.

MC PHERSON RIDGE

REYNOLDS

RD.

**July 1**

Gettysburg

Gettysburg College

CARLISLE ST.

YORK

LINCOLN SQUARE

MIDDLE

Lutheran Theological Seminary

Lincoln Room Museum

ST.

HANOVER RD.

YORK CREEK

BENNER'S HILL

**116**

To Hagerstown

**116**

Stevens

WASH.

BALTIMORE ST.

CULP'S HILL VIEW

CONFEDERATE STATES ARMORY & MUSEUM

SAMUEL COLT HERITAGE MUSEUM

**July 2**

EAST CONFEDERATE AVE.

Magic Town of Gettysburg

Gettysburg Hospital Cemetery Hill

Mr. Lincoln Returns to Gettysburg

National Civil War Wax Museum

Gettysburg National Cemetery

CULP'S HILL

Nat'l. Park Visitor Center

START TOUR

WAINWRIGHT AVE.

CONFEDERATE

RIDGE

North Carolina Memorial

**July 3 (Pickett's Charge)**

END TOUR

Cyclorama Center

BALTIMORE

PIKE

Spangler's Spring

Virginia Memorial

STEINWEHR AVE.

HANCOCK AVE.

Gen. Meade's Headquarters

Gen. Meade Statue

Gettysburg Nat'l. Battlefield Tower

High Water Mark

WEST

RD.

Ampitheater

Pitzer Woods

SICKLES AVE.

PLEASANTON AVE.

Penna. Mon.

GRANITE SCHOOLHOUSE

Eisenhower

UNITED STATES AVE.

RIDGE

N.

Rock

Creek

To Harrisburg

National

The Peach Orchard

WHEATFIELD

CEMETERY RD.

SEDGWICK AVE.

Historic

The Wheatfield

AYERS AVE.

SEMINARY

Site

**2**

WARREN AVE.

Devil's Den

LITTLE ROUND TOP

**GETTYSBURG NATIONAL MILITARY PARK**

Scale in Miles 0 — 0.7

Scale in Kilometers 0 — 1.1

Picnic Area

**July 2**

CONFEDERATE

EMMITSBURG

The Granite Farm

AVE.

BIG ROUND TOP

TANEYTOWN

**15**

Confederate Memorial

BUS. **15**

**134**

To Frederick

To Taneytown

| CONFEDERATE LINES | |
| --- | --- |
| UNION LINES | |
| TOUR ROUTE | •••••• |

2039-B

President Lincoln delivered his immortal dedication address on Nov. 19, 1863. Interpretive walks are given during the summer.

★NATIONAL PARK VISITOR CENTER, across from the National Cemetery on SR 134, serves as the starting point for tours of the battlefield. Both self-guiding and guided tours are available. Arrangements can be made for a personally conducted 2-hour tour with licensed battlefield guides for $25. Also in the visitor center are the Gettysburg Museum of the Civil War and an electric map that uses colored lights to demonstrate the progress of the 3-day battle.

Allow 1 hour minimum. Daily 8-5; closed Jan. 1, Thanksgiving and Dec. 25. Admission free. Electronic map program $2; over 62, $1.50; under 16 free.

Cyclorama Center features the famous cyclorama painting "Pickett's Charge." Completed by Paul Philippoteaux in 1884, this painting is displayed with a dramatic sound-and-light program. Exhibits and films in the building tell the story of the battle. Allow 30 minutes minimum. Daily 9-5; closed Jan. 1, Thanksgiving and Dec. 25. Admission free; sound-and-light program $2; over 61, $1.50; under 16 free.

### GREENSBURG (H-2) pop. 16,300, elev. 1,114'

In the western Pennsylvania bituminous coalfields, Greensburg was founded in 1787 and named in honor of Gen. Nathanael Greene. Another Revolutionary War general, Arthur St. Clair, is buried in St. Clair Park. The city is the site of the popular Pennsylvania Antiques Show and Sale held in late April and early November. For more event information contact the Central Westmoreland Chamber of Commerce, Toll Gate Hill, P.O. Box 240, Greensburg, PA 15601; phone (412) 834-2900.

Shopping areas: Greengate Mall, on US 30, features JCPenney, Joseph Horne and Montgomery Ward. Westmoreland Mall, US 30 and Donohoe Road, is one of the larger local shopping centers. It features The Bon-Ton, Kaufmann's and Sears.

HISTORIC HANNA'S TOWN, 3 mi. n.e. via US 119, is a reconstruction of the settlement that was the first county seat west of the Alleghenies. On their original sites are Robert Hanna's house, which served as a residence, tavern and courthouse; a one-room jail; a storage house; and the stockade fort. There also is a German log cabin and an original Conestoga wagon. Guides describe the buildings and, during the summer, interpret extensive ongoing archeological digs.

Allow 1 hour minimum. Tues.-Sun. 1-5, Memorial Day weekend-Labor Day; Sat.-Sun. 1-5, May 1-day before Memorial Day weekend and day after Labor Day-Oct. 31. Guided tours $2; ages 6-12, $1. Phone (412) 836-1800.

WESTMORELAND MUSEUM OF ART, 221 N. Main St., features American and southwestern Pennsylvanian paintings, sculpture, drawings, prints and decorative arts. The collection includes works by Mary Cassatt, Thomas Eakins, Benjamin West and Andrew Wyeth. A reference library is in the west wing. Allow 1 hour minimum. Tues.-Sat. 10-5, Sun. 1-5; closed holidays. Free. Phone (412) 837-1500.

### GREENVILLE (E-1) pop. 6,700, elev. 945'

THE CANAL MUSEUM, Lock 22, Alan Ave., chronicles the history of the Erie Extension Canal. Displays include a full-size replica of an 1840s canal boat, a working model of a canal lock and historic artifacts. Tues.-Sun. 1-5, Memorial Day-Labor Day; Sat.-Sun. 1-5, day after Labor Day-Oct. 31. Admission $1.50; ages 6-18, $1. Phone (412) 588-7540.

GREENVILLE RAILROAD MUSEUM, 314 Main St., features Engine #604—one of the larger switch engines in the world. Built in 1936, the engine hauled iron ore on the Duluth, Mesabi and Iron Range Railroad. Also on display are a coal tender, hopper car, a 1913 Empire touring car and a 1952 caboose. Allow 30 minutes minimum. Daily noon-5, Memorial Day weekend-Labor Day; Fri.-Sun. noon-5, May 1-day before Memorial Day weekend and day after Labor Day-Oct. 31; other times by appointment. Free. Phone (412) 588-4009.

### GROVE CITY (F-2) pop. 8,200, elev. 1,245'

Grove City Factory Shops, I-79 exit 31, contains more than 150 outlet stores including Ann Taylor, Bass, Bugle Boy, Jockey and Royal Doulton.

WENDELL AUGUST FORGE, 620 Madison Ave., is one of the few remaining forges in the country that produce forged aluminum, bronze, pewter and sterling silver items by hand. Visitors can tour the forge and watch craftsmen at work. Guided tours are offered Mon.-Wed. 9-noon, 12:30-3 and 4-6, Thurs.-Fri. 9-noon and 12:30-3, Sat. 9-1 and 1:30-5:30, Sun. 11-1 and 1:30-5. Free. Phone (412) 458-8360 or (800) 923-4438.

### HALIFAX (G-8) pop. 9,000

LAKE TOBIAS WILDLIFE PARK, 760 Tobias Dr., offers safari tours in a 200-acre wildlife park. Hundreds of animals are featured, including alligators, bears, buffalo, emus, llamas and monkeys. Also offered are animal and reptile shows and a petting zoo. Food is available. Allow 3 hours minimum. Mon.-Fri. 10-6, Sat.-Sun. 11-7, June-Aug.; Sat.-Sun. 11-7 in May and Sept.; Sat.-Sun. noon-5, in Oct. Last safari tour 1 hour before closing. Admission 50c. Tour $4; ages 2-12, $3. Show $1. Petting zoo 50c. Phone (717) 362-9126.

## HAMLIN (E-10) elev. 555'

One of two Pennsylvania towns called Hamlin, this Hamlin is east of Scranton at SRs 590 and 196. The other Hamlin is north of Lebanon off I-78.

**CLAWS 'N' PAWS WILD ANIMAL PARK**, 3½ mi. e. on SR 590, then ¾ mi. s. at sign, encompasses some 100 species of animals in a wooded setting. Included are bears, leopards, monkeys, tigers and wolves. Also on the grounds is a petting area where visitors can mingle with tame deer, goats and lambs; a farmyard animals exhibit; a birds of prey exhibit that includes hawks and owls; and a walk-in Lory parrot aviary. Three different live animal shows take place daily May 1-Labor Day.

Allow 2 hours minimum. Daily 10-6, May-Oct. Admission $7.50; over 65, $6.75; ages 2-11, $4.75. Phone (717) 698-6154.

## HANOVER (I-8) pop. 14,400, elev. 599'

Founded by Col. Richard McAllister, Hanover was known as both "McAllister's Town," for its founder, and "Rogue's Rest," for the many outlaws who migrated to the area due to the lack of law enforcement that resulted from the Pennsylvania-Maryland boundary dispute.

On June 30, 1863, the first Civil War battle north of the Mason-Dixon Line was fought nearby when Union generals Hugh Kilpatrick and George Custer defeated Confederate general J.E.B. Stuart and prevented him from reaching Gettysburg until the day after that major battle.

Hanover is the base for several industries, which produce such goods as shoes, yarns, furniture and textiles. The city's most famous product, however, is horses. Just south on SR 194 is Hanover Shoe Farms, one of the largest Standardbred horse breeders in the world. The 4,000-acre farm, founded in 1926, is home to some 1,800 horses, many of which are record-breaking trotters and pacers. The grounds and buildings are open for self-guiding tours.

For additional area information contact the Hanover Area Chamber of Commerce, 146 Broadway Ave., Hanover, PA 17331; phone (717) 637-6130.

**BASILICA OF THE SACRED HEART OF JESUS**—see McSherrystown.

**UTZ POTATO CHIPS**, 900 High St., allows visitors to observe the potato chip production process from an elevated, glass-enclosed observation gallery in their 500,000-square-foot plant. Allow 1 hour minimum. Mon.-Thurs. 8-4. Free. Phone (717) 637-6644.

## HARMONY (F-2) pop. 2,000, elev. 913'

George Rapp and his Harmony (or Rappite) Society set up their first communal settlement on Connoquenessing Creek in 1804. During the next 10 years about 100 members died and were buried in a little graveyard. The graves, according to custom, were numbered but not marked. This cemetery and a number of substantial brick buildings remain from the original settlement.

In 1814 the society migrated to Indiana and founded New Harmony; 10 years later they returned to Pennsylvania and established the community of Ambridge (see place listing).

**HARMONY MUSEUM**, on the Diamond in the town center, preserves relics of the Harmony Society and Mennonites, who acquired the town from the Harmonists. Items are displayed in 19th-century buildings; guided tours are offered. The original Harmonist church tower clock on display has a single hand that points to the hour. A working replica is displayed in the Grace Church.

The Dankfest, a pioneer crafts festival that celebrates the harvest, is held the fourth weekend in August. A historic house tour is held the Saturday of National Historic Preservation Week in early June and a candlelight Christmas open house takes place on the second Sunday in December.

Allow 1 hour minimum. Daily 1-4, June-Sept.; Mon., Wed., Fri. and Sun. 1-4, rest of year. Closed hoildays. Admission $3.50; ages 6-13, $1.50. Phone (412) 452-7341.

## HARRISBURG (H-7) pop. 52,400, elev. 358'

About 1710 John Harris established a trading post in the area that is now Harrisburg; in 1733 he obtained a grant of 800 acres of land. His son, John Harris Jr., began operating a ferry across the river in 1753 and had William Maclay, Pennsylvania's first U.S. senator, layout the town in 1785. A few years later he refused to sell land to the legislature until the name of the town was changed from Louisborg, for Louis XVI, to Harrisburg. In 1812, Harrisburg was chosen as the site of the state capital, and within several years the removal of the capital from Lancaster was accomplished.

Paxton Presbyterian Church, at Paxtang Boulevard and Sharon Street, is one of the older Presbyterian churches still in use in the United States. The present structure dates from 1740. In the sanctuary are the baptismal font and pulpit light holder that have been in use for more than 200 years. The archives contain a pewter communion set that was used as early as 1734.

The adjacent cemetery, which dates from the early 1700s, contains the graves of John Harris Jr.; Rev. John Elder, the "fighting parson" of the Revolution; and William Maclay. A brochure describing a self-guiding tour of the graveyard is available.

The Pennsylvania Farm Show Building covers 13 acres at Cameron and Maclay streets. Among the many events held are the Pennsylvania Farm Show and the Auto Show in January, the Eastern Sportsman Show in February, the Zembo Shrine

Circus in April and the Pennsylvania National Horse Show in October. For more area information contact the Capital Region Chamber of Commerce, P.O. Box 969, Harrisburg, PA 17108; phone (717) 232-4121.

Recreational facilities are available at nearby City Island, in the Susquehanna River; the 20 recreational facilities, including games by a AA League baseball team, are open April through September. Other facilities are in Italian Lake Park, 3rd and Division streets; Reservoir Park, 21st and Walnut streets; and Riverfront Park, along a 5-mile stretch of scenic waterfront and other city sights. The Capital Area Greenbelt, a 20-mile parkway used for biking, jogging, walking and nature studies, loops around the city and passes through many of the city's scenic parks; phone (717) 255-3020 for more information.

Several professional team sports are played at the Pennsylvania Farm Show Arena during the early spring, fall and winter months; phone (717) 783-3071 for more information.

**Shopping areas:** Shopping areas include Kline Village Shopping Center, in the 100 block of S. 25th Street, which houses more than 45 stores. Downtown's Strawberry Square, N. 3rd and Walnut streets, offers more than 85 shops, restaurants and galleries. The other 200 shops, restaurants and galleries in the heart of Harrisburg provide retail diversity. Uptown Plaza, N.

7th and Division streets, features more than 35 specialty stores.

Two local malls are Colonial Park, US 22 and Colonial Road, and Harrisburg East at I-83 and Paxton Street. The former has more than 70 stores, including Boscov's and Sears; the latter offers more than 90 stores, among them Hess's and Wanamaker's. Nearby Camp Hill has two other major malls: Camp Hill Mall at 32nd Street and Trindle Road, and Capital City at the Highland Park exit off US 15.

Center city, City Island and City-Wide Sites brochures are available free by calling or writing the Mayor's Office, 10 N. 2nd St., Harrisburg, PA 17101; phone (717) 255-3040.

**ART ASSOCIATION OF HARRISBURG,** 21 N. Front St., offers 10 exhibitions annually that feature works in all styles and media by local, national and international artists. Mon.-Thurs. 9-8, Fri. 9-4, Sat. 10-4, Sun. noon-3; closed major holidays. Free. Phone (717) 236-1432.

**FORT HUNTER MANSION** is 6 mi. n. on Front St. overlooking the Susquehanna River Valley. Built in 1787 on the site of old Fort Hunter and enlarged in 1814, the stone home is decorated with 19th-century items including pewter, pitchers, furniture, costumes, toys and the original fireplace. A 35-acre park surrounds the mansion and includes other historic buildings, playgrounds, picnic facilities and nature trails.

Allow 1 hour minimum. Tues.-Sat. 10-4:30, Sun. noon-4:30, May-Nov.; Tues.-Sun. noon-7, Dec. 1-23. Admission $4; over 60, $3; ages 6-17, $2. **Discount.** Phone (717) 599-5751. *See ad p. 99.*

**JOHN HARRIS/SIMON CAMERON MANSION,** 219 S. Front St. (enter from Washington St.), was built by the city's founder in 1766 and remodeled in 1863 by Simon Cameron, a former U.S. senator and President Lincoln's first Secretary of War. Exhibits highlight local history and art. Guided 1-hour tours are available Mon.-Fri. 11-3 (also second and fourth Sun. of the month 1-4); closed holidays. Library and archives open Mon.-Thurs. 1-4. Admission $3.50, senior citizens $2.50, students with ID $1.50. Phone (717) 233-3462.

**MUSEUM OF SCIENTIFIC DISCOVERY,** 3rd and Walnut sts. in Strawberry Square, is a hands-on science center with more than 100 exhibits covering a wide range of scientific topics. The museum also offers changing exhibits, special programs and demonstrations. Allow 2 hours minimum. Tues.-Fri. 9-5, Sat. 10-5, Sun. noon-5; closed most holidays. Admission $5; over 60 and ages 3-17, $4. MC, VI. Phone (717) 233-7969.

*PRIDE OF THE SUSQUEHANNA,* take Market St. Bridge to City Island, offers a cruise of the Susquehanna River on an authentic paddle-wheeler. A history of the city and island is given on the 40-minute narrated cruise. Dinner and special

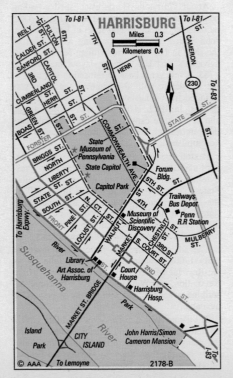

To I-81
HARRISBURG
To I-81
0  Miles  0.3
0  Kilometers  0.4
230
State Museum of Pennsylvania
State Capitol
Capitol Park
Forum Bldg.
Trailways Bus Depot
Museum of Scientific Discovery
Penn R.R Station
Library
Art Assoc. of Harrisburg
Court House
Harrisburg/Hosp.
Island
Park
CITY ISLAND
John Harris/Simon Cameron Mansion
© AAA  To Lemoyne
2178-B

event cruises also are available. Tues.-Sun. on the hour noon-4; schedule varies in May and day after Labor Day-Oct. 31. Fare $4.75; ages 3-11, $3. Wed. fare $4; ages 3-11, $2.50. Reservations are required for dinner and special event cruises. Phone (717) 234-6500.

**RIVER PARK** extends 5 mi. along the e. bank of the Susquehanna River, bordering Front St. The area contains war memorials and a sunken flower garden. At the foot of a bank on the riverside is a promenade where "Harrisburg's front steps" descend to the water's edge.

★**STATE CAPITOL** is on Capitol Hill. A magnificent building in a 13-acre park, the Capitol covers 2 acres and contains more than 600 rooms. The 272-foot dome, bronze doors, statuary, mural paintings and stained-glass windows are notable features. The marble grand staircase is designed after the one in the Paris Grand Opera House. Flanking the central entrance are two groups of statuary by the Pennsylvania-born sculptor George Grey Barnard. Guided tours are offered. Allow 30 minutes minimum. Daily 9-4. Free. Phone (717) 787-6810.

★**STATE MUSEUM OF PENNSYLVANIA,** on Third St. between North and Forster sts., chronicles Pennsylvania's history from the Earth's beginning to the present. Exhibits relate to Earth science, natural science, archeology, military history, political history, industry, technology and art. One of the world's larger paintings, "The Battle of Gettysburg: Pickett's Charge," is displayed.

Allow 2 hours minimum. Tues.-Sat. 9-5, Sun. noon-5; phone for holiday schedule. Planetarium shows Sat.-Sun. at 1 and 2:30. Museum free. Planetarium $1.50, over 60 and children $1. Phone (717) 787-4978.

## HAZLETON (F-10) pop. 24,700, elev. 1,624′

According to local legend, a deer pawing the earth uncovered the rich veins of anthracite coal on Spring Mountain in 1818. By 1837, Hazleton was founded as more and more miners migrated to the area. After the Civil War, mining was resumed on an even larger scale, until finally both the demand and supply waned. With an eye to the future, a community industrial development group known as "Can Do" formed in 1956; since then more than 30 industries have moved to the area.

Just northeast of town on SR 940 is the Sacred Heart Shrine, with depictions of the life of Christ on landscaped grounds; picnicking is permitted. The Greater Hazleton Historical Society Museum, 55 N. Wyoming St., contains exhibits relating to Indians, the mining and railroad industries, sports, the military and the life of actor and Hazleton-area native Jack Palance.

Hazleton welcomes fall with Funfest, held the weekend after Labor Day. Highlights include a car show, crafts, bed races, a flea market and a baseball card show.

For more information contact the Greater Hazleton Chamber of Commerce, 1 S. Church St., Hazleton, PA 18201; phone (717) 455-1508.

**ECKLEY MINERS' VILLAGE** is 9 mi. e. off SR 940, following signs. Set among open strip mines, this living-history museum is a 19th-century anthracite mining village with 50 buildings. Exhibits, pictures and slide shows in the visitor center depict the lives of miners and their families. Two churches and a miner's house dating from the 1850s are restored. Some houses not open to the public are occupied by retired miners. Guided walking tours are available several times daily, Memorial Day weekend-Labor Day.

Allow 2 hours minimum. Mon.-Sat. 9-5, Sun. noon-5; closed holidays, except Memorial Day, July 4 and Labor Day. Admission $3.50; over 60, $2.50; ages 6-17, $1.50. Phone (717) 636-2070.

## HELLERTOWN (G-11) pop. 5,700, elev. 278′

**LOST RIVER CAVERNS AND THE GILMAN MUSEUM** are ½ mi. e. of SR 412. The limestone cavern contains five chambers of crystal formations. One chamber, the Crystal Chapel, is used for weddings and baptisms. The formations include stalagmites, stalactites, flowstone and dripstone. Displays include a tropical garden, lapidary shop, museum of natural history, rocks, minerals, gems and antique weapons. Picnicking is permitted.

Allow 1 hour minimum. Daily 9-6, Memorial Day weekend-Labor Day; 9-5, rest of year. Closed Jan. 1, Thanksgiving and Dec. 25. Admission $7; ages 6-12, $3.50. MC, VI. **Discount.** Phone (610) 838-8767.

## HERMITAGE (E-1) pop. 15,300

**THE AVENUE OF 444 FLAGS,** 4 mi. n. of I-80 exit 1N via SR 18, following signs, is in Hillcrest Memorial Park at 2619 E. State St. A paved avenue is lined with 444 American flags, one for

each day that 53 American hostages were held captive in Iran under the reign of the Ayatollah Khomeini.

As the original flags became tattered, they were replaced by more than 1,000 from around the world. All but a few draped the coffins of American veterans who served in various military actions from the Spanish-American War to the Vietnam War. The flags fly 24 hours a day as a symbol of hope and freedom.

Also featured is a monument and eternal flame dedicated to the eight U.S. servicemen who died trying to rescue the hostages in April 1980.

**American Freedom Museum,** at the visitor center directly across from the Avenue of 444 Flags, offers a photojournalistic review of the events occurring between Nov. 4, 1979 and Jan. 20, 1981. A video presentation documents this time of patriotic resurgence. Guided tours are available. Allow 30 minutes minimum. Daily 10-5, May-Dec. Donations. Phone (412) 346-0444 or (800) 621-6744.

**KRAYNAK'S SANTA'S CHRISTMASLAND AND EASTER BUNNY LANE** are 4 mi. n. of I-80 exit 1N on SR 18, then left ½ mi. at jct. with US 62 Business Route. A nursery that has evolved into a sprawling holiday shopping center, Kraynak's has more than 175 animated figures depicting various Christmas and Easter scenes, from traditional religious themes to storybook settings. Christmas and Easter trees, each decorated in a different fashion, silk flower arrangements and a greenhouse also are displayed.

Allow 30 minutes minimum. Santa's Christmasland open Mon.-Sat. 9-9, Sun. 10-6, day after Labor Day-Dec. 24; Easter Bunny Lane open Mon.-Sat. 9-9, Sun. 10-6, mid-Feb. through Apr. 16. Free. Phone (412) 347-4511.

### HERSHEY (H-8) pop. 7,400

The aroma of chocolate pervades Hershey, a name synonymous with the confection. In the rich Lebanon Valley, the town was founded in 1903 by Milton S. Hershey, who planned and built an attractive industrial community. The Hershey Foods Corp. factory is one of the larger chocolate and cocoa plants in the world.

Pennsylvania State University's Milton S. Hershey Medical Center, US 322 at 500 University Dr., is on a 550-acre campus that includes the hospital, a medical sciences building, outpatient physicians center, animal research farm, fitness center and magnetic resonance imaging building.

Among the town's special events are the Hershey Antique Car Show in early October and Christmas Candylane in Hershey, held mid-November through Dec. 31. Also of interest is the State Police Academy, 1 mile northeast on SR 743, which offers tours by appointment.

For more information contact the Capital Region Chamber of Commerce, P.O. Box 969, Harrisburg, PA 17108; phone (717) 232-4121. Information also is available from the Harrisburg-Hershey-Carlisle Tourism and Convention Bureau, 114 Walnut St., P.O. Box 969, Harrisburg, PA 17108; phone (717) 232-1377 or (800) 995-0969.

**FOUNDERS HALL,** 1¼ mi. e. of jct. SR 743 and US 322, is a tribute to Milton Hershey and his wife, Catherine, founders of the Milton Hershey School. The building includes a banquet hall, chapel-auditorium and rotunda.

A 22-minute film about the founding of the school is shown daily. Self-guiding tours are available. Allow 1 hour minimum. Daily 10-4; closed Jan. 1, Thanksgiving, Dec. 25 and other school holidays. Free. Phone (717) 534-3500.

**HERSHEY GARDENS,** across from the Hotel Hershey, is a 23-acre botanical garden with seasonal floral displays April through October. Featured are more than 8,000 rose bushes which bloom June through September. Several theme gardens include a Japanese garden, a garden of ornamental grasses and a collection of hollies and dwarf conifers. Seasonal displays feature tulips, chrysanthemums and annuals. Mature specimen trees also are included.

Allow 1 hour minimum. Daily 9-5, mid-Apr. through Oct. 31. Admission $4.25; over 61, $3.75; ages 3-15, $2; family rate $12. Phone (717) 534-3492.

★**HERSHEY MUSEUM,** next to Hersheypark entrance, highlights the life of philanthropist Milton S. Hershey, the development of his chocolate empire and local history. Other exhibits chronicle the settlement and growth of southcentral Pennsylvania by the Pennsylvania Dutch.

Allow 1 hour minimum. Daily 10-6, Memorial Day weekend-Labor Day; 10-5, rest of year. Closed Jan. 1, Thanksgiving and Dec. 25. Admission $4.25; over 61, $3.75; ages 3-15, $2. **Discount.** Phone (717) 534-3439.

★**HERSHEYPARK,** just off SR 743 and US 422, is a 90-acre theme park. Eight areas include German, English and Pennsylvania Dutch themes. Four roller coasters, five water-related rides and children's rides are among the many attractions. Daily live entertainment includes a dolphin show.

Allow 4 hours minimum. Open daily at 10:30, Memorial Day-Labor Day; Sat.-Sun. at 10:30, selected weekends in May and Sept.; closing hours vary. All-inclusive admission, including ZooAmerica, $24.95; over 54 and ages 3-8, $15.95. Evening rates available. AE, DS, MC, VI. Phone (800) HERSHEY.

**Hersheypark Arena** seats 7,300 spectators for hockey, concerts, ice shows and other events. Public skating is available in season. AE, DS, MC, VI. Phone (717) 534-3911.

**ZooAmerica North American Wildlife Park,** on Park Ave. opposite Hersheypark, is an 11-acre zoo depicting regions of North America and the plants and animals native to each. Indoor and outdoor exhibits house more than 200 animals of 75 species. Picnicking is permitted.

Allow 1 hour minimum. Daily 10-5, with extended hours during the summer; closed Jan. 1, Thanksgiving and Dec. 25. Included in Hersheypark admission, or separately $4.50; over 54, $4; ages 3-12, $3.25. AE, DS, MC, VI. Phone (717) 534-3860.

**★HERSHEY'S CHOCOLATE WORLD,** Park Blvd., is the official visitor center of the Hershey Foods Corp. and the information center for the Hershey area. A 12-minute automated tour ride explains the chocolate-making process from harvesting the cocoa bean to packaging the finished product. There also are indoor tropical gardens and shops. Food is available.

Allow 30 minutes minimum. Daily 9-7, mid-June through Labor Day; 9-5, rest of year. Closed Jan. 1, Easter, Thanksgiving and Dec. 25. Free. Free parking is available at the Park Blvd. entrance. To confirm non-peak schedule, phone (717) 534-4900.

**INDIAN ECHO CAVERNS,** off US 322, 3 mi. w., offers a 45-minute guided tour amid the natural beauty of stalagmites, columns, flowstone and lakes. Guides narrate the history of the explorers who discovered the mysterious passageways and the tragic story of the Pennsylvania Hermit. The caverns are electronically lighted, contain level pathways and maintain a constant temperature of 52 degrees Fahrenheit. Visitors may pan for gemstones or ride in horse-drawn carriages at Gem Mill Junction. Food is available.

Daily 9-6, Memorial Day-Labor Day; 10-4, rest of year. Closed Jan. 1, Thanksgiving and Dec. 25. Admission $7; over 62, $6; ages 3-11, $3.50. MC, VI. Phone (717) 566-8131.

**PASTOR'S STUDY AND ACADEMY,** 248 E. Derry Rd. at Derry Presbyterian Church, is one of Hershey's most historic buildings. Erected in 1724, it has been enclosed in glass and can only be viewed from the outside.

## HOLTWOOD (I-9)

**MUDDY RUN INFORMATION CENTER,** 172 Bethesda Church Rd. W., offers exhibits that high-light resource conservation and information about wildlife, nuclear waste management and power generation. Audiovisual and nature programs also are presented. The center is part of a 700-acre recreation area. Picnicking is permitted. Allow 1 hour minimum. Wed.-Sun. 10-4, Apr.-Nov.; Tues.-Sat. 10-4, rest of year. Free. Phone (717) 284-2538, or 284-4325 for camping and boating information.

## HONESDALE (E-11) pop. 5,000, elev. 982'

Established in 1826 as a terminal for canal barges carrying coal to New York markets, Honesdale was the site of the first use of a steam locomotive in the United States. Imported from England to pull coal cars from the mines to the canal, the locomotive "Stourbridge Lion" made its trial run on Aug. 8, 1829. Too heavy for the rails, it was withdrawn from service. A replica can be seen in the county historical museum at 810 Main St.

Stourbridge Rail Train Excursions **(discount)** are offered by the chamber of commerce in April and June through December. For more information contact the Wayne County Chamber of Commerce, 742 Main St., Honesdale, PA 18431; phone (717) 253-1960.

**WAYNE COUNTY HISTORICAL SOCIETY MUSEUM,** 810 Main St., presents the "Movin' Energy—The History of the Delaware and Hudson Canal Co. 1828-1898" exhibit which includes a Gravity Railroad passenger car, a full-size replica of the first commercial steam engine in the U.S., paymaster's buggy and a 30-minute videotape presentation. Other displays include Indian artifacts, a dugout canoe, toys, tools and military items. A cut glass exhibit features works by Christian Dorflinger, who supplied cut glass to

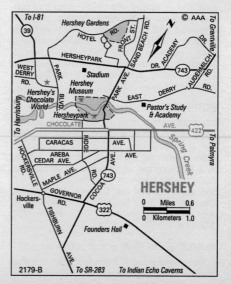

the White House; and works by renowned local artist Jennie Brownscombe. A research library also is available.

Mon.-Sat. 10-4, June-Sept.; Mon.-Sat. 1-4, Apr.-May; Mon., Wed., Fri. and Sat. 1-4, Jan. 2-Mar. 31; phone ahead for Sunday schedule. Admission $2; ages 12-18, $1. Phone (717) 253-3240.

## HOPEWELL FURNACE NATIONAL HISTORIC SITE (H-10)

One of the finer examples of an early American 18th- and 19th-century iron-making community is the 848-acre Hopewell Furnace National Historic Site, about 5 miles south of Birdsboro on SR 345. The site also is accessible via the Morgantown exit off the Pennsylvania Turnpike, using SRs 23 and 345.

Englishman William Bird was prominent in the early iron industry in Pennsylvania. His son Mark built Hopewell Furnace on French Creek in 1771. Around the furnace developed a small industrial settlement where many of the employees lived in tenant houses. A resident manager lived on the site in the ironmaster's mansion.

The furnace cast pig iron, hollowware, stoves and many other items; during the Revolutionary War it produced cannon and shot. The furnace operated until 1883, when more advanced technology made it unprofitable.

Many of the structures have been restored and refurnished. The water wheel, blast machinery, bridge house, cooling shed, barn, store, ironmaster's mansion and tenant houses can be seen. The ruin of an 1853 anthracite furnace has been uncovered and stabilized. Demonstrations of metal casting and guided tours are available.

A visitor center features an audiovisual program and an exhibit area with original iron castings produced at Hopewell Furnace and tools associated with the operation of 18th- and 19th-century cold-blast charcoal furnaces. Allow 2 hours minimum. Daily 9-5; closed Jan. 1, Thanksgiving and Dec. 25. Admission $2, under 17 free, family rate $5; free to all Dec.-Feb. Phone (610) 582-8773.

## HORSHAM (H-11) pop. 21,900

GRAEME PARK, ½ mi. w. off US 611, was the home of Sir William Keith, the provincial governor of Pennsylvania 1717-26. Built during his years as governor, the well-preserved stone house is a fine example of 18th-century architecture. Allow 1 hour minimum. Wed.-Fri. 10-4, Sat. 9-5, Sun. noon-4; closed Jan. 1, Easter, Thanksgiving, Dec. 25 and state holidays. Admission $3.50; over 60, $2.50; ages 6-17, $1.50. Phone (215) 343-0965.

## HUNTINGDON (G-6) pop. 6,800, elev. 630'

Near Huntingdon is Raystown Lake (see Recreation Chart), the largest lake wholly within Pennsylvania. Recreation available at the lake includes hunting, boating, camping, swimming and fishing, especially for small- and large-mouth bass, striped bass and lake trout. Wildlife inhabiting the area includes deer, turkeys, grouse and squirrels.

For more area information contact the chamber of commerce at 241 Mifflin St., Huntingdon, PA 16652; phone (814) 643-4322.

JUNIATA COLLEGE, n. edge of town, was founded in 1876. The L.A. Beeghly Library has an extensive collection of Pennsylvania-German printing and publications. The Shoemaker Galleries offer regular exhibits of paintings, prints and photographs; the Cloister exemplifies the Pennsylvania-German style of architecture. Galleries open Mon.-Fri. 9-5, Sat.-Sun. by appointment. Library open Mon.-Thurs. 8 a.m.-midnight, Fri. 8-8, Sat. 10-10, Sun. noon-midnight, during school sessions. Free. Phone (814) 643-4310.

LINCOLN CAVERNS, 3 mi. w. on US 22, offers interpretive tours through two crystal caverns that display a variety of rock formations. Nature trails are on the grounds. Picnicking is permitted. Guided tours also are offered in October during Ghost and Goblin Weekends. Allow 1 hour minimum. Guided tours daily 9-7, Memorial Day weekend-Labor Day; 9-5, Apr. 1-day before Memorial Day weekend and day after Labor Day-Nov. 30; Sat.-Sun. 9-5 in Mar. and Dec. Fee $7.50; over 65, $6.50; ages 4-14, $4. MC, VI. **Discount.** Phone (814) 643-0268.

SEVEN POINTS CRUISES, Seven Points Marina, offers sightseeing cruises aboard the Raystown Belle and the Raystown Queen. Each has 1½-hour cruises with music and narration. Dinner and charter cruises also are available. Allow 1 hour, 30 minutes minimum. Departures Mon.-Fri. at 2, Sat.-Sun. and holidays at 1, 2:30 and 4, June 10-Aug. 31; daily at 2 with a minimum of 10 persons, Sept.-Oct.; Sat.-Sun. at 2, May 1 to mid-June. Reservations are suggested. Fare $6; over 65, $5; under 12, $2.50. Phone (814) 658-3074.

SWIGART MUSEUM, 4 mi. e. on US 22, contains restored antique automobiles, including a 1909 Model T Ford touring car, a 1920 Carroll and a 1930 Model J Duesenberg. Displays include U.S. and foreign license plates, more than 2,000 radiator emblems and collections of horns, lights and other accessories. Allow 1 hour minimum. Daily 9-5, June-Sept.; Sat.-Sun. 9-5, in Oct. Admission $4; over 62, $3.50; ages 6-12, $2. **Discount.** Phone (814) 643-0885.

## INDIANA (G-3) pop. 15,200, elev. 1,310'

Indiana was founded in 1805 when George Clymer of Philadelphia, a signer of the Declaration of Independence, donated 250 acres of land for county buildings. Later, before the Civil War, Indiana became an important station on the underground railroad. In more recent history, the town was the birthplace and childhood home of actor Jimmy Stewart. A bronze statue of the actor, unveiled for his 75th birthday, stands on the lawn of the Indiana County Courthouse on Philadelphia Street.

Surrounding Indiana County is Amish country. Horse-drawn buggies are a common sight, especially in nearby Smicksburg.

Two historic buildings can be seen on the campus of Indiana University of Pennsylvania. John Sutton Hall, built in 1875, now houses administrative and faculty offices. Breezedale, a recently restored mansion, serves as the alumni center. The University Museum in John Sutton Hall has changing art exhibits and displays; phone (412) 357-6495.

The area presents many opportunities for hunting, fishing and boating. For information about game areas phone the Pennsylvania Game Commission regional office at (412) 238-9523, or (800) 243-8519 in Pa. For fishing information and boating regulations phone the Pennsylvania Fish and Boat Commission regional office at (814) 445-8974.

Among the special events that highlight Indiana's calendar are the New Growth Arts Festival, offering arts, crafts and ethnic foods in July; the Indiana County Fair, featuring livestock exhibits, harness racing, music and a midway, the week before Labor Day; and the Festival of Lights held late November through December.

**Self-guiding tours:** Brochures for two historic walking tours are available for 25c from the Historical Society of Indiana County in the Silas M. Clark House, S. Sixth Street and Wayne Avenue. For more information contact the Indiana County Tourist Bureau, 1019 Philadelphia St., Indiana, PA 15701; phone (412) 463-7505.

## INTERCOURSE (H-10)

In the heart of Pennsylvania Dutch Country (see place listing), Intercourse was founded in 1754. First called Cross Keys after a local tavern, the town was renamed in 1814. Its name is believed to have evolved from either the entrance to the old racecourse (the "Entercourse") just outside of town or from the joining, or intercourse, of the Old Kings Highway and the Wilmington-Erie Road.

Amish and Mennonite craftwares, including such items as quilts, toys and tablecloths, can be found at the Old Country Store on Main Street.

**THE PEOPLE'S PLACE,** 3513 Main St., is Lancaster County's center for Amish and Mennonite arts and crafts. It also interprets the story of the Amish, Mennonite and Hutterite people. "Who Are the Amish?" is a three-screen documentary slide show with music and narration; it is shown every 30 minutes 9:30-6:45, Memorial Day-Labor Day; 9:30-4:30, rest of year.

The Amish World Museum presents an inside look at the spirit and faith of the Amish. There

also are special features for children. "Hazel's People," a feature film dealing with a Mennonite family's clash of cultures, is shown at 7:30, Memorial Day-Labor Day.

Museum open Mon.-Sat. 9:30-9:30, Memorial Day-Labor Day; 9:30-5, rest of year. Closed Jan. 1 and Dec. 25. Museum $3.50; ages 7-12, $1.75. Documentary $3.50; ages 7-12, $1.75. Feature film $4; ages 2-12, $2.50. Various combination tickets are available. MC, VI. Phone (717) 768-7171. See color ad p. 107.

**The People's Place Quilt Museum,** across the street on the second floor of the Old Country Store, displays a collection of antique Amish quilts. Mon.-Sat. 9-5; closed Jan. 1, Thanksgiving and Dec. 25. Admission $4; ages 4-12, $2. MC, VI. Phone (717) 768-7101. See color ad p. 107.

## IVYLAND (H-11) pop. 500, elev. 257'

**THE WAGNER MUSEUM,** 900 Jacksonville Rd., chronicles the history of John Wagner & Sons, a manufacturer of gourmet foods, cigars and teas since the mid-1800s. Displays include photographs, business ledgers, labels and packaging, bottles, machinery, signs and a safe. Allow 30 minutes minimum. Mon.-Fri. 10-4:45, Sat. 10-2, Labor Day-Dec. 31; Mon.-Fri. 10-4:45, Sat. 9-2, Jan 1-Memorial Day; Mon.-Fri. 10-4:45, rest of year. Closed major holidays. Free. Phone (215) 674-5000.

## JAMESTOWN (E-1) pop. 800, elev. 990'

**PYMATUNING DEER PARK,** ½ mi. e. of US 322 on SR 58, is an animal park containing bears, camels, donkeys, llamas, mountain lions, monkeys, ostriches, tigers and six species of deer. A highlight is the petting zoo. Visitors can purchase food and feed the animals. Pony and train rides also are available. Allow 30 minutes minimum. Mon.-Fri. 10-5, Sat.-Sun. and holidays 10-6, Memorial Day weekend-Labor Day. Admission $3.50; over 65, $3; children $2.50. Phone (412) 932-3200.

## JEANNETTE (H-3) pop. 11,200

**BUSHY RUN BATTLEFIELD STATE HISTORICAL SITE,** SR 66 n. to SR 993W (Bushy Run Rd.), is the site of a military encounter in 1763 between the British and the Indians. The British victory at Bushy Run marked the turning point in Pontiac's War. A visitor center displays artifacts and reproductions from the period. Guided and self-guiding tours are offered. Rolling hills and woodlands are available for picnicking.

Allow 30 minutes minimum. Wed.-Sat. 9-5, Sun. noon-5; closed major holidays. Admission $2; senior citizens $1.50; ages 6-18, $1. Phone (412) 527-5584.

## JIM THORPE (F-10) pop. 5,000, elev. 531'

In the foothills of the Poconos, the town of Jim Thorpe was named after the famous Olympic athlete who won each pentathlon event but the javelin throw in the 1912 Olympic Games in Stockholm. He was later stripped of his honors because of previous "professional" sports activities.

In response to Thorpe's widow's search for a memorial for him, two Pennsylvania communities—Mauch Chunk and East Mauch Chunk—joined forces by incorporating as Jim Thorpe in the mid-1950s. The new community gave the man a final and fitting memorial, while also gaining economic stability for itself. Jim Thorpe was reinstated in the Olympic records in 1982, and the medals he won in the 1912 games were presented to his family. The Jim Thorpe Memorial is a half-mile east on SR 903.

The Harry Packer Mansion, off SR 209, features 400-pound doors made of solid walnut with bronze hardware and etched-glass panels. Guided tours are available on Sunday by appointment; phone (717) 325-8566. Mauch Chunk Lake Park *(see Recreation Chart)*, 4 miles west of town, offers recreational opportunities. Flagstaff Mountain Park, 4 miles south, offers a view of the town and surrounding valley from an observation deck. Special events in Jim Thorpe include the Fall Foliage Festival on the second weekend in October. For more area information contact the Carbon County Visitors Bureau, P.O. Box 90, Jim Thorpe, PA 18229; phone (717) 325-3673 .

**ASA PACKER MANSION,** off SR 209 on Packer Hill, was the 1860 Victorian home of the well-known 19th-century industrialist and philanthropist Asa Packer. While the exterior has changed somewhat from its original appearance, the interior remains nearly the same, containing original furnishings, woodcarvings and paintings. Allow 1 hour minimum. Daily noon-4:30, late May-Oct. 31; Sat.-Sun. noon-4:30, Apr. 1 to late May. Admission $4, students with ID $2, under 6 free. Phone (717) 325-3229.

**H.O. SCALE MODEL TRAIN DISPLAY** is on the second floor of the old Hooven Mercantile Co. building at 41 Susquehanna St. This two-level train display features 13 separate model trains pulling 60 cars over nearly 1,100 feet of winding track. The meticulously designed display includes more than 200 miniature buildings, 100 bridges, 1,000 street lights and 80 cars and trucks. Mon.-Fri. noon-5, Sat.-Sun. 10-5, July-Oct.; Sat.-Sun. noon-5, rest of year. Closed major holidays. Admission $3; over 60, $2; ages 2-16, $1. Phone (717) 325-2248.

**JIM THORPE RIVER ADVENTURES** departs ½ mi. n. of the Lehigh River Bridge on SR 903, following signs. White-water rafting on the Lehigh River is offered Mar.-Nov.; fare $42. Float trips are offered July 1 to mid-Sept.; fare $30. Minimum age or weight requirements may apply. Reservations are required. Write 1 Adventure Ln., Jim Thorpe, PA 18229. Phone (717) 325-2570.

**POCONO WHITEWATER RAFTING** trips depart 8 mi. n.e. of the Lehigh River Bridge on SR 903.

White-water rafting excursions of 4 to 6 hours are available spring and fall. Fare $44, under 10 not permitted. Fastwater trips, 3-hour runs that are slower than white water, are offered mid-May to mid-Oct. Fare $37, under 8 not permitted. Summer floats that require paddling are available July 1 to mid-Sept. Fare $29, children $19, under 5 not permitted. Reservations are recommended. Write Route 903, Jim Thorpe, PA 18229. **Discount.** Phone (717) 325-3656.

**ST. MARK'S EPISCOPAL CATHEDRAL,** on Race St., was financed largely by Sarah Packer, wife of Asa Packer. It replaced the church that originally stood on this site. The church contains altars of white Italian marble, large brass gas standards flanking the baptismal font, Tiffany stained-glass windows and one of the older operating elevators in the nation. Allow 30 minutes minimum. Daily 1-3:30, late May-Oct. 31; Sat.-Sun. 1-3:30, Apr. 1 to late May. Admission $2. Phone (717) 325-2241.

## JOHNSTOWN (H-4) pop. 28,100, elev. 1,178'

Four times disastrous floods have claimed Johnstown, which is in a deep, irregular valley formed by Stony Creek and the Little Conemaugh and Conemaugh rivers. The first two floods, in 1862 and 1889, were a result of the collapse of the South Fork Dam, about 12 miles east on the Conemaugh. Some of the older buildings still show high water marks of the 1889 disaster, one of the country's worst peacetime catastrophes. Debris held behind a stone bridge in the downtown area caught fire and added to the losses.

In 1936 a third flood caused a great deal of damage to the city and its environs. A fourth flood occurred in July 1977, when heavy rains caused rivers and streams to overflow throughout the Conemaugh Valley. Once again damage was severe.

Conemaugh Gap, a gorge cut by the Conemaugh River as it passes through Laurel Hill Ridge Mountain, extends 7 miles and is about 1,700 feet deep. For more area information contact the chamber of commerce, 111 Market St., Johnstown, PA 15901; phone (814) 536-5107.

**Shopping areas:** Richland Mall, 3200 Elton Rd., has 50 specialty stores and features Hess's, Hill's Department Store and Kmart. The Johnstown Galleria, SR 219, has more than 100 specialty stores, including Bon Ton, Boscov's, JCPenney, Sears and Wal-mart. In addition, numerous shops line Scalp Avenue.

**GRANDVIEW CEMETERY** contains the Unknown Plot, where 777 unidentified victims of the 1889 flood are buried. Daily 8-dusk. Free.

**INCLINED PLANE,** SR 56 and Johns St., is 996 feet long with a grade of 71 percent, making it one of the steeper passenger inclined planes in the country. It connects the central part of Johnstown with a residential suburb on a plateau 502 feet above the city. Both cars and pedestrians are carried. An observation platform at the top overlooks the city and showcases laser light sculptures. Food is available.

Allow 30 minutes minimum. Mon.-Thurs. 6:30 a.m.-10 p.m., Fri.-Sat. 7:30 a.m.-midnight, Sun. and holidays 9 a.m.-10 p.m., Memorial Day weekend-Labor Day; daily 6:30 a.m.-10 p.m., rest of year. Closed Jan. 1 and Dec. 25. Round-trip fare $2; ages 5-15, $1.25. Cars, vans and trucks $1.50 (plus occupants' fares); motorcycles 75c (plus riders' fare). Over 65 with ID ride free. Phone (814) 536-1816.

★JOHNSTOWN FLOOD MUSEUM, 304 Washington St. at Walnut St., features the 26-minute, 1989 Academy Award-winning documentary film "The Johnstown Flood" shown hourly. Other multimedia exhibits depict the cause of and the course of events prior to, during and after the devastating flood of May 31, 1889. A 24-foot, 3-D relief map with sound effects and fiber-optic animation shows the path of the 40-foot wall of water which traveled through the Conemaugh Valley, destroying everything in its path.

Allow 1 hour, 30 minutes minimum. Sun.-Thurs. 10-5, Fri.-Sat. 10-7, May-Oct.; daily 10-5, rest of year. Closed Jan. 1, Thanksgiving and Dec. 25. Ad-

mission $3; over 65, $2.50; ages 6-18, $2. DC, MC, VI. Phone (814) 539-1889. *See ad.*

**JOHNSTOWN FLOOD NATIONAL MEMORIAL,** 10 mi. n. via US 219, then 1½ mi. e. on SR 869 and 1½ mi. n. on Lake Rd., following signs, is on the site of the former South Fork Dam. When the dam broke and sent a 40-foot wall of water crashing through the Conemaugh Valley in 1889, Johnstown was devastated and more than 2,200 people died in about 10 minutes.

The visitor center presents a 35-minute film entitled "Black Friday" and contains a model of the dam as well as exhibits about local geography and events leading up to the flood. Ranger-conducted programs are held in summer. The dam site has a picnic area and walking trails.

Allow 1 hour minimum. Daily 9-6, Memorial Day weekend-Labor Day; 9-5, rest of year. Closed Dec. 25. Free. Phone (814) 495-4643.

**KENNETT SQUARE (I-10) pop. 5,200, elev. 260'**

★LONGWOOD GARDENS is at US 1 and SR 52. Once the country estate of entrepreneur Pierre S. Du Pont, Longwood is famous for its superb outdoor gardens, which include two lakes, woodlands, formal gardens and fountains. The 3½ acres of heated greenhouses and conservatories are particularly colorful November through April;

masses of flowering plants, some rare, adorn the conservatories all year. The chrysanthemums are usually at their best during the first 3 weeks of November.

The 1,050 acres of outdoor gardens, with tropical waterlilies and other blooms, are the main attraction in summer. The gardens nurture more than 11,000 types of plants. There are three sets of fountains: one in the Italian Water Garden, one on the stage of the Open-Air Theatre and one in front of the Main Conservatory, where half-hour color displays take place Tues., Thurs. and Sat. after dusk, June through September; the conservatories stay open 30 minutes after the fountain displays on these days.

A Fireworks With Fountains program, which requires advance tickets, is offered some Friday evenings in summer. A poinsettia and Christmas display follows in December. Organ recitals are given in the Main Conservatory and the ballroom most Sundays 2:30 to 3:30 in October and January through April. Daily in December.

Performances in the Open-Air Theatre are given June through September; a schedule is available at the visitor center or by sending a self-addressed stamped business envelope to Schedule, Longwood Gardens, P.O. Box 501, Kennett Square, PA 19348.

Allow 2 hours minimum. Conservatories open daily 10-6 (also Tues., Thurs. and Sat. 6-10:30, June-Aug.; 6-9 in Sept.). Visitor center and outdoor gardens daily 9-6, Apr.-Oct. (also Tues., Thurs. and Sat. 6-10:30, June-Aug.; 6-9 in Sept.); 9-5, rest of year. Last admission 30 minutes before closing. Admission $10, Tues. $6; ages 16-20, $6; ages 6-15, $2. Phone (610) 388-1000.

**PHILLIPS MUSHROOM MUSEUM,** 909 E. Baltimore Pike (US 1), ½ mi. s. jct. SR 52, explains the cultivation and use of mushrooms through photographs, models and a film presentation. Displays show live mushrooms in various stages of growth. Allow 30 minutes minimum. Daily 10-6; closed Jan. 1, Easter, Thanksgiving and Dec. 25. Admission $1.25; over 60, 75c; ages 7-12, 50c. Phone (610) 388-6082.

## KUTZTOWN (G-10) pop. 4,700

Kutztown was settled in 1771 by Pennsylvania Germans and named for founder George Kutz. An 1892 schoolhouse at White Oak and Normal avenues portrays a classroom and library of the era. It is open by appointment; phone (610) 683-7697. Also in town is Kutztown State University.

In early July the town celebrates its heritage with the Kutztown Folk Festival. Featured are Pennsylvania Dutch foods, arts and crafts, quilts and square dancing.

**Shopping areas:** Renningers Antique & Farmers Market, 740 Noble St., is open on weekends. Antique and collectors' shows take place in late April, late June and late September; phone (717)

385-0104 Mon.-Thurs. or (610) 683-6848 Fri.-Sat. Kutztown Antique Gallery, 272 W. Main St., is open daily and displays more than 80,000 antiques and collectibles; phone (610) 683-5033.

**CRYSTAL CAVE,** 2 mi. n. off US 222, following signs, is named for the crystalline formations found in the cavern. Geological formations resemble such objects as an ear of corn, tobacco leaves and a totem pole. Also on the grounds are a Pennsylvania Dutch food center, ice cream parlor, miniature golf course, theater, museum, rock shop and nature trail. Picnic facilities are available. Special events take place on Halloween and Thanksgiving.

Allow 1 hour, 30 minutes minimum. Mon.-Fri. 9-6, Sat.-Sun. 9-7, Memorial Day-Labor Day; Mon.-Fri. 9-5, Sat.-Sun. 9-6, day after Labor Day-Sept. 30; daily 9-5, Mar. 1-day before Memorial Day and in Nov. Admission $7; ages 4-11, $4.50. Miniature golf $2.75. Phone (610) 683-6765.

## LACKAWAXEN (E-12) pop. 2,800, elev. 687'

**ZANE GREY MUSEUM,** Scenic Dr., is situated along the Delaware River in the house where Zane Grey began his writing career. Exhibits include photographs, books and personal belongings of the Western author and his wife, Dolly. Allow 30 minutes minimum. Daily 10-4:30, Memorial Day weekend-Sept. 30; Sat.-Sun. noon-4, mid-Apr. through day before Memorial Day weekend and Oct. 1-Nov. 20. Free. Phone (717) 685-4871.

## LAHASKA (H-11)

**BUCKINGHAM VALLEY VINEYARDS AND WINERY,** s. of Buckingham on SR 413, offers tastings and self-guiding tours; questions are answered at the end of the tour. Allow 30 minutes minimum. Tues.-Fri. noon-6, Sat. 10-6, Sun. noon-4, Mar.-Dec.; Fri. noon-6, Sat. 10-6, Sun. noon-4, rest of year. Free. Phone (215) 794-7188.

**CAROUSEL WORLD,** within Peddler's Village, offers a nostalgic look at the history of the carousel amusement ride industry. The painstakingly detailed artistry of noted carousel carvers is displayed, along with miniature representations of a circus and a turn-of-the-20th-century amusement park. Rides are available on a working carousel that features carved lions and giraffes in addition to horses.

Allow 1 hour minimum. Mon.-Thurs. 10-5:30, Fri.-Sat. 10-9, Sun. 11-5:30, May 1 to mid-Nov. and late Dec.-Apr. 30; Mon.-Sat. 10-9, Sun. 11-5:30, mid-Nov. to late Dec. Closed holidays. Museum admission $3; over 65, $2.75; children $2. Museum and carousel ride $3.50, children $2.50. Carousel ride only $1.25, infants 75c. Phone (215) 794-8960.

**PEDDLER'S VILLAGE** is at US 202 and SR 263. Coops from the old Lahaska Chicken Farm have been rebuilt as a charming 42-acre shopping complex. Herringbone-patterned brick paths and landscaped gardens enhance this village of 76 shops and restaurants. Special events take place regularly. Allow 2 hours minimum. Mon.-Thurs. 10-5:30, Fri. 10-9, Sat. 10-6, Sun. noon-5:30; closed Jan. 1, Thanksgiving and Dec. 25. Phone (215) 794-4000. *See ad p. 131.*

### LANCASTER (I-9) pop. 55,600, elev. 377'

During the Revolutionary War, Lancaster was the largest inland city in the Colonies. It was capital of the nation for 1 day, Sept. 27, 1777, when Congress stopped in Lancaster as it fled Philadelphia after the Battle of Brandywine *(see Chadds Ford).* Lancaster was the state capital 1799-1812.

The city is in the heart of Lancaster County, known for its Amish and Mennonite population, its picturesque and productive farms and its heaping platters of Pennsylvania Dutch food. The Visitor Information Center, on US 30 at the Greenfield Road exit, presents a brief orientation to the area through exhibits, a multi-image program, brochures and maps.

The Long's Park Art & Craft Festival, held Labor Day weekend, features the works of nearly 200 artists. Basketry, furniture, jewelry, glass, wood, photography, watercolor, leather and musical instruments are just some of the items and crafts presented. For further information write the Long's Park Art & Craft Festival, P.O. Box 1553, Lancaster, PA 17608-1553; phone (717) 295-7001.

For additional area information contact the Pennsylvania Dutch Convention and Visitors Bureau, 501 Greenfield Rd., Lancaster, PA 17601; phone (717) 299-8901 or (800) 723-8824. *Also see Pennsylvania Dutch Country (see ads p. A151, p. A152 and p. A153).*

**Shopping areas:** Lancaster boasts a large number of factory outlets, including the Charles Chips Outlet Store at 1098 Ivy Dr.; Dansk Factory Outlet on SR 30; Hamilton Watch and Clock Shoppe at 2450 Lincoln Hwy. E.; MillStream Designer Factory Shops at 311 Outlet Dr.; and Totes Factory Store, offering umbrellas and rainwear at 220 Centerville Rd. Rockvale Square Factory Outlet Village, at SR 30E and SR 896, is another large center, containing more than 120 factory outlets.

**AMISH COUNTRY TOURS,** 5 mi. e. of SR 30 on SR 340 at 3121 Old Philadelphia Pike (grounds of the Plain and Fancy Restaurant), offers narrated bus tours of Amish farmlands and the Pennsylvania Dutch Country. Tours of Hershey and historic Philadelphia also are available. Amish Farmlands Tour departs Mon.-Sat. at 10:30, Apr.-Oct.; Sunday Sampler departs Sun. at 10:30. Winter Tour departs daily at 11:30., rest of year. Hours may vary; phone ahead. Amish Farmlands $15.95-$21.95; ages 4-12, $6.95-$7.95. Sunday Sampler $17.95; ages 4-12, $6.95.

Winter Tour $16.95; ages 4-12, $5.95. MC, VI. Reservations are recommended. **Discount.** Phone (717) 392-8622 or (800) 441-3505.

**THE AMISH FARM AND HOUSE** is 5 mi. e. on US 30. A 45-minute lecture tour explaining the Plain People's way of life is given through the 1805 house. Major local crops, barns and farm animals can be seen on the grounds. Food is available April through October. Allow 1 hour, 30 minutes minimum. Daily 8:30-6, June-Aug., 8:30-5, Apr.-May and Sept.-Oct.; 8:30-4, rest of year. Closed Dec. 25. Fee $5; senior citizens $4.50; ages 5-11, $3. AE, DS, MC, VI. Phone (717) 394-6185. *See ad p. A155.*

**ANDERSON COMPANY BAKERY,** ½ mi. e. of jct. SR 340 and US 30 at 2060 Old Philadelphia Pike, offers self-guiding tours of one of the world's larger pretzel bakeries. The tour chronicles the history of the Anderson family and the bakery. The tour winds through the facility and illustrates all phases of production. Free pretzels can be sampled at the end of the tour. Allow 30 minutes minimum. Mon.-Fri. 8:30-4; closed holidays and Good Friday. Free. Phone (717) 299-1616.

**CCINC. AUTO TAPE TOURS** offers a 3-hour taped tour of the Lancaster area, including information about the customs, culture and lifestyles of the Amish people. The audiotapes include music and sound effects; a map is provided. The tapes can be purchased for $12.95 at The Amish Farm and House, Dutch Wonderland Family Fun Park and Wax Museum of Lancaster County History *(see attraction listings),* or the tape can be purchased in advance by sending $14.95 (includes postage) to CCInc., P.O. Box 227, Allendale, NJ 07401; phone (201) 236-1666.

**DUTCH WONDERLAND FAMILY FUN PARK,** 4 mi. e. on US 30, has 44 acres of attractions, including rides, shows and gardens. Allow 4 hours minimum. Daily 10-8, July 1-Labor Day; daily 10-7, May 27-June 30; Sat. 10-6, Sun. 11-6, Apr. 15-May 26 and day after Labor Day-Oct. 8. Unlimited-ride pass $17, five-ride pass $12. Monorail $1.75. AE, DS, MC, VI. Phone (717) 291-1888. *See ad p. A155.*

**FARMERS' MARKETS** offer such delicacies as souse, schmiercase, cup cheese, schnitz, old-fashioned Bavarian pretzels and shoofly pie.

**Bird-in-Hand Farmer's Market,** on SR 340, is open Wed.-Sat. 8:30-5:30, July-Oct.; Wed. and Fri.-Sat. 8:30-5:30, Apr.-June and in Nov.; Fri.-Sat. 8:30-5:30, rest of year.

**Central Market,** Penn Sq., is one of the older enclosed markets in the country. Visitors can shop for fresh fruits, vegetables, flowers, meats and baked goods. Tues. and Fri. 6-4:30, Sat. 6-2.

**Meadowbrook Market,** 4 mi. e. on SR 23, offers fruits, vegetables, flowers, baked goods, handcrafted items and antiques. Fri. 9-7:30, Sat. 8-5.

**HANDS-ON HOUSE, CHILDREN'S MUSEUM OF LANCASTER,** in a restored Victorian farmhouse at 2380 Kissel Hill Rd., specializes in letting children learn through play. Interactive exhibit areas feature a child-size grocery store, an assembly line in the Whatcha-Ma-Giggle Co., planning and constructing a town and using light to create art. Under 16 must be with an adult. Allow 1 hour, 30 minutes minimum. Mon.-Sat. 10-5 (also Fri. 5-8), Sun. noon-5, June 15-Sept. 15; Tues.-Fri. 11-4 (also Fri. 4-8), Sat. 10-5, Sun. noon-5, rest of year. Admission $4. Phone (717) 569-5437.

**HANS HERR HOUSE** is 4 mi. s. on US 222, then ¾ mi. s. to 1849 Hans Herr Dr. Built in 1719, this is the oldest building in Lancaster County and the oldest documented Mennonite meetinghouse in America. The medieval-style Germanic stone house has been depicted in several paintings by Andrew Wyeth, a descendant of Hans Herr. The site includes the restored and furnished house, an exhibit about Mennonite farm life, a blacksmith shop, picnic tables, an orchard and a visitor center.

Allow 1 hour minimum. Mon.-Sat. 9-4, Apr.-Dec.; closed Thanksgiving and Dec. 25. Admission $3; ages 7-12, $1. Phone (717) 464-4438.

**HERITAGE CENTER MUSEUM OF LANCASTER COUNTY,** Penn Sq., occupies the historic 1798 City Hall and the Masonic Lodge Hall of the same period. The museum's exhibits of local folk and decorative arts include furniture, quilts, clocks, silver, textiles and fine art. Changing exhibits are displayed throughout the year. Allow 30 minutes minimum. Tues.-Sat. 10-4 (also Sun. 10-4 in Dec.), Apr.-Dec. Donations. Phone (717) 299-6440.

**LANCASTER COUNTY HISTORICAL SOCIETY,** 230 N. President Ave., houses items of local and national interest, including genealogical materials. Tues.-Sat. 9:30-4:30 (also Thurs. 4:30-9:30); closed holidays. Museum free; library $5. Phone (717) 392-4633.

**LANCASTER COUNTY WINERY** is 8 mi. s. off SR 272, then 1 mi. w. on Baumgardner Rd. and 2 mi. on Rawlinsville Rd. The Dickel family has operated this 60-acre farm since 1718. The stone farmhouse on the grounds, built in 1820, is surrounded by Amish farmland. Guided tours of the wine cellar are offered. Allow 30 minutes minimum. Tours on the hour (weather permitting) Mon.-Sat. 10-4, Sun. noon-4, Feb.-Dec. Fee $3. **Discount.** Phone (717) 464-3555.

**LANCASTER NEWSPAPERS NEWSEUM** is 1 blk. s. of the center square at 28 S. Queen St. Window displays depict the evolution of newspapers locally, nationally and internationally. Exhibits include major national headlines and address forms of printing and distribution. Daily 24 hours. Free. Phone (717) 291-8600.

**LANCASTER WALKING TOUR,** departing from the chamber of commerce at Queen and Vine sts., is a 90-minute tour of the city with a costumed guide who explains the cultural, economic and religious development of Lancaster. An audiovisual presentation is included. Mon.-Sat. at 10 and 1:30, Sun. and holidays at 1:30, Apr.-Oct. Fee $5. Phone (717) 392-1776.

★**LANDIS VALLEY MUSEUM** is 2½ mi. n. on Oregon Pike (SR 272). The 16-acre complex interprets Pennsylvania German rural life before 1900. The many buildings include farmsteads, a tavern and a country store. Crafts demonstrations are given May through October. Guided tours are available in April.

Allow 2 hours minimum. Tues.-Sat. 10-5, Sun. noon-5, Jan.-Oct.; closed holidays except Memorial Day, July 4 and Labor Day. Admission $7; over 60, $6; ages 6-17, $5. **Discount.** Phone (717) 569-0401.

**MENNONITE INFORMATION CENTER AND HEBREW TABERNACLE REPRODUCTION** are 4½ mi. e. at 2209 Millstream Rd., just off US 30. The information center has exhibits that explain the faith and culture of the Amish and Mennonites. A free video presentation is shown every half-hour 8-4:30. Mennonite "step-on" tour guides are available for 2-hour tours of the Amish farmlands; cars are $8.50 per hour (plus a $6 service charge per car).

Allow 30 minutes minimum. Mon.-Sat. 8-5; closed Jan. 1, Thanksgiving and Dec. 25. Free. Phone (717) 299-0954.

Adjacent is a reproduction of the Hebrew Tabernacle. Lecture tours about the tabernacle's history, construction, function and significance are given on the hour Mon.-Sat. 9-4; closed Jan. 1, Thanksgiving and Dec. 25. Fee $4; over 64, $3.25; ages 7-12, $2.

**MILL BRIDGE VILLAGE,** 4 mi. e. of jct. US 30 and SR 462, is a restored Colonial mill village with an operating 1738 water-driven gristmill that grinds corn. At the village is the longest and oldest covered bridge in Lancaster County; working craftsmen, including a blacksmith, hearth broom maker and candle dipper; and the Miller's Log Cabin, which displays Amish and Mennonite quilts and handcrafts.

Additional highlights include the Old Mill Village Store; a collection of Gay '90s nickelodeons, music boxes and memorabilia; a petting barnyard; and the old-fashioned "Gazebo in the Park." Guided tours of an Amish house, school and 1830s print shop also are available. Entertainment is provided some weekends in the fall. Also included are free horse-drawn carriage rides and picnic areas along the mill stream.

Village open daily 9:30-5:30, Memorial Day-Labor Day; daily 10-5, Apr. 1-day before Memorial Day and day after Labor Day-Oct. 31; Sat.-Sun., Nov.-Dec. Admission $10; over 55, $9; ages 6-12, $5. AE, DS, MC, VI. Phone (717) 687-6521. *See ad p. A153.*

**NORTH MUSEUM OF NATURAL HISTORY AND SCIENCE,** Franklin & Marshall College campus at College and Buchanan aves., contains natural history displays, a planetarium and a children's discovery room. Discovery room open Wed.-Sun. 1:30-4:30, late June-Aug. 31; Sat.-Sun. 1:30-4:30, rest of year. Planetarium shows Sat.-Sun. at 2 and 3. Museum open Tues.-Sat. 9-5, Sun. 1:30-5. Donations. Planetarium $2. Phone (717) 291-3941.

**THE PEOPLE'S PLACE**—*see Intercourse.*

**ROCK FORD,** in Lancaster County Park at 881 Rock Ford Rd., is the preserved 18th-century plantation of Edward Hand, adjutant general during the Revolutionary War. A museum in the barn has Zoe and Henry Kauffman's folk items. Tues.-Sat. 10-4, Sun. noon-4, Apr.-Oct. Admission $4.50; over 55, $3.50; ages 6-12, $2. **Discount.** Phone(717) 392-7223.

**TRINITY LUTHERAN CHURCH,** 31 S. Duke St., was originally constructed in 1730 and rebuilt 1761-66. The spire, with statues of apostles Matthew, Mark, Luke and John, dates from 1794. Tours are available by prior arrangement Mon.-Fri. 8:30-4:30. Guide service is available Sun. at

9:45 and noon (after services). Free. Phone (717) 397-2734.

**WAX MUSEUM OF LANCASTER COUNTY HISTORY,** 4 mi. e. on US 30, presents audiovisual scenes of historical events in Pennsylvania from the 1700s to the present. Visitors can watch a reenactment of an Amish barn raising. Allow 1 hour minimum. Daily 9-8, Apr.-Oct.; 9-6, rest of year. Admission $4.75; senior citizens $4.25; ages 5-11, $3. MC, VI. Phone (717) 393-3679. *See ad p. A155.*

★**WHEATLAND,** 1120 Marietta Ave., is the 1828 Federal mansion of James Buchanan, the only Pennsylvanian to become president of the United States. He conducted his 1856 presidential campaign from the library. Restored period rooms contain original Buchanan furnishings and decorative objects. Costumed guides conduct tours. Candlelight tours are available the first 2 weeks in December.

One-hour tours depart every 15 minutes. Daily 10-4:15, Apr.-Nov.; closed Thanksgiving. Admission $5.50; senior citizens $4.50; students with ID $3.50; ages 6-12, $1.75. Phone (717) 392-8721.

**LANGHORNE (H-12) pop. 1,400, elev. 103'**

Oxford Valley Mall, US 1 and Oxford Valley Road, is a popular place for shopping in the Langhorne area. The mall's 135 stores include JCPenney, John Wanamaker, Macy's and Sears.

**SESAME PLACE,** next to Oxford Valley Mall at US 1 and I-95, is an Anheuser-Busch family theme park with educational overtones and appearances by some of the Sesame Street characters. Water activities include inner tube rides and body flumes for children and adults. Splash pools are available for smaller children. A bathing suit is required. Non-water activities feature physical play elements on which children can jump, bounce, slide and climb. There are no mechanical rides. Indoor activities include science exhibits and electronic games.

Sesame Island features two sandy beaches, water activities and a theater in which exotic birds entertain in the Birds of Paradise show. Twiddlebug Land, themed after the tiny creatures in Bert and Ernie's flower box, is an area where all the oversized elements make its explorers feel as tiny as Twiddlebugs. Features include a wave pool, hand-powered railroad, and SkySplash.

Live entertainment includes the Sesame Street characters in walk-around appearances and the Alphabet Parade. Food is available. Picnicking is permitted.

Allow 5 hours minimum. Daily 9-8 May 15-Aug. 31; otherwise varies. Admission $21.95; over 54, $17.80; under 2 free. DS, MC, VI. **Discount.** Phone (215) 752-7070.

**LAUGHLINTOWN (H-4)**

**THE COMPASS INN MUSEUM,** on US 30, is a restored 1799 stagecoach stop. A reconstructed barn displays a Conestoga wagon, stagecoach and tools. A blacksmith shop and cookhouse contain implements of the time. Costumed docents conduct tours of the complex. Allow 1 hour, 30 minutes minimum. Tues.-Sat. 11-4, Sun. noon-4, May 1-late Oct.; candlelight tours Sat.-Sun. 2-5, Nov. 1 to mid-Dec. Admission $4; ages 6-16, $2. **Discount.** Phone (412) 238-4983.

**THE LAUREL HIGHLANDS**

The Laurel Highlands encompasses a five-county area in the Allegheny foothills of southwestern Pennsylvania. The region that once hid the exclusive resorts of wealthy Pittsburgh industrialists now yields to the modern vacationer a wide range of activities and experiences.

Excellent white-water rafting is possible on the Youghiogheny River, which runs southeastward from McKeesport to the Maryland border *(see Ohiopyle);* boating on Conemaugh Lake and Youghiogheny Reservoir also are popular. The Laurel and Chestnut ridges of the Allegheny Mountains provide for good mountain-stream fishing and hunting in season and downhill and cross-country skiing in winter. The region also offers more than 25 hiking, bicycling and bridle trails and about 30 golf courses.

The Laurel Highlands is especially scenic in the spring and fall. Wildflowers are in bloom mid-April to mid-May; the Mountain Laurel blooms at higher elevations for about 3 weeks in June. The fall foliage fireworks explode mid- to late October. Viewing is best in Forbes State Forest in the central highlands and from Mount Davis, the state's highest point, north of Springs. The scenic Pennsylvania Turnpike (I-70/76) traverses the region from east to west.

For more information contact Laurel Highlands, Inc., 120 E. Main St., Ligonier, PA 15658; phone (412) 238-5661 or (800) 925-7669 (see color ad p. 110).

Places and towns in the Laurel Highlands listed individually are Brownsville, Cresson, Dawson, Donegal, Fort Necessity National Battlefield, Greensburg, Jeannette, Johnstown, Laughlintown, Ligonier, Loretto, Mount Pleasant, Ohiopyle, Point Marion, St. Boniface, Scottdale, Somerset, Springs, Uniontown and Waynesburg.

## LEBANON (H-9) pop. 24,800, elev. 466'

A community of German agricultural and English industrial origins, Lebanon was founded in 1750 and named after the "White Mountain" of Biblical times.

Lebanon's historic churches include the 1760 Tabor United Church of Christ at 10th and Walnut streets and the 1760 Salem Lutheran Church at 8th and Willow streets. Both churches are open for tours by appointment.

North of Lebanon off SR 72 at Tunnel Hill Road is Union Canal Tunnel, one of the older tunnels in the United States. At the time it was completed, the tunneling through 729 feet of solid rock was considered an engineering marvel. The feat completed the canal between Harrisburg and Reading.

The Tulpehocken Manor Inn and Plantation, 3 miles east on US 422, is a 150-acre working farm and inn. The house, built in 1769, was remodeled in Victorian style in 1883 and is furnished with antiques. Other plantation buildings include stone cottages of Germanic Swiss Bank architecture. Half-hour tours are available by appointment.

More area information is available at the Lebanon Valley Chamber of Commerce, 252 N. 8th St., P.O. Box 899, Lebanon, PA 17042; phone (717) 273-3727.

STOY MUSEUM AND HAUCK MEMORIAL LIBRARY, 924 Cumberland St., contains such reconstructed rooms as a drugstore, doctor's office, one-room schoolhouse, toy shop and general store, as well as exhibits about early local industries and crafts. The front part of the building was constructed in 1773 as a home for Dr. William Henry Stoy. It was later used as the county courthouse, where James Buchanan, the 15th U.S. president, practiced law as a young attorney. Guided tours are available.

Allow 1 hour, 30 minutes minimum. Museum and library open Sun.-Fri. 1-4:30 (also Mon. 7-9 p.m.); closed holidays and Sun.-Mon. of holiday weekends. Last tour 1 hour, 30 minutes before closing. Fee $3; over 65, $2; ages 5-18, $1. Phone (717) 272-1473.

## LEHIGHTON (F-10) pop. 5,900, elev. 4,945'

POCONO MUSEUM UNLIMITED, ½ mi. w on SR 443 at 517 Ashtown Dr., houses an extensive model railroad collection with 16 miniature trains traveling through varied terrains, tunnels, towns and villages, an amusement park, a lake with live fish and waterfalls. Hundreds of railroad cars and "O" scale trains also are on display. Guided tours are available.

Allow 1 hour, 30 minutes minimum. Wed.-Mon. 10-5, May 1-Labor Day; Wed.-Mon. noon-5, day after Labor Day-Dec. 31; Mon. and Sat.-Sun. noon-5, rest of year. Closed Jan. 1, Easter and Dec. 25. Admission $3.75; over 60, $2.75; ages 5-12, $2. Phone (717) 386-3117.

## LENHARTSVILLE (G-10) pop. 200, elev. 369'

PENNSYLVANIA DUTCH FOLK CULTURE CENTER, ¼ mi. s. on SR 143 from jct. I-78 and US 22, features five folklife museum buildings and a library of genealogy, folklore and local history. Costumed guides give 1- to 1½-hour tours. Special exhibits and shows take place on weekends. Allow 1 hour, 30 minutes minimum. Mon.-Sat. 10-5, Sun. 1-5, Memorial Day-Labor Day; Sat. 10-4, Sun. 1-4, Apr. 1-day before Memorial Day and day after Labor Day-Oct. 31. Admission $3; ages 6-12, $1.50. Discount. Phone (610) 562-4803 or 682-7432.

## LEWISBURG (F-8) pop. 5,800, elev. 460'

Lewisburg, on the West Branch of the Susquehanna River, is noted for its late Federal and Victorian architecture. Lewisburg also is a college town: Bucknell University is a private liberal arts college.

Lewisburg is the home of White Deer Station, headquarters for the Central Pennsylvania Chapter of the National Railway Historical Society. The station has information about and relics from the railroad era of the central Susquehanna Valley.

Self-guiding tours: Brochures describing a walking tour are available from the Lewisburg Area Chamber of Commerce, 418 Market St., Lewisburg, PA 17837; phone (717) 524-2815.

Shopping areas: An interesting local shopping center is Country Cupboard, 3 miles north of town on SR 15. It offers crafts, gifts, Christmas items and specialty foods. Another unusual collection of shops is Brookpark Farm, 1 mile west of SR 15 on SR 45, offering furniture, rugs, gourmet foods, crafts, antiques, collectibles and Christmas items. Roller Mills Marketplace, 517

St. Mary St., features more than 300 antique dealers. Two miles south on SR 15 the hand-crafted wares of almost 60 artisans are displayed.

**PACKWOOD HOUSE MUSEUM**, 15 N. Water St., was begun as a log structure 1796-99. It evolved into a massive three-story building that served as a hostelry for land, river and canal travelers in the Susquehanna Valley until 1886. Its 27 rooms contain wide-ranging collections of American and central Pennsylvanian relics: textiles, ceramics, glass, art objects and period furniture.

The house is visited by guided tour only. Tours start at the adjacent Tour Center, which has an orientation exhibit and changing gallery exhibits. Allow 1 hour minimum. Museum and Tour Center open Tues.-Fri. 10-5, Sat. 1-5, Sun. 2-5; closed holidays. Last tour departs 1 hour before closing. Fee $4; over 59, $3.25; ages 6-16, $1.75. Phone (717) 524-0323.

**SLIFER HOUSE MUSEUM**, 1 mi. n. on US 15, was built in 1861 and is an excellent example of Victorian architecture. The restored mansion overlooks the Susquehanna River. Victorian furnishings and decorative arts are displayed. Allow 1 hour minimum. Guided tours Tues.-Sun. 1-4, Apr.-Dec.; Tues.-Fri. 1-4, rest of year. Fee $3; over 62, $2.50; ages 10-16, $2. Phone (717) 524-2271.

**WEST SHORE RAIL EXCURSIONS** depart from Delta Place Station, 2 mi. n. on US 15. Passengers board the Lewisburg and Buffalo Creek Railroad for a 1½-hour narrated train ride through downtown Lewisburg, past Bucknell University and along the Susquehanna River to Winfield and back. A 2½-hour ride on the West Shore Railroad winds through the Amish and Mennonite farms of the Buffalo Valley. Lunch and dinner train rides and special event trips also are available.

The Lewisburg and Buffalo Creek Railroad departs Tues.-Sat. at 11:30 and 2, Sun. at 11:30, June-Aug.; Sat. at 11:30 and 2, Sun. at 11:30, Sept.-Oct.; Sat.-Sun. at 2, Apr.-May. West Shore Railroad departs Sun. at 2, June-Oct. Lewisburg fare $7; over 60, $6; ages 3-11, $4. West Shore fare $9; over 60, $8; ages 3-11, $5. DS, MC, VI. Phone (717) 524-4337.

## LEWISTOWN (G-7) pop. 9,300, elev. 495'

Lewistown lies in a scenic region: To the east is Lewistown Narrows, a 6-mile gorge through which the Juniata River flows to meet the Susquehanna. The Stone Arch Bridge, curiously constructed without a keystone, is on the east side of US 22 at the south entrance to town. North of Lewistown is the Seven Mountain District, known for good hunting and fishing. Kishacoquillas Valley, site of an Amish community, is 6 miles north.

The Pennsylvania Fire School is in Lewistown. Firefighters from Pennsylvania and other states attend classes throughout the year.

The original county courthouse, built in the 1800s, is at Monument Square. Near the courthouse at 17 N. Main St. is the McCoy House, the 1874 birthplace and home of soldier-statesman Gen. Frank Ross McCoy. The courthouse and McCoy House are home to the Mifflin County Historical Society Museum and Library.

Goose Day, the old English custom of serving roasted goose on St. Michaelmas Day for good luck in the coming year, is celebrated on September 29. For more area information contact the Juniata Valley Area Chamber of Commerce, 19 S. Wayne St., Lewistown, PA 17044; phone (717) 248-6713.

## LIGONIER (H-4) pop. 1,600

**THE COMPASS INN MUSEUM**—see *Laughlintown.*

**FORBES ROAD GUN MUSEUM**, 2¼ mi. n. on SR 711, then 1 mi. e., exhibits firearms dating from 1450 to the present. War relics, mounted animal heads, Indian arrowheads and a butterfly collection also are shown. Guide service is available. Allow 1 hour minimum. Daily 9-5. Admission $1.50; over 62, $1.25; ages 13-16, 75c; ages 6-12, 50c. Phone (412) 238-9544.

**FORT LIGONIER**, US 30 and SR 711, is a reconstruction of the English fort built in 1758. The fort was abandoned in 1766 after serving as a major English stronghold during the French and Indian War. The museum contains interpretive exhibits from the site, two period rooms and collections of decorative arts. Fort Ligonier Days is held the second weekend in October. Allow 1 hour minimum. Mon.-Sat. 10-4:30, Sun. noon-4:30, May-Oct. Admission $5; over 62, $4.50; ages 6-14, $2.25. Phone (412) 238-9701.

**IDLEWILD PARK**, 2½ mi. w. on US 30, offers amusement rides, miniature golf, waterslides, a swimming pool, live entertainment and picnicking. Gates open Tues.-Sun. at 10, June 3-Aug. 27 (also during Memorial and Labor Day weekends); closing times vary. . All-inclusive admission $13.50; over 55, $6.50; under 2 free. Phone (412) 238-3666.

**Hootin' Holler** is a re-created Western town featuring live entertainment, steam train rides and Confusion Hill.

**Jumpin' Jungle** has a pool of balls through which visitors can swim, as well as a treehouse, rope climb, slides, Tarzan swing and raft ride.

**Mister Rogers' Neighborhood of Make-Believe** takes youngsters on a trolley ride to see life-size puppets, "X" the Owl, Henrietta Pussycat, Lady Elaine Fairchilde and King Friday XIII. There also is the Museum-Go-Round, Royal Castle and Daniel's Clock.

**Story Book Forest** is a walk-through theme park where live characters depict many familiar nursery rhymes.

## LIMERICK (H-10) pop. 6,700

**LIMERICK ENERGY INFORMATION CENTER** is at the PECO Co. nuclear power generating station, 3 mi. w. of the US 422 Limerick/Linfield exit, following signs to 298 Longview Rd. Using water from the Schuylkill and Delaware rivers, the generating station provides electricity to the Delaware Valley. The information center offers displays, films and lectures about energy, nuclear power, plant construction and environmental studies.

Allow 30 minutes minimum. Tues.-Sat. 10-4; closed holidays. Free. Phone (610) 495-6767.

## LINESVILLE (D-1) pop. 1,200, elev. 1,034'

Pymatuning Reservoir arcs through Crawford County for 16 miles, its south end near Jamestown on US 322 and its northern apex near Linesville on US 6. Its western shore curves into Ohio. Pymatuning State Park *(see Recreation Chart and Jamestown in the AAA Mideastern CampBook)* surrounds the Pennsylvania shoreline.

At the spillway in the park visitors can buy stale bread and feed the fish and ducks; the site is known as "the place where the ducks walk on the fishes' backs," since the fish are said to be so numerous that the ducks use them as stepping stones to walk across the water. The lake is stocked with bass, bluegill, crappie, muskellunge, perch and walleye.

The upper part of the reservoir near Linesville is a state waterfowl sanctuary. A number of islands mark this part of the reservoir.

**PYMATUNING VISITOR CENTER**, 2 mi. s. on Mercer St., features a number of mounted birds and animals. The center overlooks Pymatuning Lake and a bald eagle's nest. A ¼-mile nature trail has labeled exhibits. Allow 1 hour minimum. Mon.-Fri. 8-4, Sat.-Sun. 9-5, Mar.-Oct. Free. Phone (814) 683-5545.

## LITITZ (H-9) pop. 8,200, elev. 360'

Dedicated in 1756 as a Moravian community, Lititz was named for the place in Bohemia where the Moravian Church was founded in 1456. Until 1855 the entire community was owned by the church. Linden Hall, one of the older girls' residence schools in the United States, was founded by Moravians in 1746. Originally a day school, it began boarding students in 1794. The Lititz Moravian Archives and Museum, at Church Square and Main Street, provides guided tours of the church buildings Memorial Day through Labor Day. Tours are available by appointment only; phone (717) 626-8515. *Also see Pennsylvania Dutch Country.*

**Self-guiding tours:** A brochure outlining a walking tour of historic buildings and houses on E. Main Street is available from the Lititz Historical Foundation at the Johannes Mueller House *(see attraction listing),* 137-139 E. Main St., Lititz, PA 17543; phone (717) 626-7958.

**CANDY AMERICANA MUSEUM AND CANDY OUTLET** is in the Wilbur Chocolate Co. building at 48 N. Broad St. The museum displays antique confectionery equipment, including molds, tins, trays, wooden boxes and a collection of more than 200 antique chocolate pots. Visitors can watch hand-dipped candies being made. The museum has a strong aroma of chocolate from the adjoining factory. The candy outlet resembles an old country store.

Mon.-Sat. 10-5; closed Jan. 1-2, Labor Day, Thanksgiving and Dec. 25-26. Free. Phone (717) 626-3249.

**GRAVE OF GEN. JOHN A. SUTTER** is in the Moravian Cemetery behind the church on E. Main St. It was the discovery of gold on Gen. Sutter's property near Sacramento, Calif., that started the rush of 1849. Sutter lived in Lititz while battling Congress to receive compensation for the California land.

**JOHANNES MUELLER HOUSE**, 137-139 E. Main St., was built in 1792 and consists of a stone house and an adjoining log structure. The log portion contains Mueller's workshop. The stone house is furnished in period. A museum next to the house features a collection of early Lititz artifacts and paintings. Allow 30 minutes minimum. Guided tours are available Mon.-Sat. 10-4, May 1 to mid-Dec. Fee $3; over 65 and ages 6-18, $1.50. **Discount.** Phone (717) 626-7958.

**LITITZ SPRINGS PARK**, in town on SR 501, is illuminated by thousands of candles on July 4. The celebration dates from the early days of the settlement. Open daily 24 hours.

**STURGIS PRETZEL HOUSE** is at 219 E. Main St. In 1861 Julius Sturgis established what is said to be the first pretzel bakery in the United States. The bakery dates from 1784, while this first commercial pretzel factory dates from 1861. Handmade soft pretzels are baked in the 200-year-old ovens. Visitors who can successfully twist a pretzel are given a baker's hat, pretzel and diploma. Allow 30 minutes minimum. Guided tours Mon.-Sat. 9:30-4:30; closed Jan. 1, Easter, Thanksgiving and Dec. 25. Admission $1.50. Phone (717) 626-4354.

## LOCK HAVEN (F-7) pop. 9,200, elev. 563'

Lock Haven was laid out at the site of Fort Reed, which had once protected frontier settlers from the Indians. The 1778 evacuation of the fort during a fierce Indian raid became known as the "great runaway." During the 19th century Lock Haven was a major lumbering center and an important port on the Pennsylvania Canal. For more area information contact the Clinton County Chamber of Commerce, 151 Susquehanna Ave., Lock Haven, PA 17745; phone (717) 748-5782.

**Self-guiding tours:** Audio cassettes describing a walking tour of Water Street can be borrowed from the Ross Library on Main Street. The tour takes at least an hour. Tapes are available Mon. and Thurs. 9-8, Tues.-Wed. and Fri.-Sat. 9-5; phone (717) 748-3321.

**HEISEY MUSEUM,** 362 E. Water St., is in a restored two-story Victorian house that contains period rooms and furnishings as well as local memorabilia. Under 12 must be with an adult. Allow 30 minutes minimum. Tues.-Fri. 10-4; other times by appointment. Admission $2, children $1. Phone (717) 748-7254.

### LONGWOOD (I-10)

In the midst of the historic Brandywine Valley, Longwood also is in Chester County—considered the "Mushroom Capital of the World."

Brochures and information are available at the Brandywine Valley Tourist Information Center, located at the entrance to Longwood Gardens. Housed in a 19th-century Quaker meetinghouse, this historic center offers exhibits, videotape presentations and a wide range of visitor information. It is open daily 10-6, May-Sept.; 10-5, rest of year. Phone (610) 388-2900 or (800) 228-9933.

★**LONGWOOD GARDENS**—*see Kennett Square.*

SEAT BELTS ARE A MUST.

### LORETTO (G-5) pop. 1,200

**SOUTHERN ALLEGHENIES MUSEUM OF ART,** on the campus of St. Francis College, displays a fine survey of American art with emphasis on 19th- and 20th-century painting and graphics. Regional and national artists are represented in the permanent collection and changing exhibits. Allow 30 minutes minimum. Mon.-Fri. 10-4, Sat.-Sun. 1:30-4:30. Free. Phone (814) 472-6400.

### MANHEIM (H-9) pop. 5,000, elev. 400'

Baron William Stiegel, originator of Stiegel glass, founded Manheim. The remains of his house are on Main Street.

In Zion Lutheran Church, known as Red Rose Church, the Feast of Roses ceremony is held the second Sunday in June. During the ceremony, the payment of a red rose, the rent requested by Baron Stiegel, is made to a Stiegel heir.

For more area information contact the Manheim Area Chamber of Commerce, 210 S. Charlotte St., Manheim, PA 17545; phone (717) 665-6330. *Also see Pennsylvania Dutch Country.*

**MOUNT HOPE ESTATE AND WINERY** is ½ mi. s. of the Pennsylvania Tpke. exit 20 on SR 72. The restored, partially furnished Victorian mansion was built in 1800 by Henry Grubb, a wealthy ironmaster. Elaborate interior adornments include crystal chandeliers, gilded mirrors and tiled fireplaces. Ten acres of vineyards and 20 acres of formal gardens surround the mansion. Forty-five-minute tours of the mansion are given every half hour. Wine tastings also are offered.

The Pennsylvania Renaissance Faire is held Sat.-Mon., Aug. 5-Labor Day; Sat.-Sun., day after Labor Day-Oct. 16. It features 16th-century-style food, drink, theater, merchants and hundreds of costumed Elizabethan characters.

Guided tours daily 10-6, July-Aug.; Sat.-Sun. 10-5, rest of year. Closed Jan. 1, Thanksgiving and Dec. 25. Admission $5; ages 5-11, $2. Festival admission (all-inclusive) $15.95; ages 5-11, $7. **Discount.** Phone (717) 665-7021.

### MARIETTA (H-8) pop. 2,800, elev. 259'

**NISSLEY WINERY AND VINEYARDS** is 5½ mi. n. on SR 441, then ½ mi. n.e. on Wickersham Rd. Visitors can watch harvesting in the summer and fall and bottling in the spring. Tours of the vineyards and winery last 45 minutes; those under age 21 must be with a parent. Wine tastings follow the tours. Picnicking is permitted. Special events and concerts are held on the lawn of the winery; there are no tours during special events.

Mon.-Sat. 10-5, Sun. 1-4; closed Jan. 1, Easter, Thanksgiving and Dec. 25. Last tour begins 45 minutes before closing. Free. Phone (717) 426-3514.

## McSHERRYSTOWN (I-8) pop. 2,800

**BASILICA OF THE SACRED HEART OF JESUS,** 2½ mi. w. of Hanover on SR 116, then 2 mi. n. on Second St. The original 1741 log chapel was replaced in 1787 by the present stone structure. Made a minor basilica in 1962, it contains frescoes, statues and paintings. Allow 30 minutes minimum. Daily dawn-dusk. Free. Phone (717) 637-2721.

## MEADVILLE (D-2) pop. 14,300, elev. 1,078'

The invention of the hookless fastener by Whitcomb L. Judson in Chicago came to the attention of Meadville's Col. Lewis Walker in 1893. Impressed by the new idea, Walker persuaded Judson to build a machine to produce the fastener. When Judson lost interest after several years of failure, Walker moved the enterprise to Meadville. Then Gideon Sundback invented the fastener as it is currently known, as well as the machinery to produce it economically.

The fastener did not become a commercial success, however, until 1923, when the B.F. Goodrich Co. decided to put it on a new line of galoshes. The popular new galoshes were called "Zippers," a name that has evolved to mean the fastener itself.

Of interest in Meadville's historic downtown is the Unitarian Church in Diamond Park. Built in 1835, the church is a fine example of Greek Revival architecture. The Market House on Market Street has been used as an open-air marketplace since its founding about 1870 and is the cultural hub of the community. The Meadville Council on the Arts occupies the second floor.

Twelve miles northeast of Meadville via SR 77 and LR 20118S in New Richmond is the John Brown Tannery, operated by the abolitionist 1825-35. All that remains of the tannery are its 8-foot stone walls; nearby are the graves of Brown's first wife and two of their sons. More area information is available at the chamber of commerce, 211 Chestnut St., Meadville, PA 16335; phone (814) 337-8030.

**ALLEGHENY COLLEGE,** founded in 1815, is one of the older colleges west of the Allegheny Mountains. The college has a number of buildings constructed in the early 19th century, including Bentley Hall, a fine example of Federal architecture. Pelletier Library contains a notable collection of Lincoln memorabilia.

**BALDWIN-REYNOLDS HOUSE,** 639 Terrace St., was built 1841-43 for Supreme Court Justice Henry Baldwin. The building, furnished in period, houses tools, costumes and other artifacts. Adjacent is a 19th-century doctor's office. Ninety-minute tours depart every 30 minutes. Under age 16 must be with an adult. Tours Wed.-Sun. 1-5, Memorial Day-Labor Day; last tour departs 1 hour, 30 minutes before closing. Admission $3; under 16, $1.50. Phone (814) 724-6080.

## MEDIA (I-11) pop. 6,000, elev. 210'

Media, named for its central location in Delaware County, was laid out in 1848 after being designated county seat. Midway between Philadelphia and Wilmington, it has remained a thriving business and government center.

Just south of Media on Rose Valley Road in an 1840 gristmill is the 1923 Hedgerow Theatre, one of the older repertory theaters in the country. Another sign of the past still rumbles along State Street—an early 20th-century trolley that takes passengers to shops, restaurants and the Delaware County Courthouse.

Special events in Media include the Rose Tree Summer Festival, a series of free concerts in Rose Tree Park, and the Media Food and Arts Festival, which takes place the first weekend in October. For more information about Media and the surrounding area contact the Delaware County Convention and Visitors Bureau, 202 E. State St., Media, PA 19063; phone (610) 565-3679.

**FRANKLIN MINT MUSEUM,** 1 mi. s. of SR 452 on US 1, illustrates the history of The Franklin Mint, one of the world's foremost creators of fine collectibles. Fabergé jeweled pieces and works by Norman Rockwell and Andrew Wyeth are displayed. Other highlights include a collection of porcelain dolls, classic cars and Star Trek® collectibles. Items include art in bronze, porcelain, precious metals and crystal. Special events are held throughout the year. Mon.-Sat. 9:30-4:30, Sun. 1-4:30; closed holidays. Free. Phone (610) 459-6168.

**THE TYLER ARBORETUM,** 515 Painter Rd., covers 650 acres of woods and open fields, as well as special plant collections. An extensive system of trails leads among the large variety of trees, shrubs and other plants, many of which are labeled. There also is a collection of rhododendrons, an herb garden, butterfly garden and bird habitat garden. Educational programs are available. Lachford Hall and the Painter Library museums are open Sun. 2-5, Apr.-Oct. Grounds open daily 8 a.m.-dusk; extended hours in summer. Admission $3; ages 3-15, $1. Phone (610) 566-5431.

## MERCER (E-2) pop. 1,100, elev. 1,006'

Founded on the banks of the Neshannock Creek in 1803, Mercer was named for Brig. Gen. Hugh Mercer, a Scottish physician who moved to America and fought in the Revolutionary War. The city is a light industrial center in a farming region. Recreation is available at nearby Maurice K. Goddard and Pymatuning state parks *(see Recreation Chart)*. For more area information contact the chamber of commerce, P.O. Box 473, Mercer, PA 16137; phone (412) 662-4185.

**MERCER COUNTY HISTORICAL MUSEUM,** 119 S. Pitt St., chronicles the history and development of Mercer. Exhibits include clothing, dolls, furniture, photographs and toys. Primitive farm tools and machinery and a collection of Indian arrowheads also are displayed. A reference library is available. Allow 30 minutes minimum. Tues.-Sat. 10-4:30, Memorial Day weekend-Labor Day; 1-4:30, rest of year. Free. Phone (412) 662-3490.

## MERCERSBURG (I-6) pop. 1,600, elev. 581′

COWANS GAP STATE PARK, 18 acres 1 mi. n.w. off SR 16, offers fishing and picnicking. A stone monument marks the birthplace of James Buchanan, the only Pennsylvanian to become a U.S. president. Open daily dawn-dusk. Free. Phone (717) 485-3948.

MERCERSBURG ACADEMY, 1 mi. e. on SR 16, is an independent co-educational secondary school and the site of James Buchanan's log cabin birthplace, which was moved from its original location. The interior of the cabin can be viewed from the outside, May through November. Also on campus is the McFadden Railroad Museum, containing Lionel trains and accessories, including 148 engines and more than 500 cars.

The academy chapel houses a 43-bell carillon. Recitals are performed Sun. at 3. Recitals are not given and the museum is closed when school is not in session. Allow 1 hour minimum. The museum is open Sun. 1-4. Free. Phone (717) 328-2151.

## MIDDLETOWN (H-8) pop. 9,300

Due to its key position at the confluence of Swatara Creek and the Susquehanna River, midway between Lancaster and Carlisle, Middletown was the first town laid out in Dauphin County. The town boomed after the opening of the Pennsylvania and Union canals in the early 1800s.

THREE MILE ISLAND VISITORS CENTER is 3 mi. s. on SR 441. Exhibits, videotapes and staff explain nuclear energy and the TMI plant. Center open Thurs.-Sun. noon-4:30, June-Aug.; Thurs.-Sat. noon-4:30, rest of year. Closed major holidays. Free. Phone (717) 948-8829.

## MILESBURG (F-6) pop. 1,100

CURTIN VILLAGE is 3 mi. n.e. of I-80 exit 23 on SR 150. The 1830 Federal-style mansion, built by ironmaster Roland Curtin, is restored and furnished to look as it did in 1850. Pleasant Furnace was added in 1848 and consisted of a charging house, casting house, blast house and tuyere shed. Curtin's 30,000 acres provided food for the entire community, and Curtin Village became largely self-sufficient until the ironworks ceased operations in 1921.

Guided tours are available. Train rides to Curtain Village are available through Bellefonte Historic Railroad; phone (814) 355-0311.

Allow 1 hour minimum. Wed.-Sat. 10-4, Sun. 1-5, Memorial Day weekend-Labor Day; Sat. 10-4, Sun. 1-5, day after Labor Day to mid-Oct. Admission $4; under 12, $1. Phone (814) 355-1982.

## MILFORD (E-12) pop. 1,400

GREY TOWERS, off US 6, following signs, was the home of Gifford Pinchot, two-term governor of Pennsylvania and founder of the USDA Forest Service. The 45-minute tour includes three furnished rooms of memorabilia, as well as the gardens, outbuildings and terrace. Allow 1 hour minimum. Tours on the hour daily 10-4, Memorial Day weekend-Labor Day; Fri.-Mon. 10-4, by appointment Tues.-Thurs., day after Labor Day-Veterans Day; by appointment rest of year. Donations. Phone (717) 296-9630.

THE UPPER MILL, on Sawkill Creek at 150 Water St., is a restored gristmill built in the early 1800s. A three-story water wheel powers the mill. Food is available. Allow 30 minutes minimum. Daily 10-5, Easter-Thanksgiving. Free. Phone (717) 296-5141.

## MONROEVILLE (G-3) pop. 29,200

SRI VENKATESWARA TEMPLE, US 22 Business Route to Old William Penn Hwy., then 2½ mi. on Thompson Run Rd. make a right turn and 2 mi. to S. McCully Rd., then ½ mi., is one of 10 Hindu temples in the United States. It is modeled after a major temple in southern India. The ornate white towers contain representations of Hindu deities. Guided tours are available by appointment. Open Mon.-Thurs. 9-8:30, Fri. 9 a.m.-9:30 p.m., Sat.-Sun. 7:30 a.m.-8:30 p.m., Apr.-Oct.; Mon.-Thurs. 9-7:30, Fri. 9-8:30, Sat.-Sun. 7:30-7:30, rest of year. Free. Phone (412) 373-3380.

## MORRISVILLE (H-12) pop. 9,800, elev. 21′

PENNSBURY MANOR, 5 mi. s. on the Delaware River at 400 Pennsbury Memorial Rd., was the country estate of William Penn. The 43-acre historic site contains the reconstructed 1683 manor house, worker's cottage, a smokehouse, bake-and-brew house, an icehouse, blacksmith shop, stable and horse shelter, as well as farm animals and formal and kitchen gardens. The buildings display 17th- and 18th-century artifacts. Costumed guides conduct tours of the manor. Special events are held throughout the year. Picnicking is permitted in the pavilion.

Allow 1 hour, 30 minutes minimum. Tues.-Sat. 9-5, Sun. noon-5. Last tour 1 hour, 30 minutes before closing. Phone for holiday schedule. Admission $5; over 60, $4; ages 6-17, $3. Phone (215) 946-0400.

## MOUNT JEWETT (D-5) pop. 1,000, elev. 2,195'

America's First Christmas Store is housed in a turn-of-the-20th-century building about 12 miles northeast on US 6 in Smethport. A variety of unusual Christmas and other gift items is offered; phone (814) 887-5792 or (800) 841-2721.

KINZUA BRIDGE STATE PARK, 3½ mi. n.e. off US 6, covers 316 acres. The 2,053-foot bridge crosses 300 feet above Kinzua Creek. The original bridge was built to carry trains of the Erie Railroad into the Alleghenies of northern Pennsylvania to bring out lumber, coal and oil. The highest railroad viaduct in the world when completed in 1882, it was advertised as the eighth wonder of the world. Sunday excursions brought sightseers from as far away as Buffalo and Pittsburgh.

In 1900 the wrought-iron latticework was replaced with steel to accommodate heavier locomotives. The Knox Kane Railroad excursion train now utilizes the tracks; the bridge offers pedestrians an unusual view of the scenic Kinzua Valley. An information kiosk is on the grounds; picnicking, fishing and hiking are permitted. Daily dawn-dusk. Free. Phone (814) 965-2646.

## MOUNT JOY (H-8) pop. 6,200, elev. 360'

BUBE'S BREWERY, 102 N. Market St., is a 19th-century brewery that operated until Prohibition. Built by Alois Bube, a German immigrant, the brewery is 43 feet below street level in a Victorian hotel, which also houses three restaurants and an art gallery. Tours last 30 to 40 minutes and are given daily 10-5, June 15-day before Labor Day. Admission $2.50; over 65, $2; ages 6-12, $1.50. The tour is free if dining in one of the restaurants. Phone (717) 653-2056.

DONEGAL MILLS PLANTATION, 2½ mi. s.w. on SR 772, then ½ mi. w. via Musser Rd., following signs, includes a tour of a 250-year-old mansion, mill, miller's house, bake house, garden and wildlife areas. Guided tours of the historic village are available Sat.-Sun. noon-6, mid-Mar. through Dec. 31; other times by appointment. Admission $4; ages 6-12, $2. Phone (717) 653-2168.

## MOUNT PLEASANT (H-3) pop. 4,100, elev. 1,105'

L.E. SMITH GLASS CO. is e. via SR 31 to Liberty St. Visitors can observe glass artisans ply their craft. Under age 6 are not permitted. Allow 30 minutes minimum. Mon.-Fri. 9:30-2; closed holidays. Free. Phone (412) 547-3544.

## MOUNT POCONO (F-11) pop. 1,800, elev. 1,658'

From a hundred viewpoints at and near Mount Pocono, the colossal notch of the Delaware Water Gap is plainly visible, even though it is 25 miles away. Southwest of town is Pocono International Raceway, where automobile and motorcycle races are held throughout the year.

PENNSYLVANIA DUTCH FARM, 1 mi. s. on SR 611 and 1¾ mi. e. on Grange Rd., features an Amish exhibit home and farm. The house includes typical Amish clothes and furnishings. In the farmyard are buggies, wagons, sleighs, farm machinery and blacksmith and harness shops. Animals, including the smallest breed of horse, the Argentine Falabella, can be petted. Allow 30 minutes minimum. Daily 10-5, Apr. 15-Nov. 30; Sat.-Sun. 10-5, rest of year. Admission $3.50; ages 2-12, $2. **Discount.** Phone (717) 839-7680.

POCONO ADVENTURES STABLES, 1 mi. s. of Mount Pocono Meadowside Rd., offers 45-minute, 2- and 4-hour mule and horse trips into the Pocono back country. Fee for 45-minute ride $15, 2-hour ride $25, 4-hour ride $50. MC, VI. Reservations are suggested. Phone (717) 839-6333.

POCONO KNOB, ¼ mi. s. on US 611, then e. on Knob Hill Rd. to scenic overlook, is one of the more well-known viewpoints of the region. The panorama extends across the Pocono Mountains into New Jersey and New York.

## NAZARETH (G-11) pop. 5,700, elev. 530'

The area was originally part of a 5,000-acre tract of land owned as a feudal estate by the William Penn family. In 1740, evangelist George Whitefield purchased the land. He employed Peter Boehler and a small band of Moravians, a group of Protestants from Germany, to oversee the construction of what is now called the Whitfield House, located at 214 E. Center St. The house now contains the Moravian Historical Society's Museum and Research Library. The following year the Moravians bought the property and Nazareth remained exclusively a Moravian settlement for more than a century. Nazareth Hall, built in 1755, was a boys school 1759-1929.

Nearby Jacobsburg Environmental Education Center, 435 Belfast Rd., encompasses the remains of the 18th-century village of Jacobsburg *(see Recreation Chart)* and the site of the second Henry Gun Factory.

The Nazareth Speedway, SR 191, is the site of NASCAR and Indy racing in the spring. For general information phone (610) 759-9174; for race ticket information phone 759-8800.

For more information contact the Nazareth Area Chamber of Commerce, 201 N. Main St., P.O. Box 173, Nazareth, PA 18064; phone (610) 759-9188.

MARTIN GUITAR COMPANY, 510 Sycamore St., offers a one-hour guided tour through the guitar factory. The tour includes a demonstration of each step in the production process, from planing the wood to attaching the string boards. A museum displays unusual and vintage Martin guitars and memorabilia dating back to the company's founding in 1833. Allow 1 hour, 30 minutes minimum. Guided tours Mon.-Fri. at 1:15. Museum open Mon.-Fri. 9-5; closed holidays. Free. Phone (610) 759-2837.

### NEW CASTLE (F-1) pop. 28,300, elev. 806'

**HOYT INSTITUTE OF FINE ARTS,** 124 E. Leasure Ave., occupies two restored 25-room mansions built in the early 1900s; it now contains art galleries. Four acres of landscaped grounds surround the institute. Guided tours of the Alice Hoyt Mansion are offered Wednesdays, except the first Wed. of the month. Tea and cookies are included; reservations are required. Allow 1 hour minimum. Tues.-Sat. 9-4. Donations. Tour $2. Phone (412) 652-2882.

**LIVING TREASURES ANIMAL PARK,** I-79 exit 29, then 4 mi. w. on US 422, features more than 120 species of animals in a wooded setting. Included are monkeys, bears, African antelopes, elk, reindeer, kangaroos, zebras, camels and miniature horses. Visitors can feed pygmy goats, miniature sheep and llamas in a petting area. Food is available.

Allow 1 hour minimum. Daily 10-8, Memorial Day weekend-Labor Day; Sat.-Sun. 10-6, May 1-day before Memorial Day weekend and day after Labor Day-Oct. 31. Admission $4.50; over 62, $4; ages 3-11, $3.50. Phone (412) 924-9571.

### NEW HOPE (G-12) pop. 1,400, elev. 86'

The picturesque town of New Hope, an artists' and writers' colony, is a favorite spot for antique hunting. There are lovely guest homes and charming restaurants; make reservations early. 

Bucks County Playhouse is in a mill dating from the 1780s. Broadway productions are given May through December; phone (215) 862-2041. Mule-drawn barges offer hour-long canal excursions narrated by a folk singer and historian; the barges depart from the south end of New Hope on New Street above SR 32 April-November. Phone (215) 862-2842.

**NEW HOPE & IVYLAND RAIL ROAD,** jct. Bridge and Stockton sts., offers a 9-mile round-trip ride through the Pennsylvania countryside. The 1925 vintage steam train crosses over Pauline's Trestle, upon which actress Pearl White was bound in the 1914 silent film serial "The Perils of Pauline."

Allow 1 hour minimum. Train departs daily. Departure times vary; phone ahead for schedule. Closed Jan. 1, Thanksgiving and Dec. 24-25. Fare $7.50; over 61, $5.95; ages 3-11, $3.95; under 3, $1. MC, VI. Phone (215) 862-2332.

**PARRY MANSION MUSEUM,** S. Main and Ferry sts., was built in 1784 by Benjamin Parry, a wealthy lumbermill owner. The house, owned by Parry's descendants until 1966, has been furnished to reflect 125 years of decorative changes in the home. Allow 1 hour minimum. Fri.-Sun. 1-5, May-Dec. Admission $4; senior citizens $3; ages 1-12, 50c. Phone (215) 862-5148 or 862-5652.

### NORRISTOWN (H-11) pop. 30,700, elev. 83'

**ELMWOOD PARK ZOO,** on Harding Blvd., following signs, exhibits white-tailed deer, waterfowl, cougar and other animals from North America. There also are picnic areas, a children's zoo and petting barn. Animal shows are presented summer weekends. Allow 1 hour minimum. Daily 10-4; closed Jan. 1, Thanksgiving and Dec. 25. Admission $2; ages 3-12, $1. Phone (610) 277-3825.

### NORTH EAST (C-2) pop. 4,600, elev. 803'

With the help of Lake Erie's moderating effect on the climate and proper soil conditions, the area surrounding North East has developed into a prosperous winemaking area. Several area wineries offer tours and tastings. The Wine Festival, featuring wine tasting, dancing, parades, arts, crafts and entertainment, is held in late September; a live Nativity scene is staged the first 2 weekends in December.

Also of interest is the Lake Shore Railway Museum at Wall and Robinson streets. The museum is an 1889 passenger train station containing railroading relics. For more area information contact the chamber of commerce, 2 E. Main St., P.O. Box 466, North East, PA 16428; phone (814) 725-4262.

### NORTHUMBERLAND (F-8) pop. 3,900, elev. 452'

**JOSEPH PRIESTLEY HOUSE,** 472 Priestley Ave., contains the laboratory and books of Dr. Joseph Priestley, the Unitarian theologian who discovered oxygen. The house contains period furnishings. A visitor center depicts the life of Dr. Priestley, who emigrated from England in 1794. Allow 1 hour minimum. Tues.-Sat. 9-5, Sun. noon-5; closed holidays except Memorial Day, July 4 and Labor Day. Admission $3.50; over 60, $2.50; ages 6-17, $1.50. Phone (717) 473-9474.

## NOTTINGHAM (I-10)

**HERR'S SNACK FOODS,** US 1 and SR 272, offers tours that explain snack food production from vegetable washing to packaging. An audiovisual presentation and food samples are available. Allow 1 hour minimum. Mon.-Thurs. 9-3, Fri. 9-noon; closed holidays. Free. Reservations are recommended. Phone (610) 932-6401 or (800) 284-7488.

## OHIOPYLE (I-3) pop. 100, elev. 1,221'

Once a hunting area for the Delaware, Shawnee and Iroquois, Ohiopyle was named "Ohiopehhle" by the Indians for the "white frothy water" of the Youghiogheny River. George Washington had hoped to use the river as a water supply route to Fort Duquesne (now Pittsburgh), but he abandoned the idea after discovering the falls at Ohiopyle. The falls are within Ohiopyle State Park *(see Recreation Chart and the AAA Mideastern CampBook);* a day-use area provides overlook platforms.

Ohiopyle is best known as a popular starting point for white-water rafting on the "Yough." Trips can be arranged through several outfitters in town.

**BEAR RUN NATURE RESERVE,** I-76 exit 9, 3 mi. e. on SR 31, then 19 mi. s. on SR 381, next to Fallingwater, has more than 20 miles of trails traversing a variety of habitats, ranging from dense oak and hemlock forests to the spectacular Youghiogheny River gorge overlook and the sparkling waters of Bear Run and Laurel Run. The 4,000-acre reserve is open all year for hiking, photography, backpack camping and cross-country skiing. Free. Phone (412) 329-8501.

★**FALLINGWATER,** I-76 exit 9, 3 mi. e. on SR 31, then 19 mi. s. on SR 381, was a weekend home designed by Frank Lloyd Wright in 1936. Constructed of reinforced concrete and native stone, the house is dramatically cantilevered over a waterfall. This famous house blends so well with the mountainous terrain that it seems to grow out of its site.

Guided weekend tours for children and in-depth tours at 8:30 a.m. are available; reservations are required for both. Children under 9 can be left at the child care center; a nominal fee is charged. Self-guiding ground tours also are available.

Allow 1 hour minimum. Tues.-Sun. 10-4, Apr. 1 to mid-Nov.; Sat.-Sun. 10-4, rest of year. Admission Tues.-Fri. $10, Sat.-Sun. $12. Reservations are required for guides. Phone (412) 329-8501.

**LAUREL HIGHLANDS RIVER TOURS,** on SR 381, offers 6-hour white-water raft trips on the Lower Youghiogheny, Cheat, Upper Youghiogheny and Russell Fork rivers. Instruction, guides and lunch are provided, and wetsuits can be

rented. Bicycle, raft and duckie rentals, as well as paint ball games, canoe and kayak clinics and canoe trips on the Middle Youghiogheny also are available.

Raft trips depart daily, Mar.-Oct. Rates start at $19. AE, DS, MC, VI.Phone for minimum age requirements. Reservations are required. Write P.O. Box 107, Dept. PA, Ohiopyle, PA 15470. **Discount.** Phone (412) 329-8531 or (800) 4-RAFTIN. *See color ad p. 119.*

**MOUNTAIN STREAMS & TRAILS OUTFITTERS,** on SR 381, offers guided white-water raft trips on the Youghiogheny and seven other rivers; the minimum age is 6 years for the Middle Youghiogheny trip. Rafting is available for the physically impaired. Bicycle rentals are available, as are one- and two-person inflatable boats.

Trips depart daily, Apr.-Oct. Mon.-Fri. rates $19-$33 on the Middle and Lower Youghiogheny; Sat.-Sun. rates $35-$53. Other rivers might require greater paddling skills or have minimum age or weight requirements. Phone (412) 329-8810 or (800) 245-4090. *See ad p. 119.*

**WHITE WATER ADVENTURERS INC.,** Whitewater St., offers guided white-water raft trips on the Middle and Lower Youghiogheny rivers; the minimum age is 12 years. Trips depart daily, Mar. 15-Oct. 15. Rates for the 5- to 6-hour raft trip $22-$53. Trips on the Upper Youghiogheny (for experienced rafters) also are available; the minimum age is 16 years. Trips depart Mon.-Fri., Mar. 15-Oct. 15. Rates $99-$150. Trips on the Cheat River are available as well; the minimum age is 14 years. Trips depart daily, Mar.-June. Rates $35-$70.

Other activities include canoeing, bicycling and kayaking. For information and reservations write P.O. Box 31, Ohiopyle, PA 15470. Phone (412) 329-8850 for information or (800) WWA-RAFT for reservations. *See color ad.*

**WILDERNESS VOYAGEURS,** on SR 381, offers guided white-water raft trips on the Lower Youghiogheny River. The minimum age is 12 years for raft and duckie rentals; the minimum age is 6 years for raft, duckie and canoe rentals on the Middle Youghiogheny River. Lunch is provided, and wetsuit rentals are available. One- and 2-day kayak clinics for beginners through advanced paddlers also are offered. Raft trips depart daily, Apr. 1 to mid-Oct. Rates for the 3- to 5-hour trip start at $26. **Discount.** Phone (800) 272-4141.

**OIL CITY (E-2)** pop. 12,000, elev. 1,028′

The discovery of oil in 1860 precipitated the almost overnight settlement of Oil City. The narrow ravine of Oil Creek became the busiest valley on the continent and in a short time was covered with derricks from Oil City to Titusville. From 1860 to 1870, 17 million barrels of oil were shipped from this region to Pittsburgh. McClintock Well No. 1, drilled in 1861, is still producing.

The Oil Creek and Titusville Railroad (**discount**) which offers train trips between Titusville and Oil City in restored 1930s passenger cars, has a boarding stop at Rynd Farm, 4 miles north of Oil City on SR 8 *(see Titusville).*

Oil Heritage Week, held the last full week in July, includes sporting events, musical concerts, a parade, food fairs and crafts. For more information contact the Oil City Area Chamber of Commerce, 102 Center St., Oil City, PA 16301; phone (814) 676-8521.

**VENANGO MUSEUM OF ART, SCIENCE AND INDUSTRY,** 270 Seneca St., has periodic displays about early oil exploration, discovery and production in the surrounding area. SCIEN-TRIFIC offers hands-on exhibits with a scientific theme, and an annual art show spotlights the work of local high school students and professional artists. Allow 30 minutes minimum. Tues.-Sat. 10-4, Sun. 1-4. Admission $2; senior citizens and students with ID, $1; ages 6-18, 75c. Phone (814) 676-2007.

**PALMYRA (H-9)** pop. 6,900, elev. 450′

Founded by John Palm in the late 1700s, Palmyra bases its economy on food manufacturing and farming. Of interest 3 miles north of Main and Railroad streets is the 1803 Bindnagles Evangelical Lutheran Church, a two-story brick structure with round arch windows and doors. The grave of John Palm is in the churchyard.

**SELTZER'S LEBANON BOLOGNA CO. INC.** is 2 blks. n. of US 422 at 230 N. College St. The company gives tours of the final grinding, smoking and packaging processes; a videotape tour also is available. Allow 30 minutes minimum. Mon.-Fri. 8-11:45 and 12:30-3. Free. Phone (800) 282-6336.

**PAOLI (H-11)** elev. 541′

**WAYNESBOROUGH,** 1 mi. s. of US 30 via SR 252 at 2049 Waynesborough Rd., is the birthplace and former home of Revolutionary War

hero Gen. Anthony Wayne. The restored two-story Georgian-style house was built in three sections of native stone quarried on the property. The house is furnished in period and includes a collection of objects that belonged to Wayne and his family. A slide presentation tells the history of the family and the house.

Allow 30 minutes minimum. Tues. and Thurs. 10-4, Sun. 1-4, mid-Mar. to late Dec. Admission $3; over 62 and ages 7-18, $2. Phone (610) 647-1779.

**THE WHARTON ESHERICK STUDIO** is between Paoli and Valley Forge. From US 202 take SR 252 n. 1½ mi. Turn left through a covered bridge and take Yellow Springs Rd. 2½ mi. to Diamond Rock Rd. Go ½ mi. up a hill and turn right onto Horse Shoe Tr. for ¹⁄₁₀ mi. One-hour guided tours of the rustic former studio and home of the artist-craftsman feature more than 200 unique works, including paintings, woodcuts, ceramics, sculpture, furniture and utensils.

Tours Mon.-Fri. require a minimum of $25 per group. Tours Mon.-Sat. 10-4, Sun. 1-4, Mar.-Dec.; closed major holidays. Admission $5; under 12, $3. Reservations are required. **Discount.** Phone (610) 644-5822.

## PENNS CREEK (F-7)

Named for the stream that flows nearby, Penns Creek is surrounded by the rich, rolling farmland of Snyder County. Just east at US 11 and US 15 is the site where the Penns Creek Massacre occurred on Oct. 16, 1755, when Indians killed or captured 26 settlers.

**WALNUT ACRES ORGANIC FARMS** is ½ mi. e. of SR 104 on Walnut Acres Rd., 4 mi. s. of Mifflinburg. Established in 1946, Walnut Acres was one of the first organic farms in the country. Guided 30-minute tours are conducted through the cannery, bakery and mill, where whole, natural foods from the farm are prepared. Self-guiding tours also are available. Food is available. Allow 30 minutes minimum. The Annual Open House and Country Fair is held on the second Saturday in August. Guided tours Mon.-Fri. at 9:30, 11 and 1; closed holidays. Free. Phone (800) 344-9025.

## PENNSYLVANIA DUTCH COUNTRY (H-9)

The rich farmland of the Pennsylvania Dutch Country was settled in the Colonial years by several religious groups, primarily of German descent, seeking freedom of worship. The Pennsylvania Dutch have retained the convictions and customs of their ancestors. These beliefs are reflected in their dress, their work and the ways in which they spend their leisure time. The Plain People, as they are known to many, include some members of the Amish, Mennonite and Brethren faiths.

Simplicity is the keynote of the Pennsylvania Dutch, but each sect manifests it differently.

Some eschew any motive power except the horse; others do not use electricity or modern plumbing. Most dress in plain colors and clothing. But all exhibit singular speech characteristics, and all are noted for excellent foods that originated in the old countries. Souse, shoofly pie, schnitz, cup cheese, various sausages and the famous pretzels can all be sampled.

The bounty on their tables indicates the bounty of their land; few farms are as productive as these. Other regional features are hex signs—colorful radial designs painted on barns—and decorative stenciled motifs applied to furniture, tiles and household items.

Broadly, the Pennsylvania Dutch Country encompasses an area bordered by the State of Maryland, the Schuylkill and Susquehanna rivers and I-78. At the heart of this country is Lancaster. In addition to Lancaster, the cities of this region listed under their own names are Bird-in-Hand, Ephrata, Intercourse, Lititz, Manheim, Mount Joy and Strasburg.

**CCINC. AUTO TAPE TOURS** offers a 3-hour taped tour of the Pennsylvania Dutch Country, including information about the culture, customs and lifestyles of the Amish people. The audiotapes include music and sound effects; a map is provided. The tapes can be purchased for $12.95 at The Amish Farm and House, Dutch Wonderland Family Fun Park and Wax Museum of Lancaster County History (*see attraction listings in Lancaster*), or the tape can be purchased in advance by sending $14.95 (includes postage) to CCInc., P.O. Box 227, Allendale, NJ 07401; phone (201) 236-1666.

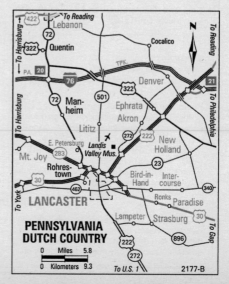

2177-B

# Philadelphia

The United States was born at the Pennsylvania State House, better known today as Independence Hall, in Philadelphia on July 4, 1776, with the adoption of the Declaration of Independence. The Constitution, drafted there in September 1787, laid the framework for the nation's future. But the seeds of independence were planted a century earlier by William Penn.

Penn, a socially prominent convert to the persecuted Society of Friends (Quakers), resolved to provide a place in which all beliefs could flourish. His opportunity arrived when he asked the king to repay a crown debt to his father with a land grant in the Colonies. Charles II, who was delighted with the prospect of easy payment while ridding the land of an embarrassing rebel, complied.

Penn's vision was simple but revolutionary—persons of all faiths living in harmony and freedom. Even in the Colonies, many of which were founded to foster religious tolerance, freedom of worship was limited to the majority sect. Penn guaranteed personal freedoms by allowing every taxpayer a vote, a prisoner the right to be heard, the accused a trial by jury and taxation only by law. Most of these "guarantees" were part of the existing system in England. The city Penn founded became known as Philadelphia, Greek for "city of brotherly love."

Rising resentment against England in the mid-1700s reached its high point in Philadelphia in 1774, where Colonial representatives met to discuss their grievances and debate their options. The fruit of their wrath was the Declaration of Independence, an open break with England and an explanation for a war that was already in progress. After the war, Philadelphia became a rallying site for the successful attempt to unify the independent states. In 1787 representatives meeting in the Pennsylvania State House produced the Constitution of the United States.

In 1790, Philadelphia became the temporary capital of the new United States. The next decade saw the fledgling government enduring numerous tests, among them the issue of the

---

## THE INFORMED TRAVELER

**POPULATION:** 1,585,600; metro 5,892,900
**ELEVATION:** 440 ft.

### Whom to Call

**Emergency:** 911

**Police (non-emergency):** 911 (calls will be transferred to the appropriate department)

**Time and Temperature:** time (215) 846-1212; temperature 936-1212

**Hospitals:** Chestnut Hill Hospital, (215) 248-8200; Children's Hospital of Philadelphia, (215) 590-1000; Hospital of the University of Pennsylvania, (215) 662-4000; Thomas Jefferson Hospital, (215) 955-6000.

### Where to Look

**Newspapers**

Philadelphia has two daily papers—the morning and Sunday Philadelphia *Inquirer* and the *Daily News*.

**Radio and TV**

Philadelphia radio station KYW (1060 AM) is an all-news/weather station; WHYY (90.1 FM) is programmed by National Public Radio.

The major TV channels are 3 (NBC), 6 (ABC), 10 (CBS), 12 (PBS) and 29 (FOX). For a complete list of radio and television programs, consult the daily newspapers.

**Visitor Information**

Information about walking tours and attractions in Philadelphia and its environs can be obtained by writing the Philadelphia Convention and Visitors Center at 16th St. and John F. Kennedy Blvd., Philadelphia, PA 19102; phone (215) 636-1666 or (800) 537-7676. The center is open daily 9-5.

Independence National Historical Park also operates a visitor center; it is at 3rd and Chestnut streets in the heart of the historical district; phone (215) 597-8974 (voice or TDD).

### What to Wear

Capricious aptly describes Philadelphia's weather. A warm January day may be followed by gray rain or winter's snowy bluster, while a sweltering summer day may turn suddenly chilly as a squall sweeps in from the sea. Temperatures range from an average low of 24 and a high of 40 in December, to an average low of 65 and high of 86 in July.

French Revolution, persistent yellow fever epidemics and rising political rivalries. In 1800, the seat of government was moved to the newly constructed city of Washington, along the Potomac between Maryland and Virginia.

Venerable landmarks rub shoulders with modern glass and steel office towers; narrow cobblestone streets intersect broad, busy boulevards; charming Colonial houses hide a few blocks from the business district. Fairmount Park presents a lush green oasis in the midst of urban bustle. Representative of past and present, the gracious elegance of Independence Hall contrasts with the strikingly modern facades of Liberty Place.

Society Hill, extending from Front to 7th streets and Walnut to Lombard streets, is the city's original residential area. Named for the Free Society of Traders, a land promotion company chartered by William Penn to develop the area, the Hill blends past and present as modern buildings mingle with hundreds of restored 18th-century houses. Germantown, in northwest Philadelphia, is another old residential section. Settled mainly by Germans and Dutch, many of its old houses are distinguished by Dutch doors and arched cellar windows.

Philadelphia's society, as legendary as its history, shows an endearingly human side. Anthony J. Drexel Biddle Sr., a colonel in World War I who taught hand-to-hand combat to Marines in World War II and raised alligators in his bathtub, inspired a best-selling novel and Broadway play. Also heralded are residents of the Main Line (once the Main Line of the Pennsylvania Railroad), a century-old swath of beautiful homes and estates rich with prestige.

The University of Pennsylvania, with its ivy-clad walls and shaded paths, dates from 1740 and numbers Benjamin Franklin among its founders. In 1765 it opened the country's first medical school and now ranks among the leading national educational centers. Contributing to the city's reputation as a force in higher education are Drexel University; LaSalle University; St. Joseph's University; Swathmore College, 11 miles southwest of Philadelphia; Temple University and Villanova University.

Philadelphia has one of the more beautiful exurban regions of any American city. Beyond the urban tangle sprawls rolling green hills studded with gems, both historical and colorful. In Montgomery County are the old company streets of Valley Forge *(see Valley Forge National Historical Park)*, where Washington's men struggled to survive the difficult winter of 1777-78.

## Approaches
### By Car

The major route from the south is I-95 to Philadelphia International Airport. Follow I-95 to I-676 to the city center; enter the business district at Market Street. From the north, I-95 leads into the northeastern section of the city. From the west, I-676/US 30 traverses the downtown area as the Vine Street Expressway, and I-76 leaves the Pennsylvania Turnpike at Valley Forge and enters Philadelphia at the Schuylkill Expressway.

US 1 (Roosevelt Boulevard) traverses northeast Philadelphia, but both the north and south entrances into town are heavily commercialized and rather slow. From the east, both the New Jersey Turnpike and I-295, which run north-south in New Jersey, provide ready access to either US 30, which enters the city center via the Benjamin Franklin Bridge and I-676, or to New Jersey SR 42 (North-South Freeway or Atlantic City Expressway), which approaches the Walt Whitman Bridge and south Philadelphia.

### By Plane, Bus and Train

Philadelphia International Airport is 6½ miles south of the business district via I-76 (Schuylkill Expressway) and SR 291 (Penrose Avenue). SEPTA's airport rail line runs daily on the half-hour 6 a.m.-midnight between Philadelphia International Airport and Market Street East Station, Suburban Station and 30th Street Station; the fare is $5. Taxis are plentiful; fares average about $20. If driving or taking a cab, allow at least 30 minutes' travel time.

The major bus terminal is Greyhound Lines Inc., (800) 231-2222, at 10th and Filbert streets. New Jersey Transit buses, (215) 569-3752, also depart for southern New Jersey and shore points.

Amtrak trains pull into both the main terminal, 30th Street Station, at 30th and Market streets, and the North Philadelphia Station at Broad Street and Glenwood Avenue. Should your destination be mid-city, disembark at 30th Street Station. Local commuter trains use 30th Street Station, Suburban Station at 17th Street and JFK Boulevard, and the Market Street East Station at 11th and Market streets. For Amtrak information phone (215) 824-1600.

## Getting Around

It would be wise to leave your automobile behind when going downtown because the old streets, though arrow straight, also are very narrow. Unless you *must* have your car, allow a bus or cab driver to negotiate the congested, often two-lane, streets.

### Street System

Most north-south streets, beginning with Front Street west of the Delaware River, are numbered; east-west streets are named. Broad Street, the major north-south artery, is the equivalent of 14th Street. All downtown north-south streets are alternate one-way with the exception of Broad, which has two lanes in each direction. Market Street is one-way eastbound between 20th and 15th streets. Westbound motorists should use JFK Boulevard at this point. Chestnut Street is

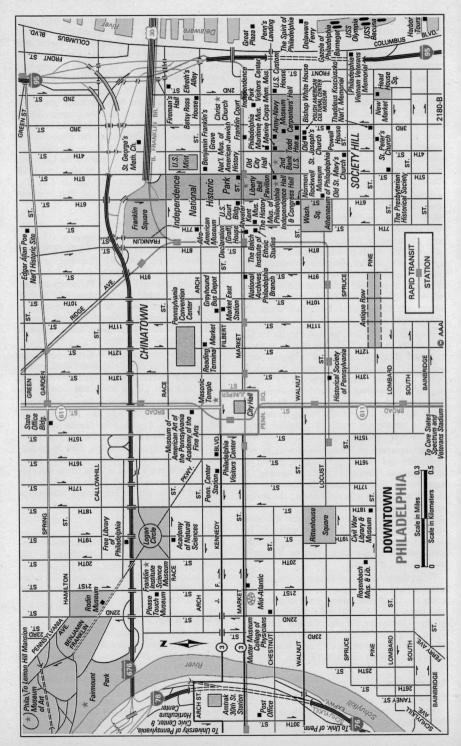

closed to all traffic except buses between 8th and 18th streets from 6 a.m. to 7 p.m.

Since Market Street is the principal east-west artery, north and south numbering begins at this street. Westward numbering begins at Front Street.

Right turns on red are permitted after a full stop, unless otherwise posted. Rush hours in general are 7-9:30 a.m. and 4-6:30 p.m. The speed limit on most streets is 25 mph, or as posted.

## Parking

Though chances of getting on-street parking on the clogged downtown streets is virtually zero, some metered parking is permitted on side streets and less traveled avenues: Parking meter rates are 25c for 15 minutes. Rates in the numerous lots and garages range from $2.50 for 30 minutes to a maximum of $11.75 for 24 hours.

## Rental Cars

Many major auto rental companies serve the Philadelphia area. Hertz, 31 S. 19th St., (800) 654-3131 or (800) 654-3080, offers discounts to AAA members. Other companies are listed in the local telephone directory.

## Taxis

Cabs do not cater to bargain hunters. Fares for United Cab Association, (215) 238-9500, are $1.80 per mile. Fares for Yellow Cab Co., (215) 922-8400, are $2.80 for the first mile and $1.80 for each additional mile. The standard tip is 15 or 20 percent.

## Public Transportation

A system of buses, streetcars, subways and elevateds (els) serves Philadelphia. Operated by the Southeastern Pennsylvania Transportation Authority (SEPTA), all vehicles charge $1.50, plus 40c for a transfer; exact change is required. Senior citizens ride free in off-peak hours. A SEPTA Daypass provides unlimited rides on all SEPTA buses, streetcars, subways and els within the city and a one-way ride on the airport line; the pass is $5. The Route 76 bus offers service between Penn's Landing and the zoo every 15 minutes daily 9-6; fare 50c.

For information about schedules, routes and locations where the Daypass and tokens may be purchased phone (215) 580-7800.

## What To See

**ACADEMY OF NATURAL SCIENCES** is at 19th St. and Benjamin Franklin Pkwy. Founded in 1812, it is the oldest continually operating institution of its kind in America. Outstanding among the natural sciences exhibits are the "Discovering Dinosaurs" exhibit, which includes dinosaur bones and eggs; "Outside-In," a hands-on nature center for children; and "What On Earth," an interactive geology exhibit. Live animal shows, films and special programs also are offered.

Allow 1 hour, 30 minutes minimum. Mon.-Fri. 10-4:30, Sat.-Sun. 10-5; closed Jan. 1, Thanksgiving and Dec. 25. Admission $6; over 65, $5.50; ages 3-12, $5. Phone (215) 299-1000.

**AFRO-AMERICAN HISTORICAL AND CULTURAL MUSEUM,** n.w. corner of 7th and Arch sts., traces the history of black culture in the Americas. The special achievements of blacks are documented through artifacts, photographs, multimedia presentations and the works of black artists. Allow 2 hours minimum. Tues.-Sat. 10-5, Sun. noon-6; closed major holidays. Admission $4; over 65 and ages 6-17, $2. Phone (215) 574-0380.

**AMERICAN SWEDISH HISTORICAL MUSEUM,** 1900 Pattison Ave. in Franklin Delano Roosevelt Park, shows contributions to America of citizens of Swedish origin. Exhibits include Swedish silver, furniture, textiles, engraved glass, paintings and sculpture. Tues.-Fri. 10-4, Sat.-Sun. noon-4; closed legal holidays. Admission $2, over 60 and students with ID $1, under 12 free with adult. Phone (215) 389-1776.

**ARMY-NAVY MUSEUM,** Chestnut St. between 3rd and 4th sts., is part of Independence National Historical Park *(see box page 126).* In a reconstruction of the 18th-century home of Quaker merchant Joseph Pemberton, the museum details the contributions made by the Army and Navy 1775-1800. Open daily 9-5; closed Jan. 1 and Dec. 25. Free. Phone (215) 597-2458, or 597-1785 TDD.

**ATHENAEUM OF PHILADELPHIA,** 219 S. 6th St., is named for Athena, the Greek goddess of wisdom. Founded in 1814, this three-story Italianate building houses a large collection of material connected with the history of America, a gallery with changing exhibits about architecture and design, as well as a library and reading room. Allow 30 minutes minimum. Mon.-Fri. 9-5; closed holidays. Library and reading room open by appointment. Free. Phone (215) 925-2688.

**ATWATER KENT MUSEUM—THE HISTORY MUSEUM OF PHILADELPHIA,** 15 S. 7th St., has hundreds of artifacts from Philadelphia's past. Featured are exhibits about the city's history, archeology, photography and Victorian doll houses. Allow 30 minutes minimum. Tues.-Sat. 10-4; closed city holidays. Admission $2, children $1. Phone (215) 922-3031.

**THE BALCH INSTITUTE FOR ETHNIC STUDIES,** 1 blk. w. of the Liberty Bell at 18 S. 7th St., documents and interprets America's varied immigrant heritage through its multicultural library, archives, museum and education center. Exhibits use photographs, clothing, household goods and other artifacts to illustrate the immigrant experience. The permanent exhibit "Discovering America: The Peopling of Pennsylvania," examines the state's immigration history. A research library has materials about more than 70 ethnic groups.

Allow 1 hour minimum. Museum open Mon.-Tues. and Thurs.-Fri. 10-4, Wed. noon-8, Sat. noon-5. Library open Mon.-Tues. and Thurs.-Fri. 9-5, Wed. noon-8. Donations. Phone (215) 925-8090.

THE BARNES FOUNDATION, 300 N. Latch's Ln. in Merion, displays the Albert C. Barnes Art Collection. Featured artists include William Glackens, Henri Matissé, Claude Monet, George Rouault and Pablo Piccaso. The foundation also displays one of the larger collections of paintings by artist Pierre Auguste Renoir. African sculpture, Indian rugs and blankets and cubist sculpture also are exhibited. Under 12 are not permitted; ages 12-15 must be with an adult. The Barnes Foundation is currently closed for renovations and is scheduled to re-open in late 1995.

Allow 2 hours minimum. Fri.-Sat. 9:30-4:30, Sun. 1-4:30, Sept.-June; closed legal holidays, Good Friday and Easter. Admission $1. Phone (215) 667-0290.

BETSY ROSS HOUSE, 239 Arch St., is where the Colonial seamstress stitched the first American flag in 1776. The restored home is furnished in the working-class manner of the period. Tues.-Sun. 10-5; closed Jan. 1, Thanksgiving and Dec. 25. Donations. Phone (215) 627-5343.

BISHOP WHITE HOUSE, 309 Walnut St., was built by Pennsylvania's first Protestant Episcopal bishop. The restored house, part of Independence National Historical Park *(see box below)*, contains many original articles. Tours daily 9-5, with extended hours in summer; closed Jan. 1 and Dec. 25. Admission by tour only; obtain free tickets at the

---

## Independence National Historical Park

The park includes buildings in Independence Square and others throughout the city that are closely associated with the Colonial period, the founding of the nation and Philadelphia's early role as national capital. The main area extends from 2nd to 6th streets between Walnut and Market streets. All buildings are open daily 9-5, with extended hours in summer. Admission is free.

The Visitor Center for Independence National Historical Park, 3rd and Chestnut streets, presents the film "Independence" throughout the day. Inquire at the center for a walking-tour map and the latest information on all the park's attractions and activities. To confirm schedules, phone (215) 597-8974 or 597-1785 TDD.

---

visitor center on 3rd and Chestnut streets. Phone (215) 597-8974, or (215) 597-1785 TDD.

BLESSED KATHARINE DREXEL SHRINE, 1663 Bristol Pike, is the gravesite of the founder of the Sisters of the Blessed Sacrament. Born into the wealthy Philadelphia Drexel family in 1858, Katharine Drexel devoted her life to the church and donated her $20 million inheritance to benefit African and Native Americans. Daily 1-5. Free. Phone (215) 244-9900.

BRYN ATHYN CATHEDRAL, SR 232 and Cathedral Rd. in Bryn Athyn, exemplifies Gothic architecture in North America. The church features fine stained-glass windows. Guided tours daily 1-4, Apr.-Oct. Cathedral open daily 11-5; grounds open daily 8-5. Free. Phone (215) 947-0266.

CARPENTERS' HALL, 320 Chestnut St., is part of Independence National Historical Park *(see box)*. It was lent by the Carpenters' Co. of Philadelphia for the First Continental Congress in 1774. Inside are a collection of early carpentry tools and chairs used by the Congress. An 11-minute videotape presentation chronicles the history of the Carpenters' Co., which still owns and operates the hall. Tues.-Sun. 10-4, Mar.-Dec.; Wed.-Sun. 10-4, rest of year. Closed Jan. 1, Easter, Thanksgiving and Dec. 25. Free. Phone (215) 925-0167.

★CHRIST CHURCH, on 2nd St. between Market and Arch sts., was the house of worship of 15 signers of the Declaration of Independence; brass plaques mark the pews once occupied by George Washington, Benjamin Franklin and Betsy Ross. Founded in 1695, the church typifies early Georgian architecture. It has one of the older Palladian windows in North America, its original chandelier and a "wine glass" pulpit. It also contains the font from which William Penn was baptized in 1644 in All-Hallows, Barking-by-the-Tower, London.

Christ Church Burial Ground, 5th and Arch streets, contains the graves of Benjamin Franklin and four other signers of the Declaration of Independence; Franklin's grave is visible from the street. Allow 30 minutes minimum. Episcopal services are held on Sunday at 9, 10 and noon. Church open Mon.-Sat. 9-5, Sun. 1-5, Mar. 15-May 31; Wed.-Sat. 9-5, Sun. 1-5, rest of year. Closed Jan. 1, Thanksgiving and Dec. 25. Donations. Phone (215) 922-1695.

CITY HALL, at Penn Sq., Broad and Market sts., was planned to be the tallest structure in the world when contruction began in 1871. However, it was surpassed in height by the Washington Monument and Eiffel Tower before its completion in 1901. A 37-foot-high bronze statue of William Penn tops the City Hall tower. The charter in Penn's left hand has the actual words of the charter inscribed upon it. One-hour guided tours of the interior of City Hall, including the tower, are offered Mon.-Fri. at 12:30; tower tours are offered every quarter-hour Mon.-Fri. 10-3. Last tour 15 minutes before closing. Closed holidays. The 1-hour tours depart from room 201. Free. Phone (215) 686-2840 for City Hall.

**CIVIL WAR LIBRARY AND MUSEUM,** 1805 Pine St., is a research library and museum of Civil War artifacts. Items on display include uniforms, weapons, medical instruments, flags and insignias. A room dedicated to Abraham Lincoln contains plaster life casts of his hands and face. Other exhibits are dedicated to Gens. George G. Meade and Ulysses S. Grant.

Allow 1 hour minimum. Mon.-Sat. 10-4, Sun. 11-4; closed holidays. Admission $3; over 65, $2; under 12 free. **Discount.** Phone (215) 735-8196.

**CLIVEDEN,** 6401 Germantown Ave., is a Georgian country house built 1763-67 for Pennsylvania Chief Justice Benjamin Chew. The house was damaged during the 1777 Battle of Germantown. Furnishings, including 18th- and 19th-century pieces, trace 2 centuries of Chew family history. Family portraits and Chinese porcelain also are featured. Allow 1 hour, 30 minutes minimum. Tues.-Sat. 10-4, Sun. 1-4, Apr.-Dec.; closed Easter, Thanksgiving and Dec. 25. Admission $6; ages 6-18, $4. **Discount.** Phone (215) 848-1777.

★**CONGRESS HALL,** 6th and Chestnut sts., was occupied by the U.S. Congress 1790-1800; it is part of Independence National Historical Park (see box page 126). On the first floor is the chamber of the House of Representatives; the second floor contains the more elaborate chamber of the Senate, and various committee rooms. The hall was the setting for the inaugurations of George Washington (his second) and John Adams. Daily 9-5, with extended summer hours; closed Jan. 1 and Dec. 25. Free. Phone (215) 597-8974, or 597-1785 TDD.

**CORE STATES SPECTRUM,** Broad St. and Pattison Ave., is Philadelphia's sports and entertainment center. Home of the Philadelphia 76ers and Philadelphia Flyers, it is the scene of special shows, concerts and athletic events. For information about scheduled events phone (215) 336-3600.

**DECLARATION (GRAFF) HOUSE,** s.w. corner of 7th and Market sts., is part of Independence National Historical Park (see box page 126). This is a reconstruction of the dwelling in which Thomas Jefferson drafted the Declaration of Independence in June 1776. An audiovisual program is shown. Daily 9-5; closed Jan. 1 and Dec. 25. Free. Phone (215) 597-8974, or 597-1785 TDD.

**DESHLER-MORRIS HOUSE,** 5442 Germantown Ave., was where George Washington spent the fall of 1793 and the summer of 1794. The restored 1772 house, now part of Independence

National Historical Park (see box page 126), is furnished in period. Tues.-Sat. 1-4, Apr. 1 to mid-Dec.; closed legal holidays. Admission $1, students with ID 50c. Phone (215) 596-1748.

**DREXEL COLLECTION,** 32nd and Chestnut sts., includes antique European and American furniture, a Rittenhouse clock, Boehm porcelain and 19th-century artworks. Mon. 11-5, Tues.-Wed. 9-10:30 and 1:30-5, Thurs.-Fri. 1:30-5; closed school holidays. Free. Phone (215) 895-2424.

**EBENEZER MAXWELL MANSION** is 6 mi. n.w. of downtown via the Schuylkill Expwy. at 200 W. Tulpehocken St. The rooms of the 1859 Victorian home, with their stenciled walls and ceilings, are furnished in period with sculpted machine-age furniture and 19th-century kitchen gadgets. The grounds feature a restored 19th-century garden; there also is a restoration resource library.

Guided tours are available. Thurs.-Sun. 1-4, Apr.-Dec. Admission $4, senior citizens $3, ages 3-12 and students with ID $2. Phone (215) 438-1861.

**EDGAR ALLAN POE NATIONAL HISTORIC SITE,** 532 N. 7th St., contains a visitor center, which has exhibits, an audiovisual show and library, and the house where Poe lived 1843-44. Guided tours daily 9-5; closed Jan. 1, Thanksgiving and Dec. 25. Free. Phone (215) 597-8780 (voice or TDD).

**ELFRETH'S ALLEY,** n. of Arch St. between Front and 2nd sts., is one of many narrow streets lined with quaint restored houses that have stood since the days of Penn's "Greene Countrie Towne." Information about other buildings in the alley is available at the Elfreth's Alley Museum. Some homes are open during the June Fete, the first weekend in June and during the Candlelight Open House, the first Friday in December. Elfreth's Alley Museum, 126 Elfreth's Alley, is open daily 10-4, mid-Feb. through Dec. Admission $1; under 5, 50c. Phone (215) 574-0560.

★**FAIRMOUNT PARK** is reached by Benjamin Franklin Pkwy. This beautiful park covers 8,579 acres along both sides of the Schuylkill River. The park is threaded by miles of scenic drives, walks, a bicycle route and bridle trails. Visitors can see sculls racing on the Schuylkill, hear band concerts in Pastorious Park or symphony orchestras at Mann Music Center, or visit the numerous museums and historic houses.

The park, founded in 1812, was the site of the Centennial Exposition in 1876. Of almost 200 buildings erected for the fair, only Memorial Hall and the Ohio House remain. Glendenning Rock Garden and Horticultural Hall Gardens are noteworthy. Within the park boundaries are several Colonial estates (see Fairmount Park Historic Houses).

The boathouses along the Schuylkill River are lit at night with strings of white lights that reflect in the water; they are best seen from the Schuylkill Expressway across the river.

**Horticulture Center,** off Montgomery Dr. on Belmont Mansion Dr., includes a landscaped arboretum with a large reflecting pool, Japanese house and garden, seasonal greenhouse displays and outdoor gardens. Allow 30 minutes minimum. Daily 9-3; closed holidays. Admission $2. Phone (215) 685-0096.

**Japanese House and Garden,** off Montgomery Dr. at Belmont Mansion Dr., are part of the Horticulture Center. A tea ceremony is held on occasional Sunday afternoons. Allow 1 hour minimum. Tues.-Sun. 11-4, May-Aug.; Sat.-Sun. 11-4, Sept.-Oct. Closed holidays. Admission $2.50; senior citizens and students with ID $2; under 12, $1. Phone (215) 878-5097.

**Laurel Hill Cemetery,** 3822 Ridge Ave., incorporates striking architecture and landscape design elements into its 95 acres. The grounds are shaded by large trees and contain interesting statuary. Tues.-Sat. 9:30-1:30. Free. Phone (215) 228-8200.

**Mann Music Center,** 52nd St. and Parkside Ave., is an outdoor amphitheater presenting summer concerts by the Philadelphia Orchestra. Concerts Mon. and Wed.-Thurs. evenings, late June-late July; Pop concerts May-Sept. Single tickets are sold at the box office. Phone (215) 878-7707.

★**Philadelphia Museum of Art,** end of Benjamin Franklin Pkwy. at 26th St., ranks among the world's major art museums. Collections range from ancient Chinese clay tomb figures to medieval armor and artifacts. There are works of the European Renaissance and contemporary American paintings, prints and photographs. Included are works by Peter Rubens, Nicolas Poussin, Pierre Auguste Renoir, Paul Cézanne, Claude Monet and Vincent Van Gogh, as well as those by modern artists. The museum displays one of the larger collections of work by Thomas Eakins. Guided tours are available hourly 11-3.

Allow 1 hour, 30 minutes minimum. Tues.-Sun. 10-5 (also Wed. 5-8:45); closed holidays. Admission $7; over 62 and ages 5-18, $4; free to all Sun. 10-1. Limited free parking. **Discount.** Phone (215) 763-8100.

**Rodin Museum,** Benjamin Franklin Pkwy. and 22nd St., contains a priceless collection of Rodin originals and casts. Allow 30 minutes minimum. Tues.-Sun. 10-5. Guided tours are available at 1 on the first and third Sat., the second and fourth Sun., and the fourth Wed. of the month. Closed legal holidays. Donations. Phone (215) 763-8100.

**Zoological Gardens,** 3400 W. Girard Ave., contains more than 1,700 mammals, birds and reptiles. A children's zoo provides both contact areas and demonstrations. Allow 2 hours minimum. Children's zoo open daily 10-4:30. Zoo open Mon.-Fri. 9:30-5, Sat.-Sun. and holidays 9:30-6; closed Jan. 1, Thanksgiving and Dec. 24-25 and 31. Zoo admission $8; over 65 and ages 2-11, $5.50. Tree house admission $1. **Discount.** Phone (215) 243-1100.

**FAIRMOUNT PARK HISTORIC HOUSES,** along the banks of the Schuylkill River, are the former homes of wealthy Philadelphians. The mansions were abandoned soon after 1822, when completion of Fairmount Dam created swampy conditions that bred mosquitoes carrying typhoid fever. Phone (215) 684-7922.

**Cedar Grove,** Lansdowne Dr., is an 18th-century Quaker farmhouse with an herb garden at its door. Tues.-Sun. 10-4. Admission $2.50; under 12, $1.

**Laurel Hill,** w. on Diamond St. until it becomes Randolph Dr., features paneling, delft tiles and an octagonal drawing room with Federal architectural details. Costumed guides conduct tours of the home. Wed., Fri. and Sun. 10-5. Admission $2.50; under 12, $1.25.

**Lemon Hill,** Kelly Dr., is a masterpiece of 19th-century architecture. Wed.-Sun. 10-4. Admission $2.50; under 12, $1.50.

**Mount Pleasant,** on Fountain Green at 35th St. and Columbia Ave., is furnished in the Chippendale style. Tues.-Sun. 10-4. Admission $2.50; under 12, $1.

**Strawberry Mansion,** near Dauphin St. entrance, is furnished in period. Tues.-Sun. 10-4. Admission $2.50; under 12, $1.

**Sweetbriar Mansion,** Lansdowne Ave. n. of Girard Ave., was restored in 1927 and is furnished in period. Tues.-Sun. 10-5. Admission $2.50; under 12, $1.

**Woodford Mansion,** 33rd and Dauphin sts., displays Colonial housewares. Tues.-Sun. 10-4. Admission $2.50; ages 6-12, $1.

**FIREMAN'S HALL—NATIONAL FIRE HOUSE AND MUSEUM OF PHILADELPHIA,** 147 N. 2nd St. above Arch St., is housed in a fire house built

in 1876. The history of firefighting is depicted using memorabilia, graphics, films and early firefighting equipment. Allow 1 hour minimum. Tues.-Sat. 9-4:30; closed holidays. Free. Phone (215) 923-1438.

**FORT MIFFLIN,** I-95 s. to Island Ave. exit, then ½ mi. s. to Fort Mifflin Rd., following signs, was built in 1772 by the British to protect the Colonies. Ironically, during the Revolutionary War it was the Americans who used the fort to protect Philadelphia and the Delaware River. The fort was used during the Civil War and for ammunition storage until 1962. Allow 1 hour minimum. Wed.-Sun. 10-4, Apr.-Nov. Admission $4, over 64 and students with ID $3.75, under 2 free. Phone (215) 492-3395.

**FRANKLIN COURT,** between 3rd, 4th, Chestnut and Market sts., is part of Independence National Historical Park *(see box page 126)*. The area was once owned by Benjamin Franklin, who lived in Philadelphia from 1722 until his death in 1790. The complex encompasses an underground theater and museum, as well as the five Market Street houses, the exteriors of which have been restored to their Franklin era appearances.

In the buildings are the refinished "Aurora" newspaper office, a working reproduction of a 1785 printing press and bindery operation, an archeological exhibit and a post office. Complex open daily 9-5, extended hours in summer; closed Jan. 1 and Dec. 25. Free. Phone (215) 597-8974, or 597-1785 TDD.

**B. Free Franklin Post Office and Museum,** 316 Market St., commemorates Franklin's 1775 appointment as first postmaster general. The only post office operated by the U.S. Postal Service that does not fly the American flag, it is named after Franklin's unique signature-cancellation. It is assumed that his use of "Free" as part of his signature referred to America's struggle for freedom. Philatelists prize the hand-canceled letters from this post office. Daily 9-5; closed Jan. 1 and Dec. 25. Free. Phone (215) 592-1289.

★**FRANKLIN INSTITUTE SCIENCE MUSEUM,** 20th St. and Benjamin Franklin Pkwy., is the national memorial to Benjamin Franklin. It contains many of his personal effects, as well as a statue by James Earle Fraser. Hands-on exhibits and demonstrations relate to science and industry, computers, physics, astronomy, geography, oceanography, meteorology, mathematics, communications and history. A computer information network helps visitors tailor their visits to suit their interests.

Allow 4 hours minimum. Daily 9:30-5; closed major holidays and Dec. 24-25. Admission (including Mandell Futures Center) $9.50; over 62 and ages 4-11, $8.50. Combination ticket including Fels Planetarium *or* Tuttleman Omniverse Theater $12; over 62 and ages 4-11, $10.50. Combination ticket including Fels Planetarium and Tuttleman Omniverse Theater $14.50; over

62 and ages 4-11, $12.50. AE, DS, MC, VI. **Discount.** Phone (215) 448-1200.

**Fels Planetarium,** opened in 1933, is among the country's oldest. Computer-generated images are projected onto the 65-foot-wide planetarium dome. For shows and times phone (215) 448-1200.

**Mandell Futures Center** displays eight exhibits that manifest how science and technology are shaping the 21st century. Visitors also can learn about future careers and preview new products made available through technology. Thurs.-Sat. 9:30-9, Sun.-Wed. 9:30-5 (also Sun. 5-6). Admission included with the Franklin Institute Science Museum. Phone (215) 448-1200.

**Tuttleman Omniverse Theater** projects films of science and adventure onto a four-story, 79-foot-wide domed screen. Diverse topics include space exploration, nature and the human body. The main feature is preceded by "Philadelphia Anthem," a short film about Philadelphia. For shows and times phone (215) 448-1200.

**FREE LIBRARY OF PHILADELPHIA,** Logan Sq. at 19th and Vine sts., has a variety of exhibits about art, architecture, photography, books and local history. Tours of the rare book room are conducted Mon.-Fri. at 11. Free concerts, films and lecture programs are presented on Sun.; phone for times. Mon.-Wed. 9-9, Thurs.-Fri. 9-6, Sat. 9-5, Sun. 1-5; closed holidays and Sun. in summer. Free. Phone (215) 686-5322.

**GERMANTOWN HISTORICAL SOCIETY,** 5501 Germantown Ave. on Market Sq., provides an overview of the history of the community from the time of settlement in 1683 to the present. Collections include toys and dolls, quilts, costumes, furniture and decorative arts. The archives and library contain collections of manuscripts, maps, land records and photographs. Guided tours are offered. Allow 2 hours minimum. Tues. and Thurs. 10-4, Sun. 1-5. Admission $3. Phone (215) 844-0514.

**GLORIA DEI (OLD SWEDES') CHURCH,** Christian St. at Christopher Columbus Blvd., is believed to be Pennsylvania's oldest church. It was built in 1700, but its congregation was founded in 1677. Sat.-Sun. 9-5 and by appointment. Phone (215) 389-1513.

**HEAD HOUSE SQUARE,** bounded by 2nd, Pine, Front and Lombard sts., was Society Hill's New Market when it opened in 1745. The square's picturesque shops include the Dickens Inn, a gourmet shop, restaurant and printshops. Mon.-Sat. 11-9, Sun. 11-6.

**HISTORIC BARTRAM'S GARDEN** is entered from Lindberg Blvd. w. of 54th St. The home of Colonial botanist John Bartram, the estate is now a public park. The house was renovated to appear the way it did in the 1700s, and the garden, filled with herbs and flowers, looks much like a Colonial kitchen garden. A guided tour of the house and gardens also includes a special slide presentation. Allow 1 hour minimum. The garden is open daily dawn-dusk. The house is open Wed.-Sun. noon-4, May-Oct.; Wed.-Fri. noon-4, rest of year. Admission free. Guided tour $4.50. Phone (215) 729-5281.

**HISTORICAL SOCIETY OF PENNSYLVANIA,** 1300 Locust St., is a museum and research center for American and Pennsylvania history and contains 15 million rare documents, books, maps, artifacts, prints and genealogical records. A permanent multimedia exhibit, "Finding Philadelphia's Past: Visions and Revisions," explores 300 years of the city's history. Among the displays are the first draft of the Constitution, William Penn's wampum belt, a trolley car theater and various artifacts from the historical society's collections. The society maintains a library.

Allow 1 hour minimum. Tues. and Thurs.-Sat. 10-5, Wed. 1-9; closed major holidays. Museum $2.50; senior citizens and ages 6-18, $1.50. Library admission charged. Phone (215) 732-6201.

★**INDEPENDENCE HALL,** between 5th and 6th sts. on Chestnut St. in Independence Square, is part of Independence National Historical Park *(see box page 126).* In this graceful 1732 brick building, the Declaration of Independence and Constitution were signed, the Second Continental Congress decided in 1775 to resist England, and George Washington accepted the role of commander in chief of the Colonial armies. Within the Assembly Room are the inkstand used in signing the Declaration and the "rising sun" chair occupied by Washington during the drafting of the Constitution.

The Assembly Room has been restored to look as it did when used by the Founding Fathers 1775-87. Across the hallway is the restored Pennsylvania Supreme Court Chamber. Upstairs, the Governor's Council Chamber, Long Room and Committee Room have been restored and furnished in period. Admission is by guided tour only; tours are offered regularly throughout the day. Daily 9-5; extended hours in summer. Free. Phone (215) 597-8974, or 597-1785 TDD.

★**LIBERTY BELL PAVILION,** 5th, 6th, Market and Chestnut sts., is part of Independence National Historical Park *(see box page 126).* A glass structure forms a permanent home for the Liberty Bell, which was moved from Independence Hall on Jan. 1, 1976. Park rangers relate the bell's history. Daily 9-5; extended hours in summer. The bell can be viewed from the exterior 24 hours a day. Free. Phone (215) 597-8974, or 597-1785 TDD.

**MARINE CORPS MEMORIAL MUSEUM,** on Chestnut between 3rd and 4th sts., is a reconstruction of a 1791 building; it is part of Independence National Historical Park *(see box page 126).* The museum commemorates the history of the Marine Corps 1775-1805. Daily 9-5; closed Jan. 1 and Dec. 25. Free. Phone (215) 597-8974, or 597-1785 TDD.

**MARIO LANZA INSTITUTE AND MUSEUM,** 416 Queen St., is in the Settlement Music School where opera and film star Mario Lanza received his early musical education. The museum displays treasures from Lanza's life, including many portraits and photographs. Among the highlights is a bust of Lanza made behind the Iron Curtain by a Hungarian sculptor. Allow 30 minutes minimum. Open Mon.-Sat. 10-3:30, Jan.-May and Sept.-Dec.; Mon.-Fri. 10-3:30, rest of year. Closed major holidays. Free. Phone (215) 468-3623.

★**MASONIC TEMPLE,** 1 N. Broad St., was built 1868-73 and is one of the city's striking architectural landmarks. Each of the temple's seven lodge halls exemplifies a different architectural style—Corinthian, Ionic, Italian Renaissance, Norman, Gothic, Oriental and Egyptian. The hallways and stairways are enhanced by chandeliers and paintings, statuary and other artworks. A large stained-glass window overlooks the marble grand staircase.

Tours of the building include the Grand Lodge Museum, a Byzantine-style room housing Masonic treasures. Included in the collection are jewels, George Washington's Masonic apron, furniture, Liverpool and Lowestoft ware, cut glass and statues by William Rush. Visitors must be accompanied by guides. Tours Mon.-Fri. at 10, 11, 1, 2 and 3, Sat. at 10 and 11; closed major holidays and Sat. in July and Aug. Donations. Phone (215) 988-1917.

**MORRIS ARBORETUM OF THE UNIVERSITY OF PENNSYLVANIA** is at 100 Northwestern Ave., between Germantown and Stenton aves. in Chestnut Hill. Within its 92 acres are 3,500 kinds of trees and shrubs, including North American, European and Asian species. Highlights include the Rose Garden, Swan Pond and Magnolia Slope. Guided tours are available Sat.-Sun. at 2.

Allow 1 hour, 30 minutes minimum. Mon.-Fri. 10-4, Sat.-Sun. 10-5 (10-4, Nov.-Mar.); closed Jan. 1, Thanksgiving and Dec. 24-31. Admission $3, over 65 and students with ID $1.50, under 6 free. **Discount.** Phone (215) 247-5777.

**MUMMERS MUSEUM,** 1100 S. 2nd St., contains audiovisual and participatory displays, costumes and musical instruments that trace the history of the Mummers and their New Year's Day parade. String band concerts are given Tues. at 8 p.m., May-Sept. (weather permitting). Allow 1 hour minimum. Tues.-Sat. 9:30-5, Sun. noon-5, Sept.-June; Tues.-Sat. 9:30-5, rest of year. Closed holidays. Admission $2.50; over 55 and ages 6-13, $2. **Discount.** Phone (215) 336-3050.

**MUSEUM OF AMERICAN ART OF THE PENNSYLVANIA ACADEMY OF THE FINE ARTS,** 118 N. Broad St. at Cherry St., is said to have been the first art museum and school in the country. Founded in 1805, the museum houses one of the more important collections of American art in the country. Featured are works by Mary Cassatt, Richard Diebenkorn, Thomas Eakins, Horace Pippin and Benjamin West. The museum building, built in 1876, is an outstanding example of high-Victorian Gothic architecture. Guided tours are available Sat.-Sun. at 12:30 and 2.

Allow 1 hour minimum. Mon.-Sat. 10-5, Sun. 11-5; closed Jan. 1, Thanksgiving and Dec. 25. Admission $5.93; over 65, students with ID, $4.95; ages 5-12, $3.95; half-price to all Sat. 10-1. Phone (215) 972-7600.

**THE MÜTTER MUSEUM OF THE COLLEGE OF PHYSICIANS OF PHILADELPHIA,** 19 S. 22nd St. between Chestnut and Market sts., contains medical instruments and an unusual collection of anatomical and pathological specimens. Founded in 1787, the museum displays a large collection of human skulls, the skeletons of a giant and a dwarf, the tumor removed from President Grover Cleveland's jaw in 1893 and a plaster cast of Siamese twins Chang and Eng. An early 20th-century doctor's office is re-created. Tues.-Fri. 10-4; closed major holidays. Admission $2, senior citizens and students with ID $1. Phone (215) 587-9919.

**NATIONAL ARCHIVES PHILADELPHIA BRANCH,** 9th and Market sts., contains records that document American history from the First Continental Congress to the present. This branch has Civil and Revolutionary War records and changing exhibitions. Allow 30 minutes minimum. Mon.-Fri. 8-5, second Sat. of each month 8-4. Free. Phone (215) 597-3000.

**NATIONAL MUSEUM OF AMERICAN JEWISH HISTORY,** 55 N. 5th St. (Independence Mall East) next to the Mikveh Israel Synagogue, offers changing exhibits depicting the contributions Jewish people have made to America. Documents and artifacts preserve the history of Jewish life. Allow 1 hour minimum. Guided tours Mon.-Thurs. 10-5, Fri. 10-3, Sun. noon-5. Admission $2.50; over 65, students with ID and ages 6-18, $1.75. Phone (215) 923-3811.

**NATIONAL SHRINE OF ST. JOHN NEUMANN,** 5th St. and Girard Ave., contains relics of the life and canonization of the saint. Featured are stained-glass windows depicting his life. His remains are in a glass casket entombed under the main altar. Allow 1 hour, 30 minutes minimum. One-hour guided tours are given Mon.-Sat. 9-4. A museum is open Mon.-Fri. 9-4, Sat.-Sun. 10-4. The church is open daily 7:30-6. Free. Phone (215) 627-3080.

**NORMAN ROCKWELL MUSEUM** is at 6th and Sansom sts. Housed in the Curtis Center on the lower level, this home of the *Saturday Evening Post* has one of the larger exhibits of Rockwell's works, including all of the *Post's* covers. Featured is a replica of the artist's studio. A film in the Four Freedoms Theatre spans his career. Allow 30 minutes minimum. Mon.-Sat. 10-4, Sun. 11-4; closed Jan. 1, Thanksgiving and Dec. 25. Admission $2; over 62, $1.50; under 12 free with adult. AE, MC, VI. Phone (215) 922-4345.

**OLD CITY HALL,** s.w. corner of 5th and Chestnut sts., was the home of the U.S. Supreme Court 1791-1800. The exterior and the room used by the Supreme Court have been restored, and the Old City Hall is now part of Independence National Historical Park *(see box page 126).* Daily 9-5; closed Jan. 1 and Dec. 25. Free. Phone (215) 597-8974, or 597-1785 TDD.

**OLD ST. JOSEPH'S CHURCH,** 321 Willings Alley, at 4th St. below Walnut St., was the first Roman Catholic church in Philadelphia. The Marquis de Lafayette and Comte de Rochambeau worshiped in its dim interior. It is part of Independence National Historical Park *(see box page 126).* Daily 6-6. Phone (215) 923-1733.

**OLD ST. MARY'S CHURCH,** 4th St. between Locust and Spruce sts., was founded in 1763 and enlarged in 1810. The second Roman Catholic church in Philadelphia, it became the city's first cathedral in 1810. Daily 9-5. Free. Phone (215) 923-7930.

**PENN'S LANDING,** between Market and Lombard sts. along the Delaware River, marks the site where William Penn landed in 1682. The 37-acre area, which has several historic ships and a sculpture garden, features concerts, festivals and special exhibitions throughout the year. Phone (215) 629-3200, or 629-6237 for program information.

*Barnegat* (**Lightship #79**), built in 1904, lighted the shipping lanes of the Port of Philadelphia for 63 years. For hours and admission prices phone (215) 923-9030.

*Gazela of Philadelphia,* built in 1883, is the last ship of the Portuguese square-rigged fishing fleet. The *Gazela* is the oldest and largest square-rigged vessel still putting out to sea. The ship

once departed Lisbon in the spring and returned about 6 months later, laden with salted cod taken from the coastal waters off Eastern Canada. For hours and admission prices phone (215) 923-9030.

**Jupiter Tugboat** was built in 1902 in Camden, N.J. For hours and admission prices phone (215) 923-9030.

**USS Becuna** is a guppy-class submarine commissioned in 1943 to serve in Adm. William Halsey's Seventh Fleet in the South Pacific. Allow 30 minutes minimum. Daily 10-4:30; closed Jan. 1 and Dec. 25. Admission, which includes the USS *Olympia* $5; over 65, $3; ages 4-12, $2. Phone (215) 922-1898.

**USS Olympia,** Adm. George Dewey's flagship during the Spanish-American War, brought back the body of the Unknown Soldier in 1921. Allow 30 minutes minimum. Open same hours as USS *Becuna;* admission included in *Becuna* fee.

**PENNSYLVANIA HORTICULTURAL SOCIETY,** 325 Walnut St., houses gardening literature. An 18th-century garden is nearby. Allow 30 minutes minimum. Mon.-Fri. 9-5; closed legal holidays. Free. Phone (215) 625-8250.

**PHILADELPHIA MARITIME MUSEUM,** 321 Chestnut St., relates the maritime heritage of the Delaware River and Bay. Featured are marine art, ship models, early navigational instruments, ship-building tools, scrimshaw, weapons, china and silver. Allow 1 hour minimum. Tues.-Sat. 10-5, Sun. 1-5; closed Jan. 1, Easter, Thanksgiving and Dec. 24-25 and 31. Admission, which includes Workshop on the Water at Penn's Landing, $2.50; senior citizens and under 12, $1. Phone (215) 925-5439.

**Workshop on the Water at Penn's Landing** is a barge where boatbuilders can be seen practicing their craft. Models, blueprints and replicas of a variety of small watercraft pay tribute to generations of boatbuilders and enthusiasts. Allow 30 minutes minimum. Wed.-Sun. 9-5. Admission $1, children 50c; admission otherwise included with Philadelphia Maritime Museum. Phone (215) 925-7589.

★**PHILADELPHIA MUSEUM OF ART**—*see Fairmount Park.*

**PLEASE TOUCH MUSEUM,** 210 N. 21st St., encourages visitors to use their senses. Children, especially those under 7, will enjoy holding, smelling, listening to and watching a variety of art, science and cultural objects. Every four children must be accompanied by one adult. Special events and weekend theater performances also are available. Allow 1 hour minimum. Daily 9-4:30; closed Jan. 1, Thanksgiving and Dec. 25. Admission $6.50; over 50, $5; under 1 free. **Discount.** Phone (215) 963-0667.

**POLISH AMERICAN CULTURAL CENTER MUSEUM,** opposite Independence National Historic Park at 308 Walnut St., maintains a portrait collection celebrating well-known Polish figures. Among the scientists, artists and leaders portrayed are freedom fighter Lech Walesa and Revolutionary War hero Gen. Casimir Pulaski. Allow 30 minutes minimum. Mon.-Sat. 10-4, May-Dec.; Mon.-Fri. 10-4, rest of year. Closed holidays. Free. Phone (215) 922-1700.

**POWEL HOUSE,** 244 S. 3rd St., is a Revolutionary War-era mansion with elegant furnishings and lovely gardens. Allow 30 minutes minimum. Tues.-Sat. 10-4, Sun. 1-4. Last tour 30 minutes before closing. Closed for special functions and holidays. Admission $3, senior citizens and students with ID $2, under 6 free. Phone (215) 627-0364.

**THE PRESBYTERIAN HISTORICAL SOCIETY,** at 5th and Lombard sts., was founded in 1852 to preserve the history of the Presbyterian Church. The museum room houses silver and pewter ware, communion tokens and artifacts from the Colonial period to the present. Other highlights include a portrait gallery featuring church leaders and paintings by such noted artists as Bass Otis, John Neagle and Rembrandt and James Peale. A research library is available. Allow 30 minutes minimum. Mon.-Fri. 8:30-4:30; closed holidays. Free. Phone (215) 627-1852.

**RODIN MUSEUM**—*see Fairmount Park.*

**ROSENBACH MUSEUM AND LIBRARY,** 2010 Delancey, exhibits more than 500 paintings, 30,000 books and 270,000 manuscripts collected by the Rosenbach brothers. Highlights include manuscripts by Geoffrey Chaucer, Charles Dickens and James Joyce, as well as books once owned by Abraham Lincoln and Herman Melville.

Allow 1 hour minimum. Tues.-Sun. 11-4, Sept.-July; closed Dec. 22-25 and major holidays. Last tour 1 hour, 15 minutes before closing. Admission $3.50; senior citizens, students with ID and under 18, $2.50. Phone (215) 732-1600.

**ST. GEORGE'S UNITED METHODIST CHURCH,** 235 N. 4th St. at the Benjamin Franklin Bridge, was dedicated in 1769. Part of Independence National Historical Park *(see box page 126),* it is the oldest Methodist church used continuously for worship. In 1784, St. George's licensed the first black Methodist preacher in the United States. The adjoining Methodist Historical Center contains church relics. For guide service ring the bell on New Street.

Allow 30 minutes minimum. Daily 10-4; closed Jan. 1, Thanksgiving and Dec. 25. Free. Phone (215) 925-7788.

**ST. PETER'S CHURCH** (Episcopal), 3rd and Pine sts., was erected in 1761. Four signers of the

Declaration of Independence worshiped at St. Peter's. If the church is locked, the key can be obtained at 313 Pine St. Tues.-Sat. 9-3. Free. Phone (215) 925-5968.

**SCHOOL GALLERY OF THE PENNSYLVANIA ACADEMY OF THE FINE ARTS,** 1301 Cherry St., has changing exhibits of multimedia works by students, faculty and alumni. Allow 30 minutes minimum. Mon.-Thurs. 9-7, Fri.-Sat. 10-4; closed holidays. Free. Phone (215) 972-7600.

★**SECOND BANK OF UNITED STATES,** 420 Chestnut St., houses Independence National Historical Park's *(see box page 126)* portrait collection. These 185 late 18th- and early 19th-century portraits, many by Charles Willson Peale, illustrate Philadelphia's role as the capital city 1790-1800. Daily 9-5; closed Jan. 1 and Dec. 25. Free. Phone (215) 597-8974, or 597-1785 TDD.

**STENTON MANSION,** 18th St. and Windrim sts., was built in 1730 by James Logan, secretary to William Penn. The house served as the Revolutionary War headquarters for both George Washington and British general Richard Howe. Allow 30 minutes minimum. Tues.-Sat. 1-4, Mar. 15-Dec. 5. Admission $3, senior citizens and students with ID $2. Phone (215) 329-7312.

**THADDEUS KOSCIUSZKO NATIONAL MEMORIAL,** 3rd and Pine sts., is part of Independence National Historical Park *(see box page 126)*. Exhibits and audiovisual presentations, in English and Polish, describe Thaddeus Kosciuszko's contributions to the American Revolution. The home's exterior has been restored. Allow 30 minutes minimum. Daily 9-5; closed Jan. 1, Thanksgiving and Dec. 25. Free. Phone (215) 597-9618.

**TODD HOUSE,** 4th and Walnut sts., was the home of Dolley Payne Todd before her marriage to James Madison, fourth president of the United States. The house is part of Independence National Historical Park *(see box page 126)*. Daily 9-5; closed Jan. 1 and Dec. 25. Obtain free tickets for tour at the park visitor center, 3rd and Chestnut streets. Phone (215) 597-8974, or 597-1785 TDD.

**UNITED STATES CUSTOM HOUSE,** 2nd and Chestnut sts., houses customs offices, appraisers' stores and other federal offices. Mon.-Fri. 8:30-5; closed holidays. Free.

**UNITED STATES MINT,** 5th and Arch sts., offers self-guiding audiotape tours that take about 45 minutes. Daily 9-4:30, July-Aug.; Mon.-Sat. 9-4:30, May-June; Mon.-Fri. 9-4:30, rest of year. Closed holidays. Coining machinery might not be operating Sat.-Sun. and Dec. 23-Jan. 3. Free. Phone (215) 597-7350.

**UNIVERSITY OF PENNSYLVANIA,** bounded by Chestnut, Pine, 32nd and 40th sts., was founded in 1740. In 1765, the country's first medical school was opened at the university and is currently considered one of the leading educational centers in the nation. Tours of the campus are available through the Office of Undergraduate Admissions, 1 College Hall. The office is open Mon.-Fri. 8:30-4:30. Free. Phone (215) 898-1000.

**Institute of Contemporary Art,** 36th and Sansom sts., presents changing exhibitions of contemporary art. Allow 1 hour minimum. Thurs.-Sun. 10-5, Wed. 10-7; closed holidays and when exhibitions are being changed. Admission $3; over 65 and students 12-18, $1; free to all Sun. 10-noon. Phone (215) 898-7108.

★**The University of Pennsylvania Museum of Archaeology and Anthropology,** 33rd and Spruce sts., displays outstanding archeological collections in the study of ancient man. Exhibits include findings from South America, Central America, the Orient, Mesopotamia, Greece, Egypt and Africa. Programs for ages 8-12 are on

Sat. at 10:30, Oct.-Mar. Tours are given Sat.-Sun. at 1:15, Oct.-May.

Allow 1 hour minimum. Tues.-Sat. 10-4:30, Sun. 1-5, Sept.-June; Tues.-Sat. 10-4:30, rest of year. Closed holidays. Admission $5, senior citizens and students with ID $2.50, under 6 free. **Discount.** Phone (215) 898-4000.

**WOODMERE ART MUSEUM,** 4 mi. s. of I-276, exit 25, at 9201 Germantown Ave., has paintings and decorative art spanning the 18th, 19th and 20th centuries. The Victorian home and art collection of Charles Knox Smith form the nucleus of the museum. Of particular interest is the collection of 19th-century American paintings, which includes works by Ottomar Anshutz, Frederick Church, Jasper Cropsey, Edward Moran and Benjamin West.

Changing exhibits often focus on local artists. The museum also presents classes, concerts, lectures and other special events. Allow 30 minutes minimum. Tues.-Sat. 10-5, Sun. 1-5; closed major holidays. Donations. Phone (215) 247-0476.

**ZOOLOGICAL GARDENS**—see Fairmount Park.

## What To Do
### Sightseeing
#### Bus, Carriage or Trolley Tours

Several companies offer tours of historic Philadelphia via trolley busses, (215) 333-2119; a 20-minute trolley ride, (215) 627-0807, along Christopher Columbus Boulevard from Penn's Landing, Christopher Columbus Boulevard and Dock Street; and horse-drawn carriage tours, (215) 923-8516, of Independence Park and Society Hill.

#### Boat Tours

Riverbus Inc. offers ferry service from Penn's Landing to the New Jersey Aquarium in Camden, N.J. The ferry departs every 30 minutes Mon.-Fri. 8 a.m.-9:45 p.m., Sat. 9 a.m.-11:45 p.m., Sun. 9-7:45, May 15-Sept. 15 (weather permitting); Mon.-Fri. 8-5:45, Sat. 9-7:45, Sun. 9-5:45, rest of year (weather permitting). Fare $2, senior citizens and children $1.50. Phone (609) 365-1400, or (800) 634-4027 outside Fla.

**THE SPIRIT OF PHILADELPHIA,** departing from Columbus Blvd. and Lombard Cir. at Penn's Landing, offers narrated, 2-hour lunch and Sunday brunch cruises on the Delaware River. Dinner and moonlight party cruises also are available. Lunch cruise Mon.-Sat. noon-2, mid-Mar. to mid-Jan. Sunday brunch cruise Sun. 1-3, mid-Mar. to mid-Jan. Closed Dec. 25. Fare $28.90; over 55, $27.80; under 13, $20.10. AE, MC, VI. Parking $6. Phone (215) 923-1419.

#### Walking Tours

The heart of historic Philadelphia lends itself to a walking tour. A stroll through the narrow cobblestone streets among restored Georgian and Colonial buildings is the best way to discover the essence of the city and to assimilate its 18th-century atmosphere. A good starting point is City Hall at Penn Square.

Walking east on Market St., you pass Wanamaker's department store on the right. A few blocks farther on Market at 9th St. is a major shopping mall, the Gallery at Market East, which includes JCPenney and Strawbridge & Clothier. Continue east on Market to 7th St., where you will find the shops and restaurants of Market Place East and the Declaration (Graff) House. Directly behind the house on 7th is the Balch Institute, which portrays the ethnic experience in the United States by means of multimedia shows.

Cross 7th St. to the Atwater Kent Museum—The History Museum of Philadelphia. Upon leaving the museum, take the walkway to the right east to 6th St. Cross 6th and turn left to the Liberty Bell Pavilion, which houses the famous symbol of American freedom. From the pavilion, walk south across Chestnut St. to Independence Hall.

Within the next three blocks of Chestnut are numerous historical buildings that are part of the Independence National Historical Park (see box page 126). They include Congress Hall and Old City Hall, which flank Independence Hall; Second Bank of United States; the Marine Corps Memorial Museum; Carpenters' Hall; Todd House; the Army-Navy Museum; and the Bishop White House. The visitor center at 3rd and Chestnut sts. has information and exhibits.

Facing Independence Mall is the renovated Philadelphia Bourse. The historic merchants' exchange now houses shops, restaurants and an information center on the first floor.

To catch a glimpse of Philadelphia's nautical past, cross Chestnut at 4th St. to the Philadelphia Maritime Museum. Just east of the museum on Chestnut is a path leading to Franklin Court where a steel frame suggests the shape of Franklin's home, destroyed in 1812. Traces of the original foundation are visible.

From Franklin Court, exit onto Market St. and walk east to 2nd St. Take 2nd north to Christ Church on the left. Continue north 1½ blocks, then stroll through Elfreth's Alley on the right. The 6-foot-wide alley is lined with a number of quaint, modest houses from the early 1700s. Farther north on 2nd is Fireman's Hall, a museum depicting the history of firefighting in America with memorabilia, graphics, films and antique equipment.

From this point do an about-face and return to Arch St. Turn right on Arch and walk a half-block to the Betsy Ross House on your right. After a visit to this home of the American flag, proceed west on Arch 1½ blocks to the United States Mint, where you can witness the making of pennies, dimes, nickels and quarters.

To end the tour, walk south to Market on 5th St. You will pass the 1783 Free Quaker Meeting

House on the right. Once on Market you can choose to walk back to the Gallery East Mall to do some shopping or perhaps rest your feet, relax and refresh at one of the many restaurants in the area. The famous Bookbinders Old Original is tucked away at Second and Walnut sts. This tour takes approximately 5 hours, which allows for a leisurely pace.

Another excellent area for the visitor on foot is Penn's Landing. There visitors can view the *Barnegat,* the USS *Becuna,* the USS *Olympia* and the *Gazela of Philadelphia,* a barkentine that participated in the U.S. Bicentennial celebration in 1982. The Philadelphia Vietnam Veterans Memorial, Christopher Columbus Blvd. and Spruce St., and A World Sculpture Garden, with sculpture given to the city during the Bicentennial, also are at Penn's Landing.

**AUDIOWALK & TOUR/HISTORIC PHILADELPHIA** rental office is in the Norman Rockwell Museum with an entrance on 6th and Sansom sts., lower level. A cassette and map for a self-guiding walking tour of Independence National Historical Park can be obtained, as well as coupons for free admission to the Norman Rockwell Museum.

Allow 3 hours minimum. Daily rentals 10-1; return by 4. Tape and equipment rentals: one person $9, two-four persons $18. AE, MC, VI. The tape can be purchased for $11.95. Write Audio-Walk & Tour, Curtis Center, 601 Walnut St., Philadelphia, PA 19106. Phone (215) 925-1234 or 922-4345.

**TALK-A-WALK** offers a tape tour entitled "Severance Park and Those 'Revolting' Americans." The self-guiding walking tour of Independence National Historical Park (*see box page 126*) can be obtained through the mail for $12.45 (includes postage and shipping) by writing Talk-A-Walk, Sound Publishers, Inc., 30 Waterside Plaza, New York, NY 10010. Phone (212) 686-0356

## Sports and Recreation

Fairmount Park caters to nearly everyone's recreational appetite, with **archery, bicycling, canoeing, fishing, golf, hiking, horseback riding, lawn bowling, sailboating** and **tennis** available. For information about other municipal facilities, consult the AAA club or the convention and visitors bureau. Running and walking maps are available at downtown hotels

Philadelphia, with a representative in every major league—**baseball, football, hockey** and **basketball**—is a paradise for spectator sports fans. The Phillies of baseball's National League and the Eagles of the National Football League play at Philadelphia's Veterans Sport Stadium at Broad and Pattison streets. The Spectrum, also at Broad and Pattison, plays host to the Philadelphia Flyers of the National Hockey League and the 76ers of the National Basketball Association.

To obtain ticket information for the Phillies, phone (215) 463-1000; the Eagles, (215) 463-5500; the 76ers, (215) 339-7676; and the Flyers, (215) 755-9700.

A familiar sight along the Schuylkill River is the scull, either one-man or crew, skimming the water. Periodic races and spectacular annual rowing regattas can be watched from Fairmount Park.

**Polo** is played by the suburban Brandywine Polo Club, (610) 268-8692, which has free games on Sunday afternoon from mid-May to September. The Hidden Pond Polo Club, (609) 767-0550, holds matches June through September; fees are adults $7, senior citizens and children $4. **Cricket** matches are held in Fairmont Park on Saturday and Sunday in the summer.

If you want to play the ponies, Philadelphia Park in Bensalem offers **Thoroughbred racing** all year; phone (215) 639-9000. Garden State Park in Cherry Hill, N.J., offers **Standardbred races** September through December and Thoroughbred races in the winter and spring; phone (609) 488-8400. Delaware Park near Wilmington, Del., offers Thoroughbred races spring through fall; phone (302) 994-2521.

**Note:** Policies concerning admittance of children to pari-mutuel betting facilities vary. Phone for information.

## Where To Shop

"Meet me at the eagle" is a time-honored request in Philadelphia, where the baroque bronze bird at John Wanamaker's department store has long marked a gathering spot for friends and been a point of reference for bewildered visitors. Practically a museum, the mellow old department store also is celebrated for its magnificent pipe organ, which soars several stories above the ground floor and booms forth in three daily concerts.

The downtown shopping district extends roughly from 8th to 18th on Market, Chestnut and Walnut streets. Besides Wanamaker's, Philadelphia has two other department stores of national repute—JCPenney and Strawbridge & Clothier. All can be found at The Gallery and Gallery II, the four-level shopping mall at Market East, between 8th, 11th and Market streets. The mall is open Mon.-Sat. 10-7 (10-8 Wed. and Fri.), Sun. noon-5. Along South Street from 2nd to 8th streets are numerous avant-garde shops, galleries and restaurants.

Another renovated historic shopping area is the Philadelphia Bourse, opposite Independence Mall on 5th Street between Chestnut and Market streets. When it opened in 1895, the Bourse housed a grain and stock exchange, industrial exhibition halls, business offices and banks. Specialty shops and restaurants open onto the Food Court, an oasis for shoppers with its 10-story atrium with live trees and plants. The Bourse is open Mon.-Sat. 10-6.

The China Town Mall, 143 N. 11th St., has Oriental food, products and goods. At the Italian Market, along 9th Street from Christian Street to Dickinson Avenue, vendors sell a variety of wares, including fresh produce, homemade pasta, clothing and spices.

The shops at Liberty Place, between 16th and 17th on Chestnut Street, comprise one of Philadelphia's more elegant malls; the mall is open Mon.-Sat. 10-7 (10-8 Wed.), Sun. noon-6. Market Place East, 701 Market St., occupies an entire city block. Built 1859-1907, this renovated building now houses fine shopping and dining establishments.

For those who get hungry while they shop, there is the Reading Terminal Market, 12th and Filbert streets. In this renovated 19th-century farmers' market, shoppers can find about 80 stalls selling everything from double-yolk eggs to fresh meats to organic vegetables. Ready-to-eat dishes from snapper soup to fried falafel meet the needs of shoppers who haven't left time for cooking after they are finished shopping. The market is open Mon.-Sat. 8-6; phone (215) 922-2317.

The upscale shopper will enjoy the Shops at Bellevue, along Broad and Walnut sts. Stores include Alfred Dunhill, Ralph Lauren and Tiffanys. Most of these shops are open Mon.-Sat. 10-6 (Wed. 10-8).

In terms of both quantity and quality, Philadelphia has one of the richest antique markets in the country. You can pick up an unusual $4 china plate or a $40,000 Chippendale highboy, barter for a mustache cup or negotiate for a priceless silver service. Bargains are found mainly in the wholesale retail district known as Antique Row, the section of Pine east of Broad between 9th and 12th streets.

Prices and quality rise and chances to barter fall in the Upper Pine Street district, along Pine west of Broad between 16th and 18th, on the numbered streets north to Chestnut and along Chestnut between 18th and 20th. In this area are the finest examples of antique art objects and furnishings, displayed in Cadillac-and-kid-glove elegance.

A short drive outside the Philadelphia city limits will take you to one of the area's more extensive malls, The Court and Plaza at King of Prussia. At the intersection of US 202 and North Gulph Road, the mall features several major stores—Bloomingdale's, JCPenney, John Wanamaker's, Macy's, Sears and Strawbridge & Clothier. Plymouth Meeting Mall, on SR 422 in Plymouth Meeting, is another suburban mall featuring Hess's, IKEA and Strawbridge & Clothier.

Franklin Mills, at the Woodhaven Road exit of I-95, is about 16 miles from the center of Philadelphia. The single-level, mile-long concourse boasts nine anchor stores including JCPenney, Marshalls, Neiman-Marcus, Nordstrom, Saks Fifth Avenue, Spiegel and Syms Outlets, and about 225 smaller outlet and discount shops, as well as six restaurants, two food courts and a 10-screen movie theater.

## Where To Dine

Though Philadelphia chefs offer English, German, French, Chinese, Lebanese and numerous other ethnic cuisines, the city's forte is seafood, especially shellfish. Most menus list an array of clams, mussels, oysters, crabs and lobsters, and a scattered few also provide turtle dishes.

To many, eating out in Philadelphia means going to Bookbinders Old Original, 2nd and Walnut streets. Often considered a must for every visitor, Bookbinders is a virtual museum of aged paneling and Currier and Ives lithographs.

If you enjoy dining in an atmosphere of early 20th-century elegance complete with wrought-iron work and oak banisters, you will enjoy La Famiglia at 8 S. Front St.

Or, if you prefer to dine even further back in history, there are Dickens Inn at 2nd and Pine streets and Romano's at 120 Lombard St., and other restaurants in Head House Square, an area of Society Hill that dates from 1745. Also nearby is the Alouette Restaurant, 334 Bainbridge St., which serves Irish-American fare. Old City Philadelphia offers the ethnic fares of Kabul, 106 Chestnut St.; Monte Carlo Living Room, 2nd and South streets; and South Street Souvlaki, 509 South St.

Among the Center City restaurants are Bookbinders Seafood House at 215 S. 15th St., D. Lullo Centro at 1407 Locust St., Deus Cheminees at 1221 Locust St., The Garden at 1617 Spruce St, Morton's of Chicago at One Logan Sq., Restaurant 210 at 210 W. Rittenhouse Sq., and Susanne Foo at 1512 Walnut St. At 10th and Race streets, the Imperial Inn is a popular Chinese restaurant in Chinatown, which is bordered by 7th, 8th, 11th, Arch and Vine streets.

At Market Fair in the Gallery at Market East, 9th and Market streets, approximately 25 eateries surround a central dining area. The selection is wide, from health foods to Chinese cuisine.

Many new restaurants have appeared in the area around South Street, with its renovated brick townhouses and converted factory buildings. Bridget Foy's, 200 South St., Cafe Nola, 328 South St., and Primavera, 146 South St., are among the standouts.

For a change of pace, Sorelle Cianfero offers a 2-hour chef's walking tour of Philadelphia's Italian Market. Nibbles as well as narration are offered; phone (215) 772-0739.

While in town, try some of the local favorites. Scrapple, a Pennsylvania Dutch concoction of peppery pork, and Pennsylvania Dutch sausage are popular breakfast treats. Cinnamon buns, which originated in Philadelphia, are widely available. Other tasty snacks are the famous Philadelphia cheese steak and the soft, salty bread pretzels served hot by street vendors and eaten with dollops of mustard.

Reservations, always prudent, are highly recommended at the most popular establishments. While some downtown restaurants require coats and ties for men, most permit casual dress.

### Nightlife

Philadelphia has a lively tradition of evening entertainment that ranges from dancing to big bands to relaxing in the intimate atmosphere of a jazz club. The Academy of Music is the home of the Philadelphia Orchestra, Philly Pops, Opera Company of Philadelphia and Pennsylvania Ballet. Along with the Core States Spectrum, it presents a varied repertoire of music and dance.

The Dock Street Brewery, 18th and Cherry streets, and Sam Adam's Brewery, 1516 Sansom St., brew their own beer. The college crowd dominates Dr. Watson's Pub, 216 S. 11th St., and Smokey Joe's, 208 S. 40th St. Everything from jazz to country can be found at J.C. Dobbs, 304 South St. and Khyber Pass Pub, 565 2nd St. For big names in rock and jazz, it's the Painted Bride Art Center, 230 Vine St.; Tower Theatre, 69th and Ludlow in Upper Darby; Theater of Living Arts, 334 South St.; and The Trocadero, 1003 Arch St.

You can laugh the evening away at The Comedy Cabaret, 126 Chestnut St. For blue's and jazz lovers there's the North Star Bar at 27th and Poplar streets. For jazz purists there are the Blue Moon Jazz Club on 4th Street, between Market and Chestnut Streets; Ortleb's Jazzhaus, 847 N. 3rd St. and Zanzibar Blue, 301 S. 11th St.

Music and dancing are available at Founders at the Hotel Atop the Bellevue, Broad and Walnut streets; Reunion Sports Bar in the Holiday Inn Independence Mall Hotel, 4th and Arch streets; Smart Alex at the Sheraton University City Hotel, Chestnut and 36th streets; and the Swann Lounge at the Four Seasons Hotel, 18th Street and Ben Franklin Parkway. Piano music can be heard at the Bar & Grill at the Ritz Carlton, 16th and Chestnut streets.

Along the waterfront are Dave and Busters, 325 N. Columbus Blvd. at Pier 19 N.; Eli's, Pier 34 at Christopher Columbus Boulevard and Fitzwater Street; Katmandu, Pier 25 and Christopher Columbus Boulevard; KoKomo Bay, 927 N. Christopher Columbus Blvd.; and Rock Lobster, Piers 13 and 15, Vine and Christopher Columbus Blvd.

For more information, check newspapers, guides or AAA Mid-Atlantic.

**Note:** The mention of any area or establishment in the preceding sections is for information only and does **not** imply endorsement by AAA.

### Theater and Concerts

The famed Philadelphia Orchestra, one of the country's finer symphonies, presents its winter series in the Academy of Music, which also presents grand opera, the Pennsylvania Ballet, the Philly Pops, musicals and special concerts; phone (215) 893-1999. In summer the orchestra's rich tones ring through Fairmount Park's Mann Music Center. Tickets are sold at the box office; phone (215) 878-7707.

Valley Forge Music Fair has performances March through December. The Police and Firemen's Band thumps out Sousa marches and other rousing favorites in several parks. During the summer, concerts are held on the Great Plaza at Penn's Landing and Kennedy Plaza, 15th Street and JFK Boulevard. Check at the visitor center for times.

Philadelphia theater is very popular. The Forrest Theater presents pre-Broadway and hit shows with name stars, while national touring companies appear at the Merriman Theatre and the Annenberg Center. The Cabaret Theatre at New Market features shows from around the world.

There also are numerous regional and community theater companies, including the American Music Festival Theatre, the Arden Theatre, the Bristol Riverside Theater, the Freedom Theater, the Hedgerow Theater, the People's Light and Theatre Company, the Philadelphia Company, the Philadelphia Festival Theatre of New Plays, the Philadelphia Drama Guild, Plays and Players, the Society Hill Playhouse, the Walnut Street Theatre and the Willma Theater. College theater can be enjoyed at Temple University's Venture Theater or Villanova University's Vasey Theater.

### Especially for Children

One of Philadelphia's fascinations for youngsters is Penn's Landing, where tugboats lie at anchor and freighters and naval vessels pass. Another delight is the variety of public conveyances to ride, especially the clanging trolleys. Sesame Place in Langhorne (see place listing) is a family-oriented theme park; it includes "Sesame Street" character appearances, a recreation of the "Sesame Street" studio set, physical play activities and water rides. At the Please Touch Museum, children can dress up in

various costumes for some memorable pictures *(see color ad p. 138)*.

For education and entertainment, visit some of the city's fine museums. Those with children's sections include the Academy of Natural Sciences and the Franklin Institute Science Museum and the Omniverse Theatre. Each year the Giant Tinkertoy Extravaganza is held at the institute during the 3 days following Thanksgiving. Older children enjoy the shows in the institute's Fels Planetarium, while all ages delight in the Children's Zoo.

For children's movies, visit the Philadelphia Museum of Art, which often screens film classics on Saturdays, or the University of Pennsylvania Museum. For details about points of interest refer to the *What To See* section; for current showings check the local newspapers.

## Special Events

Philadelphia's calendar is packed throughout the year with events ranging from the huge Mummers and Thanksgiving Day parades to quaint flower and antique shows and folk festivals.

The world-famous Mummers Parade starts off the new year and attracts some 30,000 costumed Mummers String Bands, fancies and comics. Philadelphia then settles down for the Philadelphia International Auto Show, held in January at the Pennsylvania Convention Center and the Philadelphia Boat Show, also held in January at the Civic Center. The 4-day Chinese New Year occurs sometime between January 21 and February 19 and is celebrated with 10-course banquets at the Chinese Cultural Center in mid-February.

February is Black History Month, a national event that is observed in Philadelphia with exhibitions, lectures and music at the Afro-American Historical and Cultural Museum. Presidential Jazz Weekend and the Philadelphia Home Show are held in early February. Also in February, top male players compete in the U.S. Indoor Tennis Championships.

The Philadelphia Flower Show, held March 5-12 at the Civic Center, is one of the nation's larger indoor flower shows. A culinary event not to be missed is The Book and the Cook in mid-March, when world-famous cookbook authors team up with some of Philadelphia's finer chefs to create spectacular dishes. The wearing of the green is toasted during the city's St. Patrick's Day Parade, while the Easter Promenade offers music, entertainment and celebrity guests at several locations on Easter Sunday.

The Philadelphia Antiques Show in April is conducted at the 33rd Street Armory. The Penn Relays at Franklin Field in April is one of the world's older and larger track meets. Also in the spring, the Mummers String Band Show of Shows is held at the Civic Center. In late April, Valborgsmassoafton, the traditional Swedish welcoming of spring, is observed at the American Swedish Historical Museum.

Guided walking and bus tours of selected homes, gardens and historic buildings in 10 different neighborhoods are offered during the Philadelphia Open House, which runs from April 27 to May 15. Also in May is the Africamericas Festival, celebrating African-American culture with entertainment, talent contests and a film festival at the Uptown Theater, 2240 N. Broad St. The Dad Vail Regatta is one of the larger college regattas in the country.

Additional events in May include the Rittenhouse Square Flower Market, 18th and Walnut streets; the International Theater Festival for Children at the Annenberg Center, 3680 Walnut St.; the Devon Horse Show and Country Fair, at the Devon Fairgrounds; River Blues, at Penn's Landing, which attracts aficionados of the blues on May 20-21; and Jambalaya Jam, a weekend of Creole and Cajun cooking and jazz at Penn's Landing during Memorial Day weekend.

Summer kicks off with the Rittenhouse Square Fine Arts Annual, Elfreth's Alley Fete Days and the Head House Square Crafts Fair, all held in June.

The Welcome America Festival explodes the first week in July, while August ends with the Philadelphia Folk Festival, which features folk music concerts and workshops at suburban Poole Farm in Schwenksville.

September events include the Yo! Philadelphia Festival at Penn's Landing on September 3-4, the America's Gold Cup equestrian competition at Devon Fairgrounds, the Penn's Landing In-Water Boat Show, the Harvest Show at the Horticulture Center, the Von Steuben Day Parade and The South Street Seven Arts Festival. The Pulaski Day Parade and Columbus Day Parade are in October. The Battle of Germantown is re-enacted in early October, and Super Sunday, a day of hands-on participation at all of the city's cultural and educational institutions, is celebrated in mid-month.

The Civic Center stages the Philadelphia Crafts Show in November, a major exhibition of crafts by the nation's top artisans, as well as the Philadelphia Art Show, which exhibits local, national and international works in a variety of media. Later in November, the holidays begin in grand and traditional fashion with the Philadelphia Thanksgiving Day Parade, complete with celebrities, enormous balloons and national TV coverage.

Following Thanksgiving is the Giant Tinkertoy Extravaganza at the Franklin Institute Science Museum. The Army-Navy Football Classic is held in early December at Veterans Stadium. The Colonial mansions in Fairmount Park come alive in December with all the traditional decorations for the Christmas Tours of Historic Houses. Then Christmas is celebrated in the Swedish tradition with the Lucia Fest and Julmarknad at the American Swedish Historical Museum.

# Pittsburgh

Pittsburgh is a city of pleasant surprises. Mostly hidden by the hills that surround it, the city literally bursts upon visitors who arrive through tunnels, across bridges, or along scenic hillside roadways. Famous for its Three Rivers—the Allegheny and the Monongahela meet at the "Point" to form the Ohio—Pittsburgh is a blend of modern and historic architecture. "Renaissance" is the word, and Pittsburgh's spectacular rebirth is apparent not only in new buildings, parks and transportation systems, but in philosophy as well. Believing renaissance to be a continuous process that answers to changing times and needs, Pittsburgh refuses to box itself in with an ironclad definition of goals. It continues to unfold itself: a friendly giant whose educational, cultural and recreational aspects are as important as its commercial and industrial facets. Above all, it is a livable place and proud of it.

Pittsburgh's history dates from the 18th-century dispute between the French and English over claims to the Ohio Valley. When the Canadian French established an outpost on the Allegheny River, the English quickly realized their need for a fort to defend their position in the West. Young George Washington, then a major in the Colonial army, selected the area now known as the "Golden Triangle"—the junction of the Monongahela, Allegheny and Ohio rivers. In 1758, Pittsborough was named in honor of the British statesman William Pitt.

After the Revolution, the city's position on the three rivers enhanced its commercial value, and Pittsborough—by then called Pittsburgh—grew rapidly. Coal was dug from the hills, the first glassworks was opened and Anschulz's blast furnace, built in 1792, became the precursor of the iron and steel industry. Before the 19th century, Pittsburgh boasted a post office, a network of roads and the *Pittsburgh Gazette*, the first newspaper published west of the Allegheny Mountains.

---

## THE INFORMED TRAVELER

**POPULATION:** 369,900; metro 2,242,800     **ELEVATION:** 715 ft.

### Whom to Call

**Emergency:** 911

**Police (non-emergency):** (412) 255-2916

**Time and Temperature:** (412) 391-9500

**Hospitals:** Allegheny General Hospital, (412) 359-3131; Children's Hospital of Pittsburgh, (412) 692-5325; Mercy Hospital, (412) 232-8111; North Hills Passavant Hospital, (412) 367-6700; Western Pennsylvania Hospital, (412) 578-5000.

### Where to Look

**Newspapers**
The major daily newspaper is the morning *Post-Gazette*. Smaller daily, weekly and special-interest papers also are published.

**Radio and TV**
Pittsburgh radio station KDKA (1020 AM) is a news/talk/weather station; WDUQ (90.5 FM) is serviced by National Public Radio.
The major TV channels are 2 (CBS), 4 (ABC), 11 (NBC), 13 (PBS) and 53 (FOX). For

a complete list of radio and television programs, consult the daily newspapers.

**Visitor Information**
Various maps, brochures, calendars of events and lists of sightseeing companies are available at the The Greater Pittsburgh Convention and Visitors Bureau, 4 Gateway Center, Suite 514, Pittsburgh, PA 15222; phone (412) 281-7711 or (800) 359-0758. The bureau is open all year Mon.-Fri. 9-5; closed major holidays.

### What to Wear

Pittsburghers frankly admit that their city tends to be a cloudy place. Some form of precipitation falls on about 150 days out of 365, distributing the annual 36 inches fairly evenly through the year. (If that seems like a lot, remember that the remaining 215 days can be enjoyed *sans* umbrella.) In January and February the average high temperature is only 37 and the average low temperature is 21. July and August are the warmest months, and although few days see temperatures reaching into the 90s, the average high of 83 can make quite an impression when combined with the frequently high humidity. Because the July-August average low is 61, a light sweater or other garment sometimes might be handy outdoors.

During the 19th century, Pittsburgh plunged headlong into the American industrial age; its iron and steel plants soon won it the nickname "Iron City." This industry and others continued to expand after the Civil War and throughout the early decades of the 20th century. Billows of smoke issuing from a multitude of industrial stacks earned Pittsburgh the unloved nickname "Smoky City." Following World War II, awareness of the problems found outlet in concerted, constructive action and regulation. Step by step, a lucrative but grimy past became prologue to a versatile, healthy present.

Pittsburgh's terrain is a picturesque mix of plateaus and hillsides, narrow valleys and rivers spanned by many bridges. Its urban geography is equally arresting: no fewer than 90 neighborhoods are recognized by the city's Planning Department. These areas were established as immigrants arrived to work in the factories or to open businesses; and although most of the groups have long since scattered, the comfortable feeling of neighborhood has remained a dominant, thoroughly Pittsburghian trait.

## Approaches
### By Car

The primary highway from the north or the south is I-79, which passes through the western edge of the metropolitan area. Intersecting with east-west routes I-76 (Pennsylvania Turnpike) on the north and with I-70 on the south, I-79 funnels traffic into downtown Pittsburgh via controlled-access I-279 (Parkway West) and the Fort Pitt Tunnel from Carnegie.

A second approach is I-279 (Parkway North) from Franklin Plaza, and from the south via Banksville Road and I-279. US 19 Truck Route, using East Street from the north and West Liberty Avenue from the south, carries heavy commercial and industrial traffic into the city.

I-76 carries the bulk of east-west traffic through the Pittsburgh area, interchanging en route with all major arteries; controlled-access I-376 through the eastern suburbs provides the principal link to the heart of the city, arriving downtown via Grant Street exit 3. Two other important east-west highways are US 22 and US 30, which combine upon nearing the city, then join expressways—I-279 on the west and I-376 on the east—before entering the downtown area.

SR 28, first as the Allegheny Valley Expressway, then as E. Ohio Street, follows the north bank of the Allegheny River into the city's North Side, providing a fast route from northeast suburbs. Similarly, SR 60 makes an easy connection from the northwestern suburbs along the south side of the Ohio River, picking up airport traffic before joining with US 22/30.

### By Plane, Bus and Train

The Pittsburgh International Airport, 19 miles west via I-279 and SR 60 (Airport Parkway), was completed in 1992 and is served by numerous major domestic and international carriers, as well as commuter and cargo lines. The people movers, electric trains from airside to landside, and large, shop-filled corridors help to make this modern airport user-friendly and easily negotiated.

Airlines Transportation Co., (412) 471-2250, or 471-8900 for reservations, runs limousines between the airport and major hotels downtown, in Monroeville and in South Hills; the average fare is $18. Airport Limousine Service, (412) 461-7887 or 664-4777, serves the suburbs and several neighboring communities; the average fare is $20-$23. Taxis are more expensive, averaging $28 between the airport and downtown.

Allegheny County Airport, south of the city on Lebanon Church Road in West Mifflin, handles primarily corporate or private aircraft, although air taxis and charter services also are available.

The Greyhound Lines Inc. terminal, (800) 231-2222, is at 11th Street and Liberty Avenue. Other bus companies serving the outlying areas are listed in the telephone directory.

Amtrak passenger service's station, (412) 471-6170, is on the lower level of "The Pennsylvanian," the historic former Penn Central Station, at Liberty Avenue and Grant Street. The Allegheny Port Authority operates the "T," a three-station subway that loops the city's downtown area.

## Getting Around
### Street System

Pittsburgh's topography—a maze of hills and ravines sliced at an acute angle by two rivers converging to form a third—permits no consistent geometrical street layout. Instead, there is a patchwork of patterns dictated mainly by the lay of the land. A good street map is necessary for travel in this city.

From the Golden Triangle, major thoroughfares fan out more or less parallel to the Allegheny and Monongahela rivers, with intervening streets perpendicular to the rivers near the Point but following the contours of the hills farther out. Fifth Avenue and Liberty Avenue are the primary arteries.

On the North Side, at least the sections nearest the river, the picture is more regular, with avenues running parallel to the Allegheny and streets perpendicular to it. All the major thoroughfares seem to converge on Allegheny Center, framed by N., E., S. and W. Commons. E. Ohio Street and Western Avenue feed in from the east and west, respectively; East Street, Federal Street, Brighton Avenue and Allegheny Avenue reach the center from the north.

The near edge of the hilly South Side is the only part of the city that employs the designations "East" and "West," using the Smithfield Street Bridge as the dividing line. Carson Street (SR 837), parallel to the river, is the main artery through this area.

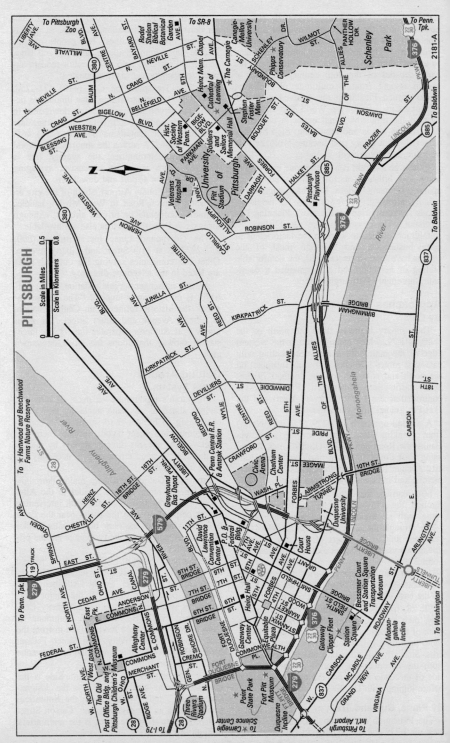

For the most part, Pittsburgh's streets are named; there are relatively few areas of consecutively numbered thoroughfares. Two such locations are on the Point, where 1st through 7th avenues are numbered northward from the Monongahela, and inland from the Allegheny River, where numbered streets increase as they proceed upstream.

The downtown speed limit, unless otherwise posted, is 25 mph, and on major thoroughfares, 35 mph. Unless a sign prohibits it, turning right at a red light after coming to a complete stop is legal. Similarly, so is turning left from one one-way street onto another. Pedestrians always have the right-of-way, particularly at marked crosswalks. Driving during rush hours, about 6:30-9 a.m. and 4-6:30 p.m., should be avoided if possible.

### Parking

As in any big city, parking downtown or near the major attractions is at a premium. On-street parking, when a space can be found, is governed by the meter system. However, commercial parking lots and garages are plentiful throughout downtown. Rates range from $2 an hour to $15 a day.

### Rental Cars

Numerous auto rental agencies operate in the Pittsburgh area. Hertz, at the Pittsburgh International Airport, offers discounts to AAA members; phone (412) 472-5955 or (800) 654-3131. In addition to downtown locations, agencies also have facilities at the airport. Other companies are listed in the telephone directory.

### Taxis

Colonial/Mayflower Cab, (412) 833-3300, People's Cab, (412) 681-3131, and Yellow Cab, (412) 665-8100, are the leading taxi companies. Cabs are metered; the standard fares range from a minimum of $1.50 to $2.50, plus $1 to $1.40 per mile. The standard tip is 15 percent of the meter reading.

### Public Transportation

Port Authority Transit (PAT) operates a fleet of buses throughout the city, suburbs and surrounding counties. The base fare is $1.25; exact change is required. Various reduced-rate passes and tickets, including weekend passes, are available at PAT's downtown service center, 534 Smithfield St. For route information phone (412) 231-5707. Bus service for the eastern suburbs is provided by the Martin Luther King Jr. East Busway.

Pittsburgh has joined the big leagues of mass transit with its launching of a downtown subway and a light rail system for the southern suburbs. The first stage of the light rail system extends 10½ miles to the South Hills Village shopping mall. Passengers ride free on the subway in the downtown zone.

## What To See

**ALLEGHENY OBSERVATORY,** off Perrysville Ave. (US 19) in Riverview Park, is one of the foremost observatories in the world. The surrounding park offers opportunities for swimming (with a city permit), picnicking and tennis. Observatory tours Thurs.-Fri. evenings by appointment, Apr.-Oct. Free. Phone (412) 321-2400.

**BEECHWOOD FARMS NATURE RESERVE** is on SR 8, ½ mi. n. of jct. SR 28, then 2 mi. n.e. on Kittanning Pike and 2½ mi. n. on Dorseyville Rd. Headquarters for the Audubon Society of Western Pennsylvania, Beechwood Farms has more than 90 acres of fields, thickets, ponds and woodlands threaded by 5 miles of hiking trails. The environmental education center has a natural history library and bird observation room.

Trails open daily dawn-dusk. Education center open Tues.-Sat. 9-5, Sun. 1-5; closed holidays. Free. Phone (412) 963-6100, or 963-0201 for events information.

**BESSEMER COURT AT STATION SQUARE,** s. end of the Smithfield St. Bridge, is an outdoor museum featuring relics of the region's industrial heritage and a 10-ton Bessemer converter built in 1930. Highlights include a 25-ton ingot mold and the sternwheel of the *Jason,* a 1940 steam-powered towboat, as well as antique railroad cars that have been converted into shops. Allow 30 minutes minimum. Museum open daily dawn-dusk. Free. Parking $1 per hour.

★**THE CARNEGIE,** 4400 Forbes Ave. across from the Cathedral of Learning, is a cultural complex in the heart of the university area. The Carnegie Performing Arts program sponsors the Music with the Masters series, Jazz Happy Hour and summer concerts in the Sculpture Court. The Carnegie Music Hall, a 2,000-seat auditorium, is home to the Y Music Society, River City Brass Band, Mendelssohn Choir, Opera Theater of Pittsburgh and the Pittsburgh Chamber Music Society. Phone (412) 622-3131.

**The Carnegie Library of Pittsburgh,** built in 1895, is one of the nation's foremost public libraries. It contains more than 4 million items, including books, magazines, newspapers, records, cassettes and photographs. The library is the state's resource library for science and technology. Cultural, educational and recreational programs also are offered.

Allow 1 hour minimum. Mon.-Wed. and Fri. 9-9, Thurs. and Sat. 9-5:30, Sun. 1-5, Nov.- Apr.; Mon.-Wed. and Fri. 9-9, Thurs. and Sat. 9-5:30, rest of year. Free. Phone (412) 622-3114.

**The Carnegie Museum of Art** displays Impressionist and post-Impressionist paintings; 19th- and 20th-century American and European paintings, sculpture and decorative arts; and contemporary art. The museum's film and videotape programs are nationally recognized, and its collection of monumental architectural casts is thought to be unique in the United States. The Heinz Architectural Center surveys past and current architectural expression through the exhibition of architectural drawings, models, photographs, and related materials. Free gallery lectures are given regularly.

Guided tours are given Sat.-Sun. at 2. Allow 3 hours minimum. Tues.-Sat. 10-5 (also Mon., July-Aug.), Sun. 1-5; closed holidays. Admission $5; senior citizens $4; students with ID and ages 3-18, $3. Guided tours are free with paid admission. **Discount.** Phone (412) 622-3131. *See color ad.*

★**The Carnegie Museum of Natural History** is the "home of the dinosaurs." Dinosaur Hall has 10 full skeletons, including a *Tyrannosaurus rex.* The Walton Hall of Ancient Egypt illustrates daily life then, using artifacts and interactive computer and videotape programs. Artifacts and displays in Polar World trace the cultural history of Inuit peoples and their adaptation to the Arctic. In Benedum Hall of Geology, interactive exhibits emphasize Pennsylvania's geology as they show how natural forces shaped the Earth. Masterpiece mineral specimens sparkle in Hillman Hall of Minerals and Gems where visitors can explore crystallography and mineral formations. The Hall of African Wildlife features mammals in their savanna, rain forest, mountain and desert habitats. The Butterfly and Insect exhibit features specimens from around the world. The Discovery Room offers hands-on displays.

Guided tours given Sat. at noon and 1, Sun. at 2 and 3. Allow 3 hours minimum. Tues.-Sat. 10-5 (also Mon., July-Aug.), Sun. 1-5; closed holidays. Admission included with Museum of Art; guided tours free with paid admission. **Discount.** Phone (412) 622-3131. *See color ad.*

★**The Carnegie Science Center,** 1 Allegheny Ave., North Shore, is an "amusement park for the mind." The Works exhibit explores natural phenomena, such as energy and matter, and how they have been applied to technical innovations in industry. A working foundry, industrial and educational robots, lasers, cryogenics and electrical equipment are displayed. Visitors can control the Aquabatics Fountain, a 30-foot interactive water sculpture that demonstrates buoyancy and hydraulic principles.

The Eating exhibit focuses on food acquisition; food processing, preservation and packaging; body processes and nutrition; and the cultural, ritual and social aspects of eating.

Ports of Discovery on the third level is composed of three areas primarily designed for children. The Early Learner's Landing, ages 3 through 6, allows visitors to explore the physical world with their hands and senses by interacting with water, animals and other objects. Science Pier, ages 7 through 13, is eight interactive modules which help visitors to understand the work

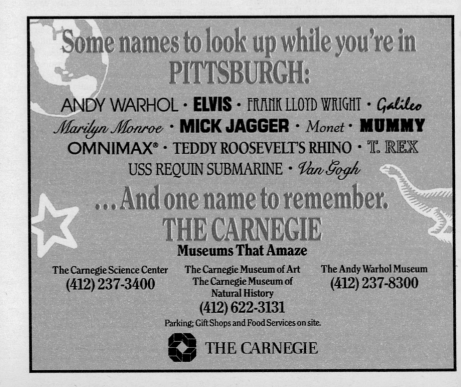

scientists perform and the ways in which science affects our daily lives. More than 100 species of ocean inhabitants are represented in the four tanks of the Pacific Coral Reef Aquarium.

The Great Miniature Railroad and Village displays the historical architectural and cultural heritage of western Pennsylvania. Trains speed through a 2,300-foot detailed miniature landscape which includes 100 animations as well as static figures and scenes.

The Henry Buhl Jr. Planetarium and Observatory probes the inner cosmos and outer space. Under age 4 are not admitted to the planetarium. The Rangos Omnimax® Theater, which includes a domed, four-story-high screen and a 56-speaker sound system, shows 45-minute to 1-hour long films about a variety of nature and science topics.

Allow 4 hours minimum. Mon.-Thurs. 10-5; Fri.-Sun. 10-6. Science center $5.75; senior citizens (Mon.-Fri.) and ages 3-18, $4.25. Combination ticket with Henry Buhl Jr. Planetarium, Rangos Omnimax Theater $12; senior citizens (Mon.-Fri.) and ages 3-18, $8.50. Parking $3. AE, MC, VI. Phone (412) 237-3400. See color ad p. 144.

USS *Requin*, in front of the Carnegie Science Center, is a 300-foot, World War II submarine. Built in May 1945, the sub reached Guam just as the war ended and therefore never saw battle action. Many guides of the 1-hour tour are former submariners, and on weekends the communications room is manned by members of an amateur radio club. There may be a waiting line, and full mobility is necessary for the tour. Allow 1 hour minimum. Mon.-Fri. noon-5, Sat.-Sun. 10-5. Admission $3.50; senior citizens and ages 3-18, $2.50. Parking $3. Phone (412) 237-1550.

★CATHEDRAL OF LEARNING, the University of Pittsburgh, is on a 14-acre quadrangle at Bigelow Blvd., 5th Ave., Bellefield Ave. and Forbes Ave. The 42-story truncated Gothic stone tower is said to be the tallest skyscraper college building in the Western Hemisphere. Encircling the Commons Room on the first and third floors are 23 nationality classrooms, reflecting styles ranging from classical, Byzantine and Romanesque to Renaissance, Tudor, Empire and folk. Each room was designed and decorated by artists and architects from nations representing Pittsburgh's ethnic heritages.

During the last 3 weeks in December the rooms are decorated in the traditional holiday manner of each nation represented. Allow 1 hour, 30 minutes minimum. Tours Mon.-Sat. 9:30-3, Sun. 11-3. Guided tour Apr.-Aug., in Dec. and Sat.-Sun. all year $2; senior citizens $1; ages 8-18, 50c. Fee 50c, rest of year. Sat.-Sun. are the best viewing times. Reservations are recommended 2 weeks in advance for guided tours; inquire at the information center on the first floor. Phone (412) 624-6000.

CIVIC ARENA, Washington Pl. at Center and Bedford aves. in the Golden Triangle, is a $22 million structure with a stainless steel retractable dome roof three times the size of the dome of St. Peter's in Rome. The multipurpose auditorium is used as a sports arena, theater, convention and concert hall. It is the home of professional hockey's Penguins. Phone (412) 642-1800 or 642-2062 for event information.

★CLAYTON, 7227 Reynolds St. in Point Breeze, is the estate of Pittsburgh industrialist Henry Clay Frick. The home features original furnishings and personal mementos of the Frick family. Also on the estate are a greenhouse; the children's playhouse, which is now the visitor center; the Carriage Museum, which exhibits 17 carriages, sleighs and vintage automobiles; and the Frick Art Museum, which contains Helen Clay Frick's collection of art. Not recommended for under age 10.

Allow 1 hour, 30 minutes minimum. Guided tours Tues.-Sat. 10-4, Sun. noon-5; closed major holidays. Admission $5, senior citizens $4, students with ID $3. Reservations are required. Phone (412) 371-0606.

Frick Art Museum is at 7227 Reynolds St. at Clayton. In a charming landscaped setting across from Frick Park, the Italian Renaissance-style building displays Italian, Flemish and French paintings from the early Renaissance through the 18th century.

Also of interest are Italian Renaissance bronzes, 16th-century tapestries and Chinese porcelains. Temporary exhibits, concerts and lectures also are presented. Allow 1 hour minimum. Tues.-Sat. 10-5:30, Sun. noon-6; closed holidays, except Easter. Free. Phone (412) 371-0600.

DUQUESNE INCLINE affords an excellent opportunity for viewing the city. The lower station is at 1197 W. Carson St., ¼ mi. w. of the s. end of the Fort Pitt Bridge. The trip ends at 1220 Grandview Ave., Mount Washington, where restaurants boast panoramas of the Golden Triangle. The incline is not accessible to the physically impaired. Trips depart Mon.-Sat. 5:30 a.m.-12:45 a.m., Sun. and holidays 7 a.m.-12:45 a.m. One-way fare $1; ages 6-11, 50c. Phone (412) 381-1665. See color ad p. A203.

★HARTWOOD, 215 Saxonburg Blvd., is a 629-acre re-creation of an English country estate. A 1¼-hour tour includes the Gothic Tudor mansion, formal gardens and stables. Allow 1 hour minimum. Guided tours are given on the hour Tues.-Sat. 10-3, Sun. noon-4, Apr.-Dec. Hour-long Old English Christmas tours are given Tues.-Sat. 10-3, Sun. noon-4, mid-Nov. to Dec. 1. Closed Thanksgiving and Dec. 25. Admission $3; over 60, $2; ages 6-12, $1. Reservations are required. Phone (412) 767-9200.

HEINZ HALL, 6th and Penn aves., is a restored 1926 movie theater. Its excellent acoustics, dramatic decor and architecture now form the backdrop for much of Pittsburgh's cultural activity.

Heinz Hall is the home of the Pittsburgh Symphony Orchestra, which presents a variety of popular series during the regular season, including Broadway, Classical, Great Performers, Pops and Summer Casual concerts. Guided tours are given by appointment. Admission $2; under 14, $1. Phone (412) 392-4800.

**HEINZ MEMORIAL CHAPEL** of the University of Pittsburgh, 5th and S. Bellefield aves. behind the Cathedral of Learning, is a modern French Gothic interdenominational chapel with 73-foot stained-glass windows. Other highlights include the organ, marble altar, carved woodwork and interior and exterior stone carvings. Special programs, concerts, recitals and half-hour guided tours are offered by appointment. Allow 1 hour minimum. Open Mon.-Fri. 9-4, Sun. 1-5; no guided tours Sun. Free. Phone (412) 624-4157 Mon.-Fri 8:30-5.

**HISTORICAL SOCIETY OF WESTERN PENNSYLVANIA**, 4338 Bigelow Blvd., contains a large collection of premier glass, including blown and etched pieces; antique furnishings; portraits and documents; a library; special exhibits; and a museum. A lecture and film series also is presented each spring and fall. Guided tours are available. Tues.-Sat. 9:30-4:30. Admission $2. Phone (412) 681-5533.

**KENNYWOOD PARK** is reached by taking the Swissvale exit off I-376, following signs. A traditional family amusement park, Kennywood has four roller coasters, a water coaster, 30 other major rides and 14 children's rides. A wooded grove with picnic shelters is available, and stage shows take place daily at Lake Kennywood. One of the few amusement parks to be named a national historic landmark, Kennywood has buildings dating from 1898. Food is available.

Allow 3 hours minimum. Daily noon-10, mid-May through Labor Day (5-10, Aug. 28-Sept. 1); Sat.-Sun. noon-10, late Apr. to mid-May. Admission $4.50, senior citizens $3.50; all-day ride pass $15, Sat.-Sun. $18. MC, VI. Phone (412) 461-0500.

**MONONGAHELA INCLINE** offers a view of the city. The lower station is on W. Carson Street across from Station Square. The terminus is on Grandview Avenue, Mount Washington. An observation deck running approximately ⅛-mile along Grandview Avenue has circular overhangs providing views of the Golden Triangle. Allow 30 minutes minimum. Mon.-Sat. 5:30 a.m.-12:45 a.m., Sun. and holidays 8:45 a.m.-midnight. One-way fare $1; ages 6-11, 50c. Phone (412) 231-5707.

**PITTSBURGH CENTER FOR THE ARTS**, 6300 5th Ave. in Mellon Park, has a school and galleries for emerging artists and special projects. Features include regional, national and international exhibitions; more than 500 classes and workshops for children, adults and the physically and emotionally impaired; concert and dance performances; lectures; an Artcamp for children; and an art shop and gallery where regional artists display their works. Tues.-Sat. 10-5:30, Sun. 1-5. Admission $3. Phone (412) 361-0873.

**PITTSBURGH CHILDREN'S MUSEUM** is ½ mi. n. via the 6th St. Bridge in the Old Post Office Building at One Landmarks Sq. (Allegheny Center). Interactive exhibits relating to human physical and social development are designed for children up to 12 years old. Highlights include puppet shows, storytelling, a hands-on silkscreen printing studio and Stuffee—a 7-foot mascot that turns inside-out to teach anatomy.

Allow 2 hours minimum. Mon.-Sat. 10-5, Sun. noon-5, mid-June through Labor Day; Tues.-Sat. 10-5, Sun. noon-5, rest of year. Closed major holidays. Admission $4, senior citizens $3, under 2 free; $2 to all Thurs. Phone (412) 322-5058.

★**PITTSBURGH ZOO** is reached by taking the Highland Park Bridge exit off SR 28, cross the bridge, then going ½ mi. w. on Butler St. and ⅛ mi. s. on Baker St. Zoo exhibits include the Tropical Forest, a fog-shrouded rain forest filled with endangered primates, including gorillas and orangutans; Asian Forest, with Siberian tigers; and African Savanna, with roaming elephants and giraffes. The Aqua Zoo contains a 92,000-gallon shark tank, a living coral reef and penguin exhibit. The insect gallery allows visitors to operate a micro video camera to zoom in for a close-up look at small details on the inhabitants. Niches of the World, with small mammals and reptiles, and Children's Farm also are featured. In all, more than 4,000 animals are displayed in a 77-acre area. Food is available.

Allow 2 hours minimum. Daily 10-6, Memorial Day weekend-Labor Day; 9-5, rest of year. Closed Dec. 25. Admission $5.75; over 59 and ages 2-13, $3. Train ride $1, carrousel ride 75c. Parking $2. To verify prices phone (412) 665-3640.

★**POINT STATE PARK**, 36 acres at the confluence of the Allegheny, Monongahela and Ohio rivers, commemorates the British settlement of this frontier outpost in 1754. In the same year, the French seized the area and built Fort Duquesne. The British regained supremacy in 1758 and erected a new fort, which they named Fort Pitt for William Pitt, prime minister of England and friend of the Colonies.

One of the larger fountains in the United states is a focal point of the Golden Triangle. The water is accented by 24 white and gold lights. The fountain, which reaches heights of 150 feet, operates daily from about Easter to mid-Nov., weather permitting. Park open daily dawn-dusk. Free. Phone (412) 471-0235.

**Fort Pitt Blockhouse**, built in 1764, is all that remains of the original Fort Pitt, the last reminder of the days when Indian, French, British and Colonial troops fought for possession of the point. Tues.-Sat. 9:30-4, Sun. noon-4. Free. Phone (412) 471-1764.

★Fort Pitt Museum, within Point State Park, focuses on the early history of western Pennsylvania and the French and Indian War through models, dioramas, a full-scale reconstructed trader's cabin and artifacts. The museum is in a reproduction of one of the original bastions. An orientation film is shown. The Royal American Regiment performs Sun. at 2:30, mid-June through Labor Day.

Allow 1 hour minimum. Tues.-Sat. 10-4:30, Sun. noon-4:30; closed major holidays, except Memorial Day, July 4 and Labor Day. Admission $4; over 64, $3; ages 6-17, $2. Phone (412) 281-9284.

RODEF SHALOM BIBLICAL BOTANICAL GARDEN, near Carnegie Mellon University at 4905 5th Ave., displays more than 150 varieties of flora—each with a biblical name or reference. The ⅓-acre setting is reminiscent of ancient Israel; a stream flowing through the garden represents the River Jordan. Parking is available behind the synagogue. Allow 30 minutes minimum. Sun.-Thurs. 10-2 (also Wed. 7-9 p.m.), Sat. noon-1, June 1-Sept. 15. Free. Phone (412) 621-6566.

SANDCASTLE, I-376 exit 8, following signs along SR 837, is a water park on the Monongahela River with 15 water slides, a lazy river, a giant hot tub, adult and children's pools, boardwalk, go-karts and a miniature golf course. Food is available. Daily 11-7, weekend after Memorial Day to late Aug. and on Labor Day weekend. Club Wet (pool, hot tub and dancing) are available to adults Wed.-Sun. 6 p.m.-1 a.m. and to minors Mon. 8 p.m.-midnight, late May-Labor Day.

Admission with slide pass $13.95. Admission with pool pass $7.95, senior citizens $4.95, under 3 free. Go-kart track $3.50. Miniature golf $3.50. Adults Fri.-Sat. evenings $3, Wed.-Thurs. and Sun. evenings $1. Minors Mon. evening $7. MC, VI. Phone (412) 462-6666.

SCHENLEY PARK, 456 acres on Schenley Dr., is one of the city's more popular green spaces. Its lake, playground, picnic areas, tennis courts, baseball fields, trails and golf course offer summer recreation; during the winter there are opportunities for ice skating and cross-country skiing. For further information phone (412) 622-6919, 7-3:30.

★Phipps Conservatory, in Schenley Park, covers 2½ acres under glass. Highlights include a Japanese Courtyard Garden, Perennial Garden, Victorian Rose Garden, Aquatic Garden and Children's Garden. During spring and fall, flower shows are open daily 9-5. A special flower show also is presented during Christmas. Guided tours are given Tues.-Sat. at 11 and 1, Sept.-June; Tues.-Sat. at 1, rest of year.

Allow 1 hour minimum. Tues.-Sun. 9-5; closed Thanksgiving, Dec. 25 and the 2 days prior to spring, fall and winter flower shows. Flower show admission $5; over 60, $3.50; ages 2-12, $2.50. Rest-of-year admission $3; over 60 and ages 2-12, $1. Phone (412) 622-6914.

SOLDIERS AND SAILORS MEMORIAL HALL, Fifth Ave. and Bigelow Blvd., honors the memory of veterans of all wars and conflicts. The 1910 building was modeled after one of the seven wonders of the ancient world, the Mausoleum of Halicarnassus. Exhibits feature black military history, Civil War memorabilia, Persian Gulf items, uniforms, photographs and weapons. Film presentations offer insights into American military conflicts and cover topics from the Revolutionary War through the Vietnam War; reservations are required for films or special tours.

Allow 1 hour minimum. Mon.-Fri. 9-4, Sat.-Sun. 1-4; closed Jan. 1, Labor Day, Thanksgiving and Dec. 25. Free. Phone (412) 621-4253.

STEPHEN FOSTER MEMORIAL, on the University of Pittsburgh campus, is dedicated to American music and to Foster, a native of Pittsburgh and composer of some of America's best-loved songs. The west wing houses a library and museum. The auditorium presents concerts, the Three Rivers Shakespeare Festival, University Theatre Department productions and Dear Friends, a program of 19th-century American music.

Library and museum open Mon.-Fri. 9-4; closed university holidays. Guided tours $1.50, senior citizens and students $1. Phone (412) 624-4100 for more information.

## What To Do

### Sightseeing

Visitors who prefer to sightsee on their own should stop at the Greater Pittsburgh Convention & Visitors Bureau's Visitor Information Center at 4 Gateway Center, (412) 281-9222 or (800) 359-0758, or the Mount Washington Center in the Grandview Avenue Branch of the Carnegie Library, (412) 381-5134. Both centers provide brochures and maps of the Golden Triangle and Mount Washington. The Pittsburgh History and Landmarks Foundation, One Station Sq., Suite 450, offers walking tours and bus tours of a range of historical sites in western Pennsylvania; phone (412) 471-5808.

### Bus Tours

GRAY LINE offers three narrated sightseeing tours: Cultural Pittsburgh, Historic Pittsburgh and Pittsburgh and its Rivers. A tour combining Cultural Pittsburgh and Historic Pittsburgh also is available. Tours depart from Station Square; pickups are made at major downtown hotels.

Fares include all applicable admission charges. AE, DS, MC, VI. Reservations are required at least 1 hour prior to departure. Phone (412) 741-2720 or 761-7000.

**The Cultural Pittsburgh Tour** is a 3-hour tour that includes stops at the West End Overlook, affording a view of the Golden Triangle; the Cathedral of Learning at the University of Pittsburgh; and PPG Place downtown. Oakland and other downtown sites are seen en route. Tour departs daily at 1 (combination tour at 9:45), Apr.-Oct. Fare $17; ages 6-11, $8. Combination tour $26; ages 6-11, $13.

**The Historic Pittsburgh Tour** is a 2-hour tour that begins with a ride on the Duquesne Incline to the top of Mount Washington. Other stops include Calvary Church and Point State Park. Historic districts, Millionaires' Row and Three Rivers Stadium are seen en route. Tour departs daily at 9:45, Apr.-Oct. Fare $14; ages 6-11, $7. Combination tour $26; ages 6-11, $13.

**Pittsburgh and its Rivers Tour** is a 5-hour tour consisting of the Historic Pittsburgh tour and a 3-hour cruise on Pittsburgh's three rivers—the Monongahela, Allegheny and Ohio. Tour departs daily at 9:45, June 1-Labor Day. Fare $24; ages 6-11, $12; ages 3-5, $4.50.

### Boat Tours

★**GATEWAY CLIPPER FLEET**, departing from the dock at Station Sq., provides scenic cruises on the city's three rivers. The 1,000-passenger *Majestic*, the 600-passenger *Gateway Party Liner*, the two 400-passenger *Belles* and the 150-passenger *Good Ship Lollipop* provide not only various narrated sightseeing cruises but Lock and Dam Cruises and Twilight Fountain Cruises as well. Dinner and moonlight dance cruises also are available.

Cruises depart daily, Memorial Day weekend-Labor Day; otherwise varies. Narrated sightseeing cruises lasting 2 to 2½ hours cost $8.50; over 60, $7.50; ages 3-12, $5.50. AE, MC, VI. Phone (412) 355-7980.

### Sports and Recreation

That Pittsburghers are avid sports lovers is well known from the city-wide celebrations that followed all the Steelers' Super Bowl victories and the Penguin's Stanley Cup victories. However, the city offers abundant and convenient opportunities for recreational pursuits as well; nearly every imaginable sport or recreational pastime is available. **Boating** is very popular on Pittsburgh's three rivers.

The focus for much recreation is the city and county parks. Frick, Highland and Schenley parks offer ballfields, tennis courts, golf courses and trails for bicycling and hiking. In winter, golf courses and hilly areas are popular for **cross-country skiing**. Information about facilities and current activities in the city parks can be obtained from the City Parks and Recreation Department; phone (412) 255-2676.

Allegheny County's North and South parks have plenty of the above activities, as well as swimming pools, nearby bicycle rentals and **ice skating** in winter, the county fairgrounds (South Park) and game preserves. In addition, North Park's lake offers **fishing**, boating and boat rentals. For more information about county park programs and activities contact Allegheny County Parks; phone (412) 392-8455.

**Bicycling** devotees have the advantage of a city bicycle route that links Highland, Mellon, Frick and Schenley parks. The City Parks and Recreation Department can provide route information; phone (412) 255-2676.

In addition to the courses in the parks, **golf** is available at a number of excellent public courses; consult the telephone directory for listings. Also inquire at your hotel, for some might have a reciprocal golf club agreement for their guests with one of the local private or semiprivate courses.

**Hiking** is popular, as the number of hiking groups and programs attest. The Sierra Club can furnish information about hiking, canoeing and camping in the area. In winter many of the city's hiking paths become **ski** trails. Besides the cross-country skiing provided by the city and county park areas, Allegheny County's Boyce Park, on Old Frankstown Road in Plum Borough, offers a downhill ski area with four tows, a snow-making machine, instruction and equipment rental. Equipment also can be rented at several ski shops, some of which also arrange ski trips and tours; check the telephone directory.

**Horseback riding** is available in South Park. Stables and riding academies are listed in the local telephone directory. Those who would rather watch the ponies than ride one can go to the **harness races** at the Meadows near Washington; phone (412) 225-9300. There is **Thoroughbred** racing throughout the year at Waterford Park near Chester, W. Va., about an hour from Pittsburgh.

**Note:** Policies concerning admittance of children to pari-mutuel betting facilities vary. Phone for information.

Among the **swimming** pools in Allegheny County, those in Boyce, Settler's Cabin and South Park provide waves for those who yearn for the surf. Fee is $3 for the wave pool, $2 for the waveless.

The county has 78 **tennis** courts; the city operates large complexes in Frick, Highland, McKinley, Mellon and Schenley parks. Courts operate on a first-come-first-served basis. Because some require permits, it is a good idea to check with the city or county parks departments first; phone (412) 255-2676, or (412) 392-8455, respectively.

The National Football League's Steelers are a household word among **football** fans; their home games are played at Three Rivers Stadium. The

Pirates are the stars during the **baseball** season. Pro **hockey** is played by the Penguins at the Civic Arena. **Soccer** and **roller hockey** also are popular with the fans. College sports also are big attractions, particularly the games played by the University of Pittsburgh's Panthers.

## Where To Shop

The Golden Triangle is the core of shopping downtown. Most heavily concentrated in the district around Market Square, 5th, 6th, Wood and Smithfield streets, stores range from specialty shops to such major department stores as Kaufmann's, Lazarus and Saks Fifth Avenue. Most of these have branches in the larger suburban shopping malls. PPG Place, at Market Square, offers shopping as well as noontime concerts in summer. High fashion is the emphasis in Oxford Centre, 301 Grant St.

If you are looking for a novel place to shop or browse, try The Strip which offers open-air and storefront shopping along several block of Penn Avenue east of the Convention Center. Purveyors offer fresh produce, meats and fish, specialty imports, bargain basement houseware, cafes and bars.

Farther out are North Hills Village, Northway Mall and Ross Park Mall—all on McKnight Road. With 67, 70 and 180 shops, respectively, the three malls include branches of most of the large department stores. On the Ohio River about 20 minutes from downtown, many Victorian homes in the old community of Sewickley now house antique and specialty shops.

Among Pittsburgh's more popular shopping places are the Shops at Station Square, across the Monongahela River at the south end of the Smithfield Street Bridge. A kaleidoscope of specialty shops, dining spots and pubs occupies the refurbished 1900s terminal complex of the Pittsburgh & Lake Erie Railroad.

The southern suburbs are served by the area's largest mall, the 190-store Century III Mall in West Mifflin. The 122 stores of South Hills Village are off US 19 between Upper St. Clair and Bethel Park. In Bethel Park at the intersection of US 19 and Fort Couch Road, Village Square offers 55 stores, including Loehmann's and Silo. Also in the South Hills off US 19 is The Galleria, which features such specialty stores as Ralph Lauren and Tiffanys.

East of downtown, some of the better known shopping areas are on Walnut Street in lively, very trendy Shadyside, where people watching is as rewarding as the fashion and fancy housewares stores; and at Forbes and Murray avenues in Squirrel Hill, where delicatessens and other specialty food shops predominate.

Of interest in Oakland is S. Craig Street, where remodeled rowhouses contain specialty shops, art galleries and restaurants. Away from the neighborhood scene on US 22 near the Pennsylvania Turnpike is Monroeville Mall; its 180 stores and other establishments are the commercial heart of this suburban region.

## Where To Dine

The gleaming modern structures in the Golden Triangle boast such noted establishments as Stouffer's Top of the Triangle, on the 62nd floor of the USX Tower at 600 Grant St., which adds a panorama of the city to its good food and gracious atmosphere.

Froggy's, at 100 Market St., is as popular as a meeting place as it is for its steaks and chops. A little farther north, at 24th Street and Penn Avenue, is a restored late 19th-century restaurant and bar with a name that tells it all: Brandy's Meeting, Eating, and Drinking Place.

Next to Market Square is PPG Place, a multibuilding, Gothic-style glass complex known for its food court, which offers treats for every palate, from seafood and salads to pastries and ice cream.

A locale with a growing list of interesting dining and drinking emporiums is Station Square, at the south end of the Smithfield Street Bridge. The restored and developed Pittsburgh & Lake Erie terminal complex is a foil for the impressive Grand Concourse, which specializes in fish and seafood but is equally noted for lamb and beef. Among the varied temptations in the complex are the Cheese Cellar, which serves omelettes, quiches, salads and similar fare amid the atmosphere of a European wine cellar, and Tequila Junction, one of the better of the city's Mexican restaurants.

On nearby Mount Washington, the Continental cuisine, panorama and the approach via glass elevator make Christopher's one of Pittsburgh's premier restaurants.

The eastern section of the city harbors some of the better places for ethnic variety. Such Middle Eastern delights as mujaddara, hummus, tabouli and shishkebab are found at Ali Baba, 404 S. Craig St. in Oakland, and Khalil's II, 4757 Baum Blvd., also in Oakland. A block away, at 317 S. Craig St., is Cafe Azure, where the provincial French offerings are gaining wide acclaim.

On the North Side there is good German fare at Max's Allegheny Tavern, an old standby at Middle and Suismon streets. One of the more popular restaurants in the western part of the city is Hyeholde, 190 Hyeholde Dr. off Parkway West; an old home on estatelike grounds, it offers good food in an Old World atmosphere.

There are two ways to find out about the myriad possibilities for dining in Pittsburgh: Consult the newspaper or the comprehensive dining guide in *Pittsburgh* magazine, or ask a resident what's good in the neighborhood. Reservations are recommended during the week and imperative on the weekends. Phone to ascertain hours, since some establishments close for lunch or dinner on certain days.

## Nightlife

Because neighborhood identities have remained stronger in Pittsburgh than in most large cities, a phenomenon that has all but died out elsewhere continues to thrive: the friendly neighborhood bar. Supposedly there is a watering hole for every 1,300 residents, so clearly this is one area where the true Pittsburgh will be revealed. And because there are so many neighborhoods, the real Pittsburgh is as multifarious in nature as any place in the country.

In addition to the bars, which range in style from comfortably seedy to polished-brass-and-fernery Victorian, there are numerous clubs and lounges offering live entertainment. A number of jazz greats hail from Pittsburgh, and the city maintains the tradition with the music at The Balcony on Walnut Street in Shadyside. Christopher's Hall of Fame on Mount Washington is a good spot for conversation as well as for some of the better lounge entertainment in the area.

A number of favorite nightspots feature Top 40 music and rock. Cahoots, in the Green Tree Marriott, is a favorite, as is The Decade, on Atwood Street in Oakland. Chauncy's and Jellyrolls Piano Bar, in Station Square, the Metropol, at 15th and Smallman streets, and The Boardwalk, at 16th Smallman streets, are additional high-energy dance places.

Devotees of country music and dancing will find both at Nashville North, on Saltsburg Road in Plum Borough and Rodeo in Parkway Center. Comedians, both known and aspiring, can be seen at the Funnybone, in Station Square, and 101 Mall Blvd. in Monroeville.

Shadyside has a nightlife style of its own, providing good food, drink and sociability. Cappy's and Mardi Gras are two of the popular nightspots.

Bars close at 2 a.m., and they are crowded fairly early, particularly on weekends. Consult the paper or *Pittsburgh* magazine for what or who is happening where.

**Note:** The mention of any establishment in the preceding sections is for information only and does **not** imply endorsement by AAA.

## Theater and Concerts

Reflecting the city's metamorphosis from industrial behemoth to corporate giant, the city's cultural scene is growing, becoming more varied, more vital and more progressive. This is perhaps most apparent in Pittsburgh's theater offerings.

While as active and excellent as ever, The Carnegie and the universities are no longer alone on the stage. The Pittsburgh Playhouse in Oakland is the site of a wide range of classical and contemporary productions. Contemporary American plays are presented by the City Theatre Company during its October through April season at the New City Theatre in Oakland. The Pittsburgh Public Theatre is now a professional Equity company; it offers classical and modern dramas, including a new play each year.

Among the popular summer series are the productions of the South Park Conservatory Theater. The Three Rivers Shakespeare Festival, held June through August, is a joyous joint effort offering three of the master's works by the City Theatre Company and the University of Pittsburgh Theater.

There are several dinner theaters in the vicinity as well. The Green Tree Marriott and the White Barn Theatre are known for their summer productions. The Fort Pitt Inn leans toward comedy productions.

Dance of many kinds, from folk to the most modern, also is available. As they have for nearly 50 years, the Duquesne University Tamburitzans bring to vivid life the folk dances of Old Europe. The acclaimed Pittsburgh Ballet Theatre performs at the Benedum Center for the Performing Arts October through April. The American Dance Ensemble, the Pittsburgh Black Theatre Dance Ensemble and several other groups stage their productions at the Pittsburgh Playhouse and similar locations.

For orchestral music at its best, the Pittsburgh Symphony has few rivals. This top-flight orchestra packs opulent Heinz Hall September through May for its regular 24-program series, as well as for its Pops, Young Peoples' and Tiny Tots' series. An outdoor courtyard with wrought-iron benches, water sculptures and lunchtime performances by local musicians has been added to Heinz Hall. The Pittsburgh Opera performs at the Benedum Center for the Performing Arts, an opulent restored theater.

Contemporary American music is the specialty of the Pittsburgh New Music Ensemble, which performs at Chatham College Chapel. Free chamber music concerts are held at the Frick Art Museum on Sundays, October through April. The Summer Concert in the Parks series provides a variety of free concerts, including bluegrass, folk and jazz in several of the city parks. At Point Park State Park the American Waterways Wind Orchestra presents concerts, folklorists, plays and puppet shows from a floating barge on the river.

The lavish Benedum Center for the Performing Arts, formerly the Stanley Theatre, is home to the Pittsburgh Opera, Civic Light Opera and Pittsburgh Ballet Theatre and also presents first-run Broadway shows.

These are only a few of the possibilities; *Pittsburgh* magazine and the newspaper carry complete listings.

## Especially for Children

The exhibits at the Pittsburgh Children's Museum are especially designed for youngsters, as are many of the hands-on exhibits at The Carnegie Science Center; the center's sky shows also are popular.

The city's many parks offer green space for youngsters needing room to run. Schenley Park has plenty of recreational facilities as well as the Phipps Conservatory; in Highland Park is that long-standing favorite, the Pittsburgh Zoo.

For a change of pace, a ride on the Duquesne or Monongahela inclines is something that can't be experienced elsewhere, and both provide a grand view of the city. The Gateway Clipper Fleet's *Good Ship Lollipop* offers a sightseeing cruise for youngsters, complete with a clown.

A consideration for a rainy day might be one of several stage presentations for children. Pittsburgh Playhouse Junior in Oakland presents plays September through May; phone (412) 621-4445. During the summer there are outdoor productions at the South Park Conservatory fairgrounds; phone (412) 831-8552. The Pittsburgh Symphony offers concert series for tots and young people.

## Special Events

Runners take to the streets of the city in early May for the Pittsburgh Marathon. In late May the David Lawrence Convention Centre is the scene of the Folk Festival, an extravaganza of international customs, costumes and cuisines. Also in May, the Shadyside Summer Arts Festival attracts artists, craftsmen, browsers and music aficionados from throughout the area.

During most of June, Pittsburgh celebrates the Three Rivers Arts Festival at Gateway Center, Station Square, Market Square and Point State Park: There are programs and productions of just about everything cultural the city has to offer, including art, dance, music, theater and mime. Also held in June is the Mellon Jazz Festival, featuring 10 days of entertainment from top jazz performers.

The Pittsburgh Three Rivers Regatta occurs the first full weekend in August. Oktoberfest, held in late September, is celebrated at Station Square. Nature's seasonal beauty is feted at Phipps Conservatory with three floral celebrations, the spring, fall and holiday flower shows.

---

## PLUMER (E-3)

**PITHOLE CITY**, 1½ mi. n. on SR 227, then 2¼ mi. e. on a paved road, was a flourishing settlement during the oil boom of the late 1860s but was subsequently abandoned as the oil reserves declined. No buildings remain, but cellar holes, streets, a reservoir and abandoned wells still mark the site of the vanished town.

The visitor center has exhibits and a brochure outlining a walking tour; other exhibits and markers are along the tour route. Guided tours are available on Sundays. Allow 1 hour minimum. Thurs.-Sun. 10-5, Wed. noon-5, Memorial Day weekend-Labor Day. Admission $2.50; over 60, $1.50; ages 6-17, 50c. Phone (814) 827-2797.

## POCONO MOUNTAINS
(E-10, E-11, F-10, F-11)

In northeastern Pennsylvania, only a 2-hour drive from New York City or Philadelphia, lie the Pocono Mountains. The 2,400 square miles of wooded hills and valleys with numerous lakes, ponds and clear, rushing rivers are spread across four counties; Carbon, Monroe, Pike and Wayne. Some of the loveliest waterfalls in the East are flanked by blossoming mountain laurel in the spring and brilliant foliage in the fall.

The Poconos are widely known as a recreational and honeymoon resort area. More than 30 golf courses provide challenging sport as well as breathtaking mountain views. Swimming, canoeing, boating and water-skiing can be enjoyed at many of the larger lakes. Lake Wallenpaupack is one of the largest lakes in Pennsylvania. The preseason stocking of lakes and streams insures the region's reputation for good fishing, particularly

for trout. Deer, bear, rabbit, squirrel, pheasant and grouse attract hunters during designated hunting seasons.

More than one million skiers annually pray for snow—the earlier the better—and flock to the Poconos' 13 developed ski areas. Many bargain packages and price specials are offered, particularly during midweek when the slopes are less crowded. Frozen lakes and ponds provide natural ice-skating rinks; cross-county skiing, snowmobiling and camping also are possible; phone (717) 421-5565 for weather and ski reports.

For more information contact the Pocono Mountains Vacation Bureau, 1004 Main St., Stroudsburg, PA 18360; phone (717) 424-6050 or (800) 762-6667. *See color ad p. A210.*

Places in the Pocono Mountains listed under their own headings are Bushkill, Canadensis, Delaware Water Gap National Recreation Area (*see N.J.*), Hamlin, Honesdale, Jim Thorpe, Milford, Mount Pocono, Shawnee on Delaware, Stroudsburg, Tannersville, White Haven and White Mills.

**Shopping areas:** Numerous factory outlet stores make the Pocono Mountains a delight for shoppers. The Pocono Outlet Complex, 9th and Anne streets in Stroudsburg, has 31 stores. The Crossings in Tannersville, I-80 exit 45, following signs, features more than 65 stores, including antique shops, American Tourister, Dansk, Etienne Aigner, London Fog, Oneida, Reebok, Toy Liquidators and Wamsutta.

## POINT MARION (I-2) pop. 1,344, elev. 817'
**FRIENDSHIP HILL NATIONAL HISTORIC SITE** is 3 mi. n. on SR 166. The scenic 340-acre site features the home that Albert Gallatin, treasury

secretary for Presidents Jefferson and Madison, built for his first wife, Sophia Allegre, in 1789. A gazebo, built in the late 1800s, typifies the lifestyle of the country gentleman. Mrs. Gallatin's gravesite is nearby.

Ten miles of nature and hiking trails wind through the site. Festifall, held the last Sunday in September, celebrates the culture of the Allegheny Plateau through food, music and crafts. Picnic facilities and self-guiding audio tours are available; guided tours are offered in summer. Allow 1 hour minimum. Daily 8:30-5; closed Dec. 25. Free. Phone (412) 725-9190.

## POINT PLEASANT (G-12)

Before its settlement in the mid-1700s, Point Pleasant was the site of Indian quarries for argillite, which was used in making arrowheads and knifeblades. Now another natural resource, the Delaware River, provides many recreational opportunities for area visitors and residents. The Bucks County River Tubing and Point Pleasant Canoe Co., which has branches in Point Pleasant and Upper Black Eddy, offers canoe, tube and raft rentals during the summer. Write Point Pleasant Canoe Co., P.O. Box 6, Point Pleasant, PA 18950. Phone (215) 297-8823.

## POTTSTOWN (H-10) pop. 21,800, elev. 144′

As early as 1714, an iron forge was established north of the present site of Pottstown, and ironmaking quickly became the area's principal industry. When Colonial ironmaster John Potts founded the city in 1752, he named it Pottsgrove. Later, in 1815, it was incorporated as Pottstown. The city remains a busy industrial and trade center. For more area information contact the Tri-County Area Chamber of Commerce, 238 High St., Pottstown, PA 19464; phone (215) 326-2900.

**Shopping areas:** Coventry Mall, SR 100 and SR 724, is the major shopping center serving the Pottstown area. It includes Boscov's, Hess's and Sears.

**POTTSGROVE MANOR,** at SR 100 and W. King St., ¾ mi. n. of jct. SR 100 and SR 422 at 100 W. King St., is the restored home of town founder and ironmaster John Potts. Built in 1752, the house contains 18th-century Pennsylvania furnishings. The home features original molding and a dining room, which is considered to be rare in homes built during that period. Allow 1 hour minimum. Tues.-Sat. 10-4, Sun. 1-4; closed major holidays. Free. Phone (610) 326-4014.

**STREITWIESER FOUNDATION TRUMPET MUSEUM** is s. on US 422 to SR 724, ¼ mi. e. on SR 724, then ½ mi. s.w. to 880 Vaughan Rd. Housed in a converted 1860 barn, the museum, purportedly the first in the world devoted to trumpets, contains more than 700 trumpets, tubas, trombones and other brass instruments, spanning 3,000 years. Displays trace the evolution of horns in musical history; also in the col-

lection are color prints, books, recordings, figurines and sheet music.

Excellent acoustics enhance the sound quality of the instruments. Museum open by appointment Tues.-Fri. 10-5, Sun. 1-5. Admission $3.50. Phone (610) 327-1351.

## POTTSVILLE (G-9) pop. 16,600, elev. 636′

Pottsville was named for John Pott, a pioneer ironworker who built a small iron furnace in 1806. The birth of the city coincided with the beginning of the vital iron and steel industry, which prospered for more than a century.

Pottsville also was the gateway to northeastern Pennsylvania's anthracite coal-mining region. Downtown Pottsville sports the 90-foot-high Henry Clay Monument, a memorial to the presidential candidate who supported legislation favorable to the area's coal industry. The monument, built in 1855, is said to be the nation's oldest cast-iron statue.

To ward off the midwinter doldrums, Pottsville holds its annual Winter Carnival from late January to early February. For more event information contact the Schuylkill Chamber of Commerce, 91 S. Progress Ave., Pottsville, PA 17901; phone (717) 622-1942.

**Shopping areas:** Schuylkill Mall, 6 mi. n. on SR 61 or at I-81 exit 36 in Frackville, has about 100 stores, including Bon Ton, Hess's, Kmart, Phar-Mor and Sears.

**YUENGLING BREWERY,** 5th and Mahantongo sts., offers tours of one of America's oldest breweries; it was established in 1829. Visitors observe all facets of the production process and sample the finished product at the tour's end. The many stairways and a few dimly lit areas might present problems for some; sandals and flip-flops are not permitted. Allow 1 hour minimum. Open Mon.-Fri. 9-4; tours depart at 10 and 1:30. Closed major holidays. Free. Phone (717) 628-4890.

## PUNXSUTAWNEY (F-3) pop. 6,800, elev. 1,236′

Each Feb. 2, the nation awaits the prognostication of one of Punxsutawney's most respected citizens: Punxsutawney Phil—the official groundhog of Groundhog Day. As they have each year since 1887, believers trek at dawn to Gobbler's Knob in Sportsman's Park and rout the rodent from his den to determine whether there will be an early spring. The legend that the groundhog's seeing his shadow on Candlemas Day (Feb. 2) presages 6 more weeks of winter was brought to this country by the German immigrants who settled the area.

Phil is honored not only on Groundhog Day but also by a life-size statue and a groundhog zoo at the Mahoning East Civic Center, a festival during the week of July 4, a Groundhog Festival each June and the Punxsutawney Groundhog Club, whose membership numbers in the thousands. For more area information contact the chamber of commerce, 124 W. Mahoning St., Punxsutawney, PA 15767; phone (814) 938-7700 or (800) 752-7445.

### QUARRYVILLE (I-9) pop. 1,600, elev. 488'

South of Quarryville on US 222 is the restored stone house where artist, inventor and engineer Robert Fulton was born in 1765. His drawings, miniature portraits and invention models, including the steamship *Clermont,* are on exhibit on weekends during the summer.

### READING (H-10) pop. 78,400, elev. 237'

Thomas and Richard Penn, sons of William Penn, founded Reading in 1748 and named it for their ancestral home in England. The settlement was a supply base for forts along the Blue Mountains during the French and Indian War. In Reading originated the first Civil War regiment, volunteer band, flag and women's aid society. Modern Reading has become a major industrial center, with many clothing manufacturers maintaining retail outlet stores in or near the city.

Reading contains a wealth of 18th- and 19th-century buildings, many noted for their elaborate use of decorative glass and wrought iron. Penn Square, the centerpiece of the city as laid out by the brothers Penn, remains the heart of downtown Reading; historic buildings now house stores and other businesses, and special activities take place on the landscaped pedestrian mall.

Reading has three historic districts: the Callowhill district, which centers on the city's commercial area; the nearby Prince district, which contains well-preserved 19th-century workers' homes, factories and commercial structures; and Centre Park, which displays some of the city's finest Victorian structures.

On the east side of Reading on the summit of Mount Penn is the Pagoda, a seven-story 1900s Japanese-style building that affords panoramas of the city and the Schuylkill Valley. About 7 miles northwest via SR 183 is the Blue Marsh Lake Recreation Area *(see Recreation Chart).*

Among the special events that take place in Reading are the Berks Jazz Fest, a 4-day music festival held at a variety of locations throughout the city in late March; the Berks County Antique Show, held in early August; and the Centre Park Historic Building Tour, an evening tour of decorated mansions held in early December. For more event information contact the Reading and Berks County Visitors Bureau, P.O. Box 6677, Reading, PA 19610; phone (800) 443-6610 *(see color ad).*

**Shopping areas:** The Reading area is known for outlet shopping and features five factory outlet complexes that carry name-brand items ranging from clothing and lingerie to baked goods and potato chips. The five complexes are Manu-facturers Outlet Mall (MOM), SR 10 at I-76 exit 22; The Outlets on Hiesters Lane, 700-800 Hiesters Ln.; Reading Outlet Center, which occupies an entire block between Windsor and Douglass streets; Reading Station, 951 N. 6th St.; and VF Factory Outlet, US 422 and Park Road *(see color ad p. A217).*

Although better known for its outlet stores, Reading also offers two other major shopping centers. Berkshire Mall, Bern Road off US 422W Bypass, features Sears and Wanamakers. Fairground Square, 2 miles north of Reading on US 222, has Boscov's and JCPenney.

**BERKS COUNTY HERITAGE CENTER** (Gruber Wagon Works), 5 mi. n.w. via SR 183 and Red Bridge Rd., is a restored late 19th-century wagon works. From 1882 to 1972, craftsmen fashioned wagons for farm and industrial use. Original tools and equipment are on display, and a short videotape presentation is offered. Crossing the grounds is the 5-mile-long Union Canal biking and walking trail; nearby is Wertz' Bridge, the longest single-span covered bridge in Pennsylvania.

The heritage center also contains the C. Howard Heister Canal Center, with displays about the history of transportation on the Union and Schuylkill canals. Allow 2 hours minimum. Tues.-Sat. and Mon. holidays 10-4, Sun. noon-5, May 1 to late Oct. Admission $2.50; over 60, $2; ages 7-18, $1.50. Phone (610) 374-8839.

**HISTORICAL SOCIETY OF BERKS COUNTY,** 940 Centre Ave., contains displays that depict local history, including fine arts, industry, transportation and Pennsylvania German arts and crafts. Highlights include the county liberty bell that was rung July 8, 1776, the Dieffenbach organ, a Conestoga wagon and a 1902 Duryea automobile. A hands-on children's museum also is featured.

Allow 1 hour minimum. Tues.-Sat. 9-4; closed holidays and holiday weekends. Admission

$2.50; senior citizens $2; ages 5-12, $1. Library $3. Phone (610) 375-4375.

**MARY MERRITT DOLL MUSEUM**, 10 mi. e. on US 422, has rare and quaint dolls dating from about 1725 to the present. Allow 1 hour minimum. Mon.-Sat. 10-4:30, Sun. 1-5; closed major holidays. Admission, including Merritt's Museum of Childhood, $3; over 60, $2.50; ages 5-12, $1.50. Phone (610) 385-3809.

**Merritt's Museum of Childhood** exhibits papers belonging to William Penn, antique toys, children's carriages, china, glassware and Pennsylvania Dutch pottery and quilts. Indian baskets, artifacts and pottery also are on display. Two rooms furnished in period reflect the 1780s. Allow 1 hour minimum. Mon.-Sat. 10-4:30, Sun. and holidays 1-5; closed major holidays. Phone (610) 385-3408.

**MID-ATLANTIC AIR MUSEUM**, SR 183 to the Reading Regional Airport, following signs, displays both military and civilian aircraft, including a 1944 Douglas DC-3 and a North American B-25 Mitchell. Of special interest is the first night fighter ever built: The 1944 Black Widow Night Fighter P-61B is one of four remaining in the world. The museum also features two classic commercial airliners, a Martin IV-O-IV and a Capitol Airways Viscount.

Allow 1 hour minimum. Daily 9:30-4; closed major holidays. Admission $5; ages 6-12, $2. MC, VI. Phone (610) 372-7333.

**READING PUBLIC MUSEUM**, 500 Museum Rd., presents art, science and history displays ranging from pre-historic times to the present. Changing exhibits, sculptural gardens and a planetarium also are featured. Open Wed.-Sat. 10-4, Sun. noon-4. Planetarium shows Sun. at 2 and 3. Closed Dec. 25. Admission $3; ages 4-17, $2. Phone (610) 371-5850.

## RED ROCK (E-9)

**RICKETTS GLEN STATE PARK** is 4 mi. n. on SR 487. In the Glens Natural Area, 22 waterfalls are formed as Kitchen Creek winds through two deep gorges. There are 21 miles of hiking trails in the park; 7 miles follow the course of Kitchen Creek. Other activities include snowmobiling, boating, fishing, camping, picnicking and swimming. Daily 8-dusk. Free; camping/cabin fee. Phone (717) 477-5675. *See Recreation Chart and the AAA Mideastern CampBook.*

## ROARING SPRING (H-5) pop. 2,600, elev. 1,200'

**BARE MEMORIAL FOUNTAIN** is in the basin of the spring for which the town of Roaring Spring was named. Varicolored sprays of water rise to a height of 25 feet. It operates Wed. 6-11 p.m. and usually all day Sat.-Sun., mid-Apr. until freezing weather. Phone (814) 224-5141.

## ROCKHILL FURNACE (H-6) pop. 400

**EAST BROAD TOP RAILROAD**, in Orbisonia, 1/4 mi. w. of jct. SR 994 and US 522, offers rail excursions on a vintage 1873 narrow-gauge steam train. The 10-mile, 50-minute round trip winds through the Pennsylvania countryside. Picnic facilities are near the station and at Colgate Grove, the turn-around point; passengers may disembark and reboard a later run. Tours through railroad shop yards also are available. Allow 1 hour minimum. Train runs Sat.-Sun., June 1-Columbus Day weekend; phone for schedule updates. Fare $9; ages 2-11, $6. Phone (814) 447-3011.

**Rockhill Trolley Museum**, across from the East Broad Top Railroad, chronicles the history of the trolley through photographs and various displays. Excursions on trolleys dating from the 1890s are offered. Open Sat. 10:30-5, Sun. 10:30-4, Memorial Day weekend-Oct. 31. Admission $3; ages 2-11, $1. MC, VI. Phone (814) 447-9576.

## ST. BONIFACE (G-5)

**SELDOM SEEN INC.**, off SR 36, offers electric train rides that carry visitors into an underground coal mine to learn about the past, present and future of coal mining. Tours include a theater presentation, a walk through a museum and the mine trip. Food is available. Allow 2 hours minimum. Daily 10-6, Memorial Day weekend-Labor Day. Admission $6; senior citizens $5.40; ages 3-12, $4.50. Phone (814) 948-4444.

## ST. MARYS (E-5) pop. 5,500, elev. 1,702'

St. Marys was founded in 1842 by a group of persecuted German Catholics from Philadelphia and Baltimore. The city is a center of light industry, dairying and farming. For more area information contact the chamber of commerce, 126 Center St., St. Marys, PA 15857; phone (814) 781-3804.

**STRAUB BREWERY**, 303 Sorg St., was founded in 1872. One of the smaller breweries in the country, Straub distributes only in Pennsylvania and eastern Ohio. Under age 12 are not permitted on tours. Allow 30 minutes minimum. Free tours and tastings Mon.-Fri. 9-noon; phone ahead for tour information. Closed holidays. Phone (814) 834-2875.

## SCHAEFFERSTOWN (H-9) elev. 491'

**MIDDLE CREEK WILDLIFE MANAGEMENT AREA**, 2 mi. e. on SR 897, then 2 mi. s. of Kleinfeltersville on Hopeland Rd., is administered by the Pennsylvania Game Commission. The 5,000-acre area, which includes a visitor center, provides a habitat for waterfowl and wildlife. The visitor center is open Tues.-Sat. 8-4, Sun. noon-5, Mar.-Nov.; closed July 4. Wildlife area open daily dawn-dusk. Free. Phone (717) 733-1512.

## SCHNECKSVILLE (G-10) elev. 669'

**TREXLER-LEHIGH COUNTY GAME PRESERVE** is 2 mi. w. on Game Preserve Rd. Its 1,500 acres contain about 50 animal species, including buffalo, elk, deer and palomino horses. A 25-acre petting zoo is on the grounds. Food is available. Picnicking is permitted. Pets are not permitted. Allow 1 hour minimum. Daily 10-5, Memorial Day weekend-Labor Day; Sat.-Sun. 10-5, May 1-day before Memorial Day weekend; Sun. 10-5, day after Labor Day to late Oct. Admission $3; over 60 and ages 2-12, $1.50. Phone (610) 799-4171.

## SCOTTDALE (H-2) pop. 5,200, elev. 1,050'

**WEST OVERTON MUSEUMS** are 1 mi. n. on SR 819. The complex includes the 1859 "Old Farm" distillery and gristmill, the 1838 Abraham Overholt Homestead, and Springhouse—the birthplace of industrialist Henry Clay Frick. The museums' displays reflect life in a 19th-century rural-industrial village. The 30-minute film "Pillars of Fire," about coke-making operations, is presented regularly.

Guided tours and archives are available. Allow 1 hour, 30 minutes minimum. Tues.-Sat. 10-4, Sun. 1-5, mid-May to mid-Oct. Admission $2.50; ages 7-12, $1. Phone (412) 887-7910.

## SCRANTON (E-10) pop. 81,800, elev. 753'

Four anthracite blast furnaces built in the 1840s and 1850s by the Scranton brothers initiated the growth of Scranton and the area's iron and coal industries. By the end of World War II, the decline of the anthracite industry, due to competition from other fuels, resulted in the development of the Scranton Plan. This plan for revitalizing the economy served as a model for other communities with similar problems.

Scranton has restored parts of its historic downtown as well. At 700 Lackawanna Ave. (I-81 exit 53) is the 1906 Lackawanna Station, a former railroad depot that has been restored and converted into a hotel. Many of the original features of the imposing French Renaissance building have been preserved, including the exterior Indiana limestone facade and the interior Siena marble walls and brass fixtures.

The Suraci and Contemporary galleries at Marywood College, feature paintings, sculpture, prints and photographs. Theater, concerts and musical presentations also are offered throughout the year; phone (717) 348-6207. For more area information contact the chamber of commerce, 222 Mulberry St., P.O. Box 431, Scranton, PA 18501; phone (717) 342-7711.

Recreational opportunities can be found at nearby Lackawanna State Park *(see Recreation Chart)*. Downhill skiing is available at Montage, off I-81 exit 51 at Montage Road and Davis Street. The Lackawanna County Stadium, also off I-81 exit 51, is below Montage Mountain.

The 10,000-seat facility presents sports events, concerts, festivals and outdoor theater; for baseball fans, it hosts the AAA league Scranton/Wilkes-Barre Red Barons from April through August.

**Shopping areas:** One of Scranton's major shopping centers is Viewmont Mall, on US 6 off I-81 exit 57A. Nearby Eynon Plaza, on US 6, is a factory outlet complex. Sugerman's, also on US 6, is another popular store. Boscov's, the Globe Store, and Montgomery Ward anchor more than 70 specialty stores in downtown Scranton in The Mall at Steamtown, at Lackawanna and Penn avenues.

**ANTHRACITE MUSEUM COMPLEX** consists of four sites: the Pennsylvania Anthracite Heritage Museum in McDade Park, the Iron Furnaces in downtown Scranton, the Museum of Anthracite Mining *(see Ashland)* and Eckley Miners' Village *(see Hazleton)*.

**Pennsylvania Anthracite Heritage Museum** is in McDade Park, 4½ mi. s. from I-81 exit 57B (North Scranton Expwy.); take Keyser Ave. exit off the expressway, following signs. The museum is dedicated to collecting, interpreting and preserving the history and culture of Pennsylvania's hard-coal region. Exhibits feature the immigrants' cultures, ethnic diversity and religion as well as their impact on the region.

Allow 1 hour minimum. Mon.-Sat. 9-5, Sun. noon-5; closed holidays. Admission $3.50; over 60, $2.50; ages 6-17, $1.50. Phone (717) 963-4804. *See color ad.*

**Scranton Iron Furnaces,** Cedar Ave. between Lackawanna Ave. and Moosic St., are four stone smokestacks of blast furnaces built in the 1840s and 1850s. These furnaces were the catalyst for development of the city; in the 1860s they were the second largest producers of iron in the nation. Daily 8 a.m.-dusk. Phone (717) 963-3208.

**EVERHART MUSEUM,** in Nay Aug Park at the e. end of Mulberry St., houses permanent exhibitions of American Folk, Native American, Oriental and primitive art. Other displays include

Dorflinger glass, a dinosaur hall, bird collection and a living beehive. The museum also presents changing exhibits, lectures and educational programs. Tues.-Fri. 10-5, Sat.-Sun. noon-5; closed major holidays. Donations. Phone (717) 346-8370.

LACKAWANNA COAL MINE TOUR is next to the Pennsylvania Anthracite Heritage Museum, 4½ mi. s. from I-81 exit 57B (North Scranton Expwy.); take Keyser Ave. exit off the expressway and follow signs to McDade Park. Visitors are taken via railcar 300 feet underground to the floor of the coal mine, then on a guided walking tour through the mine's three veins.

Underground temperatures remain at a constant 55 degrees Fahrenheit; jackets are available on loan. Above ground, the Shifting Shanty exhibit room has photomural displays, mining relics and a videotape presentation. Allow 1 hour minimum. Daily 11-4:30, Apr.-Nov. Fee $5; ages 3-12, $3.50. DS, MC, VI. Phone (717) 963-MINE or (800) 238-7245. *See color ad p. A221.*

MONTAGE SKI AND SUMMER RECREATION AREA, I-81 exit 51, has a 130-acre ski area with 20 trails, five lifts, 2 handle tows and snowmakers. Ski season runs November through April, weather permitting. Summer facilities include two waterslides and a tube slide that end with a splash in a deep pool. Summer concerts and dramas also are presented. For schedule and prices phone (717) 969-7669 or (800) GOT-SNOW.

STEAMTOWN NATIONAL HISTORIC SITE is on S. Washington Ave. (I-81 exit 53) in the former Delaware, Lackawanna and Western railyards, opposite the Chamberlain Ammunition Plant. This historic site commemorates the history of steam railroads 1850-1950 through one of the country's larger collections of period locomotives and rolling stock.

In this former transportation crossroads, visitors can see such steam locomotives as the Union Pacific 4012 "Big Boy," one of the world's larger, the Nickel Plate 759 "Bershire" and the Boston & Maine 3713 "Pacific," as well as a railway post office car, a caboose and a railroad exhibit car. Besides tours of the railyard and roundhouse, visitors can enjoy a steam train excursion during the summer and in October.

Currently under development, a visitor center and museum complex will complement the existing remnant of the original roundhouse and tell the story of American steam railroading. Until its completion in mid-1995, the park's visitor center is in the office/storage building at 150 S. Washington Ave., one block from The Mall at Steamtown.

The site is open daily 9-5; closed Jan. 1, Thanksgiving and Dec. 25. Site free. For excursion fares and reservations phone (717) 961-2035. *See color ad p. A221.*

## SHARON (E-1) pop. 17,500, elev. 854'

Evolving from a mill built on the Shenango River in 1802, Sharon is an industrial city that produces steel and steel products. For more area information contact the Shenango Valley Chamber of Commerce, 1 W. State St. Sharon, PA 16146; phone (412) 981-5880.

Shopping areas: Reyers, US 62, stocks more than 200,000 pairs of shoes and carries 300 name brands. The Winner, also on US 62, is a four-story women's clothing store.

DAFFIN'S CANDIES CHOCOLATE KINGDOM, ½ mi. e. at 496 E. State St., features large animals sculptured from chocolate, including a 700-pound rabbit and a 400-pound turtle. Numerous other unique chocolate creations are displayed, and candy-making demonstrations are available by reservation. Allow 30 minutes minimum. Mon.-Sat. 9-9, Sun. 11-5. Free. Phone (412) 342-2892.

## SHARTLESVILLE (G-9)

ROADSIDE AMERICA, on US 22 via the Shartlesville exit from I-78, is an extensive exhibit of several miniature villages and towns depicting the growth and development of rural America. The 8,000-square-foot exhibit includes model trains that represent more than a half-century's work on the part of the builder.

Allow 1 hour minimum. Daily 9-6:30, July 1-Labor Day; Mon.-Fri. 10-5, Sat.-Sun. 10-6, rest of year. Closed Dec. 25. Admission $3.75; ages 6-11, $1.25. Phone (610) 488-6241.

## SHAWNEE ON DELAWARE (F-12)

SHAWNEE PLACE PLAY AND WATER PARK, 5 mi. n. of I-80 exit 52 (Marshalls Creek) on US 209, following signs, is an elaborate outdoor play area geared toward ages 3 to 13. Daily magic shows are featured. Attractions include a chairlift ride, a waterslide, wading pool and video games, as well as a punch-bag forest, cable glide, net climb, cloud bounce, ball crawl and an adventure river ride. Picnicking is permitted.

Daily 10-5, Memorial Day weekend-Labor Day; chairlift noon-4 (weather permitting). Admission $10, adult spectators $5, under 40 inches tall free. AE, DS, MC, VI. Phone (717) 421-7231.

## SLIPPERY ROCK (F-2) pop. 3,200

The Old Stone House, built about 1822, is 4 miles south of Slippery Rock near the junction of SRs 173 and 528. The restored tavern and stagecoach stop is furnished in period. The Slippery Rock University History Department offers tours of the house Fri.-Sun., mid-Apr. to mid-Oct.; phone (412) 738-2053.

JENNINGS ENVIRONMENTAL EDUCATION CENTER, 4 mi. s. at SRs 8, 173 and 528, protects remnants of a prairie ecological system that dates back 6,000 years, when a major prairie extended out of the Midwest into Pennsylvania. The system contains a stand of blazing star, a rare, wild prairie flower that blooms in late July. Maple sugaring demonstrations begin in mid-March. Allow 30 minutes minimum. Educational center open Mon.-Fri. 8-4, Sat.-Sun. hours vary; grounds open daily dawn-dusk. Free. Phone (412) 794-6011.

## SOMERSET (H-3) pop. 6,500, elev. 2,250'

**SOMERSET HISTORICAL CENTER** is 4 mi. n. at SRs 601 and 985. The center examines southwestern Pennsylvania's rural life 1750-1950. A re-created farm includes a maple sugar camp, covered bridge and exhibit halls that contain relics and machinery from western Pennsylvania.

Tours begin in the exhibit hall with a 12-minute film about the history of the mountain barrier area. Guides demonstrate period tools and other items. Mountain Craft Days, held in mid-September, gathers more than 100 local artisans who demonstrate such skills as blacksmithing, charcoal making, coopering and apple butter making. Allow 1 hour minimum.

Exhibit hall and library open Tues.-Sat. 9-5, Sun. noon-5; other buildings daily 9-5, mid-Apr. to early Dec. Admission $3.50; over 64, $2.50; ages 7-12, $1.50. Phone (814) 445-6077.

## SPRINGS (I-3)

**SPRINGS MUSEUM,** on SR 669, depicts the lives of Casselman Valley settlers in the mid-18th century. Three buildings house domestic, farm and shop relics. Displays include an early schoolroom, post office, country store and barn. The Springs Folk Festival takes place in early October. Allow 1 hour minimum. Wed.-Sat. 1-5, Memorial Day weekend-early Oct.; by appointment, rest of year. Admission $1.50. Phone (814) 662-2625.

## SPRUCE CREEK (G-6) elev. 777'

**INDIAN CAVERNS,** 4 mi. n.e. on SR 45, contain limestone formations and Indian artifacts. The caverns are electrically lighted. Allow 1 hour minimum. Guided tours daily 9-6, Memorial Day weekend-Labor Day; daily 9-4, Apr. 1-day before Memorial Day and day after Labor Day-Oct. 31; Sat.-Sun. 9-4, rest of year. Closed Dec. 25. Admission $7.50; ages 6-12, $3.75. **Discount.** Phone (814) 632-7578.

## STATE COLLEGE (G-6) pop. 38,900, elev. 1,174'

Farmers High School was founded in the rich Nittany Valley near the geographic center of the state in 1855. The school, established to teach methods of soil conservation, became the Agricultural College of Pennsylvania in 1862, then Pennsylvania State College in 1874. The town of State College was created in 1874 by the incorporation of the two connecting townships of Benner and Harris. Additional area information is available at the local chamber of commerce, 131 S. Fraser St., State College, PA 16801; phone (814) 237-7644.

**PENNSYLVANIA STATE UNIVERSITY,** in the scenic Nittany Mountains, is noted for its large, attractive campus. For tour information contact the office of University Relations; phone (814) 865-2501.

Note: Visitors' parking is provided for a fee Mon.-Fri. until 9 p.m. (central campus) and until 5 p.m. (other areas). Metered and permit parking is available Mon.-Fri. after 5 p.m., west of Atherton Street and east of Shortlidge Road (except Eisenhower Parking Deck). Most areas do not charge Sat.-Sun. Permits are available at parking kiosks Mon.-Fri. 7 a.m.-9 p.m.

**College of Agriculture Sciences** welcomes visitors to the dairy, beef and sheep research center, deer pens, creamery and flower gardens. Allow 30 minutes minimum. Mon.-Fri. 8-5. Most facilities free.

**Earth and Mineral Sciences Museum,** in the Edward Steidle Building, contains gemstones, minerals, fossils and mineral industries-related art. Allow 30 minutes minimum. Mon.-Fri. 9-4; closed university holidays, Jan. 1. and Dec. 25-31. Free. Phone (814) 865-6427.

**Frost Entomological Museum,** Curtin Rd., houses more than 500,000 insects, including mounted, live, land and aquatic specimens. There are numerous exhibits, photographs and models. Guided tours are available on request. Allow 30 minutes minimum. Mon.-Fri. 9:30-4:30; closed major holidays. Free. Phone (814) 863-2865.

**Old Main,** one of the older buildings on the campus, was built 1857-63 and rebuilt 1929-30. It contains the Land Grant Mural, by American scene painter Henry Varnum Poor. Mon.-Fri. 8-5; closed holidays. Free. Phone (814) 865-7517.

**Palmer Museum of Art,** Curtin Rd., offers guided tours by appointment. Allow 30 minutes minimum. Tues.-Sat. 10-4:30, Sun. noon-4; closed holidays. Free. Phone (814) 865-7672.

**Penn State Football Hall of Fame,** McKean Rd. in the Greenberg Sports Complex, exhibits memorabilia of the Penn State Nittany Lions football teams, the Heisman trophy and photographs of former players. Allow 30 minutes minimum. Mon.-Fri. 8:30-4:30, Sat.-Sun. 11-3 (Sat. hours might vary during home football games); closed during semester breaks. Free. Phone (814) 865-0411.

**Penn State Room University Archives,** in the Pattee Library, offers a nostalgic look at campus history. Exhibits dating from 1855 include publications, photographs, artwork and furniture. Allow 30 minutes minimum. Mon.-Fri. 8-5, Sat. 9-1; closed major holidays. Free. Phone (814) 865-2112.

## STRASBURG (I-9) pop. 2,600

Though first settled by French Huguenots, Strasburg evolved into a community of German immigrants in the Pennsylvania Dutch Country (see place listing). The town is noted for its quaint atmosphere and the availability of Amish food, arts and crafts.

**THE AMISH VILLAGE,** 2 mi. n. on SR 896, 1 mi. s. of US 30, contains an 1840 house furnished in the Old-Order Amish style. In 20- to 25-minute educational tours, guides explain the history, clothing, furniture and Amish way of life. Other buildings include a barn, schoolhouse, blacksmith shop, store and springhouse. Picnicking is permitted. Daily 9-6, June 10-Labor Day; 9-5, March 11-June 9 and day after Labor Day-Oct. 30; 9-4, Nov.-Dec.; otherwise varies, weather permitting. Closed Mon.-Thurs. Thanksgiving week and Dec. 25. Admission $5.50; ages 6-12, $1.50. Phone (717) 687-8511. See ad p. A151.

**CHOO CHOO BARN, TRAINTOWN, U.S.A.,** e. on SR 741, is a 1,700-square-foot miniature display of Lancaster County and the Pennsylvania Dutch Country. The exhibit has 14 operating toy trains and more than 135 animated and automated figures and vehicles, as well as miniatures of many area landmarks. Allow 1 hour minimum. Daily 10-5:30, June 1-day before Labor Day; 10-4:30, Apr.-May and Labor Day-Dec. 31. Closed Jan. 1, Thanksgiving and Dec. 25. Admission $3; ages 5-12, $1.50. **Discount.** Phone (717) 687-7911.

**GAST CLASSIC MOTORCARS EXHIBIT,** 2½ mi. s. of US 30 or ½ mi. n. of SR 741 on SR 896, displays some 50 vintage vehicles ranging from an 1875 Studebaker Conestoga wagon to Michael Jackson's Rolls Royce Silver Shadow II. Other rare and classic cars exhibited are the first and last MG sports cars imported into the United States; a 1981 Lamborghini Countach; an A.C. Cobra 427; a 1957 Chevrolet BelAir convertible; a 1966 German Amphicar, an amphibious car that came with an anchor and rope as standard equipment; and a 1948 Tucker Torpedo, one of only 51 produced, as seen in the 1988 film "Tucker: The Man and His Dream."

Allow 30 minutes minimum. Daily 9-9, Memorial Day weekend-Labor Day; 9-5 (also Fri.-Sat. 5-9), Apr. 1-day before Memorial Day and day after Labor Day-Oct. 31; 9-5 (also Sat. 5-9), rest of year. Closed Jan. 1, Easter, Thanksgiving and Dec. 24-25. Admission $6; ages 7-12, $3.50. Phone (717) 687-9500.

**RAILROAD MUSEUM OF PENNSYLVANIA,** 1 mi. e. on SR 741, traces the history of railroads in Pennsylvania through restored locomotives, railcars and memorabilia. The museum takes visitors from the colorful era of 19th-century woodburning engines to modern streamliners. Exhibits include steam, diesl and electric locomotives, and passenger and freight cars. There are more than 15 cars and about 12 engines, as well as a re-created railroad station. Walking tours of the railyard are available in summer.

Allow 1 hour, 30 minutes minimum. Mon.-Sat. 9-5, Sun. noon-5, May-Oct.; Tues.-Sat. 9-5, Sun. noon-5, rest of year. Closed Jan. 1, Thanksgiving and Dec. 25. Admission $6; over 60 $5; ages 6-17, $4. Phone (717) 687-8628.

**SIGHT & SOUND ENTERTAINMENT CENTRE,** 2 mi. s. of US 30 on SR 896, presents elaborate stage productions of a biblical nature. Several productions take place throughout the early Mar.-early Jan. season. Phone for titles, show times and exact prices. Allow 2 hours minimum. Admission $21.50-$35; ages 3-12, $15.50-$35. AE, DS, MC, VI. Reservations are required. Phone (717) 687-7800.

**STRASBURG COUNTRY STORE AND CREAMERY,** Center Sq., is an early general store in a restored 18th-century building. Features include hand-carved counters and cabinets, old tins, a pot-bellied stove and an 1890 marble and silver soda fountain. Mon.-Sat. 8 a.m.-10 p.m., Sun. 11-8, Memorial Day weekend-Labor Day; daily 8-5, rest of year. Free. Phone (717) 687-0766. See ad p. A151.

**STRASBURG RAIL ROAD CO.,** 1 mi. e. on SR 741, provides a scenic 45-minute round trip through Amish country on America's oldest short line, which was chartered in 1832. Steam locomotives and wooden passenger cars are on display at the depot. Santa Claus rides the train with passengers in December. Picnicking is permitted.

Allow 1 hour minimum. Trips daily, Apr.-Oct. and Dec. 26-31; Sat.-Sun. (weather permitting), Jan. 14-Mar. 26 and Dec. 2-24. Fare $7.25; ages 3-11, $4. Phone (717) 687-7522. *See ad p. 108.*

**TOY TRAIN MUSEUM,** 1½ mi. e. on SR 741 and ¼ mi. n. on Paradise Ln., displays antique and 20th-century toy trains. Five operating layouts can be viewed. A videotape about toy trains also is presented. Allow 1 hour minimum. Daily 10-5, May-Oct.; Sat.-Sun. 10-5 in Apr. and Nov.-Dec. Admission $3; over 65, $2.75; ages 5-12, $1.50. **Discount.** Phone (717) 687-8976.

**THE VILLAGE GREENS,** 1445 Penn Grant Rd., features two miniature golf courses in a garden setting. Streams stocked with fish meander through the courses. A Christmas Spectacular, held early to mid-December, features a Christmas village and light show. Allow 2 hours minimum. Mon.-Thurs. 10-10, Fri.-Sat. and holidays 10 a.m.-11 p.m., Sun. noon-10, June-Aug.; Mon.-Thurs. 10-9, Fri.-Sat. 10-10, Sun. noon-9 in May and Sept.; Mon.-Thurs. 10-7, Fri.-Sat. 10-10, Sun. noon-7 in Apr. and Oct. The 23-hole course $5.25; under 12, $5. The 18-hole course $4; under 12, $3.75. Phone (717) 687-6933.

**STROUDSBURG (F-11) pop. 5,300, elev. 420'**

Col. Jacob Stroud, who served in the French and Indian War, settled in what is now Stroudsburg in 1769. Because of the strategic location 3 miles west of the Delaware Water Gap, Fort Penn was built around his home in 1776. Two years later the post sheltered refugees from the Wyoming Massacre *(see Wilkes-Barre)*. The town was formally established in 1799, when Stroud and his son sold lots in their spaciously platted townsite.

The 1795 Stroud Mansion, built by the colonel for his son, still stands at 9th and Main streets; it serves as headquarters for the Historical Society of Monroe County. The Quiet Valley Harvest Festival is held in mid-October and includes needlecrafts, candle dipping, woodworking, beekeeping, bread baking and basket making. For more event information contact the Pocono Mountains Vacation Bureau, 1004 Main St., Stroudsburg, PA 18360; phone (717) 424-6050.

★**QUIET VALLEY LIVING HISTORICAL FARM,** 3½ mi. s.w. on US 209 Business Route, then 1½ mi., following signs, is a re-created Pennsylvania-German farm that dates from 1765. Costumed guides conduct 1½-hour tours. Crafts are demonstrated daily. The farm is open for the Farm Animal Frolic the last two weekends in May, and for the Harvest Festival Columbus Day

weekend. Open Mon.-Sat. 9:30-5:30, Sun. 1-5:30, June 20-Labor Day. Last tour departs 1 hour, 30 minutes before closing. Admission $6; over 61, $5; ages 3-12, $3.50. **Discount.** Phone (717) 992-6161.

**SUNBURY (F-8) pop. 11,600, elev. 446'**

Sunbury, on Shamokin Creek and the Susquehanna River, was the site of Pennsylvania's largest frontier fort, Fort Augusta. The powder magazine from the 1756 fort still stands. The Hunter House, 1150 N. Front St., contains a research library and exhibits pertaining to the fort.

Sunbury boasted one of the world's first three-wire, central-station, incandescent electric lighting plants. It was built by Thomas Edison in 1883. The plant was treated with much suspicion by the townspeople, most of whom were afraid to cross the threshold to look inside.

At S. Second Street are the Blue Bird Gardens, featuring a variety of trees, azaleas and rhododendrons. The gardens reach peak bloom March through May. On SR 147 is the Shikellamy Marina & Fabridam, where a 3,000-acre lake is formed by what is said to be the world's largest inflatable dam. For more area information contact the local chamber of commerce, US 11/15, Shamokin Dam, PA 17876; phone (717) 743-4100.

**Shopping areas:** Susquehanna Valley Mall, on US 11/15, is the main local shopping center. Its major stores are The Bon Ton, Boscov's and JCPenney.

**TANNERSVILLE (F-11) elev. 1,276'**

**CAMELBACK ALPINE SLIDE AND WATERSLIDE** is 3½ mi. n.w. of I-80 exit 45, following signs. The slide includes a scenic chairlift to the top of Camelback Ski Area in Big Pocono State Park and a 3,200-foot alpine slide. The chairlift affords excellent views of the Pocono Mountains region. Waterslides, bumper boats, go-karts, a carrousel, kiddie cars, mountain biking, miniature golf, speedball and baseball batting cages and a swimming pool also are available. Free live entertainment is provided Saturday and Sunday afternoons. Food is available; picnicking is permitted.

Allow 3 hours minimum. Daily 10-6, mid-June through Labor Day; Sat.-Sun. 10-5, mid-May to mid-June and day after Labor Day to early Nov. Alpine slide $5. Five-ride waterslide ticket $5. All-day combination ticket, including alpine slide, waterslide, bumper boats and miniature golf, $19.95. Phone (717) 629-1661.

**TARENTUM (G-2) pop. 5,700, elev. 777'**

**TOUR-ED MINE & MUSEUM,** exit 14 off SR 28, then ⅛ mi. n. on Bull Creek Rd., offers guided tours of an open-pit coal mine. Old mine cars carry visitors 250 feet down into the mine. Displays feature actual equipment in working condition and illustrate the coal-mining process. A museum exhibits a company store, a miner's log cabin and coal souvenirs and jewelry. Allow 1 hour minimum. Wed.-Mon. 1-4, Memorial Day weekend-Labor Day. Admission $6; ages 3-12, $3. **Discount.** Phone (412) 224-4720.

### TITUSVILLE (D-3) pop. 6,400, elev. 1,174'

Indians used the slick film on Oil Creek to mix their war paints, and enterprising settlers bottled and sold it as a medicinal concoction called "Seneca Oil." Not until 1859, when Col. Edwin Drake drilled a well, did oil begin to revolutionize industry and spur progress around the world. Titusville became a wealthy boom town overnight. Pennsylvania was the nation's number one oil producer until 1891, when production peaked and the oil industry began striking richer fields in the West.

For more area information contact the chamber of commerce, 116 W. Central Ave., Titusville, PA 16354; phone (814) 827-2941.

★**DRAKE WELL MUSEUM** is ½ mi. s.e. on SR 8, then 1¼ mi. e. on Bloss St. to Drake Well Memorial Park. The world's first successful drilled oil well began producing in Titusville in 1859. Exhibits deal with the origin and development of the oil industry and include an oil lease display, a metal drilling rig, a working replica of Drake's derrick, a pumping jack and Densmore railroad cars. A 25-minute film details Col. Edwin Drake's efforts in drilling the well, and a library includes 10,000 early photographs of this oil region.

A 10-mile paved bicycle trail, a 15-mile hiking trail and picnic facilities also are available. During late August the anniversary of Drake's discovery is celebrated. Allow 1 hour, 30 minutes minimum. Daily 9-5, May-Oct.; Tues.-Sat. 9-5, Sun. noon-5, rest of year. Closed major holidays. Admission $4; over 60, $3; ages 6-17, $2. Phone (814) 827-2797.

**OIL CREEK AND TITUSVILLE RAILROAD**, 409 S. Perry St., offers 2½-hour train trips in restored 1930s passenger cars. A tour guide and an audio recording describe the history and scenery of the area, which is known for its 19th-century oil boom. The only operating railway post office car in the United States resumed service in 1990 after an almost 40-year absence. A renovated freight station built in 1896 also is on display.

Allow 30 minutes minimum. Train departs Sat.-Sun. at 11:45 and 3:15, mid-June through Sept. 30; Wed. at 2 and Fri.-Sun. at 11:45 and 3:15, in Oct. Trains also depart from the Drake Well Museum, south of Titusville, and Rynd Farm, north of Oil City. Fare $9; over 60, $8; ages 3-12, $5. MC, VI.Reservations are suggested. Phone (814) 676-1733.

### TOWANDA (D-9) pop. 3,200, elev. 771'

Towanda was the boyhood home of composer Stephen Collins Foster and the home of staunch

Abraham Lincoln supporter David Wilmot, who founded the Republican Party. For more area information contact the chamber of commerce, P.O. Box 146, Towanda, PA 18848; phone (717) 268-2732.

**FRENCH AZILUM**, 8 mi. s.e. on SR 187, then 3 mi. e., following signs, was founded in 1793 as a refuge for French nobility fleeing the Revolution. About 50 log buildings were erected. After Napoleon's pardon, many emigrants left the area. French Azilum is undergoing restoration. Five log cabins, a small model of the village, weaving and spinning exhibits, a yarn-dyeing display and woodworking and blacksmith tools can be seen. The 1836 Laporte House contains period furnishings and a library. Guided tours are available. Nature trails and a picnic pavilion also are featured.

Wed.-Sun. 11-4:30, June-Aug.; Sat.-Sun. 11-4:30 in May and Sept. Last tour begins 30 minutes before closing. Admission $3.50; senior citizens $3; ages 6-18, $2. Phone (717) 265-3376.

### TYRONE (G-5) pop. 1,800, elev. 909'

**BLAND'S PARK**, 12 mi. n. on Old US 220, is an 8-acre amusement park. Highlights include more than 30 rides, an 18-hole miniature golf course, go-karts and miniature train rides. Food is available. Park open Tues.-Sun. at noon (miniature golf and go-kart areas open daily), June-Aug.; Sat.-Sun. at noon, in May and Sept. Closing times vary. All-day ride pass Tues.-Thurs. $3.95, Fri.-Sun. $5.95. Miniature golf Mon.-Thurs. $2.95, Fri.-Sun. $3.50. Go-karts $3. MC, VI. Phone (814) 684-3538.

**GARDNER'S CANDY MUSEUM**, 30 W. 10th St., is in an 1890s-era candy store. A re-created candy kitchen, candy-making utensils, Easter bunny molds, candy boxes and other memorabilia are displayed. A 15-minute videotape depicts the history of the business. Food is available. Allow 1 hour minimum. Mon.-Sat. 9:30-9, Sun. 1-9; closed major holidays. Free. Phone (814) 684-0857.

### UNIONTOWN (I-3) pop. 12,000, elev. 1,022'

Uniontown, in the bituminous coking coal district of western Pennsylvania, is a major producer of coke, steel, glass and iron. The birthplace of Gen. George Marshall, Uniontown is near the grave of another general, Edward Braddock, who is buried southeast of town near Farmington (see Fort Necessity National Battlefield). About 5 miles west on US 40 is Searights Tollhouse, which was built in 1835. Tours of the tollhouse are given mid-May to mid-October. For more area information contact the Central Fayette Chamber of Business and Industry, 11 Pittsburgh St., P.O. Box 2124, Uniontown, PA 15401; phone (412) 437-4571.

**LAUREL CAVERNS** is 5½ mi. e. via US 40, then 5½ mi. s. via a marked road. A maze cave with more than 2 miles of passages, the caverns have been explored since the late 1700s. Guided tours include the "Grand Canyon" and other limestone formations. A view from Chestnut Ridge covers two states and 4,000 square miles. An indoor miniature golf course also is available.

Cavern temperatures remain at a constant 52 degrees Fahrenheit; visitors should dress accordingly. Allow 1 hour minimum. Daily 9-5, May-Oct. Admission $8; over 65, $7; ages 12-17, $6; ages 6-11, $5. **Discount.** Phone (412) 438-3003.

## UPPER DELAWARE SCENIC AND RECREATIONAL RIVER

The Upper Delaware Scenic and Recreational River comprises 73 miles of the Upper Delaware River from just north of Matamoras to Hancock, N.Y. Along this stretch the river changes from long, placid eddies to swift water and Class I and II rapids. It is paralleled on the New York side by SR 97, which has a number of scenic overlooks. The best road from which to see the river on the Pennsylvania side is the northern section of SR 191, which at times is only a few feet above the water.

The Upper Delaware was an important transportation route for Indians and early settlers. In 1828 the Delaware and Hudson Canal opened, bringing boatloads of coal from the Pennsylvania interior to the port of New York. However, problems soon developed at the point where the canal crossed the river: Slow-moving boats being towed across the river and along the canal were constantly colliding with the huge log and timber rafts that were coursing down the river to sawmills and shipyards in Trenton, N.J., and Philadelphia.

To solve the problem, the canal company approved a plan to "build the canal above the water." John Roebling, who later designed the Brooklyn Bridge, built the Delaware Aqueduct to cross the river and carry canal traffic from Lackawaxen, Pa., to Minisink Ford, N.Y. The aqueduct is considered to be the oldest existing wire suspension bridge in America. The adjacent tollhouse contains exhibits interpreting the history of the Delaware and Hudson Canal, John Roebling and the Delaware Aqueduct. It is open weekends Memorial Day weekend through mid-October.

Wildlife in the area includes bear, beaver, white-tailed deer, mink, muskrat, otter, rabbit and squirrel. Birds include the bald eagle, osprey, great egret, great blue heron, turkey vulture, Canada goose and several varieties of hawks and ducks.

On the banks of the Upper Delaware Scenic and Recreational River lies the Zane Grey Museum (see Lackawaxen). The renowned Western author began his writing career and lived at the site with his wife Dolly 1905-18.

Recreational opportunities include boating, canoeing, fishing and rafting. In summer the National Park Service offers a variety of cultural, natural history and recreational activities; phone (914) 252-3947 or (717) 685-4871.

Information stations at the public boating access sites in Narrowsburg, Ten Mile River and Skinner Falls, in New York, and at Damascus and Lackawaxen, in Pennsylvania, are open weekends 8:30-5, Memorial Day weekend through Labor Day. The Skinner Falls and Ten Mile River stations remain open weekends through September. An information center/bookstore on Main Street in Narrowsburg is open daily 9:30-4:30, mid-Apr. through Labor Day; Wed.-Sun. 9:30-4:30, day after Labor Day-Sept. 30; Sat.-Sun. 9:30-4:30, Oct. 1-Nov. 20.

## VALLEY FORGE (H-10) elev. 98'

Valley Forge began as an iron forge on Valley Creek in the 1740s. A sawmill and gristmill were added by the time of the Revolutionary War, making Valley Forge an important supply center for the Colonists. However, it did not escape the attention of the British, who destroyed the forge and mills in 1777. Only ruins marked the site when George Washington chose Valley Forge for his winter of 1777-78 encampment (see Valley Forge National Historical Park).

**FREEDOMS FOUNDATION AT VALLEY FORGE,** on SR 23, was founded in 1949 to promote responsible citizenship. The 105-acre campus features the Independence Garden, the Medal of Honor Grove, the Faith of Our Fathers Chapel and the Credo Monument. The Medal of Honor Grove and the campus are open to the public. Allow 30 minutes minimum. Mon.-Fri. 9-5. Free. Tours of the other facilities are available by reservation. Phone (610) 933-8825.

## ★VALLEY FORGE NATIONAL HISTORICAL PARK (H-10)

The 3,500-acre Valley Forge National Historical Park, extending east from the village of Valley Forge along SR 23, was the site of the 6-month winter encampment by the Continental Army. From Dec. 19, 1777, to June 19, 1778, Gen. George Washington and 12,000 soldiers kept the British Army bottled up in Philadelphia.

During that terrible winter some 2,000 troops died from disease brought on by supply shortages, severe weather and poor sanitation. Still, during those 6 months the army was reorganized, Baron von Steuben developed a uniform system of drill and the Continental Army left Valley Forge a well-trained, efficient force.

A self-guiding tour visits the reconstructed huts of Muhlenberg's Brigade, Washington's Headquarters and the original entrenchment lines and fortifications. May through September, bus tours and automobile tape tours begin at the visitor center, at the junction of SR 23 and North Gulph Road, where there are exhibits and a short film.

Allow 2 hours minimum. The park is open daily 9-5; closed Dec. 25. Free. For more information contact the Superintendent, Valley Forge

National Historical Park, Valley Forge, PA 19481; phone (610) 783-1077.

**NATIONAL MEMORIAL ARCH** commemorates the patriotism and suffering of George Washington and the men who were under his command.

**WASHINGTON'S HEADQUARTERS,** the Potts House, contains Revolutionary War-era furnishings. Allow 30 minutes minimum. Daily 9-5; closed Dec. 25. Admission $2, over 62 and under 16 free; free to all Dec.-Mar.

**WASHINGTON MEMORIAL CHAPEL** (Episcopal), on SR 23 within the park, contains relics, woodcarvings and windows depicting the history of the country. A bell tower connected with the chapel houses the 58-bell Washington Memorial National Carillon. Free recitals are given Sun. after the 11:15 service mid-Sept. to mid-June, and Wed. at 8 p.m., July-Aug. Allow 30 minutes minimum. Chapel open Mon.-Sat. 9-5, Sun. 12:30-5; closed Jan. 1 and Dec. 25. Donations. Phone (610) 783-0120.

**Valley Forge Historical Society Museum,** in the Washington Memorial Chapel, displays more than 3,000 artifacts from the winter encampment of the Continental Army 1777-78. Many other items belonged to George and Martha Washington, including a knife that doctors used to "bleed" Washington who was suffering from pneumonia at the time of his death.

Allow 1 hour minimum. Mon.-Sat. 9:30-4, Sun. 1-4; closed Jan. 1, Good Friday, Easter, Thanksgiving and Dec. 25. Admission $1.50; under 16, 50c. Phone (610) 783-0535.

**VOLANT (F-1) pop. 200, elev. 944'**

Volant grew up around a gristmill built on Neshannock Creek in 1812. The restored mill is now the centerpiece of Main Street, which is lined with quaint shops and restaurants. Amish buggies are a common sight on the roadways.

**Shopping areas:** The Volant Mill features handmade furniture, pottery, dried flowers, pictures and crafts. A nearby caboose and three train cars have been restored and also house specialty shops, as do Adadamy Square and The Barns at Potters Run Landing.

**WARREN (D-3) pop. 11,100, elev. 1,174'**

**KINZUA DAM** is 6 mi. e. of Warren via US 6 and SR 59. Several overlooks provide scenic views of the dam and reservoir. Boating, fishing and swimming are permitted. Allow 1 hour minimum. The bridge roadway spanning the dam is open to pedestrians daily (weather permitting) 10-3:30. A visitor center in the Big Bend Access Area is open daily noon-3:45, Memorial Day weekend-Labor Day; Sat.-Sun. 10-3:30, day after Labor Day-Oct. 31. Free. Phone (814) 726-0661, or 726-0164 for lake and fishing conditions.

**WARREN COUNTY HISTORICAL SOCIETY,** 210 4th Ave., is housed in an Italian Renaissance house built in 1873. Period rooms include a formal parlor, a Victorian room and a general store. A research library contains archives, genealogy records and a photograph collection. Allow 30 minutes minimum. Mon.-Fri. 9-5, Sat. 9-noon; closed holidays. Admission $1, under 18 free. Phone (814) 723-1795.

**WASHINGTON (H-1) pop. 15,900, elev. 1,039'**

The Washington and Jefferson College Memorial Library was founded by a gift from Benjamin Franklin. The college is one of the older schools for higher education west of the Allegheny Mountains.

The Duncan Miller Glass Museum, 525 Jefferson Ave., exhibits fine-pressed and hand-blown glass. Also of interest is the Arden Trolley Museum, 2 miles north in Arden on N. Main Street. The museum offers trolley rides and has displays of standard-gauge railroad equipment and trolley cars dating from 1894; phone (412) 225-9950. For more area information contact the chamber of commerce, 20 E. Beau St., Washington, PA 15301; phone (412) 225-3010.

**BRADFORD HOUSE** is at 175 S. Main St. David Bradford was a leader in the 1794 Whiskey Rebellion, a protest against high excise taxes that hurt the grain producers of western Pennsylvania. The house is furnished in 18th-century style. Candlelight tours are featured December 2-4 at 7 p.m. Wed.-Sat. 11-4, Sun. 1-4, May 1-Dec. 20. Admission $3; over 65, $2.50; ages 6-16, $1.50. Phone (412) 222-3604 or 225-7966.

**LeMOYNE HOUSE,** 49 E. Maiden St., was the home of antislavery politician and doctor, Francis LeMoyne. Built in 1812, the early Greek Revival-style stone mansion served as LeMoyne's office and apothecary shop and was a station for the underground railroad. The site now houses the Washington County Historical Society headquarters and the LeMoyne Historic Garden.

Wed.-Fri. noon-4, Feb.-Dec.; closed holidays. Admission $3; under 18, $1.50. Phone (412) 225-6740.

### ★WASHINGTON CROSSING HISTORIC PARK (H-12)

The 500 acres of Washington Crossing Historic Park are divided into two areas. The Thompson Mill section is 1½ miles southeast of New Hope via SR 32. The Washington Crossing section, 5 miles farther south on SR 32, is connected by bridge with New Jersey's Washington Crossing State Park *(see Trenton, N.J.)*. The park is dedicated to the memory of George Washington and the 2,400 soldiers who crossed the Delaware on Christmas night in 1776 to attack and capture Trenton, N.J., then garrisoned by Hessian mercenaries.

A re-enactment of the crossing of the Delaware is held at 1 p.m. on Dec. 25. Other special events include Gingerbread Days and Washington's Birthday celebrations, both in February.

Allow 2 hours minimum. The park is open daily 9-5. Buildings open Mon.-Sat. 9-5, Sun. noon-5; closed Martin Luther King's Jr.'s Birthday, Columbus Day and Thanksgiving. Last tour 1 hour, 30 minutes before closing. Park and Memorial Building free. Ticket for admission to three buildings (Thompson-Neely House, McConkey Ferry Inn and Taylor House) $2.50; over 60, $2; ages 6-17, $1. Phone (215) 493-4076.

**BOWMAN HILL WILDFOWER PRESERVE** is the more northern of the two areas. It includes a 100-acre wildflower preserve with natural history exhibits, 26 hiking trails and indoor exhibits. Mon.-Sat. 9-5, Sun. noon-5. Free. Phone (215) 862-2924.

**Bowman's Hill Tower** presents a commanding 14-mile view of the Delaware River Valley. Washington Crossing can be seen to the south. An elevator takes visitors to an observation point within the 110-foot tower; the top is then reached by stairs. Mon.-Fri. 10-5, Sat.-Sun. 10-6, Apr.-Oct.; Sat.-Sun. 10-5, in Nov. Admission $2.50; over 60 and ages 6-17, $2; ages 3-5, $1. Phone (215) 862-3166.

**Memorial Flagstaff** marks the graves of the Continental troops who died during the encampment and who were among America's first "unknown soldiers."

**Thompson-Neely House,** built in 1702, was the scene of many important conferences before the Battle of Trenton. Nearby are the Thompson-Neely Barn and Thompson's Grist Mill. Admission is included in the three-building ticket.

**WASHINGTON CROSSING SECTION** focuses on the site where Gen. George Washington and his troops embarked on their historic crossing.

**McConkey Ferry Inn** is a restored stone building, the earliest parts of which date from the 1750s. George Washington is believed to have dined at the inn before crossing the Delaware. Admission is included in the three-building ticket.

**Memorial Building** houses a copy of Emanuel Leutze's painting "Washington Crossing the Delaware" and related exhibits. A film depicting the event is shown Mon.-Sat. at 9, 10:30, noon, 1:30 and 3, Sun. at noon, 1:30 and 3; schedule is subject to change. Free.

**Taylor House** is the restored 1816 home of Mahlon Taylor, an influential businessman of the period. Guided tours are given of the first floor. Admission is included in the three-building ticket.

### WATERFORD (D-2) pop. 1,600, elev. 1,192'

Waterford, which grew up around an American post established in the area in the late 1700s, dates back to the French Fort LeBoeuf, built in 1753. A 21-year-old George Washington, then a major in the British Virginia Militia, delivered a message from Gov. Robert Dinwiddie asking the French to withdraw from the area. The French refused, and eventually tensions erupted into the French and Indian War. A model of the fort is at the Fort LeBoeuf Museum at 123 S. High St.

Also of interest on S. High Street is the Amos Judson House, a restored two-story Federal Greek Revival home built in 1820. Across the street is the restored Eagle Hotel, a Federal- and Georgian-style structure built in 1826. An old covered bridge is 1 mile off the end of East Street on a dirt road.

Waterford celebrates Community Heritage Days in mid-July. Events include an antique show, music, a historical battle re-enactment, parade and sky-diving show. Recreation is available at nearby Lake LeBoeuf *(see Recreation Chart)*.

### WAYNESBORO (I-7) pop. 9,600, elev. 713'

Tucked into rolling hills and surrounded by peach and apple orchards, Waynesboro dates back to 1749. Like many other towns in the vicinity, it lays claim to a historical footnote; abolitionist John Brown taught Sunday school nearby while preparing for his ill-fated Harper's Ferry raid. Later, Waynesboro became an early 20th-century retreat for Washington, D.C., residents seeking escape from summer heat and humidity. For more area information contact the chamber of commerce, 323 E. Main St., Waynesboro, PA 17268; phone (717) 762-7123.

**Shopping areas:** Waynesboro Factory Outlet, Barn, Walnut and Third streets, is a popular shopping center. It features Corning, Freeman Shoes, Little Red Shoehouse, Manhattan and Van Heusen Factory Store.

**RENFREW MUSEUM AND PARK,** 1010 E. Main St., houses a 300-piece pottery collection and the Nicodemus Collection of Decorative Arts, featuring ceramics, quilts, painted furniture and metalware. Special holiday programs are offered in

December; phone for schedule. The park has nature and hiking trails, a picnic area and a 150-seat pavilion. Allow 1 hour minimum.

Park open daily dawn-dusk. Museum open Thurs. and Sat.-Sun. 1-4, late Apr.-Oct. 31; closed July 4. Admission $3; over 55, $2.50; ages 7-12, $1.50. Phone (717) 762-4723.

## WAYNESBURG (I-1) pop. 4,300, elev. 938'

Waynesburg was named for Revolutionary War hero Gen. "Mad" Anthony Wayne. The town is the seat of Greene County, which was named for another Revolutionary War hero, Gen. Nathanael Greene. A statue of Greene is atop the 1850 county courthouse, a fine example of Greek Revival architecture. Also in town is Waynesburg College, one of the first colleges in the United States to grant degrees to women. For more area information contact the chamber of commerce, 26 High St., Suite 101, Waynesburg, PA 15370; phone (412) 627-5926.

GREENE COUNTY HISTORICAL MUSEUM is 3 mi. e. via I-79 exit 3 on old SR 21. The museum is housed in a 52-room mid-Victorian structure that formerly housed the county's "Poor Farm." Fourteen rooms are furnished in period—from Colonial times through the Victorian era. The exhibits include Indian artifacts, salt-glaze pottery, quilts, glassware and a country store. Picnicking is permitted. Allow 1 hour minimum. Wed-Fri. 10-4, Sat.-Sun. noon-4, May-Aug.; Thurs.-Sun. noon-4, Sept.-Oct. Admission $2.50; ages 6-12, $1.50. Phone (412) 627-3204.

## WELLSBORO (D-7) pop. 3,400, elev. 1,315'

If Wellsboro's gas-lit streets, town green and Victorian mansions seem vaguely reminiscent of Massachusetts or Vermont, it is because the town was founded by New England colonists in 1806. In the mountainous region of north-central Pennsylvania, Wellsboro is an all-year recreation center and the gateway to the "Grand Canyon" of Pennsylvania. For more area information contact the chamber of commerce, 114 Main St., P.O. Box 733, Wellsboro, PA 16901; phone (717) 724-1926.

GRAND CANYON OF PENNSYLVANIA, 10 mi. w. on SR 660, was formed by the Pine Creek River. Fifty miles long and up to 1,000 feet deep, it is the highlight of the Endless Mountain area, which includes several state parks and state-owned game lands. The area offers spectacular panoramas; Leonard Harrison and Colton Point state parks (see Recreation Chart and the AAA Mideastern CampBook) encompass the east and west rims, respectively. Many primitive areas are accessible only by narrow gravel roads. Daily dawn-dusk. Free.

## WEST CHESTER (I-10) pop. 18,500, elev. 424'

Graced by many handsome Greek Revival and Victorian homes, West Chester is surrounded by the rich farmland of Chester County. During the Revolutionary War, several major skirmishes occurred nearby, including the battles of Brandywine and Paoli. In 1842, West Chester became the home of the Jeffersonian, one of the few newspapers in the North to support the South. A rioting mob soon wrecked the paper's offices, and eventually the postmaster general prohibited its distribution by mail.

Of architectural interest is the 1704 Brinton House, 5 miles south of West Chester in Dilworthtown, a restored stone house built by a Quaker farmer. The Chester County Courthouse, downtown, was built in 1724.

Northbrook Canoe Co. in nearby Northbrook offers canoe and tube rentals for excursions on the Brandywine River; phone (610) 793-2279.

For 1 day in mid-September West Chester presents the Chester County Restaurant Festival. More than 20 restaurants from the Brandywine Valley area offer samples of their cuisines. Chester County Day, a tour of the area's historic houses, takes place on the first Saturday in October. An Old-Fashioned Christmas is celebrated the first weekend in December.

For further information contact the Chester County Tourist Bureau, 601 Westtown Rd., West Chester, PA 19382; phone (610) 344-6365.

CHESTER COUNTY HISTORICAL SOCIETY, 225 N. High St., displays early American furniture and decorative arts, including clocks, ceramics, crystal and silver. Changing exhibits feature clothing, textiles, dolls and ceramics. The research library deals with genealogy and area history. Allow 1 hour minimum. Tues. and Thurs.-Sat. 10-4, Wed. 10-6. Museum admission $2.50; under 18, $1.50. Combination library and museum admission $4; under 18, $2.50. Phone (610) 692-4800.

## WHITE HAVEN (F-10) pop. 1,100, elev. 1,120'

White Haven is a year-round outdoor recreation destination. White-water rafting is popular on the Lehigh River spring through fall, and nearby Hickory Run State Park (see Recreation Chart) offers snowmobiling and cross-country skiing in winter. Lehigh Rafting Rentals provides white-water rafts, inflatable kayaks and related equipment. Orientation and instructions for self-guiding trips also is available. For information and reservations write to P.O. Box 296, White Haven, PA 18661; phone (717) 443-4441 or (800) 291-RAFT.

WHITEWATER CHALLENGERS RAFT TOURS, 6 mi. s. of I-80 exit 40 just off Weatherly-White Haven Rd., offers white-water rafting trips on the Lehigh River that last 3 to 5 hours. Minimum age or weight restrictions may apply. White-water rafting daily 8-6, Mar.-June and Sept.-Oct. Summer rafting in calmer waters daily 8-6, July-Aug. White-water trip $46. Summer trip $29;

ages 5-17, $19; first 5-17 rate free with two paying adults. DS, MC, VI. **Discount.** Reservations are recommended. Phone (717) 443-9532 or (800) 443-RAFT.

### WHITE MILLS (E-11) elev. 922'

**DORFLINGER GLASS MUSEUM,** ½ mi. e. of US 6 on Long Ridge Rd., features more than 600 pieces of cut, engraved, etched, gilded and enameled crystal. The crystal is displayed among period antiques and items from the Dorflinger Glassworks. Allow 30 minutes minimum. Wed.-Sat. 10-4, Sun. 1-4, May 13-Oct. 29. Admission $3; over 55, $2.50; ages 6-18, $1.50. Phone (717) 253-1185.

**The Dorflinger-Suydam Wildlife Sanctuary** offers nature trails for observing indigenous wildlife and waterfowl within its 600 acres. Allow 30 minutes minimum. Daily dawn-dusk. Free. Phone (717) 253-1185.

### WILKES-BARRE (E-10) pop. 47,500, elev. 593'

In the Wyoming Valley on the Susquehanna River, Wilkes-Barre was named for John Wilkes and Isaac Barre, members of the British Parliament and Colonial sympathizers. They also are honored by a monument in Public Square.

The Wyoming Valley was the scene of the Yankee-Pennamite Wars, a land struggle between Pennsylvania and Connecticut that lasted 1769-85. Many skirmishes were fought on Wilkes-Barre's River Common, a 35-acre park on River Street between North and South streets. Within the park, which dates from 1770, are the Luzerne County Court House and numerous historic markers. Eventually Congress ruled in favor of Pennsylvania, though Connecticut did not relinquish its claims to the disputed area until 1800.

With the outbreak of the Revolution, the region's importance as a granary led to a number of attacks by Tory and Indian forces. On July 3, 1778, 1,200 Indians and renegade whites defeated 300 frontiersmen 4 miles north of Kingston near Forty Fort, leaving the settlements of the Wyoming Valley unprotected. The next day the Indians passed up and down the valley in a series of raids that became known as the Wyoming Massacre. In reprisal, Gen. John Sullivan led an expedition up the Susquehanna River, devastating the area and breaking the Indians' grip on the region.

Wilkes-Barre's "face" has changed several times since its early days. Once a center of the anthracite coal-mining region, industry is now diversified. After the city and surrounding valley were damaged by Hurricane Agnes in 1972, Wilkes-Barre underwent significant renovation.

The F.M. Kirby Center for the Performing Arts is housed in a restored 1930s Art Deco movie palace. The center is home to the Northeastern Philharmonic Orchestra and Ballet Theatre Pennsylvania. It offers a full program of drama, comedy, opera and musicals.

The Wyoming Historical and Geological Society operates a museum at 69 S. Franklin St. with exhibits about the coal-mining industry, as well as Indian artifacts, rocks, minerals and fossils of local origin; phone (717) 822-1727.

Harness racing takes place at Pocono Downs, on SR 315. Frances Slocum State Park and Harvey's Lake *(see Recreation Chart)* offer a variety of recreational facilities. Scenic Ricketts Glen State Park is 30 miles west via SR 118 in Red Rock *(see place listing).*

Special events in Wilkes-Barre include the Cherry Blossom Festival on the River Common the last weekend in April. The Fine Arts Fiesta, held Thursday through Sunday on the third weekend in May at Public Square, features displays of crafts, paintings and sculpture, as well as live performances by bands, orchestras and drama groups.

The Luzerne County Folk Festival, held in late October, is an ethnic celebration including traditional arts and crafts, entertainment and specialty foods. A farmers' market is held every Thursday afternoon at Public Square from mid-July through November. For more event information contact the chamber of commerce, 69 public Sq., Suite 600, Wilkes-Barre, PA 18710; phone (717) 823-2101.

**Shopping areas:** The Wyoming Valley Mall on Business Rte. 309 offers more than 100 stores, including Bon-Ton, Hess's, JCPenney and Sears. North on SR 315, the Leslie Fay Factory Outlet specializes in women's clothing. The Burlington Coat Factory has an outlet at the West Side Mall on US 11 in nearby Edwardsville.

**NATHAN DENISON HOUSE**—*see Forty Fort.*

**SORDONI ART GALLERY,** 150 S. River St., is on the campus of Wilkes University. The gallery displays paintings, sculpture, watercolors, photography and other media of late 19th- and 20th-century American artists. Exhibits are changed monthly; the gallery usually closes for the changeover. Daily noon-5 (also Thurs. 5-9 p.m.); closed major holidays. Free. Phone (717) 831-4325.

---

## A STARRED ATTRACTION
When you see a ★ before an attraction, it's a "must" see!

**WILLIAMSPORT (E-8)** pop. 32,300, elev. 528'

Now a manufacturing city, Williamsport was known as a great lumber center until the forests were depleted in the 1890s. Millionaires' Row, along W. Fourth Street, is lined with Victorian mansions once owned by the lumber barons.

Little League baseball originated in Williamsport in 1939, and each August the city is host to the Little League World Series. The Susquehanna Boom Festival offers a variety of activities in June. Additional event information is available at the chamber of commerce, 454 Pine St., Williamsport, PA 17701; phone (717) 326-1971 *(see ad)*.

**Shopping areas:** The Old Jail Center, 154 W. Third St., features shops and art galleries in a renovated 1868 jailhouse. Lycoming Mall, I-80 Lycoming Mall exit, features The Bon Ton, JCPenney and Sears.

**CHILDREN'S DISCOVERY WORKSHOP,** 343 W. Fourth St., is a hands-on museum for ages 3-11. Exhibits include WKID-TV, a studio, the Kid Clinic, Human Habitrail, Ice Cream Parlor, Shadow Wall and Construct-a-Space. Changing exhibits also are featured. Various programs and activities take place regularly. Allow 1 hour minimum. Tues.-Sat. 10-4, Sun. 1-4, June-Aug.; Tues.-Fri. and Sun. 1-5, Sat. 11-5, rest of year. Admission $3.50, under 2 free. **Discount.** Phone (717) 322-5437.

**HERDIC TROLLEY TOUR** acquaints visitors with Williamsport's areas of interest, including Millionaires' Row, Memorial Park and the historic Vallamont section. The 1-hour tour features taped narration on a replica of an 1891 streetcar. Tours depart from the trolley gazebo near the Sheraton Inn, Pine and W. Fourth sts. Tues. and Thurs. at 10:45, 12:15, 1:45 and 3:15, Sat. at 9, 10 and 11, Memorial Day-Labor Day. Fare $2; over 65 and ages 6-12, $1. For schedule information phone (717) 326-2500 or (800) 248-9287.

*HIAWATHA* RIVERBOAT TOURS, 4 mi. w. in Susquehanna State Park at the base of Arch St., offers 1-hour paddle-wheeler cruises along the Susquehanna River. A narrator describes the history of the river. Sightseeing cruises depart Tues.-Sat. at 11:30, 1, 2:30 and 4, Sun. at 1, 2:30 and 4, June-Aug.; Sat. at 11:30, 1, 2:30 and 4, Sun. at 1, 2:30 and 4, May 9-May 31 and Sept. 1-Oct. 22. Schedule may vary; phone ahead. Tickets are sold one hour before departure. Fare $7; over 60, $6.50; under 12, $5. Phone (717) 321-1205 or (800) 358-9900. *See ad.*

**LITTLE LEAGUE BASEBALL MUSEUM,** 1¼ mi. s. on US 15, is next to the field where the annual Little League World Series is held. Displays interpret the history and growth of Little League Baseball since its founding in 1939. Exhibits include Little League memorabilia, original uniforms and major league players' Little League items. The Hall of Excellence honors such Little League graduates as Kareem Abdul-Jabbar, Nolan Ryan, Tom Seaver and Mike Schmidt. Also featured are batting and pitching cages with videotape replay.

Allow 1 hour minimum. Mon.-Sat. 9-7, Sun. noon-7, Memorial Day-Labor Day; Mon.-Sat. 9-5, Sun. noon-5, rest of year. Closed Jan. 1, Thanksgiving and Dec. 25. Admission $4; over 62, $2; ages 5-13, $1. **Discount.** Phone (717) 326-3607. *See color ad.*

**LYCOMING COUNTY HISTORICAL MUSEUM,** off US 220 Maynard St. exit at 858 W. Fourth St., exhibits artifacts from 10,000 B.C. to early

Indian cultures and the arrival of the first settlers. Exhibits include a blacksmith shop, carpenter shop, Victorian parlor and gristmill. Displays about the lumber industry and a Shempp toy train collection also are featured. Allow 1 hour minimum. Tues.-Fri. 9:30-4, Sat. 11-4, Sun. noon-4, May-Oct.; closed major holidays. Admission $3.50; over 55, $3; ages 2-12, $1.50; free to all third Sun. of the month. MC, VI. **Discount.** Phone (717) 326-3326.

## WOMELSDORF (G-9) pop. 2,300, elev. 434'

**CONRAD WEISER HOMESTEAD,** 26 acres ½ mi. e. on US 422, was the home of Conrad Weiser, Colonial interpreter and peacemaker during the French and Indian War. Tours, a park and picnic facilities are available. Allow 1 hour minimum. Wed.-Sat. 9-5, Sun. noon-5; closed holidays, except Memorial Day, July 4 and Labor Day. Admission $2.50; over 60, $2; ages 6-17, $1. Phone (610) 589-2934.

## WOODWARD (F-7)

**WOODWARD CAVE,** 2 mi. w. on SR 45, following signs, is one of the state's larger caverns. A 1-hour, ½-mile guided tour visits five rooms. The cave maintains a constant temperature of 48 degrees Fahrenheit. Daily 9-7, May 15-Labor Day; 9-5, Mar. 15-May 14 and day after Labor Day-Nov. 15. Last tour departs 1 hour before closing. Admission $7.50; ages 5-12, $3.50. Phone (814) 349-9800 or 349-8252.

## WORTHINGTON (F-3) pop. 700

The Old Stone Tavern on Main Street dates from 1820, when it was built for use as an inn on a stagecoach route. It has been restored to its original condition, and guides in period costume conduct tours. Works by area artisans are displayed.

## WYOMING (E-10) pop. 3,300, elev. 557'

A monument at 4th Street and Wyoming Avenue marks the site of a grave for victims of the Wyoming Massacre (see Wilkes-Barre).

## YORK (I-8) pop. 42,200, elev. 375'

York served as the national capital Sept. 30, 1777, to June 27, 1778, while the British occupied Philadelphia. It was in York that Congress received the news of Gen. John Burgoyne's surrender, adopted the Articles of Confederation, issued the first National Thanksgiving Proclamation and learned that France was to send aid to the Colonies.

Many farmers' markets specialize in Pennsylvania Dutch and German cuisine, including the Central Market House, 34 W. Philadelphia St.; Farmers' Market, 380 W. Market St.; and the New Eastern Market, 201 Memory Ln.

**Self-guiding tours:** A brochure that describes a historical walking tour of York can be obtained at the York County Convention and Visitors Bureau, 1 Market Way E., York, PA 17401; phone (717) 848-4000.

**Shopping areas:** The Galleria, 2 miles east of I-83 on US 30, is the area's largest mall; anchor stores are The Bon Ton, Boscov's, JCPenney and Sears. West Manchester Mall, 1 mile west of I-83 on US 30, and York Mall Merchants, off I-83 exit 8E, are other major shopping centers. West Manchester features The Bon Ton and Wal-Mart; the major stores at York Mall Merchants are Montgomery Ward and Wal-Mart.

A number of factory outlet complexes also provide shopping opportunities. Meadowbrook Village, 2 miles east of I-83 on US 30 across from the Galleria, features Bass, Christmas Tree Hill, Doe Spun, Izod, Pewtarex, Pfaltzgraff, The Knittery and Van Heusen. East Prospect Factory Outlet, 16 W. Maple St. in East Prospect, offers Gantner Swimwear.

Old Tollgate Village, east of I-83 exit 4 on US 74, has more than two dozen shops offering specialty items, gifts and handmade crafts.

**AGRICULTURE AND INDUSTRIAL MUSEUM OF YORK COUNTY,** with locations at 480 E. Market St. and 217 W. Princess St., focuses on the history of the Golden Age of industrial development that occurred from the Civil War to World War I. Exhibits and displays highlight industrial equipment and agricultural products manufactured or used in York County. Allow 1 hour minimum. Tues.-Thurs. and Sat. 10-4; otherwise by appointment. Closed major holidays. Admission $2; ages 4-12, $1. Phone (717) 852-7007.

**Agriculture Museum** is at 480 E. Market St. Visitors can view such farm implements as thrashers, tractors, harvesters and hand plows. An antique automobile display and a replica of one of the area's first department stores also are featured.

**Industrial Museum** is at 217 W. Princess St. Various displays include pottery, antique automobiles, a gristmill and a full-size Phineas Davis locomotive model.

**BOB HOFFMAN WEIGHTLIFTING AND SOFTBALL HALL OF FAME** is off I-83N exit 11, at 3300 Board Rd. Exhibits detail the history of Olympic lifting, powerlifting, bodybuilding and strongman competitions. Mon.-Fri. 9-4, Sat. 9-3. Free. Phone (717) 767-6481.

★**HISTORICAL SOCIETY OF YORK COUNTY,** 250 E. Market St., has a gallery with changing exhibits, a museum depicting life in York County up to the 20th century and a genealogical library. The museum also has a reproduction of the original York village square.

Museum and gallery Mon.-Sat. 9-5, Sun. 1-4; library Mon.-Sat. 9-5. Closed major holidays. Museum $2; senior citizens $1.50; ages 6-13, $1. Library $4. Combination admission ticket to museum and gallery, Bonham House, Golden

Plough Tavern, General Gates House and Bobb Log House $6; senior citizens $5; ages 6-13, $3. Phone (717) 848-1587.

**Bonham House,** 152 E. Market St., depicts various periods in American life through a Victorian parlor, an early 20th-century library and a Federal dining room. The museum displays Oriental porcelains, ivories and bronzes, as well as silver, china and glass. By reservation, guided tours are offered Tues.-Sat. at 10:30 and 2:30. Fee $1; senior citizens 75c; ages 6-13, 50c. Phone (717) 848-1587.

★**Golden Plough Tavern, General Gates House and Bobb Log House,** 157 W. Market St., are restored 18th-century buildings. The half-timbered brick tavern was built in the 1740s. The stone General Gates House was the scene of the Conway Cabal meeting, at which Marquis de Lafayette prevented the overthrow of Gen. George Washington as head of the Continental Army. The log house is typical of those that characterized early York. Mon.-Sat. 10-4, Sun. 1-4; closed major holidays. Admission $3.50; senior citizens $3.25; ages 6-13, $1.75.

**RODNEY C. GOTT MUSEUM** and the Harley-Davidson assembly plant are ¾ mi. e. of jct. I-83 and US 30, at US 30 and Eden Rd. Exhibits range from the original 1903 Harley-Davidson motorcycle to current models. Racing trophies, photographs, old motorcycle ads and memorabilia trace the development of the motorcycle. In the plant, which can be visited by guided tour only, visitors can see a motorcycle roll off the assembly line about every 90 seconds. It takes aproximately two-and-one-half hours to assemble a Harley. Under 12 are not admitted to the plant.

Combined plant and museum tours are offered Mon.-Fri. at 10 and 2; plant closed holidays and during shutdown for new model changeover (phone Mar.-Aug.). Museum tours are offered Mon.-Fri. at 12:30, Sat. at 10, 11, 1 and 2; closed holidays. Free. Phone (717) 848-1177, ext. 5244.

**YORK COUNTY COLONIAL COURT HOUSE,** W. Market St. and Pershing Ave., is a reconstruction of the courthouse in which the Continental Congress voted to adopt the Articles of Confederation. A sound-and-light show is presented. Daily 10-4, and by appointment. Admission $1; ages 6-16, 50c. Phone (717) 846-1977.

**ZELIENOPLE (F-1) pop. 4,200, elev. 906′**

**PASSAVANT HOUSE** is at 243 S. Main St. Built in 1808, this is the restored home of Zelie Basse Passavant, for whom the town of Zelienople was named. The 10-room Federal period house contains historical items, furniture, 19th-century clothing and more than 7,000 original letters and documents connected with the history of Zelienople. A genealogical library is available.

Allow 1 hour minimum. House open Wed. and Sat. 1-4, May-Sept. Library also open by appointment. Closed holidays. Admission $1.50; ages 6-18, $1. Phone (412) 452-9457.

## Further Reading

The following sampling of books has been selected for the pleasure and enrichment of our members who wish to discover more about the region they are visiting. This list is not intended to be a complete survey of works available, nor does it imply AAA endorsement of a particular author, work or publisher.

**New Jersey:**

**Fleming, Thomas.** "Liberty Tavern." A historical novel about the Revolutionary War and New Jersey.

**Gillespie, Angus and Rockland, Michael.** "Looking for America on the New Jersey Turnpike." A statement about American society and values as seen through the creation and history of the New Jersey Turnpike.

**Sternlieb, George and Hughes, James.** "The Atlantic City Gamble." The results and consequences of legalized casino gambling in Atlantic City.

**Updike, John.** "The Poorhouse Fair." A story about peculiarities in a New Jersey poorhouse.

**Pennsylvania:**

**Booth, Sally Smith.** "The Women of '76." A look at some of the heroines of the American Revolution.

**Boyette, Michael.** "Let It Burn—The Philadelphia Tragedy." An examination of the man-made disaster that made national headlines.

**Brown, Rita.** "Six of One." Rivalries in a town split by the Pennsylvania-Maryland border as well as the Mason-Dixon line.

**Coover, Robert.** "The Origin of Brunists." A story about a religious cult in a western Pennsylvania mining town.

**Hartog, Jan de.** "The Peaceable Kingdom." A re-creation of Quaker life in 17th-century Pennsylvania.

**Jakes, John.** "North and South." Part of the trilogy that examines two families caught in the struggle of the Civil War.

**Lubove, Roy.** "Pittsburgh." A history of "America's most livable city."

**Meyer, Carolyn.** "Amish People—Plain Living in a Complex World." A look at the people who have lived outside the mainstream of American society for centuries.

# LODGINGS & RESTAURANTS

The Five Diamond designation assures AAA's most discriminating members that they will experience definitive luxury, service and style. AAA congratulates the lodgings and restaurants listed in this book that have met or exceeded our highest standards of excellence.

## LODGINGS

- ⬥ Hilton at Short Hills .......... SHORT HILLS, NEW JERSEY
- ⬥ Four Seasons Hotel .... PHILADELPHIA, PENNSYLVANIA
- ⬥ The Rittenhouse Hotel & Condominium
   Residences ............ PHILADELPHIA, PENNSYLVANIA

## RESTAURANTS

- ⬥ The Dining Room ............. SHORT HILLS, NEW JERSEY
   Fountain Restaurant ... PHILADELPHIA, PENNSYLVANIA
- ⬥ Le Bec-Fin .................. PHILADELPHIA, PENNSYLVANIA

# LOOK FOR THE RED

Next time you pore over a AAA TourBook in search of a lodging or restaurant, take note of the vibrant red AAA logos! These properties place a high value on the business they receive from dedicated AAA travelers.

As a member, you already turn to TourBooks for quality travel information. Now, add even more color to your itineraries — look for the special, bright red listings for lodging and dining experiences you'll long remember!

# NEW JERSEY

## ABSECON—7,300

### LODGINGS

**CAPRICE MOTOR LODGE** — Guaranteed Rates — Phone: 609/652-3322

| | | | | | | | |
|---|---|---|---|---|---|---|---|
| Fri & Sat 5/27-9/2 | 1P: $40- 95 | 2P/1B: $50- 110 | 2P/2B: $45- 105 | XP: $5 | D12 |
| Fri & Sat 5/1-5/26 & 9/3-4/30 | 1P: $40- 70 | 2P/1B: $40- 70 | 2P/2B: $40- 70 | XP: $5 | D12 |
| Sun-Thurs 5/27-9/2 | 1P: $35- 45 | 2P/1B: $35- 45 | 2P/2B: $35- 45 | XP: $5 | D12 |
| Sun-Thurs 5/1-5/26 & 9/3-4/30 | 1P: $25- 35 | 2P/1B: $25- 35 | 2P/2B: $25- 35 | XP: $5 | D12 |

Motel
**Location:** On US 30 from Garden State Pkwy n, 1/4 mi e, exit 40 southbound, exit 50 northbound then u-turn to Garden State Pkwy southbound, exit 40. 206 E White Horse Pike 08201. Fax: 609/652-9647. **Terms:** Sr. discount; reserv deposit; weekly/monthly rates; BP available; no pets. **Facility:** 22 rooms. 2 stories; exterior corridors. **All Rooms:** free movies, cable TV. **Some Rooms:** microwaves, refrigerators, whirlpools. **Cards:** AE, CB, DI, DS, MC, VI.  (D)

**DAYS INN-ABSECON/ATLANTIC CITY** — Rates Subject to Change — Phone: 609/652-2200

| | | | | | |
|---|---|---|---|---|---|
| 5/1-9/30 | 1P: $50- 130 | 2P/1B: $60- 140 | 2P/2B: $60- 140 | XP: $5 | F18 |
| 10/1-11/30 & 4/1-4/30 | 1P: $40- 85 | 2P/1B: $50- 95 | 2P/2B: $50- 95 | XP: $5 | F18 |
| 12/1-3/31 | 1P: $30- 75 | 2P/1B: $40- 85 | 2P/2B: $40- 85 | XP: $5 | F18 |

Motel
**Location:** On US 30, 1/2 mi e of Garden State Pkwy, exit 40S. 224 E White Horse Pike 08201. Fax: 609/748-8005. **Terms:** Sr. discount; check-in 4 pm; credit card guarantee; weekly/monthly rates; package plans; pets, $10, $75 dep req. **Facility:** 102 rooms. Attractively furnished motel rooms. 3 stories; exterior corridors; conference facilities; small pool. **Dining & Entertainment:** Coffee shop; 7 am-11 am, Sat & Sun to noon; cocktail lounge. **Services:** Fee: coin laundry. **All Rooms:** free movies, cable TV. **Some Rooms:** whirlpools. Fee: VCP's. **Cards:** AE, CB, DI, DS, JCB, MC, VI. (See ad p A8)  (D) ⊗

**ECONO LODGE** — Rates Subject to Change — Phone: 609/652-3300

| | | | | | |
|---|---|---|---|---|---|
| Fri & Sat 5/1-9/30 & 4/1-4/30 [CP] | 1P: $61 | 2P/1B: $75 | 2P/2B: $75 | XP: $5 |
| 10/1-3/31 [CP] | 1P: $30- 40 | 2P/1B: $40- 54 | 2P/2B: $40- 60 | XP: $5 |
| Sun-Thurs 5/1-9/30 & 4/1-4/30 [CP] | 1P: $50 | 2P/1B: $55 | 2P/2B: $55 | XP: $5 |

Motel
**Location:** On US 30; from Garden State Pkwy, 1/4 mi e exit 40 (southbound); from AC Expwy exit 12, left 2 mi; then 4 mi e on US 30. 328 White Horse Pike 08201. Fax: 609/652-8885. **Terms:** Reserv deposit; weekly rates; no pets. **Facility:** 62 rooms. Most rooms ground floor. 2 stories; exterior corridors. **All Rooms:** free movies, cable TV. **Some Rooms:** refrigerators. **Cards:** AE, CB, DI, DS, MC, VI. (See color ad below)  (D) ⊗

**HAMPTON INN** — Rates Subject to Change — Phone: 609/652-2500

| | | | | | |
|---|---|---|---|---|---|
| Fri & Sat 6/1-9/7 [CP] | 1P: $130 | 2P/1B: $98- 130 | 2P/2B: $98- 130 | |
| Fri & Sat 5/1-5/31 & 9/8-4/30 [CP] | 1P: $89- 106 | 2P/1B: $89- 106 | 2P/2B: $89- 106 | |
| Sun-Thurs 6/1-9/7 [CP] | 1P: $62- 89 | 2P/1B: $62- 89 | 2P/2B: $62- 89 | |
| Sun-Thurs 5/1-5/31 & 9/8-4/30 [CP] | 1P: $55- 82 | 2P/1B: $55- 82 | 2P/2B: $55- 82 | |

Motel
**Location:** On US 30; from Garden State Pkwy, 1/4 mi e, exit 40 (southbound); from AC Expwy exit 12, left 2 mi, then e on US 30. 240 E White Horse Pike 08201. Fax: 609/652-2212. **Terms:** Sr. discount; reserv deposit, 3 day notice; no pets. **Facility:** 129 rooms. Complimentary morning coffee & continental breakfast in lobby. Rates for up to 4 persons; 4 stories; interior corridors; meeting rooms; pool, whirlpool. **Dining:** Restaurant nearby. **Services:** area transportation, to Grand Casino. Fee: coin laundry. **All Rooms:** free movies, cable TV. **Some Rooms:** refrigerators. **Cards:** AE, CB, DI, DS, MC, VI.  (D) (S) ⊗

**MARRIOTT'S SEAVIEW RESORT** — Rates Subject to Change — Phone: 609/748-1990

| | | | | |
|---|---|---|---|---|
| 5/1-10/29 & 4/8-4/30 | 1P: $195 | 2P/1B: $195 | 2P/2B: $195 | |
| 10/30-4/7 | 1P: $115 | 2P/1B: $115 | 2P/2B: $115 | |

Resort Hotel
**Location:** On US 9; 2 1/2 mi ne of US 30, White Horse Pike. 401 S New York Rd 08201-9727. Fax: 609/652-2307. **Terms:** Sr. discount; check-in 4 pm; reserv deposit, 10 day notice, up to 30 days depending on season; weekly rates; package plans; no pets. **Facility:** 299 rooms. In operation since 1912 offering traditional atmosphere. 2 golf courses of championship golf. 3-4 stories; interior corridors; business center, conference facilities; putting green; 2 pools (2 heated, 1 indoor), saunas, whirlpool; paddle tennis; exercise room, playground, sports court, gameroom. Fee: 36 holes golf, driving range, golf learning center; 8 tennis courts (6 lighted). **Dining & Entertainment:** Dining room, restaurant; 6:30 am-11 pm; $10-$30; health conscious menu; cocktails/lounge; entertainment on weekends. **Services:** data ports, secretarial services; valet laundry. Fee: PC; childcare; massage; valet parking. **Recreation:** jogging. **All Rooms:** free pay movies, combo & shower baths, cable TV. **Some Rooms:** refrigerators. Fee: VCP's. **Cards:** AE, CB, DI, DS, JCB, MC, VI.  (D) (S) ⊗

**SUPER 8 MOTEL-ABSECON/ATLANTIC CITY** — Rates Subject to Change — Phone: 609/652-2477

| | | | | | |
|---|---|---|---|---|---|
| Fri & Sat 5/1-10/31 | 1P: $40- 120 | 2P/1B: $40- 120 | 2P/2B: $45- 125 | XP: $5 |
| Fri & Sat 11/1-4/30 | 1P: $40- 80 | 2P/1B: $40- 80 | 2P/2B: $45- 85 | XP: $5 |
| Sun-Thurs 5/1-10/31 | 1P: $35- 45 | 2P/1B: $35- 45 | 2P/2B: $40- 50 | XP: $5 |
| Sun-Thurs 11/1-4/30 | 1P: $30- 40 | 2P/1B: $30- 40 | 2P/2B: $35- 45 | XP: $5 |

Motel
**Location:** Southbound 1 1/2 mi w on US 30 or 1/2 mi e of Garden State Pkwy, exit 40; northbound return to exit 40 by reversing direction through Absecon Rest Area. 229 E White Horse Pike (US 30) 08201. Fax: 609/748-0666. **Terms:** Sr. discount; reserv deposit, 7 day notice; no pets. **Facility:** 58 rooms. Maximum occupancy 4 persons per room; 2 stories; exterior corridors. **All Rooms:** free movies, cable TV. **Some Rooms:** refrigerators. Fee: whirlpools. **Cards:** AE, CB, DI, DS, MC, VI. (See color ad p A11)  (D) ⊗

## RESTAURANT

**RAM'S HEAD INN RESTAURANT**  **Dinner:** $21-$30  **Phone:** 609/652-1700
◆◆◆◆  **Location:** On US 30, 2 3/4 mi w of US 9, exit 40 off Garden State Pkwy (southbound). 9 W White Horse
American  Pike 08201. **Hours:** noon-3 & 5-9:30 pm, Sat 5 pm-10 pm, Sun 3:30 pm-9 pm. Closed: Mon, 9/4 & 12/24.
**Reservations:** suggested. **Features:** children's menu; early bird specials; cocktails & lounge; valet parking;
a la carte. Nicely landscaped grounds. Elegant dining rooms in converted mansion. **Cards:** AE, CB, DI, DS, MC, VI.

# ALLAMUCHY

## LODGING

**THE INN AT PANTHER VALLEY**  Guaranteed Rates  **Phone:** 908/852-6000
All Year  1P: $80- 95  2P/1B: $80- 95  2P/2B: $80- 95  XP: $10 F16
⊕  **Location:** I-80 exit 19, 3/4 mi s on CR 517. CR 517 07820 (PO Box 183). **Fax:** 908/850-1503. **Terms:** Sr.
◆◆◆  discount; reserv deposit; monthly rates; no pets. **Facility:** 100 rooms. Shaded landscaped grounds around
Motor Inn  pond, in a quiet rural setting. Early American-style rooms. 8 efficiencies & fireplaces, $10 extra; 2 stories;
interior/exterior corridors; meeting rooms. **Dining & Entertainment:** Dining room, coffee shop; 6:30 am-10
pm; $5-$15; health conscious menu items; cocktails/lounge. **Services:** data ports, secretarial services; valet laundry.
**All Rooms:** free movies, cable TV. **Some Rooms:** refrigerators. **Cards:** AE, CB, DI, MC, VI.  ⒹⓈ⊗

## RESTAURANT

**MATTAR'S**  **Dinner:** $11-$20  **Phone:** 908/852-2300
◆◆◆  **Location:** I-80, exit 19; 1 mi s on CR 517. 07820. **Hours:** 11:30 am-2 & 5-10 pm, Fri-11 pm, Sat 5 pm-11
Italian  pm, Sun 2 pm-9 pm. Closed major holidays. **Reservations:** suggested; weekends. **Features:** semi-formal
attire; health conscious menu items; cocktails & lounge; entertainment; a la carte. A sophisticated dining
experience awaits; attractive dining rooms, good service & wonderfully prepared culinary treats to delight everyone's tastes.
**Cards:** AE, CB, DI, DS, MC, VI.  ⊗

# ANDOVER—700

## LODGING

**HOLIDAY MOTEL**  Rates Subject to Change  **Phone:** 201/786-5260
◆◆  All Year  1P: $65  2P/1B: $65  2P/2B: $65  XP: $6
Motel  **Location:** Westbound I-80, exit 25; then 8 mi n US 206, eastbound I-80, exit 19; then 7 mi n on CR 17 to jct
206, then 1 mi n on US 206. 708 US Hwy 206 07821. **Fax:** 201/786-7627. **Terms:** Reserv deposit; no pets.
**Facility:** 19 rooms. 1 story; exterior corridors. **Dining:** Cafeteria nearby. **Services:** data ports. **All Rooms:** shower baths,
cable TV. **Cards:** AE, DS, MC, VI.  Ⓓ⊗

# ATLANTIC CITY—38,000  (See ATLANTIC CITY ACCOMMODATIONS spotting map page A6; see index below)

To help you more easily locate accommodations in the Atlantic City area, the following
index and map show lodgings and restaurants within Atlantic City area.

**Index of Establishments on the ATLANTIC CITY ACCOMMODATIONS Spotting Map**

## Find the Hidden Money.
Read TourBook advertisements carefully;
some offer special discounts for AAA members.

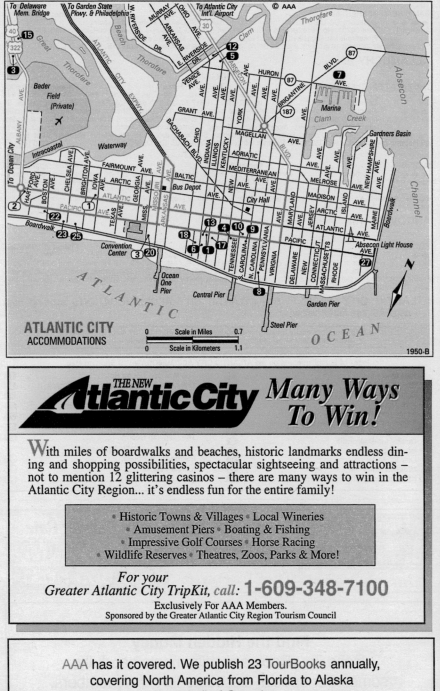

(See ATLANTIC CITY ACCOMMODATIONS spotting map page A6)

## LODGINGS

**BALA MOTOR INN**
Rates Subject to Change
Phone: 609/348-3031 **1**

| | Fri & Sat 5/1-10/31 | 1P: | $95- | 125 | | | 2P/2B: | $95- | 125 | XP: $12 | F12 |
| | Sun-Thurs 5/1-10/31 | 1P: | $75- | 100 | | | 2P/2B: | $75- | 100 | XP: $12 | F12 |
| Motel | Fri & Sat 11/1-4/30 | 1P: | $65- | 95 | | | 2P/2B: | $65- | 95 | XP: $12 | F12 |
| | Sun-Thurs 11/1-4/30 | 1P: | $50- | 85 | | | 2P/2B: | $50- | 85 | XP: $12 | F12 |

**Location:** Martin Luther King & Pacific Aves. 114 S Illinois Ave 08401. Fax: 609/347-6043. **Terms:** Reserv deposit, 3 day notice; AP, BP, MAP available; package plans; no pets. **Facility:** 108 rooms. 4 stories; interior/exterior corridors; heated pool. **Services:** Fee: childcare. **All Rooms:** cable TV. **Some Rooms:** radios. Fee: refrigerators. **Cards:** AE, CB, DI, MC, VI.   Ⓓ Ⓢ

**BALLY'S PARK PLACE CASINO HOTEL & TOWER**
Guaranteed Rates
Phone: 609/340-2000 **18**

| | 6/16-9/3 | 1P: | $125- | 215 | 2P/1B: | $125- | 215 | 2P/2B: | $125- | 215 | XP: $15 | F16 |
| | 5/1-6/15 & 9/4-12/2 | 1P: | $105- | 195 | 2P/1B: | $105- | 195 | 2P/2B: | $105- | 195 | XP: $15 | F16 |
| Hotel | 12/3-4/30 | 1P: | $75- | 165 | 2P/1B: | $75- | 165 | 2P/2B: | $75- | 165 | XP: $15 | F16 |

**Location:** Park Place & Boardwalk 08401. Fax: 609/340-4713. **Terms:** Check-in 4 pm; reserv deposit; package plans; 2 night min stay, weekends; no pets. **Facility:** 1255 rooms. Attractive public areas. 48 stories; interior corridors; oceanview; conference facilities; beach, 2 pools (2 heated, 1 indoor), steamrooms, whirlpools, inhalation room. Fee: parking; saunas, recreation facilities in summer; racquetball courts; exercise room, health club. **Dining & Entertainment:** 3 dining rooms, 2 restaurants, 2 cafeterias, coffee shop, deli; 24 hours; $6-$32; cocktails/lounge; revue show room; 24-hour room service. **Services:** secretarial services; valet laundry. Fee: massage; valet parking. **Recreation:** swimming. **All Rooms:** cable TV. Fee: movies. **Some Rooms:** honor bars, refrigerators, whirlpools. Fee: VCP's. **Cards:** AE, CB, DI, DS, MC, VI.   Ⓩ Ⓓ Ⓢ ⊗

**BEST WESTERN ENVOY INN**
Rates Subject to Change
Phone: 609/344-7117 **4**

| | 7/1-9/6 | | | | 2P/1B: | $78- | 125 | 2P/2B: | $78- | 125 | XP: $10 | F12 |
| Motel | 5/1-6/30 & 9/7-11/30 | | | | 2P/1B: | $58- | 110 | 2P/2B: | $58- | 110 | XP: $10 | F12 |
| | 12/1-4/30 | | | | 2P/1B: | $48- | 110 | 2P/2B: | $48- | 110 | XP: $10 | F12 |

**Location:** Pacific & New York aves. 1416 Pacific Ave 08401. Fax: 609/344-5659. **Terms:** Reserv deposit; CP available; no pets. **Facility:** 75 rooms. 4 stories; interior/exterior corridors. **Services:** data ports. **All Rooms:** cable TV. **Some Rooms:** whirlpools. Fee: refrigerators. **Cards:** AE, DS, MC, VI.   Ⓓ Ⓢ ⊗

**DAYS INN/ATLANTIC CITY-BOARDWALK**
Rates Subject to Change
Phone: 609/344-6101 **25**

| | Fri & Sat 5/15-9/30 | | | | 2P/1B: | $70- | 280 | 2P/2B: | $70- | 280 | XP: $10 | F16 |
| | Fri & Sat 5/1-5/14, Sun-Thurs | | | | | | | | | | | |
| | 5/15-9/30 & Fri & Sat | | | | | | | | | | | |
| Motor Inn | 10/1-4/30 | | | | 2P/1B: | $60- | 280 | 2P/2B: | $60- | 280 | XP: $10 | F16 |
| | Sun-Thurs 5/1-5/14 & | | | | | | | | | | | |
| | 10/1-4/30 | | | | 2P/1B: | $50- | 280 | 2P/2B: | $50- | 280 | XP: $10 | F16 |

**Location:** On the boardwalk. Boardwalk & Morris Ave 08401. Fax: 609/348-5335. **Terms:** Reserv deposit; 2 night min stay, weekends in season; no pets. **Facility:** 104 rooms. 5 stories; interior corridors; oceanview; pool; amusement arcade. **Dining & Entertainment:** Dining room; 7 am-10 pm; $9-$15; cocktails/lounge. **All Rooms:** cable TV. **Some Rooms:** Fee: refrigerators. **Cards:** AE, DS, MC, VI.   Ⓓ Ⓢ ⊗

**THE FLAGSHIP RESORT**
Rates Subject to Change
Phone: 609/343-7447 **27**

| | 5/1-1/2 & 4/1-4/30 | 1P: | $89- | 179 | 2P/1B: | $89- | 179 | 2P/2B: | $89- | 179 | XP: $15 | |
| | 1/3-3/31 | 1P: | $69- | 149 | 2P/1B: | $69- | 149 | 2P/2B: | $69- | 149 | XP: $15 | |

**Location:** At the boardwalk; 2 mi n on Atlantic Ave. 60 N Maine Ave 08401. Fax: 609/344-2702. **Terms:** Age restrictions may apply; check-in 4 pm; reserv deposit; package plans; no pets. **Facility:** 205 rooms. Some rooms with ocean/inlet views. Studio & 1-bedroom suites. Coffeemakers upon request. 32 stories; interior corridors; conference facilities; heated indoor pool, saunas, steamrooms, whirlpool; exercise room, video game room. **Dining & Entertainment:** Restaurant; 6:30 am-10:30 pm; deli 6 am-2 am; $6-$22; cocktails/lounge. **Services:** area transportation, to casino. Fee: childcare; coin laundry. **Recreation:** sun deck. **All Rooms:** efficiencies, no utensils, microwaves, refrigerators, cable TV. Fee: movies. **Cards:** AE, CB, DI, DS, JCB, MC, VI. *(See ad below)*   Ⓓ Ⓢ ⊗

**(See ATLANTIC CITY ACCOMMODATIONS spotting map page A6)**

**THE GRAND-A BALLY'S CASINO RESORT**  Rates Subject to Change  Phone: 609/347-7111  **22**
⊕⊕⊕  6/16-9/17  1P: $195- 215  2P/2B: $195- 215  XP: $20  F12
  5/1-6/15, 9/18-12/3 &
◆◆◆  4/10-4/30  1P: $165- 195  2P/2B: $165- 195  XP: $20  F12
Hotel  12/4-4/9  1P: $125- 165  2P/2B: $125- 165  XP: $20  F12
**Location:** On the boardwalk. Boston Ave at Pacific Ave 08401 (PO Box 1737). Fax: 609/236-7804.
**Terms:** Check-in 4 pm; reserv deposit, 3 day notice; package plans; 2 night min stay, weekends; no pets. **Facility:** 509 rooms. Large, oceanview rooms; high rise hotel. Turn-of-the-century atmosphere in public areas. 23 stories; interior corridors; beachfront; conference facilities; beach, heated indoor pool, saunas, steamrooms, whirlpools. Fee: parking; exercise room, health club, tanning beds. **Dining & Entertainment:** 3 dining rooms, 3 restaurants; 24 hours; $9-$35; cocktails/lounge; casino; 24-hour room service; entertainment. **Services:** secretarial services; valet laundry. Fee: childcare; massage; valet parking. **Recreation:** swimming. **All Rooms:** free & pay movies. **Some Rooms:** refrigerators, safes, whirlpools. Fee: VCP's. **Cards:** AE, DI, DS, MC, VI.  Ⓓ Ⓢ ⊗

**HAMPTON INN-WEST**  Rates Subject to Change  Phone: 609/484-1900  **15**
◆◆  Fri & Sat 5/26-10/9 [CP]  1P: $95- 110  2P/1B: $95- 110  2P/2B: $95- 110
Motel  Fri & Sat 5/1-5/25 &
  10/10-4/30 [CP]  1P: $79- 99  2P/1B: $79- 99  2P/2B: $79- 99
  Sun-Thurs 5/26-10/9 [CP]  1P: $62- 72  2P/1B: $62- 72  2P/2B: $62- 72
  Sun-Thurs 5/1-5/25 &
  10/10-4/30 [CP]  1P: $59- 69  2P/1B: $59- 69  2P/2B: $59- 69
**Location:** On US 40, e of Garden State Pkwy, exit 36, 2 3/4 mi e of jct US 9. 7079 Black Horse Pike 08232. Fax: 609/383-0731. **Terms:** Reserv deposit, on weekends; no pets. **Facility:** 143 rooms. Rates are for up to 4 persons; 6 stories; interior corridors; meeting rooms. **Services:** valet laundry; airport transportation. Fee: childcare, area transportation, to Grand Casino. **Recreation:** Fee: windsurfing & instruction. **All Rooms:** free movies, cable TV. **Some Rooms:** Fee: VCP's. **Cards:** AE, CB, DI, DS, MC, VI.  Ⓓ Ⓢ ⊗

**HOLIDAY INN BOARDWALK HOTEL**  Rates Subject to Change  Phone: 609/348-2200  **23**
⊕⊕⊕  6/24-9/14  1P: $100- 160  2P/1B: $100- 160  2P/2B: $100- 160  XP: $10  F19
  5/1-6/23, 9/15-10/31 &
◆◆◆  4/1-4/30  1P: $80- 130  2P/1B: $80- 130  2P/2B: $80- 130  XP: $10  F19
Hotel  11/1-11/30 & 3/1-3/30  1P: $70- 120  2P/1B: $70- 120  2P/2B: $70- 120  XP: $10  F19
  12/1-2/29  1P: $60- 110  2P/1B: $60- 110  2P/2B: $60- 110  XP: $10  F19
**Location:** On Boardwalk at Chelsea Ave. Chelsea Ave & Boardwalk 08401. Fax: 609/348-0168. **Terms:** Sr. discount; reserv deposit, 3 day notice; weekly rates; BP, CP, MAP available; package plans; 2 night min stay, weekends; no pets. **Facility:** 220 rooms. 20 stories; interior corridors; oceanview; meeting rooms; pool. **Dining:** Restaurant; 7 am-10 pm; $10-$25; cocktails. **Services:** data ports, secretarial services; valet laundry; valet parking. Fee: childcare, airport transportation. **All Rooms:** cable TV. Fee: movies. **Some Rooms:** Fee: refrigerators, VCP's. **Cards:** AE, CB, DI, DS, JCB, MC, VI. *(See color ad below)*  Ⓩ Ⓓ Ⓢ ⊗

**HOWARD JOHNSON**  Rates Subject to Change  Phone: 609/344-4193  **10**
⊕  Fri & Sat 6/22-9/15  2P/2B: $98- 175  XP: $15  F18
  Fri & Sat 5/1-6/21 &
◆◆  9/16-4/30  2P/2B: $88- 175  XP: $15  F18
Motor Inn  Sun-Thurs 6/22-9/15  2P/2B: $78- 98  XP: $15  F18
  Sun-Thurs 5/1-6/21 &
  9/16-4/30  2P/2B: $55- 75  XP: $15  F18
**Location:** At Pacific & Tennessee Aves. 1339 Pacific Ave 08401. Fax: 609/348-1263. **Terms:** Sr. discount; reserv deposit; no pets. **Facility:** 72 rooms. 1 two-bedroom unit. 3 stories; interior corridors; pool. **Dining:** Coffee shop; 7 am-4 pm, 6/22-9/15 to 9 pm; $8-$10; beer only. **Services:** valet parking. **All Rooms:** cable TV. **Some Rooms:** 4 efficiencies, no utensils, refrigerators. **Cards:** AE, CB, DI, DS, JCB, MC, VI. *(See color ad p A9)*  Ⓓ Ⓢ ⊗

**(See ATLANTIC CITY ACCOMMODATIONS spotting map page A6)**

**LIDO MOTEL**  Rates Subject to Change  Phone: 609/344-1975 **5**

| | | | | | | | |
|---|---|---|---|---|---|---|---|
| Fri & Sat 6/15-9/7 | 1P: | $60 | 2P/1B: | $60 | 2P/2B: | $70 | XP: $5 |
| Fri & Sat 5/1-6/14 & 9/8-4/30 | 1P: | $50 | 2P/1B: | $50 | 2P/2B: | $65 | XP: $5 |
| Sun-Thurs 6/15-9/7 | 1P: | $45 | 2P/1B: | $50 | 2P/2B: | $50 | XP: $5 |
| Sun-Thurs 5/1-6/14 & 9/8-4/30 | 1P: | $30 | 2P/1B: | $35 | 2P/2B: | $40 | XP: $5 |

Motel
**Location:** 1 1/2 mi w of boardwalk on US 30. 1600 Absecon Blvd 08401. **Terms:** Sr. discount; reserv deposit, 3 day notice; no pets. **Facility:** 27 rooms. All ground floor rooms. 1 story; exterior corridors; pool. **All Rooms:** combo & shower baths, cable TV. **Cards:** AE, CB, DI, DS, MC, VI. *(See color ad below)* Ⓓ

**LIDO TOO MOTEL**  Rates Subject to Change  Phone: 609/345-3555 **12**

| | | | | | | | | |
|---|---|---|---|---|---|---|---|---|
| Fri & Sat 6/15-9/7 | | | 2P/1B: | $60 | 2P/2B: | $70 | XP: $5 | D12 |
| Fri & Sat 5/1-6/14 & 9/8-4/30 | 1P: | $45 | 2P/1B: | $50 | 2P/2B: | $50 | XP: $5 | D12 |
| Sun-Thurs 6/15-9/7 | 1P: | $40 | 2P/1B: | $45 | 2P/2B: | $45 | XP: $5 | D12 |
| Sun-Thurs 5/1-6/14 & 9/8-4/30 | 1P: | $30 | 2P/1B: | $35 | 2P/2B: | $35 | XP: $5 | D12 |

Motel
**Location:** 1 1/2 mi w of boardwalk on US 30. 1400 Absecon Blvd 08401. **Terms:** Sr. discount; reserv deposit, 3 day notice; weekly rates; small pets only. **Facility:** 14 rooms. 1 story; exterior corridors; pool privileges at Lido Motel. **All Rooms:** cable TV, no phones. **Cards:** AE, CB, DI, DS, MC, VI. Ⓓ

**THE MADISON HOUSE HOTEL**  Rates Subject to Change  Phone: 609/345-1400 **17**

| | | | | | | | | |
|---|---|---|---|---|---|---|---|---|
| Fri & Sat 5/1-9/30 & 4/1-4/30 | 1P: | $85- 150 | 2P/1B: | $85- 150 | 2P/2B: | $85- 150 | XP: $10 | F16 |
| Fri & Sat 10/1-3/31 | 1P: | $45- 130 | 2P/1B: | $45- 130 | 2P/2B: | $45- 130 | XP: $10 | F16 |
| Sun-Thurs 5/1-9/30 & 4/1-4/30 | 1P: | $65- 85 | 2P/1B: | $65- 85 | 2P/2B: | $65- 85 | XP: $10 | F16 |
| Sun-Thurs 10/1-3/31 | 1P: | $35- 65 | 2P/1B: | $35- 65 | 2P/2B: | $35- 65 | XP: $10 | F16 |

Hotel
**Location:** 1/2 blk e of jct Pacific Ave & Dr Martin Luther King Blvd (Illinois Ave). 123 S Dr Martin Luther King Blvd 08401. Fax: 609/347-7265. **Terms:** Sr. discount; reserv deposit, 3 day notice; weekly rates; BP available; package plans; no pets. **Facility:** 215 rooms. Limited service hotel & compact, tastefully decorated guest rooms. 32 junior suites $85-$150; off season $60-$130; 14 stories; interior corridors. Fee: recreation facilities at the Sands Hotel. **Dining & Entertainment:** Coffee shop; 7 am-11 am; cocktail lounge. **Services:** data ports; valet laundry. **All Rooms:** combo & shower baths, cable TV. **Some Rooms:** A/C, honor bars, coffeemakers. Fee: refrigerators. **Cards:** AE, DI, DS, MC, VI.
*(See color ad p A10)* Ⓓ Ⓢ ⊘

**MERV GRIFFIN'S RESORTS CASINO HOTEL**  Rates Subject to Change  Phone: 609/344-6000 **8**

| | | | | | | | | |
|---|---|---|---|---|---|---|---|---|
| 6/19-9/17 | 1P: | $110- 205 | 2P/1B: | $110- 205 | 2P/2B: | $110- 205 | XP: $10 | F16 |
| 5/1-6/18 & 9/18-4/30 | 1P: | $80- 180 | 2P/1B: | $80- 180 | 2P/2B: | $80- 180 | XP: $10 | F16 |

Hotel
**Location:** Oceanfront, at east end of North Carolina Ave. 1133 Boardwalk 08401. Fax: 609/340-7684. **Terms:** Check-in 4 pm; reserv deposit; package plans; 2 night min stay, weekends; no pets. **Facility:** 668 rooms. Attractive marble lobby. 9-15 stories; interior corridors; beachfront; conference facilities; beach, heated indoor/outdoor pool, saunas, steamrooms, whirlpools; exercise room, health club, beauty salon, 2 eucalyptus rooms, video game room. Fee: parking. **Dining & Entertainment:** 3 dining rooms, 2 restaurants, deli; 24 hours; $12-$30; health conscious menu; cocktails/lounge; 24-hour room service; entertainment, nightclub. **Services:** data ports; valet laundry. Fee: childcare; massage; valet parking. **Recreation:** swimming. **All Rooms:** free & pay movies, cable TV. **Some Rooms:** honor bars, refrigerators, safes, whirlpools. **Cards:** AE, CB, DI, MC, VI.  Roll in showers. Ⓓ Ⓢ ⊘

Check out our **bold** listings!

**(See ATLANTIC CITY ACCOMMODATIONS spotting map page A6)**

| MIDTOWN MOTOR INN | | Rates Subject to Change | | | Phone: 609/348-3031 | 13 |
|---|---|---|---|---|---|---|
| Fri & Sat 6/1-10/31 | | 1P: $95- 125 | | | 2P/2B: $95- 125  XP: $12 | F12 |
| Sun-Thurs 6/1-10/31 | | 1P: $75- 100 | | | 2P/2B: $75- 100  XP: $12 | F12 |
| Fri & Sat 5/1-5/31 & 11/1-4/30 | | 1P: $65- 95 | | | 2P/2B: $65- 95  XP: $12 | F12 |
| Sun-Thurs 5/1-5/31 & 11/1-4/30 | | 1P: $50- 85 | | | 2P/2B: $50- 85  XP: $12 | F12 |

**Location:** Indiana & Pacific aves. 101 S Indiana Ave 08401 (PO Box 267). Fax: 609/347-6043. **Terms:** Reserv deposit, 3 day notice; $1 service charge; AP, BP, MAP available; package plans; no pets. **Facility:** 172 rooms. 7 stories; interior corridors; meeting rooms; wading pool, seasonal heated indoor pool, sun deck. **Dining:** Dining room; 24 hours; cocktails. **Services:** valet parking. Fee: childcare. **All Rooms:** cable TV. **Some Rooms:** radios. Fee: refrigerators. **Cards:** AE, CB, DI, MC, VI. *(See ad below)*

# Atlantic City's Only Victorian Hotel With An "Indoor" Connection To The Sands Casino!

★ 215 Newly Renovated Rooms & Suites
★ "Best Location"— Center City Beachblock
★ Affordable Rates & Exciting Package Plans
★ Unique National Landmark Hotel
★ Restaurant & Lounge On Premises

## The MADISON H·O·U·S·E Hotel

*Major Credit Cards Accepted*

## 1-800-458-9879

123 So. Dr. M.L.K Blvd. (Illinois Ave.)
Atlantic City, NJ 08401
609-345-1400

**Right In The Heart Of The Action!**

## Sit back and enjoy the ride.
Let our Triptik maps take the worry out of travel.

(See ATLANTIC CITY ACCOMMODATIONS spotting map page A6)

**QUALITY INN-BOARDWALK**  AAA Special Value Rates  Phone: 609/345-7070  **9**
| | | | | | | | | | |
|---|---|---|---|---|---|---|---|---|---|
| | Fri & Sat 6/16-9/3 | 1P: | $125 | | 2P/2B: | $125 | | XP: $10 | F18 |
| | Fri & Sat 5/1-6/15 & 9/4-4/30 | 1P: | $88- | 110 | 2P/2B: | $88- | 110 | XP: $10 | F18 |
| | Sun-Thurs 6/16-9/3 | 1P: | $80- | 88 | 2P/2B: | $95- | 98 | XP: $10 | F18 |
Motor Inn | Sun-Thurs 5/1-6/15 & | | | | | | | | |
| | 9/4-4/30 | 1P: | $62- | 68 | 2P/2B: | $62- | 75 | XP: $10 | F18 |

**Location:** S Carolina & Pacific aves 08401. Fax: 609/345-0633. **Terms:** Check-in 4 pm; reserv deposit; BP available; package plans; 2 night min stay, weekends in season; no pets. **Facility:** 203 rooms. Property built onto an existing Quaker school, circa late 1800. 16 stories; interior corridors; meeting rooms. **Dining & Entertainment:** Restaurant; 24 hours; $8-$15; cocktails/lounge. **Services:** valet laundry. **All Rooms:** cable TV. Fee: movies. **Some Rooms:** whirlpools. Fee: refrigerators. **Cards:** AE, CB, DI, DS, JCB, MC, VI. *(See color ad below)*  Ⓓ Ⓢ ⊗

**SANDS HOTEL & CASINO**  Rates Subject to Change  Phone: 609/441-4000  **6**
| | | | | | | | | |
|---|---|---|---|---|---|---|---|---|
| ◆◆◆ | Fri & Sat | 2P/1B: | $129- | 229 | 2P/2B: | $129- | 229 | XP: $12 F18 |
| Hotel | Sun-Thurs | 2P/1B: | $99- | 189 | 2P/2B: | $99- | 189 | XP: $12 F18 |

**Location:** Indiana Ave & Brighton Park. Fax: 609/441-4624. **Terms:** Reserv deposit; package plans; no pets. **Facility:** 534 rooms. Attractively furnished guest rooms & luxurious public areas. Rates for up to 2 persons; 20 stories; interior corridors; conference facilities; luxury level rooms; beach, indoor/outdoor pool, saunas, whirlpool; exercise room, health club. Fee: tanning beds, video game room. **Dining & Entertainment:** 4 dining rooms, restaurant, coffee shop; 24 hours; $10-$35; health conscious menu; cocktails/lounge; 24-hour room service; entertainment, nightclub. **Services:** valet laundry; valet parking. Fee: childcare; massage. **Recreation:** swimming. **All Rooms:** free & pay movies, cable TV. **Some Rooms:** refrigerators, safes, VCP's, whirlpools. **Cards:** AE, CB, DI, DS, MC, VI.  Roll in showers. 🗷 Ⓓ Ⓢ ⊗

**SUN N' SURF**  Rates Subject to Change  Phone: 609/344-2515  **3**
| | | | | | | | | |
|---|---|---|---|---|---|---|---|---|
| | Fri & Sat 6/15-9/7 | 1P: | $60 | 2P/1B: | $60 | 2P/2B: | $70 | XP:$5-10 F12 |
| | Fri & Sat 5/1-6/14 & 9/8-4/30 | 1P: | $50 | 2P/1B: | $50 | 2P/2B: | $65 | XP: $5 F12 |
| ◆ | Sun-Thurs 6/15-9/7 | 1P: | $40 | 2P/1B: | $45 | 2P/2B: | $50 | XP: $5 F12 |
| Motel | Sun-Thurs 5/1-6/14 & | | | | | | | |
| | 9/8-4/30 | 1P: | $30 | 2P/1B: | $35 | 2P/2B: | $40 | XP: $5 F12 |

**Location:** 1 1/2 mi w on US 40. 1600 Albany Ave 08401. **Terms:** Reserv deposit, 4 day notice; weekly rates; small pets only, $10 dep req. **Facility:** 25 rooms. 1 story; exterior corridors; pool. **All Rooms:** shower baths, cable TV. **Cards:** AE, DS, MC, VI. *(See color ad p A9)*  Ⓓ

# WHEN YOU'RE LIVING OUT OF A SUITCASE...

**(See ATLANTIC CITY ACCOMMODATIONS spotting map page A6)**

**TRUMP PLAZA HOTEL & CASINO**
Guaranteed Rates    Phone: 609/441-6000   **20**

6/12-9/12    1P: $185- 205   2P/1B: $185- 205   2P/2B: $185- 205   XP: $10   F18

5/1-6/11, 9/13-11/30 &

3/13-4/30    1P: $160- 185   2P/1B: $160- 185   2P/2B: $160- 185   XP: $10   F18

Hotel   12/1-3/12    1P: $120- 145   2P/1B: $120- 145   2P/2B: $120- 145   XP: $10   F18

**Location:** Mississippi & Boardwalk 08401 (PO Box 1980). Fax: 609/441-7881. **Terms:** Check-in 4 pm; reserv deposit; package plans; 2 night min stay, weekends in season; no pets. **Facility:** 556 rooms. All rooms with ocean view. 35 stories; interior corridors; business center, conference facilities; luxury level rooms; beach, heated indoor pool; 2 tennis courts; video arcade, shuffleboard. Fee: parking; saunas, whirlpools; exercise room, health club, tanning booths, skin & beauty treatments. **Dining & Entertainment:** 3 dining rooms, 3 restaurants, cafeteria, coffee shop, deli; 24 hours; $7-$50; cocktails/lounge; 24-hour room service; also, Ivana's, see separate listing; entertainment, nightclub. **Services:** data ports, secretarial services; valet laundry. Fee: PC; childcare; massage; valet parking. **Recreation:** swimming. **All Rooms:** free & pay movies, cable TV. **Some Rooms:** refrigerators, safes. Fee: VCP's, whirlpools. **Cards:** AE, CB, DI, DS, MC, VI.

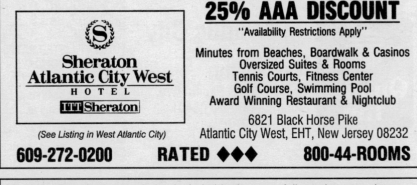
In the listings, the meal plan included in the rates follows the open dates.

**(See ATLANTIC CITY ACCOMMODATIONS spotting map page A6)**

**TRUMP'S CASTLE CASINO RESORT**          Rates Subject to Change          **Phone:** 609/441-2000      **7**
AAA
Hotel

| | 6/30-9/3 | 1P: $110- 325 | 2P/1B: $110- 325 | 2P/2B: $110- 325 | XP: $15 | F18 |
| | 5/1-6/29 & 9/4-4/30 | 1P: $80- 305 | 2P/1B: $80- 305 | 2P/2B: $80- 305 | XP: $15 | F18 |

◆◆◆ **Location:** On SR 87, 3/4 mi n of US 30; at Frank S Farley Marina. Huron Ave & Brigantine Blvd 08401. **Fax:** 609/441-8541. **Terms:** Check-in 4 pm; credit card guarantee; AP, BP, CP available; package plans; 2 night min stay, weekends in season; no pets. **Facility:** 725 rooms. Large, bayside casino. Spacious, comfortably furnished deluxe hotel rooms & suites. 23 two-bedroom units. 27 stories; interior corridors; conference facilities; luxury level rooms; heated pool, wading pool, saunas, steamroom, whirlpools; 4 lighted tennis courts; sports court, heliport, shuffleboard. Fee: parking; miniature golf; tanning booths. **Dining & Entertainment:** 3 dining rooms, restaurant, cafeteria, coffee shop, deli; 24 hours; $6-$29; cocktails; 24-hour room service; entertainment, nightclub. **Services:** secretarial services; valet laundry; area transportation. Fee: airport transportation; valet parking. **Recreation:** jogging. **All Rooms:** free & pay movies, cable TV. **Some Rooms:** honor bars, refrigerators, whirlpools. Fee: VCP's. **Cards:** AE, CB, DI, DS, JCB, MC, VI.

## RESTAURANTS

**IVANA'S**                                 **Dinner:** over $31                          **Phone:** 609/441-6000      **3**
◆◆◆ **Location:** In Trump Plaza Hotel & Casino. Mississippi & Boardwalk 08401. **Hours:** 6 pm-11 pm, Sun 10
Continental am-2 pm. Closed: Wed & Thurs. **Reservations:** required. **Features:** semi-formal attire; Sunday brunch; cocktails; fee for parking & valet parking; a la carte. Elegant dining room. Attentive, professional service. Very good wine list. **Cards:** AE, CB, DI, DS, MC, VI.

**KNIFE & FORK INN**                        **Dinner:** over $31                          **Phone:** 609/344-1133      **2**
◆◆◆ **Location:** At e end of US Rt 40. Atlantic , Albany & Pacific aves 08401. **Hours:** noon-2 & 6-10 pm. Closed:
Seafood 12/12-12/26, Sun-Wed 12/1-3/31; Sun & Mon for lunch all year. **Reservations:** suggested. **Features:** formal attire; cocktails & lounge; a la carte. Atlantic City landmark since 1912. Validated parking in lot across the street. Jackets required at dinner. **Cards:** AE, DI, DS, MC, VI.

**PEKING DUCK HOUSE**                       **Dinner:** $11-$20                           **Phone:** 609/348-1313      **1**
AAA **Location:** 2801-03 Atlantic & Iowa aves 08401. **Hours:** noon-11 pm, Fri & Sat-midnight, Sun 2 pm-11 pm.
**Reservations:** suggested; summer weekends. **Features:** casual dress; early bird specials; carryout;
◆◆◆ cocktails; a la carte. Imaginative menu. Tableside preparation. Peking duck with no advance notice.
Chinese Extensive wine list. Exotic desserts. **Cards:** AE, CB, DI, MC, VI.

# ATLANTIC HIGHLANDS

## RESTAURANT

**HOFBRAUHAUS**                             **Dinner:** $21-$30                           **Phone:** 908/291-0224
◆◆ **Location:** On Scenic Dr. 301 Scenic Dr 07716. **Hours:** 4 pm-10 pm, Sat & Sun noon-11.
Ethnic **Reservations:** suggested; weekends. **Features:** casual dress; children's menu; cocktails & lounge; entertainment; a la carte. Charming German inn serving authentic dishes in a delightful atmosphere. Entertainment on weekends. **Cards:** AE, DI, DS, MC, VI.

# AVALON—1,800

## RESTAURANT

**TORTILLA FLATS**                          **Dinner:** $11-$20                           **Phone:** 609/967-5658
◆ **Location:** Exit 13 off Garden State Pkwy, 3 1/2 mi se on CR 601, then 1/4 mi n on Dune Dr. 2540 Dune Dr
Mexican 08202. **Hours:** 5 pm-10 pm, Sat & Sun-11 pm. Closed: 4/7, 11/23 & 12/1-2/29. **Features:** casual dress; children's menu; carryout; a la carte. Great Mexican & Southwestern cuisine. Daily specials. Smoke free premises. **Cards:** AE, MC, VI.

# AVON BY THE SEA

## LODGING

**ATLANTIC VIEW INN**                       Rates Subject to Change                       **Phone:** 908/774-8505

| | 5/25-9/10 [BP] | 1P: $75- 115 | 2P/1B: $75- 115 | 2P/2B: $75- 115 | XP: $20 | D14 |
| | 5/1-5/24 & 9/11-4/30 [BP] | 1P: $60- 90 | 2P/1B: $60- 90 | 2P/2B: $60- 90 | XP: $20 | D14 |

◆◆ Historic Bed & Breakfast **Location:** One block from ocean. 20 Woodlawn Ave 07717. **Fax:** 908/775-3206. **Terms:** Reserv deposit; weekly rates; 2 night min stay, weekends in season; no pets. **Facility:** 15 rooms. Lovely Victorian inn; owners have pets. 3 stories, no elevator; interior corridors; smoke free premises; beach. **Dining:** Breakfast served 8-10:30 am; restaurants nearby. **Recreation:** swimming. **All Rooms:** no A/C, no phones. **Some Rooms:** refrigerators, combo & shower baths, shared bathrooms. **Cards:** AE, MC, VI.

# BASKING RIDGE (See NEW JERSEY METRO AREA ACCOMMODATIONS spotting map pages A40 & A41; see index starting on page A39)

## LODGING

**OLDE MILL INN**                           Rates Subject to Change                       **Phone:** 908/221-1100      **1**
◆◆◆ All Year [CP] 1P: $125    2P/1B: $135    2P/2B: $135    XP: $5    F18
Motor Inn **Location:** On US 202, jct I-287, exit 26B (second ramp). US 202 & Maple Ave 07920 (225 Rte 202). **Fax:** 908/221-1560. **Terms:** Reserv deposit; monthly rates; package plans, weekends; no pets. **Facility:** 102 rooms. Luxurious public space & guest room decor offering classic homey comfort with roaring fireplace welcoming guest to property. Suites avail; 2 stories; interior/exterior corridors; business center, meeting rooms; exercise room. **Dining:** Also, The Grain House, see separate listing. **Services:** data ports, secretarial services; valet laundry. Fee: PC, area transportation; airport transportation. **All Rooms:** cable TV. Fee: movies. **Some Rooms:** kitchen, microwaves, refrigerators, whirlpools. **Cards:** AE, CB, DI, DS, MC, VI.

## RESTAURANT

**THE GRAIN HOUSE** Historical                **Dinner:** $11-$20                          **Phone:** 908/221-1100      **1**
◆◆ **Location:** Adjacent to Olde Mill Inn. US 202 & Maple Ave 07920. **Hours:** 11:30 am-2:30 & 5:30-10 pm,
American Fri-11 pm, Sat noon-3 & 5:30-11 pm, Sun 10:30 am-9 pm. **Reservations:** suggested. **Features:** casual dress; Sunday brunch; health conscious menu items; carryout; cocktails & lounge; a la carte. Historic, converted grain mill featuring Americana cuisine served in authentic style; wonderful decorated dining rooms with early American antiques. **Cards:** AE, CB, DI, DS, MC, VI.

## BAY HEAD

### LODGINGS

**BAY HEAD GABLES**   Rates Subject to Change   **Phone: 908/892-9844**
◆●◆   6/11-9/5 [BP]   2P/1B:  $100-  185
Bed &   5/1-6/10, 9/6-12/31 &
Breakfast   4/1-4/30 [BP]   2P/1B:  $95-  140
**Location:** North end on SR 35S. 200 Main Ave 08742. Fax: 908/295-2196. **Terms:** Open 5/1-12/31 & 4/1-4/30; age restrictions may apply; reserv deposit, 10 day notice; weekly rates; 2 night min stay, weekends in season; no pets. **Facility:** 11 rooms. Charming accomodations in a tranquil setting; some rooms with ocean view. 3 stories; interior corridors; smoke free premises; meeting rooms; beach. **Dining:** Restaurant nearby. **Recreation:** swimming. **All Rooms:** combo & shower baths, no phones, no TVs. **Cards:** AE, DS, MC, VI.   Ⓓ ⊗

**CONOVERS BAY HEAD INN**   Rates Subject to Change   **Phone: 908/892-4664**
◆◆◆   All Year [BP]   2P/1B:  $85-  195
Historic Bed   **Location:** Between Forsythe & Johnson sts on SR 35S, 1 blk from ocean. 646 Main Ave 08742. **Terms:** Age
& Breakfast   restrictions may apply; reserv deposit, 14 day notice; weekly rates; 2 night min stay, weekends; no pets.
**Facility:** 12 rooms. Relax in a warm & inviting atmosphere as cordial hosts provide gracious hospitality. Unique antiques abound in cozy accomodations. Owners have a dog. Closed Mon-Thur 11/1-2/15, except 11/23 & 12/25; 3 stories, no elevator; interior corridors; designated smoking area; oceanview; meeting rooms; complimentary beach passes. **Dining:** Restaurant nearby. **Recreation:** swimming. **All Rooms:** combo & shower baths, no A/C, no phones, no TVs. **Some Rooms:** coffeemakers, refrigerators. **Cards:** AE, MC, VI.   Ⓓ ⊗

**GRENVILLE HOTEL**   Rates Subject to Change   **Phone: 908/892-3100**
◆◆◆   5/1-9/30 & 3/31-4/30   2P/1B:  $80-  205
Historic   10/1-10/29   2P/1B:  $60-  138
Country Inn   10/30-3/30   2P/1B:  $57-  107
**Location:** SR 353 at Bridge Ave, 1 blk from ocean. 345 Main Ave 08742. Fax: 908/892-0599. **Terms:** Reserv deposit, 7 day notice, 7/1-8/31; package plans; no pets. **Facility:** 31 rooms. This Victorian era country inn affords gracious hospitality in a warm & inviting atmosphere. 4 stories; interior corridors; oceanview; meeting rooms; complimentary beach passes. **Dining:** Dining room, see separate listing. **Services:** secretarial services; valet laundry. **Recreation:** swimming. **All Rooms:** combo & shower baths, cable TV. **Some Rooms:** Fee: refrigerators. **Cards:** AE, DI, DS, MC, VI.   Ⓓ Ⓢ

### RESTAURANT

**GRENVILLE BY THE SEA**   **Dinner:** $21-$30   **Phone:** 908/892-3100
◆◆   **Location:** In the Grenville Hotel. 345 Main Ave 08742. **Hours:** 11:30 am-2:30 & 5-9 pm, Fri & Sat-9:30 pm.
American   Closed: Mon except July & Aug & 12/25. **Reservations:** suggested. **Features:** casual dress; Sunday brunch; children's menu; health conscious menu items; wine only; a la carte, also prix fixe. Delightfully charming dining room serving a tempting array of house specialties. **Cards:** AE, DI, DS, MC, VI.

## BEACH HAVEN—1,500

### LODGING

**ENGLESIDE INN**   Rates Subject to Change   **Phone:** 609/492-1251
🆎   5/26-5/29 & 6/9-9/4   2P/2B:  $129-  265   XP: $10
   9/5-9/17   2P/2B:  $85-  152   XP: $7
◆◆   5/30-6/8 & 9/18-12/31   2P/2B:  $67-  133   XP: $7
Motor Inn   5/1-5/25 & 1/1-4/30   2P/2B:  $67-  133   XP: $7
**Location:** 7 1/4 mi s of SR 72 causeway to Engleside Ave, then 2 blks e. 30 Engleside Ave 08008. Fax: 609/492-9175. **Terms:** Reserv deposit, 10 day notice; 4 night min stay, weekends in season; pets, $10. **Facility:** 72 rooms. Many with balcony & patio overlooking ocean. 3 stories, no elevator; exterior corridors; beachfront; meeting rooms; beach, heated pool, sauna, whirlpool. Fee: exercise room. **Dining & Entertainment:** Restaurant; 8 am-2 & 5-9 pm; closed Mon & Tues for dinner off season; $8-$20; cocktails/lounge. **Services:** massage. **Recreation:** swimming. **All Rooms:** refrigerators, combo & shower baths, cable TV, VCP's. **Some Rooms:** 38 efficiencies, radios, whirlpools. **Cards:** AE, CB, DI, DS, MC, VI. *(See color ad below)*   Ⓓ ⊗

## BELLMAWR—12,600   (See PHILADELPHIA & VICINITY ACCOMMODATIONS spotting map pages A196 & A197; see index starting on page A193)

### LODGINGS

**BELLMAWR MOTOR INN**   AAA Special Value Rates   **Phone:** 609/931-6300   99
🆎   All Year   1P: $37   2P/1B:  $43   2P/2B:  $47   XP:  $4  F12
◆◆   **Location:** On SR 168, just n of tpk exit 3. 312 S Black Horse Pike 08031. **Terms:** Reserv deposit, 4 day
Motel   notice; weekly rates; no pets. **Facility:** 28 rooms. 2 stories; exterior corridors. **Dining:** Restaurant nearby. **All Rooms:** free movies. **Cards:** AE, DI, DS, MC, VI.   Ⓓ ⊗

(See PHILADELPHIA & VICINITY ACCOMMODATIONS spotting map pages A196 & A197)

**ECONO LODGE**    Rates Subject to Change    Phone: 609/931-2800    96
All Year    1P:  $41    2P/1B:  $47    2P/2B:  $52    XP:  $6  F18
Motel    **Location:** On SR 168, 1/4 mi n of NJ Tpk exit 3; 1/2 mi s of I-295, exit 28. 301 S Black Horse Pike 08031.
Fax: 609/931-6633. **Terms:** Sr. discount; credit card guarantee; no pets. **Facility:** 46 rooms. 2 stories; exterior
corridors;  meeting  rooms.  **Services:**  data  ports.  **All  Rooms:**  free  movies,  cable  TV.
**Some Rooms:** refrigerators. Fee: microwaves. **Cards:** AE, DI, DS, MC, VI.

**HOWARD JOHNSON**    AAA Special Value Rates    Phone: 609/931-0700    97
Fri & Sat [CP]    1P:  $60    2P/1B:  $65    2P/2B:  $65    XP:  $5  F18
Motel    Sun-Thurs [CP]    1P:  $43    2P/1B:  $48    2P/2B:  $48    XP:  $5  F18
**Location:** New Jersey Tpk, exit 3. 341 S Black Horse Pk 08031. Fax: 609/933-2808. **Terms:** Credit card
guarantee, 3 day notice; no pets. **Facility:** 90 rooms. 2 stories; interior/exterior corridors; conference facilities; heated pool.
**All Rooms:** free movies, cable TV. **Some Rooms:** refrigerators. **Cards:** AE, CB, DI, DS, MC, VI.    (D) ⊗

## RESTAURANT

**PULCINELLO'S CORAL REEF RESTURANT & LOUNGE**    **Dinner:** $21-$30    **Phone:** 609/931-3434    122
Italian    **Location:** On NJ Tpk, exit 3, & 1/2 mi s of I-295, exit 28. 317 S Black House Pike
08031. **Hours:** 11:20 am-2 am. Closed: 12/25. **Reservations:** suggested; weekends. **Features:** casual
dress; carryout; cocktails & lounge; entertainment; valet parking. Lively atmosphere, live music or DJ's
nightly. **Cards:** AE, MC, VI.    ⊗

# BELMAR—5,900

## LODGING

**BELMAR MOTOR LODGE**    Guaranteed Rates    Phone: 908/681-6600
Fri & Sat 5/25-9/4    1P:  $96    2P/1B:  $96    2P/2B:  $96    XP: $10  F12
Sun-Thurs 5/25-9/4    1P:  $82    2P/1B:  $82    2P/2B:  $82    XP: $10  F12
Motel    Fri & Sat 5/1-5/24    1P: $60-  70    2P/1B: $60-  70    2P/2B: $60-  70    XP: $10  F12
Sun-Thurs 5/1-5/24 &
9/5-4/30    1P: $50-  67    2P/1B: $50-  67    2P/2B: $50-  67    XP: $10  F12
**Location:** On SR 35; at 10th Ave, opposite Shark River Marina. 910 River Rd 07719. Fax: 908/681-6604. **Terms:** Sr.
discount; reserv deposit, 3 day notice; no pets. **Facility:** 55 rooms. Enjoy spacious accomodations is a warm friendly atmos-
phere, close proximity to docking facilities. 2 stories; interior corridors; meeting rooms; pool. **Dining:** Restaurant nearby.
**Services:** data ports, secretarial services. Fee: coin laundry. **All Rooms:** free movies, cable TV. **Some Rooms:** radios.
Fee: VCP's. **Cards:** AE, DI, MC, VI.    (D) ⊗

# BLACKWOOD

## LODGING

**HOJO INN**    AAA Special Value Rates    Phone: 609/228-4040
Fri & Sat [CP]    1P: $57-  95    2P/1B: $57-  95    2P/2B: $57-  95    XP:  $7  F18
Sun-Thurs [CP]    1P: $52-  75    2P/1B: $52-  75    2P/2B: $52-  75    XP:  $7  F18
Motel    **Location:** At jct of SR 168 & SR 42, Atlantic City Expwy. 832 N Black Horse Pike 08012.
Fax: 609/227-7544. **Terms:** Credit card guarantee; weekly rates; pets, $10. **Facility:** 100 rooms. Traditional
motel rooms, 1-bedroom suites. 3 stories, no elevator; exterior corridors; pool, whirlpool. **Services:** Fee: coin
laundry. **All Rooms:** free movies, cable TV. **Some Rooms:** whirlpools. Fee: microwaves, refrigerators. **Cards:** AE, CB, DI,
DS, JCB, MC, VI.    (D) ⊗

# BORDENTOWN—4,300

## LODGINGS

**BEST WESTERN INN**    Rates Subject to Change    Phone: 609/298-8000
All Year [CP]    1P: $60-  70    2P/1B:  $70-  80    2P/2B:  $70-  80    XP: $10  F12
Motor Inn    **Location:** Tpk exit 7, 3/4 mi n on US 206, property on s side of highway. US 206S & Dunnsmill Rd 08505.
Fax: 609/291-9757. **Terms:** Sr. discount; no pets. **Facility:** 102 rooms. Spacious accommodations; close prox-
imity to major highway. 3 stories; exterior corridors; meeting rooms; saunas, whirlpool, small heated indoor
pool; exercise room. **Dining & Entertainment:** Restaurant; 6:30 am-10 & 5-10 pm; $10-$21; health
conscious menu items; cocktails/lounge. **Services:** data ports; valet laundry. **All Rooms:** free movies, refrigerators, cable
TV. **Cards:** AE, CB, DI, DS, MC, VI. *(See color ad below)*    (D) ⊗

**DAYS INN-BORDENTOWN**     Rates Subject to Change     Phone: 609/298-6100
5/26-9/5     1P: $65- 75  2P/1B: $75- 85  2P/2B: $75- 85  XP: $10  F12
5/1-5/25 & 9/6-4/30     1P: $49- 55  2P/1B: $55- 65  2P/2B: $55- 65  XP: $10  F12
◆◆ **Location:** Tpk exit 7, US 206N. US 206N 08505. Fax: 609/298-7509. **Terms:** Sr. discount; package plans;
Motor Inn     weekends & in summer; no pets. **Facility:** 131 rooms. 2 stories; interior/exterior corridors; meeting rooms; pool.
**Dining & Entertainment:** Restaurant; 6:30 am-10 & 5-10 pm; $7-$16; health conscious menu items;
cocktails/lounge. **Services:** secretarial services; valet laundry. **All Rooms:** cable TV. Fee: movies. **Cards:** AE, CB, DI, DS,
MC, VI. *(See color ad below)*     Ⓓ ⊗

**HOLIDAY INN EXPRESS**     AAA Special Value Rates     Phone: 609/298-3200
All Year [CP]     1P: $55- 85  2P/1B: $55- 85  2P/2B: $55- 85  XP: $10  F17
◆◆◆ **Location:** Tpk exit 7, US 206N. 1083 Rt US 206N 08505. Fax: 609/298-8845. **Terms:** Weekly rates; no pets.
Motel     **Facility:** 95 rooms. 2 stories; interior corridors; meeting rooms; pool. **Services:** data ports, secretarial
services; valet laundry. **All Rooms:** free movies, cable TV. **Some Rooms:** Fee: microwaves, refrigerators,
VCP's. **Cards:** AE, CB, DI, DS, MC, VI.     Ⓓ Ⓢ ⊗

## BRIDGEPORT

**LODGING**

**HOLIDAY INN I-295 (EXECUTIVE CONFERENCE CENTER)**     AAA Special Value Rates     Phone: 609/467-3322
All Year     1P: $86- 110  2P/1B: $96- 120  2P/2B: $96- 120  XP: $10  F19
Motor Inn **Location:** Exit 10, I-295. I-295 at Center Square Rd 08014 (PO Box 304). Fax: 609/467-3031.
**Terms:** Reserv deposit; CP available; no pets. **Facility:** 149 rooms. Very contemporary rooms & excellent
public facilities. 4 stories; interior corridors; conference facilities; luxury level rooms; heated indoor pool, whirlpool; exercise
room, basketball, game room, volleyball. **Dining & Entertainment:** Restaurant; 6:30 am-10 pm; $6-$20; cocktails/lounge.
**Services:** data ports; valet laundry. Fee: airport transportation. **All Rooms:** free & pay movies, cable TV.
**Some Rooms:** microwaves, refrigerators. Fee: whirlpools. **Cards:** AE, CB, DI, DS, JCB, MC, VI.     ▨ Ⓓ Ⓢ ⊗

## BRIDGETON—18,900

**LODGING**

**DAYS INN**     Rates Subject to Change     Phone: 609/455-1500
◆◆ All Year [CP]     1P: $50- 55  2P/1B: $50- 55  2P/2B: $55     XP: $5  F12
Motel     **Location:** 1 mi e on SR 49. 500 E Broad St 08302. Fax: 609/451-1556. **Terms:** Credit card guarantee; no
pets. **Facility:** 32 rooms. Contemporary room appointments. Ground floor units with drive-up entries. 2 stories;
exterior corridors. **All Rooms:** free movies, cable TV. **Cards:** AE, CB, DI, DS, MC, VI.     Ⓓ ⊗

## BRIDGEWATER—32,500     (See NEW JERSEY METRO AREA ACCOMMODATIONS
spotting map pages A40 & A41; see index starting on page A39)

**LODGING**

**BEST WESTERN RED BULL INN**     Guaranteed Rates     Phone: 908/722-4000  ❹
Mon-Thurs [CP]     1P: $51     2P/1B: $51     2P/2B: $56     XP: $10  F
Fri-Sun [CP]     1P: $48     2P/1B: $48     2P/2B: $52     XP: $10  F
◆◆ **Location:** Westbound on US 22, 2 mi e of jct US 202 & 206; 1/4 mi w of jct I-287. 1271 Rt 22W 08807.
Motor Inn **Fax:** 908/722-4840. **Terms:** Sr. discount; reserv deposit; no pets. **Facility:** 111 rooms. Enjoy modest accom-
modations on nicely landscaped grounds; cordial staff. 2 stories; exterior corridors; pool; playground.
**Dining:** Restaurant; 11:30 am-10 pm, Sat 5 pm-10 pm, Sun 3 pm-9 pm; $9-$14; health conscious menu items; cocktails.
**Services:** data ports; valet laundry. **All Rooms:** free movies, cable TV. **Some Rooms:** Fee: VCP's. **Cards:** AE, DI, DS, MC,
VI.     Ⓓ ⊗

## BROOKLAWN—1,800     (See PHILADELPHIA & VICINITY ACCOMMODATIONS spotting
map pages A196 & A197; see index starting on page A193)

**LODGING**

**DAYS INN**     Guaranteed Rates     Phone: 609/456-6688  ⒩⒩⒩
All Year [CP]     1P: $54- 69  2P/1B: $59- 74  2P/2B: $59- 74  XP: $5  F12
◆◆◆ **Location:** From I-295, exit SR 130, 3 mi n. 801 Rt 130 08030. Fax: 609/456-1413. **Terms:** Sr. discount; no
Motel     pets. **Facility:** 115 rooms. Ground floor rooms with drive-up entries. 3 stories; exterior corridors; meeting
rooms; pool; playground. **Services:** data ports. Fee: coin laundry. **All Rooms:** free & pay movies, cable TV.
**Some Rooms:** microwaves, refrigerators. **Cards:** AE, DI, DS, MC, VI. *(See ad p A198)*     ▨ Ⓓ Ⓢ ⊗

# BUENA—4,400

## LODGING

**ECONO LODGE**   Rates Subject to Change   Phone: 609/697-9000

Fri & Sat   1P:  $58   2P/1B:  $58   2P/2B:  $68   XP:  $5   F18
Sun-Thurs   1P:  $40   2P/1B:  $45   2P/2B:  $50   XP:  $5   F18

**Location:** Jct SR 40 & SR 54. 146 Old Tuckahoe Rd 08310. Fax: 609/697-9000. **Terms:** Sr. discount; reserv deposit; weekly rates; CP available; no pets. **Facility:** 45 rooms. 2 stories; interior corridors; meeting rooms. **All Rooms:** free movies, cable TV. **Some Rooms:** whirlpools. Fee: microwaves, refrigerators. **Cards:** AE, CB, DI, DS, JCB, MC, VI.

Motel

# BURLINGTON—9,800 (See PHILADELPHIA & VICINITY ACCOMMODATIONS spotting map pages A196 & A197; see index starting on page A193)

## RESTAURANT

**CAFE GALLERY** Historical   Dinner: $11-$20   Phone: 609/386-6150   (143)

**Location:** On SR 541; 1 min n of jct US 130; 6 mi nw of NJ Tpk, exit 5; 3 mi nw of I-295, exit 47B. 219 High St 08016. **Hours:** 11:30 am-3:30 & 5-10 pm, Fri & Sat-11 pm, Sun 11:30 am-3 & 5-10 pm. Closed major holidays. **Reservations:** suggested; Sat. **Features:** casual dress; Sunday brunch; health conscious menu items; cocktails & lounge; street parking; a la carte. Casually elegant dining in 19th-century building overlooking Delaware River. Art work on display throughout; Al fresco terrace. **Cards:** AE, CB, DI, MC, VI.

Regional
French

# CAPE MAY—4,700

## LODGINGS

**THE ABBEY BED & BREAKFAST**   Rates Subject to Change   Phone: 609/884-4506

All Year [BP]   2P/1B:  $90- 200   2P/2B:  $90- 200

Historic Bed & Breakfast   **Location:** Center of historic district. 34 Gurney St at Columbia Ave 08204. **Terms:** Age restrictions may apply; reserv deposit, 30 day notice; weekly rates; no pets, owners have cat. **Facility:** 14 rooms. Beautiful Gothic villa with an imposing 60 foot tower. Closed 12/31-3/30. 3- to 4-night minimum stay 6/15-9/30. Open weekends only 4/1-4/30 & 11/1-11/30; 3 stories, no elevator; interior corridors; smoke free premises; beach chairs & passes provided. **Dining:** Afternoon tea. **All Rooms:** refrigerators, combo & shower baths, no phones, no TVs. **Some Rooms:** A/C. **Cards:** DS, MC, VI.

**THE BRASS BED INN**   Rates Subject to Change   Phone: 609/884-8075

Historic Bed & Breakfast
6/16-9/15 [BP]   2P/1B:  $85- 165   2P/2B:  $85- 165
9/16-12/31 [BP]   2P/1B:  $75- 140   2P/2B:  $75- 140
5/1-6/15 & 4/1-4/30 [BP]   2P/1B:  $80- 135   2P/2B:  $80- 135
1/1-3/31 [BP]   2P/1B:  $70- 120   2P/2B:  $70- 120

**Location:** Center. 719 Columbia Ave 08204. **Terms:** Age restrictions may apply; reserv deposit, 20 day notice; package plans; no pets. **Facility:** 8 rooms. Restored Gothic Revival Victorian cottage. Closed 11/23, 12/24 & 12/25. 3-night min stay weekends only, 2-night min stay weekends off season; 3 stories, no elevator; interior corridors; smoke free premises. **Services:** area transportation; to bus terminal. **All Rooms:** no phones, no TVs. **Some Rooms:** radios, combo & shower baths, shared bathrooms. **Cards:** MC, VI.

**CARROLL VILLA BED & BREAKFAST**   Rates Subject to Change   Phone: 609/884-9619

6/18-9/26 [BP]   2P/1B:  $90- 130   2P/2B:  $90- 130   XP: $20
5/14-6/17 & 9/27-10/17 [BP]   2P/1B:  $60- 130   2P/2B:  $60- 130   XP: $20
5/1-5/13 & 10/18-4/30 [BP]   2P/1B:  $60- 120   2P/2B:  $60- 120   XP: $20

Historic Bed & Breakfast   **Location:** Center. 19 Jackson St 08204. Fax: 609/884-0264. **Terms:** Sr. discount; reserv deposit, 30 day notice; weekly rates; CP available; no pets. **Facility:** 21 rooms. Victorian home built in 1882 on Cape May's oldest street in heart of historic district; 1/2 block from ocean. 3 stories, no elevator; interior corridors; smoke free premises. **Dining:** Dining room; 8 am-2:30 & 5:30-10 pm; $15-$21; also, The Mad Batter Restaurant, see separate listing. **Services:** data ports. **All Rooms:** combo & shower baths, no TVs. **Cards:** MC, VI.
*(See color ad below)*

**COLTON COURT MOTOR INN**   Guaranteed Rates   Phone: 609/884-5384

Motel
6/30-9/4   2P/2B:  $121- 136   XP: $15   D3
6/16-6/29 & 9/5-9/21   2P/2B:  $87- 112   XP: $15   D3
5/26-6/15   2P/2B:  $77- 92   XP: $15   D3
5/1-5/25, 9/22-10/16 & 4/1-4/30   2P/2B:  $67- 92   XP: $15   D3

**Location:** At jct Beach & Patterson aves. 105 Beach Ave 08204. **Terms:** Open 5/1-10/16 & 4/1-4/30; reserv deposit, 10 day notice; weekly rates; 3 night min stay, in season; no pets. **Facility:** 24 rooms. 2 stories; exterior corridors; oceanview; pool. **All Rooms:** free movies, refrigerators, cable TV. **Some Rooms:** coffeemakers, 14 efficiencies, microwaves. **Cards:** AE, MC, VI.

**COLVMNS BY THE SEA**   AAA Special Value Rates   Phone: 609/884-2228

All Year [BP]   1P: $120- 190   2P/1B: $120- 160   2P/2B: $115- 180   XP: $35

Historic Bed & Breakfast   **Location:** Beachfront. 1513 Beach Dr 08204. Fax: 609/884-4789. **Terms:** Age restrictions may apply; reserv deposit, 14 day notice; 3 night min stay, 4/28-10/21 weekends; no pets. **Facility:** 11 rooms. An Italianate design, antique filled country inn noted for its prominence in Cape May area. 3 stories, no elevator; interior corridors; smoke free premises; beach tags avail. **Dining:** Afternoon tea. **Recreation:** bicycles. **All Rooms:** free movies, refrigerators, combo & shower baths, cable TV, no A/C, no phones.

## HERITAGE MOTOR INN
(AAA)
◆◆ Motel

Rates Subject to Change

Phone: 609/884-7300

| | | | | |
|---|---|---|---|---|
| 6/30-9/4 | 2P/1B: $105- 115 | 2P/2B: $105- 115 | XP: $15 |
| 6/2-6/29 & 9/5-9/16 | 2P/1B: $68- 89 | 2P/2B: $68- 89 | XP: $15 |
| 5/26-6/1 & 9/17-10/9 | 2P/1B: $59- 68 | 2P/2B: $59- 68 | XP: $15 |
| 5/1-5/25, 10/10-12/31 & 4/7-4/30 | 2P/1B: $51- 59 | 2P/2B: $51- 59 | XP: $15 |

**Location:** Facing ocean at Convention Hall. 721 Beach Dr 08204. **Terms:** Open 5/1-12/31 & 4/7-4/30; reserv deposit, 21 day notice; 3 night min stay; no pets. **Facility:** 21 rooms. 7 efficiencies, $3-$5 extra; weekend nights, $10 extra; 2 stories; exterior corridors; pool. **All Rooms:** refrigerators, cable TV, no phones. **Some Rooms:** coffeemakers. **Cards:** AE, DS, MC, VI.
(D)

## HERITAGE SOUTHWINDS
(AAA)
◆◆ Motel

Rates Subject to Change

Phone: 609/884-7300

| | | | | |
|---|---|---|---|---|
| 6/30-9/4 | 2P/1B: $100- 110 | 2P/2B: $100- 110 | XP: $15 |
| 6/16-6/29 & 9/5-9/16 | 2P/1B: $79- 84 | 2P/2B: $79- 84 | XP: $15 |
| 6/2-6/15 & 9/17-10/9 | 2P/1B: $63- 73 | 2P/2B: $63- 73 | XP: $15 |
| 5/1-6/1, 10/10-12/31 & 4/7-4/30 | 2P/1B: $46- 54 | 2P/2B: $46- 54 | XP: $15 |

**Location:** 1/2 blk off Beach Dr. 14 Patterson Ave 08204. **Terms:** Open 5/1-12/31 & 4/7-4/30; reserv deposit, 21 day notice; weekly rates; package plans, off season; 3 night min stay; no pets. **Facility:** 17 rooms. Quiet rooms near ocean. 4 two-bedroom units. 10 efficiencies $5 extra; 2 bedroom units $550-$835 weekly; weekend nights $10 extra per night; 2 stories; exterior corridors. **All Rooms:** coffeemakers, refrigerators, cable TV, no phones. **Some Rooms:** A/C. **Cards:** AE, DS, MC, VI.
(D)

## THE INN ON OCEAN
◆◆◆
Historic Bed
& Breakfast

Rates Subject to Change

Phone: 609/884-7070

All Year [BP]      1P: $95- 265   2P/1B: $95- 265   2P/2B: $95- 265

**Location:** On Ocean St, 500 feet w of Beach Ave. 25 Ocean St 08204. Fax: 609/884-1384. **Terms:** Age restrictions may apply; reserv deposit, cancellation fee imposed; package plans; no pets. **Facility:** 5 rooms. 1 two-bedroom unit. 3 stories, no elevator; interior corridors; smoke free premises; billiard room. **All Rooms:** combo & shower baths, cable TV, no phones. **Some Rooms:** coffeemakers, microwaves, refrigerators, VCP's.
**Cards:** AE, CB, DI, MC, VI.
(D) ⊗

## LA MER MOTOR INN
(AAA)
◆◆◆
Motor Inn

Rates Subject to Change

Phone: 609/884-9000

| | | | | |
|---|---|---|---|---|
| 6/30-9/4 | 2P/1B: $113- 129 | 2P/2B: $121- 149 | XP:$10-15 |
| 6/16-6/29 & 9/5-9/17 | 2P/1B: $81- 111 | 2P/2B: $95- 128 | XP:$10-15 |
| 5/26-6/15 & 9/18-10/15 | 2P/1B: $63- 74 | 2P/2B: $72- 99 | XP:$10-15 |
| 5/1-5/25 & 4/20-4/30 | 2P/1B: $50- 57 | 2P/2B: $56- 67 | XP: $15 |

**Location:** 1300 blk of Beach Ave, at jct Beach & Pittsburgh aves. 1317 Beach Ave 08204. Fax: 609/884-5004. **Terms:** Open 5/1-10/15 & 4/20-4/30; reserv deposit, 14 day notice; package plans, off season; 3 night min stay, in season; no pets. **Facility:** 67 rooms. 18 efficiencies, $124-$141 in season, Fri & Sat $10 extra; 2 stories; exterior corridors; oceanview; pool, wading pool, sun deck; playground, barbecue area. **Fee:** miniature golf. **Dining:** Restaurant; 8 am-2 & 5-10 pm in season; $10-$19. **Services:** Fee: coin laundry. **Rental:** bicycles. **All Rooms:** cable TV. **Some Rooms:** microwaves, refrigerators, phones. Fee: VCP's. **Cards:** AE, CB, DI, DS, MC, VI.
(D)

## THE MAINSTAY
◆◆◆
Bed &
Breakfast

Rates Subject to Change

Phone: 609/884-8690

All Year [BP]      2P/1B: $95- 190

**Location:** Center. 635 Columbia Ave 08204. **Terms:** Age restrictions may apply; reserv deposit, 60 day notice; 3 night min stay, weekends 6/1-9/30; no pets. **Facility:** 16 rooms. An elegant Victorian country inn by the sea. 4 units in building called Officers' Quarters are open all year. 4 two-bedroom units. 2-3 stories, no elevator; interior corridors; smoke free premises; meeting rooms; croquet. **All Rooms:** comb, shower & tub baths. **Some Rooms:** A/C, coffeemakers, microwaves, refrigerators, phones, cable TV, VCP's. **Cards:** MC, VI.
(D) ⊗

## MARQUIS DE LAFAYETTE
(AAA)
◆◆
Motor Inn

Guaranteed Rates

Phone: 609/884-3431

| | | | | |
|---|---|---|---|---|
| 5/28-10/23 [BP] | 1P: $230 | 2P/1B: $238 | 2P/2B: $238 | XP: $16   F8 |
| 5/1-5/27 [BP] | 1P: $138 | 2P/1B: $146 | 2P/2B: $146 | XP: $16   F8 |
| 10/24-1/1 [BP] | 1P: $104 | 2P/1B: $112 | 2P/2B: $112 | XP: $16   F8 |
| 1/2-4/30 [BP] | 1P: $94 | 2P/1B: $102 | 2P/2B: $102 | XP: $16   F8 |

**Location:** On Beach Dr, between Decatur & Ocean sts. 501 Beach Dr 08204. Fax: 609/884-0669. **Terms:** Check-in 4 pm; reserv deposit, 14 day notice; MAP available; pets, $20, $50 dep req. **Facility:** 73 rooms. Traditional motel rooms, efficiencies & suites. 3-6 stories; interior/exterior corridors; beach view; meeting rooms; heated pool, sauna. **Dining & Entertainment:** 2 dining rooms; 8 am-10 pm; $6-$30; cocktails/lounge. **Services:** Fee: coin laundry. **All Rooms:** coffeemakers, free movies, cable TV. **Some Rooms:** 43 efficiencies, refrigerators. **Cards:** AE, CB, DI, DS, MC, VI. (See ad p A20)
(D) ⊗

## MONTREAL INN
(AAA)
◆◆◆
Apartment
Motor Inn

Rates Subject to Change

Phone: 609/884-7011

| | | | | |
|---|---|---|---|---|
| 6/16-9/3 | 2P/1B: $80- 140 | 2P/2B: $80- 140 | XP: $8 |
| 5/19-6/15 & 9/4-9/23 | 2P/1B: $50- 100 | 2P/2B: $50- 100 | XP: $5 |
| 5/5-5/18 & 9/24-10/15 | 2P/1B: $43- 80 | 2P/2B: $43- 80 | XP: $5 |
| 5/1-5/4, 10/16-11/26 & 3/3-4/30 | | 2P/2B: $30- 63 | XP: $5 |

**Location:** At jct Beach & Madison aves. 1028 Beach Ave 08204. Fax: 609/884-4559. **Terms:** Open 5/1-11/26 & 3/3-4/30; reserv deposit, 14 day notice; package plans; no pets. **Facility:** 70 rooms. Traditional motel rooms, 1 & 2-room efficiencies, every unit has a patio or balcony. 4 stories; exterior corridors; meeting rooms; miniature golf; heated pool, sauna, whirlpool; exercise room, shuffleboard, ping pong, game room. **Dining & Entertainment:** Restaurant; 8 am-10 pm 5/15-10/15; $9-$23; cocktails/lounge; ala carte brunch 8 am-3 pm. **Services:** area transportation, to bus terminal, airport transportation. Fee: coin laundry. **All Rooms:** coffeemakers, free movies, refrigerators, cable TV. **Some Rooms:** microwaves. **Cards:** AE, DS, MC, VI.
(D) ⊗

## PERIWINKLE INN
(AAA)
◆◆◆
Motel

Rates Subject to Change

Phone: 609/884-9200

| | | | |
|---|---|---|---|
| 6/30-9/17 | 2P/2B: $124- 162 | XP: $15 |
| 6/9-6/29 | 2P/2B: $89- 119 | XP: $15 |
| 5/26-6/8 | 2P/2B: $68- 74 | XP: $15 |
| 5/1-5/25, 9/18-10/22 & 4/7-4/30 | 2P/2B: $57- 68 | XP: $15 |

**Location:** Oceanfront. 1039 Beach Ave 08204 (PO Box 220). **Terms:** Open 5/1-10/22 & 4/7-4/30; reserv deposit, 14 day notice; package plans; 3 night min stay, in season; no pets. **Facility:** 50 rooms. Quiet, attractively landscaped courtyard. 3 stories; exterior corridors; pool, wading pool; barbecue grills, doll house, shuffleboard. **All Rooms:** free movies, refrigerators, cable TV, no phones. **Some Rooms:** coffeemakers, 14 efficiencies.
(D)

**THE QUEEN VICTORIA**  Guaranteed Rates  **Phone:** 609/884-8702
(AAA)
6/16-9/17 [BP]  1P: $145- 230  2P/1B: $155- 240  2P/2B: $175- 240  XP: $20
◆◆◆  5/1-6/15 & 9/18-12/31 [BP]  1P: $85- 190  2P/1B: $95- 220  2P/2B: $110- 220  XP: $20
Historic Bed  1/1-4/30 [BP]  1P: $65- 155  2P/1B: $75- 165  2P/2B: $110- 165  XP: $20
& Breakfast  **Location:** Center. 102 Ocean St 08204. **Terms:** Reserv deposit, 21 day notice; weekly rates, high season; package plans, in summer; no pets. **Facility:** 23 rooms. An authentically furnished Victorian home. Some rooms with fireplace. 3 stories; interior/exterior corridors; smoke free premises; luxury level rooms. **Recreation:** bicycles. **All Rooms:** refrigerators, combo & shower baths. **Some Rooms:** microwaves, phones, cable TV, VCP's, whirlpools. **Cards:** AE, MC, VI. *(See ad below)*  (D) ⊗

**SEA CREST INN**  Rates Subject to Change  **Phone:** 609/884-4561
(AAA)
6/18-9/6  2P/1B: $99- 185  2P/2B: $99- 199  XP: $24
◆◆◆  6/4-6/17 & 9/7-9/19  2P/1B: $85- 165  2P/2B: $88- 169  XP: $22
Motel  5/1-6/3, 9/20-10/30 &
4/29-4/30  2P/1B: $75- 140  2P/2B: $78- 149  XP: $24
10/31-11/1 & 4/25-4/28  2P/1B: $50- 79  2P/2B: $54- 84  XP: $24
**Location:** Between Patterson & Broadway aves. 101 Beach Ave 08204. **Fax:** 609/898-9675. **Terms:** Open 5/1-11/1 & 4/25-4/30; reserv deposit, 14 day notice; package plans, off season; no pets. **Facility:** 55 rooms. Some rooms facing ocean; sun deck with barbecues. 1 two-bedroom unit. 4 stories; exterior corridors; meeting rooms; heated pool, whirlpool. **Dining:** Restaurant nearby. **Services:** Fee: coin laundry. **All Rooms:** coffeemakers, efficiencies, refrigerators, cable TV. **Some Rooms:** microwaves. *(See color ad below)*  (D)

**VICTORIAN LACE INN**  Rates Subject to Change  **Phone:** 609/884-1772
◆◆  7/1-8/31 Weekly [EP]  2P/1B: $875- 1200  2P/2B: $875- 1200
Historic Bed  5/1-6/30, 9/1-10/18 &
& Breakfast  4/1-4/30 Daily [BP]  2P/1B: $95- 180  2P/2B: $95- 180  XP: $20  F
**Location:** Jct of Stockton Ave & Jefferson St, 1 blk n of beach. 901 Stockton Ave 08204. **Terms:** Open 5/1-10/18 & 4/1-4/30; reserv deposit, 14 day notice; package plans; no pets. **Facility:** 4 rooms. Suites & carriage house apartments. Working woodburning fireplaces in 2 suites & the parlor. 2 two-bedroom units. Also open 12/1-12/24, $95-$180 for 2 persons 1 bed & 2 persons 2 beds; 2-3 stories, no elevator; interior/exterior corridors; smoke free premises. **All Rooms:** coffeemakers, efficiencies, microwaves, refrigerators, combo & shower baths, no phones. **Some Rooms:** A/C, cable TV, VCP's, whirlpools.  (D) ⊗

**WHITE DOVE COTTAGE**  Rates Subject to Change  **Phone:** 609/884-0613
(AAA)
6/11-9/9 [BP]  1P: $115- 170  2P/1B: $130- 185  XP: $25
◆◆◆  5/1-6/10, 9/10-12/31 &
Historic Bed  3/27-4/30 [BP]  1P: $99- 140  2P/1B: $105- 155  XP: $25
& Breakfast  1/1-3/26 [BP]  1P: $65- 130  2P/1B: $80- 145  XP: $25
**Location:** Center. 619 Hughes St 08204. **Terms:** Age restrictions may apply; reserv deposit, 21 day notice; weekly rates; package plans; 2 night min stay, wknds & high season; no pets. **Facility:** 6 rooms. Tastefully furnished with American & European antiques. 3 stories, no elevator; interior/exterior corridors; smoke free premises. **All Rooms:** free movies, combo & shower baths, no phones. **Some Rooms:** refrigerators, cable TV, whirlpools.  (D) ⊗

## RESTAURANTS

**AXELSSONS'S BLUE CLAW RESTAURANT**  **Dinner:** $21-$30  **Phone:** 609/884-5878
(AAA)  **Location:** From southern terminus of Garden State Pkwy 1 1/4 mi e on CR 621 (Ocean Dr). 991 Ocean Dr
◆◆◆  08204. **Hours:** 5 pm-10 pm. Closed: 11/23 & 12/25. **Reservations:** suggested. **Features:** casual dress;
Steak and  children's menu; cocktails & lounge. Fine dining with a view of the restaurant's working fishing fleet. The
Seafood  Clippership pub has a northern European pub tradition. **Cards:** DI, MC, VI.  ⊗

**410 BANK ST RESTAURANT**  Historical  **Dinner:** $21-$30  **Phone:** 609/884-2127
◆◆◆  **Location:** Just n of the mall, adjacent to Welcome Center. 410 Bank St 08204. **Hours:** Open 5/15-10/17; 5
Seafood  pm-10:30 pm. **Reservations:** suggested. **Features:** No A/C; casual dress; children's menu. Cheerful, casual & bustling. New Orleans French & open fire grilled seafood & steaks. Tropical ambience, porch & garden dining in a restored 1840 carriage house. **Cards:** AE, DI, DS, MC, VI.

**FRESCOS RISTORANTE ITALIANO**  **Dinner:** $21-$30  **Phone:** 609/884-0366
◆◆◆  **Location:** Jct Bank & Broad sts. 412 Bank St 08204. **Hours:** Open 5/11-1/2; 5 pm-10 pm.
Italian  **Reservations:** suggested. **Features:** casual dress; a la carte. Seafood & homemade pastas of the South of Italy, blended with the elegant sauces & veal of the North, served in this restored 1880 Victorian cottage with its romantic candle-lit veranda. **Cards:** AE, DI, DS, MC, VI.

**LOBSTER HOUSE**  **Dinner:** $21-$30  **Phone:** 609/884-8296
(AAA)  **Location:** At the wharf; e of south end of Cold Spring Bridge. south end of Cold Spring 08204. **Hours:** 11:30
◆◆  am-3 & 5-10 pm, 6/19-9/30 11:30 am-3 & 4:30-10 pm, Sun 2 pm-9 pm, 4/6-9/30, 4 pm-10 pm. Closed: 11/23,
Seafood  12/24 & 12/25. **Features:** casual dress; children's menu; carryout; cocktails & lounge; a la carte. Overlooking harbor. Fresh fish market on property. **Cards:** AE, DS, MC, VI.

**THE MAD BATTER RESTAURANT**  Dinner: $11-$20  Phone: 609/884-5970
**Location:** In the Carroll Villa Bed & Breakfast. 19 Jackson St 08204. **Hours:** Open 5/1-12/31 & 2/5-4/30; 8 am-2:30 & 5:30-10 pm. **Reservations:** suggested. **Features:** casual dress; children's menu; carryout; fee for parking. Casual, gourmet dining experience in Victorian bed & breakfast inn. European terrace dining avail. Desserts made fresh daily. Dining room has skylight. Garden terrace dining area avail also. **Cards:** DS, MC, VI. *(See color ad p A17)*
American

**MAUREEN RESTAURANT**  Dinner: $21-$30  Phone: 609/844-3774
American  **Location:** At jct of Beach Dr & Decatur St. 429 Beach Dr 08204. **Hours:** Open 5/1-10/15 & 4/15-4/30; 5 pm-10 pm. **Reservations:** suggested. **Features:** casual dress; cocktails & lounge; minimum charge-18.00. Contemporary American cuisine served in a Victorian setting. Patio dining area offers a terrific view of the ocean & beach. Smoke free premises. **Cards:** AE, DI, DS, MC, VI.  ⊗

**MERION INN**  Dinner: $11-$20  Phone: 609/884-8363
Seafood  **Location:** Center. 106 Decatur St 08204. **Hours:** Open 5/1-10/31 & 4/20-4/30; 11:30 am-2:30 pm & 5 pm-10 pm. **Reservations:** suggested. **Features:** No A/C; casual dress; children's menu; early bird specials; carryout; cocktails & lounge. Specializing in fresh seafood & unique vegetables. Desserts prepared from own recipes. Victorian atmosphere. **Cards:** AE, CB, DI, DS, MC, VI.

**THE PETER SHIELDS RESTAURANT**  Dinner: over $31  Phone: 609/884-6491
American  **Location:** At Beach Dr & Trenton Ave. 1301 Beach Dr 08204. **Hours:** Open 5/1-12/31 & 2/1-4/30; 5 pm-10 pm. Closed: 12/25. **Reservations:** suggested. **Features:** casual dress; Sunday brunch; a la carte. Classicly elegant dining amidst the romantic ambience provided by this large turn-of-century colonial Georgian style mansion. **Cards:** AE, DI, MC, VI.

**PILOT HOUSE**  Dinner: $11-$20  Phone: 609/884-3449
Steak and  **Location:** At jct of Carpenters Ln & Decatur St; adjacent to Washington St Mall. 142 Decatur St 08204.
Seafood  **Hours:** 11:30 am-11 pm. Closed: 11/23, 12/25 & 12/26. **Reservations:** suggested. **Features:** casual dress; early bird specials; carryout; cocktails & lounge. In the center of Vistorian Historic District. Fireside or patio dining. **Cards:** AE, DS, MC, VI.  ⊗

**TOP OF THE MARQ**  Dinner: $21-$30  Phone: 609/884-3500
**Location:** Atop Marquis De Lafayette. 501 Beach Dr 08204. **Hours:** 5:30 pm-10 pm. Closed: Mon-Thurs 10/15-5/7. **Reservations:** accepted. **Features:** casual dress; children's menu; early bird specials; cocktails & lounge; a la carte. Excellent view of the ocean. **Cards:** AE, CB, DI, DS, MC, VI. *(See ad below)*  ⊗
American

**THE WASHINGTON INN**  Historical  Dinner: $11-$20  Phone: 609/884-5697
**Location:** Center. 801 Washington St 08204. **Hours:** 5 pm-10 pm; Wed-Sun 11/1-4/30 5 pm - 9 pm. Closed: 11/23, 12/24, 12/25 & 1/4-1/16. **Reservations:** suggested. **Features:** casual dress; children's menu; cocktails & lounge; a la carte. In 1848 colonial plantation home. Wine cellar with extensive collections of wines. **Cards:** AE, CB, DI, DS, MC, VI.  ⊗
American

**WATERS EDGE RESTAURANT**  Dinner: $21-$30  Phone: 609/884-1717
American  **Location:** Jct Beach & Pittsburgh aves. 1317 Beach Ave 08204. **Hours:** 8 am-2:30 & 5-10 pm, Fri & Sat-11 pm 7/1-8/31; 5/1-7/1 breakfast & lunch are served weekends only. Closed: 11/23, Mon-Thurs 10/15-4/1, Tues 4/1-6/30 & 9/1-10/14. **Reservations:** suggested. **Features:** casual dress; Sunday brunch; children's menu; carryout; cocktails & lounge; a la carte. Outstanding view of the ocean from both the casually elegant dining room & outdoor terrace. Extensive list of wines by the glass. **Cards:** AE, CB, DI, DS, MC, VI.  ⊗

## CAPE MAY COURT HOUSE

### LODGING

**HY-LAND MOTOR INN**  Guaranteed Rates  Phone: 609/465-7305

| | | 1P: | | 2P/1B: | | 2P/2B: | | XP: | F12 |
|---|---|---|---|---|---|---|---|---|---|
| 6/15-9/7 | | 1P: $65- | 75 | 2P/1B: $65- | 75 | 2P/2B: $75- | 85 | XP: $5 | F12 |
| 5/1-6/14 & 9/8-10/1 | | 1P: $50- | 55 | 2P/1B: $50- | 55 | 2P/2B: $50- | 55 | XP: $5 | F12 |
| 10/2-4/30 | | 1P: $45- | 50 | 2P/1B: $45- | 50 | 2P/2B: $45- | 50 | XP: $5 | F12 |

Motel  **Location:** On Garden State Pkwy; 1/4 mi s of Stone Harbor exit, at MM 9.6. 08210 (PO Box 97). **Terms:** Reserv deposit, 3 day notice; 2 night min stay, weekends in season; no pets. **Facility:** 34 rooms. Quiet wooded location. 1 two-bedroom unit. 10 efficiencies, $80-$90; off season $50-$60, 3-night minimum stay. Rates for up to 4 persons in season; 1-2 stories; exterior corridors; pool. **All Rooms:** combo & shower baths, cable TV. **Some Rooms:** Fee: refrigerators. **Cards:** AE, DI, MC, VI.  Ⓓ

## CARDIFF

### LODGING

**HOWARD JOHNSON**  Rates Subject to Change  Phone: 609/641-3131

| | |  | |  | |  |  |
|---|---|---|---|---|---|---|---|
| 5/1-10/29 [CP] | | 1P: $89- | 109 | 2P/2B: $89- | 109 | XP: $10 | F17 |
| 10/30-4/30 [CP] | | 1P: $59- | 79 | 2P/2B: $59- | 79 | XP: $10 | F17 |

Motel  **Location:** Atlantic City Expwy exit 9, 1 mi e on Tilton Rd. 1760 Tilton Rd 08232. Fax: 609/641-0555. **Terms:** Check-in 4 pm; credit card guarantee; weekly rates; no pets. **Facility:** 94 rooms. 2 stories; interior/exterior corridors; meeting rooms; heated pool, whirlpool. **Dining:** Dining room nearby. **Services:** airport transportation. Fee: childcare; coin laundry, area transportation, to casinos. **All Rooms:** free movies, cable TV. **Some Rooms:** Fee: microwaves, refrigerators. **Cards:** AE, CB, DI, DS, JCB, MC, VI. *(See ad p A12)*  Ⓓ ⊗

## CARLSTADT—5,500   (See NEWARK to PARAMUS ACCOMMODATIONS spotting map page A44; see index starting on page A42)

### RESTAURANT

**PRATOS**
◆◆◆
Italian

**Dinner: $21-$30**                    **Phone: 201/460-1777**  ④①
**Location:** NJ Tpk exit 16W; SR 3W to SR 17N, 1 1/2 mi n to Paterson Plank Rd, then 1/4 mi e. 335 Paterson Plank Rd 07072. **Hours:** noon-9:30 pm, Sat 5 pm-11 pm. Closed major holidays & Sun. **Reservations:** suggested. **Features:** casual dress; health conscious menu items; cocktails & lounge; entertainment; valet parking; a la carte. Sophisticated, multi-level dining rooms. **Cards:** AE, CB, DI, MC, VI.   ⊗

## CARTERET—19,000   (See NEW JERSEY METRO AREA ACCOMMODATIONS spotting map pages A40 & A41; see index starting on page A39)

### LODGING

**HOLIDAY INN**
◆◆◆
Motor Inn

AAA Special Value Rates                    **Phone: 908/541-9500**  ⑥
**All Year**        1P: $86- 118   2P/1B:  $94- 118   2P/2B:  $94- 118   XP: $8  F19
**Location:** At tpk exit 12. 1000 Roosevelt Ave 07008. Fax: 908/541-9640. **Terms:** Weekly/monthly rates; small pets only, not left unattended in rooms. **Facility:** 118 rooms. 2 stories; interior/exterior corridors; conference facilities; pool; exercise bikes. **Dining & Entertainment:** Dining room; 7 am-10 pm; seafood buffet Fri & Sat; $8-$24; health conscious menu items; cocktails; entertainment. **Services:** data ports, secretarial services; valet laundry; airport transportation, Mon-Fri. **All Rooms:** free & pay movies, cable TV, VCP's. **Some Rooms:** microwaves, refrigerators, whirlpools. **Cards:** AE, CB, DI, DS, JCB, MC, VI.   ⒹⓍ

## CEDAR GROVE   (See NEW JERSEY METRO AREA ACCOMMODATIONS spotting map pages A40 & A41; see index starting on page A39)

### RESTAURANT

**IL TULIPANO**
ⒶⒶ
◆◆◆◆
Italian
VI. (See ad p A46)

**Dinner: over $31**                    **Phone: 201/256-9300**  ①⑤②
**Location:** 1 1/2 mi s on SR 23 from jct US 46. 1131 Pompton Ave 07009. **Hours:** noon-2:30 & 6-10 pm, Sat 6 pm-10 pm, Sun 4 pm-8:30 pm. Closed: Sat, Sun & Mon for lunch. **Reservations:** suggested. **Features:** semi-formal attire; health conscious menu items; cocktails & lounge; valet parking; a la carte. A well-lit dining room highlighted by crystal tulip chandeliers & original artwork create a warm & intimate spring time atmosphere in which to enjoy wonderful house specialties. Banquet facilities. **Cards:** AE, CB, DI, MC, ⑤

## CHERRY HILL—69,300   (See PHILADELPHIA & VICINITY ACCOMMODATIONS spotting map pages A196 & A197; see index starting on page A193)

### LODGINGS

**DAYS INN**
ⒶⒶ
Motel
VI.

Rates Subject to Change                    **Phone: 609/663-0100**  ①②④
**All Year [CP]**    1P:  $50      2P/1B:  $55      2P/2B:  $60      XP: $5  F12
**Location:** I-295 exit 34B, 4 mi w on SR 70, 1/4 mi n on Cuthbert, 1/4 mi e on SR 38. 525 Cuthbert Blvd (Rt 38E) 08002. Fax: 609/663-6449. **Terms:** Sr. discount; credit card guarantee, 15 day notice; weekly rates; no pets. **Facility:** 50 rooms. 2 stories; exterior corridors. **Dining:** Restaurant nearby. **All Rooms:** free movies, cable TV. **Some Rooms:** 2 efficiencies, no utensils. Fee: refrigerators, VCP's. **Cards:** AE, CB, DI, DS, MC, ⒹⓍ

**HOLIDAY INN-CHERRY HILL**
◆◆◆
Motor Inn

Guaranteed Rates                    **Phone: 609/663-5300**  ①②③
**All Year**        1P:  $68      2P/1B:  $78      2P/2B:  $78      XP: $8  F18
**Location:** On Rt 70; 2 blks w of Haddonfield Rd; opposite Garden State Race Track. Rt 70 & Sayer Ave 08002. Fax: 609/663-5300. **Terms:** Sr. discount; reserv deposit; package plans, weekends; small pets only. **Facility:** 186 rooms. 6 stories; interior corridors; conference facilities; 2 pools (1 heated, 1 indoor); sauna; exercise room. Fee: tanning bed. **Dining & Entertainment:** Restaurant, cafeteria; 6 am-10 pm, Sat & Sun from 7 am; $9-$15; health conscious menu items; cocktails/lounge. **Services:** data ports, secretarial services. Fee: coin laundry. **All Rooms:** coffeemakers, free movies, cable TV. **Some Rooms:** refrigerators. **Cards:** AE, CB, DI, DS, MC, VI.   ⒹⓈⓍ

**RESIDENCE INN BY MARRIOTT**
◆◆◆
Apartment
Motel

Guaranteed Rates                    **Phone: 609/429-6111**  ①②⓪
**Mon-Thurs [CP]**    1P:  $92    2P/1B:  $102    2P/2B:  $130    XP: $10  F12
**Fri-Sun [CP]**      1P:  $89    2P/1B:  $89     2P/2B:  $109    XP: $10  F12
**Location:** I-295 exit 34A, 1/2 mi e on SR 70, 1/8 mi n on Old Cuthbert Rd. 1821 Old Cuthbert Rd 08034. Fax: 609/429-0345. **Terms:** Sr. discount; reserv deposit; package plans; pets, $75. **Facility:** 96 rooms. Contemporary spacious units, some with fireplace. Hospitality hour Mon-Thur. 24 two-bedroom units. 2 stories; exterior corridors; meeting rooms; heated pool, whirlpool; horseshoe pit, volleyball. **Services:** data ports, secretarial services; childcare; health club privileges. Fee: coin laundry. **All Rooms:** coffeemakers, kitchens, microwaves, free movies, refrigerators, cable TV. **Some Rooms:** Fee: VCP's. **Cards:** AE, CB, DI, DS, JCB, MC, VI.   ⓏⒹⓍ

**(See PHILADELPHIA & VICINITY ACCOMMODATIONS spotting map pages A196 & A197)**

| SHERATON INN-CHERRY HILL | | Rates Subject to Change | | | | | Phone: 609/428-2300 | **121** |
|---|---|---|---|---|---|---|---|---|
| ◆◆ Hotel | Mon-Thurs | 1P: $89- 119 | 2P/1B: $99- 129 | 2P/2B: $99- 129 | XP: $10 | F17 |
| | Fri-Sun | 1P: $74- 109 | 2P/1B: $84- 119 | 2P/2B: $84- 119 | XP: $10 | F17 |

**Location:** On SR 70, 1/4 mi w of jct I-295, exit 34B. 1450 SR 70E 08034. Fax: 609/354-7662. **Terms:** Sr. discount; reserv deposit, 3 day notice; monthly rates; package plans; no pets. **Facility:** 213 rooms. 4 stories; interior corridors; conference facilities; heated pool, wading pool; 2 tennis courts; exercise room, gameroom. **Dining & Entertainment:** Dining room; 6:30 am-11 pm, Sat & Sun from 7 am; $9-$18; health conscious menu items; cocktails/lounge. **Services:** secretarial services; valet laundry; area transportation. Fee: airport transportation. **All Rooms:** free & pay movies, cable TV. **Some Rooms:** Fee: microwaves, refrigerators. **Cards:** AE, CB, DI, DS, MC, VI. *(See ad p A188 & below)*   Ⓓ Ⓢ ⊗

## RESTAURANTS

**ANDREOTTI'S VIENNESE CAFE & PASTRY SHOP**     **Dinner:** $11-$20          **Phone:** 609/795-0172   **135**
◆◆ Continental     **Location:** I-295 exit 34B, 1/2 mi w on SR 70, in Pine Tree Plaza Shopping Center. 1442 Rt 70 08034. **Hours:** 9 am-11 pm, Fri & Sat-2 am. Closed: 11/23 & 12/25. **Reservations:** suggested; weekends. **Features:** casual dress; early bird specials; health conscious menu items; carryout; cocktails & lounge; a la carte. Charming cafe offering extensive menu. **Cards:** AE, DI, MC, VI.   ⊗

**CAFFE LAMBERTI**     **Dinner:** $11-$20          **Phone:** 609/663-1747   **134**
◆◆ Italian     **Location:** SR 70 at Haddonfield Rd, across from Garden State Park, 3 1/2 mi w of I 295 exit 34B. 2011 Rt 70W 08002. **Hours:** 11:30 am-10 pm, Fri & Sat-11 pm, Sun 1 pm-9 pm. Closed major holidays. **Reservations:** suggested. **Features:** casual dress; cocktails; a la carte. Casually elegant dining rooms featuring creative Italian & continental culinary cuisine. Patio seasonal. **Cards:** AE, DI, DS, MC, VI.   ⊗

**THE GREENBRIER**     **Dinner:** $21-$30          **Phone:** 609/665-0800   **136**
◆◆ American     **Location:** I-295, exit 34B, 2 1/4 w on SR 70 at jct of Huddon Field Rd & SR 70, across from Garden State Park. **Hours:** 11 am-1 am, Fri & Sat-1:30 am, Sun 10 am-10 pm. Closed: 12/25. **Reservations:** suggested. **Features:** casual dress; Sunday brunch; children's menu; early bird specials; carryout; cocktails & lounge; entertainment; a la carte. **Cards:** AE, CB, DI, DS, MC, VI.   ⊗

**HIDEAWAY RESTAURANT**     **Dinner:** $21-$30          **Phone:** 609/428-7379   **137**
◆◆◆ Continental     **Location:** I-295 exit 34B, 1 1/4 mi w on SR 70, 1 1/2 mi s on SR 154 (Brace Rd) 1/8 mi w on Kresson Rd. 63 Kresson Rd 08003. **Hours:** noon-3 & 5-10 pm, Sat 5 pm-11 pm, Sun 5 pm-9 pm. Closed: Mon, 1/1, 7/4. **Reservations:** suggested. **Features:** casual dress; early bird specials; health conscious menu items; carryout; cocktails & lounge; valet parking. Contemporary setting with varied menu; Wed-Fri lunch buffet noon-3 pm. **Cards:** AE, CB, DI, DS, MC, VI.   ⊗

**LA CAMPAGNE**     **Dinner:** $21-$30          **Phone:** 609/429-7647   **133**
◆◆◆ French     **Location:** 2 mi sw of Rt 70 & I-295. 312 Kresson Rd 08034. **Hours:** 11:30 am-2:30 & 5-9 pm, Sat & Sun 5 pm-9 pm. Closed: Mon, 1/1 & 12/25. **Features:** Sunday brunch; a la carte. South of France dining experience. Circa 1840 farm house with brick hearths, antiques, Oriental rugs & fresh flowers.

## CHESTER—1,200

## LODGING

| PUBLICK HOUSE INN | | AAA Special Value Rates | | | | Phone: 908/879-6878 |
|---|---|---|---|---|---|---|
| ◆◆ Historic Country Inn | All Year [CP] | 1P: $60- 90 | 2P/1B: $60- 90 | 2P/2B: $60- 90 | |

**Location:** On SR 24, 1/4 mi e jct US 206. 111 Main St 07930. Fax: 908/879-6553. **Terms:** Reserv deposit; no pets. **Facility:** 10 rooms. Quaint 1810 Inn used on stagecoach run from New York to Philadelphia; enjoy comfortable accomodations amid a bustling atmosphere. Cordial hosts strive for a pleasant stay. 2 stories; interior corridors; meeting rooms. **Dining & Entertainment:** Live entertainment Wed-Sun; dining room, see separate listing. **Services:** valet laundry. **All Rooms:** combo & shower baths, cable TV. **Some Rooms:** refrigerators. **Cards:** AE, CB, DI, DS, MC, VI.   Ⓓ

## RESTAURANTS

**LARISON'S TURKEY FARM INN**     **Dinner:** $11-$20          **Phone:** 908/879-5521
Ⓐ ◆◆ American     **Location:** Jct US 206 & SR 24. Jct US 206 & SR 24 07930. **Hours:** 11 am-9 pm. Closed: 12/24. **Features:** casual dress; children's menu; health conscious menu items; carryout; cocktails & lounge; a la carte. Country style family dining; casual atmosphere; petting farm for children & Turkey Roost Country Store, a step back in time to old fashioned country living. **Cards:** AE, DI, DS, MC, VI.   ⊗

**PUBLICK HOUSE INN   Country Inn**     **Dinner:** $11-$20          **Phone:** 908/879-6878
◆◆ American     **Location:** In Publick House Inn. 111 Main St 07930. **Hours:** 11:30 am-11 pm, Fri & Sat-midnight, Sun 9 am-11 pm. Closed: 12/25. **Reservations:** suggested. **Features:** casual dress; children's menu; early bird specials; health conscious menu items; carryout; salad bar; cocktails & lounge; entertainment; a la carte. 1810 Stagecoach Tavern. Summer veranda dining. Sun brunch 9 am-2 pm, $15.95; children $12.95; located in small village among several antique shops. **Cards:** AE, CB, DI, DS, MC, VI.   ⊗

**CLARK**—14,600   (See NEW JERSEY METRO AREA ACCOMMODATIONS spotting map pages A40 & A41; see index starting on page A39)

## LODGING

**HOWARD JOHNSON LODGE**   Rates Subject to Change   **Phone:** 908/381-6500   **9**
All Year   1P: $59- 65   2P/1B: $59- 65   2P/2B: $63- 73   XP: $6   F18
**Location:** Just w of exit 135 off Garden State Pkwy. 70 Central Ave 07066. **Fax:** 908/381-6076. **Terms:** Sr. discount; reserv deposit, 7 day notice; no pets. **Facility:** 115 rooms. 2 stories: interior/exterior corridors; meeting rooms; pool, wading pool. **Dining:** Restaurant; 11 am-11 pm, Fri & Sat to midnight; $4-$7; cocktails. **Services:** valet laundry. **All Rooms:** free movies, cable TV. **Some Rooms:** refrigerators. **Cards:** AE, CB, DI, DS, MC, VI.
Motor Inn

**CLIFTON**—71,700   (See NEWARK to PARAMUS ACCOMMODATIONS spotting map page A44; see index starting on page A42)

## LODGINGS

**HOWARD JOHNSON LODGE**   Guaranteed Rates   **Phone:** 201/471-3800   **4**
Motor Inn   All Year   1P: $62- 80   2P/1B: $65- 85   2P/2B: $75- 95   XP: $10   F18
**Location:** On SR 3W westbound; just w of Passiac Ave exit; 1 1/2 mi e of Garden State Pkwy, exit 153. 680 SR 3W at Passiac Ave 07014. **Fax:** 201/471-3800. **Terms:** Sr. discount; reserv deposit; small pets only.
**Facility:** 116 rooms. Some with balcony or patio. 4 stories; interior corridors; meeting rooms; pool. **Dining & Entertainment:** Restaurant; 7 am-11 pm, Fri & Sat-1 am; $6-$10; health conscious menu items; cocktail lounge. **Services:** data ports, secretarial services; valet laundry. **All Rooms:** free & pay movies, cable TV. **Some Rooms:** 20 efficiencies, no utensils, microwaves, refrigerators. **Cards:** AE, DI, DS, MC, VI.

**RAMADA HOTEL**   Guaranteed Rates   **Phone:** 201/778-6500   **3**
Motor Inn   Mon-Thurs   1P: $89- 125   2P/1B: $89- 125   2P/2B: $89- 125   XP: $15   F18
Fri-Sun   1P: $75- 125   2P/1B: $75- 150   2P/2B: $75- 125   XP: $15   F18
**Location:** On SR 3 eastbound; 2 1/2 mi e of Garden State Pkwy, exit 153, NJ Tpk exit 16W, 4 1/2 mi w on SR 3, then u-turn on Main Ave. 265 Rt 3E 07014. **Fax:** 201/778-8724. **Terms:** Sr. discount; reserv deposit, 3 day notice; weekly/monthly rates; small pets only. **Facility:** 183 rooms. Close to Lincoln Tunnel & Mid-town Manhattan. 4 stories; interior corridors; conference facilities; indoor pool, sauna; exercise room. **Dining & Entertainment:** Restaurant; 6:30 am-10 pm; $9-$14; health conscious menu items; cocktails/lounge; entertainment, nightclub. **Services:** data ports, PC, secretarial services; valet laundry. **All Rooms:** free & pay movies, cable TV. **Some Rooms:** 6 kitchens, microwaves, refrigerators. **Cards:** AE, CB, DI, DS, JCB, MC, VI.

## RESTAURANTS

**CAVALIER CAFE**   Dinner: $11-$20   **Phone:** 201/778-5008   **4**
American   **Location:** SR 3 w to Broad St exit, w at light on Allwood Rd, 1/4 mi to light, n on Broad St; SR 3 e to Broad St exit, n at light 1/4 mi on Broad St. 1168 Broad St 07013. **Hours:** 11:30 am-10 pm, Sat 4:30 pm-midnight. Closed: Sun, 1/1, 11/23 & 12/25. **Reservations:** suggested; weekends. **Features:** casual dress; health conscious menu items; carryout; cocktails & lounge; entertainment; a la carte. Eclectic menu featuring Italian, French, Cajun & Continental cuisines. **Cards:** AE, DI, DS, MC, VI.

**CHENGDU 46**   Dinner: $21-$30   **Phone:** 201/777-8855   **2**
Chinese   **Location:** Garden State Pkwy (NB) exit 154, 1 mi w (SB) 153B, 1 mi w. 1105 Rt 46E 07013. **Hours:** noon-3 & 5-10:30 pm, Fri-11:30 pm, Sat 5 pm-11:30 pm, Sun 1 pm-10:30 pm. Closed: 11/23. **Reservations:** suggested. **Features:** semi-formal attire; cocktails & lounge; minimum charge-$10 for dinner; a la carte. Soothing, sophisticated softly lighted dining room. Authentic Sichuan cuisine. Showy flambe dessert presentations. **Cards:** AE, DI, MC, VI.

# CLINTON—2,100

## LODGING

**HOLIDAY INN-CLINTON**   AAA Special Value Rates   **Phone:** 908/735-5111
Motor Inn   All Year   1P: $89- 93   2P/1B: $97- 101   2P/2B: $97   XP: $8   F
**Location:** Just w of exit 15 of I-78; SR 173. 111 Rt 173 08809. **Fax:** 908/730-9768. **Terms:** Credit card guarantee, 3 day notice; pets. **Facility:** 142 rooms. 5 stories; interior corridors; conference facilities; heated indoor pool, whirlpool; exercise room. **Dining & Entertainment:** Dining room; 6:30 am-2 & 5-10 pm, Sat & Sun from 7 am; $9-$15; health conscious menu items; cocktails/lounge; nightclub. **Services:** data ports, secretarial services; valet laundry. **All Rooms:** free & pay movies, cable TV. **Some Rooms:** free: microwaves, refrigerators. **Cards:** AE, DI, DS, MC, VI.

# COLTS NECK—8,600

## LODGING

**COLTS NECK INN HOTEL**   AAA Special Value Rates   **Phone:** 908/409-1200
Motel   All Year [CP]   1P: $75   2P/1B: $85   2P/2B: $85   XP: $10   F16
**Location:** Jct SR 34 & 537. 6 SR 537W 07722. **Fax:** 908/431-6640. **Terms:** Reserv deposit; package plans; no pets. **Facility:** 49 rooms. Centrally located; quiet, country setting. Limited room service hours. Suites avail, $135; 2 stories; interior corridors; meeting rooms; luxury level rooms. **Dining & Entertainment:** Restaurant; 11 am-2 am; $12-$25; cocktails/lounge; entertainment. **Services:** health club privileges; valet laundry. **All Rooms:** combo & shower baths, cable TV. **Some Rooms:** refrigerators, whirlpools. **Cards:** AE, DI, MC, VI.

# CONVENT STATION

## LODGING

**THE MADISON HOTEL**   Guaranteed Rates   **Phone:** 201/285-1800
Sun-Thurs [CP]   1P: $99   2P/1B: $99   2P/2B: $99   XP: $15   F16
Fri & Sat [CP]   1P: $89   2P/1B: $89   2P/2B: $89   XP: $15   F16
Motor Inn   **Location:** In Madison, I-287 exit 35, 1 1/2 mi e on US 24 (Madison Ave). 1 Convent Rd & Rt 24 07961. **Fax:** 201/540-0042. **Terms:** Credit card guarantee; no pets. **Facility:** 190 rooms. Rural setting with peaceful & quiet locale; traditional ambience throughout property. Victorian styling. 4 stories; interior corridors; conference facilities; heated indoor pool, sauna, whirlpool; health club. **Dining:** Restaurant; 7 am-11 pm; $13-$27; also, Rod's 1890's Restaurant, see separate listing. **Services:** data ports, PC, secretarial services; valet laundry. Fee: childcare; massage. **Recreation:** bicycles, hiking trails, jogging. **All Rooms:** free & pay movies, cable TV. **Some Rooms:** microwaves, refrigerators. **Cards:** AE, CB, DI, DS, MC, VI. (See color ad p A38)

## RESTAURANT

**ROD'S 1890'S RESTAURANT**
◆◆ American
**Dinner: $21-$30**   **Phone: 201/539-6666**
**Location:** In The Madison Hotel. Madison Ave 07961. **Hours:** 11:30 am-11 pm, Sun 11 am-3 & 4-10 pm. **Closed:** 12/25. **Reservations:** suggested; in railcars. **Features:** semi-formal attire; Sunday brunch; children's menu; early bird specials; health conscious menu items; carryout; salad bar; cocktails & lounge; entertainment; valet parking; a la carte. Presidential & Wanamaker railcars add to the Victorian charm & ambience of the many dining rooms. Jackets required for gentlemen at dinner. **Cards:** AE, CB, DI, DS, MC, VI.

# DAYTON

## LODGING

**DAYS INN OF SOUTH BRUNSWICK**   AAA Special Value Rates   **Phone: 908/329-3000**

| | | 1P: | $54 | 2P/1B: | $59 | | 2P/2B: | $59 | | XP: | $5 | F12 |
|---|---|---|---|---|---|---|---|---|---|---|---|---|

(AAA)
◆◆ Motel
**Location:** NJ Tpk, exit 8A 2 mi w on CR 32 to US 130, then 1 mi n. 2316 US 130 08810. **Fax:** 908/329-2584. **Terms:** Credit card guarantee, 3 day notice; small pets only. **Facility:** 51 rooms. 2 stories; exterior corridors. **Dining:** Restaurant nearby. **Services:** data ports. **All Rooms:** free movies, refrigerators, cable TV. **Cards:** AE, CB, DI, DS, MC, VI.   Ⓓ ⊘

# DENVILLE—13,800   (See NEW JERSEY METRO AREA ACCOMMODATIONS spotting map pages A40 & A41; see index starting on page A39)

## RESTAURANT

**THE ITALIAN CHALET**
◆◆ Italian
**Dinner: $21-$30**   **Phone: 201/366-0111**   (118)
**Location:** On SR 10W; w of Franklin Rd. 3150 SR 10W 07834. **Hours:** 11:30 am-10:30 pm, Fri & Sat-11 pm, Sun 1 pm-9:30 pm. **Closed:** 11/23 & 12/25. **Reservations:** suggested. **Features:** semi-formal attire; health conscious menu items; carryout; cocktails & lounge; a la carte. Casual dining atmosphere featuring traditional house specialities served by enjoyable staff. **Cards:** AE, DI, MC, VI.

# EAST BRUNSWICK—43,500

## LODGINGS

**BRUNSWICK HILTON AND TOWERS**   Rates Subject to Change   **Phone: 908/828-2000**

| | | 1P: | | 2P/1B: | | 2P/2B: | | XP: | |
|---|---|---|---|---|---|---|---|---|---|
| Sun-Thurs | 1P: $100- 175 | 2P/1B: $120- 195 | 2P/2B: $120- 195 | XP: $20 | F |
| Fri & Sat | 1P: $79- 175 | 2P/1B: $79- 195 | 2P/2B: $89- 130 | XP: $20 | F |

◆◆◆ Hotel
**Location:** NJ Tpk exit 9, first right on service road. 3 Tower Center Blvd 08816. **Fax:** 908/828-6958. **Terms:** Check-in 4 pm; package plans; pets. **Facility:** 405 rooms. Comtemporary accommodations in a corporate park setting. Close proximity to major highways & turnpike entrance. 15 stories; interior corridors; business center, conference facilities; luxury level rooms; heated indoor pool, sauna, whirlpool. **Dining & Entertainment:** Restaurant; 7 am-10:30 pm; $12-$27; health conscious menu items; cocktails/lounge; 24-hour room service; entertainment. **Services:** data ports, PC, secretarial services; valet laundry. **Fee:** childcare; valet parking. **All Rooms:** honor bars, free & pay movies, cable TV. **Some Rooms:** coffeemakers, microwaves, refrigerators, whirlpools. **Cards:** AE, CB, DI, DS, MC, VI.
*(See ad p 28)*   Ⓓ Ⓢ ⊘

**MCINTOSH INN OF EAST BRUNSWICK**   Rates Subject to Change   **Phone: 908/238-4900**

| | | 1P: | | 2P/1B: | | 2P/2B: | | XP: | |
|---|---|---|---|---|---|---|---|---|---|
| All Year | 1P: $45- 50 | 2P/1B: $51- 57 | 2P/2B: $51 | XP: $3 | F18 |

◆◆ Motel
**Location:** On SR 18N between Rue Ln & Racetrack Rd; 4 mi s from exit 9, NJ Tpk. 764 Rt 18 08816. **Fax:** 908/257-2023. **Terms:** Sr. discount; weekly rates; no pets. **Facility:** 107 rooms. 2 stories; interior/exterior corridors. **Dining:** Restaurant nearby. **Services:** data ports; valet laundry. **All Rooms:** free movies, cable TV. **Some Rooms:** microwaves, radios, refrigerators. **Cards:** AE, CB, DI, MC, VI. *(See ad p A53 & p A67)*   Ⓓ ⊘

## RESTAURANT

**CHI-CHI'S**
◆ Mexican
**Dinner: $11-$20**   **Phone: 908/390-1122**
**Location:** 1 1/2 mi s of NJ Tpk, exit 9 on SR 18; in Bradlees Mall. 335 Rt 18 08816. **Hours:** 11 am-11 pm, Fri & Sat-midnight, Sun-10 pm. **Closed:** 11/23 & 12/25. **Reservations:** suggested; for 8 or more. **Features:** casual dress; children's menu; health conscious menu items; carryout; salad bar; cocktails & lounge; a la carte. Luncheon buffet Mon-Sat, 11 am-2 pm. **Cards:** AE, DI, DS, MC, VI.   ⊘

# EAST HANOVER—9,900   (See NEW JERSEY METRO AREA ACCOMMODATIONS spotting map pages A40 & A41; see index starting on page A39)

## LODGING

**RAMADA HOTEL**   Rates Subject to Change   **Phone: 201/386-5622**   ⑮

| | | 1P: | | 2P/1B: | | 2P/2B: | | XP: | |
|---|---|---|---|---|---|---|---|---|---|
| Mon-Thurs | 1P: $89- 117 | 2P/1B: $89- 117 | 2P/2B: $99- 127 | XP: $10 | D18 |
| Fri-Sun | 1P: $59- 89 | 2P/1B: $59- 89 | 2P/2B: $69- 99 | XP: $10 | D18 |

(AAA)
◆◆◆ Motor Inn
**Location:** On SR 10 westbound, 3 mi e of I-287, exit 35 or 35A. 130 Rt 10 07936. **Fax:** 201/386-5724. **Terms:** Sr. discount; credit card guarantee; weekly/monthly rates; BP available; pets. **Facility:** 255 rooms. Conveniently located to nearby shopping areas; cordial & friendly staff in a relaxing atmosphere. 5 stories; interior corridors; conference facilities. **Fee:** miniature golf; driving range. **Dining & Entertainment:** Dining room; 6:30 am-midnight; $8-$18; health conscious menu items; cocktails; entertainment. **Services:** data ports, PC, secretarial services; complimentary evening beverages; health club privileges; valet laundry; area transportation. **Fee:** childcare. **All Rooms:** free & pay movies, cable TV. **Some Rooms:** microwaves, refrigerators. **Cards:** AE, CB, DI, DS, JCB, MC, VI.   Ⓓ ⊘

## RESTAURANTS

**PRIMA DONNA**
◆◆◆◆ Northern Italian
**Dinner: over $31**   **Phone: 201/887-4949**   ⑯
**Location:** On SR 10E; 3 3/4 mi e of I-287, exit 35 1 1/2 mi w of Livingston Circle. 341 SR 10 07936. **Hours:** 11:30 am-2:30 & 5-10 pm, Fri & Sat-10:30 pm. Closed major holidays & Sun. **Reservations:** suggested; weekends. **Features:** semi-formal attire; health conscious menu items; cocktails & lounge; entertainment; valet parking; a la carte. Stylish ristorante. Fish & veal specialties. Truly an enjoyable experience. **Cards:** AE, DI, MC, VI.

**RILLO'S**
◆◆ Northern Italian
**Dinner: $11-$20**   **Phone: 201/887-0580**   ⑮
**Location:** On SR 10W, 2 mi w of Livingston Cir, I-287 exit 35; 3 3/4 mi e on SR 10. 190 Rt 10 07936. **Hours:** 11:30 am-4 & 5-10 pm, Wed-Fri to 11 pm, Sat 5 pm-11 pm, Sun 4 pm-10 pm. Closed major holidays & Mon. **Reservations:** suggested; weekends. **Features:** casual dress; health conscious menu items; carryout; cocktails & lounge; valet parking; a la carte. Many pasta & veal specialties. **Cards:** AE, CB, DI, MC, VI.

## EAST RUTHERFORD—7,900 (See NEWARK to PARAMUS ACCOMMODATIONS spotting map page A44; see index starting on page A42)

### LODGINGS

**DAYS INN-MEADOWLANDS** — Guaranteed Rates — Phone: 201/507-5222
All Year — 1P: $52- 83 — 2P/1B: $60- 90 — 2P/2B: $74- 96 — XP: $10 — F16
**Location:** NJ Tpk western spur exit 16W, SR 3W to SR 17N, 1 1/2 mi n to Paterson Plank Rd (SR 120); I-80 exit 64B, 3 mi s on SR 17. 850 SR 120 07073. **Fax:** 201/507-0744. **Terms:** Sr. discount; reserv deposit, 3 day notice; weekly/monthly rates; 2 night min stay, weekends; pets, $25. **Facility:** 139 rooms. Group rate, 10 or more rooms $55 per room; 5 stories; interior corridors; meeting rooms; exercise room. **Dining:** Deli; 5 pm-midnight; $5-$8; cocktails. **Services:** data ports, secretarial services; valet laundry. **All Rooms:** free & pay movies, cable TV. **Some Rooms:** radios. **Cards:** AE, CB, DI, DS, JCB, MC, VI.

**SHERATON MEADOWLANDS** — AAA Special Value Rates — Phone: 201/896-0500
Sun-Thurs — 1P: $139 — 2P/1B: $139 — 2P/2B: $139 — XP: $20 — F17
Fri & Sat — 1P: $89 — 2P/1B: $89 — 2P/2B: $89 — XP: $20 — F17
**Location:** NJ Tpk exit 16W (from western spur), sports complex 1st right after toll (3E) to Sheraton Plaza Dr. 2 Meadowlands Plaza 07073. **Fax:** 201/896-9696. **Terms:** Reserv deposit; package plans; small pets only, must be attended. **Facility:** 425 rooms. Rooms offer panoramic views. 21 stories; interior corridors; business center, conference facilities; luxury level rooms; sauna, whirlpool, small heated indoor pool; exercise room. **Dining & Entertainment:** Dining room, restaurant; 6 am-11 pm; $8-$20; health conscious menu; cocktails/lounge. **Services:** data ports, secretarial services; valet laundry. **Fee:** airport transportation. **All Rooms:** honor bars, coffeemakers, free & pay movies, refrigerators, cable TV. **Cards:** AE, CB, DI, DS, JCB, MC, VI.

### RESTAURANT

**PARK AND ORCHARD** — Dinner: $21-$30 — Phone: 201/939-9292
**Location:** NJ Tpk exit 16W; SR 3W, 1 mi n on SR 17; after 2nd light Union Ave w to Hackensack St, then 1 blk n, southbound SR 17 Union Ave exit Rutherford. 240 Hackensack St 07073. **Hours:** noon-4 & 5-10 pm, Sat from 5 pm, Sun 2 pm-9 pm. Closed major holidays & Mon for lunch. **Features:** casual dress; children's menu; health conscious menu; cocktails & lounge. Natural foods restaurant. **Cards:** AE, DI, DS, MC, VI.

## EAST WINDSOR

### LODGINGS

**DAYS INN** — AAA Special Value Rates — Phone: 609/448-3200
5/1-9/3 — 1P: $55- 85 — 2P/1B: $55- 85 — 2P/2B: $62- 92 — XP: $10 — F12
9/4-4/30 — 1P: $49- 69 — 2P/1B: $49- 69 — 2P/2B: $55- 75 — XP: $10 — F12
**Location:** NJ E Tpk, exit 8 just e. 460 Rt 33 E 08520. **Fax:** 609/448-8447. **Terms:** Weekly/monthly rates; package plans, seasonal; small pets only, credit card number req. **Facility:** 100 rooms. Budget-oriented property in rural setting conveniently located to major highways & near-by attractions. 3 stories; interior corridors; pool. **Dining:** Restaurant nearby. **Services:** data ports. **Fee:** coin laundry. **All Rooms:** free movies, cable TV. **Some Rooms:** Fee: microwaves, refrigerators, whirlpools. **Cards:** AE, CB, DI, DS, MC, VI.

**RAMADA INN & CONFERENCE CENTER** — AAA Special Value Rates — Phone: 609/448-7000
5/1-9/3 — 1P: $65- 95 — 2P/1B: $65- 95 — 2P/2B: $72- 102 — XP: $10 — F12
9/4-4/30 — 1P: $59- 79 — 2P/1B: $59- 79 — 2P/2B: $65- 85 — XP: $10 — F12
**Location:** Exit 8, NJ E Tpk, 1/4 e on SR 33 then n on Woodside Ave 1 blk to Monmouth St. 399 Monmouth St 08520. **Fax:** 609/443-6227. **Terms:** Monthly rates; BP available; small pets only, credit card number req. **Facility:** 200 rooms. Located within minutes of historic Princeton. 4 stories; interior corridors; designated smoking area; business center, conference facilities; sauna, small pool; exercise room, playground. **Dining & Entertainment:** Dining room; 7 am-10 pm, Sat from 7:30 am, Sun 7:30 am-9 pm, Mon 7 am-9 pm; $10-$20; health conscious menu items; cocktails/lounge; entertainment, nightclub. **Services:** data ports, secretarial services; valet laundry. **Recreation:** jogging. **All Rooms:** coffeemakers, free & pay movies, cable TV. **Some Rooms:** refrigerators, VCP's, whirlpools. **Cards:** AE, CB, DI, DS, MC, VI.

## EATONTOWN—13,800

### LODGINGS

**CRYSTAL MOTOR LODGE** — Rates Subject to Change — Phone: 908/542-4900
5/1-9/6 — 1P: $56 — 2P/1B: $60 — 2P/2B: $66 — XP: $12 — F15
9/7-4/30 — 1P: $38 — 2P/1B: $44 — 2P/2B: $48 — XP: $12 — F15
**Location:** On SR 35 just n of CR 537 opposite Fort Monmouth main gate. 170 Main St (Hwy 35) 07724. **Fax:** 908/542-1718. **Terms:** Sr. discount; reserv deposit; weekly rates; pets, $10. **Facility:** 77 rooms. 2 stories; exterior corridors; playground. **Dining:** Restaurant nearby. **All Rooms:** free movies, refrigerators, cable TV. **Some Rooms:** coffeemakers. **Cards:** AE, CB, DI, DS, MC, VI.

**SHERATON HOTEL & CONFERENCE CENTER**   Guaranteed Rates      Phone: 908/542-6500
(AAA)   All Year         1P: $95- 145   2P/1B: $105- 155   2P/2B: $105- 155   XP: $10   F17
◆◆◆   **Location:** On SR 35 northbound, 1/2 mi s of jct SR 36. Industrial Way East 07724. Fax: 908/542-6607.
Hotel   **Terms:** Sr. discount; weekly/monthly rates; no pets. **Facility:** 208 rooms. Spacious, contemporary accommodations on beautifully landscaped acreage; executive level available for the corporate traveler. 6 stories; interior corridors; business center, conference facilities, convention oriented; heated indoor/outdoor pool, whirlpool;
exercise room. Fee: health club. **Dining & Entertainment:** Dining room, cafeteria; 7 am-11 pm; $14-$23; health conscious
menu items; cocktails/lounge. **Services:** data ports, PC, secretarial services; valet laundry. **All Rooms:** free & pay movies,
cable TV. **Some Rooms:** coffeemakers, whirlpools. Fee: microwaves, refrigerators. **Cards:** AE, CB, DI, DS, MC, VI.
*(See color ad p A25)*                                                                                  Ⓓ Ⓢ ⊗

# EDISON—88,700   (See NEW JERSEY METRO AREA ACCOMMODATIONS spotting map
pages A40 & A41; see index starting on page A39)

## LODGINGS

**CLARION HOTEL & TOWERS**         AAA Special Value Rates        Phone: 908/287-3500   **21**
(AAA)   Sun-Thurs [BP]   1P: $95    2P/1B: $99    2P/2B: $99    XP: $10   F18
◆◆◆   Fri & Sat [BP]    1P: $59    2P/1B: $64    2P/2B: $64    XP: $10   F18
Hotel   **Location:** I-287N exit to SR 27S, then 1 mi. 2055 Lincoln Hwy 08817. Fax: 908/287-8190. **Terms:** Reserv
deposit; AP, CP available; no pets. **Facility:** 168 rooms. 5 stories; interior corridors; conference facilities; luxury
level rooms; sauna; exercise room. **Dining & Entertainment:** Dining room; 6:30 am-10 pm, Sat & Sun from
7 am; $11-$20; health conscious menu items; cocktails/lounge; nightclub. **Services:** data ports, secretarial services;
complimentary evening beverages; valet laundry; area transportation, airport transportation. **All Rooms:** free & pay movies.
**Some Rooms:** refrigerators. **Cards:** AE, CB, DI, DS, MC, VI.                                        Ⓓ Ⓢ ⊗

**CROWNE PLAZA AT RARITAN CENTER**     Rates Subject to Change       Phone: 908/225-8300   **19**
(AAA)   All Year         1P: $125    2P/1B: $125    2P/2B: $125    XP: $5
◆◆◆   **Location:** 1/2 mi se of tpk, exit 10; on CR 514 keep right after tolls. 125 Raritan Center Pkwy 08837.
Hotel   Fax: 908/225-0037. **Terms:** Sr. discount; credit card guarantee; monthly rates; small pets only. **Facility:** 274
rooms. Enjoy comfortable accomodations with friendly staff in a warm & inviting atmosphere. Corporate park
environment. 12 stories; interior corridors; conference facilities, convention oriented; heated indoor pool,
saunas, whirlpool; exercise room. **Dining & Entertainment:** Restaurant; 6:30 am-11 pm, Sun-10 pm; $7-$20; health
conscious menu items; cocktail lounge. **Services:** data ports, secretarial services; valet laundry. **All Rooms:** free & pay
movies, cable TV. **Some Rooms:** refrigerators. **Cards:** AE, CB, DI, DS, MC, VI.

**RED ROOF INN**                   Rates Subject to Change       Phone: 908/248-9300   **22**
◆◆   All Year         1P: $36- 40   2P/1B: $43- 47   2P/2B: $50- 57   XP: $7   F18
Motel   **Location:** Northbound on I-287, exit Durham Ave & return to I-287 southbound, exit Metuchen & New
Durham Rd. 860 New Durham Rd 08817. Fax: 908/248-9326. **Terms:** Credit card guarantee; pets.
**Facility:** 132 rooms. Meeting rooms. **Dining:** Deli nearby. **Services:** data ports; valet laundry. **All Rooms:** free movies,
cable TV. **Cards:** AE, CB, DI, DS, MC, VI.                                                             Ⓓ ⊗

**WELLESLEY INN**                   Guaranteed Rates            Phone: 908/287-0171   **20**
(AAA)   All Year [CP]     1P: $46- 66   2P/1B: $46- 60   2P/2B: $50- 71   XP: $5   F18
◆◆◆   **Location:** On US 1 southbound; 1 mi s of I-287. 831 US 1S 08817. Fax: 908/287-8364. **Terms:** Sr. discount;
Motel   monthly rates; small pets only. **Facility:** 101 rooms. 3 stories; interior corridors; meeting rooms. Fee: health
club privileges. **Services:** data ports, secretarial services; valet laundry. **All Rooms:** coffeemakers, free &
pay movies, cable TV. **Some Rooms:** refrigerators. **Cards:** AE, CB, DI, DS, JCB, MC, VI.              Ⓓ Ⓢ ⊗

### RESTAURANT

**JACK COOPER'S**                   Dinner: $11-$20             Phone: 908/549-4580   **19**
◆   **Location:** 1/4 mi w of US 1; located in Tano Mall. 1199 Amboy Ave 08837. **Hours:** 9 am-9 pm. **Closed:** Mon.
American   **Features:** casual dress; Sunday brunch; children's menu; health conscious menu items; carryout; a la carte.
**Cards:** AE, CB, DI, MC, VI.

# ELIZABETH   (See NEWARK to PARAMUS ACCOMMODATIONS spotting map page A44;
see index starting on page A42)

## LODGINGS

**CLARION HOTEL NEWARK AIRPORT**       Rates Subject to Change       Phone: 908/527-1600   **27**
(AAA)   All Year         1P: $79    2P/1B: $92    2P/2B: $92    XP: $10   F18
◆◆◆   **Location:** Exit 13A off NJ Tpk on US 1 & 9 northbound, adjacent to airport. 901 Spring St 07201.
Hotel   Fax: 908/527-1327. **Terms:** Credit card guarantee; package plans; small pets only. **Facility:** 258 rooms. Some
units, $104-125; 11 stories; interior corridors; meeting rooms; heated indoor/outdoor pool. Fee: parking.
**Dining & Entertainment:** Dining room; 6:30 am-11 pm; $10-$23; cocktails/lounge; entertainment.
**Services:** data ports, secretarial services; valet laundry; area transportation, airport transportation. **All Rooms:** free & pay
movies, cable TV. **Some Rooms:** coffeemakers, microwaves, refrigerators. **Cards:** AE, DI, DS, MC, VI.
*(See ad p A45)*                                                                                        Ⓓ Ⓢ ⊗

**HAMPTON INN-NEWARK AIRPORT**         Rates Subject to Change       Phone: 908/355-0500   **26**
◆◆◆   Sun-Thurs [CP]    1P: $67- 77   2P/1B: $72- 87   2P/2B: $87
Motel   Fri & Sat [CP]    1P: $64    2P/1B: $64    2P/2B: $64
**Location:** Exit 13A NJ Tpk on US 1 & 9N, u-turn on McClellan St opposite Newark Airport. 1128-38 Spring
St 07207. Fax: 908/355-4343. **Terms:** Credit card guarantee; no pets. **Facility:** 152 rooms. Security controlled parking area.
5 stories; interior corridors; meeting rooms; exercise room. **Services:** data ports, secretarial services; valet laundry; area
transportation, to area restaurants, airport transportation. **All Rooms:** free movies, cable TV. **Some Rooms:** refrigerators.
**Cards:** AE, DI, DS, MC, VI.                                                                           Ⓓ Ⓢ ⊗

**HOLIDAY INN-JETPORT**             Rates Subject to Change       Phone: 908/355-1700   **29**
◆◆   Mon-Thurs        1P: $79- 99   2P/1B: $89- 109   2P/2B: $89- 109   XP: $10   F18
Hotel   Fri-Sun          1P: $69- 89   2P/1B: $79- 99   2P/2B: $79- 99   XP: $10   F18
**Location:** Exit 13A off NJ Tpk on US 1 & 9N, u-turn on McClellan St, opposite Newark Airport. 1000 Spring
St 07201. Fax: 908/355-1741. **Terms:** Sr. discount; reserv deposit; weekly/monthly rates; small pets only. **Facility:** 392 rooms.
9 two-bedroom units. 10 stories; interior corridors; conference facilities; heated indoor pool, saunas; exercise room.
**Dining & Entertainment:** Dining room; 6 am-11 pm, Sat & Sun from 7 am; $14-$20; health conscious menu items;
cocktails/lounge; entertainment. **Services:** data ports, secretarial services; valet laundry; area transportation, to Penn Station
Newark, airport transportation. **All Rooms:** free & pay movies, cable TV. **Some Rooms:** coffeemakers, refrigerators.
**Cards:** AE, CB, DI, DS, JCB, MC, VI.                                                                   Ⓓ Ⓢ ⊗

**(See NEWARK to PARAMUS ACCOMMODATIONS spotting map page A44)**

**NEWARK AIRPORT HILTON HOTEL**    AAA Special Value Rates     **Phone:** 908/351-3900   **28**
| | | | | | |
|---|---|---|---|---|---|
| Mon-Thurs | 1P: $135 | 2P/1B: $135 | 2P/2B: $135 | XP: $10 | F |
| Fri-Sun | 1P: $99 | 2P/1B: $99 | 2P/2B: $99 | XP: $10 | F |

Hotel   **Location:** 1 mi from main terminal, 3 mi sw of exit , on US 1 & 9, local at McClellan St. 1170 Spring St 07201. **Fax:** 908/351-9556. **Terms:** Weekly/monthly rates; AP, BP, CP, MAP available; no pets. **Facility:** 376 rooms. Contemporary marble lobby. Inviting atmosphere. Access to major highways. 12 stories; interior corridors; business center, conference facilities; heated indoor pool, sauna, steamroom, whirlpool; exercise room. **Dining & Entertainment:** Restaurant; 6:30 am-11 pm, Sat & Sun from 7 am; $13-$20; health conscious menu items; cocktails/lounge. **Services:** data ports, PC, secretarial services; valet laundry; airport transportation. Fee: massage. **All Rooms:** coffeemakers, free & pay movies, cable TV. **Some Rooms:** refrigerators, whirlpools. Fee: VCP's. **Cards:** AE, CB, DI, DS, MC, VI. A Hilton Hotel. *(See ad p 28 & p A46)*   ⊘ Ⓓ Ⓢ ⊘

# ENGLEWOOD—24,900   (See NEWARK to PARAMUS ACCOMMODATIONS spotting map page A44; see index starting on page A42)

## LODGING

**RADISSON HOTEL ENGLEWOOD**     Guaranteed Rates     **Phone:** 201/871-2020   **8**
| | | | | | |
|---|---|---|---|---|---|
| Sun-Thurs | 1P: $129- 149 | 2P/1B: $149- 169 | 2P/2B: $149- 169 | XP: $20 | F18 |
| Fri & Sat | 1P: $89- 109 | 2P/1B: $89- 109 | 2P/2B: $89- 109 | XP: $20 | F18 |

Hotel   **Location:** Van Brunt exit, off SR 4. 401 S Van Brunt St 07631. **Fax:** 201/871-7116. **Terms:** Sr. discount; credit card guarantee, 3 day notice; weekly/monthly rates; package plans; small pets only. **Facility:** 192 rooms. 9 stories; interior corridors; conference facilities; luxury level rooms; heated indoor pool; exercise room. **Dining & Entertainment:** Dining room; 6:30 am-10 pm; $6-$15; health conscious menu items; cocktails/lounge. **Services:** data ports, secretarial services; area transportation, to local businesses. Fee: coin laundry, airport transportation. **All Rooms:** free & pay movies, cable TV. **Some Rooms:** coffeemakers, microwaves, refrigerators. **Cards:** AE, CB, DI, DS, JCB, MC, VI.   Ⓓ Ⓢ ⊘

# FAIRFIELD—7,600   (See NEW JERSEY METRO AREA ACCOMMODATIONS spotting map pages A40 & A41; see index starting on page A39)

## LODGINGS

**BEST WESTERN FAIRFIELD EXECUTIVE INN**   AAA Special Value Rates   **Phone:** 201/575-7700   **11**
| | | | | | |
|---|---|---|---|---|---|
| All Year | 1P: $84- 150 | 2P/1B: $97- 163 | 2P/2B: $97- 163 | XP: $13 | F18 |

Motor Inn   **Location:** I-80 westbound exit 52 & 1 1/2 mi w on US 46 (on eastbound 46), I-80 eastbound exit 47B & 5 1/2 mi e on US 46. 216-234 Rt 46E 07004. **Fax:** 201/575-4653. **Terms:** Credit card guarantee; weekly/monthly rates; weekend rates available; no pets. **Facility:** 150 rooms. 4 stories; interior corridors; conference facilities; heated indoor pool, sauna, whirlpool; exercise room. **Dining & Entertainment:** Restaurant; 7 am-11 pm, Sat & Sun from 8 am; $10-$20; health conscious menu items; cocktails/lounge; entertainment. **Services:** data ports, secretarial services; complimentary evening beverages; valet laundry; area transportation, to local businesses. **All Rooms:** coffeemakers, free & pay movies, cable TV. **Some Rooms:** microwaves, refrigerators, whirlpools. **Cards:** AE, CB, DI, DS, MC, VI.   Ⓓ Ⓢ ⊘

**RADISSON HOTEL & SUITES**     Rates Subject to Change     **Phone:** 201/227-9200   **12**
| | | | | | |
|---|---|---|---|---|---|
| All Year | 1P: $140- 175 | 2P/1B: $145- 185 | 2P/2B: $140- 185 | XP: $10 | F17 |

Hotel   **Location:** Westbound I-80 exit 52, eastbound exit Caldwells 47B, then 7 mi e on US 46. 690 US 46E 07004. **Fax:** 201/227-4308. **Terms:** Sr. discount; credit card guarantee; small pets only, $50 dep req. **Facility:** 204 rooms. 5 stories; interior corridors; conference facilities; heated indoor pool, sauna; exercise room. **Dining & Entertainment:** Dining room; 6:30 am-10 pm, Fri-Sun from 7 am; $14-$25; health conscious menu items; cocktails/lounge; entertainment. **Services:** data ports, secretarial services; complimentary evening beverages; valet laundry. **All Rooms:** free & pay movies, cable TV. **Some Rooms:** coffeemakers, 12 efficiencies, microwaves, refrigerators. **Cards:** AE, CB, DI, DS, JCB, MC, VI.   Ⓓ Ⓢ ⊘

**RAMADA INN**     AAA Special Value Rates     **Phone:** 201/575-1742   **13**
| | | | | | |
|---|---|---|---|---|---|
| Mon-Thurs | 1P: $89- 109 | 2P/1B: $89- 119 | 2P/2B: $89- 119 | XP: $10 | F12 |
| Fri-Sun | 1P: $62- 89 | 2P/1B: $62- 89 | 2P/2B: $62- 89 | XP: $10 | F12 |

Motor Inn   **Location:** I-80 westbound exit 52; I-80 eastbound, exit Caldwells 47B, 7 mi e on US 46, exit Passaic Ave. 38 Two Bridges Rd 07004. **Fax:** 201/575-9567. **Terms:** Reserv deposit, 14 day notice; BP available; no pets. **Facility:** 176 rooms. 2 stories; interior corridors; conference facilities; heated indoor/outdoor pool; exercise room. Fee: 6 indoor tennis courts. **Dining & Entertainment:** Dining room; 6:30 am-10 pm; $10-$15; health conscious menu items; cocktails/lounge; entertainment. **Services:** data ports, secretarial services; valet laundry. **All Rooms:** free & pay movies, cable TV. **Some Rooms:** coffeemakers, 11 efficiencies, no utensils, microwaves, refrigerators. **Cards:** AE, DI, DS, MC, VI.   Ⓓ ⊘

# FANWOOD—7,100   (See NEW JERSEY METRO AREA ACCOMMODATIONS spotting map pages A40 & A41; see index starting on page A39)

## LODGING

**THE MANSION BEST WESTERN**     AAA Special Value Rates     **Phone:** 908/654-5200   **25**
| | | | | | |
|---|---|---|---|---|---|
| All Year | 1P: $85- 95 | 2P/1B: $95- 105 | 2P/2B: $95- 105 | XP: $10 | F18 |

Motor Inn   **Location:** 1 1/4 mi s of US 22 (Fanwood) on Park Ave, e on South Ave (SR 28). 295 South Ave 07023. **Fax:** 908/789-0451. **Terms:** Reserv deposit; monthly rates; no pets. **Facility:** 71 rooms. 4 stories; interior corridors; meeting rooms. **Dining & Entertainment:** Dining room; 7-9:30 am, noon-2:30 & 5-10 pm, Sat 7:30 am-10 & 5-10 pm, Sun 7:30 am-10:30 & 5-10 pm; $10-$20; health conscious menu items; cocktails/lounge. **Services:** data ports; health club privileges; valet laundry; area transportation, airport transportation. **All Rooms:** free movies, cable TV. **Some Rooms:** 26 efficiencies, refrigerators, whirlpools. Fee: VCP's. **Cards:** AE, CB, DI, DS, JCB, MC, VI.   Ⓓ ⊘

# FLEMINGTON—4,000

## LODGINGS

**THE BEL-AIR INN & CONFERENCE CENTER**     Rates Subject to Change     **Phone:** 908/782-7472
| | | | | | |
|---|---|---|---|---|---|
| All Year | 1P: $72 | 2P/1B: $72 | 2P/2B: $72 | XP: $8 | F |

Motor Inn   **Location:** On US 202 & SR 31; 1/2 mi s of the circle. 250 Hwy US 202 & SR 31 08822. **Fax:** 908/782-1975. **Terms:** Credit card guarantee, 3 day notice; no pets. **Facility:** 104 rooms. 2 stories; exterior corridors; meeting rooms; pool. **Dining:** Restaurant; 11:30 am-11 pm; $6-$19; cocktails. **Services:** Fee: coin laundry. **Some Rooms:** 23 efficiencies, kitchen, no utensils, refrigerators. **Cards:** AE, CB, DI, DS, MC, VI.   Ⓓ

**CABBAGE ROSE INN**  Guaranteed Rates  Phone: 908/788-0247
◆◆◆  Fri-Sun [BP]  1P: $80- 120  2P/1B: $80- 120  XP: $15
Bed &  Mon-Thurs [BP]  1P: $70- 100  2P/1B: $70- 100  XP: $15
Breakfast  **Location:** Center. 162 Main St 08822. **Terms:** Reserv deposit, 7 day notice; no pets. **Facility:** 5 rooms. Victorian town home, circa 1891. Convenient location to shops & boutiques. Owners have a dog. Interior corridors; smoke free premises. **Dining:** Restaurant nearby. **Services:** data ports. **All Rooms:** combo & shower baths, no TVs.
**Cards:** AE, MC, VI.  Ⓓ ⊗

**JERICA HILL-A BED & BREAKFAST INN**  Guaranteed Rates  Phone: 908/782-8234
⊕  All Year [CP]  1P: $70- 110  2P/1B: $70- 110  XP: $20
  **Location:** 2 blks e of Main St between Church & Williams sts. 96 Broad St 08822. **Terms:** Reserv deposit,
◆◆◆  10 day notice; weekly rates; 2 night min stay, on most weekends; no pets. **Facility:** 5 rooms. Turn-of-the-
Historic Bed  Century Victorian home featuring beautiful center hall staircase; Colonial antique decor, living room with fire-
& Breakfast  place & TV, & screened porch. Owner has cats. Interior corridors; smoke free premises; Nearby recreational
  facilities. **Dining:** Breakfast served 7:30 am-9 am, Sat, Sun & holidays; 8:30 am-9:30 am. **All Rooms:** free
movies, combo & shower baths. **Some Rooms:** phones, cable TV. **Cards:** AE, MC, VI.  Ⓓ ⊗

## RESTAURANT
**IL RUSTICO**  Dinner: $11-$20  Phone: 908/782-5488
◆◆◆  **Location:** 4 mi w of Flemington Cir via SR 12, on CR 579, at Texaco. 300 Old Croton Rd 08822.
Italian  **Hours:** noon-2:30 & 5-9:30 pm, Fri-10:30 pm, Sat 5 pm-10:30 pm, Sun 4 pm-9 pm. Closed major holidays &
  Mon. **Reservations:** suggested. **Features:** casual dress; health conscious menu items; cocktails & lounge;
entertainment; a la carte. Delightful house specialties served in a country setting. **Cards:** AE, MC, VI.  ⊗

# FLORHAM PARK—8,500  (See NEW JERSEY METRO AREA ACCOMMODATIONS
spotting map pages A40 & A41; see index starting on page A39)

## LODGING
**HAMILTON PARK EXECUTIVE CONFERENCE CENTER**  Guaranteed Rates  Phone: 201/377-2424  **27**
◆◆◆  Sun-Thurs  1P: $130  2P/1B: $130  2P/2B: $150  XP: $10  F18
Hotel  Fri & Sat  1P: $85  2P/1B: $85  2P/2B: $85
  **Location:** 2 mi w on CR 510, 1 mi s on CR 623 (Park Ave). 175 Park Ave 07932. Fax: 201/377-6108.
**Terms:** Reserv deposit, 3 day notice; AP, BP available; package plans; small pets only. **Facility:** 209 rooms. Corporate park
central location. 5 stories; interior corridors; business center, conference facilities; 2 pools (2 heated, 1 indoor), saunas, whirlpools; racquetball courts, 2 lighted tennis courts; health club, volleyball. **Dining & Entertainment:** Dining room; 6:45-9:30
am, ll:30-2 & 5:30-10 pm, Sun brunch 11 am-2 pm; $20-$35; health conscious menu items; cocktails/lounge. **Services:** data
ports, PC, secretarial services; valet laundry; area transportation, within 10 mi. **Fee:** childcare; massage; airport
transportation. **Recreation:** jogging. **All Rooms:** free & pay movies, cable TV. **Some Rooms:** refrigerators. **Fee:** VCP's.
**Cards:** AE, CB, DI, DS, MC, VI.  Ⓓ Ⓢ

## RESTAURANT
**THE AFTON**  Dinner: $11-$20  Phone: 201/377-1871  **28**
⊕  **Location:** Opposite Auto Club at S Orange Ave & Hanover Rd. 2 Hanover Rd 07932. **Hours:** 11:30 am-2:30
  & 5-9 pm, Sat 11:30 am-3 & 5-9 pm, Sun noon-8 pm. Closed: Mon & 12/25. **Reservations:** suggested.
◆◆  **Features:** casual dress; Sunday brunch; children's menu; carryout; cocktails & lounge; a la carte. Family
American  owned colonial inn. **Cards:** AE, CB, DI, MC, VI.  ⊗

# FORKED RIVER

## RESTAURANT
**CAPTAIN'S INN**  Dinner: $11-$20  Phone: 609/693-3351
◆◆  **Location:** Garden State Pkwy exit 74 (southbound), 3 mi e on Lacey Rd; exit 69 (northbound) 2 mi on 532E;
Seafood  n 4 mi on US 9, e on Lacey Rd to dock. 08731. **Hours:** 11:45 am-10 pm. Closed: 12/25. **Features:** casual
  dress; children's menu; early bird specials; health conscious menu items; carryout; cocktails & lounge; a la
carte. Extensive seafood menu; overlooking Forked River, docking facilities avail. **Cards:** AE, DI, MC, VI.

# FORT LEE—32,000  (See NEWARK to PARAMUS ACCOMMODATIONS spotting map
page A44; see index starting on page A42)

## LODGINGS
**DAYS INN**  AAA Special Value Rates  Phone: 201/944-5000  **10**
⊕  All Year  1P: $70- 80  2P/1B: $80- 92  2P/2B: $80- 92  XP: $10  F18
  **Location:** 1 mi w of GW Bridge on SR 4E; u-turn on Jones Rd; eastbound I-80 & I-95 local lanes exit Broad
◆◆  Ave-Leonia (exit 71) to Broad Ave, 1/2 mi to SR 4, 1/2 mi e. 2339 Rt 4 07024. Fax: 201/944-0623.
Motor Inn  **Terms:** Monthly rates; no pets. **Facility:** 175 rooms. 6 stories; interior corridors; meeting rooms. **Dining &
  Entertainment:**  Coffee shop; 7 am-2 pm; health conscious menu items; cocktails/lounge.
**Services:** secretarial services; valet laundry. **All Rooms:** free movies, cable TV. **Some Rooms:** radios. **Cards:** AE, CB, DI,
DS, JCB, MC, VI.  Ⓓ ⊗

**THE FORT LEE HILTON HOTEL**  Rates Subject to Change  Phone: 201/461-9000  **11**
⊕  All Year  1P: $135  2P/1B: $147  2P/2B: $147  XP: $12  F18
  **Location:** On SR 4E; 1 mi w of GW Bridge; u-turn on Jones Rd; I-95 & I-80 eastbound, local lanes exit 71
◆◆◆  Broad Ave-Leonia to Broad Ave then 1/2 mi e on SR 4. 2117 Rt 4 E 07024. Fax: 201/585-9807. **Terms:** Sr.
Hotel  discount; reserv deposit, 3 day notice; weekly rates; AP, BP, CP available; package plans; no pets.
  **Facility:** 235 rooms. Convenient access to George Washington Bridge. 15 stories; interior corridors; business
center, conference facilities; luxury level rooms; heated indoor pool, sauna, whirlpool; exercise room. **Dining &
Entertainment:** Dining room; 6:30 am-11 pm; $12-$28; health conscious menu items; cocktails/lounge; 24-hour room
service; nightclub. **Services:** data ports, PC, secretarial services; valet laundry; area transportation. **Fee:** airport
transportation. **All Rooms:** free movies, cable TV. **Some Rooms:** refrigerators, whirlpools. **Cards:** AE, CB, DI, DS, JCB,
MC, VI.  Ⓓ Ⓢ ⊗

# FRENCHTOWN

## LODGING

HUNTERDON HOUSE ◆◆◆
Historic Bed & Breakfast

AAA Special Value Rates

| | | |
|---|---|---|
| Fri & Sat [BP] | 2P/1B: $110- 145 | XP: $15 |
| Sun-Thurs [BP] | 2P/1B: $85- 100 | XP: $15 |

Phone: 908/996-3632

**Location:** Center of town, 2 blks w of jct SR 12. 12 Bridge St 08825. **Terms:** Age restrictions may apply; reserv deposit, 10 day notice; weekly rates; no pets. **Facility:** 7 rooms. Casually elegant. Italianate brick Victorian, circa 1865. Large dining room, study/library with fireplace; porch, garden with patio. Interior corridors; smoke free premises; mountain view. **Dining:** Breakfast 8 am-9:30 am. **Recreation:** Fee: river rafting & tubing; downhill & cross country skiing. **All Rooms:** combo & shower baths, no TVs. **Some Rooms:** phones. **Cards:** AE, MC, VI.   Ⓓ Ⓢ ⊗

# GLEN ROCK (See NEWARK to PARAMUS ACCOMMODATIONS spotting map page A44; see index starting on page A42)

## RESTAURANT

GLEN ROCK INN ⑭
◆◆
American

Dinner: $11-$20

Phone: 201/445-2362   ⑥⓪

**Location:** SR 208 to CR 507 (Maple Ave), 1 mi n to Rock Rd, w 1/4 mi. 222 Rock Rd 07452. **Hours:** 11:30 am-midnight, Sun from 11 am. Closed: 12/25. **Reservations:** suggested; weekends. **Features:** casual dress; Sunday brunch; children's menu; early bird specials; health conscious menu items; carryout; cocktails & lounge; street parking; a la carte. Casual dining in a cozy atmosphere. **Cards:** AE, CB, DI, DS, MC, VI.

# HACKENSACK—37,000 (See NEWARK to PARAMUS ACCOMMODATIONS spotting map page A44; see index starting on page A42)

## RESTAURANT

STONY HILL INN   Historical
◆◆◆◆
Continental

Dinner: over $31

Phone: 201/342-4085   ㊼

**Location:** I-80 westbound local lanes from GW Bridge exit 64B & right; I-80 eastbound local lane exit 64 (SR 17S), exit Terrace Ave, then 1/4 mi n on Polifly Rd 231. 231 Polifly Rd 07601. **Hours:** 11:30 am-3 & 5:30-10:30 pm, Sat seatings 5:30 pm-7 pm & after 9:15 pm, Sun 3 pm-10 pm. Closed: 12/25. **Reservations:** suggested. **Features:** semi-formal attire; health conscious menu items; cocktails & lounge; entertainment; valet parking; a la carte, also prix fixe. Elegant classic Georgian; on National Register of Historic Places. **Cards:** AE, CB, DI, MC, VI.

# HAMMONTON—12,200

## LODGING

RAMADA INN OF HAMMONTON ⑭
◆◆◆
Motor Inn

Rates Subject to Change

All Year          2P/2B:   $45-  95   XP: $10  F18

Phone: 609/561-5700

**Location:** Exit 28 of Atlantic City Expwy, 3 mi n on SR 54, then 1 mi e on SR 30, White Horse Pike. 308 White Horse Pike 08037. Fax: 609/561-2392. **Terms:** Sr. discount; reserv deposit, 3 day notice; weekly/monthly rates; BP available; package plans; no pets. **Facility:** 103 rooms. 2 two-bedroom units. 2 stories; exterior corridors; meeting rooms; heated pool, wading pool. **Dining & Entertainment:** Restaurant; 6 am-11 pm; $6-$15; cocktails/lounge. **Services:** complimentary evening beverages. **All Rooms:** combo & shower baths, cable TV. **Some Rooms:** refrigerators. Fee: VCP's. **Cards:** AE, DI, DS, MC, VI.   Ⓓ ⊗

# HARDYSTON

## RESTAURANT

HAYLOFT RESTAURANT ◆
American

Dinner: $11-$20

Phone: 201/209-1816

**Location:** On SR 94, 3/4 mi n jct SR 23. Rt 94 07428. **Hours:** noon-2:30 pm, also Tue-Fri 5 pm-10 pm, Sat 5 pm-10 pm, Sun noon-9 pm. Closed: 12/25. **Features:** casual dress; children's menu; health conscious menu items; carryout; cocktails & lounge; a la carte. Early bird specials Mon-Fri. Rural locale. **Cards:** AE, MC, VI.   ⊗

# HASBROUCK HEIGHTS—11,500 (See NEWARK to PARAMUS ACCOMMODATIONS spotting map page A44; see index starting on page A42)

## LODGINGS

HOLIDAY INN ⑭
◆◆◆
Motor Inn

Rates Subject to Change

| | | | | |
|---|---|---|---|---|
| Mon-Thurs | 1P: $82- 107 | 2P/1B: $90- 115 | 2P/2B: $90- 115 | XP: $10  F12 |
| Fri-Sun | 1P: $70-  87 | 2P/1B: $70-  87 | 2P/2B: $70-  87 | XP: $10  F12 |

Phone: 201/288-9600   ⑭

**Location:** On SR 17 southbound; 1 mi s of jct I-80, exit 64B westbound, exit 64 eastbound. 283 Rt 17S 07604. Fax: 201/288-4527. **Terms:** Reserv deposit; no pets. **Facility:** 248 rooms. Close proximity to mid-town Manhattan. 2-5 stories; interior corridors; business center, conference facilities; pool, sauna; exercise room. **Dining & Entertainment:** Restaurant; 6:30 am-2:30 & 4-10 pm, Sat & Sun from 7 am; $12-$20; health conscious menu items; cocktails/lounge; entertainment, nightclub. **Services:** data ports, secretarial services; valet laundry; area transportation, to local businesses. Fee: airport transportation. **All Rooms:** free & pay movies, combo & shower baths, cable TV. **Some Rooms:** coffeemakers, refrigerators. **Cards:** AE, DI, DS, JCB, MC, VI. *(See ad below)*   Ⓓ ⊗

**(See NEWARK to PARAMUS ACCOMMODATIONS spotting map page A44)**

SHERATON HASBROUCK HEIGHTS HOTEL   Guaranteed Rates   Phone: 201/288-6100   🔟
  Sun-Thurs   1P:  $89- 109   2P/1B: $99- 119   2P/2B: $99- 119   XP: $10  F16
  Fri & Sat   1P:  $60-  70   2P/1B: $60-  70   2P/2B: $60-  70   XP: $10  F16
♦♦♦   **Location:** E of SR 17 northbound; s of I-80 local lanes exit SR 17S. 650 Terrace Ave 07604.
Hotel   **Fax:** 201/288-4717. **Terms:** Sr. discount; reserv deposit, 3 day notice; BP available; package plans; pets.
**Facility:** 349 rooms. Skyline view from roof-top restaurant & lounge. 12 stories; interior corridors; conference
facilities; heated pool, saunas, whirlpool; exercise room. **Dining & Entertainment:** Dining room, coffee shop; 6:30 am-11
pm; $11-$20; cocktails; entertainment. **Services:** secretarial services; valet laundry. **All Rooms:** free & pay movies, cable
TV. **Some Rooms:** coffeemakers, refrigerators. **Cards:** AE, DI, DS, JCB, MC, VI.   Ⓓ Ⓢ ⊗

# HAZLET—22,000

## LODGING

WELLESLEY INN   Rates Subject to Change   Phone: 908/888-2800
♦♦   All Year   1P:  $53-  63   2P/1B: $55-  72   2P/2B: $64-  79   XP: $5   F
Motel   **Location:** Exit 117 off Garden State Pkwy, 1 1/2 mi s on SR 35, u-turn Hazlet Ave. 3215 SR 35N 07730.
**Fax:** 908/888-2902. **Terms:** Sr. discount; reserv deposit; small pets only, $3. **Facility:** 89 rooms. 3 stories; in-
terior corridors; meeting rooms. **Dining:** Restaurant nearby. **Services:** data ports; area transportation, to local businesses.
Fee: coin laundry. **All Rooms:** free movies, cable TV. **Some Rooms:** microwaves. **Cards:** AE, DI, DS, MC, VI.   Ⓓ Ⓢ ⊗

# HIGHTSTOWN—5,100

## LODGING

TOWN HOUSE MOTEL   AAA Special Value Rates   Phone: 609/448-2400
⚫   All Year [CP]   1P:  $55- 115   2P/1B: $55- 125   2P/2B: $65-  95   XP: $10  F16
♦♦   **Location:** NJ Tpk exit 8, on SR 33W. SR 33 08520. **Fax:** 609/443-0395. **Terms:** Reserv deposit, 3 day
Motor Inn   notice; weekly rates; pets. **Facility:** 105 rooms. Budget property. Some smaller economy rooms. 2 stories;
interior/exterior corridors; meeting rooms; pool. **Dining:** Restaurant nearby. **Services:** secretarial services;
valet laundry. **All Rooms:** free movies, refrigerators, combo & shower baths. **Some Rooms:** microwaves,
VCP's, whirlpools. **Cards:** AE, CB, DI, DS, MC, VI.   Ⓓ

### RESTAURANT

JACK BAKER'S LOBSTER SHANTY   Dinner: $11-$20   Phone: 609/443-6600
♦♦   **Location:** On SR 33, 4 1/4 mi e of tpk exit 8. Rt 33 & Perrineville Rd 08520. **Hours:** 11:30 am-2 & 4:30-9
Seafood   pm, Sat-10 pm, Sun 1 pm-8:30 pm; in summer Fri-10 pm, Sat-10:30 pm. Closed: 12/25.
**Reservations:** suggested; for 8 or more. **Features:** casual dress; children's menu; early bird specials; health
conscious menu; carryout; cocktails & lounge; a la carte. Casual family dining in an informal atmosphere offering a varied
selection of fish & seafood. **Cards:** AE, CB, DI, MC, VI.   ⊗

# HILLSBOROUGH

## LODGING

DAYS INN HILLSBOROUGH EXECUTIVE CENTER   AAA Special Value Rates   Phone: 908/685-9000
♦♦   All Year [CP]   1P:  $78   2P/1B: $78   2P/2B:  $78   XP: $10  F18
Motel   **Location:** 2 3/4 mi s on Sommerville Cir on US 206. 118 Rt 206S 08876. **Fax:** 908/685-0601.
**Terms:** Reserv deposit; no pets. **Facility:** 100 rooms. 2 stories; interior corridors; meeting rooms; pool, whirl-
pool; exercise room. **Dining:** Cocktails; restaurant nearby. **Services:** data ports; health club privileges; valet laundry.
**All Rooms:** free movies, cable TV. **Some Rooms:** refrigerators, VCP's, whirlpools. **Cards:** AE, CB, DI, DS, MC, VI.
Ⓓ Ⓢ ⊗

### RESTAURANT

JASPERS   Dinner: $11-$20   Phone: 908/526-5584
♦♦   **Location:** 2 3/4 mi s of Somerville Cir on US 206. 150 Rt 206S 08876. **Hours:** 11:30 am-2:30 & 5-9:30 pm,
Continental   Fri-10 pm, Sat 5 pm-10 pm, Sun 4 pm-8 pm. Closed major holidays. **Reservations:** suggested.
**Features:** casual dress; children's menu; health conscious menu items; carryout; cocktails & lounge.
Northern Italian & French cuisine. Homemade pasta specialties. **Cards:** AE, DI, DS, MC, VI.

# HOBOKEN—33,400   (See NEWARK to PARAMUS ACCOMMODATIONS spotting map
page A44; see index starting on page A42)

### RESTAURANTS

ARTHUR'S TAVERN   Dinner: $11-$20   Phone: 201/656-5009   🔢
♦♦   **Location:** Corner Washington & 3rd St. 237 Washington 07030. **Hours:** 11:30 am-11 pm, Fri & Sat-midnight,
Steakhouse   Sun 2 pm-10 pm. Closed: 11/23 & 12/25. **Features:** casual dress; cocktails & lounge. A bustling tavern.
Steaks, burgers & sandwiches in a relaxing casual atmosphere. **Cards:** AE, DI, DS, MC, VI.

THE BRASS RAIL   Dinner: $21-$30   Phone: 201/659-7074   🔢
♦♦♦   **Location:** Corner Washington & 2nd St. 135 Washington 07030. **Hours:** 11:30 am-10 pm, Sat-midnight.
Continental   Closed: Mon, 1/1, 12/24 & 12/25. **Reservations:** suggested; weekends. **Features:** casual dress; Sunday
brunch; health conscious menu items; carryout; cocktails & lounge; street parking. Brasserie on 1st floor
open for lunch & dinner; fine dining room on 2nd floor, dinner only 5:30 pm-10 pm. **Cards:** AE, DI, MC, VI.   ⊗

RISTORANTE GERRINO   Dinner: $11-$20   Phone: 201/656-7731   🔢
♦♦   **Location:** On corner of 1st & River sts. 96 River St 07030. **Hours:** noon-10 pm, Fri & Sat-11 pm. Closed
Italian   major holidays & Sun. **Reservations:** suggested; for 4 or more. **Features:** casual dress; health conscious
menu items; carryout; cocktails & lounge; street parking; a la carte. A popular, relaxing bistro. Rooftop dining
in the summer months. **Cards:** AE, CB, DI, MC, VI.   ⊗

# HO-HO-KUS—3,900

### RESTAURANT

CLAUDE'S HO-HO-KUS INN   Historical   Dinner: $21-$30   Phone: 201/445-4115
♦♦♦   **Location:** Southbound SR 17 1 mi w via Race Track Rd; northbound W Linwood Ave-Ridgewood exit, 1 1/2
French   mi w then 1 mi n on Maple. Franklin Tpk & Sheridan Ave 07423. **Hours:** noon-2 & 5-9 pm, Fri-9:30 pm, Sat
5 pm-10 pm, Sun noon-2 & 3-8 pm. Closed: 1/1 & 12/25. **Reservations:** suggested. **Features:** semi-formal
attire; Sunday brunch; health conscious menu; cocktails & lounge; valet parking; a la carte. Charming historical landmark.
Formal service, valet parking for dinner. **Cards:** AE, CB, DI, MC, VI.

# HOPE—1,700

## LODGING

**INN AT MILLRACE POND**
◆◆◆
Historic
Country Inn

Guaranteed Rates                                    **Phone: 908/459-4884**
All Year [CP]         1P:  $85- 170  2P/1B:  $85- 150  2P/2B:  $85- 150  XP: $20
**Location:** I-80 exit 12, 1 mi S on CR 521, then left at blinker on CR 519. Rt 519 07844 (PO Box 359). **Terms:** Sr. discount; reserv deposit, 7 day notice; 2 night min stay, weekends; no pets. **Facility:** 17 rooms. Charming historic grist mill. Moravian colonial. 1 two-bedroom unit. 3 stories, no elevator; interior corridors; designated smoking area; meeting rooms; 1 tennis court. **Dining & Entertainment:** Dining room; 8-10 am guests only, Sun 8-9:30 am guests only; $19-$23; health conscious menu items; cocktails/lounge; dining room, see separate listing. **All Rooms:** no TVs. **Some Rooms:** whirlpools. **Cards:** AE, DI, MC, VI.                        ⒹⓈ⊗

## RESTAURANT

**INN AT MILLRACE POND**   Country Inn
◆◆◆
American

DI, MC, VI.

**Dinner: $21-$30**                                **Phone: 908/459-4884**
**Location:** In the Inn at Millrace Pond. Rt 519 07844. **Hours:** 5 pm-9:30 pm, Fri & Sat-10 pm, Sun noon-8 pm. **Reservations:** suggested; weekends. **Features:** casual dress; health conscious menu items; cocktails & lounge; a la carte. Seasonal menu featuring original cuisine, fresh-baked bread & dessert. **Cards:** AE, CB,
♿ ⊗

# JERSEY CITY—228,500   (See NEWARK to PARAMUS ACCOMMODATIONS spotting map page A44; see index starting on page A42)

## LODGINGS

**ECONO LODGE**
Ⓐ
◆
Motel

Rates Subject to Change                            **Phone: 201/420-9040**  ㉑
All Year            1P:  $50      2P/1B:  $55- 60  2P/2B:  $55- 60  XP: $5  F18
**Location:** 1 mi n, jct US 1 & 9. 750-760 Tonnelle Ave 07306. Fax: 201/420-9040. **Terms:** Sr. discount; credit card guarantee; CP available; no pets. **Facility:** 37 rooms. Located in industrial area between Holland & Lincoln Tunnels. 2 stories; interior corridors. **Dining:** Restaurants nearby. **Some Rooms:** refrigerators. Fee: whirlpools. **Cards:** AE, DI, DS, MC, VI. *(See color ad below)*                        ⒹⓈ⊗

**HOLLAND MOTOR LODGE**
◆
Motel

AAA Special Value Rates                            **Phone: 201/963-6200**  ⑱
All Year [CP]       1P:  $45- 54  2P/1B:  $49- 59  2P/2B:  $49- 59
**Location:** New Jersey Tpk (I-95) exit 14C, then 3 mi e following signs to Holland Tunnel, at New Jersey entrance to tunnel. Holland Tunnel Plaza E 07302. Fax: 201/420-5091. **Terms:** Reserv deposit, 5 day notice; weekly rates; no pets. **Facility:** 71 rooms. 3 stories; interior corridors. **Dining:** Coffee shop nearby. **Services:** data ports. **All Rooms:** free movies, refrigerators, combo & shower baths, cable TV. **Some Rooms:** microwaves. **Cards:** AE, CB, DI, DS, MC, VI.                        Ⓓ

**QUALITY INN**
Ⓐ
◆◆
Motor Inn

Guaranteed Rates                                  **Phone: 201/653-0300**  ⑳
All Year            1P:  $72      2P/1B:  $77      2P/2B:  $79      XP: $5  F18
**Location:** Entrance to Holland Tunnel. 180 12th St 07302. Fax: 201/659-1963. **Terms:** Sr. discount; credit card guarantee; monthly rates; no pets. **Facility:** 148 rooms. Budget property located in high traffic area entering Holland Tunnel. 2 stories; interior corridors; meeting rooms; pool. **Dining:** Dining room; 7 am-10:30 pm; $8-$16; cocktails. **Services:** valet laundry. **All Rooms:** free movies, cable TV. **Some Rooms:** radios. **Cards:** AE, CB, DI, DS, MC, VI.                        Ⓓ⊗

# KENDALL PARK

## RESTAURANT

**SHOGUN 27 JAPANESE CUISINE**
◆◆
Ethnic

**Dinner: $11-$20**                                **Phone: 908/422-1117**
**Location:** SR 27 at corner Sand Hill Rd. 3376 Hwy 27 08824. **Hours:** 11:30 am-2:30 & 4:30-10 pm, Fri-11 pm, Sat 4:30 pm-11 pm, Sun 4 pm-9:30 pm. Closed major holidays. **Reservations:** suggested; weekends. **Features:** casual dress; children's menu; early bird specials; health conscious menu items; carryout; cocktails & lounge; a la carte. Individual dining in tatami rooms, hibachi dining & sushi bar. **Cards:** AE, DI, MC, VI.          ⊗

# KENILWORTH—7,600   (See NEW JERSEY METRO AREA ACCOMMODATIONS spotting map pages A40 & A41; see index starting on page A39)

## LODGING

**KENILWORTH INN**
◆◆
Motor Inn

Rates Subject to Change                            **Phone: 908/241-4100**  ㉜
All Year            1P:  $64- 72  2P/1B:  $78      2P/2B:  $78      XP: $6  F18
**Location:** Just w of Garden State Pkwy, exit 138. S 31st St & Garden State Pkwy 07033. Fax: 908/241-1413. **Terms:** Credit card guarantee; small pets only. **Facility:** 120 rooms. 2 stories; interior corridors; conference facilities; pool. **Dining & Entertainment:** Dining room; 6:30 am-2:30 & 5-10 pm; $7-$15; health conscious menu items; cocktails/lounge. **Services:** data ports, secretarial services; valet laundry. **All Rooms:** free & pay movies, cable TV. **Cards:** AE, DI, DS, JCB, MC, VI.                        Ⓓ⊗

## RESTAURANT

**GOLDEN PALACE**
◆◆
Chinese

**Dinner: $11-$20**                                **Phone: 908/276-8884**  ㉜
**Location:** Center; Garden State Pkwy exit 136, 3/4 mi e on Boulevard; between N 20th & N 21st. 504 Boulevard 07033. **Hours:** 11:30 am-9:30 pm, Fri & Sat-10:30 pm, Sun noon-9:30 pm. **Reservations:** suggested; weekends. **Features:** casual dress; health conscious menu items; carryout; street parking; a la carte. Delightfully charming dining room serving gourmet dishes. A wonderful experience in Chinese dining. **Cards:** AE, MC, VI.

# KEYPORT

## RESTAURANT

YE COTTAGE INN
◆◆
Seafood

**Dinner:** $11-$20                                    **Phone:** 908/264-1263
**Location:** W Front St, 1/4 mi s CR 6. 149 W Front St 07735. **Hours:** noon-10 pm, Fri & Sat-11 pm.
**Reservations:** suggested; for 6 or more. **Features:** casual dress; children's menu; early bird specials; health conscious menu items; carryout; cocktails & lounge. Wonderful view of pier & harbor. **Cards:** AE, DI, DS, MC, VI.                                                                  ⊗

# LAKEWOOD—45,000

## LODGING

BEST WESTERN LEISURE INN
🅐🅐🅐
◆◆
Motor Inn

|  | Rates Subject to Change |  |  |  |  | **Phone:** 908/367-0900 |
|---|---|---|---|---|---|---|
| 6/1-9/30 [CP] | 1P: | $85- 95 | 2P/1B: | $95 | 2P/2B: | $95 | XP: $10  F16 |
| 5/1-5/31 & 10/1-4/30 [CP] | 1P: | $53- 66 | 2P/1B: | $57- 76 | 2P/2B: | $53- 66 | XP: $10  F16 |

**Location:** On SR 70, w of Garden State Pkwy exit 88 southbound; 2 1/2 mi e of US 9. 1600 Rt 70 08701.
**Fax:** 908/370-4928. **Terms:** Sr. discount; reserv deposit, 3 day notice; weekly/monthly rates; small pets only, must be on leash. **Facility:** 105 rooms. 2 stories; interior/exterior corridors; meeting rooms; pool; exercise room. **Dining & Entertainment:** Restaurant; 6:30 am-10:30 pm, Sat & Sun from 7:30 am; $6-$14; health conscious menu items; cocktails/lounge. **Services:** data ports. Fee: coin laundry. **All Rooms:** free movies, cable TV. **Some Rooms:** microwaves, refrigerators, whirlpools. **Cards:** AE, CB, DI, DS, MC, VI.                    ⒟ ⊗

## RESTAURANT

THE CASTLE
◆◆
Continental

**Dinner:** $11-$20                                    **Phone:** 908/905-3700
**Location:** US 9S, 1 mi n of jct SR 70. 945 River Ave 08701. **Hours:** 11:30 am-9 pm, Fri & Sat-9:30 pm, Sun 10:30 am-9 pm. **Reservations:** suggested. **Features:** casual dress; Sunday brunch; children's menu; early bird specials; health conscious menu items; carryout; cocktails & lounge; a la carte. Serving a variety of European classic dishes. **Cards:** AE, DS, MC, VI.                                           ⊗

# LAMBERTVILLE—3,900

## LODGING

THE INN AT LAMBERTVILLE STATION
🅐🅐🅐
◆◆◆
Motor Inn

|  | Rates Subject to Change |  |  | **Phone:** 609/397-4400 |
|---|---|---|---|---|
| Fri & Sat [CP] | 2P/1B: | $100- 150 | 2P/2B: | $115- 170 | XP: $15 |
| Sun-Thurs [CP] | 2P/1B: | $80- 90 | 2P/2B: | $90 | XP: $15 |

**Location:** Center, s of the Free Bridge. 11 Bridge St 08530. **Fax:** 609/397-9744. **Terms:** Credit card guarantee; package plans; no pets. **Facility:** 45 rooms. Serene accommodations. Individually antique decorated rooms with river view, some with fireplace. Suites, $125-$225; 3 stories; interior corridors; meeting rooms. **Dining & Entertainment:** $12-$20; cocktails/lounge; also, The Lambertville Station, see separate listing. **Services:** secretarial services; valet laundry. **All Rooms:** cable TV. **Some Rooms:** refrigerators, whirlpools. **Cards:** AE, CB, DI, MC, VI.                                                                          ⒟

## RESTAURANT

THE LAMBERTVILLE STATION   Historical
◆◆
American

**Dinner:** $11-$20                                    **Phone:** 609/397-8300
**Location:** In the Inn at Lambertville Station. 11 Bridge St 08530. **Hours:** 11:30 am-3 & 4-10 pm, Fri & Sat-11 pm, Sun 10:30 am-3 & 4-10 pm. **Reservations:** suggested; 6 or more. **Features:** casual dress; Sunday brunch; children's menu; early bird specials; health conscious menu items; cocktails & lounge; a la carte. Restored train station alongside scenic Delaware River. **Cards:** AE, CB, DI, MC, VI.                          ⊗

# LAWRENCEVILLE

## LODGINGS

HOWARD JOHNSON
🅐🅐🅐
◆◆◆
Motel

|  | AAA Special Value Rates |  |  |  |  | **Phone:** 609/896-1100 |
|---|---|---|---|---|---|---|
| All Year | 1P: | $65- 85 | 2P/1B: | $75- 95 | 2P/2B: | $75- 95 | XP: $10  F18 |

**Location:** On US 1 southbound, 1/2 mi s of I-295. 2995 Brunswick Pike 08648. **Fax:** 609/895-1325. **Terms:** Credit card guarantee; weekly/monthly rates; BP available; pets, $10 must be attended at all times. **Facility:** 104 rooms. Enjoy spacious rooms in a warm & friendly atmosphere with beautifully landscaped grounds, convenient to major highways. 2 stories; interior/exterior corridors; meeting rooms; pool, wading pool. **Dining:** Restaurant nearby. **Services:** data ports, secretarial services; valet laundry. **All Rooms:** free & pay movies, cable TV. **Some Rooms:** microwaves, refrigerators. **Cards:** AE, CB, DI, DS, JCB, MC, VI.                        ⒟ ⊗

MCINTOSH INN OF PRINCETON
◆◆
Motel

|  | Rates Subject to Change |  |  |  |  | **Phone:** 609/896-3700 |
|---|---|---|---|---|---|---|
| All Year | 1P: | $40- 48 | 2P/1B: | $47- 55 | 2P/2B: | $52 | XP: $3  F18 |

**Location:** 1/4 mi n of exit 67A off I-295, on US 1 adjacent to Quaker Bridge Mall. 3270 Brunswick Pike 08648. **Fax:** 609/896-2544. **Terms:** Sr. discount; weekly rates; no pets. **Facility:** 115 rooms. 4 stories; interior corridors; meeting rooms. **Dining:** Restaurant nearby. **Services:** data ports. **All Rooms:** free movies. **Some Rooms:** microwaves, radios, refrigerators. **Cards:** AE, CB, DI, MC, VI. *(See ad p A53 & p A67)*                    ⒟ ⊗

RED ROOF INN
◆◆
Motel

|  | Rates Subject to Change |  |  |  |  | **Phone:** 609/896-3388 |
|---|---|---|---|---|---|---|
| All Year | 1P: | $36- 47 | 2P/1B: | $43- 54 | 2P/2B: | $47- 57 | XP: $7  F18 |

**Location:** On US 1, just n of exit 67A of I-295. 3203 Brunswick Pike 08648. **Fax:** 609/896-3388. **Terms:** Credit card guarantee; small pets only. **Facility:** 149 rooms. 2 stories; exterior corridors; meeting rooms. **Dining:** Restaurant nearby. **Services:** data ports. **All Rooms:** free movies, cable TV. **Cards:** AE, CB, DI, DS, MC, VI.                                                                          ⒟ ⊗

# LEDGEWOOD   (See NEW JERSEY METRO AREA ACCOMMODATIONS spotting map pages A40 & A41; see index starting on page A39)

## LODGING

DAYS INN
◆◆
Motor Inn

|  | Rates Subject to Change |  |  |  | **Phone:** 201/347-5100  🄴 |
|---|---|---|---|---|---|
| All Year | 1P: | $68 | 2P/1B: | $68- 76 | 2P/2B: | $68- 76 | XP: $10  F12 |

**Location:** Westbound I-80, exit 27B, 2 mi e on 46E; eastbound I-80, exit 27 (thru 206N & 183N), 2 mi e on 46E. 1691 US 46W 07852. **Fax:** 201/347-6356. **Terms:** Sr. discount; no pets. **Facility:** 98 rooms. 2 stories; interior corridors; meeting rooms; pool; 2 tennis courts. **Dining & Entertainment:** Dining room; 7 am-9 pm, Sat & Sun from 8 am; $10-$18; cocktails/lounge. **Services:** data ports; valet laundry. **All Rooms:** cable TV. **Some Rooms:** microwaves, refrigerators. Fee: VCP's. **Cards:** AE, CB, DI, DS, MC, VI.                                ⒟ ⊗

# LIVINGSTON—26,600   (See NEW JERSEY METRO AREA ACCOMMODATIONS spotting map pages A40 & A41; see index starting on page A39)

## LODGING

**THE LIVINGSTON HOTEL**
AAA Special Value Rates   Phone: 201/994-3500   **36**

| | | | | | | | |
|---|---|---|---|---|---|---|---|
| Mon-Thurs | 1P: | $62- 84 | 2P/1B: | $62- 89 | 2P/2B: | $62- 89 | XP: $10 F |
| Fri-Sun | 1P: | $59- 65 | 2P/1B: | $59- 74 | 2P/2B: | $59- 79 | XP: $10 F |

Motor Inn
**Location:** On SR 10W; 2 mi w of jct CR 527; 2 1/2 mi s of I-280 exit 4A & w of circle. 550 W Mt Pleasant Ave 07039. Fax: 201/535-6321. **Terms:** Credit card guarantee, 7 day notice; weekly/monthly rates; no pets. **Facility:** 178 rooms. 3 stories; interior corridors; conference facilities; heated indoor pool; exercise room. **Dining & Entertainment:** Dining room; 7 am-2 & 5-10 pm; $6-$14; health conscious menu items; cocktails/lounge. **All Rooms:** free & pay movies, cable TV. **Some Rooms:** microwaves, refrigerators. **Cards:** AE, CB, DI, DS, MC, VI.   Ⓓ Ⓢ ⊗

# LONG BRANCH—28,700

## LODGING

**OCEAN PLACE HILTON RESORT & SPA**
Rates Subject to Change   Phone: 908/571-4000

Hotel

| | | | | | | | |
|---|---|---|---|---|---|---|---|
| 5/20-9/8 | 1P: | $170- 205 | 2P/1B: | $190- 225 | 2P/2B: | $190- 225 | XP: $20 F |
| 5/1-5/19, 9/9-11/17 & | | | | | | | |
| 3/29-4/30 | 1P: | $130- 160 | 2P/1B: | $150- 180 | 2P/2B: | $150- 180 | XP: $20 F |
| 11/18-3/28 | 1P: | $110- 140 | 2P/1B: | $130- 160 | 2P/2B: | $130- 160 | XP: $20 F |

**Location:** Corner Broadway & Ocean Blvd, Garden State Pkwy, exit 105. 1 Ocean Blvd 07740. Fax: 908/571-3314. **Terms:** Check-in 4 pm; weekly/monthly rates; no pets. **Facility:** 255 rooms. 5 two-bedroom units. 12 stories; interior corridors; oceanview; business center, conference facilities, convention oriented; beach, 2 pools (2 heated, 1 indoor), saunas, steamrooms, whirlpools; 2 lighted tennis courts; exercise room. Fee: health club. **Dining & Entertainment:** Dining room, 2 restaurants; 6:30 am-11 pm; $8-$28; health conscious menu items; cocktails/lounge; nightclub. **Services:** data ports, PC, secretarial services; valet laundry. Fee: massage. **Recreation:** social program; swimming. **All Rooms:** free & pay movies, cable TV. Fee: VCP. **Some Rooms:** coffeemakers, 2 efficiencies, microwaves, refrigerators. **Cards:** AE, CB, DI, DS, JCB, MC, VI. *(See ad p 28)*   Ⓓ Ⓢ ⊗

# LYNDHURST—18,300   (See NEWARK to PARAMUS ACCOMMODATIONS spotting map page A44; see index starting on page A42)

## LODGINGS

**NOVOTEL MEADOWLANDS**
Rates Subject to Change   Phone: 201/896-6666   **23**

| | | | | | |
|---|---|---|---|---|---|
| All Year | 2P/1B: | $85 | 2P/2B: | $95 | XP: $10 F16 |

Hotel
**Location:** NJ Tpk western spur exit 16W, w on SR 3 & s on SR 17. 1 Polito Ave 07071. Fax: 201/896-1309. **Terms:** Reserv deposit; pets. **Facility:** 219 rooms. 6 stories; interior corridors; heated indoor pool, sauna, whirlpool; exercise room. **Dining:** Restaurant; 6 am-midnight; $10-$20; cocktails. **Services:** data ports, secretarial services; valet laundry; airport transportation. **All Rooms:** free & pay movies, cable TV. **Some Rooms:** refrigerators, safes. **Cards:** AE, DI, DS, MC, VI.   Ⓓ Ⓢ ⊗

**QUALITY INN-SPORTS COMPLEX**
Rates Subject to Change   Phone: 201/933-9800   **24**

| | | | | | | |
|---|---|---|---|---|---|---|
| All Year | 1P: | $63- 75 | 2P/1B: | $66- 85 | 2P/2B: | $66- 85   XP: $6 F18 |

Motor Inn
**Location:** NJ Tpk western spur (George Washington) exit 16W, SR 3W, then s on SR 17. 10 Polito Ave 07071. Fax: 201/933-0658. **Terms:** Sr. discount; weekly/monthly rates; no pets. **Facility:** 145 rooms. Budget property near Lincoln Tunnel. 2 stories; interior corridors; business center, conference facilities; pool. **Dining & Entertainment:** Dining room; 6:30 am-11 pm; $8-$17; health conscious menu items; cocktails/lounge; entertainment. **Services:** data ports; valet laundry. Fee: childcare, area transportation; airport transportation. **All Rooms:** free & pay movies, cable TV. **Some Rooms:** VCP's. Fee: microwaves, refrigerators. **Cards:** AE, CB, DI, DS, JCB, MC, VI.   Ⓓ ⊗

## RESTAURANT

**LA DOLCE VITA**
Dinner: $21-$30   Phone: 201/935-4260   **23**

Italian
**Location:** From SR 3W exit Ridge Rd, 3/4 mi s (5 lights), then w on Valley Brook Ave 1/2 mi. 316 Valley Brook Ave 07071. **Hours:** noon-10:30 pm, Fri-11 pm, Sat 5 pm-11:30 pm, Sun 1 pm-10 pm. **Reservations:** suggested. **Features:** casual dress; health conscious menu items; cocktails & lounge; a la carte. Traditional cuisine. **Cards:** AE, DI, DS, MC, VI.   ⊗

# MADISON   (See NEW JERSEY METRO AREA ACCOMMODATIONS spotting map pages A40 & A41; see index starting on page A39)

## RESTAURANTS

**CREATIONS**
Dinner: $21-$30   Phone: 201/966-0252   **158**

American
**Location:** Center on Main St (SR 24A). 54 Main St 07940. **Hours:** 11:30 am-2:30 & 5-10 pm, Sat from 5 pm, Sun 5 pm-9 pm. Closed major holidays. **Reservations:** suggested. **Features:** semi-formal attire; health conscious menu items; cocktails & lounge; entertainment; minimum charge-$20; a la carte. Enjoy a variety of unique & creative American cuisine, exclusively prepared by chef. Cordial & pleasant staff in warm atmosphere. Cafe menu Mon for dinner & daily in lounge. **Cards:** AE, CB, DI, MC, VI.   ⊗

**L'ALLEGRIA**
Dinner: over $31   Phone: 201/377-6808   **159**

Italian
**Location:** Center, at jct Prospect & Main sts. 9-11 Prospect St 07940. **Hours:** 11:30 am-3 & 5-11 pm, Sat from 5 pm, Sun 1 pm-8 pm. Closed: 11/24, 12/25 & 1/1. **Reservations:** suggested. **Features:** casual dress; health conscious menu items; cocktails & lounge; a la carte. Ambience of a casually sophisticated Mediterranean courtyard. **Cards:** AE, CB, DI, MC, VI.   ⊗

**3 CENTRAL**
Dinner: $21-$30   Phone: 201/514-1333   **161**

American
**Location:** Center, jct of Central & Main. 3 Central Ave 07940. **Hours:** 11:30 am-2:30 & 5-9:30 pm, Fri-10 pm, Sat 5 pm-10 pm. Closed major holidays & Sun. **Reservations:** suggested; weekends. **Features:** casual dress; health conscious menu items; carryout; street parking. Bistro-style dining room, bright & cheerful. Assortment of fresh seafoods. Fine pasta dishes. Guests encouraged to bring their own wine or spirits. **Cards:** AE, CB, DI, MC, VI.   ⊗

## MAHWAH—17,900

### LODGINGS

**COMFORT INN-MAHWAH**   Rates Subject to Change   Phone: 201/512-0800
◆◆ All Year [CP]   1P: $52   2P/1B: $58   2P/2B: $55   XP: $6   F14
Motel   **Location:** On SR 17S; 2 mi s of I-287, exit 66. 160 Rt 17S 07430. Fax: 201/512-0800. **Terms:** Sr. discount; reserv deposit; no pets. **Facility:** 77 rooms. Enjoy attractively decorated rooms in a warm & friendly environment. 3 stories; interior corridors. **Services:** data ports; valet laundry. **All Rooms:** free movies, cable TV. **Some Rooms:** Fee: microwaves, refrigerators. **Cards:** AE, CB, DI, DS, MC, VI.   ⅅ Ⓢ ⊗

**COURTYARD BY MARRIOTT**   Rates Subject to Change   Phone: 201/529-5200
◆◆◆ Mon-Thurs   1P: $89   2P/1B: $99   2P/2B: $99
Motor Inn   Fri-Sun   1P: $49-  74   2P/1B: $54-  79   2P/2B: $69
   **Location:** SR 17S, 1 1/4 mi s of I-287 exit 66. 140 SR 17S 07430. Fax: 201/529-1991. **Terms:** Sr. discount; reserv deposit; weekly/monthly rates; no pets. **Facility:** 146 rooms. 3 stories; interior corridors; meeting rooms; heated indoor pool, whirlpool. **Dining & Entertainment:** Restaurant; 6:30 am-10 pm; $8-$14; cocktail lounge. **Services:** data ports; valet laundry. **All Rooms:** free movies, cable TV. **Some Rooms:** microwaves, refrigerators. **Cards:** AE, DI, DS, MC, VI. *(See color ad below)*   ⅅ Ⓢ ⊗

**RAMADA INN**   AAA Special Value Rates   Phone: 201/529-5880
◆◆◆ Sun-Thurs   1P: $84-  99   2P/1B: $94- 109   2P/2B: $84-  98   XP: $10   F19
Motor Inn   Fri & Sat   1P: $68-  94   2P/1B: $68-  94   2P/2B: $68-  94   XP: $10   F19
   **Location:** On SR 17S; 2 mi s of I-287, exit 66. 180 Rt 17S 07430. Fax: 201/529-4767. **Terms:** Credit card guarantee; monthly rates; small pets only. **Facility:** 129 rooms. Main highway property with close proximity to major interstates, shopping centers & office parks. 4 stories; interior corridors; conference facilities; heated indoor pool. **Dining:** Dining room; 6:30 am-3 & 5-10 pm, Sat & Sun from 7 am; $7-$16; health conscious menu items; cocktails. **Services:** data ports, secretarial services; complimentary evening beverages; valet laundry. **All Rooms:** free & pay movies, cable TV. **Some Rooms:** 12 efficiencies, refrigerators. **Cards:** AE, CB, DI, DS, JCB, MC, VI.   ⅅ ⊗

**SHERATON CROSSROADS HOTEL AND TOWERS**   Guaranteed Rates   Phone: 201/529-1660
◆◆◆ Sun-Thurs   1P: $99- 135   2P/1B: $119- 155   2P/2B: $119- 155   XP: $20   D18
Hotel   Fri & Sat   1P: $79- 109   2P/1B: $79- 109   2P/2B: $79- 109   XP: $20   D18
   **Location:** At jct SR 17N & exit 66 of I-287. 1 International Blvd, Rt 17 07495. Fax: 201/529-4709. **Terms:** Sr. discount; credit card guarantee; package plans; small pets only, signed damage rel. & not left unattended. **Facility:** 225 rooms. At base of Ramapo Mountains in newly developed corporate park. 22 stories; interior corridors; business center, conference facilities; luxury level rooms; heated indoor pool, saunas, whirlpool; 2 tennis courts (1 lighted); exercise room. **Dining & Entertainment:** Dining room, coffee shop; 6 am-10 pm, Fri & Sat-11 pm; $15-$21; health conscious menu items; cocktail lounge; entertainment, nightclub. **Services:** data ports, PC, secretarial services; complimentary evening beverages; valet laundry; area transportation, to local businesses. **Recreation:** jogging. **All Rooms:** honor bars, coffeemakers, free & pay movies, cable TV. **Cards:** AE, DI, DS, MC, VI.   ⅅ Ⓢ ⊗

## MANCHESTER

### LODGING

**ECONO LODGE OF MANCHESTER**   Rates Subject to Change   Phone: 908/657-7100
◆◆ 7/1-9/3   1P: $57-  80   2P/1B: $57-  80   2P/2B: $62-  90   XP: $10   F18
Motel   5/1-6/30 & 9/4-10/31   1P: $52-  70   2P/1B: $52-  70   2P/2B: $57-  80   XP: $6   F18
   11/1-4/30   1P: $47-  50   2P/1B: $47-  50   2P/2B: $52-  55   XP: $6   F18
**Location:** Garden State Pkwy exit 82A, 5 mi w on SR 37, then Rt 70 to jct Rt 37 1 mi e. 2016 Rt 37W 08733. Fax: 908/657-1672. **Terms:** Sr. discount; credit card guarantee, 3 day notice; no pets. **Facility:** 45 rooms. 2 stories; interior corridors; meeting rooms. **Dining:** Restaurants nearby. **Services:** data ports, secretarial services. Fee: coin laundry. **Some Rooms:** Fee: refrigerators, VCP's. **Cards:** AE, CB, DI, DS, JCB, MC, VI.   ⅅ ⊗

## MEDFORD (See PHILADELPHIA & VICINITY ACCOMMODATIONS spotting map pages A196 & A197; see index starting on page A193)

### RESTAURANT

**BEAU RIVAGE RESTAURANT**   Dinner: $21-$30   Phone: 609/983-1999   ⑴⑺⑼
◆◆◆ **Location:** From jct of SR 70 & 73 1 mi s to Marlton Pkwy (CR544), 4 mi e to Taunton Rd (CR623), then 1
French   mi n; 1/4 mi s of jct Taunton Blvd & Tuckerton Rd. 128 Taunton Blvd 08055. **Hours:** 11:30 am-2:30 & 5:30-9:30 pm, Sat from 5:30 pm, Sun 4 pm-8 pm. Closed major holidays & last 2 weeks in Aug. **Reservations:** suggested. **Features:** formal attire; cocktails; a la carte. Fine dining in a setting of understated elegance. Varied menu features daily specials. Emphasis on French country dining. **Cards:** AE, CB, DI, DS, MC, VI.   ⊗

## MENDHAM—4,900 (See NEW JERSEY METRO AREA ACCOMMODATIONS spotting map pages A40 & A41; see index starting on page A39)

### RESTAURANT

**THE BLACK HORSE INN AND PUB**   Historical   Dinner: $11-$20   Phone: 201/543-7300   ⑴⑵⑵
◆◆ **Location:** Center; on SR 24. 1 W Main St 07945. **Hours:** 11:30 am-11 pm, Sun 10 am-8 pm. Closed: 12/25.
American   **Reservations:** suggested. **Features:** children's menu; health conscious menu items; carryout; cocktails & lounge; entertainment; valet parking; a la carte. Quaint historic coach inn. **Cards:** AE, CB, DI, MC, VI.   ⊗

## MIDDLETOWN—68,200

### LODGING

**HOWARD JOHNSON LODGE** — Guaranteed Rates — **Phone: 908/671-3400**
All Year   1P: $61- 90   2P/1B: $66- 95   2P/2B: $71- 100   XP: $6   F18
**Location:** Adjacent to Bradlee's Shopping Center. 750 Hwy 35S 07748. Fax: 908/671-3911. **Terms:** Pets, $5. **Facility:** 81 rooms. 2 stories; interior corridors; meeting rooms; pool, wading pool. **Dining & Entertainment:** Restaurant; 7 am-10 pm, Fri & Sat-11 pm; $5-$13; health conscious menu items; cocktails/lounge. **Services:** data ports, secretarial services; valet laundry; winter plug-ins. **All Rooms:** free movies, cable TV. **Some Rooms:** coffeemakers, refrigerators. **Cards:** AE, CB, DI, DS, MC, VI. *(See ad below)* Ⓓ ⊗

Motor Inn ◆◆◆

## MILLBURN—18,600   (See NEW JERSEY METRO AREA ACCOMMODATIONS spotting map pages A40 & A41; see index starting on page A39)

### RESTAURANT

**40 MAIN STREET RESTAURANT AND CAFE MAIN** — Dinner: $21-$30 — **Phone: 201/376-4444** ⑫⑥
◆◆◆   **Location:** 40 Main St 07041. **Hours:** 11:30 am-2 & 5:30-10 pm, Fri-11 pm, Sat 5:30 pm-11 pm. Closed
American   major holidays, Sun & Mon. **Reservations:** suggested. **Features:** casual dress; children's menu; health conscious menu items; cocktails; street parking; a la carte. Charming dining room serves creative gourmet cuisine. Livlier cafe features pastas, burgers & pizza. **Cards:** AE, MC, VI. ⊗

## MILLVILLE—26,000

### LODGING

**COUNTRY INN BY CARLSON** — AAA Special Value Rates — **Phone: 609/825-3100**
All Year   1P: $60- 67   2P/1B: $65- 72   2P/2B: $65- 72   XP: $5   F18
**Location:** From SR 55 exit 26 (Wheaton Village), 1/2 mi w following signs. 1125 Village Dr & Wade Blvd
Motor Inn   08332. Fax: 609/825-1317. **Terms:** Credit card guarantee; monthly rates; package plans; no pets.
◆◆◆   **Facility:** 100 rooms. Quiet, country setting overlooking small lake. 4 suites, $110-$120; 2 stories; interior corridors; meeting rooms; heated pool. **Dining & Entertainment:** Restaurant; 7 am-9 pm, Fri & Sat-10 pm; $5-$13; cocktails/lounge. **Services:** valet laundry. **All Rooms:** coffeemakers, free movies, cable TV. **Some Rooms:** Fee: VCP's. **Cards:** AE, CB, DI, DS, MC, VI. *(See color ad below)* ⚏ Ⓓ Ⓢ ⊗

## MONMOUTH JUNCTION

### LODGINGS

**DAYS INN** — AAA Special Value Rates — **Phone: 908/329-4555**
5/25-6/13   1P: $80   2P/1B: $90- 95   2P/2B: $90- 95   XP: $10   F12
5/1-5/24 & 6/14-4/30   1P: $40- 50   2P/1B: $55- 65   2P/2B: $65- 90   XP: $7   F12
**Location:** On US 1 southbound, 3/4 mi n of Raymond Rd. 4191, Rt 1 08852. Fax: 908/329-1041.
Motel ◆◆   **Terms:** Reserv deposit; weekly/monthly rates; no pets. **Facility:** 73 rooms. 2 stories; exterior corridors; meeting rooms. **Dining:** Coffee shop; 6:30 am-7 pm, Sat & Sun 8 am-3 pm. **All Rooms:** cable TV. **Some Rooms:** Fee: VCP's, whirlpools. **Cards:** AE, DI, DS, MC, VI. Ⓓ ⊗

**RED ROOF INN/NORTH PRINCETON** — Rates Subject to Change — **Phone: 908/821-8800**
All Year   1P: $34- 46   2P/1B: $38- 51   2P/2B: $46- 57   XP: $6-8   F18
Motel ◆◆   **Location:** On US 1 southbound at New Rd. 208 New Rd 08852. Fax: 908/821-5171. **Terms:** Credit card guarantee; small pets only. **Facility:** 119 rooms. Some smaller rooms. 3 stories; exterior corridors. **Services:** data ports. **All Rooms:** free movies, cable TV. **Cards:** AE, CB, DI, DS, MC, VI. Ⓓ Ⓢ ⊗

**RESIDENCE INNS BY MARRIOTT**
◆◆◆     AAA Special Value Rates     **Phone:** 908/329-9600
    Mon-Fri [BP]     1P: $134    2P/1B: $134     2P/2B: $154
Apartment     Sat & Sun [BP]     1P: $89    2P/1B: $89     2P/2B: $109
Motel     **Location:** On US 1 southbound, 1/2 mi s of Raymond Rd. 4225 Rt 1 08540 (PO Box 8388, PRINCETON, 08543). Fax: 908/329-8422. **Terms:** Reserv deposit; weekly/monthly rates; CP available; pets, $10 daily, up to $50. **Facility:** 208 rooms. 2 stories; interior/exterior corridors; meeting rooms; heated pool, whirlpool; sports court. **Services:** data ports; health club privileges; valet laundry. **All Rooms:** kitchens, microwaves, free movies, refrigerators, cable TV. **Some Rooms:** coffeemakers. Fee: VCP's. **Cards:** AE, DI, DS, MC, VI. *(See ad p A53)*   Ⓓ ⊗

# MONROE

## LODGING

**HOLIDAY INN CENTER POINT**     AAA Special Value Rates     **Phone:** 609/655-4775
◆◆◆     All Year     1P: $99- 165   2P/1B: $109- 165   2P/2B: $109- 165   XP: $10   F12
Motor Inn     **Location:** NJ Tpk exit 8A, follow sign for Monroe/Jamesburg. 390 Forsgate Dr 08831. Fax: 609/655-5254. **Terms:** Reserv deposit; package plans, weekends & seasonal; no pets. **Facility:** 150 rooms. 6 stories; interior corridors; conference facilities; heated indoor pool, sauna; racquetball courts; exercise room. **Dining & Entertainment:** Dining room; 6:30 am-10 pm; $11-$25; health conscious menu items; cocktails/lounge. **Services:** data ports, secretarial services; valet laundry. Fee: airport transportation. **All Rooms:** free & pay movies, cable TV. **Some Rooms:** 10 efficiencies, refrigerators. **Cards:** AE, CB, DI, DS, JCB, MC, VI.   Ⓓ Ⓢ ⊗

# MORRIS PLAINS—5,200   (See NEW JERSEY METRO AREA ACCOMMODATIONS spotting map pages A40 & A41; see index starting on page A39)

## RESTAURANT

**ARTHUR'S**     **Dinner:** $11-$20     **Phone:** 201/455-9705   ⑬⓪
◆◆     **Location:** Center on US 202; across from train station. 700 Speedwell Ave 07950. **Hours:** 11:30 am-2:30 & 5-11 pm, Sun 3 pm-9 pm. Closed: 11/23 & 12/25. **Features:** casual dress; carryout; cocktails & lounge; street parking; a la carte. Pub atmosphere. No credit cards accepted.
Steakhouse

# MORRISTOWN—16,200   (See NEW JERSEY METRO AREA ACCOMMODATIONS spotting map pages A40 & A41; see index starting on page A39)

## LODGINGS

**BEST WESTERN MORRISTOWN INN**     AAA Special Value Rates     **Phone:** 201/540-1700   ④⓪
Ⓐ     Sun-Thurs     1P: $89- 97   2P/1B: $99- 107   2P/2B: $99- 107   XP: $10   F18
    Fri & Sat     1P: $79   2P/1B: $79   2P/2B: $79   XP: $10   F18
◆◆◆     **Location:** I-287 exit 35, 1 blk w on US 24, 1 blk s on South St. 270 South St 07960. Fax: 201/267-0241.
Motor Inn     **Terms:** Reserv deposit; monthly rates; no pets. **Facility:** 59 rooms. 3 stories; interior corridors; meeting rooms; sauna; exercise room. **Dining:** Restaurant; 6:30-10 am, 11-2 & 5:30-9:30 pm, Sun brunch, 11:30 am-2:30 pm; $11-$18. **Services:** data ports, secretarial services; airport transportation, to Newark Int'l. Fee: coin laundry. **All Rooms:** free movies, cable TV. **Some Rooms:** coffeemakers, 14 efficiencies, refrigerators. Fee: VCP's. **Cards:** AE, CB, DI, DS, JCB, MC, VI.   Ⓓ ⊗

**GOVERNOR MORRIS HOTEL & CONFERENCE CENTER**     Rates Subject to Change     **Phone:** 201/539-7300   ④①
◆◆◆     Sun-Thurs     1P: $137- 157   2P/1B: $147- 167   2P/2B: $147- 167   XP: $10   F18
Hotel     Fri & Sat     1P: $89- 104   2P/1B: $99- 119   2P/2B: $99- 119   XP: $10   F18
    **Location:** I-287, southbound exit 36, left lane to light, left to stop & left 1 mi to hotel; northbound exit 36A thru Morris Ave, 1/4 mi following signs. 2 Whippany Rd 07960. Fax: 201/984-1036. **Terms:** Sr. discount; reserv deposit; monthly rates; package plans; no pets. **Facility:** 198 rooms. 1 two-bedroom unit. 6 stories; interior corridors; business center, conference facilities, convention oriented; pool; exercise room, playground; sports court. **Dining & Entertainment:** Dining room; 6:30 am-11 pm, cafe 11:30 am-2 am; $10-$30; health conscious menu items; cocktails/lounge; entertainment. **Services:** data ports, PC, secretarial services; valet laundry; area transportation. Fee: childcare, airport transportation. **Recreation:** jogging. **All Rooms:** free & pay movies, cable TV. **Some Rooms:** 8 efficiencies, refrigerators. Fee: microwaves, VCP's. **Cards:** AE, CB, DI, DS, MC, VI.   Ⓓ ⊗

## RESTAURANT

**CALALOO CAFE**     **Dinner:** $11-$20     **Phone:** 201/993-1100   ④②
◆◆     **Location:** Center on SR 24. 190 South St 07960. **Hours:** 11:30 am-11 pm, Fri & Sat-midnight, Sun 11 am-3 & 4-10 pm. Closed major holidays. **Reservations:** suggested; for Sun brunch. **Features:** casual dress; health conscious menu items; cocktails & lounge; entertainment; a la carte. Featuring fresh fish & pasta. Popular, bustling atmosphere. Comedy cafe Fri & Sat. Reservations req for all shows. **Cards:** AE, DI, MC, VI.   ⊗
American

# MOUNTAIN LAKES—3,800   (See NEW JERSEY METRO AREA ACCOMMODATIONS spotting map pages A40 & A41; see index starting on page A39)

## RESTAURANT

**THE BLACK BULL INN**     **Dinner:** $11-$20     **Phone:** 201/335-8585   ⑬④
◆◆     **Location:** Denville exit off I-80, 2 mi e on US 46. Rt 46 07046. **Hours:** 11:30 am-10 pm, Sat 5 pm-11 pm. Closed major holidays & Sun. **Reservations:** suggested; large parties. **Features:** casual dress; children's menu; carryout; salad bar; cocktails & lounge. Specialties are beef, ribs & seafood. **Cards:** AE, CB, DI, DS, MC, VI.
Steakhouse

# MOUNT ARLINGTON—3,600

## LODGING

**SHERATON INN**     Guaranteed Rates     **Phone:** 201/770-2000
◆◆◆     5/1-10/31 & 3/1-4/30     1P: $95- 119   2P/1B: $103- 119   2P/2B: $98- 119   XP: $10   F17
Hotel     11/1-2/29     1P: $80- 90   2P/1B: $95- 105   2P/2B: $90- 100   XP: $10   F17
    **Location:** Just n of I-80, exit 30. 15 Howard Blvd 07856. Fax: 201/770-2000. **Terms:** Sr. discount; weekly rates; BP available; small pets only. **Facility:** 124 rooms. Nestled in the Hopatcong Valley in a small corporate park. 5 stories; interior corridors; conference facilities; heated indoor pool; exercise room. **Dining & Entertainment:** Dining room; 6:30 am-10 pm, Sat & Sun from 7 am; $8-$16; health conscious menu items; cocktails/lounge. **Services:** data ports, secretarial services; complimentary evening beverages; valet laundry. Fee: childcare. **All Rooms:** free & pay movies, cable TV. **Some Rooms:** 40 efficiencies, microwaves, refrigerators. **Cards:** AE, CB, DI, DS, MC, VI.   Ⓓ Ⓢ ⊗

## MOUNT HOLLY—10,600   (See PHILADELPHIA & VICINITY ACCOMMODATIONS spotting map pages A196 & A197; see index starting on page A193)

### LODGINGS

**BEST WESTERN MOTOR INN** — Rates Subject to Change — **Phone:** 609/261-3800 **156**
All Year — 1P: $49- 59 — 2P/1B: $55- 65 — 2P/2B: $55- 65 — XP: $8 F12
**Location:** NJ Tpk, exit 5, on CR 541. Box 2020 Rt 541, RD 1 08060. Fax: 609/267-0958. **Terms:** Sr. discount; reserv deposit, 14 day notice; pets, $5. **Facility:** 62 rooms. At turnpike ramp; charming roadside inn with upgrade accommodations. 2 stories; interior corridors; meeting rooms; exercise room. **Dining:** Coffee shop nearby. **All Rooms:** free movies, cable TV. **Cards:** AE, CB, DI, DS, MC, VI. ⓓ ⊗
*Motel*

**HOWARD JOHNSON MOTOR LODGE** — Rates Subject to Change — **Phone:** 609/267-6550 **155**
All Year — 1P: $49- 86 — 2P/1B: $54- 86 — 2P/2B: $59- 84 — XP: $7
**Location:** At tpk exit 5; on CR 541 between Burlington & Mount Holly rds. 08060 (PO Box 73). Fax: 609/267-2575. **Terms:** CP available; pets. **Facility:** 90 rooms. At turnpike ramp. 2 stories; interior/exterior corridors; meeting rooms; pool, saunas, whirlpool; playground. **Dining & Entertainment:** Restaurant; 6 am-9 pm, Fri & Sat-10 pm; $5-$9; cocktail lounge. **Services:** valet laundry. **All Rooms:** free movies.
*Motel*
**Some Rooms:** whirlpools. **Cards:** AE, CB, DI, DS, MC, VI. ⓓ ⊗

## MOUNT LAUREL—30,300   (See PHILADELPHIA & VICINITY ACCOMMODATIONS spotting map pages A196 & A197; see index starting on page A193)

### LODGINGS

**CLARION HOTEL AT MOUNT LAUREL** — Guaranteed Rates — **Phone:** 609/234-7300 **137**
All Year — 1P: $59 — 2P/1B: $69 — 2P/2B: $69 — XP: $10 F18
**Location:** On SR 73; 1/4 mi nw of tpk exit 4, se of jct I-295, exit 36A. 915 Rte 73 & I-295 08054. Fax: 609/866-9401. **Terms:** Sr. discount; reserv deposit, 3 day notice; weekly/monthly rates; package plans; small pets only. **Facility:** 283 rooms. 2-10 stories; interior corridors; conference facilities; luxury level rooms; pool; 2 lighted tennis courts; exercise room, gameroom. **Dining & Entertainment:** Dining room; 6:30 am-2 & 5-10 pm, Sat & Sun from 7 am; lite fare in lounge; $10-$23; health conscious menu items; cocktails/lounge. **Services:** data ports, secretarial services; area transportation, within 5 mi. Fee: coin laundry. **All Rooms:** free & pay movies, cable TV. Fee: VCP. **Some Rooms:** refrigerators, whirlpools. **Cards:** AE, CB, DI, DS, JCB, MC, VI. *(See color ad below)* ⓓⓈ⊗
*Hotel*

**COURTYARD BY MARRIOTT** — Rates Subject to Change — **Phone:** 609/273-4400 **135**
Sun-Thurs — 1P: $85 — 2P/1B: $95 — 2P/2B: $95
Fri & Sat — 1P: $69 — 2P/1B: $69 — 2P/2B: $79
*Motor Inn*
**Location:** Just nw of tpk exit 4; from I-295 exit 36A, 1 blk se on SR 73, 1/2 blk s on Fellowship Rd. 1000 Century Pkwy 08054. Fax: 609/273-2889. **Terms:** Sr. discount; reserv deposit, 3 day notice; weekly rates; no pets. **Facility:** 151 rooms. In-room coffee service. 4 stories; interior corridors; heated indoor pool, whirlpool, sundeck; exercise room. **Dining & Entertainment:** Restaurant; 6:30 am-9:30 am, Sat & Sun 7 am-noon; $8-$14; cocktail lounge; lounge 4 pm-11 pm, Mon-Fri. **Services:** data ports. Fee: coin laundry. **All Rooms:** free & pay movies, cable TV. **Some Rooms:** refrigerators. **Cards:** AE, CB, DI, DS, MC, VI. *(See color ad below)* ⓓⓈ⊗

**ECONO LODGE** — Rates Subject to Change — **Phone:** 609/722-1919 **149**
All Year — 1P: $40 — 2P/1B: $46 — 2P/2B: $54 — XP: $6 F18
**Location:** Just nw of tpk exit 4; also from I-295 exit 36A, 1 blk se on SR 73, 1 blk s on Fellowship Rd. 611 Fellowship Rd 08054. Fax: 609/722-0116. **Terms:** Sr. discount; credit card guarantee; weekly/monthly rates; small pets only. **Facility:** 66 rooms. 2 stories; exterior corridors. **Dining:** Restaurant nearby. **Services:** valet laundry. **All Rooms:** free movies, cable TV. **Some Rooms:** Fee: refrigerators, VCP's. **Cards:** AE, CB, DI, DS, JCB, MC, VI. ⓓ ⊗
*Motel*

**(See PHILADELPHIA & VICINITY ACCOMMODATIONS spotting map pages A196 & A197)**

GUEST QUARTERS SUITE HOTEL — Rates Subject to Change — Phone: 609/778-8999 **146**
◆◆◆ All Year [BP] 1P: $108- 112 2P/1B: $108- 122 2P/2B: $108- 122 XP: $15 F12
Suite Hotel **Location:** Nw of tpk exit 4; also I-295 exit 36A, 1 blk e on SR 73, 2 blks n on Fellowship Rd. 515 Fellowship Rd 08054. Fax: 609/778-9720. **Terms:** Monthly rates; package plans; no pets. **Facility:** 129 rooms. Some units with patio or balcony. Corporate park setting. 3 stories; interior corridors; meeting rooms; indoor/outdoor pool, whirlpool; exercise room. **Dining & Entertainment:** Restaurant; 6:30 am-10:30 pm, Sat 6:30 am-11:30 & 5-10 pm, Sun 6:30 am-11:30 am, room service 11:30 am-10 pm; $10-$17; cocktails/lounge; entertainment. **Services:** data ports, secretarial services; complimentary evening beverages, Mon-Sat; health club privileges. Fee: coin laundry. **All Rooms:** coffeemakers, microwaves, refrigerators, cable TV, VCP's. **Cards:** AE, DI, DS, MC, VI. *(See ad p A199)* Ⓓ Ⓢ ⊗

HAMPTON INN — Guaranteed Rates — Phone: 609/778-5535 **144**
◆◆◆ All Year [CP] 1P: $65 2P/1B: $65 2P/2B: $65
Motel **Location:** From tpk exit 4, 1 mi e on SR 73 (behind Chili's); from I-295 exit 36A, 1 1/4 mi se on SR 73. 4000 Crawford Place 08054. Fax: 609/778-0377. **Terms:** Credit card guarantee; no pets. **Facility:** 127 rooms. Valet laundry also avail. Long term rates avail; 4 stories; interior corridors; meeting rooms; pool. **Dining:** Restaurant nearby. **Services:** data ports; health club privileges. Fee: coin laundry. **All Rooms:** free & pay movies, cable TV. Fee: VCP. **Some Rooms:** refrigerators. **Cards:** AE, CB, DI, DS, MC, VI. *(See ad below)* Ⓓ Ⓢ ⊗

MCINTOSH INN OF MOUNT LAUREL — Rates Subject to Change — Phone: 609/234-7194 **141**
◆◆ All Year 1P: $35- 41 2P/1B: $37- 45 2P/2B: $45 XP: $3 F18
Motel **Location:** On SR 73, 1/4 mi se of tpk exit 4; 3/4 mi se of I-295, exit 36A. SR 73 & Church Rd 08054. Fax: 609/231-8516. **Terms:** Sr. discount; weekly rates; no pets. **Facility:** 93 rooms. 2 stories; exterior corridors. **Dining:** Restaurant nearby. **All Rooms:** free movies. **Some Rooms:** microwaves, radios, refrigerators. **Cards:** AE, CB, DI, DS, MC, VI. *(See ad p A53, p A67 & p A185)* Ⓓ ⊗

**RED CARPET INN** — Rates Subject to Change — Phone: 609/235-5610 **142**
AAA All Year 1P: $36- 40 2P/1B: $40- 44 2P/2B: $44- 48 XP: $4 F11
◆◆ **Location:** On SR 73; just se of NJ Tpk, exit 4; I-295, exit 36A. 1104 SR 73S 08054. Fax: 609/235-6713.
Motel **Terms:** Sr. discount; no pets. **Facility:** 71 rooms. Comfortable accomodations in a friendly atmosphere; cordial hospitable staff; convenient location to turnpike ramp. 3 family units, $66; 2 stories; exterior corridors; meeting rooms. **Dining:** Restaurant nearby. **Services:** data ports. **All Rooms:** free movies. **Some Rooms:** refrigerators. **Cards:** AE, DI, DS, MC, VI. Ⓓ ⊗

RED ROOF INN — Rates Subject to Change — Phone: 609/234-5589 **138**
◆◆ All Year 2P/1B: $41- 57 2P/2B: $57 XP: $7 F18
Motel **Location:** On SR 73, just nw of tpk exit 4; 1/4 mi se of jct I-295, exit 36A. 603 Fellowship Rd 08054. Fax: 609/234-4063. **Terms:** Credit card guarantee; small pets only. **Facility:** 109 rooms. 2 stories; exterior corridors. **Dining:** Cafeteria nearby. **Services:** data ports. **All Rooms:** free movies. **Cards:** AE, CB, DI, DS, MC, VI. Ⓓ ⊗

**(See PHILADELPHIA & VICINITY ACCOMMODATIONS spotting map pages A196 & A197)**

**TRACK & TURF MOTEL**                 Guaranteed Rates                        Phone: 609/235-6500   **136**
    All Year          1P: $30- 36   2P/1B: $30- 36   2P/2B: $35- 44   XP: $4   F12
♦    **Location:** On SR 73; 3/4 mi nw of tpk exit 4; I-295 exit 36B 1/8 mi nw. 809 SR 73 08054. **Terms:** Reserv
Motel   deposit; weekly rates; small pets only. **Facility:** 30 rooms. On busy major highway. 1 story; exterior corridors.
    **Dining:** Restaurant nearby. **All Rooms:** free movies, cable TV. **Cards:** AE, CB, DI, DS, MC, VI.
    *(See color ad p A38)*                                                                        **(D)**

**TRAVELODGE HOTEL AND CONFERENCE CENTER**   Rates Subject to Change   Phone: 609/234-7000   **139**
    All Year          1P: $59              2P/1B: $59         2P/2B: $59         XP: $5   F18
♦♦    **Location:** On SR 73, se of tpk exit 4, 1/2 mi se of jct I-295, exit 36A. 1111 SR 73 08054. Fax: 609/235-3909.
Hotel   **Terms:** Reserv deposit, 3 day notice; small pets only, $25. **Facility:** 240 rooms. Suites, $150-$250; 9 stories;
   interior corridors; conference facilities; luxury level rooms; heated indoor pool, saunas, whirlpool; exercise
   room. **Dining & Entertainment:** Dining room; 6:30-10 am; Mon-Fri 7-11 am; Sat & Sun 11:30 am-2 & 5-10
pm; $17-$24; health conscious menu items; cocktails/lounge. **Services:** data ports, secretarial services; valet laundry.
**All Rooms:** coffeemakers, cable TV. **Fee:** movies. **Some Rooms:** microwaves, refrigerators. **Fee:** VCP's. **Cards:** AE, CB,
DI, DS, JCB, MC, VI.                                                                       **(D) (S) ⊗**

# NEW JERSEY METRO—(See NEW JERSEY METRO ACCOMMODATIONS spotting map pages A40 & A41; see index below)

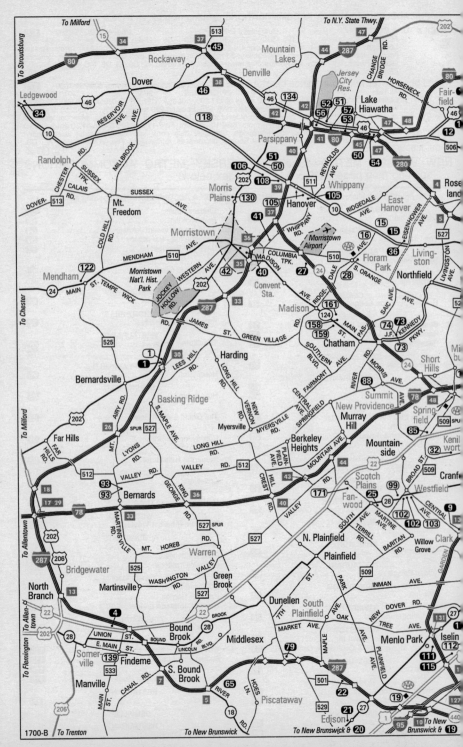

1700-B  To Trenton

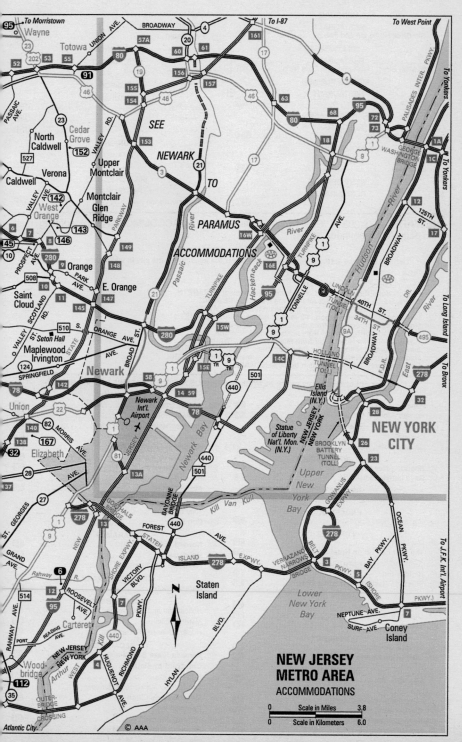

**NEW JERSEY METRO AREA**

ACCOMMODATIONS

Scale in Miles    0 — 3.8
Scale in Kilometers    0 — 6.0

© AAA

# NEWARK—275,200

(See NEWARK to PARAMUS ACCOMMODATIONS spotting map page A44; see index below)

## Airport Accommodations

Listings for these establishments are found under the heading for the city in which they are located.

**NEWARK**

Airport Marriott, at airport/NEWARK
Clarion Hotel Newark Airport, 1 mi from main terminal/ELIZABETH
Courtyard by Marriott, 1 1/2 mi from main terminal/NEWARK
Days Inn-Newark Airport, 1/2 mi from main terminal/NEWARK
Hampton Inn-Newark Airport, 1/2 mi n of main terminal/ELIZABETH
Holiday Inn-Jetport, 3 mi from main terminal/ELIZABETH
Holiday Inn-North, 2 1/2 mi from main terminal/NEWARK
Howard Johnson Hotel, 2 mi from main terminal/NEWARK
Newark Airport Hilton Hotel, 1 mi n from main terminal/ELIZABETH
Radisson Hotel Newark Airport, 2 mi ne from main terminal/NEWARK
Ramada Hotel, 1/4 mi from main terminal/NEWARK

## Index of Establishments on the NEWARK to PARAMUS ACCOMMODATIONS Spotting Map

(See NEWARK to PARAMUS ACCOMMODATIONS spotting map page A44)


**CARLSTADT**

RESTAURANT

Pratos ........................................ ㊶

**HACKENSACK**

RESTAURANT

Stony Hill Inn ................................ ㊼

**HOBOKEN**

RESTAURANTS

Ristorante Gerrino ............................ (51)
Arthur's Tavern ............................... (52)
The Brass Rail ................................ (54)

**GLEN ROCK**

RESTAURANT

AAA **Glen Rock Inn** .......................... (60)


## LODGINGS

AIRPORT MARRIOTT — Rates Subject to Change — **Phone:** 201/623-0006 ㊵

◆◆◆ Hotel

Mon-Thurs 1P: $159 2P/1B: $159 2P/2B: $159 XP: $20
Fri-Sun 1P: $95 2P/1B: $95 2P/2B: $95

**Location:** Northbound NJ Tpk exit 13A, southbound exit 14 to airport. Newark International Airport 07114. Fax: 201/623-7618. **Terms:** Check-in 4 pm; weekly/monthly rates; no pets. **Facility:** 590 rooms. 10 stories; interior corridors; business center, conference facilities; luxury level rooms; heated indoor/outdoor pool, saunas, whirlpool; exercise room. **Dining & Entertainment:** Dining room, restaurant; 6 am-11 pm; Sat & Sun from 7 am; $14-$25; health conscious menu items; cocktails/lounge; buffet breakfast & lunch avail; 24-hour room service. **Services:** data ports, PC, secretarial services; valet laundry; airport transportation. Fee: massage; valet parking. **All Rooms:** free & pay movies, cable TV. **Some Rooms:** refrigerators. **Cards:** AE, DI, DS, JCB, MC, VI. (D) (S) ⊗

COURTYARD BY MARRIOTT — Rates Subject to Change — **Phone:** 201/643-8500 ㊲

◆◆◆ Motor Inn

Sun-Thurs 1P: $104 2P/1B: $114 2P/2B: $114 XP: $10 F12
Fri & Sat 1P: $74 2P/1B: $74 2P/2B: $74

**Location:** NJ Tpk exit 14, 1 mi SW via US I-9S; I-78 exit 58B to US 1 & 9S, local lanes. 600 US Rt 1 & US 9S 07114. Fax: 201/648-0662. **Terms:** Credit card guarantee; no pets. **Facility:** 146 rooms. 3 stories; interior corridors; meeting rooms; heated indoor pool, whirlpool; exercise room. **Dining:** Restaurant; 6:30 am-11 & 5-10 pm, Mon-Fri to 11 pm; $8-$15; health conscious menu items; cocktails. **Services:** data ports, secretarial services; valet laundry; airport transportation. Fee: childcare. **All Rooms:** free & pay movies, cable TV. **Some Rooms:** microwaves, refrigerators. **Cards:** AE, CB, DI, DS, MC, VI. *(See color ad below)* (D) (S) ⊗

**DAYS INN-NEWARK AIRPORT** — Guaranteed Rates — **Phone:** 201/242-0900 ㉟

AAA ◆◆◆ Motor Inn

All Year 1P: $65- 85 2P/1B: $70- 90 2P/2B: $70- 90 XP: $5 F12

**Location:** Exit 14 of NJ Tpk & 1 1/2 mi on US I-9S. 450 US Rt 1S 07114. Fax: 201/242-8480. **Terms:** Sr. discount; no pets. **Facility:** 191 rooms. 8 stories; interior corridors; meeting rooms; exercise room. **Dining & Entertainment:** Restaurant; 6:30 am-midnight, Fri & Sat from 7 am; $9-$18; cocktails/lounge. **Services:** data ports, secretarial services; valet laundry; airport transportation. **All Rooms:** free & pay movies, cable TV. **Some Rooms:** microwaves, refrigerators. **Cards:** AE, CB, DI, DS, MC, VI. *(See ad below)* (D) (S) ⊗

**HILTON GATEWAY** — Guaranteed Rates — **Phone:** 201/622-5000 ㊳

AAA ◆◆◆ Hotel

All Year 1P: $79 2P/1B: $79 2P/2B: $79

**Location:** 3 mi w of exit 15E of NJ Tpk via Raymond Blvd, connecting to Penn Station, NJ Transit, Path & Amtrak. Gateway Center-Raymond Blvd 07102. Fax: 201/622-2644. **Terms:** Package plans; no pets. **Facility:** 253 rooms. 15 stories; interior corridors; business center, meeting rooms; luxury level rooms; seasonal rooftop pool; health club. **Dining & Entertainment:** Dining room, restaurant; 6 am-11 pm; $10-$20; health conscious menu items; cocktails/lounge; also Pizza Hut & Taco Bell on premises. **Services:** data ports, PC, secretarial services; valet laundry; airport transportation; valet parking. **All Rooms:** coffeemakers, free & pay movies, cable TV. **Some Rooms:** refrigerators. **Cards:** AE, CB, DI, DS, JCB, MC, VI. *(See ad p 28 & p A46)* (D) (S) ⊗

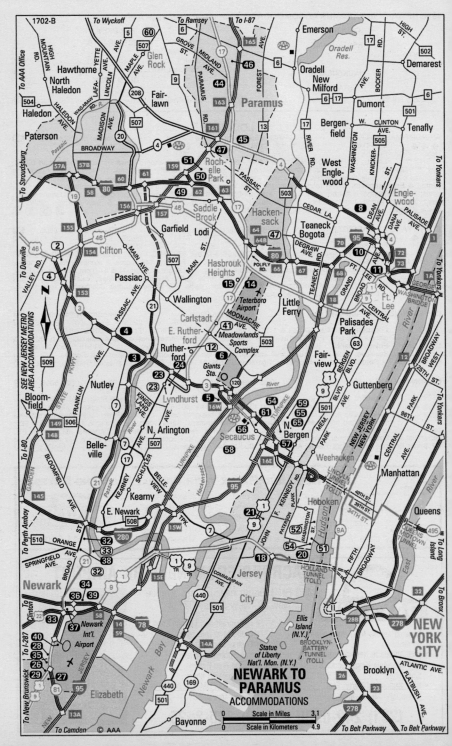

(See NEWARK to PARAMUS ACCOMMODATIONS spotting map page A44)

**HOLIDAY INN-NORTH**       Rates Subject to Change       Phone: 201/589-1000   36
(AAA)    Mon-Thurs      1P: $79- 99   2P/1B:   $84- 104   2P/2B:   $84      XP:   $5   F19
◆◆     Fri-Sun       1P: $69     2P/1B:   $69      2P/2B:   $69      XP:   $5   F19
Hotel    **Location:** NJ Tpk exit 14 via service road; 2nd right after toll booth; I-78, exit 58B, following signs to Frontage Rd. 160 Holiday Plaza 07114. Fax: 201/589-2799. **Terms:** Sr. discount; reserv deposit; monthly rates; BP available; pets, $25, $25 dep req. **Facility:** 234 rooms. 10 stories; interior corridors; conference facilities; pool; 2 tennis courts. **Dining & Entertainment:** Dining room; 6:30 am-10:30 pm, Sat & Sun 7 am-10 pm; $11-$19; health conscious menu items; cocktails/lounge. **Services:** secretarial services; valet laundry; airport transportation. **All Rooms:** free & pay movies, cable TV. **Some Rooms:** whirlpools. **Cards:** AE, DI, DS, JCB, MC, VI.    Ⓓ ⊗

**HOWARD JOHNSON HOTEL**      AAA Special Value Rates      Phone: 201/344-1500   39
(AAA)    All Year      1P:   $70- 75          2P/2B:   $75- 80
◆◆◆   **Location:** Tpk exit 14, 2nd right after toll booth via service road & right 1/4 mi. 50 Port St 07114.
Motor Inn   Fax: 201/344-3311. **Terms:** Package plans; no pets. **Facility:** 171 rooms. Long-term secure valet parking. 3 stories; interior corridors; meeting rooms. **Dining & Entertainment:** Coffee shop; 6 am-midnight; $7-$15; cocktails/lounge. **Services:** data ports, secretarial services; valet laundry; airport transportation, 24 hours. **All Rooms:** free movies, cable TV. **Cards:** AE, CB, DI, DS, MC, VI. *(See ad p A46)*    Ⓓ ⊗

**(See NEWARK to PARAMUS ACCOMMODATIONS spotting map page A44)**

**RADISSON HOTEL NEWARK AIRPORT**  AAA Special Value Rates  Phone: 201/690-5500  **34**
◆◆◆  Sun-Thurs  1P: $119- 149  2P/1B: $129- 164  2P/2B: $129- 164  XP: $10  F18
Hotel  Fri & Sat  1P: $69  2P/1B: $79  2P/2B: $79  XP: $10  F18
**Location:** NJ Tpk exit 14; via service road, 2nd right after toll booth. 128 Frontage Rd 07114. Fax: 201/465-7195. **Terms:** Small pets only. **Facility:** 502 rooms. 12 stories; interior corridors; business center, conference facilities, convention oriented; luxury level rooms; heated indoor pool, whirlpool; exercise room. **Dining & Entertainment:** Dining room, restaurant; 6:30 am-11:30 pm; $15-$25; health conscious menu items; cocktails/lounge; entertainment. **Services:** data ports, PC, secretarial services; valet parking; airport transportation, to Newark Airport. **All Rooms:** free & pay movies, cable TV. **Some Rooms:** microwaves, refrigerators. **Cards:** AE, CB, DI, DS, MC, VI.  Ⓓ Ⓢ ⊗

**RAMADA HOTEL**  AAA Special Value Rates  Phone: 201/824-4000  **33**
(AAA)  All Year  1P: $70- 90  2P/1B: $80- 100  2P/2B: $80- 100  XP: $5  F18
**Location:** On US 1 & 9 southbound, exit 14 off NJ Tpk. US 1 & 9S 07114. Fax: 201/824-2034. **Terms:** BP
◆◆◆  available; pets. **Facility:** 342 rooms. 5 stories; interior corridors; business center, meeting rooms; pool; exer-
Motor Inn  cise room. **Dining & Entertainment:** Restaurant, coffee shop; 6 am-1 am; $10-$16; cocktails/lounge. **Services:** secretarial services; valet laundry; area transportation, airport transportation. **All Rooms:** free & pay movies, cable TV. **Cards:** AE, DI, DS, JCB, MC, VI.  ⑦ Ⓓ Ⓢ ⊗

**ROBERT TREAT HOTEL**  AAA Special Value Rates  Phone: 201/622-1000  **32**
(AAA)  All Year  1P: $90  2P/1B: $95  2P/2B: $95  XP: $7  F16
**Location:** 3 mi w of NJ Tpk exit 15E, on Raymond Blvd to center; (Park Pl) east side of Military Park. 50
Hotel  Park Pl 07102. Fax: 201/622-6410. **Terms:** No pets. **Facility:** 168 rooms. 15 stories; interior corridors; meeting
◆◆  rooms; exercise room. **Dining:** Coffee shop; 7 am-11 pm; $6-$12; health conscious menu items; cocktails. **Services:** secretarial services; airport transportation. **Fee:** coin laundry. **All Rooms:** cable TV. **Fee:** movies. **Some Rooms:** refrigerators, whirlpools. **Cards:** AE, CB, DI, DS, MC, VI.  Ⓓ Ⓢ ⊗

The TourBook & the AAA state map: Together they make beautiful travel music.

**(See NEWARK to PARAMUS ACCOMMODATIONS spotting map page A44)**

## RESTAURANTS

**DON PEPE**                    Dinner: $11-$20                    Phone: 201/623-4662    [33]
Ⓐ    **Location:** 1 blk n of Raymond Blvd. 844 McCarter (US 22) Hwy 07102. **Hours:** 11:30 am-10 pm, Fri &
◆◆    Sat-11 pm, Sun 1 pm-10 pm. Closed: 11/23 & 12/25. **Reservations:** suggested; weekends. **Features:** casual
Ethnic    dress; cocktails & lounge; valet parking; a la carte. **Cards:** AE, DI, DS, MC, VI.

**TONY DA CANECA**                    Dinner: $11-$20                    Phone: 201/589-6882    [32]
◆◆    **Location:** On corner of Elm Rd & Houston St; in Ironbound section. 72 Elm Rd 07105. **Hours:** 11:30 am-10
Ethnic    pm, Fri & Sat-11 pm, Sun noon-10 pm. **Reservations:** suggested; weekends. **Features:** casual dress;
children's menu; health conscious menu items; carryout; cocktails & lounge; street parking; a la carte.
Authentic Portuguese & Spanish cuisine. Featuring pork with clams Alentejana, rabbit stew & suckling pig with pepper
sauce. **Cards:** AE, DI, DS, MC, VI.

# NEW BRUNSWICK—41,700

## LODGING

**ECONO LODGE**                    AAA Special Value Rates                    Phone: 908/828-8000
Ⓐ    All Year [CP]        1P:  $45-  76  2P/1B:  $47-  81  2P/2B:  $55-  87  XP: $3-5  F18
◆    **Location:** On US 1, just n of SR 18. 26 US 1 N 08901. Fax: 908/220-0314. **Terms:** Credit card guarantee, 3
Motel    day notice; weekly rates; pets, $5. **Facility:** 112 rooms. 2 stories; exterior corridors; pool. **Dining:** Restaurant
nearby. **Services:** Fee: coin laundry. **All Rooms:** free movies, cable TV. **Some Rooms:** radios, refrigerators.
**Cards:** AE, CB, DI, DS, JCB, MC, VI.                                    Ⓓ ⊗

## RESTAURANTS

**THE FROG AND THE PEACH**  Historical        Dinner: $21-$30        Phone: 908/846-3216
◆◆◆    **Location:** Just e of jct SR 27 & 18 via Neilson St. 29 Dennis St 08901. **Hours:** 11:30 am-2:30 & 5:30-10:30
Nouvelle    pm, Sat from 5:30 pm, Sun 4:30 pm-9:30 pm. Closed major holidays. **Reservations:** suggested.
American    **Features:** semi-formal attire; health conscious menu items; cocktails & lounge; a la carte. Charming intimate
dining in restored brownstone. **Cards:** AE, CB, DI, DS, MC, VI.                        ⊗

**LA FONTANA RISTORANTE**                    Dinner: over $31                    Phone: 908/249-7500
◆◆◆    **Location:** Downtown, corner George & Albany sts. 120 Albany St 08901. **Hours:** 11:30 am-2:30 & 5-10 pm,
Italian    Sat 5 pm-11 pm. Closed: Sun. **Reservations:** suggested. **Features:** semi-formal attire; cocktails; valet
parking; a la carte. Old world romantic ambience. Professionally attentive, yet friendly wait staff. Classic
preparation of entrees from all regions of Italy. Excellent wine list, including many half-bottles. **Cards:** AE, DI, MC, VI.    ⊗

**PANICO'S**                    Dinner: over $31                    Phone: 908/545-6100
◆◆◆    **Location:** Downtown, just e of jct George St & Church St. 103 Church St 08901. **Hours:** 11:30 am-2:30 &
Italian    5:30-10 pm, Sat 5:30 pm-11 pm. Closed major holidays & Sun. **Reservations:** suggested.
**Features:** semi-formal attire; cocktails; fee for parking; a la carte. Creative cuisine; all made on premises.
Award winning wine list. Excellent professional wait staff. Simple elegance with a touch of sophistication. Public parking lot
opposite. **Cards:** AE, DI, DS, MC, VI.                                ⊗

# NEW PROVIDENCE

## LODGING

**BEST WESTERN MURRAY HILL INN**        AAA Special Value Rates        Phone: 908/665-9200
Ⓐ    Sun-Thurs        1P:  $96- 105  2P/1B: $106- 115  2P/2B: $106- 115  XP: $10  F18
Fri & Sat        1P:  $79        2P/1B:  $79        2P/2B:  $79        XP: $10  F18
◆◆◆    **Location:** I-78 eastbound exit 44, westbound exit 43, 1 1/2 mi n New Providence; in Murray Hill Office Park
Motor Inn    at intersection of South St & Central Ave. 535 Central Ave 07974. Fax: 908/665-9562. **Terms:** Reserv
deposit; monthly rates; no pets. **Facility:** 76 rooms. 3 stories; interior corridors; meeting rooms; sauna; exercise room. Fee: racquetball court, 6 lighted tennis courts; squash court privileges. **Dining:** Dining room; 6:30-10:30 am,
11:30-1:30 & 5:30-9:30 pm, Sat 7:30 am-10:30 & 5:30-9:30 pm, Sun 7 am-noon; $13-$16; health conscious menu items.
**Services:** data ports, secretarial services; valet laundry. **All Rooms:** free movies, cable TV. **Some Rooms:** 17 efficiencies,
refrigerators, whirlpools. Fee: VCP's. **Cards:** AE, CB, DI, DS, JCB, MC, VI. Best Western Motels.            Ⓓ ⊗

# NORTH BRUNSWICK—31,300

## RESTAURANT

**ARTHUR'S TAVERN**                    Dinner: $11-$20                    Phone: 908/828-1117
◆◆    **Location:** Exit 9 of NJ Tpk, Rt 18W 1 mi, 2 mi s on US 1, then n on Georges Rd 1/2 mi. 644 Georges Rd
Steakhouse    08902. **Hours:** 11:30 am-11 pm, Fri-midnight, Sat noon-midnight, Sun 2 pm-10 pm. Closed: 11/23 & 12/25.
**Features:** casual dress; carryout; cocktails & lounge; a la carte. Inviting pub atmosphere. **Cards:** AE, DI,
MC, VI.

# NORTHFIELD

## RESTAURANT

**GIOVANNI'S, THE BEST OF ITALY**            Dinner: up to $10            Phone: 609/383-1155
◆    **Location:** Garden State Pkwy exit 36, 1/4 mi n on Fire Rd, then 1 mi e on Tilton Ave. 801 Tilton Ave 08225.
Italian    **Hours:** 11 am-10:30 pm. Closed: 1/1, 4/7 & 11/23. **Features:** casual dress; children's menu; carryout.

# NORTH WILDWOOD

## LODGINGS

**EUROPEAN**                    Guaranteed Rates                    Phone: 609/729-4622
◆◆    6/30-8/26 & 9/1-9/4        2P/1B:  $82    2P/2B:  $94    XP: $10    F3
Motel    6/23-6/29 & 8/27-8/31        2P/1B:  $70    2P/2B:  $85    XP: $8    F3
6/9-6/22 & 9/5-10/1        2P/1B:  $40    2P/2B:  $48    XP: $8    F3
5/6-6/8                2P/1B:  $36    2P/2B:  $40    XP: $8    F3
**Location:** 3rd St & Ocean Ave. 300 Ocean Ave 08260. **Terms:** Open 5/6-10/1; reserv deposit, 14 day notice; weekly rates;
package plans, low season; no pets. **Facility:** 20 rooms. 1-& 2-room efficiencies. 2 stories; exterior corridors; heated pool,
wading pool. **All Rooms:** coffeemakers, refrigerators, cable TV. **Cards:** AE, DS, MC, VI.            Ⓓ

**ISLE OF CAPRI MOTEL**

Phone: 609/522-1991

| | Guaranteed Rates | | | | | | | |
|---|---|---|---|---|---|---|---|---|
| 6/26-9/6 | 1P: | $64- | 70 | 2P/1B: | $68- | 76 | 2P/2B: | $76- | 90 | XP: $8 |
| 6/12-6/25 & 9/7-9/20 | 1P: | $40 | | 2P/1B: | $42- | 44 | 2P/2B: | $46- | 54 | XP: $6 |
| 5/1-6/11 & 9/21-10/1 | 1P: | $38 | | 2P/1B: | $40- | 42 | 2P/2B: | $40- | 46 | XP: $8 |

**Location:** From Garden State Pkwy exit 6, 3 mi se on SR 147, to 5th Ave, 4 blks. Ocean Ave At 5th Ave 08260. **Terms:** Open 5/1-10/1; reserv deposit, 14 day notice; 3 night min stay, 6/25-9/7; no pets. **Facility:** 20 rooms. In quiet residential neighborhood. Family oriented. 1 block from beach. 2 stories; exterior corridors; heated pool, wading pool. **All Rooms:** cable TV, no phones. **Some Rooms:** 5 efficiencies, refrigerators. **Cards:** MC, VI. *(See color ad p A72)* (D)

**LONG BEACH LODGE**

Phone: 609/522-1520

| | Rates Subject to Change | | | | |
|---|---|---|---|---|---|
| 7/14-8/20 | 2P/1B: | $75- | 79 | 2P/2B: | $99- | 130 | XP: $10 |
| 6/23-7/13 & 8/21-9/6 | 2P/1B: | $60- | 69 | 2P/2B: | $80- | 118 | XP: $10 |
| 5/26-6/22 & 9/7-9/19 | 2P/1B: | $40- | 49 | 2P/2B: | $56- | 100 | XP: $8 |
| 5/1-5/25 & 9/20-10/18 | 2P/1B: | $40- | 49 | 2P/2B: | $40- | 49 | XP: $8 |

**Location:** Garden State Pkwy exit 6, s on SR 147 to New Jersey Ave, s 1/2 mi to 9th Ave, e 4 blks. 539 E 9th Ave 08260. Fax: 609/523-1583. **Terms:** Open 5/1-10/18; reserv deposit, 14 day notice; package plans; no pets. **Facility:** 24 rooms. Large outside decks. Picnic area with gas barbecue. 3 two-bedroom units. Rates for up to 6 persons in season; 3 stories; exterior corridors; heated pool, wading pool. **Services:** Fee: coin laundry. **All Rooms:** efficiencies, cable TV. **Cards:** AE, DS, MC, VI. *(See color ad p A72)* (D)

**MEDITERRANEAN MOTEL**

Phone: 609/522-0112

| | Guaranteed Rates | | | | | | | |
|---|---|---|---|---|---|---|---|---|
| 6/30-8/26 & 9/1-9/4 | 1P: | $65 | 2P/1B: | $65 | | 2P/2B: | $70- | 94 | XP:$8-10 | F3 |
| 6/23-6/29 & 8/27-8/31 | 1P: | $50 | 2P/1B: | $55 | | 2P/2B: | $70- | 85 | XP: $8 | F3 |
| 6/9-6/22 & 9/5-10/1 | 1P: | $36 | 2P/1B: | $38 | | 2P/2B: | $40- | 48 | XP: $8 | F3 |
| 5/6-6/8 | 1P: | $30 | 2P/1B: | $34 | | 2P/2B: | $36- | 40 | XP: $8 | F3 |

**Location:** Exit 6 off Garden State Pkwy, 3 mi se on SR 147 (which becomes New Jersey Ave) to 5th Ave, then e 5 blks. 405 Ocean Ave 08260. **Terms:** Open 5/6-10/1; reserv deposit, 14 day notice; package plans; 3 night min stay, weekends in season; no pets. **Facility:** 33 rooms. Sun deck & barbecue grill. 1 block to beach. Open Fri-Sun only 5/7-5/15. Winter phone number (215) 271-6882; 3 stories; exterior corridors; heated pool, wading pool. **Services:** Fee: coin laundry. **All Rooms:** free movies, cable TV. Fee: VCP. **Some Rooms:** 22 efficiencies, refrigerators. **Cards:** AE, DS, MC, VI. *(See ad p A74)* (D)

**SURF SONG MOTEL**

Phone: 609/523-0003

| | Guaranteed Rates | | | | | |
|---|---|---|---|---|---|---|
| 7/9-8/28 | 2P/1B: | $89- | 115 | | | XP: $10 | F5 |
| 6/11-7/8 & 8/29-9/2 | 2P/1B: | $55- | 79 | | | XP: $10 | F5 |
| 5/1-5/23, 9/19-11/1 & 3/15-4/30 | 2P/1B: | $29- | 39 | | | XP: $6 | F5 |
| 5/24-6/10 & 9/3-9/18 | 2P/1B: | $45- | 52 | | | XP: $6 | F5 |

**Location:** Garden State Pkwy exit 6, 3 1/2 mi se on SR 147 which becomes New Jersey Ave to 18th Ave, then e 4 blks. 1800 Ocean Ave 08260. Fax: 609/522-3966. **Terms:** Open 5/1-11/1 & 3/15-4/30; reserv deposit, 15 day notice; package plans; no pets. **Facility:** 60 rooms. Contemporary 2-room efficiency suites. Rates are for up to 4 persons; 5 stories; exterior corridors; pool, wading pool. **Services:** Fee: coin laundry. **All Rooms:** cable TV. **Cards:** AE, DS, MC, VI.

## RESTAURANT

**PIRO'S VILLAGE RESTAURANT**

**Dinner: $11-$20**

Phone: 609/729-0401

**Location:** Garden State Pkwy exit 6, 3 mi se on SR 147 which becomes New Jersey Ave to 19th Ave, then 1 block w. 1901 New York Ave 08260. **Hours:** Open 5/1-10/15; 5 pm-10 pm. **Reservations:** suggested. **Features:** casual dress; children's menu; carryout; cocktails & lounge. **Cards:** MC, VI.

# OCEAN CITY—15,500

## LODGINGS

**BEACH CLUB HOTEL**

Phone: 609/399-8555

| | Rates Subject to Change | | | |
|---|---|---|---|---|
| 6/17-9/4 | 2P/2B: | $148- | 225 | XP: $10 |
| 9/5-9/16 | 2P/2B: | $90- | 140 | XP: $10 |
| 5/11-6/16 & 9/17-10/9 | 2P/2B: | $74- | 126 | XP: $10 |
| 5/5-5/10 | 2P/2B: | $60- | 104 | XP: $10 |

**Location:** Oceanfront, at 13th St & Ocean Ave. 1280 Boardwalk Ave 08226. Fax: 609/398-4379. **Terms:** Open 5/5-10/9; reserv deposit, 7 day notice; package plans; 3 night min stay, in season; no pets. **Facility:** 82 rooms. Most rooms with private balcony. 1 two-bedroom unit. 4 stories; interior corridors; meeting rooms; beach, heated pool, wading pool. **Dining:** Restaurant; 7 am-9 pm; $6-$16. **Services:** Fee: coin laundry. **Recreation:** swimming. **All Rooms:** refrigerators, cable TV. Fee: movies. **Some Rooms:** 2 kitchens. **Cards:** AE, DI, MC, VI. (D) ⊗

**CROSSINGS MOTOR INN**

Phone: 609/398-4433

| | Rates Subject to Change | | | | | | | |
|---|---|---|---|---|---|---|---|---|
| 7/15-8/29 [CP] | 1P: | $98- | 125 | 2P/1B: | $98- | 125 | 2P/2B: | $98- | 125 | XP: $7 | F12 |
| 6/25-7/14 & 8/30-9/5 [CP] | 1P: | $78- | 109 | 2P/1B: | $78- | 109 | 2P/2B: | $78- | 109 | XP: $7 | F12 |
| 6/10-6/24 & 9/6-9/17 [CP] | 1P: | $59- | 91 | 2P/1B: | $59- | 91 | 2P/2B: | $59- | 91 | XP: $7 | F12 |
| 5/1-6/9 & 9/18-10/15 [CP] | 1P: | $47- | 72 | 2P/1B: | $47- | 72 | 2P/2B: | $47- | 72 | XP: $7 | F12 |

**Location:** Garden State Pkwy exit 25, 2 mi e on CR 54. 3420 Haven Ave 08226. Fax: 609/525-0490. **Terms:** Open 5/1-10/15; reserv deposit, 7 day notice; weekly/monthly rates; package plans; 2 night min stay, weekends, July & Aug; pets, $15, off season only. **Facility:** 70 rooms. 3 stories; exterior corridors; meeting rooms; heated pool, wading pool. **Services:** Fee: coin laundry. **All Rooms:** coffeemakers, free movies, refrigerators, cable TV. **Some Rooms:** microwaves. **Cards:** AE, DI, DS, MC, VI. (D) ⊗

**THE FORUM MOTOR INN**

Phone: 609/399-8700

| | Rates Subject to Change | | | |
|---|---|---|---|---|
| 6/16-9/11 | 2P/2B: | $76- | 130 | XP: $8 | F4 |
| 5/24-6/15 & 9/12-9/18 | 2P/2B: | $66- | 96 | XP: $8 | F4 |
| 5/1-5/23 & 9/19-10/9 | 2P/2B: | $54- | 86 | XP: $8 | F4 |

**Location:** 8th St between Ocean & Atlantic aves. 8th St & Atlantic Ave 08226 (Box 448). Fax: 609/399-8704. **Terms:** Open 5/1-10/9; reserv deposit, 7 day notice, cancellation fee imposed; 3 night min stay, 7/1-8/31; no pets. **Facility:** 55 rooms. Well-maintained property. Offering personalized service. 2-3 stories; interior/exterior corridors; heated pool, wading pool. **Dining:** Coffee shop; 7 am-3 pm 5/15-9/15. **Services:** Fee: coin laundry. **All Rooms:** refrigerators, cable TV. **Cards:** MC, VI.

**IMPALA ISLAND INN**  Rates Subject to Change  Phone: 609/399-7500

| | 6/16-9/4 | | 2P/2B: | $99- | 135 | XP: | $8 | F16 |
| --- | --- | --- | --- | --- | --- | --- | --- | --- |
| | 9/5-9/17 | | 2P/2B: | $60- | 85 | XP: | $8 | F16 |
| ◆◆ | 5/1-6/15 & 9/18-4/30 | | 2P/2B: | $55- | 66 | XP: | $8 | F16 |

Motor Inn  **Location:** Center, at Ocean Ave & 10th St. 1001 Ocean Ave 08226. Fax: 609/398-4379. **Terms:** Reserv deposit, 7 day notice; 2 night min stay, weekends in season; no pets. **Facility:** 109 rooms. 2 two-bedroom units. 2 stories; exterior corridors; meeting rooms; 3 pools (1 heated), wading pool. **Dining:** Restaurant; 8 am-8 pm, closed 10/31-3/1; $6-$15. **Services:** Fee: coin laundry. **All Rooms:** cable TV. Fee: movies. **Some Rooms:** coffeemakers, 8 kitchens, microwaves, refrigerators. **Cards:** AE, DI, MC, VI.  Ⓓ Ⓧ

**NORTHWOOD INN**  Rates Subject to Change  Phone: 609/399-6071

| ◆◆ | 6/1-10/1 [CP] | 2P/1B: | $85- | 105 | 2P/2B: | $105 | | XP: $15 |
| --- | --- | --- | --- | --- | --- | --- | --- | --- |
| Historic Bed | 5/1-5/31, 10/2-1/2 & | | | | | | | |
| & Breakfast | 1/22-4/30 [CP] | 2P/1B: | $75- | 95 | 2P/2B: | $95 | | XP: $15 |

**Location:** Garden State Pkwy exit 30, continue over 9th St Bridge to Wesley Ave N 1/2 mi. 401 Wesley Ave 08226. Fax: 609/398-5553. **Terms:** Open 5/1-1/2 & 1/22-4/30; credit card guarantee, 7 day notice; weekly rates; BP available, weekends; package plans; 2 night min stay, weekends; no pets. **Facility:** 8 rooms. Charming & relaxed setting. 1894 Victorian home. 1 suite, $135-$145; 3 stories, no elevator; interior corridors; designated smoking area; pool table. **Dining:** Full breakfast served weekends. **Services:** area transportation, to train & bus terminals, airport transportation. **All Rooms:** combo & shower baths, no phones. **Some Rooms:** cable TV, VCP's. **Cards:** AE, MC, VI.  Ⓓ Ⓢ Ⓧ

**PORT-O-CALL HOTEL**  AAA Special Value Rates  Phone: 609/399-8812

| | 6/16-9/4 | | | | 2P/2B: | $149- | 204 | XP: $15 | F12 |
| --- | --- | --- | --- | --- | --- | --- | --- | --- | --- |
| ◆◆◆ | 5/26-6/15 & 9/5-10/9 | 1P: | $99- | 105 | 2P/2B: | $99- | 169 | XP: $15 | F12 |
| Motor Inn | 10/10-4/5 | 1P: | $69- | 99 | 2P/2B: | $99- | 159 | XP: $15 | F12 |
| | 5/1-5/25 & 4/17-4/30 | 1P: | $69- | 99 | 2P/2B: | $89- | 139 | XP: $15 | F12 |

**Location:** Between 15th & 16th sts. 1500 Boardwalk 08226 (PO Box 89). Fax: 609/399-0387. **Terms:** Reserv deposit, 7 day notice; weekly rates; package plans; 3 night min stay, weekends; no pets. **Facility:** 99 rooms. Some with balcony. 1 two-bedroom unit, 1 three-bedroom unit. 10 stories; interior corridors; meeting rooms; beach, pool, saunas; exercise room, beauty salon. **Dining:** Dining room; 8 am-11, noon-2 & 5:30-9 pm; 9/16-5/26 to 8 pm; $10-$16. **Services:** data ports. Fee: coin laundry, area transportation, Atlantic City Casinos. **Recreation:** swimming. **All Rooms:** coffeemakers, refrigerators, cable TV. Fee: movies. **Some Rooms:** microwaves, whirlpools. **Cards:** AE, CB, DI, DS, MC, VI.  Ⓓ Ⓢ Ⓧ

**TOP O' THE WAVES**  Rates Subject to Change  Phone: 609/399-0477

| ◆◆ | 7/1-9/7 [CP] | 2P/1B: | $110- | 185 | 2P/2B: | $155- | 185 | XP:$10-19 |
| --- | --- | --- | --- | --- | --- | --- | --- | --- |
| Bed & | 9/8-12/31 [CP] | 2P/1B: | $95- | 110 | 2P/2B: | $135- | 160 | XP:$10-19 |
| Breakfast | 5/1-6/30 & 1/1-4/30 [CP] | 2P/1B: | $95- | 110 | 2P/2B: | $95- | 110 | XP:$10-19 |

**Location:** From Garden State Pkwy, exit 25, e on Roosevelt Blvd right on Central Ave, to 55th St. 5447 Central Ave 08226. Fax: 609/399-6964. **Terms:** Sr. discount; reserv deposit, 14 day notice, in summer; weekly rates; 3 night min stay, in season; no pets. **Facility:** 8 rooms. Beachfront pensionne with charming rooms, good view. 1 two-bedroom unit. 3 stories; interior/exterior corridors; smoke free premises; beach. **Services:** area transportation. Fee: coin laundry. **Recreation:** swimming. **All Rooms:** coffeemakers, microwaves, free movies, refrigerators, combo & shower baths, cable TV. **Some Rooms:** 7 efficiencies, kitchen, VCP's, whirlpools. **Cards:** AE, DI, DS, MC, VI.  Ⓓ Ⓧ

**WATSON'S REGENCY SUITES**  AAA Special Value Rates  Phone: 609/398-4300

| ◆◆◆ | 6/25-9/6 | | | | 2P/2B: | $199- | 225 | XP: $15 | F3 |
| --- | --- | --- | --- | --- | --- | --- | --- | --- | --- |
| Suite Motel | 5/1-6/24 & 9/7-10/9 | | | | 2P/2B: | $129- | 159 | XP: $10 | F3 |
| | 10/10-12/31 | 2P/1B: | $70- | 115 | 2P/2B: | $109- | 129 | XP: $10 | F3 |
| | 1/1-4/30 | 2P/1B: | $60- | 95 | 2P/2B: | $89- | 109 | XP: $10 | F3 |

**Location:** Garden State Pkwy exit 30 over 9th St Bridge to Ocean Ave S. 901 Ocean Ave 08226. Fax: 609/398-0197. **Terms:** Check-in 4 pm; reserv deposit; weekly rates; package plans; no pets. **Facility:** 79 rooms. Spacious 1-bedroom suites with full kitchens, all units have private balcony. Each unit equipped with sleep sofa & sleep chair in living room. Rates for up to 5 persons; 5 stories; interior corridors; meeting rooms; heated indoor/outdoor pool, whirlpool. **Dining:** Coffee shop nearby. **Services:** Fee: coin laundry. **All Rooms:** coffeemakers, kitchens, microwaves, free movies, refrigerators, cable TV, VCP's. **Cards:** AE, DS, MC, VI.  Ⓓ Ⓢ Ⓧ

## RESTAURANT

**THE CULINARY GARDEN**  Dinner: $11-$20  Phone: 609/399-3713

**Location:** 9th St & Central Ave. 841 Central Ave 08226. **Hours:** 8 am-2 & 5-9 pm 6/1-9/4, 11 am-2 & 5-8 pm 3/5-5/31 Sun 8 am-2 & 5-9 pm. **Reservations:** suggested; in summer. **Features:** casual dress; children's menu; early bird specials; carryout; a la carte. Selection of gourmet to downhome cookin, unique Continental  preparation, homemade desserts. **Cards:** AE, DS, MC, VI.  Ⓧ

# PARAMUS—25,100  (See NEWARK to PARAMUS ACCOMMODATIONS spotting map page A44; see index starting on page A42)

## LODGINGS

**HOLIDAY INN**  Guaranteed Rates  Phone: 201/843-5400  **45**

All Year  1P: $70- 100  2P/1B: $75- 100  2P/2B: $75- 100  XP: $3  F19

**Location:** On SR 17 northbound, n of jct SR 4; Garden State Pkwy northbound exit 161, southbound exit 163. 50 Rt 17 07652. Fax: 201/712-0434. **Terms:** Sr. discount; credit card guarantee; no pets. **Facility:** 80 rooms. 2 stories; interior corridors; meeting rooms; pool. **Dining:** Restaurant; 7 am-10 pm; $8-$20; health Motor Inn  conscious menu items. **Services:** data ports, secretarial services; health club privileges; valet laundry. **All Rooms:** free movies, cable TV. **Cards:** AE, CB, DI, DS, JCB, MC, VI.  Ⓓ Ⓢ Ⓧ

**HOWARD JOHNSON LODGE**  AAA Special Value Rates  Phone: 201/265-4200  **44**

All Year  1P: $65- 70  2P/1B: $65- 70  2P/2B: $73- 80  XP: $7  F18

**Location:** On SR 17 southbound, 1/2 mi n of Garden State Pkwy northbound exit 163, u-turn on Midland Ave-Glen Rock to 17S; Garden St Pkwy southbound, exit 16S 4 mi s on SR. 393 SR 17 07652. Motor Inn  Fax: 201/265-0247. **Terms:** Credit card guarantee; small pets only. **Facility:** 81 rooms. In very busy commercial area. Most units with balcony. 3 stories; interior corridors; meeting rooms; pool. **Dining:** Restaurant; 7 am-11:30 pm, Fri & Sat-midnight, Sun 7:30 am-11:30 pm; $5-$9. **Services:** valet laundry. **All Rooms:** free movies, cable TV. **Cards:** AE, CB, DI, DS, JCB, MC, VI.  Ⓓ Ⓢ Ⓧ

**(See NEWARK to PARAMUS ACCOMMODATIONS spotting map page A44)**

**RADISSON INN PARAMUS**     Guaranteed Rates          Phone: 201/262-6900  **46**
◆◆◆   All Year          1P: $125     2P/1B: $135     2P/2B: $145     XP: $10  F16
Motor Inn  **Location:** On service road (From Rd) w of Garden State Pkwy exit 165; northbound Ridgewood exit (shopping center), southbound Oradell (shopping center). 601 From Rd 07652. Fax: 201/262-4955. **Terms:** Reserv deposit, 3 day notice; small pets only. **Facility:** 119 rooms. 2 stories; interior corridors; meeting rooms; pool. **Dining:** Dining room; 6:30 am-10 pm; $6-$16; cocktails. **Services:** data ports, secretarial services; health club privileges; valet laundry. **All Rooms:** free & pay movies, cable TV. **Some Rooms:** coffeemakers, refrigerators. **Cards:** AE, CB, DI, DS, JCB, MC, VI.     Ⓓ Ⓢ ⊗

## PARK RIDGE—8,100

### LODGING

**MARRIOTT HOTEL**     Rates Subject to Change          Phone: 201/307-0800
◆◆◆   Sun-Thurs [EP]     1P: $112     2P/1B: $124     2P/2B: $124
Hotel   Fri & Sat [BP]      1P: $84      2P/1B: $84      2P/2B: $84
**Location:** Southbound Garden State Pkwy, u-turn thru Food Fuel Service Plaza to Garden State Pkwy northbound, exit 172, right 300 yds on Grand Ave & 1/2 mi s on Mercedes. 300 Brae Blvd 07656. Fax: 201/307-0859. **Terms:** Sr. discount; check-in 4 pm; reserv deposit; weekly/monthly rates; package plans; small pets only. **Facility:** 289 rooms. Country office park setting. 4 stories; interior corridors; conference facilities; luxury level rooms; heated indoor/outdoor pool, sauna, whirlpool; exercise room. **Dining & Entertainment:** 2 dining rooms; 6:30-10 am, 11-2:30 & 5-10 pm; $9-$24; cocktails; entertainment. **Services:** data ports, secretarial services; valet laundry. **All Rooms:** free & pay movies, cable TV. **Some Rooms:** refrigerators. **Cards:** AE, DI, DS, MC, VI.     Ⓓ Ⓢ ⊗

## PARSIPPANY—48,500   (See NEW JERSEY METRO AREA ACCOMMODATIONS spotting map pages A40 & A41; see index starting on page A39)

### LODGINGS

**DAYS INN-PARSIPPANY**     AAA Special Value Rates          Phone: 201/335-0200  **57**
◆◆◆   All Year          1P: $66      2P/1B: $71      2P/2B: $71      XP: $5  F12
Motor Inn  **Location:** On US 46; 1/4 mi w of jct I-287 & US 202; I-80 exit 42, 1/2 mi e. 3159 Rt 46 07054. Fax: 201/263-3094. **Terms:** Reserv deposit; weekly/monthly rates; pets. **Facility:** 120 rooms. On busy highway. 2 stories; interior/exterior corridors; meeting rooms; pool, wading pool. **Dining:** Restaurant nearby. **Services:** valet laundry. **All Rooms:** free movies, cable TV. **Some Rooms:** 4 kitchens. Fee: microwaves. **Cards:** AE, CB, DI, DS, MC, VI.     Ⓓ Ⓢ ⊗

**EMBASSY SUITES**     Guaranteed Rates          Phone: 201/334-1440  **52**
◆◆◆   Sun-Thurs [BP]     1P: $149     2P/1B: $169     2P/2B: $169     XP: $20  F11
Suite Hotel  Fri & Sat [BP]      1P: $104     2P/1B: $104     2P/2B: $104     XP: $20  F11
**Location:** On US 202; 1/4 mi n of jct US 46, 1 mi n of I-287, exit 35 to US 202N. 909 Parsippany Blvd 07054. Fax: 201/402-1188. **Terms:** Sr. discount; reserv deposit; monthly rates; small pets only, $250. **Facility:** 274 rooms. Kids activity club on weekends. 2 two-bedroom units. 5 stories; interior corridors; business center, conference facilities; sauna, whirlpool, small heated indoor pool; exercise room. **Dining:** Also, Caffe' Sport, see separate listing. **Services:** data ports, PC, secretarial services; valet laundry. Fee: childcare. **All Rooms:** efficiencies, microwaves, free & pay movies, cable TV. **Some Rooms:** coffeemakers. **Cards:** AE, CB, DI, DS, JCB, MC, VI.     Ⓓ Ⓢ ⊗

**HAMPTON INN - PARSIPPANY**     Rates Subject to Change          Phone: 201/263-0095  **56**
◆◆◆   Sun-Thurs     1P: $83- 99     2P/1B: $95- 109     2P/2B: $93
Motor Inn  Fri & Sat     1P: $59      2P/1B: $59      2P/2B: $59
**Location:** At jct SR 46 & Cherry Hill Rd; 1 mi n of I-80, exit 42. 3535 Rt 46 07054. Fax: 201/263-6133. **Terms:** Weekly/monthly rates; package plans; small pets only. **Facility:** 100 rooms. Suburban location near commercial area; inviting, contemporary atmosphere; large rooms, stylishly furnished; convenient to major highways, interstates & shopping areas. 18 efficiencies, $10 extra; 4 stories; interior corridors; meeting rooms; sauna; exercise room. **Dining:** Dining room; 5 pm-10 pm; $6-$15; cocktails. **Services:** data ports, PC, secretarial services; valet laundry. **All Rooms:** free & pay movies, combo & shower baths, cable TV. **Some Rooms:** coffeemakers, microwaves, refrigerators. Fee: whirlpools. **Cards:** AE, DI, DS, MC, VI. *(See ad below)*

**HOJO INN BY HOWARD JOHNSON**     Rates Subject to Change          Phone: 201/882-8600  **54**
◆◆   All Year          1P: $45- 47     2P/1B: $47- 53     2P/2B: $47- 53     XP: $6  F18
Motel   **Location:** I-80 westbound exit 47, eastbound exit 45, 1 mi e on US 46. 625 Rt 46E 07054. Fax: 201/882-3493. **Terms:** Sr. discount; weekly/monthly rates; pets. **Facility:** 120 rooms. 3 stories; exterior corridors. **Dining:** Continental breakfast Mon-Fri. **Services:** guest laundry. **All Rooms:** free movies, cable TV. **Some Rooms:** microwaves, refrigerators. Fee: VCP's. **Cards:** AE, CB, DI, DS, JCB, MC, VI.     Ⓓ ⊗

**HOLIDAY INN-PARSIPPANY**     AAA Special Value Rates          Phone: 201/263-2000  **50**
◆◆◆   Sun-Thurs     1P: $59- 109     2P/1B: $59- 109     2P/2B: $59- 109
Motel   Fri & Sat     1P: $49      2P/1B: $49      2P/2B: $49
**Location:** On US 46; just w of jct I-80; westbound exit 47, eastbound exit 45 then 3/4 mi e. 707 Rt 46E 07054. Fax: 201/299-9029. **Terms:** Reserv deposit; BP available; no pets. **Facility:** 153 rooms. Conveniently located to major highways. Suites, $99-$159; 4 stories; interior corridors; conference facilities; pool. **Dining & Entertainment:** Restaurant; 7 am-11 pm, Sat & Sun-midnight; cocktails/lounge. **Services:** data ports, secretarial services; health club privileges; valet laundry. Fee: airport transportation. **All Rooms:** free & pay movies, cable TV. **Some Rooms:** coffeemakers, microwaves, refrigerators. **Cards:** AE, CB, DI, DS, JCB, MC, VI.     Ⓓ Ⓢ ⊗

**(See NEW JERSEY METRO AREA ACCOMMODATIONS spotting map pages A40 & A41)**

**PARSIPPANY HILTON**
Rates Subject to Change — Phone: 201/267-7373 — **51**
Mon-Thurs 1P: $110 2P/1B: $120 2P/2B: $120 XP: $10 F
Fri-Sun 1P: $70 2P/1B: $70 2P/2B: $70

Hotel **Location:** In Hilton Court, I-287 northbound exit 35, southbound exit 35B, 1 1/4 mi w on SR 10. 1 Hilton Court 07054. Fax: 201/984-6853. **Terms:** Reserv deposit; package plans; small pets only, must be caged. **Facility:** 508 rooms. Suburban location set back off highway in wooded area of corporate office park. Gracious atmosphere with spacious public areas & cordial staff. Conveniently located to interstates. 6 stories; interior corridors; business center, conference facilities; 2 pools (1 heated, 1 indoor), whirlpool; 2 lighted tennis courts; exercise room, playground, sports court. **Dining & Entertainment:** 2 dining rooms; 6:30 am-11:45 pm, Sat & Sun from 7 am; $10-$35; cocktails; also, Livingston's Chop House, see separate listing; entertainment. **Services:** data ports, PC, secretarial services; valet laundry. Fee: childcare. **Recreation:** bicycles, jogging. **All Rooms:** free & pay movies, cable TV. **Some Rooms:** refrigerators. **Cards:** AE, CB, DI, DS, MC, VI. *(See ad p 28)*

**RED ROOF INN**
Rates Subject to Change — Phone: 201/334-3737 — **53**
All Year 1P: $45- 48 2P/1B: $53- 56 2P/2B: $55- 60 XP: $8 F18
Motel **Location:** On US 46; w of I-80, westbound exit 47, eastbound exit 45 then 1/2 mi e. 855 US 46E 07054. Fax: 201/334-1984. **Terms:** Credit card guarantee; pets. **Facility:** 108 rooms. Budget-oriented property featuring reasonable rates; convenient location to shopping areas & easy access to major highways & interstates. 2 stories; exterior corridors. **Dining:** Restaurant nearby. **All Rooms:** free movies, cable TV. **Cards:** AE, CB, DI, DS, MC, VI.

## RESTAURANTS

**CAFFE' SPORT**
Dinner: $11-$20 — Phone: 201/402-8080 — **51**
Italian **Location:** In Embassy Suites. 909 Parsippany Blvd 07054. **Hours:** 11 am-11 pm. Closed: 12/25. **Features:** casual dress; Sunday brunch; children's menu; health conscious menu items; carryout; cocktails & lounge; a la carte. **Cards:** AE, CB, DI, JCB, MC, VI.

**LIVINGSTON'S CHOP HOUSE**
Dinner: over $31 — Phone: 201/267-3881 — **50**
Continental **Location:** In Parsippany Hilton. One Hilton Court 07054. **Hours:** 5:30 pm-10:30 pm, Sat-11 pm, Sun 10:30 am-3 pm. **Reservations:** suggested; weekends. **Features:** casual dress; cocktails & lounge; a la carte. Fine dining open for dinner & Sun brunch only, Continental culinary treats served in a traditional atmosphere. **Cards:** AE, DI, DS, MC, VI.

# PENNS GROVE

## LODGING

**WELLESLEY INN & SUITES**
Guaranteed Rates — Phone: 609/299-3800
6/3-6/5 & 9/16-9/18 [CP] 1P: $75 2P/1B: $80 2P/2B: $80 XP: $5 F17
Mon-Thurs 5/1-6/2, 6/6-9/15
& 9/19-4/30 [CP] 1P: $51 2P/1B: $56 2P/2B: $56 XP: $5 F17
Motel Fri-Sun 5/1-6/2, 6/6-9/15 &
9/19-4/30 [CP] 1P: $49 2P/1B: $49 2P/2B: $54

**Location:** 1 mi e of Delaware Memorial Bridge, jct US 40 & NJ Tpk exit 1, off I-295, exit 2B. 10 Howard Johnson Ln 08069. Fax: 609/299-6982. **Terms:** Sr. discount; reserv deposit, 4 day notice; pets. **Facility:** 140 rooms. 2 stories; interior corridors; meeting rooms; heated indoor pool; exercise room. **Dining & Entertainment:** Cocktail lounge; restaurant nearby. **Services:** Fee: coin laundry. **All Rooms:** coffeemakers, free & pay movies, cable TV. **Some Rooms:** microwaves, refrigerators. **Cards:** AE, CB, DI, DS, JCB, MC, VI.

# PISCATAWAY—47,100 (See NEW JERSEY METRO AREA ACCOMMODATIONS spotting map pages A40 & A41; see index starting on page A39)

## LODGING

**EMBASSY SUITES HOTEL**
AAA Special Value Rates — Phone: 908/980-0500 — **65**
Sun-Thurs [BP] 1P: $145 2P/1B: $165 2P/2B: $165 XP: $20 F18
Hotel Fri & Sat [BP] 1P: $99 2P/1B: $109 2P/2B: $109 XP: $20 F18
**Location:** I-287 exit 5 (SR 18), Highland Park to Centennial Ave, in Office Park. 121 Centennial Ave 08854. Fax: 908/980-9473. **Terms:** Reserv deposit; weekly/monthly rates; small pets only, $50, also $50 dep req. **Facility:** 220 rooms. Enjoy spacious accommodations; beautiful atrium public area with tropical atmosphere. Conveniently located off interstate. 5 stories; interior corridors; conference facilities; heated indoor pool, sauna, whirlpool; exercise room. **Dining & Entertainment:** Restaurant; 6-9:30 am, 11-2 & 5-10 pm, Fri-Sun from 7 am; $9-$20; health conscious menu items; cocktails/lounge. **Services:** data ports, secretarial services; valet laundry; area transportation, to local businesses. **All Rooms:** microwaves, free & pay movies, refrigerators, cable TV. **Some Rooms:** coffeemakers. **Cards:** AE, CB, DI, DS, JCB, MC, VI.

# PLEASANTVILLE—16,000

## LODGING

**DAYS INN ATLANTIC CITY-PLEASANTVILLE**
Guaranteed Rates — Phone: 609/641-4500
7/1-9/9 [CP] 1P: $69- 130 2P/2B: $74- 135 XP: $5 F12
5/1-6/30 [CP] 1P: $60- 95 2P/2B: $65- 105 XP: $5 F12
9/10-12/31 [CP] 1P: $50- 85 2P/2B: $55- 90 XP: $5 F12
Motel 1/1-4/30 [CP] 1P: $45- 80 2P/2B: $50- 85 XP: $5 F12
**Location:** Exit 36 of Garden State Pkwy at Tilton Rd; on CR 563, 1 blk s of US 40. 6708 Tilton Rd 08232. Fax: 609/645-8295. **Terms:** Sr. discount; reserv deposit; no pets. **Facility:** 117 rooms. Deluxe continental breakfast served off lobby area. 5 stories; interior corridors; meeting rooms; pool; exercise room. **Dining:** Restaurant nearby. **Services:** data ports; area transportation, to casino. Fee: coin laundry. **All Rooms:** free & pay movies, cable TV. **Some Rooms:** efficiency, microwaves, refrigerators. **Cards:** AE, CB, DI, DS, MC, VI. *(See ad below)*

## RESTAURANT

**SHORE DINER**  **Dinner:** $11-$20  **Phone:** 609/641-3669
◆
American  **Location:** From Garden State Pkwy, exit 36. 6710 Tilton Rd 08232. **Hours:** 7 am-midnight. Closed: 12/25. **Features:** casual dress; children's menu; carryout; cocktails; a la carte. Casual, family dining, offering large portions. **Cards:** AE, DS, MC, VI.  ⊗

# POINT PLEASANT BEACH—5,100

## LODGINGS

**MARINER'S COVE MOTOR INN**  Rates Subject to Change  **Phone:** 908/899-0060

| | | 1P | | 2P/1B | | 2P/2B | | XP | | |
|---|---|---|---|---|---|---|---|---|---|---|
| Fri & Sat 6/25-9/5 | 1P: | $118 | 2P/1B: | $118 | 2P/2B: | $118 | XP: | $7-15 | F12 |
| Sun-Thurs 6/25-9/5 | 1P: | $95 | 2P/1B: | $95 | 2P/2B: | $95 | XP: | $15 | F12 |
| Fri & Sat 5/1-6/24 & 9/6-9/30 | 1P: | $80 | 2P/1B: | $80 | 2P/2B: | $80 | XP: | $7 | F12 |
| Sun-Thurs 5/1-6/24, 9/6-9/30, 10/1-12/31 & 2/1-4/30 | 1P: | $35- 50 | 2P/1B: | $35- 50 | 2P/2B: | $35- 50 | XP: | $7 | F12 |

Motel  **Location:** 3/4 mi e of SR 35 following signs to beach. 50 Broadway 08742. **Terms:** Open 5/1-12/31 & 2/1-4/30; reserv deposit, 7 day notice; weekly rates; 2 night min stay, weekends in season; no pets. **Facility:** 24 rooms. Complimentary beach pass. Closed 1/1-1/31; 2 stories; exterior corridors; beach, pool. **Dining:** Restaurant nearby. **Recreation:** swimming. **All Rooms:** refrigerators, cable TV. **Cards:** AE, MC, VI.  Ⓓ

**SURFSIDE MOTEL**  Rates Subject to Change  **Phone:** 908/899-1109

| | | 2P/1B | | 2P/2B | | XP | | |
|---|---|---|---|---|---|---|---|---|
| Fri & Sat 7/1-8/31 | | 2P/1B: $127 | 2P/2B: | $137 | XP: | $10 | F12 |
| Fri & Sat 5/1-6/30 & 9/1-4/30 | | | 2P/2B: | $38- 118 | XP: | $10 | F12 |
| Sun-Thurs 7/1-8/31 | | 2P/1B: $88 | 2P/2B: | $97 | XP: | $10 | F12 |
| Sun-Thurs 5/1-6/30 & 9/1-4/30 | | | 2P/2B: | $28- 57 | XP: | $10 | F12 |

Motel  **Location:** 2 blks from ocean; 1/4 mi e jct SR 35. 101 Broadway 08742. **Terms:** Reserv deposit, 7 day notice; weekly/monthly rates; package plans, off season; no pets. **Facility:** 27 rooms. Conveniently located to beach & fishing. 2 stories; exterior corridors; beach, heated pool, complimentary beach pass; basketball court. **Dining:** Restaurant nearby. **Recreation:** swimming. **All Rooms:** refrigerators, combo & shower baths, cable TV. **Cards:** AE, DS, MC, VI.  Ⓓ

## RESTAURANTS

**BARMORES SHRIMP BOX**  **Dinner:** $11-$20  **Phone:** 908/899-1637
◆◆
Seafood  **Location:** 1/2 mi e of US 35 via Broadway & left at inlet. 75 Inlet Dr 08742. **Hours:** 11:30 am-10 pm, Sun 2 pm-9 pm, 9/2-6/14 from 11 am. Closed: Mon & Tues 9/2-6/14. **Features:** casual dress; children's menu; early bird specials; health conscious menu items; carryout; salad bar; cocktails & lounge; also prix fixe. Overlooking Manasquan Inlet. Sun brunch, Sept-June. **Cards:** AE, DI, MC, VI.  ⊗

**JACK BAKER'S WHARFSIDE**  **Dinner:** $11-$20  **Phone:** 908/892-9100
◆◆
Seafood  **Location:** 1/2 mi e of SR 35, follow signs to beach area, left on Boston. 101 Channel Dr 08742. **Hours:** 11:30 am-9:30 pm, Fri-10 pm, Sat-10:30 pm, Sun-9 pm; in winter noon-9 pm, Fri-9:30 pm, Sat-10 pm, Sun-8:30 pm. Closed: 11/23 & 12/25. **Features:** casual dress; children's menu; early bird specials; health conscious menu items; carryout; cocktails & lounge. Overlooking Manasquan Inlet. **Cards:** AE, CB, DI, MC, VI.  ⊗

# PRINCETON—12,000

## LODGINGS

**HOLIDAY INN-PRINCETON**  Guaranteed Rates  **Phone:** 609/452-2400

| | | 1P | | 2P/1B | | 2P/2B | | XP | |
|---|---|---|---|---|---|---|---|---|---|
| Fri-Sun | 1P: | $79 | 2P/1B: | $79 | 2P/2B: | $79 | XP: | $15 | F18 |
| Mon-Thurs | 1P: | $69 | 2P/1B: | $69 | 2P/2B: | $69 | XP: | $15 | F18 |

Motor Inn  **Location:** On US 1 southbound, jct Ridge Rd; 3 mi n of CR 571. 4355 US 1 at Ridge Rd 08540. **Fax:** 609/452-2494. **Terms:** Sr. discount; reserv deposit, 5 day notice; weekly/monthly rates; BP available; no pets. **Facility:** 240 rooms. 6 stories; interior corridors; conference facilities, meeting rooms; heated indoor pool. **Dining & Entertainment:** Dining room; 6:30 am-11 pm, Sun from 7 am; $10-$22; health conscious menu items; cocktails/lounge; entertainment. **Services:** secretarial services; valet laundry. **All Rooms:** free & pay movies, cable TV. **Some Rooms:** 10 efficiencies, microwaves, refrigerators. **Cards:** AE, CB, DI, DS, MC, VI.  Ⓓ Ⓢ ⊗

**HYATT REGENCY-PRINCETON**  Rates Subject to Change  **Phone:** 609/987-1234

| | | 1P | | 2P/1B | | 2P/2B | |
|---|---|---|---|---|---|---|---|
| Mon-Thurs | 1P: | $129- 161 | 2P/1B: | $129- 161 | 2P/2B: | $129- 161 |
| Fri-Sun | 1P: | $79- 104 | 2P/1B: | $79- 104 | 2P/2B: | $79- 104 |

Hotel  **Location:** On US 1 northbound; 1/2 mi s of CR 571; in Carnegie Office Complex. 102 Carnegie Center 08540. **Fax:** 609/987-2584. **Terms:** Sr. discount; credit card guarantee; weekly/monthly rates; no pets. **Facility:** 348 rooms. 4 stories; interior corridors; conference facilities; heated indoor pool, saunas, whirlpool; 2 tennis courts. **Dining & Entertainment:** Cocktails/lounge; also, Crystal Garden Restaurant, see separate listing; entertainment, nightclub. **Services:** data ports, secretarial services; valet laundry. **Fee:** valet parking. **All Rooms:** free & pay movies, cable TV. **Some Rooms:** coffeemakers, refrigerators. **Fee:** VCP's. **Cards:** AE, CB, DI, DS, MC, VI.  Ⓓ Ⓢ ⊗

**NASSAU INN**  Rates Subject to Change  **Phone:** 609/921-7500

| | | 1P | | 2P/1B | | 2P/2B | |
|---|---|---|---|---|---|---|---|
| All Year | 1P: | $140 | 2P/1B: | $140 | 2P/2B: | $140 |

Motor Inn  **Location:** Palmer Sq town center. 10 Palmer Sq 08542. **Fax:** 609/921-9385. **Terms:** Reserv deposit; package plans; no pets. **Facility:** 215 rooms. Some smaller rooms. 1 two-bedroom unit. 5 stories; interior corridors; conference facilities. **Dining & Entertainment:** Dining room, restaurant, coffee shop; 7 am-10:30 pm; $8-$18; cocktails/lounge; also, Palmer's, see separate listing; entertainment. **Services:** data ports, secretarial services; health club privileges; valet laundry. **Fee:** childcare, airport transportation. **All Rooms:** free & pay movies, cable TV. **Fee:** VCP. **Some Rooms:** refrigerators. **Cards:** AE, MC, VI.  Ⓓ Ⓢ ⊗

**NOVOTEL HOTEL**  AAA Special Value Rates  **Phone:** 609/520-1200

| | | 1P | | 2P/1B | | 2P/2B | | XP | |
|---|---|---|---|---|---|---|---|---|---|
| Sun-Thurs | 1P: | $99- 109 | 2P/1B: | $109- 119 | 2P/2B: | $109- 119 | XP: | $10 | F16 |
| Fri & Sat | 1P: | $74 | 2P/1B: | $74 | 2P/2B: | $74 | XP: | $10 | F16 |

Motor Inn  **Location:** On US 1; exit 67 off I-295, 3 mi n of jct CR 526 & 571; in Princeton Corporate Center. 100 Independence Way 08540. **Fax:** 609/520-0594. **Terms:** Credit card guarantee; monthly rates; BP available; small pets only, must be attended. **Facility:** 180 rooms. Close proximity to corporate parks, attractions & shopping centers. 4 stories; interior corridors; meeting rooms; pool, whirlpool. **Dining & Entertainment:** Restaurant; 6 am-midnight; $9-$14; health conscious menu items; cocktails/lounge. **Services:** data ports, PC, secretarial services; complimentary evening beverages; valet laundry. **All Rooms:** free & pay movies, cable TV. **Some Rooms:** microwaves, refrigerators. **Cards:** AE, CB, DI, DS, JCB, MC, VI.  Ⓓ Ⓢ ⊗

**PALMER INN-BEST WESTERN**
AAA Special Value Rates
Phone: 609/452-2500

Motor Inn

Sun-Thurs [CP]   1P: $78- 92   2P/1B: $88- 102   2P/2B: $88- 102   XP: $10   F18
Fri & Sat [CP]   1P: $72   2P/1B: $72   2P/2B: $72   XP: $10   F18
**Location:** On US 1 southbound, 2 mi s of jct CR 526 & 571. 3499 US 1S 08540. Fax: 609/452-1371.
**Terms:** Reserv deposit; monthly rates; no pets. **Facility:** 105 rooms. 2 stories: interior/exterior corridors; meeting rooms; pool, sauna. **Dining & Entertainment:** Dining room; 6:30 am-9 & 11:30-2 pm, Fri & Sat-10 pm, Sat & Sun 7:30-10 am; $8-$15; health conscious menu items; cocktails/lounge. **Services:** secretarial services; valet laundry. **All Rooms:** cable TV. **Some Rooms:** coffeemakers, 6 efficiencies, microwaves, refrigerators. Fee: VCP's.
**Cards:** AE, CB, DI, DS, MC, VI.   ⓄⓈⓍ

**PRINCETON MARRIOTT FORRESTAL VILLAGE**
Rates Subject to Change
Phone: 609/452-7900

Hotel

Sun-Thurs   1P: $125   2P/1B: $125   2P/2B: $125
Fri & Sat   1P: $99   2P/1B: $99   2P/2B: $99
**Location:** On US 1 southbound, 1 1/2 mi n of CR 571. 201 Village Blvd; Forrestal V 08540.
Fax: 609/452-0927. **Terms:** Check-in 4 pm; credit card guarantee; package plans, weekend & seasonal; no pets.
**Facility:** 294 rooms. Some balconies. Many rooms overlooking the Forrestal Village. 6 stories; interior corridors; business center, conference facilities; luxury level rooms; saunas, whirlpool, small heated indoor/outdoor pool; 2 tennis courts; sports court. **Dining & Entertainment:** Dining room, restaurant; 6 am-11 pm; $7-$25; health conscious menu items; cocktails/lounge; entertainment, nightclub. **Services:** data ports, PC, secretarial services; valet laundry. **Recreation:** jogging.
**All Rooms:** free & pay movies, cable TV. **Some Rooms:** refrigerators. **Cards:** AE, CB, DI, DS, JCB, MC, VI.   ⓄⓈⓍ

**THE SCANTICON-PRINCETON CONFERENCE CENTER HOTEL**
Guaranteed Rates
Phone: 609/452-7800

Hotel

All Year   1P: $110- 145   2P/1B: $130- 160   2P/2B: $130- 160   XP: $25   F
**Location:** Off US 1, northbound 2 1/2 mi n of CR 571; in the Princeton Forrestal Center. 100 College Rd E 08540. Fax: 609/452-7883. **Terms:** Sr. discount; BP available; package plans; no pets. **Facility:** 300 rooms.
On 25 acres of peaceful wooded grounds. 3-4 stories; interior corridors; business center, conference facilities; heated indoor pool, saunas, whirlpool; 4 lighted tennis courts; health club. **Dining & Entertainment:** 2 dining rooms, coffee shop; 7-9 am, 11-2:30 & 6-11 pm; $11-$24; health conscious menu items; cocktails/lounge; also, Tivoli Gardens, The Black Swan, see separate listing. **Services:** data ports, PC, secretarial services; valet laundry; valet parking. **Recreation:** jogging. Rental: bicycles. **All Rooms:** honor bars, cable TV. Fee: movies. **Some Rooms:** kitchen, refrigerators.
Fee: VCP's. **Cards:** AE, DI, JCB, MC, VI.   ⓄⓈⓍ

**SUMMERFIELD SUITES HOTEL**
Rates Subject to Change
Phone: 609/951-0009

Suite Motel

Sun-Thurs [CP]   1P: $149   2P/1B: $149- 179   2P/2B: $179
Fri & Sat [CP]   1P: $89   2P/1B: $89- 109   2P/2B: $119
**Location:** US 1S just past Ridge Rd. 4375 US 1 S 08543. Fax: 609/951-0696. **Terms:** Credit card guarantee; weekly/monthly rates; package plans; pets, $8, also $125 dep req . **Facility:** 124 rooms. Some units with fireplace. 56 two-bedroom units. 2 stories; interior corridors; meeting rooms; pool; exercise room. **Dining:** Restaurant nearby. **Services:** data ports, secretarial services; valet laundry; area transportation, within 3-5 mi. **All Rooms:** kitchens, microwaves, free movies, refrigerators, cable TV, VCP's. **Some Rooms:** coffeemakers. **Cards:** AE, DI, DS, MC, VI.   ⓄⓈⓍ

## RESTAURANTS

**THE BLACK SWAN**
Dinner: over $31
Phone: 609/452-7800

French

**Location:** In The Scanticon-Princeton Conference Center Hotel. 100 College Rd E 08540. **Hours:** 6 pm-11 pm. Closed major holidays, Sun & Mon. **Reservations:** suggested. **Features:** semi-formal attire; health conscious menu items; cocktails & lounge; valet parking; a la carte. Intimate dining in a romantic atmosphere. Wonderfully prepared cuisine presented with an artistic flair. **Cards:** AE, CB, DI, DS, JCB, MC, VI.   Ⓧ

**CRYSTAL GARDEN RESTAURANT**
Dinner: $21-$30
Phone: 609/987-1234

American

**Location:** In the Hyatt Regency-Princeton. 102 Carnegie Ctr 08540. **Hours:** 6:30 am-11 pm. **Reservations:** suggested. **Features:** casual dress; Sunday brunch; children's menu; health conscious menu items; cocktails & lounge; valet parking; a la carte. Patio restaurant offering unique cuisine. **Cards:** AE, DI, DS, MC, VI.   Ⓧ

**LAHIERE'S**
◆◆◆
French

Dinner: $21-$30
Phone: 609/921-2798
**Location:** On Witherspoon at Nassau St (SR 27). 5-11 Witherspoon 08542. **Hours:** 11:30 am-2:30 & 5-9:30 pm, Fri-10 pm, Sat 11:30 am-2 & 5-10 pm. Closed major holidays & Sun. **Reservations:** suggested. **Features:** casual dress; health conscious menu items; cocktails & lounge; entertainment; street parking; a la carte. Located in the center of historic Princeton. Charming dining rooms attended by a cordial & accommodating staff serving intriguing French cuisine. **Cards:** AE, CB, DI, MC, VI. ⊗

**PALMER'S**
◆◆
American

Dinner: $21-$30
Phone: 609/921-7500
**Location:** In Nassau Inn. 10 Palmer Sq 08542. **Hours:** 6 pm-10 pm. **Closed:** Sun & Mon. **Reservations:** suggested. **Features:** semi-formal attire; health conscious menu items; cocktails & lounge; entertainment; street parking; a la carte. Smoke free premises. **Cards:** AE, CB, DI, MC, VI. ⊗

**THE RUSTY SCUPPER**
◆◆
Seafood

Dinner: $11-$20
Phone: 609/921-3276
**Location:** 1/2 mi e on Alexander Rd; 3/4 mi w on Alexander Rd from US 1. 378 Alexander Rd 08540. **Hours:** 11:30 am-2:30 & 5-10 pm, Fri & Sat 5 pm-11 pm, Sun 4 pm-9 pm. **Closed:** 12/25. **Reservations:** suggested; weekends. **Features:** casual dress; children's menu; health conscious menu items; carryout; salad bar; cocktails & lounge. Seasonal patio. **Cards:** AE, CB, DI, DS, MC, VI. ⊗

**TIVOLI GARDENS**
◆◆
Continental

Dinner: $11-$20
Phone: 609/452-7800
**Location:** In The Scanticon-Princeton Conference Center Hotel. 100 College Rd E 08540. **Hours:** 11 am-2:30 & 6-11 pm, Sun 6 pm-9:30 pm. **Closed:** Fri for dinner & Sat. **Reservations:** suggested. **Features:** casual dress; children's menu; health conscious menu items; cocktails & lounge; valet parking; a la carte. Luncheon buffet Mon-Fri. **Cards:** AE, CB, DI, DS, JCB, MC, VI. ⊗

# RAMSEY—13,200

## LODGINGS

**HOWARD JOHNSON MOTOR LODGE**
Ⓐ
◆◆
Motor Inn

AAA Special Value Rates
Phone: 201/327-4500
All Year          1P: $45-  80  2P/1B: $55-  90  2P/2B: $55-  90  XP: $10  F18
**Location:** From I-287, 1 1/2 mi s on SR 17 southbound. 1255 Rt 17S 07446. **Fax:** 201/327-4745. **Terms:** Credit card guarantee; weekly/monthly rates; pets. **Facility:** 50 rooms. Some rooms with balcony or patio facing interior courtyard; Japanese-American restaurant. 2 stories; exterior corridors; meeting rooms. **Dining:** Restaurant; 11:30 am-2:30 & 4:30-10 pm, Fri-Sun to 11 pm; $8-$20. **Services:** valet parking. **All Rooms:** free movies, cable TV. **Some Rooms:** microwaves. **Cards:** AE, CB, DI, DS, MC, VI. ⒹⓍ

**THE INN AT RAMSEY**
Ⓐ
◆◆◆
Motor Inn

AAA Special Value Rates
Phone: 201/327-6700
All Year          1P: $47- 110  2P/1B: $52- 110  2P/2B: $52- 110  XP: $5  F
**Location:** On SR 17. 1315 SR 17S 07446. **Fax:** 201/327-6709. **Terms:** Weekly/monthly rates; pets. **Facility:** 81 rooms. In foothills of Ramapo Mountains; specialty rooms avail, lively sports lounge. 2 stories; interior corridors; meeting rooms; pool. **Dining & Entertainment:** Restaurant; 7 am-midnight; $5-$20; cocktails/lounge; entertainment. **Services:** data ports; secretarial services; valet laundry. **All Rooms:** free movies, combo & shower baths, cable TV. **Some Rooms:** microwaves, refrigerators. Fee: VCP's, whirlpools. **Cards:** AE, CB, DI, DS, MC, VI. ⒹⓍ

**WELLESLEY INN**
◆◆
Motel

AAA Special Value Rates
Phone: 201/934-9250
All Year [CP]     1P: $55-  70  2P/1B: $57-  72  2P/2B: $57-  75  XP: $5  F18
**Location:** Rt 17 at Airmont Rd. 946 Rt 17N 07446. **Fax:** 201/934-9719. **Terms:** Pets, $5. **Facility:** 90 rooms. 3 stories; interior corridors. **Dining:** Restaurant nearby. **Services:** data ports, secretarial services; valet laundry. **All Rooms:** coffeemakers, free & pay movies, combo & shower baths, cable TV. **Some Rooms:** refrigerators. **Cards:** AE, CB, DI, DS, JCB, MC, VI. ⒹⓈⓍ

## RESTAURANTS

**CAFE PANCHE**
◆◆◆
French

Dinner: $21-$30
Phone: 201/934-0030
**Location:** Center. 130 E Main 07446. **Hours:** noon-2:30 & 5:30-9 pm, Fri-10 pm, Sat seatings at 6:30 pm & 9 pm, Sun 5 pm-8 pm. Closed major holidays. **Reservations:** suggested. **Features:** semi-formal attire; health conscious menu items; a la carte. Intimate dining room. **Cards:** AE, CB, DI, MC, VI. ⊗

**EL TORITO**
◆
Mexican

Dinner: up to $10
Phone: 201/327-5331
**Location:** SR 17 northbound, 1 mi s of Franklin Tpk. 706 SR 17 07446. **Hours:** 11:30 am-10:30 pm, Fri & Sat-midnight, Sun 11 am-10 pm. **Closed:** 11/24 & 12/25. **Reservations:** suggested; weekends. **Features:** casual dress; Sunday brunch; children's menu; health conscious menu items; carryout; cocktails & lounge. **Cards:** AE, CB, DI, DS, MC, VI. ⊗

**GUILIO'S RISTORANTE**
◆◆
Italian

Dinner: $11-$20
Phone: 201/327-4772
**Location:** On SR 17N, just n of Franklin Tpk. 1206 Rt 17N 07446. **Hours:** noon-3 & 5-10 pm, Fri & Sat-11 pm, Sun 1 pm-9 pm. **Closed:** 12/25. **Reservations:** suggested; weekends. **Features:** casual dress; children's menu; health conscious menu items; carryout; cocktails & lounge. Fine pasta & veal dishes; casual dining atmosphere & friendly staff. **Cards:** AE, MC, VI. ⊗

# RANDOLPH

## RESTAURANT

**CASA DE PASTA**
◆◆
Italian

Dinner: $11-$20
Phone: 201/584-3700
**Location:** 1/4 mi n jct Dover-Chester Rd & Sussex Tpk. 1438 Sussex Tpk 07969. **Hours:** 11:30 am-3:30 & 5-11 pm, Sat 5 pm-11 pm, Sun 4 pm-10 pm. **Closed:** Mon, 11/23, 12/25, & 12/24 for dinner. **Features:** casual dress; health conscious menu items; carryout; cocktails & lounge. Bustling rustic inn. **Cards:** AE, DS, MC, VI.

# RED BANK—10,600

## LODGINGS

**COURTYARD BY MARRIOTT**
◆◆◆
Motor Inn

Rates Subject to Change
Phone: 908/530-5552
Fri & Sat 5/1-10/31   1P: $95      2P/1B: $95      2P/2B: $100   XP: $10  F16
Sun-Thurs             1P: $87      2P/1B: $97      2P/2B: $97    XP: $10  F16
Fri & Sat 11/1-4/30   1P: $70-  80  2P/1B: $70-  80  2P/2B: $70-  80  XP: $10  F16
**Location:** 1/4 mi e of Garden State Pkwy, exit 109. 245 Half Mile Rd 07701. **Fax:** 908/530-5756. **Terms:** Sr. discount; check-in 4 pm; reserv deposit; no pets. **Facility:** 146 rooms. In rural setting. 3 stories; interior corridors; meeting rooms; heated indoor pool, whirlpool; exercise room. **Dining:** Restaurant; 6:30 am-9:30 & 5-10 pm, Sat & Sun 7:30 am-1 & 6-10 pm; $9-$14; cocktails. **Services:** data ports; valet laundry. Fee: childcare. **All Rooms:** free & pay movies, cable TV. **Some Rooms:** refrigerators. **Cards:** AE, DI, DS, MC, VI. *(See color ad p A55)*   ⒹⓈⓍ

**THE OYSTER POINT HOTEL**
◆◆◆ All Year     Rates Subject to Change     Phone: 908/530-8200
Motor Inn.    1P: $95- 115   2P/1B: $95- 115   2P/2B: $95- 115
**Location:** 1 blk from SR 35 on Navesink River. 146 Bodman Place 07701. **Fax:** 908/747-1875. **Terms:** Credit card guarantee; package plans, weekends; no pets. **Facility:** 58 rooms. On the Navesink River. 5 stories; interior corridors; beachfront; whirlpool; boat dock, marina; exercise room. **Dining:** Dining room; 6:30 am-9:30 pm, Fri & Sat-10 pm; $10-$25; cocktails. **Services:** PC, secretarial services; valet laundry. **Fee:** childcare. **Recreation:** fishing. **All Rooms:** coffeemakers, free movies, cable TV. **Some Rooms:** honor bars, refrigerators, whirlpools. **Cards:** AE, DI, DS, MC, VI.     ⒹⓈ

## ROCHELLE PARK—5,600    (See NEWARK to PARAMUS ACCOMMODATIONS spotting map page A44; see index starting on page A42)

### LODGING

**RAMADA HOTEL**
Ⓐ    Rates Subject to Change     Phone: 201/845-3400   ㊼
Mon-Thurs    1P: $90- 118   2P/1B: $110- 138   2P/2B: $110- 138   XP: $10   F18
Fri-Sun    1P: $60- 95   2P/1B: $60- 95   2P/2B: $60- 95   XP: $10   F18
◆◆◆ Motor Inn   **Location:** At Garden State Pkwy exit 160 northbound; from exit 163 southbound, 3/4 mi s on SR 17, exit Century Rd, 1 mi to Paramus Rd, then left 1 1/2 mi n. 375 W Passaic St 07662. **Fax:** 201/845-0412. **Terms:** Credit card guarantee; pets. **Facility:** 175 rooms. 5 stories; interior corridors; conference facilities; heated indoor pool; exercise room. **Dining & Entertainment:** Dining room; 7 am-10 pm; $9-$22; cocktails; entertainment. **Services:** secretarial services; valet laundry. **All Rooms:** free & pay movies, cable TV. **Some Rooms:** 2 efficiencies, microwaves, refrigerators. **Cards:** AE, CB, DI, DS, MC, VI.     Ⓓ⊘

## ROCKAWAY—6,200    (See NEW JERSEY METRO AREA ACCOMMODATIONS spotting map pages A40 & A41; see index starting on page A39)

### LODGINGS

**HOWARD JOHNSON LODGE**
Ⓐ    AAA Special Value Rates     Phone: 201/625-1200   ㊺
All Year    1P: $66- 79   2P/1B: $76- 89   2P/2B: $76- 89   XP: $10   F
◆◆ Motel   **Location:** I-80, exit 37, 1/4 mi n. 14 Green Pond Rd 07866. **Fax:** 201/625-1200. **Terms:** Weekly/monthly rates; small pets only. **Facility:** 64 rooms. 2 stories; interior corridors; pool. **Dining:** Restaurants nearby. **Services:** data ports; valet laundry. **All Rooms:** free & pay movies, cable TV. **Some Rooms:** microwaves, refrigerators. **Cards:** AE, CB, DI, DS, MC, VI.     Ⓓ⊘

**MOUNTAIN INN OF ROCKAWAY**
Ⓐ    AAA Special Value Rates     Phone: 201/627-8310   ㊻
Sun-Thurs [CP]    1P: $40- 60   2P/1B: $40- 60   2P/2B: $45- 60   XP: $5   F12
Fri & Sat [CP]    1P: $40- 50   2P/1B: $40- 50   2P/2B: $40- 50
◆◆ Motel   **Location:** From I-80, Denville exit to Rt 46, w 1 mi. 156 Rt 46E 07866 (Rt 46). **Fax:** 201/627-0556. **Terms:** Credit card guarantee; weekly/monthly rates; no pets. **Facility:** 110 rooms. 16 efficiencies, $5 extra; 12 apartments with kitchen, $65; 2 stories; interior corridors; meeting rooms; pool. **Dining:** Restaurant; $10-$20; health conscious menu items; cocktails. **Services:** valet laundry. **All Rooms:** free movies, cable TV. **Some Rooms:** refrigerators. **Cards:** AE, DI, DS, MC, VI.     Ⓓ⊘

## ROSELLE PARK

### RESTAURANT

**COSTAS RESTAURANT**
◆◆ Italian    Dinner: $11-$20     Phone: 908/241-1131
**Location:** Garden State Pkwy exit 137, 1 1/4 mi e on SR 28, 1/2 blk n. 120 Chestnut St 07204. **Hours:** noon-3 & 5-10 pm, Sat 4 pm-11 pm, Sun 2 pm-10 pm. Closed: 1/1 & 12/25. **Reservations:** suggested; weekends. **Features:** casual dress; children's menu; health conscious menu items; carryout; cocktails & lounge; street parking; a la carte. Casual elegance serving freshly prepared cuisine. Banquet hall. **Cards:** AE, DI, MC, VI.

## RUMSON

### RESTAURANT

**FROMAGERIE**
◆◆◆ French    Dinner: $21-$30     Phone: 908/842-8088
**Location:** Jct SR 34 (Ridge Rd) & Two Rivers Ave. 26 Ridge Rd 07760. **Hours:** 11:30 am-2:30 & 5-10 pm, Fri & Sat-11 pm, Sun 4 pm-10 pm. Closed: 12/25. **Reservations:** suggested. **Features:** semi-formal attire; cocktails. Warm rustic elegance for fine dining. Comfortable yet professional wait staff. Excellent wine list. Our own great desserts. **Cards:** AE, DI, MC, VI.

## RUNNEMEDE—9,000    (See PHILADELPHIA & VICINITY ACCOMMODATIONS spotting map pages A196 & A197; see index starting on page A193)

### LODGING

**COMFORT INN**
Ⓐ    Guaranteed Rates     Phone: 609/939-6700   ⑮
All Year [CP]    1P: $45- 90   2P/1B: $50- 95   2P/2B: $55- 95   XP: $5   F18
◆◆ Motel   **Location:** 1/4 mi se on SR 168, from NJ Tpk, exit 3; 2 blks e on 9th Ave; 1 mi se of I-295, Mt Emphraim-Runnemede exit 28. 101 9th Ave 08078. **Fax:** 609/939-6700. **Terms:** Sr. discount; reserv deposit, 5 day notice; weekly/monthly rates; small pets only, $5. **Facility:** 42 rooms. 2 stories; interior corridors; meeting rooms; exercise room. **Dining:** Restaurant nearby. **Services:** data ports. **All Rooms:** free movies, cable TV. **Some Rooms:** microwaves, refrigerators, whirlpools. **Fee:** VCP's. **Cards:** AE, CB, DI, DS, JCB, MC, VI. *(See color ad p A199)*     Ⓓ⊘

## SADDLE BROOK—13,300   (See NEWARK to PARAMUS ACCOMMODATIONS spotting map page A44; see index starting on page A42)

### LODGINGS

**HOLIDAY INN AND CONFERENCE CENTER**   Guaranteed Rates   Phone: 201/843-0600   **49**
◆◆◆    Mon-Thurs   1P: $83   2P/1B: $83   2P/2B: $83
Hotel    Fri-Sun   1P: $65   2P/1B: $65   2P/2B: $65
**Location:** I-80 exit 62, to Midland Ave, Garden State Pkwy exit 159, direction Saddle Brook, e 1 blk on Kenny Pl. 50 Kenney Pl 07662. Fax: 201/843-7172. **Terms:** Sr. discount; reserv deposit, 3 day notice; BP available; small pets only. **Facility:** 144 rooms. Rooftop nightclub with panoramic view of skyline. 12 stories; interior corridors; conference facilities; pool, wading pool; exercise room. **Dining & Entertainment:** Restaurant; 6:30 am-10 pm; $9-$17; cocktails/lounge; entertainment, nightclub. **Services:** data ports, secretarial services; valet laundry; area transportation, local shops & restaurants. Fee: airport transportation. **All Rooms:** coffeemakers, free & pay movies, cable TV. **Some Rooms:** refrigerators. **Cards:** AE, CB, DI, DS, MC, VI.   Ⓓ Ⓢ ⊗

**HOWARD JOHNSON PLAZA HOTEL**   Rates Subject to Change   Phone: 201/845-7800   **51**
◆◆    Mon-Thurs [CP]   1P: $69- 99   2P/1B: $79- 99   2P/2B: $79- 99   XP: $10   F18
Hotel    Fri-Sun [CP]   1P: $64   2P/1B: $74   2P/2B: $74   XP: $10   F18
**Location:** Jct I-80 exit 62 direction Saddle Brook, right at Pehle Ave E; Garden State Pkwy exit 159, direction Saddle Brook. 129 Pehle Ave 07663. Fax: 201/845-7061. **Terms:** Sr. discount; reserv deposit, 10 day notice; weekly rates; pets. **Facility:** 147 rooms. Some smaller rooms. 8 stories; interior corridors; conference facilities; heated indoor pool, wading pool, sauna, steamroom; health club. **Dining & Entertainment:** Restaurant; 7 am-10:30 pm; $8-$20; health conscious menu items; cocktails/lounge. **Services:** data ports, PC, secretarial services; valet laundry; area transportation, airport transportation. Fee: massage. **All Rooms:** free & pay movies, cable TV. **Some Rooms:** coffeemakers, microwaves, refrigerators, whirlpools. Fee: VCP's. **Cards:** AE, DI, DS, MC; VI.   Ⓓ Ⓢ ⊗

**MARRIOTT HOTEL**   Rates Subject to Change   Phone: 201/843-9500   **50**
◆◆◆    Sun-Thurs   1P: $115   2P/1B: $115   2P/2B: $115   XP: $20   F
Hotel    Fri & Sat   1P: $74- 84   2P/1B: $74- 84   2P/2B: $74- 84   XP: $20   F
**Location:** I-80, exit 62 (Midland Ave) & Garden State Pkwy, exit 159. Jct I-80 & Garden State Pkwy 07662. Fax: 201/843-3539. **Terms:** Sr. discount; reserv deposit; package plans; pets, $25. **Facility:** 281 rooms. 12 stories; interior corridors; conference facilities; 2 pools (2 heated, 1 indoor), saunas, whirlpool; exercise room. **Dining & Entertainment:** Restaurant; 6:30 am-midnight; $7-$22; cocktails/lounge. **Services:** PC, secretarial services; valet laundry. Fee: childcare, area transportation, airport transportation. **All Rooms:** coffeemakers, free & pay movies, cable TV. **Some Rooms:** microwaves, refrigerators. **Cards:** AE, CB, DI, DS, JCB, MC, VI.   Ⓓ Ⓢ ⊗

## SCOTCH PLAINS   (See NEW JERSEY METRO AREA ACCOMMODATIONS spotting map pages A40 & A41; see index starting on page A39)

### RESTAURANT

**STAGE HOUSE INN**   Historical   Dinner: over $31   Phone: 908/322-4224   **171**
◆◆◆    **Location:** Corner Park Ave & Front St, 1/4 mi e jct US 22. 366 Park Ave 07076. **Hours:** 11:30 am-2:30 &
American    5:30-9:30 pm, Fri-10 pm. Sat 5:30 pm-10 pm, Sun 4 pm-8 pm. Closed major holidays & Mon. **Reservations:** suggested. **Features:** semi-formal attire; health conscious menu items; cocktails & lounge; a la carte. A 1746 stagecoach retreat. Converted into a charming inn with an elegantly appointed dining room creating a romantic mood to enjoy wonderfully prepared cuisine. **Cards:** AE, DS, MC, VI.   ⊗

## SECAUCUS—14,100   (See NEWARK to PARAMUS ACCOMMODATIONS spotting map page A44; see index starting on page A42)

### LODGINGS

**COURTYARD BY MARRIOTT**   AAA Special Value Rates   Phone: 201/617-8888   **55**
Ⓐ    All Year   1P: $99   2P/1B: $109   2P/2B: $109   XP: $10   F18
Hotel    **Location:** Between the eastern & western spurs of NJ Tpk exits 16E, 17, or 16W via SR 3 to Harmon Meadow Blvd. 455 Harmon Meadow Blvd 07094. Fax: 201/617-0035. **Terms:** Credit card guarantee; no pets. **Facility:** 165 rooms. 7 stories; interior corridors; meeting rooms; exercise room. Fee: passes for nearby health club. **Dining & Entertainment:** Restaurant; 6:30 am-11 pm, Sat & Sun from 7 am; $7-$9; cocktails/lounge. **Services:** data ports; valet laundry. Fee: airport transportation. **All Rooms:** coffeemakers, free & pay movies, safes, cable TV. **Some Rooms:** microwaves. Fee: refrigerators. **Cards:** AE, DI, DS, MC, VI.
*(See color ad p A57)*   Ⓓ Ⓢ ⊗

**EMBASSY SUITES-MEADOWLANDS**   Rates Subject to Change   Phone: 201/864-7300   **65**
◆◆◆    Sun-Thurs [BP]   1P: $119- 159   2P/1B: $119- 159   2P/2B: $129- 179   XP: $10   F12
Suite Hotel    Fri & Sat [BP]   1P: $109   2P/1B: $109   2P/2B: $119   XP: $10   F12
**Location:** Between eastern & western spurs of NJ Tpk exits 16E, 17, or 16W via SR 3, exit Harmon Meadow Blvd. 455 Plaza Dr 07094. Fax: 201/864-5391. **Terms:** Reserv deposit; no pets. **Facility:** 261 rooms. Beautiful atrium area, highlighted by tropical plants & waterfall makes for a relaxing, charming stay. 2 two-bedroom units. 9 stories; interior corridors; business center, meeting rooms; heated indoor pool, sauna, whirlpool; exercise room. **Dining & Entertainment:** Dining room; 6 am-9:30 & 11:30-11 pm, Sat & Sun 7 am-10:30 & 11:30-11 pm; $7-$20; health conscious menu items; cocktails/lounge. **Services:** data ports, PC, secretarial services; complimentary evening beverages; valet laundry. Fee: childcare. **All Rooms:** microwaves, free & pay movies, refrigerators, cable TV. **Some Rooms:** coffeemakers, 235 efficiencies, VCP's. **Cards:** AE, CB, DI, DS, JCB, MC, VI.   Ⓓ Ⓢ ⊗

**HAMPTON INN**   Rates Subject to Change   Phone: 201/867-4400   **59**
◆◆◆    Sun-Thurs [CP]   1P: $72   2P/1B: $82   2P/2B: $82
Motel    Fri & Sat [CP]   1P: $68   2P/1B: $68   2P/2B: $68
**Location:** Eastern Tpk spur, northbound exit 16E, southbound exit 17, 1/4 mi w on SR 3. 250 Harmon Meadow Blvd 07094. Fax: 201/865-7932. **Terms:** Sr. discount; no pets. **Facility:** 151 rooms. Close access into New York City via Lincoln Tunnel. 5 stories; interior corridors; sauna; exercise room. **Dining:** Restaurants nearby. **Services:** data ports; valet laundry. **All Rooms:** free & pay movies, cable TV. **Cards:** AE, CB, DI, DS, MC, VI.   Ⓓ Ⓢ ⊗

---

Look for the Ⓐ in our listings!

**(See NEWARK to PARAMUS ACCOMMODATIONS spotting map page A44)**

**THE HOLIDAY INN HARMON MEADOW**   Rates Subject to Change   Phone: 201/348-2000   **57**
◆◆◆   7/1-9/6 & 1/1-3/15 &   1P:  $89- 105  2P/1B:  $99- 115  2P/2B:  $99- 115  XP: $10  F12
Hotel   5/1-6/30, 9/7-12/31 &
   3/16-4/30   1P: $105   2P/1B: $115   2P/2B: $115   XP: $10  F12
**Location:** Between eastern & western spurs of NJ Tpk, exits 16E, 17, or 16W via SR 3 to Harmon Meadow Blvd. 300 Plaza Dr 07094. Fax: 201/348-6035. **Terms:** Sr. discount; reserv deposit, 30 day notice; weekly/monthly rates; BP available; small pets only. **Facility:** 160 rooms. Spacious accomodations, a stylish atmosphere; adjacent to Harmon Meadow Convention Center & Shopping Mall. 8 stories; interior corridors; conference facilities, convention oriented; exercise room. Fee: parking. **Dining & Entertainment:** Restaurant, cafeteria; 6:30 am-10 pm; $6-$18; health conscious menu items; cocktails/lounge. **Services:** data ports, PC, secretarial services; health club privileges; valet laundry; area transportation, to shopping & businesses. Fee: airport transportation. **All Rooms:** free & pay movies, cable TV. **Some Rooms:** coffeemakers, microwaves, refrigerators. **Cards:** AE, CB, DI, DS, MC, VI.   ⒹⓈ⊗

**HOWARD JOHNSON**   AAA Special Value Rates   Phone: 201/864-1400   **61**
Ⓐ   All Year   1P:  $55- 70  2P/1B:  $60- 75  2P/2B:  $70- 85  XP: $10  F18
   **Location:** Service road off Rt 3 to NJ Tpk. 875 Patterson Plank Rd 07094. Fax: 201/864-9845. **Terms:** No
◆◆   pets. **Facility:** 62 rooms. On busy road. Close to large shopping & entertainment centers. 2 stories; interior
Motel   corridors; pool, wading pool. **Dining:** Restaurant nearby. **Services:** data ports; valet laundry.
   **All Rooms:** free movies, cable TV. **Cards:** AE, DI, DS, JCB, MC, VI.   Ⓓ⊗

**MEADOWLANDS HILTON**   AAA Special Value Rates   Phone: 201/348-6900   **58**
Ⓐ   Sun-Thurs 1/1-4/30   1P: $150   2P/1B: $150   2P/2B: $150   XP: $10  F17
   Sun-Thurs 5/1-12/31   1P: $145   2P/1B: $145   2P/2B: $145   XP: $10  F17
◆◆◆   Fri & Sat 1/1-4/30   1P:  $99   2P/1B:  $99   2P/2B:  $99   XP: $10  F17
Hotel   Fri & Sat 5/1-12/31   1P:  $84   2P/1B:  $84   2P/2B:  $84   XP: $10  F17
   **Location:** Between eastern & western spurs of NJ Tpk exits 16E, 17 or 16W via SR 3 exit Meadowlands Pkwy. 2 Harmon Plaza 07094. Fax: 201/348-4436. **Terms:** Small pets only, cannot be left unattended. **Facility:** 296 rooms. Comfortable accommodations in a vibrant atmosphere; overlooks Meadowlands Sports Complex. 14 stories; interior corridors; business center, conference facilities, convention oriented; pool, sauna, whirlpool; exercise room. **Dining & Entertainment:** Dining room; 6:30 am-11 pm; $12-$21; health conscious menu items; cocktails/lounge. **Services:** data ports, PC, secretarial services; valet laundry; valet parking. Fee: childcare, airport transportation. **Recreation:** jogging. **All Rooms:** free & pay movies, cable TV. **Some Rooms:** coffeemakers, refrigerators. **Cards:** AE, CB, DI, DS, JCB, MC, VI.
*(See ad p 28)*   ⒹⓈ⊗

**RAMADA PLAZA SUITE HOTEL**   Rates Subject to Change   Phone: 201/863-8700   **54**
Ⓐ   Sun-Thurs   1P: $119- 149  2P/1B: $129- 159  2P/2B: $129- 159  XP: $20  F18
◆◆◆   Fri & Sat   1P:  $99- 129  2P/1B:  $99- 129  2P/2B:  $99- 129  XP: $20  F18
Hotel   **Location:** In Mill Creek Mall, between eastern & western spurs of NJ Tpk exits 16E, 17 or 16W via SR 3 & Harmon Meadow Blvd. 350 Rt 3W, Mill Creek Dr 07094. Fax: 201/863-6209. **Terms:** Sr. discount; reserv deposit, 7 day notice; package plans; small pets only. **Facility:** 151 rooms. Spacious accommodations in a friendly atmosphere. Central location in large shopping center. 9 stories; interior corridors; conference facilities; luxury level rooms; heated indoor pool; exercise room. **Dining & Entertainment:** Dining room; 6:30 am-3 & 4-10 pm; $9-$20; health conscious menu items; cocktails/lounge. **Services:** data ports, secretarial services; complimentary evening beverages; valet laundry; area transportation, to local businesses. Fee: airport transportation. **All Rooms:** coffeemakers, free & pay movies, refrigerators, cable TV. **Some Rooms:** 50 efficiencies, microwaves, whirlpools. **Cards:** AE, DI, MC, VI.   ⒹⓈ⊗

**RED ROOF INN**   Rates Subject to Change   Phone: 201/319-1000   **56**
◆◆   All Year   1P:  $50- 68  2P/1B:  $58- 76  2P/2B:  $64- 83  XP: $8  F18
Motel   **Location:** Between eastern & western spurs of NJ Tpk, exits 16E, 17 or 16W via SR3 exit Meadowlands Pkwy. 15 Meadowlands Pkwy 07094. Fax: 201/319-1097. **Terms:** Credit card guarantee; small pets only. **Facility:** 172 rooms. Access to Manhattan via the Lincoln Tunnel. 3 stories; exterior corridors. **Dining:** Restaurants nearby. **Services:** data ports. **All Rooms:** free movies. **Some Rooms:** microwaves, refrigerators. **Cards:** AE, CB, DI, DS, MC, VI.   Ⓓ⊗

## SHORT HILLS (See NEW JERSEY METRO AREA ACCOMMODATIONS spotting map pages A40 & A41; see index starting on page A39)

### LODGING

**HILTON AT SHORT HILLS**          Rates Subject to Change          **Phone:** 201/379-0100  🖼73
All Year                    1P: $205- 265   2P/1B: $225- 285   2P/2B: $225- 285   XP: $20   F18
**Location:** Exit 142 off Garden State Pkwy to I-78W, 4 mi then exit SR 24, 2 1/2 mi to Kennedy Pkwy exit.
◆◆◆◆ 41 John F Kennedy Pkwy 07078. **Fax:** 201/379-6870. **Terms:** Weekly/monthly rates; package plans,
Hotel            weekends; no pets. **Facility:** 300 rooms. Tranquil setting backs onto a forested wetlands refuge. Gracious
public areas with stunning floral displays. Outstanding room appointments. 8 stories; interior corridors; business center, conference facilities; luxury level rooms; 2 pools (1 heated, 1 indoor), saunas, whirlpool; health club, aerobic instruction. Fee: personal trainer. **Dining:** Afternoon tea; also, The Dining Room, The Terrace, see separate listing. **Services:** data ports, PC; valet laundry; area transportation, to mall, airport transportation, to Newark Airport. Fee: childcare; massage; valet parking. **All Rooms:** free & pay movies, cable TV. **Some Rooms:** 5 efficiencies, refrigerators. Fee: VCP's.
**Cards:** AE, CB, DI, DS, JCB, MC, VI. *(See color ad p A45 & ad p 28)*          🖼 Ⓓ Ⓢ ⊗

### RESTAURANTS

**THE DINING ROOM**          **Dinner:** over $31          **Phone:** 201/379-0100  🖼73
**Location:** In Hilton at Short Hills. 41 John F Kennedy Pkwy 07078. **Hours:** 5:30 pm-11 pm, Sat 6 pm-11
◆◆◆◆◆ pm. Closed: Sun & Mon. **Reservations:** required. **Features:** health conscious menu items; cocktails &
Continental     lounge; street parking & valet parking; a la carte. Intimate, formal dining room. Harpist provides peaceful
background music nightly. Imaginative menu reflects seasonal influences with stunning food presentations.
**Cards:** AE, CB, DI, DS, JCB, MC, VI.          ⊗

**THE TERRACE**          **Dinner:** over $31          **Phone:** 201/379-0100  🖼74
◆◆◆ **Location:** In Hilton at Short Hills. 41 John F Kennedy Pkwy 07078. **Hours:** 6:30 am-11 pm.
Continental  **Reservations:** required; for brunch. **Features:** casual dress; children's menu; health conscious menu items;
cocktails & lounge; valet parking; a la carte. Elegant, multi-purpose restaurant offers a casual atmosphere
with a formal edge. Extensive menu selection to suit all tastes. Stunning food presentations. Lavish Sun brunch buffet.
**Cards:** AE, CB, DI, DS, JCB, MC, VI.          ⊗

## SHREWSBURY—3,100

### RESTAURANT

**THE SHADOWBROOK RESTAURANT**          **Dinner:** over $31          **Phone:** 908/747-0200
◆◆◆ **Location:** 1/2 blk n of jct White St & SR 35. SR 35 07702. **Hours:** 5:30 pm-9 pm, Sat-10 pm, Sun 3 pm-9
Continental  pm. Closed: Mon & 12/24. **Reservations:** suggested. **Features:** semi-formal attire; children's menu; health
conscious menu items; cocktails & lounge; valet parking; a la carte. Oak & Regency rooms in converted
Georgian mansion overlooking gardens. **Cards:** AE, MC, VI.

## SMITHVILLE

### RESTAURANT

**SMITHVILLE INN**  Historical          **Dinner:** $21-$30          **Phone:** 609/652-7777
◆◆ **Location:** On US 9, n of jct CR 561A; southbound exit 48 off Garden State Pkwy. 3 N New York Rd 08201.
American  **Hours:** noon-9 pm, Sun 10 am-2 pm. Closed: 12/25. **Reservations:** suggested; for dinner. **Features:** casual
dress; Sunday brunch; children's menu; cocktails & lounge; a la carte. Charming country inn with Early
American atmosphere. Smoking permitted in lounge only. Dining room is smoke free. **Cards:** AE, DI, MC, VI.

## SOMERSET

### LODGINGS

**HOLIDAY INN-SOMERSET**          AAA Special Value Rates          **Phone:** 908/356-1700
Mon-Thurs              1P: $95- 99   2P/1B: $95- 99   2P/2B: $95- 99
Fri-Sun                1P: $79- 99   2P/1B: $79- 99   2P/2B: $79- 99
◆◆◆ **Location:** From I-287 exit 6, 1/4 mi n on CR 527, (direction Bound Brook) then 1/2 mi w on Davidson Ave.
Hotel      195 Davidson Ave 08873. **Fax:** 908/356-0939. **Terms:** Credit card guarantee, 7 day notice; package plans;
pets. **Facility:** 280 rooms. 6 stories; interior corridors; conference facilities; pool; exercise room. **Dining &
Entertainment:** Dining room; 6:30 am-10:30 pm; $10-$20; health conscious menu items; cocktails/lounge. **Services:** data
ports, secretarial services; valet laundry; area transportation, to businesses. Fee: airport transportation.
**All Rooms:** coffeemakers, free & pay movies, cable TV. **Some Rooms:** microwaves, refrigerators. **Cards:** AE, CB, DI, DS,
JCB, MC, VI. *(See ad below)*          Ⓓ Ⓢ ⊗

**MADISON SUITES HOTEL**          Rates Subject to Change          **Phone:** 908/563-1000
Sun-Thurs [BP]        1P: $85- 105   2P/1B: $85- 105   2P/2B:  $85- 105   XP: $10   F18
Fri & Sat [BP]        1P: $65- 85    2P/1B: $65- 85    2P/2B:  $65- 85    XP: $10   F18
◆◆◆ **Location:** I-287, exit 6; 1/4 mi se on CR 527 (direction New Brunswick) to Cedar Grove Ln. 25 Cedar Grove
Motel      Ln 08873. **Fax:** 908/563-0352. **Terms:** Sr. discount; credit card guarantee, 3 day notice; weekly/monthly
rates; AP available; no pets. **Facility:** 83 rooms. 2 stories; interior corridors; meeting rooms. **Dining:** Dining
room; 6:30 am-10 am, Sat & Sun from 8 am, room service 5 pm-10 pm. **Services:** data ports, secretarial services; valet
laundry. **All Rooms:** coffeemakers, free movies, cable TV. **Some Rooms:** 40 efficiencies, microwaves, refrigerators.
**Cards:** AE, CB, DI, MC, VI.          Ⓓ ⊗

**QUALITY INN-SOMERSET**  AAA Special Value Rates  **Phone:** 908/469-5050
All Year  1P: $55- 68  2P/1B: $55- 68  2P/2B: $62  XP: $5
**Location:** Just s of I-287, exit 6; (direction New Brunswick) on CR 527. 1850 Easton Ave 08873.
Fax: 908/469-6870. **Terms:** Monthly rates; no pets. **Facility:** 112 rooms. 2 stories; interior/exterior corridors;
Motor Inn  conference facilities; heated indoor pool, saunas, whirlpool. **Dining & Entertainment:** Dining room; 6:30
am-2 & 5-10 pm, Sun-9 pm; $6-$12; health conscious menu items; cocktails/lounge. **Services:** data ports,
secretarial services; health club privileges; valet laundry. Fee: childcare. **All Rooms:** free movies, cable TV.
**Some Rooms:** 6 efficiencies, microwaves, refrigerators. **Cards:** AE, CB, DI, DS, MC, VI.  (D) ⊗

**RADISSON HOTEL SOMERSET**  Rates Subject to Change  **Phone:** 908/469-2600
All Year  1P: $105  2P/1B: $120  2P/2B: $120  XP: $15
**Location:** From I-287 exit 6; 1/4 mi n on CR 527, then 1/2 mi w on Davidson Ave; in Atrium Corp Park. 200
Hotel  Atrium Dr 08873. Fax: 908/469-4617. **Terms:** Credit card guarantee; package plans, weekends & seasonal;
small pets only, $50 dep req. **Facility:** 361 rooms. Enjoy contemporary accommodations in an inviting atmos-
phere. 6 stories; interior corridors; business center, conference facilities, convention oriented; luxury level
rooms; 2 pools (1 heated, 1 indoor), saunas, whirlpool; 2 lighted tennis courts; exercise room. **Dining & Entertainment:**
Dining room, 2 restaurants; 6:30 am-11:30 pm; $11-$25; health conscious menu items; cocktails/lounge; Sun brunch;
entertainment. **Services:** data ports, PC, secretarial services; valet laundry; area transportation. Fee: airport transportation,
to local businesses. **Recreation:** jogging. **All Rooms:** free & pay movies, cable TV. **Some Rooms:** coffeemakers,
refrigerators. **Cards:** AE, CB, DI, DS, MC, VI.  (D)(S)⊗

**RAMADA INN SOMERSET**  AAA Special Value Rates  **Phone:** 908/560-9880
Mon-Thurs  1P: $70- 100  2P/1B: $80- 110  2P/2B: $60- 100  XP: $10  F18
Motor Inn  Fri-Sun  1P: $49- 70  2P/1B: $59- 69  2P/2B: $49- 70  XP: $10  F18
**Location:** Just w of I-287 exit 7. Weston Canal Rd & Rt 287 08873 (60 Cottontail Ln). Fax: 908/356-7455.
**Terms:** Monthly rates; package plans, weekends; small pets only. **Facility:** 126 rooms. Corporate property accomodating local
area business travelers; located at interstate ramp. 5 stories; interior corridors; conference facilities; heated indoor pool, sauna;
exercise room. **Dining & Entertainment:** Dining room; 6:30 am-10 pm, Sat & Sun from 7 am; $9-$20; health conscious
menu items; cocktails/lounge. **Services:** data ports, secretarial services; valet laundry; area transportation, to local
businesses. Fee: childcare, airport transportation. **All Rooms:** coffeemakers, free & pay movies, refrigerators, cable TV.
**Some Rooms:** 7 efficiencies, microwaves. **Cards:** AE, CB, DI, DS, MC, VI.  (D)⊗

**SOMERSET MARRIOTT HOTEL**  Rates Subject to Change  **Phone:** 908/560-0500
Sun-Thurs  1P: $120- 135  2P/1B: $120- 135  2P/2B: $120- 135  XP: $15  F16
Hotel  Fri & Sat  1P: $99  2P/1B: $99  2P/2B: $99  XP: $15  F16
**Location:** From I-287 exit 6, 1/4 mi n on CR 527, (direction Bound Brook) then 1/4 mi w on Davidson Ave.
110 Davidson Ave 08873. Fax: 908/560-3669. **Terms:** Credit card guarantee; no pets. **Facility:** 434 rooms. 3-11 stories; interior corridors; conference facilities; luxury level rooms; heated indoor/outdoor pool, saunas, whirlpool; 2 lighted tennis courts;
exercise room. **Dining & Entertainment:** 2 dining rooms; 6:30 am-10 pm; $6-$29; health conscious menu items;
cocktails/lounge; entertainment. **Services:** data ports, secretarial services; valet laundry; area transportation. Fee: airport
transportation. **All Rooms:** free & pay movies, cable TV. **Some Rooms:** refrigerators. **Cards:** AE, CB, DI, DS, JCB, MC, VI.
(D)(S)⊗

**SUMMERFIELD SUITES HOTEL**  Rates Subject to Change  **Phone:** 908/356-8000
All Year [CP]  1P: $95- 170  2P/1B: $95- 170  2P/2B: $95- 170
Suite Motel  **Location:** I-287 exit 6, to Davidson Ave, 1/4 mi n. 260 Davidson Ave 08873. Fax: 908/356-0782.
**Terms:** Check-in 4 pm; credit card guarantee; small pets only, $5, also $100 dep req. **Facility:** 140 rooms. 85
two-bedroom units. 2 stories; interior/exterior corridors; meeting rooms; heated pool, whirlpool; exercise room, sports court.
**Services:** data ports, secretarial services; valet laundry; area transportation, to local businesses. Fee: childcare.
**All Rooms:** coffeemakers, kitchens, microwaves, free movies, refrigerators, cable TV, VCP's. **Cards:** AE, CB, DI, DS, MC,
VI.  (D)(S)⊗

## RESTAURANT

**THE MCATEERS**  Dinner: $11-$20  **Phone:** 908/469-2522
Continental  **Location:** I-287 exit 6, direction New Brunswick, 3/4 mi s. 1714 Easton Ave 08873. **Hours:** 11:30 am-3:30 &
5-10:30 pm, Fri-11:30 pm, Sat 5 pm-11:30 pm, Sun 1 pm-9 pm. Closed: 12/25. **Reservations:** suggested.
**Features:** casual dress; children's menu; early bird specials; health conscious menu items; carryout;
cocktails & lounge; entertainment. Complete dinners from 4:30 pm-7 pm Mon-Fri & 1 pm-5 pm on Sun. Valet parking dinner
only. **Cards:** AE, DI, DS, MC, VI.

# SOMERS POINT—11,200

## LODGING

**RESIDENCE INN BY MARRIOTT AT GREATE BAY RESORT & COUNTRY CLUB**  Rates Subject to Change
**Phone:** 609/927-6400
5/15-9/24 [CP]  2P/1B: $120- 130  2P/2B: $180  XP: $10  F12
5/1-5/14 & 9/25-11/19 [CP]  2P/1B: $94- 104  2P/2B: $134  XP: $10  F12
Apartment  12/31-4/30 [CP]  2P/1B: $89  2P/2B: $89- 119  XP: $10  F12
Motel  11/20-12/30 [CP]  2P/1B: $89  2P/2B: $119  XP: $10  F12
**Location:** 1 mi e of Garden State Pkwy, exit 30 (southbound only) or 1 mi e of Garden State Pkwy, exit 29
(northbound only). 900 Mays Landing Rd 08244. Fax: 609/926-0145. **Terms:** Reserv deposit; weekly/monthly
rates; package plans; 2 night min stay, weekends in season; small pets only, $150 dep req, $50 non-refundable.
**Facility:** 120 rooms. Residential, townhouse atmosphere. Spacious units, some bi-level. Fireplace in some units. 2 stories; ex-
terior corridors; meeting rooms; heated pool; exercise room, sports court. Fee: golf privileges. **Dining:** Restaurant nearby.
**Services:** Fee: coin laundry. **All Rooms:** coffeemakers, kitchens, microwaves, free movies, refrigerators, cable TV.
**Some Rooms:** Fee: VCP's. **Cards:** AE, CB, DI, DS, JCB, MC, VI.  ⊠ (D)(S)⊗

## RESTAURANT

**CRAB TRAP RESTAURANT**  Dinner: $21-$30  **Phone:** 609/927-7377
**Location:** Exit 30; 1 1/2 mi e of Garden State Pkwy (southbound only) at circle; jct SR 52 & CR 559; on the
circle. 2 Broadway 08244. **Hours:** 11 am-10 pm, Fri & Sat-11 pm. Closed: 12/25. **Features:** casual dress;
American  children's menu; early bird specials; carryout; cocktails & lounge; entertainment; a la carte. Featuring a
variety of seafood dishes & steaks; homemade baked goods. Overlooking Great Egg Harbor Bay.
**Cards:** AE, CB, DI, DS, MC, VI.  ⊗

## SOMERVILLE—11,600 (See NEW JERSEY METRO AREA ACCOMMODATIONS spotting map pages A40 & A41; see index starting on page A39)

### RESTAURANT

**LA CUCINA**     **Dinner: $21-$30**     **Phone: 908/526-4907**   139
◆◆◆   **Location:** Downtown, on east end of Pathmark Shopping Center. 125 W Main 08876. **Hours:** 11:30 am-3 &
Northern   5:30-10 pm, Fri-11 pm, Sat 5 pm-11 pm, Sun 5 pm-9 pm. Closed major holidays. **Reservations:** suggested.
Italian   **Features:** casual dress; health conscious menu items; carryout; cocktails & lounge; street parking; a la carte.
House specialties in a romantic dining room with a neo-classical elegance & a touch of the old country. Patio
dining avail in season. **Cards:** AE, CB, DI, MC, VI.

## SOUTH AMBOY—7,900

### LODGING

**PARKWAY MOTOR INN**     Rates Subject to Change     **Phone: 908/525-1770**
◆   All Year    1P: $40- 45   2P/1B: $40- 45   2P/2B: $45- 55
Motel   **Location:** Exit 125 Garden State Pkwy, 1/4 mi s on SR 35. 7089 SR 35S 08879. Fax: 908/525-1770.
    **Terms:** Credit card guarantee; no pets. **Facility:** 114 rooms. 2 stories; exterior corridors.
**Dining:** Restaurants nearby. **Services:** Fee: coin laundry. **All Rooms:** free movies, cable TV. **Some Rooms:**
Fee: whirlpools. **Cards:** AE, DI, MC, VI.    Ⓓ ⊗

## SOUTH PLAINFIELD—20,500 (See NEW JERSEY METRO AREA ACCOMMODATIONS spotting map pages A40 & A41; see index starting on page A39)

### LODGING

**HOLIDAY INN**     Guaranteed Rates     **Phone: 908/753-5500**   79
◆◆   Sun-Thurs    1P: $77- 99   2P/1B: $84- 106   2P/2B: $77- 106   XP: $7   F18
Motor Inn   Fri & Sat    1P: $56- 62   2P/1B: $56- 62   2P/2B: $56- 62
    **Location:** 1-287 northbound, left off Durham Ave exit ramp, first right, 1 mi w on Hadley Rd, southbound exit
Edison; adjacent Middlesex Mall. 4701 Stelton Rd 07080. Fax: 908/753-5500. **Terms:** Sr. discount; monthly rates; small pets
only. **Facility:** 173 rooms. 4 stories; interior corridors; conference facilities; luxury level rooms; heated indoor/outdoor pool,
sauna, whirlpool; exercise room. **Dining & Entertainment:** Dining room; 6:30 am-10 pm, Sat & Sun from 7 am; $9-$20;
cocktails/lounge. **Services:** data ports, secretarial services; valet laundry. **All Rooms:** free & pay movies, refrigerators, cable
TV. **Some Rooms:** microwaves. **Cards:** AE, CB, DI, DS, JCB, MC, VI.    Ⓓ ⊗

## SPARTA

### RESTAURANT

**KROGH'S RESTAURANT**   Historical     **Dinner:** $11-$20     **Phone:** 201/729-8428
🔺   **Location:** Center town, jct Winona Pkwy. 23 White Deer Plaza 07871. **Hours:** 11:30 am-4:30 & 5-10 pm,
◆   Sun noon-9 pm. Closed major holidays. **Reservations:** suggested. **Features:** casual dress; children's menu;
American   carryout; cocktails & lounge; a la carte. Pub-style atmosphere; view of Lake Mohawk. **Cards:** AE, CB, DI,
DS, MC, VI.

## SPRINGFIELD—13,400 (See NEW JERSEY METRO AREA ACCOMMODATIONS spotting map pages A40 & A41; see index starting on page A39)

### LODGING

**HOLIDAY INN**     AAA Special Value Rates     **Phone:** 201/376-9400   85
◆◆   All Year    1P: $68- 71   2P/1B: $71   2P/2B: $68   XP: $10   F19
Motor Inn   **Location:** On SR 22 westbound, 4 mi w of Garden State Pkwy; northbound exit 140, southbound exit 140A.
304 Rt 22W 07081. Fax: 201/376-9534. **Terms:** Credit card guarantee; monthly rates; pets. **Facility:** 194
rooms. 4 stories; interior corridors; conference facilities; heated indoor pool, sauna, whirlpool. **Dining & Entertainment:**
Dining room; 6:30 am-10 pm, Sat-Mon from 7 am; $12-$18; health conscious menu items; cocktails/lounge. **Services:** data
ports, secretarial services; valet laundry. **All Rooms:** free & pay movies, shower baths, cable TV.
**Some Rooms:** refrigerators. **Cards:** AE, CB, DI, DS, JCB, MC, VI.    Ⓓ Ⓢ ⊗

## SPRING LAKE—3,500

### LODGINGS

**ASHLING COTTAGE**     Rates Subject to Change     **Phone:** 908/449-3553
◆◆◆   5/19-9/17 [BP]    2P/1B: $98- 150
Historic Bed   5/1-5/18 & 9/18-1/1 [BP]    2P/2B: $79- 125
& Breakfast   **Location:** 1 blk from ocean. 106 Sussex Ave 07762. **Terms:** Open 5/1-1/1; reserv deposit, 14 day notice;
weekly rates; no pets. **Facility:** 10 rooms. A genteel 19th century residence nestled under sentinal sycamores
for more than 100 years. Tastefully decorated rooms with antiques of the period, each with an individual charm. 2-3 night
minimum some weekends; 3 stories, no elevator; interior corridors; smoke free premises; beach pass avail. **Dining:** Buffet
breakfast 8:30-10 am. **Recreation:** boating; bicycles. **All Rooms:** no A/C, no phones, no TVs. **Some Rooms:** combo &
shower baths, shared bathrooms. *(See ad p A61)*    Ⓓ ⊗

**THE BREAKERS HOTEL**     Rates Subject to Change     **Phone:** 908/449-7700
◆◆◆   6/20-9/14    2P/1B: $135- 160   2P/2B: $135- 160   XP: $30   F14
Historic Hotel   5/1-6/19 & 9/15-4/30    2P/1B: $80- 110   2P/2B: $80- 110   XP: $30   F14
    **Location:** Across from beach. 1507 Ocean Ave 07762. Fax: 908/449-0161. **Terms:** Reserv deposit, 10 day
notice; no pets. **Facility:** 64 rooms. Rooms range in size from compact to spacious. 4 stories; interior corridors; beach view;
street parking only; conference facilities; beach, pool, whirlpool, complimentary beach passes. **Dining & Entertainment:**
Dining room; 8 am-4 & 5-10 pm, Mon-8 pm, Fri & Sat-11 pm, Sun 8 am-9 pm, closed 12/20-1/31; $12-$22; cocktails/lounge;
entertainment. **Services:** data ports; valet parking. **Recreation:** Fee: bicycles. **All Rooms:** refrigerators, combo & shower
baths. **Some Rooms:** VCP's, whirlpools. **Cards:** AE, CB, DI, MC, VI. *(See ad p A61)*    Ⓓ

---

**TRAVEL WITH CONFIDENCE: CONFIRM YOUR RESERVATIONS.**

**THE CHATEAU**

AAA Special Value Rates — Phone: 908/974-2000

| | 1P: | 2P/1B: | 2P/2B: | XP | |
|---|---|---|---|---|---|
| 6/16-9/9 | $95- 110 | $105- 145 | $130- 145 | $15 | F12 |
| 5/1-6/15, 9/10-10/28 & 4/26-4/30 | $55- 75 | $65- 99 | $79- 99 | $15 | F12 |
| 10/29-4/25 | $49- 62 | $59- 72 | $65- 72 | $15 | F12 |

Historic Country Inn **Location:** W of lake & Divine Park. 5th & Warren Ave 07762. Fax: 908/974-0007. **Terms:** Reserv deposit, 10 day notice; weekly/monthly rates; package plans, off season; no pets. **Facility:** 38 rooms. Beautifully appointed Victorian era inn, circa 1888. Gracious hosts reflect a warm & inviting hospitality. Charming breakfast room & parlor with scenic vistas of parks, lake & gazeboes. Ideal for a romantic interlude. 3-night min stay weekends when including Sat 7/1-8/31, 2-night min stay weekends 4/29-6/26 & 9/9-10/30; 3 stories; interior corridors; lake view; meeting rooms; beach, complimentary beach & tennis passes; complimentary trolley passes in summer. **Dining:** Continental breakfast 4/14-10/29, weekends 10/30-4/13, complimentary breakfast Mon-Fri during winter. **Services:** data ports; valet laundry. **Recreation:** swimming. Rental: bicycles. **All Rooms:** free movies, refrigerators, combo & shower baths, cable TV, VCP's. **Some Rooms:** 2 kitchens. **Cards:** AE, DI, MC, VI. *(See color ad p A62)* Ⓓ

**COMFORT INN**

Rates Subject to Change — Phone: 908/449-6146

| | 1P: | 2P/1B: | 2P/2B: | XP | |
|---|---|---|---|---|---|
| 6/21-9/7 [CP] | $85- 125 | $85- 125 | $85- 125 | $10 | F18 |
| 5/1-6/20 & 9/8-4/30 [CP] | $50- 80 | $50- 80 | $50- 80 | $10 | F18 |

Motel **Location:** Exit 98 off Garden State Pkwy to I-195 & to Wall Township, 1 1/2 mi s on SR 35. 1909 SR 35 07719 (PO Box 14, 07762). Fax: 908/449-6556. **Terms:** Sr. discount; reserv deposit; weekly rates; pets, $5 dep req. **Facility:** 70 rooms. 2 stories; interior/exterior corridors; meeting rooms; pool; exercise room. **Dining:** Restaurant nearby. **Services:** data ports. **All Rooms:** free movies, cable TV. **Some Rooms:** 8 efficiencies, no utensils, refrigerators. **Cards:** AE, CB, DI, DS, MC, VI. Ⓓ ⊗

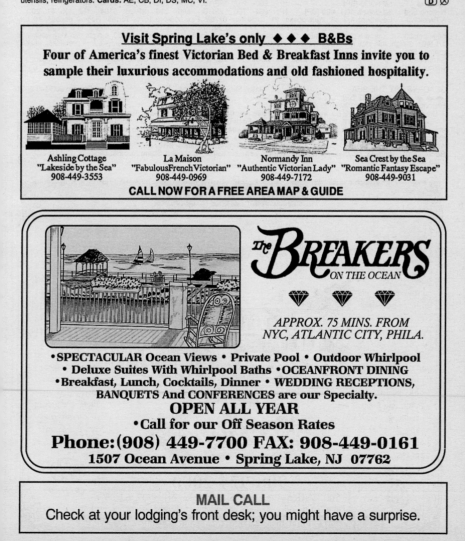
**MAIL CALL**
Check at your lodging's front desk; you might have a surprise.

**THE HEWITT WELLINGTON HOTEL**

Rates Subject to Change                                    Phone: 908/974-1212
5/24-5/26 & 6/10-9/12 [CP]          2P/1B:  $110- 220                    XP: $10
5/1-5/23, 5/27-6/9,
9/13-10/31 & 4/1-4/30 [CP]          2P/1B:  $70- 150                    XP: $10

Historic Hotel **Location:** On s side of lake at 2nd Ave. 200 Monmouth Ave 07762. Fax: 908/974-2338. **Terms:** Open 5/1-10/31 & 4/1-4/30; age restrictions may apply; credit card guarantee, 7 day notice; weekly rates; 2 night min stay, in season; no pets. **Facility:** 29 rooms. Grand Victorian style lakefront & oceanview hotel. Maximum rates for up to 4 persons; 3 stories, no elevator; interior corridors; lake view; meeting rooms; beach, heated pool, complimentary beach pass. **Dining:** Dining room; 11:30 am-2:30 & 5:30-9:30 pm, Fri & Sat 11:30 am-2:30 & 5-10 pm; $14-$24. **All Rooms:** refrigerators, cable TV. **Cards:** AE, MC, VI.                                            (D)

**LA MAISON**

Guaranteed Rates                                    Phone: 908/449-0969
5/24-9/21 [BP]                 2P/1B:  $119- 175                    XP: $35
5/1-5/20 & 9/22-4/30 [BP]       2P/1B:  $95- 145                    XP: $35

Historic Bed **Location:** 4 blks from ocean. 404 Jersey Ave 07762. Fax: 908/449-4860. **Terms:** Age restrictions may apply; & Breakfast reserv deposit, 10 day notice; weekly rates; package plans; 2 night min stay, weekends; no pets. **Facility:** 9 rooms. Offers a peaceful & memorable getaway, pampered in an authentic Victorian style. Cottage unit, seasonal only; 3 stories, no elevator; interior corridors; smoke free premises; meeting rooms; complimentary beach & tennis passes. **Dining:** Breakfast 8:30-10:30 am. **Services:** complimentary evening beverages. **Recreation:** swimming; bicycles. **All Rooms:** comb, shower & tub baths, cable TV. **Cards:** AE, DI, DS, MC, VI. *(See ad p A61)*                   (D) ⊗

**NORMANDY INN**

AAA Special Value Rates                                    Phone: 308/449-7172
5/21-9/30 [BP]            1P:  $80- 242   2P/1B: $108- 252   2P/2B: $130- 141   XP:$10-20
5/1-5/20 & 10/1-4/30 [BP]   1P:  $64- 190   2P/1B:  $86- 200   2P/2B: $104- 112   XP:$10-20

Historic Bed **Location:** 1/2 blk from ocean. 21 Tuttle Ave 07762. Fax: 908/449-1070. **Terms:** Reserv deposit, 10 day & Breakfast notice; weekly rates; no pets. **Facility:** 17 rooms. An 1888 Victorian inn reflecting the charm & elegance of its origin; distinct rooms with period antiques. Owner has pets. 2-night min stay weekends 3/1-11/30, 4-night min stay weekends 1/1-8/31, 2-night min stay mid-week 7/1-8/31. Rental TV, $2 daily; 3 stories; interior corridors; smoke free premises; meeting rooms. Fee: daily beach & pool passes. **Dining:** Dining room; breakfast only 8:30-10:30 am; 9/3-6/15 to 10 am. **Services:** data ports. **Recreation:** bicycles. **All Rooms:** combo & shower baths. **Some Rooms:** kitchen, refrigerators, whirlpools. **Cards:** AE, CB, DI, DS, MC, VI. *(See ad p A61)*                   (D) ⊗

**SEACREST BY THE SEA**

Rates Subject to Change                                    Phone: 908/449-9031
5/16-9/30 [BP]                 2P/1B:  $139- 179
5/1-5/15 & 10/1-4/30 [BP]       2P/1B:  $92- 129

Historic Bed **Location:** 1/2 blk from ocean. 19 Tuttle Ave 07762. Fax: 908/974-0403. **Terms:** Age restrictions may apply; & Breakfast reserv deposit, 30 day notice; no pets. **Facility:** 11 rooms. Charming & gracious hosts delight in providing uniquely decorated rooms in a romantic atmosphere. Relax year-round on magnificent wrap-around porch. Owner has pets. 8 rooms with gas fireplace. 2 room suite $195-$219; 3 stories, no elevator; interior corridors; smoke free premises; meeting rooms; beach, complimentary beach & tennis passes. **Dining:** Breakfast 9-10 am; afternoon tea; restaurant nearby. **Recreation:** swimming; bicycles. **All Rooms:** combo & shower baths, no phones. **Some Rooms:** cable TV. **Cards:** MC, VI. *(See ad p A61)*                   (D) ⊗

## SPRING LAKE HEIGHTS—5,300

### RESTAURANT

**OLD MILL INN**
◆◆◆
American
**Dinner: $11-$20**
**Location:** On Old Mill Rd, at Ocean Rd, between SR 35 & 71. Old Mill Rd 07762. **Hours:** 11:30 am-10 pm,
Fri & Sat-11 pm, Sun 11 am-10 pm. **Reservations:** suggested. **Features:** casual dress; children's menu;
early bird specials; health conscious menu items; cocktails & lounge; a la carte, also prix fixe. Pleasant
dining rooms overlooking Old Mill Pond. Large selection. Reservations advised for Sun brunch. **Cards:** AE, DI, MC, VI.
**Phone:** 908/449-1800

## STANHOPE

### LODGING

**THE WHISTLING SWAN INN**
◆◆◆
Bed &
Breakfast
**Rates Subject to Change**
All Year [BP]   1P:  $80- 105   2P/1B:   $85- 110
**Location:** Center; I-80 exit 27B, SR 183/206N 1 mi to Main St, 1/2 mi w. 110 Main St 07874.
Fax: 201/347-3391. **Terms:** Credit card guarantee; weekly/monthly rates; no pets. **Facility:** 10 rooms.
Charming Victorian-era residence converted to delightful inn offering a gentle atmosphere. 3 stories, no el-
evator; interior corridors; smoke free premises; meeting rooms. **Dining:** Restaurant nearby. **Services:** data ports, secretarial
services; valet laundry. **All Rooms:** free movies, combo & shower baths. **Some Rooms:** cable TV. **Cards:** AE, DS, MC, VI.
**Phone:** 201/347-6369
XP: $20
Ⓓ ⊗

### RESTAURANT

**BLACK FOREST INN**
◆◆◆
Continental
**Dinner: $21-$30**
**Location:** I-80, exit 25 to US 206N, 1 mi n on right. 249 US 206 N 07874. **Hours:** 11:30 am-2 & 5-10 pm,
Sun 1 pm-9 pm. Closed: Tues. **Reservations:** suggested. **Features:** casual dress; health conscious menu
items; cocktails & lounge; a la carte. Delightful Old World charm; authentic German cuisine. House
specialties are superb; save room for an array of fresh-made desserts. **Cards:** AE.
**Phone:** 201/347-3344
♿ ⊗

## SUMMIT—19,800   (See NEW JERSEY METRO AREA ACCOMMODATIONS spotting map pages A40 & A41; see index starting on page A39)

### LODGING

**THE GRAND SUMMIT HOTEL**
◆◆◆
Historic Hotel
**Guaranteed Rates**
All Year   1P: $140   2P/1B: $140   2P/2B: $149   XP: $15
**Location:** 1/2 mi w of center (Summit Ave) on Springfield Ave. 570 Springfield Ave 07901.
Fax: 908/273-4228. **Terms:** Sr. discount; reserv deposit; monthly rates; no pets. **Facility:** 144 rooms. Charming
& inviting atmosphere. Spacious grounds. 4 stories; interior corridors; business center, conference facilities; pool, wading pool;
exercise room. **Dining & Entertainment:** Dining room; 7 am-10 pm; $16-$24; health conscious menu items;
cocktails/lounge; entertainment. **Services:** data ports, PC, secretarial services; health club privileges; valet laundry; area
transportation, airport transportation, to Newark Int. Fee: childcare; massage. **Recreation:** jogging. **All Rooms:** free movies,
combo & shower baths, cable TV. **Some Rooms:** coffeemakers, microwaves, refrigerators, whirlpools. **Cards:** AE, DI, DS,
MC, VI.
**Phone:** 908/273-3000   ⑧⑧
F
Ⓓ ⊗

## THOROFARE

### LODGING

**QUALITY INN WEST DEPTFORD**
⒜⒜
◆◆◆
Motor Inn
**AAA Special Value Rates**
All Year   1P:  $65   2P/1B:  $70   2P/2B:  $65   XP:  $5  F18
**Location:** I-295, exit 20 (Thorofare). 101 Grove Rd 08086. Fax: 609/845-8977. **Terms:** Reserv deposit;
weekly/monthly rates; no pets. **Facility:** 100 rooms. Attractively furnished traditional motel rooms. 2 stories; in-
terior corridors; meeting rooms; pool; exercise room. **Dining & Entertainment:** Restaurant; 6:30 am-10 pm,
Sun 6:30 am-noon; $9-$25; cocktails/lounge. **Services:** complimentary evening beverages. Fee: coin
laundry. **All Rooms:** free movies, cable TV. **Some Rooms:** Fee: refrigerators. **Cards:** AE, CB, DI, DS, JCB, MC, VI. Ⓓ ⊗
**Phone:** 609/848-4111

## TINTON FALLS—12,400

### LODGINGS

**COURTYARD BY MARRIOTT**
◆◆◆
Motor Inn
**Rates Subject to Change**
5/1-9/30 & Sun-Thurs
10/1-4/30   1P: $76   2P/1B:  $76- 86   2P/2B:  $76- 86   XP: $10   F
Fri & Sat 10/1-4/30   1P:  $49- 69   2P/1B:  $49- 69   2P/2B:  $49- 69   XP: $10   F
**Location:** Garden State Pkwy, exit 105, 1st jughandle after toll, then n on Hope Rd. 600 Hope Rd 07724.
Fax: 908/389-1727. **Terms:** Check-in 4 pm; reserv deposit, 3 day notice; small pets only, no cats. **Facility:** 120 rooms. Stately
manor with beautifully landscaped grounds. Breakfast buffet avail. 3 stories; interior corridors; meeting rooms; pool; exercise
room. **Dining:** Dining room nearby. **Services:** data ports, PC, secretarial services; valet laundry. Fee: childcare.
**All Rooms:** free & pay movies, cable TV. **Some Rooms:** refrigerators. **Cards:** AE, DI, DS, MC, VI.
*(See color ad below)*
**Phone:** 908/389-2100
Ⓓ Ⓢ ⊗

**HOLIDAY INN AT TINTON FALLS**
⒜⒜
◆◆◆
Hotel
**Rates Subject to Change**
All Year   1P:  $75- 95   2P/1B:  $85- 125   2P/2B:  $85- 125   XP: $10   F17
**Location:** Garden State Pkwy, exit 105, Hope Rd S. 700 Hope Rd 07724. Fax: 908/544-8049. **Terms:** Sr.
discount; reserv deposit; monthly rates; no pets. **Facility:** 171 rooms. 5 stories; interior corridors; conference
facilities; pool, sauna; exercise room. **Dining & Entertainment:** Dining room; 6:30 am-10:30 pm; $10-$20;
health conscious menu items; cocktails/lounge. **Services:** data ports, PC, secretarial services; valet laundry.
Fee: childcare. **All Rooms:** free & pay movies, cable TV. **Some Rooms:** microwaves, refrigerators. **Cards:** AE, CB, DI, DS,
MC, VI. *(See ad p A64)*
**Phone:** 908/544-9300
Ⓓ Ⓢ ⊗

**RESIDENCE INN BY MARRIOTT**  Rates Subject to Change  Phone: 908/389-8100
◆◆◆  5/1-9/30 [CP]  1P: $112  2P/1B: $112  2P/2B: $122
Apartment  10/1-4/30 [CP]  1P: $99  2P/1B: $99  2P/2B: $109
Motel  **Location:** Garden State Pkwy, exit 105, first jughandle after toll, immediate left before Courtyard by Marriott. 90 Park Rd 07724. Fax: 908/389-1573. **Terms:** Sr. discount; small pets only, $150, min 7 night stay. **Facility:** 96 rooms. Rural setting. 24 two-bedroom units. 2 stories; exterior corridors; meeting rooms; pool, whirlpool; sports court. **Services:** data ports, secretarial services; valet laundry. **All Rooms:** kitchens, microwaves, free movies, refrigerators, cable TV. **Some Rooms:** coffeemakers. Fee: VCP's. **Cards:** AE, CB, DI, DS, JCB, MC, VI.  Ⓓ ⊗

# TOMS RIVER

## LODGINGS

**HOLIDAY INN**  Guaranteed Rates  Phone: 908/244-4000
◆◆◆  5/25-9/6  1P: $89- 107  2P/1B: $99- 107  2P/2B: $99- 107  XP:$8-10 F19
Motor Inn  5/1-5/24 & 9/7-4/30  1P: $74- 85  2P/1B: $84- 95  2P/2B: $84  XP: $10 F19
**Location:** Garden State Pkwy exit 82, 1 mi e on SR 37. 290 Hwy 37E 08753. Fax: 908/244-4000. **Terms:** Sr. discount; reserv deposit, 3 day notice; AP available; small pets only. **Facility:** 123 rooms. 4 stories; interior corridors; meeting rooms; luxury level rooms; heated indoor pool, sauna, whirlpool. **Dining & Entertainment:** Dining room; 6:30 am-10 pm, Sat & Sun from 7:30 am; $9-$17; health conscious menu items; cocktails/lounge. **Services:** secretarial services; health club privileges; valet laundry. **All Rooms:** free & pay movies, refrigerators, cable TV. **Some Rooms:** microwaves. **Cards:** AE, CB, DI, DS, JCB, MC, VI.  Ⓓ Ⓢ ⊗

**HOWARD JOHNSON MOTOR LODGE-TOMS RIVER**  Rates Subject to Change  Phone: 908/244-1000
Ⓐ  7/1-9/15  1P: $75- 85  2P/1B: $85- 98  2P/2B: $110  XP: $6 F18
  5/25-6/30  1P: $80  2P/1B: $90  2P/2B: $107  XP: $6 F18
◆◆  5/1-5/24 & 3/31-4/30  1P: $65  2P/1B: $75  2P/2B: $85  XP: $6 F18
Motor Inn  9/16-3/30  1P: $60  2P/1B: $75  2P/2B: $85  XP: $6 F18
**Location:** Jct SR 37 & Hooper Ave, 1 mi e of Garden State Pkwy exit 82. 955 Hooper Ave 08753. Fax: 908/505-3194. **Terms:** Credit card guarantee; small pets only, $10. **Facility:** 96 rooms. 2 stories; interior corridors; meeting rooms; heated indoor pool. **Dining & Entertainment:** Dining room; 11:30 am-9 pm; $7-$19; health conscious menu items; cocktails/lounge; entertainment. **Services:** data ports, secretarial services; health club privileges; valet laundry. **All Rooms:** free movies, cable TV. **Some Rooms:** Fee: refrigerators, VCP's. **Cards:** AE, DI, DS, MC, VI.  Ⓓ ⊗

**QUALITY INN**  Rates Subject to Change  Phone: 908/341-2400
Ⓐ  6/29-9/3  1P: $85  2P/1B: $85  2P/2B: $95  XP: $10 F18
◆◆◆  5/1-6/28 & 9/4-4/30  1P: $69- 75  2P/1B: $69- 75  2P/2B: $80- 88  XP: $10 F18
Motor Inn  **Location:** 1 1/2 mi w of Garden State Pkwy, exit 82A, on SR 37. 815 SR 37 08755. Fax: 908/341-6469. **Terms:** Sr. discount; credit card guarantee, 3 day notice; no pets. **Facility:** 100 rooms. 2 stories; interior corridors; meeting rooms; pool, saunas; exercise room. **Dining & Entertainment:** Restaurant; 7-11 am, 11:30-3 & 5-9 pm; $10-$24; health conscious menu items; cocktails/lounge. **Services:** data ports, secretarial services; valet laundry. **All Rooms:** free movies, cable TV. **Some Rooms:** whirlpools. Fee: refrigerators, VCP's. **Cards:** AE, CB, DI, JCB, MC, VI.  Ⓓ Ⓢ ⊗

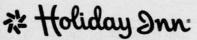

**RAMADA HOTEL-TOMS RIVER/LAKEWOOD**          AAA Special Value Rates          Phone: 908/905-2626

| | | | | | | | | | | |
|---|---|---|---|---|---|---|---|---|---|---|
| | 5/26-9/7 | 1P: | $75- 95 | 2P/1B: | $80- 100 | 2P/2B: | $75- 95 | XP: $10 | F12 |
| | 5/1-5/25 & 9/8-4/30 | 1P: | $62- 69 | 2P/1B: | $69 | 2P/2B: | $62 | XP: $10 | F12 |

Motor Inn          **Location:** At jct US 9 & SR 70, 2 1/2 mi w of exit 88 of Garden State Pkwy southbound, 3 1/2 mi n of exit 83 northbound on US 9. 2373 Rt 9 08755. Fax: 908/905-8735. **Terms:** Small pets only. **Facility:** 102 rooms. 3 stories; interior corridors; meeting rooms; pool; whirlpool; exercise room. **Dining & Entertainment:** Dining room; 7 am-10 pm, Sat from 7:30 am, Sun 7:30 am-9 pm; $8-$21; health conscious menu items; cocktails/lounge. **Services:** data ports, secretarial services. **All Rooms:** free & pay movies, cable TV. **Some Rooms:** whirlpools. Fee: refrigerators. **Cards:** AE, CB, DI, DS, MC, VI.          Ⓓ Ⓢ ⊗

## RESTAURANT

**JACK BAKER'S LOBSTER SHANTY**          Dinner: $11-$20          Phone: 908/240-4800

◆◆
Seafood          **Location:** 1/2 mi e of Garden State Pkwy exit 81A; just e of jct SR 166, overlooking Toms River across from Huddy Park. Robbins Pkwy 08753. **Hours:** 11:30 am-9 pm; in summer-9:30 pm, Sat-10:30 pm. **Features:** casual dress; children's menu; early bird specials; health conscious menu items; carryout; salad bar; cocktails & lounge. Variety of daily specials, raw bar. Overlooking Toms River Basin. **Cards:** AE, CB, DI, MC, VI. Ⓐ ⊗

# TOTOWA—10,200    (See NEW JERSEY METRO AREA ACCOMMODATIONS spotting map pages A40 & A41; see index starting on page A39)

## LODGING

**HOLIDAY INN-TOTOWA**          Guaranteed Rates          Phone: 201/785-9000  Ⓖ①

| | | | | | | | | |
|---|---|---|---|---|---|---|---|---|
| | Mon-Thurs | 1P: | $90 | 2P/1B: | $89 | 2P/2B: | $89 | XP: $6 F18 |
| Motor Inn | Fri-Sun | 1P: | $68 | 2P/1B: | $68 | 2P/2B: | $68 | XP: $6 F18 |

**Location:** On US 46W; 2 1/2 mi w of jct SR 3; I-80 westbound exit 55A at 1st left, I-80 eastbound to US 46E, to Totowa Union Blvd exit, then 1st right. 1 US 46 W 07512. Fax: 201/785-3031. **Terms:** Sr. discount; reserv deposit, 3 day notice; weekly/monthly rates; no pets. **Facility:** 155 rooms. 5 stories; interior corridors; conference facilities; pool; exercise room. Fee: 8 indoor tennis courts. **Dining & Entertainment:** Dining room; 7 am-10 pm; $8-$18; health conscious menu items; cocktails/lounge; entertainment. **Services:** data ports, secretarial services; complimentary evening beverages; health club privileges; valet laundry; area transportation, to local businesses. **All Rooms:** free & pay movies, cable TV. **Some Rooms:** refrigerators. **Cards:** AE, DI, DS, JCB, MC, VI.          Ⓓ ⊗

# TRENTON—88,700

## RESTAURANT

**LARRY PERONI'S WATERFRONT**          Dinner: $11-$20          Phone: 609/882-0303

◆◆
Continental          **Location:** On SR 29; 3/4 mi n of I-95, exit 1. SR 29, River Rd 08628. **Hours:** 11:30 am-10 pm, Fri & Sat-11 pm, Sun 11:30 am-9 pm. Closed: 12/25. **Reservations:** suggested; weekends. **Features:** casual dress; Sunday brunch; children's menu; health conscious menu; carryout; cocktails & lounge; valet parking; a la carte. Quaint dining rooms with rustic ambience. Large selection of continental cuisine. **Cards:** AE, CB, DI, DS, MC, VI.

# UNION    (See NEW JERSEY METRO AREA ACCOMMODATIONS spotting map pages A40 & A41; see index starting on page A39)

## RESTAURANT

**MARIO'S TRATTORIA**          Dinner: $11-$20          Phone: 908/687-3250  ①⑥⑦

◆
Italian          **Location:** Garden State Pkwy exit 139, 1/2 mi e on Chestnut St. 495 Chestnut St 07083. **Hours:** 11 am-11 pm, Fri-midnight, Sat 4 pm-midnight, Sun 3 pm-10 pm. Closed: 12/25. **Reservations:** suggested; weekends. **Features:** casual dress; children's menu; early bird specials; health conscious menu items; carryout; cocktails & lounge; a la carte. Charming bistro. **Cards:** AE, CB, DI, MC, VI.

# VERNON

## LODGING

**APPALACHIAN MOTEL**          Rates Subject to Change          Phone: 201/764-6070

| | | | | | | | | |
|---|---|---|---|---|---|---|---|---|
| | Fri & Sat 5/30-9/5 & 12/15-3/15 | 1P: | $70 | 2P/1B: | $70 | 2P/2B: | $70 | XP: $5 |
| ◆◆ Motel | Sun-Thurs 5/30-9/5 & 12/15-3/15 | 1P: | $65 | 2P/1B: | $65 | 2P/2B: | $65 | XP: $5 |
| | Fri & Sat 5/1-5/29, 9/6-12/14 & 3/16-4/30 | 1P: | $60 | 2P/1B: | $60 | 2P/2B: | $60 | XP: $5 |
| | Sun-Thurs 5/1-5/29, 9/6-12/14 & 3/16-4/30 | 1P: | $55 | 2P/1B: | $55 | 2P/2B: | $55 | XP: $5 |

**Location:** On SR 94, 1 mi n jct CR 515. 367 Rt 94 07462. **Terms:** Reserv deposit; weekly rates; no pets. **Facility:** 10 rooms. 1 story; exterior corridors; valley view. **Services:** data ports. **All Rooms:** shower baths, cable TV. **Cards:** DS, MC, VI. Ⓓ ⊗

# VOORHEES—24,600

## LODGING

**HAMPTON INN**          AAA Special Value Rates          Phone: 609/346-4500

| | | | | | | |
|---|---|---|---|---|---|---|
| | All Year [CP] | 1P: $71- 78 | 2P/1B: | $71- 78 | 2P/2B: | $76- 83 |

Motel          **Location:** I-295 exit 32, 2 1/4 mi e on Haddonfield-Berlin Rd, then s on White Horse Rd, 1/4 mi to Laurel Oak Rd in Voorhees Corporate Center. 121 Laurel Oak Rd 08043. Fax: 609/346-0452. **Terms:** Small pets only, dogs must be leashed. **Facility:** 120 rooms. Charming location next to public parks; close proximity to shopping centers & interstate. 4 stories; interior corridors; meeting rooms; pool. **Dining:** Restaurant nearby. **Services:** data ports, secretarial services; health club privileges; valet laundry. **All Rooms:** free & pay movies, combo & shower baths, cable TV. **Some Rooms:** refrigerators. **Cards:** AE, CB, DI, DS, MC, VI. (See ad p A21)          Ⓓ Ⓢ ⊗

## RESTAURANT

**MAMA VENTURA'S**          Dinner: $21-$30          Phone: 609/767-7400

◆◆◆
Italian          **Location:** On SR 73, 4 mi s of SR 70. 178 SR 73 08043. **Hours:** 11:30 am-3 & 4-10 pm, Fri-11 pm, Sat 4 pm-11 pm, Sun 3 pm-10 pm. Closed: 12/25. **Reservations:** suggested; weekends. **Features:** semi-formal attire; children's menu; early bird specials; cocktails & lounge; entertainment; valet parking; a la carte. Panoramic window seating overlooking waterfall garden. Varied selection of seafood. Enjoy outdoor dining on the terrace in season. Luncheon buffet $6.95. Valet Wed, Fri & Sat. **Cards:** AE, CB, DI, DS, MC, VI.

## WARREN—10,800   (See NEW JERSEY METRO AREA ACCOMMODATIONS spotting map pages A40 & A41; see index starting on page A39)

### LODGING

**SOMERSET HILLS HOTEL**     Guaranteed Rates     Phone: 908/647-6700   93

| | | | |
|---|---|---|---|
| Sun-Thurs | 1P: $150 | 2P/1B: $160 | 2P/2B: $160 | XP: $10 F16 |
| Fri & Sat | 1P: $99 | 2P/1B: $99 | 2P/2B: $99 | XP: $10 F16 |

(AAA)
◆◆◆   **Location:** I-78 exit 33; 1/4 mi n CR 525. 200 Liberty Corner Rd 07059. Fax: 908/647-8053. **Terms:** Sr.
Hotel   discount; credit card guarantee; monthly rates; package plans; small pets only. **Facility:** 111 rooms. Rural setting. 5 stories; interior corridors; meeting rooms; pool; bocci court; exercise room. **Dining:** Also, Christine's, see separate listing. **Services:** data ports; secretarial services; area transportation, within 5 mi. Fee: coin laundry, airport transportation. **All Rooms:** free movies, combo & shower baths, cable TV. **Some Rooms:** honor bars, coffeemakers, 9 efficiencies, microwaves, refrigerators, whirlpools. Fee: VCP's. **Cards:** AE, DI, MC, VI.   (D) (S) ⊗

### RESTAURANT

**CHRISTINE'S**     **Dinner: over $31**     Phone: 908/647-6700   93
◆◆◆   **Location:** In Somerset Hills Hotel. 200 Liberty Corner Rd 07059. **Hours:** 11 am-3 & 5-10 pm, Fri-11 pm, Sat
Continental   5 pm-11 pm, Sun 10:30 am-2:30 pm. Closed major holidays & Sun for dinner. **Reservations:** suggested; weekends. **Features:** casual dress; Sunday brunch; cocktails & lounge; entertainment; a la carte. Elegant dining featuring unique & creative cuisine. Valet parking avail for dinner meals. **Cards:** AE, CB, DI, MC, VI.

## WAYNE—47,000   (See NEW JERSEY METRO AREA ACCOMMODATIONS spotting map pages A40 & A41; see index starting on page A39)

### LODGING

**HOWARD JOHNSON MOTOR LODGE**     AAA Special Value Rates     Phone: 201/696-8050   95

| | | | |
|---|---|---|---|
| All Year | 1P: $62- 69 | 2P/1B: $72- 79 | 2P/2B: $75 | XP: $10 F18 |

(AAA)
◆◆   **Location:** 3 1/2 mi n of I-80, Butler N exit at SR 23 & Ratzer Rd service road. 1850 Rt 23 & Ratzer Rd
Motel   07470. Fax: 201/696-8050. **Terms:** Credit card guarantee, 3 day notice; weekly rates; small pets only; no pets.
**Facility:** 151 rooms. 2 stories; interior corridors; pool; wading pool. **Dining:** Restaurant nearby. **Services:** valet laundry; area transportation. **All Rooms:** free movies, cable TV.
**Some Rooms:** microwaves, refrigerators. **Cards:** AE, CB, DI, DS, MC, VI.   (D) ⊗

## WEEHAWKEN

### LODGING

**RAMADA SUITE HOTEL**     Guaranteed Rates     Phone: 201/617-5600

| | | | |
|---|---|---|---|
| All Year [CP] | 1P: $119- 189 | 2P/1B: $119- 189 | 2P/2B: $119- 189 | XP: $20 F18 |

(AAA)
◆◆◆   **Location:** In Lincoln Harbor Complex. 500 Harbor Blvd 07087. Fax: 201/617-5627. **Terms:** Sr. discount;
Suite Hotel   reserv deposit, 14 day notice; monthly rates; package plans; small pets only, $100 dep req. **Facility:** 244 rooms. Overlooking New York Harbor with magnificent view of Midtown Manhattan skyline; conveniently located to Lincoln Tunnel & Lincoln Harbor Ferry which departs to Midtown & Lower Manhattan daily from hotel dock. 10 stories; interior corridors; conference facilities; indoor pool; exercise room. **Dining & Entertainment:** Dining room; 11 am-3:30 & 5-11 pm, Sat & Sun 5 pm-11 pm; $18-$25; cocktails/lounge; 24-hour room service; entertainment. **Services:** data ports, secretarial services; complimentary evening beverages; valet laundry; area transportation. Fee: PC; childcare, airport transportation. **All Rooms:** microwaves, free & pay movies, refrigerators, cable TV. **Some Rooms:** coffeemakers. **Cards:** AE, CB, DI, DS, JCB, MC, VI.   (D) (S) ⊗

## WEST ATLANTIC CITY

### LODGINGS

**COMFORT INN-ATLANTIC CITY/WEST**     AAA Special Value Rates     Phone: 609/645-1818

| | | | |
|---|---|---|---|
| 7/2-8/31 | 1P: $59- 149 | 2P/1B: $59- 149 | 2P/2B: $59- 149 | XP: $10 F18 |
| 9/1-10/31 | 1P: $55- 139 | 2P/1B: $55- 139 | 2P/2B: $55- 139 | XP: $10 F18 |
| 5/1-7/1 | 1P: $49- 129 | 2P/1B: $49- 129 | 2P/2B: $49- 129 | XP: $10 F18 |
| 11/1-4/30 | 1P: $39- 119 | 2P/1B: $39- 119 | 2P/2B: $39- 119 | XP: $10 F18 |

(AAA)
◆◆   **Location:** On US 40; e of Garden State Pkwy exit 36; at Dover Pl. 7095 Black Horse Pike 08232.
Motel   Fax: 609/383-0228. **Terms:** Check-in 4 pm; reserv deposit, weekends; package plans; no pets. **Facility:** 189 rooms. 2-3 stories; interior corridors; heated pool; exercise room; game room. **Dining:** Coffee shop; 7 am-11 am, Sat & Sun-11:30 am; cocktails. **Services:** data ports; airport transportation. Fee: coin laundry, area transportation, to casino. **All Rooms:** free & pay movies, cable TV. **Some Rooms:** coffeemakers. Fee: refrigerators. **Cards:** AE, CB, DI, DS, MC, VI.
*(See color ad p A11)*   (D) ⊗

**COMFORT INN VICTORIAN**     AAA Special Value Rates     Phone: 609/646-8880

| | | | |
|---|---|---|---|
| All Year [CP] | 1P: $50- 150 | 2P/1B: $50- 150 | 2P/2B: $50- 150 | XP: $10 F16 |

(AAA)
◆◆◆   **Location:** Rts 40 & 322; 1/2 mi w of Rt 9. 6817 Black Horse Pike 08232. Fax: 609/272-9176. **Terms:** Reserv
Motel   deposit, 3 day notice; no pets. **Facility:** 117 rooms. 2 stories; interior corridors; meeting rooms; putting green; small pool; exercise room. **Services:** data ports. Fee: coin laundry, area transportation, to casino. **All Rooms:** cable TV. Fee: movies. **Cards:** AE, CB, DI, DS, MC, VI.   (D) ⊗

**HOLIDAY INN EXPRESS-ATLANTIC CITY WEST**     Rates Subject to Change     Phone: 609/484-1500

| | | | |
|---|---|---|---|
| 5/1-10/29 [CP] | 1P: $99- 109 | 2P/1B: $99- 109 | 2P/2B: $99- 109 | XP: $15 F18 |
| 10/30-4/30 [CP] | 1P: $79 | 2P/1B: $79 | 2P/2B: $79 | XP: $15 F18 |

(AAA)
◆◆◆   **Location:** US Rt 40 & 322, 1/2 mi w of US Rt 9. 6811 Black Horse Pike 08232. Fax: 609/645-9657.
Motel   **Terms:** Check-in 4 pm; no pets. **Facility:** 196 rooms. Woodburning fireplace with ample adjacent seating in lobby. 4 stories; interior corridors; meeting rooms; putting green; small heated pool; 2 tennis courts; exercise room, game room, basketball court. Fee: 9 holes golf. **Dining:** Dining room nearby. **Services:** data ports; area transportation, airport transportation. Fee: childcare; coin laundry. **Recreation:** jogging. **All Rooms:** free & pay movies, cable TV. **Some Rooms:** Fee: microwaves, refrigerators. **Cards:** AE, CB, DI, DS, JCB, MC, VI. *(See ad p A12)*   (D) (S) ⊗

---

**Distances indicated are from the center of town unless otherwise designated.**

**SHERATON HOTEL-ATLANTIC CITY WEST**
◆◆◆  5/1-10/29   1P: $110
Hotel  10/30-4/30   1P: $99
Rates Subject to Change
2P/2B: $110   XP: $15 F17
2P/2B: $99   XP: $15 F17
**Phone:** 609/272-0200
**Location:** On US 40; Black Horse Pike, 1/2 mi w of jct US 9. 6821 Black Horse Pike 08232.
Fax: 609/646-3703. **Terms:** Check-in 4 pm; reserv deposit; weekly/monthly rates; package plans; no pets. **Facility:** 213 rooms. Many 2-room suites. 6 stories; interior corridors; conference facilities; putting green; pool; 2 lighted tennis courts; exercise room, basketball court. Fee: 9 holes golf. **Dining & Entertainment:** Restuarant; 6:30 am-10:30 pm; $11-$15; cocktails/lounge; 24-hour room service. **Services:** data ports, secretarial services; valet laundry; airport transportation. Fee: childcare, area transportation, to casinos. **All Rooms:** coffeemakers, free & pay movies, cable TV. Fee: refrigerators. **Some Rooms:** whirlpools. Fee: microwaves, VCP's. **Cards:** AE, CB, DI, DS, MC, VI. *(See ad p A12)*   Ⓓ Ⓢ ⊗

**WESTFIELD**—28,900   (See NEW JERSEY METRO AREA ACCOMMODATIONS spotting map pages A40 & A41; see index starting on page A39)

## LODGING

**WESTFIELD INN-BEST WESTERN**
ⒶⒶ   All Year [CP]
◆◆   Motel
AAA Special Value Rates
1P: $85- 93 2P/1B: $95- 103 2P/2B: $97- 103 XP: $10 F18
**Phone:** 908/654-5600   **102**
**Location:** On SR 28; 4 mi w of Garden State Pkwy, exit 137. 435 North Ave W 07090. Fax: 908/654-6483.
**Terms:** Reserv deposit; no pets. **Facility:** 40 rooms. Charming rooms. Centrally located in colonial town. 2 stories; interior corridors; meeting rooms. **Dining:** Restaurant nearby. **Services:** data ports, secretarial services; valet laundry. **All Rooms:** free movies, combo & shower baths, cable TV. **Some Rooms:** 16 efficiencies, refrigerators. **Cards:** AE, CB, DI, DS, JCB, MC, VI.   Ⓓ Ⓢ ⊗

## RESTAURANTS

**CHEZ CATHERINE**
◆◆◆   French
**Dinner:** over $31
**Phone:** 908/232-1680   **102**
**Location:** Adjoining Westfield Inn-Best Western, on SR 28. 431 North Ave. **Hours:** noon-2 & 5:30-9 pm, Fri-9:30 pm, Sat seatings at 5:30 pm, 7:30 & 9:30 pm. Closed major holidays, Sun & Mon for lunch. **Reservations:** suggested. **Features:** semi-formal attire; health conscious menu items; cocktails; also prix fixe. Intimately elegant dining room offering a relaxed ambience, while serving innovative cuisine with professional, thoughtful service. **Cards:** AE, CB, DI, MC, VI.

**KEN MARCOTTE**
◆◆◆   American
**Dinner:** $21-$30
**Phone:** 908/233-2309   **99**
**Location:** Downtown. 115 Elm St 07090. **Hours:** 11:30 am-2:30 & 5:30-9 pm, Fri-10 pm, Sat 5:30 pm-10 pm, Sun 4:30 pm-8 pm. Closed major holidays. **Reservations:** suggested. **Features:** semi-formal attire; health conscious menu; cocktails; street parking; a la carte. Contemporary, creative entrees emphasizing fresh indredients. Good wine list. Espresso, cappuccino. Understated elegance of old bank building with art deco touches. **Cards:** AE, DI, MC, VI.   ⊗

**NORTHSIDE TRATTORIA**
◆   Regional Italian
**Dinner:** $11-$20
**Phone:** 908/232-7320   **103**
**Location:** Between North Ave & Broad St. 16 Prospect St. **Hours:** 11:30 am-10 pm, Fri & Sat-11 pm, Sun 5 pm-9 pm. Closed major holidays. **Features:** casual dress; health conscious menu items; carryout; street parking; a la carte. Lively bistro. Imported pasta house specials, homemade stuffed pizza & foccacio.   ⊗

**WEST LONG BRANCH**—7,700

## LODGING

**McINTOSH INN OF WEST LONG BRANCH**
◆◆   5/1-9/4   1P: $47- 59 2P/1B: $53- 65 2P/2B: $58   XP: $3 F18
Motel  9/5-4/30   1P: $43- 53 2P/1B: $48- 59 2P/2B: $54   XP: $3 F18
Rates Subject to Change
**Phone:** 908/542-7900
**Location:** Garden State Pkwy exit 105, 4 mi e on SR 36; 1 mi e of jct SR 35. 294 Rt 36E 07764. Fax: 908/542-7356. **Terms:** Sr. discount; weekly rates; no pets. **Facility:** 117 rooms. 4 stories; interior corridors; meeting rooms. **Services:** data ports. **All Rooms:** free movies, cable TV. **Some Rooms:** microwaves, radios, refrigerators. **Cards:** AE, CB, DI, MC, VI. *(See ad p A53 & below)*   Ⓓ ⊗

**WEST ORANGE**—39,100   (See NEW JERSEY METRO AREA ACCOMMODATIONS spotting map pages A40 & A41; see index starting on page A39)

## RESTAURANTS

**HIGHLAWN PAVILION**   Historical
◆◆◆   American
**Dinner:** over $31
**Phone:** 201/731-3463   **143**
**Location:** 1/4 mi n of I-280 exit 8B, 1/4 mi e on Eagle Rock Ave; in Eagle Rock Reservation. Eagle Rock Ave 07052. **Hours:** noon-3 & 5:30-9:30 pm, Fri-10:30 pm, Sat 5 pm-11 pm, Sun 5 pm-9:30 pm. Closed: 12/24. **Reservations:** required. **Features:** semi-formal attire; health conscious menu items; cocktails & lounge; entertainment; valet parking; a la carte. 1900's casino on 412 acre park site. Magnificent view of northern New Jersey & Manhattan skyline. Outdoor patio. **Cards:** AE, DI, DS, MC, VI.   ⊗

**(See NEW JERSEY METRO AREA ACCOMMODATIONS spotting map pages A40 & A41)**

THE MANOR    **Dinner: $21-$30**    Phone: 201/731-2360    (142)
◆◆◆◆    **Location:** On CR 577; 1 mi n of I-280, exit 8B. 111 Prospect Ave 07052. **Hours:** noon-3 & 6-10 pm, Sat
Continental    from 6 pm, Sun noon-8 pm, lobster buffet Tues-Sat $34, Sun candlelight buffet noon-7 pm $27, Wed lunch
buffet noon-3 pm $16. **Closed:** Mon & 12/24. **Reservations:** suggested. **Features:** semi-formal attire;
cocktails & lounge; entertainment; valet parking; a la carte. Extensive menu; elegant dining rooms. **Cards:** AE, CB, DI, DS,
MC, VI.

PALS CABIN    **Dinner: $21-$30**    Phone: 201/731-4000    (146)
(AAA)    **Location:** 1/8 mi n of I-280, exit 8B. Prospect & Eagle Rock aves 07052. **Hours:** 7:30 am-11 pm,
Fri-midnight, Sat 8 am-midnight. **Reservations:** suggested; weekends. **Features:** casual dress; children's
◆◆    menu; early bird specials; carryout; cocktails & lounge; entertainment; valet parking; a la carte. Landmark
American    restaurant, rustic decor. Family-owned since 1932. **Cards:** AE, CB, DI, DS, MC, VI.    ⊗

THE RUSTY SCUPPER    **Dinner: $11-$20**    Phone: 201/736-9890    (145)
◆◆    **Location:** I-280 exit 8A, 1/4 mi s on CR 577; in Essex Green Shopping Plaza. 3 Essex Green Plaza 07052.
Seafood    **Hours:** 11:30 am-2:30 & 5-10 pm, Fri & Sat-11 pm, Sun 11 am-2:30 & 4-9 pm. **Closed:** 11/23 & 12/25.
**Reservations:** suggested. **Features:** casual dress; Sunday brunch; children's menu; early bird specials;
health conscious menu items; salad bar; cocktails & lounge; valet parking; buffet. Attractive multi-level dining rooms, with
potted greens & skylights. **Cards:** AE, CB, DI, MC, VI.    ⊗

# WHIPPANY (See NEW JERSEY METRO AREA ACCOMMODATIONS spotting map pages A40 & A41; see index starting on page A39)

## LODGINGS

COURTYARD BY MARRIOTT    Rates Subject to Change    Phone: 201/887-8700    (105)
◆◆◆    Sun-Thurs    1P:  $99    2P/1B:  $109    2P/2B:  $109    XP: $10    F
Motor Inn    Fri & Sat    1P:  $69    2P/1B:  $79    2P/2B:  $79    XP: $10    F
**Location:** From I-287, 1 1/2 mi e on SR 10. 157 SR 10E 07981. **Fax:** 201/887-8068. **Terms:** Sr. discount;
package plans; no pets. **Facility:** 149 rooms. Convenient location in commercial area; rural setting. 3 stories; interior corridors;
meeting rooms; luxury level rooms; heated indoor pool, whirlpool; exercise room. **Dining:** Restaurant; 6:30 am-10 & 5-10
pm, Sat & Sun 7 am-2 pm; $8-$19. **Services:** data ports; valet laundry. Fee: childcare. **All Rooms:** free & pay movies,
cable TV. **Some Rooms:** honor bars, refrigerators. **Cards:** AE, CB, DI, DS, MC, VI. *(See color ad below)*    Ⓓ Ⓢ ⊗

HANOVER MARRIOTT    Rates Subject to Change    Phone: 201/538-8811    (106)
◆◆◆    Sun-Thurs [EP]    1P: $130    2P/1B: $130    2P/2B: $130
Hotel    Fri & Sat [BP]    1P:  $79    2P/1B:  $79    2P/2B:  $79
**Location:** On SR 10, 1/2 mi w of I-287, southbound exit 35B, northbound exit 35. 1401 Rt 10E 07981.
**Fax:** 201/538-0291. **Terms:** Check-in 4 pm; monthly rates; no pets. **Facility:** 353 rooms. 8 stories; interior corridors; business
center, conference facilities; luxury level rooms; heated indoor/outdoor pool, saunas, whirlpool; exercise room. **Dining &
Entertainment:** Dining room, restaurant; 6:30 am-11 pm, Sat & Sun from 7 am; $7-$14; health conscious menu items;
cocktails/lounge; entertainment. **Services:** data ports, PC, secretarial services; valet laundry. Fee: childcare.
**Recreation:** jogging. **All Rooms:** cable TV. Fee: movies. **Some Rooms:** refrigerators. **Cards:** AE, CB, DI, DS, JCB, MC, VI.    Ⓓ Ⓢ ⊗

HOWARD JOHNSON LODGE    AAA Special Value Rates    Phone: 201/539-8350    (108)
(AAA)    All Year    1P:  $75    2P/1B:  $85    2P/2B:  $85    XP: $10    F
**Location:** Exit 39B, I-287. 1255 Rt 10E 07981. **Fax:** 201/539-9338. **Terms:** Reserv deposit; weekly/monthly
◆◆    rates; package plans, weekends; small pets only. **Facility:** 108 rooms. 2 stories; interior corridors; meeting
Motel    rooms; pool. **Dining & Entertainment:** Restaurant; 6 am-11 pm, Fri & Sat-2 am; $8-$15; health conscious
menu items; cocktails/lounge. **Services:** data ports, secretarial services; valet laundry; area transportation, to
nearby businesses. **All Rooms:** free & pay movies, cable TV. **Some Rooms:** coffeemakers, efficiency, microwaves,
refrigerators. **Cards:** AE, CB, DI, DS, JCB, MC, VI.    Ⓓ ⊗

## RESTAURANT

IL CAPRICCIO    **Dinner: over $31**    Phone: 201/884-9175    (105)
◆◆◆◆    **Location:** 1 mi e of I-287; on SR 10E. 633 SR 10 07981. **Hours:** 11:30 am-3 & 5-10 pm, Fri-11 pm, Sat 5
Italian    pm-11 pm. **Closed** major holidays & Sun. **Reservations:** suggested. **Features:** semi-formal attire; cocktails;
entertainment; valet parking. Enjoy classic & creative cuisine amid a sophisticated ambience. **Cards:** AE, DI,
MC, VI.    ⊗

# WHITEHOUSE

## RESTAURANT

THE RYLAND INN    **Dinner: over $31**    Phone: 908/534-4011
◆◆◆    **Location:** On SR 22 W, 1 mi e. **Hours:** 11:30 am-2 & 5:30-9 pm, Fri & Sat-10 pm, Sun 2 pm-8 pm. Closed
French    major holidays. **Reservations:** suggested. **Features:** semi-formal attire; cocktails; a la carte. Grand country
manor with intimate elegant dining rooms. Modern regional French cuisine using own garden herbs &
vegetables. Jackets required at dinner. Valet parking Fri & Sat evenings. **Cards:** AE, DI, DS, MC, VI.

## WHITE HOUSE STATION

### LODGING

**HOLLY THORN HOUSE**

Rates Subject to Change

All Year [BP]   1P: $90   2P/1B: $90   2P/2B: $90   XP: $25   Phone: 908/534-1616

♦♦♦♦
Historic Bed
& Breakfast

**Location:** 3 mi s of US 22; on CR 620 4 mi e of jct CR 523. 143 Readington Road 08889. Fax: 908/534-9017. **Terms:** Age restrictions may apply; reserv deposit, 7 day notice; no pets. **Facility:** 4 rooms. Rurally located, rustically decorated public areas. Variety of room themes with quality furnishings & gracious hospitality offered by innkeepers. 2 stories; interior corridors; smoke free premises; meeting rooms; pool, whirlpool; exercise room, billiard room. **Dining:** Breakfast 7-9 am, buffet after 9 am on weekends. **All Rooms:** combo & shower baths, no phones, no TVs. **Some Rooms:** radios. **Cards:** AE, DS, MC, VI.   Ⓓ ⊗

## WILDWOOD—4,500

### LODGINGS

**AA HEART OF WILDWOOD MOTELS**

Rates Subject to Change

Phone: 609/522-4090

♦♦
Motel

| | 2P/1B | | 2P/2B | | XP | F16 |
|---|---|---|---|---|---|---|
| 7/16-8/19 & 9/1-9/3 5/26-5/28, 6/23-7/15 & | $70- | 92 | $82- | 140 | $10 | F16 |
| 8/20-8/31 5/29-6/22 | $65- | 82 | $75- | 120 | $10 | F16 |
| 5/1-5/25, 9/4-10/15 & | $47- | 72 | $57- | 100 | $5 | F16 |
| 4/18-4/30 | $34- | 85 | $45- | 85 | $5 | F16 |

**Location:** Garden State Pkwy exit 4B, 3 mi se on SR 47, 1/2 mi n on Ocean Ave. 3915 & 4002 Ocean Ave 08260. Fax: 609/522-4224. **Terms:** Open 5/1-10/15 & 4/18-4/30; reserv deposit, 14 day notice; package plans; 3 night min stay, weekends in season; no pets. **Facility:** 74 rooms. Standard motel rooms, 35 one & two room efficiency units. Third floor level pool & sundeck provide an excellent view of the beach, boardwalk & amusement park. 5 two-bedroom efficiencies, $65-$140; 2 stories; exterior corridors; 2 heated pools, wading pool. **All Rooms:** free movies, combo & shower baths, cable TV. **Some Rooms:** refrigerators. **Cards:** AE, CB, DI, DS, MC, VI. *(See color ad below)*   Ⓓ

**DAYS INN**

Rates Subject to Change

Phone: 609/522-0331

♦♦
Motel

| | 2P/2B | | XP | F12 |
|---|---|---|---|---|
| 7/1-7/4, 7/15-8/27 & 9/2-9/5 [CP] | $145- | 165 | $10 | F12 |
| 7/5-7/14 & 8/28-9/1 [CP] | $129- | 139 | $8 | F12 |
| 6/10-6/30 & 9/6-9/24 [CP] 5/1-6/9, 9/25-10/16 & | $85- | 95 | $5-8 | F12 |
| 4/8-4/30 [CP] | $55- | 82 | $5-8 | F12 |

**Location:** 4B exit off Garden State Pkwy, 3 mi se on SR 47, then 1/4 mi n on Ocean Ave. 4610 Ocean Ave 08260. Fax: 609/522-2018. **Terms:** Sr. discount; Open 5/1-10/16 & 4/15-4/30; reserv deposit, 3 day notice; weekly rates; package plans; 3 night min stay, 7/15-8/27; no pets. **Facility:** 36 rooms. 5 stories; exterior corridors; oceanview; heated pool, wading pool; game room. **Services:** Fee: coin laundry. **All Rooms:** refrigerators, cable TV. **Some Rooms:** coffeemakers, 35 efficiencies. **Cards:** AE, CB, DI, DS, JCB, MC, VI.   Ⓓ ⊗

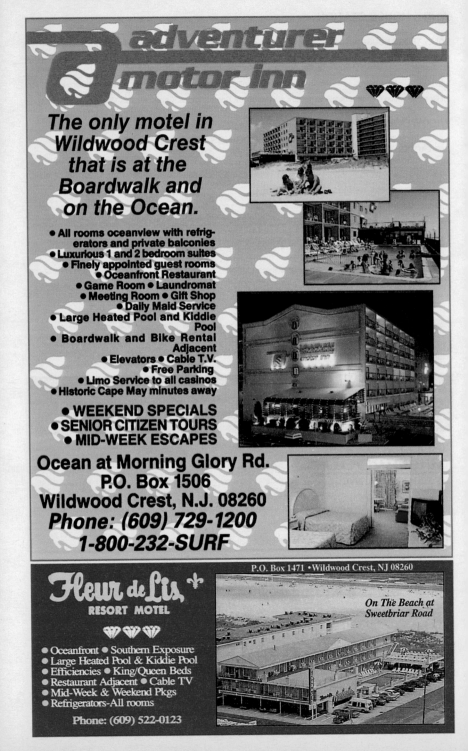

**KNOLL'S RESORT MOTEL**          AAA Special Value Rates          Phone: 609/522-8211

| | | | | | |
|---|---|---|---|---|---|
| (AAA) | 7/7-8/20 | | 2P/2B: | $89- 109 | XP: $10 D12 |
| ◆ ◆ | 6/25-7/6 & 8/21-9/3 | | 2P/2B: | $79- 99 | XP: $10 D12 |
| Motel | 6/1-6/24 & 9/4-9/16 | | 2P/2B: | $59- 79 | XP: $10 D12 |
| | 5/1-5/31 & 9/17-4/30 | | 2P/2B: | $39- 49 | XP: $10 D12 |

**Location:** From exit 4B off Garden State Pkwy; 2 mi se on SR 47, then 1/2 n mi on Atlantic Ave. 4111 Atlantic Ave 08260. Fax: 609/522-0687. **Terms:** Reserv deposit, 14 day notice; weekly rates; package plans; 3 night min stay, in season; no pets. **Facility:** 40 rooms. 1 blk to beach & boardwalk. Closed 12/31 & 1/1. 3 stories; exterior corridors; heated pool. **Services:** area transportation, to bus terminal. **All Rooms:** coffeemakers, free movies, refrigerators, cable TV. **Some Rooms:** microwaves, VCP's. **Cards:** AE, DS, MC, VI. *(See color ad p A69)*                    Ⓓ ⊗

**PINK CHAMPAGNE MOTEL**

Rates Subject to Change

Phone: 609/522-4857

| | | | | | | |
|---|---|---|---|---|---|---|
| 7/12-9/6 | 2P/1B: | $70- 80 | 2P/2B: | $80- 85 | XP: $9 | F5 |
| 6/14-7/11 | 2P/1B: | $60- 70 | 2P/2B: | $70- 75 | XP: $9 | F5 |
| 5/16-6/13 & 9/7-9/30 | 2P/1B: | $40- 50 | 2P/2B: | $50 | XP: $9 | F5 |

**Location:** From exit 4B of Garden State Pkwy, 3 mi se on SR 47, then 1/2 blk s on Atlantic Ave. 4910 Atlantic Ave 08260. Fax: 609/522-9374. **Terms:** Sr. discount; Open 5/16-9/30; reserv deposit, 7 day notice; weekly rates; package plans; 2 night min stay, weekends; no pets. **Facility:** 25 rooms. Traditional motel rooms. 4 two-bedroom units. 2-room efficiency units for up to 4 persons, $85-$120; 3 stories, no elevator; exterior corridors; saltwater pool, sun deck; barbecue grills. **Services:** Fee: coin laundry. **All Rooms:** free movies, refrigerators, combo & shower baths, cable TV. **Cards:** AE, DS, MC, VI.

DON'T BE A NO-SHOW.

If you must cancel a reservation that you have guaranteed or for which you have paid a deposit, notify the establishment before the cancellation deadline. This will prevent you from being billed for the room or losing your deposit.

## ROYAL CANADIAN MOTEL

Guaranteed Rates   Phone: 609/522-0950

| | | | | | | | |
|---|---|---|---|---|---|---|---|
| 7/7-8/20 | 2P/1B: | $85- 125 | 2P/2B: | $85- 125 | XP:$5-10 | D |
| 6/24-7/6 & 8/21-8/31 | 2P/1B: | $70- 103 | 2P/2B: | $70- 103 | XP: $8 | D |
| 6/2-6/23 & 9/1-9/16 | 2P/1B: | $60- 83 | 2P/2B: | $60- 83 | XP: $5 | D |
| 5/1-6/1, 9/17-10/30 & 4/1-4/30 | 2P/1B: | $40- 60 | 2P/2B: | $40- 60 | XP: $5 | D |

**Location:** From exit 4B off Garden State Pkwy, 3 mi se on SR 47, 1 mi n on Atlantic Ave. 3300 Atlantic Ave 08260 (PO Box 856). Fax: 609/522-3290. **Terms:** Sr. discount; Open 5/1-10/30 & 4/1-4/30; reserv deposit, 5 day notice; weekly rates; package plans; no pets. **Facility:** 86 rooms. 45 two-bedroom units. 4 stories; exterior corridors; heated pool, wading pool. Fee: miniature golf. **Dining:** Restaurant nearby. **Services:** Fee: coin laundry. **All Rooms:** cable TV. **Some Rooms:** 32 efficiencies, radios, refrigerators. **Cards:** AE, CB, DI, DS, MC, VI.   (D)

## SEA-N-SUN MOTEL

Guaranteed Rates   Phone: 609/522-2826

| | | | |
|---|---|---|---|
| 7/1-8/21 | 2P/2B: | $98- 120 | XP:$6-12 |
| 6/10-6/30 & 8/22-8/31 | 2P/2B: | $78- 105 | XP:$6-12 |
| 5/26-6/9 & 9/1-9/14 | 2P/2B: | $58- 78 | XP:$6-12 |
| 5/1-5/25 & 9/16-9/30 | 2P/2B: | $52- 68 | XP:$6-12 |

**Location:** From exit 4B of Garden State Pkwy, 3 mi se on SR 47, then 1/2 mi n on Ocean Ave. 3909 Ocean Ave 08260 (PO Box 127). Fax: 609/522-3992. **Terms:** Open 5/1-9/30; reserv deposit, 14 day notice; package plans; no pets. **Facility:** 21 rooms. Weekends $10 extra 5/1-6/30 & 9/1-9/30; 2 stories; exterior corridors; beachfront; beach, small pool. **Recreation:** swimming. **All Rooms:** free movies, cable TV. **Some Rooms:** coffeemakers, 4 efficiencies, microwaves, refrigerators. **Cards:** AE, DS, MC, VI.   (D)

## TOWER MOTEL

Rates Subject to Change   Phone: 609/522-5800

| | | | | | | |
|---|---|---|---|---|---|---|
| 6/30-8/26 | 2P/1B: | $49- 59 | 2P/2B: | $59- 74 | XP: $6 | F18 |
| 8/27-10/1 | 2P/1B: | $25- 42 | 2P/2B: | $30- 49 | XP: $6 | F18 |
| 5/12-6/29 | 2P/1B: | $25- 40 | 2P/2B: | $30- 45 | XP: $6 | F18 |

**Location:** Garden State Pkwy exit 4B, SR 47 (Rio Grande Ave) s 2 1/2 mi 430 W Rio Grande Ave 08260. **Terms:** Open 5/12-10/1; reserv deposit, 14 day notice; package plans; 2 night min stay, weekends, 7/1-8/31; no pets. **Facility:** 30 rooms. Traditional motel rooms. Located 8 mi from the Cape May Lewes Ferry. 2 stories; exterior corridors; pool, wading pool; game room, barbecue grill area. **Services:** area transportation, to bus terminal. **All Rooms:** free movies, refrigerators, cable TV. **Some Rooms:** coffeemakers, microwaves. **Cards:** AE, DS, MC, VI.   (D) ⊗

# RESTAURANTS

## BOATHOUSE RESTAURANT

Dinner: $11-$20   Phone: 609/729-5301

**Location:** Garden State Pkwy exit 4B, SR 47 s to se side of bridge. 506 W Rio Grande Ave 08260. **Hours:** Open 5/1-10/15 & 4/15-4/30; 11:30 am-10 pm. **Features:** casual dress; children's menu; early bird specials; cocktails & lounge; valet parking. Comfortable dining room, also deck dining overlooking bay. Lunch is served on the crab deck only. **Cards:** AE, CB, DI, DS, MC, VI.

## CHIARELLA'S RISTORANTE & SIDEWALK CAFE

Dinner: $21-$30   Phone: 609/522-4117

**Location:** Garden State Pkwy exit 4B, SR 47 s to NJ Ave; n to Taylor Ave. 100 E Taylor Ave 08260. **Hours:** 11:30 am-11 pm; Wed-Fri 10/16-3/31, from 4 pm; late night menu 11 pm-2 am. Closed: Mon & Tues 10/16-3/31. **Features:** casual dress; children's menu; carryout; cocktails & lounge; a la carte. Family oriented. Family owned & operated for 25 years. **Cards:** AE, CB, DI, DS, MC, VI.   ⊗

## THE CRAB HOUSE AT TWO MILE LANDING

Dinner: up to $10   Phone: 609/522-1341

**Location:** 1 mi s of Wildwood Crest on Ocean Dr. Ocean Dr 08260. **Hours:** Open 5/19-9/24; noon-10 pm. **Features:** casual dress; children's menu; cocktails & lounge; a la carte. Traditional Maryland crab house with a diversified menu. Additional deck dining area overlooks the marina. **Cards:** AE, CB, DI, DS, MC, VI.

## THE TWO MILE INN RESTAURANT

Dinner: $11-$20   Phone: 609/522-1341

**Location:** 1 mi s of Wildwood Crest on Ocean Dr. Ocean Dr 08260. **Hours:** Open 5/5-10/8; 4:30 pm-10 pm. **Features:** casual dress; children's menu; cocktails & lounge. Great view & very good seafood in comfortable setting. **Cards:** AE, CB, DI, DS, MC, VI.

The best reservation is a *confirmed* reservation.

# WILDWOOD CREST

## LODGINGS

**ACACIA MOTOR INN**   Rates Subject to Change   **Phone:** 609/729-2233

(AAA)

◆◆
Motel

| | | | | |
|---|---|---|---|---|
| 7/1-8/25 | 2P/2B: | $95- 140 | XP:$7-9 | F10 |
| 6/16-6/30 & 8/26-9/7 | 2P/2B: | $83- 105 | XP: $9 | F10 |
| 5/15-6/15 & 9/8-9/30 | 2P/2B: | $36- 74 | XP: $7 | F10 |

**Location:** Garden State Pkwy exit 4B; SR 47 se 3 mi to Atlantic Ave, then 2 mi s. 9101 Atlantic Ave 08260. Fax: 609/522-2294. **Terms:** Open 5/15-9/30; reserv deposit, 14 day notice, cancellation fee imposed; no pets. **Facility:** 52 rooms. 1 & 2 room efficiency suites. 2 oceanfront sundecks. 3 two-bedroom units. Rates for up to 4 persons, in season; 4 stories; exterior corridors; beachfront; meeting rooms; beach, heated pool; ping pong, barbecue grills. **Services:** Fee: coin laundry. **Recreation:** swimming. **All Rooms:** coffeemakers, microwaves, refrigerators, combo & shower baths, cable TV. **Some Rooms:** VCP's. **Cards:** MC, VI.   Ⓓ

---

**ADVENTURER MOTOR INN**   Rates Subject to Change   **Phone:** 609/729-1200

(AAA)

◆◆◆
Motor Inn

| | | | | |
|---|---|---|---|---|
| 7/8-8/20 & 9/2-9/5 | 2P/2B: | $118- 175 | XP:$6-12 | F3 |
| 6/25-7/7 & 8/21-9/1 | 2P/2B: | $98- 140 | XP:$6-10 | F3 |
| 5/1-6/24, 9/6-10/16 & | | | | |
| 4/29-4/30 | 2P/2B: | $56- 80 | XP: $10 | F3 |

**Location:** Ocean Ave & Morning Glory; exit 4B off Garden State Pkwy, 3 mi se on SR 47, 1/4 mi s on Ocean Ave. 5401 Ocean Ave 08260 (PO Box 1506). Fax: 609/729-3935. **Terms:** Open 5/1-10/16 & 4/29-4/30; reserv deposit, 21 day notice; package plans; no pets. **Facility:** 104 rooms. All rooms have private balcony. Rates for up to 4 persons; 6 stories; interior corridors; beachfront; meeting rooms; beach, heated pool, wading pool. **Dining:** Restaurant; 7 am-9 pm; $5-$14. **Services:** Fee: coin laundry. **Recreation:** swimming. **All Rooms:** cable TV. **Some Rooms:** 75 efficiencies, refrigerators. Fee: VCP's. **Cards:** AE, MC, VI. *(See color ad p A70)*   Ⓓ⊗

---

**AMERICAN SAFARI MOTEL**   Rates Subject to Change   **Phone:** 609/522-0157

(AAA)

◆◆
Motel

| | | | | |
|---|---|---|---|---|
| 7/15-8/19 | 2P/2B: | $90- 139 | XP:$5-8 | |
| 7/1-7/14 & 8/20-8/26 | 2P/2B: | $72- 110 | XP: $5 | |
| 6/16-6/30 & 8/27-9/4 | 2P/2B: | $64- 98 | XP: $5 | |
| 5/1-6/15 & 9/5-10/9 | 2P/2B: | $40- 78 | XP: $5 | |

**Location:** From Garden State Pkwy exit 4B, 3 mi se on SR 47, 1/2 mi s on Ocean Ave. 5610 Ocean Ave 08260. **Terms:** Open 5/1-10/9; reserv deposit, 21 day notice; package plans; no pets. **Facility:** 25 rooms. 8 two-bedroom units. Rates for up to 4 persons; 3 stories; exterior corridors; heated pool; sun deck. **Dining:** Restaurant nearby. **Services:** Fee: coin laundry. **All Rooms:** coffeemakers, free movies, refrigerators, cable TV. **Some Rooms:** 12 efficiencies. **Cards:** AE, DS, MC, VI.   Ⓓ

---

**AQUA BEACH RESORT**   Rates Subject to Change   **Phone:** 609/522-6507

(AAA)

◆◆◆
Complex

| | | | | | | |
|---|---|---|---|---|---|---|
| 7/9-8/21 | 2P/1B: | $113- 124 | 2P/2B: | $114- 170 | XP:$5-10 | |
| 8/22-9/15 & 10/16-11/1 | 2P/1B: | $45- 100 | 2P/2B: | $44- 153 | XP: $5 | |
| 6/14-7/8 | 2P/1B: | $68- 110 | 2P/2B: | $68- 134 | XP: $10 | |
| 5/1-6/13, 9/16-10/15 & | | | | | | |
| 4/1-4/30 | 2P/1B: | $41- 77 | 2P/2B: | $40- 100 | XP: $5 | |

**Location:** Exit 4B Garden State Pkwy, 3 mi se on SR 47, 1/4 mi s on Ocean Ave. 5501 Ocean Ave 08260. Fax: 609/522-8535. **Terms:** Open 5/1-11/1 & 4/1-4/30; reserv deposit, 14 day notice; weekly rates; BP available; package plans; no pets. **Facility:** 123 rooms. Traditional motel rooms, cottages & efficiencies. Large sun deck faces the ocean. Patio & balcony. 3 two-bedroom suites. In-season rates for 4-6 persons; 5 stories; exterior corridors; beachfront; beach, heated pool, wading pool, whirlpool; game room. **Dining:** Coffee shop; 6 am-4 pm. **Services:** Fee: coin laundry. **Recreation:** social program; swimming. **All Rooms:** free movies, refrigerators, cable TV. **Some Rooms:** whirlpools. **Cards:** DS, MC, VI. *(See color ad below)*   Ⓓ

---

**ATTACHE RESORT MOTEL**   Rates Subject to Change   **Phone:** 609/522-0241

(AAA)

◆◆◆
Motel

| | | | | |
|---|---|---|---|---|
| 7/13-8/29 | | | | |
| 6/20-7/12 & 8/30-9/6 | 2P/2B: | $115- 165 | XP:$5-12 | |
| 5/30-6/19 & 9/7-9/19 | 2P/2B: | $85- 135 | XP:$5-12 | |
| 5/1-5/29, 9/20-10/15 & | 2P/2B: | $60- 90 | XP:$5-12 | |
| 4/29-4/30 | 2P/2B: | $45- 65 | XP:$5-12 | |

**Location:** From Garden State Pkwy, exit 4B, 3 mi se on SR 47, then 1/4 mi s on Ocean Ave to Heather Rd. Heather Rd & Beach 08260 (Dept A). **Terms:** Open 5/1-10/15 & 4/29-4/30; reserv deposit, 21 day notice; package plans, off season; no pets. **Facility:** 42 rooms. 2 sun decks have a southern exposure. Rates 6/20-9/6 for up to 4 persons; 3 stories; exterior corridors; beachfront; beach, heated pool, wading pool. **Services:** Fee: coin laundry. **Recreation:** swimming. **All Rooms:** coffeemakers, refrigerators, combo & shower baths, cable TV. **Some Rooms:** microwaves. **Cards:** AE, CB, DI, DS, MC, VI.   Ⓓ

## BEACH COLONY MOTEL

Rates Subject to Change     Phone: 609/522-4037

| | | | | | |
|---|---|---|---|---|---|
| 7/14-8/19 | | 2P/2B: | $85- | 105 | XP: $8 |
| 6/2-7/13 & 8/20-9/16 | | 2P/2B: | $52- | 62 | XP: $5 |
| 5/1-6/1 & 9/17-10/22 | | 2P/2B: | $38- | 50 | XP: $5 |

Motel **Location:** Exit 4B off Garden State Pkwy, 3 mi se on SR 47, 2 mi s on Ocean Ave to Stockton Ave. 500 E Stockton Ave 08260. **Terms:** Open 5/1-10/22; reserv deposit, 21 day notice; weekly rates; package plans; no pets. **Facility:** 26 rooms. 8 two-bedroom units. Weekend rate in season $7 extra; 2 stories; exterior corridors; pool, heated pool; shuffleboard. **Dining:** Restaurant nearby. **Services:** Fee: coin laundry. **All Rooms:** microwaves, refrigerators, cable TV. **Some Rooms:** 14 efficiencies. *(See color ad p A71)* Ⓓ

## BEAU RIVAGE MOTOR INN

Rates Subject to Change     Phone: 609/729-2121

| | | | | | |
|---|---|---|---|---|---|
| 7/16-8/20 | | 2P/2B: | $105- | 155 | XP: $8 |
| 7/2-7/15 & 8/21-9/4 | | 2P/2B: | $90- | 135 | XP: $8 |
| 6/4-7/1 & 9/5-9/10 | | 2P/2B: | $50- | 130 | XP: $6 |
| 5/1-6/3, 9/11-10/15 & 4/28-4/30 | | 2P/2B: | $45- | 65 | XP: $6 |

Apartment Motel **Location:** Exit 4B off Garden State Pkwy, 3 mi se on SR 47, 2 1/2 mi s on Atlantic Ave. 9103 Atlantic Ave 08260. **Terms:** Open 5/1-10/15 & 4/28-4/30; reserv deposit, 21 day notice; package plans; 3 night min stay, in season; no pets. **Facility:** 49 rooms. 2- & 3-room efficiency suites. Oceanfront units have private balcony. 4 stories; exterior corridors; beachfront; beach, heated pool, wading pool; game room. **Dining:** Coffee shop; 8 am-4 pm. **Services:** Fee: coin laundry. **Recreation:** recreation program; swimming. **All Rooms:** coffeemakers, microwaves, refrigerators, cable TV. **Some Rooms:** radios. **Cards:** MC, VI.

## BEL-AIR MOTEL

Rates Subject to Change     Phone: 609/522-4235

| | | | | | | |
|---|---|---|---|---|---|---|
| 7/15-8/20 | | 2P/2B: | $105- | 142 | XP: $7 | F16 |
| 6/24-7/14 | | 2P/2B: | $77- | 130 | XP: $7 | F16 |
| 8/21-9/4 | | 2P/2B: | $78- | 124 | XP: $7 | F16 |
| 5/1-6/23 & 9/5-10/8 | | 2P/2B: | $45- | 92 | XP: $5 | F16 |

Motel **Location:** From exit 4B of Garden State Pkwy, 3 mi se on SR 47, then 1/4 mi s on Ocean Ave. 5510 Ocean Ave 08260. **Terms:** Open 5/1-10/8; reserv deposit, 21 day notice; package plans; no pets. **Facility:** 27 rooms. Traditional motel rooms, 2-room suite, 1- & 2-room efficiencies. Rates for up to 4 persons in season; 2 stories; exterior corridors; heated pool, wading pool. **Dining:** Restaurant nearby. **Services:** Fee: coin laundry. **All Rooms:** coffeemakers, free movies, refrigerators, combo & shower baths, cable TV. **Some Rooms:** 12 efficiencies. **Cards:** MC, VI. *(See ad p A71)* Ⓓ

## BISCAYNE MOTEL

Rates Subject to Change     Phone: 609/522-4444

| | | | | | |
|---|---|---|---|---|---|
| 7/9-8/20 | | 2P/2B: | $85- | 110 | XP:$6-10 |
| 6/24-7/8 & 8/21-9/3 | | 2P/2B: | $75- | 90 | XP: $8 |
| 6/17-6/23 | | 2P/2B: | $48- | 75 | XP: $6 |
| 5/1-6/16 & 9/4-10/1 | | 2P/2B: | $42- | 60 | XP: $6 |

Apartment Motel **Location:** Garden State Pkwy, exit 4B; 3 mi se on SR 47, then 1 1/2 mi s on Atlantic Ave. 7807 Atlantic Ave 08260. **Terms:** Open 5/1-10/1; reserv deposit, 21 day notice; weekly rates; no pets. **Facility:** 33 rooms. Family oriented. 1 three-bedroom unit, 6 two-bedroom units. 7 night min stay in housekeeping apartments & 3 night in motel units, in season; 3 stories, no elevator; exterior corridors; heated pool, wading pool, sundeck. **Services:** Fee: coin laundry. **All Rooms:** free movies, refrigerators, cable TV. **Some Rooms:** 20 efficiencies, microwaves. **Cards:** MC, VI. *(See ad p A71)* Ⓓ

## BLUE WATER MOTEL

Rates Subject to Change     Phone: 609/522-8340

| | | | | | |
|---|---|---|---|---|---|
| 7/17-8/25 | | 2P/2B: | $85- | 110 | XP: $10 |
| 6/19-7/16 & 8/26-9/17 | | 2P/2B: | $60- | 75 | XP: $10 |
| 5/1-6/18 & 9/18-9/30 | | 2P/2B: | $25- | 55 | XP: $10 |

Motel **Location:** SR 47, exit 4B off Garden State Pkwy 3 mi se, then 1 1/2 mi s on Atlantic Ave. 8600 Atlantic Ave 08260. **Terms:** Open 5/1-9/30; reserv deposit, 14 day notice; 3 night min stay, 7/2-9/5; no pets. **Facility:** 30 rooms. 1- & 2-room efficiency suites. Large sun deck. Attractive landscaping & picnic area with barbecue. 2 stories; exterior corridors; heated pool, wading pool; game area, pool table. **Dining:** Restaurant nearby. **Services:** Fee: coin laundry. **All Rooms:** refrigerators, cable TV, no phones. **Some Rooms:** microwaves. **Cards:** AE, MC, VI. Ⓓ ⊗

## BRISTOL PLAZA MOTOR INN

Rates Subject to Change     Phone: 609/729-1234

| | | | | | | | |
|---|---|---|---|---|---|---|---|
| 7/10-8/19 | | 2P/1B: | $121- | 168 | 2P/2B: | $121- 168 | XP:$6-10 | F3 |
| 7/3-7/9 & 8/20-8/31 | | 2P/1B: | $102- | 147 | 2P/2B: | $102- 147 | XP: $10 | F3 |
| 6/16-7/2 | | 2P/1B: | $70- | 124 | 2P/2B: | $70- 124 | XP:$6-10 | F3 |
| 5/1-6/15, 9/1-10/31 & 4/1-4/30 | | 2P/1B: | $36- | 85 | 2P/2B: | $36- 85 | XP: $6 | F3 |

Motel **Location:** Exit 4B off Garden State Pkwy, 3 mi se on SR 47, 1/2 mi s on Ocean Ave. 6407 Ocean Ave 08260. **Fax:** 609/729-9363. **Terms:** Open 5/1-10/31 & 4/1-4/30; reserv deposit, 14 day notice; package plans; no pets. **Facility:** 55 rooms. Modern contemporary rooms. Private balcony. Oceanfront sun deck. 5 stories; exterior corridors; beachfront; meeting rooms; beach, heated pool; game room. **Dining:** Restaurant nearby. **Services:** Fee: coin laundry. **Recreation:** swimming. **All Rooms:** free movies, refrigerators, cable TV. **Some Rooms:** 40 efficiencies, microwaves, radios. **Cards:** DS, MC, VI. *(See ad p A77)* Ⓓ ⊗

## CARIBBEAN MOTEL

Rates Subject to Change     Phone: 609/522-8292

| | | | | | |
|---|---|---|---|---|---|
| 6/12-9/5 | | 2P/2B: | $63- | 109 | XP: $10 |
| 5/1-6/11 & 4/16-4/30 | | 2P/2B: | $45- | 65 | XP: $6 |
| 9/6-10/15 | | 2P/2B: | $52- | 65 | XP: $6 |

Motel **Location:** From exit 4B off Garden State Pkwy, 3 1/2 mi se on SR 47, 1/4 mi s on Ocean Ave. 5600 Ocean Ave 08260. **Terms:** Open 5/1-10/15 & 4/16-4/30; reserv deposit, 21 day notice; weekly/monthly rates; package plans; no pets. **Facility:** 30 rooms. Rates for up to 4 persons in season; 2 stories; exterior corridors; meeting rooms; wading pool, small heated pool; game room, shuffleboard. **Dining:** Restaurant nearby. **Services:** Fee: coin laundry. **All Rooms:** coffeemakers, refrigerators, cable TV. **Some Rooms:** 9 efficiencies. **Cards:** MC, VI. Ⓓ

## CARRIAGE STOP MOTEL

Rates Subject to Change     Phone: 609/522-6400

| | | | | | | | |
|---|---|---|---|---|---|---|---|
| 7/1-7/4 & 7/15-8/14 | | 2P/1B: | $100- | 121 | 2P/2B: | $114- 131 | XP: $10 | F12 |
| 7/5-7/14 & 8/15-9/4 | | 2P/1B: | $79- | 100 | 2P/2B: | $82- 112 | XP:$7-10 | F12 |
| 5/26-5/29 & 6/17-6/30 | | 2P/1B: | $69- | 89 | 2P/2B: | $75- 99 | XP: $7 | F12 |
| 5/1-5/25, 5/30-6/16 & 9/5-10/18 | | 2P/1B: | $38- | 64 | 2P/2B: | $40- 67 | XP: $5 | F12 |

Motel **Location:** Garden State Pkwy, exit 4B, 3 mi se on SR 47, 1 1/2 mi s on Atlantic Ave. 400 E St Paul Ave 08260. **Fax:** 609/523-1583. **Terms:** Open 5/1-10/18; reserv deposit, 7 day notice; weekly rates; package plans; 3 night min stay, 7/1-8/31; pets, $25. **Facility:** 31 rooms. 1- & 2-room efficiency units. Rates for up to 4 persons; 3 stories, no elevator; exterior corridors; heated pool, wading pool, sun deck; barbecue grills, shuffleboard. **All Rooms:** coffeemakers, efficiencies, refrigerators, cable TV, no phones. **Cards:** AE, DS, MC, VI. Ⓓ

**COMMANDER BY THE SEA**

| | Guaranteed Rates | | | | Phone: 609/522-2802 |
|---|---|---|---|---|---|

| | | | | |
|---|---|---|---|---|
| 7/9-8/20 | 2P/1B: | $79 | 2P/2B: | $125- 140  XP: $10  F6 |
| 6/16-7/8 & 8/21-9/4 | 2P/1B: | $65 | 2P/2B: | $98- 125  XP: $8  F6 |
| 5/26-6/15 & 9/5-9/17 | 2P/1B: | $55 | 2P/2B: | $75- 105  XP: $8  F6 |
| 5/1-5/25 & 9/18-10/15 | 2P/1B: | $45 | 2P/2B: | $47- 70  XP: $7  F6 |

Apartment
Motel

**Location:** SR 47 exit 4B off Garden State Pkwy, 3 mi se, then 1 1/2 mi s on Atlantic Ave. 8803 Atlantic Ave 08260. **Terms:** Open 5/10/15; reserv deposit, 14 day notice; package plans; 3 night min stay; no pets. **Facility:** 40 rooms. Most units with sitting rooms. A family oriented motel. Complimentary morning coffee. Rates for up to 4 persons in season; 3 stories; exterior corridors; beach, heated pool, wading pool; video games, pool table. **Dining:** Restaurant nearby. **Services:** Fee: coin laundry. **Recreation:** recreation program; swimming. **All Rooms:** free movies, refrigerators, cable TV, no phones. **Some Rooms:** 31 efficiencies, microwaves. **Cards:** MC, VI.  (D) ⊗

## *Compass Motor Inn*

### A *family* resort located in beautiful Wildwood Crest

N  W  E  S

We welcome you to enjoy uncompromising hospitality at a family resort located just steps from the beautiful white beaches of Wildwood Crest. Ask about our Weekend, Holiday, and Summer money-saving specials.

♦ Efficiencies & Motel Rooms
♦ Game Room, Pool Table
♦ Shuffleboard, Ping Pong
♦ Major Credit Cards Welcome

♦ Miniature Golf Course
♦ Daily Maid Service
♦ Direct Dial Telephones
♦ Much Much More!

♦ Olympic Size Heated Pool
♦ Barbecue Grills

Winter Hours: 9 Am to 5 Pm

For a color brochure, or to make reservations call *toll free* **(800) 624-2530**

## Bristol *Plaza*

6407 Ocean Avenue
Wildwood Crest, NJ, 08260
**Call Toll FREE: 800-433-9731**
Winter Hours: 9am-5pm

*Located Directly on the glistening sands of the Wildwood Crest beach, amidst the panoramic view of the Atlantic Ocean. elegant accommodations await you and your family...*

•*Deluxe Motel Rooms, Fully equipped 2-Room Efficiencies & 2 Room Suites*

•A/C & Heat
•Oceanfront
•Cable color TV
•Elevator

•Direct Dial Phones
•Refrigerators in room
•Meeting Room
*Bar-B-Que

•Game Room
•Southern exposure
•Laundromat
•Heated Pool

•Kiddie Pool
•Sundeck
•Major Credit Cards

*Weekend, Holiday & Summer Packages Available!*
No other motel in the Wildwood's rated higher

AAA APPROVED

---

## AAA'S REDUCING PLAN.
AAA **Special Value Rates** means a 10-percent minimum reduction off the rates printed in the TourBook.

**COMPASS MOTOR INN**  
(AAA)  
7/12-8/20  
5/1-7/11, 8/21-10/31 &  
4/15-4/30  
Motel  
Rates Subject to Change  
2P/1B: $92- 114 2P/2B: $92- 114 XP:$4-8 F3  

2P/1B: $35- 62 2P/2B: $35- 62 XP: $4 F3  
Phone: 609/522-6948  

**Location:** Exit 4B off Garden State Pkwy, 3 mi se on SR 47, then 1 mi s on Atlantic Ave. 6501 Atlantic Ave 08260. Fax: 609/729-9363. **Terms:** Open 5/1-10/31 & 4/15-4/30; reserv deposit, 14 day notice; weekly rates; package plans; no pets. **Facility:** 50 rooms. Rates are for up to 4 persons, 7/13-8/21, 9/6-10/15 & 4/15-5/26; 3 stories, no elevator; exterior corridors; meeting rooms; miniature golf; heated pool, wading pool; game room, shuffleboard. **Services:** Fee: coin laundry. **All Rooms:** coffeemakers, refrigerators, cable TV. **Some Rooms:** 25 efficiencies, microwaves. **Cards:** DS, MC, VI. *(See ad p A77)*  (D) ⊗

**CRUSADER RESORT MOTOR INN**  
(AAA)  
7/11-9/4  
6/24-7/10  
Motor Inn  
5/27-6/23 & 9/5-9/17  
5/1-5/26, 9/18-10/16 &  
4/2-4/30  
Rates Subject to Change  
2P/1B: $129- 136 2P/2B: $149- 188 XP:$6-12  
2P/1B: $107- 122 2P/2B: $144- 155 XP: $12  
2P/1B: $74- 90 2P/2B: $95- 107 XP: $6  

2P/1B: $45- 70 2P/2B: $62- 84 XP: $6  
Phone: 609/522-6991  

**Location:** At Ocean Ave & Cardinal Rd, Exit 4B off Garden State Pkwy 3 mi se on SR 47, then 1/2 mi s on Ocean Ave. 6101 Ocean Ave 08260 (PO Box 1308). Fax: 609/522-2280. **Terms:** Open 5/1-10/16 & 4/2-4/30; reserv deposit, 14 day notice; BP, CP available, off season; package plans; no pets. **Facility:** 60 rooms. 3 stories; exterior corridors; beachfront; meeting rooms; beach, heated pool, wading pool, sauna; beach volleyball. **Dining:** Restaurant; 7 am-9 pm; $4-$9. **Services:** data ports. Fee: coin laundry, area transportation. **Recreation:** swimming. **All Rooms:** coffeemakers, microwaves, free movies, refrigerators, combo & shower baths, cable TV. **Some Rooms:** 39 efficiencies. **Cards:** AE, MC, VI.  (D)

**DIAMOND CREST MOTEL**  
(AAA)  
7/10-8/22  
6/11-7/9  
Apartment  
Motel  
8/23-10/10  
5/8-6/10  
Rates Subject to Change  
2P/2B: $110- 115 XP:$5-7 D8  
2P/2B: $50- 100 XP:$5-7 D8  
2P/2B: $52- 79 XP:$5-7 D8  
2P/2B: $32- 61 XP:$5-7 D8  
Phone: 609/522-0974  

**Location:** 4B exit off Garden State Pkwy; 3 mi se on SR 47, 1 1/2 mi s on Atlantic Ave. 7011 Atlantic Ave 08260. **Terms:** Open 5/8-10/10; reserv deposit, 14 day notice; package plans; no pets. **Facility:** 53 rooms. 3 stories, no elevator; exterior corridors; putting green; heated pool, wading pool. **Services:** Fee: coin laundry. **All Rooms:** refrigerators, cable TV. **Some Rooms:** 39 efficiencies. **Cards:** AE, DS, MC, VI. *(See ad p A72)*  (D)

**EL CORONADO MOTOR INN**  
(AAA)  
7/10-8/28  
6/2-7/9  
Motor Inn  
8/29-10/15  
5/5-6/1 & 4/15-4/30  
Rates Subject to Change  
2P/1B: $117- 127 2P/2B: $155- 224 XP: $10 F12  
2P/1B: $73- 106 2P/2B: $91- 224 XP: $10 F12  
2P/1B: $47- 116 2P/2B: $59- 218 XP: $5 F12  
2P/1B: $51- 81 2P/2B: $59- 158 XP: $5 F12  
Phone: 609/729-1000  

**Location:** Garden State Pkwy exit 4B to SR 47, 3 mi se on Atlantic Ave, then 1 1/2 mi s on Atlantic Ave. 8501 Atlantic Ave 08260. Fax: 609/729-6557. **Terms:** Open 5/5-10/15 & 4/15-4/30; reserv deposit, 14 day notice; package plans; no pets. **Facility:** 113 rooms. Traditional motel rooms. 8 two-bedroom units. 6 stories; interior corridors; beachfront; meeting rooms; heated pool, wading pool, saunas, whirlpool. **Dining:** Coffee shop; 7:30 am-4 pm. **Services:** Fee: coin laundry. **Recreation:** children's program, social program. **All Rooms:** free movies, refrigerators, cable TV. **Some Rooms:** coffeemakers, 63 efficiencies, radios. **Cards:** AE, DS, MC, VI. *(See color ad below)*  (D)

**FLEUR DE LIS**  
(AAA)  
7/14-8/19  
6/23-7/13 & 8/20-8/31  
Apartment  
Motel  
5/26-6/22 & 9/1-9/16  
5/1-5/25, 9/17-10/16 &  
4/14-4/30  
Rates Subject to Change  
1P: $95- 150 2P/1B: $95- 150 2P/2B: $95- 150 XP:$5-10  
1P: $90- 130 2P/1B: $90- 130 2P/2B: $90- 130 XP: $10  
1P: $55- 80 2P/1B: $55- 80 XP: $8  

1P: $38- 55 2P/1B: $38- 55 XP: $6  
Phone: 609/522-0123  

**Location:** 3 mi se on SR 47, exit 4B off Garden State Pkwy, then 1/2 mi s on Ocean Ave. 6105 Ocean Ave 08260. **Terms:** Open 5/1-10/16 & 4/14-4/30; reserv deposit, 21 day notice; package plans; no pets. **Facility:** 44 rooms. Guests may choose from traditional motel rooms, 2-bedroom suites, oceanfront efficiencies, 2-bedroom efficiencies & 3-bedroom efficiency suites. Oceanfront sun decks. 3 night min stay in season, 4 night min stay in efficiencies. Rates for up to 4 persons in season. Weekends $10 extra in season; $5 off season; 3 stories; exterior corridors; beachfront; meeting rooms; beach, heated pool, wading pool. **Services:** Fee: coin laundry. **Recreation:** swimming. **All Rooms:** cable TV. **Some Rooms:** refrigerators. **Cards:** AE, MC, VI. *(See color ad p A70)*  (D) ⊗

**CHECK-IN TIME?** It is noted in the listing if it is after 3 p.m.

**GONDOLIER MOTEL**      Guaranteed Rates      Phone: 609/522-6974

| | | | |
|---|---|---|---|
| 7/14-8/19 | 2P/2B: | $105- 219 | XP:$7-10 |
| 6/30-7/13 & 8/20-9/4 | 2P/2B: | $79- 185 | XP: $10 |
| 5/30-6/29 & 9/5-9/16 | 2P/2B: | $50- 119 | XP: $7 |
| 5/1-5/29 & 9/17-10/9 | 2P/2B: | $42- 89 | XP: $7 |

Motel

**Location:** On the beach at Lavender Rd. 5701 Ocean Ave 08260. Fax: 609/523-8379. **Terms:** Open 5/1-10/9; reserv deposit, 14 day notice; package plans; no pets. **Facility:** 43 rooms. 2nd floor sundeck overlooks the beach. 1 two-bedroom unit. Rates are for up to 4 persons; 3 stories; interior/exterior corridors; beachfront; beach, heated pool, wading pool; barbecue grills. **Dining:** Coffee shop nearby. **Services:** area transportation, to bus terminal, airport transportation. Fee: coin laundry. **Recreation:** swimming. **All Rooms:** coffeemakers, refrigerators, cable TV. **Some Rooms:** 25 efficiencies. **Cards:** DI, DS, MC, VI.   Ⓓ

**GRANADA MOTEL**      Rates Subject to Change      Phone: 609/522-9020

| | | | | | |
|---|---|---|---|---|---|
| 7/1-8/26 | 2P/1B: | $79 | 2P/2B: | $129- 165 | XP: $10 F6 |
| 6/16-6/30 & 8/27-8/31 | 2P/1B: | $69 | 2P/2B: | $99- 129 | XP: $10 F6 |
| 5/26-6/15 & 9/1-9/18 | 2P/1B: | $42- 51 | 2P/2B: | $62- 99 | XP: $8 F6 |
| 5/1-5/25, 9/19-10/16 & 4/14-4/30 | 2P/1B: | $39 | 2P/2B: | $49- 82 | XP: $8 F6 |

Apartment
Motel

**Location:** SR 47 exit 4B off Garden State Pkwy; 3 mi se, then 1 1/2 mi s on Atlantic Ave. 8801 Atlantic Ave at Topeka Ave 08260. Fax: 609/523-1583. **Terms:** Open 5/1-10/16 & 4/14-4/30; reserv deposit; package plans; 3 night min stay, in season; no pets. **Facility:** 37 rooms. 21 efficiency units, most with sitting room. Oceanfront rooms with private sun deck. Rates for up to 4 persons; 3 stories; exterior corridors; beachfront; beach, heated pool, wading pool; beach volleyball, ping pong, shuffleboard. **Dining:** Restaurant nearby. **Services:** data ports. Fee: coin laundry. **Recreation:** swimming. **All Rooms:** refrigerators, combo & shower baths, cable TV. **Some Rooms:** Fee: microwaves. **Cards:** AE, DS, MC, VI. *(See ad p A73)*   Ⓓ ⊗

**HAWAII KAI MOTOR INN**      Rates Subject to Change      Phone: 609/522-8181

| | | | | | |
|---|---|---|---|---|---|
| 7/17-8/13 & 9/1-9/4 | 2P/1B: | $88- 110 | 2P/2B: | $88- 110 | XP: $10 |
| 6/26-7/16 & 8/14-8/31 | 2P/1B: | $70- 85 | 2P/2B: | $70- 85 | XP: $10 |
| 5/1-6/25, 9/5-9/30 & 4/25-4/30 | 2P/1B: | $45- 65 | 2P/2B: | $45- 65 | XP: $10 |

Motel

**Location:** Garden State Pkwy, exit 4B, 3 mi se on SR 47, 1 1/2 mi s on Ocean Ave. 7504 Ocean Ave 08260. **Terms:** Open 5/1-9/30 & 4/25-4/30; reserv deposit, 21 day notice; package plans; 2 night min stay, weekends, 7/1-8/31; no pets. **Facility:** 30 rooms. Traditonal motel rooms, 1- & 2-room efficiencies. 3 stories; exterior corridors; wading pool, small pool. **Services:** Fee: coin laundry. **All Rooms:** refrigerators, cable TV, no phones. **Cards:** AE, MC, VI.   Ⓓ

**HIALEAH RESORT MOTEL**

Guaranteed Rates

Phone: 609/522-6655

| | | | | | |
|---|---|---|---|---|---|
| 7/10-8/19 | | 2P/2B: | $80- 100 | XP: $5 | F3 |
| 6/30-7/9 & 8/20-8/31 | | 2P/2B: | $70- 91 | XP: $5 | F3 |
| 5/25-6/29 & 9/1-9/17 | | 2P/2B: | $45- 66 | XP: $5 | F3 |
| Apartment 5/1-5/24, 9/18-10/30 & | | | | | |
| Motel 4/15-4/30 | | 2P/2B: | $35- 50 | XP: $5 | F3 |

**Location:** Exit 4B off Garden State Pkwy 3 mi se on SR 47, 1/2 mi s on Atlantic Ave. 6211 Atlantic Ave at Wisteria Rd 08260. **Terms:** Open 5/1-10/30 & 4/15-4/30; reserv deposit, 14 day notice; package plans; no pets. **Facility:** 52 rooms. 3 stories, no elevator; exterior corridors; meeting rooms; heated pool, wading pool; game room. **Services:** Fee: coin laundry. **All Rooms:** free movies, refrigerators, combo & shower baths, cable TV. **Some Rooms:** coffeemakers, 42 efficiencies. **Cards:** AE, DS, MC, VI. Ⓓ

**IMPERIAL 500 MOTEL**

Rates Subject to Change

Phone: 609/522-6063

| | | | | |
|---|---|---|---|---|
| 6/30-7/4, 7/7-8/20 & 9/1-9/4 | | 2P/2B: | $90- 105 | XP: $5 |
| Motel 6/23-6/29, 7/5-7/6 & | | | | |
| 8/21-8/31 | | 2P/2B: | $70- 85 | XP: $5 |
| 5/29-6/22 & 9/5-9/24 | | 2P/2B: | $45- 60 | XP: $5 |
| 5/1-5/28, 9/25-10/15 & | | | | |
| 4/1-4/30 | | 2P/2B: | $45- 55 | XP: $5 |

**Location:** Garden State Pkwy exit 4B, SR 47 se to Atlantic Ave, then 1 mi s. 6601 Atlantic Ave 08260. **Terms:** Open 5/1-10/15 & 4/1-4/30; reserv deposit, 45 day notice; package plans; no pets. **Facility:** 45 rooms. 13 two-bedroom units. Rates for up to 4 persons 7/2-9/2; 3 stories, no elevator; exterior corridors; meeting rooms; heated pool, wading pool; shuffleboard, horseshoes, pool tables, game room. **Services:** Fee: coin laundry. **All Rooms:** refrigerators, cable TV. **Some Rooms:** 26 efficiencies, microwaves. **Cards:** DS, MC, VI.

**JOLLY ROGER MOTEL**

Guaranteed Rates

Phone: 609/522-6915

| | | | | |
|---|---|---|---|---|
| 7/15-8/19 | 2P/2B: | $94- 149 | XP: $7 | F5 |
| Motel 6/30-7/14 & 8/20-8/26 | 2P/2B: | $89- 126 | XP: $5 | F5 |
| 6/2-6/29 & 8/27-9/16 | 2P/2B: | $83- 115 | XP: $5 | F5 |
| 5/19-6/1 & 9/17-9/23 | 2P/2B: | $48- 70 | XP: $3 | F5 |

**Location:** Exit 4B off Garden State Pkwy 3 mi se on SR 47, then 1 mi s on Atlantic Ave. 6805 Atlantic Ave 08260. **Terms:** Open 5/19-9/23; reserv deposit, 14 day notice; package plans; 3 night min stay, in season; no pets. **Facility:** 74 rooms. Private balcony. 2 two-bedroom units. 3 stories, no elevator; exterior corridors; meeting rooms; heated pool, wading pool, sun-deck; 1 tennis court; game room, shuffleboard, social program 7/1-9/4, barbecue grills. **Dining:** Coffee shop; 8 am-4 pm in season. **Services:** Fee: coin laundry. **Recreation:** children's program. **All Rooms:** refrigerators, combo & shower baths, cable TV. **Some Rooms:** coffeemakers, 30 efficiencies, microwaves. **Cards:** MC, VI. Ⓓ

**LOTUS MOTOR INN**

Rates Subject to Change

Phone: 609/522-6300

| | | | |
|---|---|---|---|
| 6/30-8/19 & 9/1-9/3 [CP] | 2P/2B: | $100- 140 | XP: $10 |
| 8/20-8/31 [CP] | 2P/2B: | $85- 125 | XP: $10 |
| Motel 6/23-6/29 [CP] | 2P/2B: | $70- 95 | XP: $10 |
| 5/1-6/22, 9/4-10/29 & | | | |
| 4/14-4/30 [EP] | 2P/2B: | $40- 80 | XP:$5-10 |

**Location:** Exit 4B off Garden State Pkwy, 3 mi se on Ocean Ave. 6900 Ocean Ave 08260. **Fax:** 609/729-0203. **Terms:** Open 5/1-10/29 & 4/14-4/30; reserv deposit, 14 day notice; package plans; 2 night min stay, weekends, July & Aug; no pets. **Facility:** 62 rooms. Motel rooms & 2-room efficiencies, many with private balcony. 3 stories; exterior corridors; heated pool, wading pool; sun deck. **Services:** Fee: coin laundry. **All Rooms:** microwaves, free movies, refrigerators, cable TV. **Some Rooms:** coffeemakers, 52 efficiencies. **Cards:** AE, DI, DS, MC, VI. Ⓓ ⊗

**MADRID OCEAN RESORT**

Rates Subject to Change

Phone: 609/729-1600

| | | | | | |
|---|---|---|---|---|---|
| 7/1-8/25 & 9/1-9/16 | 2P/1B: | $95 | 2P/2B: | $125- 140 | XP: $10 |
| 6/20-6/30 & 8/26-8/31 | 2P/1B: | $85 | 2P/2B: | $95- 110 | XP: $10 |
| 5/13-6/19 | 2P/1B: | $60 | 2P/2B: | $65- 80 | XP: $10 |
| Motor Inn 9/17-10/1 | 2P/1B: | $40 | 2P/2B: | $45- 60 | XP: $10 |

**Location:** Off 8000 blk of Atlantic Ave; exit 4B off Garden State Pkwy, 3 mi se on SR 47, 1 1/2 mi s on Atlantic Ave to Miami Ave. 427 Miami Ave 08260. **Fax:** 609/729-8483. **Terms:** Open 5/13-10/1; reserv deposit, 21 day notice; package plans; no pets. **Facility:** 54 rooms. 5 stories; exterior corridors; beachfront; meeting rooms; beach, heated pool, wading pool, beach volleyball; game room, shuffleboard. **Dining:** Restaurant; 7 am-10 pm; off season to 6 pm; $3-$13. **Services:** Fee: coin laundry. **Recreation:** swimming. **All Rooms:** free movies, refrigerators, cable TV. **Some Rooms:** coffeemakers, 24 efficiencies. **Cards:** AE, MC, VI. Ⓓ

**THE MARINER RESORT MOTEL**

Rates Subject to Change

Phone: 609/522-1849

| | | | | | | | | |
|---|---|---|---|---|---|---|---|---|
| 7/1-8/20 | 1P: | $83 | 2P/1B: | $83- 88 | 2P/2B: | $91- 107 | XP: $8 |
| 8/21-9/5 | 1P: | $70 | 2P/1B: | $72- 77 | 2P/2B: | $86- 102 | XP: $8 |
| Motel 5/1-6/30 & 9/6-4/30 | 1P: | $45 | 2P/1B: | $45- 66 | 2P/2B: | $50- 72 | XP: $8 |

**Location:** From exit 4B off Garden State Pkwy on SR 47, then 1 1/2 mi s on Atlantic Ave. 407 E Monterey Ave 08260. **Terms:** Reserv deposit, 14 day notice; package plans; no pets. **Facility:** 14 rooms. Family oriented. 1 two-bedroom unit. Maximum rates for up to 4 persons, 7/11-8/23; 2 stories; exterior corridors; heated pool; sun deck. **Services:** Fee: coin laundry. **All Rooms:** coffeemakers, efficiencies, microwaves, refrigerators, combo & shower baths, cable TV. **Some Rooms:** VCP's. **Cards:** AE, DS, MC, VI. Ⓓ

DIAMONDS tell the story—read Using Your TourBook.

**MONTA CELLO MOTEL**        Rates Subject to Change                    Phone: 609/522-4758

(AAA)
    7/1-9/4                                        2P/2B:  $62-  87  XP:$3-6  F5
    5/13-6/30                                      2P/2B:  $22-  59  XP:$2-4  F5
◆ ◆
Motel   9/5-9/24                                      2P/2B:  $53-  59  XP:$2-4  F5

**Location:** Garden State Pkwy exit 4B, 3 mi se on SR 47, then 1 mi s on Seaview Ave to jct with Denver Ave. 8400 Seaview Ave 08260. **Terms:** Open 5/13-9/24; reserv deposit, 14 day notice, cancellation fee imposed; 3 night min stay, for efficiencies; no pets. **Facility:** 21 rooms. Rates for up to 6 persons; 5/13-9/24 efficiency suite $36-$123; 2 stories; exterior corridors; heated pool, wading pool. **Services:** Fee: coin laundry. **All Rooms:** refrigerators, combo & shower baths, cable TV, no phones. **Some Rooms:** microwaves. **Cards:** MC, VI.     (D)

---

**NASSAU INN**        Guaranteed Rates                    Phone: 609/729-9077

(AAA)
    6/30-9/4                     2P/1B:  $95-  115   2P/2B:  $130-  163  XP:  $10  D3
    6/16-6/29                    2P/1B:  $80          2P/2B:  $90-   100  XP:  $7   D3
◆ ◆ ◆
Apartment 5/31-6/15 & 9/5-9/16       2P/1B:  $65          2P/2B:  $75-   85   XP:  $7   D3
Motel   5/1-5/30, 9/17-10/10 &
    4/28-4/30                    2P/1B:  $55          2P/2B:  $65-   75   XP:  $7   D3

**Location:** From exit 4B off Garden State Pkwy, 3 mi se on SR 47, then 1/2 mi s on Ocean Ave. 6201 Ocean Ave at Sweetbriar Rd 08260. **Terms:** Open 5/1-10/10 & 4/28-4/30; reserv deposit, 14 day notice; package plans; no pets. **Facility:** 56 rooms. Attractively furnished motel suites & efficiency apartments. Private balcony & oceanfront sun deck. 2 two-bedroom units. 7/2-9/6 maximum rates for up to 4 persons; 5 stories; exterior corridors; beachfront; beach, heated pool, wading pool. **Dining:** Coffee shop nearby. **Services:** Fee: coin laundry. **Recreation:** swimming. **All Rooms:** cable TV. **Some Rooms:** 40 efficiencies, refrigerators. **Cards:** DS, MC, VI. *(See color ad p A71)*

---

**PAN AMERICAN HOTEL**        Guaranteed Rates                    Phone: 609/522-6936

(AAA)
    6/30-9/4                     2P/1B:  $120         2P/2B:  $146-  180  XP:$6-12  F4
    6/9-6/29                     2P/1B:  $76-  102    2P/2B:  $86-   150  XP:  $12  F4
◆ ◆ ◆
Motor Inn 6/2-6/8 & 9/5-9/16          2P/1B:  $76          2P/2B:  $79-   106  XP:  $6   F4
    5/5-6/1 & 9/17-10/8          2P/1B:  $58          2P/2B:  $65-   83   XP:  $6   F4

**Location:** At Crocus Rd; exit 4B off Garden State Pkwy, 3 mi se on SR 47, then 1/2 mi s on Ocean Ave. 5901 Ocean Ave 08260. Fax: 609/522-6937. **Terms:** Open 5/5-10/8; reserv deposit, 14 day notice, cancellation fee imposed; package plans, off season; no pets. **Facility:** 78 rooms. Maximum rates 6/26-9/6 for up to 4 persons; 4 stories; interior corridors; beachfront; meeting rooms; beach, heated pool, wading pool, sauna. **Dining:** Dining room; 7:30 am-9 pm in season; $3-$17. **Services:** Fee: coin laundry. **Recreation:** children's program, social program; swimming. **All Rooms:** free movies, refrigerators, combo & shower baths, cable TV. **Some Rooms:** 49 efficiencies, microwaves, VCP's. **Cards:** MC, VI. *(See ad p A73)*     (D)

---

**PORT ROYAL HOTEL**        Guaranteed Rates                    Phone: 609/729-2000

(AAA)
    6/30-9/4                     2P/1B:  $121-  130   2P/2B:  $145-  178  XP:  $12
    6/23-6/29                    2P/1B:  $102-  108   2P/2B:  $122-  151  XP:  $12
◆ ◆ ◆
Motor Inn 6/16-6/22                   2P/1B:  $91-   95    2P/2B:  $101-  122  XP:  $6
    5/12-6/15 & 9/5-10/8         2P/1B:  $78-   82    2P/2B:  $86-   106  XP:  $6

**Location:** Exit 4B off Garden State Pkwy, 3 mi se on SR 47, then 1 mi s on Ocean Ave. 6801 Ocean Ave 08260. Fax: 609/729-2051. **Terms:** Open 5/12-10/8; package plans; 4 night min stay, in season; no pets. **Facility:** 100 rooms. Ocean suites, efficiency apartments & motel rooms avail with private balcony. 50 efficiencies, $168-$173 in season; 6 stories; interior corridors; beachfront; meeting rooms; beach, heated pool, wading pool, sauna; social program 7/1-8/30. Fee: parking. **Dining:** Dining room; 8 am-3 pm; 6/15-9/6 to 8 pm; $9-$16. **Services:** Fee: coin laundry. **Recreation:** swimming. **All Rooms:** refrigerators, cable TV. **Some Rooms:** coffeemakers, microwaves. **Cards:** MC, VI. *(See ad p A73)*     (D)

---

**SIESTA MOTELS**        Rates Subject to Change                    Phone: 609/522-2527

(AAA)
    7/8-8/20                                       2P/2B:  $99-  206  XP:  $15
    6/24-7/7                                       2P/2B:  $85-  202  XP:  $15
◆ ◆
Complex 8/21-9/3                                   2P/2B:  $85-  160  XP:$6-7
    5/1-6/23, 9/4-10/31 &
    4/1-4/30                                       2P/2B:  $37-  147  XP:$6-7

**Location:** At Ocean & Morning glory aves; from the Garden State Pkwy, exit 4B; 3 mi se on SR 47, then 1/4 mi s on Ocean Ave. 5410 Ocean Ave 08260. Fax: 609/522-4662. **Terms:** Open 5/1-10/31 & 4/1-4/30; reserv deposit, 21 day notice; weekly rates; BP available; package plans; no pets. **Facility:** 55 rooms. Traditional motel units, 1 & 2-room efficiencies; 1, 2 & 3-bedroom apartments; 1, 2 & 4-bedroom cottages. Attractive courtyard with gazebo in the cottage area. Rates based on 4 person occupancy; 13 cottages & 5 apartments avail 6/20-9/19, $292-$1270 weekly; 2 stories; exterior corridors; heated pool. **Dining:** Restaurant nearby. **Services:** Fee: coin laundry. **All Rooms:** cable TV. **Some Rooms:** coffeemakers, microwaves, refrigerators. Fee: VCP's. **Cards:** AE, CB, DI, DS, MC, VI.     (D)

---

**TANGIERS MOTEL**        Rates Subject to Change                    Phone: 609/522-1414

(AAA)
    7/14-8/20     1P:  $98-  114   2P/1B:  $98-  114   2P/2B:  $98-  114  XP:  $10   F6
    6/30-7/13 & 8/21-9/3  1P:  $80-  92   2P/1B:  $80-  92   2P/2B:  $80-  92   XP:  $10   F6
◆ ◆
Motel   6/16-6/29     1P:  $67-  81   2P/1B:  $67-  81   2P/2B:  $67-  81   XP:$7-10  F6
    5/1-6/15 & 9/4-10/16  1P:  $36-  61   2P/1B:  $36-  61   2P/2B:  $36-  61   XP:  $5   F6

**Location:** At Sweet Briar Rd & Atlantic Ave. 6201 Atlantic Ave 08260. Fax: 609/523-1583. **Terms:** Open 5/1-10/16; reserv deposit, 14 day notice; package plans; 3 night min stay, 7/15-8/21; no pets. **Facility:** 50 rooms. Traditional motel rooms. 1- & 2-bedroom efficiencies. Complimentary coffee in lobby. 3 stories, no elevator; exterior corridors; heated pool, wading pool; game room, ping pong, shuffleboard. **Dining:** Coffee shop; 7 am-9 pm; 4/1-4/30 & 10/1-10/31 7 am-10 am; 5/1-6/30 & 9/7-9/30 7 am-2 pm; $3-$5. **All Rooms:** refrigerators, combo & shower baths, cable TV. **Some Rooms:** Fee: microwaves. **Cards:** AE, DI, MC, VI.     (D) ⊗

---

## When making reservations, state:

1. Your AAA/CAA membership.          4. Type of accommodations desired.
2. Number of persons in your party.   5. Rate preferred.
3. Ages of any children.             6. Date and estimated arrival time.
       7. Length of stay.

**WATERWAYS MOTEL**          Guaranteed Rates          **Phone: 609/522-2845**

◆◆     7/1-9/3                                   2P/2B:   $65-   104

Motel     5/29-6/30 & 9/4-9/30                   2P/2B:   $40-   55

           5/1-5/28 & 10/1-10/15                 2P/2B:   $30-   40

**Location:** Garden State Pkwy exit 4B, 3 mi se on SR 47 to Ocean Ave, s 1 1/4 mi. 7204 Ocean Ave 08260. **Terms:** Open 5/1-10/15; reserv deposit, 40 day notice; package plans; no pets. **Facility:** 25 rooms. Rates for up to 4 persons in efficiencies & 2-room suites, 3 persons in motel rooms, 5/25-6/30 for 2 persons; 3 stories, no elevator; exterior corridors; meeting rooms; miniature golf; beach access, heated pool, wading pool; game room, sun deck. **Services:** Fee: coin laundry. **All Rooms:** free movies, refrigerators, cable TV. **Some Rooms:** coffeemakers, 20 efficiencies, microwaves. **Cards:** AE, DS, MC, VI. *(See color ad p A80)* Ⓓ

## RESTAURANTS

**THE CAPTAIN'S TABLE RESTAURANT**          **Dinner:** $11-$20          **Phone: 609/522-2939**

⊛         **Location:** From SR 47 exit 4B, 3 mi se, then 1/2 mi s on Atlantic Ave. 8701 Atlantic Ave W 08260.

           **Hours:** Open 5/8-9/20; 8 am-noon & 4:30-10 pm, Sun 8 am-1 & 4:30-10 pm. **Reservations:** suggested.

◆◆        **Features:** casual dress; children's menu; early bird specials; carryout; minimum charge-$10; a la carte.

American     Family oriented. Dining room offers a nice view of the beach. **Cards:** AE, CB, DI, DS, MC, VI.   ⊗

**DUFFY'S ON THE LAKE**          **Dinner:** $11-$20          **Phone: 609/522-1815**

           **Location:** From Garden State Pkwy, exit 4B, 2 3/4 mi se on SR 47, then 1 1/2 mi s on New Jersey Ave.

American     7601 New Jersey Ave 08260. **Hours:** Open 5/30-9/15; 4:30 pm-9:30 pm. **Reservations:** suggested.

           **Features:** casual dress; children's menu; early bird specials; a la carte. Family oriented. Dining room offers an excellent view of the bay. **Cards:** MC, VI.

# WOODBRIDGE—93,100   (See NEW JERSEY METRO AREA ACCOMMODATIONS spotting map pages A40 & A41; see index starting on page A39)

## LODGINGS

| | | | | |
|---|---|---|---|---|
| **BUDGET MOTOR LODGE** | Guaranteed Rates | | **Phone: 908/636-4000** 🉑112 | |

◆◆     All Year       1P: $48- 75   2P/1B: $48- 75   2P/2B: $58- 80   XP: $5   F14

Motor Inn   **Location:** NJ Tpk exit 11, 1 mi s on Rt 9N. 350 Rt 9N 07095. Fax: 908/636-0636. **Terms:** Sr. discount; no pets. **Facility:** 168 rooms. 5 stories; interior corridors; conference facilities; exercise room. **Dining & Entertainment:** Restaurant; 6:30 am-2 & 4-10 pm; $9-$20; cocktails/lounge. **Services:** valet laundry. **All Rooms:** free movies, cable TV. **Some Rooms:** Fee: VCP's. **Cards:** AE, CB, DI, DS, MC, VI.   Ⓓ ⊗

**DAYS INN**          Rates Subject to Change          **Phone: 908/634-4200** 🉑114

⊛     All Year [CP]    1P: $50- 60   2P/1B: $60- 70   2P/2B: $70- 80   XP: $10   F12

           **Location:** Garden State Pkwy exit 130, 1 1/2 mi on Rt 1; NJ Tpk exit 11, 1 1/2 mi n on Rt 35, to Rt 1S. US

Motel     Rt 1S 08830. Fax: 908/634-7840. **Terms:** Sr. discount; reserv deposit, 3 day notice; small pets only.

           **Facility:** 78 rooms. 2 stories; interior/exterior corridors. **All Rooms:** free movies, cable TV. **Some Rooms:** radios. Fee: VCP's, whirlpools. **Cards:** AE, CB, DI, DS.   Ⓓ Ⓢ ⊗

**SHERATON AT WOODBRIDGE PLACE**     Rates Subject to Change     **Phone: 908/634-3600** 🉑115

◆◆◆   Sun-Thurs [EP]   1P: $98- 135   2P/1B: $108- 135   2P/2B: $108- 135   XP: $10   F12

Hotel     Fri & Sat [BP]    1P: $69        2P/1B: $69        2P/2B: $69       XP: $10   F12

           **Location:** On US 1 southbound, 2 mi s of jct SR 9; diagonal to Woodbridge Center. 515 Rt 1S 08830. Fax: 908/634-0258. **Terms:** Credit card guarantee; monthly rates; package plans; weekends & seasonal; no pets. **Facility:** 253 rooms. Enjoy comfortable accommodations in a friendly & inviting atmosphere; cordial staff. Convenient to large shopping areas. 7 stories; interior corridors; conference facilities, convention oriented; luxury level rooms; 2 pools (2 heated, 1 indoor), whirlpool; exercise room. **Dining & Entertainment:** Dining room, restaurant; 6 am-11 pm; $6-$30; health conscious menu items; cocktails/lounge; entertainment, nightclub. **Services:** data ports, secretarial services; valet laundry; area transportation. **All Rooms:** free & pay movies, cable TV. **Some Rooms:** microwaves, refrigerators. **Cards:** AE, CB, DI, DS, JCB, MC, VI.   Ⓓ Ⓢ ⊗

**WOODBRIDGE HILTON**     AAA Special Value Rates     **Phone: 908/494-6200** 🉑111

⊛     Mon-Thurs    1P: $103- 135   2P/1B: $115- 147   2P/2B: $115- 147   XP: $12   F

           Fri-Sun       1P: $74       2P/1B: $86        2P/2B: $86        XP: $12   F

◆◆◆   **Location:** Exit 131A of Garden State Pkwy; NJ Tpk exit 11 to Garden State Pkwy N. 120 Wood Ave S

Hotel     08830. Fax: 908/603-7777. **Terms:** Reserv deposit, 3 day notice; monthly rates; package plans; no pets. **Facility:** 200 rooms. 11 stories; interior corridors; business center, conference facilities; heated indoor pool, sauna, whirlpool; exercise room. Fee: racquetball court. **Dining & Entertainment:** Dining room, restaurant, coffee shop; 6 am-11 pm; $10-$19; health conscious menu items; cocktails/lounge; entertainment. **Services:** data ports, PC, secretarial services; valet laundry. Fee: massage. **All Rooms:** free movies, cable TV, VCP's. **Some Rooms:** Fee: refrigerators. **Cards:** AE, DI, DS, MC, VI. *(See ad p 28)*   Ⓓ Ⓢ ⊗

## RESTAURANT

**CHI-CHI'S**          **Dinner:** up to $10          **Phone: 908/636-5200** 🉑112

           **Location:** In Iselin; on US 1; opposite Woodbridge Center. 625 Rt 1 at Gill Ln 08830. **Hours:** 11 am-11 pm,

Mexican    Fri & Sat-midnight, Sun noon-10 pm. Closed: 11/23 & 12/25. **Reservations:** suggested; 6 or more.

           **Features:** casual dress; children's menu; senior's menu; health conscious menu items; carryout; cocktails & lounge; a la carte. Relaxing atmosphere with south of the border flair; cordial service; varied menu. Lunch buffet, $4.99. **Cards:** AE, CB, DI, MC, VI.   ⊗

# WOODCLIFF LAKE—5,300

## LODGING

**WOODCLIFF LAKE HILTON**     Rates Subject to Change     **Phone: 201/391-3600**

⊛     All Year       1P: $87        2P/1B: $102        2P/2B: $105        XP: $15   F

◆◆◆   **Location:** Southbound Garden State Pkwy u-turn thru Food/Fuel Service Plaza to Garden State Pkwy N exit

Hotel     171, 1/4 mi w & 1 mi s on Chestnut Ridge Rd. 200 Tice Blvd 07675. Fax: 201/391-4572. **Terms:** Sr. discount; reserv deposit, 3 day notice; monthly rates; BP available; package plans; weekends; small pets only. **Facility:** 334 rooms. Continental breakfast included on Fri & Sat; 4 stories; interior corridors; business center, conference facilities; luxury level rooms; putting green; 2 pools (2 heated, 1 indoor), wading pool, saunas, whirlpool; health club, playground, sports court. Fee: racquetball courts, 2 lighted tennis courts. **Dining & Entertainment:** 2 dining rooms; 6:30 am-11 pm, Sat & Sun from 7 am; $8-$26; health conscious menu items; cocktails; Sun brunch; entertainment, nightclub. **Services:** data ports, PC, secretarial services; valet laundry; area transportation. Fee: massage, airport transportation. **Recreation:** jogging. **All Rooms:** free & pay movies, cable TV. **Some Rooms:** coffeemakers, microwaves, refrigerators, safes. **Cards:** AE, DI, DS, MC, VI. *(See ad p 28)*   Ⓓ ⊗

---

**PATRONIZE AAA/CAA ESTABLISHMENTS**

# PENNSYLVANIA

## ABBOTTSTOWN—500

### LODGING

**THE INN AT THE ALTLAND HOUSE**   AAA Special Value Rates   Phone: 717/259-9535

◆◆◆
Historic
Hotel

All Year [CP]   1P: $68   2P/1B: $74   XP: $8   D
**Location:** Center. Center Sq 17301. **Fax:** 717/259-9956. **Terms:** Reserv deposit, 3 day notice; no pets.
**Facility:** 5 rooms. 18th-century structure; in continued use as a hotel or restaurant; very attractive public areas
in Victorian atmosphere. Charming rural area. 3 stories; interior corridors; meeting rooms. **Dining &
Entertainment:** Cocktail lounge; dining room, see separate listing. **All Rooms:** combo & shower baths,
cable TV. **Cards:** AE, DS, MC, VI.   Ⓓ

### RESTAURANT

**THE INN AT ALTLAND HOUSE**   Historical   **Dinner:** $11-$20   Phone: 717/259-9535

◆◆◆
American

**Location:** In The Inn at the Altland House. Center Sq Rt 30 17301. **Hours:** 11 am-9 pm, Fri & Sat-11 pm,
Sun 11:30 am-7 pm. **Closed:** Mon & 12/25. **Reservations:** suggested; weekends. **Features:** casual dress;
Sunday brunch; children's menu; carryout; cocktails & lounge. Inviting decor in 200 year-old landmark.
Homemade soups, breads & desserts. Smoke free premises. **Cards:** AE, DS, MC, VI.   ⊗

## ADAMSTOWN

### LODGINGS

**ADAMSTOWN INN**   Guaranteed Rates   Phone: 717/484-0800

◆◆◆
Historic Bed
& Breakfast

All Year [CP]   1P: $59- 100   2P/1B: $65- 110
**Location:** Center. 62 W Main St 19501. **Terms:** Reserv deposit, 14 day notice; weekly rates; no pets.
**Facility:** 4 rooms. Victorian architecture, in relaxed small town setting. 2 stories; interior corridors; smoke free
premises. **All Rooms:** no phones, no TVs. **Some Rooms:** whirlpools. **Cards:** MC, VI.   Ⓓ ⊗

**BLACK FOREST INN**   Rates Subject to Change   Phone: 717/484-4801

ⒶⒶⒶ
◆
Motel

5/1-11/30 & 4/1-4/30 [CP]   2P/1B: $42- 85   2P/2B: $42- 85   XP: $5   F12
Fri & Sat 12/1-3/31 [CP]   2P/1B: $37- 54   2P/2B: $42- 58   XP: $5   F12
Sun-Thurs 12/1-3/31 [CP]   2P/1B: $35- 44   2P/2B: $39- 46   XP: $5   F12
**Location:** On US 272; 2 3/4 mi n of Tpk, exit 21. US Rt 272 19501 (PO Box 457). **Terms:** Credit card
guarantee, 3 day notice; 3 night min stay; pets. **Facility:** 19 rooms. Well-maintained property. 1 story; exterior
corridors. **Dining:** Restaurant nearby. **All Rooms:** shower baths, cable TV. **Cards:** DS, MC, VI.   Ⓓ ⊗

### RESTAURANT

**BLACK ANGUS STEAK HOUSE**   **Dinner:** $21-$30   Phone: 717/484-4385

ⒶⒶⒶ
◆◆◆
Steakhouse

**Location:** 2 3/4 mi n of tpk exit 21 on SR 272. 19501. **Hours:** 5 pm-11 pm, Sun noon-9 pm. **Closed:** 1/1,
11/23 & 12/25. **Reservations:** suggested. **Features:** casual dress; children's menu; cocktails & lounge.
Victorian decor. German beer garden, weekends in summer. Authentic selection of German cuisine.
Micro-brewery on premises. Homemade beer bread & soups. **Cards:** AE, CB, DI, MC, VI.   ⊗

## AKRON—3,900

### LODGINGS

**BOXWOOD INN**   Rates Subject to Change   Phone: 717/859-3466

◆◆◆
Historic Bed
& Breakfast

5/1-12/31 & 2/1-4/30 [BP]   1P: $75- 135   2P/1B: $75- 135   2P/2B: $75- 135   XP: $10
**Location:** From SR 272, 3/4 mi e on Main & Diamond sts to corner of Tobacco Rd. 12 Tobacco Rd 17501
(Box 203). **Fax:** 717/859-4507. **Terms:** Open 5/1-12/31 & 2/1-4/30; reserv deposit; 2 night min stay, for
carriage house; no pets. **Facility:** 5 rooms. 1768 stone farmhouse. Separate carriage house. 3 stories; interior
corridors; smoke free premises; meeting rooms; croquet. **Dining:** Afternoon tea. **All Rooms:** free movies, shower baths, no
phones. **Some Rooms:** honor bars, refrigerators, cable TV, whirlpools. **Cards:** MC, VI.   Ⓓ ⊗

**MOTEL AKRON**   Rates Subject to Change   Phone: 717/859-1654

ⒶⒶ
◆◆
Motel

6/21-10/31   1P: $38- 42   2P/1B: $38- 42   2P/2B: $42- 48   XP: $5
5/1-6/20 & 4/1-4/30   2P/1B: $36- 40   2P/2B: $40- 46   XP: $5
11/1-3/31   2P/1B: $30- 35   2P/2B: $34- 39
**Location:** 2 blks s on SR 272. 116 S 7th St 17501. **Terms:** Reserv deposit, 7 day notice; no pets.
**Facility:** 23 rooms. Well-maintained property & rooms. 1 story; exterior corridors; smoke free premises.
**Dining:** Restaurant nearby. **All Rooms:** combo & shower baths, cable TV. **Cards:** MC, VI.
*(See color ad p A113 & p A149)*   Ⓓ ⊗

## RESTAURANT

**AKRON RESTAURANT**  **Dinner:** up to $10  **Phone:** 717/859-1181

◆  **Location:** 1/2 mi s on SR 272. 333 S 7th St 17501. **Hours:** 6 am-8 pm, Sun 11 am-7 pm. Closed major
American  holidays. **Features:** casual dress; children's menu; early bird specials. Home-style cooking & atmosphere;
also counter service. **Cards:** DS, MC, VI.  ⊗

## ALLENTOWN—105,100

## LODGINGS

**ALLENTOWN COMFORT SUITES**  AAA Special Value Rates  **Phone:** 610/437-9100

⍟  5/1-10/31 & 4/1-4/30 [CP]  1P: $89- 99  2P/1B:  $99- 109  2P/2B:  $99- 109  XP: $10  F18
11/1-3/31 [CP]  1P: $79- 89  2P/1B:  $89- 99  2P/2B:  $79- 89  XP: $10  F18
◆◆◆  **Location:** Hamilton Blvd, exit off I-78, then 1/2 mi n opposite Dorney Park. 3712 Hamilton Blvd 18103.
Motor Inn  **Fax:** 610/437-0221. **Terms:** Reserv deposit; monthly rates; package plans; no pets. **Facility:** 122 rooms.
Large, attractive rooms. 4 stories; interior corridors; meeting rooms; exercise room. **Dining &**
**Entertainment:** Dining room; 11 am-1 am; $10-$20; cocktails/lounge. **Services:** data ports; valet laundry; airport
transportation. **All Rooms:** microwaves, free movies, refrigerators, cable TV. **Some Rooms:** VCP's, whirlpools. **Cards:** AE,
CB, DI, DS, JCB, MC, VI.  Ⓓ Ⓢ ⊗

**ALLENTOWN HILTON**  Rates Subject to Change  **Phone:** 610/433-2221

⍟  Mon-Thurs [EP]  1P: $84- 104  2P/1B:  $94- 114  2P/2B:  $94- 114  XP: $10  F18
Fri-Sun [CP]  1P: $70  2P/1B:  $70  2P/2B:  $70  XP: $10  F18
◆◆◆  **Location:** 9th & Hamilton sts. 904 Hamilton Mall 18101. **Fax:** 610/433-6455. **Terms:** Sr. discount; reserv
Hotel  deposit; package plans; no pets. **Facility:** 224 rooms. Attractively furnished guest rooms & public areas. 9 sto-
ries; interior corridors; meeting rooms; heated indoor pool, sauna; game room; exercise room. **Fee:** parking.
**Dining & Entertainment:** Dining room; 6:30 am-2:30 & 5:30-10 pm; $5-$29; cocktails/lounge. **Services:** valet laundry;
airport transportation. **All Rooms:** coffeemakers, free movies, cable TV. **Some Rooms:** refrigerators. **Cards:** AE, CB, DI,
DS, MC, VI. *(See ad p 28)*  ⧄ Ⓓ Ⓢ ⊗

**ALLENWOOD MOTEL**  Rates Subject to Change  **Phone:** 610/395-3707

⍟  All Year  2P/2B:  $39  XP: $3
◆◆  **Location:** 1/2 mi e on US 22 from tpk exit 33, 3/4 mi s on SR 309, w on Tilghman St to light, 3/4 mi n on
Motel  Hausman Rd to dead end, then turn left. 1058 Hausman Rd 18104. **Terms:** Credit card guarantee; pets.
**Facility:** 22 rooms. Spacious shaded grounds. Large rooms. 1 story; exterior corridors. **All Rooms:** cable
TV. **Cards:** AE, DS, MC, VI.  Ⓓ ⊗

**COMFORT INN**  Rates Subject to Change  **Phone:** 610/391-0344

◆◆◆  5/1-10/31 [CP]  1P: $38- 85  2P/1B:  $38- 85  2P/2B:  $38- 85  XP: $5  F18
Motor Inn  11/1-4/30 [CP]  1P: $35- 85  2P/1B:  $35- 85  2P/2B:  $35- 85  XP: $5  F18
**Location:** Exit SR 100N, off I-78 exit 14B. 7625 Imperial Way 18106. **Fax:** 610/391-0974. **Terms:** Credit card
guarantee, 30 day notice; weekly/monthly rates; package plans; pets, $10. **Facility:** 127 rooms. 1 efficiency, $55-$85; 3 rooms
with whirlpool bath, $80-$150; 5 stories; interior corridors; meeting rooms; exercise room. **Dining & Entertainment:**
Restaurant; 4 pm-11 pm; $3-$7; cocktails/lounge. **Services:** data ports; area transportation, within 15 mi, airport
transportation. **Fee:** coin laundry. **All Rooms:** coffeemakers, free movies, cable TV. **Some Rooms:** microwaves,
refrigerators. **Fee:** VCP's, whirlpools. **Cards:** AE, CB, DI, DS, JCB, MC, VI.  Ⓓ Ⓢ ⊗

**DAYS INN**  Rates Subject to Change  **Phone:** 610/797-1234

⍟  5/1-9/30  1P: $65- 99  2P/1B:  $65- 99  2P/2B:  $65- 99  XP: $5  F12
10/1-4/30  1P: $55- 75  2P/1B:  $60- 75  2P/2B:  $60- 75  XP: $5  F12
◆◆  **Location:** Just n of jct I-78/SR 309, exit 18 (Lehigh St). 2622 Lehigh St 18103. **Fax:** 610/797-1234.
Motel  **Terms:** Sr. discount; reserv deposit, 3 day notice; no pets. **Facility:** 36 rooms. 2 stories; interior corridors.
**Dining:** Restaurant nearby. **All Rooms:** microwaves, free movies, refrigerators, cable TV.
**Some Rooms:** whirlpools. **Cards:** AE, CB, DI, DS, MC, VI.  Ⓓ ⊗

**DAYS INN CONFERENCE CENTER**  Rates Subject to Change  **Phone:** 610/395-3731

⍟  All Year  1P: $54- 71  2P/1B:  $54- 79  2P/2B:  $54- 79  XP: $6  F12
◆◆  **Location:** 4 1/2 mi w on SR 309, n of jct US 22; 1/2 mi e of tpk exit 33; off SR 309 via Bulldog Dr access
Motor Inn  road. 1151 Bulldog Dr 18104. **Fax:** 610/395-9899. **Terms:** Check-in 4 pm; credit card guarantee; small pets
only, $6. **Facility:** 282 rooms. Very attractive landscaping. 1 two-bedroom unit. Extended stay rooms avail with
refrigerator & microwave, $900-1000 monthly; 1-2 stories; interior/exterior corridors; conference facilities; pool;
beach volleyball. **Dining & Entertainment:** Dining room; 6:30 am-10 pm, Sat & Sun from 7 am; $6-$12; cocktails/lounge.
**Services:** airport transportation. **Fee:** coin laundry. **All Rooms:** free movies, safes, cable TV. **Some Rooms:** coffeemakers,
microwaves, radios, refrigerators. **Fee:** VCP's. **Cards:** AE, CB, DI, DS, MC, VI. *(See color ad below)*  Ⓓ ⊗

**ECONO LODGE**

(AAA) ◆◆ Motel

| | Rates Subject to Change | | | |
|---|---|---|---|---|
| All Year | 1P: $51 | 2P/1B: $56 | 2P/2B: $61 | XP: $5 D18 |

Phone: 610/797-2200

**Location:** SR 309/I-78, exit 18, 3/4 mi n on Lehigh St. 2115 Downyflake Ln 18103. **Fax:** 610/797-2818. **Terms:** Sr. discount; credit card guarantee; CP available; package plans; no pets. **Facility:** 49 rooms. Comfortably decorated rooms. 1 handicap suite $51; 4 whirlpool suites, $95; 2 stories; interior/exterior corridors. **All Rooms:** free & pay movies, cable TV. **Cards:** AE, DI, DS, JCB, MC, VI. (D) ⊗

**HOLIDAY INN EXPRESS**

(AAA) ◆◆◆ Motel

| | Rates Subject to Change | | | |
|---|---|---|---|---|
| Fri & Sat 6/1-9/30 [CP] | 1P: $64- 80 | 2P/1B: $64- 80 | 2P/2B: $64- 80 | XP: $5 F18 |
| Sun-Thurs 6/1-9/30 [CP] | 1P: $60- 80 | 2P/1B: $60- 80 | 2P/2B: $60- 80 | XP: $5 F18 |
| Sun-Thurs 5/1-5/31 & 10/1-4/30 [CP] | 1P: $54- 80 | 2P/1B: $54- 80 | 2P/2B: $54- 80 | XP: $5 F18 |
| Fri & Sat 5/1-5/31 & 10/1-4/30 [CP] | 1P: $55- 80 | 2P/1B: $55- 80 | 2P/2B: $55- 80 | XP: $5 F18 |

Phone: 610/435-7880

**Location:** US 22, 15th St exit, 1/4 mi n on Plaza Ln. 1715 Plaza Ln 18104. **Fax:** 610/432-2555. **Terms:** Sr. discount; package plans; no pets. **Facility:** 83 rooms. 4 stories; interior corridors; meeting rooms. **Services:** data ports; valet laundry. **All Rooms:** free movies, cable TV. **Some Rooms:** microwaves. **Fee:** refrigerators. **Cards:** AE, CB, DI, DS, JCB, MC, VI. 🈳 (D) ⊗

**HOWARD JOHNSON LODGE**

(AAA) ◆◆ Motel

| | Rates Subject to Change | | | |
|---|---|---|---|---|
| 6/15-9/6 | 1P: $56- 65 | 2P/1B: $56- 75 | 2P/2B: $75- 95 | XP: $5 F12 |
| 5/1-6/14 & 9/7-12/31 | 1P: $40- 48 | 2P/1B: $48- 52 | 2P/2B: $52- 60 | XP: $5 F12 |
| 1/1-4/30 | 1P: $39- 44 | 2P/1B: $44- 48 | 2P/2B: $48- 52 | XP: $5 F12 |

Phone: 610/439-4000

**Location:** Hamilton Blvd, exit 16 off I-78; then 1/2 mi n. 3220 Hamilton Blvd 18103. **Fax:** 610/439-4000. **Terms:** Reserv deposit; 3 day notice; no pets. **Facility:** 43 rooms. 2 stories; interior corridors. **Dining:** Restaurant nearby. **Services:** valet laundry. **All Rooms:** microwaves, free movies, refrigerators, cable TV. **Some Rooms:** whirlpools. **Cards:** AE, CB, DI, DS, MC, VI. (D) ⊗

**MCINTOSH INN OF ALLENTOWN**

◆◆ Motel

| | Rates Subject to Change | | | |
|---|---|---|---|---|
| All Year | 1P: $37- 49 | 2P/1B: $45- 57 | 2P/2B: $48 | XP: $3 F18 |

Phone: 610/264-7531

**Location:** US 22, exit Airport Rd S. US 22 & Airport Rd 18103. **Fax:** 610/264-5474. **Terms:** Sr. discount; weekly rates; no pets. **Facility:** 107 rooms. 2 stories; interior/exterior corridors. **Dining:** Restaurant nearby. **Services:** data ports. **All Rooms:** free movies, combo & shower baths, cable TV. **Some Rooms:** microwaves, radios, refrigerators. **Cards:** AE, CB, DI, MC, VI. *(See ad p A132)*       Roll in showers. 🈳 (D) ⊗

**MICROTEL-ALLENTOWN**

(AAA) ◆◆ Motel

| | Rates Subject to Change | |
|---|---|---|
| 5/1-6/16 | 1P: $36 | 2P/1B: $40 |
| 6/17-10/31 | 1P: $35 | 2P/1B: $39 |
| 11/1-4/30 | 1P: $31 | 2P/1B: $35 |

Phone: 610/266-9070

**Location:** At Airport Rd S exit of US 22. 1880 Steelstone Rd 18103. **Fax:** 610/266-0377. **Terms:** Credit card guarantee; small pets only. **Facility:** 105 rooms. 3 stories; interior corridors. **All Rooms:** free & pay movies, combo & shower baths, cable TV. **Cards:** AE, CB, DI, DS, MC, VI.       Roll in showers. 🈳 (D) (S) ⊗

**RAMADA INN-ALLENTOWN/WHITEHALL**

(AAA) ◆◆◆ Motor Inn

| | Rates Subject to Change | | |
|---|---|---|---|
| Mon-Thurs [CP] | 1P: $80 | 2P/1B: $85 | 2P/2B: $85 | XP:$5-10 F18 |
| Fri-Sun [CP] | 1P: $70 | 2P/1B: $75 | 2P/2B: $75 | XP: $10 F18 |

Phone: 610/439-1037

**Location:** US 22, MacArthur Rd N exit to Grape St exit, turn around, hotel 1/4 mi on right. 1500 MacArthur Rd 18052. **Fax:** 610/770-1425. **Terms:** Credit card guarantee, 3 day notice; weekly/monthly rates; package plans; no pets. **Facility:** 123 rooms. 2 stories; interior corridors; conference facilities; pool, wading pool. **Dining & Entertainment:** Restaurant; 6:30 am-10 pm; $6-$19; cocktails/lounge; entertainment. **Services:** data ports; complimentary evening beverages; health club privileges; valet laundry; area transportation, within 5 mi; airport transportation. **All Rooms:** free movies, cable TV. **Some Rooms:** **Fee:** refrigerators, VCP's. **Cards:** AE, DS, JCB, MC, VI. (D) ⊗

**RED ROOF INN**

◆◆ Motel

| | Rates Subject to Change | | | |
|---|---|---|---|---|
| All Year | 1P: $30- 40 | 2P/1B: $40- 63 | 2P/2B: $50- 63 | XP: $8 F18 |

Phone: 610/264-5404

**Location:** Just s of US 22, exit Airport Rd S. 1846 Catasauqua Rd 18103. **Fax:** 610/264-5404. **Terms:** Credit card guarantee; pets. **Facility:** 116 rooms. 3 stories; exterior corridors. **Dining:** Restaurant nearby. **Services:** data ports. **All Rooms:** free movies, cable TV. **Cards:** AE, CB, DI, DS, MC, VI. 🈳 (D) (S) ⊗

## RESTAURANTS

**AMBASSADOR RESTAURANT**

(AAA) ◆◆◆ Continental

Dinner: $11-$20       Phone: 610/432-2025

**Location:** 1/4 mi e of I-78 exit 16. 3750 Hamilton Blvd 18103. **Hours:** 11:30 am-2:30 & 5-10 pm. Closed major holidays & Sun. **Reservations:** suggested; weekends. **Features:** casual dress; children's menu; carryout; cocktails & lounge; a la carte. Very well prepared steak & seafood in a pleasant Spanish atmosphere. Some Spanish selections. **Cards:** AE, CB, DS, MC, VI.

**THE BRASS RAIL RESTAURANT**

(AAA) ◆ American

Dinner: up to $10       Phone: 610/797-1927

**Location:** S on Lehigh St at jct I-78, exit 18. 3015 Lehigh St 18103. **Hours:** 7 am-midnight, Fri & Sat-1 am, Sun 8 am-10 pm. **Closed:** 4/7, 11/23 & 12/25. **Features:** casual dress; children's menu; carryout; cocktails & lounge; a la carte. Complete breakfast menu. **Cards:** MC, VI. *(See ad below)*       ⊗

**BRASS RAIL RESTAURANT**

(AAA) ◆ American

Dinner: up to $10       Phone: 610/434-9383

**Location:** Downtown, at jct 12th St & Hamilton St. 1137 Hamilton St 18101. **Hours:** 7 am-midnight, Fri & Sat-1 am, Sun 8 am-9 pm. **Closed:** 4/7, 11/23 & 12/25. **Features:** casual dress; children's menu; carryout; cocktails & lounge; a la carte. Family dining in historic area. Ample portions. Complete breakfast menu. **Cards:** MC, VI. *(See ad below)*       ⊗

**FINLEY'S AMERICAN RESTAURANT**          Dinner: $11-$20                    Phone: 610/965-8447
◆                    **Location:** Lehigh St exit off SR 309, 1/2 mi sw. 3400 Lehigh St 18103. **Hours:** 11 am-10 pm, Fri & Sat-11
Steak and            pm. Closed: 11/23 & 12/25. **Features:** casual dress; children's menu; carryout; cocktails; a la carte. Casual
Seafood              family dining. Seasonally updated specialties. **Cards:** AE, DI, DS, MC, VI.                              ⊗

**WALP'S RESTAURANT**                     Dinner: $11-$20                    Phone: 610/437-4841
Ⓐ                   **Location:** 1 1/2 mi s of US 22 at corner of Union Blvd & Airport Rd (SR 987). 911 Union Blvd 18103.
                     **Hours:** 6:30 am-10 pm, Mon-9 pm. Closed: 7/4 & 12/25. **Reservations:** suggested. **Features:** casual dress;
◆                    children's menu; early bird specials; carryout; cocktails & lounge; a la carte. Casual family style restaurant.
American             Pennsylvania Dutch style cooking. Family owned & operated since 1936. **Cards:** AE, DS, MC, VI.        ⊗

# ALTOONA

## LODGINGS

**DAYS INN**                          Rates Subject to Change                       Phone: 814/944-9661
Ⓐ              All Year          1P: $53- 63   2P/1B: $58- 68   2P/2B: $58- 68   XP: $5  F13
               **Location:** 2 1/4 mi e on US 220; 2 1/4 mi n of jct US 32. 3306 Pleasant Valley Blvd 16602.
◆◆◆            Fax: 814/944-9661. **Terms:** Sr. discount; no pets. **Facility:** 111 rooms. Large comfortable rooms. 2 stories; in-
Motel          terior corridors; meeting rooms; whirlpool; exercise room. **Dining:** Restaurant nearby. **Services:** Fee: coin
               laundry. **All Rooms:** coffeemakers, free movies, cable TV. **Some Rooms:** microwaves, refrigerators.
Fee: VCP's. **Cards:** AE, CB, DI, DS, JCB, MC, VI.                                                          Ⓓ ⊗

**ECONO LODGE**                       Guaranteed Rates                              Phone: 814/944-3555
Ⓐ              All Year          1P: $37- 39   2P/1B: $41        2P/2B: $44        XP: $5  F18
               **Location:** 1 1/2 mi n on Old US 220 from US 220 Plank Rd exit; 1/2 mi n from SR 36 on Old US 220. 2906
◆◆             Pleasant Valley Blvd 16602. Fax: 814/946-3258. **Terms:** Sr. discount; reserv deposit, 3 day notice; pets.
Motel          **Facility:** 69 rooms. Convenient to attractions. 2 stories; exterior corridors. **Dining:** Restaurant nearby.
               **Services:** data ports. **All Rooms:** cable TV. **Some Rooms:** 2 efficiencies, no utensils, microwaves,
refrigerators. Fee: VCP's. **Cards:** AE, CB, DI, DS, JCB, MC, VI.                                           Ⓓ ⊗

**HOJO INN**                          AAA Special Value Rates                       Phone: 814/946-7601
◆◆             All Year [BP]     1P: $42- 47   2P/1B: $49        2P/2B: $47        XP: $5  F12
Motel          **Location:** Plank Rd at US 220, behind shopping center. 1500 Sterling St 16602. Fax: 814/946-5162.
               **Terms:** Check-in 4 pm; reserv deposit, 5 day notice; weekly/monthly rates; CP available; pets. **Facility:** 112
               rooms. Budget oriented traveler. 1 story; exterior corridors; pool. **Dining:** Restaurant nearby. **All Rooms:** free movies, cable
TV. Fee: VCP. **Some Rooms:** 11 kitchens, microwaves, radios, refrigerators. **Cards:** AE, CB, DI, DS, JCB, MC, VI.   Ⓓ ⊗

**HOLIDAY INN**                       AAA Special Value Rates                       Phone: 814/944-4581
Ⓐ              5/1-8/31         1P: $66- 70   2P/1B: $71- 75   2P/2B: $74        XP: $5  F18
               9/1-4/30         1P: $61- 68   2P/1B: $65- 70   2P/2B: $66        XP: $5  F18
◆◆◆            **Location:** 2 1/2 mi n of jct US 22 on US 220 Bus. 2915 Pleasant Valley Blvd 16602. Fax: 814/943-4996.
Motor Inn      **Terms:** BP available; no pets. **Facility:** 142 rooms. Renovated in 1993. Attractive courtyard & patio. 2 stories;
               exterior corridors; meeting rooms; pool; exercise room. **Dining & Entertainment:** Restaurant; 7 am-2 & 5-10
pm, Sun-8 pm; $9-$15; cocktails/lounge; entertainment. **Services:** data ports, PC. Fee: coin laundry.
**All Rooms:** coffeemakers, free & pay movies, cable TV. **Some Rooms:** microwaves, refrigerators, whirlpools. **Cards:** AE,
CB, DI, DS, JCB, MC, VI. *(See ad below)*                                                                    Ⓓ ⊗

## RESTAURANTS

**ALLEGRO**                               Dinner: $21-$30                    Phone: 814/946-5216
◆◆                   **Location:** Broad Ave & 40th St. 3926 Broad Ave 16601. **Hours:** 4 pm-9:30 pm, Sat-10 pm. Closed major
Italian              holidays & Sun. **Features:** casual dress; children's menu; carryout; cocktails & lounge. Extensive menu
                     includes steaks & seafood. **Cards:** AE, DI, DS, MC, VI.                                            ⊗

**LAUREL ROOM**                           Dinner: $21-$30                    Phone: 814/946-1631
◆◆◆                  **Location:** On US 220, 1/2 mi s of jct SR 36. 1 Sheraton Dr 16601. **Hours:** 5:30 pm-10 pm, Sat-11 pm.
American             Closed major holidays & Sun. **Reservations:** suggested; weekends. **Features:** casual dress; children's
                     menu; cocktails & lounge; a la carte. Steaks, seafood & flambe' dining. **Cards:** AE, DI, DS, MC, VI.    ⊗

# ANNVILLE—4,300

## LODGING

**SWATARA CREEK INN**                 AAA Special Value Rates                       Phone: 717/865-3259
Ⓐ              5/1-11/30 & 3/1-4/30 [BP]   1P: $40- 65   2P/1B: $50- 75              XP:$5-10  D3
               12/1-2/29 [BP]             1P: $34- 55   2P/1B: $43- 64              XP:$4-9   D3
◆◆◆            **Location:** On Jonestown Rd; from I-81, 1/2 mi s on SR 934, 1 blk w at Harper's Tavern. (RD 2, Box 692).
Bed &          **Terms:** Reserv deposit; weekly/monthly rates; no pets. **Facility:** 10 rooms. Country setting. Inviting rooms, with
Breakfast      sun dried sheets. 1 two-bedroom unit. 3 stories, no elevator; interior corridors; smoke free premises.
               **Dining:** Restaurant nearby. **All Rooms:** combo & shower baths, no phones, no TVs. **Cards:** AE, DI, DS,
MC, VI.                                                                                                      Ⓓ ⊗

# ARCHBALD (See POCONO MOUNTAINS & VICINITY ACCOMMODATIONS spotting
map pages A212 & A213; see index starting on page A210)

## RESTAURANT

**BARRETT'S FAMILY RESTAURANT**          Dinner: up to $10                   Phone: 717/876-2503   Ⓐ⑤
◆                    **Location:** 1 mi n on Main St. 474 Main St 18403. **Hours:** 11 am-11 pm. Closed: 4/7, 7/4, 11/23 & 12/25.
American             **Reservations:** suggested; weekends. **Features:** casual dress; children's menu; carryout; cocktails & lounge;
                     a la carte. Family style dining room with adjacent Irish pub. **Cards:** AE, MC, VI.

# AAAFFORDABLE RATES

**Altoona**                               ✻ Holiday Inn
2915 Pleasant Valley Blvd.                STAY WITH SOMEONE YOU KNOW.˙
(814) 944-4581          **FOR RESERVATIONS CALL 1-800-HOLIDAY OR YOUR TRAVEL AGENT.**
                       Rooms limited and subject to availability. Not valid during blackout dates.

## ARDMORE (See PHILADELPHIA & VICINITY ACCOMMODATIONS spotting map pages A196 & A197; see index starting on page A193)

### RESTAURANT

**THAI PEPPER RESTAURANT**          **Dinner: $11-$20**                **Phone:** 215/642-5951     [153]
Location: Center on US 30. 64 E Lancaster Ave 19003. **Hours:** noon-3 & 5-10 pm, Fri-10:30 pm, Sat noon-3 & 5-10:30 pm, Sun 4 pm-9:30 pm. Closed: 7/4 & 9/4. **Reservations:** suggested; weekend.
Ethnic   **Features:** casual dress; carryout; street parking; a la carte. Extensive menu with variety of Thai specialties including tofu, curry dishes. Smoke free premises. **Cards:** AE, DI, DS, MC, VI.          ⊗

## BALA-CYNWYD (See PHILADELPHIA & VICINITY ACCOMMODATIONS spotting map pages A196 & A197; see index starting on page A193)

### RESTAURANT

**HOULIHAN'S RESTAURANT & BAR**          **Dinner: $11-$20**                **Phone:** 215/667-9717     [159]
◆◆   Location: On US 1 at Presidential St, just w off jct I-76, exit 33. 555 City Line Ave 19004. **Hours:** 11:30
American   am-midnight, Fri & Sat-1 am, Sun-10 pm. Closed: 12/25. **Features:** casual dress; Sunday brunch; children's menu; carryout; cocktails & lounge; a la carte. **Cards:** AE, DI, DS, MC, VI.          ⊗

## BALDWIN

### LODGING

**HOWARD JOHNSON LODGE**          AAA Special Value Rates                **Phone:** 412/884-6000
◆   All Year [BP]          1P: $65- 85  2P/1B: $75- 90  2P/2B: $80- 90  XP: $10 F18
Motel   **Location:** 1/4 mi n of Lebanon Church Rd (Yellow Belt) on US 51. 5300 Clairton Blvd 15236.
Fax: 412/884-6000. **Terms:** Reserv deposit; pets. **Facility:** 95 rooms. 2 stories; interior corridors; meeting rooms; pool. **Dining:** Restaurant nearby. **Services:** valet laundry. **All Rooms:** free & pay movies, cable TV.
**Some Rooms:** coffeemakers, radios, refrigerators. **Cards:** AE, DI, DS, MC, VI.          Ⓓ ⊗

## BALLIETTSVILLE

### RESTAURANT

**BALLIETSVILLE INN**   Historical          **Dinner: $21-$30**                **Phone:** 610/799-2435
◆◆◆◆   Location: 6 mi n of US 22 (15th St exit) via Mauch Chunk Rd. 2700 Balliet St 18037. **Hours:** 5 pm-9:30 pm.
French   Closed: Sun, 5/29, 7/4, 9/4, 12/24 & 12/25. **Reservations:** suggested. **Features:** semi-casual dress; cocktails & lounge; a la carte. Fine food served in French country setting. Extensive wine list. Smoke free premises. **Cards:** AE, CB, DI, MC, VI.          ⊗

## BARKEYVILLE—300

### LODGING

**DAYS INN**          Rates Subject to Change          **Phone:** 814/786-7901
◆◆   All Year          1P: $44- 53  2P/1B: $49          2P/2B: $51          XP: $6 F18
Motel   **Location:** From I-80 exit 3, 1/8 mi n on SR 8. I-80 & Rt 8 16038 (PO Box 98A). Fax: 814/786-9693.
**Terms:** Sr. discount; reserv deposit; pets. **Facility:** 83 rooms. 2 stories; exterior corridors. **All Rooms:** free movies, cable TV. **Cards:** AE, DS, JCB, MC, VI.          Ⓓ ⊗

## BARTONSVILLE (See POCONO MOUNTAINS & VICINITY ACCOMMODATIONS spotting map pages A212 & A213; see index starting on page A210)

### LODGINGS

**COMFORT INN-POCONO**          AAA Special Value Rates                **Phone:** 717/476-1500     [76]
Fri & Sat 5/17-10/21 &
12/26-3/17 [CP]          1P: $70- 110  2P/1B: $70- 110  2P/2B: $80          XP: $7 F18
◆◆   Sun-Thurs, 10/22-12/25,
Motel   3/18-4/30 & [CP]          1P: $46- 100  2P/1B: $46- 100  2P/2B: $50          XP: $7 F18
**Location:** From I-80 exit 46B, 1/2 mi n on SR 611. Rt 611 18321 (Box 184). Fax: 717/476-0985.
**Terms:** Reserv deposit, 14 day notice; pets, $50 dep req. **Facility:** 120 rooms. 2 stories; interior corridors; meeting rooms; pool; game room. **Dining & Entertainment:** Restaurant; 6 am-10:30 & 5:30-10:30 pm, Fri & Sat-midnight; $6-$9; cocktails/lounge. **Services:** Fee: coin laundry. **All Rooms:** safes, cable TV. **Some Rooms:** Fee: VCP's, whirlpools.
**Cards:** AE, CB, DI, DS, JCB, MC, VI.          Ⓓ ⊗

**HOLIDAY INN**          Rates Subject to Change                **Phone:** 717/424-6100     [75]
◆◆   5/28-10/31 & 12/26-3/15   1P: $72- 92  2P/1B: $79- 99  2P/2B: $79- 99  XP: $7 F19
Motor Inn   5/1-5/27, 11/1-12/25 &
3/16-4/30          1P: $62- 92  2P/1B: $69- 99  2P/2B: $69- 99  XP: $7 F19
**Location:** 1/4 mi s on SR 611 from I-80, exit 46B. Rt 611 & I-80 18321. Fax: 717/421-4293. **Terms:** Sr. discount; credit card guarantee; BP available; package plans; small pets only. **Facility:** 151 rooms. 2 stories; interior corridors; conference facilities; heated indoor pool; exercise room. **Dining & Entertainment:** Restaurant; 7 am-2 & 5-10 pm; $7-$16; cocktails/lounge. **Services:** data ports. Fee: coin laundry. **All Rooms:** free movies, cable TV. **Some Rooms:** Fee: refrigerators, whirlpools.
**Cards:** AE, CB, DI, DS, JCB, MC, VI.          Ⓓ ⊗

## BEAVER—5,000

### RESTAURANT

**THE WOODEN ANGEL**          **Dinner: $21-$30**                **Phone:** 412/774-7880
◆◆   Location: In West Bridgewater, from jct SR 68 (at w end of bridge), 1/2 mi n on SR 51, then 1/4 mi w under
American   the underpass & up the hill. Sharon Rd & Leopard Ln 15009. **Hours:** 11:30 am-11 pm, Sat from 5 pm.
Closed major holidays, Sun & Mon. **Reservations:** suggested. **Features:** casual dress; children's menu; carryout; cocktails & lounge; a la carte. Candlelight atmosphere. Extensive American wine list. Foreign language & Braille menus. Also family-style dining room. **Cards:** AE, DI, DS, MC, VI.          ⊗

## BEAVER FALLS—10,700

### LODGINGS

**BEAVER VALLEY MOTEL**     Rates Subject to Change     Phone: 212/843-0630
All Year     1P: $37    2P/1B: $44     2P/2B: $52     XP: $8   F18
**Location:** On SR 18, 1/2 mi n of Tpk exit 2. SR 18 15010. **Fax:** 412/843-1610. **Terms:** Reserv deposit, 5 day notice; weekly rates; small pets only, $5. **Facility:** 27 rooms. Exterior corridors. **All Rooms:** free movies, refrigerators, combo & shower baths, cable TV. **Some Rooms:** 4 efficiencies, utensil deposit. **Cards:** AE, CB, DI, DS, MC, VI.   (D)
*Motel*

**CONLEY INN**     AAA Special Value Rates     Phone: 412/843-9300
All Year     1P: $50    2P/1B: $60     2P/2B: $60     XP: $8   F13
**Location:** On SR 18; 1/4 mi s of tpk exit 2. Rt 18 15010. **Terms:** Reserv deposit, 3 day notice; weekly/monthly rates; small pets only. **Facility:** 58 rooms. 2 stories; exterior corridors. **Dining:** Restaurant; 7 am-10 pm; $6-$15; cocktails. **All Rooms:** cable TV. **Some Rooms:** 4 efficiencies, refrigerators. **Cards:** CB, DI, DS, MC, VI.   (D) (S)
*Motor Inn*

**HOLIDAY INN**     AAA Special Value Rates     Phone: 412/846-3700
5/1-10/31    1P: $70- 79   2P/1B: $70- 79   2P/2B: $70- 79
11/1-4/30    1P: $65- 74   2P/1B: $65- 74   2P/2B: $65- 74   XP: $8   F18
**Location:** On SR 18; 1/4 mi n of I-76 exit 2. (PO Box 696). **Fax:** 412/846-3700. **Terms:** Credit card guarantee, 3 day notice; 15% service charge; monthly rates; pets. **Facility:** 156 rooms. 3 stories; interior corridors; conference facilities; miniature golf; heated indoor pool, sauna, whirlpool. **Dining:** Dining room; 6:30 am-2 & 5-10 pm, Sat & Sun from 7 am; $10-$20; cocktails. **Services:** data ports. **Fee:** coin laundry. **All Rooms:** free movies. **Cards:** AE, CB, DI, DS, MC, VI.   (D) (S)
*Motor Inn*

**LARK MOTEL**     Rates Subject to Change     Phone: 412/846-6507
5/1-10/31    1P: $38    2P/1B: $44     2P/2B: $50     XP: $7
11/1-4/30    1P: $34    2P/1B: $40     2P/2B: $45     XP: $7
**Location:** On SR 18; 1/2 mi n of tpk exit 2. SR 18 15010. **Terms:** Reserv deposit, 7 day notice; no pets. **Facility:** 12 rooms. Well-maintained property. Exterior corridors. **All Rooms:** refrigerators, cable TV. **Cards:** AE, DS, MC, VI.   (D) (S)
*Motel*

### RESTAURANT

**GIUSEPPE'S ITALIAN RESTAURANT**     Dinner: $11-$20     Phone: 412/843-5656
**Location:** Just s on SR 18 off tpk exit 2. Rt 18, Box 852 15010. **Hours:** 11 am-11 pm, Sun-10 pm. **Closed:** 1/1, 11/23 & 12/25. **Features:** carryout; cocktail lounge; a la carte. Casual dining; also featuring steaks, seafood & daily specials. **Cards:** AE, DI, DS, MC, VI.   (S)
*Italian*

## BEDFORD—3,100

### LODGINGS

**BEST WESTERN HOSS'S INN**     AAA Special Value Rates     Phone: 814/623-9006
5/1-10/31    1P: $44- 54   2P/1B: $52- 62   2P/2B: $52- 62   XP: $8   F18
11/1-4/30    1P: $38- 48   2P/1B: $46- 56   2P/2B: $46- 56   XP: $8   F18
**Location:** On US 220 Business Rt, 1/4 mi n of Tpk I-70 & I-76, exit 11. (RD 2, Box 33B). **Fax:** 814/623-7120. **Terms:** Reserv deposit; pets, $50 dep req. **Facility:** 107 rooms. 1-2 stories; exterior corridors; meeting rooms; pool, sauna, whirlpool; exercise room. **Dining & Entertainment:** Restaurant; 6:30 am-11 & 5-10 pm, Sat & Sun 6:30 am-10 pm; $7-$13; cocktails/lounge. **All Rooms:** free movies, cable TV. **Some Rooms:** radios, refrigerators, whirlpools. **Fee:** VCP's. **Cards:** AE, DI, DS, MC, VI. *(See color ad below)*   (D) (S)
*Motor Inn*

**FRIENDSHIP INN**     AAA Special Value Rates     Phone: 814/623-5174
5/1-10/31 & 4/1-4/30   1P: $36   2P/1B: $42   2P/2B: $42   XP: $6   F16
11/1-3/31    1P: $32    2P/1B: $38     2P/2B: $38     XP: $6   F16
**Location:** 1/4 mi n on US 220 from I-70 & I-76 Tpk. Rd 2, US 220N 15522. **Fax:** 814/623-5455. **Terms:** BP available; small pets only, $25 dep req. **Facility:** 32 rooms. 2 stories; interior corridors. **Dining & Entertainment:** Restaurant; 24 hours; $4-$10; cocktail lounge. **All Rooms:** free movies, cable TV. **Cards:** AE, CB, DI, DS, JCB, MC, VI.   (D) (S)
*Motor Inn*

**JANEY LYNN MOTEL**     AAA Special Value Rates     Phone: 814/623-9515
5/1-10/31    1P: $27- 31   2P/1B: $31- 35   2P/2B: $35- 39   XP: $4   F6
11/1-4/30    1P: $23- 27   2P/1B: $27- 31   2P/2B: $31- 35   XP: $4   F6
**Location:** On US 220 Business Rt, 1 1/2 mi s of Tpk I-70 & I-76, exit 11, turn right. (RD 5, Box 367). **Terms:** Reserv deposit; small pets only, $4. **Facility:** 21 rooms. Attractive decor, well-maintained property with balcony view at rear. 1 two-bedroom unit. 2 stories; exterior corridors. **All Rooms:** free movies, cable TV. **Some Rooms:** microwaves, radios, refrigerators, phones. **Cards:** AE, CB, DI, DS, MC, VI.   (D) (S)
*Motel*

**JUDY'S MOTEL-PA DUTCH HERITAGE**     Guaranteed Rates     Phone: 814/623-9118
All Year     1P: $24    2P/1B: $28- 28   2P/2B: $32     XP: $3
**Location:** On US 220 Business Rt, 1 1/2 mi s of Tpk I-70 & I-76, exit 11. Business Rt 220 15522 (Rd 5 Box 370). **Terms:** Credit card guarantee; AP available; package plans; no pets. **Facility:** 12 rooms. Budget oriented traveler, reservations recommended. In room courtesy coffee; 1 story; exterior corridors. **Dining:** Restaurant nearby. **All Rooms:** coffeemakers, free movies, combo & shower baths, cable TV. **Some Rooms:** refrigerators, phones. **Cards:** DS, MC, VI.   (D) (S)
*Motel*

**MIDWAY MOTEL**

Rates Subject to Change      Phone: 814/623-8107

Ⓐ
5/1-11/25   1P: $29- 32   2P/1B: $34- 38   2P/2B: $42- 47   XP: $3 F10
11/26-4/30   1P: $22- 27   2P/1B: $27- 30   2P/2B: $34- 40   XP: $3 F10

◆
Motel
**Location:** On US 220 Business Rt, at jct Pa Tpk, I-70 & 76 exit 11. RD 2, Box 13A 15522. **Terms:** Credit card guarantee; no pets. **Facility:** 33 rooms. 1-2 stories; exterior corridors. **Dining:** Restaurant nearby. **All Rooms:** free movies, cable TV. **Cards:** AE, DI, DS, MC, VI. ⊗

**MOTEL TOWN HOUSE**

Rates Subject to Change      Phone: 814/623-5138

Ⓐ
Fri & Sat 5/1-10/31   1P: $32- 42   2P/1B: $40- 50   2P/2B: $45- 55   XP: $5 F14
Sun-Thurs 5/1-10/31   1P: $32- 40   2P/1B: $37- 45   2P/2B: $40- 50   XP: $5 F14
11/1-4/30   1P: $30- 35   2P/1B: $32- 37   2P/2B: $35- 40   XP: $5 F14

◆◆◆
Motel
**Location:** On US 220 Business Rt, 2 1/2 mi s of Tpk I-70 & I-76, exit 11. 200 S Richard St 15522.
**Facility:** 19 rooms. Interim, budget oriented. 2 stories; exterior corridors. **Dining:** Restaurant nearby. **Services:** data ports.
**All Rooms:** free movies, cable TV. **Some Rooms:** microwaves, refrigerators. **Cards:** AE, CB, DI, DS, JCB, MC, VI.
*(See color ad below)* Ⓓ⊗

**QUALITY INN BEDFORD**

AAA Special Value Rates      Phone: 814/623-5188

Ⓐ
6/1-10/31   1P: $61   2P/1B: $67   2P/2B: $67   XP: $6 F18
5/1-5/31 & 11/1-4/30   1P: $54   2P/1B: $60   2P/2B: $60   XP: $6 F18

◆◆◆
Motor Inn
**Location:** On US 220 Business Rt; 1/4 mi n of Tpk I-70 & I-76, exit 11. 15522 (RD 2, Box 171). **Terms:** Reserv deposit, 3 day notice; pets. **Facility:** 66 rooms. 2 stories; interior/exterior corridors; meeting rooms; heated pool; playground. **Dining:** Also, The Arena, see separate listing. **Services:** data ports. **All Rooms:** free movies, cable TV. **Some Rooms:** microwaves, radios, refrigerators. **Cards:** AE, CB, DI, DS, JCB, MC, VI.
*(See ad below)* Ⓓ⊗

**SUPER 8 MOTEL**

Rates Subject to Change      Phone: 814/623-5880

◆◆
Motel
All Year   1P: $42   2P/1B: $46   2P/2B: $48   XP: $5 F12
**Location:** 1/4 mi n on US 220 Business Rt from I-70 & I-76 Tpk, exit 11. 15522 (RD 2, Box 32A). Fax: 814/623-5880. **Terms:** Sr. discount; small pets only. **Facility:** 57 rooms. 3 stories; interior corridors; whirlpool; exercise room. **Dining:** Restaurant nearby. **All Rooms:** free movies, cable TV. **Some Rooms:** refrigerators. Fee: VCP's. **Cards:** AE, CB, DI, DS, JCB, MC, VI. Ⓓ⊗

## RESTAURANTS

**THE ARENA**

Dinner: $11-$20      Phone: 814/623-8074

Ⓐ
◆◆◆
American
**Location:** In Quality Inn Bedford. 15522. **Hours:** 7 am-10 pm, Sun-9 pm. Closed: 1/1, 12/25 & 12/26. **Reservations:** suggested; weekends. **Features:** casual dress; children's menu; health conscious menu; carryout; salad bar; cocktails & lounge; a la carte. Very attractive modern dining rooms with relaxing & contemporary atmosphere. Lunch buffet Mon-Sat. **Cards:** AE, CB, DI, DS, MC, VI. *(See ad below)* ⊗

**ED'S STEAK HOUSE**

Dinner: $11-$20      Phone: 814/623-8894

Ⓐ
◆
Steakhouse
**Location:** On US 220 Business Rt, 1/4 mi n of Tpk I-70 & I-76, exit 11. 15522. **Hours:** 7 am-9:30 pm, Sun-9 pm; winter hours may vary. Closed: 12/25. **Features:** casual dress; children's menu; carryout; cocktails & lounge; a la carte. Popular locally. **Cards:** AE, MC, VI. ⊗

**SLICK'S IVY STONE RESTAURANT**

Dinner: up to $10      Phone: 814/276-3131

Ⓐ
◆◆
American
**Location:** Near Osterburg, 9 mi n, 2 mi n of US 220, Osterburg/St Clairsville exit on unmarked old US 220, 1/4 mi n of Osterburg. 16667. **Hours:** Open 5/1-12/23 & 4/1-4/30; 11 am-8:30 pm, Sat 4 pm-8:30 pm, Sun 11 am-8 pm. Closed: Mon. **Features:** casual dress; children's menu; salad bar; a la carte. Colonial atmosphere. Featuring family-style meals. Homemade soups, breads & desserts, famous for fried chicken, roast turkey & waffles. Ample portions. ⊗

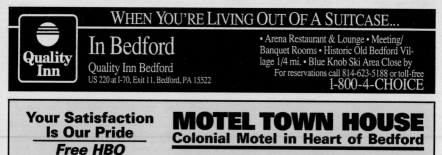

# BELLE VERNON—1,200

## RESTAURANTS

THE BACK PORCH RESTAURANT  Historical             **Dinner:** $11-$20          **Phone:** 412/483-4500
◆ ◆          **Location:** Exit 17, I-70, located under exit bridge on river by marina (take Charleroi-Allenport exit). 114
American     Speers St 15012. **Hours:** 11:30 am-10 pm, Fri-11 pm, Sat 5 pm-11 pm, Sun 4 pm-9 pm. **Closed:** Mon, 1/1,
12/24 & 12/25. **Reservations:** suggested; for dinner. **Features:** casual dress; children's menu; cocktails &
lounge. Restored 1806 home, historical landmark built by the founders of Belle Vernon. **Cards:** AE, DS, MC, VI.    ⊗

PEASANT VILLAGE                                   **Dinner:** $11-$20          **Phone:** 412/929-9424
◆            **Location:** 2 mi n on SR 51 from I-70, under overpass at jct SR 51 & SR 201. PO Box 722 15012.
American     **Hours:** 11 am-9 pm, Fri & Sat-10:30 pm. **Closed:** Mon & 12/24-12/26. **Reservations:** suggested; weekends.
**Features:** casual dress; children's menu; carryout; cocktails & lounge. Italian dishes also served. Hearty
portions. **Cards:** MC, VI.     ⊗

SNOOTERS GALLEY & PUB                             **Dinner:** $11-$20          **Phone:** 412/483-6000
◆ ◆          **Location:** I-70, exit 17 e 1/4 mi under bridge near Marina. 119 River Rd 15012. **Hours:** 11:30 am-10 pm.
American     **Closed:** 1/1, 11/23 & 12/25. **Reservations:** required; weekends. **Features:** casual dress; children's menu;
early bird specials; carryout; cocktails & lounge. Casual dining with excellent scenic views of river &
surrounding countryside. **Cards:** AE, DS, MC, VI.     ⊗

# BELMONT HILLS  (See PHILADELPHIA & VICINITY ACCOMMODATIONS spotting map pages A196 & A197; see index starting on page A193)

## RESTAURANT

LA COLLINA RESTAURANT                             **Dinner:** $11-$20          **Phone:** 610/668-1780   (150)
◆ ◆ ◆        **Location:** I-76 exit 31 Belmont Ave 1/10 mi s, Jefferson Ave 2/10 mi s. 37-41 Ashland Ave 19004.
Northern     **Hours:** 11:30 am-2:30 & 5:30-10 pm, Fri-11 pm, Sat 5:30 pm-11:30 pm. **Closed** major holidays & Sun.
Italian      **Reservations:** suggested. **Features:** semi-formal attire; cocktails & lounge; valet parking; a la carte. Elegant
dining with Italian ambience. Seafood is a specialty. **Cards:** AE, DI, MC, VI.     ⊗

# BENSALEM  (See PHILADELPHIA & VICINITY ACCOMMODATIONS spotting map pages A196 & A197; see index starting on page A193)

## LODGINGS

COMFORT INN                    Rates Subject to Change              **Phone:** 215/245-0100   (30)
(AAA)         All Year [CP]          1P: $62-  99  2P/1B:  $72-  99                      XP: $7  F18
◆ ◆ ◆        **Location:** On SR 132, E Street Rd, jct US 1, exit SR 132E; from PA Tpk, exit 28. 3660 Street Rd 19020.
Motel        **Fax:** 215/245-0100. **Terms:** Sr. discount; package plans; pets. **Facility:** 141 rooms. King suite, $110; 3 stories;
interior/exterior corridors; meeting rooms; exercise room, arcade. **Dining & Entertainment:** Cocktails/lounge;
restaurant nearby; entertainment. **Services:** data ports; valet laundry. **All Rooms:** free movies, cable TV.
**Some Rooms:** whirlpools. Fee: VCP's. **Cards:** AE, CB, DI, DS, JCB, MC, VI.     🖪 Ⓓ ⊗

COURTYARD BY MARRIOTT BENSALEM    AAA Special Value Rates           **Phone:** 215/639-9100   (31)
◆ ◆ ◆        5/1-9/30          1P:  $85      2P/1B:  $95       2P/2B:  $95
Motor Inn    10/1-4/30         1P:  $75      2P/1B:  $85       2P/2B:  $85
**Location:** On SR 132; 2 mi e of jct US 1, exit SR 132E, from PA Tpk exit 28. 3327 Street Rd 19020.
**Fax:** 215/639-4598. **Terms:** Weekly/monthly rates; package plans; no pets. **Facility:** 167 rooms. Thoughtfully decorated rooms
& public areas. Reading room. 6 stories; interior corridors; meeting rooms; sauna, whirlpool, small heated pool; exercise room.
**Dining:** Dining room; 11 am-2 & 5-9 pm; $9-$14. **Services:** data ports. Fee: coin laundry. **All Rooms:** coffeemakers, free &
pay movies, cable TV. **Some Rooms:** refrigerators. **Cards:** AE, CB, DI, DS, JCB, MC, VI.
*(See color ad below)*                                                                    🖪 Ⓓ Ⓢ ⊗

HAMPTON INN PHILADELPHIA NORTH EAST    AAA Special Value Rates       **Phone:** 215/245-5222   (33)
(AAA)         All Year           1P: $70-  85  2P/1B:  $75-  95  2P/2B:  $75-  95
◆ ◆ ◆        **Location:** Jct US 13 & I-95, Woodhaven Rd exit, then 1/4 mi w on US 13, Bristol Pike. 1329 Bristol Pike
Motor Inn    19020. **Fax:** 215/245-1314. **Terms:** Credit card guarantee, 3 day notice; no pets. **Facility:** 141 rooms. Com-
fortably furnished rooms. 3 stories; interior corridors; meeting rooms; pool; exercise room. **Dining &
Entertainment:** Cocktails/lounge. **Services:** valet laundry. **All Rooms:** free movies, cable TV. Fee: VCP.
**Some Rooms:** coffeemakers, refrigerators, whirlpools. **Cards:** AE, CB, DI, DS, MC, VI. *(See ad p A200)*   🖪 Ⓓ Ⓢ ⊗

HOLIDAY INN-PHILADELPHIA NORTHEAST    Rates Subject to Change        **Phone:** 215/638-1500   (34)
(AAA)         5/29-9/7           1P: $85- 105  2P/1B:  $85- 105  2P/2B:  $85- 105  XP: $10  F17
◆ ◆ ◆        5/1-5/28 & 9/8-4/30   1P: $69      2P/1B:  $85       2P/2B:  $77       XP: $10  F17
Motor Inn    **Location:** On SR 132, 1/4 mi e of jct US 1, 3/4 mi se of tpk, exit 28. 3499 Street Rd 19020.
**Fax:** 215/638-8547. **Terms:** Sr. discount; reserv deposit, 30 day notice; package plans; no pets. **Facility:** 117
rooms. Contemporary furnishings in lobby & rooms. Suites, $195; 2 stories; interior/exterior corridors; meeting
rooms; pool, wading pool. **Dining:** Dining room; 6:30 am-2 & 5-10 pm, Sun 5 pm-9 pm; $6-$15; cocktails; Sun brunch
Oct-Dec. **Services:** data ports; secretarial services; health club privileges. Fee: coin laundry. **All Rooms:** free & pay movies,
cable TV. **Some Rooms:** coffeemakers. Fee: refrigerators. **Cards:** AE, CB, DI, DS, JCB, MC, VI.
*(See ad p A91)*                                                                          🖪 Ⓓ ⊗

**(See PHILADELPHIA & VICINITY ACCOMMODATIONS spotting map pages A196 & A197)**

MCINTOSH INN OF BENSALEM
◆◆ Motel

| | | | | | | | | | |
|---|---|---|---|---|---|---|---|---|---|
| | Rates Subject to Change | | | | | | Phone: 215/245-0111 | | 37 |
| Fri & Sat 6/25-9/3 | 1P: | $50- | 57 | 2P/1B: | $57 | | 2P/2B: | $62 | XP: | $3 | F18 |
| Fri & Sat 5/1-6/24 & 9/4-4/30 | 1P: | $48- | 55 | 2P/1B: | $55 | | 2P/2B: | $60 | XP: | $3 | F18 |
| Sun-Thurs 5/1-9/3 | 1P: | $44- | 51 | 2P/1B: | $51 | | 2P/2B: | $56 | XP: | $3 | F18 |
| Sun-Thurs 9/4-4/30 | 1P: | $44- | 49 | 2P/1B: | $51 | | 2P/2B: | $55 | XP: | $3 | F18 |

**Location:** From PA Tpk, exit 28, s on US 1 to SR 132E (Street Rd). 3671 E Street Rd 19020. Fax: 215/244-4999.
**Terms:** Sr. discount; weekly rates; no pets. **Facility:** 111 rooms. 5 stories; interior corridors; meeting rooms.
**Dining:** Restaurant nearby. **Services:** data ports. **All Rooms:** free movies, combo & shower baths, cable TV.
**Some Rooms:** microwaves, radios, refrigerators. **Cards:** AE, CB, DI, MC, VI.
*(See ad p A185)*                                                    Roll in showers. (symbols)

## RESTAURANT

FISHER'S TUDOR HOUSE                **Dinner:** $11-$20                **Phone:** 215/244-9777   85
◆◆
Seafood   **Location:** On SR 132, 1 mi w of jct I-95. 1858 Street Rd 19020. **Hours:** 11 am-10 pm, Sun 1 pm-9 pm.
**Closed:** Mon, 11/23 & 12/25. **Reservations:** suggested. **Features:** casual dress; children's menu; early bird
specials; health conscious menu; carryout; cocktails & lounge; a la carte. Popular restaurant serving nicely
prepared food. Bakery. **Cards:** AE, MC, VI.                                        (symbol)

# BETHEL PARK

## LODGING

HOLIDAY INN PITTSBURGH SOUTH          Guaranteed Rates                **Phone:** 412/833-5300
◆◆◆

| | | | | | | | | |
|---|---|---|---|---|---|---|---|---|
| Fri & Sat | 1P: | $69 | 2P/1B: | $69 | 2P/2B: | $69 | XP: | $10 | F19 |
| Sun-Thurs | 1P: | $59 | 2P/1B: | $59 | 2P/2B: | $59 | XP: | $10 | F19 |

Motor Inn   **Location:** 1 mi n on US 19, opposite South Hills Village Mall. 164 Ft Couch Rd 15241. Fax: 412/831-8539.
**Terms:** Sr. discount; BP, CP, MAP available; small pets only. **Facility:** 210 rooms. 2-7 stories; interior corridors; conference
facilities; pool. **Dining & Entertainment:** Dining room; 6:30 am-11 pm; $7-$15; cocktails/lounge. **Services:** health club
privileges. Fee: coin laundry, airport transportation. **All Rooms:** free & pay movies, combo & shower baths, cable TV.
**Some Rooms:** microwaves, refrigerators. **Cards:** AE, CB, DI, DS, JCB, MC, VI.                   (symbols)

# BETHLEHEM—71,400

## LODGINGS

COMFORT INN          AAA Special Value Rates                **Phone:** 610/865-6300
(AAA)

| | | | | | | | | |
|---|---|---|---|---|---|---|---|---|
| All Year [CP] | 1P: | $52- | 69 | 2P/1B: | $62- | 79 | 2P/2B: | $62- | 79 | XP: | $6 | F18 |

◆◆ Motel   **Location:** Just s of US 22, exit SR 191. 3191 Highfield Dr 18017. Fax: 610/865-6300. **Terms:** Reserv
deposit, 7 day notice; pets. **Facility:** 116 rooms. 2 stories; interior/exterior corridors; meeting rooms.
**Dining & Entertainment:** Cocktails/lounge; restaurant nearby. **Services:** data ports; valet laundry.
**All Rooms:** free movies, cable TV, VCP's. **Some Rooms:** Fee: whirlpools. **Cards:** AE, CB, DI, DS, JCB,
MC, VI.                                                                            (symbols)

COMFORT SUITES          AAA Special Value Rates                **Phone:** 610/882-9700
(AAA)

| | | | | | | | |
|---|---|---|---|---|---|---|---|
| All Year | 1P: | $71- | 75 | 2P/1B: | $85- | 99 | XP: | $8 | F18 |

◆◆◆ Suite Motel   **Location:** Center, w 3rd & Broadhead sts (3rd St exit from SR 378). 120 W 3rd St 18015.
Fax: 610/882-9700. **Terms:** Credit card guarantee, 3 day notice; pets. **Facility:** 124 rooms. 4 stories; interior
corridors; conference facilities; exercise room. **Dining & Entertainment:** Restaurant; 10 am-10 pm;
cocktails/lounge. **Services:** data ports; valet laundry; airport transportation. **All Rooms:** microwaves, free
movies, refrigerators, cable TV. **Some Rooms:** Fee: whirlpools. **Cards:** AE, CB, DI, DS, MC, VI.   (symbols)

**ECONO LODGE**
◆◆ Motel
All Year — Rates Subject to Change
1P: $39- 65  2P/1B: $46- 65  2P/2B: $46- 65  XP: $5  F18
Phone: 215/867-8681
**Location:** 3/4 mi se off US 22 (Airport Rd S exit) on Catasauqua Rd. 2140 Motel Dr 18018 (US 22, Airport Rd S). Fax: 215/867-6426. **Terms:** Sr. discount; reserv deposit; CP available; no pets. **Facility:** 119 rooms. Large rooms. 1 story; exterior corridors; meeting rooms; pool; 2 tennis courts. **Dining:** Restaurant nearby. **Services:** data ports. Fee: coin laundry. **All Rooms:** cable TV. **Some Rooms:** coffeemakers. Fee: microwaves, refrigerators, VCP's, whirlpools. **Cards:** AE, CB, DI, DS, JCB, MC, VI. Ⓓ ⊗

**HOLIDAY INN HOTEL & CONFERENCE CENTER**
◆◆◆ Motor Inn
All Year — Rates Subject to Change
1P: $85- 98  2P/1B: $108  2P/2B: $108  XP: $10  F19
Phone: 610/866-5800
**Location:** Off US 22, Center St & SR 512 exit. US 22 & 512 18017. Fax: 610/867-9120. **Terms:** Sr. discount; reserv deposit, 3 day notice; no pets. **Facility:** 192 rooms. 1 two-bedroom unit. 2 stories; interior/exterior corridors; conference facilities; pool, wading pool; exercise room. **Dining & Entertainment:** Restaurant; 6:30 am-10 pm, Sat & Sun from 7 am; $10-$19; cocktails/lounge. **Services:** data ports; valet laundry; airport transportation. **Recreation:** jogging. **All Rooms:** free movies, cable TV. **Some Rooms:** VCP's. Fee: microwaves, refrigerators, whirlpools. **Cards:** AE, CB, DI, DS, JCB, MC, VI.
Roll in showers. ☒ Ⓓ ⊗

**WYDNOR HALL INN**
◆◆◆ Historic Bed & Breakfast
Fri-Sun [CP] — Guaranteed Rates
1P: $100- 120  2P/1B: $110- 130  XP: $20  F8
Mon-Thurs [CP]
1P: $75- 85  2P/1B: $85- 95  XP: $20  F8
Phone: 610/867-6851
**Location:** I-78 exit 20, 1/4 mi s to Savcon Valley Rd. 2 1/4 mi e to SR 378, 1 1/2 mi n to Black River Rd, 1/4 mi w to Old Philadelphia Pk, then 1/4 mi s. 3612 Old Philadelphia Pk 18015. Fax: 610/866-2062. **Terms:** Reserv deposit, 10 day notice; package plans; no pets. **Facility:** 5 rooms. Circa 1812 late Georgian-style fieldstone manor home. Tastefully decorated in antiques. 2 night min stay weekends 5/1-6/30 & 9/1-10/31; 3 stories, no elevator; interior corridors; meeting rooms; putting green. **Dining:** Afternoon tea. **All Rooms:** cable TV. **Cards:** AE, CB, DI, MC, VI. Ⓓ ⊗

## RESTAURANT

**THE SUN INN**
◆◆ American
Dinner: $11-$20
Phone: 610/974-9451
**Location:** Downtown, in historic district. 564 Main St 18018. **Hours:** 11:30 am-2 & 5-8 pm. Closed: Sun, Mon, 1/1, 7/4, 12/24 & 12/25. **Reservations:** suggested. **Features:** casual dress; cocktails; a la carte. Traditional dining in an authentic Colonial setting; serving guest since 1758. Smoke free premises. ⊗
**Cards:** AE, MC, VI.

# BIRD IN HAND

## LODGINGS

**AMISH COUNTRY MOTEL**
Ⓐ
◆◆ Motel
Rates Subject to Change
Phone: 717/768-8396
6/30-9/3                2P/2B: $73   XP: $8  F16
9/4-10/28               2P/2B: $65   XP: $8  F16
5/17-6/29               2P/2B: $62   XP: $8  F16
5/1-5/16, 10/29-11/25 &
3/31-4/30               2P/2B: $49- 53  XP: $8  F16
**Location:** 1 mi e on SR 340; 4 3/4 mi e of US 30. 17505 (PO Box 73). **Terms:** Open 5/1-11/25 & 3/31-4/30; reserv deposit, 3 day notice; no pets. **Facility:** 25 rooms. Located in rural area in view of Amish farmlands. Weekends, $5 extra 9/1-11/31; 2 stories; exterior corridors; pool. **Dining:** Restaurant nearby. **All Rooms:** cable TV. **Some Rooms:** coffeemakers. **Cards:** AE, DS, MC, VI. Ⓓ ⊗

**BIRD-IN-HAND FAMILY INN**
Ⓐ
◆◆◆ Motor Inn
Rates Subject to Change
Phone: 717/768-8271
6/16-9/3                2P/2B: $81   XP: $8  F16
9/4-10/28               2P/2B: $73   XP: $8  F16
5/12-6/15               2P/2B: $65   XP: $8  F16
5/1-5/11 & 10/29-4/30   2P/2B: $49- 59  XP: $8  F16
**Location:** 1/4 mi e on SR 340, 3 3/4 mi e of US 30. 17505 (PO Box 402). Fax: 717/768-1117. **Terms:** Reserv deposit, 3 day notice; package plans; no pets. **Facility:** 100 rooms. Weekends, $5 extra 9/1-11/30; 2 stories; interior/exterior corridors; designated smoking area; meeting rooms; 2 pools (2 heated, 1 indoor), whirlpool; 2 lighted tennis courts; playground. **Dining:** Restaurant; 6 am-9 pm, in winter-8 pm, closed Sun; $6-$9; health conscious menu items. **Services:** data ports. Fee: coin laundry. **All Rooms:** coffeemakers, cable TV. **Some Rooms:** efficiency, refrigerators. Fee: VCP's, whirlpools. **Cards:** AE, CB, DI, DS, MC, VI. *(See ad starting on p A152)* Ⓓ ⊗

**VILLAGE INN OF BIRD-IN-HAND**
Ⓐ
◆◆ Historic Bed & Breakfast
Rates Subject to Change
Phone: 717/293-8369
6/30-10/27 [CP]          2P/1B: $79- 139  XP: $10  F3
5/1-6/29 & 10/28-4/30 [CP]  2P/1B: $59- 119  XP: $10  F3
**Location:** Center; on SR 340. 2695 Old Philadelphia Pike 17505 (PO Box 253). **Terms:** Reserv deposit, 3 day notice; no pets. **Facility:** 11 rooms. Restored 1852 inn, attractively furnished. Closed 1/1-1/15 & 12/11-12/26. Weekends, $5 extra 9/1-10/31; 3 stories; interior corridors. **All Rooms:** cable TV. **Some Rooms:** whirlpools. **Cards:** AE, DS, MC, VI. Ⓓ ⊗

## RESTAURANT

**PLAIN & FANCY FARM DINING ROOM**
Ⓐ
◆ American
Dinner: $11-$20
Phone: 717/768-8281
**Location:** 2 mi e on SR 340, from SR 896. 17505. **Hours:** 11:30 am-8 pm; 1/1-3/31 noon-7 pm. Closed: Sun & 12/25. **Reservations:** suggested; weekends. **Features:** casual dress; buffet. Family-style. No menu. Children 4-11 years, $4.95. Small parties share tables. Smoke free premises. **Cards:** MC, VI. ⊗
*(See ad starting on p A152)*

# BLAIRSVILLE—3,600

## LODGING

**COMFORT INN**
◆◆◆ Motel
All Year [CP] — Rates Subject to Change
1P: $50- 69  2P/1B: $70- 84  2P/2B: $65  XP: $5  F18
Phone: 412/459-7100
**Location:** On US 22 & US 119. (RR 1 Box 22). Fax: 412/459-7192. **Terms:** Package plans; no pets. **Facility:** 72 rooms. 2 stories; interior corridors; meeting rooms; heated indoor pool. **Dining:** Restaurant nearby. **Services:** data ports; winter plug-ins. Fee: coin laundry. **All Rooms:** cable TV. **Some Rooms:** microwaves, refrigerators, whirlpools. **Cards:** AE, DI, DS, MC, VI. Ⓓ Ⓢ ⊗

## RESTAURANT

**CHESTNUT RIDGE CRYSTAL ROOM**
◆◆◆ American
Dinner: $11-$20
Phone: 412/459-7191
**Location:** 2 mi e on US 119, 2 blks s of jct US 22, in Chestnut Ridge Inn on the Green. 15717. **Hours:** 5 pm-10 pm, Fri & Sat-11 pm, Sun-9 pm. Closed major holidays. **Reservations:** suggested; weekends. **Features:** cocktails & lounge. Attractive country inn on public golf course complex. **Cards:** AE, DI, DS, MC, VI.

# BLAWNOX (See PITTSBURGH ACCOMMODATIONS spotting map page A207; see index starting on page A206)

## LODGING

**HOLIDAY INN-R I D C PARK**     Rates Subject to Change          **Phone:** 412/963-0600  🆙
◆◆          All Year [AP]          1P:   $90- 150   2P/1B:   $90- 150   2P/2B:   $90- 175   XP: $10   F18
Motor Inn     **Location:** Off SR 28, RIDC, exit 10; 3 1/4 mi s of I-76, exit 5. 180 Gamma Dr 15238. **Fax:** 412/963-7852.
**Terms:** Sr. discount; reserv deposit; 10% service charge; weekly/monthly rates; no pets. **Facility:** 225 rooms.
2 stories; interior corridors; meeting rooms; pool; exercise room. **Dining:** Dining room; 6 am-10 pm, Sat & Sun from 7 am;
$11-$17; cocktails. **Services:** data ports; valet laundry. **All Rooms:** free movies, combo & shower baths.
**Some Rooms:** A/C, coffeemakers, microwaves. **Cards:** AE, DI, DS, JCB, MC.          Ⓓ ⊗

# BLOOMSBURG—12,400

## LODGINGS

**BUDGET HOST PATRIOT INN**     Rates Subject to Change          **Phone:** 717/387-1776
🆔          All Year          1P:   $42- 55   2P/1B:   $47- 65   2P/2B:   $47- 65   XP:$5-10   F16
          **Location:** On US 11, 1/2 mi s of jct 36S. 6305 US 11 17815 (6305 New Berwick Hwy).
◆◆          **Fax:** 717/387-9611. **Terms:** No pets. **Facility:** 30 rooms. 1 story; interior corridors; meeting rooms. **Dining &**
Motor Inn     **Entertainment:** Restaurant; 6 am-10 pm, Fri & Sat-11 pm; $6-$14; cocktails/lounge. **All Rooms:** free
          movies, cable TV. Fee: VCP. **Some Rooms:** Fee: microwaves, refrigerators. **Cards:** AE, CB, DI, DS, MC, VI.
(See color ad p A83)          Ⓓ ⊗

**ECONO LODGE AT BLOOMSBURG**     Rates Subject to Change          **Phone:** 717/387-0490
🆔          All Year          1P:   $43- 56   2P/1B:   $49- 63   2P/2B:   $51- 63   XP: $5   F18
          **Location:** I-80 exit 34; on SR 42. 189 Columbia Mall Dr 17815. **Terms:** Sr. discount;
◆◆          pets, $10. **Facility:** 80 rooms. Next to Mall. 1 two-bedroom unit. 2 stories; interior corridors.
Motel     **Dining:** Restaurant nearby. **All Rooms:** free movies, cable TV. **Cards:** AE, CB, DI, DS, JCB, MC, VI.
          🖼 Ⓓ ⊗

**THE INN AT TURKEY HILL**     Rates Subject to Change          **Phone:** 717/387-1500
🆔          All Year [CP]          1P:   $76- 140          2P/2B:   $88- 170   XP: $15   F12
          **Location:** I-80 westbound, exit 35S; eastbound, exit 35, just e of stoplight. 991 Central Rd 17815.
◆◆◆          **Fax:** 717/784-3718. **Terms:** Credit card guarantee; monthly rates; pets, $15. **Facility:** 18 rooms. Inn amid
Country Inn     rolling hills & farmlands of central Pennsylvania. Rooms decorated with handmade furnishings. 2 rooms with
          whirlpool & fireplace $100-$170; 1-2 stories; interior/exterior corridors; meeting rooms. **Dining:** Dining room,
see separate listing. **Services:** valet laundry. **All Rooms:** cable TV. **Some Rooms:** VCP's, whirlpools. **Cards:** AE, CB, DI,
DS, MC, VI.          Ⓓ ⊗

**QUALITY INN**     Guaranteed Rates          **Phone:** 717/784-5300
🆔          All Year          1P:   $45- 65   2P/1B:   $50- 70   2P/2B:   $55- 70   XP: $5   F18
          **Location:** On SR 42 at I-80 exit 34. 1 Buckhorn Rd 17815. **Fax:** 717/387-0367. **Terms:** Sr. discount; reserv
◆◆          deposit; pets. **Facility:** 120 rooms. 2 stories; interior corridors. **Dining & Entertainment:** Restaurant; 6
Motor Inn     am-10 pm; $6-$14; cocktails/lounge. **All Rooms:** free movies, cable TV. **Some Rooms:** radios, refrigerators.
          **Cards:** AE, CB, DI, DS, JCB, MC, VI.          Ⓓ ⊗

## RESTAURANT

**THE INN AT TURKEY HILL**          Dinner: $11-$20          **Phone:** 717/387-1500
◆◆◆     **Location:** In The Inn At Turkey Hill. 991 Central Rd 17815. **Hours:** 5 pm-9 pm, Fri & Sat-10 pm.
Regional     **Reservations:** suggested. **Features:** casual dress; Sunday brunch; cocktails & lounge; a la carte. Intimate
American     country dining with gourmet touch. 3 distinct dining rooms overlooking beautiful landscaped courtyard.
          **Cards:** AE, CB, DI, DS, MC, VI.          ⊗

# BLUE BELL

## RESTAURANT

**BLUE BELL INN**  Historical          Dinner: $21-$30          **Phone:** 215/646-2010
◆◆◆     **Location:** On SR 73, 1 1/2 mi e of jct US 202. 601 Skippack Pike 19422. **Hours:** 11:30 am-2:30 & 4:30-10
American     pm, Sat-10:30 pm. Closed major holidays, Sun & Mon. **Reservations:** suggested. **Features:** semi-formal
          attire; children's menu; early bird specials; health conscious menu; carryout; cocktails & lounge;
entertainment. Well-prepared food served in historic inn. Sun & Mon private parties only by reservation. **Cards:** AE, MC, VI.
          ⊗

Guestroom fire alarm installations
are indicated by:

Ⓓ—smoke detector

Ⓢ—sprinkler system.

## BLUE MOUNTAIN

### LODGING

**KENMAR MOTEL**  Rates Subject to Change  Phone: 717/423-5915
All Year [CP]  1P: $36- 40  2P/1B: $40- 48  2P/2B: $45- 55  XP: $5
**Location:** 1/4 mi e of I-76 exit 15, on SR 997N. 17788 Cumberland Hwy 17240. **Terms:** Sr. discount; reserv deposit, 4 day notice; weekly rates; small pets only. **Facility:** 15 rooms. Well-maintained property. 1 unit with 3 double beds, $65-$85; 1 story; exterior corridors; pool. **All Rooms:** free movies, cable TV. **Some Rooms:** radios, refrigerators. **Cards:** AE, DS, MC, VI.  (D) (X)

Motel

## BOYERTOWN—3,800

### LODGINGS

**MEL-DOR MOTEL**  Guaranteed Rates  Phone: 610/367-2626
All Year [CP]  1P: $35- 40  2P/1B: $38- 40  2P/2B: $45  XP: $5 F12
**Location:** 1 mi n of Boyertown at New Berlinville exit. 494 Swamp Creek Rd 19545 (PO Box 349, NEW BERLINVILLE). **Terms:** Reserv deposit; weekly rates; small pets only, $5. **Facility:** 16 rooms. 1 story; exterior corridors. **All Rooms:** free movies, combo & shower baths, cable TV. **Some Rooms:** Fee: microwaves, refrigerators. **Cards:** AE, DS, MC, VI.  (D)

Motel

**TWIN TURRETS INN**  Rates Subject to Change  Phone: 610/367-4513
All Year [BP]  1P: $60- 100  2P/1B: $80- 120  2P/2B: $80- 120  XP: $10 F3
Historic Bed  **Location:** Off SR 100 Boyertown exit, 2 mi w on SR 73. 11 E Philadelphia Ave 19512. Fax: 610/369-7898.
& Breakfast  **Terms:** Sr. discount; age restrictions may apply; reserv deposit, 14 day notice; weekly/monthly rates; no pets. **Facility:** 10 rooms. Victorian home built in 1865 for Horace Boyer of founding family, furnished with antiques & modern amenities. 3 stories; interior corridors. **All Rooms:** free movies, shower baths, cable TV. **Cards:** AE, DS, MC, VI.  (D) (X)

## BRADDOCK HILLS

### LODGING

**HOLIDAY INN PARKWAY EAST**  AAA Special Value Rates  Phone: 412/247-2700
All Year  1P: $84- 99  2P/1B: $84- 99  2P/2B: $84- 99
Motor Inn  **Location:** Rt 8 exit 11 off Rt 376, 1/4 mi n. 915 Brinton Rd 15221. Fax: 412/371-9619. **Terms:** $1 service charge; monthly rates; small pets only. **Facility:** 180 rooms. 11 stories; interior corridors; meeting rooms; heated indoor pool. **Dining:** Restaurant; 6:30 am-11 pm; $12-$20. **Services:** data ports; valet laundry. Fee: airport transportation. **All Rooms:** free & pay movies. **Some Rooms:** microwaves, refrigerators. **Cards:** AE, CB, DI, DS, JCB, MC, VI.  (D) (X)

## BRADFORD—9,600

### LODGING

**HOWARD JOHNSON MOTOR LODGE**  AAA Special Value Rates  Phone: 814/362-4501
All Year  1P: $66- 76  2P/1B: $68- 86  2P/2B: $68- 86  XP: $10 F18
**Location:** 1 blk s, southbound off US 219, Forman St exit, northbound off US 219, Elm St exit. 100 Davis St 16701 (PO Box 523). Fax: 814/362-2709. **Terms:** Credit card guarantee, 3 day notice; no pets. **Facility:** 120
Motor Inn  rooms. 3 stories; interior/exterior corridors; conference facilities; pool. **Dining:** Dining room; 7 am-2 & 5-9:30 pm; $6-$12; cocktails. **Services:** health club privileges; valet laundry. **All Rooms:** free movies, cable TV. **Cards:** AE, CB, DI, DS, JCB, MC, VI.  (D) (X)

## BREEZEWOOD

### LODGINGS

**COMFORT INN OF BREEZEWOOD**  Rates Subject to Change  Phone: 814/735-2200
All Year [CP]  1P: $40- 60  2P/1B: $50- 70  2P/2B: $50- 75  XP: $6 F18
**Location:** On US 30 at jct I-70, at Tpk I-76, exit 12. I-70 & US 30 15533 (PO Box 309). Fax: 814/735-4910.
Motor Inn  **Terms:** Sr. discount; reserv deposit; weekly/monthly rates; small pets only, $5. **Facility:** 118 rooms. Commercial location. 2 stories; interior/exterior corridors; meeting rooms; pool. **Dining & Entertainment:** Restaurant; 6:30 am-10 pm; $6-$16; cocktails/lounge. **Services:** data ports; winter plug-ins. **All Rooms:** free movies, cable TV. **Some Rooms:** Fee: VCP's. **Cards:** AE, CB, DI, DS, JCB, MC, VI. *(See color ad below)*  (D) (X)

**ECONO LODGE**                    AAA Special Value Rates                              Phone: 814/735-4341

|          |       |         |        |          |       |       |     |     |
|----------|-------|---------|--------|----------|-------|-------|-----|-----|
| Thurs-Sat 5/1-12/31 | 1P: | $45 | 2P/1B: | $51 | 2P/2B: | $56 | XP: $6 | F12 |
| Sun-Wed 5/1-12/31 | 1P: | $39 | 2P/1B: | $45 | 2P/2B: | $51 | XP: $6 | F12 |
| Thurs-Sat 1/1-4/30 | 1P: | $35 | 2P/1B: | $41 | 2P/2B: | $45 | XP: $6 | F12 |
| Sun-Wed 1/1-4/30 | 1P: | $30 | 2P/1B: | $35 | 2P/2B: | $39 | XP: $6 | F12 |

**Location:** On US 30 at jct I-70, w of Tpk I-76, exit 12. I-70 & Rt 30 15533 (RD 1, Box 101A).
Fax: 814/735-3958. **Terms:** Reserv deposit; no pets. **Facility:** 64 rooms. 1 story; exterior corridors; pool. **Dining:** Restaurant
nearby. **All Rooms:** free movies, cable TV. **Cards:** AE, CB, DI, DS, MC, VI.    Ⓓ ⊗

**PENN-AIRE MOTEL**                   Rates Subject to Change                          Phone: 814/735-4351

|          |           |        |          |       |     |
|----------|-----------|--------|----------|-------|-----|
| 5/1-10/31 & 4/1-4/30 | 2P/1B: $36- 40 | 2P/2B: $42- 46 | XP: $4 |
| 11/1-3/31 | 2P/1B: $28- 34 | 2P/2B: $36 | XP: $4 |

**Location:** On US 30, w of jct I-70, 1/4 mi w of tpk I-76 exit 12. I-70 & Rt 30 15533 (PO Box 156).
**Terms:** Credit card guarantee; pets. **Facility:** 31 rooms. 2 two-bedroom units. 1 story; exterior corridors; pool.
**Dining:** Restaurant nearby. **Services:** winter plug-ins. **All Rooms:** free movies, cable TV. **Cards:** AE, DI,
DS, MC, VI. (See ad below)    Ⓓ ⊗

**QUALITY INN-BREEZE MANOR**                                    Phone: 814/735-4311

AAA Special Value Rates

| | | 1P: | | 2P/1B: | | 2P/2B: | | XP: | |
|---|---|---|---|---|---|---|---|---|---|
| | 5/1-10/31 | 1P: | $43- 56 | 2P/1B: | $49- 56 | 2P/2B: | $56 | XP: $5 | F18 |
| | 3/1-4/30 | 1P: | $40- 50 | 2P/1B: | $45- 50 | 2P/2B: | $50 | XP: $5 | F18 |
| | 11/1-2/29 | 1P: | $38- 48 | 2P/1B: | $42- 48 | 2P/2B: | $48 | XP: $5 | F18 |

Motel   **Location:** On US 30 at Tpk I-76 exit 12, 1/4 mi e of jct I-70. I-70 & US 30 (RD 1, Box 36). **Terms:** No pets. **Facility:** 50 rooms. 1-2 stories; exterior corridors; heated pool, wading pool; playground. **Dining:** Restaurant nearby. **Services:** winter plug-ins. **Fee:** coin laundry. **Recreation:** jogging. **All Rooms:** free movies, cable TV. **Cards:** AE, CB, DI, DS, JCB, MC, VI. *(See color ad p A95)*   Ⓓ Ⓧ

**RAMADA INN**                                    Phone: 814/735-4005

AAA Special Value Rates

| | | 1P: | | 2P/1B: | | 2P/2B: | | XP: | |
|---|---|---|---|---|---|---|---|---|---|
| | 5/1-10/31 | 1P: | $57 | 2P/1B: | $65 | 2P/2B: | $65 | XP: $8 | F18 |
| | 11/1-4/30 | 1P: | $41 | 2P/1B: | $49 | 2P/2B: | $49 | XP: $8 | F18 |

Motor Inn   **Fax:** 814/735-3228. **Terms:** BP available; small pets only. **Facility:** 125 rooms. Commercial location. 2 stories; interior corridors; meeting rooms; heated indoor pool, sauna, whirlpool; exercise room, playground. **Dining:** Also, Prime Rib Restaurant, see separate listing. **All Rooms:** free movies, cable TV. **Some Rooms:** **Fee:** VCP's. **Cards:** AE, CB, DI, DS, JCB, MC, VI. *(See color ad p A95)*   **Location:** 1/10 mi e on US 30 from I-70 & 76 (turnpike), exit 12. Jct I-70 & Rt 30 15533 (PO Box 157).   Ⓓ Ⓧ

**WILTSHIRE MOTEL**                                    Phone: 814/735-4361

Rates Subject to Change

| | |  | |  | |  | |
|---|---|---|---|---|---|---|---|
| | 5/1-10/31 | 1P: | $28- 30 | 2P/2B: | $32- 36 | XP: $4 | |
| | 11/1-4/30 | 1P: | $24- 26 | 2P/2B: | $30- 32 | XP: $4 | |

Motel   **Location:** On US 30, w of jct I-70, 1/4 mi w of Tpk I-76 exit 12. Star Rt 2, Box 1 15533. **Terms:** Reserv deposit; small pets only. **Facility:** 12 rooms. 1 story; exterior corridors. **Dining:** Restaurant nearby. **All Rooms:** free movies, cable TV. **Cards:** AE, DS, MC, VI.   Ⓓ

## RESTAURANTS

**BOB EVAN'S GENERAL STORE RESTAURANT**          Dinner: up to $10          Phone: 814/735-4020

American   **Location:** At jct I-70 & US 30. 15533. **Hours:** 6 am-10 pm, Fri & Sat-11 pm. Closed: 11/23 & 12/25. **Features:** casual dress; children's menu; carryout. **Cards:** AE, MC, VI.

**PRIME RIB RESTAURANT**          Dinner: $11-$20          Phone: 814/735-4005

**Location:** Located in the Ramada Inn. US Rt 30E 15533. **Hours:** 6:30 am-10 pm. Closed: 12/25. **Features:** casual dress; children's menu; salad bar; cocktails & lounge. Casual dining experience. **Cards:** AE, CB, DI, DS, JCB, MC, VI. *(See color ad p A95)*

Steakhouse   Ⓧ

---

# BRIDGEVILLE—5,400    (See PITTSBURGH ACCOMMODATIONS spotting map page A207; see index starting on page A206)

## LODGING

**KNIGHTS INN-PITTSBURGH-BRIDGEVILLE**          Rates Subject to Change          Phone: 412/221-8110   **55**

| | | 1P: | | 2P/1B: | | 2P/2B: | | XP: | |
|---|---|---|---|---|---|---|---|---|---|
| | All Year | 1P: | $39 | 2P/1B: | $45 | 2P/2B: | $45 | XP: $6 | F18 |

Motel   **Location:** At jct I-79, exit 11 & SR 50. 111 Hickory Grade Rd 15017. **Fax:** 412/257-1020. **Terms:** Sr. discount; reserv deposit; weekly rates; pets. **Facility:** 105 rooms. 11 efficiencies, $38-$44; 1 story; exterior corridors; meeting rooms; small pool. **All Rooms:** free movies. **Some Rooms:** **Fee:** microwaves, refrigerators, VCP's. **Cards:** AE, CB, DI, DS, MC, VI.

## RESTAURANT

**PETERS PLACE**          Dinner: $11-$20          Phone: 412/221-5000   **50**

American   **Location:** From I-79, Kirwin Heights exit 12, then 1/4 mi w on US 50. 1199 Washington Pike 15017. **Hours:** 11 am-10 pm, Fri & Sat-midnight, Sun 11 am-8:30 pm. Closed major holidays. **Reservations:** suggested; weekends. **Features:** casual dress; children's menu; early bird specials; health conscious menu items; carryout; cocktails & lounge. Specializing in seafood & veal dishes. **Cards:** AE, DI, DS, MC, VI.   Ⓧ

---

# BROOKVILLE—4,200

## LODGINGS

**BUDGET HOST GOLD EAGLE INN**          Guaranteed Rates          Phone: 814/849-7344

| | | 1P: | | 2P/1B: | | 2P/2B: | | XP: | |
|---|---|---|---|---|---|---|---|---|---|
| | All Year | 1P: | $30- 38 | 2P/1B: | $32- 45 | 2P/2B: | $35- 47 | XP: $5 | |

Motor Inn   **Location:** Jct SR 28, 36 & 322; 1/2 mi s of I-80, exit 13. 250 W Main St 15825. **Fax:** 814/849-7345. **Terms:** Credit card guarantee, 3 day notice; weekly/monthly rates; small pets only. **Facility:** 29 rooms. Convenient to interstate for budget traveller. 1 two-bedroom unit. 2 stories; exterior corridors. **Dining:** Also, Gold Eagle Restaurant, see separate listing. **All Rooms:** combo & shower baths, cable TV. **Some Rooms:** 3 efficiencies. **Cards:** AE, DS, MC, VI. *(See color ad p A83 & ad below)*

**HOJO INN**                                    Phone: 814/849-3335

AAA Special Value Rates

| | | 1P: | | 2P/1B: | | 2P/2B: | | XP: |
|---|---|---|---|---|---|---|---|---|
| | All Year | 1P: | $26- 44 | 2P/1B: | $31- 49 | 2P/2B: | $31- 49 | XP: $6 |

Motel   **Location:** At I-80 exit 13. 245 Allegheny Blvd 15825. **Fax:** 814/849-5259. **Terms:** Reserv deposit, 3 day notice; weekly/monthly rates; no pets. **Facility:** 40 rooms. Popular with truckers. 2 stories; interior/exterior corridors. **Dining:** Restaurant nearby. **Services:** **Fee:** coin laundry. **All Rooms:** free movies, cable TV. **Cards:** AE, DS, MC, VI.   Ⓓ Ⓧ

**RAMADA LIMITED**                                    Phone: 814/849-8381

AAA Special Value Rates

| | | 1P: | | 2P/1B: | | 2P/2B: | | XP: | |
|---|---|---|---|---|---|---|---|---|---|
| | 5/1-10/31 [CP] | 1P: | $41- 46 | 2P/1B: | $47- 65 | 2P/2B: | $47- 65 | XP: $5 | F18 |
| | 11/1-4/30 [CP] | 1P: | $29- 39 | 2P/1B: | $35- 45 | | | XP: $5 | F18 |

Motel   **Location:** On SR 36, 1/4 mi s of I-80 exit 13. 235 Allegheny Blvd 15825-8213. **Terms:** Credit card guarantee; small pets only, $5. **Facility:** 69 rooms. Convenient to interstate & downtown. 3 stories, no elevator; interior corridors; meeting rooms. **Dining:** Restaurant nearby. **Services:** **Fee:** coin laundry. **All Rooms:** free movies, cable TV. **Cards:** AE, CB, DI, DS, JCB, MC, VI.   Ⓓ Ⓧ

# Before you hit the open road,

# tear along the dotted line.

Cut your travel expenses before you hit the road. Just clip the attached coupons and get $5 off the AAA room rate at participating Holiday Inn® hotels, where you'll always find a clean, comfortable room at an exceptional value.

Then relax. Enjoy the freedom of the open highway. And the extra savings in your pocket.

STAY WITH SOMEONE YOU KNOW.®  *Holiday Inn*®

## CALL 1-800-HOLIDAY OR YOUR TRAVEL AGENT.

# Check out these participating Holiday Inn® hotels:

## NEW JERSEY
**Atlantic City**-West ◊
(609) 484-1500

**Bordentown** ◊
(609) 298-3200

**Clinton**
(908) 735-5111

**Jamesburg**-Cranbury Area
(Exit 8A-NJ Tnpk)
(609) 655-4775

**Newark**
International Airport North
(201) 589-1000

Jetport-International
Airport West
(908) 355-1700

**Paramus**
(201) 843-5400

**Parsippany**
(201) 263-2000

**Secaucus**-Meadowlands
(201) 348-2000

**South Plainfield**-Piscataway
(908) 753-5500

**Tinton Falls**-Eatontown
(908) 544-9300

**Toms River**
(908) 244-4000

## NEW YORK
**New York City**-LaGuardia Airport †
(718) 457-6300

## PENNSYLVANIA
**Allentown**-Lehigh Valley (I-78)
(610) 391-1000

**Bartonsville**-Pocono Area
(717) 424-6100

**Erie**
Downtown
(814) 456-2961

South
(814) 864-4911

**Exton**-Downington
(610) 363-1100

**Harrisburg**
Hershey Area (I-81)
(717) 469-0661

West
(717) 697-0321

**Hazleton** (Rt 309)
(717) 455-2061

**Indiana**
(412) 463-3561

**Lancaster County**
(717) 336-7541

**Lewistown**
(717) 248-4961

**Philadelphia Area**
Bridgeport-Pureland
Industrial Park (I-295)
(609) 467-3322

Bucks County (PA Tnpk & Rt 132)
(215) 364-2000

### Philadelphia Area cont.
City Line (I-76, Exit 33)
(215) 477-0200

King of Prussia-
Valley Forge Area (Exit 24)
(610) 265-7500

Northeast (PA Tnpk Exit 28
& SR 132 East)
(215) 638-1500

Stadium
(215) 755-9500

**Philadelphia Dwtn Area**
City Centre (18th & Market)
(215) 561-7500

Independence Mall-Historic Area
(215) 923-8660

**Pittsburgh Area**
Allegheny Valley-R.I.D.C. Park Exit
(412) 963-0600

Beaver Falls (Exit 2 PA Tnpk.)
(412) 846-3700

Central-Greentree
(412) 922-8100

McKnight Road-North Hills Area
(412) 366-5200

Monroeville
(412) 372-1022

Parkway East-Braddock Hills
(412) 247-2700

South Hills Area
(412) 833-5300

### Pittsburgh Area cont.
University Center-Oakland
(412) 682-6200

Washington-Meadow Lands
(412) 222-6200

**Pottstown** ◊
(215) 327-3300

**Reading** (Rt. 222 North)
(610) 929-4741

**Scranton**-East (Dunmore)
(717) 343-4771

**Sharon**- Hermitage
(412) 981-1530

**Somerset**
(814) 445-9611

**State College**-
Penn State University Area
(814) 238-3001

**York**
Arsenal Road (I-83 & Rt 30)
(717) 845-5671

Market Street (Rt 462)
(717) 755-1966

West Manchester Mall
(US 30 at Rt 74)
(717) 846-9500

◊ Denotes Holiday Inn Express® hotel location. † Denotes Holiday Inn Crowne Plaza® hotel location.

---

Valid at participating New Jersey/Pennsylvania/
New York Holiday Inn® hotels (see list). One coupon per
room, per single or multiple night stay; no copies or
facsimiles accepted. Not valid for groups or in
conjunction with any other discount, promotion or
special event as established by each independent operator.
Not valid with employee or travel industry discounts.
Blackout dates apply. Rooms limited and subject to
availability. Void where taxed, restricted or otherwise
prohibited by law. Coupon has no cash value. Offer valid
May 1, 1995 through April 30, 1996.

NJ95AA

Valid at participating New Jersey/Pennsylvania/
New York Holiday Inn® hotels (see list). One coupon per
room, per single or multiple night stay; no copies or
facsimiles accepted. Not valid for groups or in
conjunction with any other discount, promotion or
special event as established by each independent operator.
Not valid with employee or travel industry discounts.
Blackout dates apply. Rooms limited and subject to
availability. Void where taxed, restricted or otherwise
prohibited by law. Coupon has no cash value. Offer valid
May 1, 1995 through April 30, 1996.

NJ95AA

Valid at participating New Jersey/Pennsylvania/
New York Holiday Inn® hotels (see list). One coupon per
room, per single or multiple night stay; no copies or
facsimiles accepted. Not valid for groups or in
conjunction with any other discount, promotion or
special event as established by each independent operator.
Not valid with employee or travel industry discounts.
Blackout dates apply. Rooms limited and subject to
availability. Void where taxed, restricted or otherwise
prohibited by law. Coupon has no cash value. Offer valid
May 1, 1995 through April 30, 1996.

NJ95AA

SUPER 8 MOTEL
◆◆ Motel
All Year [CP]   Rates Subject to Change   1P: $37- 42 2P/1B: $44- 50 2P/2B: $44- 50 XP: $6 F12   Phone: 814/849-8840
**Location:** On SR 36; 1/4 mi n of I-80, exit 13. 251 Allegheny Blvd 15825. Fax: 814/849-8840. **Terms:** Sr. discount; credit card guarantee, 5 day notice; small pets only. **Facility:** 57 rooms. Convenient to interstate & downtown. 3 stories; interior corridors. **Dining:** Restaurant nearby. **Services:** Fee: coin laundry. **All Rooms:** free movies, cable TV. **Some Rooms:** Fee: VCP's. **Cards:** AE, CB, DI, DS, MC, VI.   ⒹⓈ⊗

## RESTAURANTS

GOLD EAGLE RESTAURANT
◆◆ Seafood
Dinner: $11-$20   Phone: 814/849-8251
**Location:** In Budget Host Gold Eagle Inn. 250 W Main St 15825. **Hours:** 4 pm-9:30 pm, Fri & Sat-10 pm, Sun 4 pm-9 pm. Closed major holidays. **Reservations:** suggested; weekends. **Features:** casual dress; children's menu; cocktails & lounge; a la carte. Older architecture & decor, with atmosphere, "Memories of yesteryear". **Cards:** AE, DS, MC, VI. *(See ad p A96)*   ⊗

THE MEETING PLACE
⑯ ◆◆ American
Dinner: up to $10   Phone: 814/849-2557
**Location:** Town Center across from courthouse. 209 Main St 15825. **Hours:** 8 am-9 pm, Fri-10 pm, Sat 9 am-9 pm, Sun 10 am-3 pm. Closed major holidays. **Features:** casual dress; children's menu; cocktails & lounge; street parking. Located in the heart of town, built in 1871. **Cards:** AE, DS, MC, VI.   ⊗

# BURNHAM—2,200

## LODGING

LEWISTOWN SUPER 8 MOTEL
⑯ ◆◆ Motel
All Year [CP]   Rates Subject to Change   1P: $44 2P/1B: $44 2P/2B: $49 XP: $5 F12   Phone: 717/242-8888
**Location:** On US 322 at Burnham exit. 19 Windmill Hill 17009. Fax: 717/242-9401. **Terms:** Sr. discount; reserv deposit, 7 day notice; no pets. **Facility:** 57 rooms. 2 stories, no elevator; interior corridors; meeting rooms. **Dining:** Restaurant nearby. **Services:** data ports. **All Rooms:** free & pay movies, combo & shower baths, cable TV. **Some Rooms:** microwaves, refrigerators, whirlpools. **Cards:** AE, DI, DS, MC, VI.
Roll in showers. ♿ 🗂 Ⓓ⊗

## RESTAURANT

LUBA'S RESTAURANT
◆◆ American
Dinner: $11-$20   Phone: 717/248-4566
**Location:** From US 322 Burnham exit, 3/4 mi e on E Ferguson Rd/W Freedom Ave. 205 W Freedom Ave 17009. **Hours:** 4 pm-9 pm, Fri & Sat-10 pm. Closed: Sun. **Features:** casual dress; children's menu; health conscious menu; carryout; cocktails & lounge. Special preparation for the individual. **Cards:** MC, VI.   ⊗

# BUSHKILL—5,500   (See POCONO MOUNTAINS & VICINITY ACCOMMODATIONS spotting map pages A212 & A213; see index starting on page A210)

## LODGING

FERNWOOD RESORT AND COUNTRY CLUB
⑯ ◆◆ Resort Motor Inn
All Year [MAP]   Rates Subject to Change   2P/1B: $198 2P/2B: $98- 198 XP:$8-30 F12   Phone: 717/588-9500 ⑮
**Location:** On US 209, 11 mi ne of I-80, exit 52. Rt 209 18324. Fax: 717/588-6680. **Terms:** Check-in 4 pm; reserv deposit; AP, BP, EP available; package plans; no pets. **Facility:** 177 rooms. 37 rooms with steambath. 2-3 stories; interior/exterior corridors; conference facilities; miniature golf; 2 pools (1 heated, 1 indoor), wading pool, sauna, whirlpool; 10 tennis courts (6 indoor, 4 lighted); exercise room, playground. Fee: 18 holes golf. **Dining & Entertainment:** 3 restaurants, coffee shop; 6 am-midnight; 5/30-10/12 to 1 am; $9-$22; cocktails/lounge; entertainment. **Services:** secretarial services; valet laundry. Fee: childcare. **Recreation:** children's program, nature program, social program; fishing, paddleboats; bicycles. Fee: cross country skiing, snowmobiling, tobogganing; horseback riding. **All Rooms:** cable TV. **Some Rooms:** radios, refrigerators, whirlpools. Fee: VCP's. **Cards:** AE, DS, MC, VI. *(See ad below)*   🗂 Ⓓ⊗

# BUTLER—15,700

## LODGINGS

DAYS INN
⑯ ◆ Motor Inn
All Year   Guaranteed Rates   1P: $35- 75 2P/1B: $35- 75 2P/2B: $35- 75 XP: $5 F17   Phone: 412/287-6761
**Location:** 2 mi s on SR 8. 139 Pittsburgh Rd 16001. Fax: 412/287-4307. **Terms:** Sr. discount; monthly rates; package plans; small pets only, $25 dep req. **Facility:** 139 rooms. 2 stories; interior/exterior corridors; meeting rooms; heated indoor pool, whirlpool. **Dining & Entertainment:** Dining room; 6 am-2 & 5-10 pm, Sat 7 am-noon & 5-10 pm, Sun 7 am-8 pm; $7-$15; cocktails/lounge. **Services:** Fee: coin laundry. **All Rooms:** free movies, cable TV. Fee: safes. **Some Rooms:** Fee: VCP's. **Cards:** AE, CB, DI, DS, MC, VI. *(See color ad p A98)*   🗂 Ⓓ⊗

Checkout time
is noted in the listing if the required time is before 10 a.m.

**SUPER 8 MOTEL**  ·  AAA Special Value Rates  ·  **Phone:** 412/287-8888
◆◆  All Year [CP]  1P:  $38  2P/1B:  $44  2P/2B:  $44  XP:$2-4  F12
Motel  **Location:** 2 mi s on SR 8. 128 Pittsburgh/Rt 8 16001. **Fax:** 412/287-8888. **Terms:** Credit card guarantee, 3 day notice; no pets. **Facility:** 66 rooms. 3 stories, no elevator; interior corridors; meeting rooms. **Dining:** Restaurant nearby. **Services:** data ports; valet laundry. **All Rooms:** free movies, cable TV. **Some Rooms:** Fee: microwaves, refrigerators, VCP's. **Cards:** AE, CB, DI, DS, JCB, MC, VI.  🅰 🅓 🅢 ⊗

## CAMPBELLTOWN

### LODGING

**VILLAGE MOTEL**  ·  Guaranteed Rates  ·  **Phone:** 717/838-4761
🅰🅰  6/30-9/3  1P:  $48  2P/1B:  $52  2P/2B:  $60  XP:  $4
  5/26-6/29  1P:  $44  2P/1B:  $48  2P/2B:  $56  XP:  $4
◆  5/1-5/25 & 9/4-4/30  1P:  $32  2P/1B:  $36  2P/2B:  $40  XP:  $4
Motel  **Location:** 4 mi e of Hershey on US 322. 17010 (PO Box 76). **Terms:** Reserv deposit, 3 day notice; weekly/monthly rates, off season; no pets. **Facility:** 32 rooms. Rural setting. 2 stories; exterior corridors; pool; 1 tennis court; playground. **Services:** Fee: coin laundry. **All Rooms:** cable TV. **Some Rooms:** efficiency, phones. **Cards:** DS, MC, VI. *(See color ad p A140)*  🅓 ⊗

## CANADENSIS  (See POCONO MOUNTAINS & VICINITY ACCOMMODATIONS spotting map pages A212 & A213; see index starting on page A210)

### LODGINGS

**BROOKVIEW MANOR BED & BREAKFAST**  ·  Rates Subject to Change  ·  **Phone:** 717/595-2451  🔟
◆  Fri & Sat [BP]  1P:  $75- 125  2P/1B:  $85- 135  XP: $20
Historic Bed  Sun-Thurs [BP]  1P:  $60- 100  2P/1B:  $70- 115  XP: $20
& Breakfast  **Location:** On SR 447, 1 mi s of jct SR 390. (RR 1 Box 365). **Terms:** Age restrictions may apply; reserv deposit, 14 day notice; weekly rates; no pets. **Facility:** 6 rooms. Frame house, built in 1911, sits on a hill in a rural area. 3 rooms with glassed-in sun porch. 1 two-bedroom unit, 1 three-bedroom unit. 3 stories, no elevator; interior corridors; smoke free premises; recreation room. **All Rooms:** combo & shower baths, no A/C, no phones, no TVs. **Some Rooms:** refrigerators. **Cards:** AE, CB, DI, DS, MC, VI.  🅓 ⊗

**HILLSIDE LODGE & RESORT**  ·  Rates Subject to Change  ·  **Phone:** 717/595-7551  🔟
🅰🅰  All Year [MAP]  1P:  $96- 118  2P/1B:  $128- 158  2P/2B:  $128- 158  XP:$13-50
◆  **Location:** 1 mi n on SR 390. 18325 (PO Box 268). **Terms:** Reserv deposit, 14 day notice; weekly rates; no pets. **Facility:** 33 rooms. Motel rooms & 5 cottages with living room & fireplace. Heart-shaped bathtub & 2 person jacuzzi; 1-2 stories; interior/exterior corridors; miniature golf; heated pool; 1 lighted tennis court; playground, basketball court, bocci court, horseshoes, shuffleboard, softball diamond, volleyball. **Dining & Entertainment:** Restaurant; 8:30 am-10 & 6-7:30 pm; cocktails/lounge. **Recreation:** nature program, recreation program, social program; ice skating, sledding. **All Rooms:** combo & shower baths, cable TV, no phones. **Some Rooms:** coffeemakers, microwaves, refrigerators, whirlpools. Fee: VCP's. **Cards:** DS, MC, VI.  🅓 ⊗

# CARBONDALE—10,700

## RESTAURANTS

**BEN-MAR RESTAURANT**   **Dinner:** $11-$20   Phone: 717/282-5970
⊛   **Location:** Center, on US 6. 89 N Main St 18407. **Hours:** 8 am-11 pm, Sun 11:30 am-9:30 pm. Closed:
◆◆   12/25. **Reservations:** suggested; Sat. **Features:** casual dress; children's menu; carryout; cocktails & lounge.
American   Warm inviting atmosphere. Selections of seafood, beef, veal & poultry. **Cards:** AE, CB, DI, DS, MC, VI.   ⊗

**GRIFF'S CORNER RESTAURANT**   **Dinner:** up to $10   Phone: 717/282-2052
◆   **Location:** In town, corner of Lincoln & N Church, 1 blk e of US 6. 49 N Church St 18407. **Hours:** 6:30 am-8
American   pm, Sun-2 pm. Closed major holidays. **Features:** No A/C; casual dress; children's menu; senior's menu;
carryout; street parking.

# CARLISLE—18,400

## LODGINGS

**APPALACHIAN MOTOR INN**   Rates Subject to Change   Phone: 717/245-2242
⊛   All Year   2P/1B:   $40-   50   2P/2B:   $45-   55   XP:   $5   F12
◆◆   **Location:** On US 11, 1/2 mi n of I-81, exit 17; 1 1/4 mi n of PA Tpk, I-76 exit 16. 1825 Harrisburg Pike
Motor Inn   17013. Fax: 717/258-4881. **Terms:** Sr. discount; credit card guarantee, 3 day notice; no pets. **Facility:** 200
rooms. Located along busy commercial highway. 2 stories; interior corridors; meeting rooms; pool room.
**Dining:** Restaurant;   5 am-1 am;   $8-$12;   cocktails.   **All Rooms:**   free movies,   cable TV.
**Some Rooms:** coffeemakers, radios, whirlpools. **Cards:** AE, CB, DI, DS, MC, VI.   ⒹⓈ⊗

**BEST WESTERN INN OF THE BUTTERFLY**   Rates Subject to Change   Phone: 717/243-5411
⊛   7/1-10/31   1P:   $57-   67   2P/2B:   $64-   74   XP:   $7   F18
   5/1-6/30 & 4/1-4/30   1P:   $53-   63   2P/2B:   $63-   73   XP:   $7   F18
◆◆◆   11/1-3/31   1P:   $51-   61   2P/2B:   $60-   70   XP:   $7   F18
Motor Inn   **Location:** On US 11, 3/4 mi n of Tpk I-76, exit 16; 1/4 mi s of jct I-81, exit 17. 1245 Harrisburg Pike 17013.
Fax: 717/243-0778. **Terms:** Sr. discount; small pets only. **Facility:** 130 rooms. 3 two-bedroom units. 2 stories;
interior/exterior corridors; meeting rooms; pool. **Dining:** Restaurant; 6:30 am-9 pm; $5-$12; cocktails. **All Rooms:** free
movies. **Some Rooms:** microwaves. **Cards:** AE, DI, DS, MC, VI.   Ⓓ⊗

**COAST TO COAST BUDGET HOST INN**   AAA Special Value Rates   Phone: 717/243-8585
⊛   All Year   1P:   $32-   56   2P/1B:   $38-   66   2P/2B:   $44-   76   XP:   $5   F18
◆   **Location:** Jct I-81 exit 17 & US 11, 1 mi n of tpk, exit 16, I-76; on US 11. 1252 Harrisburg Pike 17013.
Motor Inn   Fax: 717/2439711. **Terms:** Reserv deposit, 4 day notice; pets. **Facility:** 71 rooms. Located at busy commercial
highway intersection. 2 stories; interior/exterior corridors. **Dining:** Restaurant; 6:30 am-11 & 5-9 pm; Sat-7
am; Sun 7-11 am; closed Mon; $5-$10. **All Rooms:** free movies, cable TV. **Some Rooms:** radios.
Fee: VCP's. **Cards:** AE, DS, MC, VI. *(See color ad p A83 & below)*   Ⓓ⊗

**DAYS INN CARLISLE**   AAA Special Value Rates   Phone: 717/258-4147
⊛   All Year [CP]   1P:   $50-   75   2P/2B:   $55-   75   XP:   $5   F18
◆◆◆   **Location:** From I-81, exit 13; w on Walnut Bottom Rd; n on Alexander Spring Rd. 101 Alexander Spring Rd
Motel   17013. Fax: 717/258-4147. **Terms:** Credit card guarantee, 3 day notice; BP available; small pets only, $5 in
smoking rooms only. **Facility:** 95 rooms. 2 stories; interior corridors; meeting rooms; pool; exercise room.
**All Rooms:** free movies, cable TV. **Some Rooms:** microwaves, refrigerators. Fee: VCP's. **Cards:** AE, CB,
DI, DS, JCB, MC, VI.   ⓏⒹ⊗

**ECONO LODGE**   AAA Special Value Rates   Phone: 717/249-7775
⊛   All Year   1P:   $38-   65   2P/1B:   $42-   65   2P/2B:   $45-   70   XP:   $5   F18
◆◆   **Location:** On US 11 at jct I-81, exit 17; Tpk I-76, 3/4 mi n from exit 16. 1460 Harrisburg Pike 17013.
Motel   Fax: 717/249-7775. **Terms:** Reserv deposit, 3 day notice; small pets only, $5, smoking rooms only.
**Facility:** 72 rooms. Located along busy commercial highway. 2 stories; exterior corridors. **All Rooms:** free
movies, cable TV. **Cards:** AE, CB, DI, DS, MC, VI.   Ⓓ⊗

**HOLIDAY INN**   Guaranteed Rates   Phone: 717/245-2400
⊛   All Year   1P:   $55-   65   2P/1B:   $58-   67   2P/2B:   $62-   72   XP:   $7   F18
◆◆◆   **Location:** On US 11 at jct I-81 exit 17; 3/4 mi n of Tpk I-76 exit 16. 1450 Harrisburg Pike 17013.
Motor Inn   Fax: 717/245-2400. **Terms:** Sr. discount; reserv deposit; BP available; small pets only. **Facility:** 100 rooms. 2
stories; interior corridors; meeting rooms; pool. **Dining:** Restaurant; 6:30 am-2 & 5-10 pm; $9-$16; cocktails.
**Services:** Fee: coin laundry. **All Rooms:** free movies, cable TV. **Some Rooms:** microwaves, refrigerators.
**Cards:** AE, DI, DS, MC, VI.   Ⓓ⊗

**HOWARD JOHNSON LODGE**
AAA Special Value Rates     Phone: 717/243-6000
All Year     1P: $39- 65   2P/1B: $46- 80   2P/2B: $45- 80   XP: $7   F
Motel
**Location:** On US 11 at jct I-81, exit 17; 3/4 mi n of Tpk I-76, exit 16. 1255 Harrisburg Pike 17013. Fax: 717/258-4123. **Terms:** Credit card guarantee; weekly rates; pets. **Facility:** 96 rooms. Located along busy commercial highway. 2 stories; interior corridors; pool, wading pool. **Dining & Entertainment:** Cocktail lounge; restaurant nearby. **Services:** data ports. **All Rooms:** free movies, cable TV.
**Some Rooms:** microwaves, refrigerators, whirlpools. **Cards:** AE, CB, DI, DS, JCB, MC, VI.   Ⓓ ⊗

**KNIGHTS INN**
Rates Subject to Change     Phone: 717/249-7622
All Year     1P: $39- 72   2P/1B: $44- 82   2P/2B: $41- 83   XP:$5-10 F16
Motel
**Location:** Just s of PA Tpk, exit 16; on US 11. 1153 Harrisburg Pike 17013. Fax: 717/249-0597. **Terms:** Reserv deposit; weekly rates; pets, $5. **Facility:** 119 rooms. Located near historic Carlisle Fairgrounds. 12 kitchens, $9-$12 extra for up to 2 persons; 1 story; exterior corridors; pool. **All Rooms:** free movies, cable TV. **Some Rooms:** microwaves, refrigerators. **Cards:** AE, DI, DS, MC, VI.   Ⓓ ⊗

**PHEASANT FIELD BED & BREAKFAST**
Guaranteed Rates     Phone: 717/258-0717
All Year [BP]     1P: $60- 90   2P/1B: $65- 95     XP: $10
Historic Bed & Breakfast
**Location:** I-81, exit 17; 1 mi s on US 11, 2 3/10 mi se on S Middlesex Rd (turn at Rodeway Inn), 4/10 mi e on Ridge Rd, 2/10 mi s on Hickorytown Rd. 150 Hickorytown Rd. Fax: 717/258-0717. **Terms:** Age restrictions may apply; check-in 4 pm; credit card guarantee, 3 day notice; weekly rates; no pets. **Facility:** 4 rooms. Rural location on farm in quiet, serene area. Comfortable, average sized rooms. A stop on the underground railroad. 2 stories; interior corridors; smoke free premises; 1 tennis court; stable for overnight horse boarding. **All Rooms:** no phones, no TVs. **Some Rooms:** radios, shared bathrooms. **Cards:** AE, MC, VI.   Ⓓ ⊗

**RODEWAY INN**
AAA Special Value Rates     Phone: 717/249-2800
6/15-10/15 [CP]    1P: $42   2P/1B: $47   2P/2B: $48   XP: $5 D18
5/1-6/14 & 4/28-4/30 [CP]   1P: $39   2P/1B: $44   2P/2B: $45   XP: $5 D18
10/16-4/27 [CP]    1P: $39   2P/1B: $44   2P/2B: $45   XP: $5 D18
Motel
**Location:** On US 11; 3/4 mi n of Tpk I-76, exit 16; 1/4 mi s of I-81, exit 17. 1239 Harrisburg Pike 17013. Fax: 717/249-9444. **Terms:** Reserv deposit, 3 day notice; weekly/monthly rates; small pets only. **Facility:** 101 rooms. Located along busy commerical highway. 10 efficiencies, $49-$54 for 2 persons; 1 story; exterior corridors; pool. **Dining:** Restaurant nearby. **All Rooms:** free movies, cable TV. **Some Rooms:** microwaves, radios, refrigerators. **Cards:** AE, CB, DI, DS, JCB, MC, VI.   Ⓓ ⊗

**SUPER 8 MOTEL**
Rates Subject to Change     Phone: 717/249-7000
5/1-10/31 [CP]    1P: $33   2P/1B: $35   2P/2B: $38   XP: $3 D11
11/1-4/30 [CP]    1P: $33   2P/1B: $35   2P/2B: $35   XP: $3 D11
Motel
**Location:** On US 11, 1/2 mi n of jct I-81 exit 17; 1 1/4 mi n of tpk exit 16. 1800 Harrisburg Pike 17013. Fax: 717/249-9070. **Terms:** Sr. discount; credit card guarantee; no pets. **Facility:** 112 rooms. Located along busy commercial highway. 2 stories; exterior corridors. **Dining:** Restaurant nearby. **Services:** Fee: coin laundry. **All Rooms:** free movies, cable TV. **Some Rooms:** 16 efficiencies, microwaves, refrigerators. **Cards:** AE, CB, DI, DS, MC, VI.
Roll in showers.   Ⓓ ⊗

## RESTAURANTS

**CALIFORNIA CAFE**
Dinner: $11-$20     Phone: 717/249-2028
American
**Location:** Downtown. 52 W Pomfret St 17013. **Hours:** 11 am-2 & 5-9 pm. Closed major holidays, Sun & Mon. **Features:** casual dress; children's menu; carryout; cocktails; street parking. California style cuisine. **Cards:** AE, DI, DS, MC, VI.   ⊗

**RILLOS**
Dinner: $11-$20     Phone: 717/243-6141
Italian
**Location:** 3/4 mi e on High St, 1/2 mi s on SR 74 (York Rd); 1/4 mi e on Spruce. 50 Pine St 17013. **Hours:** 5 pm-10 pm, Fri & Sat-11 pm. Closed: Mon, 1/1, 11/23 & 12/25. **Reservations:** suggested; weekends. **Features:** casual dress; children's menu; senior's menu; cocktails & lounge; a la carte. Pleasant atmosphere. **Cards:** AE, DI, MC, VI.   ⊗

**SUNNYSIDE RESTAURANT**
Dinner: $21-$30     Phone: 717/243-5712
American
**Location:** On US 11, 4 mi s of I-81, exit 17. 850 N Hanover St 17013. **Hours:** 11 am-10 pm. Closed major holidays & Sun. **Features:** casual dress; children's menu; carryout; cocktails & lounge. Across from Army War College. Specializing in steaks & seafood. **Cards:** AE, DS, MC, VI.

# CASHTOWN

## LODGING

**CASHTOWN INN**
Rates Subject to Change     Phone: 717/334-9722
All Year [CP]     1P: $80- 135   2P/1B: $80- 135     XP: $12   D
Historic Country Inn
**Location:** 10 minutes from Gettysburg on old US 30. 1325 Old Rt 30 17310 (PO Box 103). **Terms:** Age restrictions may apply; reserv deposit, 5 day notice; no pets. **Facility:** 5 rooms. 1797 inn was Confederate headquarters during the Gettysburg Campaign. Reservations strongly advised; 3 stories; interior corridors. **Dining & Entertainment:** Dining room; Thurs-Sat 5 pm-9 pm, reservations advised; $10-$18; cocktails/lounge. **All Rooms:** no phones. **Some Rooms:** combo & shower baths, shared bathrooms. **Cards:** AE, DS, MC, VI.   Ⓓ ⊗

# CENTER SQUARE

## RESTAURANT

**TIFFANY DINING PLACE & GAZEBO**
Dinner: $11-$20     Phone: 215/272-1888
American
**Location:** On US 202, 1/4 mi ne of jct SR 73. 799 Dekalb Pike 19422. **Hours:** 5 pm-10 pm, Fri-11 pm, Sat 4:15 pm-11 pm, Sun 10:30 am-2 & 3:30-10 pm. Closed: 12/25. **Reservations:** suggested. **Features:** casual dress; Sunday brunch; children's menu; early bird specials; health conscious menu; salad bar; cocktails & lounge. Popular eatery in Victorian style dining rooms. Featuring some mesquite grill items. Fresh fish. Extensive salad bar. **Cards:** AE, DI, DS, MC, VI.   ⊗

# CHADDS FORD

## LODGING

**BRANDYWINE RIVER HOTEL**
AAA Special Value Rates     Phone: 610/388-1200
All Year [CP]     1P: $109- 129   2P/1B: $119- 139   2P/2B: $140   XP: $10 F12
Motel
**Location:** 2 mi w of US 202, at jct US 1 & SR 100. US 1 & SR 100 19317 (PO Box 1058). Fax: 610/388-1200. **Terms:** Reserv deposit, 3 day notice; weekly/monthly rates; small pets only, $25, $50 dep req. **Facility:** 40 rooms. Colonial ambience in historic setting; Queen Anne cherrywood furnishings. 10 suites with whirlpool bath & fireplace, $130; 2 stories; interior corridors; meeting rooms. **Dining:** Afternoon tea; restaurant nearby. **Services:** valet laundry. **All Rooms:** cable TV. **Some Rooms:** refrigerators. **Cards:** AE, DI, DS, MC, VI.   Ⓓ ⊗

## RESTAURANT

**CHADDS FORD INN RESTAURANT** Historical     **Dinner:** $11-$20     **Phone:** 610/388-7361
◆◆     **Location:** On US 1 at jct SR 100. **Hours:** 11:30 am-2 & 5:30-10 pm, Fri & Sat 5 pm-10:30 pm, Sun 11 am-2
American     & 4-9 pm. Closed: 1/1, 7/4, 12/24 & 12/25. **Reservations:** suggested. **Features:** casual dress; children's
menu; carryout; cocktails & lounge; a la carte. Dating from 1736, several dining rooms with Brandywine
decor. Innovative menu. **Cards:** AE, CB, DI, MC, VI.     ⊗

# CHALKHILL

## LODGING

**THE LODGE AT CHALK HILL**     Rates Subject to Change     **Phone:** 412/438-8880
Ⓐ     Fri & Sat [CP]     1P: $71     2P/2B: $71     XP: $10  F14
    Sun-Thurs [CP]     1P: $49     2P/2B: $60     XP: $10  F14
◆◆     **Location:** Across US 40 from Chalkhill Post Office. (Rt 40E, Box 240). Fax: 412/438-1685. **Terms:** Check-in
Motel     4 pm; reserv deposit; weekly/monthly rates; pets, $5. **Facility:** 61 rooms. Very contemporary, well-appointed
motel in beautiful woodland setting. Convenient to area attractions. 6 kitchens, $65; Fri & Sat, $81; 1 story; ex-
terior corridors; meeting rooms; volleyball. **Recreation:** nature program; fishing; hiking trails. **All Rooms:** free movies, cable
TV. **Some Rooms:** microwaves. **Cards:** AE, DS, MC, VI. *(See color ad p A231)*     Ⓓ ⊗

# CHAMBERSBURG—16,600

## LODGINGS

**CHAMBERSBURG TRAVELODGE**     AAA Special Value Rates     **Phone:** 717-264-4187
Ⓐ     All Year     1P: $46     2P/1B: $52     2P/2B: $57     XP: $7  F18
    **Location:** On US 30, 3/4 mi w of I-81 exit 6. 565 Lincoln Way E 17201. Fax: 717/264-2446. **Terms:** Reserv
◆◆◆     deposit, 3 day notice; small pets only. **Facility:** 51 rooms. Attractively decorated rooms. 3 stories; exterior cor-
Motel     ridors; meeting rooms. **All Rooms:** coffeemakers, free movies, combo & shower baths, cable TV.
**Some Rooms:** refrigerators. **Cards:** AE, CB, DI, DS, JCB, MC, VI. *(See ad below)*     Ⓓ ⊗

**COMFORT INN-CHAMBERSBURG**     Rates Subject to Change     **Phone:** 717/263-6655
Ⓐ     All Year [CP]     1P: $47- 59     2P/1B: $54- 69     2P/2B: $54- 69     XP: $5  F18
◆◆◆     **Location:** I-81 exit 8, 1/10 mi s on SR 696, 1 blk e. 3301 Blackgap Rd 17201. Fax: 717/263-6655.
Motel     **Terms:** Sr. discount; reserv deposit; small pets only, $5. **Facility:** 69 rooms. 2 stories; interior corridors;
meeting rooms; indoor pool, whirlpool; exercise room. **Dining:** Restaurant nearby. **Services:** data ports.
**All Rooms:** free movies, cable TV. **Some Rooms:** microwaves, refrigerators, whirlpools. **Cards:** AE, CB, DI,
DS, JCB, MC, VI. *(See color ad below)*     ⒹⓈ⊗

**DAYS INN**     Rates Subject to Change     **Phone:** 717/263-1288
Ⓐ     5/1-9/28, 10/2-10/31,
◆◆◆     4/1-4/19 & 4/23-4/30     1P: $48     2P/2B: $56     XP: $8  F18
Motel     11/1-3/31     1P: $42     2P/2B: $50
    4/20-4/22     1P: $65     2P/1B: $65
    9/29-10/1     1P: $65     2P/1B: $65
**Location:** I-81 exit 6, on US 30. 30 Falling Spring Rd 17201. Fax: 717/263-6514. **Terms:** Small pets only. **Facility:** 107 rooms.
Located along busy commercial highway. 3 stories; interior corridors; meeting rooms. **Dining:** Restaurant nearby.
**Services:** data ports. **All Rooms:** free movies, cable TV. **Some Rooms:** microwaves, refrigerators. Fee: VCP's. **Cards:** AE,
CB, DI, DS, MC, VI. *(See color ad below)*     Ⓓ⊗

Pull out the AAA state map to enhance navigation to your TourBook destination.

**ECONO LODGE**
Rates Subject to Change
Phone: 717/264-8005

| | | | | | |
|---|---|---|---|---|---|
| 9/23-10/31 | 1P: $43 | 2P/1B: $46 | 2P/2B: $50 | XP: $3 | F18 |
| 5/1-9/22 | 1P: $41 | 2P/1B: $44 | 2P/2B: $48 | XP: $3 | F18 |
| 4/1-4/30 | 1P: $40 | 2P/1B: $43 | 2P/2B: $44 | XP: $3 | F18 |
| 11/1-3/31 | 1P: $38 | 2P/1B: $41 | 2P/2B: $42 | XP: $3 | F18 |

Motel    **Location:** On SR 316; just w of I-81, exit 5. 1110 Sheller Ave 17201. Fax: 717/263-7720. **Terms:** Sr. discount; reserv deposit; no pets. **Facility:** 61 rooms. Located in busy commercial district. 2 stories; interior corridors; meeting rooms. **Dining:** Restaurant nearby. **Services:** Fee: coin laundry. **All Rooms:** cable TV. **Some Rooms:** refrigerators. Fee: VCP's. **Cards:** AE, DI, DS, JCB, MC, VI.   (D) ⊗

**FRIENDSHIP INN**
Rates Subject to Change
Phone: 717/264-4108

| | | | | | |
|---|---|---|---|---|---|
| 5/1-12/31 & 4/1-4/30 | 1P: $35- 38 | 2P/1B: $35- 38 | 2P/2B: $42 | XP: $3 | F18 |
| 1/1-3/31 | 1P: $30 | 2P/1B: $32 | 2P/2B: $37 | XP: $3 | F18 |

Motel    **Location:** On US 30, 1 1/4 mi e of jct I-81, exit 6. 1620 Lincoln Way E 17201. Fax: 717/268-7720. **Terms:** Sr. discount; reserv deposit; small pets only, $5 dep req. **Facility:** 40 rooms. 1-2 stories; exterior corridors; meeting rooms. **Dining:** Restaurant nearby. **All Rooms:** combo & shower baths, cable TV. **Some Rooms:** refrigerators. **Cards:** AE, DI, DS, JCB, MC, VI.   (D) ⊗

**HAMPTON INN**
Guaranteed Rates
Phone: 717/261-9185

| | | | |
|---|---|---|---|
| All Year [CP] | 1P: $46- 59 | 2P/1B: $54- 64 | 2P/2B: $52- 62 |

Motel ♦♦♦    **Location:** 1 blk e on SR 316 from I-81, exit 5. 955 Lesher Rd 17201. Fax: 717/261-1984. **Terms:** Monthly rates; no pets. **Facility:** 84 rooms. Very attractive public areas. 3 stories; interior corridors; meeting rooms; exercise room. **Dining:** Restaurant nearby. **Services:** data ports. **All Rooms:** free movies, refrigerators, cable TV. **Cards:** AE, CB, DI, DS, MC, VI.   (D) (S) ⊗

**HOLIDAY INN**
Rates Subject to Change
Phone: 717/263-3400

| | | | | |
|---|---|---|---|---|
| All Year | 1P: $55- 65 | 2P/1B: $62- 72 | 2P/2B: $62- 72 | XP: $7 F19 |

Motor Inn ♦♦♦    **Location:** Jct I-81 SR 316, exit 5. 1095 Wayne Ave 17201. Fax: 717/263-3400. **Terms:** Sr. discount; BP available; pets. **Facility:** 139 rooms. Very attractive public areas. 2 stories; interior corridors; meeting rooms; pool, wading pool. **Dining:** Restaurant; 6 am-2 & 5-10 pm; $9-$16; cocktails. **All Rooms:** free movies, cable TV. **Some Rooms:** refrigerators. **Cards:** AE, CB, DI, DS, JCB, MC, VI.   (D) ⊗

**HOWARD JOHNSON LODGE**
AAA Special Value Rates
Phone: 717/263-9191

| | | | | |
|---|---|---|---|---|
| All Year | 1P: $44- 57 | 2P/1B: $52- 67 | 2P/2B: $53- 69 | XP: $7 F18 |

Motor Inn ♦♦♦    **Location:** On US 30 at jct I-81 exit 6. 1123 Lincoln Hwy E 17201. Fax: 717/263-4752. **Terms:** Reserv deposit; monthly rates; no pets. **Facility:** 132 rooms. Located in busy commercial district. 3 stories; interior corridors; meeting rooms; heated indoor pool, sauna. **Dining:** Restaurant; 6 am-11 pm, Fri & Sat-midnight; $6-$10. **Services:** data ports. **All Rooms:** coffeemakers, refrigerators, cable TV. **Some Rooms:** Fee: VCP's. **Cards:** AE, CB, DI, DS, JCB, MC, VI.

**SHULTZ VICTORIAN MANSION B & B**
Rates Subject to Change
Phone: 717/263-3371

| | | | | |
|---|---|---|---|---|
| All Year [BP] | 1P: $55- 73 | 2P/1B: $60- 78 | 2P/2B: $65 | XP: $10 |

Historic Bed ♦♦♦ & Breakfast    **Location:** On US 11, 3/4 mi n of jct US 30. 756 Philadelphia Ave 17201. **Terms:** Age restrictions may apply; check-in 4 pm; reserv deposit, 4 day notice; weekly/monthly rates; no pets. **Facility:** 5 rooms. Tree shaded 1880 Victorian mansion. 3 stories, no elevator; interior corridors; smoke free premises. **All Rooms:** combo & shower baths, no phones, no TVs. **Cards:** MC, VI.   (D) ⊗

## RESTAURANTS

**COPPER KETTLE RESTAURANT**
Dinner: $21-$30
Phone: 717/264-3109

♦♦♦ American    **Location:** On US 30, 1/4 mi w of I-81, exit 6. 1049 Lincoln Way E 17201. **Hours:** 5 pm-9:30 pm. Closed major holidays & Sun. **Features:** casual dress; children's menu; cocktails & lounge. Small, attractively decorated dining rooms. **Cards:** AE, DI, MC, VI.   (&) ⊗

**SCHOENBERG'S**
Dinner: $21-$30
Phone: 717/263-1137

♦♦ American    **Location:** On US 30, 1 1/4 mi w of I-82, exit 6. 346 Lincoln Way E 17201. **Hours:** 5 pm-10 pm, Sun from noon. Closed: Mon, 1/1, 12/24 & 12/25. **Features:** casual dress; children's menu; carryout; cocktails & lounge. Since 1936. Specialties are steaks & seafood. **Cards:** AE, CB, DI, DS, MC, VI.   ⊗

# CLARION—6,500

## LODGINGS

**HOLIDAY INN**
Rates Subject to Change
Phone: 814/226-8850

| | | | | |
|---|---|---|---|---|
| 6/1-10/15 [BP] | 1P: $66- 86 | 2P/1B: $66- 86 | 2P/2B: $66- 86 | |
| 5/1-5/31 & 10/16-4/30 [BP] | 1P: $66- 80 | 2P/1B: $66- 80 | 2P/2B: $66- 80 | |

Motor Inn ♦♦♦    **Location:** At I-80 exit 9, on SR 68. Rt 68 & I-80 16214. Fax: 814/226-8850. **Terms:** Sr. discount; credit card guarantee, 3 day notice; monthly rates; AP available; pets. **Facility:** 122 rooms. 2 stories; interior corridors; meeting rooms; heated indoor pool, saunas; indoor recreation area. Fee: 18 holes golf. **Dining:** Dining room; 7 am-10 pm; $10-$20; cocktails. **Services:** data ports; health club privileges. Fee: coin laundry. **All Rooms:** free movies, cable TV. **Cards:** AE, CB, DI, DS, JCB, MC, VI.   (D) ⊗

**SUPER 8**
Rates Subject to Change
Phone: 814/226-4550

| | | | | |
|---|---|---|---|---|
| All Year | 1P: $42- 55 | 2P/1B: $47- 55 | 2P/2B: $49- 65 | XP: $5 F18 |

Motel ♦♦    **Location:** On SR 68 at jct I-80, exit 9. Rt 3 16214 (Box 253). Fax: 814/227-2337. **Terms:** Sr. discount; reserv deposit, 7 day notice; weekly/monthly rates; pets. **Facility:** 100 rooms. Nicely landscaped grounds. All units ground level. 9 efficiencies, $43.95-$48.95; 1 story; exterior corridors; meeting rooms; pool. **Dining:** Restaurant nearby. **Services:** data ports. **All Rooms:** free movies, cable TV. **Some Rooms:** refrigerators. Fee: VCP's. **Cards:** AE, CB, DI, DS, MC, VI.   (D) ⊗

## RESTAURANT

**CLARION CLIPPER RESTAURANT**
Dinner: up to $10
Phone: 814/226-7950

♦ American    **Location:** From I-80 exit 9, 1 1/4 mi n on SR 68. 16214. **Hours:** 6:30 am-10 pm. Closed: 11/23 & 12/25. **Features:** Sunday brunch; children's menu; senior's menu; carryout; salad bar; cocktails & lounge. Family dining. Generous portions. Convenient parking. Homemade soups, broasted chicken local favorite, fresh baked cookies. **Cards:** AE, DS, MC, VI.

## CLARK—600

### LODGING

**TARA-A COUNTRY INN**
Rates Subject to Change                                  **Phone:** 412/962-3535
◆◆◆◆           Sat. [BP]                 1P: $175- 355    2P/1B: $175- 355                XP:$263-413
Country Inn    Sun-Fri [BP]              1P: $150- 325    2P/1B: $150- 325                XP:$263-338
◆◆◆◆    **Location:** Exit 1N from I-80, 8 mi n on Rt 18. 3665 Valley View Rd 16113. **Fax:** 412/962-3250.
Country Inn    **Terms:** Reserv deposit, 7 day notice; MAP available; package plans; no pets. **Facility:** 27 rooms. Elegant
rooms with rare antiques & original works of art. Gone With The Wind theme. 3 stories, no elevator; interior
corridors; conference facilities; pool, sauna, whirlpool, indoor mineral bath. **Dining:** 3 dining rooms; 11 am-3 & 5-8 pm, Sun
noon-7 pm; cocktails. **Recreation:** bicycles. **All Rooms:** free movies, combo & tub baths, cable TV, VCP's. **Cards:** AE, DS,
MC, VI.                                                                                                       Ⓓ Ⓢ ⊗

### RESTAURANT

**ASHLEY'S**
**Dinner:** over $31                                      **Phone:** 412/962-2992
◆◆◆◆    **Location:** I-80 exit 1N, 8 mi n on Rt 18. 3665 Valley View Rd 16113. **Hours:** 11:30 am-2:30 & 6-8 pm, Fri &
American     Sat-8:30 pm. **Closed:** 12/25. **Reservations:** required. **Features:** formal attire; health conscious menu;
cocktails & lounge; prix fixe. An elegant & sophisticated setting with skilled attentive service. Smoke free
premises. **Cards:** AE, DS, MC, VI.                                                                          ⊗

## CLARKS SUMMIT—5,400    (See POCONO MOUNTAINS & VICINITY ACCOM-
MODATIONS spotting map pages A212 & A213; see index starting on page A210)

### LODGINGS

**THE INN AT NICHOLS VILLAGE**
Rates Subject to Change                                  **Phone:** 717/587-1135  94
⬛        All Year              1P: $78- 145    2P/1B: $88- 155    2P/2B: $98- 155    XP: $10   F18
◆◆◆◆    **Location:** On US 6 & 11, 1/2 mi w of tpk exit 38 & I-81 exit 58. 1101 Northern Blvd 18411.
Motor Inn    **Fax:** 717/586-7140. **Terms:** Sr. discount; reserv deposit; weekly/monthly rates; package plans; no pets.
**Facility:** 134 rooms. Patios, courtyards & gardens. Beautifully furnished rooms, immaculately kept. 2-4 stories;
interior corridors; business center, meeting rooms; heated indoor pool, saunas; exercise room.
**Dining:** Coffee shop; also, Ryah House, So-Journer, see separate listing. **Services:** data ports, PC, secretarial services;
valet laundry; area transportation, airport transportation. **All Rooms:** free movies, cable TV. **Some Rooms:** coffeemakers,
microwaves, refrigerators, whirlpools. Fee: VCP's. **Cards:** AE, CB, DI, DS, MC, VI. *(See ad p A220)*          🗗 Ⓓ ⊗

**RAMADA INN**
Rates Subject to Change                                  **Phone:** 717/586-2730  95
◆◆           5/1-10/31              1P: $66- 71                       2P/2B: $76- 81    XP: $7   F18
Motor Inn    1/1-4/30               1P: $59- 64                       2P/2B: $69- 74    XP: $7   F18
11/1-12/31              1P: $58- 63                       2P/2B: $68- 73    XP: $7   F18
**Location:** On US 6 & 11, 1/4 mi w of tpk exit 38 & I-81 exit 58. Rts 6 & 11 18411. **Fax:** 717/587-0740. **Terms:** Sr. discount;
credit card guarantee, 3 day notice; no pets. **Facility:** 108 rooms. Comfortable rooms 6 mi from downtown Scranton. 5 stories;
interior corridors; meeting rooms; heated pool. **Dining & Entertainment:** Restaurant; 6:30 am-10 pm; $11-$19;
cocktails/lounge. **All Rooms:** cable TV. **Some Rooms:** refrigerators. Fee: VCP's. **Cards:** AE, CB, DI, DS, MC, VI.
🗗 Ⓓ ⊗

### RESTAURANTS

**RYAH HOUSE**
**Dinner:** $11-$20                                       **Phone:** 717/587-4124  50
◆◆◆    **Location:** In The Inn At Nichols Village. 1101 Northern Blvd 18411. **Hours:** 4:30 pm-10 pm, Sat-11 pm.
Regional     Closed major holidays & Sun. **Reservations:** suggested. **Features:** casual dress; health conscious menu;
American     cocktails & lounge. Rustic, formal dining room. Fine wine list. 6 mi northwest of downtown Scranton.
**Cards:** AE, CB, DI, DS, MC, VI.                                                                          ⊗

**SO-JOURNER**
**Dinner:** $11-$20                                       **Phone:** 717/586-5517  51
◆◆           **Location:** In The Inn At Nichols Village. 1101 Northern Blvd 18411. **Features:** casual
American     dress; children's menu; health conscious menu; carryout; beer & wine only. Informal family dining in
contemporary atmosphere. Specializing in freshly made entrees, homemade breads & desserts. 6 mi
northwest of Scranton. **Cards:** AE, CB, DI, DS, MC, VI.                                                       ⊗

## CLEARFIELD—6,600

### LODGINGS

**BEST WESTERN MOTOR INN**
Rates Subject to Change                                  **Phone:** 814/765-2441
⬛           All Year       1P: $51- 58    2P/1B: $55- 64    2P/2B: $60- 68    XP: $4   F
◆◆    **Location:** 1/4 mi n of I-80 exit 19, SR 879. (PO Box 286). **Fax:** 814/765-5221. **Terms:** Sr. discount; small
Motor Inn    pets only. **Facility:** 120 rooms. 2 stories; interior corridors; meeting rooms; heated indoor pool closed 12/1-
4/15. **Dining & Entertainment:** Restaurant; 6 am-10 pm; $9-$15; cocktails/lounge; entertainment.
**All Rooms:** cable TV. **Some Rooms:** radios. **Cards:** AE, CB, DI, DS, MC, VI.                               Ⓓ ⊗

**DAYS INN**
Rates Subject to Change                                  **Phone:** 814/765-5381
⬛           All Year [AP]  1P: $39- 65    2P/1B: $45- 65    2P/2B: $44- 75    XP: $6   F18
◆◆    **Location:** 1/4 mi s of I-80, exit 19 on SR 879. 16830 (RR 2, Box 245B). **Fax:** 814/765-7885. **Terms:** Sr.
Motor Inn    discount; credit card guarantee; weekly rates; MAP available; small pets only. **Facility:** 119 rooms. 2 stories;
exterior corridors; meeting rooms; pool. **Dining & Entertainment:** Restaurant; 4/15-12/1 6 am-9 pm;
12/2-4/14 6 pm-9 pm; $6-$16; cocktails/lounge; entertainment. **All Rooms:** cable TV. **Some Rooms:**
Fee: VCP's. **Cards:** AE, CB, DI, DS, MC, VI.                                                                 Ⓓ ⊗

**FRIENDSHIP INN**
Rates Subject to Change                                  **Phone:** 814/765-7587
⬛           All Year [CP]  1P: $38- 50    2P/1B: $43- 50    2P/2B: $45- 65    XP: $4   F18
◆◆    **Location:** Off I-80, exit 19; 2 mi s via SR 879, 2 mi e on US 322. 16830 (RD 2, Box 297B).
Motel     **Fax:** 814/765-7885. **Terms:** Sr. discount; credit card guarantee; weekly rates; small pets only. **Facility:** 34
rooms. Close to downtown. 2-3 stories; exterior corridors. **Dining:** Restaurant nearby. **All Rooms:** cable TV.
**Some Rooms:** refrigerators. **Cards:** AE, CB, DI, DS, MC, VI.                                                Ⓓ ⊗

**ROYAL 9 MOTOR INNS**
Rates Subject to Change                                  **Phone:** 814/765-2639
⬛           All Year       1P: $25- 28    2P/1B: $28- 30    2P/2B: $32- 36    XP: $4   F10
◆     **Location:** From I-80 exit 19, 2 mi w via SR 879, 2 mi e on US 322. RD 2, Rt 322 E, Box 297 16830.
Motel     **Terms:** Sr. discount; credit card guarantee, 3 day notice; weekly rates; pets, $4. **Facility:** 29 rooms. Budget
oriented traveler. 1 story; interior/exterior corridors; playground. **Dining:** Restaurant nearby.
**All Rooms:** cable TV. **Cards:** AE, DS, MC, VI.                                                            Ⓓ ⊗

### RESTAURANT

**DUTCH PANTRY**  **Dinner:** up to $10  **Phone:** 814/765-2127
◆◆  **Location:** I-80, exit 19. Rd 2 Box 244 16830. **Hours:** 6 am-10 pm. Closed: 12/25. **Features:** casual dress;
American  children's menu; senior's menu; carryout. Casual family dining, homemade soups; some homemade
desserts. **Cards:** AE, DS, MC, VI.  ⊗

## CLYMER

### RESTAURANT

**LUIGI'S RISTORANTE**  **Dinner:** up to $10  **Phone:** 412/254-4777
◆◆  **Location:** Center on SR 286. 31 Rear 6th St 15728. **Hours:** 8 am-10 pm, Fri & Sat-11 pm, Sun noon-9 pm.
Italian  Closed major holidays. **Features:** casual dress; children's menu; carryout; cocktails; street parking. Very
popular, specializing in expertly prepared Southern Italian homemade pasta dishes, soups & desserts.
Friendly service & hearty portions. **Cards:** DS, MC, VI.  ⊗

## CONCORDVILLE

### LODGING

**BEST WESTERN CONCORDVILLE HOTEL & CONFERENCE CTR**  AAA Special Value Rates  **Phone:** 610/358-9400
  All Year [CP]  1P: $85- 95  2P/1B: $95- 105  2P/2B: $95- 105  XP: $15  F11
(AAA)  **Location:** At jct US 322S & US 1. US 322 & US 1 19331. **Fax:** 610/358-9381. **Terms:** Reserv deposit; no
◆◆◆  pets. **Facility:** 117 rooms. English country style hotel. Spacious deluxe guest rooms, suites & parlors. 5 sto-
Hotel  ries; interior corridors; conference facilities; heated indoor pool, sauna, whirlpool; exercise room, aerobic in-
struction, tanning beds. **Dining & Entertainment:** Cocktail lounge; also, Concordville Inn, see separate
listing. **Services:** data ports; valet laundry; airport transportation. **All Rooms:** free movies, combo & shower baths, cable TV.
**Some Rooms:** refrigerators. Fee: VCP's, whirlpools. **Cards:** AE, DI, DS, MC, VI.  ⒟Ⓢ⊗

### RESTAURANT

**CONCORDVILLE INN**  **Dinner:** $11-$20  **Phone:** 610/459-2230
◆◆  **Location:** Adjacent to Best Western Concordville Hotel & Conference Ctr. 780 Baltimore Pike 19331.
American  **Hours:** 11 am-3 & 5-10 pm, Sun 1 pm-9 pm. Closed: 12/25. **Reservations:** suggested. **Features:** casual
dress; children's menu; carryout; cocktails & lounge. Rustic decor. **Cards:** AE, DI, DS, MC, VI.  ⊗

## CONNEAUT LAKE—700

### RESTAURANT

**MAMA BEAR'S COUNTRY INN RESTAURANT**  **Dinner:** up to $10  **Phone:** 814/382-3115
  **Location:** 1 mi w on US 6, 1 1/2 mi n on Rt 618. 16316. **Hours:** Open 5/26-9/10; 8 am-10 pm.
(AAA)  **Features:** No A/C; children's menu; carryout; salad bar; a la carte. Home-style cooking with a family
◆  atmosphere, breakfast served to 3 pm. **Cards:** MC, VI.
American

## CONSHOHOCKEN  (See PHILADELPHIA & VICINITY ACCOMMODATIONS spotting map
pages A196 & A197; see index starting on page A193)

### RESTAURANT

**SPRING MILL CAFE**  **Dinner:** $21-$30  **Phone:** 610/828-2550  (169)
◆◆◆  **Location:** Rt 76W, Conshohocken exit, over Fayette Bridge right on Elm St, left on Sandy St, right on
French  Heather St, right on Barren Hill Rd. 164 Barren Hill Rd 19428. **Hours:** 9 am-10 pm. Closed: Mon, Tues, 7/4,
11/23 & 12/25. **Features:** a la carte. Intimate bistro. Housed in a rustic building that was once a grist mill.

## CONYNGHAM

### LODGINGS

**ECONO LODGE**  Rates Subject to Change  **Phone:** 717/788-5887
  Fri & Sat  1P: $50- 55  2P/1B: $50- 60  2P/2B: $55- 65  XP: $7  F10
(AAA)  Sun-Thurs 5/1-11/29  1P: $40- 45  2P/1B: $45- 50  2P/2B: $48- 52  XP: $7  F10
◆◆  Sun-Thurs 11/30-4/30  1P: $35  2P/1B: $35- 40  2P/2B: $40- 45  XP: $7  F10
Motel  **Location:** On SR 93, 1 blk s of jct I-80, exit 38 or I-81 exit 41, then 4 mi n. 18222 (RR 2, Box 304,
DRUMS). **Fax:** 717/788-3929. **Terms:** Sr. discount; reserv deposit; 7 day notice; weekly/monthly rates; CP
available; small pets only, $5. **Facility:** 63 rooms. 5 suites, $65-$85; 3 stories, no elevator; interior corridors.
**All Rooms:** free movies, cable TV. **Some Rooms:** refrigerators. **Cards:** AE, DI, DS, MC, VI.  ⒟⊗

**LOOKOUT MOTOR LODGE**  AAA Special Value Rates  **Phone:** 717/788-4131
  5/1-10/31 [CP]  1P: $41  2P/2B: $46  XP: $5  F8
(AAA)  11/1-4/30 [CP]  1P: $36  2P/2B: $40  XP: $5  F8
◆◆  **Location:** On SR 93 (Hazleton-Berwick Hwy), 1 1/4 mi n of jct I-80 exit 38, 6 1/4 mi n of jct I-81 exit 41.
Motel  18222 (RD 2, Box 130, DRUMS). **Terms:** Reserv deposit; no pets. **Facility:** 19 rooms. Mountainside location.
1 story; exterior corridors. **Dining:** Restaurant nearby. **All Rooms:** cable TV. **Some Rooms:** refrigerators.
**Cards:** AE, DS, MC, VI. *(See ad p A135)*  ⒟⊗

## COOKSBURG

### LODGING

**CLARION RIVER LODGE**  Rates Subject to Change  **Phone:** 814/744-8171
  All Year [CP]  1P: $67- 114  2P/1B: $67- 114  XP: $15  F
(AAA)  **Location:** N on River Rd, along Clarion River, 5 1/8 mi. 16217 (HC 1 Box 22D). **Fax:** 814/744-8553.
◆◆◆  **Terms:** Sr. discount; reserv deposit, 7 day notice; weekly rates; BP available; no pets. **Facility:** 20 rooms.
Lodge  Comfortable lodgings set along scenic Clarion River in quiet setting with numerous outdoor activities nearby. 2
stories; interior corridors; meeting rooms. **Dining:** Dining room; 11:30 am-8 pm, Sat & Sun from 8 am;
$9-$20; cocktails. **Recreation:** nature program; canoeing, fishing; hiking trails. **All Rooms:** free movies, refrigerators, cable
TV. **Some Rooms:** Fee: VCP's. **Cards:** AE, MC, VI.  ⒟⊗

# CORAOPOLIS (See PITTSBURGH ACCOMMODATIONS spotting map page A207; see index starting on page A206)

## LODGINGS

**COURTYARD BY MARRIOTT**  Rates Subject to Change  Phone: 412/264-5000  **21**
◆◆◆
Motor Inn | Sun-Thurs | 1P: $84 | 2P/1B: $94 | 2P/2B: $94 | XP: $10 | F
Fri & Sat | 1P: $69 | 2P/1B: $79 | 2P/2B: $92 | XP: $10 | F
**Location:** Business Rt 60 at Coraopolis/Sewickley exit. 450 Cherrington Pkwy 15108. Fax: 412/264-7979. **Terms:** Sr. discount; no pets. **Facility:** 148 rooms. 2-3 stories; interior corridors; meeting rooms; heated pool, whirlpool; exercise room. **Dining & Entertainment:** Restaurant; 6:30 am-10:30 & 6-10:30 pm, Fri, Sat & Sun have limited dinner menu hours; $8-$13; cocktail lounge. **Services:** data ports; valet laundry; airport transportation. **All Rooms:** free & pay movies. **Fee:** VCP. **Some Rooms:** refrigerators. **Cards:** AE, DI, DS, MC, VI. *(See color ad p A205)*  Ⓓ Ⓢ ⊗

**DAYS INN-PITTSBURGH AIRPORT**  Rates Subject to Change  Phone: 412/269-0990  **28**
◆◆
Motel | All Year [CP] | 1P: $56 | | 2P/2B: $60 | XP: $8 | F18
**Location:** Business Rt 60 to Coraopolis/Sewickley exit to Thorn Run Rd. 1170 Thorn Run Rd Ext 15108. Fax: 412/269-0462. **Terms:** Sr. discount; monthly rates; package plans; small pets only, $8. **Facility:** 99 rooms. Convenient to airport office park. 2 stories; interior corridors; meeting rooms. **Dining:** Restaurant nearby. **Services:** area transportation, airport transportation. **Fee:** coin laundry. **All Rooms:** free movies, cable TV. **Some Rooms:** microwaves, refrigerators, VCP's. **Cards:** AE, CB, DI, DS, JCB, MC, VI.  Ⓓ ⊗

**EMBASSY SUITES-PITTSBURGH INTERNATIONAL AIRPORT** AAA Special Value Rates Phone: 412/269-9070 **26**
Ⓐ
◆◆◆
Suite Hotel | Mon-Thurs [BP] | 1P: $135 | 2P/1B: $145 | 2P/2B: $145 | XP: $15 | F16
Fri-Sun [BP] | 1P: $109 | 2P/1B: $109 | 2P/2B: $109 | XP: $15 | F16
**Location:** From SR 60 Coraopolis/Sewickley exit, just e to Cherrington Pkwy. 550 Cherrington Pkwy 15108. Fax: 412/262-4119. **Terms:** Reserv deposit; package plans; pets. **Facility:** 223 rooms. Beautiful atrium landscaping with running stream, waterfall, & live trout. Very attractive country theme & furnishing throughout. 2-line phones. 5 stories; interior corridors; conference facilities, convention oriented; heated indoor pool, sauna, whirlpool; exercise room. **Dining & Entertainment:** Restaurant; 6:30 am-midnight; $7-$24; cocktails/lounge. **Services:** data ports, secretarial services; complimentary evening beverages; valet laundry; airport transportation. **Fee:** PC; childcare. **All Rooms:** microwaves, free movies, refrigerators, VCP's. **Some Rooms:** coffeemakers. **Cards:** AE, CB, DI, DS, MC, VI. *(See ad p A204)*  Ⓓ Ⓢ ⊗

**HAMPTON INN HOTEL AIRPORT**  AAA Special Value Rates  Phone: 412/264-0020  **24**
◆◆◆
Motel | All Year [CP] | 1P: $60- 62 | 2P/1B: $63- 68 | 2P/2B: $68 | XP: $5 | F18
**Location:** 1 mi n of Business Rt 60 on Beers School Rd. 1420 Beers School Rd 15108. Fax: 412/264-0020. **Terms:** Reserv deposit, 3 day notice; package plans; pets, $25 dep req. **Facility:** 128 rooms. 5 stories; interior corridors; meeting rooms. **Dining:** Restaurant nearby. **Services:** data ports; valet laundry; airport transportation. **All Rooms:** free movies, cable TV. **Cards:** AE, CB, DI, DS, MC, VI.  Ⓓ Ⓢ ⊗

**LA QUINTA INN-AIRPORT**  Rates Subject to Change  Phone: 412/269-0400  **23**
◆◆◆
Motel | All Year [CP] | 1P: $50- 57 | 2P/1B: $59- 63 | 2P/2B: $57 | XP: $7 | F18
**Location:** 1 mi n of Business Rt 60 on Beers School Rd. 1433 Beers School Rd 15108-2509. Fax: 412/269-9258. **Terms:** Small pets only. **Facility:** 129 rooms. 3 stories; interior corridors; meeting rooms; heated pool; exercise room. **Dining:** Restaurant nearby. **Services:** data ports; airport transportation. **Fee:** coin laundry. **All Rooms:** free movies. **Cards:** AE, CB, DI, DS, MC, VI.  Ⓓ ⊗

**PITTSBURGH AIRPORT INN BEST WESTERN**  AAA Special Value Rates  Phone: 412/262-3800  **20**
Ⓐ
◆◆
Motor Inn | Mon-Thurs [BP] | 1P: $75- 125 | 2P/1B: $85- 120 | 2P/2B: $85- 120 | XP: $10 | F18
Fri-Sun [BP] | 1P: $59 | 2P/1B: $59 | 2P/2B: $59 | XP: $10 | F18
**Location:** Business Rt 60 at Montour Run exit. 1 Airport Exp 15231 (PO Box 12411, PITTSBURGH). Fax: 412/695-1068. **Terms:** Reserv deposit; $2 service charge; small pets only. **Facility:** 140 rooms. 4 stories; interior corridors; meeting rooms; luxury level rooms; heated pool, wading pool; racquet club privileges; exercise room. **Dining & Entertainment:** Dining room; 6:30 am-10 pm, Sat & Sun from 7 am; $12-$18; cocktails/lounge. **Services:** valet laundry; area transportation, airport transportation. **All Rooms:** free & pay movies, cable TV. **Some Rooms:** coffeemakers. **Cards:** AE, CB, DI, DS, MC, VI.  Ⓓ Ⓢ ⊗

**PITTSBURGH AIRPORT MARRIOTT**  Rates Subject to Change  Phone: 412/788-8800  **22**
◆◆◆
Hotel | Sun-Thurs | 1P: $145 | 2P/1B: $160 | 2P/2B: $160 |
Fri & Sat | 1P: $99 | 2P/1B: $99 | 2P/2B: $99 |
**Location:** SR 60 at Montour Run exit. 100 Aten Rd 15108. Fax: 412/788-0743. **Terms:** Credit card guarantee; $2 service charge; small pets only. **Facility:** 314 rooms. Elegant but casual hotel accommodations. 15 stories; interior corridors; conference facilities, meeting rooms; luxury level rooms; 2 pools (1 heated, 1 indoor), sauna, whirlpool; exercise room. **Dining:** Dining room; 6 am-11 pm; $15-$28. **Services:** data ports, secretarial services; valet laundry; airport transportation. **Fee:** childcare. **Recreation:** jogging. **All Rooms:** free & pay movies. **Some Rooms:** refrigerators. **Fee:** VCP's. **Cards:** AE, CB, DI, DS, JCB, MC, VI.  🖪 Ⓓ Ⓢ ⊗

**RED ROOF INN PITTSBURGH AIRPORT**  Rates Subject to Change  Phone: 412/264-5678  **25**
◆◆
Motel | All Year | 1P: $41 | 2P/1B: $47- 52 | 2P/2B: $50- 55 | XP: $5 | F18
**Location:** 1 mi n of Business Rt 60 on Beers School Rd. 1454 Beers School Rd 15108. Fax: 412/264-8034. **Terms:** Reserv deposit; pets. **Facility:** 119 rooms. 3 stories; exterior corridors; meeting rooms. **Dining:** Restaurant nearby. **Services:** airport transportation. **Fee:** coin laundry. **All Rooms:** free movies, cable TV. **Cards:** AE, CB, DI, DS, MC, VI.  Ⓓ ⊗

## RESTAURANTS

**CLARK'S**  Dinner: $21-$30  Phone: 412/269-9100  **22**
◆◆
American
**Location:** 1 mi n of Coraopolis/Sewickley exit off Business Rt 60 on Rouser Rd. 333 Rouser Rd 15108. **Hours:** 11 am-11 pm, Fri-midnight, Sat 5-midnight. Closed major holidays & Sun. **Features:** casual dress; cocktails & lounge; a la carte. Attractive old English pub lounge with greenhouse style dining room. **Cards:** AE, DI, DS, MC, VI.  ⊗

**HYEHOLDE RESTAURANT**  Dinner: over $31  Phone: 412/264-3116  **21**
◆◆◆
Continental
**Location:** Coraopolis Heights Rd at Beauvel Grade Rd. 190 Hyeholde Dr 15108. **Hours:** 11:30 am-2 & 5-10 pm, Sat from 5 pm. Closed major holidays & Sun. **Reservations:** suggested; preferred. **Features:** semi-formal attire; cocktails; valet parking; a la carte. Fine dining in French country setting. Authentic medieval farmhouse re-creation provides old ambience. **Cards:** AE, DI, DS, MC, VI.  ⊗

**THE ITALIAN OVEN**  Dinner: up to $10  Phone: 412/262-5657  **20**
◆
Italian
**Location:** In Moon Plaza Shopping Center. 800 Narrows Run 15108. **Hours:** 11 am-10 pm, Fri & Sat-11 pm. Closed major holidays. **Features:** casual dress; children's menu; carryout; beer & wine only; a la carte. Braille menu. Complimentary babyfood. **Cards:** AE, DI, MC, VI.  ⊗

## CORRY—7,200

### LODGING

**DAY LILY INN BED & BREAKFAST**  Rates Subject to Change  Phone: 814/664-9047
◆◆◆  All Year [BP]  1P: $50-  60  2P/1B:  $50-  60  2P/2B: $60-  70  XP: $10
Bed &  **Location:** 1 blk n, w on W Smith St. 49 W Smith St 16407. **Terms:** Reserv deposit; 7 day notice; weekly
Breakfast  rates; no pets. **Facility:** 7 rooms. Homey atmosphere in a quiet setting. 3 stories, no elevator; interior corridors; designated smoking area; exercise room. **All Rooms:** free movies, combo & shower baths, cable TV.
**Some Rooms:** phones. **Cards:** AE, DS, MC, VI.  Ⓓ ⊗

## COUDERSPORT

### LODGING

**WESTGATE INN**  AAA Special Value Rates  Phone: 814/274-0400
⊕  All Year  2P/1B:  $56  2P/2B:  $60  Phone: 814/274-0400
◆◆  **Location:** 1 mi w on US 6. US 6W 16915. **Fax:** 814/274-8607. **Terms:** Check-in 3:30 pm; reserv deposit; no
Motel  pets. **Facility:** 34 rooms. 1 two-bedroom unit. Interior corridors; meeting rooms. **Dining:** Restaurant nearby.
**Services:** data ports. **All Rooms:** coffeemakers, free movies, cable TV. **Some Rooms:** microwaves,
refrigerators. **Cards:** AE, CB, DI, DS, MC, VI.  Ⓓ ⊗

## COVENTRYVILLE

### RESTAURANT

**COVENTRY FORGE INN RESTAURANT**  Country Inn  **Dinner: $21-$30**  Phone: 610/469-6222
◆◆◆  **Location:** 5 mi s of Pottstown, 1 1/2 mi w of jct SR 100, off SR 23, on Coventryville Rd. 3360 Coventryville
French  Rd 19465. **Hours:** 5:30 pm-9 pm, Sat 5 pm-10 pm. Closed major holidays, Sun & Mon.
**Reservations:** suggested. **Features:** cocktails; a la carte. Fine cuisine served in 18th-century inn. Extensive
wine cellar. Sat prix fixe, $38.50. **Cards:** AE, CB, DI, MC, VI.  ⊗

## CRABTREE

### RESTAURANT

**CARBONE'S**  **Dinner: $11-$20**  Phone: 412/834-3430
◆◆  **Location:** Center, on US 119, 3 mi s of US 22. **Hours:** 4:30 pm-9 pm, Fri & Sat-10 pm. Closed major
Italian  holidays & Sun. **Features:** casual dress; children's menu; cocktails & lounge; a la carte. Some American
dishes; many homemade desserts. Homemade soups & sauces. **Cards:** AE, CB, DI, MC, VI.  ⊗

## CRAFTON—7,200  (See PITTSBURGH ACCOMMODATIONS spotting map page A207; see index starting on page A206)

### LODGING

**DAYS INN**  AAA Special Value Rates  Phone: 412/922-0120  ㉚
⊕  All Year [CP]  1P: $36-  43  2P/1B:  $42-  49  2P/2B:  $44-  51  XP: $6  F18
◆  **Location:** On SR 60, from I-79N, exit 16, from I-79S, exit 16B. 100 Kisow Dr 15205. **Fax:** 412/922-0125.
Motel  **Terms:** Credit card guarantee; weekly/monthly rates; pets. **Facility:** 117 rooms. 2 stories; exterior corridors.
**Dining:** Restaurant nearby. **All Rooms:** free movies. **Some Rooms:** radios. **Cards:** AE, DI, DS, MC, VI.
Ⓓ ⊗

## CRESCO  (See POCONO MOUNTAINS & VICINITY ACCOMMODATIONS spotting map pages A212 & A213; see index starting on page A210)

### LODGING

**CRESCENT LODGE**  Rates Subject to Change  Phone: 717/595-7486  ㊿
⊕  Fri & Sat  2P/1B:  $100-  265  2P/2B:  $150  XP: $15
  Sun-Thurs  2P/1B:  $85-  265  2P/2B:  $120  XP: $15
◆◆◆  **Location:** 3 mi s on SR 191, at jct SR 940. Paradise Valley 18326. **Terms:** Reserv deposit, 14 day notice;
Country Inn  MAP available; no pets. **Facility:** 30 rooms. Some excellent units with whirlpool, sun deck & fireplace. Luxury
accommodations tastefully appointed. 2 two-bedroom housekeeping cottages, $950-$1100 6/15-9/15; 1-3 stories, no elevator; interior/exterior corridors; meeting rooms; heated pool; 1 tennis court. **Dining:** Dining room, see separate
listing. **Recreation:** jogging. **All Rooms:** cable TV. **Some Rooms:** microwaves, refrigerators. Fee: VCP's. **Cards:** AE, CB,
DI, DS, MC, VI. *(See color ad p A211)*  Ⓓ ⊗

### RESTAURANTS

**CRESCENT LODGE**  **Dinner: $11-$20**  Phone: 717/595-7486  ㊵
⊕  **Location:** In Crescent Lodge. Paradise Valley 18326. **Hours:** 8 am-11 & 5:30-9 pm, Fri & Sat-10 pm, Sun 3
pm-8 pm. Closed: 12/25, Mon & Tues 11/1-4/30. **Reservations:** suggested. **Features:** casual dress;
◆◆◆  children's menu; cocktails & lounge. Attractive country atmosphere. **Cards:** AE, CB, DI, DS, MC, VI.
Continental  *(See color ad p A211)*  ⊗

**THE HOMESTEAD INN**  **Dinner: $21-$30**  Phone: 717/595-3171  ㊶
◆◆◆  **Location:** 2 1/2 mi n of jct SR 191 & 940 following signs. Sandspring Dr 18326. **Hours:** 5 pm-9 pm, Sun
American  from 4 pm. **Reservations:** suggested; in season. **Features:** casual dress; children's menu; health conscious
menu; carryout; cocktails & lounge. Fine dining in a relaxed country atmosphere. **Cards:** AE, MC, VI.

## CRYSTAL LAKE

### RESTAURANT

**OLIVERI'S RESTAURANT AND LAKESIDE CAFE**  **Dinner: $11-$20**  Phone: 717/876-1931
⊕  **Location:** At Oliveri's Crystal Lake Hotel. RD 1 18407. **Hours:** 9 am-midnight. Closed: 12/24 & 12/25.
**Reservations:** suggested; weekends. **Features:** casual dress; children's menu; carryout; cocktails & lounge.
◆◆◆  Italian influence. All dishes made to order, including pastas, salads, veal, pastry & unique ice creams.
American  Family-owned & operated for nearly 50 years. **Cards:** AE, MC, VI.  ⊗

## CUMRU TOWNSHIP

### RESTAURANT

**ALPENHOF BAVARIAN RESTAURANT**
Dinner: up to $10   Phone: 610/373-1624
(AAA)
**Location:** On SR 10, 1 1/4 mi s of jct US 222. Morgantown Rd 19607. **Hours:** 11:30 am-2 & 5-8:30 pm, Sat 5 pm-9 pm, Sun 11:30 am-7 pm. **Closed:** Mon for dinner, 1/1 & 12/25. **Reservations:** suggested; for dinner.
◆ **Features:** casual dress; children's menu; cocktails & lounge; a la carte. Bavarian gasthaus & bierstube
German decor. Varied menu. **Cards:** AE, MC, VI. ⊗

## DALLAS—7,600

### LODGING

**PONDA-ROWLAND BED & BREAKFAST**
Guaranteed Rates   Phone: 717/639-3245
(AAA)
All Year [BP]   1P: $55- 95   2P/1B: $55- 95   XP:$15-30D12
**Location:** 6 mi n on SR 309 from jct SR 415. 18612 (RR 1 Box 349). **Fax:** 717/639-5531. **Terms:** Check-in
◆◆ 4 pm; credit card guarantee, 14 day notice; no pets. **Facility:** 3 rooms. Colonial-American country antiques,
Bed & nestled in the Endless Mountains. Family oriented. 2 stories; interior corridors; smoke free premises.
Breakfast **Recreation:** nature program; fishing. **All Rooms:** shower baths, no A/C, no phones, no TVs. **Cards:** AE, DS,
MC, VI. ⒹⓈ⊗

### RESTAURANTS

**OVERBROOK**
Dinner: $21-$30   Phone: 717/675-2223
◆◆ **Location:** 1 mi s on Pioneer Ave, 1/2 mi w on Overbrook Rd; from SR 309 Trucksville, left at Chrysler
Italian dealer, 1 1/2 mi n on Pioneer Ave then 1/2 mi w on Overbrook Rd. Overbrook Rd 18612. **Hours:** 5 pm-11
pm. **Closed:** Sun, 1/1, 11/23, 12/24 & 12/25. **Reservations:** suggested; weekends. **Features:** casual dress;
children's menu; carryout; cocktails & lounge. Specializing in seafood, veal & pasta. Cozy, intimate atmosphere. **Cards:** MC,
VI.

**PEKING CHEF-WEST**
Dinner: $11-$20   Phone: 717/675-0555
(AAA) **Location:** Center, on SR 309, in Dallas Shopping Ctr. Dallas Shopping Ctr 18612. **Hours:** 11:30 am-9:30
pm, Fri & Sat-10:30 pm & Sun noon-9 pm. **Closed:** 11/23 & 12/25. **Reservations:** suggested; weekends.
◆◆ **Features:** casual dress; children's menu; health conscious menu; carryout; cocktails & lounge. Specializing
Chinese in General Wong's Chicken, Sesame Shrimp & Beef With Orange Flavoring. **Cards:** AE, DI, MC, VI. ⊗

## DANVILLE—5,200

### LODGING

**THE PINE BARN INN**
Guaranteed Rates   Phone: 717/275-2071
(AAA) All Year   1P: $40- 55   2P/1B: $44- 65   2P/2B: $52- 70   XP: $4 F12
**Location:** 1/2 mi n of US 11, follow signs to Geisinger Medical Center. 1 Pine Barn Pl 17821.
◆◆◆ **Fax:** 717/275-3248. **Terms:** Reserv deposit; no pets. **Facility:** 64 rooms. Main building is a converted barn.
Motor Inn Rustic atmosphere; country inn decor. 2 stories; interior/exterior corridors; meeting rooms. **Dining &**
**Entertainment:** Dining room; 7 am-10 pm, Sat from 8 am, Sun 8 am-8 pm; $12-$19; cocktails/lounge;
dining room, see separate listing. **All Rooms:** combo & shower baths, cable TV. **Some Rooms:** radios, whirlpools.
**Cards:** AE, CB, DI, DS, MC, VI. Ⓓ⊗

### RESTAURANTS

**THE OLD HARDWARE RESTAURANT**
Dinner: $11-$20   Phone: 717/275-6615
(AAA) **Location:** Downtown, 1/2 blk s of US 11. 336 Mill St 17821. **Hours:** 11 am-8 pm, Fri & Sat-9 pm, Sun 11
am-2 pm. **Closed:** major holidays except 4/16 & 5/14. **Features:** casual dress; children's menu; carryout;
◆◆ street parking; a la carte. Well-prepared entrees served in attractive, country atmosphere for a taste of the
American past. **Cards:** MC, VI. ⊗

**PINE BARN INN RESTAURANT**
Dinner: $11-$20   Phone: 717/275-2071
◆◆ **Location:** In The Pine Barn Inn. 1 Pine Barn Pl 17821. **Hours:** 7 am-10 pm, Sat from 8 am, Sun 8 am-8
American pm. **Closed:** major holidays. **Reservations:** suggested; Sat. **Features:** casual dress; children's menu;
carryout; salad bar; cocktails & lounge; a la carte. Rustic country atmosphere in a converted barn;
specializing in New England seafood with live Maine lobsters. Desserts baked on premises. **Cards:** AE, CB, DI, DS, MC, VI.
⊗

## DELAWARE WATER GAP—700 (See POCONO MOUNTAINS & VICINITY ACCOMMODATIONS spotting map pages A212 & A213; see index starting on page A210)

### LODGING

**RAMADA INN**
AAA Special Value Rates   Phone: 717/476-0000 **12**
(AAA)
Fri & Sat 5/27-10/31 &
12/26-4/30   1P: $74- 99   2P/1B: $79- 99   2P/2B: $79- 99   XP: $10 F18
◆◆◆ Sun-Thurs 5/27-10/31 &
Motor Inn 12/26-4/30   1P: $62- 79   2P/1B: $68- 85   2P/2B: $68- 85   XP: $10 F18
5/1-5/26 & 11/1-12/25   1P: $52- 69   2P/1B: $58- 75   2P/2B: $58- 75   XP: $10 F18
**Location:** I-80 exit 53, 1/4 mi s on SR 611. 18327 (PO Box 270). **Fax:** 717/476-6260. **Terms:** Reserv deposit, 4 day notice;
weekly/monthly rates; package plans; small pets only, $50 dep req. **Facility:** 104 rooms. Attractively furnished large rooms. 2
stories; interior/exterior corridors; meeting rooms. 2 pools (2 heated, 1 indoor), wading pool. **Dining & Entertainment:**
Restaurant; 7 am-10 pm, Fri & Sat-11 pm; $9-$13; cocktails/lounge. **Services:** valet laundry. **All Rooms:** cable TV.
Fee: movies. **Cards:** AE, DI, DS, MC, VI. *(See color ad p A210)* Ⓓ⊗

## DELMONT—2,000

### LODGING

**SUPER 8 MOTEL**
AAA Special Value Rates   Phone: 412/468-4888
◆◆ All Year   1P: $40   2P/1B: $47   2P/2B: $47   XP: $5 F12
Motel **Location:** On SR 66, just s of US 22. 180 Sheffield Dr 15626. **Fax:** 412/468-4888. **Terms:** Reserv deposit,
10 day notice; pets. **Facility:** 46 rooms. Modern property. Whirlpool units $75 for up to 2 persons; 2 stories;
interior corridors. **Dining:** Restaurant nearby. **Services:** valet laundry; winter plug-ins. **All Rooms:** free & pay movies, cable
TV. **Some Rooms:** refrigerators, whirlpools. Fee: VCP's. **Cards:** AE, CB, DI, DS, MC, VI. ⒹⓈ⊗

## RESTAURANT

**LAMPLIGHTER RESTAURANT**                   Dinner: $11-$20                   Phone: 412/468-4545
Location: On US 22, w of jct SR 66. 330 Rt 22 15626. **Hours:** 7 am-10:30 pm, Fri & Sat-11:30 pm,
Sun-8:30 pm. Closed major holidays. **Reservations:** suggested. **Features:** casual dress; children's menu;
cocktails & lounge. Inviting coffee shop & very attractive dining room. Dinner theatre 6/1-10/31. Homemade
American   soup, bread & dessert. **Cards:** AE, CB, DI, MC, VI.                                   ⊗

# DENVER—2,900

## LODGINGS

**BLACK HORSE LODGE AND SUITES**        Rates Subject to Change             Phone: 717/336-7563
        5/1-11/30 & 4/1-4/30 [CP]        2P/1B:   $59-  99   2P/2B:   $69-  119   XP: $10  F18
        12/1-3/31 [CP]                   2P/1B:   $57-  79   2P/2B:   $62-  89    XP: $10  F18
Motor Inn  **Location:** 1 mi n of tpk exit 21, on SR 272. 2180 N Reading Rd 17517 (PO Box 343). Fax: 717/336-1110.
**Terms:** Sr. discount; reserv deposit; weekly/monthly rates; pets. **Facility:** 74 rooms. Contemporary rooms with
balcony or patio. 2 stories; interior/exterior corridors; luxury level rooms; pool; playground, outdoor health stations, picnic pavilion. **Dining:** Dining room, see separate listing. **Services:** Fee: coin laundry. **All Rooms:** coffeemakers, free
movies, cable TV. **Some Rooms:** honor bars, 2 efficiencies, 4 kitchens, microwaves, refrigerators. Fee: whirlpools.
**Cards:** AE, CB, DI, DS, MC, VI. *(See color ad p A157 & p A215)*                          Ⓓ⊗

**COMFORT INN**                         Rates Subject to Change             Phone: 717/336-4649
        7/1-10/31 [CP]            1P:   $45- 110   2P/1B:   $55- 110   2P/2B:   $55- 110   XP: $8  F12
Motel   5/1-6/30 [CP]            1P:   $40-  60   2P/1B:   $55- 100   2P/2B:   $55- 100   XP: $8  F12
        11/1-4/30 [CP]           1P:   $40-  50   2P/1B:   $50-  60   2P/2B:   $50-  60   XP: $8  F12
**Location:** On SR 272. 2015 N Reading Rd 17517. Fax: 717/336-5501. **Terms:** Sr. discount; reserv deposit, 3 day notice;
weekly/monthly rates; pets, $8. **Facility:** 45 rooms. Quiet rural location. 2-night minimum stay, last weekend in April, June &
Sept; 2 stories; interior corridors. **Dining:** Restaurant nearby. **All Rooms:** free movies, cable TV. **Cards:** AE, DI, DS, MC, VI.
                                                                                       Ⓓ⊗

**HOLIDAY INN-LANCASTER COUNTY**        Rates Subject to Change             Phone: 717/336-7541
        Fri & Sat                 1P:   $49-  91   2P/1B:   $49- 106   2P/2B:   $49- 106   XP: $8  F19
        Sun-Thurs                 1P:   $49-  87   2P/1B:   $49-  98   2P/2B:   $49-  98   XP: $8  F19
Motor Inn  **Location:** W of jct I-76 (PA Tpk) exit 21, on SR 272. 17517 (PO Box 129). Fax: 717/336-0515. **Terms:** Sr.
discount; reserv deposit, 3 day notice; monthly rates; pets. **Facility:** 110 rooms. Located in rural setting. 2-night
minimum stay 4/28-4/29 & 9/22-9/23; 2 stories; interior corridors; meeting rooms; pool. **Dining:** Dining room,
6:30 am-2 & 5-10 pm; $9-$13; cocktails. **Services:** Fee: coin laundry. **All Rooms:** free movies, cable TV.
**Some Rooms:** coffeemakers. Fee: VCP's. **Cards:** AE, CB, DI, DS, JCB, MC, VI.               Ⓓ⊗

**PENNSYLVANIA DUTCH MOTEL**            Rates Subject to Change             Phone: 717/336-5559
        5/1-10/31 & 4/1-4/30             2P/1B:   $46        2P/2B:   $50        XP: $3  F10
        11/1-3/31                        2P/1B:   $36        2P/2B:   $40        XP: $3  F10
Motel   **Location:** 1 1/2 mi n on SR 272 from I-76, tpk exit 21. 2275 N Reading Rd 17517. **Terms:** Reserv deposit;
pets. **Facility:** 20 rooms. Quiet location. 1 story; exterior corridors. **Dining:** Restaurant nearby.
**All Rooms:** cable TV. **Cards:** MC, VI.                                                     Ⓓ

## RESTAURANT

**THE BLACK HORSE RESTAURANT & TAVERN**      Dinner: $11-$20               Phone: 717/336-6555
**Location:** In The Black Horse Lodge & Suites. 2170 N Reading Rd 17517. **Hours:** 11:30 am-10 pm, Sun-9
pm. Closed: 11/23 & 12/25. **Reservations:** suggested. **Features:** casual dress; children's menu; cocktails &
lounge; a la carte. Homemade soups & desserts; specialties are Maryland crab cakes, barbecued ribs & pork
American   tenderloins. All beef is certified Angus. **Cards:** AE, DI, DS, MC, VI. *(See color ad below)*   ⊗

# DICKSON CITY  (See POCONO MOUNTAINS & VICINITY ACCOMMODATIONS spotting map pages A212 & A213; see index starting on page A210)

## LODGING

**PASONICK HOTEL & CONVENTION CENTER**   Rates Subject to Change           Phone: 717/383-9979   85
        6/1-8/31                  1P:   $60   2P/1B:   $65        2P/2B:   $75        XP: $10  F18
        5/1-5/31 & 9/1-4/30       1P:   $50   2P/1B:   $55        2P/2B:   $65        XP: $10  F18
Hotel   **Location:** I-81 exit 57A, 2 mi e on US 6. From PA tpk NE ext, Clarks Summit exit, 4 1/2 mi e on US 6.
(1946 Scranton-Carbondale Hwy, SCRANTON). Fax: 717/383-1756. **Terms:** Sr. discount; credit card
guarantee; package plans; no pets. **Facility:** 85 rooms. 4 stories; interior corridors; mountain view; conference
facilities; whirlpool, small heated indoor pool; exercise room, game room. **Dining & Entertainment:** Dining room; 6 am-10
pm; $5-$27; cocktails/lounge; entertainment. **Services:** data ports; valet laundry; area transportation, within 10 mi; airport
transportation. **All Rooms:** cable TV. **Some Rooms:** Fee: VCP's. **Cards:** AE, DS, MC, VI. *(See color ad p A219)*   Ⓓ⊗

# DONEGAL—2,400

## LODGINGS

**DAYS INN AT DONEGAL**                 AAA Special Value Rates            Phone: 412/593-7536
        12/15-3/15               1P:   $68   2P/1B:   $68        2P/2B:   $68        XP: $5  F12
Motel   5/1-12/14 & 3/16-4/30    1P:   $54-  65   2P/1B:   $54-  65   2P/2B:   $54-  65   XP: $5  F12
**Location:** On SR 31E at I-70/76, exit 9. Rt 31 15628 (PO Box 184). Fax: 412/593-6165. **Terms:** Reserv
deposit, 3 day notice; CP available; no pets. **Facility:** 34 rooms. 2 stories; exterior corridors; heated pool; shuffleboard, volleyball. **Dining:** Restaurant nearby. **All Rooms:** free movies, combo & shower baths, cable TV. **Cards:** AE, MC, VI.   Ⓓ⊗

**MOUNTAIN VIEW BED & BREAKFAST**   Guaranteed Rates   Phone: 412/593-6349
All Year [BP]   1P: $75- 100   2P/1B:   $95- 125   2P/2B: $125- 1500   XP: $15
Historic Bed & Breakfast
**Location:** Off SR 31; 1 mi e of exit 9 (PA Tpk), 1/2 mi s on Mountain View Rd. Mountain View Rd 15628. **Terms:** Age restrictions may apply; credit card guarantee, 7 day notice; no pets. **Facility:** 7 rooms. Restored mid-1800's farmhouse & barn with period furnishings. Antiques avail for purchase. 2 stories; interior/exterior corridors; smoke free premises. **All Rooms:** cable TV. **Some Rooms:** combo & shower baths, shared bathrooms, phones. **Cards:** AE, CB, DI, DS, MC, VI.   (D) ⊗

### RESTAURANT
**CANDLELIGHT RESTAURANT**   Dinner: up to $10   Phone: 412/593-6301
American
**Location:** SR 31, 1/4 mi w of I-76, tpk exit 9. 15628. **Hours:** 7 am-9 pm, Fri & Sat-10 pm. Closed: 11/23 & 12/25. **Features:** casual dress; Sunday brunch; children's menu; carryout; cocktails. Casual dining atmosphere. Dinner buffet Fri & Sat. Lunch/dinner buffet on Sun. **Cards:** DS, MC, VI.   ⊗

# DOUGLASSVILLE

### LODGING
**ECONO LODGE**   AAA Special Value Rates   Phone: 610/385-3016
5/1-11/30 [CP]   1P: $43- 63   2P/1B:   $47- 67   2P/2B:   $54- 69   XP: $10  F14
12/1-4/30 [CP]   1P: $38- 56   2P/1B:   $45- 61   2P/2B:   $49- 68   XP: $10  F14
Motel
**Location:** on Rt 422, from Pottstown 422 W 10 mi, from Reading 422 E 10 mi. 387 Ben Franklin Hwy 19518. Fax: 610/385-3016. **Terms:** Credit card guarantee, 3 day notice; weekly rates; no pets. **Facility:** 24 rooms. 2 stories; exterior corridors. **All Rooms:** free movies, cable TV. **Some Rooms:** Fee: microwaves, refrigerators. **Cards:** AE, DS, MC, VI.   (D) ⊗

# DOYLESTOWN—8,600

### RESTAURANT
**CONTI CROSS KEYS INN**   Dinner: $11-$20   Phone: 215/348-9600
American
**Location:** 1 mi n on SR 611, exit SR 313, 2 blks n. SR 611 & SR 313 18901. **Hours:** 11:30 am-10 pm, Sat from 5 pm. Closed major holidays & Sun. **Reservations:** suggested. **Features:** casual dress; children's menu; cocktails & lounge; a la carte. Popular restaurant, variety of dining areas. Also Italian cuisine. **Cards:** AE, CB, DI, DS, MC, VI.   ⊗

# DRINKER   (See POCONO MOUNTAINS & VICINITY ACCOMMODATIONS spotting map pages A212 & A213; see index starting on page A210)

### RESTAURANT
**MY BROTHERS PLACE**   Dinner: $21-$30   Phone: 717/689-4410   (77)
American
**Location:** 3/4 mi w on SR 590; 5 mi e of jct SR 590 & 435 at Elmhurst. 18444. **Hours:** 4 pm-10 pm, Sun from 1 pm. Closed: Tues & 1/1-2/14. **Features:** casual dress; children's menu; carryout; salad bar; cocktails & lounge. Cozy atmosphere; good selection of seafood & beef. Prime rib specials on weekends. **Cards:** AE, CB, DI, DS, MC, VI.

# DRUMS

### LODGING
**ECONO LODGE**   Rates Subject to Change   Phone: 717/788-4121
Fri & Sat 5/17-10/31   1P: $45- 50   2P/2B:   $49- 55   XP: $7  F18
Sun-Thurs 5/17-10/31   1P: $45- 46   2P/2B:   $47- 49   XP: $7  F18
5/1-5/16 & 11/1-4/30   1P: $33- 36   2P/2B:   $38- 40   XP: $7  F18
Motel
**Location:** I-80 exit 39, 1/4 mi n on SR 309, I-81 exit 42, e to 309S, following signs. (RR 1, Box 1470). **Terms:** Sr. discount; reserv deposit, 3 day notice; no pets. **Facility:** 43 rooms. 2 stories; exterior corridors; pool. **Dining:** Complimentary morning coffee & doughnuts; restaurant nearby. **All Rooms:** free movies, cable TV. **Cards:** AE, DS, JCB, MC, VI. *(See color ad p A135)*   (D) ⊗

# DU BOIS—8,300

### LODGINGS
**DUBOIS MANOR MOTEL**   Rates Subject to Change   Phone: 814/371-5400
All Year   1P: $35- 40.   2P/1B:   $40- 45   2P/2B:   $40- 45   XP: $4
Motel
**Location:** On US 219, 1/2 blk s of SR 255, between I-80 exits 1 & 17. 525 Liberty Blvd 15801. **Terms:** Sr. discount; reserv deposit; small pets only, $5. **Facility:** 45 rooms. 2 stories; exterior corridors. **Dining:** Restaurant nearby. **All Rooms:** combo & shower baths, cable TV. **Cards:** AE, DS, MC, VI. *(See ad p A110)*   (D) ⊗

**HOLIDAY INN**   Rates Subject to Change   Phone: 814/371-5100
All Year   1P: $54- 69   2P/1B:   $54- 75   2P/2B:   $54- 75   XP: $6  F19
Motor Inn
**Location:** On US 219, 1/4 mi s of I-80, exit 16. US 219 & I-80 15801. Fax: 814/375-0230. **Terms:** Sr. discount; pets. **Facility:** 161 rooms. 2 stories; interior corridors; meeting rooms; pool, wading pool. **Dining & Entertainment:** Cocktail lounge; also, Fogarty's, see separate listing. **Services:** airport transportation. Fee: coin laundry. **All Rooms:** free & pay movies, cable TV. **Cards:** AE, CB, DI, DS, MC, VI. *(See ad p A110)*   (D) ⊗

**PENN ROSE MOTOR INN-BEST WESTERN**   Rates Subject to Change   Phone: 814/371-6200
All Year   1P: $43- 51   2P/1B:   $49- 57   2P/2B:   $49- 57   XP: $6  F12
Motel
**Location:** Jct US 219 & SR 255; between I-80 exits 16 & 17. 82 N Park Pl 15801. Fax: 814/371-4608. **Terms:** Sr. discount; reserv deposit, 5 day notice; no pets. **Facility:** 60 rooms. Opposite DuBois campus, Penn State. 3 stories; interior corridors; playground. **Dining:** Restaurant nearby. **All Rooms:** free movies, combo & shower baths, cable TV. **Some Rooms:** refrigerators. **Cards:** AE, CB, DI, DS, MC, VI.   (D) ⊗

**RAMADA INN**   Guaranteed Rates   Phone: 814/371-7070
All Year   1P: $50- 65   2P/2B:   $60- 75   XP: $10  F18
Motor Inn
**Location:** At I-80, exit 17, on SR 255. Rt 255 & I-80 15801-9682. Fax: 814/371-1055. **Terms:** Sr. discount; credit card guarantee; small pets only. **Facility:** 96 rooms. Convenient to interstate. 3 stories; interior corridors; meeting rooms; heated indoor pool, saunas. **Dining & Entertainment:** Dining room; 6:30 am-2 & 5-10 pm; $9-$16; cocktails/lounge; 24-hour room service; entertainment. **Services:** airport transportation. Fee: coin laundry. **All Rooms:** cable TV. **Cards:** AE, DI, DS, MC, VI.   (D) ⊗

## RESTAURANTS

**FOGARTY'S**
◆◆
American
DS, MC, VI.
**Dinner: $11-$20**            **Phone: 814/371-5100**
**Location:** In Holiday Inn. US 219 & I-80 15801. **Hours:** 6:30 am-2 & 5-10 pm, Sat & Sun from 7 am.
**Features:** casual dress; children's menu; early bird specials; health conscious menu; salad bar; cocktails & lounge; buffet. Intimate dining section; daily buffet, $4.25; Sun brunch 11 am-2 pm, $6.95. **Cards:** AE, DI, DS, MC, VI. ⊗

**THUNDERBIRD RESTAURANT & LOUNGE**
◆◆
American
**Dinner: $11-$20**            **Phone: 814/371-0799**
**Location:** In Reynoldsville; from Dubois, 2 1/2 mi s on US 219 from US 255, 1 mi s on US 119, 1 mi w on US 322. 15851. **Hours:** 5 pm-9 pm. **Closed:** Sun, Mon & 12/25. **Reservations:** suggested; weekends.
**Features:** casual dress; children's menu; cocktails & lounge. Steaks, seafood & chops. Casual family dining; rustic atmosphere with fireplace. **Cards:** AE, DS, MC, VI.

# DUNCANSVILLE

## LODGING

**WYE MOTOR LODGE**       Rates Subject to Change       **Phone: 814/695-4407**

| | | 1P: | | 2P/1B: | | 2P/2B: | | XP: | |
|---|---|---|---|---|---|---|---|---|---|
| 5/1-10/31 | | $27- | 29 | $32- | 34 | $33- | 36 | $3 | D |
| 11/1-4/30 | | $27- | 28 | $30- | 32 | $30- | 34 | $3 | D |

⊛
◆◆
Motel
refrigerators. **Cards:** AE, DS, MC, VI.
**Location:** On US 22, e from US 220, Plank Rd exit 2 1/2 mi toward Hollidaysburg. US 22 & Old US 220 16635. **Terms:** Reserv deposit; weekly rates; no pets. **Facility:** 38 rooms. Well-maintained property. 1 story; exterior corridors. **All Rooms:** combo & shower baths, cable TV. **Some Rooms:** microwaves, radios, ⒟ ⊗

# DUNMORE—15,400   (See POCONO MOUNTAINS & VICINITY ACCOMMODATIONS spotting map pages A212 & A213; see index starting on page A210)

## LODGINGS

**DAYS INN**       Rates Subject to Change       **Phone: 717/348-6101**  **❶**

◆◆
Motel
All Year [CP]            1P: $54- 59   2P/1B: $64- 74   2P/2B: $69- 79   XP: $5  F12
**Location:** Jct SR 347 & I-81, exit 55A. 1226 O'Neil Hwy 18512. Fax: 717/348-5064. **Terms:** Sr. discount; package plans; pets. **Facility:** 90 rooms. Very decorative rooms. 4 stories; interior corridors.
**Dining:** Restaurant nearby. **All Rooms:** microwaves, free movies, refrigerators, combo & shower baths, cable TV.
**Some Rooms:** whirlpools. Fee: VCP's. **Cards:** AE, CB, DI, DS, JCB, MC, VI. ⒟ ⊗

**ECONO LODGE**       Rates Subject to Change       **Phone: 717/346-8782**  **❹**

| | | 1P: | | 2P/1B: | | 2P/2B: | | XP: | |
|---|---|---|---|---|---|---|---|---|---|
| 5/1-10/31 & 4/1-4/30 [CP] | | $40- | 75 | $50- | 75 | $50- | 95 | $5 | F13 |
| 11/1-3/31 [CP] | | $40- | 60 | $50- | 75 | $50- | 75 | $5 | F13 |

⊛
◆◆
Motel
VI.
**Location:** On SR 347, 1/4 mi e of I-81, exit 55A (Throop exit). 1027 O'Neill Hwy 18512. Fax: 717/344-7825. **Terms:** Sr. discount; reserv deposit, 3 day notice; package plans; no pets. **Facility:** 32 rooms. 2 stories; exterior corridors. **Dining:** Restaurant nearby. **All Rooms:** free movies, cable TV. **Cards:** AE, CB, DI, DS, MC, ⒟ ⊗

**HOLIDAY INN-EAST**       Rates Subject to Change       **Phone: 717/343-4771**  **❸**

| | | 1P: | 2P/1B: | 2P/2B: | | XP: | |
|---|---|---|---|---|---|---|---|
| 11/1-4/30 | | $86 | $96 | $96 | | $10 | F |
| 7/1-10/31 | | $85 | $95 | $95 | | $10 | F |
| 5/1-6/30 | | $79 | $89 | $89 | | $10 | F |

⊛
◆◆◆
Motor Inn
**Location:** I-380/84 at exit 1 (Tigue St), 1/4 mi e of jct I-81. 200 Tigue St 18512 (PO Box 132). Fax: 717/343-5171. **Terms:** Sr. discount; credit card guarantee; BP available; package plans; no pets.
**Facility:** 139 rooms. Suites, $125-$135; 3 stories; interior/exterior corridors; meeting rooms; heated indoor pool, whirlpool; exercise room, game room. **Dining & Entertainment:** Restaurant; 6:30 am-10 pm; $9-$18; cocktails/lounge. **Services:** data ports; valet laundry; area transportation, to Keystone Industrial Pk, airport transportation. **All Rooms:** free movies, cable TV.
**Some Rooms:** whirlpools. Fee: refrigerators. **Cards:** AE, CB, DI, DS, JCB, MC, VI. *(See color ad p A220)* ⒟ ⊗

## RESTAURANT

**BILLY'S SEAFOOD AND STEAKHOUSE**     **Dinner: $11-$20**     **Phone: 717/961-1130**  ②
⊛
◆◆
Steak and
Seafood
**Location:** From I-81 exit 55B; 1 1/2 mi s. Rear 618 S Blakely St 18510. **Hours:** 11 am-11 pm, Sat from 4:30 pm, Sun noon-9 pm. **Closed:** 12/25. **Reservations:** suggested; major holidays & weekends.
**Features:** casual dress; children's menu; early bird specials; health conscious menu; carryout; cocktails & lounge. Also Italian cuisine. **Cards:** AE, DI, DS, MC, VI. ⊗

# EAGLES MERE—100

## LODGING

**SHADY LANE BED & BREAKFAST**  Guaranteed Rates  Phone: 717/525-3394
◆◆  All Year [BP]  1P: $60  2P/1B: $75  2P/2B: $75  XP: $15
Bed &  **Location:** 1 blk s on Allegheny Ave. Allegheny Ave 17731 (PO Box 314). **Terms:** Sr. discount; age
Breakfast  restrictions may apply; reserv deposit, 10 day notice; weekly rates; package plans; no pets. **Facility:** 8 rooms.
Reservations suggested 11/1-4/30, Mon-Thur. 1 carriage house, $100-$115; 1 story; interior corridors; smoke
free premises; lake privileges. **Dining:** Afternoon tea. **All Rooms:** combo & shower baths, no A/C, no phones, no TVs.
**Some Rooms:** coffeemakers, efficiency, radios, refrigerators.  (D) ⊗

# EASTON—26,300

## LODGINGS

**BEST WESTERN EASTON INN**  Rates Subject to Change  Phone: 610/253-9131
▨  6/21-11/25 [CP]  1P: $70- 85  2P/1B: $80- 85  2P/2B: $80- 85  XP: $10 F12
5/1-6/20 & 4/1-4/30 [CP]  1P: $65- 75  2P/1B: $75- 80  2P/2B: $75- 80  XP: $10 F12
◆◆◆  1/1-3/31 [CP]  1P: $55- 60  2P/1B: $65- 70  2P/2B: $65- 70  XP: $10 F12
Motel  11/26-12/31 [CP]  1P: $49- 59  2P/1B: $59- 65  2P/2B: $59- 65  XP: $10 F12
**Location:** US 22, 4th St (SR 611) exit, 1 blk s to 3rd St, then 1/2 mi s; or I-78 exit 22, 1 mi n following
signs. 185 S Third St 18042. Fax: 610/252-5145. **Terms:** Sr. discount; reserv deposit, 3 day notice; weekly rates; small pets
only, $50 dep req. **Facility:** 85 rooms. Comfortably furnished guest rooms. 4 stories; interior corridors; conference facilities;
heated indoor pool; game room. **Dining & Entertainment:** Cocktail lounge; restaurant nearby. **Services:** data ports.
**All Rooms:** microwaves, refrigerators, cable TV. **Cards:** AE, CB, DI, DS, MC, VI.  ▨ (D) ⊗

**DAYS INN**  Guaranteed Rates  Phone: 610/253-0546
▨  All Year [CP]  1P: $45- 56  2P/1B: $56- 70  2P/2B: $56- 70  XP: $4  F
**Location:** US 22, exit 25th St, 1/4 mi e on N Service Rd. 2555 Nazareth Rd 18042. Fax: 610/252-8952.
◆◆  **Terms:** Sr. discount; reserv deposit, 3 day notice; pets, $5. **Facility:** 84 rooms. Well-kept property convenient
Motel  to shopping area. 4 stories; interior corridors; game room. **Dining:** Restaurant nearby. **All Rooms:** free
movies, combo & shower baths, cable TV. **Cards:** AE, DS, JCB, MC, VI.  (D) (S) ⊗

## RESTAURANTS

**SILVER DOLLAR CAFE**  Dinner: $11-$20  Phone: 610/253-7795
◆  **Location:** US 22, 13th St exit, e 1 blk to 12th St, 2 blks n to Chidsey St, 1 blk w. 1220 Chidsey St 18042.
Steak and  **Hours:** 4 pm-10 pm, Sun-9 pm. Closed: Mon & 11/23. **Features:** casual dress; carryout; salad bar; cocktails
Seafood  & lounge. **Cards:** DS, MC, VI.

**THE WINDMILL RESTAURANT**  Dinner: $11-$20  Phone: 610/252-1541
◆◆  **Location:** From SR 33 Stockertown exit, SR 191 n to Main St, right 2 blks to Lefevre, 2 mi to Youngs Hill
American  Rd, 3/4 mi e. 769 Young's Hill Rd 18042. **Hours:** 5 pm-9 pm, Fri & Sat-9 pm, Sat 5 pm-9:30 pm, Sun
noon-7:30 pm. Closed: Mon, Tues, 1/1, 7/4, 12/24 & 12/25. **Reservations:** suggested. **Features:** casual
dress; children's menu; cocktails & lounge; a la carte. Specializing in fresh seafood, veal & prime rib. Family style dining Sun
for 4 or more. Panoramic view, 704 feet above sea level. **Cards:** AE, CB, DI, DS, MC, VI.  ⊗

# EAST PETERSBURG—4,200

## RESTAURANT

**HAYDN ZUG'S**  Historical  Dinner: $11-$20  Phone: 717/569-5746
◆◆  **Location:** On the square; jct of SR 72 & 722, 2 3/4 mi n of US 30. 1987 State St 17520. **Hours:** 11:30 am-2
American  & 5-9 pm, Sat from 5 pm. Closed major holidays & Sun. **Reservations:** suggested. **Features:** casual dress;
children's menu; cocktails & lounge; cafeteria. Well-prepared meals served in colonial atmosphere. Built in
1852. Half-dinners avail. **Cards:** AE, MC, VI.  ⊗

# EAST STROUDSBURG—8,800  (See POCONO MOUNTAINS & VICINITY ACCOMMODATIONS spotting map pages A212 & A213; see index starting on page A210)

## LODGINGS

**BUDGET MOTEL**  Rates Subject to Change  Phone: 717/424-5451  **41**
▨  Fri-Sun  1P: $44- 50  2P/1B: $44- 52  2P/2B: $50- 65
Mon-Thurs  1P: $33- 43  2P/1B: $38- 46  2P/2B: $40- 50
◆◆  **Location:** At jct I-80 exit 51, just se on Greentree Rd. 18301 (PO Box 216, STROUDSBURG).
Motor Inn  Fax: 717/424-0389. **Terms:** Weekly/monthly rates; package plans; pets, $20 dep req. **Facility:** 115 rooms.
Rates for up to 5 persons; 2-3 stories; interior/exterior corridors; meeting rooms. **Dining & Entertainment:**
Restaurant; 7 am-11 & 5-10 pm, Sun-9 pm; $8-$14; cocktails/lounge. **Services:** data ports. **All Rooms:** cable TV.
**Some Rooms:** microwaves, refrigerators. Fee: VCP's. **Cards:** AE, DI, DS, MC, VI. *(See color ad p A229)*  (D) ⊗

**SUPER 8 MOTEL**  Rates Subject to Change  Phone: 717/424-7411  **42**
▨  All Year  1P: $42- 48  2P/1B: $49- 55  2P/2B: $51- 57  XP: $7 F12
**Location:** At jct I-80, exit 51, just se on Greentree Dr. 340 Green Tree Dr 18301. Fax: 717/424-7411.
◆  **Terms:** Credit card guarantee; weekly rates; pets, $10 dep req. **Facility:** 57 rooms. 3 stories, no elevator; in-
Motel  terior corridors; whirlpool. **Dining:** Restaurant nearby. **All Rooms:** free movies, cable TV. **Some Rooms:**
Fee: VCP's. **Cards:** AE, CB, DI, DS, MC, VI.  (D) ⊗

## RESTAURANT

**PEPPE'S**  Dinner: $11-$20  Phone: 717/421-4460  **35**
◆◆◆  **Location:** At jct Business Rt 209 & SR 447N, at the Eagle Valley Mall. Eagle Valley Mall 18360.
Northern  **Hours:** 11:30 am-2:30 & 5:30-10:30 pm, Sun 3 pm-9 pm. Closed: 4/16, 11/23 & 12/25.
Italian  **Reservations:** suggested. **Features:** casual dress; children's menu; carryout; cocktails & lounge; a la carte.
Roman arches, inviting atmosphere; tableside preparation. **Cards:** AE, CB, DI, MC, VI.  ⊗

## EBENSBURG—3,900

### LODGINGS

**COMFORT INN**
◆◆◆    Guaranteed Rates    Phone: 814/472-6100
Motel    All Year [CP]    1P: $49- 55   2P/1B: $55- 61   2P/2B: $55- 61   XP: $6   F17
**Location:** On US 22, 1/4 mi e of jct US 219. 111 Cook Rd 15931 (Rt 22 Box 63). Fax: 814/472-4960.
**Terms:** Sr. discount; credit card guarantee, 3 day notice; monthly rates; pets, $50 dep req. **Facility:** 78 rooms.
3 stories; interior corridors; meeting rooms; heated indoor pool, whirlpool; exercise room. **Dining:** Restaurant nearby.
**Services:** data ports. Fee: coin laundry. **All Rooms:** free movies, combo & shower baths, cable TV.
**Some Rooms:** microwaves, refrigerators, whirlpools. Fee: VCP's. **Cards:** AE, CB, DI, DS, JCB, MC, VI.
Roll in showers. ⓩ Ⓓ Ⓢ ⊗

**THE COTTAGE RESTAURANT & INN**    AAA Special Value Rates    Phone: 814/472-8002
ⒶⒶ    All Year [CP]    1P: $39- 59   2P/1B: $44- 58   2P/2B: $48- 64   XP: $5   F12
**Location:** 1 mi e of jct US 219 on US 22. 15931 (RD 4, Box 50). Fax: 814/472-9795. **Terms:** Pets.
◆◆    **Facility:** 56 rooms. 1 two-bedroom unit. 2 stories; interior corridors; meeting rooms; pool. **Dining &**
Motor Inn    **Entertainment:** Restaurant; 6:30 am-10 pm, Sat from 7 am, Sun 7 am-10 pm; $10-$15; cocktails/lounge.
**All Rooms:** free movies, cable TV, VCP's. **Some Rooms:** refrigerators. **Cards:** AE, DI, MC, VI.
Independent. *(See ad below)*    Ⓓ ⊗

**THE NOON-COLLINS INN**    AAA Special Value Rates    Phone: 814/472-4311
ⒶⒶ    5/1-10/31 [BP]    1P: $55   2P/1B: $60   2P/2B: $60   XP: $15   F3
    11/1-4/30 [BP]    1P: $50   2P/1B: $55   2P/2B: $55   XP: $15   F3
◆◆◆    **Location:** Jct SR 219, SR 422 & Business Rt SR 22. 114 E High St 15931. **Terms:** Reserv deposit, 7 day
Historic Bed    notice; no pets. **Facility:** 7 rooms. Restored historic inn originally constructed in 1834 with an addition built on
& Breakfast    in 1900. Phones avail; 2 stories; interior corridors. **Dining:** Restaurant; 11 am-2 & 5-9 pm; $8-$14; cocktails.
**All Rooms:** shower baths. **Cards:** AE, CB, DI, MC, VI.    Ⓓ ⊗

## EDINBORO—7,700

### LODGING

**EDINBORO INN**    Rates Subject to Change    Phone: 814/734-5650
◆    5/1-10/9    1P: $73   2P/1B: $78   2P/2B: $78   XP:$5-15   F19
Motor Inn    10/10-4/30    1P: $50   2P/1B: $55   2P/2B: $55   XP: $5   F19
**Location:** 2 mi e of I-79. Rt 6N 16412. Fax: 814/734-7532. **Terms:** Sr. discount; check-in 4 pm; credit card
guarantee; weekly/monthly rates; package plans; pets. **Facility:** 105 rooms. 2 stories; interior corridors; meeting rooms; heated
indoor pool, saunas. Fee: 18 holes golf. **Dining & Entertainment:** Dining room; 7 am-2 & 5-9 pm; $6-$18; cocktails/lounge.
**Services:** secretarial services. Fee: childcare; coin laundry. **All Rooms:** free & pay movies. **Some Rooms:** Fee: VCP's.
**Cards:** AE, CB, DI, DS, MC, VI.    Ⓓ ⊗

## ELIZABETHTOWN—10,000

### LODGING

**WEST RIDGE GUEST HOUSE**    Rates Subject to Change    Phone: 717/367-7783
ⒶⒶ    All Year [BP]    1P: $60- 90   2P/1B: $60- 90   2P/2B: $60   XP: $15   D11
**Location:** 5 1/2 mi se from I-283 via Rt 743N, Rt 230S, Rt 743S, then w on West Ridge Rd. 1285 W Ridge
◆◆◆    Rd 17022. **Terms:** Reserv deposit, 7 day notice, cancellation fee imposed; weekly rates; no pets. **Facility:** 9
Bed &    rooms. Tranquil, rural setting with luxurious period-decorated theme rooms, 3 with gas fireplace. 2 stories; in-
Breakfast    terior corridors; smoke free premises; meeting rooms; exercise room, video library. **All Rooms:** cable TV.
**Some Rooms:** refrigerators, VCP's, whirlpools. **Cards:** AE, DS, MC, VI.    Ⓓ ⊗

## EMLENTON—800

### LODGING

**WHIPPLE TREE INN & FARM**    Guaranteed Rates    Phone: 412/867-9543
◆◆    All Year [BP]    1P: $45- 60   2P/1B: $50- 60   2P/2B: $45- 55   XP: $10   F3
Bed &    **Location:** Exit 5 off I-80, e 1 mi on SR 208, n 1 mi on Big Bend Rd. Big Bend Rd (Rd #3, Box 285).
Breakfast    **Terms:** Reserv deposit, 7 day notice; weekly rates; no pets. **Facility:** 4 rooms. 2 stories; interior corridors.
**All Rooms:** no phones, no TVs. **Some Rooms:** shower baths, shared bathrooms.    Ⓓ ⊗

## EMMAUS—11,200

### LODGING

**LEIBERT GAP MANOR BED & BREAKFAST**    AAA Special Value Rates    Phone: 610/967-1242
ⒶⒶ    All Year [BP]    1P: $75- 140   2P/1B: $85- 150
**Location:** Rt 9 PA Tpk exit 32, e on SR 663 to SR 309N exit 17, SR 29S (Cedar Crest Blvd), 1 blk e on
◆◆◆    Chestnut to 10th St & 1 mi s. 4502 S Mountain Dr 18049 (PO Box 623). **Terms:** Age restrictions may apply;
Bed &    reserv deposit; no pets. **Facility:** 4 rooms. Warm hospitality. Tastefully furnished in antiques. 3 stories; interior
Breakfast    corridors; smoke free premises; game room. **Services:** airport transportation. **Recreation:** bicycles, hiking
trails. **All Rooms:** combo & shower baths, no phones, no TVs. **Some Rooms:** whirlpools. **Cards:** AE, CB,
DI, MC, VI.    Ⓓ ⊗

### RESTAURANT

**THE FARMHOUSE RESTAURANT**    Dinner: $21-$30    Phone: 610/967-6225
◆◆◆    **Location:** I-78, exit 17; 3 mi s on SR 29 (Cedar Crest Blvd), 1/3 mi w on Chestnut St. 1449 Chestnut St
French    18049. **Hours:** 11:30 am-2 & 5-9 pm, Fri & Sat-10 pm, Sun 10:30 am-2 & 5-9 pm. Closed: 1/1 & 12/25.
**Reservations:** suggested. **Features:** casual dress; Sunday brunch; carryout; cocktails & lounge; a la carte.
Intimate dining in a early 1800's farmhouse. Smoke free premises. **Cards:** AE, DS, MC, VI.    ⊗

**ENOLA** (See HARRISBURG ACCOMMODATIONS spotting map page A129; see index starting on page A128)

## LODGING

**QUALITY INN SUMMERDALE** — AAA Special Value Rates — Phone: 717/732-0785 **51**

Motel
5/1-10/31 & 4/1-4/30    1P: $59-  67  2P/1B:  $65-  73  2P/2B:  $65-  73  XP: $6  F18
11/1-3/31    1P: $49-  57  2P/1B:  $55-  63  2P/2B:  $55-  63  XP: $6  F18
**Location:** 4 1/2 mi n on US 11 & 15; 1 mi s of I-81 exit 21. 501 N Enola Rd 17025. Fax: 717/732-7860.
**Terms:** Reserv deposit, 3 day notice; CP available; pets. **Facility:** 72 rooms. Located along busy commercial highway. 2 stories; interior corridors; pool. **Dining:** Restaurant nearby. **All Rooms:** free movies, cable TV.
**Some Rooms:** coffeemakers, radios. Fee: VCP's. **Cards:** AE, CB, DI, DS, MC, VI.   ⒹⓍ

## EPHRATA—12,100

## LODGINGS

**CLEARVIEW FARM BED & BREAKFAST** — Guaranteed Rates — Phone: 717/733-6333

Historic Bed & Breakfast
All Year [BP]    2P/1B:  $95-  115
**Location:** 4 mi w on US 322 from jct SR 272, 1 mi n on Clearview Rd. 355 Clearview Rd 17522.
**Terms:** Age restrictions may apply; check-in 4 pm; reserv deposit, 10 day notice; 2 night min stay; no pets. **Facility:** 5 rooms. A touch of elegance in 1814 limestone farmhouse. Rooms well-appointed with antiques. 2 stories; interior corridors; smoke free premises. **All Rooms:** combo & shower baths, no phones, no TVs. **Cards:** DS, MC, VI. *(See ad starting on p A152)*   ⒹⓍ

**DUTCHMAID MOTEL** — Rates Subject to Change — Phone: 717/733-1720

Motel
5/1-11/1 & 4/1-4/30    2P/2B:  $40-  44  XP: $4
11/2-3/31    2P/2B:  $35-  39  XP: $4
**Location:** On SR 272, 1/4 mi n of US 322; 3 1/4 mi nw of jct US 222 & 322. 222 N Reading Rd 17522.
**Terms:** Reserv deposit; small pets only. **Facility:** 20 rooms. Located along busy commercial highway. 1 story; exterior corridors. **Dining & Entertainment:** Cocktail lounge. **All Rooms:** combo & shower baths, cable TV.
**Cards:** AE, MC, VI.   ⒹⓍ

**HISTORIC SMITHTON COUNTRY INN** — Rates Subject to Change — Phone: 717/733-6094

Historic Country Inn
Fri-Sun [BP]    1P: $85-  125  2P/1B:  $95-  135  XP:$20-35
Mon-Thurs [BP]    1P: $55-  95  2P/1B:  $65-  105  XP:$20-35
**Location:** On SR 322; 5 mi s of PA Tpk, exit 21; corner Main St & Academy Dr. 900 W Main St 17522.
**Terms:** Age restrictions may apply; check-in 3:30 pm; reserv deposit, 14 day notice; 2 night min stay; pets. **Facility:** 8 rooms. Historic 1763 stagecoach inn; all units with fireplace. Courtesy phones by request. 3 stories; interior corridors; smoke free premises. **All Rooms:** combo & shower baths, no phones, no TVs.
**Some Rooms:** refrigerators, whirlpools. **Cards:** AE, MC, VI.   ⒹⓍ

## RESTAURANTS

**FAMILY TIME RESTAURANT** — Dinner: up to $10 — Phone: 717/738-4231

American
**Location:** On US 322, 1 3/4 mi w of jct SR 272. 1737 W Main St 17522. **Hours:** 11 am-8 pm, Fri & Sat-9 pm. **Closed:** 12/25. **Features:** casual dress; children's menu. Pennsylvania Dutch smorgasbord. Seafood buffet, Tues 4 pm-8 pm & Fri 4 pm-9 pm; Sat from 3 pm-9 pm, $12.50. Smoke free premises. **Cards:** DS, MC, VI.   Ⓧ

**ISAAC'S RESTAURANT & DELI** — Dinner: up to $10 — Phone: 717/733-7777

American
**Location:** Rts 272 & 322 in the Cloister Shopping Center. 120 N Reading Rd 17522. **Hours:** 10 am-9 pm, Fri & Sat-10 pm, Sun 11 am-9 pm. **Closed:** 1/1, 11/23 & 12/25. **Features:** casual dress; children's menu; carryout. Grilled sandwiches, named after birds, plants & flowers. Each sandwich has a unique personality. **Cards:** AE, DS, MC, VI.

**THE RESTAURANT AT DONECKERS** — Dinner: $21-$30 — Phone: 717/738-9501

French
**Location:** 2 mi w of jct SR 222 & 322 via SR 322, then 1/2 mi n on State St. 333 N State St 17522. **Hours:** 11 am-10 pm, Sun 11:30 am-3 pm. Closed major holidays & Wed. **Reservations:** suggested; weekends. **Features:** Sunday brunch; children's menu; health conscious menu items; cocktails. Relaxed dining. Expertly prepared entrees. Varied menu. Homemade desserts, breads, soups, ice creams & sauces. Braille & large print menus. No smoking during lunch. **Cards:** AE, DI, DS, MC, VI.   Ⓧ

## ERIE—108,700

## LODGINGS

**COMFORT INN** — Rates Subject to Change — Phone: 814/866-6666

Motel
5/1-10/31 & 3/1-4/30 [CP]    1P: $80-  99  2P/1B:  $90-  120  2P/2B:  $90-  120  XP: $6  F18
11/1-2/29 [CP]    1P: $60-  80  2P/1B:  $75-  110  2P/2B:  $75-  110  XP: $6  F18
**Location:** Exit 6 from I-90, 1/8 mi s. 8051 Peach St 16509. Fax: 814/866-6666. **Terms:** Sr. discount; small pets only, $15 dep req. **Facility:** 110 rooms. 2 stories; interior corridors; meeting rooms; luxury level rooms; heated pool, whirlpool; exercise room. **Dining:** Restaurant nearby. **Services:** data ports; valet laundry.
**All Rooms:** free movies, shower baths, VCP's. **Some Rooms:** microwaves, refrigerators, whirlpools. **Cards:** AE, CB, DI, DS, MC, VI.   ⒹⓍ

**DAYS INN** — Rates Subject to Change — Phone: 814/868-8521

Motel
5/1-10/31 [CP]    1P: $80    2P/1B:  $100  2P/2B:  $100  XP: $5  F18
11/1-4/30 [CP]    1P: $50    2P/1B:  $70  2P/2B:  $70  XP: $5  F18
**Location:** On SR 97, at jct I-90, exit 7. 7415 Schultz Rd 16509. Fax: 814/868-8521. **Terms:** Sr. discount; reserv deposit, 3 day notice; pets. **Facility:** 113 rooms. 4 stories; interior corridors; meeting rooms; heated pool. **Dining:** Restaurant nearby. **All Rooms:** free movies. **Some Rooms:** refrigerators. **Cards:** AE, CB, DI, DS, JCB, MC, VI. *(See ad p A114)*   ⒹⓍ

**ECONO LODGE**
Rates Subject to Change
Phone: 814/866-5544

| | | | | | |
|---|---|---|---|---|---|
| 5/1-10/31 [CP] | 1P: $69- 130 | 2P/1B: $89- 130 | 2P/2B: $89- 130 | XP: $6 | F18 |
| 11/1-4/30 [CP] | 1P: $59- 120 | 2P/1B: $79- 120 | 2P/2B: $79- 120 | XP: $6 | F18 |

**Location:** Exit 6 off I-90, 1/8 mi s. 8050 Peach St 16509. **Fax:** 814/866-3557. **Terms:** Sr. discount; reserv deposit; weekly/monthly rates; no pets. **Facility:** 97 rooms. 3 stories; interior corridors; meeting rooms; heated indoor pool, sauna, whirlpool; exercise room. **Services:** data ports; valet laundry; airport transportation. **All Rooms:** free movies, combo & shower baths. **Some Rooms:** refrigerators. Fee: VCP's. **Cards:** AE, DI, DS, MC, VI.   Ⓓ Ⓢ ⊗

**GLASS HOUSE INN**
Guaranteed Rates
Phone: 814/833-7751

| | | | |
|---|---|---|---|
| 6/30-9/4 [CP] | 2P/1B: $55- 65 | 2P/2B: $79- 89 | XP: $5-7 |
| 5/26-6/29 [CP] | 2P/1B: $50- 60 | 2P/2B: $65- 75 | XP: $5 |
| 5/1-5/25 & 9/5-4/30 [CP] | 2P/1B: $45- 55 | 2P/2B: $65- 65 | XP: $5 |

**Location:** On US 20, 1/4 mi w of jct SR 832, 1 mi w of I-79 exit 43. 3202 W 26th St 16506. **Fax:** 814/833-4222. **Terms:** Reserv deposit; no pets. **Facility:** 30 rooms. Bed & breakfast style motel by 3rd generation owner. Colonial motif. Weekend special rates, 9/7-5/26; 1 story; exterior corridors; heated pool, sauna. **All Rooms:** cable TV. **Cards:** AE, CB, DI, DS, MC, VI. *(See color ad below)*   Ⓓ ⊗

**HAMPTON INN ERIE**
Rates Subject to Change
Phone: 814/835-4200

| | | | |
|---|---|---|---|
| 5/14-9/10 [CP] | 1P: $82 | 2P/1B: $82 | 2P/2B: $80 |
| 5/1-5/13 & 9/11-4/30 [CP] | 1P: $62 | 2P/1B: $69 | 2P/2B: $69 |

**Location:** Exit 44B off I-79, w 1 3/4 mi on Rt 5. 3041 W 12th St 16505. **Fax:** 814/835-5212. **Terms:** Reserv deposit; no pets. **Facility:** 100 rooms. 3 stories; interior corridors; heated pool. **Services:** data ports; valet laundry; airport transportation. **All Rooms:** free movies. **Cards:** AE, CB, DI, DS, MC, VI.   Ⓓ Ⓢ ⊗

**HOLIDAY INN-DOWNTOWN**
AAA Special Value Rates
Phone: 814/456-2961

| | | | | | |
|---|---|---|---|---|---|
| 5/27-9/5 | 1P: $67- 89 | 2P/1B: $67- 89 | 2P/2B: $67- 89 | XP: $6 | F19 |
| 5/1-5/26 & 9/6-4/30 | 1P: $49- 80 | 2P/1B: $49- 80 | 2P/2B: $49- 80 | XP: $6 | F19 |

**Location:** 1 mi s at 18th & Peach sts. 18 W 18th St 16501. **Fax:** 814/456-7067. **Terms:** Reserv deposit, 3 day notice; small pets only. **Facility:** 134 rooms. 4 stories; interior/exterior corridors; meeting rooms; heated pool. **Dining & Entertainment:** Dining room; 6:30 am-2 & 5-10 pm; $6-$14; cocktails/lounge. **Services:** data ports; guest laundry. **All Rooms:** cable TV. Fee: movies. **Some Rooms:** coffeemakers, refrigerators. **Cards:** AE, CB, DI, DS, JCB, MC, VI.   ⌚ Ⓓ ⊗

**HOLIDAY INN-SOUTH**
Rates Subject to Change
Phone: 814/864-4911

| | | | | | |
|---|---|---|---|---|---|
| All Year | 1P: $65- 74 | 2P/1B: $69- 74 | 2P/2B: $69- 73 | XP: $6 | F18 |

**Location:** On SR 97, at I-90 exit 7. 8040 Perry Hwy 16509. **Fax:** 814/864-3743. **Terms:** Sr. discount; reserv deposit, 3 day notice; package plans; pets. **Facility:** 216 rooms. 2-4 stories; interior/exterior corridors; meeting rooms; heated pool; complimentary health club privileges. **Dining & Entertainment:** Dining room, restaurant; 6:30 am-10 pm; $10-$22; cocktails; entertainment. **Services:** data ports, secretarial services; valet laundry; airport transportation. Fee: childcare. **All Rooms:** cable TV. Fee: movies. **Some Rooms:** coffeemakers, 2 kitchens. Fee: microwaves, refrigerators, VCP's. **Cards:** AE, CB, DI, DS, JCB, MC, VI.   ⌚ Ⓓ ⊗

**HOWARD JOHNSON**
Rates Subject to Change
Phone: 814/864-4811

| | | | | | |
|---|---|---|---|---|---|
| All Year | 1P: $49- 86 | 2P/1B: $59- 96 | 2P/2B: $54- 96 | XP: $10 | F17 |

**Location:** Jct I-90 exit 6 & SR 19. 7575 Peach St 16509. **Fax:** 814/864-4811. **Terms:** Sr. discount; credit card guarantee, 4 day notice; pets. **Facility:** 111 rooms. 2 stories; interior corridors; meeting rooms; heated indoor pool, wading pool, sauna. **Dining:** Restaurant nearby. **Services:** data ports; valet laundry; airport transportation. **All Rooms:** free & pay movies. **Some Rooms:** microwaves, radios, refrigerators. **Cards:** AE, CB, DI, DS, MC, VI.   ⌚ Ⓓ ⊗

**KNIGHTS INN**
Rates Subject to Change
Phone: 814/868-0879

| | | | | | |
|---|---|---|---|---|---|
| 5/1-10/31 & 4/15-4/30 [CP] | 1P: $39 | 2P/1B: $45 | 2P/2B: $46 | XP: $6 | F18 |
| 11/1-4/14 [CP] | 1P: $36 | 2P/1B: $41 | 2P/2B: $43 | XP: $6 | F18 |

**Location:** On SR 97, at I-90 exit 7. 7455 Schultz Rd 16509. **Fax:** 814/866-5974. **Terms:** Check-in 4 pm; credit card guarantee; pets. **Facility:** 104 rooms. 11 efficiencies, $9-$12 extra for up to 2 persons; 1 story; exterior corridors; meeting rooms; small pool. **Dining:** Restaurant nearby. **All Rooms:** free movies, cable TV. **Some Rooms:** 11 efficiencies. Fee: VCP's. **Cards:** AE, DI, DS, MC, VI.   Ⓓ ⊗

**MICROTEL ERIE**
Rates Subject to Change
Phone: 814/864-1010

| | | | | |
|---|---|---|---|---|
| 7/1-8/31 | 1P: $46 | 2P/1B: $50 | XP: $4 | F18 |
| 5/1-6/30 | 1P: $40 | 2P/1B: $44 | XP: $4 | F18 |
| 11/1-4/30 | 1P: $33 | 2P/1B: $37 | XP: $4 | F18 |
| 9/1-10/31 | 1P: $40 | 2P/1B: $44 | XP: $4 | F18 |

**Location:** 1/4 mi s on SR 19 from I-90 exit 6. 8100 Peach St 16509. **Fax:** 814/866-6661. **Terms:** Reserv deposit; small pets only. **Facility:** 101 rooms. 3 stories; interior corridors. **Dining:** Restaurant nearby. **Services:** data ports; valet laundry. **All Rooms:** free & pay movies, cable TV. **Cards:** AE, CB, DI, DS, MC, VI.   Roll in showers. Ⓓ Ⓢ ⊗

**RAMADA INN**

| | | 1P: | | | 2P/1B: | | 2P/2B: | | XP: | |
|---|---|---|---|---|---|---|---|---|---|---|
| 5/15-9/15 | | $49- | 59 | | $59- | 72 | $64- | 75 | $8 | F16 |
| 9/16-12/31 | | $45- | 50 | | $50- | 55 | $55- | 60 | $8 | F16 |
| 5/1-5/14 & 1/1-4/30 | | $40- | 45 | | $45- | 50 | $50- | 55 | $8 | F16 |

Rates Subject to Change   Phone: 814/825-3100

Motor Inn   **Location:** On SR 8, at I-90 exit 8. 6101 Wattsburg Rd 16509. Fax: 814/825-0857. **Terms:** Reserv deposit, 3 day notice; weekly/monthly rates; pets, $5. **Facility:** 122 rooms. 2 stories; interior corridors; business center, meeting rooms; heated pool, wading pool; playground. **Dining:** Dining room; 6:30 am-2 & 5-10 pm; $6-$13; cocktails. **Services:** data ports, PC, secretarial services. Fee: coin laundry. **All Rooms:** free movies. **Some Rooms:** Fee: VCP's. **Cards:** AE, CB, DI, DS, MC, VI.   ⒟ ⊗

**RED ROOF INN**

| | 1P: | | 2P/1B: | | 2P/2B: | | XP: | |
|---|---|---|---|---|---|---|---|---|
| 7/1-8/31 | $56 | | $64 | | $70 | | $8 | F18 |
| 5/1-6/30 & 9/1-9/30 | $39 | | $47 | | $53 | | $8 | F18 |
| 10/1-12/31 & 1/1-4/30 | $33 | | $41 | | $44 | | $8 | F18 |

Rates Subject to Change   Phone: 814/868-5246

Motel   **Location:** On SR 97, at I-90 exit 7. 7865 Perry Hwy 16509. Fax: 814/868-5450. **Terms:** Credit card guarantee; small pets only. **Facility:** 110 rooms. 2 stories; interior/exterior corridors. **Dining:** Restaurant nearby. **All Rooms:** free movies, cable TV. **Cards:** AE, CB, DI, DS, MC, VI.   ⒟ ⊗

**RESIDENCE INN BY MARRIOTT**   Phone: 814/864-2500

Suite Motel   Under construction; **Location:** Exit 6, off I-90; 1/8 mi s. 8061 Peach St 16509. **Facility:** 78 rooms. Rating withheld pending completion of construction December, 1994. **All Rooms:** cable TV.

**SPENCER HOUSE BED & BREAKFAST**

| | | 1P: | | 2P/1B: | | 2P/2B: | | XP: | |
|---|---|---|---|---|---|---|---|---|---|
| 5/15-10/15 [BP] | | $75- | 130 | $75- | 130 | $75- | 130 | $15 | F10 |
| 5/1-5/14 & 10/16-4/30 [BP] | | $65- | 120 | $65- | 120 | $65- | 130 | $15 | F10 |

Rates Subject to Change   Phone: 814/456-5091

Bed &   **Location:** W of downtown on 6th St. 519 W 6th St 16507. Fax: 814/456-5019. **Terms:** Reserv deposit, 7 day
Breakfast   notice; weekly/monthly rates; small pets only. **Facility:** 5 rooms. 3 stories; interior corridors; smoke free premises. **Services:** data ports; guest laundry. **All Rooms:** combo & shower baths, cable TV, VCP's, no A/C. **Cards:** AE, DS, MC, VI.   ⒟ ⊗

## RESTAURANTS

**THE MARKETPLACE GRILL**   **Dinner:** $11-$20   Phone: 814/455-7272

American   **Location:** 3 blks s of public docks. 319 State St 16507. **Hours:** 11:30 am-10 pm. Fri & Sat-11 pm. Closed major holidays & Sun. **Reservations:** accepted. **Features:** casual dress; children's menu; early bird specials; senior's menu; health conscious menu items; carryout; cocktails & lounge; street parking; a la carte. Casual dining in renovated factory. Validated parking in Hamot Parking on 3rd St. **Cards:** AE, DI, DS, MC, VI.

**THE OLIVE GARDEN ITALIAN RESTAURANT**   **Dinner:** $11-$20   Phone: 814/866-1105

Italian   **Location:** 1 1/4 mi n I-90 exit 6. 5945 Peach St 16509. **Hours:** 11 am-10 pm, Fri & Sat-11 pm. Closed: 11/23 & 12/25. **Reservations:** accepted. **Features:** casual dress; children's menu; health conscious menu items; carryout; cocktails & lounge; a la carte. **Cards:** AE, DI, DS, MC, VI.

**PUFFERBELLY RESTAURANT**   **Dinner:** $11-$20   Phone: 814/454-1557

American   **Location:** 3 blks se of public dock. 414 French St 16507. **Hours:** 11 am-10 pm, Fri & Sat-midnight, Sun-8 pm. **Reservations:** accepted. **Features:** casual dress; children's menu; health conscious menu items; carryout; cocktails & lounge; a la carte. Historic 1907 fire station. **Cards:** AE, MC, VI.   ⊗

# ESSINGTON (See PHILADELPHIA & VICINITY ACCOMMODATIONS spotting map pages A196 & A197; see index starting on page A193)

## LODGINGS

**COMFORT INN AIRPORT**   Guaranteed Rates   Phone: 610/521-9800   **74**

| | | 1P: | | 2P/1B: | | 2P/2B: | | XP: | |
|---|---|---|---|---|---|---|---|---|---|
| All Year [CP] | | $59- | 119 | $59- | 119 | $59- | 119 | $5 | F18 |

Motel   **Location:** On SR 291, just s of jct SR 420, 1/4 mi s of I-95 Essington exit SR 420. 53 Industrial Hwy 19029. Fax: 610/521-4847. **Terms:** Sr. discount; credit card guarantee; small pets only, $5. **Facility:** 150 rooms. Comfortably decorated units & public areas with contemporary decor. 5 stories; interior corridors; meeting rooms; exercise room. **Dining:** Restaurant nearby. **Services:** data ports; health club privileges; valet laundry; airport transportation. **All Rooms:** free & pay movies, cable TV. **Some Rooms:** Fee: microwaves, refrigerators, whirlpools. **Cards:** AE, CB, DI, DS, JCB, MC, VI. *(See ad p A200)*   ⒟ Ⓢ ⊗

**HOLIDAY INN-AIRPORT**   Guaranteed Rates   Phone: 610/521-2400   **71**

| | 1P: | | 2P/1B: | | 2P/2B: | | XP: | |
|---|---|---|---|---|---|---|---|
| Mon-Thurs | $89 | | $89 | | $89 | | $10 | F |
| Fri-Sun | $79 | | $79 | | $79 | | $10 | F |

Motor Inn   **Location:** On SR 291 at jct SR 420; 1/4 mi se of I-95, Essington 420 exit 9A. 45 Industrial Hwy 19029. Fax: 610/521-1605. **Terms:** Sr. discount; pets. **Facility:** 303 rooms. 6 stories; interior corridors; conference facilities; pool; exercise room. **Dining & Entertainment:** Dining room, coffee shop; 5:30 am-2 & 5-10 pm, Sat & Sun from 7 am; $13-$18; cocktails/lounge. **Services:** secretarial services; valet laundry; airport transportation. **All Rooms:** coffeemakers, free & pay movies, cable TV. **Cards:** AE, CB, DI, DS, MC, VI. *(See color ad p A186)*   🖻 ⒟ ⊗

**RAMADA INN-PHILADELPHIA INTERNATIONAL AIRPORT**   Rates Subject to Change   Phone: 610/521-9600   **70**

| | 1P: | | 2P/1B: | | 2P/2B: | | |
|---|---|---|---|---|---|---|---|
| All Year | $49- | 109 | $49- | 109 | $49- | 109 | |

Hotel   **Location:** I-95, exit 9A; 1/2 mi w on SR 291. 76 Industrial Blvd 19029. Fax: 610/521-9388. **Terms:** Credit card guarantee; weekly/monthly rates; package plans; pets. **Facility:** 292 rooms. 7 stories; interior corridors; conference facilities; putting green; heated pool; exercise room. **Dining & Entertainment:** Dining room; 6 am-10 pm; $10-$17; cocktails/lounge. **Services:** data ports; valet laundry; area transportation, within 15 mi, airport transportation. **All Rooms:** free movies, cable TV. **Some Rooms:** coffeemakers, radios, refrigerators. **Cards:** AE, CB, DI, DS, JCB, MC, VI. *(See color ad p A187)*   🖻 ⒟ ⊗

**RED ROOF INN-AIRPORT**   Rates Subject to Change   Phone: 610/521-5090   **73**

| | 1P: | | 2P/1B: | | 2P/2B: | | XP: | |
|---|---|---|---|---|---|---|---|
| All Year | $56 | | $56 | | $56- | 62 | $6 | F18 |

Motel   **Location:** On SR 291, just s of jct SR 420; 1/4 mi se of I-95, Essington SR 420 exit 9A. 49 Industrial Hwy 19029. Fax: 610/521-5090. **Terms:** Credit card guarantee; small pets only. **Facility:** 134 rooms. 2-3 stories; exterior corridors; meeting rooms. **Dining:** Restaurant nearby. **Services:** data ports. **All Rooms:** free movies, cable TV. **Cards:** AE, CB, DI, DS, MC, VI.   🖻 ⒟ ⊗

## RESTAURANT

**THE LOGOON RESTAURANT & NITE CLUB**   **Dinner:** $11-$20   Phone: 610/521-3636   **117**

Seafood   **Location:** 5 blks s of I-95, exit 9A, on SR 420. 101 Taylor Ave 19029. **Hours:** 11 am-11 pm. Closed: 12/25. **Reservations:** suggested. **Features:** casual dress; carryout; cocktails & lounge; entertainment; fee for valet parking; a la carte. Lively atmosphere. Luncheon buffet. **Cards:** AE, DI, DS, MC, VI.   ⊗

## EVANS CITY—2,000 (See PITTSBURGH ACCOMMODATIONS spotting map page A207; see index starting on page A206)

### RESTAURANT

**CRANBERRY HALL FAMILY RESTAURANT**  **Dinner:** $11-$20  **Phone:** 412/776-9930  (72)
American
**Location:** In Evans City on US 19; 1 mi w of I-79, 1 mi n of I-76 exit 3. 16033. **Hours:** 4 pm-8:30 pm, Sat from 4 pm, Sun from noon. **Closed:** Mon & 12/25. **Features:** casual dress; children's menu; carryout; a la carte. Dinners cheerfully served in pleasant surroundings. Smoke free premises. **Cards:** DS, MC, VI.

## EXETER

### LODGING

**DUTCH COLONY INN**  Rates Subject to Change  **Phone:** 610/779-2345

| | | | | | | | | | |
|---|---|---|---|---|---|---|---|---|---|
| 5/1-11/30 | 1P: | $58- | 73 | | | 2P/2B: | $63- | 78 | XP: $5 F18 |
| 12/1-4/30 | 1P: | $51- | 66 | | | 2P/2B: | $56- | 71 | XP: $5 F18 |

Motor Inn
**Location:** On US 422 1/4 mi e of jct US 422 business route. (4635 Perkiomen Ave). Fax: 610/779-8348. **Terms:** Sr. discount; credit card guarantee; weekly rates; small pets only, $5. **Facility:** 77 rooms. Nicely landscaped grounds. Comfortable guest rooms. 2-3 stories; interior/exterior corridors; meeting rooms; heated pool; exercise room, playground. **Dining & Entertainment:** Restaurant; 7 am-10 pm, Sun 7 am-1 pm; 1/1-3/30 7 am-9 pm, Mon & Sat from 8 am, Sun 8 am-1 pm; $6-$15; cocktails/lounge. **Services:** Fee: coin laundry. **All Rooms:** free movies, cable TV. **Some Rooms:** microwaves, radios, refrigerators. Fee: VCP's. **Cards:** AE, CB, DI, DS, MC, VI.
*(See color ad p A216)*

## EXTON

### LODGINGS

**DULING-KURTZ HOUSE & COUNTRY INN**  Rates Subject to Change  **Phone:** 610/524-1830

| | | | | | | | | | |
|---|---|---|---|---|---|---|---|---|---|
| Fri & Sat [CP] | 1P: | $80- | 120 | 2P/1B: | $80- | 120 | 2P/2B: | $80- | 120 XP: $15 |
| Sun-Thurs [CP] | 1P: | $55- | 79 | 2P/1B: | $55- | 79 | 2P/2B: | $55- | 79 XP: $15 |

Country Inn
**Location:** 1 mi w on SR 30, from jct with SR 100, 1/2 mi s on Whitford Rd. 146 S Whitford Rd 19341. Fax: 610/524-6258. **Terms:** Age restrictions may apply; reserv deposit; no pets. **Facility:** 14 rooms. Historical country inn named after Edith-Duling Carr & Lena Kurtz-Knour. 3 stories; interior corridors; meeting rooms. **Dining & Entertainment:** Dining room; 11:30 am-2 & 5-10 pm, Sun 3 pm-8:30 pm; $15-$24; cocktails/lounge. **Services:** valet laundry. **All Rooms:** free movies, combo & shower baths, cable TV. **Cards:** AE, DI, DS, MC, VI.

**HOLIDAY INN EXPRESS**  AAA Special Value Rates  **Phone:** 610/524-9000

| | | | | | | | |
|---|---|---|---|---|---|---|---|
| All Year [CP] | 1P: | $65 | | 2P/1B: | $70 | 2P/2B: | $70 XP: $5 F18 |

Motel
**Location:** Jct US 30 & SR 100, 4 mi s of PA Tpk, exit 23. 120 N Pottstown Pike 19341. Fax: 610/524-7259. **Terms:** Credit card guarantee; pets. **Facility:** 124 rooms. Comfortably furnished guest rooms. 4 stories; interior corridors; meeting rooms; pool; exercise room. **Dining:** Restaurant nearby. **Services:** data ports; valet laundry. **All Rooms:** cable TV. Fee: movies. **Some Rooms:** Fee: microwaves, refrigerators. **Cards:** AE, CB, DI, DS, JCB, MC, VI.

### RESTAURANT

**CHINA ROYAL**  **Dinner:** $11-$20  **Phone:** 610/363-1553
Chinese
**Location:** Jct US 30 & SR 100, 4 mi s of PA Tpk, exit 23. 201-30 W Lincoln Hwy 19341. **Hours:** 11:30 am-9:30 pm, Sat-10 pm, Sun noon-9 pm. **Closed:** 11/23 & 12/25. **Reservations:** suggested. **Features:** casual dress; a la carte. Attractive restaurant, with an extensive menu selection. **Cards:** AE, DI, DS, MC, VI.

## FAIRFIELD—500

### RESTAURANT

**THE HISTORIC FAIRFIELD INN**  Historical  **Dinner:** $11-$20  **Phone:** 717/642-5410
American
**Location:** Center, on SR 116. 15 W Main St 17320. **Hours:** 11 am-2 & 5-8:30 pm. Closed major holidays, Sun & Mon. **Reservations:** suggested; evenings. **Features:** casual dress; children's menu; carryout; cocktails & lounge; cafeteria. Historic inn circa 1757. Serving well-prepared food. 19th-century stagecoach stop frequented by Mamie Eisenhower. In operation since 1823. **Cards:** AE, MC, VI.

## FAIRVIEW

### LODGING

**BEST WESTERN-PRESQUE ISLE COUNTRY INN**  Rates Subject to Change  **Phone:** 814/838-7647

| | | | | | | | |
|---|---|---|---|---|---|---|---|
| 7/1-9/10 | 1P: | $52- | 62 | 2P/2B: | $62- | 72 | XP: $6 F16 |
| 5/1-6/30 | 1P: | $36- | 46 | 2P/2B: | $46- | 56 | XP: $6 F16 |
| 9/11-4/30 | 1P: | $28- | 38 | 2P/2B: | $38- | 48 | XP: $6 F16 |

Motor Inn
**Location:** I-90, exit 5; 1/4 mi s on SR 832. 6467 Sterrettania Rd 16415. Fax: 814/838-7647. **Terms:** Sr. discount; reserv deposit, 10 day notice; no pets. **Facility:** 120 rooms. 17 efficiencies, no utensils; 2 stories; interior corridors; meeting rooms; heated pool. **Dining & Entertainment:** Dining room; 6 am-2 & 5-9 pm; $7-$14; cocktails/lounge; entertainment. **All Rooms:** free movies. **Some Rooms:** 8 efficiencies. **Cards:** AE, DI, DS, MC, VI.

## FAIRVILLE

### LODGING

**FAIRVILLE INN**  Rates Subject to Change  **Phone:** 610/388-5900

| | | | | | | | |
|---|---|---|---|---|---|---|---|
| All Year [CP] | 1P: | $100- | 175 | 2P/1B: | $100- | 175 | 2P/2B: | $100- 175 XP: $10 |

Country Inn
**Location:** 2 mi s on SR 52 from US 1. Rt 52 19357 (PO Box 219, MENDENHALL). Fax: 610/388-5902. **Terms:** Age restrictions may apply; reserv deposit; no pets. **Facility:** 15 rooms. Charming country inn. Some rooms with fireplace. 2 stories; interior/exterior corridors. **Services:** valet laundry. **All Rooms:** cable TV. **Cards:** AE, DS, MC, VI.

# FARMINGTON

## LODGING

**SUMMIT INN RESORT**   Rates Subject to Change   **Phone:** 412/438-8594
5/1-11/1   1P: $60- 71  2P/1B: $70- 81  2P/2B: $86- 96  XP: $10  F12
**Location:** 5 1/2 mi e on US 40; adjacent to Laurel Caverns. US 40, 2 Skyline Dr 15437. Fax: 412/438-3917.
**Terms:** Open 5/1-11/1; check-in 4 pm; reserv deposit, 4 day notice; BP, MAP available; package plans; 2 night min stay, weekends; small pets only. **Facility:** 94 rooms. Scenic mountain view. Mostly furnished rooms in beautiful alpine-style resort. Spectacular mountain setting. 4 stories; interior corridors; meeting rooms; 2 pools (1 heated, 1 indoor), whirlpools; 2 lighted tennis courts; exercise room, indoor recreation area, volleyball, shuffleboard. Fee: 9 holes golf. **Dining:** Restaurant; 8 am-11, noon-2 & 6-8:30 pm; $12-$16. **Services:** childcare. Fee: airport transportation. **Recreation:** social program 7/1-9/7; hiking trails. **All Rooms:** free movies, cable TV. **Some Rooms:** refrigerators. Fee: VCP's. **Cards:** AE, DS, MC, VI. *(See ad below)*   Ⓓ Ⓢ ⊗

*Resort*
*Country Inn*

## RESTAURANT

**THE GOLDEN TROUT**   **Dinner:** $21-$30   **Phone:** 412/329-8555
**Location:** In Nemacolin Woodlands. 15437. **Hours:** 6 pm-10 pm, Sun 11 am-2 & 6-10 pm. No children under 12 after 6 pm. **Reservations:** suggested. **Features:** Sunday brunch; cocktails; valet parking; area transportation; a la carte. Fine dining in elegant surroundings. **Cards:** AE, DI, MC, VI.   ⊗

*Continental*

# FAYETTEVILLE

## LODGING

**RITE SPOT MOTEL**   Guaranteed Rates   **Phone:** 717/352-2144
5/1-10/31 & 4/1-4/30   1P: $36   2P/1B: $39   2P/2B: $42   XP: $3
11/1-3/31   1P: $33   2P/1B: $36   2P/2B: $38   XP: $3
**Location:** On US 30; 5 1/2 mi e of jct I-81, exit 6. 5651 Lincoln Way E 17222. **Terms:** Reserv deposit, 7 day notice; weekly/monthly rates; small pets only, $1. **Facility:** 20 rooms. Clean & well maintained property. Restaurant on premises. 1 story; exterior corridors. **All Rooms:** cable TV. **Cards:** AE, MC, VI.   Ⓓ

*Motel*

# FLEETWOOD—3,400

## RESTAURANT

**MOSELEM SPRINGS INN**   **Dinner:** $11-$20   **Phone:** 610/944-8213
**Location:** On US 222 at jct SR 662. 19522. **Hours:** 11:30 am-9 pm, Fri & Sat-10 pm, Sun-8 pm. Closed: 12/24 & 12/25. **Reservations:** suggested. **Features:** casual dress; senior's menu; cocktails & lounge; also prix fixe. Colonial atmosphere of a country inn. Featuring a variety of country smoked meats, smoked on premises since 1852. **Cards:** AE, CB, DI, MC, VI.   ⊗

*American*

# FOGELSVILLE

## LODGINGS

**CLOVERLEAF MOTEL**   Rates Subject to Change   **Phone:** 610/395-3367
All Year   2P/1B: $39- 43  2P/2B: $39- 43  XP: $4  F12
**Location:** On SR 100, s of US 22, left first traffic light & immediate left on service road, at end of service road. 327 Star Rd 18051 (PO Box 213). **Terms:** Credit card guarantee; weekly rates; pets. **Facility:** 29 rooms. Spacious grounds. 1 story; exterior corridors. **Dining:** Restaurant nearby. **All Rooms:** combo & shower baths, cable TV. **Some Rooms:** coffeemakers, radios. **Cards:** AE, DS, MC, VI. *(See ad p A84)*   Ⓓ ⊗

*Motel*

**GLASBERN**   Rates Subject to Change   **Phone:** 610/285-4723
All Year [BP]   1P: $90- 235  2P/1B: $105- 235  2P/2B: $100- 170  XP: $15
**Location:** From US 22/I-78, exit 14B (SR 100); 1/4 mi n to first light turn left (w), on Main St, 1/2 mi w on Church St, 1/2 mi nw to Pack House Rd then 1 mi nw. 2141 Pack House Rd 18051. Fax: 610/285-2862.
**Terms:** Age restrictions may apply; check-in 4 pm; credit card guarantee, 7 day notice; no pets. **Facility:** 23 rooms. Renovated 19th-century bank barn on 110 acres transformed into an elegant country inn. 2-3 stories, no elevator; interior/exterior corridors; meeting rooms; heated pool; 2 mi hiking trail. **Dining:** Dining room; dinner by reservation, seating 6-8 pm; $18-$38. **Services:** valet laundry. **All Rooms:** free movies, refrigerators, combo & shower baths, cable TV, VCP's. **Some Rooms:** coffeemakers, microwaves, whirlpools. **Cards:** MC, VI.   Ⓓ ⊗

*Country Inn*

**HAMPTON INN-ALLENTOWN**   AAA Special Value Rates   **Phone:** 610/391-1500
All Year [CP]   1P: $60- 75  2P/1B: $60- 75  2P/2B: $60- 75
**Location:** Jct SR 100 & US 22/I-78; exit SR 100S, 1/4 mi; Wm Penn Business Center. 7471 Keebler Way 18106. Fax: 610/391-0386. **Terms:** No pets. **Facility:** 124 rooms. 5 stories; interior corridors; business center, meeting rooms; sauna; exercise room. **Services:** valet laundry; area transportation, within 15 mi. **Recreation:** jogging. **All Rooms:** free & pay movies, cable TV. **Some Rooms:** microwaves. Fee: refrigerators. **Cards:** AE, CB, DI, DS, MC, VI.   Ⓓ Ⓢ ⊗

*Motel*

**HOLIDAY INN CONFERENCE CENTER**   Rates Subject to Change   **Phone:** 610/391-1000
All Year   1P: $81- 85  2P/1B: $91- 95  2P/2B: $91   XP: $10  F18
**Location:** 1/4 mi s of jct I-78 exit 14A & 100S. 18002 (PO Box 22226, LEHIGH VALLEY). Fax: 610/391-1664. **Terms:** Sr. discount; reserv deposit, 3 day notice; no pets. **Facility:** 182 rooms. 3 stories; interior corridors; conference facilities; pool; exercise room. **Dining & Entertainment:** Dining room; 6:30 am-10 pm; $10-$15; cocktails/lounge; entertainment. **Services:** data ports; area transportation, within 10 mi, airport transportation. Fee: coin laundry. **All Rooms:** coffeemakers, free & pay movies, cable TV. **Some Rooms:** whirlpools. Fee: VCP's. **Cards:** AE, CB, DI, DS, JCB, MC, VI.   🆓 Ⓓ ⊗

*Motor Inn*

# FRACKVILLE—4,700

## LODGINGS

**CENTRAL MOTEL**  Guaranteed Rates  Phone: 717/874-3176
(AAA)  All Year  1P: $30  2P/2B: $34  XP: $3  F4
◆◆  **Location:** Off I-81 via exit 36W, 1/4 mi nw on SR 61, then 1/4 mi n on Altamont Blvd. 17931 (PO Box D).
Motel  **Terms:** Reserv deposit; CP available; no pets. **Facility:** 55 rooms. 1-2 stories; interior/exterior corridors.
**Dining:** Restaurant nearby. **All Rooms:** combo & shower baths, cable TV. **Cards:** AE, DS, MC, VI.  (D) ⊗

**ECONO LODGE**  Rates Subject to Change  Phone: 717/874-3838
(AAA)  All Year [CP]  1P: $30-  76  2P/1B: $35-  76  2P/2B: $35-  76  XP: $5  F18
◆◆  **Location:** On SR 61N, exit 36W off I-81. 501 S Middle St 17931. Fax: 717/874-4660. **Terms:** Sr. discount;
Motel  weekly rates; small pets only, $5. **Facility:** 39 rooms. 2 stories; exterior corridors. **Dining:** Restaurant
nearby. **All Rooms:** free movies, cable TV. **Cards:** AE, DI, DS, MC, VI.  ⊘ (D) ⊗

# FRANKLIN—4,100

## LODGINGS

**IDLEWOOD MOTEL**  Rates Subject to Change  Phone: 814/437-3003
(AAA)  All Year  1P: $25  2P/1B: $28  2P/2B: $31  XP: $2  F10
◆  **Location:** 1 1/2 mi s on US 62 & SR 8. 16323 (RD 2, Box 2). **Terms:** Reserv deposit; no pets. **Facility:** 17
Motel  rooms. 1 efficiency unit, $34 for 2 persons; exterior corridors; pool. **Dining:** Restaurant nearby.
**All Rooms:** combo & shower baths, cable TV. **Cards:** AE, DI, DS, MC, VI.  (D)

**THE INN AT FRANKLIN**  AAA Special Value Rates  Phone: 814/437-3031
(AAA)  All Year  1P: $60  2P/1B: $65  2P/2B: $70  XP: $5  F12
◆◆  **Location:** Center. 1411 Liberty St 16323. Fax: 814/432-7481. **Terms:** Reserv deposit, 3 day notice; $15
Motor Inn  service charge; weekly rates; small pets only. **Facility:** 85 rooms. 6 stories; interior corridors; meeting rooms.
**Dining:** Dining room; 6 am-2 & 5-10 pm; $8-$16; cocktails. **Services:** data ports; valet laundry; airport
transportation. **All Rooms:** cable TV. **Some Rooms:** coffeemakers. Fee: VCP's. **Cards:** AE, DI, DS, MC, VI.
(D) ⊗

**QUO VADIS BED & BREAKFAST**  Guaranteed Rates  Phone: 814/432-4208
(AAA)  All Year [BP]  1P: $60-  80  2P/1B: $60-  80  2P/2B: $80  XP: $10
◆◆  **Location:** Corner of 15th & Liberty sts. In historic district. 1501 Liberty St 16323. **Terms:** Credit card
Bed &  guarantee, 7 day notice; weekly rates; no pets. **Facility:** 6 rooms. Quiet relaxing atmosphere. Victorian el-
Breakfast  egance with heirloom antiques. 2 stories; interior corridors. **Services:** Fee: coin laundry. **All Rooms:** combo
& shower baths, no phones, no TVs. **Cards:** AE, MC, VI.  (D) ⊗

# FRAZER—1,400

## LODGINGS

**MCINTOSH INN OF MALVERN**  Rates Subject to Change  Phone: 610/651-0400
◆◆  All Year  1P: $50-  52  2P/1B: $57  2P/2B: $59  XP: $3  F18
Motel  **Location:** On US 30 at jct SR 29. One Moorehall Rd 19355. Fax: 610/647-9434. **Terms:** Sr. discount;
weekly rates; no pets. **Facility:** 91 rooms. 12 large rooms with microwave & refrigerator, $55.95-$72; 4 stories;
interior corridors. **Dining:** Restaurant nearby. **Services:** data ports; valet laundry. **All Rooms:** free movies, cable TV.
**Some Rooms:** radios. **Cards:** AE, CB, DI, MC, VI. *(See ad p A185)*  ⊘ (D) ⊗

**SHERATON GREAT VALLEY HOTEL**  Rates Subject to Change  Phone: 610/524-5500
◆◆◆  Sun-Thurs  1P: $85-  120  2P/1B: $85-  120  2P/2B: $85-  120  XP: $15  F17
Motor Inn  Fri & Sat  1P: $69-  79  2P/1B: $69-  79  2P/2B: $59-  69  XP: $15  F17
**Location:** On SR 30 & jct SR 202. 707 Lancaster Pike 19355. Fax: 610/524-1808. **Terms:** Check-in 4 pm;
credit card guarantee, 3 day notice; small pets only. **Facility:** 155 rooms. Restored 1763 limestone inn. Colonial theme. Presidential suite, $395 for up to 5 persons; drawing room suites, $175; 5 stories; interior corridors; conference facilities; heated
indoor pool, whirlpool; exercise room. **Dining & Entertainment:** Restaurant; 6:30 am-2 & 5:30-10:30 pm; $14-$24;
cocktails/lounge. **Services:** data ports; valet laundry. **All Rooms:** honor bars, coffeemakers, free & pay movies, cable TV.
**Some Rooms:** Fee: whirlpools. **Cards:** AE, DI, DS, MC, VI.  ⊘ (D) (S) ⊗

# FRYSTOWN

## LODGING

**MOTEL OF FRYSTOWN**  Guaranteed Rates  Phone: 717/933-4613
◆  All Year  1P: $30  2P/1B: $35  2P/2B: $40  XP: $5  F12
Motel  **Location:** Jct I-78 & SR 645 exit 2, 1/4 mi e on service road. 90 Fort Motel Dr 17067. **Terms:** Reserv
deposit; pets. **Facility:** 13 rooms. Located along busy highway. 1 story; exterior corridors.
**Dining:** Restaurant nearby. **All Rooms:** combo & shower baths. **Cards:** DS, MC, VI.  (D)

# GAP

## RESTAURANT

**BEECHTREE INN**  Dinner: $11-$20  Phone: 717/442-9000
(AAA)  **Location:** On US 30. 5267 Lincoln Hwy 17527. **Hours:** 11 am-9 pm. Closed: Mon, 1/1, 7/4 & 12/25.
**Reservations:** suggested. **Features:** casual dress; children's menu; carryout; cocktails & lounge; a la carte.
◆◆◆  Casual dining. Lunch menu served to 5 pm; lite fare menu avail Tues-Fri & Sun 5 pm-9 pm. **Cards:** CB, DI,
American  DS, MC, VI.  ⊗

# GETTYSBURG—7,000

## LODGINGS

**BALADERRY INN AT GETTYSBURG**  Guaranteed Rates  Phone: 717/337-1342
(AAA)  All Year [BP]  1P: $68-  85  2P/1B: $78-  95  2P/2B: $78-  95  XP: $15
◆◆◆  **Location:** 2 mi s on Baltimore St, right on McAllister Mill Rd, 1/2 mi left on Blacksmith Rd, just left on
Historic Bed  Hospital Rd. 40 Hospital Rd 17325. **Terms:** Sr. discount; reserv deposit, 5 day notice; 2 night min stay; no
& Breakfast  pets. **Facility:** 9 rooms. Attractive public area & well-maintained, spacious grounds. Located close to battle-
fields. 2 stories; interior corridors; designated smoking area; meeting rooms; 1 tennis court. **Services:** data
ports. **All Rooms:** combo & shower baths, no TVs. **Some Rooms:** phones, whirlpools. **Cards:** AE, DI, MC,
VI.  (D) ⊗

**BEST WESTERN GETTYSBURG HOTEL EST. 1797**     AAA Special Value Rates     **Phone:** 717/337-2000

| | | | | | | | | | |
|---|---|---|---|---|---|---|---|---|---|
| 6/26-9/6 | 1P: | $79- | 119 | 2P/1B: | $79- | 129 | 2P/2B: | $89- | 129 | XP: | $5 | F16 |
| 5/1-6/25 & 9/7-10/31 | 1P: | $69- | 109 | 2P/1B: | $69- | 119 | 2P/2B: | $79- | 119 | XP: | $5 | F16 |
| 11/1-4/30 | 1P: | $65- | 105 | 2P/1B: | $65- | 105 | 2P/2B: | $65- | 105 | XP: | $5 | F16 |

◆◆◆
Historic
Hotel

**Location:** Center. 1 Lincoln Sq 17325. **Fax:** 717/337-2075. **Terms:** Credit card guarantee, 3 day notice; no pets. **Facility:** 83 rooms. Completely restored historic hotel. 6 stories; interior corridors; meeting rooms; pool; 20 units with gas fireplace. **Dining:** Restaurant; 7:15 am-9:30 & 5-9 pm; $14-$15; cocktails. **Services:** health club privileges. **All Rooms:** cable TV. **Some Rooms:** whirlpools. Fee: refrigerators, VCP's. **Cards:** AE, CB, DI, DS, JCB, MC, VI. *(See color ad below)* Ⓓ Ⓢ ⊗

**BLUE SKY MOTEL**     Guaranteed Rates     **Phone:** 717/677-7736

| | | | | | |
|---|---|---|---|---|---|
| 6/9-9/3 | 2P/1B: | $48 | 2P/2B: | $49 | XP: | $4 |
| 5/1-6/8, 9/4-10/31 & 4/1-4/30 | 2P/1B: | $36 | 2P/2B: | $39 | XP: | $4 |
| 11/1-3/31 | 2P/1B: | $29 | 2P/2B: | $34 | XP: | $4 |

◆
Motel

**Location:** 4 1/2 mi n on SR 34. 2585 Biglerville Rd 17325. **Fax:** 717/677-6794. **Terms:** Reserv deposit; weekly rates; no pets. **Facility:** 16 rooms. 1 two-bedroom unit. 1 story; exterior corridors; heated pool; exercise room, playground. **All Rooms:** free movies, combo & shower baths, cable TV. **Some Rooms:** efficiency. Fee: microwaves, refrigerators. **Cards:** AE, CB, DI, DS, MC, VI. *(See color ad below)* Ⓓ

**BUDGET HOST THREE CROWNS MOTOR LODGE**     Rates Subject to Change     **Phone:** 717/334-3168

| | | | | | | | |
|---|---|---|---|---|---|---|---|
| 6/23-8/26 | 1P: | $69 | 2P/1B: | $69 | 2P/2B: | $69 | XP: | $5 |
| 6/1-6/22 & 8/27-10/21 | 1P: | $50 | 2P/1B: | $55 | 2P/2B: | $55 | XP: | $5 |
| 5/1-5/31 & 4/1-4/30 | 1P: | $45 | 2P/1B: | $50 | 2P/2B: | $50 | XP: | $5 |
| 10/22-3/31 | 1P: | $35 | 2P/1B: | $40 | 2P/2B: | $40 | XP: | $5 |

◆
Motel

**Location:** 1/2 mi s on US 15 (Business). 205 Steinwehr Ave 17325. **Terms:** Reserv deposit, 3 day notice; no pets. **Facility:** 29 rooms. Located along busy commercial highway. 1 story; exterior corridors; pool. **Dining:** Restaurant nearby. **All Rooms:** cable TV. **Some Rooms:** Fee: refrigerators. **Cards:** AE, DS, MC, VI. *(See color ad below & p A83)* Ⓓ ⊗

**COLLEGE MOTEL**  Rates Subject to Change  Phone: 717/334-6731

| | | | | | | | | | | | |
|---|---|---|---|---|---|---|---|---|---|---|---|
| 6/9-9/3 | | 2P/1B: | $68- | 76 | 2P/2B: | $68- | 76 | XP: | $5 | F17 |
| 5/1-6/8 & 9/4-10/28 | | 2P/1B: | $58- | 66 | 2P/2B: | $58- | 66 | XP: | $5 | F17 |
| 3/30-4/30 | | 2P/1B: | $49- | 58 | 2P/2B: | $49- | 58 | XP: | $5 | F17 |
| 10/29-3/29 | | 2P/1B: | $38- | 48 | 2P/2B: | $38- | 48 | XP: | $5 | F17 |

Motel

**Location:** 3 1/2 blks n on US 15 business route. 345 Carlisle St 17325. **Terms:** Sr. discount; reserv deposit; no pets. **Facility:** 21 rooms. Well-kept rooms. 1 story; exterior corridors; small pool. **All Rooms:** cable TV. **Some Rooms:** radios. **Cards:** AE, MC, VI. *(See ad p A121)*  Ⓓ

**COLONIAL MOTEL**  Rates Subject to Change  Phone: 717/334-3126

| | | | | | | | | | | | |
|---|---|---|---|---|---|---|---|---|---|---|---|
| 6/9-9/3 | | 2P/1B: | $64- | 72 | 2P/2B: | $64- | 72 | XP: | $5 | F17 |
| 5/1-6/8 & 9/4-10/28 | | 2P/1B: | $58- | 66 | 2P/2B: | $58- | 66 | XP: | $5 | F17 |
| 3/30-4/30 | | 2P/1B: | $49- | 58 | 2P/2B: | $49- | 58 | XP: | $5 | F17 |
| 10/29-3/29 | | 2P/1B: | $38- | 48 | 2P/2B: | $38- | 48 | XP: | $5 | F17 |

Motel

**Location:** 2 blks n on US 15 business route. 157 Carlisle St 17325. **Terms:** Sr. discount; reserv deposit; no pets. **Facility:** 30 rooms. Many rooms are attractively appointed. 2 stories; exterior corridors. **All Rooms:** cable TV. **Cards:** AE, MC, VI. *(See ad p A121)*  Ⓓ Ⓧ

**COMFORT INN**  AAA Special Value Rates  Phone: 717/337-2400

| | | | | | | | | | | | |
|---|---|---|---|---|---|---|---|---|---|---|---|
| 6/12-9/6 | 1P: | $67- | 79 | 2P/1B: | $77- | 89 | 2P/2B: | $77- | 89 | XP: | $6 | F18 |
| 5/1-6/11 & 9/7-10/31 | 1P: | $51- | 63 | 2P/1B: | $61- | 75 | 2P/2B: | $61- | 75 | XP: | $6 | F18 |
| 4/1-4/30 | 1P: | $47- | 57 | 2P/1B: | $57- | 72 | 2P/2B: | $57- | 72 | XP: | $6 | F18 |
| 11/1-3/31 | 1P: | $40- | 45 | 2P/1B: | $45- | 51 | 2P/2B: | $45- | 51 | XP: | $6 | F18 |

Motel

**Location:** On US 30, 2 1/2 mi e. 871 York Rd 17325. Fax: 717/337-1400. **Terms:** Reserv deposit; no pets. **Facility:** 81 rooms. Commercial location. Battlefield tours from the motel. 2 stories; interior corridors; heated indoor pool, whirlpool. **Dining:** Restaurant nearby. **All Rooms:** free movies, cable TV. **Some Rooms:** microwaves, radios, refrigerators, whirlpools. **Cards:** AE, CB, DI, DS, JCB, MC, VI. *(See color ad below)*  Ⓓ Ⓢ Ⓧ

**CRITERION MOTOR LODGE**  Rates Subject to Change  Phone: 717/334-6268

| | | | | | | | | | | | |
|---|---|---|---|---|---|---|---|---|---|---|---|
| 6/9-9/3 | | 2P/1B: | $56- | 64 | 2P/2B: | $60- | 68 | XP: | $5 | F17 |
| 5/1-6/8 & 9/4-10/28 | | 2P/1B: | $54- | 60 | 2P/2B: | $56- | 62 | XP: | $5 | F17 |
| 3/31-4/30 | | 2P/1B: | $47- | 56 | 2P/2B: | $49- | 58 | XP: | $5 | F17 |
| 10/29-11/19 | | 2P/1B: | $38- | 46 | 2P/2B: | $38- | 48 | XP: | $5 | F17 |

Motel

**Location:** 3 blks n on US 15 (Business). 337 Carlisle St 17325. **Terms:** Sr. discount; Open 5/1-11/19 & 3/31-4/30; reserv deposit. **Facility:** 14 rooms. Located along busy commercial highway. 1 story; exterior corridors. **All Rooms:** cable TV. **Some Rooms:** radios. **Cards:** AE, MC, VI.  Ⓓ

**DAYS INN GETTYSBURG**  Rates Subject to Change  Phone: 717/334-0030

| | | | | | | | | | | | |
|---|---|---|---|---|---|---|---|---|---|---|---|
| 6/8-9/3 & 9/29-10/31 | 1P: | $70- | 85 | 2P/1B: | $80- | 95 | 2P/2B: | $80- | 95 | XP: | $5 | F18 |
| 5/1-6/7 & 9/4-9/28 | 1P: | $61- | 71 | 2P/1B: | $71- | 81 | 2P/2B: | $71- | 81 | XP: | $5 | F18 |
| 4/1-4/30 | 1P: | $56- | 66 | 2P/1B: | $66- | 76 | 2P/2B: | $66- | 76 | XP: | $5 | F18 |
| 11/1-3/31 | 1P: | $48- | 50 | 2P/1B: | $53- | 55 | 2P/2B: | $53- | 55 | XP: | $5 | F18 |

Motel

**Location:** On US 30, 2 1/2 mi e. 865 York Rd 17325. Fax: 717/337-1002. **Terms:** Sr. discount; credit card guarantee; package plans; no pets. **Facility:** 113 rooms. Tastefully furnished rooms. 5 stories; interior corridors; meeting rooms; pool; exercise room. **Dining:** Restaurant nearby. **Services:** area transportation. Fee: coin laundry. **All Rooms:** free movies, cable TV. **Some Rooms:** Fee: refrigerators, VCP's. **Cards:** AE, CB, DI, DS, JCB, MC, VI.  Ⓓ Ⓢ Ⓧ
*(See ad p A121)*

**ECONO LODGE**  AAA Special Value Rates  Phone: 717/334-6715

| | | | | | | | | | | | |
|---|---|---|---|---|---|---|---|---|---|---|---|
| 6/9-9/4 | 1P: | $65- | 76 | 2P/1B: | $69 | | 2P/2B: | $76 | | XP: | $5 | F18 |
| 9/29-10/28 | 1P: | $52- | 66 | 2P/1B: | $57- | 62 | 2P/2B: | $61- | 66 | XP: | $5 | F18 |
| 5/1-6/8, 9/5-9/28 & 4/28-4/30 | 1P: | $48- | 62 | 2P/1B: | $52- | 58 | 2P/2B: | $57- | 62 | XP: | $5 | F18 |
| 10/29-4/27 | 1P: | $33 | | 2P/1B: | $36 | | 2P/2B: | $39 | | XP: | $5 | F18 |

Motel

**Location:** 1/2 mi s on SR 97. 945 Baltimore Pike 17325. Fax: 717/334-6580. **Terms:** Reserv deposit; 2 night min stay; no pets. **Facility:** 42 rooms. Weekend rates 5/1-6/9 & 9/7-10/31; 2 stories; interior/exterior corridors; pool. **Dining:** Restaurant nearby. **All Rooms:** cable TV. **Some Rooms:** radios. Fee: VCP's. **Cards:** AE, CB, DI, DS, MC, VI.  Ⓓ Ⓧ
*(See color ad below)*

**FARNSWORTH HOUSE INN**  Guaranteed Rates  Phone: 717/334-8838

| | | | | | | | | |
|---|---|---|---|---|---|---|---|---|
| 5/1-11/6 & 3/16-4/30 [BP] | 1P: | $65- | 75 | 2P/1B: | $75- | 85 | | |
| 11/7-3/15 [BP] | 1P: | $55- | 65 | 2P/1B: | $65- | 75 | XP: | $10 |

Historic Bed & Breakfast

**Location:** 4 blks s on US 15 business route. 401 Baltimore St 17325. **Terms:** Age restrictions may apply; credit card guarantee, 3 day notice; no pets. **Facility:** 4 rooms. Circa 1810. Individually decorated rooms in Victorian style; 19th-century antiques. 3 stories; interior corridors; designated smoking area. **Dining:** Dining room, see separate listing. **All Rooms:** no phones, no TVs. **Cards:** AE, DS, MC, VI.  Ⓓ Ⓧ

**FRIENDSHIP INN PENN EAGLE**

⊛
◆◆
Motel

| | | | | | | | | | | | |
|---|---|---|---|---|---|---|---|---|---|---|---|
| 6/9-9/4 | 1P: | $65- | 70 | 2P/1B: | $65- | 70 | 2P/2B: | $70- | 74 | XP: $4 | F18 |
| 9/5-11/4 | 1P: | $50- | 66 | 2P/1B: | $56- | 66 | 2P/2B: | $63- | 68 | XP: $4 | F18 |
| 5/1-6/8 | 1P: | $50- | 64 | 2P/1B: | $56- | 60 | 2P/2B: | $60- | 64 | XP: $4 | F18 |
| 11/5-4/30 | 1P: | $37- | 40 | 2P/1B: | $37- | 40 | 2P/2B: | $40- | 45 | XP: $4 | F18 |

Rates Subject to Change          Phone: 717/334-1804

**Location:** 1 1/4 mi e on US 30. 1031 York Rd. **Terms:** Reserv deposit; no pets. **Facility:** 21 rooms. 2 stories; exterior corridors; pool. **Dining:** Restaurant nearby. **All Rooms:** free movies, cable TV. **Some Rooms:** radios, refrigerators. **Cards:** AE, DI, DS, MC, VI.  Ⓓ ⊗

**GASLIGHT INN**
Bed &
Breakfast

Rates Subject to Change          Phone: 717/337-9100

All Year [BP]          1P: $85- 110   2P/1B: $85- 110   2P/2B: $95          XP: $20
Too new to rate; **Location:** Downtown. 33 E Middle St 17325. **Terms:** age restrictions may apply; reserv deposit, 7 day notice; no pets. **Facility:** 8 rooms. Rating withheld pending completion of construction. Scheduled to open in the fall. 3 stories, no elevator; interior corridors; smoke free premises. **Dining:** Restaurant nearby. **Services:** health club privileges. **All Rooms:** combo & shower baths, cable TV. **Some Rooms:** VCP's, whirlpools. **Cards:** AE, DS, MC, VI.          Roll in showers. Ⓓ ⊗

**GETTYSTOWN INN BED & BREAKFAST**
◆◆
Bed &
Breakfast

Rates Subject to Change          Phone: 717/334-2100

5/1-11/30 & 3/1-4/30 [BP]          2P/1B: $85- 105          XP: $6
12/1-2/29 [BP]          2P/1B: $55- 75          XP: $6
**Location:** Adjacent to the Dobbin House Tavern; 1/2 blk n of jct SR 134 & US 15. 89 Steinwehr Ave 17325. Fax: 717/334-6905. **Terms:** Sr. discount; age restrictions may apply; reserv deposit; no pets. **Facility:** 5 rooms. Period antique furnishings. 2 stories; interior corridors; smoke free premises. **Dining & Entertainment:** Cocktail lounge; also, The Dobbin House Restaurant & Tavern (1776), see separate listing. **All Rooms:** refrigerators, no phones. **Some Rooms:** cable TV. **Cards:** AE, MC, VI. *(See ad p A121)*          Ⓓ

**HERITAGE MOTOR LODGE**

⊛
◆◆
Motel

| | | | | | | | | |
|---|---|---|---|---|---|---|---|---|
| 6/6-9/8 | 1P: | $45 | 2P/1B: | $48- | 50 | 2P/2B: | $50- | 56 |
| 5/11-6/5 & 9/9-11/20 | 1P: | $35 | 2P/1B: | $40- | 42 | 2P/2B: | $42- | 48 |
| 5/1-5/10 & 4/13-4/30 | 1P: | $32 | 2P/1B: | $38- | 40 | 2P/2B: | $40- | 44 |

Rates Subject to Change          Phone: 717/334-9281

**Location:** At jct US 15 Business Rt & SR 97. 64 Steinwehr Ave 17325. Fax: 717/334-6913. **Terms:** Sr. discount; Open 5/1-11/20 & 3/1-4/30; reserv deposit; small pets only, $4. **Facility:** 28 rooms. Close to battlefields. 4 two-bedroom units. 1 story; exterior corridors. **Dining:** Restaurant nearby. **All Rooms:** free movies, combo & shower baths, cable TV. **Cards:** AE, DS, MC, VI. *(See ad below)*          Ⓓ

**HERR TAVERN & PUBLICK HOUSE**
⊛
◆◆◆
Historic Bed
& Breakfast

AAA Special Value Rates          Phone: 717/334-4332

All Year          1P: $65- 170   2P/1B: $65- 170          XP: $10
**Location:** On Rt 30, 1 1/2 mi w. 900 Chambersburg Rd 17325. Fax: 717/334-3332. **Terms:** Age restrictions may apply; check-in 4 pm; reserv deposit, 14 day notice; weekly rates; BP available; no pets. **Facility:** 5 rooms. 3 stories, no elevator; interior corridors; designated smoking area. **Dining & Entertainment:** Cocktail lounge; dining room, see separate listing. **Services:** data ports. **All Rooms:** combo & shower baths, cable TV. **Some Rooms:** microwaves, refrigerators, VCP's, whirlpools. **Cards:** AE, DS, MC, VI.

*(See color ad below)*          Ⓓ ⊗

**HICKORY BRIDGE FARM BED & BREAKFAST**
◆◆◆
Cottage

Rates Subject to Change          Phone: 717/642-5261

Fri & Sat [BP]          1P: $60          2P/2B: $89
Sun-Thurs [BP]          1P: $50          2P/2B: $79
**Location:** S end of town. 96 Hickory Bridge Rd 17353. **Terms:** Reserv deposit, 7 day notice; 2 night min stay, weekends; no pets. **Facility:** 7 rooms. Cozy wooded rural farm location. All units with fireplace. 1 story; exterior corridors; smoke free premises. **Dining:** Restaurant, see separate listing. **Recreation:** fishing; bicycles. **All Rooms:** no phones, no TVs. **Some Rooms:** combo & shower baths, shared bathrooms. **Cards:** MC, VI.          Ⓓ

**HOLIDAY INN-BATTLEFIELD**

⊛
◆◆◆
Motor Inn

| | | | | | | | | | | | |
|---|---|---|---|---|---|---|---|---|---|---|---|
| 5/26-9/3 | 1P: | $88- | 98 | 2P/1B: | $88- | 98 | 2P/2B: | $88- | 98 | XP: $7 | F19 |
| 5/1-5/25 & 9/4-10/31 | 1P: | $78- | 88 | 2P/1B: | $78- | 88 | 2P/2B: | $78- | 88 | XP: $7 | F19 |
| 4/1-4/30 | 1P: | $68- | 78 | 2P/1B: | $68- | 78 | 2P/2B: | $68- | 78 | XP: $7 | F19 |
| 11/1-3/31 | 1P: | $49- | 59 | 2P/1B: | $49- | 59 | 2P/2B: | $49- | 59 | XP: $7 | F19 |

Rates Subject to Change          Phone: 717/334-6211

**Location:** At jct US 15 business route & SR 97. 516 Baltimore St 17325. Fax: 717/334-7183. **Terms:** Sr. discount; pets. **Facility:** 100 rooms. Downtown location. Weekend rates 4/1-10/31; 3 stories; exterior corridors; meeting rooms; pool. **Dining:** Restaurant; 7 am-10 pm, Sun 7 am-2 & 5-10 pm; $12-$19; cocktails; 24-hour room service. **Services:** data ports. **All Rooms:** free movies, cable TV. **Cards:** AE, CB, DI, DS, JCB, MC, VI. *(See ad p A121)*          Ⓓ ⊗

## HOLIDAY INN EXPRESS OF GETTYSBURG
Rates Subject to Change      Phone: 717/337-1400

| | | | | | | | | | | | |
|---|---|---|---|---|---|---|---|---|---|---|---|
| 6/12-9/6 [CP] | 1P: | $75- | 85 | 2P/1B: | $85- | 95 | 2P/2B: | $85- | 95 | XP: $10 | F20 |
| 5/1-6/11 & 9/7-10/31 [CP] | 1P: | $59- | 69 | 2P/1B: | $69- | 79 | 2P/2B: | $69- | 79 | XP: $10 | F20 |
| 4/1-4/30 [CP] | 1P: | $54- | 64 | 2P/1B: | $64- | 74 | 2P/2B: | $64- | 74 | XP: $10 | F20 |
| 11/1-3/31 [CP] | 1P: | $42- | 52 | 2P/1B: | $52- | 62 | 2P/2B: | $52- | 62 | XP: $10 | F20 |

Motel

**Location:** On US 30; 2 1/2 mi e. 869 York Rd 17325. **Fax:** 717/337-1400. **Terms:** Sr. discount; no pets. **Facility:** 51 rooms. Commercial location. Battlefield tours from motel. Weekend rates 4/1-9/5 $2 increase; 2 stories; interior corridors; heated indoor pool, whirlpool; exercise room. **All Rooms:** free movies, cable TV. **Some Rooms:** efficiency, no utensils, refrigerators. **Cards:** AE, CB, DI, DS, MC, VI. *(See color ad below)* Ⓓ Ⓢ ⊗

## HOMESTEAD MOTOR LODGE
Rates Subject to Change      Phone: 717/334-3866

| | | | | | | | | |
|---|---|---|---|---|---|---|---|---|
| 6/9-9/5 | | | 2P/1B: | $46- | 58 | 2P/2B: | $52- | 66 | XP: $8 |
| 5/1-6/8 & 9/6-11/30 | | | 2P/1B: | $38- | 46 | 2P/2B: | $44- | 58 | XP: $8 |

Motel

**Location:** On US 30, 1/2 mi e of jct US 15 bypass. 1650 York Rd 17325. **Terms:** Open 5/1-11/30; reserv deposit, 7 day notice; no pets. **Facility:** 10 rooms. Well-maintained property. 1 story; exterior corridors. **Some Rooms:** Fee: refrigerators. **Cards:** DS, MC, VI. Ⓓ ⊗

## HOWARD JOHNSON LODGE
Rates Subject to Change      Phone: 717/334-1188

| | | | | | | | | | | |
|---|---|---|---|---|---|---|---|---|---|---|
| 5/1-10/21 & 3/29-4/30 | 1P: | $51- | 66 | 2P/1B: | $57- | 72 | 2P/2B: | $57- | 72 | XP: $6 F17 |
| 10/22-3/28 | 1P: | $37- | 47 | 2P/1B: | $46- | 53 | 2P/2B: | $46- | 53 | XP: $6 F17 |

Motel

**Location:** 1 mi s on US 15 business route. 301 Steinwehr Ave 17325. **Fax:** 717/334-1103. **Terms:** Sr. discount; small pets only. **Facility:** 77 rooms. Variety of rooms. Some with balcony. Opposite Gettysburg visitor center. 2 stories; interior/exterior corridors; pool. **Dining & Entertainment:** Cocktail lounge; restaurant nearby. **All Rooms:** free movies, cable TV. **Some Rooms:** efficiency. **Cards:** AE, CB, DI, DS, MC, VI. *(See ad p 94)* Ⓓ ⊗

## THE OLD APPLEFORD INN
Rates Subject to Change      Phone: 717/337-1711

| | | | | | | | | |
|---|---|---|---|---|---|---|---|---|
| 5/1-12/31 & Fri & Sat | | | | | | | | |
| 1/1-4/30 [BP] | 1P: | $88- | 98 | 2P/1B: | $103- | 113 | 2P/2B: | $123 | XP: $15 |
| Sun-Thurs 1/1-4/30 [BP] | 1P: | $78- | 88 | 2P/1B: | $83- | 93 | 2P/2B: | $103 | XP: $10 |

Historic Bed & Breakfast

**Location:** 2 blks n on US 15 (business). 218 Carlisle St 17325. **Fax:** 717/334-6228. **Terms:** Age restrictions may apply; reserv deposit, 10 day notice; 2 night min stay, 5/1-10/31 weekends; no pets. **Facility:** 11 rooms. Victorian mansion; all rooms & public areas furnished with period antiques. Very nice antique camera collection & display. 3 stories, no elevator; interior corridors; smoke free premises. **All Rooms:** comb, shower & tub baths, no phones, no TVs. **Cards:** AE, DS, MC, VI. Ⓓ ⊗

## PERFECT REST MOTEL
Rates Subject to Change      Phone: 717/334-1345

| | | | | | | | | | | |
|---|---|---|---|---|---|---|---|---|---|---|
| 6/1-9/3 | 1P: | $50 | | 2P/1B: | $55 | | 2P/2B: | $60- | 64 | XP: $4 F10 |
| 5/10-5/31 & 9/4-10/31 | 1P: | $46 | | 2P/1B: | $50 | | 2P/2B: | $58 | | XP: $4 F10 |
| 5/1-5/9 & 3/29-4/30 | 1P: | $38- | 40 | 2P/1B: | $42- | 44 | 2P/2B: | $46- | 48 | XP: $4 F10 |
| 11/1-3/28 | 1P: | $34 | | 2P/1B: | $38 | | 2P/2B: | $42 | | XP: $4 F10 |

Motel

**Location:** 4 1/2 mi s on US 15 business route. 2450 Emmitsburg Rd 17325. **Terms:** Reserv deposit, 3 day notice; weekly rates; no pets. **Facility:** 25 rooms. Semi-rural location. 1 two-bedroom unit. 1 story; exterior corridors; pool. **All Rooms:** combo & shower baths, cable TV, no phones. **Cards:** AE, CB, DI, DS, MC, VI. *(See ad p A121)* Ⓓ ⊗

## QUALITY INN GETTYSBURG MOTOR LODGE
Rates Subject to Change      Phone: 717/334-1103

| | | | | | | | | | | |
|---|---|---|---|---|---|---|---|---|---|---|
| 5/1-10/21 & 3/29-4/30 | 1P: | $58- | 71 | 2P/1B: | $64- | 77 | 2P/2B: | $64- | 77 | XP: $6 F17 |
| 10/22-3/28 | 1P: | $39- | 52 | 2P/1B: | $48- | 58 | 2P/2B: | $48- | 58 | XP: $6 F17 |

Motel

**Location:** 1 mi s on US 15 business route. 380 Steinwehr Ave 17325. **Fax:** 717/334-1103. **Terms:** Sr. discount; small pets only. **Facility:** 104 rooms. Variety of rooms, attractive exterior. Adjacent to Gettysburg visitor center. 2 stories; exterior corridors; putting green; pool, sauna, whirlpool; exercise room. **Dining & Entertainment:** Cocktail lounge; restaurant nearby. **Services:** data ports. Fee: coin laundry. **All Rooms:** free movies, combo & shower baths, cable TV. **Some Rooms:** efficiency, kitchen, no utensils, refrigerators. **Cards:** AE, CB, DI, DS, MC, VI. *(See ad p 92)* Ⓓ ⊗

## QUALITY INN LARSON'S
Rates Subject to Change      Phone: 717/334-3141

| | | | | | | | |
|---|---|---|---|---|---|---|---|
| 6/2-9/3 | 1P: | $60 | 2P/1B: | $68 | 2P/2B: | $78 | XP: $5 F18 |
| Fri & Sat 5/1-6/1, 9/4-10/28 & 4/1-4/30 | 1P: | $56 | 2P/1B: | $64 | 2P/2B: | $72 | XP: $5 F18 |
| Sun-Thurs 5/1-6/1, 9/4-10/28 & 4/1-4/30 | 1P: | $52 | 2P/1B: | $56 | 2P/2B: | $62 | XP: $5 F18 |
| 10/29-3/31 | 1P: | $38 | 2P/1B: | $46 | 2P/2B: | $46 | XP: $5 F18 |

Motor Inn

**Location:** 3/4 mi w on US 30. 401 Buford Ave 17325. **Terms:** Sr. discount; credit card guarantee; no pets. **Facility:** 41 rooms. Exceptionally well maintained property. 1 story; exterior corridors; putting green; pool. **Dining:** Also, General Lee's Family Restaurant, see separate listing. **All Rooms:** cable TV. **Cards:** AE, CB, DI, DS, MC, VI. *(See ad p A121)* Ⓓ ⊗

## RAMADA INN-GETTYSBURG
Rates Subject to Change      Phone: 717/334-8121

| | | | | | | | | |
|---|---|---|---|---|---|---|---|---|
| 5/1-10/31 & 4/1-4/30 | 1P: | $87- | 130 | | | 2P/2B: | $87- | 130 | XP: $7 F18 |
| 11/1-3/31 | 1P: | $73- | 120 | | | 2P/2B: | $73- | 120 | XP: $7 F18 |

Motor Inn

**Location:** 5 mi s on US 15 Business Rt. 2634 Emmitsburg Rd 17325. **Fax:** 717/334-6066. **Terms:** Reserv deposit, 14 day notice; 2 night min stay; no pets. **Facility:** 203 rooms. Spacious grounds. Impressive courtyard setting. Very attractive public areas. 2 stories; interior corridors; conference facilities; putting green; heated indoor pool, sauna, whirlpools; racquetball courts, 2 tennis courts; exercise room. **Dining & Entertainment:** Restaurant, deli; 6:30 am-10 pm; $9-$18; cocktails/lounge; 24-hour room service. **Services:** Fee: coin laundry. **Recreation:** fishing. **All Rooms:** cable TV. Fee: movies. **Some Rooms:** coffeemakers, microwaves, refrigerators. **Cards:** AE, CB, DI, DS, MC, VI. Ⓓ ⊗

## RESTAURANTS

**THE DOBBIN HOUSE RESTAURANT & TAVERN (1776)** Historical   **Dinner:** $11-$20   **Phone:** 717/334-2100
Ⓐ   **Location:** In Gettystown Inn Bed & Breakfast. #89 Steinwehr Ave 17325. **Hours:** 11:30 am-10 pm tavern, dining room 5 pm-9 pm. **Closed:** 1/1, 11/23, 12/24 & 12/25. **Reservations:** suggested; in dining room.
◆◆   **Features:** casual dress; children's menu; cocktails & lounge; cafeteria. Early-American fare served in
American   authentic colonial tavern. Sandwich menu at lunch. **Cards:** AE, MC, VI. *(See ad p A121)*   ⊗

**FARNSWORTH HOUSE** Historical   **Dinner:** $11-$20   **Phone:** 717/334-8838
Ⓐ   **Location:** In Farnsworth House Inn. 401 Baltimore St 17325. **Hours:** 5 pm-9:30 pm. **Closed:** 1/1, 11/23 &
12/25. **Reservations:** suggested. **Features:** casual dress; children's menu; cocktails & lounge; cafeteria.
◆◆   Civil War period house with summer garden. **Cards:** AE, DS, MC, VI.   ⊗
American

**GENERAL LEE'S FAMILY RESTAURANT**   **Dinner:** $11-$20   **Phone:** 717/334-2200
Ⓐ   **Location:** In Quality Inn Larson's. 401 Buford Ave 17325. **Hours:** 7 am-9 pm. **Closed:** 12/25.
◆◆   **Features:** casual dress; children's menu; cocktails & lounge; cafeteria. Early American ambience with many
antiques & Civil War relics. **Cards:** AE, DS, MC, VI. *(See ad p A121)*   ⊗
American

**THE HERR TAVERN & PUBLICK HOUSE** Historical   **Dinner:** $11-$20   **Phone:** 717/334-4332
Ⓐ   **Location:** In Herr Tavern & Publick House. 900 Chambersburg Rd 17325. **Hours:** 11 am-9 pm, Sat from
11:30 am, Sun from 5 pm. **Closed:** 1/1, 12/24 & 12/25. **Reservations:** suggested; weekends.
◆◆◆   **Features:** casual dress; children's menu; cocktails & lounge; cafeteria. Relaxed dining in comfortable
American   atmosphere of 1816 public house. Adjacent to battlefield. **Cards:** AE, DS, MC, VI.
*(See color ad p A122)*   ⊗

**HICKORY BRIDGE FARM RESTAURANT**   **Dinner:** $11-$20   **Phone:** 717/642-5261
◆◆   **Location:** In Hickory Bridge Farm Bed & Breakfast. 96 Hickory Bridge Rd 17353. **Hours:** 5 pm-8 pm, Sun
American   noon-3 pm. **Closed:** Mon-Thurs. **Reservations:** suggested. **Features:** casual dress; children's menu; health
conscious menu items; cafeteria. Farm-style service; 140 year-old barn. Smoking not permitted. Price
includes choice of appetizers, salads, entrees, beverage & dessert, all homemade. Smoke free premises. **Cards:** MC, VI.   ⊗

## GIBSONIA (See PITTSBURGH ACCOMMODATIONS spotting map page A207; see index starting on page A206)

## LODGING

**COMFORT INN NORTH**   Rates Subject to Change   **Phone:** 412/444-8700   **⑩⑨**
◆◆   All Year [CP]   1P: $46- 55   2P/1B:   $52- 60   2P/2B:   $54- 60   XP: $6   F18
Motel   **Location:** Exit 4 off I-76 tpk, 1/8 mi n on Rt 8. 5137 Rt 8 15044. Fax: 412/444-8727. **Terms:** Sr. discount;
reserv deposit; no pets. **Facility:** 63 rooms. 3 stories; exterior corridors. **Services:** valet laundry.
**All Rooms:** cable TV. **Cards:** AE, DI, DS, JCB, MC, VI.   Ⓓ Ⓢ ⊗

## GINTHER

## LODGING

**PINES MOTEL**   Rates Subject to Change   **Phone:** 717/668-0100
Ⓐ   Fri & Sat 5/1-10/31   1P: $35- 45   2P/1B:   $38- 45   2P/2B:   $45- 55   XP: $4
Sun-Thurs 5/1-10/31   1P: $35   2P/1B:   $38   2P/2B:   $38   XP: $4
◆   11/1-4/30   1P: $28   2P/1B:   $32   2P/2B:   $38   XP: $4
Motel   **Location:** 2 mi s on SR 309 from I-81 exit 39 (McAdoo). SR 309 18252 (RD 4 Box 349A, TAMAQUA).
**Terms:** Sr. discount; reserv deposit; weekly/monthly rates; no pets. **Facility:** 20 rooms. 1 story; exterior corri-
dors; pool. **All Rooms:** free movies, combo & shower baths, cable TV. **Some Rooms:** radios. **Cards:** AE, DS, MC, VI.   Ⓓ

## GLEN ROCK—1,700

## LODGING

**ROCKY RIDGE MOTEL**   Guaranteed Rates   **Phone:** 717/235-5646
Ⓐ   5/1-10/31 & 4/1-4/30   1P: $30   2P/1B:   $34   2P/2B:   $38   XP: $2   F6
11/1-3/31   1P: $28   2P/1B:   $32   2P/2B:   $36   XP: $2   F6
◆   **Location:** At exit 2, I-83. Rt 216, Seaks Run Rd 17327 (RD 2, Box 243). **Terms:** Sr. discount; reserv
Motel   deposit, 7 day notice; weekly rates; small pets only, $3. **Facility:** 18 rooms. Rural setting. RV sites avail.
Waterbed, $37; 2 stories; exterior corridors. **Dining:** Restaurant nearby. **All Rooms:** combo & shower baths,
cable TV. **Some Rooms:** coffeemakers, refrigerators. **Cards:** AE, DI, DS, MC, VI.   Ⓓ ⊗

## GLENSIDE (See PHILADELPHIA & VICINITY ACCOMMODATIONS spotting map pages A196 & A197; see index starting on page A193)

## RESTAURANT

**ALFIO'S RESTAURANT**   **Dinner:** $11-$20   **Phone:** 215/885-3787   **⑰③**
◆◆   **Location:** PA Turnpike, exit 27 (Willow Grove), 5 mi s on Easton Rd, 1/2 mi w on Glenside, 2 blks n on
Italian   Limekiln Pike. 15 Limekiln Pike 19038. **Hours:** 11:30 am-10 pm, Fri-11 pm, Sat 4 pm-11 pm, Sun 4 pm-9
pm. **Closed** major holidays, Mon & 8/27-9/11. **Reservations:** suggested; weekends. **Features:** casual dress;
health conscious menu; carryout; cocktails. Pasta, seafood & veal entrees. Ceasar salad is a specialty. **Cards:** AE, DI, DS,
MC, VI.   ⊗

## GRANTVILLE—800

## LODGINGS

**ECONO LODGE**   Rates Subject to Change   **Phone:** 717/469-0631
Ⓐ   5/1-9/30 & 4/1-4/30   1P: $45- 65   2P/1B:   $45- 75   2P/2B:   $45- 75   XP: $5   F18
10/1-3/31   1P: $40- 50   2P/1B:   $40- 50   2P/2B:   $40- 50   XP: $5   F18
◆◆   **Location:** I-81, exit 28. 17028 (RD 1, Box 5005). Fax: 717/469-0843. **Terms:** Sr. discount; reserv deposit;
Motel   CP available; no pets. **Facility:** 100 rooms. Busy commercial location. Convenient interstate access. 4 rooms
with whirlpool $70-$110 for 2 persons; 3 stories; exterior corridors. **All Rooms:** free movies, cable TV.
**Some Rooms:** refrigerators. Fee: VCP's. **Cards:** AE, CB, DI, DS, MC, VI.   Ⓓ ⊗

**HOLIDAY INN HARRISBURG-HERSHEY AREA, I-81**   Rates Subject to Change   **Phone: 717/469-0661**

◆◆◆ Motor Inn

| | | | | | |
|---|---|---|---|---|---|
| Fri & Sat 6/30-9/3 | 1P: $118- | 170 | 2P/2B: $128- | 170 | XP: $10 F18 |
| Sun-Thurs 6/30-9/3 | 1P: $108- | 160 | 2P/2B: $118- | 160 | XP: $10 F18 |
| 5/1-6/29 & 9/4-10/28 | 1P: $105- | 160 | 2P/2B: $100- | 160 | XP: $10 F18 |
| 10/29-4/30 | 1P: $95- | 150 | 2P/2B: $100- | 150 | XP: $10 F18 |

**Location:** At I-81, exit 28. 17028 (PO Box 179). Fax: 717/469-7755. **Terms:** Sr. discount; reserv deposit, 3 day notice; BP, CP available; pets. **Facility:** 195 rooms. Busy commercial location. Convenient interstate access. 4 stories; interior corridors; conference facilities; 2 pools (2 heated, 1 indoor), sauna, whirlpool; exercise room. **Dining & Entertainment:** Dining room, restaurant; 6:30 am-10 pm; $7-$20; cocktails/lounge; 24-hour room service; entertainment. **Services:** data ports. Fee: coin laundry. **All Rooms:** coffeemakers, free & pay movies, combo & shower baths, cable TV. **Some Rooms:** refrigerators, whirlpools. **Cards:** AE, CB, DI, DS, JCB, MC, VI. *(See ad p A138 & p A132)*   Roll in showers. &#x1F6BF; &#x24D3; &#x2297;

## GREENCASTLE—3,600

### LODGING

**COMFORT INN**   AAA Special Value Rates   **Phone: 717/597-8164**

&#x24D3;

◆◆◆ Motor Inn

| | | | | | | |
|---|---|---|---|---|---|---|
| All Year [CP] | 1P: $46- | 51 | 2P/1B: $54- | 59 | 2P/2B: $54- | 59 XP: $6 F18 |

**Location:** At jct I-81 & US 11E, I-81 exit 2. 50 Pine Dr 17225. Fax: 717/597-5050. **Terms:** No pets. **Facility:** 71 rooms. Convenient to interstate with sports activities. 3 stories; interior corridors; meeting rooms; saunas, whirlpools; health club, aerobics instruction. Fee: racquetball courts. **Dining:** Dining room; 6 am-10 pm; $5-$14; 24-hour room service. **Recreation:** jogging. **All Rooms:** free & pay movies, cable TV. Fee: VCP. **Cards:** AE, CB, DI, DS, JCB, MC, VI.   &#x24D3; &#x2297;

### RESTAURANT

**ANTRIM HOUSE**   Dinner: up to $10   **Phone: 717/597-8111**

&#x24D3;

◆◆ American

**Location:** I-81, exit 3; 1 mi w on SR 16. 104 E Baltimore St 17725. **Hours:** 6 am-9 pm. Closed: 1/1, 12/24, 12/25 & 12/31. **Features:** casual dress; children's menu; carryout; salad bar; buffet. Homestyle cooking for both buffet items & plate items. Homemade desserts & pies. Sat breakfast buffet. **Cards:** AE, DS, MC, VI.   &#x2297;

## GREENSBURG—16,300

### LODGINGS

**COMFORT INN**   AAA Special Value Rates   **Phone: 412/832-2600**

&#x24D3;

◆◆◆ Motel

| | | | | | | |
|---|---|---|---|---|---|---|
| 5/1-5/25 & 9/10-4/30 [CP] | 1P: $64- | 84 | 2P/1B: $69- | 94 | 2P/2B: $69- | 94 XP: $5 F18 |
| 5/26-9/9 [CP] | 1P: $59- | 84 | 2P/1B: $64- | 84 | 2P/2B: $59- | 84 XP: $5 F18 |

**Location:** 3 mi e on US 30 on hilltop opposite Eastgate Shopping Center. 1129 E Pittsburgh St 15601. Fax: 412/834-3442. **Terms:** No pets. **Facility:** 77 rooms. Very upscale public areas. All rooms are well-appointed. 3 stories; interior corridors; meeting rooms; heated pool. **Dining:** Restaurant nearby. **Services:** data ports; valet laundry. **All Rooms:** free movies, cable TV. **Some Rooms:** radios, refrigerators, whirlpools. Fee: microwaves, VCP's. **Cards:** AE, CB, DI, DS, JCB, MC, VI.   &#x24D3; &#x24C8; &#x2297;

**KNIGHTS INN-GREENSBURG**   Guaranteed Rates   **Phone: 412/836-7100**

&#x24D3;

◆◆ Motel

| | | | | | |
|---|---|---|---|---|---|
| All Year | 1P: $47 | 2P/1B: $53 | 2P/2B: $57 | XP: $6 F18 |

**Location:** At US 119 & US 30 bypass. 1215 S Main St 15601. Fax: 412/837-5390. **Terms:** Sr. discount; reserv deposit; weekly/monthly rates; no pets. **Facility:** 110 rooms. Attractive landscaping. 11 efficiencies, $6 extra for up to 2 persons; 1 story; exterior corridors; meeting rooms; small pool. **Dining:** Restaurant nearby. **Services:** Fee: coin laundry. **All Rooms:** free & pay movies, cable TV. **Some Rooms:** refrigerators. Fee: VCP's. **Cards:** AE, CB, DI, DS, MC, VI.   &#x24D3; &#x2297;

**MOUNTAIN VIEW INN**　　　　Rates Subject to Change　　　　Phone: 412/834-5300
All Year　　1P: $55- 110　2P/1B: $63- 119　2P/2B: $88- 112　XP: $8 F16
Location: 4 1/2 mi e on US 30. 1001 Village Dr 15601. Fax: 412/834-5304. Terms: Sr. discount; reserv
Country Inn　deposit; monthly rates; no pets. Facility: 56 rooms. Restored 1924 historic motor inn with antiques, hand-
somely appointed rooms & a modern newer section. 2 stories; interior corridors; meeting rooms; heated pool.
Dining & Entertainment: Dining room; 6:30 am-9 pm, Fri & Sat-10 pm, Sun 7:30 am-8 pm; $12-$22;
cocktails/lounge. All Rooms: free movies, cable TV. Cards: AE, CB, DI, DS, MC, VI. *(See color ad p A125)*　(D)(S)

### RESTAURANT

**VALLOZZI'S**　　　　　　Dinner: $11-$20　　　　　　Phone: 412/836-7663
Italian　　Location: 3 mi e, on US 30. 15601. Hours: 11 am-10 pm, Fri-11 pm, Sat 4 pm-11 pm. Closed major
holidays & Sun. Reservations: suggested; weekends. Features: casual dress; children's menu; cocktails &
lounge. Northern Italian specialties & seafood. Relaxed dining. Cards: AE, DI, MC, VI.

## GREENTREE—4,900　(See PITTSBURGH ACCOMMODATIONS spotting map page A207; see index starting on page A206)

### LODGINGS

**BEST WESTERN-PARKWAY CENTER INN**　Rates Subject to Change　Phone: 412/922-7070　46
Sun-Thurs　1P: $75- 95　2P/1B: $81- 99　2P/2B: $81- 99　XP: $9 F12
Fri & Sat　1P: $60- 70　2P/1B: $60- 70　2P/2B: $60- 70　XP: $9 F12
Motel　Location: 3 mi sw via I-279, 1/2 mi nw of I-279, northbound exit 4 & Greentree Rd, southbound
exit 5 & Parkway Center Dr. 875 Greentree Rd 15220. Fax: 412/922-4949. Terms: Sr. discount; pets, $25
dep req. Facility: 138 rooms. 6 stories; interior corridors; meeting rooms; heated indoor pool, saunas; exercise
room, men's steamroom. Services: data ports; airport transportation. Fee: coin laundry. All Rooms: free movies, cable TV.
Some Rooms: coffeemakers, 44 efficiencies, microwaves, refrigerators. Cards: AE, CB, DI, DS, MC, VI.

**HAMPTON INN HOTEL GREENTREE**　Rates Subject to Change　Phone: 412/922-0100　49
Motel　All Year [CP]　1P: $64- 69　2P/1B: $69- 74　2P/2B: $71- 73
Location: 3 mi sw via I-279, US 22 & 30, exit 4, 1 mi nw via Mansfield Ave. 555 Trumbull Dr 15205.
Fax: 412/922-0100. Terms: Reserv deposit; pets. Facility: 133 rooms. 6 stories; interior corridors; meeting
rooms. Services: valet laundry; airport transportation. All Rooms: free movies. Cards: AE, CB, DI, DS, JCB, MC, VI.
(D)(S)

**HAWTHORN SUITES HOTEL**　　AAA Special Value Rates　　Phone: 412/279-6300　50
Apartment　All Year [CP]　1P: $119　2P/1B: $119　2P/2B: $149
Motel　Location: 3 mi sw via I-279, US 22 & 30, exit 4; 1 1/2 mi nw via Mansfield Ave. 700 Mansfield Ave 15205.
Fax: 412/279-4993. Terms: Credit card guarantee; weekly/monthly rates; pets, $6, $50 dep req. Facility: 152
rooms. In quiet area. 1 & 2-bedroom units with living room & kitchen; many with fireplace. 2 stories; exterior
corridors; meeting rooms; heated pool, whirlpool; sports court. Services: data ports. Fee: coin laundry.
All Rooms: coffeemakers, microwaves, free movies, refrigerators, cable TV. Cards: AE, CB, DI, DS, JCB, MC, VI.　(D)

**PITTSBURGH GREEN TREE MARRIOTT**　Rates Subject to Change　Phone: 412/922-8400　45
Hotel　Sun-Thurs　1P: $107　2P/1B: $107　2P/2B: $107　XP: $15 F18
Fri & Sat　1P: $67　2P/1B: $67　2P/2B: $67　XP: $15 F18
Location: 3 mi sw via I-279, US 22 & 30; exit 4, 1 mi nw via Mansfield Ave. 101 Marriott Dr 15205.
Fax: 412/922-8981. Terms: Reserv deposit, 3 day notice; 15% service charge; monthly rates; package plans; weekend rates
available; small pets only. Facility: 467 rooms. 5 stories; interior corridors; conference facilities; convention oriented; luxury
level rooms; 3 pools (2 heated, 1 indoor/outdoor), sauna, whirlpool; 2 lighted tennis courts, racquet club privileges; exercise
room. Dining & Entertainment: Dining room, coffee shop; 6:30 am-midnight, snack menu-2 am; $10-$25; cocktails/lounge;
entertainment. Services: data ports, secretarial services; valet laundry; airport transportation. All Rooms: free & pay
movies. Some Rooms: honor bars, coffeemakers. Fee: refrigerators, VCP's. Cards: AE, CB, DI, DS, MC, VI.　(D)

### RESTAURANT

**PICCOLO MONDO**　　　Dinner: $11-$20　　　Phone: 412/922-0920　44
Location: Exit 4 (Greentree) off I-279, n on route 121 to Mansfield Ave, 3/4 m to Anderson Dr. 661 Andersen
Dr 15220. Hours: 11:30 am-10 pm, Fri-11 pm, Sat 4 pm-11 pm. Closed major holidays & Sun.
Reservations: required; for 6 or more. Features: carryout; cocktails & lounge; cafeteria. Varied menu in a
Northern　relaxing atmsophere. Cards: AE, DI, DS, MC, VI.
Italian

## GROVE CITY—8,200

### LODGINGS

**LYNNROSE BED & BREAKFAST**　　Guaranteed Rates　　Phone: 412/458-6425
Bed &　All Year [BP]　1P: $50- 65　2P/1B: $50- 65　2P/2B: $50- 65　XP: $10 F9
Breakfast　Location: 2 blks s of downtown. 114 W Main St 16127. Terms: Sr. discount; reserv deposit; no pets.
Facility: 5 rooms. 2 stories; interior corridors; smoke free premises. All Rooms: coffeemakers, free movies,
combo & shower baths, no phones. Some Rooms: A/C, cable TV. Cards: DS, MC, VI.　(D)

**SNOW GOOSE INN**　　　Rates Subject to Change　　　Phone: 412/458-4644
All Year [BP]　1P: $55　2P/1B: $55　2P/2B: $55　XP: $5
Location: Across from entrance to Grove City College. 112 E Main St 16127. Terms: Reserv deposit;
weekly rates; no pets. Facility: 4 rooms. 2 stories; interior corridors. All Rooms: no phones, no TVs.
Bed &　Cards: MC, VI.　(D)
Breakfast

## GWYNEDD

### RESTAURANT

**WILLIAM PENN INN**　　　Dinner: $21-$30　　　Phone: 215/699-9272
Continental　Location: At jct US 202 & Sumneytown Pike. 1017 Dekalb Pl 19436. Hours: 11:30 am-2 & 5-10 pm, Sat
11:30 am-2 & 4:30-10 pm, Sun 10:30 am-8 pm. Closed: 12/25. Reservations: suggested; weekends.
Features: formal attire; children's menu; early bird specials; health conscious menu; carryout; cocktails &
lounge; a la carte. Long established; serving extensive menu of international dishes. Sun brunch, 10:30 am-2:30 pm. Smoke
free premises. Cards: AE, CB, DI, DS, MC, VI.

# HALLSTEAD—1,300

## LODGING

**COLONIAL BRICK MOTEL**  Rates Subject to Change  **Phone:** 717/879-2162
All Year  1P: $36- 49  2P/1B: $44- 55  2P/2B: $44- 55  XP: $7  D12
**Location:** On US 11, at jct I-81, Great Bend-Hallstead exit 68. 18822 (PO Box AD). Fax: 717/879-2162.
Motel  **Terms:** Reserv deposit; weekly/monthly rates; package plans; no pets. **Facility:** 54 rooms. 2 stories; interior corridors; meeting rooms. **Dining:** Restaurant nearby. **All Rooms:** cable TV. **Some Rooms:** 7 efficiencies, radios. **Cards:** AE, DS, MC, VI. *(See color ad below)*  (D) ⊗

# HAMLIN—800   (See POCONO MOUNTAINS & VICINITY ACCOMMODATIONS spotting map pages A212 & A213; see index starting on page A210)

## LODGING

**COMFORT INN**  Rates Subject to Change  **Phone:** 717/689-4148  55
5/12-10/31 [CP]  1P: $59- 94  2P/1B: $58- 94  2P/2B: $68- 94  XP: $7  F17
5/1-5/11 & 11/1-4/30 [CP]  1P: $46- 69  2P/1B: $49- 74  2P/2B: $58- 79  XP: $7  F17
◆◆◆  **Location:** I-84, exit 5; 1/8 mi n. 18436 (RD 5, LAKE ARIEL). Fax: 717/698-3043. **Terms:** Sr. discount; reserv
Motel  deposit; weekly/monthly rates; package plans; pets, $5. **Facility:** 124 rooms. Immaculate rooms in Pocono Mountain area. 2 stories; interior corridors; meeting rooms; sauna; whirlpool; exercise room. **Dining &**
**Entertainment:**  Cocktails/lounge; restaurant nearby. **Services:** Fee: coin laundry. **All Rooms:** cable TV.
**Some Rooms:** honor bars, refrigerators, whirlpools. Fee: VCP's. **Cards:** AE, CB, DI, DS, JCB, MC, VI.
*(See color ad below)*  (D) ⊗

# HANOVER—3,500

## LODGING

**BEECHMONT INN**  Guaranteed Rates  **Phone:** 717/632-3013
◆◆◆  All Year [BP]  1P: $80- 135  2P/1B: $80- 135  2P/2B: $95  XP: $10
Historic Bed  **Location:** 3 blks n on SR 194 from SR 94. 315 Broadway 17331. Fax: 717/632-3988. **Terms:** Age
& Breakfast  restrictions may apply; reserv deposit, 3 day notice; package plans; no pets. **Facility:** 7 rooms. 1830 home with Federal period ambience. 2 stories; interior corridors. **Dining:** Restaurant nearby. **All Rooms:** combo & shower baths. **Some Rooms:** refrigerators, cable TV, whirlpools. **Cards:** AE, DI, MC, VI.  (D)

# HARFORD

## LODGING

**9 PARTNERS INN BED & BREAKFAST**  Guaranteed Rates  **Phone:** 717/434-2233
◆◆  All Year [BP]  1P: $85  2P/1B: $85  2P/2B: $85
Historic Bed  **Location:** I-81, exit 65; 2 1/2 mi s on SR 547. 1 N Harmony Rd 18823 (PO Box 300). Fax: 717/434-2801.
& Breakfast  **Terms:** Age restrictions may apply; reserv deposit, 14 day notice; weekly rates; package plans; 2 night min stay, on weekends; no pets. **Facility:** 3 rooms. 3 stories, no elevator; interior corridors; smoke free premises.
**All Rooms:** combo & shower baths, no A/C, no TVs. **Some Rooms:** phones. **Cards:** AE, DS, MC, VI.  (D) ⊗

# HARLANSBURG

## RESTAURANT

**THE VILLAGE INN**  Historical  **Dinner:** $11-$20  **Phone:** 412/654-6851
◆◆  **Location:** On SR 108, 3 mi w of I-79 exit 30, at jct US 19. RD 1, Box 316 New Castle 16101. **Hours:** 4
American  pm-8 pm, Sun noon-7 pm. Closed: Mon & Tues. **Reservations:** suggested; weekends. **Features:** children's menu; beer only; a la carte. Country style dining in restored country home. Smoke free premises.
**Cards:** MC, VI.  ⊗

# HARMARVILLE   (See PITTSBURGH ACCOMMODATIONS spotting map page A207; see index starting on page A206)

## LODGINGS

**COMFORT INN**  AAA Special Value Rates  **Phone:** 412/828-9400  96
Motel  All Year [CP]  1P: $58  2P/1B: $64  2P/2B: $64  XP: $6
Too new to rate; **Location:** 1/8 mi s jof Pa Tpk, exit 5, on Freeport Rd. 10 Landings Dr 15238. **Terms:** no pets. **Facility:** 63 rooms. 1 story; heated indoor pool; video game room. **All Rooms:** cable TV.  (D) ⊗

**SUPER 8 MOTEL**  **Phone:** 412/828-8900  97
Motel  Under construction; **Location:** 1/8 mi s of Pa Tpk, exit 5, on Freeport Rd. 8 Landings Dr 15238. **Terms:** no pets. **Facility:** 61 rooms. Scheduled to open November, 1994. 1 story.  (D)

(See **PITTSBURGH ACCOMMODATIONS** spotting map page A207)

## RESTAURANT

**BOB EVANS**
◆
American
**Dinner:** up to $10                    Phone: 412/828-2004  ⑥⓪
**Location:** Exit 5 off PA Tpk, 1/2 mi w on SR 28. 1 Mariner Ct 15238. **Hours:** 6 am-10 pm, Fri & Sat-11:30 pm. **Closed:** 11/23 & 12/25. **Features:** children's menu; carryout; a la carte. Family dining, also serving breakfast. **Cards:** MC, VI.  ⊗

# HARRISBURG—52,400   (See HARRISBURG ACCOMMODATIONS spotting map page A129; see index below)

To help you more easily locate accommodations in the Harrisburg area, the following index and map show lodgings and restaurants in multiple cities. Listings for these establishments are found under the heading for the city in which they are located. The Harrisburg area comprises: Enola, Harrisburg and New Cumberland.

### Index of Establishments on the HARRISBURG ACCOMMODATIONS Spotting Map

## LODGINGS

**BEST WESTERN CAPITAL PLAZA**        Rates Subject to Change                Phone: 717/545-9089  ㊲
🏨
◆◆
Motel

| | | 1P: | $45 | 2P/1B: | $49 | 2P/2B: | $53 | XP: | $4 | F18 |

**All Year**
**Location:** I-81; exit 24. 150 Nationwide Dr 17110. Fax: 717/545-7926. **Terms:** Sr. discount; reserv deposit, 7 day notice; small pets only. **Facility:** 121 rooms. Located along busy interstate highway. 3 stories; interior/exterior corridors; meeting rooms. **Dining:** Restaurant nearby. **Services:** Fee: coin laundry. **All Rooms:** free movies, cable TV. **Some Rooms:** refrigerators. **Cards:** AE, CB, DI, DS, JCB, MC, VI.  ⒟⊗

**BEST WESTERN COUNTRY OVEN**        Rates Subject to Change                Phone: 717/652-7180  ㊶
🏨
◆◆◆
Motor Inn

| | | | | | | | | | | |
|---|---|---|---|---|---|---|---|---|---|---|
| 6/3-11/4 | 1P: | $73- | 83 | 2P/1B: | $73- | 83 | 2P/2B: | $73- | 83 | XP: $3 F13 |
| 5/1-6/2 | 1P: | $61- | 71 | 2P/1B: | $61- | 71 | 2P/2B: | $66- | 76 | XP: $3 F13 |
| 11/5-4/30 | 1P: | $51- | 57 | 2P/1B: | $56- | 66 | 2P/2B: | $61- | 71 | XP: $3 F13 |

**Location:** At I-81, exit 26W. 300 N Mountain Rd 17112. Fax: 717/541-8991. **Terms:** Sr. discount; reserv deposit, 3 day notice; weekly/monthly rates; pets. **Facility:** 49 rooms. Attractive public areas, gardens in back. 2 stories; interior corridors. **Dining & Entertainment:** Coffee shop; $10-$20; cocktails/lounge; also, Country Oven Restaurant, see separate listing. **All Rooms:** free movies, cable TV. **Cards:** AE, CB, DI, DS, MC, VI.
*(See color ad p A130)*                                                                            ⒟⊗

**BEST WESTERN HOTEL CROWN PARK**      Rates Subject to Change                Phone: 717/558-9500  ㊵
🏨
◆◆◆
Motor Inn

| | | 1P: | $79- | 99 | 2P/1B: | $89- | 109 | 2P/2B: | $89- | 109 | XP: $10 | F18 |

**All Year**
**Location:** I-283, exit 1 & SR 441. 765 Eisenhower Blvd 17111. Fax: 717/558-8956. **Terms:** Sr. discount; reserv deposit, 3 day notice; pets. **Facility:** 167 rooms. Very attractive & well-appointed rooms. 6 stories; interior corridors; meeting rooms; heated pool, sauna, whirlpool; exercise room. **Dining & Entertainment:** Dining room; 6-10 am, 11-1:30 & 4:30-10 pm; $8-$14; health conscious menu items; cocktails/lounge. **Services:** data ports; valet laundry; airport transportation. **All Rooms:** coffeemakers, free & pay movies, cable TV. **Some Rooms:** Fee: microwaves, refrigerators. **Cards:** AE, CB, DI, DS, JCB, MC, VI.  ⒟Ⓢ⊗

**BUDGETEL INN**                Guaranteed Rates                Phone: 717/540-9339  ⓯
🏨
◆◆◆
Motel

| | | 1P: | $51- | 59 | 2P/1B: | $59- | 69 | 2P/2B: | $59- | 69 |

**All Year [CP]**
**Location:** I-81, exit 26E. 200 N Mountain Rd 17112. Fax: 717/540-9486. **Terms:** Sr. discount; pets. **Facility:** 67 rooms. 3 stories; interior corridors; meeting rooms. **Dining:** Restaurant nearby. **Services:** data ports. Fee: coin laundry. **All Rooms:** coffeemakers, free movies, cable TV. **Some Rooms:** microwaves, refrigerators. **Cards:** AE, CB, DI, DS, MC, VI.  ⒟Ⓢ⊗

**BUDGETEL INN**                Rates Subject to Change                Phone: 717/939-8000  ㉑
◆◆
Motel

| | | 1P: | $42- | 53 | 2P/1B: | $49- | 60 | 2P/2B: | $52 |

**All Year [CP]**
**Location:** I-283, exit 1; 1 mi s of jct I-83 & US 322. 990 Eisenhower Blvd 17111. Fax: 717/939-0500. **Terms:** Sr. discount; small pets only. **Facility:** 114 rooms. Located near Harrisburg International Airport. Rates for up to 4 persons; 3 stories; interior corridors; meeting rooms. **Dining:** Restaurant nearby. **Services:** data ports. Fee: coin laundry, airport transportation. **All Rooms:** coffeemakers, free & pay movies, cable TV. **Some Rooms:** microwaves, refrigerators. **Cards:** AE, CB, DI, DS, MC, VI.  ⒟Ⓢ⊗

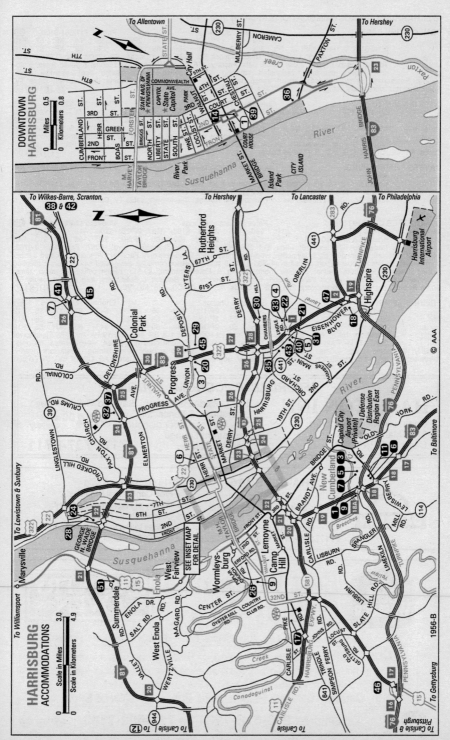

**(See HARRISBURG ACCOMMODATIONS spotting map page A129)**

**COMFORT INN EAST**    AAA Special Value Rates    Phone: 717/561-8100   ⑳

6/1-10/31 [CP]   1P: $62- 67   2P/1B: $69- 74   2P/2B: $69- 74   XP: $7   F18
5/1-5/31 & 11/1-4/30 [CP]   1P: $59- 62   2P/1B: $66- 69   2P/2B: $66- 69   XP: $7   F18
**Location:** I-83, exit 29; 1 blk w on Union Deposit Rd. 4021 Union Deposit Rd 17109. Fax: 717/561-1357.
Motel **Terms:** Reserv deposit, 3 day notice; pets. **Facility:** 116 rooms. Well-appointed rooms & public areas. 5 stories; interior corridors; designated smoking area; meeting rooms; heated pool; exercise room.
**Dining:** Restaurant nearby. **Services:** airport transportation. Fee: coin laundry. **All Rooms:** free movies, cable TV. **Some Rooms:** microwaves, refrigerators. Fee: VCP's. **Cards:** AE, CB, DI, DS, JCB, MC, VI.   ⓐ Ⓓ Ⓢ ⊗

**DAYS INN NORTH**    Guaranteed Rates    Phone: 717/233-3100   ㉔

5/1-10/31 [CP]   1P: $49- 65   2P/1B: $59- 74   2P/2B: $54- 74   XP: $5   F12
11/1-4/30 [CP]   1P: $42- 65   2P/1B: $48- 74   2P/2B: $48- 74   XP: $5   F12
**Location:** I-81, exit 22; 1/4 mi n on N Front St. 3919 N Front St 17110. Fax: 717/233-6415. **Terms:** Sr. discount; no pets. **Facility:** 116 rooms. Some rooms with view of river. 3 stories; exterior corridors; pool; playground. **Dining:** Restaurant nearby. **All Rooms:** free & pay movies. **Some Rooms:** Fee: refrigerators.
**Cards:** AE, CB, DI, DS, JCB, MC, VI. *(See ad below)*   Ⓓ Ⓢ ⊗

**DAYSTOP HARRISBURG**    AAA Special Value Rates    Phone: 717/652-9578   ㊳

All Year   1P: $49   2P/1B: $55   XP: $6   F18
**Location:** I-81 & SR 39 exit 27, adjacent to truck stop. 7848 Linglestown Rd 17112. Fax: 717/657-5012.
Motor Inn **Terms:** Reserv deposit; no pets. **Facility:** 31 rooms. 2 stories; exterior corridors. **Dining:** Restaurant; 24 hours; $7-$10. **Services:** Fee: coin laundry. **All Rooms:** free movies, cable TV. **Cards:** AE, DI, DS, MC, VI.
Ⓓ ⊗

**DOUBLETREE CLUB HOTEL**    Rates Subject to Change    Phone: 717/939-1600   ⑱

6/1-9/6 [BP]   1P: $90- 105   2P/1B: $100- 115   2P/2B: $100- 115   XP: $10   F18
5/1-5/31 & 9/7-4/30 [BP]   1P: $80- 95   2P/1B: $90- 105   2P/2B: $90- 105   XP: $10   F18
**Location:** I-76, exit 19; I-283 exit 2W (Highspire). 815 Eisenhower Blvd 17057. Fax: 717/939-8763.
**Terms:** Sr. discount; reserv deposit, 3 day notice; weekly/monthly rates; small pets only. **Facility:** 176 rooms. Located 3 miles from Harrisburg International Airport. Suites avail, $85-$120; 6 stories; interior corridors; designated smoking area; meeting rooms; heated indoor pool, sauna; exercise room. **Dining & Entertainment:** $9-$15; health conscious menu items; cocktails/lounge. **Services:** airport transportation. Fee: coin laundry. **All Rooms:** coffeemakers, free movies, cable TV. **Some Rooms:** microwaves, refrigerators. Fee: VCP's. **Cards:** AE, CB, DI, DS, JCB, MC, VI.   Ⓓ Ⓢ ⊗

**FRIENDSHIP INN**    Rates Subject to Change    Phone: 717/561-1885   ㉟

10/1-10/15   1P: $35- 80   2P/1B: $40- 85   2P/2B: $45- 85   XP: $5   F12
5/1-9/30   1P: $35- 55   2P/1B: $40- 65   2P/2B: $45- 70   XP: $5   F12
10/16-4/30   1P: $35- 55   2P/1B: $40- 60   2P/2B: $45- 65   XP: $5   F12
**Location:** 1/4 mi n on Eisenhower Blvd from jct I-283, exit 1 & SR 441, exit 19 PA Tpk. 495 Eisenhower Blvd 17111. Fax: 717/561-2054. **Terms:** Sr. discount; credit card guarantee; weekly rates; no pets.
**Facility:** 30 rooms. Large rooms. 2 stories; interior corridors; designated smoking area. **Dining:** Restaurant nearby. **Services:** Fee: airport transportation. **All Rooms:** cable TV. **Some Rooms:** Fee: VCP's. **Cards:** AE, CB, DI, MC, VI. Ⓓ ⊗

(See HARRISBURG ACCOMMODATIONS spotting map page A129)

**HAMPTON INN CAMP HILL/MECHANICSBURG**     Guaranteed Rates     Phone: 717/737-6711   **17**
All Year     1P: $34     2P/1B: $39     2P/2B: $44     XP: $5   F12
**Location:** In Camp Hill, 3/4 mi w of US 15 on Carlisle Pike (Market St extended). 3721 Market St 17011.
**Fax:** 717/737-6514. **Terms:** Sr. discount; credit card guarantee, 3 day notice; weekly rates; no pets.
Motor Inn     **Facility:** 58 rooms. Budget traveler oriented, occasional entertainment. 3 two-bedroom units. 2 stories; interior/exterior corridors; designated smoking area; whirlpool. **Dining & Entertainment:** Restaurant; 11 am-11 pm; $4-$14; cocktails/lounge. **Services:** Fee: airport transportation. **All Rooms:** combo & shower baths, cable TV.
**Cards:** AE, CB, DI, MC, VI. *(See ad p A130)*     Ⓓ

**HAMPTON INN HARRISBURG EAST**     AAA Special Value Rates     Phone: 717/545-9595   **45**
5/1-10/27 & 4/1-4/30 [CP]     1P: $63- 73     2P/1B: $68- 78     2P/2B: $68- 78
10/28-3/31 [CP]     1P: $60- 70     2P/1B: $64- 74     2P/2B: $64- 74
Motel     **Location:** Exit 29 off I-83, 1 blk e. 4230 Union Deposit Rd 17111. **Fax:** 717/545-6907. **Terms:** Reserv deposit, 3 day notice; weekly/monthly rates; no pets. **Facility:** 145 rooms. Handsomely decorated public areas. 5 stories; interior corridors; designated smoking area; meeting rooms; heated pool, whirlpool; exercise room.
**Dining:** Restaurant nearby. **Services:** data ports; airport transportation. Fee: coin laundry. **All Rooms:** free movies, cable TV. **Some Rooms:** microwaves, refrigerators. **Cards:** AE, CB, DI, DS, MC, VI.     Ⓓ Ⓢ ⊗

**HARRISBURG HILTON & TOWERS**     Rates Subject to Change     Phone: 717/233-6000   **14**
1/1-4/30     1P: $149     2P/1B: $159     2P/2B: $159     XP: $10   F
5/1-12/31     1P: $154     2P/1B: $154     2P/2B: $154     XP: $10   F
Hotel     **Location:** Center. One North 2nd St 17101. **Fax:** 717/233-6271. **Terms:** Sr. discount; credit card guarantee, 3 day notice; package plans; weekend rates available; no pets. **Facility:** 341 rooms. Attractive public areas. 15 stories; interior corridors; conference facilities; luxury level rooms; heated indoor pool; exercise room.
Fee: health club privileges. **Dining & Entertainment:** Dining room, restaurant; 6:30 am-11 pm, Sat & Sun from 7 am; $9-$22; health conscious menu items; cocktail lounge; also, The Golden Sheaf, see separate listing; entertainment.
**Services:** data ports, secretarial services; valet laundry; area transportation, to Amtrak station, airport transportation.
Fee: valet parking. **All Rooms:** free & pay movies, combo & shower baths, cable TV. **Some Rooms:** Fee: microwaves, refrigerators. **Cards:** AE, CB, DI, DS, MC, VI. *(See ad p 28)*     Ⓓ Ⓢ ⊗

**THE HARRISBURG HOTEL ON MARKET SQUARE**     Guaranteed Rates     Phone: 717/234-5021   **39**
All Year     1P: $69- 99     2P/1B: $69- 119     2P/2B: $69- 119     XP: $10   F16
**Location:** 2nd & Chestnut sts. 23 S 2nd St 17101. **Terms:** Sr. discount; reserv deposit, 3 day notice; no pets. **Facility:** 261 rooms. Some smaller units. Occasional weekend entertainment. 10 sto-
Hotel     ries; interior corridors; meeting rooms; heated indoor pool; exercise room. **Dining & Entertainment:** Dining room; 6:30 am-2 & 5-10 pm, Sat & Sun from 7 am; $10-$18; health conscious menu items; cocktails/lounge.
**Services:** health club privileges. Fee: coin laundry, airport transportation. **All Rooms:** free movies, cable TV.
**Some Rooms:** refrigerators. **Cards:** AE, CB, DI, DS, MC, VI. *(See ad below)*     Ⓓ Ⓢ ⊗

**HARRISBURG MARRIOTT**     Rates Subject to Change     Phone: 717/564-5511   **33**
Motor Inn     All Year     1P: $84     2P/1B: $84     2P/2B: $84     XP: $14   F18
**Location:** Exit 1 (Swatara) off I-283 at jct of SR 441. 4650 Lindle Rd 17111. **Fax:** 717/564-6173. **Terms:** Sr. discount; reserv deposit; package plans; no pets. **Facility:** 348 rooms. Very attractive public areas. 10 stories; interior corridors; conference facilities; luxury level rooms; heated indoor/outdoor pool, sauna, whirlpool; health club.
**Dining & Entertainment:** Dining room, restaurant; 6 am-11 pm; $6-$20; health conscious menu items; cocktails/lounge; also, Ashley's, see separate listing; entertainment. **Services:** data ports; valet laundry; airport transportation.
**All Rooms:** free & pay movies. **Cards:** AE, CB, DI, DS, MC, VI.     Roll in showers. 📶 Ⓓ Ⓢ ⊗

(See HARRISBURG ACCOMMODATIONS spotting map page A129)

**HOLIDAY INN HARRISBURG EAST-AIRPORT**   AAA Special Value Rates   Phone: 717/939-7841   ㉒
All Year   1P: $107   2P/1B: $119   2P/2B: $119   XP: $12   F19
**Location:** I-283 & SR 441 exit 1; 1 mi s of jct I-83 & US 322. 4751 Lindle Rd 17111. Fax: 717/939-9317.
**Terms:** Reserv deposit; small pets only. **Facility:** 299 rooms. Excellent room size. 3 stories; interior corridors; conference facilities; luxury level rooms; 2 pools (2 heated, 1 indoor), whirlpool; 3 lighted tennis courts; exercise room, basketball court, outdoor shuffleboard, pitch & putt. **Dining & Entertainment:** Dining room; 6:30 am-2 & 5-10 pm; $10-$19; cocktails/lounge. **Services:** data ports, secretarial services; valet laundry; airport transportation. **All Rooms:** free & pay movies, cable TV, whirlpools. **Some Rooms:** coffeemakers. **Cards:** AE, CB, DI, DS, JCB, MC, VI. *(See color ad p A131)*   ⓓ ⊗

**HOMEWOOD SUITES**   Rates Subject to Change   Phone: 717/697-4900   ㊻
Suite Motel   All Year [CP]   1P: $89   2P/1B: $89   2P/2B: $89
Too new to rate; **Location:** PA Tpk exit 17, 1 mi n on US 15, exit Rossmoyne Rd. (5001 Ritter Rd, MECHANICSBURG). Fax: 717/697-9101. **Terms:** reserv deposit; weekly/monthly rates; no pets. **Facility:** 84 rooms. Scheduled to open February 1995. 6 two-bedroom units. 2 stories; interior corridors; designated smoking area; business center, meeting rooms; heated pool; exercise room, sports court. **Dining:** Restaurant nearby. **Services:** data ports; complimentary evening beverages, Mon-Thurs. Fee: coin laundry; airport transportation. **All Rooms:** coffeemakers, kitchens, microwaves, free movies, refrigerators, cable TV, VCP's. **Cards:** AE, CB, DI, DS, MC, VI.   ⓓ ⓢ ⊗

**QUALITY INN - RIVERFRONT**   AAA Special Value Rates   Phone: 717/233-1611   ㊱
5/1-10/31   1P: $60   2P/1B: $65   2P/2B: $70   XP: $5   F16
11/1-4/30   1P: $45   2P/1B: $50   2P/2B: $55   XP: $5   F16
**Location:** Center, 1/2 mi n of I-83 exit 23. 525 S Front St 17104. Fax: 717/233-1611. **Terms:** Pets, $5. **Facility:** 124 rooms. Overlooking Susquehanna River. 2 stories; interior/exterior corridors; meeting rooms; pool. **Dining & Entertainment:** Restaurant; 7 am-2 & 5-10 pm; $9-$17; health conscious menu items; cocktails/lounge. **Services:** valet laundry. Fee: airport transportation. **All Rooms:** free movies, cable TV. **Cards:** AE, CB, DI, DS, JCB, MC, VI.   ⓓ ⊗

**(See HARRISBURG ACCOMMODATIONS spotting map page A129)**

**RADISSON PENN HARRIS HOTEL & CONVENTION CENTER** AAA Special Value Rates    Phone: 717/763-7117    26

Motor Inn
◆◆◆
| | | | |
|---|---|---|---|
| 5/1-11/30 | 1P: $79 | 2P/1B: $89 | 2P/2B: $89 |
| 12/1-4/30 | 1P: $69 | 2P/1B: $79 | 2P/2B: $79 |

**Location:** 1 1/2 mi w on US 11 & 15 in Camp Hill; Erford Rd exit off Camp Hill Expwy. 1150 Camp Hill By-Pass 17011. Fax: 717/763-4518. **Terms:** Reserv deposit, 4 day notice; package plans; small pets only, $25. **Facility:** 258 rooms. Located near state capitol. 2-3 stories; interior/exterior corridors; designated smoking area; conference facilities; pool. **Dining & Entertainment:** Dining room, coffee shop; 6:30 am-10 pm, Fri & Sat-11 pm; $9-$15; cocktails/lounge; entertainment. **Services:** secretarial services; valet laundry; area transportation, within 2 mi, airport transportation. **All Rooms:** combo & shower baths, cable TV. **Fee:** movies. **Some Rooms:** coffeemakers. **Fee:** refrigerators. **Cards:** AE, CB, DI, DS, MC, VI. *(See color ad below)*    Roll in showers.  (D) ⊗

**RED ROOF INN-NORTH**    Rates Subject to Change    Phone: 717/657-1445    32
◆◆
Motel
All Year    2P/1B: $38-  42   2P/2B: $47-  51   XP: $3   F18

**Location:** At I-81 exit 24, Progress Ave. 400 Corporate Cir 17110. Fax: 717/657-2775. **Terms:** Credit card guarantee; pets. **Facility:** 110 rooms. Located along busy interstate highway. 2 stories; interior/exterior corridors. **Dining:** Restaurant nearby. **Services:** data ports. **All Rooms:** free movies, cable TV. **Cards:** AE, CB, DI, DS, MC, VI.
(D) ⊗

**RED ROOF INN-SOUTH**    Rates Subject to Change    Phone: 717/939-1331    31
◆◆
Motel
| | | | | |
|---|---|---|---|---|
| 7/1-8/31 | 1P: $42 | 2P/1B: $49 | 2P/2B: $51 | XP: $7  F18 |
| 5/1-6/30, 9/1-10/31 & 3/1-4/30 | 1P: $38 | 2P/1B: $44 | 2P/2B: $47 | XP: $7  F18 |
| 11/1-12/31 & 1/1-2/29 | 1P: $30 | 2P/1B: $36 | 2P/2B: $40 | XP: $7  F18 |

**Location:** I-283 exit 1; 1 mi s of jct I-83 & US 322. 950 Eisenhower Blvd 17111. Fax: 717/939-8266. **Terms:** Credit card guarantee; pets. **Facility:** 110 rooms. Located along busy commercial highway. 2 stories; interior/exterior corridors. **Dining:** Restaurant nearby. **Services:** Fee: airport transportation. **All Rooms:** free movies, cable TV. **Cards:** AE, CB, DI, DS, MC, VI.
(D) ⊗

**RESIDENCE INN BY MARRIOTT HARRISBURG-HERSHEY**    Guaranteed Rates    Phone: 717/561-1900    30
◆◆◆
Apartment
Motel
All Year [BP]    1P: $98    2P/1B: $107    2P/2B: $134

**Location:** I-83 at US 322; US 322 e & w, exit Penhar Dr. 4480 Lewis Rd 17111. Fax: 717/561-8617. **Terms:** Sr. discount; reserv deposit; pets, $5, $50 dep req. **Facility:** 80 rooms. Many with fireplace. Light evening meals Mon-Thurs, 5:30-7 pm. 20 two-bedroom units. 2 stories; exterior corridors; designated smoking area; meeting rooms; pool, whirlpool; sports court, volleyball court & picnic area. **Services:** health club privileges. Fee: coin laundry. **All Rooms:** kitchens, free movies, cable TV. **Some Rooms:** VCP's. **Cards:** AE, CB, DI, DS, MC, VI.  (D) ⊗

**RODEWAY INN**    AAA Special Value Rates    Phone: 717/939-4147    47
◆◆
Motel
| | | | | |
|---|---|---|---|---|
| 6/21-10/9 [CP] | 1P: $47 | 2P/1B: $53 | 2P/2B: $55 | XP: $5  F18 |
| 5/1-6/20 [CP] | 1P: $44 | 2P/1B: $50 | 2P/2B: $53 | XP: $5  F18 |
| 10/10-4/30 [CP] | 1P: $40 | 2P/1B: $45 | 2P/2B: $50 | XP: $5  F18 |

**Location:** I-76, exit 19; I-283, exit 2W (Highspire). 800 Eisenhower Blvd 17057. Fax: 717/939-5291. **Terms:** Reserv deposit, 3 day notice; weekly/monthly rates; small pets only, $20 dep req. **Facility:** 82 rooms. Rooms have contempry decor. 2 stories; exterior corridors; designated smoking area; meeting rooms. **Services:** health club privileges; area transportation, within 10 mi, airport transportation. **All Rooms:** cable TV. **Some Rooms:** coffeemakers. Fee: VCP's. **Cards:** AE, CB, DI, DS, JCB, MC, VI.  (D) ⊗

**SHERATON INN HARRISBURG**    AAA Special Value Rates    Phone: 717/561-2800    29
◆◆◆
Hotel
| | | | | |
|---|---|---|---|---|
| 5/1-10/31 | 1P: $85- 125 | 2P/1B: $95- 135 | 2P/2B: $95- 135 | XP: $10  F18 |
| 11/1-4/30 | 1P: $75- 110 | 2P/1B: $85- 125 | 2P/2B: $85- 125 | XP: $10  F18 |

**Location:** I-83, exit 29; 2 blks e on Union Deposit Rd, 1/2 mi s on East Park Dr. 800 East Park Dr 17111. Fax: 717/561-8398. **Terms:** Reserv deposit; package plans; pets. **Facility:** 174 rooms. Spacious, very attractive public areas; voice mail. 3 stories; interior corridors; conference facilities; heated indoor pool, sauna, whirlpool; health club. **Dining & Entertainment:** Dining room; 6:30-10:30 am, 11:30-2 & 5-10 pm; $10-$17; cocktails/lounge. **Services:** data ports; valet laundry; airport transportation. **All Rooms:** free & pay movies, combo & shower baths, cable TV. **Cards:** AE, CB, DI, DS, MC, VI.  (D) (S) ⊗

**SLEEP INN HARRISBURG HERSHEY**    Rates Subject to Change    Phone: 717/540-9100    42
◆◆
Motel
| | | | | |
|---|---|---|---|---|
| 6/2-9/4 [CP] | 2P/1B: $49- 59 | 2P/2B: $56- 66 | XP: $7  F18 |
| 5/1-6/1 & 3/31-4/30 [CP] | 2P/1B: $46- 56 | 2P/2B: $53- 63 | XP: $7  F18 |
| 9/5-3/30 [CP] | 2P/1B: $39- 49 | 2P/2B: $46- 56 | XP: $7  F18 |

Too new to rate; **Location:** I-81, exit 27. 7930 Linglestown Rd 17112. Fax: 717/671-8514. **Terms:** sr. discount; reserv deposit, 7 day notice; no pets. **Facility:** 42 rooms. 2 stories; interior corridors; designated smoking area; meeting rooms. **Dining:** Restaurant nearby. **Services:** data ports; guest laundry. **All Rooms:** free movies, combo & shower baths, cable TV. **Cards:** AE, DI, DS, JCB, MC, VI.  (D) (S) ⊗

**(See HARRISBURG ACCOMMODATIONS spotting map page A129)**

**SUPER 8 MOTEL HARRISBURG/HERSHEY**        Guaranteed Rates        Phone: 717/564-7790    **43**
6/9-9/30 [EP]        1P:  $43-  47    2P/1B:  $53        2P/2B:  $53        XP:  $5    F12
5/1-6/8 & 9/1-4/30 [CP]    1P:  $34-  38    2P/1B:  $45        2P/2B:  $45        XP:  $5    F12
◆◆        **Location:** Exit 1 (Swatara) off I-283, 1/2 blk w, 1/2 mi n. 4131 Executive Park Dr 17111. Fax: 717/564-7790.
Motel        **Terms:** Credit card guarantee, 3 day notice, 6/1-8/31; no pets. **Facility:** 48 rooms. 2 stories; interior corridors;
designated smoking area. Fee: private club pool. **Dining:** Restaurant nearby. **Services:** Fee: airport
transportation. **All Rooms:** free movies, cable TV. **Cards:** AE, CB, DI, DS, MC, VI.        (D) ⊗

**SUPER 8 MOTEL-NORTH**        Rates Subject to Change        Phone: ]17/233-5891    **28**
All Year        1P:  $40-  45    2P/1B:  $48-  54    2P/2B:  $52-  58    XP:  $5    F
◆◆        **Location:** 3/4 mi n of I-81, exit 22, Front St. 4125 N Front St 17110. Fax: 717/233-5891. **Terms:** Sr.
Motor Inn        discount; weekly rates; pets. **Facility:** 58 rooms. Opposite Susquehanna River. 2 stories; exterior corridors;
meeting rooms; pool. **Dining & Entertainment:** Restaurant; 7-11 am, 11:30-2 & 5-9 pm, Fri & Sat-9 pm, Sun
8 am-11:30 am; $10-$17; cocktail lounge. **Services:** data ports. **All Rooms:** free movies, cable TV.
**Some Rooms:** refrigerators. Fee: VCP's. **Cards:** AE, DI, DS, MC, VI.        (D) ⊗

## RESTAURANTS

**ASHLEY'S**        **Dinner:** $11-$20        Phone: 717/564-5511    **4**
◆◆◆        **Location:** In Harrisburg Marriott. 4560 Lindle Rd 17111. **Hours:** 6 am-11 pm, Fri & Sat-midnight, Sun 7
American        am-11 pm. **Reservations:** suggested. **Features:** casual dress; Sunday brunch; children's menu; senior's
menu; health conscious menu items; cocktails & lounge. Daily lunch buffet $7.25 & Sun buffet $15.95.
**Cards:** AE, CB, DI, DS, JCB, MC, VI.        ⊗

**BOB EVANS FARM RESTAURANT**        **Dinner:** up to $10        Phone: 717/986-0163    **5**
◆        **Location:** I-283 exit 1, 1 blk w. 771 Eisenhower Blvd 17111. **Hours:** 6 am-10 pm, Fri & Sat-11:30 pm.
American        Closed: 11/23 & 12/25. **Features:** casual dress; children's menu; senior's menu; health conscious menu
items; carryout. Budget traveler & family oriented. Smoke free premises. **Cards:** MC, VI.

**CASA RILLO**        **Dinner:** $11-$20        Phone: 717/761-8617    **9**
◆◆◆        **Location:** US 11 & 15N to N 21st St, 1 blk w on N 21st St. 451 N 21st St 17011. **Hours:** 11:30 am-10 pm,
Italian        Fri-11 pm, Sat 5 pm-11 pm, Sun 5 pm-10 pm. Closed major holidays. **Reservations:** suggested; weekends.
**Features:** children's menu; carryout; cocktails & lounge; a la carte. Homemade pastas & desserts, also
seafood entrees, award winning restaurant. **Cards:** AE, CB, DI, DS, MC, VI.

**COUNTRY OVEN RESTAURANT**        **Dinner:** $11-$20        Phone: 717/652-7180    **7**
◆◆◆        **Location:** In Best Western Country Oven; exit 26W off I-81. 300 N Mountain Rd 17112. **Hours:** 6:30 am-9
American        pm, Fri & Sat-9:30 pm, Sun-8 pm. Closed: 12/25. **Reservations:** suggested. **Features:** casual dress;
children's menu; carryout; cocktails & lounge. Popular dining, also serving regional specialties. Homemade
soup & dessert. **Cards:** AE, CB, DI, DS, MC, VI. *(See color ad p A130)*        ⊗

**FINLEY'S AMERICAN RESTAURANT**        **Dinner:** $11-$20        Phone: 717/564-4270    **3**
◆        **Location:** 1/4 mi w of I-83, exit 29 (Union Deposit Rd). 3951 Union Deposit Rd 17109. **Hours:** 11 am-10
Steakhouse        pm, Fri & Sat-11 pm. Closed: 11/23 & 12/25. **Features:** casual dress; children's menu; senior's menu; health
conscious menu; carryout. Casual family dining. Seasonally updated specialties. **Cards:** AE, DI, DS, MC, VI.        ⊗

**THE GOLDEN SHEAF**        **Dinner:** $21-$30        Phone: 717/237-6400    **1**
◆◆◆◆        **Location:** In Harrisburg Hilton & Towers. One N 2nd St 17101. **Hours:** 5:30 pm-10 pm. Closed: Sun &
American        12/25. **Reservations:** suggested. **Features:** casual dress; senior's menu; cocktails; entertainment; fee for
valet parking. Seasonal specialty menu, intimate fine dining. Winemaker specialty dinners hosted monthly.
Member Chaine des Rotisseurs. Smoking in lounge only. **Cards:** AE, CB, DI, DS, JCB, MC, VI.

**MAVERICK RESTAURANT**        **Dinner:** $11-$20        Phone: 717/233-7688    **6**
◆◆        **Location:** Cameron St exit off I-81, then 1 mi s to Rt 22, 1/2 mi e. 18th & Rt 22 17103. **Hours:** 11 am-10
Continental        pm, Sat 4:30 pm-10:30 pm. Closed major holidays & Sun. **Reservations:** suggested. **Features:** casual
dress; children's menu; cocktails & lounge. Family owned since 1961. Fresh seafood, aged beef, lamb &
veal capably served in warm, comfortable supper club ambience. **Cards:** AE, CB, DI, MC, VI.

**VISAGGIO'S RISTORANTE**        **Dinner:** $21-$30        Phone: 717/697-8082    **12**
◆◆◆        **Location:** I-81 exit 20, 3 4/10 mi on SR 944W. 6990 Wertzville Rd 17025. **Hours:** 5 pm-9 pm, Sun 4 pm-8
Italian        pm, 5/14 & 6/18 noon-6 pm & 11 am-9 pm 12/1-12/23. Closed major holidays & Sun 6/1-8/31.
**Reservations:** suggested. **Features:** casual dress; carryout; cocktails & lounge. Fine Italian cuisine, in a
relaxing atmosphere Very good wine list, mostly Italian. **Cards:** AE, MC, VI.        ⊗

# HAWLEY—1,200

## LODGING

**THE SETTLERS INN AT BINGHAM PARK**        AAA Special Value Rates        Phone: 717/226-2993
7/1-10/31 [BP]        1P:  $60-  75    2P/1B:  $75- 110    2P/2B:  $80-  95    XP:  $15    D6
5/1-6/30 & 11/1-4/30 [BP]    1P:  $55-  70    2P/1B:  $70- 100    2P/2B:  $75-  90    XP:  $15    D6
◆◆◆        **Location:** 1/4 mi w on US 6. 4 Main Ave 18428. Fax: 717/226-1874. **Terms:** Reserv deposit, 3 day notice;
Historic        package plans; no pets. **Facility:** 18 rooms. 3 stories, no elevator; interior corridors; meeting rooms; horse-
Country Inn        shoes. **Dining & Entertainment:** Dining room; $16-$27; cocktails/lounge. **All Rooms:** combo & shower
baths. **Some Rooms:** coffeemakers, 2 efficiencies, refrigerators, phones, cable TV, VCP's. **Cards:** AE, MC,
VI.        (D) (S) ⊗

## RESTAURANT

**EHRHARDT'S LAKESIDE RESTAURANT**        **Dinner:** $11-$20        Phone: 717/226-2124
◆◆        **Location:** 1 mi s of US Rt 6 on SR 507. 18428. **Hours:** 11 am-9 pm, Fri & Sat-11 pm, Sun 9 am-9 pm;
American        6/16-9/29  11 am-10 pm, Fri & Sat-11 pm, Sun 9 am-10 pm. Closed: 11/23 & 12/25.
**Reservations:** suggested. **Features:** casual dress; Sunday brunch; children's menu; carryout; cocktails &
lounge. Casual dining with scenic tranquil lakeside view. **Cards:** AE, DS, MC, VI.        ⊗

# HAZLETON—24,700

## LODGINGS

**BEST WESTERN GENETTI MOTOR LODGE**   Rates Subject to Change   **Phone:** 717/454-2494

| | | | 1P: | | | 2P/1B: | | | 2P/2B: | | XP: | |
|---|---|---|---|---|---|---|---|---|---|---|---|---|
| | 5/1-10/31 [CP] | | $50- | 59 | | $55- | 65 | | $65- | 75 | $7 | F12 |
| | 11/1-4/30 [CP] | | $39- | 51 | | $49- | 55 | | $60- | 65 | $7 | F12 |

**Location:** 2 mi n on SR 309, 6 mi s on SR 309 from I-80 exit 39. 32nd & N Church St 18201 (RR 2, Box 37). **Fax:** 717/455-7793. **Terms:** Sr. discount; credit card guarantee; weekly/monthly rates; small pets only. **Facility:** 89 rooms. Well-appointed guest rooms. 7 suites with whirlpool tub, $83-$105; 3 stories; interior/exterior corridors; meeting rooms; heated pool; playground. **Dining:** Restaurant nearby. **Services:** Fee: coin laundry. **All Rooms:** combo & shower baths, cable TV. **Some Rooms:** microwaves, refrigerators. Fee: VCP's. **Cards:** AE, CB, DI, DS, MC, VI. *(See color ad below)*

**COMFORT INN-WEST HAZLETON**   AAA Special Value Rates   **Phone:** 717/455-9300

| | | | 1P: | | | 2P/1B: | | | 2P/2B: | | XP: | |
|---|---|---|---|---|---|---|---|---|---|---|---|---|
| | 11/1-4/1 [CP] | | $57- | 87 | | $70- | 87 | | $73- | 87 | $8 | F18 |
| | 5/1-10/31 [CP] | | $56- | 85 | | $69- | 85 | | $72- | 85 | $8 | F18 |
| | 4/2-4/30 [CP] | | $53- | 82 | | $66- | 82 | | $69- | 82 | $8 | F18 |

**Location:** I-81 exit 41, 1/4 mi se on SR 93. SR 93 & Kiwanis Blvd 18201 (RR 1, Box 301). **Fax:** 717/455-8720. **Terms:** Pets. **Facility:** 119 rooms. Atrium lobby. 3 stories; interior corridors; meeting rooms. **Dining & Entertainment:** Coffee shop; 5 pm-10 pm; $3-$6; cocktail lounge. **Services:** valet laundry. **All Rooms:** free movies, cable TV. **Some Rooms:** refrigerators. Fee: VCP's, whirlpools. **Cards:** AE, CB, DI, VI.

**FOREST HILL INN**   AAA Special Value Rates   **Phone:** 717/459-2730

| | | 1P: | | 2P/1B: | | 2P/2B: | | XP: | |
|---|---|---|---|---|---|---|---|---|---|
| | All Year | $45 | | $50 | | $50 | | $5 | F |

**Location:** I-81, exit 41; 1/4 mi se on SR 93. Rt 93 18201 (RD 1, Box 262). **Terms:** Reserv deposit, 7 day notice; weekly rates; pets. **Facility:** 40 rooms. Located atop a mountain, every unit offers a scenic view of the adjacent valley & mountains opposite. 2 stories; exterior corridors. **Dining:** Restaurant nearby. **Services:** valet laundry. **All Rooms:** cable TV. **Cards:** AE, CB, DI, DS, MC, VI.

**HAMPTON INN**   Rates Subject to Change   **Phone:** 717/454-3449

| | | 1P: | | 2P/1B: | | 2P/2B: | |
|---|---|---|---|---|---|---|---|
| | All Year [CP] | $59- | 89 | $69- | 89 | $69- | 89 |

**Location:** Jct I-81, exit 41 & SR 93. I 81 & Hwy 93 18201 (RR 1, Box 273A). **Fax:** 717/454-3396. **Terms:** Credit card guarantee; package plans; pets. **Facility:** 123 rooms. Attractive well kept rooms. Some with extraordinary view of valley. 3 stories; interior corridors; meeting rooms; pool; exercise room. **Dining:** Restaurant nearby. **Services:** data ports; valet laundry. **All Rooms:** free movies, combo & shower baths, cable TV. **Some Rooms:** microwaves, refrigerators. **Cards:** AE, CB, DI, DS, MC, VI.   Roll in showers.

**HOLIDAY INN**   AAA Special Value Rates   **Phone:** 717/455-2061

| | | 1P: | | 2P/1B: | | 2P/2B: | |
|---|---|---|---|---|---|---|---|
| | All Year | $69- | 75 | $69- | 75 | $69- | 75 |

**Location:** 2 mi n on SR 309; 6 mi s on SR 309 from I-80 exit 39; From I-81, exit 41, 1/2 mi s on SR 93, 1 mi e on Airport Rd, then 3/4 mi s on SR 309. 18201 (Rt 309). **Fax:** 717/455-9387. **Terms:** Credit card guarantee; pets. **Facility:** 107 rooms. Large, attractive rooms. 2 stories; exterior corridors; meeting rooms; pool, wading pool; horseshoes, picnic area with barbeque grills, volleyball. **Dining & Entertainment:** Restaurant; 6 am-2 & 5-10 pm; $7-$20; cocktails/lounge. **Services:** data ports. Fee: coin laundry. **All Rooms:** free & pay movies, cable TV. **Some Rooms:** Fee: microwaves, refrigerators. **Cards:** AE, CB, DI, DS, JCB, MC, VI. *(See color ad p A136)*

## RESTAURANTS

**CARMEN'S**   **Dinner:** $11-$20   **Phone:** 717/455-5521

**Location:** Center. 44 E Broad St 18201. **Hours:** 11 am-9 pm, Sun 8 am-8 pm. **Closed:** 12/25. **Reservations:** suggested; weekends. **Features:** casual dress; children's menu; carryout; cocktails & lounge; buffet. Homemade desserts. Seafood, fowl & steak specialties. **Cards:** AE, DI, MC, VI.

**EDGEWOOD IN THE PINES RESTAURANT**            Dinner: $11-$20          Phone: 717/788-1101
⬙⬙⬙
**Location:** From jct I-80, exit 39, 1 mi s on SR 309, 3/4 mi w on Edgewood Rd. 18201. **Hours:** 5 pm-10 pm,
Sun noon-8 pm. Closed: Mon, Tues, 1/1, 12/24 & 12/25. **Reservations:** suggested; weekends.
◆◆◆    **Features:** casual dress; children's menu; carryout; cocktails & lounge. Very attractive setting. **Cards:** MC, VI.
American                                                                              ⊗

**MIKE DUBATTO'S LIBRARY LOUNGE RESTAURANT**     Dinner: $11-$20          Phone: 717/455-3920
⬙⬙⬙
**Location:** E on SR 93, behind Dubatto's Family Restaurant. 615 E Broad St 18201. **Hours:** 4:30 pm-11 pm.
Closed major holidays. **Reservations:** required. **Features:** casual dress; carryout; cocktails & lounge.
◆◆    Attractive atmosphere. Traditional Northern cuisine. Fresh fish nightly. **Cards:** AE, MC, VI.
Italian

**SCATTON'S RESTAURANT**                          Dinner: $11-$20          Phone: 717/455-6630
⬙⬙⬙
**Location:** From I-81, exit 40, 3 mi n on SR 924 to Center City, then 1 mi n on SR 309, 1 blk w on 22nd St;
from I-80 exit 30, 6 mi s on SR 309 to 22nd St. 1008 N Vine St 18201. **Hours:** 5 pm-10 pm, also Thurs
◆◆◆    11:30 am-2 pm. Closed: Sun, 1/1, 11/23 & 12/25. **Reservations:** suggested; weekends. **Features:** casual
Italian    dress; carryout; cocktails & lounge; a la carte. Featuring homemade pastas, chicken, veal & beef.
Chef/owner. **Cards:** AE, CB, DI, MC, VI.

# HEIDELBERG—3,800    (See PITTSBURGH ACCOMMODATIONS spotting map page A207; see index starting on page A206)

## RESTAURANT

**WRIGHT'S SEAFOOD INN**                          Dinner: $11-$20          Phone: 412/279-7900   ⑺⑻
◆◆
**Location:** In Heidelberg, exit 12 off I-79, 1 mi e on Rt 50, then 2 blks s on Collier & Washington St. 1837
Seafood   Washington St 15106. **Hours:** 11 am-10 pm, Fri & Sat-11 pm, Sun 4 pm-9 pm. Closed major holidays.
**Reservations:** suggested. **Features:** children's menu; early bird specials; senior's menu; health conscious
menu; carryout; cocktails & lounge; a la carte. Relaxed family dining. **Cards:** AE, DI, DS, MC, VI.      ⊗

# HERMITAGE—15,300

## LODGINGS

**COLLINS MOTEL**                   Rates Subject to Change                Phone: 412/981-6150
⬙
All Year            1P:  $35-  40  2P/1B:  $38-  43  2P/2B:  $42-  47  XP:  $5
**Location:** On US 62; 3/4 mi e of jct SR 18. 4036 E State St 16148. **Terms:** Reserv deposit, 7 day notice; no
◆    pets. **Facility:** 13 rooms. Quiet location. 1 story; exterior corridors. **All Rooms:** free movies, shower baths,
Motel    cable TV. **Some Rooms:** Fee: refrigerators. **Cards:** MC, VI.                        ⒟⊗

**HOLIDAY INN-SHARON/HERMITAGE**     AAA Special Value Rates               Phone: 412/981-1530
◆◆◆
5/1-9/30         1P:  $69-  75  2P/1B:  $75-  80  2P/2B:  $75-  80  XP:  $6  F19
Motor Inn    10/1-4/30        1P:  $69       2P/1B:  $75       2P/2B:  $75       XP:  $6  F19
**Location:** On SR 18, at jct I-80 exit 1N. 3200 S Hermitage Rd 16159. Fax: 412/981-1518. **Terms:** $15
service charge; monthly rates; package plans; pets. **Facility:** 180 rooms. Good variety of rooms. 3 stories; interior corridors;
conference facilities; heated pool. **Dining:** Dining room; 6:30 am-10 pm; $10-$20; cocktails. **Services:** data ports. Fee: coin
laundry. **All Rooms:** Fee: movies. **Some Rooms:** Fee: refrigerators, VCP's. **Cards:** AE, CB, DI, DS, JCB, MC, VI.   ⒟⊗

**ROYAL MOTEL**                     Rates Subject to Change                Phone: 412/347-5546
⬙
All Year            1P:  $35       2P/1B:  $38       2P/2B:      $45       XP:  $5  F14
**Location:** Jct SR 18 & US 62. 301 S Hermitage Rd 16148. **Terms:** Reserv deposit, 3 day notice; small pets
◆    only. **Facility:** 23 rooms. 2 stories; exterior corridors. **Dining:** Restaurant nearby. **All Rooms:** combo &
Motel    shower baths, cable TV. **Some Rooms:** Fee: refrigerators. **Cards:** AE, CB, DI, DS, MC, VI.      ⒟⊗

# HERSHEY

## LODGINGS

**BEST WESTERN INN-HERSHEY**        AAA Special Value Rates                Phone: 717/533-5665
⬙
6/30-9/3 [CP]    1P:  $115      2P/1B:  $120      2P/2B:  $115      XP:  $10  F18
5/1-6/29 [CP]    1P:  $99       2P/1B:  $104      2P/2B:  $99       XP:  $10  F18
◆◆◆    9/4-4/30 [CP]    1P:  $69       2P/1B:  $74       2P/2B:  $69       XP:  $10  F18
Motel    **Location:** 2 mi w on US 422. US 422 & Sipe Ave 17033 (PO Box 364). Fax: 717/533-5675. **Terms:** Credit
card guarantee; package plans; no pets. **Facility:** 123 rooms. 3 stories; interior/exterior corridors; meeting
rooms; pool, wading pool. **Dining:** Restaurant nearby. **Services:** data ports. Fee: coin laundry. **All Rooms:** free movies,
refrigerators, cable TV. **Some Rooms:** Fee: microwaves, VCP's. **Cards:** AE, DI, DS, MC, VI.
*(See color ad p A137)*                                                          ⒟⊗

**CHOCOLATETOWN MOTEL**  Rates Subject to Change  Phone: 717/533-2330

|  |  | 2P/1B: | $72 |  | 2P/2B: | $78 |  | XP: | $5 |
|---|---|---|---|---|---|---|---|---|---|
| 7/1-8/26 |  | 2P/1B: | $72 |  | 2P/2B: | $78 |  | XP: | $5 |
| 6/10-6/30 & 8/27-9/3 |  | 2P/1B: | $52- | 56 | 2P/2B: | $60- | 64 | XP: | $5 |
| 5/1-6/9, 9/4-10/22 & 4/1-4/30 |  | 2P/1B: | $39- | 43 | 2P/2B: | $45- | 49 | XP: | $5 |
| 10/23-12/17 & 3/1-3/31 |  | 2P/1B: | $37- | 39 | 2P/2B: | $40- | 43 |  |  |

(AAA) ◆◆ Motel

**Location:** 2 mi e on US 422. 1806 E Chocolate Ave 17033. **Terms:** Open 5/1-12/17 & 3/1-4/30; reserv deposit, 3 day notice; no pets. **Facility:** 26 rooms. 2 stories; interior/exterior corridors; designated smoking area; heated pool. **Dining:** Restaurant nearby. **All Rooms:** combo & shower baths, cable TV. **Some Rooms:** Fee: refrigerators. **Cards:** DS, MC, VI. *(See color ad below)*   (D)

**COCOA MOTEL**  Rates Subject to Change  Phone: 717/534-1243

| 7/1-9/5 | 1P: | $55 | 2P/1B: | $55- | 60 | 2P/2B: | $68- | 75 | XP: | $5 |
|---|---|---|---|---|---|---|---|---|---|---|
| 5/1-6/30, 9/6-10/23 & 3/26-4/30 | 1P: | $38- | 48 | 2P/1B: | $38- | 48 | 2P/2B: | $48- | 58 | XP: | $5 |
| 10/24-3/25 | 1P: | $34 | 2P/1B: | $34 | | 2P/2B: | $44 | | XP: | $5 |

(AAA) ◆ Motel

**Location:** Jct US 322 & SR 743. 914 Cocoa Ave 17033. Fax: 717/533-4822. **Terms:** Reserv deposit, 3 day notice; weekly rates; no pets. **Facility:** 14 rooms. 1 story; exterior corridors; designated smoking area. **Dining:** Restaurant nearby. **All Rooms:** cable TV. **Some Rooms:** refrigerators. **Cards:** AE, DS, MC, VI.   (D) ⊗

**COMFORT INN**         Rates Subject to Change         Phone: 717/566-2050

| | | | | |
|---|---|---|---|---|
| 6/30-9/4 [BP] | 1P: $105- 125 | 2P/1B: $115- 135 | 2P/2B: $115- 135 | XP: $10  F18 |
| 5/26-6/29 [BP] | 1P: $75- 100 | 2P/1B: $85- 110 | 2P/2B: $85- 110 | XP: $10  F18 |
| 1/1-4/30 [BP] | 1P: $55- 90 | 2P/1B: $65- 100 | 2P/2B: $65- 100 | XP: $10  F18 |
| 5/1-5/25 & 9/5-12/31 [BP] | 1P: $55- 80 | 2P/1B: $65- 90 | 2P/2B: $65- 90 | XP: $10  F18 |

**Location:** At jct SR 322, 422 & US 39; just off Hershey Park Dr. (1200 Mae St, HUMMELSTOWN). **Fax:** 717/566-8656. **Terms:** Sr. discount; check-in 4 pm; no pets. **Facility:** 125 rooms. 6 two-bedroom units. 7 stories; interior corridors; designated smoking area; meeting rooms; heated indoor pool. **Dining & Entertainment:** Cocktail lounge; restaurant nearby. **Services:** data ports; area transportation, airport transportation, within 5 mi. Fee: coin laundry. **Some Rooms:** coffeemakers, 18 efficiencies, microwaves, refrigerators. Fee: VCP's. **Cards:** AE, CB, DI, DS, MC, VI. *(See color ad below)*

**DAYS INN HERSHEY**         AAA Special Value Rates         Phone: 717/534-2162

| | | | | |
|---|---|---|---|---|
| 6/15-9/5 [CP] | 1P: $80- 113 | 2P/1B: $90- 118 | 2P/2B: $90- 118 | XP: $5  F17 |
| 5/1-6/14 [CP] | 1P: $55- 99 | 2P/1B: $65- 109 | 2P/2B: $65- 109 | XP: $5  F17 |
| 9/6-10/15 [CP] | 1P: $55- 91 | 2P/1B: $65- 101 | 2P/2B: $65- 101 | XP: $5  F17 |
| 10/16-4/30 [CP] | 1P: $49- 75 | 2P/1B: $59- 80 | 2P/2B: $59- 80 | XP: $5  F17 |

**Location:** Center, on Rt 422. 350 W Chocolate Ave 17033. **Fax:** 717/533-6409. **Terms:** Reserv deposit; no pets. **Facility:** 75 rooms. Located in close proximity to Hershey Park. 4 stories; interior corridors. **Dining:** Restaurant nearby. **Services:** valet laundry; airport transportation, with 3 day notice. **All Rooms:** free movies, combo & shower baths, cable TV. **Some Rooms:** refrigerators. Fee: VCP's. **Cards:** AE, CB, DI, DS, JCB, MC, VI. *(See ad below)*

**ECONO LODGE HERSHEY**         Rates Subject to Change         Phone: 717/533-2515

| | | | | |
|---|---|---|---|---|
| 10/2-10/9 | 1P: $107 | 2P/2B: $107 | XP: $5  F18 |
| 5/26-10/1 | 1P: $88 | 2P/2B: $98 | XP: $5  F18 |
| 5/1-5/25 | 1P: $50 | 2P/2B: $60 | XP: $5  F18 |
| 10/10-4/30 | 1P: $45 | 2P/2B: $50 | XP: $5  F18 |

**Location:** Jct US 422 & US 322. 115 Lucy Ave 17033 (PO Box 737). **Fax:** 717/533-2543. **Terms:** Reserv deposit; small pets only, $25. **Facility:** 48 rooms. Located near Hershey Medical Center. 3 stories; exterior corridors. **Dining:** Restaurant nearby. **All Rooms:** cable TV. **Cards:** AE, DS, MC, VI.

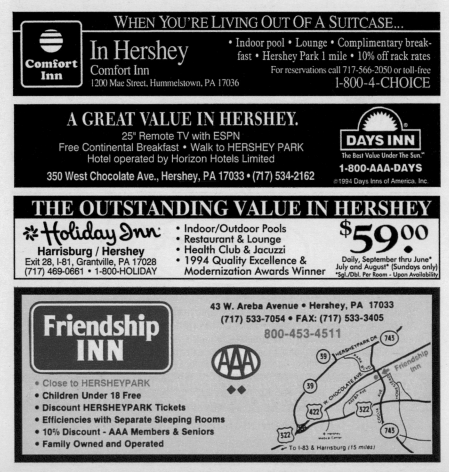

**FRIENDSHIP INN HERSHEY**
Rates Subject to Change
Phone: 717/533-7054

Motel ◆◆

| | | | | | |
|---|---|---|---|---|---|
| 7/1-9/4 | 2P/2B: | $85- | 150 | XP: $5 | F18 |
| 5/1-6/30 & 3/16-4/30 | 2P/2B: | $60- | 135 | XP: $5 | F18 |
| 9/5-10/15 | 2P/2B: | $55- | 115 | XP: $5 | F18 |
| 10/16-12/18 & 1/2-3/15 | 2P/2B: | $50- | 105 | XP: $5 | F18 |

**Location:** 3 blks s of SR 422 (Chocolate Ave) on SR 743, then 1/2 blk w. 43 W Areba Ave 17033. **Fax:** 717/533-3405. **Terms:** Sr. discount; Open 5/1-12/18 & 1/2-4/30; no pets. **Facility:** 24 rooms. Pleasant rooms in quiet residential area. 2 stories; exterior corridors; designated smoking area. **Dining:** Restaurant nearby. **All Rooms:** cable TV. **Some Rooms:** coffeemakers, 6 efficiencies, 4 kitchens, no utensils, microwaves, refrigerators. **Cards:** AE, CB, DI, DS, JCB, MC, VI. *(See color ad p A138)*  Ⓓ ⊗

**HERSHEY LODGE & CONVENTION CENTER**
Rates Subject to Change
Phone: 717/533-3311

Resort Motor Inn ◆◆◆

| | | | | | | | |
|---|---|---|---|---|---|---|---|
| 5/26-9/3 | 1P: $122- | 132 | 2P/2B: | $128- | 138 | XP: $15 | F17 |
| 9/4-10/20 | 1P: $112- | 122 | 2P/2B: | $112- | 128 | XP: $15 | F17 |
| 5/1-5/25 & 4/1-4/30 | 1P: $102- | 112 | 2P/2B: | $100- | 118 | XP: $15 | F17 |
| 10/21-3/31 | 1P: $93- | 103 | 2P/2B: | $99- | 109 | XP: $15 | F17 |

**Location:** 1 1/2 mi w on US 322 & 422. W Chocolate Ave & Univ Dr 17033-0446 (PO Box 446). **Fax:** 717/533-9642. **Terms:** Sr. discount; check-in 4 pm; reserv deposit; MAP available; package plans; no pets. **Facility:** 457 rooms. Hearing impaired kits avail. Very attractive public areas & grounds; well-appointed rooms. 2 stories; interior/exterior corridors; conference facilities, convention oriented; putting green; 2 pools (1 heated, 1 indoor), wading pool, saunas, whirlpool; 4 lighted tennis courts; exercise room, playground. Fee: 9 hole pitch & putt; movie theatre. **Dining & Entertainment:** Dining room; 7 am-9 pm, Fri & Sat-10 pm; $6-$25; cocktails/lounge; also, The Tack Room, Hearth Restaurant, see separate listing; nightclub. **Services:** secretarial services; valet laundry; airport transportation. **Recreation:** recreation program; jogging. Fee: bicycles. **All Rooms:** coffeemakers, free movies, cable TV. **Some Rooms:** Fee: refrigerators. **Cards:** AE, CB, DI, DS, MC, VI. *(See ad p A141)*  Ⓓ ⊗

---

**GOING UP?**
Expect elevators in establishments of four or more stories.
We tell you in the listings if there are none.

**HOTEL HERSHEY**     Guaranteed Rates     Phone: 717/533-2171

| | | 1P: | 2P/1B: | 2P/2B: | XP: | F18 |
|---|---|---|---|---|---|---|
| | 5/26-9/3 | $185- 245 | $195- 255 | $195- 255 | $15 | F18 |
| | 9/4-10/21 | $165- 225 | $175- 235 | $175- 235 | $15 | F18 |
| ◆◆◆ | 5/1-5/25 | $155- 215 | $165- 225 | $165- 225 | $15 | F18 |
| Resort Hotel | 10/22-4/30 | $145- 205 | $155- 215 | $155- 215 | $15 | F18 |

**Location:** 1 1/2 mi n via SR 39 w from US 322, off Hershey Park Dr. Hotel Rd 17033 (PO Box 400). Fax: 717/534-8887. **Terms:** Sr. discount; check-in 4 pm; reserv deposit; BP, MAP available; package plans; 3 night min stay; no pets. **Facility:** 241 rooms. A historical hotel. 5 stories; interior corridors; business center, conference facilities; 9 holes golf; 2 pools (1 heated, 1 indoor), wading pool, saunas, whirlpool; 4 tennis courts; exercise room, balloon rides, bocci, lawn bowling. Fee: carriage rides. **Dining & Entertainment:** Restaurant; $10-$35; health conscious menu items; cocktails/lounge; live entertainment Thur-Sun; 24-hour room service; also, The Circular Dining Room, see separate listing. **Services:** valet laundry; area transportation; airport transportation; valet parking. Fee: massage. **Recreation:** children's program, nature trails. Fee: cross country skiing, tobogganing. Rental: bicycles. **All Rooms:** cable TV. Fee: movies. **Some Rooms:** whirlpools. Fee: refrigerators. **Cards:** AE, CB, DI, DS, MC, VI. *(See ad p A141)*     Ⓓ ⊗

**J. SPINNER'S MOTOR INN**

Rates Subject to Change  Phone: 717/533-9157

| | | | | | | | |
|---|---|---|---|---|---|---|---|
| 7/7-9/3 [CP] | 2P/1B: | $80 | 2P/2B: | $80- | 90 | XP: | $5 |
| 6/9-7/6 [CP] | 2P/1B: | $59 | 2P/2B: | $60- | 68 | XP: | $5 |
| 5/1-6/8, 9/4-10/31 & | | | | | | | |
| 4/11-4/30 [CP] | 2P/1B: | $50 | 2P/2B: | $45- | 55 | XP: | $5 |
| 11/1-4/10 [CP] | 2P/1B: | $45 | 2P/2B: | $40- | 49 | XP: | $5 |

Motor Inn

**Location:** 1 mi e on US 422. 845 E Chocolate Ave 17033. Fax: 717/534-1189. **Terms:** Reserv deposit, 3 day notice; no pets. **Facility:** 52 rooms. 2 stories; exterior corridors; meeting rooms; heated pool. **Dining:** Restaurant, see separate listing. **All Rooms:** free movies, combo & shower baths, cable TV. **Cards:** AE, CB, DI, MC, VI. *(See color ad p A137)* D ⊗

**MILTON MOTEL**

Rates Subject to Change  Phone: 717/533-4533

| | | | | | | |
|---|---|---|---|---|---|---|
| 7/7-8/26 | 2P/1B: | $66 | 2P/2B: | $79 | XP: $5 | D |
| 6/9-7/6 & 8/27-9/3 | 2P/1B: | $59 | 2P/2B: | $69 | XP: $5 | D |
| 5/1-6/8 & 9/4-4/30 | 2P/1B: | $39 | 2P/2B: | $49 | XP: $5 | D |

Motel

**Location:** 2 mi e on US 422. 1733 E Chocolate Ave 17033. Fax: 717/533-0369. **Terms:** Sr. discount; reserv deposit; weekly rates; 2 night min stay, weekends 6/15-8/31; no pets. **Facility:** 31 rooms. Attractive guest rooms with appealing room decor. 2 stories; interior/exterior corridors; designated smoking area; heated pool. **Dining:** Restaurant nearby. **All Rooms:** free movies, cable TV. **Some Rooms:** refrigerators. **Cards:** AE, DS, MC, VI. *(See color ad p A139)* D ⊗

**UNION CANAL HOUSE COUNTRY INN**

Rates Subject to Change  Phone: 717/566-0054

| | | | | | | |
|---|---|---|---|---|---|---|
| 5/1-10/1 [CP] | 1P: | $78 | 2P/1B: | $88 | 2P/2B: | $89 | XP:$10-15 |
| 10/2-4/30 [CP] | 1P: | $45 | 2P/1B: | $55 | 2P/2B: | $70 | XP: $10 |

Country Inn

**Location:** 1 1/4 mi w on SR 39 (Hershey Park Dr) from jct US 322, 1/4 mi s via Union Deposit exit (Hanover St). 107 S Hanover St 17033. Fax: 717/566-5867. **Terms:** Sr. discount; reserv deposit; weekly/monthly rates; BP available; no pets. **Facility:** 6 rooms. Built in 1751. 2 stories; interior corridors. **Dining:** Restaurant, see separate listing. **All Rooms:** combo & shower baths, cable TV, no phones. **Cards:** AE, DI, MC, VI. *(See color ad p A140)* D ⊗

**WHITE ROSE MOTEL**

Guaranteed Rates  Phone: 717/533-9876

| | | | | |
|---|---|---|---|---|
| 7/8-9/3 | 2P/2B: | $85 | XP: | $5 |
| 6/10-7/7 | 2P/2B: | $62 | XP: | $5 |
| 5/1-6/9, 9/4-10/31 & 4/1-4/30 | 2P/2B: | $42- | 47 XP: | $5 |
| 11/1-3/31 | 2P/2B: | $39- | 44 XP: | $5 |

Motel

**Location:** 1 1/4 mi e on US 422. 1060 E Chocolate Ave 17033. Fax: 717/533-6923. **Terms:** Sr. discount; reserv deposit; weekly/monthly rates; no pets. **Facility:** 24 rooms. 2 stories; interior/exterior corridors; designated smoking area; heated pool. **Dining:** Restaurant nearby. **Services:** data ports. **All Rooms:** coffeemakers, free movies, refrigerators, combo & shower baths, cable TV. **Some Rooms:** efficiency. **Cards:** AE, DI, MC, VI. *(See color ad p A140)* D ⊗

## RESTAURANTS

THE CIRCULAR DINING ROOM  **Dinner:** over $31  Phone: 717/533-2171

Continental

**Location:** In Hotel Hershey. 17033. **Hours:** 7-10 am, 11:30-2 & 5:30-10:30 pm. **Reservations:** required; for dinner. **Features:** semi-formal attire; Sunday brunch; children's menu; cocktails & lounge; valet parking; a la carte, buffet. Mediterranean atmosphere with grand hotel style dining. Live entertainment Thurs-Sun. Nightly prix fixe menu avail. Smoke free premises. **Cards:** AE, CB, DI, DS, JCB, MC, VI. ⊗

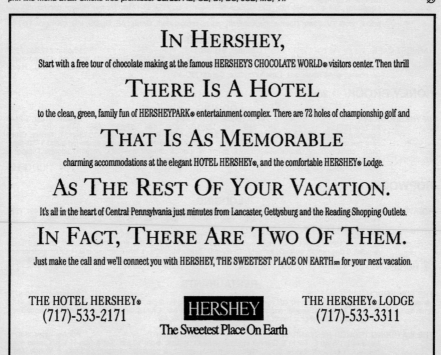

**FRIENDLY FAMILY RESTAURANT**     **Dinner:** up to $10     **Phone:** 717/533-4190
◆
American    **Location:** 1 1/2 mi w on US 322 & US 422. 1000 Reese Ave 17033. **Hours:** 6 am-11 pm, Fri & Sat-midnight. **Closed:** 12/25. **Features:** casual dress; children's menu; carryout. Budget traveler & family oriented. **Cards:** AE, DS, MC, VI. ⊗

**HEARTH RESTAURANT**     **Dinner:** $11-$20     **Phone:** 717/533-3311
◆◆
American    **Location:** In Hershey Lodge & Convention Center. W Chocolate Ave & Univ Dr 17033-0446. **Hours:** 7-11 am, 11:30-2 & 5-9 pm, Fri & Sat-10 pm, Sun 7 am-9 pm. **Features:** casual dress; children's menu; salad bar; cocktails. Luncheon buffet Mon-Sat. Early American decor. Smoke free premises. **Cards:** AE, DI, DS, MC, VI.

**J. SPINNER'S RESTAURANT**     **Dinner:** $11-$20     **Phone:** 717/533-9050
Ⓐ
◆◆◆    **Location:** In J. Spinner's Motor Inn. 845 E Chocolate Ave 17033. **Hours:** 5 pm-10 pm. Closed major holidays, Sun & Mon. **Reservations:** suggested. **Features:** casual dress; children's menu; cocktails & lounge. Williamsburg decor. Traditional beef, veal & seafood favorites. **Cards:** AE, CB, DI, MC, VI.
American    *(See color ad p A137)*    ⊗

**THE TACK ROOM**     **Dinner:** $21-$30     **Phone:** 717/533-3311
◆◆◆
American    **Location:** In Hershey Lodge & Convention Center. W Chocolate Ave & Univ Dr 17033-0446. **Hours:** 11:30 am-2 & 5-10 pm, Sun 11 am-2 pm. **Closed:** Mon. **Features:** semi-formal attire; Sunday brunch; children's menu; cocktails. Baked walleye & signature snapper soup. Some tableside cooking. **Cards:** AE, DI, DS, MC, VI. ⊗

**UNION CANAL HOUSE**   Historical     **Dinner:** $11-$20     **Phone:** 717/566-0054
◆◆
American    **Location:** In Union Canal House Country Inn. 107 S Hanover St 17033. **Hours:** 4 pm-10 pm. Closed major holidays & Sun. **Reservations:** suggested. **Features:** casual dress; children's menu; health conscious menu items; cocktails & lounge. Old English pub atmosphere specializing in steak & seafood, a friendly place to dine. **Cards:** AE, DI, MC, VI. *(See color ad p A140)* ⊗

## HOLLIDAYSBURG—5,600

### RESTAURANT

**THE DREAM FAMILY RESTAURANT**     **Dinner:** up to $10     **Phone:** 814/696-3384
◆◆
American    **Location:** 1 mi e on SR 22. 1500 Allegheny St 16648. **Hours:** 7 am-9 pm, Fri & Sat-10 pm. Closed major holidays. **Features:** casual dress; children's menu; buffet. Additional selection of Italian dishes & seafood. Bakery. **Cards:** AE, DS, MC, VI. ⊗

## HONESDALE—5,000

### LODGING

**FIFE & DRUM MOTOR INN**     Rates Subject to Change     **Phone:** 717/253-1392

| | | 1P: | $35- | 55 | 2P/1B: | $46- | 75 | 2P/2B: | $60- | 65 | XP: | $6 | F9 |
|---|---|---|---|---|---|---|---|---|---|---|---|---|---|
| 7/1-8/31 | | 1P: | $32- | 43 | 2P/1B: | $39- | 51 | 2P/2B: | $46- | 51 | XP: | $6 | F9 |

5/1-6/30 & 9/1-4/30

Ⓐ
◆
Motel    **Location:** Just s on SR 191. 100 Terrace St 18431. Fax: 717/253-1716. **Terms:** Reserv deposit, 30 day notice; pets, $6 dep req. **Facility:** 28 rooms. 2 stories; exterior corridors. **All Rooms:** combo & shower baths, cable TV. **Some Rooms:** microwaves, radios, refrigerators. **Cards:** AE, DI, DS, MC, VI. Ⓓ⊗

### RESTAURANT

**HARVEST CAFE**     **Dinner:** $11-$20     **Phone:** 717/253-2530
◆
American    **Location:** Downtown, 1/2 blk off US 6 & SR 191. 112 10th St 18431. **Hours:** 11 am-8 pm. Closed major holidays & Sun. **Features:** casual dress; children's menu; carryout; salad bar; street parking. Nicely decorated, small restaurant. Light lunch fare. **Cards:** MC, VI. ⊗

## HONEY BROOK—1,200

### LODGING

**WAYNEBROOK INN**     AAA Special Value Rates     **Phone:** 610/273-2444
Ⓐ

| | | 1P: | $69- | 145 | 2P/1B: | $69- | 145 | 2P/2B: | $95- | 145 | XP: | $8 | F18 |
|---|---|---|---|---|---|---|---|---|---|---|---|---|---|
| All Year [CP] | | | | | | | | | | | | | |

◆◆◆
Bed &
Breakfast    **Location:** Jct of US 322 & SR 10. Rts 10 & 322 19344 (PO Box 490). Fax: 610/273-2137. **Terms:** Credit card guarantee, 3 day notice; no pets. **Facility:** 21 rooms. Operated continually as an inn since 1738. Spacious, contemporary rooms with colonial decor. 4 stories; interior corridors; meeting rooms. **Dining &** **Entertainment:** Cocktail lounge. **All Rooms:** combo & shower baths. **Cards:** AE, MC, VI.   Ⓓ⑤⊗
   *(See color ad p A156)*

## HOPWOOD

### LODGING

**HOPWOOD MOTEL**     Guaranteed Rates     **Phone:** 412/437-7591
Ⓐ

| | | 1P: | $36- | 38 | 2P/1B: | $42- | 44 | 2P/2B: | $46- | 50 | XP: | $3 |
|---|---|---|---|---|---|---|---|---|---|---|---|---|
| Fri & Sat 5/1-10/31 | | | | | | | | | | | | |
| Sun-Thurs & Fri & Sat 11/1-4/30 | | 1P: | $32- | 34 | 2P/1B: | $40- | 42 | 2P/2B: | $44- | 46 | XP: | $3 |

◆
Motel    **Location:** 1/2 mi e on US 40, Hopwood Business Rt. 15401 (RD 2, Box 661, UNIONTOWN). **Terms:** Reserv deposit, 3 day notice; no pets. **Facility:** 15 rooms. Variety of rooms. 1 two-bedroom unit. 1 story; exterior corridors. **Dining:** Restaurant nearby. **All Rooms:** combo & shower baths, cable TV. **Some Rooms:** refrigerators. **Cards:** AE, DS, MC, VI.   Ⓓ

### RESTAURANTS

**THE SUN PORCH**     **Dinner:** up to $10     **Phone:** 412/439-5734
◆◆
American    **Location:** 1/2 mi w on Rt 40. 15445. **Hours:** 11 am-8 pm, Fri-9 pm, Sat 4 pm-9 pm. **Closed:** Mon 1/1, 11/23 & 12/25. **Features:** casual dress; children's menu; salad bar. Casual dining in light, cheerful surroundings. Offers extensive buffet at lunch & dinner. **Cards:** CB, DI, DS, MC, VI.

**THE WATERING TROUGH RESTAURANT**     **Dinner:** $11-$20     **Phone:** 412/438-9716
Ⓐ    **Location:** US 40 E. Rt 40 E Summit Mountain 15445. **Hours:** 4 pm-10 pm, Sat & Sun-11 pm. Closed major holidays. **Features:** casual dress; children's menu; early bird specials; carryout; cocktails & lounge. Many pasta & seafood specialties. **Cards:** DI, MC, VI. ⊗
◆
American

## HORSHAM (See PHILADELPHIA & VICINITY ACCOMMODATIONS spotting map pages A196 & A197; see index starting on page A193)

### LODGINGS

**HORSHAM DAYS INN**  AAA Special Value Rates  Phone: 215/674-2500  [62]
All Year [CP]  1P: $73- 79  2P/1B: $77- 85  2P/2B: $79- 85  XP: $6  F18
**Location:** On SR 611N, exit 27 off tpk, 1 mi n on SR 611 (Easton Rd). 245 Easton Rd 19044.
Fax: 215/674-0145. **Terms:** Weekly/monthly rates, upon request; no pets. **Facility:** 171 rooms. Rooms with
Motel  contemporary decor. Nicely landscaped entrance with stone garden. Rates for up to 4 persons; 4 stories; interior corridors; meeting rooms; whirlpool; exercise room. **Dining:** Restaurant nearby. **Services:** data ports.
Fee: coin laundry, airport transportation. **All Rooms:** free & pay movies, cable TV. **Some Rooms:** whirlpools.
Fee: microwaves, refrigerators. **Cards:** AE, CB, DI, DS, MC, VI.  (D) (S) ⊗

**RESIDENCE INN BY MARRIOTT-WILLOW GROVE**  AAA Special Value Rates  Phone: 215/443-7330  [60]
All Year [CP]  1P: $125  2P/1B: $125  2P/2B: $159
Apartment  **Location:** From PA Tpk exit 27, 1 mi n on SR 611, then 1 1/4 mi w on Dresher Rd. 3 Walnut Grove Dr
Motel  19044. Fax: 215/443-7330. **Terms:** Reserv deposit, 3 day notice; weekly/monthly rates; pets. **Facility:** 118
rooms. 1- & 2-bedroom suites with living room & kitchen; many with fireplace. Residential atmosphere. 28 two-
bedroom suites, $144; 2 stories; exterior corridors; meeting rooms; pool, whirlpool; exercise room, sports court.
Fee: coin laundry, airport transportation. **All Rooms:** free movies, cable TV. **Some Rooms:** Fee: VCP's. **Cards:** AE, CB, DI,
DS, JCB, MC, VI.  ⊡ (D) (S) ⊗

## HUNTINGDON—6,800

### LODGINGS

**DAYS INN-RAYSTOWN LAKE**  Rates Subject to Change  Phone: 814/643-3934
Fri & Sat  1P: $44- 49  2P/1B: $51- 56  2P/2B: $51- 56  XP: $5  F12
Sun-Thurs  1P: $39- 44  2P/1B: $46- 51  2P/2B: $46- 51  XP: $5  F12
Motor Inn  **Location:** US 22. Rt 22 & 4th St 16652 (RD 1, Box 353). **Terms:** Credit card guarantee;
weekly/monthly rates; small pets only, $5. **Facility:** 76 rooms. Close to lake. 3 stories; interior/exterior corridors;
meeting rooms. **Dining & Entertainment:** Restaurant; 6 am-10 pm; Fri & Sat-11 pm in summer; $5-$10;
cocktails/lounge. **All Rooms:** combo & shower baths, cable TV. **Some Rooms:** Fee: VCP's. **Cards:** AE, CB, DI, DS, MC,
VI.  (D) ⊗

**HUNTINGDON MOTOR INN**  Rates Subject to Change  Phone: 814/643-1133
All Year  1P: $35- 40  2P/1B: $44- 50  2P/2B: $52- 54  XP: $5  F12
**Location:** On US 22 at jct SR 26. Rt 22 & 26 16652 (PO Box 353). Fax: 814/643-1331. **Terms:** Reserv
Motor Inn  deposit; small pets only, $5. **Facility:** 48 rooms. Variety of room decor. 2 stories; exterior corridors.
**Dining:** Restaurant; 11 am-2 & 5-10 pm, Sat 5 pm-9 pm, closed Sun & major holidays; $9-$17; cocktails.
**All Rooms:** cable TV. Fee: VCP. **Cards:** AE, CB, DI, DS, MC, VI.  (D) ⊗

## INDIANA—15,200

### LODGINGS

**BEST WESTERN UNIVERSITY INN**  AAA Special Value Rates  Phone: 412/349-9620
All Year  1P: $50  2P/1B: $55  2P/2B: $55  XP: $5  F16
**Location:** 3 mi s on US 119. 1545 Wayne Ave 15701. Fax: 412/349-2620. **Terms:** No pets. **Facility:** 107
Motor Inn  rooms. Convenient to University of PA. 2 stories; interior corridors; meeting rooms; heated pool. **Dining &**
**Entertainment:** Restaurant; 6:30 am-1 & 5-9 pm, Sat 8 am-1 & 5-9 pm, Sun 8 am-1 pm; $6-$13;
cocktails/lounge. **All Rooms:** coffeemakers, free & pay movies, cable TV. **Cards:** AE, CB, DI, DS, MC, VI.
(D) ⊗

**HOLIDAY INN**  Guaranteed Rates  Phone: 412/463-3561
All Year  1P: $65- 75  2P/1B: $75- 85  2P/2B: $75- 85  XP: $8
Motor Inn  **Location:** 2 1/4 mi s; US 119 at jct US 422. 1395 Wayne Ave 15701. Fax: 412/463-8006. **Terms:** Sr.
discount; small pets only. **Facility:** 159 rooms. Attractive indoor courtyard. 2 stories; interior/exterior corridors;
meeting rooms; miniature golf; heated indoor pool, sauna, whirlpool; indoor recreation area. **Dining & Entertainment:**
Restaurant; 6 am-10 pm, Sat & Sun from 7 am; $6-$18; cocktails/lounge; Sun brunch. **Services:** data ports; airport
transportation. Fee: coin laundry. **All Rooms:** free movies, cable TV. **Some Rooms:** Fee: refrigerators. **Cards:** AE, CB, DI,
DS, JCB, MC, VI.  (D) ⊗

### RESTAURANTS

**DEAN'S RESTAURANT**  Dinner: $11-$20  Phone: 412/349-3326
American  **Location:** Downtown. 533 Philadelphia St 15701. **Hours:** 6:30 am-9 pm. Closed: 12/25. **Features:** casual
dress; children's menu; early bird specials; salad bar; street parking. Good selection. Seafood also featured.
**Cards:** DS, MC, VI.  ⊗

**PONDEROSA STEAK HOUSE**  Dinner: up to $10  Phone: 412/465-2641
Steakhouse  **Location:** 1 1/2 mi w on SR 286. 1972 SR 286W 15701. **Hours:** 11 am-9 pm, Fri & Sat-10 pm. Closed:
11/23 & 12/25. **Features:** casual dress; children's menu; senior's menu; salad bar. Popular; hearty portions,
mega salad/hot bar & homemade soups. **Cards:** DS, MC, VI.  ⊗

**ROUKI'S RESTAURANT & DELI**  Dinner: up to $10  Phone: 412/465-7200
American  **Location:** Downtown. 665 Philadelphia St 15701. **Hours:** 7:30 am-8 pm. Closed major holidays & Sun.
**Features:** casual dress; children's menu; health conscious menu; carryout; street parking; a la carte.
Specialty sandwiches. **Cards:** AE, DS, MC, VI.  ⊗

## INDUSTRY—2,100

### LODGING

**WILLOWS INN**  Rates Subject to Change  Phone: 412/643-4500
All Year  1P: $36- 42  2P/1B: $47  2P/2B: $41  XP: $5  F16
**Location:** Midland exit off Rt 60, 4 mi w on SR 68. 1830 Beaver-Midland Rd 15052. Fax: 412/643-1765.
Motor Inn  **Terms:** Reserv deposit; no pets. **Facility:** 30 rooms. 2 stories; exterior corridors; meeting rooms.
**Dining:** Also, Willows Inn Family Smorgasbord, see separate listing. **Services:** data ports. **All Rooms:** cable
TV. **Some Rooms:** microwaves, refrigerators, VCP's. **Cards:** AE, DS, MC, VI.  (D)

## RESTAURANT

**WILLOWS INN FAMILY SMORGASBORD**　　**Dinner:** up to $10　　　　　　　Phone: 412/643-4500
◆◆ **Location:** In Willows Inn. 1830 Beaver-Midland Rd 15052. **Hours:** 11:30 am-3 & 3:30-8:30 pm, Tues & Sat
American　3:30 pm-8:30 pm, Sun 10:30 am-6:30 pm. **Closed:** Mon, 1/1, 7/4 & 12/25. **Features:** casual dress; Sunday
brunch; senior's menu; salad bar; cocktails. Casual family atmosphere. **Cards:** AE, DS, MC, VI.　　　🔧 ⊘

# INTERCOURSE

## LODGINGS

**BEST WESTERN INTERCOURSE VILLAGE MOTOR INN**　Rates Subject to Change　　Phone: 717/768-3636

| | | | | |
|---|---|---|---|---|
| 6/15-10/29 | 2P/2B: | $79- | 99 | XP: $6 F12 |
| 5/1-6/14 & 4/1-4/30 | 2P/2B: | $69- | 89 | XP: $6 F12 |
| 10/30-3/31 | 2P/2B: | $49- | 69 | XP: $6 F12 |

Motor Inn　**Location:** On SR 772, 1/2 blk s of SR 340. Rt 340 & 772 17534 (PO Box 40). **Terms:** Credit card
guarantee; no pets. **Facility:** 40 rooms. Good sized rooms, well-maintained grounds. 5 efficiencies, $20 extra;
2 stories; exterior corridors; game room. **Dining:** Restaurant; 6 am-8 pm; $4-$9. **Services:** data ports. Fee: coin laundry.
**All Rooms:** cable TV. **Some Rooms:** coffeemakers, microwaves, refrigerators. **Cards:** AE, DI, DS, MC, VI.
*(See ad starting on p A152)*　　　　　　　　　　　　　　　　　　　　　　　　　　　　　　Ⓓ ⊘

**TRAVELERS REST MOTEL**　　　Rates Subject to Change　　　　　　　Phone: 717/768-8731

| | | | | |
|---|---|---|---|---|
| 6/30-9/3 [CP] | 2P/2B: | $73 | | XP: $8 F16 |
| 9/4-10/28 [CP] | 2P/2B: | $65 | | XP: $8 F16 |
| 5/17-6/29 [CP] | 2P/2B: | $62 | | XP: $8 F16 |
| 5/1-5/16 & 10/29-4/30 [CP] | 2P/2B: | $39- | 53 | XP: $8 F16 |

Motel　**Location:** 1/2 mi e on SR 340. 3701 Old Philadelphia Pike 17534 (PO Box 128). **Terms:** Reserv deposit, 3
day notice; no pets. **Facility:** 40 rooms. Nestled in the heart of Lancaster County's rolling farmlands. 1 story; exterior corridors.
**All Rooms:** cable TV. **Some Rooms:** coffeemakers. **Cards:** AE, DS, MC, VI. *(See ad starting on p A152)*　　Ⓓ ⊘

# IRWIN—4,600

## RESTAURANTS

**BOB EVANS FARMS RESTAURANT**　　**Dinner:** up to $10　　　　　　Phone: 412/864-4446
◆ **Location:** 1/2 mi w on US 30, 1/2 mi w of I-76 tpk exit 7, in Murphys Mart Shopping Center. 8989 Rt 30
American　15642. **Hours:** 6 am-10 pm, Fri & Sat-11:30 pm. **Closed:** 11/23 & 12/25. **Features:** casual dress; children's
menu. Budget traveler & family oriented. **Cards:** MC, VI.　　　　　　　　　　　　　　　　⊘

**NORWIN DINER**　　　　　**Dinner:** $11-$20　　　　　　　　　Phone: 412/863-2941
◆ **Location:** On Rt 30, 2 1/4 mi w of PA Tpk, exit 7 (I-76). 10640 Rt 30 15642. **Hours:** 24 hours. **Closed:** 4/16,
American　11/23 & 12/25. **Features:** casual dress; children's menu; salad bar. Homemade pies & rolls; fresh meats
from in-house butcher shop. **Cards:** AE, CB, DI, DS, MC, VI.　　　　　　　　　　　　　⊘

# JENNERSTOWN—600

## RESTAURANT

**GREEN GABLES**　　　　　**Dinner:** $11-$20　　　　　　　　　Phone: 814/629-9412
◆◆ **Location:** 1/2 mi n on SR 985. 15547. **Hours:** Open 5/1-12/31 & 3/18-4/30; noon-9 pm, Sun-7 pm. **Closed:**
American　Mon, 12/25 & Tues 9/4-10/16. **Reservations:** suggested. **Features:** casual dress; cocktails. Picturesque
country setting with early 1800's grist mill on property. Dinner theater. Open weekends only from 10/16-12/31
& 3/18-5/21, call for times. **Cards:** AE, DI, DS, MC, VI.　　　　　　　　　　　　　　　⊘

# JERMYN—2,300　　(See POCONO MOUNTAINS & VICINITY ACCOMMODATIONS
spotting map pages A212 & A213; see index starting on page A210)

## RESTAURANTS

**WINDSOR INN**　　　　　**Dinner:** up to $10　　　　　　　　Phone: 717/876-4600　Ⓖ⓪
⊕ **Location:** On SR 107, 1/4 mi s of jct US 6. 669-671 Washington Ave 18433. **Hours:** 9 am-11:30 pm, Sun &
Mon 4 pm-10 pm. **Closed:** 4/7, 7/4, 12/24 & 12/25. **Features:** casual dress; children's menu; carryout;
◆ cocktails & lounge. Famous for hot wings. Rustic decor. **Cards:** DS, MC, VI.
American

**WOODLAND INN**　　　　　**Dinner:** $11-$20　　　　　　　　Phone: 717/876-1672　⓪③
◆◆◆ **Location:** From US 6, 1/2 mi se on SR 107, 1 1/4 mi s on Washington Ave. 1 S Washington Ave 18433.
Continental　**Hours:** 4 pm-10 pm, Sun 3 pm-9 pm. **Closed:** Mon, 1/1, 7/4, 12/24 & 12/26. **Reservations:** suggested; Fri &
Sat. **Features:** casual dress; cocktails & lounge. Leisurely dining featuring excellent variety of entrees.
**Cards:** DS, MC, VI.

# JIM THORPE—5,000

## LODGING

**THE INN AT JIM THORPE**　　Guaranteed Rates　　　　　　　Phone: 717/325-2599
◆◆ All Year [CP]　　　1P: $65- 90 2P/1B: $65- 90 2P/2B: $90- 100 XP: $10 D5
Historic　**Location:** Downtown. 24 Broadway 18229. Fax: 717/325-9145. **Terms:** Sr. discount; reserv deposit, 3 day
Country Inn　notice; 2 night min stay, some weekends; no pets. **Facility:** 22 rooms. Victorian decor with modern amenities.
2 stories; interior corridors; meeting rooms. **Dining & Entertainment:** Restaurant; 11:30 am-9 pm; $9-$18;
cocktails/lounge. **All Rooms:** free movies, combo & shower baths, cable TV. **Cards:** AE, DI, DS, MC, VI.　Ⓓ Ⓢ ⊘

## RESTAURANT

**HOTEL SWITZERLAND RESTAURANT**　Historical　　**Dinner:** $11-$20　　　Phone: 717/325-4563
◆◆ **Location:** Off SR 209 on Hazard Square. 5 Hazard Square 18229. **Hours:** 11 am-9 pm, Sun noon-7 pm,
American　dinner only Fri & Sat 1/96-4/96 & Thurs-Sat, 5/95-12/95. **Closed:** major holidays & Mon.
**Reservations:** suggested. **Features:** casual dress; children's menu; carryout; cocktails & lounge; street
parking; a la carte. The oldest remaining structure from the early glory days of Hazard Square. Cozy Victorian atmosphere.
**Cards:** MC, VI.　　　　　　　　　　　　　　　　　　　　　　　　　　　　　　　　⊘

## JOHNSTOWN—28,100

### LODGINGS

**COMFORT INN**  Rates Subject to Change  **Phone: 814/266-3678**
◆◆◆   All Year [CP]   1P: $51- 57   2P/1B: $56- 62   2P/2B: $57   XP: $6  F18
Motel   **Location:** 1 blk e of US 219, exit Elton Rd. 455 Theatre Dr 15904. Fax: 814/266-9783. **Terms:** Sr. discount; weekly/monthly rates; small pets only. **Facility:** 117 rooms. Hilltop location, across from Richland Mall. 27 whirlpool suites, $85-$95; 5 stories; interior corridors; meeting rooms; heated indoor pool, whirlpool; exercise room. **Dining:** Restaurant nearby. **Services:** airport transportation. Fee: coin laundry. **All Rooms:** cable TV, VCP's. Fee: movies. **Some Rooms:** microwaves, radios, refrigerators. Fee: whirlpools. **Cards:** AE, CB, DI, DS, JCB, MC, VI.
*(See ad below)*  Ⓓ Ⓢ ⊗

**HOLIDAY INN**  Guaranteed Rates  **Phone: 814/535-7777**
◆◆   All Year   1P: $59- 69   2P/1B: $69- 79   2P/2B: $69- 79
Motor Inn   **Location:** Downtown; corner Market & Vine sts. 250 Market St 15901. Fax: 814/535-7777. **Terms:** Sr. discount; monthly rates; BP available; pets. **Facility:** 164 rooms. Convenient downtown location. 6 stories; interior corridors; meeting rooms; heated indoor pool, sauna, whirlpool; exercise equipment. **Dining & Entertainment:** Restaurant; seasonal sidewalk cafe; 7 am-10 pm; $10-$16; cocktails/lounge. **Services:** data ports; valet laundry; airport transportation. **All Rooms:** cable TV. Fee: movies. **Some Rooms:** refrigerators. Fee: VCP's. **Cards:** AE, CB, DI, DS, JCB, MC, VI. *(See ad p 105)*  Ⓓ ⊗

**MURPHY INN**  Rates Subject to Change  **Phone: 814/266-4800**
◆◆   All Year   1P: $44   2P/1B: $44   2P/2B: $54   XP: $5  F12
Motel   **Location:** 1/4 mi s off US 219 (SR 756, Elton exit), then 1 blk n on Donald Ln to Penmar Ln. 3203 Penmar Ln 15904. **Terms:** Sr. discount; credit card guarantee; weekly/monthly rates; no pets. **Facility:** 15 rooms. Close to Richland Mall. 2 stories; interior corridors. **All Rooms:** cable TV. **Some Rooms:** 9 efficiencies, no utensils, microwaves, refrigerators. **Cards:** AE, CB, DI, DS, MC, VI.  Ⓓ

**SUPER 8 MOTEL**  Guaranteed Rates  **Phone: 814/266-8789**
◆◆   All Year   1P: $40- 50   2P/1B: $45- 55   2P/2B: $45- 55   XP: $5  F16
Motel   **Location:** 8 1/4 mi se on SR 56; 1/4 mi e of US 219. 1440 Scalp Ave 15904. Fax: 814/266-5285. **Terms:** Sr. discount; reserv deposit; weekly/monthly rates; pets. **Facility:** 105 rooms. Budget traveller oriented. 3 stories; interior corridors. **Services:** airport transportation. Fee: coin laundry. **All Rooms:** cable TV. **Some Rooms:** honor bars. Fee: microwaves, VCP's. **Cards:** AE, CB, DS, JCB, MC, VI.  🖨 Ⓓ Ⓢ ⊗

### RESTAURANT

**LOMBARDO'S**  **Dinner:** $11-$20  **Phone: 814/266-4247**
◆◆   **Location:** 3/4 mi w of US 219, exit SR 56. 935 Scalp Ave 15904. **Hours:** 11 am-10 pm, Sat 4 pm-11 pm,
Italian   Sun 11 am-8 pm. Closed major holidays. **Reservations:** suggested; wkends. **Features:** casual dress; children's menu; cocktails. Good selections of American cuisine & many seafood items. **Cards:** AE, DI, DS, MC, VI.  ⊗

## KANE—4,600

### LODGING

**KANE VIEW MOTEL**  Guaranteed Rates  **Phone: 814/837-8600**
Ⓐ   All Year   1P: $33   2P/1B: $44   2P/2B: $48   XP: $5  F11
   **Location:** 1 mi e on US 6. 16735 (RD 1, Box 91A). **Terms:** Reserv deposit; weekly rates; pets. **Facility:** 19
◆   rooms. Spacious grounds with wooded area. 1 story; exterior corridors. **Recreation:** nature trails; cross
Motel   country skiing. **All Rooms:** combo & shower baths, cable TV. **Cards:** AE, DI, DS, MC, VI.  Ⓓ ⊗

## KENNETT SQUARE—5,200

### LODGINGS

**LONGWOOD INN**  Rates Subject to Change  **Phone: 610/444-3515**
Ⓐ   All Year [CP]   1P: $69   2P/1B: $75   2P/2B: $75   XP: $6  F16
◆◆   **Location:** On US 1, 1/2 mi s of Longwood Gardens. 815 E Baltimore Pike 19348. Fax: 610/444-4285.
Motor Inn   **Terms:** Reserv deposit; no pets. **Facility:** 28 rooms. Very attractive landscaping in season. 2 stories; exterior corridors; meeting rooms. **Dining & Entertainment:** Dining room; 7 am-9 pm, Fri & Sat-9:30 pm; $11-$19; cocktails/lounge. **All Rooms:** Fee: VCP. **Cards:** AE, DI, DS, MC, VI.  Ⓓ ⊗

**SCARLETT HOUSE**  Rates Subject to Change  **Phone: 610/444-9592**
Ⓐ   All Year [CP]   1P: $65- 100   2P/1B: $65- 100   2P/2B: $110   XP: $10
   **Location:** 5 blks w. 503 W State St 19348. **Terms:** Age restrictions may apply; check-in 4 pm; reserv
◆◆◆   deposit, 3 day notice; weekly rates; no pets. **Facility:** 4 rooms. Stone manor built in Foursquare architectural
Historic Bed   style. Attractively furnished with Victorian antiques circa late 1800's. 3 stories; interior corridors; smoke free
& Breakfast   premises. **All Rooms:** no TVs. **Some Rooms:** phones.  Ⓓ ⊗

## KING OF PRUSSIA

### LODGINGS

**COMFORT INN VALLEY FORGE**  AAA Special Value Rates  **Phone: 610/962-0700**
Ⓐ   5/1-6/30 & 9/1-10/31 [CP]   1P: $65- 99   2P/1B: $70- 104   2P/2B: $75- 109   XP: $5  F18
   7/1-8/31 & 11/1-4/30 [CP]   1P: $55- 94   2P/1B: $60- 94   2P/2B: $65- 104   XP: $5  F18
◆◆◆   **Location:** On US 202N, 3/4 mi ne of I-76, exit 26B, from PA Tpk exit 24 (Valley Forge) 1 mi ne. 550 W
Motor Inn   Dekalb Pike 19406. Fax: 610/962-0218. **Terms:** Credit card guarantee; weekly/monthly rates; small pets only. **Facility:** 121 rooms. 5 stories; interior corridors; meeting rooms; exercise room. **Dining:** Restaurant nearby. **Services:** data ports; valet laundry. Fee: airport transportation. **All Rooms:** honor bars, free movies, combo & shower baths, cable TV, VCP's. **Cards:** AE, CB, DI, DS, JCB, MC, VI.  Roll in showers. 🖨 Ⓓ Ⓢ ⊗

**HAMPTON INN** Rates Subject to Change **Phone:** 610/962-8111

AAA ◆◆◆ Motel

Sun-Thurs [CP] 1P: $69- 77 2P/1B: $76- 84 2P/2B: $79
Fri & Sat [CP] 1P: $69 2P/1B: $69 2P/2B: $69

**Location:** On US 202N; 3/4 mi ne of I-76, exit 26B, from PA Tpk exit 24 (Valley Forge), 1 mi ne. 530 Dekalb Pike 19406. Fax: 610/962-5494. **Terms:** Credit card guarantee; weekly/monthly rates; no pets. **Facility:** 148 rooms. Comfortably furnished guest rooms. 7 stories; interior corridors; meeting rooms; sauna; exercise room. **Dining:** Restaurant nearby. **Services:** data ports; valet laundry. **All Rooms:** free movies, cable TV. **Some Rooms:** refrigerators. **Cards:** AE, CB, DI, DS, MC, VI.

HOLIDAY INN OF KING OF PRUSSIA Guaranteed Rates **Phone:** 610/265-7500

◆◆◆ Motor Inn

All Year 1P: $95- 99 2P/1B: $100- 104 2P/2B: $105 XP: $10 F16

**Location:** 1 blk w off US 202N, 1 1/2 mi e of tpk exit 24. 260 Mall Blvd 19406. Fax: 610/265-4076. **Terms:** Sr. discount; monthly rates; package plans; pets, $10. **Facility:** 305 rooms. Comfortable guestrooms; located adjacent to a large shopping mall. 5 stories; interior corridors; conference facilities; sauna, whirlpool, heated indoor lap pool; racquetball courts; health club, indoor track. **Dining & Entertainment:** Dining room; 6:30 am-10 pm, Sat & Sun from 7 am; $9-$16; cocktails/lounge; entertainment. **Services:** data ports; valet laundry. Fee: airport transportation. **All Rooms:** cable TV. Fee: movies. **Some Rooms:** refrigerators. **Cards:** AE, CB, DI, DS, JCB, MC, VI.

**HOWARD JOHNSON LODGE** Rates Subject to Change **Phone:** 610/265-4500

AAA ◆◆◆ Motel

All Year [CP] 1P: $55- 87 2P/1B: $55- 92 2P/2B: $55- 97 XP: $10 F18

**Location:** On US 202N & S Gulph Rd, 1 1/4 mi e of tpk exit 24, e of I-76 exit 26A westbound, 26B eastbound. 127 S Gulph Rd 19406. Fax: 610/337-0672. **Terms:** Sr. discount; weekly/monthly rates; no pets. **Facility:** 168 rooms. 2-story garden type property. Weekend rates for up to 4 persons. 18 executive rooms with upgraded amenities; 2 stories; interior/exterior corridors; meeting rooms; pool. **Dining:** Restaurant nearby. **Services:** data ports. Fee: coin laundry, airport transportation. **All Rooms:** free & pay movies, cable TV. **Some Rooms:** Fee: whirlpools. **Cards:** AE, CB, DI, DS, MC, VI. *(See ad below)*

MCINTOSH INN OF KING OF PRUSSIA Rates Subject to Change **Phone:** 610/768-9500

◆◆ Motel

All Year 1P: $48- 53 2P/1B: $55 2P/2B: $60 XP: $3 F18

**Location:** 1/2 mi n of jct US 202 on SR 363, exit 24 off PA Tpk, US 202N to first traffic light turn left. 260 N Gulph Rd 19406. Fax: 610/768-0225. **Terms:** Sr. discount; weekly rates; no pets. **Facility:** 212 rooms. Some balconies. Adjacent to one of the nation's largest shopping malls. 7 stories; interior corridors. **Dining:** Restaurant nearby. **Services:** data ports; valet laundry. **All Rooms:** free movies, combo & shower baths, cable TV. **Some Rooms:** radios. Fee: microwaves, refrigerators. **Cards:** AE, CB, DI, MC, VI. *(See ad p A185)*

**THE PARK RIDGE AT VALLEY FORGE** AAA Special Value Rates **Phone:** 610/337-1800

AAA ◆◆◆ Hotel

All Year 1P: $125- 145 2P/1B: $135- 155 2P/2B: $145- 165 XP: $10 F

**Location:** On SR 363 (N Gulph Rd) 1/4 mi w of I-76, exit 24. 480 N Gulph Rd 19406. Fax: 610/337-4506. **Terms:** Credit card guarantee; weekly/monthly rates; no pets. **Facility:** 289 rooms. 6 stories; interior corridors; conference facilities; luxury level rooms; pool; 2 lighted tennis courts; exercise room, heliport. **Dining & Entertainment:** Dining room; 6:30 am-11 pm, Sun from 7 am; $6-$20; cocktails/lounge; 24-hour room service; entertainment. **Services:** data ports; valet laundry. Fee: airport transportation. **All Rooms:** free & pay movies, cable TV. **Some Rooms:** honor bars, refrigerators. **Cards:** AE, CB, DI, DS, JCB, MC, VI.

**RESIDENCE INN BY MARRIOTT**
◆◆◆     All Year [BP]     Rates Subject to Change     Phone: 610/640-9494
Apartment     All Year [BP]     1P: $115     2P/1B: $115     2P/2B: $135
Motel     **Location:** From US 202, Devon exit, then SR 252 (Swedesford Rd) 1 mi s. 600 W Swedesford Rd 19312. **Fax:** 610/993-0330. **Terms:** Sr. discount; reserv deposit, 3 day notice; pets, $100, $6 daily. **Facility:** 88 rooms. Residential townhouse style complex. Many units with fireplace. 2 stories; exterior corridors; meeting rooms; heated pool, whirlpool; sports court. **Dining:** Restaurant nearby. **Services:** data ports; health club privileges. Fee: coin laundry. **All Rooms:** kitchens, free movies, cable TV. **Some Rooms:** Fee: VCP's. **Cards:** AE, CB, DI, DS, JCB, MC, VI.
Ⓓ ⊗

**VALLEY FORGE HILTON**
(AAA)     Guaranteed Rates     Phone: 610/337-1200
◆◆◆     All Year     1P: $79- 119     2P/1B: $89- 129     2P/2B: $89- 129     XP: $10     F
Hotel     **Location:** On US 202N, 1 1/4 mi ne of I-76 exit 24A. 251 W Dekalb Pike 19406. **Fax:** 610/337-2224. **Terms:** Sr. discount; AP, BP, CP, MAP available; no pets. **Facility:** 340 rooms. Attractive public areas. 3 two-bedroom units. 9 stories; interior corridors; conference facilities; luxury level rooms; heated indoor/outdoor pool, saunas, whirlpool; exercise room. **Dining & Entertainment:** 2 dining rooms; 6:30 am-11 pm; $10-$26; cocktails/lounge; also, Kobe, see separate listing; entertainment, nightclub. **Services:** data ports; valet laundry; area transportation, The Court & Plaza Malls. Fee: airport transportation. **All Rooms:** free & pay movies, cable TV. **Some Rooms:** honor bars, coffeemakers, refrigerators. Fee: whirlpools. **Cards:** AE, CB, DI, DS, MC, VI.
*(See ad p 28)*
🎦 Ⓓ Ⓢ ⊗

## RESTAURANTS

**THE BARONS INNE**
◆◆◆     **Dinner:** $21-$30     Phone: 610/265-2550
Continental     **Location:** On SR 363, 1/4 mi w of I-76, exit 24. 499 N Gulph Rd 19406. **Hours:** 11 am-2:30 & 5-10:30 pm, Fri & Sat 5 pm-11 pm. Closed major holidays & Sun. **Reservations:** suggested. **Features:** casual dress; health conscious menu; carryout; cocktails & lounge. Elegant dining in Old World charm. **Cards:** AE, CB, DI, MC, VI.

**CHARLEY'S PLACE**
◆     **Dinner:** $11-$20     Phone: 610/337-8620
American     **Location:** On SR 363, (N Gulph Rd) 1/2 mi n of jct US 202. N Gulph Rd & Mall Blvd 19406. **Hours:** 11:30 am-10:30 pm, Fri-11 pm, Sat noon-11 pm, Sun noon-9:30 pm. **Reservations:** suggested. **Features:** casual dress; children's menu; early bird specials; carryout; cocktails & lounge. Brandywine decor. Casual family dining. **Cards:** AE, CB, DI, DS, MC, VI.
⊗

**KENNEDY SUPPLEE MANSION RESTAURANT**     Historical     **Dinner:** $21-$30     Phone: 215/337-3777
Continental     **Location:** From I-76 exit 24, 3/4 mi w on SR 363 n Gulph Rd to SR 23W, 1/4 mi on right side. 1100 W Valley Forge Rd 19406. **Hours:** 11:30 am-2 & 5:30-10 pm, Sat 5:30-10:30 pm. Closed: 12/25 & Sun. **Reservations:** suggested. **Features:** semi-formal attire; cocktails & lounge; valet parking. Built in 1852 with Italian architectural detail. Elegant setting for very well prepared entrees. Private dining rooms avail. **Cards:** AE, MC, VI.

**KOBE**
◆◆◆     **Dinner:** $11-$20     Phone: 610/337-1200
Ethnic     **Location:** In Valley Forge Hilton. 251 W DeKalb Pike 19406. **Hours:** 6 pm-10 pm, Sun 5 pm-9 pm. Closed: 1/1, 11/23 & 12/25. **Reservations:** suggested. **Features:** casual dress; children's menu; senior's menu; cocktails & lounge; valet parking; buffet. A very entertaining Japanese Hibachi house featuring the chef as the star attraction. Continental to Japanese fare. Smoke free premises. **Cards:** AE, CB, DI, DS, JCB, MC, VI.
⊗

**PASTABILITIES**
(AAA)     **Dinner:** up to $10     Phone: 610/265-8772
◆◆     **Location:** On US 202N, 1 mi ne of I-76, exit 26B. 435 W DeKalb Pike 19406. **Hours:** 11:30 am-10 pm, Fri & Sat-midnight, Sun 9 am-10 pm. **Reservations:** suggested. **Features:** casual dress; children's menu; carryout; cocktails & lounge; buffet. Generous portions. **Cards:** AE, CB, DI, DS, MC, VI.
Italian     ⊗

# KINTNERSVILLE

## LODGINGS

**THE BUCKSVILLE HOUSE**
◆◆◆     Rates Subject to Change     Phone: 610/847-8948
Historic Bed     All Year [BP]     1P: $100- 130     2P/1B: $100- 130     XP: $35
& Breakfast     **Location:** 2 mi n on SR 412 (Durham Rd) from jct SR 611. 4501 Durham Rd, Rt 412 18930-1610. **Terms:** Age restrictions may apply; reserv deposit, 7 day notice; weekly rates; no pets. **Facility:** 5 rooms. Tranquil rural setting. Circa 1795, restored with antiques & reproductions. Hearty breakfast served in outdoor gazebo. Inviting gardens & patio. 3 stories; interior/exterior corridors; smoke free premises. **All Rooms:** combo & shower baths, no phones, no TVs. **Cards:** AE, DS, MC, VI.
Ⓓ ⊗

**LIGHTFARM**
◆◆◆     Rates Subject to Change     Phone: 610/847-3276
Historic Bed     All Year [BP]     1P: $81- 115     2P/1B: $81- 115     2P/2B: $115- 150     XP: $10   F12
& Breakfast     **Location:** 3/4 mi s on Berger Rd from SR 412. 2042 Berger Rd 18930. **Fax:** 610/847-2926. **Terms:** Sr. discount; reserv deposit, 7 day notice; weekly rates; small pets only, $15. **Facility:** 3 rooms. 1815 farm with original floors. Very attractive public areas with period furnishings. Working farm. 1 two-bedroom unit. 3 stories; interior corridors; smoke free premises; meeting rooms; whirlpool. **Recreation:** hiking trails. **All Rooms:** combo & shower baths, cable TV, no phones. **Some Rooms:** VCP's. **Cards:** AE, MC, VI.
Ⓓ ⊗

# KITTANNING—5,100

## LODGINGS

**FRIENDSHIP INN KITTANNING**
(AAA)     AAA Special Value Rates     Phone: 412/543-1100
◆     All Year     1P: $42- 44     2P/1B: $46- 48     2P/2B: $48- 52     XP: $12   F18
Motel     **Location:** Rt 28N exit 19, 5 mi e on SR 422. 16201 (RD 6, Box 2796). **Fax:** 412/543-1526. **Terms:** Reserv deposit, 3 day notice; weekly rates; no pets. **Facility:** 20 rooms. 2 stories; exterior corridors; meeting rooms. **Services:** data ports; valet laundry. **All Rooms:** combo & shower baths, cable TV. Fee: VCP. **Some Rooms:** coffeemakers, radios. Fee: microwaves, refrigerators. **Cards:** AE, CB, DI, DS, JCB, MC, VI.
Ⓓ ⊗

**QUALITY INN ROYLE**
(AAA)     AAA Special Value Rates     Phone: 412/543-1159
◆◆◆     All Year [CP]     1P: $50     2P/1B: $54     2P/2B: $54     XP: $4   F18
Motel     **Location:** 1 3/4 mi w via US 422, at jct SR 268. 405 Butler Rd 16201. **Fax:** 412/543-1159. **Terms:** Reserv deposit, 3 day notice; no pets. **Facility:** 58 rooms. Exceptionally well maintained property. 2 stories; interior/exterior corridors. **Dining:** Restaurant nearby. **Services:** valet laundry. **All Rooms:** cable TV. **Some Rooms:** coffeemakers, refrigerators. Fee: VCP's. **Cards:** AE, CB, DI, DS, JCB, MC, VI.
Ⓓ ⊗

## KNOX—700

### RESTAURANT

**WOLF'S DEN RESTAURANT**
◆◆ American
**Dinner: $11-$20**
**Phone: 814/797-1105**
**Location:** At I-80 exit 7. 16232. **Hours:** 11:30 am-9 pm, Fri & Sat-10 pm, Sun 11 am-9 pm. Closed: 1/1, 11/23 & 12/25. **Features:** Sunday brunch; children's menu; carryout; cocktails & lounge; a la carte. Served in attractively remodeled 1831 barn. **Cards:** AE, DS, MC, VI. ⊗

## KULPSVILLE

### LODGING

**HOLIDAY INN-KULPSVILLE**
◆◆◆ Motor Inn

| | | | | | | | |
|---|---|---|---|---|---|---|---|
| Sun-Thurs | 1P: | $74 | 2P/1B: | $79- | 84 | 2P/2B: | $79 | XP: $5 F18 |
| Fri & Sat | 1P: | $64 | 2P/1B: | $64 | | 2P/2B: | $64 | XP: $5 F18 |

Rates Subject to Change   **Phone: 215/368-3800**
**Location:** Exit 31, NE Ext PA Tpk. 1750 Sumneytown Pike 19443. Fax: 215/368-7824. **Terms:** Reserv deposit, 3 day notice; pets. **Facility:** 184 rooms. 4 stories; interior corridors; conference facilities; pool; exercise room, basketball, horseshoes, volleyball. **Dining & Entertainment:** Restaurant; 6:45 am-2 & 5:30-10 pm; $5-$15; health conscious menu; cocktails/lounge; entertainment. **Services:** valet laundry. **All Rooms:** cable TV. Fee: movies. **Some Rooms:** coffeemakers, 9 efficiencies. Fee: refrigerators, VCP's. **Cards:** AE, CB, DI, DS, JCB, MC, VI. ⒹⓈ⊗

## KUTZTOWN—4,700

### LODGINGS

**CAMPUS INN**
ⒶⒶ
◆◆ Motel
AAA Special Value Rates   **Phone: 610/683-8721**

| | | | | | | | |
|---|---|---|---|---|---|---|---|
| All Year | 1P: | $40- 70 | 2P/1B: | $50- 75 | 2P/2B: | $50- 75 | XP: $5 F10 |

**Location:** US 222 Kutztown/Virginsville exit, 1 mi e. 15080 Kutztown Rd 19530. Fax: 610/683-8721. **Terms:** Reserv deposit, 3 day notice; CP available; small pets only. **Facility:** 29 rooms. 2 stories; exterior corridors; pool. **Services:** data ports. **All Rooms:** cable TV. **Some Rooms:** microwaves, refrigerators. Fee: whirlpools. **Cards:** AE, DI, DS, MC, VI. *(See color ad p A215)* ⒹⓈ⊗

**LINCOLN MOTEL**
ⒶⒶ
◆◆ Motel
AAA Special Value Rates   **Phone: 610/683-3456**

| | | | | | | | |
|---|---|---|---|---|---|---|---|
| All Year | 1P: | $35- 65 | 2P/1B: | $45- 70 | 2P/2B: | $45- 70 | XP: $5 F10 |

**Location:** US 222, Kutztown/Virginsville exit. Main St 19530 (RD 4 Box 171). **Terms:** Reserv deposit, 3 day notice; weekly rates; small pets only. **Facility:** 14 rooms. Cozy rooms with contemporary appointments. 1 story; exterior corridors. **All Rooms:** combo & shower baths, cable TV. **Some Rooms:** radios. **Cards:** AE, DI, DS, MC, VI. ⒹⓈ⊗

## LAHASKA

### LODGING

**GOLDEN PLOUGH INN**
ⒶⒶ
◆◆◆ Motor Inn
All Year [CP]   Rates Subject to Change   **Phone: 215/794-4004**

| | | | | | | | |
|---|---|---|---|---|---|---|---|
| | 1P: | $95- 300 | 2P/1B: | $95- 300 | 2P/2B: | $95- 300 | XP: $15 F12 |

**Location:** On SR 202 in Peddlers Village. SR 202 & Street Rd 18931. Fax: 215/794-4001. **Terms:** Sr. discount; reserv deposit; MAP available; package plans; no pets. **Facility:** 60 rooms. Spacious guest rooms with accent on elegant country style furnishings. Some rooms with fireplace. Suites, $175-$300; 3 stories; interior corridors; meeting rooms. **Dining:** Dining room; 7 am-11 pm; $11-$16; cocktails. **Services:** data ports; valet laundry. **All Rooms:** refrigerators, cable TV. **Some Rooms:** 4 kitchens, whirlpools. **Cards:** AE, CB, DI, DS, MC, VI. ⒹⓈ⊗

### RESTAURANT

**COCK 'N BULL RESTAURANT**
ⒶⒶ
◆◆ American
**Dinner: $11-$20**
**Phone: 215/794-4010**
**Location:** On SR 202 in Peddlers Village. SR 263 & Street Rd 18931. **Hours:** 11 am-3 & 5-9 pm, Sat 11 am-3 & 4-10 pm, Sun 10 am-3 & 4-8 pm. Closed: 1/1, 12/25 & evening of 12/24. **Reservations:** suggested. **Features:** casual dress; children's menu; cocktails & lounge; buffet. Murder Mystery Fri & Sat, call for time & dates. Sun brunch. **Cards:** AE, CB, DI, DS, MC, VI. ⊗

## LAMAR—2,300

### LODGING

**COMFORT INN OF LAMAR-LOCK HAVEN**
◆◆ Motel
All Year [CP]   Rates Subject to Change   **Phone: 717/726-4901**

| | | | | | | | |
|---|---|---|---|---|---|---|---|
| | 1P: | $39- 62 | 2P/1B: | $44- 80 | 2P/2B: | $49- 80 | XP: $5 F18 |

**Location:** On SR 64, at I-80 exit 25. 17751 (RR 3, Box 600, MILL HALL). Fax: 717/726-3617. **Terms:** Age restrictions may apply; credit card guarantee; pets. **Facility:** 155 rooms. Convenient to the interstate. 2-3 stories; interior corridors; meeting rooms; pool, wading pool; playground. **Dining & Entertainment:** Cocktail lounge; restaurant nearby. **Services:** Fee: coin laundry. **All Rooms:** free movies, cable TV. **Some Rooms:** whirlpools. **Cards:** AE, CB, DI, DS, JCB, MC, VI. ⒹⓈ⊗

## LAMPETER

### LODGINGS

**BED & BREAKFAST-THE MANOR**
◆◆ Bed & Breakfast
Guaranteed Rates   **Phone: 717/464-9564**

| | | | | | |
|---|---|---|---|---|---|
| 5/15-10/31 [BP] | 2P/1B: | $79- 99 | 2P/2B: | $79- 99 | XP: $30 D12 |
| 5/1-5/14 & 11/1-4/30 [BP] | 2P/1B: | $69- 89 | 2P/2B: | $69- 89 | XP: $30 D12 |

**Location:** 1/4 mi w on SR 741. 830 Village Rd 17537 (PO Box 416). **Terms:** Reserv deposit, 7 day notice, cancellation fee imposed; weekly/monthly rates; no pets. **Facility:** 6 rooms. Cozy farmhouse in a rural setting. 2 stories; interior corridors; smoke free premises; pool; lawn games. **Services:** area transportation, airport transportation. **All Rooms:** no phones, no TVs. **Some Rooms:** combo & shower baths, shared bathrooms. **Cards:** MC, VI. ⒹⓈ⊗

**THE WALKABOUT INN BED & BREAKFAST**

(AAA) ◆◆◆
Historic Bed & Breakfast

| | | | | | |
|---|---|---|---|---|---|
| 11/1-3/31 [BP] | 1P: $70 | 2P/1B: $85 | 2P/2B: $139 | XP: $25 |
| 5/1-10/31 & 4/1-4/30 [BP] | 1P: $75 | 2P/1B: $95 | 2P/2B: $95 | XP: $25 |

Rates Subject to Change          Phone: 717/464-0707

**Location:** From US 30, exit Rt 462 (Lincoln Hwy) w 1 blk; 2 mi s on Strasburg Pike, 1 mi w on Pioneer Rd, 1/2 mi s on Lampeter Rd, 1/4 mi w on SR 741. 837 Village Rd 17537 (PO Box 294). **Terms:** Reserv deposit, 7 day notice; package plans, Sun-Thurs; no pets. **Facility:** 5 rooms. Attractive rooms with many antiques. Authentic British-style bed & breakfast inn. Rural village setting. 3 stories; exterior corridors; smoke free premises; playground. **All Rooms:** combo & shower baths, cable TV, no phones. **Some Rooms:** VCP's, whirlpools. **Cards:** AE, MC, VI. *(See color ad p A148)*                    (D) ⊗

# LANCASTER—55,600

## LODGINGS

**BEST WESTERN EDEN RESORT INN & CONFERENCE CENTER**

(AAA) ◆◆◆
Motor Inn

| | | | | | | |
|---|---|---|---|---|---|---|
| 7/1-10/29 | 1P: $99- 124 | 2P/2B: $99- 139 | XP: $10 | F |
| 5/1-6/30 | 1P: $89- 118 | 2P/2B: $89- 118 | XP: $10 | F |
| 10/3-4/30 | 1P: $84- 99 | 2P/2B: $84- 99 | XP: $10 | F |

Rates Subject to Change          Phone: 717/569-6444

**Location:** At jct US 30 & SR 272, 1/4 mi n on SR 272. 222 Eden Rd 17601. Fax: 717/569-4208. **Terms:** Sr. discount; reserv deposit; weekly/monthly rates; AP, BP, CP available; small pets only. **Facility:** 274 rooms. Spacious public areas. 16 two-bedroom units. 3 stories; interior/exterior corridors; business center, conference facilities; luxury level rooms; 2 pools (1 heated, 1 indoor), wading pool, saunas, whirlpool; 1 lighted tennis court; exercise room, playground, basketball, shuffleboard. **Dining & Entertainment:** 2 dining rooms; 6:30 am-11 pm, Sun brunch 10:30 am-2 pm; $10-$20; cocktails; entertainment. **Services:** PC, secretarial services; area transportation, to train station, airport transportation. Fee: coin laundry. **All Rooms:** coffeemakers, free & pay movies, cable TV. **Some Rooms:** 40 kitchens, microwaves, refrigerators, whirlpools. **Cards:** AE, CB, DI, DS, MC, VI. *(See ad p A150)*                    (D) ⊗

**CLASSIC INN**

(AAA) ◆◆◆
Motel

| | | | | | | |
|---|---|---|---|---|---|---|
| 6/24-11/13 | 1P: $59- 69 | 2P/1B: $59- 79 | 2P/2B: $69- 89 | XP:$5-6 F16 |
| 5/1-6/23 & 11/14-4/30 | 1P: $59- 69 | 2P/1B: $49- 59 | 2P/2B: $59- 69 | XP:$5-6 F16 |

Rates Subject to Change          Phone: 717/291-4576

**Location:** On SR 30. 2302 Lincoln Hwy E 17602. Fax: 717/291-1762. **Terms:** Credit card guarantee, 5 day notice; no pets. **Facility:** 18 rooms. Very attractive rooms. 2 stories; interior/exterior corridors; smoke free premises. **All Rooms:** combo & shower baths, cable TV. **Some Rooms:** coffeemakers, efficiency, microwaves, refrigerators, VCP's, whirlpools. **Cards:** AE, DS, MC, VI.                    (D) ⊗

**COMFORT INN-SHERWOOD KNOLL**

(AAA) ◆◆◆
Motor Inn

| | | | | | | |
|---|---|---|---|---|---|---|
| 7/1-10/31 [CP] | 1P: $60- 74 | 2P/1B: $70- 94 | 2P/2B: $94 | XP: $6 F18 |
| 11/1-4/30 [CP] | 1P: $59- 69 | 2P/1B: $69- 85 | 2P/2B: $85 | XP: $6 F18 |
| 5/1-6/30 [CP] | 1P: $58- 70 | 2P/1B: $68- 84 | 2P/2B: $84 | XP: $6 F18 |

AAA Special Value Rates          Phone: 717/898-2431

**Location:** 5 mi w on US 30, at Centerville exit. 500 Centerville Rd 17601. Fax: 717/898-2344. **Terms:** Credit card guarantee, 3 day notice; small pets only. **Facility:** 166 rooms. Located along busy interstate highway. 4 rooms with whirlpool, $98 for 2 persons; 3 stories; interior corridors; meeting rooms; pool; exercise room. **Dining & Entertainment:** Dining room; 7 am-9:30 pm, Sun-8 pm; $7-$14; cocktails; entertainment. **All Rooms:** free & pay movies, cable TV. **Some Rooms:** refrigerators. **Cards:** AE, CB, DI, DS, MC, VI.                    (D) ⊗

**CONTINENTAL MOTOR INN**

(AAA) ◆◆
Motor Inn

| | | | | |
|---|---|---|---|---|
| 6/18-9/4 5/1-6/17, 9/5-11/25 & | 2P/1B: $69- 78 | 2P/2B: $81- 92 | XP: $10 F15 |
| 4/2-4/30 | 2P/1B: $52- 62 | 2P/2B: $62- 72 | XP: $7 F15 |
| 11/26-4/1 | 2P/1B: $48- 50 | 2P/2B: $52- 54 | XP:$7-10 F15 |

Rates Subject to Change          Phone: 717/299-0421

**Location:** 5 mi e on US 30. 2285 Lincoln Hwy E 17602. Fax: 717/293-8512. **Terms:** Reserv deposit; no pets. **Facility:** 165 rooms. Right next to Dutch Wonderland. 2 stories; exterior corridors; meeting rooms; 2 pools (1 heated, 1 indoor), 2 wading pools, sauna, whirlpool; 2 tennis courts( Fee: 2 lighted); playground. **Dining & Entertainment:** Dining room; 7:30 am-10:30 & 6-9 pm, Fri-9:30 pm, Sat 8 am-11:30 & 6-10 pm, Sun 8 am-11:30 & 6-9 pm; $9-$15; health conscious menu items; cocktails/lounge. **Services:** Fee: coin laundry. **All Rooms:** coffeemakers, cable TV. **Some Rooms:** refrigerators. Fee: VCP's. **Cards:** AE, DI, DS, MC, VI. *(See color ad p A150)*                    (D) ⊗

**COUNTRY LIVING MOTOR INN**
◆◆◆
Motel

6/8-10/28
5/1-6/7 & 2/9-4/30
10/29-2/8

Rates Subject to Change

Phone: 717/295-7295

| | | | | |
|---|---|---|---|---|
| 2P/2B: | $68- 75 | XP: $5 | F5 |
| 2P/2B: | $51- 65 | XP: $5 | F5 |
| 2P/2B: | $41- 59 | XP: $5 | F5 |

**Location:** 2 mi w on SR 340; 2 mi e of jct US 30 & SR 340. 2406 Old Philadelphia Pike 17602. **Terms:** Reserv deposit; no pets. **Facility:** 34 rooms. Country theme setting with good sized rooms & well-kept grounds. 2 stories; interior corridors. **Dining:** Continental breakfast 5/1-10/31 weekends only. **All Rooms:** cable TV. **Some Rooms:** radios, refrigerators. Fee: whirlpools. **Cards:** MC, VI.  Ⓓ ⊗

**DAYS INN-LANCASTER**
AAA Special Value Rates
Phone: 717/299-5700

5/1-12/31 & 4/1-4/30    1P: $76-  89        2P/2B: $86-  99  XP: $10 F12
1/1-3/31                1P: $70-  76        2P/2B: $80-  86  XP: $10 F12
Motor Inn

**Location:** 1/2 mi s off US 30, on US 222S, 1/4 blk w on Keller Ave. 30 Keller Ave 17601. **Fax:** 717/295-1907. **Terms:** Reserv deposit; no pets. **Facility:** 193 rooms. Located in busy commercial district. Convenient to train station. 2-3 stories; interior/exterior corridors; meeting rooms; 2 pools (1 heated, 1 indoor), wading pool, sauna; 3 lighted tennis courts; playground. **Dining & Entertainment:** Dining room; 7 am-10 pm; $8-$15; cocktails/lounge. **Services:** Fee: coin laundry. **Recreation:** jogging. **All Rooms:** free & pay movies, cable TV. Fee: safes. **Some Rooms:** Fee: refrigerators. **Cards:** AE, DI, DS, MC, VI.    Ⓓ ⊗

**ECONO LODGE NORTH**
Rates Subject to Change
Phone: 717/299-6900

6/16-8/31    1P: $59-  75   2P/1B: $59-  75   2P/2B: $59-  75   XP: $5  F18
9/1-10/31    1P: $44-  75   2P/1B: $47-  75   2P/2B: $53-  75   XP: $5  F18
11/1-4/30    1P: $32-  60   2P/1B: $33-  60   2P/2B: $36-  60   XP: $5  F18
5/1-6/15     1P: $39-  60   2P/1B: $41-  60   2P/2B: $41-  60   XP: $5  F18
Motel

**Location:** 4 1/2 mi e on US 30. 2165 US Hwy 30 E 17602. **Fax:** 717/299-6900. **Terms:** Sr. discount; reserv deposit; weekly rates; no pets. **Facility:** 49 rooms. Modern room decor. 2 stories; interior corridors. **Dining:** Restaurant nearby. **All Rooms:** refrigerators, cable TV. **Cards:** AE, DS, MC, VI.    Ⓓ ⊗

**ECONO LODGE SOUTH**  Rates Subject to Change  Phone: 717/397-1900

| | | | | | | | | | | | | |
|---|---|---|---|---|---|---|---|---|---|---|---|---|
| | 6/16-8/31 | 1P: | $59- | 75 | 2P/1B: | $59- | 75 | 2P/2B: | $59- | 75 | XP: $5 | F18 |
| | 9/1-10/31 | 1P: | $44- | 75 | 2P/1B: | $47- | 75 | 2P/2B: | $53- | 75 | XP: $5 | F18 |
| | 5/1-6/15 | 1P: | $39- | 60 | 2P/1B: | $41- | 60 | 2P/2B: | $41- | 60 | XP: $5 | F18 |
| Motel | 11/1-4/30 | 1P: | $32- | 60 | 2P/1B: | $33- | 60 | 2P/2B: | $36- | 60 | XP: $5 | F18 |

**Location:** 4 1/2 mi e on US Hwy 30E. 2140 US Hwy 30E 17602. Fax: 717/299-6900. **Terms:** Sr. discount; reserv deposit; weekly rates; no pets. **Facility:** 44 rooms. Modern rooms. 1 two-bedroom unit. 2 stories; interior corridors. **Dining:** Restaurant nearby. **All Rooms:** refrigerators, cable TV. **Some Rooms:** whirlpools. **Cards:** AE, DS, MC, VI. ⒹⓍ

**FRIENDSHIP INN-ITALIAN VILLA**

| | | | | | | | | |
|---|---|---|---|---|---|---|---|---|
| | 5/1-9/10 | 1P: | $68 | 2P/1B: | $68 | 2P/2B: | $68 | XP: $6 F12 |
| | 9/11-10/31 | 1P: | $58 | 2P/1B: | $58 | 2P/2B: | $58 | XP: $6 F12 |
| | 11/1-12/31 & 4/1-4/30 | 1P: | $48 | 2P/1B: | $48 | 2P/2B: | $48 | XP: $6 F12 |
| Motel | 1/1-3/31 | 1P: | $38 | 2P/1B: | $38 | 2P/2B: | $38 | XP: $6 F12 |

Rates Subject to Change  Phone: 717/397-4973

**Location:** 5 mi e on US 30. 2331 Lincoln Hwy E 17602. Fax: 717/393-7819. **Terms:** Sr. discount; credit card guarantee, 4 day notice; no pets. **Facility:** 60 rooms. Located along busy commercial highway. 2 stories; interior/exterior corridors; pool. **Dining:** Restaurant; 4 pm-10 pm; $10-$15. **All Rooms:** free movies, cable TV. **Some Rooms:** radios, refrigerators. **Cards:** AE, DS, MC, VI. *(See ad below)*   Ⓓ ⊗

**GARDEN SPOT MOTEL**

| | | | | | | |
|---|---|---|---|---|---|---|
| | 6/23-9/3 | | | 2P/1B: | $49 | 2P/2B: | $57 | XP: $4-5 |
| | 5/1-6/22, 9/4-11/4 & 4/28-4/30 | 2P/1B: | $45 | 2P/2B: | $49 | XP: $4-5 |
| Motel | 11/5-11/26 & 3/31-4/27 | 2P/1B: | $39 | 2P/2B: | $43 | XP: $4-5 |

Rates Subject to Change  Phone: 717/394-4736

**Location:** 5 mi e on US 30. 2291 US 30E 17602. **Terms:** Open 5/1-11/26 & 3/31-4/30; reserv deposit; no pets. **Facility:** 19 rooms. Attractive public areas. 1 story; exterior corridors. **Dining:** Coffee shop; 7:30 am-11 am. **All Rooms:** cable TV. **Cards:** AE, DS, MC, VI.   Ⓓ ⊗

**HAMPTON INN**

| | | | | | | | | Phone: 717/299-1200 |
|---|---|---|---|---|---|---|---|---|

| | | Rates Subject to Change | | | | | |
|---|---|---|---|---|---|---|---|

◆◆◆     6/16-10/31 [CP]     1P: $78- 96   2P/1B:   $96    2P/2B:   $88    XP: $10   F18
Motel      4/16-4/30 [CP]     1P: $72- 89   2P/1B:   $89    2P/2B:   $82    XP: $10   F18
         5/1-6/15 [CP]     1P: $69- 87   2P/1B:   $85    2P/2B:   $77    XP: $10   F18
         11/1-4/15 [CP]     1P: $58- 76   2P/1B:   $76    2P/2B:   $68    XP: $10   F18

**Location:** 3 1/4 mi e on US 30 at Greenfield Rd exit. 545 Greenfield Rd 17601. Fax: 717/299-1155. **Terms:** Sr. discount; reserv deposit, 3 day notice; no pets. **Facility:** 129 rooms. Located close to Greenfield Corporate Center. Rates for up to 4 persons; 4 stories; interior corridors; meeting rooms; heated pool, whirlpool; exercise room. **Dining:** Restaurant nearby. **Services:** data ports. Fee: coin laundry. **All Rooms:** free movies, cable TV. **Some Rooms:** microwaves, refrigerators. **Cards:** AE, CB, DI, DS, MC, VI.

**HOLIDAY INN-EAST**        AAA Special Value Rates        **Phone:** 717/299-2551
      All Year [CP]     1P: $85- 89   2P/1B:   $85- 89   2P/2B:   $85- 89   XP: $10   F19
◆◆   **Location:** 2 1/4 mi e on US 30 at Greenfield Rd exit. 521 Greenfield Rd 17602. Fax: 717/397-0220.
Motor Inn     **Terms:** Small pets only. **Facility:** 189 rooms. Adjacent to the Pennsylvania Dutch Convention & Vistors Bureau. 2-4 stories; interior/exterior corridors; meeting rooms; 2 pools (1 heated, 1 indoor), wading pool; 2 tennis courts. **Dining & Entertainment:** Dining room; 6 am-2 & 5-10 pm; $6-$16; health conscious menu items; cocktails/lounge; complimentary hors d'oeuvres Tues-Thurs. **Services:** data ports; health club privileges; guest laundry. **All Rooms:** free & pay movies, cable TV. **Some Rooms:** coffeemakers, refrigerators. **Cards:** AE, CB, DI, DS, JCB, MC, VI.
*(See color ad below)*

**HOLIDAY INN-NORTH** AAA Special Value Rates Phone: 717/393-0771
5/1-10/31 1P: $85- 89 2P/1B: $85- 89 2P/2B: $85- 89 XP: $10 F19
11/1-4/30 1P: $79- 85 2P/1B: $79- 85 2P/2B: $79- 85
◆◆◆ **Location:** 1 mi n on SR 501 & US 222; 1/2 mi s of US 30. 1492 Lititz Pike 17601. Fax: 717/299-6238.
Motor Inn **Terms:** Credit card guarantee; no pets. **Facility:** 160 rooms. Located in busy commercial district. 2 stories; exterior corridors; meeting rooms; pool, wading pool. **Dining:** Dining room; 6 am-1 & 5-10 pm; $9-$16; cocktails. **Services:** data ports. **All Rooms:** free & pay movies, cable TV. **Some Rooms:** coffeemakers. **Cards:** AE, CB, DI, DS, JCB, MC, VI. *(See ad p A224 & color ad p A156)* Ⓓ ⊗

**HOTEL BRUNSWICK** AAA Special Value Rates Phone: 717/397-4801
5/1-10/31 1P: $60- 78 2P/1B: $70- 88 2P/2B: $75- 83 XP: $6 F18
11/1-4/30 1P: $52- 70 2P/1B: $62- 80 2P/2B: $65- 75 XP: $6 F18
◆◆◆ **Location:** Corner of Chestnut & Queen sts. 17608 (PO Box 749). Fax: 717/397-4991. **Terms:** Reserv
Hotel deposit, 3 day notice; monthly rates; small pets only, $100 dep req. **Facility:** 225 rooms. 9 stories; interior corridors; conference facilities; heated indoor pool; exercise room. **Dining:** Restaurant; 7 am-1:30 & 5-9 pm; breakfast & lunch buffet Mon-Fri; $6-$18; cocktails. **Services:** secretarial services. Fee: coin laundry. **All Rooms:** combo & shower baths, cable TV. Fee: movies. **Cards:** AE, DI, DS, MC, VI. Ⓓ Ⓢ ⊗

**HOWARD JOHNSON LODGE** Rates Subject to Change Phone: 717/397-7781
6/17-10/31 1P: $51- 66 2P/1B: $66- 71 2P/2B: $79- 85 XP: $7 F18
5/1-6/16 & 11/1-4/30 1P: $35- 41 2P/1B: $39- 57 2P/2B: $42- 61 XP: $7 F18
◆ **Location:** 4 mi e on US 30. 2100 Lincoln Hwy E 17602. Fax: 717/397-6340. **Terms:** Sr. discount; reserv
Motor Inn deposit; no pets. **Facility:** 112 rooms. Balcony or patio. 2 stories; interior corridors; designated smoking area; meeting rooms; heated indoor pool, wading pool. **Dining & Entertainment:** Restaurant; 6 am-midnight, Fri & Sat-1 am; $5-$16; cocktails/lounge. **All Rooms:** free movies, cable TV. **Cards:** AE, DI, DS, MC, VI. Ⓓ ⊗

**THE KING'S COTTAGE** Guaranteed Rates Phone: 717/397-1017
All Year [BP] 2P/1B: $80- 135 XP: $25
◆◆◆ **Location:** 1 1/2 mi e on US 462. 1049 E King St 17602. **Terms:** Age restrictions may apply; check-in 4 pm;
Historic Bed reserv deposit, 7 day notice; weekly rates; 2 night min stay, weekends; no pets. **Facility:** 8 rooms. 1900's pe-
& Breakfast riod architecture & furnishings. Elegant accommodations. 3 stories; interior corridors; smoke free premises. **All Rooms:** combo & tub baths, no phones, no TVs. **Cards:** DS, MC, VI. Ⓓ ⊗

**LANCASTER HILTON GARDEN INN** Rates Subject to Change Phone: 717/560-0880
◆◆◆ 7/1-11/14 [CP] 1P: $99- 129 2P/1B: $104- 134 2P/2B: $104- 134 XP: $10 F
Motor Inn 5/1-6/30 [CP] 1P: $89- 114 2P/1B: $94- 119 2P/2B: $94- 119 XP: $10 F
2/16-4/30 [CP] 1P: $84- 99 2P/1B: $89- 104 2P/2B: $89- 104 XP: $10 F
11/15-2/15 [CP] 1P: $74- 89 2P/1B: $84- 94 2P/2B: $84- 94 XP: $10 F
**Location:** On SR 72; jct SR 72 & 283. 101 Granite Run Dr 17601. Fax: 717/560-5400. **Terms:** Reserv deposit, 3 day notice; no pets. **Facility:** 155 rooms. Attractive public areas. 2 stories; interior corridors; business center, meeting rooms; heated indoor pool, whirlpool; exercise room. **Dining:** Restaurant; 7 am-11 pm; $6-$11. **Services:** data ports, secretarial services. **All Rooms:** coffeemakers, free & pay movies, cable TV. **Cards:** AE, CB, DI, DS, MC, VI. *(See ad p 28)* Ⓓ Ⓢ ⊗

**LANCASTER HOST RESORT** AAA Special Value Rates Phone: 717/299-5500
5/26-9/5 1P: $139- 159 2P/1B: $154- 174 2P/2B: $154- 174 XP: $15 F18
5/1-5/25 & 9/6-4/30 1P: $99- 149 2P/1B: $114- 164 2P/2B: $114- 164 XP: $15 F18
◆◆◆ **Location:** 5 mi e on US 30. 2300 Lincoln Hwy E 17602. Fax: 717/295-5139. **Terms:** Check-in 4 pm; reserv
Resort Motor deposit, 7 day notice; BP available; package plans; no pets. **Facility:** 331 rooms. Attractive rooms & public
Inn areas. 2 two-bedroom units. 4 stories; interior corridors; designated smoking area; conference facilities; 2 pools (2 heated, 1 indoor); sauna; fitness level. Fee: 27 holes golf; 12 tennis courts (4 indoor, 8 lighted). **Dining & Entertainment:** 2 dining rooms; 6:30 am-10 pm; $13-$18; health conscious menu items; cocktails/lounge. **Services:** data ports; area transportation, within 5 mi; airport transportation. Fee: coin laundry. Rental: bicycles. **All Rooms:** free & pay movies, cable TV. **Cards:** AE, CB, DI, DS, MC, VI. *(See color ad p A158)* Ⓓ Ⓢ

**LANCASTER KNIGHTS INN** AAA Special Value Rates Phone: 717/299-8971
6/15-10/31 1P: $65 2P/1B: $65 2P/2B: $77 XP: $5 F18
5/1-6/14, 11/1-11/30 &
3/1-4/30 1P: $55 2P/1B: $55 2P/2B: $67 XP: $5 F18
◆◆ 12/1-2/29 1P: $39 2P/1B: $39 2P/2B: $49 XP: $5 F18
Motel **Location:** 4 1/2 mi e on US 30. 2151 Lincoln Hwy E 17602. Fax: 717/299-9216. **Terms:** Credit card guarantee; no pets. **Facility:** 66 rooms. 3 stories; interior/exterior corridors; pool. **All Rooms:** free movies, combo & shower baths, cable TV. **Cards:** AE, DS, MC, VI. Ⓓ ⊗

# YEAR-ROUND VALUE IN THE HEART OF PENNSYLVANIA DUTCH COUNTRY

**25%** *AAA & SENIOR DISCOUNTS OFF LISTED RATES*

**$59** * *SUNDAYS AAA & SENIORS*

## 365 Days A Year, AAA Members Get Great Value In Lancaster County's Full Service Hotel

### The Lancaster Host Resort Features:

- 200 factory outlet stores within 1 mile of hotel
- Directly across from Dutch Wonderland Amusement Park; Hershey Park 35 minutes
- 330 spacious and comfortable guest rooms
- Seasonal "Kids World" program
- 27 holes of championship golf
- Indoor/outdoor tennis
- Indoor & outdoor pools, sauna & Fitness Trail
- Two restaurants & lounges with entertainment

*For Value And A Whole Lot More All Year Long, Call The Host!* 1(800)233-0121 or (717)299-5500

# LANCASTER HOST
## RESORT
2300 Lincoln Highway East • Lancaster, PA 17602

*Rates subject to availability. Not available to groups. Not valid with any other discount. Certain blackout dates may apply. Rates are per room, per night based on double occupancy.

**MCINTOSH INN OF LANCASTER**
◆◆ Motel

| | | | | | | | | |
|---|---|---|---|---|---|---|---|---|
| 6/23-9/3 | 1P: | $63- 74 | 2P/1B: | $72- 83 | 2P/2B: | $77 | XP: $3 | F18 |
| 9/4-10/28 | 1P: | $50- 58 | 2P/1B: | $57- 65 | 2P/2B: | $59 | XP: $3 | F18 |
| 5/1-6/22 | 1P: | $39- 47 | 2P/1B: | $46- 54 | 2P/2B: | $48 | XP: $3 | F18 |
| 10/29-4/30 | 1P: | $32- 40 | 2P/1B: | $37- 45 | 2P/2B: | $39 | XP: $3 | F18 |

Rates Subject to Change   Phone: 717/299-9700
**Location:** 5 mi e on US 30. 2307 Lincoln Hwy E 17602. Fax: 713/392-3576. **Terms:** Sr. discount; weekly rates; no pets. **Facility:** 98 rooms. Well maintained property. 3 stories; interior/exterior corridors; heated pool. **Dining:** Restaurant nearby. **All Rooms:** free movies, cable TV. **Some Rooms:** microwaves, refrigerators. **Cards:** AE, CB, DI, MC, VI.
*(See ad p A132)*   ⒹⓈ⊗

**OREGON BED & BREAKFAST**
◆◆ Bed & Breakfast

AAA Special Value Rates   Phone: 717/656-2644

| | | | | | | |
|---|---|---|---|---|---|---|
| 5/1-10/31 [BP] | 2P/1B: | $55- 77 | 2P/2B: | $55- 77 | XP: $12 | |
| 11/1-4/30 [BP] | 2P/1B: | $44- 66 | 2P/2B: | $44- 66 | XP: $12 | |

**Location:** At jct SR 272 & 722; 1 mi n from US 222, Oregon Pike exit. 1500 Oregon Rd 17540. **Terms:** Reserv deposit, 3 day notice; weekly/monthly rates; no pets. **Facility:** 4 rooms. 19th-century home built around circa 1774. Large squirrel-tail bake oven still in operation. 1 two-bedroom unit. 2 stories; interior corridors; smoke free premises. **All Rooms:** B/W TV, no phones. **Some Rooms:** combo & shower baths, shared bathrooms. **Cards:** DS, MC, VI.
Ⓓ⊗

**QUALITY INN & SUITES**
(AAA)
◆◆ Motor Inn

AAA Special Value Rates   Phone: 717/569-0477

| | | | | | | | |
|---|---|---|---|---|---|---|---|
| 7/1-10/31 | 1P: | $72- 92 | 2P/1B: | $79- 99 | 2P/2B: | $79- 99 | XP: $6 F18 |
| 5/1-6/30 | 1P: | $59- 79 | 2P/1B: | $69- 89 | 2P/2B: | $69- 89 | XP: $6 F18 |
| 11/1-4/30 | 1P: | $49- 69 | 2P/1B: | $49- 69 | 2P/2B: | $49- 69 | XP: $6 F18 |

**Location:** On SR 272; 2 mi n of jct US 30. 2363 Oregon Pike 17601. Fax: 717/569-6479. **Terms:** Reserv deposit; small pets only, $25 dep req. **Facility:** 82 rooms. Quiet rural setting. Rooms with hot tub, $140; 1 story; interior/exterior corridors; meeting rooms; pool. **Dining:** Dining room; 7-10:30 am, 11:30-2 & 5-10 pm; $8-$14; cocktails. **All Rooms:** cable TV. **Some Rooms:** microwaves, refrigerators. Fee: VCP's. **Cards:** AE, DS, MC, VI.
*(See color ad p A157)*   Ⓓ⊗

**ROCKVALE VILLAGE INN**
(AAA)
◆◆◆ Motel

Rates Subject to Change   Phone: 717/293-9500

| | | | | | | | |
|---|---|---|---|---|---|---|---|
| 6/30-11/4 | 1P: | $69- 79 | 2P/1B: | $75- 95 | 2P/2B: | $75- 95 | XP: $5 F15 |
| 5/1-6/29, 11/5-12/31 & 4/2-4/30 | 1P: | $59- 69 | 2P/1B: | $59- 79 | 2P/2B: | $59- 79 | XP: $5 F15 |
| 1/1-4/1 | 1P: | $45- 55 | 2P/1B: | $45- 65 | 2P/2B: | $45- 65 | XP: $5 F15 |

**Location:** 6 1/2 mi e on US 30; in Rockvale Square Shopping Center. 24 S Willowdale Dr 17602. Fax: 717/293-8558. **Terms:** No pets. **Facility:** 113 rooms. Located near Rockvale shopping outlets. 2 stories; interior corridors; meeting rooms; pool. **Dining & Entertainment:** Coffee shop; 7 am-3 pm; cocktail lounge. **All Rooms:** free movies, cable TV. **Some Rooms:** Fee: VCP's. **Cards:** AE, DI, DS, MC, VI.
Ⓓ⊗

**THE 1722 MOTOR LODGE**
(AAA)
◆◆ Motel

Rates Subject to Change   Phone: 717/397-4791

| | | | | |
|---|---|---|---|---|
| 6/16-9/3 [CP] | 2P/2B: | $59 | XP: $5 F10 |
| 9/4-11/11 [CP] | 2P/2B: | $43- 53 | XP: $5 F10 |
| 5/1-6/15 & 4/1-4/30 [CP] | 2P/2B: | $39- 48 | XP: $5 F10 |
| 11/12-3/31 [CP] | 2P/2B: | $29- 34 | XP: $5 F10 |

**Location:** 3/4 mi w on SR 340 from US 30. 1722 Old Philadelphia Pike 17602. **Terms:** Reserv deposit; no pets. **Facility:** 21 rooms. Quiet residential location. 1 story; interior corridors. **Services:** Fee: coin laundry. **All Rooms:** combo & shower baths, cable TV. **Cards:** AE, MC, VI.
Ⓓ⊗

**SUNSET VALLEY MOTEL**
◆◆ Motel

Rates Subject to Change   Phone: 717/656-2091

| | | | |
|---|---|---|---|
| 5/24-10/31 5/1-5/23, 11/1-11/15 & | 2P/2B: | $55 | XP: $5 |
| 3/15-4/30 | 2P/2B: | $51 | XP: $5 |
| 11/16-3/14 | 2P/2B: | $41 | XP: $5 |

**Location:** 5 mi e on SR 23; 3 mi e of US 30. 2288 New Holland Pike 17601. **Terms:** Reserv deposit; no pets. **Facility:** 20 rooms. Quiet farm setting. 1 story; exterior corridors. **All Rooms:** cable TV. **Some Rooms:** radios. **Cards:** MC, VI.
Ⓓ⊗

**SUPER 8 MOTEL**
◆◆ Motel

AAA Special Value Rates   Phone: 717/393-8888

| | | | | | | |
|---|---|---|---|---|---|---|
| 6/15-10/31 | 1P: | $52 | 2P/1B: | $61 | 2P/2B: | $67 | XP: $6 F16 |
| 5/1-6/14 & 11/1-4/30 | 1P: | $35 | 2P/1B: | $41 | 2P/2B: | $45 | XP: $6 F16 |

**Location:** 2 mi e on SR 30. 2129 E Lincoln Hwy 17602. Fax: 717/393-8888. **Terms:** Reserv deposit, 3 day notice; weekly rates; pets, $10. **Facility:** 101 rooms. Modern & attractive room decor. 3 stories; interior corridors. **Dining:** Restaurant nearby. **All Rooms:** free movies, cable TV. **Cards:** AE, CB, DI, DS, MC, VI.
ⒹⓈ⊗

**TRAVELODGE**
(AAA)
◆ Motor Inn

AAA Special Value Rates   Phone: 717/397-4201

| | | | | | | |
|---|---|---|---|---|---|---|
| 7/17-11/14 | 1P: | $66 | 2P/1B: | $70 | 2P/2B: | $74 | XP:$4-6 F17 |
| 5/1-7/16 | 1P: | $52 | 2P/1B: | $62 | 2P/2B: | $68 | XP:$4-6 F17 |
| 11/15-12/31 | 1P: | $44 | 2P/1B: | $47 | 2P/2B: | $50 | XP:$4-6 F17 |
| 1/1-4/30 | 1P: | $38 | 2P/1B: | $42 | 2P/2B: | $46 | XP:$4-6 F17 |

**Location:** 3 mi w on SR 462. 2101 Columbia Ave 17603. Fax: 717/397-7842. **Terms:** Pets, $5, $50 dep req. **Facility:** 58 rooms. Located near Franklin & Marshall College. 2 stories; exterior corridors; small pool. **Dining:** Dining room; 11:30 am-2 & 5:30-9:30 pm, Fri-10 pm, Sat & Sun from 5 pm; $9-$16; cocktails. **All Rooms:** coffeemakers, combo & shower baths, cable TV. **Some Rooms:** refrigerators. Fee: VCP's. **Cards:** AE, CB, DI, DS, JCB, MC, VI.
Ⓓ⊗

**WILLOW VALLEY FAMILY RESORT & CONFERENCE CENTER**
(AAA)
◆◆◆ Resort Motor Inn

Rates Subject to Change   Phone: 717/464-2711

| | | | | | | |
|---|---|---|---|---|---|---|
| 6/16-9/3 [MAP] | 1P: | $97- 132 | 2P/1B: | $97- 132 | 2P/2B: | $97- 132 | XP: $10 D18 |
| 9/4-10/28 [MAP] | 1P: | $85- 120 | 2P/1B: | $85- 120 | 2P/2B: | $85- 120 | XP: $10 D18 |
| 5/1-6/15 & 10/29-11/25 [MAP] | 1P: | $75- 110 | 2P/1B: | $75- 110 | 2P/2B: | $75- 110 | XP: $10 D18 |
| 11/26-4/30 [MAP] | 1P: | $65- 100 | 2P/1B: | $65- 100 | 2P/2B: | $65- 100 | XP: $10 D18 |

**Location:** 3 3/4 mi s on US 222. 2416 Willow St Pike 17602. Fax: 717/464-4784. **Terms:** Sr. discount; reserv deposit; package plans; no pets. **Facility:** 353 rooms. Well-appointed guest rooms. Family oriented. 2-5 stories; interior/exterior corridors; conference facilities; 3 pools (3 heated, 2 indoor), saunas, whirlpools; 2 lighted tennis courts; exercise room, playground. Fee: 9 holes golf. **Dining:** 2 restaurants; 6 am-9 pm, closed 12/25; $6-$15; Sun Brunch. **Services:** secretarial services; guest laundry; area transportation, to train station, airport transportation. **All Rooms:** cable TV. **Some Rooms:** refrigerators, whirlpools. Fee: VCP's. **Cards:** AE, CB, DI, DS, MC, VI.
*(See color ad p A160)*   ⒹⓈ⊗

**YOUR PLACE COUNTRY INN**
(AAA)
◆◆◆ Motor Inn

Rates Subject to Change   Phone: 717/393-3413

| | | | | | | |
|---|---|---|---|---|---|---|
| 6/15-10/31 [CP] | 1P: | $69 | 2P/1B: | $79- 89 | 2P/2B: | $79- 89 | XP: $10 F16 |
| 5/1-6/14 & 11/1-4/30 [CP] | 1P: | $49 | 2P/1B: | $49- 69 | 2P/2B: | $49- 69 | XP: $10 F16 |

**Location:** 4 1/2 mi e on US 30. 2133 Lincoln Hwy E 17602. Fax: 717/393-2889. **Terms:** Reserv deposit; no pets. **Facility:** 79 rooms. Country decor & furnishings. 2 stories; interior corridors; meeting rooms; heated pool. **Dining:** Restaurant; 11 am-2 am; $5-$10; cocktails. **All Rooms:** cable TV. **Some Rooms:** refrigerators. Fee: VCP's. **Cards:** AE, DS, MC, VI. *(See color ad p A154)*
ⒹⓈ⊗

You can see one of two Lancaster Counties. The one most tourists settle for. Or the one you're looking for. The one where people treat you like a guest in their own home. And show you around

# THE REAL LANCASTER COUNTY

like friends in the country should. That's the one you'll find at Willow Valley. Always could. Even back when we were a simple farmer's market stand in 1943, we were giving folks a good deal on food, good conversation, and good directions to all the local attractions. Still are. To find the heart of Lancaster County, head three miles south of Lancaster on Route 222.

| |
|---|
| AAA ◆◆◆ rating |
| 353 air-conditioned rooms, some nonsmoking |
| Two restaurants |
| Breakfast, lunch, and dinner smorgasbords and menu dining |
| Free tours of Pennsylvania Dutch country |
| Three heated pools, two indoors |
| Nine-hole executive golf course |
| Fitness center/spa |
| Lighted outdoor tennis courts |
| Discounts available to AAA members |
| Special packages and off-season rates available |
| **Coming Summer 1995** 65-acre working Amish farm with horse-and-buggy rides, and farm animal petting area |

**Free Lancaster County Tour Kit.**
*Our free Real Lancaster County Tour Kit will help you find the county's most rewarding destinations.*

FAMILY RESORT
**Willow Valley**  The Real Lancaster County.

2416 Willow Street Pike • Lancaster, PA 17602 • 717 464-2711, 800 444-1714

# RESTAURANTS

**CENTER CITY GRILLE**  Dinner: $11-$20  Phone: 717/299-3456
American
◆◆
**Location:** Corner of King & Prince sts. 10 S Prince St 17601. **Hours:** 11:30 am-midnight, Sat from 5 pm, Sun 5 pm-9 pm. Closed major holidays. **Reservations:** suggested. **Features:** casual dress; children's menu; carryout; cocktails & lounge; street parking; a la carte. Very good fare served amidst Victorian decor. **Cards:** AE, DI, DS, MC, VI. ⊗

**FAMILY STYLE RESTAURANT**  Dinner: up to $10  Phone: 717/393-2323
◆
American
**Location:** 4 mi from center. 2323 Lincoln Hwy E 17602. **Hours:** 8 am-8 pm, Fri & Sat-9 pm summer only. Closed: 12/25 & Mon-Thurs 1/1-2/29. **Features:** casual dress; Sunday brunch; beer & wine only; buffet. **Cards:** AE, DI, DS, MC, VI.

**FINLEY'S AMERICAN RESTAURANT**  Dinner: $11-$20  Phone: 717/392-7801
◆
Steakhouse
**Location:** 5 mi e on US 30. 2175 Lincoln Hwy E 17602. **Hours:** 11 am-10 pm, Fri & Sat-11 pm. Closed: 11/23 & 12/25. **Features:** casual dress; children's menu; senior's menu; carryout; a la carte. Seasonally updated specialties. **Cards:** AE, DI, DS, MC, VI. ⊗

**FINLEY'S AMERICAN RESTAURANT**  Dinner: $11-$20  Phone: 717/393-0611
◆
Steakhouse
**Location:** 2 mi e; 1/4 mi e of jct SR 741 & 462. 2020 Columbia Ave 17603. **Hours:** 11 am-10 pm, Fri & Sat-11 pm. Closed: 11/23 & 12/25. **Features:** casual dress; children's menu; senior's menu; carryout; a la carte. Casual family dining. Seasonally updated specialties. **Cards:** AE, DI, DS, MC, VI.

**HORSE INN RESTAURANT**  Dinner: $11-$20  Phone: 717/392-5528
◆
Steakhouse
**Location:** Access via 200 blk of N Marshall St in alley. 225 N Marshall St, rear alley 17602. **Hours:** 5 pm-10 pm, Fri & Sat-10:30 pm, Sun-9 pm. Closed major holidays & Mon. **Reservations:** suggested. **Features:** casual dress; children's menu; carryout; cocktails. Very rustic & casual atmosphere in a 2-story building; specializing in steaks & tenderloin tips. Some vegetarian entrees avail. **Cards:** AE, DI, DS, MC, VI.

**ISAAC'S RESTAURANT & DELI**  Dinner: up to $10  Phone: 717/394-4441
◆
American
**Location:** 1/2 blk n of Town Square. 44 N Queen St 17603. **Hours:** 10 am-9 pm. Closed: Sun, 1/1, 11/23 & 12/25. **Features:** casual dress; children's menu; carryout. Grilled sandwiches, named after birds, plants & flowers. **Cards:** AE, DS, MC, VI.

**ISAAC'S RESTAURANT & DELI**  Dinner: up to $10  Phone: 717/560-7774
◆
American
**Location:** From Rt 30 at exit 72N. 1559 Manheim Pike 17601. **Hours:** 10 am-9 pm, Fri & Sat-10 pm, Sun from 11 am. Closed: 1/1, 11/23 & 12/25. **Features:** casual dress; children's menu; carryout. Grilled sandwiches, named after birds, plants & flowers. **Cards:** AE, DS, MC, VI.

**ISAAC'S RESTAURANT & DELI**  Dinner: up to $10  Phone: 717/393-6067
◆
American
**Location:** From Rt 30, n 1/4 mi; at Greenfield Rd exit. 555 Greenfield Rd 17601. **Hours:** 10 am-9 pm, Fri & Sat-10 pm, Sun from 11 am. Closed: 1/1, 11/23 & 12/25. **Features:** casual dress; children's menu; carryout. Grilled sandwiches, named after birds, plants & flowers. **Cards:** AE, DS, MC, VI.

**ISAAC'S RESTAURANT & DELI**  Dinner: up to $10  Phone: 717/393-1199
◆
American
**Location:** From US 30 at Centerville Rd exit, s 1/4 mi on Centerville Rd. 245 Centerville Rd 17603. **Hours:** 10 am-9 pm, Fri & Sat-10 pm, Sun from 11 am. Closed: 11/23 & 12/25. **Features:** casual dress; children's menu; carryout. Grilled sandwiches, named after birds, plants & flowers. **Cards:** AE, DS, MC, VI. ⊗

**KOUNTRY KITCHEN**  Dinner: up to $10  Phone: 717/394-2291
◆
American
**Location:** On SR 501; 1/2 mi s of US 30. 1500 Oregon Pike 17601. **Hours:** 7 am-8:30 pm. Closed: 12/25. **Features:** casual dress; children's menu; carryout; a la carte. Country-style cooking served in country atmosphere. Ample portions; homemade soups & some desserts. Smoke free premises. ⊗

**MARKET FARE RESTAURANT**  Dinner: $11-$20  Phone: 717/299-7090
Nouvelle
American
◆◆◆
**Location:** At corner of Grant & Market sts. 25 W King St 17603. **Hours:** 11 am-2:30 & 5-10 pm, Mon-9 pm, Sat from 5 pm, Sun 11 am-2 & 5-9 pm. Closed major holidays. **Reservations:** suggested. **Features:** casual dress; Sunday brunch; children's menu; carryout; cocktails & lounge; fee for parking; a la carte. Good food in a contemporary decor. Seafood & pasta entrees are specialties. **Cards:** AE, DI, DS, MC, VI. ⊗

**OLDE GREENFIELD INN**  Dinner: $11-$20  Phone: 717/393-0668
American
◆◆
**Location:** 3 1/2 mi e on US 30 at Greenfield Rd exit, 1/2 mi n. 595 Greenfield Rd 17601. **Hours:** 11 am-2 & 5-10 pm, Mon from 5 pm, Sat from 8 am, Sun 8 am-2 pm. Closed major holidays. **Reservations:** suggested. **Features:** casual dress; Sunday brunch; health conscious menu items; cocktails. Gracious country dining in historic atmosphere of the 1800's. **Cards:** AE, DI, DS, MC, VI.

**STOCKYARD INN**  Dinner: $11-$20  Phone: 717/394-7975
American
◆◆◆
**Location:** 1/2 mi s off US 30; on US 222S. 1147 Lititz Pike 17601. **Hours:** 11:30 am-9 pm, Fri-9:30 pm, Sat 4 pm-9:30 pm, Sun-8 pm. Closed: Mon, 1/1 & 12/25. **Reservations:** suggested. **Features:** casual dress; children's menu; cocktails; a la carte. Former home of President James Buchanan. Casual dining with homemade soups & some desserts. Some continental entrees. **Cards:** AE, MC, VI. ⊗

**WINDOWS ON STEINMAN PARK**  Dinner: $21-$30  Phone: 717/295-1316
French
◆◆◆
**Location:** 1/2 blk w of Center Sq. 16-18 W King St 17603. **Hours:** 11:30 am-2 & 5-9 pm, Fri-10 pm, Sat 5 pm-10 pm, Sun 11:30 am-2:30 & 5-9 pm. Closed major holidays. **Reservations:** suggested. **Features:** semi-formal attire; Sunday brunch; cocktails; entertainment; valet parking; a la carte. Elegant dining, overlooking Steinman Park. **Cards:** AE, CB, DI, MC, VI.

## LANGHORNE—1,400  (See PHILADELPHIA & VICINITY ACCOMMODATIONS spotting map pages A196 & A197; see index starting on page A193)

# LODGINGS

**RED ROOF INN-OXFORD VALLEY**  Rates Subject to Change  Phone: 215/750-6200  [108]
◆
Motel

| | | | | | |
|---|---|---|---|---|---|
| 7/1-8/31 | 1P: $53 | 2P/1B: $60 | 2P/2B: $73 | XP: $6 | F18 |
| 5/1-6/30 & 4/1-4/30 | 1P: $53 | 2P/1B: $60 | 2P/2B: $67 | XP: $6 | F18 |
| 9/1-3/31 | 1P: $45 | 2P/1B: $48 | 2P/2B: $56 | XP: $6 | F18 |

**Location:** Jct Oxford Valley Rd & Cabot Blvd W, Oxford Valley Rd, exit off I-95; 1/2 mi from Sesame Pl. 3100 Cabot Blvd W 19047. Fax: 215/750-6205. **Terms:** Credit card guarantee; AP available; small pets only. **Facility:** 91 rooms. 3 stories; exterior corridors. **Services:** data ports. **All Rooms:** free movies, cable TV. **Cards:** AE, CB, DI, DS, MC, VI. ⊘ Ⓓ ⊗

**(See PHILADELPHIA & VICINITY ACCOMMODATIONS spotting map pages A196 & A197)**

**SHERATON BUCKS COUNTY HOTEL**    Rates Subject to Change    **Phone:** 215/547-4100   110

Hotel

| | | | |
|---|---|---|---|
| 7/2-9/5 | 1P: $155 | 2P/1B: $170 | 2P/2B: $155 | XP: $15 | F16 |
| 5/2-7/1 & 9/9-12/31 | 1P: $79- 145 | 2P/1B: $79- 160 | 2P/2B: $79- 145 | XP: $15 | F16 |
| 5/1-5/1 & 9/6-4/30 | 1P: $79- 125 | 2P/1B: $79- 125 | 2P/2B: $79- 140 | XP: $15 | F16 |

**Location:** From US 1, Oxford Valley exit, opposite Sesame Pl, adjacent to Oxford Valley Mall. 400 Oxford Valley Rd 19047. **Fax:** 215/547-4100. **Terms:** Sr. discount; reserv deposit, 3 day notice, 5/1-10/10; package plans; no pets. **Facility:** 167 rooms. Attractive public areas. 15 stories; interior corridors; conference facilities; heated indoor pool, wading pool, saunas, steamrooms, whirlpool; health club, hair salon, arcade. **Dining & Entertainment:** Restaurant; 6:30 am-10 pm, Fri-11 pm, Sat 7 am-11 pm, Sun 7 am-10 pm, Sun brunch 11 am-2:30 pm; $10-$20; cocktails/lounge. **Services:** data ports, secretarial services. Fee: PC; coin laundry, airport transportation. **All Rooms:** coffeemakers, free & pay movies, combo & shower baths, cable TV. **Some Rooms:** Fee: microwaves, refrigerators. **Cards:** AE, CB, DI, DS, MC, VI. *(See color ad p A194)*    Roll in showers. ⊘ Ⓓ Ⓢ ⊗

### RESTAURANT

**FINLEY'S AMERICAN RESTAURANT**    **Dinner:** $11-$20    **Phone:** 215/750-7003   128

Steakhouse

**Location:** From US 1, Oxford Valley Rd exit, 1/2 mi on Oxford Valley Rd, then 1/3 nw on N Buckstown Rd to Middletown Blvd, opposite Macy's. 610 Middletown Blvd 19047. **Hours:** 11 am-10 pm, Fri & Sat-11 pm. **Closed:** 11/23 & 12/25. **Features:** casual dress; children's menu; senior's menu; carryout; cocktails; a la carte. Seasonally updated specialties. **Cards:** AE, DI, DS, MC, VI.

## LATROBE—9,300

### RESTAURANT

**BAR-B-QUE & ALE LTD**    **Dinner:** up to $10    **Phone:** 412/539-7427

American

**Location:** On US 30, 1/2 mi e of jct SR 981. Rt 30E 15650. **Hours:** 11 am-9 pm, Fri & Sat-11 pm. **Closed:** 4/16, 11/23 & 12/25. **Features:** casual dress; children's menu; salad bar; beer only; a la carte. Barbecue & seafood items. **Cards:** DS, MC, VI.    ⊗

## LEBANON—24,800

### LODGING

**QUALITY INN LEBANON VALLEY**    AAA Special Value Rates    **Phone:** 717/273-6771

Motor Inn

| | | | |
|---|---|---|---|
| 6/30-9/4 | 1P: $77- 85 | 2P/1B: $91- 93 | 2P/2B: $92- 99 | XP: $7 | F18 |
| 9/5-10/31 | 1P: $75- 77 | 2P/1B: $81- 83 | 2P/2B: $82- 98 | XP: $7 | F18 |
| 5/1-6/29 | 1P: $72- 83 | 2P/1B: $78- 83 | 2P/2B: $79- 89 | XP: $7 | F18 |
| 11/1-4/30 | 1P: $65- 74 | 2P/1B: $73- 85 | 2P/2B: $74- 85 | XP: $7 | F18 |

**Location:** 1/2 mi s on SR 72. 625 Quentin Rd 17042. **Fax:** 717/273-4882. **Terms:** Reserv deposit; weekly/monthly rates; no pets. **Facility:** 130 rooms. Convenient midtown location. 5 stories; interior/exterior corridors; conference facilities; pool, wading pool. **Dining & Entertainment:** Dining room; 7 am-1:30 & 5-9 pm, Sun 7 am-11, noon-2 & 5-8 pm; $7-$17; cocktails/lounge; weekend entertainment. **Services:** data ports; valet laundry. **All Rooms:** cable TV. **Cards:** AE, CB, DI, DS, JCB, MC, VI. *(See color ad p A140)*    Ⓓ ⊗

## LEWISBURG—5,800

### LODGINGS

**BEST WESTERN COUNTRY CUPBOARD INN**    Rates Subject to Change    **Phone:** 717/524-5500

Motor Inn

All Year [CP]    1P: $67- 129   2P/1B: $73- 129   2P/2B: $66- 129   XP: $6   F18

**Location:** 2 1/2 mi n on US 15, I-80 exit 30A (Lewisburg), 4 mi s. 17837 (PO Box 46). **Fax:** 717/524-4291. **Terms:** Reserv deposit, 3 day notice; no pets. **Facility:** 107 rooms. Luxurious Colonial theme decor rooms. Attractive public areas. Closed 12/24 & 12/25. 2-3 stories; interior corridors; meeting rooms; heated pool; exercise room, playground. **Dining:** Restaurant, see separate listing. **Services:** data ports. Fee: coin laundry. **All Rooms:** free movies, cable TV. Fee: VCP. **Some Rooms:** refrigerators, whirlpools. **Cards:** AE, CB, DI, DS, MC, VI. *(See ad p A163)*    Ⓓ ⊗

AAA CampBooks — valuable additions for members who enjoy outdoor vacations.

**BRYNWOOD INN**  Rates Subject to Change  Phone: 717/524-2121
All Year [CP]  1P: $49- 65  2P/1B: $65- 70  2P/2B: $54- 70  XP: $5  F16
**Location:** Jct US 15 & SR 45. US 15 & SR 45 17837. **Terms:** Reserv deposit; small
pets only. **Facility:** 17 rooms. Modestly appointed rooms. 2 stories; interior corridors; meeting rooms.
Motel  **Dining:** Restaurant nearby. **All Rooms:** cable TV. **Some Rooms:** refrigerators. **Cards:** AE, CB, DI, MC, VI.
(D) ⊗

**LEWISBURG-DAYS INN**  Rates Subject to Change  Phone: 717/523-1171
All Year  1P: $53- 126  2P/1B: $59- 126  2P/2B: $64- 126  XP: $6  F16
**Location:** On US 15; 1/2 mi n of jct SR 45. US Rt 15 17837 (PO Box 253). Fax: 717/524-4667. **Terms:** Sr.
discount; reserv deposit, 3 day notice; small pets only. **Facility:** 108 rooms. Modestly appointed rooms. 2 suites
Motel  with whirlpool, $120; 2 stories; exterior corridors; pool; exercise room. **Dining:** Restaurant nearby.
**All Rooms:** cable TV. **Cards:** AE, CB, DI, DS, JCB, MC, VI. *(See ad p A162)*  (D) ⊗

### RESTAURANT
**COUNTRY CUPBOARD RESTAURANT**  Dinner: up to $10  Phone: 717/523-3211
**Location:** In Best Western Country Cupboard Inn. 17837. **Hours:** 7 am-9 pm. **Closed:** 12/25.
**Features:** casual dress; children's menu; carryout; buffet. Popular, colonial style family restaurant, also
American  regional specialties. Smoke free premises. **Cards:** DS, MC, VI. *(See ad below)*  ⊗

## LEWISTOWN—9,300

### LODGING
**HOLIDAY INN OF LEWISTOWN**  Rates Subject to Change  Phone: 717/248-4961
All Year  1P: $39- 65  2P/1B: $53- 65  2P/2B: $50- 65  XP: $5  F18
Motor Inn  **Location:** On US 322 at Burnham exit, 2 1/2 mi n of jct US 22. (Rt 322, BURNHAM). Fax: 717/242-3013.
**Terms:** Credit card guarantee; weekly rates; pets. **Facility:** 121 rooms. Semi rural location. 2 stories; exterior
corridors; meeting rooms; pool. **Dining & Entertainment:** Restaurant; 6 am-2 & 5-10 pm; $7-$11; cocktails/lounge.
**Services:** data ports. Fee: coin laundry. **All Rooms:** free movies, cable TV. **Cards:** AE, CB, DI, DS, JCB, MC, VI.  (D) ⊗

### RESTAURANT
**KIRBY'S RESTAURANT**  Historical  Dinner: $11-$20  Phone: 717/248-4468
**Location:** 1 mi ne. 55 Chestnut St 17044. **Hours:** 5 pm-9 pm, Fri & Sat-10 pm. **Closed:** Sun, Mon, 1/1 &
American  12/25. **Reservations:** suggested; for dinner. **Features:** casual dress; children's menu; cocktails. Restored
1870's Victorian mansion. Prime rib, seafood, steak & Northern Italian specialties; homemade soups &
desserts. **Cards:** AE, CB, DI, MC, VI.  ⊗

## LIGHT STREET

### RESTAURANT
**LIGHTSTREET RESTAURANT**  Historical  Dinner: $21-$30  Phone: 717/784-1070
**Location:** I-80 exit 35, 1/2 mi n, corner Ridge Rd & Main St. **Hours:** 11 am-9 pm, Fri & Sat-10 pm, Sun-8
pm. Closed major holidays. **Reservations:** suggested. **Features:** casual dress; children's menu; carryout;
American  cocktails & lounge. Circa 1856. In a pre-Civil War hotel/tavern. Well known for hotel clam chowder & crab
cakes. **Cards:** AE, DS, MC, VI.  ⊗

Respect Property—Public and Private.

## LIGONIER—1,600

### LODGING

**GRANT HOUSE BED & BREAKFAST**
♦♦♦   All Year [CP]   1P: $75- 80   2P/1B: $75- 80   2P/2B: $75- 80   XP: $20   **Phone:** 412/238-5135
Historic Bed   **Location:** 1 blk n on SR 711, then 2 blks w on Church St. 244 W Church St 15658. **Terms:** Age restrictions
& Breakfast   may apply; reserv deposit, 14 day notice; no pets. **Facility:** 3 rooms. Meticulously restored late Victorian home.
2 stories; interior corridors; smoke free premises. **All Rooms:** no phones, no TVs. **Some Rooms:** shower
baths, shared bathrooms.   Ⓓ ⊗

### RESTAURANTS

**COLONIAL INN**   **Dinner:** $11-$20   **Phone:** 412/238-6604
♦♦   **Location:** 1 1/2 mi w on US 30. 15658. **Hours:** 11:30 am-2:30 & 5-10 pm, Fri & Sat-11 pm, Sun noon-9 pm.
American   Closed: Mon, 1/1, 11/23 & 12/25. **Reservations:** suggested; weekends. **Features:** casual dress; cocktails &
lounge. Quiet country dining. Nouvelle dishes & seafood specialties. Homemade soup & dessert, dutch apple
pie speciality. Lunch buffet daily except Sunday. **Cards:** AE, MC, VI.   ⊗

**LIGONIER TAVERN**   **Dinner:** $11-$20   **Phone:** 412/238-4831
Ⓐ   **Location:** Center, 1 blk w. 137 W Main St 15658. **Hours:** 11:30 am-9 pm, Fri & Sat-10 pm, Sun 1 pm-8 pm.
Closed: 1/1, 11/23 & 12/25. **Reservations:** suggested; weekends. **Features:** casual dress; children's menu;
♦♦   carryout; cocktails & lounge; street parking. Family owned since 1935. Homemade soups & desserts. Smoke
American   free premises. **Cards:** DS, MC, VI.   ⊗

## LINE LEXINGTON

### RESTAURANT

**ZOTO'S RESTAURANT**   **Dinner:** up to $10   **Phone:** 215/822-1948
♦   **Location:** On SR 309. Rt 309 & Hilltown Pike 18932. **Hours:** 7 am-11 pm, Fri & Sat-midnight, Sun-10 pm.
American   Closed: 12/25. **Features:** casual dress; children's menu; early bird specials; health conscious menu; a la
carte, buffet. Family style restaurant. Banquet facilities. **Cards:** MC, VI.

## LIONVILLE

### LODGINGS

**EXTON COMFORT INN**   Rates Subject to Change   **Phone:** 610/524-8811
♦♦   All Year [CP]   1P: $58- 60   2P/1B: $60- 64   2P/2B: $60- 64   XP: $5   F18
Motel   **Location:** Jct SR 113 & SR 100; 1/2 mi s of tpk, exit 23. 5 N Pottstown Pike 19341. Fax: 610/524-0562.
**Terms:** Credit card guarantee; pets. **Facility:** 104 rooms. 4 stories; interior corridors; meeting rooms; small
heated indoor pool; exercise room. **Services:** Fee: coin laundry. **All Rooms:** free movies, cable TV. **Some Rooms:**
Fee: microwaves, refrigerators, whirlpools. **Cards:** AE, CB, DI, DS, JCB, MC, VI.   Ⓓ Ⓢ ⊗

**HAMPTON INN**   AAA Special Value Rates   **Phone:** 610/363-5555
♦♦♦   All Year [CP]   1P: $55- 67   2P/1B: $60- 72   2P/2B: $65- 72
Motel   **Location:** Jct SR 113 & 100; 1/2 mi s of tpk, exit 23. 4 N Pottstown Pike 19341. Fax: 610/363-4969.
**Terms:** Credit card guarantee, 3 day notice; weekly/monthly rates; pets. **Facility:** 122 rooms. Comfortably fur-
nished guest rooms. 4 stories; interior corridors; meeting rooms; small pool. **Dining:** Restaurant nearby. **Services:** valet
laundry. **All Rooms:** free & pay movies, cable TV. **Some Rooms:** microwaves, refrigerators. **Cards:** AE, CB, DI, DS, MC,
VI.   Ⓓ Ⓢ ⊗

**HOLIDAY INN HOTEL & CONFERENCE CENTER**   AAA Special Value Rates   **Phone:** 610/363-1100
Ⓐ   All Year [CP]   1P: $59- 109   2P/1B: $67- 117   2P/2B: $67- 117   XP: $8   F20
**Location:** Jct SR 113 & 100, 1 1/5 mi s of tpk, exit 23. 815 N Pottstown Pike 19341-1597.
♦♦   Fax: 610/524-2329. **Terms:** Credit card guarantee; weekly/monthly rates; MAP available; small pets only.
Motor Inn   **Facility:** 213 rooms. 4 stories; interior corridors; conference facilities; 2 pools (1 heated, 1 indoor), whirlpool.
**Dining & Entertainment:** Restaurant; 6:30 am-2 & 5:30-10 pm; $9-$18; cocktails/lounge; entertainment.
**Services:** data ports; health club privileges. Fee: coin laundry. **All Rooms:** coffeemakers, free & pay movies, cable TV.
**Some Rooms:** microwaves, refrigerators. **Cards:** AE, CB, DI, DS, JCB, MC, VI.   Ⓓ ⊗

### RESTAURANT

**BAGEL EMPORIUM AT THE GRAPEVINE**   **Dinner:** up to $10   **Phone:** 610/524-8711
♦   **Location:** From jct SR 100, 1 mi n on US 113. 255 Gordon Dr 19341. **Hours:** 7 am-3 pm. Closed: 11/23 &
American   12/25. **Features:** casual dress. Specializing in homemade soups & bagels.   ⊗

## LITITZ—8,300

### LODGINGS

**GENERAL SUTTER INN**   Guaranteed Rates   **Phone:** 717/626-2115
♦♦♦   All Year   1P: $65- 90   2P/1B: $75- 100   2P/2B: $75- 100   XP: $4
Historic   **Location:** On the square, SR 501. 14 E Main St 17543. **Terms:** Reserv deposit; small pets only. **Facility:** 12
Country Inn   rooms. Early 19th century inn. Attractive rooms furnished with antiques, some smaller units. Closed 1/1, 12/24
& 12/25. 2 two-bedroom units. 3 stories; interior corridors; meeting rooms. **Dining & Entertainment:** Dining
room, coffee shop; 7 am-9 pm, Fri & Sat-9:30 pm, Sun-8 pm; $12-$16; cocktail lounge. **All Rooms:** comb, shower & tub
baths. **Cards:** AE, DS, MC, VI.   Ⓓ

**SWISS WOODS BED & BREAKFAST**   Guaranteed Rates   **Phone:** 717/627-3358
♦♦♦   All Year [BP]   1P: $65- 105   2P/1B: $79- 125   2P/2B: $79   XP: $15
Bed &   **Location:** 4 mi n on Rt 501, 1 mi w on Brubaker Valley Rd. 500 Blantz Rd 17543. Fax: 717/627-3483.
Breakfast   **Terms:** Age restrictions may apply; credit card guarantee; no pets. **Facility:** 7 rooms. A rural inn features au-
thentic Swiss decor. Tucked into the woods overlooking Speedwell Lake. Closed 12/24-12/26. 2 stories; inte-
rior corridors; smoke free premises. **All Rooms:** no phones, no TVs. **Some Rooms:** whirlpools. **Cards:** DS, MC, VI.   Ⓓ ⊗

## LOCK HAVEN—9,200

### LODGING

**DAYS INN**   AAA Special Value Rates   **Phone:** 717/748-3297
♦♦   5/1-12/1 [CP]   1P: $52- 82   2P/1B: $57- 87   2P/2B: $57- 87   XP: $5   F12
Motel   12/2-4/30 [CP]   1P: $47- 77   2P/1B: $52- 82   2P/2B: $52- 82   XP: $5   F12
**Location:** US 220, SR 120W exit, 2 blks s on E Walnut St. 101 E Walnut St 17745. Fax: 717/748-5390.
**Terms:** Check-in 4 pm; pets, $3. **Facility:** 60 rooms. 4 stories; interior corridors; meeting rooms. **Services:** valet laundry;
airport transportation. **All Rooms:** free movies, cable TV. **Some Rooms:** Fee: microwaves, refrigerators, VCP's. **Cards:** AE,
CB, DI, DS, MC, VI.   ⓼ ⓩ Ⓓ ⊗

## LUMBERVILLE

### LODGING

**1740 HOUSE**
Rates Subject to Change
Phone: 215/297-5661
All Year [BP]   1P: $70- 110   2P/1B: $70- 110   2P/2B: $70- 110   XP: $15
**Location:** On SR 32. River Rd 18933. Fax: 215/297-5243. **Terms:** Age restrictions may apply; reserv deposit; 2 night min stay, Sat; no pets. **Facility:** 24 rooms. Attractive & spacious rooms all with balcony or terrace overlooking Delaware River. Living room with large stone working fireplace. 2 stories; interior corridors; meeting rooms; small pool. **Dining:** Dining room; 7 pm-8 pm, Fri & Sat only; $23-$30; includes appetizer & dessert; afternoon tea. **Recreation:** canoeing; bicycles, hiking trails. **All Rooms:** combo & shower baths, no phones, no TVs. (See ad p A175)   (D)

Country Inn

### RESTAURANT

**CUTTALOSSA INN**
**Dinner:** $21-$30
Phone: 215/297-5082
**Location:** On Rt 32. River Rd 18933. **Hours:** 11 am-2 & 5-9 pm. Closed: Sun, 1/1, 12/24 & 12/25.
American   **Reservations:** suggested; in winter. **Features:** casual dress; health conscious menu; cocktails & lounge. Several dining rooms overlook waterfall. Outdoor bar & colorful garden. Jacket required during the winter.
**Cards:** AE, MC, VI.   ⊗

## LUZERNE

### RESTAURANT

**ANDY PERUGINO'S RESTAURANT**
**Dinner:** $11-$20
Phone: 717/287-9315
**Location:** From Cross Valley Expwy southbound exit 5, right on Bennett 5 blks to Carpenter, right on
Italian   Carpenter, right on Charles St; northbound exit 6, back to exit 5. 258 Charles St 18709. **Hours:** 11 am-2 & 4-11 pm, Sat from 4 pm. Closed: Sun, 1/1, 11/23, 12/25 & 8/1-8/8. **Reservations:** suggested; weekends.
**Features:** casual dress; children's menu; carryout; cocktails & lounge. Also American dishes; hearty portions. **Cards:** MC, VI.   ⊗

## MACUNGIE—2,600

### LODGING

**SYCAMORE INN BED & BREAKFAST**
Rates Subject to Change
Phone: 610/966-5177
All Year [BP]   1P: $70- 80   2P/1B: $70- 80   2P/2B: $70- 80   XP: $10
Historic Bed   **Location:** Center, on SR 100. 165 E Main St 18062. **Terms:** Sr. discount; age restrictions may apply;
& Breakfast   check-in 4 pm; reserv deposit, 5 day notice; weekly/monthly rates; no pets. **Facility:** 5 rooms. Stone house built in 1835. 2 stories; interior corridors; smoke free premises. **Dining:** Restaurant nearby. **All Rooms:** no phones, no TVs. **Some Rooms:** combo & shower baths, shared bathrooms, whirlpools. **Cards:** MC, VI.   (D) ⊗

## MALVERN—2,900

### LODGING

**THE DESMOND, GREAT VALLEY HOTEL**
Rates Subject to Change
Phone: 610/296-9800
Mon-Thurs   1P: $95- 135   2P/1B: $110- 150   2P/2B: $110- 150   XP: $15   F
Hotel   Fri-Sun   1P: $79   2P/1B: $79   2P/2B: $79   XP: $15   F
**Location:** 1/2 mi w of US 202, SR 29 exit. In Great Valley Corporate Center. 1 Liberty Blvd 19355.
Fax: 610/889-9869. **Terms:** Sr. discount; credit card guarantee; no pets. **Facility:** 201 rooms. 4 stories; interior corridors; conference facilities; heated indoor pool, wading pool, whirlpool; 2 tennis courts; exercise room. **Dining & Entertainment:** Dining room; 6:30 am-10 pm, Sat 7 am-11 pm, Sun 7 am-10 pm; $8-$23; cocktails/lounge. **Services:** data ports; valet laundry. **Fee:** airport transportation. **Recreation:** bicycles. **All Rooms:** free movies, refrigerators, cable TV. **Some Rooms:** Fee: VCP's. **Cards:** AE, CB, DI, DS, JCB, MC, VI. (See ad p A146)   🖪 (D) (S) ⊗

## MANSFIELD—3,500

### LODGINGS

**COMFORT INN**
AAA Special Value Rates
Phone: 717/662-3000
10/1-10/31 [CP]   1P: $59- 75   2P/1B: $69- 85   2P/2B: $69- 85   XP: $6   F18
5/1-9/30 & 4/1-4/30 [CP]   1P: $55- 75   2P/1B: $55- 75   2P/2B: $55- 75   XP: $6   F18
11/1-3/31 [CP]   1P: $55- 70   2P/1B: $56- 70   2P/2B: $56- 70   XP: $6   F18
Motel   **Location:** Jct US 15 & US 6. 300 Gateway Dr 16933. Fax: 717/662-2551. **Terms:** Reserv deposit; package plans; pets. **Facility:** 100 rooms. King rooms have recliner & desk. 2 stories; interior corridors; exercise room.
**All Rooms:** free movies, cable TV. **Some Rooms:** Fee: VCP's, whirlpools. **Cards:** AE, CB, DI, DS, JCB, MC, VI.   (D) (S) ⊗

**MANSFIELD INN**
Rates Subject to Change
Phone: 717/662-2136
5/1-12/1 [CP]   1P: $49   2P/1B: $59   2P/2B: $65   XP: $5   F
12/2-4/30 [CP]   1P: $45   2P/1B: $55   2P/2B: $60
Motel   **Location:** 1 blk s on US 15. 26 S Main St 16933. Fax: 717/662-2067. **Terms:** Reserv deposit, 5 day notice; pets, $5. **Facility:** 26 rooms. Attractively appointed rooms. Closed 1/1, 12/24 & 12/25. 1 two-bedroom unit. 1 story; exterior corridors. **All Rooms:** coffeemakers, free movies, cable TV. **Cards:** AE, CB, DI, DS, MC, VI.
(See color ad below)   (D) ⊗

**OASIS MOTEL**
Rates Subject to Change
Phone: 717/659-5576
All Year [CP]   2P/1B: $40   2P/2B: $45   XP: $5   F10
**Location:** 2 mi s on US 15. 16933 (RD 1, Box 90). **Terms:** Reserv deposit; weekly rates; small pets only.
Motel   **Facility:** 12 rooms. 1 story; exterior corridors. **Dining:** Restaurant nearby. **All Rooms:** free movies, cable TV. **Some Rooms:** refrigerators. **Cards:** DS, MC, VI.   (D) ⊗

**WEST'S DELUXE MOTEL** — Rates Subject to Change — **Phone:** 717/659-5141
(AAA) — All Year — 1P: $32 — 2P/1B: $40 — 2P/2B: $45 — XP: $5 F10
◆◆ — **Location:** 3 1/2 mi s on US 15. 16933 (RD 1, Box 97). **Terms:** Reserv deposit; pets. **Facility:** 20 rooms. 1
Motel — story; exterior corridors; pool. **Dining:** Restaurant nearby. **All Rooms:** coffeemakers, combo & shower baths,
cable TV. **Some Rooms:** refrigerators. **Cards:** AE, DS, MC, VI. (D) ⊗

## MARS—1,700   (See PITTSBURGH ACCOMMODATIONS spotting map page A207; see index starting on page A206)

### LODGINGS

**FAIRFIELD INN** — Rates Subject to Change — **Phone:** 412/772-0600 — **59**
◆◆◆ — 5/23-9/11 [CP] — 1P: $46- 51 — 2P/1B: $52- 66 — 2P/2B: $52- 66 — XP: $7 F12
Motel — 5/1-5/22 & 9/12-4/30 [CP] — 1P: $43- 49 — 2P/1B: $50- 66 — 2P/2B: $50- 66 — XP: $7 F12
**Location:** Exit 3 off I-76, tpk 1/4 mi n on Rt 19; exit 25 of I-79 then 1/2 mi n on US 19. 30 St. Francis Way
16046. Fax: 412/772-0600. **Terms:** Sr. discount; credit card guarantee, 3 day notice; no pets. **Facility:** 105 rooms. Quiet setting. 3 stories; interior/exterior corridors; meeting rooms; heated pool. **Services:** data ports; valet laundry. **All Rooms:** free
movies. **Cards:** AE, DI, DS, MC, VI. *(See color ad p A205)* ⓩ (D) (S) ⊗

**HAMPTON INN CRANBERRY** — Rates Subject to Change — **Phone:** 412/776-1000 — **60**
◆◆◆ — All Year [CP] — 1P: $55- 63 — 2P/1B: $63- 71 — 2P/2B: $73
Motel — **Location:** Tpk exit 3, 1/2 mi n on US 19, 1/4 mi w on Freedom Rd; exit 25 off I-79 1 mi n on US 19, 1/4 mi
w on Freedom Rd; sbound I-79, exit 25; 1/2 mi w on Freedom Rd. 210 Executive Dr 16046.
Fax: 412/776-6699. **Terms:** Sr. discount; no pets. **Facility:** 118 rooms. Fax & copy service avail; free local calls. 4 stories; in-
terior corridors; meeting rooms; heated indoor pool, sauna, whirlpool; exercise room. **Fee:** tanning bed. **Dining:** Restaurant
nearby. **Services:** data ports; valet laundry. **All Rooms:** free movies, cable TV. **Cards:** AE, CB, DI, DS, JCB, MC, VI.
ⓩ (D) (S) ⊗

**RED ROOF INN-CRANBERRY** — Rates Subject to Change — **Phone:** 412/776-5670 — **61**
◆◆ — All Year — 1P: $50- 57 — 2P/1B: $58 — 2P/2B: $65 — XP: $8 F18
Motel — **Location:** I-76 & I-79 at SR 19. 20009 Rt 19 16066. Fax: 412/776-5687. **Terms:** Credit card guarantee;
small pets only. **Facility:** 109 rooms. 2 stories; exterior corridors. **Dining:** Restaurant nearby. **Services:** data
ports. **Fee:** coin laundry. **All Rooms:** free movies. **Cards:** AE, CB, DI, DS, MC, VI.

**SHERATON INN-PITTSBURGH NORTH** — Rates Subject to Change — **Phone:** 412/776-6900 — **63**
◆◆◆ — All Year — 1P: $97- 107 — 2P/1B: $97- 107 — XP: $10 F16
Hotel — **Location:** I-79 exit 25 Mars, US 19N & tpk I-76 exit 3. 910 Sheraton Dr 16046. Fax: 412/776-1115.
**Terms:** Sr. discount; 15% service charge; weekly/monthly rates; weekend rates available; no pets.
**Facility:** 191 rooms. 4 suites, $180; 5 stories; interior corridors; conference facilities; 18 hole golf privleges avail;
indoor/outdoor pool, saunas, whirlpool; exercise room. **Dining & Entertainment:** Coffee shop; 6:30 am-11 pm, Sat & Sun
from 7 am; $5-$10; cocktails/lounge; also, Tremont House, see separate listing; entertainment; nightclub. **Services:** data
ports, secretarial services; childcare; valet laundry. **All Rooms:** coffeemakers, free & pay movies. **Fee:** VCP's.
**Some Rooms:** Fee: refrigerators. **Cards:** AE, CB, DI, DS, JCB, MC, VI. (D) ⊗

### RESTAURANT

**TREMONT HOUSE** — **Dinner:** $21-$30 — **Phone:** 412/776-6900 — **56**
◆◆◆ — **Location:** In Sheraton Inn-Pittsburgh North. 910 Sheraton Dr 16046. **Hours:** 6:30 am-11 pm, Sat from 7 am,
American — Sun 7 am-10 pm. **Features:** semi-formal attire; Sunday brunch; children's menu; senior's menu; health
conscious menu items; carryout; cocktails. Fine dining in a relaxed atmosphere. **Cards:** AE, DI, DS, JCB,
MC, VI. (&) ⊗

## MATAMORAS—1,900

### LODGINGS

**BEST WESTERN INN AT HUNT'S LANDING** — AAA Special Value Rates — **Phone:** 717/491-2400
(AAA) — 5/1-10/31 — 1P: $69- 85 — 2P/1B: $77- 85 — 2P/2B: $77- 85 — XP: $6 F11
— 11/1-4/30 — 1P: $55- 61 — 2P/1B: $63- 69 — 2P/2B: $63- 69 — XP: $6 F11
◆◆◆ — **Location:** On US 6 & 209 at jct I-84 exit 11, 1/2 mi w on US 6 & 209. 900 Rt 6 & 209 18336.
Motor Inn — Fax: 717/491-2422. **Terms:** Reserv deposit, 3 day notice; package plans; pets. **Facility:** 108 rooms. Borders
Delaware River, spectacular views of Delaware Valley from some rooms. Contemporary decor. 4 stories; inte-
rior corridors; mountain view; meeting rooms; heated indoor pool, saunas; exercise room; shuffleboard courts. **Dining &
Entertainment:** Restaurant, cafeteria; 6:30 am-9 pm, Fri & Sat-10 pm, Sun from 7 am; $7-$22; cocktails/lounge. **Services:**
Fee: coin laundry. **All Rooms:** free movies, cable TV. **Some Rooms:** whirlpools. **Fee:** refrigerators, VCP's. **Cards:** AE, CB,
DI, DS, MC, VI. (D) (S) ⊗

**BLUE SPRUCE MOTEL** — Guaranteed Rates — **Phone:** 717/491-4969
(AAA) — 5/1-10/31 — 1P: $40- 55 — 2P/1B: $50- 75 — 2P/2B: $50- 75 — XP: $5-8
— 11/1-4/30 — 1P: $35- 45 — 2P/1B: $40- 45 — 2P/2B: $40- 50 — XP: $5-8
◆◆ — **Location:** On US 6 & 209, 1/2 mi w of jct I-84, exit 11. 550 Rts 6 & 209 18336. **Terms:** Sr. discount; reserv
Motel — deposit; no pets. **Facility:** 15 rooms. Quiet & cozy atmosphere. Attractive well maintained rooms & cottages.
1 story; exterior corridors. **All Rooms:** shower baths, cable TV. **Cards:** AE, DS, MC, VI. (D) ⊗

## MAYFIELD—1,900

### RESTAURANT

**ALEXANDER'S FAMILY RESTAURANT** — **Dinner:** $11-$20 — **Phone:** 717/876-9993
(AAA) — **Location:** on US 6. 18433. **Hours:** 8 am-2 am, Fri & Sat open 24 hours. Closed: 12/24 & 12/25.
**Reservations:** accepted. **Features:** casual dress; children's menu; carryout; cocktails & lounge. Family
◆◆ — restaurant featuring fresh seafood, beef & pork. On-premise baking. **Cards:** AE, MC, VI. ⊗
American

## MEADVILLE—14,300

### LODGINGS

**DAYS INN OF MEADVILLE** — Guaranteed Rates — **Phone:** 814/337-4264
(AAA) — All Year — 1P: $39- 72 — 2P/1B: $39- 72 — 2P/2B: $39- 72 — XP: $6 F
— **Location:** On US 6 & 322; from I-79 exit 36, 1/2 mi e. 240 Conneaut Lake Rd 16335. Fax: 814/337-7304.
◆◆ — **Terms:** Sr. discount; weekly/monthly rates; package plans; small pets only, $10 dep req. **Facility:** 163 rooms.
Motor Inn — 2 stories; interior corridors; meeting rooms; heated indoor pool, whirlpool. **Dining:** Dining room; 7 am-2 &
5-10 pm; $8-$15; cocktails. **Services:** valet laundry. **All Rooms:** free movies, cable TV. **Fee:** safes.
**Some Rooms:** radios. Fee: VCP's. **Cards:** AE, CB, DI, DS, JCB, MC, VI. *(See color ad p A167)* ⓩ (D) ⊗

**HOLIDAY INN EXPRESS** Rates Subject to Change Phone: 814/724-6012
Motel All Year [CP] 1P: $65- 75 2P/1B: $73- 83 2P/2B: $73- 83 XP: $8 F18
Too new to rate; **Location:** Exit 36B off I-79, 1/4 mi w on US 322. 290 Conneaut Lake Rd 16335.
Fax: 814/337-2617. **Terms:** sr. discount; no pets. **Facility:** 68 rooms. Suites & apartments $75-$165; 3 stories; interior/exterior corridors; meeting rooms. **Dining:** Restaurant nearby. **Services:** data ports. Fee: coin laundry. **All Rooms:** cable TV. **Some Rooms:** coffeemakers, microwaves, refrigerators. Fee: VCP's. **Cards:** AE, CB, DI, DS, JCB, MC, VI. Ⓓ Ⓢ ⊗

**SUPER 8 MOTEL** Rates Subject to Change Phone: 814/333-8883
◆◆ All Year 1P: $42 2P/1B: $48 2P/2B: $48 XP: $6 F14
Motel **Location:** Exit 36B off I-79, 1/2 mi w on US 322. 845 Conneaut Lake Rd 16335. Fax: 814/333-8883.
**Terms:** Sr. discount; reserv deposit, 7 day notice; CP available; small pets only, $50 dep req.
**Facility:** 62 rooms. Weekends 5/1-11/1 rates $5 higher; 3 stories; interior/exterior corridors. **All Rooms:** free movies, cable TV. **Some Rooms:** refrigerators. Fee: VCP's. **Cards:** AE, CB, DI, DS, JCB, MC, VI. Ⓓ Ⓢ ⊗

## RESTAURANT

**SANDALINI'S** Dinner: $11-$20 Phone: 814/724-1286
◆◆ **Location:** Exit 36B off I-79, 1/4 mi w on US 322. 300 Conneaut Lake Rd 16335. **Hours:** 11 am-1 am.
American Closed major holidays. **Features:** casual dress; children's menu; early bird specials; health conscious menu; cocktails. Bistro cafe atmosphere. **Cards:** AE, DS, MC, VI. ⊗

# MECHANICSBURG—9,500

## LODGINGS

**AMBER INN** Rates Subject to Change Phone: 717/766-9006
(AAA) All Year 1P: $30- 37 2P/1B: $37- 44 2P/2B: $40- 47 XP: $5 F12
◆◆ **Location:** PA Tpk exit 17, 1/2 mi n on US 15 to Wesley Dr exit, 1 blk w to light, then s on Gettysburg Rd, 1
Motel blk to Audubon Rd (left). 1032 Audubon Rd 17055. **Terms:** Credit card guarantee, 3 day notice; no pets. **Facility:** 15 rooms. Located on access road off interstate. 1 story; exterior corridors. **Some Rooms:** efficiency, microwaves, refrigerators. **Cards:** DS, MC, VI. Ⓓ ⊗

**BEST WESTERN PLANTATION INN** Rates Subject to Change Phone: 717/766-0238
(AAA) 5/1-11/1 & 4/15-4/30 [CP] 1P: $62- 75 2P/2B: $68- 85 XP: $5 F12
◆◆◆ 11/2-4/14 [CP] 1P: $52- 75 2P/2B: $58- 72 XP: $5 F12
Motel **Location:** On US 15 at I-76 tpk exit 17. 325 E Winding Hill Rd 17055. **Terms:** Sr. discount; reserv deposit, 7 day notice; no pets. **Facility:** 35 rooms. Spacious well maintained grounds. Attractive rooms. 2 stories; exterior corridors; 18 holes golf, par 3; pool; 1 tennis court. **Dining:** Restaurant nearby. **All Rooms:** combo & shower baths, cable TV. **Some Rooms:** microwaves, refrigerators. **Cards:** AE, CB, DI, DS, MC, VI. ⊗

**COMFORT INN WEST** Rates Subject to Change Phone: 717/790-0924
(AAA) All Year [CP] 1P: $57- 66 2P/1B: $63- 71 2P/2B: $63- 71 XP: $6 F18
◆◆◆ **Location:** On US 11; 6 mi w of Harrisburg & 8 mi e of Carlisle. 6325 Carlisle Pike 17055.
Motel Fax: 717/790-0924. **Terms:** Sr. discount; reserv deposit; weekly/monthly rates; no pets. **Facility:** 125 rooms. Located in busy commercial district. 4 stories; interior corridors; meeting rooms; exercise room. **Dining:** Restaurant nearby. **Services:** Fee: coin laundry. **All Rooms:** free movies, refrigerators, cable TV. **Some Rooms:** microwaves. **Cards:** AE, CB, DI, DS, JCB, MC, VI. Ⓓ Ⓢ ⊗

**HAMPTON INN WEST**  Rates Subject to Change  Phone: 717/691-1300
◆◆◆  3/2-4/30 [CP]  1P: $70- 79  2P/1B: $81- 87  2P/2B: $78  XP: $8  F18
Motel  5/1-3/1 [CP]  1P: $67- 76  2P/1B: $77- 84  2P/2B: $75  XP: $8  F18
**Location:** PA Tpk exit 17, 1 mi on US 15 exit Rossmoyne Rd. 4950 Ritter Rd 17055. Fax: 717/691-9692. **Terms:** No pets. **Facility:** 129 rooms. Easily accessible to State Capitol. Rates for up to 4 persons; 4 stories; interior corridors; meeting rooms; heated pool, whirlpool; exercise room. **Dining:** Cafeteria nearby. **Services:** data ports. **Fee:** coin laundry. **All Rooms:** free movies, cable TV. **Some Rooms:** refrigerators. **Cards:** AE, CB, DI, DS, MC, VI.  (D)(S)⊗

**HOLIDAY INN HARRISBURG-WEST**  Rates Subject to Change  Phone: 717/697-0321
(AAA)  9/25-10/8  1P: $95  2P/1B: $105  2P/2B: $105  XP: $10  F18
  5/1-9/24  1P: $79  2P/1B: $89  2P/2B: $89  XP: $10  F18
◆◆◆  4/15-4/30  1P: $79  2P/1B: $89  2P/2B: $89  XP: $10  F18
Motor Inn  10/9-4/14  1P: $75  2P/1B: $85  2P/2B: $85  XP: $10  F18
**Location:** I-83, exit 20; 4 3/4 mi w on SR 581 at jct Carlisle Pike & SR 581. 5401 Carlisle Pike 17055. Fax: 717/697-7594. **Terms:** Sr. discount; reserv deposit; pets, $50 dep req. **Facility:** 222 rooms. Located in busy commercial district. 2 stories; exterior corridors; meeting rooms; pool, wading pool; exercise room. **Fee:** miniature golf; driving range. **Dining & Entertainment:** Dining room; 6:30 am-10 pm, Sun 7 am-9 pm; $4-$13; cocktails/lounge; entertainment. **All Rooms:** free & pay movies, cable TV. **Some Rooms:** whirlpools. **Cards:** AE, CB, DI, DS, JCB, MC, VI.
*(See color ad p A132)*  (D)⊗

## RESTAURANTS

**FINLEY'S AMERICAN RESTAURANT**  Dinner: $11-$20  Phone: 717/763-5626
◆  **Location:** On Carlisle Pike, 1 1/2 mi sw of Camp Hill. 4956 Carlisle Pike 17055. **Hours:** 11 am-10 pm, Fri & American  Sat-11 pm. Closed: 11/23, 12/25 & 12/24 for dinner. **Features:** casual dress; children's menu; senior's menu; buffet. Casual family dining. Sesonally updated specialties. **Cards:** AE, DI, DS, MC, VI.  ⊗

**ISAAC'S RESTAURANT & DELI**  Dinner: up to $10  Phone: 717/766-1111
◆  **Location:** 1 mi n on US 15, from I-76 exit 17, at Rossmoyne Rd. 4940 Ritter Rd 17055. **Hours:** 10 am-9 American  pm, Fri & Sat-10 pm, Sun 11 am-9 pm. **Features:** casual dress; carryout. Specializing in gourmet sandwiches. **Cards:** AE, DS, MC, VI.  ⊗

# MEDIA—6,000

## LODGING

**MCINTOSH INN OF MEDIA**  Rates Subject to Change  Phone: 610/565-5800
◆◆  All Year  1P: $42- 50  2P/1B: $47- 55  2P/2B: $49  XP: $3  F18
Motel  **Location:** On SR 352, at jct US 1, just s on SR 352 from US 1. Rt US 1 & 352 19063. Fax: 610/565-7748. **Terms:** Sr. discount; weekly rates; no pets. **Facility:** 84 rooms. 2-3 stories; exterior corridors. **Dining:** Restaurant nearby. **Services:** data ports. **All Rooms:** free movies, cable TV. **Some Rooms:** microwaves, radios, refrigerators. **Cards:** AE, CB, DI, MC, VI. *(See ad p A185)*  (⊿)(D)⊗

# MENDENHALL

## LODGING

**MENDENHALL INN HOTEL & CONFERENCE CENTER**  Rates Subject to Change  Phone: 610/388-2100
◆◆◆  All Year [CP]  1P: $81  2P/1B: $91  2P/2B: $91  XP: $15  F12
Motor Inn  **Location:** On SR 52, 1 mi s of jct US 1. Rt 52 Kennett Pike 19357 (PO Box 606). Fax: 610/388-1184. **Terms:** Credit card guarantee; no pets. **Facility:** 70 rooms. Country setting in heart of Brandywine area. Comfortably decorated rooms. 4 two-bedroom units. 4 suites, $125-$160; 3 stories; interior/exterior corridors; conference facilities; exercise room. **Dining & Entertainment:** Dining room; 11:30 am-2:30 & 5-10 pm, Sun 10 am-2 & 4-8 pm; $14-$28; cocktails/lounge; dining room, see separate listing. **Services:** data ports; valet laundry; area transportation, within 5 mi. **Fee:** airport transportation, to Philadelphia. **All Rooms:** free movies, cable TV. **Some Rooms:** Fee: VCP's, whirlpools. **Cards:** AE, CB, DI, DS, MC, VI.  (⊿)(D)(S)⊗

## RESTAURANT

**MENDENHALL INN**  Dinner: $21-$30  Phone: 610/388-1181
◆◆◆  **Location:** On SR 52, 1 mi s of US 1. 52 South 19357. **Hours:** 11:30 am-2:30 & 5-10 pm, Sun 10 am-2 & Continental  4-8 pm. Closed: 12/25. **Reservations:** suggested. **Features:** casual dress; children's menu; cocktails & lounge; valet parking; buffet. Elegant dining in traditional style; menu features various game birds. **Cards:** AE, CB, DI, DS, MC, VI.  ⊗

# MERCER—2,400

## LODGINGS

**COLONIAL INN MOTEL**  Rates Subject to Change  Phone: 412/662-5600
(AAA)  5/1-9/30 & 4/1-4/30  1P: $27  2P/1B: $31  2P/2B: $36  XP: $5
  10/1-3/31  1P: $22- 25  2P/1B: $25- 28  2P/2B: $28- 32  XP: $5
◆  **Location:** 1 1/4 mi n on US 19. 383 N Perry Hwy 16137 (Rt 19N). **Terms:** Sr. discount; reserv deposit; Motel  weekly rates; pets. **Facility:** 21 rooms. Quiet location. 1 story; interior/exterior corridors. **All Rooms:** cable TV. **Cards:** AE, DS, MC, VI. *(See ad below)*  (D)⊗

**HOWARD JOHNSON MOTOR LODGE**  AAA Special Value Rates  Phone: 412/748-3030
(AAA)  All Year  1P: $64  2P/1B: $68  2P/2B: $71  XP: $6  F18
◆◆◆  **Location:** On US 19, at I-80 exit 2. 835 Perry Hwy 16137. Fax: 412/748-3484. **Terms:** Reserv deposit; Motor Inn  package plans; pets. **Facility:** 102 rooms. 2 stories; interior corridors; meeting rooms; heated pool, saunas; exercise room, playground. **Dining:** Restaurant; 6 am-midnight; $5-$10; cocktails. **Services:** Fee: coin laundry. **All Rooms:** free movies, cable TV. **Some Rooms:** VCP's. **Cards:** AE, CB, DI, DS, MC, VI.
*(See ad p A169)*  (D)⊗

## RESTAURANTS

**GIUSEPPE'S RESTAURANT**  **Dinner:** $11-$20  **Phone:** 412/748-3589
*Location:* From I-80 exit 2, 1 1/2 mi s on US 19. 16137. **Hours:** 11 am-11 pm, Sun-10 pm. **Reservations:** suggested. **Features:** carryout; cocktails; a la carte. **Cards:** AE, DI, DS, MC, VI.
Italian

**TIMBERS**  Historical  **Dinner:** $11-$20  **Phone:** 412/662-4533
*Location:* 2 mi n on Rt 19 off I-80, exit 2, then 1 mi sw on SR 62. 16137. **Hours:** 11:30 am-10 pm, Fri & Sat-11 pm, Sun-8 pm. Closed: 1/1, 11/23 & 12/25. **Reservations:** suggested; weekends. **Features:** casual dress; Sunday brunch; children's menu; cocktails & lounge; a la carte. 1872 restored farm & country store, featuring steaks & seafood. **Cards:** AE, DS, MC, VI.
American

## MERCERSBURG—1,600

## LODGING

**THE MERCERSBURG INN**  Rates Subject to Change  **Phone:** 717/328-5231
All Year [BP]  2P/1B: $110- 180  2P/2B: $110- 180  XP: $25
*Location:* I-81 exit 3, 10 mi w on US 16. 405 S Main 17236. Fax: 717/328-3403. **Terms:** Reserv deposit, 14 day notice; package plans; no pets. **Facility:** 15 rooms. Restored mansion circa 1910. Some rooms with fireplace. 3 stories; interior corridors; smoke free premises; cable TV in game room. **Dining:** Dining room; prix fixe, Fri & Sat 8 pm seating only; $45; cocktails. **All Rooms:** combo & shower baths, no TVs. **Cards:** DS, MC, VI.
Historic Country Inn

## MIDDLETOWN—9,300

## RESTAURANT

**ALFRED'S VICTORIAN RESTAURANT**  **Dinner:** $11-$20  **Phone:** 717/944-5373
*Location:* On SR 441, 3 1/4 mi s of SR 230. 38 N Union St 17057. **Hours:** 11:30 am-2 & 5-10 pm, Sat from 5 pm, Sun 3 pm-9 pm. Closed major holidays. **Reservations:** suggested. **Features:** semi-formal attire; cocktails; street parking; a la carte. Original Victorian decor. Extensive menu. Italian specialties. Owner/chef.
American
**Cards:** AE, DI, DS, MC, VI.

## MIFFLINTOWN—900

## LODGING

**ECONO LODGE**  Rates Subject to Change  **Phone:** 717/436-5981
All Year  1P: $42- 44  2P/1B: $44- 47  2P/2B: $44- 47  XP: $4 F18
*Location:* At jct US 322/22 & SR 35. 17059-0202 (PO Box 202). Fax: 717/436-5574. **Terms:** Sr. discount; reserv deposit; weekly/monthly rates; no pets. **Facility:** 47 rooms. Very attractive rooms. 2 stories; interior/exterior corridors. **Dining:** Restaurant nearby. **Services:** data ports. **All Rooms:** cable TV. **Some Rooms:** efficiency, refrigerators, whirlpools. Fee: microwaves, VCP's. **Cards:** AE, CB, DI, DS, JCB, MC, VI.
Motel

## MIFFLINVILLE

## LODGING

**SUPER 8 MOTEL**  Rates Subject to Change  **Phone:** 717/759-6778
All Year  1P: $40  2P/2B: $50  XP: $5 F12
*Location:* Just n of I-80, exit 37. I-80, exit 37 18631. **Terms:** Sr. discount; reserv deposit, 7 day notice; small pets only. **Facility:** 30 rooms. 1 story; exterior corridors. **Dining & Entertainment:** Restaurant; 8 am-9 pm; Fri & Sat-10 pm; $7-$24; cocktails/lounge. **All Rooms:** cable TV. **Cards:** AE, DI, DS, MC, VI.
Motor Inn

## MILESBURG—1,100

### LODGING

**DAYS INN**
Rates Subject to Change
Phone: 814/355-7521
All Year    1P: $48    2P/2B: $58    XP: $5  F12

Motor Inn
**Location:** 1/4 mi n on SR 150 from I-80, exit 23. 16853 (PO Box 538). Fax: 814/355-7521. **Terms:** Sr. discount; age restrictions may apply; small pets only, $5. **Facility:** 115 rooms. 2 stories; interior corridors; meeting rooms; pool. **Dining & Entertainment:** Restaurant; 6 am-10 & 5-10 pm; $6-$12; cocktails/lounge. **Services:** Fee: coin laundry. **All Rooms:** free movies, cable TV. **Some Rooms:** Fee: VCP's. **Cards:** AE, CB, DI, DS, MC, VI.    (D) ⊗

## MILFORD—1,100

### LODGINGS

**MYER MOTEL**
AAA Special Value Rates
Phone: 717/296-7223
All Year [CP]    1P: $40- 50  2P/1B: $45- 70  2P/2B: $50- 70  XP: $5  F10

Cottage
**Location:** 1/2 mi ne on US 6 & 209. 18337 (RR 4, Box 8030). **Terms:** Credit card guarantee; pets. **Facility:** 19 rooms. Spacious grounds, well maintained property. Country feel. Duplex cottages without kitchens. 1 kitchen, $20 extra; 1 story; exterior corridors. **Dining:** Restaurant nearby. **All Rooms:** combo & shower baths, cable TV, no phones. **Some Rooms:** refrigerators. **Cards:** AE, CB, DI, DS, MC, VI.    (D) ⊗

**PINE HILL FARM BED & BREAKFAST**
Guaranteed Rates
Phone: 717/296-7395
All Year [BP]    1P: $75- 100  2P/1B: $85- 110    XP: $25

Bed & Breakfast
**Location:** I-84 exit 11, 3 mi s on Rt 209; w on Cummins Hill Rd. Cummins Hill Rd 18337 (PO Box 1001). **Terms:** Age restrictions may apply; reserv deposit, 7 day notice; no pets. **Facility:** 5 rooms. Panoramic views of the Delaware River. Rooms with country & formal American antiques. 2 stories; interior corridors; mountain view. **Recreation:** nature trails; cross country skiing; hiking trails. **All Rooms:** no phones. **Some Rooms:** radios. **Cards:** DS, MC, VI.

**TOURIST VILLAGE MOTEL**
Rates Subject to Change
Phone: 717/491-4414
Fri & Sat 5/1-11/1    1P: $38- 48  2P/1B: $48- 58    XP: $6
Sun-Thurs 5/1-11/1   1P: $28- 38  2P/1B: $38- 48    XP: $6
11/2-4/30            1P: $28      2P/1B: $38         XP: $6

Motel
**Location:** 1 mi s of I-84, exit 11. US 6 & 209 18337 (PO Box 487). Fax: 717/491-4178. **Terms:** Sr. discount; reserv deposit; pets. **Facility:** 18 rooms. 1 story; exterior corridors. **Dining:** Restaurant nearby. **Services:** Fee: coin laundry. **All Rooms:** combo & shower baths, cable TV. **Some Rooms:** kitchen. **Cards:** AE, DI, DS, MC, VI.    (D) ⊗

## MONROEVILLE—29,100   (See PITTSBURGH ACCOMMODATIONS spotting map page A207; see index starting on page A206)

### LODGINGS

**DAYS INN-MONROEVILLE**
Rates Subject to Change
Phone: 412/856-1610   **74**
All Year    1P: $48- 57  2P/1B: $54- 63  2P/2B: $55- 63  XP: $6  F18

Motel
**Location:** 1 mi w of I-76 (PA Tpk) exit 6, on SR 48S; 1 mi s of I-376, exit 16A. 2727 Mosside Blvd 15146. Fax: 412/856-1628. **Terms:** Sr. discount; small pets only, in smoking rooms only. **Facility:** 107 rooms. 2-3 stories; exterior corridors. **Dining:** Restaurant nearby. **All Rooms:** free movies, cable TV. **Cards:** AE, CB, DI, DS, MC, VI. *(See ad below)*    (D) ⊗

**HARLEY HOTEL**
AAA Special Value Rates
Phone: 412/244-1600   **70**
All Year    1P: $103- 113  2P/1B: $123    2P/2B: $123    XP: $10  F18

Motor Inn
**Location:** 8 mi e on I-376 & US 22, exit 15. 699 Rodi Rd 15235. Fax: 412/829-2334. **Terms:** Credit card guarantee; 15% service charge; weekly/monthly rates; no pets. **Facility:** 152 rooms. Unusually good pool facilities. 3 stories; interior corridors; conference facilities; 2 pools (2 heated, 1 indoor), saunas, whirlpool; 3 lighted tennis courts; exercise room. **Dining & Entertainment:** Dining room; 6:30 am-2 & 5:30-10 pm, Fri & Sat-11 pm, Sun 7 am-2 & 5:30-10 pm; $9-$20; cocktails; entertainment. **Services:** data ports. Fee: coin laundry, airport transportation. **All Rooms:** cable TV. Fee: movies. **Some Rooms:** refrigerators. **Cards:** AE, CB, DI, DS, MC, VI. *(See ad p A208)*    (D) ⊗

**HOLIDAY INN**
Rates Subject to Change
Phone: 412/372-1022   **73**
All Year    1P: $109    2P/1B: $119    2P/2B: $109    XP: $15  F19

Motor Inn
**Location:** I-76 exit 6, 2/10 mi w on US Business 22, 1/10 mi s on SR 48. 2750 Mosside Blvd 15146. Fax: 412/373-4065. **Terms:** Sr. discount; check-in 4 pm; 15% service charge; no pets. **Facility:** 189 rooms. Modestly appointed rooms. 4 stories; interior corridors; meeting rooms; pool. **Dining & Entertainment:** Dining room; 6 am-10 pm; $10-$20; cocktail lounge; entertainment. **Services:** data ports. Fee: coin laundry. **All Rooms:** free movies. **Some Rooms:** coffeemakers, microwaves, refrigerators. **Cards:** AE, CB, DI, DS, JCB, MC, VI.    (D) ⊗

**RED ROOF INN-MONROEVILLE**
Rates Subject to Change
Phone: 412/856-4738   **76**
5/1-10/31    1P: $47- 60  2P/1B: $47- 60  2P/2B: $47- 60  XP: $7  F18
1/1-4/30     1P: $45- 60  2P/1B: $45- 60  2P/2B: $45- 60  XP: $7  F18
11/1-12/31   1P: $43- 60  2P/1B: $43- 60  2P/2B: $43- 60  XP: $7  F18

Motel
**Location:** 3/4 mi s on SR 48 from exit 6, PA Tpk I-76; exit 16A from I-376. 2729 Mosside Blvd 15146. Fax: 412/856-4758. **Terms:** Credit card guarantee; pets. **Facility:** 117 rooms. 3 stories; exterior corridors; meeting rooms. **Dining:** Restaurant nearby. **Services:** data ports; valet laundry. **All Rooms:** free movies. **Cards:** AE, CB, DI, DS, MC, VI.    (D) ⊗

(See PITTSBURGH ACCOMMODATIONS spotting map page A207)

**WM PENN MOTEL**    Rates Subject to Change    Phone: 412/373-0700   **71**
(AAA)    All Year    1P: $39- 45   2P/1B: $44    2P/2B: $48- 50   XP: $7   F16
◆    **Location:** 1/4 mi w of tpk exit 6 on US 22 business rt. 4139 Wm Penn Hwy 15146. **Terms:** Sr. discount;
Motel    reserv deposit, 7 day notice; weekly rates; small pets only, $10. **Facility:** 22 rooms. 1 two-bedroom unit. 1
story; exterior corridors. **Dining:** Restaurant nearby. **All Rooms:** combo & shower baths. **Cards:** AE, CB, DI,
MC, VI. *(See color ad p A206)*    ⓓ

# MONTGOMERY—4,600

## LODGING

**NORTHWOOD MOTEL**    Rates Subject to Change    Phone: 717/547-6624
(AAA)    All Year    1P: $35   2P/1B: $37    2P/2B: $39    XP: $2   D
◆    **Location:** 8 mi s of Williamsport on US 15. 17752 (RD 2, Box 583). **Terms:** Sr. discount; reserv deposit;
Motel    weekly rates; no pets. **Facility:** 10 rooms. Quiet rural location. 1 story; exterior corridors; Two 18-hole public
golf courses across the street; pool. **All Rooms:** microwaves, free movies, refrigerators, cable TV.
**Cards:** AE, DS, MC, VI.    ⓓ ⊗

# MONTGOMERYVILLE

## LODGING

**COMFORT INN**    AAA Special Value Rates    Phone: 215/361-3600
(AAA)    All Year [CP]    1P: $75- 109   2P/1B: $94    2P/2B: $80    XP: $5   F
◆◆◆    **Location:** On SR 309, 1/4 mi n of jct SR 309, 463 & US 202. 678 Bethlehem Pike 18936 (PO Box 88).
Motel    **Fax:** 215/361-7949. **Terms:** Reserv deposit; no pets. **Facility:** 84 rooms. Tastefully decorated rooms. Red brick
pillored exterior. 3 stories; interior corridors; meeting rooms. **Dining:** Restaurant nearby. **Services:** data
ports; health club privileges. Fee: coin laundry, airport transportation. **All Rooms:** cable TV. **Some Rooms:** 6
efficiencies, no utensils. Fee: VCP's, whirlpools. **Cards:** AE, DI, DS, MC, VI.    ⓓ Ⓢ ⊗

# MONTOURSVILLE—5,000

## RESTAURANT

**HILLSIDE RESTAURANT**    **Dinner:** $11-$20    Phone: 717/326-6779
◆◆    **Location:** From I-180 (US 220), Faxon exit, 1 mi n on North Way Rd, 1 mi e on Four Mile Dr. 2725 Four
American    Mile Dr 17754. **Hours:** 11 am-11 pm, Sat from 4:30 pm. Closed: Sun, major holidays & 12/24-12/26.
**Reservations:** suggested; weekends. **Features:** casual dress; children's menu; health conscious menu
items; carryout; cocktails & lounge. Attractive, 2 level dining room with lovely view. Also some Continental fare. **Cards:** AE,
DI, MC, VI.    ⊗

# MONTROSE—2,000

## LODGING

**RIDGE HOUSE**    Rates Subject to Change    Phone: 717/278-4933
◆◆    All Year [CP]    1P: $35   2P/1B: $45    XP: $10
Historic Bed    **Location:** I-81 exit 67, 1/2 mi w on SR 492, 1/2 mi s on US 11, 9 mi w on SR 706. 6 Ridge St 18801.
& Breakfast    **Terms:** Reserv deposit, 3 day notice; weekly rates; small pets only, in pet carrier. **Facility:** 5 rooms. Circa 1866
Eastlake Octagonal Victorian house. Furnished in antiques. 2 stories; interior corridors. **All Rooms:** no A/C,
no phones, no TVs. **Some Rooms:** radios, combo & shower baths, shared bathrooms. **Cards:** AE, MC, VI.    ⓓ ⊗

## RESTAURANT

**THE MONTROSE HOUSE RESTAURANT & INN**    **Dinner:** $11-$20    Phone: 717/278-1124
◆◆    **Location:** On SR 29, 1/2 blk s of jct SR 706. 26 S Main St 18801. **Hours:** 11 am-2 & 5-9 pm, Fri-10 pm, Sat
American    5 pm-10 pm, Sun noon-8 pm. Closed: 10/1-4/30 closed Sun & Mon, 1/1, 5/29, 7/4, 9/4 & 12/25.
**Reservations:** suggested. **Features:** casual dress; carryout; cocktails & lounge. Fine dining in a rustic
atmosphere in the heart of the Endless Mountains. **Cards:** CB, DI, DS, MC, VI.    ⊗

**MOOSIC** (See POCONO MOUNTAINS & VICINITY ACCOMMODATIONS spotting map
pages A212 & A213; see index starting on page A210)

## LODGING

**DAYS INN-MONTAGE**    Rates Subject to Change    Phone: 717/457-6713   **70**
(AAA)    All Year [CP]    1P: $45- 59   2P/1B: $45- 59   2P/2B: $50- 65   XP: $5   F16
◆◆    **Location:** I-81 exit 51, US 11 s 2 mi, I-81 exit 50, US 11 n 1/4 mi. 4130 Birney Ave 18507.
Motel    **Fax:** 717/457-4479. **Terms:** Sr. discount; weekly/monthly rates; small pets only. **Facility:** 44 rooms. Some large
rooms. 1 two-bedroom unit. 2 stories; interior/exterior corridors; meeting rooms. **Services:** Fee: coin laundry.
**All Rooms:** free movies, combo & shower baths, cable TV. **Some Rooms:** microwaves, refrigerators,
whirlpools. Fee: VCP's. **Cards:** AE, CB, DI, DS, JCB, MC, VI.    ⓓ ⊗

# MORGANTOWN

## LODGING

**HOLIDAY INN-HOLIDOME**    AAA Special Value Rates    Phone: 610/286-3000
◆◆◆    All Year    1P: $79- 89   2P/1B: $99- 109    XP: $10   F19
Motor Inn    **Location:** Just s of exit 22 off PA Tpk & SR 10. Exit 22 PA Tpk 19543. **Fax:** 610/286-0520. **Terms:** Reserv
deposit; monthly rates; small pets only. **Facility:** 196 rooms. Direct access to Manufacture Outlet Mall. 4 sto-
ries; interior corridors; conference facilities; heated indoor pool, sauna, whirlpools, paddlepool; exercise room, gameroom.
**Dining & Entertainment:** Restaurant; 6 am-11 & 5-10 pm, Sat & Sun 6 am-2 & 5-10 pm; $6-$17; cocktails/lounge.
**Services:** data ports. Fee: coin laundry. **All Rooms:** free movies, cable TV. **Some Rooms:** refrigerators. **Cards:** AE, CB, DI,
DS, MC, VI.    ▣ ⓓ Ⓢ ⊗

## RESTAURANT

**THE WINDMILL RESTAURANT**    **Dinner:** up to $10    Phone: 610/286-5980
(AAA)    **Location:** On SR 10 & 23, 1/2 mi w of jct Hwy 76. Rts 10 & 23 19543. **Hours:** 7 am-10 pm, Fri & Sat-11
◆    pm. Closed: 11/23 & 12/25. **Features:** casual dress; children's menu; early bird specials; senior's menu;
American    carryout. Casual dining. Features homemade pie & bread. **Cards:** AE, DS, MC, VI.    ⊗

# MOUNT JOY—2,800

## LODGING

**CAMERON ESTATE INN**          Guaranteed Rates                                    Phone: 717-653-1773
⚑⚑⚑
5/1-11/30 & 3/1-4/30 [CP]          2P/1B:   $65-  110                              XP: $10
12/1-2/29 [CP]                    2P/1B:   $60-  90                               XP: $10
◆◆◆          **Location:** Rheems exit SR 283, 3 1/2 mi s on Cloverleaf & Colebrook rds, 1/4 mi w on Donegal Springs Rd;
Historic          adjacent to Donegal Presbyterian Church. 1895 Donegal Springs Rd 17552. Fax: 717/653-9432. **Terms:** Age
Country Inn          restrictions may apply; reserv deposit, 3 day notice; 2 night min stay, in season; no pets. **Facility:** 18 rooms.
          Early 19th-century rural manor house on spacious grounds. Some fireplaces. 3 stories; interior corridors;
meeting rooms. **Dining:** Dining room, see separate listing. **All Rooms:** no phones, no TVs. **Cards:** AE, DI, DS, MC, VI.  Ⓓ

## RESTAURANTS

**ALOIS'S RESTAURANT**  Historical          **Dinner:** $21-$30          Phone: 717/653-2057
⚑          **Location:** 1/4 mi w on SR 230, 1 blk n on N Market St. 102 N Market St 17552. **Hours:** 5:30 pm-9 pm, Fri &
          Sat-9:45 pm, Sun-8 pm. Closed major holidays & Mon. **Reservations:** suggested. **Features:** semi-formal
◆◆          attire; cocktails & lounge; prix fixe. Fine gourmet dining in restored 1800's Victorian hotel/brewery.
American          **Cards:** AE, DS, MC, VI.          ⊗

**CAMERON ESTATE INN DINING ROOM**  Historical          **Dinner:** $11-$20          Phone: 717/653-1773
◆◆◆          **Location:** In Cameron Estate Inn. 17552. **Hours:** 6 pm-8:30 pm, Fri & Sat 5:30 pm-9:30 pm, Sun 10:30
American          am-1:30 pm. Closed: 12/24 & 12/25. **Reservations:** suggested. **Features:** semi-formal attire; Sunday
          brunch; cocktails; a la carte. French & American country cuisine; candlelight dining. In early 19th century
manorhouse. **Cards:** AE, DI, DS, MC, VI.

**THE CATACOMBS**  Historical          **Dinner:** $21-$30          Phone: 717/653-2056
⚑          **Location:** 1/4 mi w on SR 230, 1 blk n on Market St. 102 N Market St 17552. **Hours:** 5:30 pm-9 pm, Fri &
          Sat 5 pm-10 pm, Sun 5 pm-9:45 pm. Closed major holidays. **Reservations:** required. **Features:** casual
◆◆          dress; children's menu; cocktails & lounge. Underground lagering cellars of 19th-century brewery; outdoor
American          bier garten in summer. Hearty portions. Medieval feast on selected Sun, 5 pm-9 pm, $30. Smoke free
          premises. **Cards:** AE, DI, DS, MC, VI.          ⊗

**GROFF'S FARM**  Historical          **Dinner:** $11-$20          Phone: 717/653-2048
⚑          **Location:** 1/2 mi w on Marietta Ave (SR 772), 1 mi s on Pinkerton Rd. 650 Pinkerton Rd 17552.
          **Hours:** 11:30 am-1:30 pm, also seatings at 5 pm or 7:30 pm, Sat seatings at 5 pm or 8 pm. Closed: Sun,
◆◆◆          Mon, 12/24 & 12/25. **Reservations:** required; for evening seatings. **Features:** casual dress; children's menu;
American          cocktails; a la carte. Authentic Pennsylvania fare served in original 1756 farm house. Individual family-style
          seatings. Homemade breads, soups & desserts. **Cards:** AE, DI, DS, MC, VI.

**THE WATERING TROUGH**          **Dinner:** $11-$20          Phone: 717/653-6181
◆◆          **Location:** On SR 230, W Main St. 905 W Main St 17552. **Hours:** 11 am-2 & 5-10 pm, Sun 11 am-10 pm.
American          Closed: 1/1, 11/23 & 12/25. **Features:** casual dress; carryout; cocktails & lounge; entertainment. Casual, fine
          dining from "wings to filet". **Cards:** MC, VI.          ⊗

# MOUNT PLEASANT—4,100

## RESTAURANT

**NINO'S RESTAURANT**          **Dinner:** $11-$20          Phone: 412/547-2900
⚑          **Location:** 3 mi e on SR 31, 1 blk e of jct SR 982. SR 31 15666. **Hours:** 11 am-3 & 5-10 pm, Sat 11 am-11
          pm, Sun 11 am-9 pm. Closed: Mon, 1/1, 11/23, 12/24 & 12/25. **Reservations:** suggested. **Features:** casual
◆◆          dress; Sunday brunch; children's menu; salad bar; cocktails & lounge; fee for valet parking. Also, nicely
Italian          prepared American dishes, homemade. Dinner buffet on Tues. **Cards:** AE, CB, DI, DS, MC, VI.

# MOUNT POCONO—1,800   (See POCONO MOUNTAINS & VICINITY ACCOMMODATIONS spotting map pages A212 & A213; see index starting on page A210)

## LODGINGS

**FARMHOUSE BED & BREAKFAST**          Rates Subject to Change          Phone: 717/839-0796   45
◆◆          All Year [BP]          1P:  $55-  85   2P/1B:  $85-  105          XP: $25
Historic Bed          **Location:** 2 1/4 mi e on SR 940, 1/4 mi s on Grange Rd. 18344. (HCR 1, Box 6B). **Terms:** Reserv deposit,
& Breakfast          14 day notice; package plans; no pets. **Facility:** 3 rooms. Restored farmhouse, circa 1850 on 6 acres. Nestled
          beneath giant evergreens in Paradise Valley. All rooms have fireplace. 2 or more night stay mid-week save $15
per night; 2 stories; exterior corridors; smoke free premises. **All Rooms:** coffeemakers, refrigerators, cable TV, VCP's.
**Some Rooms:** radios. **Cards:** DS, MC, VI.          Ⓓ ⊗

**POCONO FOUNTAIN MOTEL**          Guaranteed Rates          Phone: 717/839-7728   47
⚑          5/27-9/5          1P:  $52-  150   2P/1B:  $56-  150   2P/2B:  $59-  69   XP: $5   F12
          5/1-5/26 & 9/6-4/30          1P:  $42-  125   2P/1B:  $45-  125   2P/2B:  $52-  69   XP: $5   F12
◆◆          **Location:** 2 mi s on SR 611. 18344. (HCR 1, Box 115). Fax: 717/839-7728. **Terms:** Sr. discount; reserv
Motor Inn          deposit, 7 day notice; weekly rates; package plans; no pets. **Facility:** 38 rooms. 2- to 3-night minimum stay
          weekends in season; 1 story; exterior corridors; heated pool. **Dining & Entertainment:** Restaurant; 6 am-10
pm; $4-$11; cocktails/lounge. **All Rooms:** free movies, combo & shower baths, cable TV. **Some Rooms:** 2 efficiencies, no
utensils, whirlpools. Fee: refrigerators, VCP's. **Cards:** AE, CB, DI, DS, MC, VI.          Ⓓ ⊗

## RESTAURANT

**HAMPTON COURT INN RESTAURANT**          **Dinner:** $11-$20          Phone: 717/839-2119   40
⚑          **Location:** On SR 940, 2 mi e of jct SR 940 & SR 611. 18344. **Hours:** 5 pm-10 pm, Fri & Sat-11 pm. Closed:
          Tues, 11/23, 12/24 & 12/25. **Reservations:** required; Sat. **Features:** casual dress; carryout; cocktails;
◆◆◆          minimum charge-$9. Century-old converted farm house, quaint, intimate Henry VIII ambience. Featuring
Continental          fresh seafood & steaks. Desserts made on premises. **Cards:** AE, CB, DI, MC, VI.          ⊗

## MOUNT UNION—2,900

### LODGING

**MOTEL 22**  
(AAA)  
◆ Motel  
Rates Subject to Change    Phone: 814/542-2571

| | | 1P: | 2P/1B: | | 2P/2B: | | XP: | |
|---|---|---|---|---|---|---|---|---|
| Fri & Sat 5/1-10/31 | | $28 | $39- | 42 | $39- | 42 | $5 | D |
| Sun-Thurs & Fri & Sat | | | | | | | | |
| 11/1-12/31 | | $26 | $34 | | $34 | | $5 | D |
| Fri & Sat 1/1-4/30 | | $25 | $33 | | $33 | | $5 | D |

**Location:** On US 22, 3 1/4 mi w of jct US 522. 17052 (RD 1 Box 1900, MAPLETON DEPOT). **Fax:** 814/542-2571. **Terms:** Sr. discount; reserv deposit, 7 day notice; weekly/monthly rates; no pets. **Facility:** 32 rooms. Country atmosphere. 1 story; exterior corridors; pool. **Dining & Entertainment:** Cocktail lounge; restaurant nearby. **All Rooms:** combo & shower baths, cable TV. **Cards:** AE, DI, DS, MC, VI.    (D)

## MUHLENBERG

### LODGINGS

**COMFORT INN**  
(AAA)  
◆◆◆ Motel  
Rates Subject to Change    Phone: 610/371-0500

| | | 1P: | | 2P/1B: | | 2P/2B: | | XP: | |
|---|---|---|---|---|---|---|---|---|---|
| All Year [CP] | | $45- | 115 | $45- | 115 | $55- | 115 | $5 | F18 |

**Location:** On US 222 business route at jct US 222 (5th St). (2200 Stacy Dr, READING). **Fax:** 610/478-9421. **Terms:** Sr. discount; reserv deposit; no pets. **Facility:** 60 rooms. Traditional motel rooms. 2 stories; interior corridors; meeting rooms; exercise room. **Dining:** Restaurant nearby. **Services:** data ports; valet laundry. **All Rooms:** free movies, cable TV. **Some Rooms:** microwaves, refrigerators. **Fee:** VCP's, whirlpools. **Cards:** AE, CB, DI, DS, JCB, MC, VI. (See color ad p A216)    ⊘ (D) ⊗

**HOLIDAY INN**  
◆◆◆ Motor Inn  
Guaranteed Rates    Phone: 610/929-4741

| | | 1P: | | 2P/1B: | | 2P/2B: | | XP: | |
|---|---|---|---|---|---|---|---|---|---|
| 5/1-11/30 | | $77- | 119 | $87- | 129 | $87- | 129 | $10 | F18 |
| 12/1-4/30 | | $64- | 69 | $74- | 79 | $74- | 79 | $10 | F18 |

**Location:** 2 1/2 mi n on US 222 business route at jct US 222, s of Warren St bypass. (2545 5th St). **Fax:** 610/929-5237. **Terms:** Sr. discount; credit card guarantee; weekly rates; small pets only. **Facility:** 140 rooms. 2 stories; interior corridors; meeting rooms; pool. **Dining & Entertainment:** Dining room; 6:30 am-10 pm; $4-$10; cocktails/lounge. **Services:** Fee: coin laundry. **All Rooms:** free & pay movies, cable TV. **Some Rooms:** microwaves, refrigerators. **Cards:** AE, CB, DI, DS, JCB, MC, VI.    ⊘ (D) ⊗

## MUNCY—2,700

### LODGING

**WALTON HOUSE BED & BREAKFAST**  
(AAA)  
◆ Historic Bed & Breakfast  
Rates Subject to Change    Phone: 717/546-8114

| | | 1P: | | 2P/1B: | | 2P/2B: | | XP: |
|---|---|---|---|---|---|---|---|---|
| All Year [BP] | | $40- | 55 | $40- | 55 | $45 | | $5 |

**Location:** 1/2 mi w on SR 405. 172 W Water St 17756. **Terms:** Credit card guarantee, 7 day notice; no pets. **Facility:** 4 rooms. 2 stories; interior corridors; smoke free premises; whirlpool; sports court, badminton, horseshoes & volleyball. **Recreation:** bicycles. **All Rooms:** no phones, no TVs. **Some Rooms:** A/C, radios, combo & shower baths, shared bathrooms. **Cards:** AE, MC, VI.    (D) ⊗

## MURRYSVILLE—17,000

### RESTAURANT

**SPADARO'S RESTAURANT**  
◆◆ Italian  
Dinner: up to $10    Phone: 412/327-5955

**Location:** On US 22, 1/4 mi e of School Rd. 4430 Wm Penn Hwy 15668. **Hours:** 11 am-10 pm, Fri & Sat-11 pm, Sun noon-8 pm. **Closed:** 1/1 & 12/25. **Reservations:** suggested; weekends. **Features:** casual dress; children's menu; cocktails & lounge. Distinctively creative Italian & American cuisine. Lunch buffet Mon-Fri. **Cards:** AE, DI, DS, MC, VI.    ⊗

## MYERSTOWN—3,200

### LODGINGS

**LANTERN LODGE MOTOR INN**  
(AAA)  
◆◆◆ Motor Inn  
AAA Special Value Rates    Phone: 717/866-6536

| | | 1P: | | 2P/1B: | 2P/2B: | | XP: | |
|---|---|---|---|---|---|---|---|---|
| 5/1-10/31 & 4/15-4/30 | | $54- | 85 | $65 | $85 | | $10 | D12 |
| 11/1-4/14 | | $45- | 75 | $55 | $65- | 70 | $10 | D12 |

**Location:** 1 blk n of US 422, on SR 501. 411 N College St 17067. **Fax:** 717/866-6536. **Terms:** Reserv deposit; no pets. **Facility:** 79 rooms. Renowned for its summer gardens. Well furnished rooms. Few smaller units. Weekend entertainment. 1 two-bedroom unit. 3-bedroom homes, $125-$150 for up to 2 persons, $20 extra person. 1 whirlpool suite, $225 for up to 4 persons; 2 stories; interior corridors; designated smoking area; meeting rooms; luxury level rooms. **Dining:** Dining room, see separate listing. **Services:** valet laundry. **Fee:** massage. **All Rooms:** coffeemakers, combo & shower baths, cable TV. **Some Rooms:** 2 kitchens, VCP's. **Cards:** AE, CB, DI, DS, MC, VI.    (D) ⊗

**MOTEL SKANDIA**  
(AAA)  
◆◆ Motel  
AAA Special Value Rates    Phone: 717/866-6447

| | | 1P: | 2P/1B: | | 2P/2B: | | XP: | |
|---|---|---|---|---|---|---|---|---|
| Fri & Sat 5/1-1/1 & 3/1-4/30 | | $42 | $47 | | $52 | | $5 | F12 |
| Sun-Thurs 5/1-1/1 & 3/1-4/30 | | $39 | $44 | | $49 | | $5 | F12 |

**Location:** 2 mi e on SR 422. 922 E Lincoln Ave 17067. **Terms:** Open 5/1-1/1 & 3/1-4/30; reserv deposit, 3 day notice; no pets. **Facility:** 8 rooms. Country setting. Well landscaped grounds. 1 story; exterior corridors. **All Rooms:** coffeemakers, cable TV, no phones. **Cards:** AE, MC, VI.    (D)

### RESTAURANT

**LANTERN LODGE DINING ROOM**  
◆◆◆ Continental  
Dinner: $11-$20    Phone: 717/866-6536

**Location:** In Lantern Lodge Motor Inn. 411 N College St 17067. **Hours:** 7-11 am, 11:30-2 & 5-10 pm, Sun-9 pm. **Closed:** major holidays at 5 pm. **Reservations:** suggested. **Features:** casual dress; Sunday brunch; children's menu; cocktails & lounge. Weekend entertainment. **Cards:** AE, DI, DS, MC, VI.    ⊗

## NAZARETH—5,700

### LODGING

**CLASSIC VICTORIAN BED & BREAKFAST**  
◆◆ Historic Bed & Breakfast  
Rates Subject to Change    Phone: 610/759-8276

| | | 1P: | | 2P/1B: | | 2P/2B: | | XP: | |
|---|---|---|---|---|---|---|---|---|---|
| All Year [BP] | | $65- | 75 | $65- | 75 | $65- | 75 | $10 | D21 |

**Location:** 5 mi n on SR 191 from US 22; 1/2 mi from town center in historic district. 35 N New St 18064. **Fax:** 610/434-1889. **Terms:** Check-in 4 pm; reserv deposit, 10 day notice; no pets. **Facility:** 3 rooms. 1905 historical property. Blend of Victorian & Colonial antique furnishings in all rooms. 2 stories; interior corridors; smoke free premises. **Some Rooms:** combo & shower baths, shared bathrooms, cable TV. **Cards:** AE, MC, VI.    (D) ⊗

## RESTAURANT

**NEWBURG INN**                                    **Dinner:** $11-$20                                    **Phone:** 610/759-8528
◆◆                **Location:** On SR 191, 2 mi n of US 22. 4357 Newburg Rd 18064. **Hours:** 11:30 am-3 & 5-9:30 pm, Sat
American          from 5 pm, Sun noon-7:30 pm. Closed major holidays. **Reservations:** suggested. **Features:** casual dress;
                  children's menu; carryout; salad bar; cocktails & lounge. Specializing in seafood & steak. Wed prime rib
luncheon special. Hot bar served at lunch Mon-Fri. **Cards:** AE, CB, DI, DS, MC, VI.                              ⊗

# NEW BERLIN—900

## LODGING

**THE INN AT OLDE NEW BERLIN**              Rates Subject to Change                     **Phone:** 717/966-0321
(AAA)             All Year [BP]            1P: $75-  85  2P/1B:  $75-  85                    XP: $15
                  **Location:** Center of town at intersection of SR 304 & SR 204, 8 mi w of US Rt 15. 321 Market St
◆◆◆           17855-0390 (PO Box 390). Fax: 717/966-9557. **Terms:** Check-in 4 pm; reserv deposit, 7 day notice; no pets.
Historic          **Facility:** 5 rooms. Victorian architecture, in a quiet small town setting. 3 stories; interior corridors; smoke free
Country Inn       premises. **Dining:** Restaurant; Wed-Sun 10 am-2 & 4:30-8:30 pm; $9-$14. **All Rooms:** combo & shower
                  baths, no phones, no TVs. **Cards:** MC, VI.                                                    Ⓓ

# NEW CASTLE—28,300

## LODGING

**COMFORT INN**                            Rates Subject to Change                     **Phone:** 412/658-7700
(AAA)             All Year [CP]            1P: $52-  58  2P/1B:  $63-  66  2P/2B:  $57-  60  XP: $5  F18
                  **Location:** Exit 29 off I-79, 11 mi w on US 422 or exit Rt 60S off I-80 to US 422E, continue 7 mi to New
◆◆◆           Castle exit. 1740 New Butler Rd 16101. Fax: 412/658-7727. **Terms:** Sr. discount; reserv deposit;
Motel             weekly/monthly rates; small pets only, $6. **Facility:** 79 rooms. 2 stories; interior corridors; meeting rooms; ex-
                  ercise room. **Services:** data ports. **All Rooms:** free movies. **Some Rooms:** radios. Fee: refrigerators,
VCP's. **Cards:** AE, CB, DI, DS, JCB, MC, VI.                                                          Ⓓ Ⓢ ⊗

# NEW COLUMBIA

## LODGING

**NEW COLUMBIA COMFORT INN**              Rates Subject to Change                     **Phone:** 717/568-8000
(AAA)             All Year            1P: $49-  59  2P/1B:  $56-  64  2P/2B:  $54                XP: $5  F18
                  **Location:** I-80 exit 30A, Rt 15/New Columbia exit. 17856 (PO Box 62). Fax: 717/568-0660. **Terms:** Sr.
◆◆                discount; reserv deposit; pets. **Facility:** 120 rooms. Tasteful decor. 2 stories; interior/exterior corridors; meeting
Motor Inn         rooms; pool. **Dining & Entertainment:** Cafeteria; 7 am-9 pm; cocktail lounge. **Services:** Fee: coin laundry.
                  **All Rooms:** free & pay movies, cable TV. **Cards:** AE, CB, DI, DS, JCB, MC, VI.              Ⓓ Ⓢ ⊗

# NEW CUMBERLAND—7,700   (See HARRISBURG ACCOMMODATIONS spotting map
page A129; see index starting on page A128)

## LODGINGS

| **BEST WESTERN CONFERENCE CENTER** | Rates Subject to Change | | | | | **Phone:** 717/774-1100 | ❶ |
|---|---|---|---|---|---|---|---|

◆◆
Motor Inn
| 5/30-10/31 | 1P: $55 | 2P/1B: $65 | | 2P/2B: $75 | XP: $10 | F18 |
| 5/1-5/29 & 3/1-4/30 | 1P: $45 | 2P/1B: $55 | | 2P/2B: $65 | XP: $10 | F18 |
| 11/1-2/29 | 1P: $35 | 2P/1B: $45 | | 2P/2B: $55 | XP: $10 | F18 |

**Location:** I-83 exit 18A (Limekiln Rd); 1/8 mi e. 10 Limekiln Rd 17070. Fax: 717/774-0634. **Terms:** Sr. discount; credit card
guarantee, 3 day notice; small pets only, $10 dep req. **Facility:** 99 rooms. Comfortable guest rooms. 1 story; interior/exterior
corridors; pool. **Dining & Entertainment:** Cocktail lounge; restaurant nearby. **All Rooms:** free movies, cable TV.
**Some Rooms:** Fee: VCP's. **Cards:** AE, CB, DI, DS, MC, VI.                                              Ⓓ ⊗

**DAYS INN**                               AAA Special Value Rates                     **Phone:** 717/774-4156   ❻
(AAA)             6/1-10/31            1P: $55                      2P/2B:  $65         XP: $5  F12
                  5/1-5/31 & 11/1-4/30  1P: $39                      2P/2B:  $49         XP: $5  F12
                  **Location:** On SR 114 at I-83 exit 18; 1/2 mi s of tpk exit 18. 353 Lewisberry Rd 17070. Fax: 717/774-2040.
◆◆                **Terms:** MAP available; no pets. **Facility:** 62 rooms. Convenient to State Capitol-Harrisburg. 2 stories; interior
Motor Inn         corridors; pool; playground. **Dining & Entertainment:** Restaurant; 7 am-11 & 5-9 pm; $5-$9;
                  cocktails/lounge. **All Rooms:** free movies, cable TV. **Some Rooms:** Fee: VCP's. **Cards:** AE, CB, DI, DS, MC, VI.  Ⓓ Ⓢ

**FAIRFIELD INN HARRISBURG WEST**         Rates Subject to Change                     **Phone:** 717/774-6200   ❺
◆◆◆           6/13-9/11            1P: $39-  57  2P/1B:  $50-  57  2P/2B:  $53-  57  XP: $6
Motel             5/1-6/12, 9/12-12/31 &
                  1/1-4/30              1P: $36-  41  2P/1B:  $45-  50  2P/2B:  $45-  48  XP: $6
**Location:** I-76, toll exit 18, I-83 to exit 18A (Limekiln Rd). 175 Beacon Hill Blvd 17070. Fax: 717/774-6200. **Terms:** Reserv
deposit; no pets. **Facility:** 105 rooms. Convenient to state capitol & Hershey. 3 stories; interior/exterior corridors; meeting
rooms; pool. **Dining:** Restaurant nearby. **All Rooms:** free movies, cable TV. **Some Rooms:**
Fee: refrigerators. **Cards:** AE, DI, DS, MC, VI. *(See color ad p A131)*                                  Ⓓ Ⓢ ⊗

**FARM FORTUNE BED & BREAKFAST**          Guaranteed Rates                     **Phone:** 717/774-2683   ❸
◆◆◆           All Year [BP]           1P: $57-  77  2P/1B:  $65-  85  2P/2B:  $65-  85  XP: $15
Historic Bed      **Location:** I-83 s at exit 18A Limekiln Rd. 204 Limekiln Rd 17070. **Terms:** Age restrictions may apply; reserv
& Breakfast       deposit, 7 day notice; no pets. **Facility:** 4 rooms. 1 story; interior corridors; smoke free premises.
                  **Dining:** Restaurant nearby. **Services:** guest laundry. **All Rooms:** no TVs. **Some Rooms:** microwaves,
refrigerators. **Cards:** AE, CB, DI, DS, MC, VI.                                                          Ⓓ ⊗

**KEYSTONE INN**                           AAA Special Value Rates                     **Phone:** 717/774-1310   ⓫
◆◆                6/1-3/31            1P: $35  2P/1B:  $48         2P/2B:  $59         XP: $5  F12
Motel             5/1-5/31 & 4/1-4/30  1P: $24  2P/1B:  $34         2P/2B:  $30         XP: $5  F12
                  **Location:** On SR 114; at I-83, exit 18, 1/2 mi s of tpk, exit 18. 353 Lewisberry Rd 17070.
**Terms:** Weekly/monthly rates; MAP available; pets. **Facility:** 58 rooms. Convenient to state capitol-Harrisburg. 1 story; exterior
corridors; playground. **Dining:** Restaurant nearby. **All Rooms:** free movies, combo & shower baths, cable TV.
**Some Rooms:** 9 efficiencies, 2 kitchens, radios. **Cards:** AE, CB, DI, DS, MC, VI.                      Ⓓ

**KNIGHTS INN**                            Rates Subject to Change                     **Phone:** 717/774-5990   ❾
(AAA)             All Year [CP]           1P: $30  2P/1B:  $36         2P/2B:  $38         XP: $5  F18
                  **Location:** At jct I-83, exit 18A; 1/4 mi n of I-76 tpk exit 18. 300 Commerce Dr 17070. Fax: 717/774-3056.
◆◆                **Terms:** Sr. discount; reserv deposit, 3 day notice; weekly rates; pets. **Facility:** 117 rooms. Located near state
Motel             capitol. 11 efficiencies, $9-$12 extra for up to 2 persons; 1 story; exterior corridors; small pool.
                  **Dining:** Restaurant nearby. **Services:** data ports. **All Rooms:** free movies, cable TV.
**Some Rooms:** microwaves, refrigerators. Fee: VCP's. **Cards:** AE, CB, DI, DS, MC, VI.                    Ⓓ ⊗

**(See HARRISBURG ACCOMMODATIONS spotting map page A129)**

**MCINTOSH INN**
◆◆◆
Motel

| | | 1P: | | 2P/1B: | | 2P/2B: | | XP: | | |
|---|---|---|---|---|---|---|---|---|---|---|
| Rates Subject to Change | | | | | | Phone: 717/774-8888 | | | | **7** |
| Fri & Sat 6/23-9/3 | | 1P: $53- 55 | 2P/1B: $53 | | | 2P/2B: $55 | | XP: $3 | | F18 |
| 5/1-6/22, Sun-Thurs 6/23-9/3 & 9/4-10/28 | | 1P: $40- 46 | 2P/1B: $46 | | | 2P/2B: $52 | | XP: $3 | | F18 |
| 10/29-4/30 | | 1P: $37- 41 | 2P/1B: $44 | | | 2P/2B: $48 | | XP: $3 | | F18 |

**Location:** I-76, toll exit 18, I-83 at exit 18A, (Limekiln Rd). 130 Limekiln Rd 17070. Fax: 717/774-7717. **Terms:** Sr. discount; weekly rates; no pets. **Facility:** 89 rooms. Well maintained property. 3 stories; interior/exterior corridors; heated pool. **All Rooms:** free movies, cable TV. **Some Rooms:** microwaves, refrigerators. **Cards:** AE, CB, DI, MC, VI.
*(See ad p A132)*   Ⓓ Ⓢ ⊗

# NEW HOLLAND—4,500

## LODGINGS

**COMFORT INN**
Ⓐ
◆◆
Motel

AAA Special Value Rates   **Phone: 717/355-9900**

| | 1P: | 2P/1B: | | 2P/2B: | | XP: | | |
|---|---|---|---|---|---|---|---|---|
| 5/1-10/31 & 4/17-4/30 [CP] | 1P: $59 | 2P/1B: $65 | | 2P/2B: $77 | | XP: $7 | F16 |
| 11/1-11/28 [CP] | 1P: $57 | 2P/1B: $63 | | 2P/2B: $69 | | XP: $7 | F16 |
| 11/29-4/16 [CP] | 1P: $55 | 2P/1B: $59 | | 2P/2B: $65 | | XP: $5 | F16 |

**Location:** 1/2 mi w on SR 23. 626 W Main St 17557. Fax: 717/354-4193. **Terms:** Reserv deposit; no pets. **Facility:** 70 rooms. Located in heart of Pennsylvania Dutch Country. 2 stories; interior corridors; exercise room. **Dining:** Restaurant nearby. **All Rooms:** cable TV. **Some Rooms:** Fee: whirlpools. **Cards:** AE, DI, DS, MC, VI.   Ⓓ Ⓢ ⊗

**COUNTRY SQUIRE MOTOR INN**
Ⓐ
◆
Motel

Rates Subject to Change   **Phone: 717/354-4166**

| |  | |  | |  | |
|---|---|---|---|---|---|---|
| 6/10-11/10 | 1P: $55 | | 2P/2B: $59 | | XP: $5 | F12 |
| 5/1-6/9, 11/11-12/6 & 3/1-4/30 | 1P: $45 | | 2P/2B: $49 | | XP: $5 | F12 |
| 12/7-2/29 | 1P: $35 | | 2P/2B: $39 | | XP: $5 | F12 |

**Location:** 3/4 mi e on SR 23. 504 E Main St 17557. Fax: 917/354-8697. **Terms:** Credit card guarantee; weekly rates; no pets. **Facility:** 24 rooms. Located in heart of Pennsylvania Dutch Country. 1 story; exterior corridors. **Dining:** Coffee shop; breakfast only 6 am-11 am. **All Rooms:** cable TV. Fee: movies. **Cards:** AE, DS, MC, VI.   Ⓓ ⊗

**THE HOLLANDER MOTEL**
◆
Motel

Guaranteed Rates   **Phone: 717/354-4377**

| | 1P: | 2P/1B: | | 2P/2B: | | XP: | |
|---|---|---|---|---|---|---|---|
| 5/1-11/12 | 1P: $52 | 2P/1B: $52 | | 2P/2B: $55 | | XP: $5 | F6 |
| 11/13-4/30 | 1P: $34 | 2P/1B: $36 | | 2P/2B: $39 | | XP: $5 | F6 |

**Location:** 2 blks e on E Main St. 320 E Main St 17557. Fax: 717/355-9714. **Terms:** Sr. discount; reserv deposit, 3 day notice; pets, $20 dep req. **Facility:** 17 rooms. 1 story; exterior corridors. **All Rooms:** cable TV. **Cards:** AE, CB, DI, DS, MC, VI.   Ⓓ ⊗

## RESTAURANT

**PEOPLE'S RESTAURANT**
Ⓐ
◆◆
American

Dinner: up to $10   **Phone: 717/354-2276**

**Location:** Town center; on SR 23. 140 W Main St 17557. **Hours:** 7 am-8 pm, Sun 11 am-7 pm. Closed: Sat, 5/31, 9/6 & 12/24-1/2. **Features:** casual dress; children's menu; senior's menu; health conscious menu; carryout. Established 1907. Home cooked meals; homemade soups & desserts. French fried eggplant a specialty. Roast turkey dinners Fri & Sun. Smoke free premises. **Cards:** MC, VI.   ⊗

# NEW HOPE—1,400

## LODGINGS

**AARON BURR HOUSE**
◆◆◆
Historic Bed
& Breakfast

Guaranteed Rates   **Phone: 215/862-2343**

| | 1P: | 2P/1B: | | 2P/2B: | |
|---|---|---|---|---|---|
| All Year [CP] | 1P: $90- 170 | 2P/1B: $90- 190 | | | |

**Location:** Center, corner of Chestnut St. 80 W Bridge St 18938. Fax: 215/862-2570. **Terms:** Reserv deposit, 10 day notice; weekly/monthly rates; BP available; 2 night min stay, weekends; no pets. **Facility:** 7 rooms. 19th-century ambience & modern comfort, antique filled rooms. 3 stories, no elevator; interior corridors; designated smoking area; meeting rooms; horse & carriage rides, pool & tennis privileges. **Dining:** Afternoon tea. **All Rooms:** free movies, combo & shower baths. **Some Rooms:** phones, cable TV, VCP's. **Cards:** AE, DS, MC, VI.   Ⓓ ⊗

**BEST WESTERN NEW HOPE INN**
Ⓐ
◆◆
Motor Inn

AAA Special Value Rates   **Phone: 215/862-5221**

| | 1P: | | 2P/1B: | | 2P/2B: | | XP: |
|---|---|---|---|---|---|---|---|
| Fri & Sat | 1P: $105- 120 | | 2P/1B: $105- 120 | | 2P/2B: $105- 120 | | |
| Sun-Thurs | 1P: $89- 99 | | 2P/1B: $89- 99 | | 2P/2B: $89- 99 | | XP: $20 |

**Location:** 2 mi s on US 202, 1 mi w of jct SR 179. 6426 Lower York Rd 18938. Fax: 215/862-5847. **Terms:** Reserv deposit; BP available; small pets only, $20. **Facility:** 152 rooms. 3 stories; exterior corridors; conference facilities; heated pool; 1 tennis court; shuffleboard. **Dining & Entertainment:** Coffee shop; 6-10 am, Sat & Sun 7-11 am; cocktails/lounge. **Services:** Fee: coin laundry. **All Rooms:** cable TV. **Cards:** AE, CB, DI, DS, MC, VI. *(See color ad below)*   Ⓓ ⊗

**THE FOX & HOUND BED & BREAKFAST**   Rates Subject to Change   Phone: 215/862-5082
Fri & Sat [BP]   1P: $110- 120   2P/1B: $110- 120   2P/2B: $110- 120   XP: $20
Sun-Thurs [BP]   1P: $60- 75   2P/1B: $60- 75   2P/2B: $60- 75   XP:$10-20
**Location:** 1 mi s on SR 179. 246 W Bridge St 18938. **Terms:** Reserv deposit, 10 day notice; weekly rates; 2 night min stay, weekends; no pets. **Facility:** 3 rooms. Elegant 1850's stone manor located on 2 acres of parkline setting. 3 stories, no elevator; interior corridors. **All Rooms:** shower baths, no phones. **Cards:** AE, CB, DI, MC, VI.
◆ ◆
Bed & Breakfast

**NEW HOPE MOTEL IN THE WOODS**   Rates Subject to Change   Phone: 215/862-2800
All Year   2P/1B: $55- 65   2P/2B: $60- 65   XP: $9
**Location:** 1 mi s on SR 179, e of jct US 202. 400 W Bridge St 18938. **Terms:** Reserv deposit, 14 day notice; no pets. **Facility:** 28 rooms. Wooded grounds. 2- to 3-night minimum stay weekends; 1 story; exterior corridors; heated pool. **All Rooms:** combo & shower baths, cable TV. **Cards:** CB, DI, DS, MC, VI.
◆
Motel

**THE WEDGWOOD INN**   Guaranteed Rates   Phone: 215/862-2570
All Year [CP]   1P: $70- 180   2P/1B: $75- 190   XP: $20
**Location:** Center on SR 179, w of jct SR 32. 111 W Bridge St 18938. Fax: 215/862-2570. **Terms:** Reserv deposit, 10 day notice; weekly/monthly rates; package plans; 2 night min stay, weekends; no pets. **Facility:** 12 rooms. 1870 Victorian home; rap-around veranda, porte cochere, gazebo; 1833 plastered fieldstone classic revival manor house. On National Register of Historic Places. 2 stories; interior corridors; smoke free premises; meeting rooms. Fee: horse & carriage rides. **Dining:** Afternoon tea. **Services:** area transportation, bus terminal. **Recreation:** Fee: pool & tennis privileges. **All Rooms:** free movies, combo & shower baths. **Some Rooms:** coffeemakers, kitchen, microwaves, refrigerators, phones, cable TV, VCP's. **Cards:** AE, MC, VI.
◆ ◆ ◆
Historic Bed & Breakfast

## RESTAURANTS

**CENTRE BRIDGE INN**   Country Inn   **Dinner:** $21-$30   Phone: 215/862-2048
**Location:** 4 mi n, at jct SR 32 & 263. 18938. **Hours:** 5:30 pm-9:30 pm, Fri & Sat-10 pm, Sun 3 pm-9 pm. **Closed:** 12/25. **Reservations:** suggested. **Features:** semi-formal attire; cocktails & lounge. Informal dining in a quaint rustic setting. Friendly, attentive service. Features fresh fish & homemade desserts. Patio dining in season. **Cards:** AE, MC, VI.
◆ ◆ ◆
Continental

**LA BONNE AUBERGE**   **Dinner:** over $31   Phone: 215/862-2462
**Location:** 1 mi w off Mechanic St at rear of Village 2 townhouse complex. Village 2 18938. **Hours:** 6 pm-10 pm, Sun 5:30 pm-9 pm. **Closed:** Mon, Tues, 11/23, 12/25 & 3/1-3/18. **Reservations:** suggested. **Features:** cocktails & lounge; a la carte, buffet. Fine dining in a beautifully landscaped 18th-century farmhouse. Gracious dining room appointments. Unpretentious, attentive service, classic food. **Cards:** AE.
◆ ◆ ◆ ◆
French

# NEW KENSINGTON—15,900   (See PITTSBURGH ACCOMMODATIONS spotting map page A207; see index starting on page A206)

## LODGING

**DAYS INN OF NEW KENSINGTON**   AAA Special Value Rates   Phone: 412/335-9171   **80**
5/1-9/8   1P: $55- 65   2P/1B: $60- 75   2P/2B: $60- 75   XP: $5   F18
9/9-4/30   1P: $50- 60   2P/1B: $55- 65   2P/2B: $55- 65   XP: $5   F18
**Location:** On SR 366; 1 1/2 mi s of SR 28, exit 14; at s end of Tarentum Bridge. 300 Tarentum Bridge Rd 15068. Fax: 412/335-6642. **Terms:** 15% service charge; pets. **Facility:** 111 rooms. 2 stories; interior corridors; conference facilities; heated pool. **Dining:** Dining room; 7 am-2 & 5-9:30 pm, Sun 7 am-9 pm; $6-$14; cocktails. **Services:** Fee: coin laundry. **All Rooms:** free movies, safes, cable TV. **Some Rooms:** Fee: microwaves, refrigerators. **Cards:** AE, CB, DI, DS, MC, VI.
◆ ◆
Motor Inn

# NEW SMITHVILLE

## LODGING

**SUPER 8 MOTEL**   Rates Subject to Change   Phone: 610/285-4880
All Year   1P: $42   2P/1B: $45   2P/2B: $49   XP: $4
**Location:** I-78, exit 13. 2160 Golden Key Rd 19530 (Box 2160E RR 2, KUTZTOWN). Fax: 610/285-4452. **Terms:** Reserv deposit; weekly rates; BP available; no pets. **Facility:** 38 rooms. Queen suite, $52.88; 2 stories; interior corridors. **All Rooms:** free movies, cable TV. **Cards:** AE, DI, DS, MC, VI.
◆ ◆
Motel

# NEW STANTON—2,100

## LODGINGS

**CARDINAL MOTEL**   Guaranteed Rates   Phone: 412/925-2162
All Year   1P: $32   2P/1B: $36- 38   2P/2B: $40- 42   XP: $4   D12
**Location:** 1/2 mi sw of I-76, exit 8, off I-70, exit 26. 115 Byers Ave 15672. **Terms:** Reserv deposit, 3 day notice; no pets. **Facility:** 20 rooms. 1 story; exterior corridors. **All Rooms:** combo & shower baths, cable TV. **Cards:** AE, DI, DS, MC, VI.
◆
Motel

**CONLEY'S MOTOR INN**   AAA Special Value Rates   Phone: 412/925-3541
All Year [BP]   1P: $40   2P/1B: $50   2P/2B: $50   XP: $8   F12
**Location:** 1/2 mi sw of I-76, tpk exit 8, off I-70, exit 26. 15672 (PO Box 444). **Terms:** Reserv deposit, 3 day notice; weekly/monthly rates; no pets. **Facility:** 73 rooms. Monthly rental only in 5 efficiencies; 3 stories, no elevator; exterior corridors; pool. **Dining & Entertainment:** Restaurant; 5:30 am-9:30 & 5-9:30 pm; $8-$15; cocktails/lounge. **All Rooms:** cable TV. **Some Rooms:** refrigerators. **Cards:** AE, CB, DI, DS, MC, VI.
◆ ◆
Motor Inn

**HOWARD JOHNSON LODGE**
AAA Special Value Rates
Phone: 412/925-3511

|  |  | 2P/1B: | 2P/2B: | XP: |  |
|---|---|---|---|---|---|
| 5/1-9/11 [CP] | | $52- 62 | $60- 71 | $5 | F18 |
| 9/12-10/31 & 4/1-4/30 [CP] | | $49- 56 | $57- 64 | $5 | F18 |
| 11/1-3/31 [CP] | | $49- 54 | $52- 58 | $5 | F18 |

Motel **Location:** 1/2 mi sw of I-76 & tpk exit 8, off I-70, exit 26. 15672 (PO Box 214). Fax: 412/925-3511. **Terms:** Reserv deposit; weekly/monthly rates; pets, $5. **Facility:** 87 rooms. 2 stories; interior/exterior corridors; heated pool; playground. **Dining:** Restaurant nearby. **All Rooms:** cable TV. Fee: VCP. **Some Rooms:** microwaves. Fee: refrigerators. **Cards:** AE, CB, DI, DS, MC, VI. *(See color ad p A176)*  Ⓓ ⊗

# NEWTOWN—2,600

## LODGINGS

**THE BRICK HOTEL**
Rates Subject to Change
Phone: 215/860-8313

◆◆◆  All Year [CP]  1P:  $85- 125

Historic Country Inn **Location:** I-95 Newtown exit, 3 mi w to S State St, then 9/10 mi n to Center; Corner Washington Ave & State St. 1 E Washington Ave 18940. Fax: 215/860-8084. **Terms:** Sr. discount; credit card guarantee, 3 day notice; weekly/monthly rates; no pets. **Facility:** 13 rooms. Elegant hotel circa 1764. Once owned by Joseph Archambault an aide of Napoleon Bonaparte & used by George Washington. 3 stories, no elevator; interior corridors; meeting rooms. **Dining & Entertainment:** Dining room; 11:30 am-2 & 5:30-9 pm, Fri-10 pm, Sat 7:30-10 am, 11:30-2 & 5:30-10 pm, Sun 10 am-2 & 4:30-8:30 pm; $13-$21; cocktails/lounge. **All Rooms:** cable TV. **Cards:** AE, DS, MC, VI.  Ⓓ Ⓢ ⊗

**HOLLILEIF BED & BREAKFAST**
Rates Subject to Change
Phone: 215/598-3100

◆◆  All Year [BP]  1P:  $80- 130  2P/1B:  $80- 130  XP: $20

Historic Bed & Breakfast **Location:** 4 mi n on SR 413. (677 Durham Rd, WRIGHTSTOWN). **Terms:** Sr. discount; reserv deposit, 7 day notice; no pets. **Facility:** 5 rooms. 18th-century respite on 5 1/2 acres of countryside. Romantic ambience & gracious service. 3 stories, no elevator; interior corridors; smoke free premises. **All Rooms:** combo & shower baths, no phones, no TVs. **Cards:** AE, DS, MC, VI.  Ⓓ Ⓢ

**YE OLDE TEMPERANCE HOUSE**
AAA Special Value Rates
Phone: 215/860-0474

◆◆◆  All Year [CP]  1P:  $95- 135  2P/1B:  $95- 135  2P/2B: $135

Historic Country Inn **Location:** I-95 Newtown exit, 3 mi w to S State St, 9/10 mi n to center. 5-11 S State St 18940. Fax: 215/860-7773. **Terms:** Reserv deposit; package plans; no pets. **Facility:** 13 rooms. A post-revolutionary inn, often the site of temperance gatherings in 1772. Rooms renovated to reflect the ambience of the 18th & early 19th centuries. 3 stories, no elevator; interior corridors; meeting rooms. **Dining & Entertainment:** Dining room; 11:30 am-2 & 4-10 pm, Sat 6 pm-11 pm, Sun 10 am-8 pm; $12-$22; cocktails/lounge. **All Rooms:** cable TV. **Cards:** AE, DI, MC, VI.  Ⓓ Ⓢ

# NEW WILMINGTON—2,700

## RESTAURANT

**THE TAVERN**  Historical
Dinner: $11-$20
Phone: 412/946-2020

◆◆ **Location:** On SR 208, at jct SR 158 & 956. 108 N Market St 16142. **Hours:** 11:30 am-2 & 5-8 pm, Sun noon-6:30 pm. **Closed:** Tues, 7/4, 11/23 & 12/25. **Reservations:** suggested. **Features:** children's menu; American health conscious menu; a la carte. Good down home country fare, sticky rolls & calling the menu, long standing traditions. Afternoon tea & weekend breakfast buffet avail.

# NOTTINGHAM

## RESTAURANT

**NOTTINGHAM INN**
Dinner: $11-$20
Phone: 610/932-4050

◆◆ **Location:** On US 272, 1/2 mi s of jct US 1. 190 Baltimore Pike 19362. **Hours:** 11:30 am-3 & 5-9 pm, Fri & Continental Sat-10 pm, Sun 3 pm-8 pm. **Closed:** Mon & 12/25. **Reservations:** required; weekends. **Features:** casual dress; children's menu; carryout; cocktails & lounge. Fine dining in 1939 restored home. Country setting. Very good varied menu. Specializing in grilled seafood & uniquely prepared steaks. **Cards:** AE, MC, VI.  ⊗

# OAKDALE—1,800  (See PITTSBURGH ACCOMMODATIONS spotting map page A207; see index starting on page A206)

## LODGING

**COMFORT INN-PARKWAY WEST**
Rates Subject to Change
Phone: 412/787-2600  🆔

◆◆  All Year  1P:  $53- 88  2P/1B:  $58- 93  2P/2B:  $58- 93  XP: $5  F18

Motor Inn **Location:** On US 22 & 30, at jct SR 60; 4 mi w of I-279 & I-79. 7011 Old Steubenville Pk Rd 15071. Fax: 412/787-3590. **Terms:** Sr. discount; credit card guarantee; weekly rates; pets, $8. **Facility:** 75 rooms. Distinctively styled rooms. 2 stories; interior corridors; meeting rooms; exercise room. **Dining:** Restaurant; 7 am-10 pm, Fri & Sat-11 pm, Sun-9 pm; closed 1/1, 11/23 & 12/25; $6-$10; cocktails. **Services:** data ports; valet laundry; airport transportation. **All Rooms:** coffeemakers, free movies, cable TV. **Some Rooms:** microwaves, refrigerators. Fee: VCP's. **Cards:** AE, CB, DI, DS, JCB, MC, VI. *(See color ad p A204)*  Ⓓ ⊗

# OAKLAND—1,500

## LODGINGS

**HAMPTON INN-UNIVERSITY CENTER**
Rates Subject to Change
Phone: 412/681-1000

◆◆◆  All Year [CP]  1P:  $69- 79  2P/1B:  $77- 84  2P/2B:  $84- 89

Motel **Location:** Jct Forbes & Kraft aves. 3315 Hamlet St 15213. Fax: 412/681-1000. **Terms:** Credit card guarantee, 10 day notice; pets. **Facility:** 133 rooms. 8 stories; interior corridors. **Services:** data ports; valet laundry; area transportation; to downtown. Fee: airport transportation. **All Rooms:** free movies, combo & shower baths. **Some Rooms:** refrigerators. Fee: VCP's. **Cards:** AE, CB, DI, DS, MC, VI.  Ⓓ Ⓢ ⊗

**HOLIDAY INN AT UNIVERSITY CENTER**
AAA Special Value Rates
Phone: 412/682-6200

| | | 2P/1B: | 2P/2B: | XP: | |
|---|---|---|---|---|---|
| ◆◆◆ 1/1-4/30 | 1P: $140 | $153 | $166 | $13 | F18 |
| Motor Inn 5/1-12/31 | 1P: $135 | $147 | $159 | $13 | F18 |

**Location:** 5 mi e on 5th Ave; Oakland exit on I-376 (Pkwy); adjacent to Syria Mosque. 100 Lytton Ave 15213. Fax: 412/682-5745. **Terms:** Reserv deposit; pets. **Facility:** 253 rooms. 10 stories; interior corridors; conference facilities; heated indoor pool, sauna; exercise room. Fee: parking. **Dining & Entertainment:** Dining room; 6:30 am-10 pm; $13-$23; cocktails; entertainment. **Services:** data ports; secretarial services; area transportation, to attractions. Fee: coin laundry; airport transportation. **All Rooms:** coffeemakers, free & pay movies, combo & shower baths, cable TV. **Some Rooms:** refrigerators. **Cards:** AE, CB, DI, DS, JCB, MC, VI.  Ⓓ Ⓢ ⊗

## OAKMONT—7,000   (See PITTSBURGH ACCOMMODATIONS spotting map page A207; see index starting on page A206)

### LODGING

**THE INN AT OAKMONT**   Guaranteed Rates   Phone: 412/828-0410   **101**
All Year [BP]   1P:  $95- 120  2P/1B: $130- 140  2P/2B: $130- 140  XP:  $5
**Location:** 1 mi e on Hulton Rd, jct SR 909 & Hulton Rd. (PO Box 103). Fax: 412/828-1358. **Terms:** Reserv deposit, 3 day notice; no pets. **Facility:** 8 rooms. 2 stories; interior corridors; exercise room. **Cards:** DS, MC, VI.
Bed & Breakfast

## OIL CITY—11,900

### LODGING

**HOLIDAY INN**   Rates Subject to Change   Phone: 814/677-1221
All Year   1P:  $61- 97  2P/1B:  $71- 76  2P/2B:  $73- 78  XP: $10  F18
**Location:** Downtown. 1 Seneca St 16301. Fax: 814/677-0492. **Terms:** Sr. discount; reserv deposit; 15% service charge; package plans; pets. **Facility:** 104 rooms. 5 stories; exterior corridors; meeting rooms; luxury level rooms; heated pool. **Dining & Entertainment:** Dining room; 7 am-2 & 5-10 pm; $8-$16; cocktails; entertainment. **Services:** data ports; valet laundry. **All Rooms:** cable TV. Fee: movies.
**Some Rooms:** coffeemakers. Fee: whirlpools. **Cards:** AE, CB, DI, DS, JCB, MC, VI. *(See ad below)*
Motor Inn

## ONO

### RESTAURANT

**COUNTRY APPLE RESTAURANT**   Dinner: $11-$20   Phone: 717/865-7163
**Location:** 1/4 mi e on US 22. 17077. **Hours:** 6 am-9 pm. Closed: 7/4 & 12/25. **Features:** casual dress; children's menu; senior's menu; carryout; buffet. Pennsylvania Dutch cuisine. **Cards:** AE, MC, VI.
American

## ORWIGSBURG—2,800

### LODGING

**FORT MOTEL**   Rates Subject to Change   Phone: 717/366-2091
All Year   1P:  $32   2P/1B:  $38   2P/2B:  $45   XP:  $5  F10
**Location:** On SR 61, 2 mi s of jct SR 443. RD 1, Box 1223 17961. **Terms:** Reserv deposit; weekly/monthly rates; no pets. **Facility:** 12 rooms. 1 two-bedroom unit. 1 story; exterior corridors. **All Rooms:** coffeemakers, cable TV. **Cards:** DS, MC, VI.
Motel

### RESTAURANT

**LEIBENSPERGER'S DEER LAKE INN**   Dinner: $11-$20   Phone: 717/366-1135
**Location:** On SR 61, 4 1/2 mi s of jct SR 443. 17961. **Hours:** 11 am-2 & 5-9 pm, Fri & Sat-10 pm, Sun noon-9 pm. Closed: 12/25 & Mon. **Reservations:** suggested; Sat. **Features:** casual dress; children's menu; carryout; cocktails; a la carte. Specializing in roast duckling with orange sauce, crabmeat imperial & roast prime rib of beef; served in a warm, congenial & cozy atmosphere. **Cards:** AE, CB, DI, DS, MC, VI.
American

## PALMYRA—6,900

### LODGING

**PALMYRA MOTEL**   Guaranteed Rates   Phone: 717/838-1324
5/20-9/4   1P:  $47- 67           2P/2B:  $66- 76  XP:  $5  D3
5/1-5/19 & 9/5-10/31   1P:  $38- 48           2P/2B:  $48- 58  XP:  $5  D3
11/1-4/30   1P:  $38- 48           2P/2B:  $38- 48  XP:  $5  D3
**Location:** 1 mi e on US 422. 1071 E Main St 17078. **Terms:** Sr. discount; reserv deposit; weekly rates; no pets. **Facility:** 30 rooms. Variety of rooms, some attractively appointed. 2 stories; interior/exterior corridors; heated pool; playground. **Dining:** Restaurant nearby. **Services:** data ports. **All Rooms:** cable TV.
**Some Rooms:** refrigerators. **Cards:** AE, DS, MC, VI. *(See color ad p A139)*
Motel

## PARADISE—4,400

### LODGING

**BEST WESTERN REVERE MOTOR INN**   Rates Subject to Change   Phone: 717/687-7683
5/26-5/28 & 6/9-9/3   1P:  $72   2P/1B:  $79   2P/2B:  $79   XP:  $5  F12
9/4-11/25   1P:  $59   2P/1B:  $68   2P/2B:  $68   XP:  $5  F12
5/1-5/25, 5/29-6/8 & 3/22-4/30   1P:  $54   2P/1B:  $59   2P/2B:  $59   XP:  $5  F12
11/26-3/21   1P:  $44   2P/1B:  $49   2P/2B:  $49   XP:  $5  F12
**Location:** On US 30. 3063 Lincoln Hwy E 17562 (PO Box 336). Fax: 717/687-6141. **Terms:** Sr. discount; credit card guarantee; no pets. **Facility:** 29 rooms. Good sized rooms, well-maintained grounds. Suites, $85-$135; 2 stories; exterior corridors; heated pool. **Dining & Entertainment:** Dining room, coffee shop; 8 am-2 & 5-10 pm, Sun 4 pm-9 pm; $10-$17; cocktails/lounge. **All Rooms:** free movies, refrigerators, cable TV. **Some Rooms:** whirlpools. **Cards:** AE, CB, DI, DS, MC, VI.
Motor Inn

### RESTAURANT

**MILLER'S SMORGASBORD**   Dinner: $11-$20   Phone: 717/687-6621
**Location:** In Ronks; 1 1/2 mi w on US 30; 1 1/2 mi e of SR 896. 2811 Lincoln Hwy E 17572. **Hours:** 8 am-8 pm; 11/1-5/31, noon-8 pm, Sat 8 am-8:30 pm. Closed: 12/24 & 12/25. **Features:** casual dress; children's menu; buffet. Informal dining, children prices avail. Smoke free premises. **Cards:** AE, MC, VI.
*(See ad starting on p A152)*
American

# PENNSYLVANIA DUTCH COUNTRY (See PENNSYLVANIA DUTCH COUNTRY map below)

# PHILADELPHIA—1,585,600   (See DOWNTOWN PHILADELPHIA ACCOMMODATIONS spotting map page A181; see index below)

To help you more easily locate accommodations in the Greater Philadelphia area, the following two indexes and maps show lodgings and restaurants in multiple cities. Listings for these establishments are found under the heading for the city in which they are located. The Philadelphia area comprises: Ardmore, Bala-Cynwyd, Bellmawr, NJ, Belmont Hills, Bensalem, Brooklawn, Burlington, NJ, Cherry Hill, NJ, Essington, Horsham, Langhorne, Mount Laurel, NJ, Mount Holly, NJ, Philadelphia, Plymouth Meeting, Runnemede, NJ, Trevose, Voorhees and Willow Grove.

### Airport Accommodations
Listings for these establishments are found under the heading for the city in which they are located.

**PHILADELPHIA**

- Comfort Inn Airport, 2 1/2 mi sw of airport/ESSINGTON
- Courtyard By Marriott Airport, on Bartram Ave 1 1/2 mi n of terminal/PHILADELPHIA
- Days Inn/Philadelphia Int'l Airport, at entrance to airport/PHILADELPHIA
- Embassy Suites-Philadelphia Airport, 1 1/2 mi nw of airport/PHILADELPHIA
- Guest Quarters Suite Hotel, at entrance to airport/PHILADELPHIA
- Holiday Inn-Airport, 2 1/2 mi sw of airport/ESSINGTON
- Philadelphia Airport Hilton, at entrance to airport/PHILADELPHIA
- Philadelphia Airport Residence Inn, 1 1/2 mi e of terminal on SR 291/PHILADELPHIA
- Radisson Hotel Philadelphia Airport, 2 mi sw of airport/PHILADELPHIA
- Ramada Inn-Philadelphia International Airport, SR 291, 2 1/4 mi w of terminal/ESSINGTON
- Red Roof Inn-Airport, 2 3/4 mi sw of airport/ESSINGTON

### Index of Establishments on the DOWNTOWN PHILADELPHIA ACCOMMODATIONS Spotting Map

| | |
|---|---|
| Penn's View Inn .......................... **1** | Best Western Independence Park Inn ........ **18** |
| The Warwick .............................. **2** | Sheraton Society Hill ..................... **19** |
| Wyndham Franklin Plaza Hotel ............ **3** | The Thomas Bond House .................. **20** |
| Four Seasons Hotel ....................... **4** | Omni Hotel at Independence Park .......... **21** |
| Abigail Adams Bed & Breakfast ........... **5** | The Ritz-Carlton, Philadelphia ............ **22** |
| Holiday Inn-Independence Mall ........... **6** | Holiday Inn Philadelphia Stadium .......... **23** |
| Holiday Inn Select Centre City ........... **7** | **RESTAURANTS** |
| Sheraton University City ................. **8** | Ruth's Chris Steak House ................. **1** |
| The Latham .............................. **9** | Founder's ............................... **2** |
| Comfort Inn Penns Landing .............. **10** | Fountain Restaurant ..................... **3** |
| Holiday Inn-Express Midtown ............ **11** | La Famiglia ............................. **4** |
| The Rittenhouse Hotel & Condominium | Bookbinder's Old Original ................ **5** |
|   Residences .......................... **12** | Morton's of Chicago Steak House ......... **7** |
| The Doubletree Hotel Philadelphia ....... **13** | Alouette Restaurant ..................... **8** |
| Shippen Way Inn ........................ **14** | South Street Souvlaki .................... **9** |
| Korman Suites .......................... **15** | Ralphs' Italian Restaurant ............... **10** |
| Penn Tower Hotel ....................... **16** | London Grill ............................ **11** |
| Embassy Suites Center City .............. **17** | Le Bec-Fin .............................. **12** |

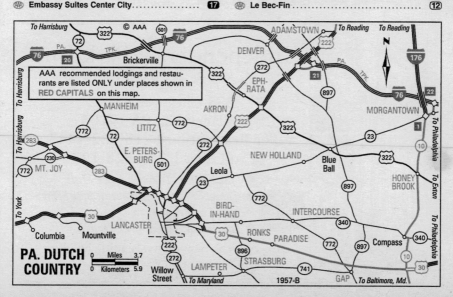

AAA recommended lodgings and restaurants are listed ONLY under places shown in RED CAPITALS on this map.

PA. DUTCH COUNTRY

0   Miles   3.7
0   Kilometers   5.9

(See DOWNTOWN PHILADELPHIA ACCOMMODATIONS spotting map page A181)

| | | | | |
|---|---|---|---|---|
| Jack's Firehouse Restaurant | ⑭ | Dimitri's | ㊻ |
| The Garden | ⑮ | Dock Street Brewing Company Brewery & | |
| Deux Cheminees | ⑯ | Restaurant | ㊼ |
| Bookbinder's Sea Food House | ⑰ | Essene Cafe | ㊾ |
| Di Lullo Centro | ⑱ | Fez | ㊿ |
| Susanna Foo | ⑲ | Imprial Inn | ㊷ |
| Restaurant 210 | ⑳ | The Inn Philadelphia | ㊿③ |
| The Monte Carlo Living Room | ㉑ | Kabul, Cuisine of Afghanistan | ㊾④ |
| The Ritz-Carlton Dining Room | ㉒ | Kat Man Du & Elizabeth at Kat Man Du | ㊾⑥ |
| Palm Restaurant | ㉔ | La Bella Vita at the Main Event | ㊿⑦ |
| Aglio | ㉕ | La Truffe | ㊿⑨ |
| Arizona | ㉖ | Mia's | ㊿⓪ |
| Azalea | ㉗ | Mick's Downstairs at the Bellevue | ㊿② |
| Bertucci's | ㉙ | Milano's | ㊿③ |
| Bistro Romano | ㉛ | Overtures | ㊿④ |
| Brasil's | ㉞ | Palladium Restaurant | ㊿⑤ |
| Cafe Nola | ㉟ | Pamplona | ㊿⑧ |
| Carolina's | ㊱ | Passage To India | ㊿⓪ |
| Chanterelles | ㊲ | Rangoon | ㊿① |
| Ciboulette | ㊴ | Ristorante Primavera | ㊿② |
| Circa | ㊶ | The Ritz-Carlton Grill Room | ㊿③ |
| City Tavern | ㊷ | Singapore Vegetarian Chinese Restaurant | ㊿④ |
| Cutter's Grand Cafe | ㊸ | Striped Bass | ㊿⑤ |
| Dickens Inn | ㊺ | Swann Lounge & Cafe | ㊿⑦ |
| | | Tsui Hang Chun | ㊿⑨ |

## LODGINGS

**ABIGAIL ADAMS BED & BREAKFAST**  Rates Subject to Change   Phone: 215/546-7336  ⑤
◆◆  All Year [CP]   1P: $80- 110  2P/1B: $80- 110  2P/2B: $80- 110  XP: $15  F13
Historic Bed  **Location:** Downtown, between 12th & 13th sts. 1208 Walnut St 19107. Fax: 215/546-7573. **Terms:** Credit
& Breakfast  card guarantee, 3 day notice; no pets. **Facility:** 32 rooms. 7 stories; interior corridors; smoke free premises;
meeting rooms. **Fee:** parking. **Services:** valet laundry. **All Rooms:** combo & shower baths, cable TV.
**Cards:** AE, CB, DI, DS, MC, VI.  Ⓓ Ⓢ ⊗

**BEST WESTERN INDEPENDENCE PARK INN**  Rates Subject to Change   Phone: 215/922-4443  ⑱
ⒶⒶⒶ  All Year [CP]   1P: $125- 145  2P/1B: $135- 155  2P/2B: $135- 155  XP: $10
◆◆◆  **Location:** In Independence Park Historic District. 235 Chestnut St 19106. Fax: 215/922-4487. **Terms:** Sr.
Hotel  discount; credit card guarantee, 3 day notice; no pets. **Facility:** 36 rooms. Circa mid 1800's. High ceilings with
touches of Victorian in the rosewood & cherrywood lobby. 4 stories; interior corridors; meeting rooms.
**Fee:** parking. **Dining:** Afternoon tea; restaurant nearby. **Services:** data ports; valet laundry.
**All Rooms:** cable TV. **Some Rooms:** Fee: VCP's. **Cards:** AE, CB, DI, DS, JCB, MC, VI. *(See color ad below)*  Ⓓ Ⓢ ⊗

**COMFORT INN PENNS LANDING**  Rates Subject to Change   Phone: 215/627-7900  ⑩
ⒶⒶⒶ  All Year [CP]   1P: $69- 109  2P/1B: $79- 119  2P/2B: $79- 119  XP: $10  F18
◆◆  **Location:** From I-95, Historic Area exit, to Columbus Blvd & Race St. 100 N Columbus Blvd 19106.
Motel  Fax: 215/238-0809. **Terms:** Sr. discount; monthly rates; no pets. **Facility:** 185 rooms. 10 stories; interior cor-
ridors; meeting rooms. **Fee:** health club. **Dining:** Restaurant nearby. **Services:** valet laundry; area
transportation. **Fee:** airport transportation. **All Rooms:** coffeemakers, free & pay movies, cable TV.
**Fee:** VCP. **Some Rooms:** whirlpools. **Cards:** AE, CB, DI, DS, JCB, MC, VI. *(See ad p A182)*  Ⓩ Ⓓ Ⓢ ⊗

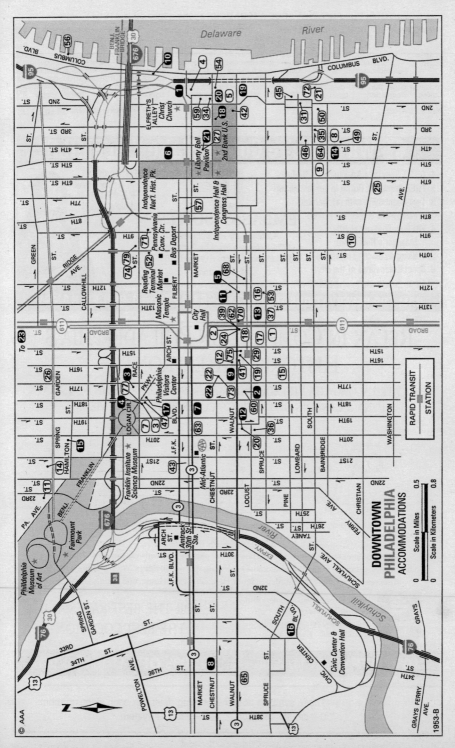

**(See DOWNTOWN PHILADELPHIA ACCOMMODATIONS spotting map page A181)**

**THE DOUBLETREE HOTEL PHILADELPHIA**
Rates Subject to Change     **Phone:** 215/893-1600   **13**

| | | | | |
|---|---|---|---|---|
| Sun-Thurs | 1P: $108 | 2P/1B: $108 | 2P/2B: $108 | XP: $15  F18 |
| Fri & Sat | 1P: $98 | 2P/1B: $98 | 2P/2B: $98 | XP: $15  F18 |

**Location:** Broad & Locust sts 19107. Fax: 215/893-1663. **Terms:** Sr. discount; package plans; no pets. **Facility:** 427 rooms. Convenient to theater district. 26 stories; interior corridors; business center, conference facilities; luxury level rooms; heated indoor pool, saunas, whirlpool; exercise room, 2 steamrooms. Fee: parking; racquetball courts; tanning salon. **Dining & Entertainment:** Dining room; 6:30 am-10:30 pm; $8-$18; cocktails/lounge. **Services:** data ports, PC, secretarial services; childcare; valet laundry. Fee: airport transportation; valet parking. **Recreation:** jogging. **All Rooms:** free & pay movies, combo & shower baths, cable TV. **Some Rooms:** coffeemakers, refrigerators. **Cards:** AE, CB, DI, DS, MC, VI.
*(See ad p A183)*

Roll in showers. Ⓓ Ⓢ

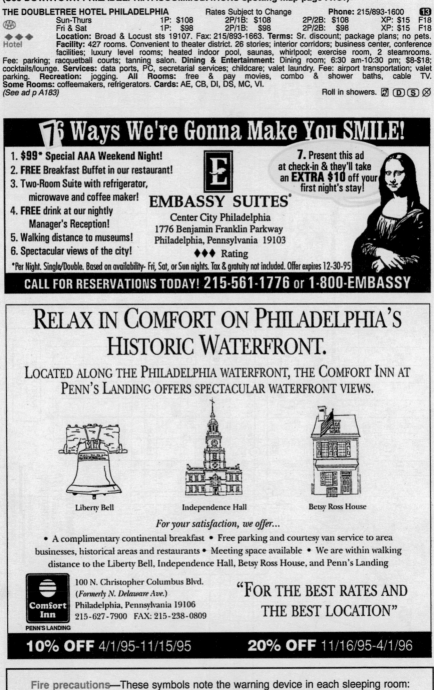
Fire precautions—These symbols note the warning device in each sleeping room:
Ⓓ—smoke detector     Ⓢ—sprinkler system

**(See DOWNTOWN PHILADELPHIA ACCOMMODATIONS spotting map page A181)**

**EMBASSY SUITES CENTER CITY**      Rates Subject to Change      Phone: 215/561-1776   **17**
      Mon-Thurs [BP]      1P: $169- 189    2P/1B: $184- 204    2P/2B: $184- 204    XP: $15   D12
      Fri-Sun [BP]      1P: $99- 129    2P/1B: $114- 144    2P/2B: $114- 144    XP: $15   D12
◆◆◆    **Location:** Downtown, at 18th St & Benjamin Franklin Pkwy. 1776 Benjamin Franklin Pkwy 19103.
Suite Hotel   **Fax:** 215/963-0122. **Terms:** Sr. discount; check-in 4 pm; reserv deposit, 3 day notice; package plans; no pets. **Facility:** 288 rooms. Well-appointed guest rooms. 28 stories; interior corridors; meeting rooms; sauna; exercise room, children's playroom. **Dining & Entertainment:** Restaurant; 6:30 am-1 am; $6-$17; cocktails/lounge. **Services:** data ports, PC, secretarial services; complimentary evening beverages; valet laundry. **All Rooms:** coffeemakers, microwaves, free & pay movies, refrigerators, cable TV. **Cards:** AE, CB, DI, DS, JCB, MC, VI.
*(See color ad p A182)*                  🅙 ⒟ Ⓢ ⊗

**FOUR SEASONS HOTEL**      Rates Subject to Change      Phone: 215/963-1500   **4**
      Sun-Thurs      1P: $250- 325    2P/1B: $250- 325    2P/2B: $280- 355    XP: $30   F18
      Fri & Sat      1P: $175- 245    2P/1B: $175- 245    2P/2B: $175- 245    XP: $30   F18
◆◆◆◆◆    **Location:** At corner 18th & Ben Franklin Pkwy. 1 Logan Sq 19103. **Fax:** 215/963-9506. **Terms:** AP, CP
Hotel   available; package plans; small pets only. **Facility:** 371 rooms. Exceptionally well appointed rooms. A luxury, service-oriented operation. 8 stories; interior corridors; business center, conference facilities; heated indoor pool, saunas, whirlpool; health club. **Dining & Entertainment:** seasonal outdoor cafe; 24-hour room service; afternoon tea; also, Fountain Restaurant, Swann Lounge & Cafe, see separate listing; entertainment. **Services:** data ports, secretarial services; valet laundry; area transportation, to Central City. **Fee:** PC; childcare; massage, airport transportation; valet parking. **Recreation:** children's program. **All Rooms:** honor bars, free & pay movies, refrigerators, safes, cable TV. **Some Rooms:** VCP's, whirlpools. **Cards:** AE, CB, DI, DS, JCB, MC, VI.       🅙 ⒟ Ⓢ ⊗

**HOLIDAY INN-EXPRESS MIDTOWN**      Guaranteed Rates      Phone: 215/735-9300   **11**
      All Year [CP]      1P: $85    2P/1B: $85    2P/2B: $85    XP: $10
◆◆◆    **Location:** 1 1/2 blks e of Broad St. 1305 Walnut St 19107. **Fax:** 215/732-2682. **Terms:** Sr. discount; no pets.
Motel   **Facility:** 161 rooms. Conveniently located to historic, cultural & shopping districts. 20 stories; interior corridors; meeting rooms; rooftop pool with southern exposure. **Fee:** parking. **Services:** data ports, secretarial services; valet laundry. **Fee:** valet parking. **All Rooms:** free movies, cable TV. **Cards:** AE, CB, DI, DS, JCB, MC, VI.
*(See color ad p A184)*                  ⒟ ⊗

**HOLIDAY INN-INDEPENDENCE MALL**      Rates Subject to Change      Phone: 215/923-8660   **6**
      All Year      1P: $85    2P/1B: $85    2P/2B: $85    XP: $10   F19
◆◆◆    **Location:** In historic district between 4th & 5th sts. 400 Arch St 19106. **Fax:** 215/923-4633. **Terms:** Sr.
Hotel   discount; check-in 4 pm; reserv deposit, 3 day notice; monthly rates; BP available; package plans; no pets. **Facility:** 364 rooms. Traditional American decor. 8 stories; interior corridors; business center, conference facilities; pool. **Fee:** parking. **Dining & Entertainment:** Dining room, coffee shop; 6:30 am-10:30 pm; $5-$25; cocktails/lounge; entertainment. **Services:** data ports, PC, secretarial services. **Fee:** coin laundry, airport transportation. **All Rooms:** free & pay movies, cable TV. **Some Rooms:** refrigerators. **Fee:** VCP's. **Cards:** AE, CB, DI, DS, JCB, MC, VI.
*(See color ad p A184)*                  🅙 ⒟ Ⓢ ⊗

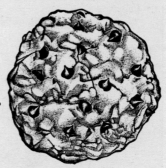

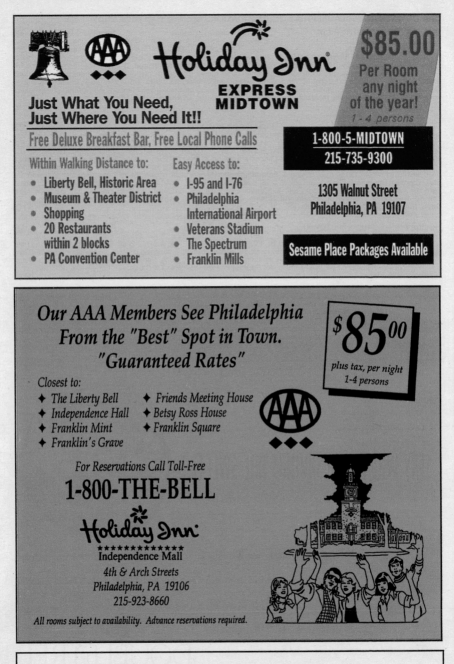

**(See DOWNTOWN PHILADELPHIA ACCOMMODATIONS spotting map page A181)**

**HOLIDAY INN PHILADELPHIA STADIUM**     Guaranteed Rates     **Phone:** 215/755-9500   **23**
(AAA)     All Year     1P: $79    2P/1B: $79    2P/2B: $79    XP: $10   F18
◆◆◆     **Location:** At jct of I-76 & I-95, at w end of Walt Whitman Bridge. 10th St & Packer Ave 19148.
Hotel     Fax: 215/462-6947. **Terms:** Sr. discount; weekly/monthly rates; no pets. **Facility:** 238 rooms. Nicely appointed
public areas & guest rooms. 11 stories; interior corridors; conference facilities; heated pool; exercise room.
**Dining & Entertainment:** Dining room, restaurant; 6:30 am-midnight; $9-$30; cocktails/lounge;
entertainment, nightclub. **Services:** data ports, secretarial services; valet laundry; airport transportation. **All Rooms:** free &
pay movies, cable TV. **Cards:** AE, CB, DI, DS, MC, VI. *(See color ad below)*    Ⓓ Ⓢ ⊗

**HOLIDAY INN SELECT CENTRE CITY**    Rates Subject to Change     **Phone:** 215/561-7500   **7**
(AAA)     Mon-Thurs    1P: $99    2P/1B: $99    2P/2B: $99    XP: $10   F19
◆◆◆     Fri-Sun    1P: $89    2P/1B: $89    2P/2B: $89
Hotel     **Location:** 18th & Market sts 19103. Fax: 215/561-4484. **Terms:** Reserv deposit; no pets. **Facility:** 445 rooms.
Attractive rooms & public areas. 25 stories; interior corridors; conference facilities; luxury level rooms; pool; exercise room. **Dining & Entertainment:** Dining room; 6:30 am-11 pm; $9-$17; cocktails/lounge.
**Services:** data ports. Fee: coin laundry, airport transportation; valet parking. **All Rooms:** free & pay movies, cable TV.
**Some Rooms:** coffeemakers, whirlpools. Fee: refrigerators. **Cards:** AE, CB, DI, DS, MC, VI.    🄵 Ⓓ Ⓢ Ⓕ

**KORMAN SUITES**     Rates Subject to Change     **Phone:** 215/569-7000   **15**
◆◆◆     Sun-Thurs    1P: $139    2P/1B: $139    2P/2B: $189    XP: $10-15 F16
Hotel     Fri & Sat    1P: $99    2P/1B: $99    2P/2B: $149    XP: $10-15 F16
**Location:** 20th St at Hamilton St. 2001 Hamilton St 19130. Fax: 215/569-1422. **Terms:** Credit card
guarantee; monthly rates; no pets. **Facility:** 99 rooms. Upscale facility offers bright, spacious rooms & multi-room suites, all
with washer/dryer. Some luxury services. 24 stories; interior corridors; conference facilities; pool, whirlpool; health club.
**Dining & Entertainment:** Restaurant; 6:30-10:30 am, 11-2:30 & 5:30-10:30 pm; $8-$20; health conscious menu;
cocktails/lounge. **Services:** data ports; valet laundry; area transportation, mid city shuttle. Fee: massage, airport
transportation. **All Rooms:** free movies, cable TV. **Some Rooms:** 80 efficiencies, 19 kitchens, VCP's. **Cards:** AE, CB, DI,
MC, VI.    Ⓓ Ⓢ

**THE LATHAM**     AAA Special Value Rates     **Phone:** 215/563-7474   **9**
(AAA)     All Year    1P: $150- 185    2P/1B: $170- 190    2P/2B: $170- 190    XP: $20   F18
◆◆◆     **Location:** Center. 135 S 17th St at Walnut St 19103. Fax: 215/563-4034. **Terms:** Reserv deposit; monthly
Hotel     rates; BP, CP available; package plans; no pets. **Facility:** 138 rooms. Elegant small European style hotel. 14
stories; interior corridors; meeting rooms. **Dining & Entertainment:** Dining room; 6:30 am-10:30 pm, Sat &
Sun from 7 am; $11-$23; cocktails/lounge. **Services:** secretarial services; health club privileges; valet
laundry. Fee: airport transportation; valet parking. **All Rooms:** free & pay movies, cable TV. **Some Rooms:** honor bars,
microwaves, safes. **Cards:** AE, CB, DI, DS, MC, VI. *(See ad p A186)*    Ⓓ Ⓢ ⊗

**(See DOWNTOWN PHILADELPHIA ACCOMMODATIONS spotting map page A181)**

**OMNI HOTEL AT INDEPENDENCE PARK**  Rates Subject to Change  Phone: 215/925-0000  **21**
◆◆◆◆  All Year  1P: $160  2P/1B: $160  2P/2B: $160
Hotel  **Location:** Chestnut St at 4th St. 401 Chestnut St 19106. Fax: 215/925-1263. **Terms:** Sr. discount; reserv deposit; package plans; no pets. **Facility:** 145 rooms. Beautifully appointed guest rooms. 14 stories; interior corridors; meeting rooms; sauna, whirlpool, small heated indoor pool; exercise room. Fee: parking. **Dining & Entertainment:** Cocktails/lounge; 24-hour room service; also, Azalea, see separate listing; entertainment. **Services:** data ports, PC, secretarial services; valet laundry. Fee: airport transportation; valet parking. **All Rooms:** honor bars, free & pay movies, cable TV. **Some Rooms:** whirlpools. Fee: VCP's. **Cards:** AE, CB, DI, DS, JCB, MC, VI.  🖵 Ⓓ Ⓢ ⊗

**PENN'S VIEW INN**  AAA Special Value Rates  Phone: 215/922-7600  **1**
Ⓐ  All Year [CP]  2P/1B: $100- 175  XP: $15  F12
◆◆◆  **Location:** At Front & Market sts; from I-95, Old City exit, on Front St. 14 N Front St 19106.
Historic Hotel  Fax: 215/922-7642. **Terms:** Reserv deposit, 3 day notice; package plans, weekends; no pets. **Facility:** 27 rooms. Tastefully appointed rooms in converted, restored warehouse. Closed 12/24 & 12/25. 5 stories; interior corridors; meeting rooms. Fee: parking; health club privileges. **Dining & Entertainment:** Restaurant; noon-10 pm; $8-$16; cocktails/lounge. **Services:** data ports; valet laundry. Fee: airport transportation. **All Rooms:** free movies, combo & shower baths, cable TV. **Some Rooms:** refrigerators, whirlpools. **Cards:** AE, CB, DI, MC, VI.  Ⓓ Ⓢ ⊗

(See DOWNTOWN PHILADELPHIA ACCOMMODATIONS spotting map page A181)

**PENN TOWER HOTEL**   Guaranteed Rates   Phone: 215/387-8333  **16**
All Year   1P: $105- 145   2P/1B: $115- 165   2P/2B: $115   XP: $10  F18
**Location:** W of I-76 South St exit, facing civic center. Civic Center Blvd & 34th St 19104-4385.
◆◆◆  **Fax:** 215/386-8306. **Terms:** Weekly/monthly rates; no pets. **Facility:** 175 rooms. A variety of modest to well ap-
Hotel   pointed rooms. 20 stories; interior corridors; conference facilities; luxury level rooms. Fee: parking. **Dining &**
**Entertainment:** Dining room; 6:30 am-11 & 11:30-8:30 pm; $7-$17; cocktails/lounge. **Services:** data ports,
secretarial services; health club privileges; valet laundry. Fee: airport transportation. **All Rooms:** free & pay movies, cable TV.
**Some Rooms:** coffeemakers. Fee: refrigerators. **Cards:** AE, CB, DI, MC, VI. *(See ad below)*   🅿 Ⓓ Ⓢ ⊗

**(See DOWNTOWN PHILADELPHIA ACCOMMODATIONS spotting map page A181)**

THE RITTENHOUSE HOTEL & CONDOMINIUM RESIDENCES Rates Subject to Change **Phone:** 215/546-9000  ⑫
        Sun-Thurs        1P: $205- 250  2P/1B: $225- 275  2P/2B: $225- 275  XP: $25  F16
        Fri & Sat          1P: $150- 160  2P/1B: $150- 160  2P/2B: $150- 160  XP: $25  F16
◆◆◆◆◆ **Location:** On Rittenhouse Sq. 210 W Rittenhouse Sq 19103. Fax: 215/732-3364. **Terms:** Reserv deposit;
Hotel    monthly rates; package plans; pets. **Facility:** 98 rooms. Elegant, open lobby area features works of local artists. Timeless, classic & luxurious room decor. Service oriented. 33 stories; interior corridors; business center,
conference facilities; heated indoor pool, sauna, steamroom. Fee: exercise room. **Dining & Entertainment:** Dining room;
6:30 am-11 pm, Fri & Sat-1 am; $12-$35; cocktails/lounge; 24-hour room service; afternoon tea; also, Restaurant 210, see
separate listing. **Services:** data ports, secretarial services; valet laundry; area transportation, downtown. Fee: PC; childcare;
massage, airport transportation; valet parking. **All Rooms:** honor bars, free movies, combo & shower baths, cable TV,
VCP's. **Cards:** AE, CB, DI, DS, MC, VI. A Preferred Hotel.    🅿 ⓓ ⓢ ⊗

THE RITZ-CARLTON, PHILADELPHIA      Rates Subject to Change      **Phone:** 215/563-1600  ㉒
◆◆◆◆    All Year          1P: $195- 265  2P/1B: $195- 265  2P/2B: $195- 265
Hotel    **Location:** 17th & Chestnut St at Liberty Pl 19103. Fax: 215/567-2822. **Terms:** Reserv deposit; no pets.
    **Facility:** 290 rooms. Charming, elegant decor. Fireplace in lobby lounge. Most attentive, gracious guest serv-
ices. Located in the fine downtown shopping district. 15 stories; interior corridors; conference facilities; luxury level rooms;
saunas; exercise room, health club. **Dining & Entertainment:** 24-hour room service; afternoon tea; also, The Ritz-Carlton
Dining Room, The Ritz-Carlton Grill Room, see separate listing; entertainment. **Services:** data ports, secretarial services;
valet laundry; area transportation, to downtown area. Fee: PC; childcare; massage, airport transportation; valet parking.
**All Rooms:** honor bars, free movies, cable TV. Fee: VCP. **Cards:** AE, CB, DI, DS, JCB, MC, VI.    🅿 ⓓ ⓢ ⊗

SHERATON SOCIETY HILL        Rates Subject to Change      **Phone:** 215/238-6000  ⑲
        All Year          1P: $103- 215  2P/1B: $103- 215  2P/2B: $103- 215  XP: $20  F17
    **Location:** Off I-95, Historic District Center City exit 16, 1/2 mi n on Delaware St to Dock St; at 2nd & Walnut
◆◆◆    sts. One Dock St 19106. Fax: 215/922-2709. **Terms:** Reserv deposit; package plans; no pets. **Facility:** 365
Hotel    rooms. Adjacent to historic area. Atrium lobby. 4 stories; interior corridors; business center, conference facili-
ties; heated indoor pool, wading pool, saunas, whirlpool; exercise room. Fee: parking. **Dining &**
**Entertainment:** Restaurant; 6:30 am-10:30 pm; $11-$26; cocktails/lounge; 24-hour room service; entertainment.
**Services:** data ports, PC, secretarial services; valet laundry. Fee: airport transportation; valet parking. **All Rooms:** honor
bars, coffeemakers, free & pay movies, cable TV. **Some Rooms:** refrigerators, whirlpools. **Cards:** AE, CB, DI, DS, MC, VI.
*(See ad below)*    🅿 ⓓ ⓢ ⊗

---

Your AAA Travel Information System combines the best maps with
the best books. Don't use one without the other.

**(See DOWNTOWN PHILADELPHIA ACCOMMODATIONS spotting map page A181)**

**SHERATON UNIVERSITY CITY**
◆◆◆   Rates Subject to Change   **Phone:** 215/387-8000   **8**
Motor Inn   All Year   1P: $125   2P/1B: $135   2P/2B: $135   XP: $10   F17
**Location:** 1/2 mi w of I-76. Chestnut & 36th Sts 19104. Fax: 215/387-7920. **Terms:** Sr. discount; credit card guarantee; monthly rates; BP available; no pets. **Facility:** 377 rooms. Convenient location. 13 suites, $195-$275; 20 stories; interior corridors; conference facilities; heated pool. Fee: parking; health club privileges. **Dining & Entertainment:** Dining room; 7 am-11 pm; $5-$19; cocktails/lounge. **Services:** data ports; valet laundry. Fee: airport transportation. **All Rooms:** coffeemakers, free & pay movies, cable TV. **Some Rooms:** Fee: refrigerators. **Cards:** AE, CB, DI, DS, MC, VI.   ⊘ Ⓓ Ⓢ ⊗

**SHIPPEN WAY INN**
◆◆   Guaranteed Rates   **Phone:** 215/627-7266   **14**
Historic Bed   All Year [CP]   1P: $70-  95   2P/1B: $70- 105   2P/2B: $90   XP: $10
& Breakfast   **Location:** Between 4th & 5th sts. 418 Bainbridge St 19147. **Terms:** Check-in 3:30 pm; reserv deposit, 3 day notice; weekly rates; no pets. **Facility:** 9 rooms. In row house section with roots dating back to 1750. Each unit appointed in colonial, country or southwest style. 3 stories, no elevator; interior/exterior corridors; smoke free premises. Fee: parking. **All Rooms:** shower baths. **Some Rooms:** cable TV. **Cards:** AE, MC, VI.   Ⓓ ⊗

**THE THOMAS BOND HOUSE**
Ⓐ   AAA Special Value Rates   **Phone:** 215/923-8523   **20**
◆◆   All Year [CP]   2P/1B: $80- 150   2P/2B: $80- 150   XP: $10   F7
Historic Bed   **Location:** In historic district. 129 S 2nd St 19106. Fax: 215/923-8504. **Terms:** Reserv deposit, 3 day notice; weekly/monthly rates; BP available; package plans; 2 night min stay, weekends 11/1-2/29; no pets.
& Breakfast   **Facility:** 12 rooms. A restored, early American guest house, listed in National Register of Historic Places; some small rooms. 4 stories, no elevator; interior corridors. Fee: health club privileges. **Dining:** Full breakfast on weekends; restaurant nearby. **Services:** valet laundry. **All Rooms:** combo & shower baths.
**Some Rooms:** whirlpools. **Cards:** AE, DS, MC, VI.   Ⓓ

**THE WARWICK**
◆◆◆   AAA Special Value Rates   **Phone:** 215/735-6000   **2**
Hotel   5/1-5/31, 9/14-11/14 &
3/2-4/30   1P: $130- 170   2P/1B: $145- 180   2P/2B: $145- 180   XP: $15   F12
6/1-9/13 & 11/15-3/1   1P: $125- 145   2P/1B: $140- 165   2P/2B: $140- 165   XP: $15   F12
**Location:** 17th St at Locust. 1701 Locust St 19103-6179. Fax: 215/790-7766. **Terms:** Reserv deposit, 4 day notice; monthly rates; no pets. **Facility:** 180 rooms. Landmark city hotel with rooms that vary in appointments from older vintage to upscale contemporary. Some luxury services. 20 stories; interior corridors; conference facilities. Fee: parking. **Dining & Entertainment:** Restaurant, coffee shop; 6:30 am-11 pm; $8-$26; cocktails/lounge; also, Mia's, see separate listing. **Services:** data ports, secretarial services; health club privileges; valet laundry. Fee: childcare; massage; airport transportation; valet parking. **All Rooms:** honor bars, free & pay movies, cable TV. **Some Rooms:** 10 efficiencies, 20 kitchens. **Cards:** AE, CB, DI, MC, VI.   Ⓓ ⊗

**Choose an establishment with the Ⓐ next to its listing!**

**(See DOWNTOWN PHILADELPHIA ACCOMMODATIONS spotting map page A181)**

| WYNDHAM FRANKLIN PLAZA HOTEL | Rates Subject to Change | | | Phone: 215/448-2000 | 3 |
|---|---|---|---|---|---|
| ◆◆◆  Mon-Thurs | 1P: $145 | 2P/1B: $145 | 2P/2B: $145 | XP: $20 | F18 |
| Hotel  Fri-Sun | 1P: $89- 99 | 2P/1B: $89- 99 | 2P/2B: $89- 99 | XP: $20 | F18 |

**Location:** 17th at Race & Vine sts. 2 Franklin Plaza 19103. **Fax:** 215/448-2864. **Terms:** Credit card guarantee; package plans; no pets. **Facility:** 760 rooms. Modern hotel. 27 stories; interior corridors; conference facilities; heated indoor pool, saunas, whirlpool; exercise room, sports court, tanning salon. **Fee:** parking; racquetball courts, 1 tennis court; squash & handball-4 courts. **Dining & Entertainment:** Dining room, cafeteria; 6:30 am-11 pm; $8-$30; health conscious menu; cocktails/lounge; 24-hour room service. **Services:** data ports; valet laundry. **Fee:** PC; massage, airport transportation; valet parking. **Recreation:** jogging. **All Rooms:** coffeemakers, combo & shower baths, cable TV. **Fee:** movies. **Some Rooms:** Fee: refrigerators. **Cards:** AE, CB, DI, DS, JCB, MC, VI.
*(See ad p A189)*                                                    Roll in showers. 🗗 Ⓓ Ⓢ ⊗

## RESTAURANTS

**AGLIO**                    **Dinner: $21-$30**                    **Phone: 215/336-8008** 25
◆◆◆  **Location:** Between Carpenter & Christian. 937 E Passyunk Ave 19147. **Hours:** 5:30 pm-11 pm, Fri & Sat-1
Italian   am, Sun 4:30 pm-9 pm. Closed major holidays. **Reservations:** accepted. **Features:** valet parking; a la carte. A delicious break from tradition. Food takes taste buds to paradise.

**ALOUETTE RESTAURANT**        **Dinner: $21-$30**                   **Phone: 215/629-1126** 8
◆◆◆  **Location:** South St area. 334 Bainbridge St 19147. **Hours:** 11:30 am-2:30 & 5:30-10 pm, Fri & Sat-10:30
French   pm. Closed major holidays & Tues. **Reservations:** suggested. **Features:** casual dress; Sunday brunch; cocktails & lounge; fee for parking; a la carte. Intimate, cozy dining room. **Cards:** AE, MC, VI.

**ARIZONA**                   **Dinner: up to $10**                  **Phone: 215/567-5555** 26
◆◆  **Location:** Corner 16th & Spring Garden. 1543 Spring Garden St 19130. **Hours:** 11:30 am-3 pm. Closed
Southwest major holidays, Sat & Sun. **Features:** A quick-lunch spot where creative dining is enhanced by colorful,
American  unusual & surprisingly light fare.

**AZALEA**                    **Dinner: $21-$30**                    **Phone: 215/925-0000** 27
◆◆◆◆  **Location:** In Omni Hotel at Independence Park. 401 Chestnut St 19106. **Hours:** 7-11:30 am, noon-2 &
American  5:30-9:30 pm, Sun 7 am-2 pm. **Reservations:** suggested. **Features:** casual dress; Sunday brunch; children's menu; cocktails & lounge; entertainment; fee for parking & valet parking; a la carte, also prix fixe. Contemporary American restaurant serving exceptional regional foods. Smoke free premises. **Cards:** AE, CB, DI, DS, MC, VI.

**BERTUCCI'S**                **Dinner: up to $10**                  **Phone: 215/731-1400** 29
◆  **Location:** Between 15th & 16th sts. 1515 Locust St 19102. **Hours:** 11 am-11 pm, Fri & Sat-midnight, Sun
Italian  noon-11 pm. Closed major holidays. **Features:** a la carte. Wood burning pizza oven. **Cards:** AE, MC, VI.

**BISTRO ROMANO**             **Dinner: $11-$20**                   **Phone: 215/925-8880** 31
ⒶⒶ  **Location:** On Lombard St, between Front & Second sts. 120 Lombard St 19147. **Hours:** 4:30 pm-11 pm, Fri
& Sat-midnight & Sun til 10 pm. Closed: 12/25. **Reservations:** suggested; weekends. **Features:** casual
◆◆  dress; children's menu; health conscious menu; carryout; cocktails & lounge; street parking; area
Italian  transportation; a la carte. Mystery Cafe dinner theatre on Fri & Sat. **Cards:** AE, CB, DI, DS, MC, VI.  ⊗

**BOOKBINDER'S OLD ORIGINAL** Historical    **Dinner: over $31**    **Phone: 215/925-7028** 5
ⒶⒶ  **Location:** At 2nd St. 125 Walnut St 19106. **Hours:** 11:45 am-10 pm, Sat noon-10 pm, 7/4-9/6 from 3 pm,
Sun 3 pm-9 pm. Closed: 11/23, 12/24 for dinner & 12/25. **Reservations:** suggested. **Features:** casual dress;
◆◆  children's menu; carryout; cocktails & lounge; fee for valet parking. Famous restaurant established in 1865.
Seafood  Large selection of seafood. Free valet parking at lunch. **Cards:** AE, DI, DS, MC, VI.                 ⊗

**BOOKBINDER'S SEA FOOD HOUSE**   **Dinner: $21-$30**              **Phone: 215/545-1137** 17
ⒶⒶ  **Location:** 215 S 15th St 19102. **Hours:** 11:30 am-10 pm, Sat 4 pm-11 pm, Sun 3 pm-10 pm. Closed: 11/23
& 12/25. **Reservations:** suggested. **Features:** casual dress; children's menu; carryout; cocktails; fee for
◆  parking; a la carte. Well-known family operation. **Cards:** AE, CB, DI, DS, MC, VI.                         ⊗
Seafood

**BRASIL'S**                  **Dinner: $11-$20**                   **Phone: 215/413-1700** 34
◆◆  **Location:** Off I-95 exit Independence Hall, s until 8th & Chestnut, e on Chestnut. 112 Chestnut St 19106.
Ethnic  **Hours:** 5 pm-10 pm, Fri & Sat-midnight, Sun 3 pm-10 pm. Closed major holidays. **Features:** a la carte.
Philadelphia's only Brazilian restaurant, which evokes that colorful country & culture. Night club Fri & Sat 10
pm-2 am. **Cards:** AE, CB, DS, MC, VI.

**CAFE NOLA**                 **Dinner: $21-$30**                   **Phone: 215/627-2590** 35
◆◆  **Location:** South St. District. 328 South St 19147. **Hours:** Noon-2:45 & 5-10:45 pm, Fri & Sat-midnight,
Ethnic  Sun-10 pm. **Features:** casual dress; Sunday brunch; cocktails & lounge; fee for parking; a la carte. Authentic
Cajun-Creole cuisine served in a Mardi Gras atmosphere. Intimate antique-mirrored dining room with festive
Art Deco oyster bar. Sun a Plantation breakfast or Champagne brunch is served. **Cards:** AE, CB, DI, DS, MC, VI.  ⊗

**CAROLINA'S**                **Dinner: $11-$20**                   **Phone: 215/545-1000** 36
◆◆◆  **Location:** Between Locust & Spruce sts. 261 S 20th St 19103. **Hours:** 11:45 am-2:30 & 5:30-10 pm, Fri &
American  Sat 5:30 pm-11 pm. Closed major holidays. **Features:** Sunday brunch; a la carte. Casual, affordable dining
in comfortable setting.

**CHANTERELLES**              **Dinner: $21-$30**                   **Phone: 215/735-7551** 37
◆◆◆◆  **Location:** Between 13th & Broad sts. 1312 Spruce St 19107. **Hours:** 5:30 pm-10 pm, Fri & Sat-11 pm.
French  Closed major holidays & Sun. **Reservations:** suggested. **Features:** a la carte. Sophisticated atmosphere.
Prix fixe $29. **Cards:** AE, CB, DI, MC, VI.

**CIBOULETTE**                **Dinner: $21-$30**                   **Phone: 215/790-1210** 39
◆◆◆◆  **Location:** Between Walnut & Broad sts, in the Bellevue Building. 200 S Broad St 19102. **Hours:** noon-2 &
French  5:30-9 pm, Mon from 5:30 pm, Fri noon-2 & 5:30-10:30 pm, Sat 5:30 pm-10:30 pm. Closed: 1/1 & 12/24.
**Features:** fee for valet parking; a la carte. Provencial French. Grand food with a setting to match. 1904
French Renaissance decor. **Cards:** AE, MC, VI.

**CIRCA**                     **Dinner: $11-$20**                   **Phone: 215/545-6800** 41
◆◆◆  **Location:** Between 15th & 16th sts. 1518 Walnut St 19102. **Hours:** 11:30 am-2:30 & 5-10 pm, Thurs-Sat-11
American  pm. Closed: Sun, call for hours on holidays. **Features:** a la carte. Affordable high style. The grand
marble-walled building once housed a bank. A downstairs dining room is inside the old bank vault.
**Cards:** AE, MC, VI.

**(See DOWNTOWN PHILADELPHIA ACCOMMODATIONS spotting map page A181)**

**CITY TAVERN**
Dinner: $21-$30
Phone: 215/413-1443  ㊷
◆◆
American
**Location:** Corner of 2nd & Walnut sts. 138 S 2nd St 19106. **Hours:** 11:30 am-10 pm, Fri & Sat-11 pm, Sun-8 pm. **Features:** a la carte. Faithful re-creation of a colonial tavern. A culinary experience inspired by the customs & foods of the 18th century. Colonial American. Costumed wait staff.

**CUTTER'S GRAND CAFE**
Dinner: $11-$20
Phone: 215/851-6262  ㊸
◆◆
Chinese
**Location:** In the Commerce Square building on Market St. 2005 Market St 19103. **Hours:** 11 am-2:30 & 5-10 pm, Fri & Sat-11 pm, Sun 5 pm-9 pm. Closed major holidays. **Features:** valet parking; a la carte. Eager to please brasserie. **Cards:** AE, DI, DS, MC, VI.

**DEUX CHEMINEES**
Dinner: over $31
Phone: 215/790-0200  ⑯
Ⓐ
◆◆◆◆
Regional
French
**Location:** Downtown. 1221 Locust St 19107. **Hours:** 5:30 pm-8:30 pm, Sat-9 pm. Closed major holidays, Sun & Mon. **Reservations:** suggested. **Features:** cocktails; fee for parking. Intimate Victorian elegance. Gracious attentive service. Traditional classic cuisine. Extensive wine list. **Cards:** AE, CB, DI, MC, VI.  ⊗

**DICKENS INN**
Dinner: $21-$30
Phone: 215/928-9307  ㊺
◆◆◆
Continental
**Location:** At Head House Square. 421 S 2nd St 19147. **Hours:** 11:30 am-3 & 5-10 pm, Sun dinner 3 pm-9 pm. Closed: 1/1 & 12/25. **Reservations:** suggested. **Features:** casual dress; Sunday brunch; cocktails & lounge; fee for parking; a la carte. Traditional English foods as well as dishes with a European flair served in a 1780 building renovated to portray the era of Charles Dickens. Illustrations from his novels decorate the walls. Imported ales & beers. **Cards:** AE, CB, DI, DS, MC, VI.  ⊗

**DI LULLO CENTRO**
Dinner: over $31
Phone: 215/546-2000  ⑱
◆◆◆
Northern
Italian
**Location:** Opposite Academy of Music. 1407 Locust St 19102. **Hours:** 11:45 am-1:45 & 5:30-10 pm, Sat 5:30 pm-10 pm. Closed major holidays, Sun, 12/24 for dinner & for lunch 7/1-9/1. **Reservations:** suggested. **Features:** casual dress; cocktails & lounge; fee for parking; a la carte. Elegant surroundings. **Cards:** AE, CB, DI, MC, VI.

**DIMITRI'S**
Dinner: $11-$20
Phone: 215/625-0556  ㊻
◆◆
Greek
**Location:** 3rd & Catherine, in Queens Village area. 795 S 3rd St 19147. **Hours:** 5:30 pm-11 pm. Closed: 11/23, 8/28-9/5 & 12/24-1/1. **Features:** a la carte. Festive & comfortable. Open kitchen from dining room.

**DOCK STREET BREWING COMPANY BREWERY & RESTAURANT**
Dinner: $11-$20
Phone: 215/496-0413  ㊼
◆◆
American
**Location:** In Two Logan Square Bldg, at 18th & Cherry sts. Two Logan Sq 19103. **Hours:** 11:30 pm-midnight, Fri-2 am, Sat noon-2 am, Sun noon-11 pm. Closed: 9/4, 11/23 & 12/25. **Reservations:** suggested; for 6 or more. **Features:** casual dress; children's menu; carryout; cocktail lounge; beer only; a la carte. Philadelphia's only full-grain brewery serving classic brewed on premise beers & ales. A savory menu of moderately priced English, American & European brasserie cuisine. **Cards:** AE, CB, DI, DS, MC, VI.  ⊗

**ESSENE CAFE**
Dinner: $11-$20
Phone: 215/928-3722  ㊾
◆◆
American
**Location:** Sw Corner of Monroe & 4th, near South St. 719 S 4th St 19147. **Hours:** 11 am-3 & 5:30 pm-9 pm, Fri & Sat-10 pm. Closed: Tues. **Features:** a la carte. Cheerfully laid-back. Vegetarian menu. **Cards:** MC, VI.

**FEZ**
Dinner: $11-$20
Phone: 215/925-5367  ㊿
◆◆◆
Ethnic
**Location:** Between South & Bainbridge sts. 620 S 2nd St 19147. **Hours:** 5:30 pm-11 pm. Closed: 11/23 & 12/25. **Features:** prix fixe. Moroccan hideaway. Choose from a 6 or 8-course feast. Allow at least 3 hours of dining pleasure. **Cards:** AE, DS, MC, VI.

**FOUNDER'S**
Dinner: over $31
Phone: 215/893-1776  ②
Ⓐ
◆◆◆◆
Continental
**Location:** Center; Corner of Broad & Walnut sts. 1415 Chancellor Ct 19102. **Hours:** 5 pm-11 pm, Sun 10:30 am-11 pm. **Reservations:** suggested. **Features:** semi-formal attire; Sunday brunch; children's menu; early bird specials; health conscious menu; carryout; cocktails & lounge; entertainment; fee for parking & valet parking; a la carte. Elegant classical decor. Gracious service. **Cards:** AE, CB, DI, DS, MC, VI.  ⊗

**FOUNTAIN RESTAURANT**
Dinner: over $31
Phone: 215/963-1500  ③
◆◆◆◆◆
Continental
**Location:** In Four Seasons Hotel. One Logan Sq 19103. **Hours:** 6:30 am-2:30 & 6-11 pm, Sat & Sun from 7 am. **Reservations:** suggested. **Features:** semi-formal attire; Sunday brunch; children's menu; health conscious menu; cocktails & lounge; entertainment; fee for valet parking; a la carte, also prix fixe. Rich African mahogony accents & gracious table appointments; refined elegance. Innovative menu changes seasonally Table d'hote menu daily. **Cards:** AE, CB, DI, DS, JCB, MC, VI.  ⊗

**THE GARDEN**
Dinner: $11-$20
Phone: 215/546-4455  ⑮
◆◆◆
American
MC, VI.
**Location:** 1617 Spruce St 19103. **Hours:** 11:30 am-1:30 & 5:30-9 pm, Sat 5:30 pm-9:30 pm. Closed major holidays & Sun. **Reservations:** suggested. **Features:** casual dress; early bird specials; cocktails & lounge; fee for valet parking; a la carte. Converted townhouse with garden dining in summer. **Cards:** AE, CB, DI,

**IMPERIAL INN**
Dinner: $11-$20
Phone: 215/627-2299  ㊼② (52)
◆◆
Chinese
**Location:** In Chinatown. 142-46 N 10th St 19107. **Hours:** 11 am-12:30 am, Fri & Sat-2 am, Sun-midnight. **Reservations:** suggested. **Features:** casual dress; carryout; cocktails; minimum charge-$3; fee for parking; a la carte. Variety of Szechuan, Mandarin & Cantonese dishes. Authentic Dim Sum table served buffet 11 am-3 pm. **Cards:** AE, CB, DI, MC, VI.  ⊗

**THE INN PHILADELPHIA**
Dinner: $11-$20
Phone: 215/732-8630  ㉛ (31)
◆◆◆
American
**Location:** Between Locust & Spruce sts, 1 1/2 blks e of the Academy of Music. 251-253 S Camac St 19107. **Hours:** 5:30 pm-10:30 pm. Closed: 12/25. **Features:** Sunday brunch; cocktail lounge. Three exceedingly tasteful dining areas. The Green Room is an intimately-scaled formal room. The Great Room is a traditional room with 2 fireplaces, The Gallery is contempory. **Cards:** AE, CB, DI, DS, MC, VI.

**JACK'S FIREHOUSE RESTAURANT**
Dinner: $11-$20
Phone: 215/232-9000  ⑭
◆◆
American
MC, VI.
**Location:** 1/2 blk e of jct 22nd St & Fairmont Ave. 2130 Fairmount Ave 19130. **Hours:** 11:30 am-2:30 & 5-10:30 pm, Sat from 5 pm. Closed major holidays. **Reservations:** suggested. **Features:** casual dress; Sunday brunch; cocktails & lounge; a la carte. Converted firehouse. Casual atmosphere. **Cards:** AE, CB, DI,

**KABUL, CUISINE OF AFGHANISTAN**
Dinner: $11-$20
Phone: 215/922-3676  ㊴ (54)
◆◆
Ethnic
**Location:** Between 2nd & Front sts. 106 Chestnut St 19106. **Hours:** 4:30 pm-10 pm, Fri & Sat 5 pm-11 pm, Sun 4:30 pm-9 pm. Closed: Mon. **Reservations:** suggested. **Features:** casual dress; carryout; fee for parking. Featuring traditional kabobs of marinated chicken, lamb or beef. Appetizers such as scallion-filled dumplings with yogurt sauce. Many vegetable dishes. **Cards:** AE, DI, DS, MC, VI.  ⊗

**(See DOWNTOWN PHILADELPHIA ACCOMMODATIONS spotting map page A181)**

**KAT MAN DU & ELIZABETH AT KAT MAN DU**  Dinner: $11-$20  Phone: 215/629-7400  ⑤⑥
◆◆  **Location:** On Columbus Blvd, between Spring Garden & Callowhill sts, Pier 25 N. 417 N Columbus Blvd
American  19123. **Hours:** 11:30 am-11 pm. light fare 11 pm-1 am. Closed major holidays, Mon & Tues.
**Reservations:** suggested. **Features:** casual dress; Sunday brunch; carryout; cocktails & lounge;
entertainment; fee for valet parking; a la carte. Lively American bistro with a Gulf Coast Creole & Caribbean flair. **Cards:** AE,
CB, DI, DS, MC, VI.

**LA BELLA VITA AT THE MAIN EVENT**  Dinner: up to $10  Phone: 215/413-1776  ⑤⑦
◆  **Location:** Downtown, in Market East Shopping Mall, Concourse level. 8th & Market sts 19106. **Hours:** 11
Italian  am-2 pm, Thurs & Fri-10 pm, Sat 4 pm-10 pm. **Closed:** Sun. **Reservations:** accepted. **Features:** casual
dress; children's menu; carryout; salad bar; cocktails & lounge; fee for parking; a la carte. Pleasant family
style Italian eatery. **Cards:** AE, CB, DI, DS, MC, VI.  ⊗

**LA FAMIGLIA**  Dinner: over $31  Phone: 215/922-2803  ④
◆◆◆  **Location:** Center. 8 S Front St 19106. **Hours:** noon-2 & 5:30-9:30 pm, Sat 5:30 pm-10 pm, Sun 4:30 pm-9
Regional  pm. Closed major holidays, Mon & 12/24, 12/31 & 1/6. **Reservations:** suggested. **Features:** formal
Italian  attire; cocktails; fee for parking; a la carte. Family owned & operated. Outstanding wine cellar. **Cards:** AE,
CB, DI, MC, VI.  ⊗

**LA TRUFFE**  Dinner: $21-$30  Phone: 215/925-5062  ⑤⑨
◆◆◆  **Location:** In Society Hill District. 10 S Front St 19106. **Hours:** Noon-2 & 5:30-10:30 pm. **Closed:** Sun.
French  **Reservations:** suggested. **Features:** casual dress; cocktails & lounge; prix fixe. Intimately elegant romantic
setting.  ⊗

**LE BEC-FIN**  Dinner: over $31  Phone: 215/567-1000  ⑫
⌘  **Location:** Between 15th & 16th sts. 1523 Walnut St 19102. **Hours:** Lunch seatings at 11:30 am & 1:30 pm
Mon-Fri, dinner seatings Mon-Thurs at 6 pm & 9 pm & Fri & Sat 6 pm & 9:30 pm. Closed major holidays, Sun
◆◆◆◆◆  & last week in Aug. **Reservations:** required. **Features:** formal attire; cocktails & lounge; fee for valet parking;
French  prix fixe. Formal dining in a lavish setting; Louis XVI decor. Exquisite table appointments. Menu changes
seasonally & offers outstanding variety. **Cards:** AE, CB, DI, DS, MC, VI.  ⊗

**LONDON GRILL**  Dinner: $11-$20  Phone: 215/978-4545  ⑪
⌘  **Location:** 1/2 blk w of jct 22nd St & Fairmount Ave. 2301 Fairmount Ave 19130. **Hours:** 11:30 am-3 &
5:30-10:30 pm, Sun 4 pm-9 pm. **Closed:** 1/1, 11/23 & 12/25. **Reservations:** suggested. **Features:** casual
◆◆  dress; Sunday brunch; children's menu; carryout; cocktails & lounge; minimum charge-$15; a la carte.
American  Friendly neighborhood dining. Lighter fare menu avail. Eclectic menu. **Cards:** AE, CB, DI, DS, MC, VI.  ⊗

**MIA'S**  Dinner: $21-$30  Phone: 215/545-4655  ⑥⓪
◆◆◆  **Location:** In The Warwick. 1701 Locust St 19103-6179. **Hours:** 6:30 am-11 pm. **Reservations:** suggested.
Continental  **Features:** casual dress; Sunday brunch; cocktails & lounge; fee for parking & valet parking; a la carte. Cozy,
sophisticated dining, specializing in "Mezzano", cuisines of the Middle East & its Mediterranean neighbors.
**Cards:** AE, CB, DI, MC, VI.  ⊗

**MICK'S DOWNSTAIRS AT THE BELLEVUE**  Dinner: $11-$20  Phone: 215/732-7997  ⑥②
◆  **Location:** Center; corner of Broad & Walnut sts. 200 S Broad St 19102. **Hours:** 11 am-10 pm, Fri & Sat-11
American  pm, Sun noon-9 pm. **Closed:** 11/23 & 12/25. **Features:** a la carte. Upscale looks, but family-friendly.

**MILANO'S**  Dinner: up to $10  Phone: 215/851-8722  ⑥③
◆◆  **Location:** Corner of 20th & Market sts. 2001 Market St 19103. **Hours:** 11 am-10 pm, Fri-11 pm, Sat 4 pm-11
Italian  pm, Sun 3 pm-9 pm. Closed major holidays. **Features:** a la carte. Slick-looking but affordable. Look & feel of
a high-style gourmet shop. **Cards:** AE, MC, VI.

**THE MONTE CARLO LIVING ROOM**  Dinner: over $31  Phone: 215/925-2220  ②①
⌘  **Location:** South St at 2nd St. 150 South St 19147. **Hours:** 6 pm-10:30 pm, Sat 5:30 pm-10:30 pm, Sun 5
pm-9:30 pm. Closed major holidays. **Reservations:** suggested. **Features:** semi-formal attire; cocktails &
◆◆◆◆  lounge; fee for valet parking; a la carte. Intimate dining room in trendy Queen's Village area. Reserved
Italian  atmosphere. Features fresh domestic & imported seafood. Formal service. **Cards:** AE, CB, DI, MC, VI.  ⊗

**MORTON'S OF CHICAGO STEAK HOUSE**  Dinner: $21-$30  Phone: 215/557-0724  ⑦
◆◆  **Location:** At corner of 19th & Cherry sts. 1 Logan Sq 19103. **Hours:** 11:30 am-2:30 & 5:30-11 pm, Sun 5
American  pm-10 pm. Closed major holidays. **Reservations:** suggested. **Features:** semi-formal attire; cocktails &
lounge; valet parking; a la carte. Jackets suggested. Large portions served in attractive dining room.
Well-prepared steak & seafood dishes. **Cards:** AE, CB, DI, MC, VI.  ⊗

**OVERTURES**  Dinner: $11-$20  Phone: 215/627-3455  ⑥④
◆◆◆  **Location:** Between Bainbridge & South sts & between 4th & 5th sts. 609 E Passyunk Ave 19147. **Hours:** 6
Provincial  pm-10:30 pm. Closed major holidays & Mon. **Features:** Old World atmosphere. **Cards:** AE, MC, VI.
French

**PALLADIUM RESTAURANT**  Dinner: $11-$20  Phone: 215/387-3463  ⑥⑤
⌘  **Location:** I-76 exit 38, 1/2 mi w on Market St, 1/2 mi s on 36th St to campus parking, then 1 blk walk s.
3601 Locust Walk 19104. **Hours:** 11:30 am-2:30 & 5-10 pm, Sun-Tues to 9 pm. **Closed:** 6/15-9/1 Sun;
◆◆  8/16-8/22 & 12/23-1/3. **Reservations:** suggested. **Features:** casual dress; carryout; cocktails & lounge; a la
Continental  carte. Located on the University of PA campus in a restored Collegiate Gothic building. Late-night menu avail
Tues-Sat to midnight in basement wine cellar. **Cards:** AE, CB, DI, DS, MC, VI.  ⊗

**PALM RESTAURANT**  Dinner: $21-$30  Phone: 215/546-7256  ②④
◆◆  **Location:** Corner of Walnut & Broad sts. 200 S Broad St 19102. **Hours:** 11:30 am-11 pm, Sat 5 pm-11 pm,
American  Sun 4:30 pm-9 pm. Closed major holidays. **Reservations:** suggested. **Features:** casual dress; cocktails &
lounge; fee for parking & valet parking; a la carte. In shops at the Bellevue. Upbeat, high-energy
atmosphere. **Cards:** AE, CB, DI, MC, VI.  ⊗

**PAMPLONA**  Dinner: $11-$20  Phone: 215/627-9059  ⑥⑧
◆◆◆  **Location:** Corner of 12th & Locust sts. 12th & Locust 19107. **Hours:** 11:30 am-2:30 & 5:30-11 pm, Sun 5:30
Ethnic  pm-10 pm. Closed major holidays. **Features:** a la carte. Spanish. Gloriously theatrical space dominated by
oversized Picasso-inspired murals. Sleek, yet relaxed. Tapas style menu. **Cards:** AE, MC, VI.

**PASSAGE TO INDIA**  Dinner: $11-$20  Phone: 215/732-7300  ⑦⓪
◆◆  **Location:** Corner of Juniper & Walnut sts. 1320 Walnut St 19107. **Hours:** 11:30 am-2:30 & 5-10 pm, Fri &
Ethnic  Sat-11 pm. **Features:** a la carte. Buffet $7.99.

**RALPHS' ITALIAN RESTAURANT**  Dinner: $11-$20  Phone: 215/627-6011  ⑩
◆  **Location:** South Philadelphia. 760 S 9th St 19147. **Hours:** Noon-9:45 pm, Fri & Sat-10:45 pm. **Closed:**
South Italian  11/23 & 12/25. **Reservations:** suggested. **Features:** casual dress; carryout; cocktails; a la carte. Family run
operation in the Italian Market area since the early 1900's. Offering simple, home cooked cuisine.  ⊗

**(See DOWNTOWN PHILADELPHIA ACCOMMODATIONS spotting map page A181)**

**RANGOON**  **Dinner:** up to $10  **Phone:** 215/829-8939  (71)
◆
Ethnic  **Location:** In Chinatown, Between Cherry & Race sts. 145 N 9th St 19107. **Hours:** 11:30 am-9 pm, Fri-10 pm, Sat 1 pm-10 pm, Sun 1 pm-9 pm. Closed major holidays. **Features:** a la carte. Burmese cuisine. The menu combines ingredients from Indian, Thia & Chinese cooking traditions, with distinctive & delicious results.

**RESTAURANT 210**  **Dinner:** over $31  **Phone:** 215/546-9000  (20)
◆◆◆◆
French  **Location:** In The Rittenhouse Hotel & Condominium Residences. 210 W Rittenhouse Sq 19103. **Hours:** 11:30 am-2 & 5:30-11 pm, Fri & Sat-1 am. Closed: Sun. **Reservations:** suggested. **Features:** cocktails; fee for valet parking; a la carte. Award-winning classical cuisine prepared from fresh regional markets. Elegant ambience. Gracious service. Extensive wine list. **Cards:** AE, CB, DI, DS, JCB, MC, VI.  ⊗

**RISTORANTE PRIMAVERA**  **Dinner:** $11-$20  **Phone:** 215/925-7832  (72)
♨
◆◆  **Location:** South St. District. 146 South St 19147. **Hours:** 5:30 pm-10:30 pm, Sun-9:30 pm, Fri & Sat-11 pm. Closed: 1/1, 5/29, 9/4, 11/23 & 12/25. **Features:** casual dress; carryout; cocktails; fee for parking & valet parking; a la carte. Homemade pastas & fish specials daily.
Italian

**THE RITZ-CARLTON DINING ROOM**  **Dinner:** over $31  **Phone:** 215/563-1600  (22)
◆◆◆◆
Continental  **Location:** In The Ritz-Carlton, Philadelphia. 17th & Chestnut St at Liberty Pl 19103. **Hours:** 6:30-11 am, 11:30-2:30 & 6-10 pm, Sun 10:30 am-2:30 pm. Closed: Sun & Mon for dinner. **Reservations:** suggested. **Features:** formal attire; Sunday brunch; cocktails & lounge; fee for valet parking; a la carte. Charming, elegant decor. Creative contemporary cuisine. Extensive wine list. Prix fixe dinner $50-75. **Cards:** AE, CB, DI, DS, JCB, MC, VI.  ⊗

**THE RITZ-CARLTON GRILL ROOM**  **Dinner:** over $31  **Phone:** 215/563-1600  (73)
◆◆◆◆
American  **Location:** In The Ritz-Carlton, Philadelphia. 17th & Chestnut St at Lib Pl 19103. **Hours:** 11:30 am-2:30 & 5:30-10:30 pm, Sun 6:30 am-11:30 & 5:30-10:30 pm. **Reservations:** suggested. **Features:** semi-formal attire; health conscious menu; cocktails & lounge; fee for valet parking; a la carte. Regional fare, including hearty steaks, chops & seafood served in a club-like setting, enhanced with rich mahogany & oil paintings. **Cards:** AE, CB, DI, DS, JCB, MC, VI.

**RUTH'S CHRIS STEAK HOUSE**  **Dinner:** $21-$30  **Phone:** 215/790-1515  (1)
◆◆◆
Steakhouse  **Location:** Corner of Broad & Spruce sts. 260 S Broad St 19102. **Hours:** 5 pm-11:30 pm, Fri noon-11:30 pm. **Reservations:** suggested. **Features:** casual dress; cocktails & lounge; fee for parking & valet parking; a la carte. Fine dining featuring fresh seafood & custom-aged, corn-fed beef brought to your table sizzling. **Cards:** AE, DI, DS, MC, VI.

**SINGAPORE VEGETARIAN CHINESE RESTAURANT**  **Dinner:** up to $10  **Phone:** 215/922-3288  (74)
◆◆
Chinese  **Location:** Corner of 11th & Race sts, in Chinatown. 1029 Race St 19107. **Hours:** 11:30 am-11 pm. **Features:** a la carte. Dishes based on fresh & dried vegetables along with mock meat & seafood dishes made from grains, glutens & soy product. **Cards:** AE, DS, MC, VI.

**SOUTH STREET SOUVLAKI**  **Dinner:** up to $10  **Phone:** 215/925-3026  (9)
♨
◆  **Location:** 509 South St 19147. **Hours:** 11 am-10 pm, Fri & Sat-11 pm, Sun noon-10 pm. Closed: Mon, 1/1, 11/23 & 12/25. **Reservations:** accepted. **Features:** casual dress; carryout; cocktails; a la carte. Informal dining atmosphere. Traditionally prepared cuisine made-on premises.  ⊗
Greek

**STRIPED BASS**  **Dinner:** $21-$30  **Phone:** 215/732-4444  (75)
◆◆◆
Seafood  **Location:** Sw corner of 15th & Walnut sts. 1500 Walnut St 19102. **Hours:** 11:30 am-2:30 & 5-11 pm, Fri & Sat-11:30 pm, Sun 5 pm-10 pm. Closed major holidays. **Features:** fee for valet parking; a la carte. Stylish, marble pillars. 30-foot marquetry ceiling, colorful Oriental rug, potted palms & spectacular flower arrangements set the mood. **Cards:** AE, DI, MC, VI.

**SUSANNA FOO**  **Dinner:** $21-$30  **Phone:** 215/545-2666  (19)
◆◆◆
Chinese  **Location:** Between 15th & 16th sts. 1512 Walnut St 19102. **Hours:** 11:30 am-2:30 & 5-10 pm, Fri-11 pm, Sat 5 pm-11 pm. Closed major holidays & Sun. **Reservations:** suggested. **Features:** semi-formal attire; carryout; cocktails; fee for parking & valet parking; a la carte. Excellent selection of imaginative & unorthodox preparations that offer an adventure in gastronomy. Atmosphere has a formal edge. **Cards:** AE, CB, DI, MC, VI.  ⊗

**SWANN LOUNGE & CAFE**  **Dinner:** $11-$20  **Phone:** 215/963-1500  (77)
◆◆◆◆
Continental  **Location:** In Four Seasons Hotel. One Logan Sq 19103. **Hours:** 7 am-1 am, Sun from 9 am, Mon from 11 am. **Reservations:** accepted. **Features:** casual dress; Sunday brunch; children's menu; health conscious menu; cocktails & lounge; entertainment; fee for valet parking; a la carte. Relaxed elegant environment with view of Logan Circle. Seasonal menu changes. **Cards:** AE, CB, DI, DS, JCB, MC, VI.  ⊗

**TSUI HANG CHUN**  **Dinner:** $11-$20  **Phone:** 215/925-8901  (79)
◆◆
Ethnic  **Location:** Between 9th & 10th sts, in Chinatown. 911-913 Race St 19107. **Hours:** 11 am-2 am. **Features:** a la carte. Handsome Chinese restaurant. Dim-Sum 11 am-3 pm. **Cards:** AE, DI, DS, MC, VI.

# GREATER PHILADELPHIA (See PHILADELPHIA & VICINITY ACCOMMODATIONS spotting map pages A196 & A197; see index below)

---

### Index of Establishments on the PHILADELPHIA & VICINITY ACCOMMODATIONS Spotting Map

**(See PHILADELPHIA & VICINITY ACCOMMODATIONS spotting map pages A196 & A197)**

**(See PHILADELPHIA & VICINITY ACCOMMODATIONS spotting map pages A196 & A197)**

## LODGINGS

**ADAM'S MARK HOTEL**   Guaranteed Rates   Phone: 215/581-5000   **40**
Mon-Thurs   1P: $105   2P/1B: $120   2P/2B: $157   XP: $12   F18
Fri-Sun   1P: $89   2P/1B: $89   2P/2B: $89   XP: $12   F18
◆◆◆   **Location:** On US 1 (City Ave), 2 blks s of I-76, Schuylkill Expwy, exit 33. City Ave at Monument Rd 19131.
Hotel   Fax: 215/581-5089. **Terms:** Sr. discount; reserv deposit; package plans; no pets. **Facility:** 515 rooms. Impressive public areas. Comfortably appointed rooms. Hair salon, travel agency & car rentals avail on premises. 3 two-bedroom units. 23 stories; interior corridors; business center, conference facilities; 2 pools (2 heated, 1 indoor), saunas, whirlpool; racquetball courts; exercise room. **Dining & Entertainment:** Dining room, restaurant; 6:30 am-11 pm; $8-$30; cocktails/lounge; also, The Marker, see separate listing; entertainment. **Services:** data ports, PC, secretarial services; valet laundry; area transportation. Fee: childcare, airport transportation, within 2 mi; valet parking. **All Rooms:** cable TV. Fee: movies. **Some Rooms:** coffeemakers, whirlpools. Fee: refrigerators, VCP's. **Cards:** AE, CB, DI, DS, MC, VI.
☑ Ⓓ Ⓢ ⊗

**BEST WESTERN HOTEL PHILADELPHIA NORTHEAST**   Rates Subject to Change   Phone: 215/464-9500   **53**
All Year [CP]   1P: $85   2P/1B: $90   2P/2B: $95   XP: $10   F18
◆◆◆   **Location:** 3 mi s on US 1, from PA Tpk exit 28. 11580 Roosevelt Blvd 19116. Fax: 215/464-8511.
Motor Inn   **Terms:** Credit card guarantee; weekly/monthly rates; package plans; no pets. **Facility:** 100 rooms. 2 stories; interior corridors; conference facilities; pool, wading pool, beach volleyball; exercise room, playground, shuffleboard. **Dining & Entertainment:** Coffee shop; 9 am-9 pm, Sun noon-midnight; $4-$8; cocktails/lounge.
**Services:** secretarial services; area transportation. Fee: coin laundry. **All Rooms:** free movies, cable TV. **Some Rooms:** 6 efficiencies, no utensils, microwaves, refrigerators, whirlpools. **Cards:** AE, DI, DS, MC, VI. *(See ad below)*   Ⓓ ⊗

**CHESTNUT HILL HOTEL**   Rates Subject to Change   Phone: 215/242-5905   **47**
◆◆◆   All Year [CP]   1P: $80- 120   2P/1B: $90- 120   2P/2B: $90- 120   XP: $10   F12
Historic Hotel   **Location:** From I-276 exit 25; 5 1/2 mi e on Germantown Pike. 8229 Germantown Ave 19118.
Fax: 215/242-8778. **Terms:** Credit card guarantee; package plans; no pets. **Facility:** 28 rooms. Colonial-style hotel with 18th-century style furnishings. Individually decorated rooms. 2-4 stories; interior corridors; meeting rooms. **Dining:** Also, Pollo Rosso, see separate listing. **Services:** valet laundry. Fee: airport transportation. **All Rooms:** free movies, combo & shower baths, cable TV. **Cards:** AE, DI, MC, VI.   Ⓓ

**COURTYARD BY MARRIOTT AIRPORT**   AAA Special Value Rates   Phone: 215/365-2200   **54**
◆◆◆   5/1-12/31   1P: $95   2P/1B: $105   2P/2B: $105
Motor Inn   Mon-Thurs 1/1-4/30   1P: $92   2P/1B: $102   2P/2B: $102
Fri-Sun 1/1-4/30   1P: $65   2P/1B: $65   2P/2B: $65
**Location:** I-95 southbound exit 10 (airport), bearing right on exit ramp to light, then 1 mi n, I-95 northbound exit 10, follow 291E signs until light, then 1 mi n. 8900 Bartram Ave 19153. Fax: 215/365-6905. **Terms:** Weekly rates; no pets. **Facility:** 152 rooms. Courtyard with pagota. 12 suites, $110-$120. Long term stay (7 day minimum) $80 per night; 4 stories; interior corridors; meeting rooms; heated indoor pool, whirlpool; exercise room. **Dining & Entertainment:** Restaurant; 6:30 am-1 & 5-10 pm, room service 5 pm-9:30 pm; $9-$17; cocktails/lounge. **Services:** data ports; airport transportation. Fee: coin laundry. **All Rooms:** coffeemakers, free & pay movies, cable TV. Fee: VCP. **Some Rooms:** refrigerators. **Cards:** AE, CB, DI, DS, MC, VI. *(See color ad p A198)*   Ⓓ Ⓢ ⊗

**DAYS INN**   AAA Special Value Rates   Phone: 215/289-9200   **42**
12/31-1/1 [CP]   1P: $70- 80   2P/1B: $85   2P/2B: $85   XP:$7-10   F12
5/1-12/30 & 1/2-4/30 [CP]   1P: $50   2P/1B: $50   2P/2B: $55   XP:$7-10   F12
◆◆   **Location:** I-76 exit 34 US 1N (Roosevelt Blvd), 5 3/10 mi n, or PA Tpk exit 28, 12 mi s on US 1. 4200
Motel   Roosevelt Blvd 19124. Fax: 215/289-9200. **Terms:** Reserv deposit, 3 day notice; weekly rates; no pets. **Facility:** 116 rooms. 2 stories; interior corridors; meeting rooms. **Dining:** Restaurant nearby.
**All Rooms:** free movies, cable TV. **Some Rooms:** Fee: whirlpools. **Cards:** AE, CB, DI, DS, JCB, MC, VI.   ☑ Ⓓ ⊗

**DAYS INN/PHILADELPHIA INT'L AIRPORT**   Rates Subject to Change   Phone: 215/492-0400   **44**
5/1-10/31 & 2/1-4/30   1P: $87- 97   2P/1B: $99- 109   2P/2B: $99- 109   XP: $15   F17
11/1-1/31   1P: $69   2P/1B: $69   2P/2B: $69   XP: $15   F17
◆◆   **Location:** Jct I-95 & SR 291 exit 10. 4101 Island Ave 19153. Fax: 215/365-6035. **Terms:** Monthly rates; BP
Motor Inn   available; package plans; no pets. **Facility:** 177 rooms. 5 stories; interior corridors; meeting rooms; pool. **Dining & Entertainment:** Dining room; 6 am-2 & 5-10 pm; $9-$16; health conscious menu; cocktails/lounge; 24-hour room service. **Services:** complimentary evening beverages; health club privileges; airport transportation. Fee: coin laundry. **Recreation:** jogging. **All Rooms:** coffeemakers, free & pay movies, cable TV. **Some Rooms:** microwaves, refrigerators. Fee: VCP's. **Cards:** AE, CB, DI, DS, MC, VI. *(See ad p A198)*   Ⓓ Ⓢ ⊗

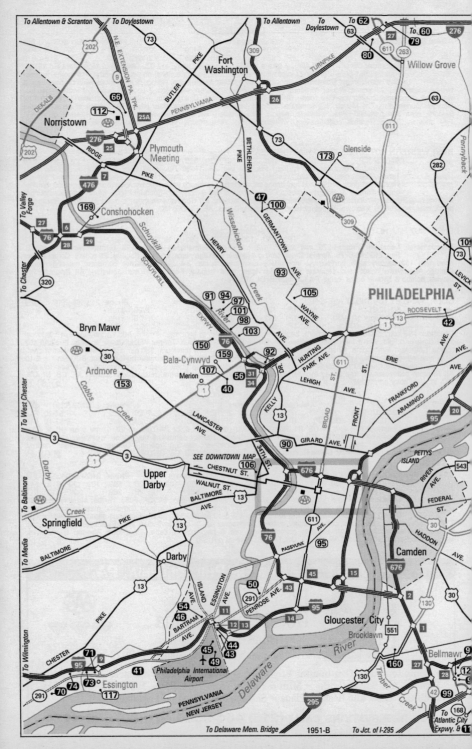

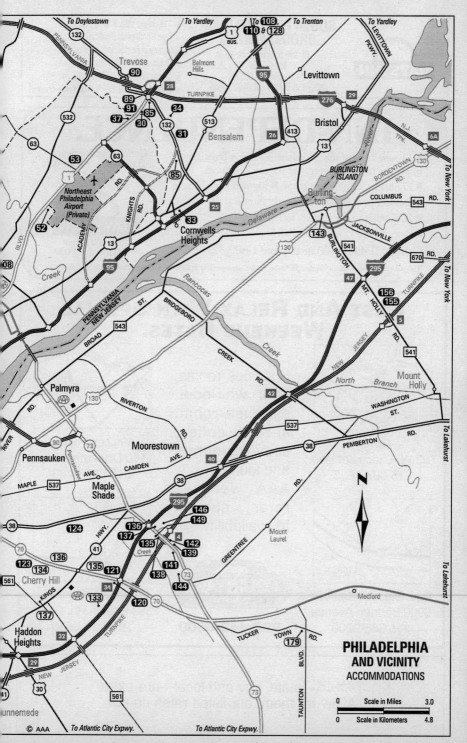

PHILADELPHIA
**AND VICINITY**
ACCOMMODATIONS

TAXES—state, city and local—are extra.
Allow for them, our listed rates do not.

**(See PHILADELPHIA & VICINITY ACCOMMODATIONS spotting map pages A196 & A197)**

EMBASSY SUITES-PHILADELPHIA AIRPORT    AAA Special Value Rates    **Phone:** 215/365-4500   **46**
◆◆◆    All Year [BP]    1P: $159    2P/1B: $159    2P/2B: $169
Hotel    **Location:** From jct I-95 & Essington Ave, 2 blks n on Essington Ave, then 5 blks w on Bartram Ave. 9000 Bartram Ave 19153. Fax: 215/365-3195. **Terms:** Reserv deposit, 7 day notice; package plans; weekend rates available; no pets. **Facility:** 265 rooms. Tropically landscaped sunken atrium area with park-like setting. Small waterfalls with goldfish & duck pond. Comfortably furnished suites. 5 stories; interior corridors; business center, conference facilities; heated indoor pool, sauna, whirlpool; exercise room. **Dining & Entertainment:** Dining room; 11 am-11 pm; $8-$15; cocktails/lounge. **Services:** data ports; airport transportation. Fee: coin laundry. **All Rooms:** coffeemakers, microwaves, free & pay movies, refrigerators, cable TV. **Some Rooms:** Fee: VCP's. **Cards:** AE, DI, DS, JCB, MC, VI.    Roll in showers. Ⓐ Ⓓ Ⓢ ⊗

GUEST QUARTERS SUITE HOTEL    Rates Subject to Change    **Phone:** 215/365-6600   **43**
◆◆◆    Mon-Thurs [EP]    1P: $114    2P/1B: $114    2P/2B: $114    XP: $20   F18
Suite Hotel    Fri-Sun [CP]    1P: $85    2P/1B: $85    2P/2B: $85    XP: $20   F18
   **Location:** Jct I-95 & SR 291 exit 11. 4101 Island Ave 19153. Fax: 215/492-8471. **Terms:** Sr. discount; weekly/monthly rates; no pets. **Facility:** 251 rooms. Atrium style hotel at Gateway Center. 1-bedroom suites with living room. 1 two-bedroom unit. 8 stories; interior corridors; business center, conference facilities; heated indoor pool, sauna, steamroom, whirlpool; exercise room, beach volleyball, game room, horseshoes. **Dining & Entertainment:** Restaurant; 6 am-11 pm; $9-$21; cocktails/lounge. **Services:** data ports, PC, secretarial services; valet laundry; airport transportation. Fee: childcare. **Recreation:** jogging. **All Rooms:** coffeemakers, free & pay movies, refrigerators, cable TV. **Some Rooms:** honor bars, microwaves, whirlpools. Fee: VCP's. **Cards:** AE, CB, DI, DS, MC, VI. *(See ad below)* Ⓓ Ⓢ ⊗

HOLIDAY INN CITY LINE    AAA Special Value Rates    **Phone:** 215/477-0200   **56**
(AAA)    All Year    1P: $99    2P/1B: $115    2P/2B: $115    XP: $15   F
◆◆◆    **Location:** On US 1, 1 blk s of I-76, Schuylkill Expwy, exit 33. 4100 Presidential Blvd 19131.
Hotel    Fax: 215/473-5510. **Terms:** Credit card guarantee, 5 day notice; monthly rates; BP, CP available; no pets. **Facility:** 344 rooms. Comfortably furnished rooms with contemporary decor. Nicely appointed public areas. 8 stories; interior corridors; conference facilities; heated indoor pool, whirlpool; exercise room. **Dining & Entertainment:** Dining room; 6:30 am-10:30 pm, Sat & Sun from 7 am; $7-$18; cocktails/lounge. **Services:** data ports, secretarial services. Fee: PC; coin laundry, airport transportation. **All Rooms:** free & pay movies, cable TV. **Some Rooms:** coffeemakers. Fee: refrigerators, VCP's. **Cards:** AE, CB, DI, DS, MC, VI. Ⓐ Ⓓ ⊗

(See **PHILADELPHIA & VICINITY ACCOMMODATIONS** spotting map pages A196 & A197)

PHILADELPHIA AIRPORT HILTON  Rates Subject to Change  Phone: 215/365-4150  **45**
◆◆◆  Sun-Thurs  1P: $136  2P/1B: $146  2P/2B: $146  XP: $10  F12
Hotel  Fri & Sat  1P: $79  2P/1B: $79  2P/2B: $79  XP: $10  F12
**Location:** Jct I-95 & SR 291 exit 10. 4509 Island Ave 19153. Fax: 215/365-3875. **Terms:** Credit card guarantee; weekly/monthly rates; package plans; pets. **Facility:** 330 rooms. Large spacious public areas with marble tile. 9 stories; interior corridors; conference facilities; luxury level rooms; heated indoor pool, whirlpool; exercise room, game room. **Dining & Entertainment:** Dining room, 2 restaurants; 6 am-1 am; $7-$28; health conscious menu; cocktails/lounge; 24-hour room service. **Services:** data ports, secretarial services; airport transportation. Fee: coin laundry. **All Rooms:** coffeemakers, free & pay movies, cable TV. **Some Rooms:** refrigerators. **Cards:** AE, CB, DI, DS, MC, VI. *(See ad p 28)*  (D)(S)⊗

PHILADELPHIA AIRPORT RESIDENCE INN  AAA Special Value Rates  Phone: 215/492-1611  **49**
◆◆◆  Mon-Thurs [CP]  1P: $125  2P/1B: $125  2P/2B: $145
Apartment  Fri-Sun [CP]  1P: $69  2P/1B: $69  2P/2B: $112
Motel  **Location:** From I-95 (Northbound, exit 11 or Southbound, exit 10), 1/4 mi e on SR 291. 4630 Island Ave 19153. Fax: 215/492-1665. **Terms:** Reserv deposit, 3 day notice; weekly/monthly rates; BP available; pets, $100, $6 daily. **Facility:** 102 rooms. Comfortably appointed suite units. 24 two-bedroom units. 2 stories; exterior corridors; meeting rooms; heated pool, whirlpool; exercise room, sports court. **Dining:** Evening social Mon-Thurs; restaurant nearby. **Services:** data ports; childcare; area transportation, within 15 mi, airport transportation. Fee: coin laundry. **All Rooms:** coffeemakers, kitchens, microwaves, free movies, refrigerators, cable TV. **Some Rooms:** Fee: VCP's. **Cards:** AE, CB, DI, DS, JCB, MC, VI.  Roll in showers. (D)(S)⊗

PHILADELPHIA TRAVELODGE HOTEL-AIRPORT/STADIUM  Guaranteed Rates  Phone: 215/755-6500  **50**
(AAA)  All Year  1P: $75  2P/1B: $85  2P/2B: $75  XP: $6  F17
◆◆  **Location:** I-76 exit 43A (eastbound) or I-76 exit 44 (westbound), 1 blk e on Hartranft St, then 1 blk n on Hotel  Penrose Ave. 2015 Penrose Ave 19145. Fax: 215/465-7517. **Terms:** Sr. discount; reserv deposit; weekly/monthly rates; small pets only. **Facility:** 203 rooms. 17 stories; interior corridors; meeting rooms; heated pool, wading pool; exercise room, gameroom. **Dining & Entertainment:** Restaurant; 6:30 am-10 pm; $6-$12; cocktails/lounge. **Services:** data ports, secretarial services; valet laundry; area transportation, to train station, airport transportation. **All Rooms:** coffeemakers, free & pay movies, safes, cable TV. **Some Rooms:** refrigerators. Fee: microwaves. **Cards:** AE, CB, DI, DS, JCB, MC, VI. *(See color ad p A201)*  ⊠(D)⊗

**(See PHILADELPHIA & VICINITY ACCOMMODATIONS spotting map pages A196 & A197)**

RADISSON HOTEL PHILADELPHIA AIRPORT    Rates Subject to Change    Phone: 610/521-5900   **41**
◆◆◆    Sun-Thurs    1P: $119- 139   2P/1B: $129- 149   2P/2B: $129- 149   XP: $10   F18
Hotel    Fri & Sat    1P: $79- 99   2P/1B: $79- 99   2P/2B: $79- 99   XP: $10   F18
      **Location:** On SR 291, 1 mi e of jct SR 420, I-95 Essington/SR 420 exit 9A. 500 Stevens Dr 19113.
Fax: 610/521-4362. **Terms:** Check-in 4 pm; credit card guarantee; no pets. **Facility:** 353 rooms. Upscale, contemporary designed rooms & public areas. 12 stories; interior corridors; conference facilities; heated indoor pool; whirlpool; exercise room, video arcade. **Dining & Entertainment:** Restaurant; 6:30 am-11 pm; $8-$19; health conscious menu; cocktails/lounge; entertainment. **Services:** data ports, secretarial services; valet laundry; airport transportation. Fee: PC. **All Rooms:** cable TV. Fee: movies. **Some Rooms:** refrigerators. **Cards:** AE, CB, DI, DS, MC, VI.   ⒟ ⓢ ⊗

SHERATON INN-PHILADELPHIA NORTHEAST    Guaranteed Rates    Phone: 215/671-9600   **52**
Ⓐ    All Year    1P: $67    2P/1B: $77    2P/2B: $77    XP: $10   F17
      **Location:** 5 mi s on US 1, from PA Tpk exit 28. 9461 Roosevelt Blvd 19114. Fax: 215/464-7759. **Terms:** Sr.
◆◆◆    discount; reserv deposit, 3 day notice; no pets. **Facility:** 188 rooms. Nicely appointed public areas & rooms
Motor Inn    with quality cherry finish furnishings. 4 suites available; 6 stories; interior corridors; conference facilities; heated indoor pool; exercise room. **Dining & Entertainment:** Dining room; 6:30 am-2:30 & 5-10 pm, Sat & Sun from 7 am; $8-$18; cocktails/lounge. **Services:** data ports; area transportation, within 5 mi, airport transportation, Northeast Airport only. Fee: coin laundry. **All Rooms:** free & pay movies, cable TV. **Some Rooms:** coffeemakers, microwaves, refrigerators. **Cards:** AE, CB, DI, DS, MC, VI. *(See ad below)*   ⒟ ⓢ ⊗

## RESTAURANTS

CAFE FLOWER SHOP    **Dinner:** $11-$20    Phone: 215/232-1076   **90**
◆    **Location:** 25th St just n of Fairmount Ave. 2501 Meredith St 19130. **Hours:** 11 am-10 pm, Sat from 9 am,
Continental    Sun 9 am-9 pm. Closed major holidays, Mon & Tues. **Features:** a la carte. Indoor Garden. **Cards:** MC, VI.

CAFE ZESTY    **Dinner:** $11-$20    Phone: 215/483-6226   **91**
◆◆    **Location:** In Manayunk, off of Interstate 76, exit 31. 4382 Main St 19127. **Hours:** 11 am-10 pm, Fri & Sat-11
Ethnic    pm. Closed major holidays & Mon. **Features:** a la carte. The open kitchen & brick pizza oven are in full view of the dining room. Smoke free premises. **Cards:** AE, DI, DS, MC, VI.   ⊗

CATFISH CAFE & STEAKHOUSE    **Dinner:** $11-$20    Phone: 215/229-9999   **92**
◆◆    **Location:** Corner of Ridge Ave & Scots Ln. 4007 Ridge Ave 19129. **Hours:** 11:30 am-2:30 & 5:30-10 pm, Fri
Steak and    & Sat-11, Sun 5:30 pm-9 pm. Closed major holidays. **Features:** a la carte. Located in a charmingly
Seafood    old-fashioned century-old building. **Cards:** AE, MC, VI.

COUNTRY CLUB RESTAURANT    **Dinner:** up to $10    Phone: 215/722-0500   **109**
Ⓐ    **Location:** On SR 73, 1 mi w of jct US 1 (Roosevelt Blvd). 1717 Cottman Ave 19111. **Hours:** 7 am-1 am, Fri
◆    & Sat 24 hours. Closed: 12/25. **Reservations:** suggested; for 6 or more. **Features:** casual dress; children's
American    menu; early bird specials; health conscious menu; cocktails; a la carte. Family owned since 1955. Bakery on premises. **Cards:** AE, DI, DS, MC, VI.

FISHERS SEAFOOD RESTAURANT    **Dinner:** up to $10    Phone: 215/725-6201   **108**
◆◆    **Location:** Jct US 1 & SR 73 (Cottman Ave), 3/4 mi w on SR 73, 1/4 mi n on Castor Ave. 7312 Castor Ave
Seafood    19152. **Hours:** 11 am-9 pm, Fri & Sat-10 pm, Sun noon-9 pm. Closed: Mon, 11/23 & 12/25.
      **Reservations:** suggested; for 5 or more. **Features:** casual dress; children's menu; early bird specials; health conscious menu; carryout; cocktails & lounge; a la carte. Popular. Nicely prepared food served in attractive dining rooms. Bakery. **Cards:** AE, MC, VI.   ⊗

ITALIAN OVEN    **Dinner:** up to $10    Phone: 215/242-4450   **93**
◆    **Location:** Corner of Moreland & Germantown Ave. 7700 Germantown Ave 19118. **Hours:** 11 am-10 pm, Fri
Italian    & Sat-11 pm. Closed major holidays. **Features:** a la carte. Upscale pizzeria & much more. **Cards:** MC, VI.

**(See PHILADELPHIA & VICINITY ACCOMMODATIONS spotting map pages A196 & A197)**

**JAKE'S** — Dinner: $11-$20 — Phone: 215/483-0444 ⑨④
◆◆◆ American — **Location:** In Manayunk, between Levering & Grape sts. 4365 Main St 19127. **Hours:** 11:30 am-2:30 & 5:30-9:30 pm, Fri-10:30 pm, Sat 5:30 pm-10:30 pm, Sun 5 pm-9 pm. Closed: 11/23. **Features:** Sunday brunch; a la carte. New American. Dining room is as much a gallery as a restaurant. Decorative sculpture & pottery is for sale. The love of color carries over to the plates & every delicious dish makes an effort to delight the eye. **Cards:** AE, DI, MC, VI.

**JOSEPH'S** — Dinner: $11-$20 — Phone: 215/755-2770 ⑨⑤
◆◆ Italian — **Location:** Between 13th & Passyunk Ave. 1915 E Passyunk Ave 19148. **Hours:** noon-3 & 5-10 pm. Closed major holidays. **Features:** a la carte. South Philly friendly, with bountiful portions. **Cards:** CB, MC, VI.

**KANSAS CITY PRIME** — Dinner: $21-$30 — Phone: 215/482-3700 ⑨⑦
◆◆◆ Steakhouse — **Location:** In Manayunk district; I-76 exit 31, 1/4 mi n on Green Ln, then 1/4 mi e on Main St. 4417 Main St 19127. **Hours:** 11:30 am-2:30 & 5:30-11 pm, Sat from 5:30, Sun 5 pm-10 pm. **Reservations:** suggested. **Features:** casual dress; carryout; cocktails & lounge; fee for valet parking; a la carte. Specializing in char-grilled steaks & seafood presented in a comfortably sophisticated atmosphere. **Cards:** AE, CB, DI, DS, MC, VI. ⊗

**LE BUS** — Dinner: $11-$20 — Phone: 215/487-0643 ⑨⑧
◆ American — **Location:** From I-76, exit 31, 1/4 mi n on Green Ln & 1/4 mi e on Main St. 4266 Main St 19127. **Hours:** Mon & Tues, 11 am-10 pm, Wed-Fri 11 am-11 pm, Sat 9:30 am-11:30 pm & Sun 9:30 am-10 am. Closed major holidays. **Reservations:** required; for 6 persons. **Features:** casual dress; Sunday brunch; children's menu; carryout; cocktails & lounge; street parking; a la carte. Lively, family oriented atmosphere. Homestyle breads, pasta, pastries & desserts. **Cards:** MC, VI.

**THE MARKER** — Dinner: $21-$30 — Phone: 215/581-5010 ⑩⑦
◆◆◆ American — **Location:** In the Adams Mark Hotel. City Ave at Monument Rd 19131. **Hours:** 11:30 am-2:30 & 5:30-10:30 pm, Fri & Sat-11 pm; Sun brunch 10:30 am & 1:30 pm seatings reservations required. **Reservations:** suggested. **Features:** semi-formal attire; early bird specials; cocktails; valet parking; a la carte. Fine dining in elegant atmosphere. Nicely presented entrees. **Cards:** AE, CB, DI, DS, MC, VI. ⊗

**POLLO ROSSO** — Dinner: $11-$20 — Phone: 215/248-9338 ⑩⓪
◆◆ Italian — **Location:** In the Chestnut Hill Hotel. 8229 Germantown Ave 19118. **Hours:** 5 pm-10 pm, Fri & Sat-11 pm, Sun-9 pm. **Features:** a la carte. Features a wood-burning pizza oven & a menu built around pastas & simple grilled dishes. Smoke free premises. **Cards:** AE, CB, DI, MC, VI. ⊗

**SONOMA** — Dinner: $11-$20 — Phone: 215/483-9400 ⑩①
◆◆ Italian — **Location:** In Manayunk district; I-76 exit 31, 1/4 mi n on Green Ln, then 1/4 mi e on Main St. 4411 Main St 19127. **Hours:** 11 am-11 pm, Fri & Sat-midnight. **Reservations:** suggested; for big parties. **Features:** casual dress; Sunday brunch; early bird specials; health conscious menu; carryout; cocktails & lounge; fee for valet parking; a la carte. "Italifornia" cuisine which combines the fresh herbs, olive oil & vegetable components of Italian cooking with the fun & casual elements of California eating. **Cards:** AE, DI, DS, MC, VI.

**STEPHEN'S** — Dinner: $21-$30 — Phone: 215/487-3136 ⑩③
◆◆ Italian — **Location:** 1 blk off of Main St, in Manayunk. 105 Shurs Ln 19127. **Hours:** 5:30 pm-10 pm, Fri & Sat 5:30 pm-11 pm, Sun 5 pm-9 pm. Closed major holidays & Mon. **Reservations:** suggested. **Features:** cocktail lounge; a la carte. A white-tablecloth restaurant without the tablecloths, dressed up with fresh flowers & candles. Located in a nicely renovated Victorian building. **Cards:** MC, VI.

**UMBRIA** — Dinner: $21-$30 — Phone: 215/242-6470 ⑩⑤
◆◆◆ Italian — **Location:** Between Germantown, Mount Pleasant & Mount Airy. 7131 Germantown Ave 19119. **Hours:** 6 pm-9 pm. Closed major holidays & Mon. **Features:** a la carte. Chic trattoria.

**ZOCALO** — Dinner: $11-$20 — Phone: 215/895-0139 ⑩⑥
◆◆◆ Regional Mexican — **Location:** 1 blk n of Market St. 3600 Lancaster Ave 19104. **Hours:** noon-2:30 & 5:30-10 pm, Fri-11 pm, Sat 5:30 pm-11 pm, Sun 5 pm-9:30 pm. Closed major holidays. **Features:** a la carte. Bright bold South West decor. Philadelphia's only hand made corn tortillas.

# PHILIPSBURG—3,000

## LODGING

**MAIN LINER MOTEL** — Rates Subject to Change — Phone: 814/342-2004
🌸 ◆ Motel — All Year — 1P: $28 — 2P/1B: $31- 39 — 2P/2B: $33 — XP: $6 — D9
**Location:** 1 3/4 mi w on US 322. 16866 (RD 3, Box 115). **Terms:** Sr. discount; reserv deposit; weekly/monthly rates; small pets only, $6. **Facility:** 21 rooms. Located outside of town, quiet. 1 story; exterior corridors. **Dining:** Restaurant nearby. **All Rooms:** cable TV. **Cards:** AE, DS, MC, VI. Ⓓ ⊗

# PINE GROVE—3,700

## LODGINGS

**COMFORT INN** — Guaranteed Rates — Phone: 717/345-8031

| ◆◆ Motel | | 1P | | 2P/1B | | 2P/2B | | XP | |
|---|---|---|---|---|---|---|---|---|---|
| 10/4-10/7 | | 1P: $115 | | 2P/1B: $115 | | 2P/2B: $115 | | XP: $5 | F17 |
| 5/1-10/3 | | 1P: $50- | 75 | 2P/1B: $55- | 80 | 2P/2B: $55- | 80 | XP: $5 | F17 |
| 11/1-4/30 | | 1P: $40- | 60 | 2P/1B: $45- | 65 | 2P/2B: $45- | 65 | XP: $5 | F17 |
| 10/8-10/31 | | 1P: $45- | 55 | 2P/1B: $50- | 60 | 2P/2B: $50- | 60 | XP: $5 | F17 |

**Location:** I-81, exit 31. 17963 (PO Box 327). Fax: 717/345-2308. **Terms:** Sr. discount; reserv deposit; pets, $10. **Facility:** 68 rooms. 3 stories; exterior corridors; heated indoor pool; exercise room. **Dining:** Restaurant nearby. **All Rooms:** cable TV. **Some Rooms:** Fee: VCP's. **Cards:** AE, CB, DI, DS, MC, VI. *(See ad below)* Ⓓ Ⓢ ⊗

## ECONO LODGE

| | Rates Subject to Change | | | Phone: 717/345-4099 |
|---|---|---|---|---|

(AAA)
◆◆
Motel

5/1-9/30    1P: $40- 50   2P/1B: $45- 60   2P/2B: $45- 60   XP: $5
10/1-4/30   1P: $35- 45   2P/1B: $40- 50   2P/2B: $40- 50   XP: $5
**Location:** I-81 exit 31, 1 blk e on Rt 443. 17963 (RD 1, Box 581). Fax: 717/345-4984. **Terms:** Reserv deposit; pets, $3. **Facility:** 50 rooms. Convenient interstate access. Mountain setting. 2 stories; interior/exterior corridors. **Dining:** Restaurant nearby. **All Rooms:** free movies, cable TV. **Some Rooms:** refrigerators.
Fee: VCP's. **Cards:** AE, CB, DI, DS, MC, VI.  Ⓓ ⊗

# PITTSBURGH—369,900   (See DOWNTOWN PITTSBURGH ACCOMMODATIONS spotting map page A204; see index below)

> To help you more easily locate accommodations in the Greater Pittsburgh area, the following two indexes and maps show lodgings and restaurants in multiple cities. Listings for these establishments are found under the heading for the city in which they are located. The Pittsburgh area comprises: Blawnox, Bridgeville, Coraopolis, Crafton, Evans City, Gibsonia, Greentree, Harmarville, Heidelberg, Mars, Monroeville, New Kensington, Oakdale, Oakmont, Pittsburgh, Pleasant Hills, Robinson and Wexford.

### Airport Accommodations

Listings for these establishments are found under the heading for the city in which they are located.

**PITTSBURGH**

Courtyard by Marriott, 6 mi e of airport/CORAOPOLIS
Days Inn-Pittsburgh Airport, 6 1/2 mi e of airport/CORAOPOLIS
(AAA) Embassy Suites-Pittsburgh International Airport, 6 mi e of airport/CORAOPOLIS
(AAA) Hampton Inn Hotel Airport, 6 1/2 mi n of airport/CORAOPOLIS
(AAA) La Quinta Inn-Airport, 6 1/2 mi n of airport/CORAOPOLIS
(AAA) Pittsburgh Airport Inn Best Western, 6 mi se of airport/CORAOPOLIS
(AAA) Pittsburgh Airport Marriott, 1 1/4 mi se of airport/CORAOPOLIS
(AAA) Red Roof Inn Pittsburgh Airport, 6 1/2 mi n of airport/CORAOPOLIS
(AAA) Red Roof Inn South Airport, 9 mi e of airport via SR 60S/PITTSBURGH

## LODGINGS

### HYATT REGENCY PITTSBURGH AT CHATHAM CENTER

| | Rates Subject to Change | Phone: 412/471-1234 | ❹ |
|---|---|---|---|

(AAA)
◆◆◆
Hotel

Sun-Thurs   1P: $112- 175   2P/1B: $112- 175   2P/2B: $137- 175   XP: $25  F18
Fri & Sat    1P: $89- 99    2P/1B: $89- 99     2P/2B: $89- 99      XP: $25  F18
**Location:** On Center Ave, just e of Crosstown Blvd, opposite Civic Arena. 112 Washington Pl 15219. Fax: 412/355-0315. **Terms:** Sr. discount; reserv deposit; 15% service charge; no pets. **Facility:** 400 rooms. Presidential suite $350 for 1-bedroom, $500 2-bedroom, whirlpool, wet bar, kitchenette; 21 stories; interior corridors; conference facilities; heated indoor pool, saunas, whirlpools; exercise room. Fee: parking. **Dining & Entertainment:** Dining room; 6:30 am-2 am; $10-$22; cocktails/lounge. **Services:** data ports, secretarial services; valet laundry. Fee: childcare; massage; valet parking. **All Rooms:** cable TV. Fee: movies, VCP. **Some Rooms:** coffeemakers. **Cards:** AE, CB, DI, DS, MC, VI.  ⚏ Ⓓ Ⓢ ⊗

### PITTSBURGH HILTON & TOWERS

| | AAA Special Value Rates | Phone: 412/391-4600 | ❷ |
|---|---|---|---|

(AAA)
◆◆◆
Hotel

Mon-Thurs   1P: $124- 174   2P/1B: $149- 199   2P/2B: $149- 199   XP: $25  F18
Fri-Sun     1P: $89- 99    2P/1B: $89- 99     2P/2B: $89- 99      XP: $25  F18
**Location:** In Gateway Center, on Commonwealth Pl, opposite Point State Park. Gateway Center 15222. Fax: 412/594-5161. **Terms:** Credit card guarantee, 3 day notice; package plans; small pets only, $100 dep req. **Facility:** 712 rooms. Some units with in-room fax. 24 stories; interior corridors; business center, conference facilities; exercise room. Fee: parking. **Dining & Entertainment:** 2 dining rooms; 6:30 am-11:30 pm; $7-$28; cocktails/lounge. **Services:** data ports; valet laundry. Fee: valet parking. **All Rooms:** honor bars, free & pay movies, cable TV. **Some Rooms:** coffeemakers, VCP's. **Cards:** AE, CB, DI, DS, JCB, MC, VI. *(See ad p 28)*  ⬚ ⚏ Ⓓ Ⓢ Ⓢ ⊗

### THE PRIORY-A CITY INN

| | Rates Subject to Change | Phone: 412/231-3338 | ❶ |
|---|---|---|---|

(AAA)
◆◆◆
Historic Bed
& Breakfast

Sun-Thurs [CP]   1P: $68- 100   2P/1B: $95- 110            XP: $12  F7
Fri & Sat [CP]   1P: $90        2P/1B: $90                 XP: $12  F7
**Location:** 614 Pressley St 15212. Fax: 412/231-4838. **Terms:** Reserv deposit; package plans, Sat & Sun; no pets. **Facility:** 24 rooms. Historic Inn built in 1888 to house Benedictine priests traveling through Pittsburgh. Restored to 19th-century elegance with added modern appointments. 3 stories, no elevator; interior corridors. **Services:** complimentary evening beverages; area transportation, 7-11 am weekdays. **All Rooms:** combo & shower baths, cable TV. **Cards:** AE, CB, DI, DS, MC, VI. *(See color ad p A205)*  Ⓓ Ⓢ

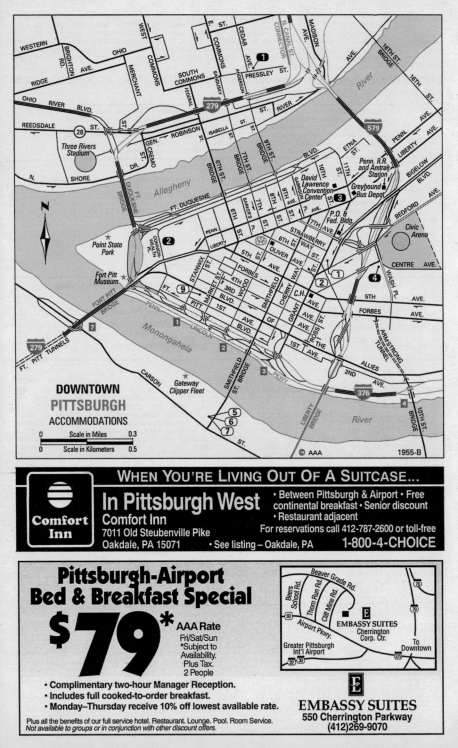

DOWNTOWN
PITTSBURGH
ACCOMMODATIONS

Scale in Miles 0 — 0.3
Scale in Kilometers 0 — 0.5

© AAA

1955-B

**(See DOWNTOWN PITTSBURGH ACCOMMODATIONS spotting map page A204)**

VISTA INTERNATIONAL HOTEL PITTSBURGH ◆◆◆ All Year
Hotel
Guaranteed Rates     Phone: 412/281-3700 **3**
1P: $153- 196   2P/1B: $175- 210   2P/2B: $175- 210   XP: $20   F12
**Location:** At Liberty Center. 1000 Penn Ave 15222. Fax: 412/227-4500. **Terms:** Sr. discount; reserv deposit, 7 day notice; $1 service charge; package plans; small pets only. **Facility:** 616 rooms. 26 stories; interior corridors; business center, conference facilities; heated indoor pool, saunas, steamrooms, whirlpool. Fee: parking; exercise room. **Dining & Entertainment:** 2 restaurants; 6:30 am-10:30 pm, limited menu-2 am; $10-$25; cocktails/lounge; nightclub. **Services:** secretarial services; valet laundry; area transportation, area restaurants. Fee: childcare, airport transportation; valet parking. **All Rooms:** honor bars, cable TV. Fee: movies. **Some Rooms:** 6 kitchens, microwaves, refrigerators. Fee: VCP's. **Cards:** AE, CB, DI, DS, MC, VI.   Ⓓ Ⓢ ⊗

## RESTAURANTS

CHEESE CELLAR RESTAURANT ◆◆
American
**Dinner:** up to $10     Phone: 412/471-3355 ⑦
**Location:** At Station Square, Smithfield & Carson sts. 25 Freight House Shops 15219. **Hours:** 11:30 am-midnight, Fri & Sat-1 am, Sun 10:30 am-11 pm. Closed: 12/25. **Features:** casual dress; children's menu; health conscious menu items; carryout; cocktails & lounge; fee for parking; a la carte. Variety of cheese & pasta dishes. **Cards:** AE, DI, DS, MC, VI.

GRAND CONCOURSE RESTAURANT   Historical ◆◆◆
American
**Dinner:** $11-$20     Phone: 412/261-1717 ⑤
**Location:** S end of Smithfield St Bridge, Grant St exit from I-376, in Pittsburgh & Lake Erie Railroad Terminal Bldg, at Station Square. 1 Station Square 15219. **Hours:** 11:30 am-2:30 & 4:30-10 pm, Fri-11 pm, Sat 4:30 pm-11 pm, Sun 10 am-2:30 & 4:30-9 pm. Closed: 1/1 & 12/25. **Reservations:** suggested. **Features:** Sunday brunch; children's menu; senior's menu; carryout; cocktails & lounge; entertainment; fee for parking; a la carte. Impressive dining rooms in restored 1901 railroad terminal. Baroque styling typical of transition between Victorian & Edwardian eras. Seafood featured. **Cards:** AE, DI, DS, MC, VI.   ⊗

RUTH'S CHRIS STEAK HOUSE ◆◆◆
Steakhouse
**Dinner:** $21-$30     Phone: 412/391-4800 ⑨
**Location:** On the plaza at PPG Place. 6 PPG Pl 15222. **Hours:** 11:30 am-3 & 5-10:30 pm, Fri-11 pm, Sat 5 pm-11 pm, Sun 5 pm-9 pm. Closed major holidays. **Reservations:** suggested. **Features:** semi-formal attire; cocktails & lounge; fee for parking; a la carte. Serves US prime beef as a standard. **Cards:** AE, DI, MC, VI.

TEQUILA JUNCTION ◆
Mexican
**Dinner:** $11-$20     Phone: 412/261-3265 ⑥
**Location:** Station Square Shops, Carson & Smithfield sts. 31 Station Sq 15219. **Hours:** 11:30 am-10 pm, Fri & Sat-midnight, Sun noon-10 pm. Closed: 1/1, 4/3 & 12/25. **Features:** casual dress; children's menu; carryout; cocktails & lounge; fee for parking; a la carte. Southwestern decor, located on 2nd floor, overlooking mall. **Cards:** AE, DI, DS, MC, VI.

THE TERRACE ROOM ◆◆
Continental
**Dinner:** $21-$30     Phone: 412/281-7100 ②
**Location:** Opposite Mellon Square, between Oliver St & 6th Ave, in The Westin Wiliam Penn. 530 William Penn Pl 15219. **Hours:** 6:30 am-11 pm, Sat-midnight. **Reservations:** suggested. **Features:** Sunday brunch; children's menu; cocktails & lounge; fee for parking; a la carte. A fine dining experience. American cuisine also featured. **Cards:** AE, DI, DS, MC, VI.   ⊗

TOP OF THE TRIANGLE ◆◆◆
American
DS, MC, VI.
**Dinner:** $21-$30     Phone: 412/471-4100 ①
**Location:** On 62nd floor of USX Tower. 600 Grant St 15219. **Hours:** 11:30 am-3 & 5:30-10 pm, Sat noon-3 & 5:30-11 pm, Sun 4 pm-9 pm. Closed: 9/4 & 12/25. **Reservations:** suggested. **Features:** semi-formal attire; children's menu; carryout; cocktails & lounge; fee for parking; a la carte. Panoramic city view. **Cards:** AE, DI, ⊗

**FIRE SAFETY MEANS FIRE SENSE.**
Read Hotel and Motel Fire Safety.

## GREATER PITTSBURGH (See PITTSBURGH ACCOMMODATIONS spotting map page A207; see index below)

Our **bold type** listings have a special interest in serving you!

(See PITTSBURGH ACCOMMODATIONS spotting map below)

## LODGINGS

**DAYS INN PITTSBURGH**   Rates Subject to Change   **Phone:** 412/531-8900   **33**
All Year   1P: $50   2P/1B: $55   2P/2B: $55   XP: $5   F16
**Location:** 3 1/2 mi s on US 19. 1150 Banksville Rd 15216. **Fax:** 412/531-7630. **Terms:** Credit card guarantee, 3 day notice; weekly rates; no pets. **Facility:** 70 rooms. 2 stories; interior/exterior corridors; meeting rooms; pool. **Services:** airport transportation. **All Rooms:** free movies, cable TV. **Cards:** AE, CB, DI, DS, MC, VI. *(See color ad below)*

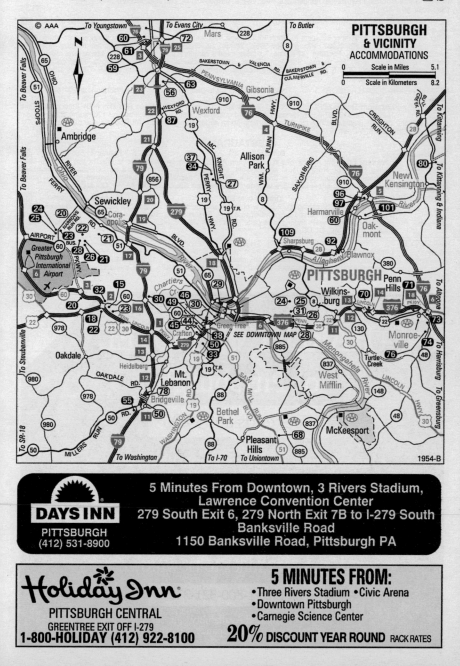

**(See PITTSBURGH ACCOMMODATIONS spotting map page A207)**

**HOLIDAY INN-PITTSBURGH CENTRAL (GREENTREE)**   Rates Subject to Change   **Phone:** 412/922-8100   38
All Year          1P: $79- 114   2P/1B: $87- 124   2P/2B: $87- 124   XP: $10   F18
Motor Inn   **Location:** 3 mi sw via I-279, US 22 & 30, exit 4, 1 mi nw via Mansfield Ave. 401 Holiday Dr 15220.
**Fax:** 412/922-6511. **Terms:** Credit card guarantee; 15% service charge; package plans; weekend rates available; pets. **Facility:** 200 rooms. 4 stories; interior corridors; meeting rooms; heated pool; exercise room, racket club privileges. **Dining:** Dining room; 6:30 am-11 pm; $9-$15; cocktails. **Services:** data ports; valet laundry; area transportation, within 5 miles, airport transportation. **Fee:** childcare. **All Rooms:** coffeemakers, free & pay movies. **Some Rooms:** microwaves, refrigerators. **Fee:** VCP's. **Cards:** AE, DI, DS, JCB, MC, VI.
*(See color ad p A207)*                                                                                    Ⓓ ⊗

**HOLIDAY INN PITTSBURGH-MCKNIGHT ROAD**   Rates Subject to Change   **Phone:** 412/366-5200   34
◆◆◆   All Year          1P: $69- 109   2P/1B: $69- 109   2P/2B: $69- 109   XP: $10   F18
Motor Inn   **Location:** 7 mi n; adjacent to North Hills Village Mall, enter at n end of plaza by the appliance store. 4859 McKnight Rd 15237. **Fax:** 412/366-5682. **Terms:** Sr. discount; 15% service charge; monthly rates; BP available; package plans; pets. **Facility:** 147 rooms. 7 stories; interior corridors; conference facilities; luxury level rooms; pool. **Dining:** Dining room; 6:30 am-10 pm, Sun from 7 am; $7-$18; cocktails. **Services:** data ports. **Fee:** coin laundry. **All Rooms:** coffeemakers, free & pay movies. **Some Rooms:** microwaves, refrigerators. **Cards:** AE, CB, DI, DS, MC, VI.
                                                                                                           Ⓓ ⊗

**RED ROOF INN SOUTH AIRPORT**   Rates Subject to Change   **Phone:** 412/787-7870   32
◆◆   All Year          1P: $35- 41   2P/1B: $42- 48   2P/2B: $52- 58   XP: $6   F18
Motel   **Location:** On SR 60, 2 blks e of jct US 22 & 30; 3 1/2 mi w of I-79, Moon Run exit. 6404 Steubenville Pike 15205. **Fax:** 412/787-8392. **Terms:** Credit card guarantee; small pets only. **Facility:** 120 rooms. 2 stories; exterior corridors. **Dining:** Restaurant nearby. **Services:** data ports; airport transportation. **All Rooms:** free movies, cable TV. **Cards:** AE, CB, DI, DS, MC, VI.                                                                      Ⓓ ⊗

## RESTAURANTS

**THE BALCONY**          **Dinner:** $11-$20          **Phone:** 412/687-0110   25
◆◆   **Location:** From 5th Ave, 3 blks n on S Aiken Ave, 3 blks e on Walnut St; in the Theatre Building. 5520
American   Walnut St 15232. **Hours:** 11:30 am-midnight, Fri & Sat-1 am, Sun 11 am-3 pm. Closed major holidays. **Reservations:** suggested; 6 or more only. **Features:** casual dress; Sunday brunch; children's menu; carryout; cocktails; entertainment; street parking; a la carte. New American cuisine. **Cards:** AE, DI, DS, MC, VI.

**CHRISTOPHER'S**          **Dinner:** over $31          **Phone:** 412/381-4500   30
   **Location:** Atop Mt Washington, 2 blks w of Duquesne Incline. 1411 Grandview Ave 15211. **Hours:** 5 pm-10
◆◆◆   pm, Fri & Sat-11 pm. Closed major holidays & Sun. **Reservations:** suggested. **Features:** semi-formal attire;
American   cocktails & lounge; valet parking; a la carte. Panoramic view. Continental as well as New American/Western cuisine. **Cards:** AE, DI, DS, MC, VI.                                                                      ⊗

**GULLIFTY'S**          **Dinner:** $11-$20          **Phone:** 412/521-8222   26
◆◆   **Location:** 3 blks s of Forbes Ave, 1 mi n of I-376, Squirrel Hill exit. 1922 Murray Ave 15217. **Hours:** 11
American   am-midnight, Fri & Sat-1 am, Sun 10 am-midnight. **Closed:** 11/23 & 12/25. **Features:** casual dress; Sunday brunch; children's menu; carryout; cocktails & lounge; street parking. Large menu selection. **Cards:** AE, DI,
DS, MC, VI.                                                                                                 ⊗

**(See PITTSBURGH ACCOMMODATIONS spotting map page A207)**

**JIMMY TSANG'S CHINESE RESTAURANT**    Dinner: $11-$20    Phone: 412/661-4226    (24)
Location: Jct Centre & Negley aves, 3 blks n of 5th Ave. 5700 Centre Ave 15206. Hours: 11:30 am-10 pm,
Fri & Sat-11 pm, Sun 3:30 pm-9 pm. Closed: 7/4 & 11/23. Reservations: suggested. Features: casual
dress; early bird specials; carryout; cocktails; a la carte. A variety of Oriental cuisines including Mandarin,
Chinese    Szechuan, Cantonese, Hunan & Korean. Cards: AE, CB, DI, MC, VI. *(See color ad below)*    ⊗

**LE MONT RESTAURANT**    Dinner: over $31    Phone: 412/431-3100    (29)
Location: Atop Mt Washington, adjacent to the Duquesne Incline. 1114 Grandview Ave 15211. Hours: 5
pm-11 pm, Fri & Sat-midnight, Sun 4 pm-10 pm. Closed major holidays. Reservations: suggested.
Features: semi-formal attire; children's menu; health conscious menu items; carryout; cocktails & lounge; fee
Continental    for valet parking. Continental decor. Panoramic view of downtown area. Cards: AE, DI, DS, JCB, MC, VI.    ⊗

**LONG NECKER'S**    Dinner: $11-$20    Phone: 412/366-5200    (37)
Location: 7 mi n, adjacent to North Hills Village Mall, enter at n end of plaza by appliance store. 4859
Seafood    McKnight Rd 15237. Hours: 6:30 am-10 pm. Reservations: suggested. Features: casual dress; Sunday
brunch; children's menu; early bird specials; senior's menu; carryout; salad bar; cocktails. Seafood buffet on
Fri. Cards: AE, CB, DI, DS, JCB, MC, VI.    & ⊗

**OLD COUNTRY BUFFET**    Dinner: up to $10    Phone: 412/369-8801    (27)
Location: In North Hills Village Mall. 4801 McKnight Rd 15237. Hours: 11 am-8 pm, Fri & Sat-9 pm, Sun 8
American    am-8 pm. Closed: 12/25. Features: casual dress. Budget traveler & family oriented.    ⊗

**PASTA PIATTO**    Dinner: $11-$20    Phone: 412/621-5547    (31)
Location: 5 mi e on 5th Ave, 2 blks n on S Aiken, 1 blk e on Walnut-Shadyside District. 736 Bellefonte
15232. Hours: 11:30 am-3 & 4:30-10 pm, Wed, Fri & Sat-11 pm, Sun 3 pm-9 pm. Closed major holidays.
Features: children's menu; early bird specials; carryout; cocktails & lounge; a la carte. A variety of pasta
Italian    made fresh on premises. Very popular. Cards: AE, MC, VI.    ⊗

**POLI RESTAURANT**    Dinner: $11-$20    Phone: 412/521-6400    (28)
Location: I-376, 1/4 mi n of exit 8, following signs to Squirrel Hill. 2607 Murray Ave 15217. Hours: 11:30
am-11 pm, Sun 11 am-9:30 pm. Closed: Mon, 11/23 & 12/25. Features: casual dress; Sunday brunch; early
bird specials; carryout; cocktails & lounge; fee for valet parking; a la carte. Popular. Family-run since 1921.
Seafood    Extensive menu. Cards: AE, CB, DI, MC, VI.    ⊗

**RED BULL INN**    Dinner: $11-$20    Phone: 412/787-2855    (23)
Location: 7 mi w on I-279, US 22 & 30 exit, 1 blk n on SR 60, then e on Campbell's Run Rd. 5205
American    Campbell's Run Rd 15205. Hours: 11 am-11 pm, Fri-midnight, Sat 4 pm-midnight, Sun 4 pm-9 pm. Closed:
12/25. Features: casual dress; children's menu; salad bar; cocktails; a la carte. Traditional casual dining with
prime rib featured. Cards: AE, DI, DS, MC, VI.    ⊗

## PITTSTON—9,400

### RESTAURANT

**COOPER'S ON THE WATERFRONT**    Dinner: $11-$20    Phone: 717/654-6883
Location: Center. 304 Kennedy Blvd 18640. Hours: 11 am-11 pm, 4 pm-11 pm Mon-Tues, Fri 11
am-midnight, Sun 10 am-9 pm. Closed: 4/7, 5/29, 7/4 11/23 & 12/25. Features: casual dress; children's
menu; carryout; cocktails & lounge. Large variety of fresh seafood & meat entrees. Cards: DS, MC, VI.    ⊗
South French

## PLEASANT HILLS—8,900    (See PITTSBURGH ACCOMMODATIONS spotting map page A207; see index starting on page A206)

### RESTAURANT

**OLDE COUNTRY BUFFET**    Dinner: up to $10    Phone: 412/653-2422    (68)
Location: 10 mi s on SR 51, in Southland Shopping Center, 1/4 mi s of Century III Mall. 591 Clairton Blvd
American    15216. Hours: 11 am-8:30 pm, Fri-9 pm, Sat 8 am-9 pm, Sun 8 am-8:30 pm. Closed: 12/25.
Features: children's menu. Budget traveler & family oriented.    ⊗

## PLEASANT MOUNT

### RESTAURANT

**FIELDSTONE INN & RESTAURANT II**    Dinner: up to $10    Phone: 717/448-2623
Location: 8 mi e on SR 371, 3 mi n on Dixon Valley Rd. Hours: 10 am-10 pm, Fri & Sat-11 pm, Sun 7:30
American    am-9 pm. Closed: Mon & 12/25. Features: casual dress; children's menu; carryout. Family oriented, daily
specials. Cards: MC, VI.

## PLEASANTVILLE—200

### LODGING

**WEST VU MOTEL**                    Guaranteed Rates                              **Phone:** 814/839-2632
   All Year              1P:  $25        2P/1B:  $30        2P/2B:  $34        XP:  $4        D
   **Location:** On SR 56, just e of jct SR 96. (Rd 1, Box 366). **Terms:** Reserv deposit, 3 day notice;
◆   weekly/monthly rates; pets, $5. **Facility:** 16 rooms. Well-maintained grounds, spacious rooms. 1 two-bedroom
Motel  unit. 6 kitchen units, $34-$42; 1 story; exterior corridors. **All Rooms:** free movies, cable TV, no phones.
   **Some Rooms:** refrigerators. **Cards:** AE, DS, MC, VI.                    Ⓓ ⊗

**PLYMOUTH MEETING**  (See PHILADELPHIA & VICINITY ACCOMMODATIONS spotting
  map pages A196 & A197; see index starting on page A193)

### LODGING

**GUEST QUARTERS**                   Rates Subject to Change                      **Phone:** 610/834-8300   Ⓖ⑥
◆◆◆   Fri-Sun            1P:  $94        2P/1B:  $94        2P/2B:  $94        XP:  $10    F17
Suite Hotel  Mon-Thurs        1P:  $145- 155  2P/1B:  $155- 165                  XP:  $10    F17
   **Location:** I-276, exit 25, 2/10 mi w on Plymouth Rd, 1/4 mi n on Germantown Pike; then 2/10 mi e on
Hickory Rd. 640 W Germantown Pike 19462. Fax: 610/834-7813. **Terms:** Sr. discount; reserv deposit, 3 day notice; no pets.
**Facility:** 252 rooms. Large tropically landscaped atrium center with suites bordering. 1 two-bedroom unit. 7 stories; interior
corridors; business center, conference facilities; heated indoor pool, wading pool, sauna, whirlpool; exercise room. **Dining &**
**Entertainment:** Dining room; 6:30 am-10:30, 11-2:30 & 5-10:30 pm; $10-$21; cocktails/lounge. **Services:** secretarial
services; area transportation, within 1 mi. Fee: coin laundry. **All Rooms:** free & pay movies, cable TV. **Some Rooms:** honor
bars, microwaves, refrigerators, whirlpools. **Cards:** AE, CB, DI, DS, JCB, MC, VI. *(See ad p A199)*   Ⓐ Ⓓ Ⓢ ⊗

### RESTAURANT

**HOULIHAN'S RESTAURANT**            **Dinner:** $11-$20                           **Phone:** 610/825-2537   ⑪②
◆◆    **Location:** On US 422, 1/2 mi n of tpk exit 25. 601 W Germantown Pike 19462. **Hours:** 11:30 am-11 pm, Fri-
American   11:30 pm, Sat 11 am-11:30 pm, Sun noon-10 pm. Closed: 12/25. **Reservations:** suggested; weekends.
   **Features:** casual dress; children's menu; early bird specials; health conscious menu; carryout; cocktails &
lounge; a la carte. Well-prepared portions served in a lively setting. **Cards:** AE, CB, DI, DS, MC, VI.                ⊗

## POCONO MOUNTAINS

> To help you more easily locate accommodations in the Pocono Mountains area, the fol-
> lowing index and map show lodgings and restaurants in multiple cities. Listings for
> these establishments are found under the heading for the city in which they are located.
> The Pocono Mountains area comprises: Archbald, Bartonsville, Bushkill, Canadensis,
> Clarks Summit, Cresco, Delaware Water Gap, Drinker, Dickson City, Dunmore, East
> Stroudsburg, Hamlin, Jermyn, Moosic, Mount Pocono, Oakdale, Scranton, Snydersville,
> Stroudsburg, Swiftwater, White Haven and Wilkes-Barre.

## Crescent Lodge

Experience the charm of a romantic Country Inn with flowered walkways, sparkling outdoor pool, hiking and fitness trails. Central to all winter sports.
 Enjoy a newly refurbished room in the Inn or a private cottage with whirlpool tub, log burning fireplace and private sun deck.
 Dine in one of the finest restaurants in the Pocono Mts.

Located 90 miles from New York City and Philadelphia in Paradise Valley, Cresco, Pa. 18326

◆◆◆ *A Classic Country Inn*

**Reservations and Free Brochure 800-392-9400**

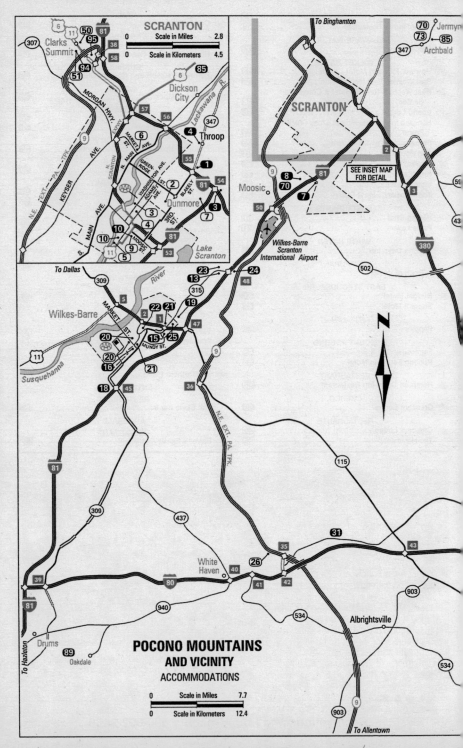

POCONO MOUNTAINS
**AND VICINITY**
ACCOMMODATIONS

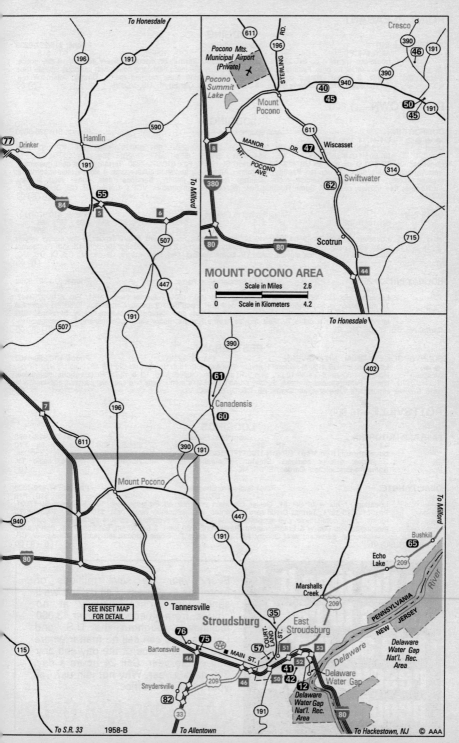

MOUNT POCONO AREA

| 0 | Scale in Miles | 2.6 |
| 0 | Scale in Kilometers | 4.2 |

# POINT PLEASANT

## LODGING

**TATTERSALL INN**
Guaranteed Rates
Phone: 215/297-8233
All Year [CP]　1P: $60- 99　2P/1B: $70- 109　XP: $15
**Location:** 1/2 mi n on SR 32. 16 Cafferty Rd 18950. **Terms:** Sr. discount; reserv deposit, 10 day notice; weekly rates; no pets. **Facility:** 6 rooms. 18th-century plastered fieldstone house with spacious antique filled
Historic Bed rooms. 2 stories; interior corridors; designated smoking area; meeting rooms. **Dining:** Afternoon tea.
& Breakfast **All Rooms:** combo & shower baths, no phones, no TVs. **Cards:** AE, DS, MC, VI.　Ⓓ ⊗

# POTTSTOWN—21,800

## LODGINGS

**COMFORT INN**
AAA Special Value Rates
Phone: 610/326-5000
Motel　5/1-11/14, Mon-Thurs
11/15-3/30 & 3/31-4/30 [CP]　1P: $59- 69　2P/1B: $59- 69　2P/2B: $59- 69　XP: $7　F18
Fri-Sun 11/15-3/30 [CP]　1P: $54- 61　2P/1B: $54- 61　2P/2B: $54- 61　XP: $7　F18
**Location:** On SR 100, 1 mi n of jct US 422. 99 Robinson St 19464. **Fax:** 610/970-7230. **Terms:** Credit card guarantee; weekly/monthly rates; pets, $25 dep req. **Facility:** 121 rooms. Attractively furnished guest rooms. 4 stories; interior corridors; meeting rooms; heated pool; exercise room. **Dining:** Restaurant nearby. **Services:** data ports; valet laundry. **All Rooms:** free movies, cable TV. **Some Rooms:** Fee: microwaves, refrigerators, VCP's. **Cards:** AE, CB, DI, DS, JCB, MC, VI.　Ⓓ Ⓢ ⊗

**DAYS INN**
Rates Subject to Change
Phone: 610/970-1101
5/1-10/31 [CP]　1P: $43　2P/1B: $43　2P/2B: $55- 85　XP: $5
11/1-4/30 [CP]　1P: $34　2P/1B: $34　2P/2B: $45　XP: $5
Motel **Location:** 29 High St 19464. **Fax:** 610/327-8643. **Terms:** Sr. discount; reserv deposit, 3 day notice; weekly rates; small pets only, $10, $10 dep req. **Facility:** 60 rooms. 2 stories; exterior corridors. **Dining:** Restaurant nearby. **All Rooms:** free movies, cable TV. **Some Rooms:** Fee: refrigerators. **Cards:** AE, CB, DI, DS, MC, VI.　Ⓓ ⊗

**HOLIDAY INN EXPRESS**
AAA Special Value Rates
Phone: 610/327-3300
All Year [CP]　1P: $64　2P/1B: $64　2P/2B: $64　XP: $5　F19
**Location:** Jct US 422 & Armand Hammer Blvd exit. 1600 Industrial Hwy 19464. **Fax:** 610/327-9447.
Motel **Terms:** Reserv deposit; weekly rates; small pets only. **Facility:** 119 rooms. Comfortably furnished traditional motel rooms. 4 stories; interior corridors; meeting rooms; pool. **Dining:** Restaurant nearby. **Services:** valet laundry. **All Rooms:** cable TV. Fee: movies. **Some Rooms:** honor bars, coffeemakers. Fee: refrigerators.
**Cards:** AE, CB, DI, DS, MC, VI.　Ⓩ Ⓓ Ⓢ ⊗

## RESTAURANT

**SUNNYBROOK COLONIAL INN & TAVERN**
Dinner: $21-$30
Phone: 610/326-6400
American **Location:** Jct US 422, at Armand Hammer Blvd exit, e to High St, right on Old US 422. Old US 422 19464.
**Hours:** 11:30 am-2 & 4:30-10 pm, Sun 9:30 am-2 pm. **Closed:** Mon, 1/1 & 12/25. **Reservations:** suggested; dinner. **Features:** casual dress; Sunday brunch; children's menu; early bird specials; carryout; cocktails; a la carte. Colonial atmosphere. Daily specials. **Cards:** AE, CB, DI, DS, MC, VI.

# POTTSVILLE—16,600

## LODGINGS

**FAIRLANE MOTOR INN**
Guaranteed Rates
Phone: 717/429-1696
All Year　1P: $29　2P/1B: $36　2P/2B: $36　XP: $9　F10
**Location:** 1 mi n on SR 61. SR 61N 17901 (PO Box 600). **Terms:** Reserv deposit; no pets. **Facility:** 23 rooms.
Motel 2 stories; exterior corridors. **Dining:** Restaurant nearby. **All Rooms:** free movies, cable TV.
**Some Rooms:** kitchen. **Cards:** AE, DS, MC, VI.　Ⓓ

**QUALITY HOTEL**
Rates Subject to Change
Phone: 717/622-4600
All Year　1P: $71　2P/1B: $81　2P/2B: $81　XP: $10　F18
**Location:** 1 blk w of SR 61, Center City-Main entrance off Progress Ave. 100 S Center St 17901.
Motor Inn **Fax:** 717/628-5971. **Terms:** Credit card guarantee; weekly/monthly rates; pets, $10 dep req. **Facility:** 70 rooms. Large, comfortable, well appointed rooms. Originally a department store. 4 stories; interior corridors; meeting rooms. **Dining & Entertainment:** Restaurant; 6:30 am-2 & 5-9:30 pm, Sat from 7 am, Sun 7 am-2 pm; $8-$19; cocktails/lounge. **Services:** valet laundry. **All Rooms:** cable TV. **Some Rooms:** refrigerators. **Cards:** AE, CB, DI, DS, JCB, MC, VI.　Ⓓ Ⓢ ⊗

# PUNXSUTAWNEY—6,800

## LODGINGS

**COUNTRY VILLA MOTEL** — Rates Subject to Change — Phone: 814/938-8330
All Year — 1P: $30- 34 — 2P/1B: $36- 40 — 2P/2B: $40- 44 — XP: $4 — D6
**Motor Inn** — **Location:** 1 1/2 mi s on US 119. (RD 1, Box 77). **Terms:** Reserv deposit; weekly/monthly rates; pets, $4. **Facility:** 27 rooms. Budget traveler oriented, in the outskirts of town. 2 two-bedroom units. 2 stories; exterior corridors. **Dining & Entertainment:** Restaurant; 6 am-9 pm, Sun 8:30 am-7:30 pm; $5-$16; cocktail lounge. **All Rooms:** combo & shower baths, cable TV. **Some Rooms:** 2 efficiencies. **Cards:** AE, DI, DS, MC, VI.

**PANTALL HOTEL** — Rates Subject to Change — Phone: 814/938-6600
All Year — 1P: $39- 85 — 2P/1B: $47- 93 — 2P/2B: $47- 93 — XP: $8 — D12
**Historic Hotel** — **Location:** Town Center; on US 119 & SR 36. 135 E Mahoning St 15767. Fax: 814/938-8592. **Terms:** Reserv deposit, 7 day notice; weekly/monthly rates; pets. **Facility:** 57 rooms. Older architecture, built in 1888. 4 stories; interior corridors; meeting rooms; Recreation facilities avail at nearby parks. Fee: parking. **Dining & Entertainment:** Dining room, restaurant; 7 am-9 pm; $5-$11; cocktails/lounge. **All Rooms:** combo & shower baths, cable TV. **Cards:** AE, DS, MC, VI.

# QUAKERTOWN—9,000

## LODGING

**BEST WESTERN MOTOR INN** — Guaranteed Rates — Phone: 215/536-2500
All Year — 1P: $60- 172 — 2P/1B: $68- 80 — 2P/2B: $68- 80 — XP: $8 — F12
**Motel** — **Location:** E of jct SR 313 & 309. 1446 W Broad St 18951. Fax: 215/536-2508. **Terms:** Sr. discount; reserv deposit; no pets. **Facility:** 40 rooms. Comfortably furnished guest rooms. 2 stories; interior corridors; meeting rooms; exercise room. **Dining:** Breakfast room for guests only, 6-10 am. **Services:** data ports. Fee: coin laundry. **All Rooms:** cable TV. **Cards:** AE, CB, DI, DS, MC, VI. *(See ad below)*

# READING—78,400

## RESTAURANT

**WIDOW FINNEYS** Historical — Dinner: $11-$20 — Phone: 610/378-1776
**Location:** Center at 4th & Cherry St. 30 S 4th St 19602. **Hours:** 5 pm-9 pm, Fri & Sat-9:30 pm. Closed: Sun, Mon, 1/1 & 12/25. **Reservations:** suggested. **Features:** casual dress; children's menu; carryout; cocktails; street parking; a la carte. Colonial dining in a restored 18th-century log house. Named in honor of Reading's first settlers. **Cards:** AE, CB, DI, MC, VI.

## WE'RE ON YOUR SIDE

AAA is concerned with motorists' rights. Legislation and regulatory measures are constantly being evaluated and acted upon by AAA lobbyists to ensure that automobile drivers are not the targets of discriminatory legislation.

## RIDGWAY—4,800

### LODGING

**FAIRCROFT BED & BREAKFAST**  Rates Subject to Change  **Phone:** 814/776-2539
◆ &  All Year [BP]  1P: $45- 50  2P/1B: $45- 50  2P/2B: $45- 50  XP: $10
Bed &  **Location:** 2 mi s on SR 948. Box 17 Montmorenci Rd 15853. **Terms:** Reserv deposit, 7 day notice; no pets.
Breakfast  **Facility:** 3 rooms. Rural setting. 2 stories; interior corridors; smoke free premises. **All Rooms:** no TVs.
**Some Rooms:** combo & shower baths, shared bathrooms.  (D) ⊗

## RIEGELSVILLE—900

### RESTAURANT

**THE RIEGELSVILLE HOTEL & INN**  Historical  **Dinner:** $21-$30  **Phone:** 610/749-2469
◆◆◆  **Location:** Off SR 611 on Delaware Rd. 10-12 Delaware Rd 18077. **Hours:** 4 pm-10 pm, Fri & Sat-11:30 pm,
Continental  Sun noon-9 pm. **Closed:** Mon 1/1, 7/4 & 12/25. **Reservations:** suggested. **Features:** casual dress; Sunday
brunch; cocktails & lounge; a la carte. Restored 1838 hotel offering country elegance & seasonal entrees.
French influence. **Cards:** AE, MC, VI.  ⊗

## ROBESONIA—1,900

### RESTAURANT

**HEIDELBERG FAMILY RESTAURANT**  **Dinner:** up to $10  **Phone:** 215/693-5060
(AAA)  **Location:** 1 1/2 mi w on US 422. 19551. **Hours:** 6 am-8:30 pm. **Closed:** 1/1 & 12/25. **Features:** casual
dress; children's menu; carryout; salad bar; minimum charge-$10; buffet. Pennsylvania Dutch specialties;
◆  homemade soups, breads, desserts & in-house bakery. Counter service. **Cards:** DS, MC, VI.  ⊗
American

## ROBINSON—2,200   (See PITTSBURGH ACCOMMODATIONS spotting map page A207; see index starting on page A206)

### LODGING

**CLUBHOUSE INN**  Rates Subject to Change  **Phone:** 412/788-8400  **15**
◆◆◆  Sun-Thurs [BP]  1P: $73  2P/1B: $83  2P/2B: $83  XP: $10  F10
Motel  Fri & Sat [BP]  1P: $56  2P/1B: $56  2P/2B: $56  XP: $10  F10
**Location:** Pkwy w to Moon Run exit, w 1/4 mi. 5311 Campbell's Run Rd 15205. **Fax:** 412/788-2577.
**Terms:** Reserv deposit, 14 day notice; weekly rates; no pets. **Facility:** 152 rooms. Very attractively appointed rooms & suites.
3 stories; interior corridors; meeting rooms; heated pool, whirlpool; exercise room. **Dining:** Restaurant nearby.
**Services:** airport transportation. Fee: coin laundry. **All Rooms:** free movies. **Some Rooms:** coffeemakers, 2 efficiencies,
microwaves, refrigerators. **Cards:** AE, DI, DS, MC, VI. *(See color ad p A206)*  (D) ⊗

## RONKS

### LODGINGS

**BLACK FOREST COUNTRY LODGE**  Rates Subject to Change  **Phone:** 717/393-2550
(AAA)  7/1-10/31  2P/2B: $59- 85  XP: $5
  5/1-6/30  2P/1B: $55  2P/2B: $49- 65  XP: $5
◆ ◆  11/1-12/5 & 2/10-4/30  2P/2B: $39- 62  XP: $5
Motel  **Location:** On SR 896, just n of SR 30. 21 Eastbrook Rd 17572. **Fax:** 717/291-1080. **Terms:** Open 5/1-12/5
& 2/10-4/30; reserv deposit, 4 day notice; no pets. **Facility:** 54 rooms. Located near Rockvale Square outlets.
2 stories; interior corridors. **Dining:** Restaurant nearby. **All Rooms:** cable TV. **Some Rooms:** refrigerators. **Cards:** AE, DS,
MC, VI.  (D)(S) ⊗

**CHERRY LANE MOTOR INN**  Rates Subject to Change  **Phone:** 717/687-7646
(AAA)  6/2-9/5  2P/1B: $62- 82  2P/2B: $67- 82  XP: $6  F12
  9/6-10/31  2P/1B: $52- 82  2P/2B: $52- 82  XP: $6  F12
◆ ◆  5/1-6/1 & 3/29-4/30  2P/1B: $48- 52  2P/2B: $52- 68  XP: $6  F12
Motel  11/1-3/28  2P/1B: $41- 59  2P/2B: $41- 61  XP: $6  F12
**Location:** 1/4 mi n on Ronks from Rt 30E. 84 N Ronks Rd 17572. **Terms:** Sr. discount; reserv deposit, 7
day notice; no pets. **Facility:** 41 rooms. 1 efficiency, $56 extra; 2 stories; interior/exterior corridors; pool; mini farm.
**Dining:** Coffee shop. **Services:** Fee: coin laundry. **All Rooms:** combo & shower baths, cable TV, no phones.
**Some Rooms:** refrigerators. **Cards:** AE, DS, MC, VI. *(See color ad p A149)*  (D) ⊗

**DAYS INN**  Rates Subject to Change  **Phone:** 717/390-1800
(AAA)  5/1-10/31 & 4/1-4/30 [CP]  1P: $44- 79  2P/1B: $52- 79  2P/2B: $52- 79  XP: $5  F17
  11/1-3/31 [CP]  1P: $43- 52  2P/1B: $49- 52  2P/2B: $49- 54  XP: $5  F17
◆◆◆  **Location:** From SR 30 n on Rt 896 1 blk. 34 E Brooks Rd 17572. **Fax:** 717/390-1800. **Terms:** Sr. discount;
Motel  reserv deposit, 3 day notice; weekly rates; no pets. **Facility:** 52 rooms. Commercial location. Close to outlet
shops in the Rockvale shopping mall. 2 stories; interior corridors. **Dining:** Restaurant nearby. **Services:** data
ports. **All Rooms:** free movies, refrigerators, cable TV. **Some Rooms:** microwaves, whirlpools. **Cards:** AE, DS, MC, VI.
(D)(S) ⊗

**OLDE AMISH INN**  Rates Subject to Change  **Phone:** 717/393-3100
(AAA)  6/22-9/5  2P/2B: $62- 70  XP: $5  F12
  9/6-11/1  2P/2B: $58- 65  XP: $5  F12
◆◆◆  5/1-6/21 & 3/31-4/30  2P/2B: $51- 62  XP: $5  F12
Motel  11/2-12/22 & 2/1-3/30  2P/2B: $39- 49  XP: $5  F12
**Location:** Jct US 30 & SR 896N. 33 Eastbrook Rd 17572. **Terms:** Open 5/1-12/22 & 2/1-4/30; reserv
deposit; no pets. **Facility:** 25 rooms. Family owned & operated. 2 stories; interior/exterior corridors. **Dining:** Restaurant
nearby. **All Rooms:** cable TV. **Cards:** AE, DS, MC, VI. *(See ad starting on p A152)*  (D) ⊗

**QUIET HAVEN MOTEL**  Rates Subject to Change  **Phone:** 717/397-6231
(AAA)  6/15-10/31  2P/2B: $56  XP: $3
  5/1-6/14 & 4/1-4/30  2P/2B: $48  XP: $3
◆  11/1-3/31  2P/2B: $36  XP: $3
Motel  **Location:** 3/4 mi w on SR 340, 1/2 mi s on SR 896, then 1/4 mi e on Siegrist Rd. 2556 Siegrist Rd 17572.
**Terms:** No pets. **Facility:** 15 rooms. Quiet rural area. 1 story; exterior corridors. **All Rooms:** no phones. (D)

**WEATHERVANE MOTOR COURT**
Rates Subject to Change
Phone: 717/397-3398

Motel
5/1-10/31 [CP]         2P/2B: $45- 60   XP: $5   F12
11/1-4/30 [CP]         2P/2B: $32- 40   XP: $5   F12
**Location:** Jct SR 896 & US 30. 15 Eastbrook Rd 17572 (PO Box 281). **Terms:** Reserv deposit, 3 day notice; no pets. **Facility:** 34 rooms. 1 story; exterior corridors. **Dining:** Restaurant nearby. **All Rooms:** cable TV. **Cards:** MC, VI.   Ⓓ⊗

## RESTAURANT

**HERSHEY FARM RESTAURANT OF FAMILY TIME**
Dinner: $11-$20
Phone: 717/687-8635

American
**Location:** From SR 30, 1 1/2 mi s on SR 896. 240 Hartman Bridge Rd 17572. **Hours:** 8 am-8 pm, Sun 11:30 am-7 pm. **Closed:** 12/25. **Reservations:** suggested. **Features:** casual dress; children's menu; carryout; salad bar; buffet. Pennsylvania Dutch home cooked meals from the menu, smorgasbord or family style dining. Smoke free premises. **Cards:** DS, MC, VI.   ⊗

# ST. DAVIDS

## LODGING

**RADNOR HOTEL**
AAA Special Value Rates
Phone: 610/688-5800

Motor Inn
All Year     1P: $120    2P/1B: $120     2P/2B: $120     XP: $10   F12
**Location:** 1/4 mi w of intersection I-476 exit 5 & US 30. 591 E Lancaster Ave 19087. **Fax:** 610/341-3299. **Terms:** Reserv deposit, 3 day notice; weekly/monthly rates; no pets. **Facility:** 170 rooms. 4 stories; interior corridors; meeting rooms; pool, wading pool; exercise room. **Dining & Entertainment:** Dining room; 6:30 am-10 pm; $7-$19; cocktails/lounge; 24-hour room service; entertainment. **Services:** data ports; valet laundry. **All Rooms:** combo & shower baths, cable TV. Fee: movies. **Some Rooms:** 2 efficiencies, microwaves, refrigerators. Fee: VCP's. **Cards:** AE, CB, DI, DS, MC, VI.   Ⓓ⊗

# ST. MARYS—5,500

## LODGING

**TOWNE HOUSE INN**
AAA Special Value Rates
Phone: 814/781-1556

Country Inn
All Year     1P: $48- 90   2P/1B: $54- 90   2P/2B: $54- 90   XP: $7   F12
**Location:** 1/2 blk w of SR 255 & 120. 138 Center St 15857. **Fax:** 814/834-4449. **Terms:** Reserv deposit; CP available, Sat & Sun; no pets. **Facility:** 43 rooms. Conventional rooms & some handsomely appointed rooms in converted Victorian house. Some motel rooms. 3 stories, no elevator; interior/exterior corridors; meeting rooms; exercise room. **Dining:** Coffee shop; 7 am-1:30 pm, closed Sat & Sun. **Services:** data ports. **All Rooms:** coffeemakers, free movies, combo & shower baths, cable TV. **Some Rooms:** whirlpools. Fee: microwaves, refrigerators. **Cards:** AE, DI, DS, MC, VI.   Ⓓ⊗

## RESTAURANT

**BAVARIAN INN**
Dinner: up to $10
Phone: 814/834-2161

Ethnic
**Location:** Downtown. 33 S St. Marys St 15857. **Hours:** 7 am-10 pm, Sat from 5 pm. **Closed:** Sun & 12/25. **Reservations:** suggested. **Features:** children's menu; carryout; salad bar; cocktails & lounge. Bavarian cuisine & decor. Some American entrees including fresh seafood & steaks. **Cards:** AE, MC, VI.

# SCENERY HILL

## RESTAURANT

**CENTURY INN DINING ROOM**   Historical
Dinner: $11-$20
Phone: 412/945-6600

American
**Location:** Center, on US 40. US 40 15360. **Hours:** Open 5/1-12/30 & 3/14-4/30; noon-3 & 4:30-8 pm, Fri & Sat-9 pm, Sun noon-3 & 3:30-7 pm. **Reservations:** suggested. **Features:** casual dress; children's menu; cocktails & lounge. Historic 1794 inn with dining room restored to period. Homemade breads, soups & desserts.   ⊗

# SCHENLEY

## RESTAURANT

**LEWIS & CLARK**
Dinner: $11-$20
Phone: 412/681-9080

Italian
**Location:** Jct Bigelow Blvd & N Dithridge St. 3955 Bigelow Blvd 15213. **Hours:** 11 am-10 pm, Fri-11 pm, Sat 4 pm-11 pm. **Closed:** Sun, 11/23 & 12/25. **Reservations:** suggested. **Features:** children's menu; carryout; cocktails; valet parking; a la carte. Italian & Continental offerings. **Cards:** AE, DI, DS, MC, VI.   ⊗

# SCRANTON—81,800   (See POCONO MOUNTAINS & VICINITY ACCOMMODATIONS spotting map pages A212 & A213; see index starting on page A210)

## LODGINGS

**ECONO LODGE**
Rates Subject to Change
Phone: 717/348-1000   **8**

Motor Inn
All Year [CP]    1P: $40- 75   2P/1B: $45- 75   2P/2B: $45- 75   XP: $6   F16
**Location:** I-81 exit 51, 1/2 mi n. 1175 Kane St 18505. **Fax:** 717/348-0683. **Terms:** Credit card guarantee; package plans; pets, $6. **Facility:** 64 rooms. 2 stories; interior corridors; pool, whirlpool. **Dining & Entertainment:** Restaurant; 5 pm-10 pm; $8-$19; cocktails/lounge. **All Rooms:** free movies, cable TV. **Some Rooms:** radios, whirlpools. Fee: VCP's. **Cards:** AE, CB, DI, DS, MC, VI.   ⊘Ⓓ⊗

**(See POCONO MOUNTAINS & VICINITY ACCOMMODATIONS spotting map pages A212 & A213)**

**HAMPTON INN-SCRANTON**   Rates Subject to Change   Phone: 717/342-7002  **7**
◆◆◆   All Year [CP]   1P: $63- 69 2P/1B: $71- 77 2P/2B: $68- 72
Motel   **Location:** I-81, exit 51. 22 Montage Mountain Rd 18507. Fax: 717/342-7012. **Terms:** Package plans; no pets. **Facility:** 129 rooms. 8 fireplace/whirlpool suites $90-$125; 4 stories; interior corridors; mountain view; meeting rooms; heated indoor pool, whirlpool; exercise room. **Services:** data ports; valet laundry; area transportation, airport transportation. **All Rooms:** free movies, combo & shower baths, cable TV. **Some Rooms:** Fee: refrigerators. **Cards:** AE, CB, DI, DS, MC, VI.   Roll in showers. ⓓ Ⓓ Ⓢ ⊗

**LACKAWANNA STATION HOTEL**   AAA Special Value Rates   Phone: 717/342-8300  **10**
(AAA)   All Year   1P: $89- 179 2P/1B: $99- 189 2P/2B: $99- 189 XP: $10 F18
◆◆◆   **Location:** From I-81 exit 53, at the confluence of Lackawanna Ave, Jefferson Ave & Spruce St. 700
Historic Hotel   Lackawanna Ave 18503. Fax: 717/342-0380. **Terms:** Reserv deposit; monthly rates; no pets. **Facility:** 145 rooms. Elegant public areas, very appealing & comfortable rooms. Historical downtown converted train station. 18 luxurious suites, $109-$179; 6 stories; interior corridors; conference facilities; heated indoor pool, sauna, steamroom, whirlpool; racquetball courts; exercise room, game room. **Dining & Entertainment:** Dining room, restaurant; 6:30 am-midnight; $9-$22; cocktails/lounge; Sun brunch 10 am-2 pm; also, Carmen's, see separate listing; entertainment. **Services:** data ports, PC, secretarial services; valet laundry; airport transportation; valet parking. **All Rooms:** free & pay movies, cable TV. **Some Rooms:** Fee: microwaves, refrigerators, VCP's, whirlpools. **Cards:** AE, MC, VI.
*(See color ad p A221)*   Ⓓ Ⓢ ⊗

**(See POCONO MOUNTAINS & VICINITY ACCOMMODATIONS spotting map pages A212 & A213)**

## RESTAURANTS

**CARMELLA'S RESTAURANT**  Dinner: $11-$20  Phone: 717/961-3070 ⑦
Italian
**Location:** From I-81, exit 55B; 1/2 mi s on Blakely, left at Drinker, an immediate right on Chestnut, 3/4 mi to Mill St, then follow signs. 140 Erie St 18512. **Hours:** 11 am-3 & 4-10:30 pm, Fri & Sat-11 pm, Sun 1 pm-9 pm. Closed: 1/1, 7/4, 12/24 & 12/25. **Reservations:** suggested; weekends. **Features:** casual dress; children's menu; carryout; cocktails & lounge. Buses welcome at lunch & dinner. **Cards:** AE, CB, DI, DS, MC, VI. ⊗

**CARMEN'S**  Dinner: $21-$30  Phone: 717/342-8300 ⑨
Continental
**Location:** In Lackawanna Station Hotel. 700 Lackawanna Ave 18503. **Hours:** 6:30 am-11 & 5-10 pm, Sun 10 am-2 pm. **Reservations:** suggested. **Features:** casual dress; Sunday brunch; health conscious menu; cocktails & lounge; entertainment; valet parking. Fine dining in an elegant atmosphere amid Italian marble & an authentic vaulted Tiffany glass ceiling. **Cards:** AE, CB, DI, DS, MC, VI. ⊗

**COOPER'S SEAFOOD HOUSE & SHIP'S PUB**  Dinner: $11-$20  Phone: 717/346-6883 ③
Seafood
**Location:** Center at Washington Ave & Pine St. 701 N Washington Ave 18509. **Hours:** 11 am-midnight, Fri & Sat-1 am, Sun 1 pm-9 pm. Closed major holidays. **Features:** casual dress; children's menu; carryout; cocktails & lounge; entertainment. New replica of turn-of-the-century sailing vessel serving a large variety of fresh seafood & meat entrees. Lite fare & music in ships pub. **Cards:** DS, MC, VI.
*(See color ad p A221)* ⊗

**FARLEY'S**  Dinner: $11-$20  Phone: 717/346-3000 ④
American
**Location:** Center; corner Adams Ave & Linden St. 300 Adams Ave 18503. **Hours:** 11 am-11 pm, Fri & Sat-midnight. **Reservations:** suggested; weekends. **Features:** casual dress; children's menu; carryout; cocktails & lounge. Contemporary atmosphere. Raw bar. **Cards:** DS, MC, VI. ⊗

**SMITHS RESTAURANT**  Dinner: $11-$20  Phone: 717/961-9192 ⑤
American
**Location:** I-81, exit 51, w to US 11, then 1 1/2 mi n. 1402 Cedar Ave 18505. **Hours:** 5:30 am-11 pm, Sat-8 pm. Closed major holidays & Sun. **Features:** casual dress; children's menu; health conscious menu; carryout; cocktails. Home cooking, family atmosphere. Family owned for 59 years. ⊗

**STRAZZERI'S RESTAURANT**  Dinner: up to $10  Phone: 717/961-8455 ⑥
Italian
**Location:** I-81 exit 56 Main Ave, 1 1/2 mi s. 1911 N Main Ave 18508. **Hours:** 11 am-9 pm, Sat & Sun-9:30 pm. Closed major holidays. **Features:** casual dress; children's menu; carryout; cocktails & lounge. Casual family atmosphere. Italian specialties.

**TOM & JERRY'S RESTAURANT**  Dinner: up to $10  Phone: 717/344-1771 ⑩
American
**Location:** At jct Pittston Ave & Birch St; from I-81, exit 51 to SR 11, 2 mi n. 731 Pittston Ave 18505. **Hours:** 11 am-1 am. Closed major holidays. **Features:** casual dress; children's menu; carryout; cocktails. Family oriented restaurant. Wall mounted cartoon characters will intrigue the children. **Cards:** AE, DS, MC, VI. ⊗

# SELINSGROVE—5,400

## LODGINGS

**COMFORT INN**  AAA Special Value Rates  Phone: 717/374-8880
Motor Inn

| | | 1P: | | 2P/2B: | | XP: | |
|---|---|---|---|---|---|---|---|
| 5/1-10/31 [CP] | | 1P: $48- 75 | | 2P/2B: $50- 75 | | XP: $5 | F18 |
| 11/1-4/30 [CP] | | 1P: $39- 60 | | 2P/2B: $39- 60 | | XP: $5 | F18 |

**Location:** 1 mi n on US 11 & 15. US Rts 11 & 15 17870 (PO Box 299). **Fax:** 717/374-8880. **Terms:** Reserv deposit, 3 day notice; pets, $25 dep req. **Facility:** 62 rooms. 3 two-bedroom units. 2 stories; interior corridors; arcade room. **Dining & Entertainment:** Dining room; 11 am-10 pm, Sun 7 am-noon; $5-$16; cocktail lounge. **All Rooms:** cable TV. **Some Rooms:** radios, refrigerators. Fee: VCP's. **Cards:** AE, DI, DS, JCB, MC, VI. ⒹⓍ

**PHILLIPS MOTEL, INC**  Rates Subject to Change  Phone: 717/743-3100
Motel

| | | 1P: | | 2P/1B: | | 2P/2B: | | XP: | |
|---|---|---|---|---|---|---|---|---|---|
| All Year | | 1P: $38- 45 | | 2P/1B: $44- 54 | | 2P/2B: $46- 58 | | XP: $4 | |

**Location:** 4 mi n on US 11 & 15. 17876 (PO Box 191, SHAMOKIN DAM). **Terms:** Reserv deposit; **Facility:** 47 rooms. Distinctively decorated, well-maintained rooms. Many with antique furnishings. 1 story; exterior corridors. **Dining:** Restaurant nearby. **All Rooms:** cable TV. **Cards:** AE, CB, DI, DS, MC, VI.
*(See color ad below)* ⒹⓍ

# SHAMOKIN DAM—1,700

## LODGING

**DAYS INN-SUNBURY-SELINSGROVE**  Rates Subject to Change  Phone: 717/743-1111
Motor Inn

| | | 1P: | | 2P/1B: | | 2P/2B: | | XP: | |
|---|---|---|---|---|---|---|---|---|---|
| All Year | | 1P: $39- 60 | | 2P/1B: $49- 65 | | 2P/2B: $44- 68 | | XP: $5 | F12 |

**Location:** 4 1/4 mi n on US 11 & 15. (Rt 11-15, Box 487). **Fax:** 717/743-1190. **Terms:** Credit card guarantee; pets, $5. **Facility:** 151 rooms. 2 stories; exterior corridors; pool, open 5/1-9/5. **Dining & Entertainment:** Dining room; 6:30 am-11 & 5:30-10 pm, Sat & Sun 7 am-11 & 5:30-10 pm; $7-$15; cocktail lounge; entertainment. **All Rooms:** free & pay movies, cable TV. **Cards:** AE, DI, DS, JCB, MC, VI. ⒹⓍ

## RESTAURANT

**TEDD'S LANDING**  Dinner: $11-$20  Phone: 717/743-1591
American
**Location:** 1/2 mi n at jct US 11 & 15. 17876. **Hours:** 11 am-10 pm, Sat 4 pm-11 pm, Sun 4 pm-9 pm. Closed major holidays. **Features:** casual dress; children's menu; cocktails & lounge. Rustic ambience, family operation, fresh seafood specialty. Good river views. In-house baker & butcher. Homemade breads, pastries & soups. **Cards:** AE, MC, VI. ⊗

# SHARON—17,500

## RESTAURANT

**SEAFOOD EXPRESS**
◆◆
Seafood
**Dinner:** up to $10     **Phone:** 412/981-3123
**Location:** Downtown. 110 Connelly Blvd 16146. **Hours:** 4:30 pm-10 pm, Fri & Sat-10:30 pm, Sun noon-7:30 pm. **Closed:** Mon & 12/25. **Features:** children's menu; carryout; salad bar; cocktails & lounge; a la carte. Fresh seafood. **Cards:** AE, DI, DS, MC, VI. ⊗

# SHARTLESVILLE—3,800

## LODGING

**DUTCH MOTEL**
🅰🅰
◆
Motel
**Rates Subject to Change**     **Phone:** 215/488-1479
5/1-12/31 & 3/1-4/30   1P: $30- 35   2P/1B: $35- 40   2P/2B: $40- 45   XP: $7   F8
**Location:** Nw of Shartlesville exit off I-78 & US 22 on Motel Rd. 19554 (PO Box 25). **Terms:** Open 5/1-12/31 & 3/1-4/30; reserv deposit, 4 day notice; small pets only, $3. **Facility:** 14 rooms. 1 story; exterior corridors. **Dining:** Restaurant nearby. **All Rooms:** combo & shower baths, cable TV, no phones. **Cards:** AE, MC, VI. Ⓓ

# SHILLINGTON—5,000

## LODGING

**DAYS INN**
◆◆
Motel
**Rates Subject to Change**     **Phone:** 610/777-7888
All Year [CP]   1P: $62   2P/1B: $68   2P/2B: $68   XP: $5 F18
**Location:** On US 222, 5 mi s of US 422 & US 222 business route exit. 415 Lancaster Pike W 19607. **Fax:** 610/777-5138. **Terms:** Sr. discount; reserv deposit; no pets. **Facility:** 142 rooms. Contemporary rooms. 4 stories; interior corridors; meeting rooms; pool; 3 rooms with exercise equipment. **Dining:** Restaurant nearby. **Services:** data ports. **Fee:** coin laundry. **All Rooms:** free movies, cable TV. **Some Rooms:** Fee: microwaves, refrigerators. **Cards:** AE, DI, DS, MC, VI. *(See color ad p A217)* Ⓓ ⊗

# SHIPPENSBURG—5,300

## RESTAURANT

**RUSTIC INN**
◆◆
American
**Dinner:** $11-$20     **Phone:** 717/532-3716
**Location:** 1/4 mi w on King St. 105 W King St 17257. **Hours:** 11 am-10 pm, Sun-8 pm. **Closed:** 1/1, 5/25 & 12/25. **Reservations:** suggested; weekends. **Features:** casual dress; children's menu; carryout; cocktails; buffet. Well-prepared meals in a relaxing atmosphere. **Cards:** AE, DS, MC, VI. ⊗

# SLIPPERY ROCK—3,000

## LODGING

**EVENING STAR MOTEL**
◆
Motel
**Rates Subject to Change**     **Phone:** 412/794-3211
All Year   1P: $37   2P/1B: $41   2P/2B: $41   XP: $3 F10
**Location:** On SR 108; 1/2 mi e of I-79, exit 30. 16057 (RD 3, Box 380A). **Terms:** Reserv deposit; no pets. **Facility:** 18 rooms. Well-maintained. **All Rooms:** coffeemakers, shower baths, cable TV. **Cards:** AE, DS, MC, VI. Ⓓ

# SMOKETOWN

## LODGINGS

**MILL STREAM MOTOR LODGE**
🅰🅰
◆◆◆
Motel
**Rates Subject to Change**     **Phone:** 717/299-0931

| | | | | | | |
|---|---|---|---|---|---|---|
| 6/16-9/3 | 1P: $75 | | 2P/2B: $75 | XP: $7 | F5 |
| 9/4-10/28 | 1P: $73 | | 2P/2B: $73 | XP: $7 | F5 |
| 5/1-6/15 & 4/28-4/30 | 1P: $63 | | 2P/2B: $63 | XP: $7 | F5 |
| 10/29-4/27 | 1P: $55 | | 2P/2B: $55 | XP: $7 | F5 |

**Location:** 3/4 mi w on SR 340, 1/4 mi s on SR 896. 170 Eastbrook Rd 17576. **Fax:** 717/295-9326. **Terms:** Reserv deposit; package plans; no pets. **Facility:** 52 rooms. Countryside setting. 2-3 stories; exterior corridors; meeting rooms. **Dining:** Coffee shop; 7 am-1:30 pm, closed Sun & 12/25, except for complimentary continental breakfast Sun 8-10 am. **All Rooms:** cable TV. **Some Rooms:** Fee: refrigerators, VCP's. **Cards:** AE, DS, MC, VI. Ⓓ ⊗

**SMOKETOWN MOTOR LODGE**
🅰🅰
◆◆
Motel
**Rates Subject to Change**     **Phone:** 717/397-6944

| | | | | | |
|---|---|---|---|---|---|
| 6/16-9/3 | 2P/1B: $54- 62 | 2P/2B: $54- 62 | XP: $5 |
| 9/4-10/31 | 2P/1B: $49- 58 | 2P/2B: $49- 58 | XP: $5 |
| 5/1-6/15 & 4/1-4/30 | 2P/1B: $42- 52 | 2P/2B: $42- 52 | XP: $5 |
| 11/1-3/31 | 2P/1B: $32- 48 | 2P/2B: $32- 48 | XP: $5 |

**Location:** 1/4 mi s on 896 from Rt 340. 190 Eastbrook Rd 17576. **Terms:** Reserv deposit, 7 day notice; weekly/monthly rates, off season; no pets. **Facility:** 17 rooms. 2 stories; interior corridors. **Dining:** Restaurant nearby. **All Rooms:** refrigerators, cable TV, no phones. **Some Rooms:** 3 efficiencies, radios. **Cards:** MC, VI. Ⓓ ⊗

## RESTAURANTS

**GAVIN'S HOME ON THE RANGE**
🅰🅰
◆◆
American
**Dinner:** up to $10     **Phone:** 717/399-2194
**Location:** From jct SR 896 & SR 340, 1/4 mi w on SR 340. 2481 Old Philadephia Pike 17576. **Hours:** 7 am-9 pm, 5/1-12/1, 11 am-8 pm 12/2-4/30, Fri & Sat 7 am-8 pm. **Closed:** Sun, 11/23 & 12/25. **Reservations:** suggested; weekends. **Features:** casual dress; children's menu; health conscious menu; carryout. Casual family dining. Smoke free premises. **Cards:** MC, VI. ⊗

**GOOD N PLENTY RESTAURANT**
🅰🅰
◆
American
**Dinner:** $11-$20     **Phone:** 717/394-7111
**Location:** 1 mi n on SR 896 from US 30. Eastbrook Rd (SR 896) 17576. **Hours:** 11:30 am-8 pm. **Closed:** Sun & 12/20-2/5. **Features:** casual dress. Pennsylvania Dutch fare. Original farmhouse dates from 1871. Small parties share tables. Family style. Smoke free premises. **Cards:** MC, VI.
*(See ad starting on p A152)* ⊗

# SNYDERSVILLE (See POCONO MOUNTAINS & VICINITY ACCOMMODATIONS spotting map pages A212 & A213; see index starting on page A210)

## RESTAURANT

**THE STONE BAR INN**
◆◆
American
**Dinner:** $21-$30     **Phone:** 717/992-6634   ⑧②
**Location:** Center on US 209 Business Rt. Rt 209 18360. **Hours:** 4 pm-10 pm, Fri & Sat-11 pm. Closed major holidays. **Reservations:** suggested; weekends. **Features:** casual dress; children's menu; early bird specials; carryout; cocktails & lounge. **Cards:** AE, CB, DI, DS, MC, VI. ⊗

## SOMERSET—6,500

### LODGINGS

**BUDGET HOST INN**
Rates Subject to Change          Phone: 814/445-7988
Fri & Sat          1P: $40- 50   2P/1B: $40- 55   2P/2B: $45- 60   XP: $5  F11
Sun-Thurs        1P: $33- 38   2P/1B: $33- 40   2P/2B: $33- 40   XP: $5  F11
Location: 1/4 mi s of I-70, 76 & PA tpk exit 10. 799 N Center Ave 15501. Terms: Sr. discount; reserv deposit; small pets only, $5. Facility: 28 rooms. 2 stories; exterior corridors. Dining: Restaurant nearby.
Motel
All Rooms: free movies, combo & shower baths, cable TV. Some Rooms: refrigerators. Cards: AE, CB, DI, DS, MC, VI. *(See color ad p A83)*

**DAYS INN-SOMERSET**
Rates Subject to Change          Phone: 814/445-9200
Fri & Sat 12/24-3/31 [CP]   1P: $65   2P/1B: $65   2P/2B: $69   XP: $6  F18
Motel
5/1-12/23, Sun-Thurs
12/24-3/31 & 4/1-4/30 [CP]  1P: $44- 59   2P/1B: $49- 65   2P/2B: $51- 64   XP: $6  F18
Location: At tpk entrance, I-76 & I-70, exit 10. 220 Waterworks Rd 15501. Fax: 814/445-9222. Terms: Sr. discount; reserv deposit; pets. Facility: 106 rooms. 2 stories; exterior corridors. Dining: Restaurant nearby. All Rooms: free movies, cable TV. Some Rooms: microwaves, refrigerators. Cards: AE, CB, DI, DS, MC, VI. *(See ad below)*

**DOLLAR INN**
Rates Subject to Change          Phone: 814/445-2977
Fri & Sat          1P: $25- 35   2P/1B: $30- 40   2P/2B: $35- 45   XP: $5
Sun-Thurs        1P: $25- 32   2P/1B: $28- 35   2P/2B: $32- 40   XP: $5
Motel
Location: 1/2 mi n on SR 601. 15501 (RD 2, Box 0, SR 601). Terms: Reserv deposit, 7 day notice; weekly/monthly rates; pets, $5. Facility: 15 rooms. 1 story; exterior corridors. Dining: Restaurant nearby.
All Rooms: free movies, cable TV. Some Rooms: refrigerators. Cards: AE, DS, MC, VI.

**ECONOMY INN**
Rates Subject to Change          Phone: 814/445-4144
Fri & Sat          1P: $50- 65   2P/1B: $50- 65   2P/2B: $65- 70   XP: $5  F12
Sun-Thurs        1P: $35- 40   2P/1B: $35- 40   2P/2B: $35- 40   XP: $5  F12
Location: 1/2 mi n on SR 601. 15501 (RD 2, Box 5, SR 601). Fax: 814/445-3763. Terms: Sr. discount; reserv deposit, 7 day notice; weekly rates; no pets. Facility: 19 rooms. 1 story; exterior corridors.
Motel
Dining: Restaurant nearby. Services: Fee: coin laundry. All Rooms: free movies, refrigerators, combo & shower baths, cable TV. Cards: AE, DS, MC, VI.

**HOLIDAY INN**
AAA Special Value Rates          Phone: 814/445-9611
Fri & Sat          1P: $65- 95   2P/1B: $100- 115   2P/2B: $100- 115   XP: $10  F19
Sun-Thurs        1P: $65- 80   2P/1B: $75- 90   2P/2B: $75- 90   XP: $10  F19
Motor Inn
Location: At tpk entrance, I-76 & I-70, exit 10. 202 Shaffer St 15501 (PO Box 191). Fax: 814/445-5815. Terms: Reserv deposit; small pets only. Facility: 102 rooms. Modestly appointed rooms. 3 stories; interior corridors; pool, wading pool. Dining & Entertainment: Restaurant; 6:30 am-2 & 5-10 pm; $8-$16; cocktails/lounge; entertainment. Services: data ports. Fee: coin laundry. All Rooms: free movies, cable TV. Some Rooms: coffeemakers. Fee: VCP's. Cards: AE, CB, DI, DS, JCB, MC, VI. *(See ad below)*

**THE INN AT GEORGIAN PLACE**
Guaranteed Rates          Phone: 814/443-1043
All Year [BP]    1P: $85- 165   2P/1B: $85- 165   2P/2B: $85- 165   XP: $10
Historic Bed
& Breakfast
Location: I-70 & I-76 exit 10, e on Waterworks Rd, n 1/3 mi on SR 601. 800 Georgian Pl 15501. Fax: 814/443-1043. Terms: Age restrictions may apply; credit card guarantee, 7 day notice; small pets only. Facility: 11 rooms. 1915 mansion on hilltop with superb view. 3 stories, no elevator; interior corridors; meeting rooms. All Rooms: free movies, comb, shower & tub baths, cable TV, VCP's. Cards: AE, DS, MC, VI.

**KNIGHTS INN**
AAA Special Value Rates          Phone: 814/445-8933
Fri & Sat 12/17-3/12   1P: $46   2P/1B: $56   2P/2B: $58   XP: $10  F18
Motel
5/1-12/16, Sun-Thurs
12/17-3/12 & 3/13-4/30   1P: $38   2P/1B: $45   2P/2B: $47   XP: $7  F18
Location: At tpk entrance, I-76 & I-70, exit 10. I-70 & I-76 at exit 10 15501. Fax: 814/445-9745. Terms: Reserv deposit; weekly/monthly rates; no pets. Facility: 112 rooms. 10 efficiencies; $43.95-$51.95; 1 story; exterior corridors; pool. Dining: Restaurant nearby. Services: Fee: coin laundry. All Rooms: free movies, cable TV. Some Rooms: microwaves, refrigerators. Cards: AE, CB, DI, DS, MC, VI.

**RAMADA INN**
AAA Special Value Rates          Phone: 814/443-4646
All Year          1P: $58- 80   2P/1B: $68- 90   2P/2B: $68- 90   XP: $10  F17
Location: At Tpk entrance, I-76 & I-70, exit 10. 15501 (PO Box 511). Fax: 814/445-7539. Terms: Reserv deposit, 7 day notice; weekly/monthly rates; small pets only. Facility: 152 rooms. Attractive enclosed courtyard.
Motor Inn
2 stories; interior corridors; heated indoor pool, saunas, whirlpool. Dining: Also, Myron's, see separate listing. All Rooms: free movies, cable TV. Some Rooms: refrigerators. Fee: VCP's. Cards: AE, CB, DI, DS, MC, VI.

## RESTAURANTS

**MYRON'S**
◆◆
American

**Dinner: $11-$20**

**Phone: 814/443-4646**

**Location:** In Ramada Inn. 15501. **Hours:** 6:30 am-11, 11:30-2 & 5-10 pm, Sun from 4 pm. **Features:** casual dress; children's menu; salad bar; cocktails & lounge; entertainment; buffet. Relaxed dining in attractive surroundings. **Cards:** AE, DI, DS, MC, VI.  ⊗

**OAKHURST TEA ROOM**
⊛
◆◆
American

**Dinner: $11-$20**

**Phone: 814/443-2897**

**Location:** 6 mi w on SR 31. 15501. **Hours:** 11 am-10 pm, Sun-8 pm; smorgasbord Tues-Sat 4 pm-9 pm, Sun 11 am-8 pm; Tues-Sat luncheon buffet 11:3 0 am-3 pm, $6.50.Closed: Mon & 12/25. **Features:** casual dress; children's menu; carryout; cocktails & lounge; buffet. Country dining serving smorgasbord & family-style meals. Sun brunch. Homemade soups, breads & desserts; popular bread stuffing ball. **Cards:** DS, MC, VI.  ⊗

## STAHLSTOWN

## RESTAURANT

**THE BRASS DUCK**
◆◆
American

**Dinner: $21-$30**

**Phone: 412/593-7440**

**Location:** SR 130, 1/4 mi e of jct SR 130 & 711. **Hours:** 11 am-10 pm, Sun-9 pm. Closed: Tues, 11/23 & 12/25. **Reservations:** suggested; weekends. **Features:** casual dress; children's menu; cocktails & lounge. Specializing in duck. Patio dining, weather permitting. **Cards:** AE, CB, DI, DS, MC, VI.  ⊗

## STARLIGHT

## LODGING

**THE INN AT STARLIGHT LAKE**
⊛
◆◆
Historic
Country Inn

Rates Subject to Change

**Phone: 717/798-2519**

All Year [MAP]   1P:  $64- 93   2P/1B:  $110- 154   2P/2B:  $110- 154   XP: $53
**Location:** Off SR 370, 2 mi n following signs. 18461 (PO Box 27). Fax: 718/798-2672. **Terms:** Reserv deposit, 14 day notice; weekly rates; BP available; no pets. **Facility:** 26 rooms. 1 two-bedroom unit, 1 three-bedroom unit. 1-3 stories; interior/exterior corridors; lake view; meeting rooms; beach; 1 lighted tennis court. **Dining & Entertainment:** Restaurant; 8 am-10, noon-1:30 & 6-9 pm, Sun 8 am-2 & 3-8 pm; $10-$21; cocktails/lounge. **Recreation:** nature program; swimming, boating, canoeing, fishing; cross country skiing, ice skating; bicycles. **All Rooms:** no A/C, no phones. **Some Rooms:** kitchen, combo & shower baths, shared bathrooms, cable TV, whirlpools. **Cards:** MC, VI.  Ⓓ

## STARRUCCA—200

## LODGING

**THE NETHERCOTT INN B&B**
◆◆
Historic Bed
& Breakfast

Rates Subject to Change

**Phone: 717/727-2211**

All Year [BP]   1P:  $75   2P/1B:  $75   2P/2B:  $90   XP: $15   F3
**Location:** Center. 1 Main St 18462 (PO Box 26). **Terms:** Reserv deposit, 3 day notice; no pets. **Facility:** 5 rooms. Circa 1893 Victorian home furnished with antiques. Small, rural town location. 2 units for families only. 3 stories, no elevator; interior corridors; smoke free premises. **All Rooms:** combo & shower baths, no A/C.
**Some Rooms:** phones, cable TV, VCP's. **Cards:** AE, DS, MC, VI.  Ⓓ ⊗

## STATE COLLEGE—38,900

## LODGINGS

**ATHERTON HILTON**
⊛
◆◆◆
Hotel

AAA Special Value Rates

**Phone: 814/231-2100**

All Year   1P:  $85   2P/1B:  $95   2P/2B:  $95   XP: $10   F18
**Location:** Downtown, 1 blk s of Penn State campus. 125 S Atherton St 16801. Fax: 814/231-2100. **Terms:** Reserv deposit; AP, BP, CP available; no pets. **Facility:** 150 rooms. 8 stories; interior corridors; meeting rooms. **Dining & Entertainment:** Dining room; 6:30 am-2 & 5-10 pm; $11-$19; cocktails/lounge; entertainment. **Services:** data ports; airport transportation; valet parking. **All Rooms:** free movies, cable TV.
**Some Rooms:** refrigerators, whirlpools. **Cards:** AE, CB, DI, DS, JCB, MC, VI. *(See ad p 28)*  Ⓓ Ⓢ ⊗

**AUTOPORT MOTEL**
⊛
◆◆
Motor Inn

AAA Special Value Rates

**Phone: 814/237-7666**

6/1-8/31   1P:  $50- 70   2P/1B:  $69- 79   2P/2B:  $69- 79   XP: $10   F16
5/1-5/31 & 9/1-4/30   1P:  $55- 65   2P/1B:  $59- 69   2P/2B:  $59- 69   XP: $5   F16
**Location:** 1 1/2 mi e on US 322 business route. 1405 S Atherton St 16801. Fax: 814/237-7456. **Terms:** Reserv deposit, 7 day notice; no pets. **Facility:** 86 rooms. Located along busy commercial highway. 1 two-bedroom unit. 2 stories; interior/exterior corridors; meeting rooms; golf & tennis privileges; heated pool. **Dining & Entertainment:** Restaurant, coffee shop; 6 am-midnight; $12-$18; cocktails/lounge. **Services:** data ports. Fee: coin laundry. **All Rooms:** coffeemakers, free movies, cable TV. **Some Rooms:** 11 efficiencies, microwaves, refrigerators. Fee: VCP's. **Cards:** AE, CB, DI, DS, MC, VI.  Ⓓ ⊗

**BEST WESTERN STATE COLLEGE INN**
⊛
◆◆◆
Motel

Rates Subject to Change

**Phone: 814/237-8005**

All Year [CP]   1P:  $52   2P/1B:  $57   2P/2B:  $57   XP: $5   F18
**Location:** 1 3/4 mi e on US 322 business route. 1663 S Atherton St 16801. Fax: 814/238-8805. **Terms:** Sr. discount; reserv deposit, 3 day notice; weekly/monthly rates; no pets. **Facility:** 139 rooms. 24 efficiencies, $10 extra. 3 suites with whirlpool bath, $75; speical event weekends $125; 4 stories; interior corridors; meeting rooms; sauna, whirlpool; exercise room. **Dining:** Restaurant nearby. **Services:** data ports. **All Rooms:** free & pay movies, cable TV. **Some Rooms:** coffeemakers, microwaves, refrigerators, whirlpools. **Cards:** AE, CB, DI, DS, MC, VI. *(See color ad p A226)*  ⓈⒷ Ⓩ Ⓓ Ⓢ ⊗

**BREWMEISTER'S BED & BREAKFAST MOTEL**
◆
Motel

Rates Subject to Change

**Phone: 814/238-0015**

All Year [CP]   1P:  $40   2P/1B:  $49   2P/2B:  $49   XP: $7   F12
**Location:** On SR 26, 2 1/2 mi s of jct US 322 bus rt. 2070 Cato Ave 16801. **Terms:** No pets. **Facility:** 16 rooms. 1 story; exterior corridors. **Dining:** Restaurant nearby. **All Rooms:** microwaves, refrigerators, cable TV. **Cards:** AE, DI, DS, MC, VI.  Ⓓ

**DAYS INN PENN STATE** ◆◆◆ Hotel — Rates Subject to Change — Phone: 814/238-8454
All Year 1P: $55- 90    2P/2B: $65- 95  XP: $10  F17
**Location:** From jct US 322 business route, 5 blks n on SR 26 (northbound); 1 blk e of SR 26 on S Pugh St. 240 S Pugh St 16801. Fax: 814/234-3377. **Terms:** Package plans; small pets only, $7. **Facility:** 184 rooms. 1 blk from Penn State campus. 6 stories; interior corridors; business center, meeting rooms; heated indoor pool, sauna; exercise room. **Dining & Entertainment:** Dining room; 6:30-midnight, Sun from 8 am; $6-$16; cocktails/lounge; 24-hour room service; entertainment. **Services:** secretarial services; airport transportation. **All Rooms:** cable TV. Fee: movies. **Cards:** AE, CB, DI, DS, MC, VI. *(See color ad p A227)*  Ⓓ ⊗

**FRIENDSHIP INN** ⒶⒶ ◆◆ Motel — Rates Subject to Change — Phone: 814/238-6783
All Year 1P: $36- 46   2P/1B: $41- 46   2P/2B: $46- 64  XP: $5  F18
**Location:** 3/4 mi w on US 322. 1101 E College Ave 16801. 2 blks w of Penn State campus. 1040 N Atherton St 16803. Fax: 814/238-4519. **Terms:** Sr. discount; no pets. **Facility:** 29 rooms. Located along busy commercial highway. 2 stories; interior/exterior corridors; **Dining:** Restaurant nearby. **All Rooms:** free movies, combo & shower baths, cable TV. **Some Rooms:** refrigerators. **Cards:** AE, CB, DI, DS, JCB, MC, VI.  Ⓓ ⊗

**HAMPTON INN** ◆◆◆ Motel — Rates Subject to Change — Phone: 814/231-1590
All Year [BP] 1P: $52- 76   2P/1B: $52- 76   2P/2B: $63- 75
**Location:** 2 mi s on SR 26. 1101 E College Ave 16801. **Terms:** Sr. discount; reserv deposit; monthly rates; small pets only. **Facility:** 121 rooms. Good sized rooms. 3 stories; interior corridors; heated pool. **Dining:** Restaurant nearby. **Services:** data ports; airport transportation. **All Rooms:** free & pay movies, cable TV. **Cards:** AE, CB, DI, DS, MC, VI.  Ⓓ Ⓢ ⊗

**HOLIDAY INN** ⒶⒶ ◆◆ Motor Inn — Rates Subject to Change — Phone: 814/238-3001
All Year 1P: $58    2P/1B: $65    2P/2B: $65  XP: $7  F
**Location:** 1 1/2 mi e on US 322 business route. 1450 S Atherton St 16801. Fax: 814/237-1345. **Terms:** Sr. discount; weekly/monthly rates; small pets only. **Facility:** 288 rooms. Located along busy commerical highway. 2 stories; exterior corridors; meeting rooms; 2 pools; 2 lighted tennis courts. **Dining & Entertainment:** Restaurant; 7 am-2 & 5-10 pm; $6-$14; cocktails/lounge; entertainment. **All Rooms:** free movies, cable TV. **Cards:** AE, CB, DI, DS, JCB, MC, VI.

**IMPERIAL MOTOR INN** ⒶⒶ ◆ Motel — Rates Subject to Change — Phone: 814/237-7686
All Year 1P: $45- 100   2P/1B: $50- 125   2P/2B: $55- 135  XP: $5  F16
**Location:** Downtown on US 322 business route; 1 blk s of Penn State campus. 118 S Atherton St 16801. Fax: 814/237-4406. **Terms:** Sr. discount; reserv deposit, 7 day notice; small pets only, $5. **Facility:** 37 rooms. Located in busy downtown area. 2 stories; exterior corridors; pool. **Dining:** Restaurant nearby. **All Rooms:** free movies, cable TV. **Some Rooms:** efficiency. **Cards:** AE, CB, DI, DS, JCB, MC, VI.
*(See ad p A225)*  Ⓓ ⊗

**NITTANY BUDGET MOTEL** ⒶⒶ ◆ Motel — Rates Subject to Change — Phone: 814/237-7638
All Year 1P: $30    2P/1B: $38    2P/2B: $40  XP: $7
**Location:** 1 mi w on US 322. 1274 N Atherton St 16803. **Terms:** Reserv deposit, 3 day notice; weekly/monthly rates; no pets. **Facility:** 47 rooms. Located in busy commercial district. 2 stories; interior/exterior corridors. **Dining:** Restaurant nearby. **All Rooms:** combo & shower baths, cable TV. **Some Rooms:** 10 efficiencies, refrigerators. **Cards:** AE, CB, DI, DS, MC, VI. *(See ad p A227)*  Ⓓ ⊗

**TOFTREES HOTEL RESORT & CONFERENCE CENTER**   Rates Subject to Change   **Phone:** 814/234-8000
◆◆◆ Resort Motor Inn

| | | | | | | | | |
|---|---|---|---|---|---|---|---|---|
| 5/1-10/31 & 4/2-4/30 | 1P: | $95- 110 | 2P/1B: | $110- 150 | 2P/2B: | $110- 150 | XP: $15 | F12 |
| 11/1-4/1 | 1P: | $49- 69 | 2P/1B: | $49- 69 | 2P/2B: | $49- 69 | XP: $15 | F12 |

**Location:** From jct SR 26, 4 1/2 mi w on US 322, Toftrees exit, 1/4 mi n, following signs. 1 Country Club Ln 16803. **Fax:** 814/238-4404. **Terms:** Credit card guarantee; package plans; no pets. **Facility:** 131 rooms. Well-appointed rooms. 22 two-bedroom units. 1- & 2-bedroom efficiency apartments, $89-$160; 2-3 stories; interior corridors; conference facilities; heated pool, wading pool; exercise room, jogging & fitness trail. Fee: 18 holes golf; 4 lighted tennis courts. **Dining & Entertainment:** Dining room, restaurant; 6:30 am-10 pm; $9-$20; cocktails/lounge; 24-hour room service; entertainment. **Services:** data ports, secretarial services; airport transportation. Fee: massage. **Recreation:** children's program in summer, social program in summer. Fee: bicycles. **All Rooms:** coffeemakers, free & pay movies, cable TV. **Some Rooms:** honor bars, microwaves, refrigerators. Fee: VCP's. **Cards:** AE, DI, DS, MC, VI.
*(See ad p A226)*   Ⓓ ⊗

## RESTAURANTS

**MARIO & LUIGI'S ITALIAN RESTAURANT**   **Dinner:** $11-$20   **Phone:** 814/237-0374
◆◆ Italian

**Location:** Located near Penn State Campus in town between College & Beaver sts. 112 S Garner St 16801. **Hours:** 4 pm-10 pm, Sat noon-11 pm, Sun noon-10 pm. **Closed:** 11/23 & 12/25. **Features:** casual dress; children's menu; health conscious menu; carryout; cocktails; street parking. Fresh house pasta. Veal, chicken & seafood specialties. Homemade soups, breads & desserts. Woodburning ovens & rotisserie in view. **Cards:** AE, DI, DS, MC, VI.   ⊗

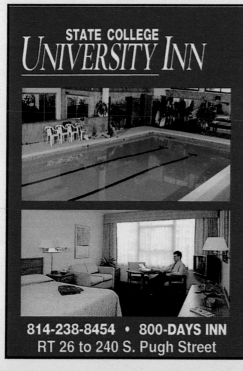

**THE TAVERN RESTAURANT**      Dinner: $11-$20      Phone: 814/238-6116
◆◆   **Location:** On SR 26 (southbound), 5 blks n of US 322 business route. 220 E College Ave 16805. **Hours:** 5
American   pm-10:30 pm, Sun-8:30 pm. Closed major holidays. **Features:** casual dress; children's menu; cocktails &
lounge; street parking. Established, popular tavern with informal colonial atmosphere. Homemade desserts. ⊗
**Cards:** AE, DI, DS, MC, VI.

**THE VICTORIAN MANOR RESTAURANT**      Dinner: $21-$30      Phone: 814/238-5534
◆◆◆   **Location:** In Lemont; 1 3/4 mi e on US 322, 2 mi ne via E Branch Rd. 901 Pike St 16851. **Hours:** 5:30
Continental   pm-9 pm. Closed major holidays. **Reservations:** suggested. **Features:** semi-formal attire; cocktails & lounge.
Dining in converted residence. Smoke free premises. **Cards:** AE, DI, DS, MC, VI. ⊗

**ZIMM'S FAMILY RESTAURANT**      Dinner: up to $10      Phone: 814/234-2447
◆◆   **Location:** 4 mi n on SR 26. 2541 E College Ave 16801. **Hours:** 7 am-9 pm, Fri & Sat-9 pm, Sun 8 am-8
American   pm, senior discount Mon & Tues only. Closed major holidays. **Features:** casual dress; children's menu;
carryout; salad bar; buffet. Hearty portions with homemade pies & desserts. Famous homemade soups. ⊗
**Cards:** AE, DI, DS, MC, VI.

# STRAFFORD

## RESTAURANT

**MILEPOST INN**   Historical      Dinner: $11-$20      Phone: 610/688-5640
◆   **Location:** Center, on US 30. 644 W Lancaster Ave 19087. **Hours:** 11:30 am-10 pm, Sat 11:30 am-3 &
American   4:30-11 pm, Sun 4 pm-9 pm. Closed: 12/25. **Reservations:** suggested; weekends. **Features:** casual dress;
cocktails & lounge; a la carte. Old turnpike coaching inn. **Cards:** AE, CB, DI, MC, VI. ⊗

# STRASBURG—2,600

## LODGINGS

**AMISH LANTERNS MOTEL**      Rates Subject to Change      Phone: 717/687-7839

| | | 2P/1B: | | 2P/2B: | | XP: |
|---|---|---|---|---|---|---|
| 6/9-9/3 | | $50- | 62 | $60- | 70 | $6 |
| 5/1-6/8, 9/4-11/4 & 3/29-4/30 | | $40- | 52 | $50- | 60 | $6 |
| 11/5-3/28 | | $34 | | $38- | 44 | $6 |

Motel   **Location:** 1/4 mi n on SR 896; 2 1/2 mi s of US 30. 17579 (PO Box 16). **Terms:** Reserv deposit, 7 day
notice; no pets. **Facility:** 33 rooms. Located in historic village. 2 stories; exterior corridors; heated pool.
**Dining:** Breakfast room 7-11 am, 3/15-11/15. **All Rooms:** cable TV. **Some Rooms:** phones. **Cards:** AE, DS, MC, VI.
*(See ad starting on p A152)*     Ⓓⓧ

**CARRIAGE HOUSE MOTOR INN**      Rates Subject to Change      Phone: 717/687-7651

| | | 2P/2B: | | XP: | |
|---|---|---|---|---|---|
| 7/1-10/29 | | $69- | 89 | $6 | F12 |
| 5/1-6/30 & 4/1-4/30 | | $49- | 69 | $6 | F12 |
| 10/30-3/31 | | $29- | 49 | $6 | F12 |

Motel   **Location:** 1/4 mi e on SR 896 & 741. 144 E Main St 17579. **Terms:** No pets. **Facility:** 14 rooms. Good sized
rooms, well-maintained. 1 story; exterior corridors; playground. **Dining:** Restaurant nearby. **All Rooms:** cable
TV. **Cards:** AE, DS, MC, VI.     Ⓓ

**DUTCH TREAT MOTEL**      Rates Subject to Change      Phone: 717/687-7998

| | | 2P/1B: | | 2P/2B: | | XP: |
|---|---|---|---|---|---|---|
| 6/30-9/3 | | $48- | 58 | $58- | 64 | $5 |
| 5/1-6/29, 9/4-11/4 & 4/5-4/30 | | $38- | 48 | $48- | 56 | $5 |
| 11/5-4/4 | | $30- | 34 | $34- | 44 | $5 |

Motel   **Location:** 2 mi s of Rt 30, off Rt 896. (265 Herr Rd, RONKS). **Terms:** Reserv deposit, 5 day notice; no pets.
**Facility:** 25 rooms. Well-maintained rooms & grounds. 1 two-bedroom unit. 1 story; exterior corridors; heated
pool. **All Rooms:** combo & shower baths, cable TV. **Some Rooms:** refrigerators. **Cards:** AE, DS, MC, VI.   Ⓓⓧ

**HISTORIC STRASBURG INN**      Rates Subject to Change      Phone: 717/687-7691

| | 1P: | | 2P/1B: | | 2P/2B: | | XP: | |
|---|---|---|---|---|---|---|---|---|
| 6/15-10/31 [CP] | 1P: | $89 | 2P/1B: | $89 | 2P/2B: | $89 | $12 | F12 |
| 5/1-6/14, 11/1-11/30 & | | | | | | | | |
| 4/1-4/30 [CP] | 1P: | $79 | | $79 | | $79 | $12 | F12 |
| 12/1-3/31 [CP] | 1P: | $59 | | $59 | | $59 | $12 | F12 |

Country Inn   **Location:** 1/2 mi n on SR 896, 2 1/2 mi s of US 30. SR 896 Historic Dr 17579. Fax: 717/687-6098.
**Terms:** Reserv deposit, 3 day notice; package plans; small pets only, $5, $25 dep req. **Facility:** 103 rooms. Colonial setting
on spacious grounds. Fri & Sat $10 extra. Suites $20 extra; 2 stories; exterior corridors; meeting rooms; heated pool; exercise
room, playground, information center, antique portrait center, horse drawn wagon rides, horseshoes, shuffleboard, volleyball.
**Dining & Entertainment:** Dining room, cafeteria, 7-10 am, 11:30-2 & 5-9 pm, Fri & Sat-10 pm; $13-$33; cocktails/lounge;
entertainment weekends in season; afternoon tea; entertainment. **Recreation:** social program. Fee: bicycles.
**All Rooms:** cable TV. **Some Rooms:** coffeemakers, refrigerators. Fee: VCP's. **Cards:** AE, CB, DI, DS, MC, VI.
*(See color ad p A154)*     Ⓓⓧ

**PJ'S GUEST HOME**      Guaranteed Rates      Phone: 717/687-8800

| | 1P: | | 2P/1B: | | XP: | |
|---|---|---|---|---|---|---|
| All Year [CP] | 1P: | $27- | 43 | $32- | 48 | $10   D |

Historic Bed   **Location:** 1/4 mi w on SR 741, from jct SR 896. 101 W Main St 17579. **Terms:** Reserv deposit, 5 day
& Breakfast   notice; weekly rates; no pets. **Facility:** 3 rooms. Circa 1824. 2 stories; interior corridors; smoke free premises;
whirlpool, small pool. **Dining:** Restaurant nearby. **All Rooms:** cable TV, no phones. **Cards:** AE, DS, MC, VI.
    Ⓓⓧ

**STRASBURG VILLAGE INN**      Rates Subject to Change      Phone: 717/687-0900

| | 2P/1B: | | 2P/2B: | | XP: | |
|---|---|---|---|---|---|---|
| 6/10-10/28 [BP] | $79- | 129 | $79- | 129 | $10 | F5 |
| 5/1-6/9 [BP] | $64- | 114 | $64- | 114 | $10 | F5 |
| 10/29-4/30 [BP] | $54- | 99 | $54- | 99 | $10 | F5 |

Historic Bed   **Location:** Center; at jct SR 741 & 896. 1 W Main St, Center Sq 17579. **Terms:** Sr. discount; reserv deposit,
& Breakfast   5 day notice; no pets. **Facility:** 11 rooms. Elegantly appointed Williamsburg rooms, circa 1788. 2 stories; inte-
rior corridors; smoke free premises. **Dining:** Continental breakfast on Sunday; restaurant nearby.
**All Rooms:** cable TV, no phones. **Cards:** AE, DS, MC, VI. *(See ad starting on p A152)*     Ⓓⓧ

## RESTAURANT

**ISAAC'S RESTAURANT & DELI**      Dinner: up to $10      Phone: 717/687-7699
◆   **Location:** RT 741 E 17579. **Hours:** 10 am-9 pm, Fri & Sat-9 pm, Sun-8 pm. Closed: 11/23, 12/25 & Easter.
American   **Features:** casual dress; children's menu; carryout. Friendly deli with atmosphere. Smoke free premises.
**Cards:** AE, DS, MC, VI.     ⊗

## STROUDSBURG—5,300 (See POCONO MOUNTAINS & VICINITY ACCOMMODATIONS spotting map pages A212 & A213; see index starting on page A210)

### RESTAURANT

**GLADSTONE'S SIDE STREET GRILLE**
◆◆ American
**Dinner:** $11-$20  **Phone:** 717/424-9120  (57)
**Location:** Center, at Quaker Plaza. 5th & Sarah sts 18360. **Hours:** 11:30 am-9:30 pm, Fri & Sat-10:30 pm, Sun 3 pm-8:30 pm. **Closed:** 11/23 & 12/25. **Reservations:** suggested; Saturday. **Features:** casual dress; children's menu; carryout; cocktails & lounge. Specializing in their own marinated London Broil & hickory smoked ribs. **Cards:** AE, DS, MC, VI. ⊗

## SUNBURY—11,600

### RESTAURANT

**THE AUGUSTA HOUSE FAMILY RESTAURANT**
◆◆ American
**Dinner:** $11-$20  **Phone:** 717/286-9979
**Location:** 3 blks s at corner of 2nd & Walnut sts. 212 Walnut St 17801. **Hours:** 7 am-8 pm, Sun 11 am-2 pm. **Closed:** major holidays. **Features:** casual dress; children's menu; carryout; buffet. Family style, homemade soups & desserts. Attractive foyer & dining room. **Cards:** MC, VI. ⊗

## SWIFTWATER (See POCONO MOUNTAINS & VICINITY ACCOMMODATIONS spotting map pages A212 & A213; see index starting on page A210)

### RESTAURANT

**FANUCCI'S**
◆◆◆ Italian
**Dinner:** $11-$20  **Phone:** 717/839-7097  (62)
**Location:** On SR 611, 2 3/4 mi n of I-80 exit 44. SR 611 18370. **Hours:** 4 pm-11 pm, Sun from 11 am. **Closed:** 11/23, 12/24 & 12/25. **Reservations:** suggested. **Features:** casual dress; children's menu; early bird specials; carryout; cocktails & lounge; a la carte. Also American entrees. **Cards:** AE, CB, DI, DS, MC, VI. ⊗

## TOWN HILL

### LODGING

**DAYS INN-BREEZEWOOD-WARFORDSBURG**
◆◆◆ Motor Inn
**Guaranteed Rates**  **Phone:** 814/735-3860
All Year  1P: $40  2P/1B: $46  XP: $4  F12
**Location:** At exit 31, I-70. 17267 (RD 2, Box 1595, WARFORDSBURG). Fax: 814/735-3841. **Terms:** Sr. discount; reserv deposit; no pets. **Facility:** 64 rooms. 2 stories; interior corridors; mountain view. **Dining:** Also, Four Seasons Restaurant, see separate listing. **All Rooms:** free movies. **Cards:** AE, DI, DS, MC, VI. (D) ⊗

### RESTAURANT

**FOUR SEASONS RESTAURANT**
◆ American
**Dinner:** up to $10  **Phone:** 814/735-4347
**Location:** In Days Inn-Breezewood-Warfordsburg. 17267. **Hours:** 24 hours. **Features:** casual dress; children's menu; carryout; salad bar; cocktails & lounge; buffet. Homemade soups & pies. **Cards:** AE, DI, DS, MC, VI. ⊗

## TREVOSE (See PHILADELPHIA & VICINITY ACCOMMODATIONS spotting map pages A196 & A197; see index starting on page A193)

### LODGINGS

**HOLIDAY INN BUCKS COUNTY** — Guaranteed Rates — **Phone:** 215/364-2000 **90**

| | | 1P: | | 2P/1B: | | | 2P/2B: | | XP: | |
|---|---|---|---|---|---|---|---|---|---|---|
| | 5/1-12/15 | 1P: $89- | 119 | 2P/1B: $99- | 129 | | 2P/2B: $99- | 129 | XP: $10 | F18 |
| | 12/16-4/30 | 1P: $79- | 119 | 2P/1B: $89- | 129 | | 2P/2B: $89- | 129 | XP: $10 | F18 |

Motor Inn
**Location:** On SR 132; 1 mi nw of I-276 (PA Tpk), exit 28 via US 1S. 4700 Street Rd 19053. **Fax:** 215/364-7197. **Terms:** Sr. discount; credit card guarantee, 3 day notice; weekly/monthly rates; package plans; no pets. **Facility:** 215 rooms. Attractive public areas. Upscale modern exterior with nicely landscaped grounds. Contemporary decor in rooms. Suites, $225; 6 stories; interior corridors; conference facilities; luxury level rooms; heated indoor pool, sauna, whirlpool; exercise room. **Dining & Entertainment:** Restaurant; 6:30 am-10 pm, Sat & Sun from 7 am; children 12 & under eat free; $8-$20; cocktails/lounge. **Services:** data ports, secretarial services. Fee: coin laundry, airport transportation. **All Rooms:** coffeemakers, free & pay movies, cable TV. **Some Rooms:** Fee: microwaves, refrigerators, VCP's. **Cards:** AE, CB, DI, DS, MC, VI. *(See ad p A200)* Ⓓ Ⓢ ⊗

**HOWARD JOHNSON HOTEL** — AAA Special Value Rates — **Phone:** 215/638-4554 **85**

| | | 1P: | | 2P/1B: | | 2P/2B: | |
|---|---|---|---|---|---|---|---|
| | 5/1-9/8 | 1P: $55- | 70 | 2P/1B: $55- | 80 | 2P/2B: $55- | 80 |
| Motor Inn | 9/9-4/30 | 1P: $45- | 60 | 2P/1B: $45- | 60 | 2P/2B: $45- | 60 |

**Location:** US 1, 1/2 mi s of PA Turnpike, exit 28. 2779 Rt 1N 19053. **Fax:** 215/638-7085. **Terms:** Credit card guarantee, 3 day notice; weekly rates; package plans; small pets only. **Facility:** 88 rooms. 3 stories; interior corridors; meeting rooms; pool; game room. **Dining & Entertainment:** Restaurant; 6:30 am-11 pm; $10-$15; cocktails/lounge. **Services:** valet laundry. **All Rooms:** free movies, cable TV. **Some Rooms:** honor bars, refrigerators, whirlpools. **Cards:** AE, CB, DI, DS, MC, VI. *(See ad p A199)* Ⓓ Ⓢ ⊗

**RADISON HOTEL & CONFERENCE CENTER** — AAA Special Value Rates — **Phone:** 215/638-8300 **91**

| | | 1P: | | 2P/1B: | | 2P/2B: | | XP: | |
|---|---|---|---|---|---|---|---|---|---|
| | All Year | 1P: $80- | 110 | 2P/1B: $90- | 120 | 2P/2B: $90- | 120 | XP: $10 | F18 |

Hotel
**Location:** On US 1; 1 mi s of tpk exit 28, jct Roosevelt Blvd & Old Lincoln Hwy. 2400 Old Lincoln Hwy 19053. **Fax:** 215/638-4377. **Terms:** Reserv deposit, 3 day notice; weekly rates; package plans; no pets. **Facility:** 286 rooms. 6 stories; interior corridors; business center; conference facilities; luxury level rooms; heated indoor/outdoor pool, steamroom; exercise room, hair salon; arcade; activities room; shoe shining. **Dining & Entertainment:** Dining room, coffee shop; 7 am-10 pm; $15-$25; cocktails/lounge; Sun brunch 10 am-2 pm; 24-hour room service; entertainment. **Services:** data ports; complimentary evening beverages. Fee: childcare; coin laundry, airport transportation, by reservation. **All Rooms:** free & pay movies, cable TV. **Some Rooms:** Fee: microwaves, refrigerators, VCP's. **Cards:** AE, DI, DS, MC, VI. ⒵ Ⓓ Ⓢ ⊗

**RED ROOF INN** — Rates Subject to Change — **Phone:** 215/244-9422 **89**

| | | 1P: | | 2P/1B: | | 2P/2B: | | XP: | |
|---|---|---|---|---|---|---|---|---|---|
| | All Year | 1P: $28- | 40 | 2P/1B: $35- | 59 | 2P/2B: $40- | 61 | XP: $7 | F18 |

Motel
**Location:** On US 1; 1/2 mi s from exit 28 off PA Tpk. 3100 Lincoln Hwy 19053. **Fax:** 215/244-9469. **Terms:** Credit card guarantee; package plans; small pets only. **Facility:** 162 rooms. 2 stories; exterior corridors. **Services:** data ports. **All Rooms:** free movies, cable TV. **Cards:** AE, CB, DI, DS, MC, VI. ⒵ Ⓓ ⊗

## TUNKHANNOCK—2,300

### LODGING

**SHARPE'S HOUSE BED & BREAKFAST** — Rates Subject to Change — **Phone:** 717/836-4900

| | |  | |  | |
|---|---|---|---|---|---|
| | All Year [BP] | 1P: $40 | | 2P: $50 | |

Historic Bed
& Breakfast
**Location:** From jct SR 29, 3 3/4 mi w on US 6, 1 mi n on Bartron Rd. Bartron Rd 18657 (PO Box L). **Fax:** 717/836-6107. **Terms:** Age restrictions may apply; check-in 4 pm; reserv deposit, 10 day notice; no pets. **Facility:** 2 rooms. 2 stories; interior corridors; smoke free premises. **All Rooms:** no phones, no TVs. **Cards:** MC, VI. Ⓓ ⊗

## UNIONTOWN—12,000

### LODGING

**MOUNT VERNON INN** — Rates Subject to Change — **Phone:** 412/437-2704

| | | 1P: | | 2P/1B: | | 2P/2B: | | XP: | |
|---|---|---|---|---|---|---|---|---|---|
| | All Year [CP] | 1P: $40- | 56 | 2P/1B: $45- | 62 | 2P/2B: $45- | 60 | XP: $5 | D10 |

Motor Inn
**Location:** 1/2 mi w on US 40. 180 W Main St 15401. **Fax:** 412/437-2737. **Terms:** Reserv deposit, 3 day notice; weekly rates; no pets. **Facility:** 60 rooms. Completing renovation. Many rooms well-appointed. Convenient downtown location. 1-3 stories; exterior corridors; meeting rooms. **Dining & Entertainment:** Restaurant; 11 am-10 pm; $8-$16; cocktails/lounge. **All Rooms:** combo & shower baths, cable TV, **Some Rooms:** radios, refrigerators. **Cards:** AE, CB, DI, DS, MC, VI. *(See ad below)* Ⓓ ⊗

For <u>guaranteed</u> rates, you MUST show your membership card.

## RESTAURANTS

**COAL BARON RESTAURANT**  **Dinner:** $11-$20  Phone: 412/439-0111
◆◆◆  **Location:** 4 mi w on US 40. Rt 40 W 15401. **Hours:** 4 pm-11 pm, Sun noon-8 pm. Closed: Mon, 1/1, 11/23
Steakhouse  & 12/25. **Reservations:** suggested. **Features:** casual dress; children's menu; carryout; cocktails & lounge;
valet parking. Flambe desserts, popular for prime rib & veal dishes. Extensive wine list. **Cards:** AE, CB, DI,
MC, VI.

**MELONI'S**  **Dinner:** up to $10  Phone: 412/437-2061
⊕  **Location:** Center. 105 W Main St 15401. **Hours:** 11 am-10 pm, Fri & Sat-11 pm, Sun noon-9 pm. Closed
◆  major holidays. **Features:** casual dress; children's menu; carryout; cocktails & lounge. Casual atmosphere
Italian  with Italian specialties. **Cards:** MC, VI.

# WARMINSTER—32,800

## LODGING

**REGENCY 265 MOTOR INN**  Guaranteed Rates  Phone: 215/674-2200
⊕  All Year  1P: $50  2P/1B: $55  2P/2B: $60  XP: $5
◆◆  **Location:** On SR 132, 1 3/4 mi se of jct SR 263. 265 E Street Rd 18974. Fax: 215/443-7854. **Terms:** Sr.
Motel  discount; credit card guarantee; weekly/monthly rates; no pets. **Facility:** 52 rooms. 2 stories; interior/exterior
corridors; meeting rooms; exercise room. **Dining:** Restaurant nearby. **All Rooms:** free movies, cable TV.
**Some Rooms:** Fee: refrigerators. **Cards:** AE, CB, DI, DS, MC, VI.  Ⓓ⊗

# WARREN—11,100

## LODGINGS

**HOLIDAY INN OF WARREN**  Rates Subject to Change  Phone: 814/726-3000
⊕  5/1-10/31  1P: $63- 65  2P/1B: $69- 71  2P/2B: $69- 71  XP: $6 F16
11/1-4/30  1P: $55- 60  2P/1B: $60- 65  2P/2B: $60- 65  XP: $6 F16
◆◆  **Location:** 1 1/2 mi w on US 6; at Ludlow St exit. 210 Ludlow St 16365. Fax: 814/726-3720. **Terms:** Sr.
Motor Inn  discount; reserv deposit, 3 day notice; no pets. **Facility:** 110 rooms. 4 stories; interior corridors; conference fa-
cilities; heated indoor pool, sauna; exercise room, game room. **Dining:** Dining room; 6:30 am-2 & 5-9 pm;
Fri-10 pm; Sat 7:30 am-2 & 5-10 pm; Sun 8 am-2 & 5-8 pm; $7-$15; cocktails. **Services:** valet laundry.
**All Rooms:** coffeemakers, free movies, cable TV. **Some Rooms:** refrigerators. **Cards:** AE, CB, DI, DS, JCB, MC, VI.  Ⓓ⊗

**WARREN SUPER 8 MOTEL**  Rates Subject to Change  Phone: 814/723-8881
◆◆  All Year [CP]  1P: $41  2P/1B: $47  2P/2B: $47  XP: $5 F12
Motel  **Location:** 1 1/2 mi w on US 6, at Ludlow St exit. 204 Struthers St 16365. Fax: 814/723-8881. **Terms:** Sr.
discount; small pets only, in smoking rooms; $25 dep req. **Facility:** 56 rooms. 3 stories; interior/exterior corri-
dors; meeting rooms. **Dining:** Restaurant nearby. **Services:** data ports. **All Rooms:** free movies, cable TV.
**Some Rooms:** microwaves, refrigerators. Fee: VCP's. **Cards:** AE, CB, DI, DS, MC, VI.  ⒹⓈ⊗

## RESTAURANT

**THE JEFFERSON HOUSE & PUB**  Historical  **Dinner:** $11-$20  Phone: 814/723-2268
◆◆  **Location:** Center; on US 62. 119 Market St 16365. **Hours:** 11:30 am-2:30 & 5:30-9 pm. Closed major
American  holidays, Sun & Mon. **Reservations:** suggested. **Features:** children's menu; carryout; cocktails & lounge.
Restored 1890 home. Mostly mesquite grilled entrees. Imaginative sandwich creations. **Cards:** MC, VI.  ⊗

## WASHINGTON—15,900

### LODGINGS

**BEST WESTERN WASHINGTON MOTOR INN**　　Rates Subject to Change　　**Phone:** 412/222-6500
All Year [CP]　　1P: $44- 64　2P/1B: $54- 74　2P/2B: $54- 80　XP: $6　F18
**Location:** On US 40, e of I-70, exit 4. 1385 W Chestnut St 15301. Fax: 412/222-7671. **Terms:** Sr. discount;
no pets. **Facility:** 62 rooms. 1-2 stories; exterior corridors. **Dining:** Restaurant nearby. **Services:** childcare;
Motel　valet laundry. **All Rooms:** free movies, cable TV. **Cards:** AE, CB, DI, DS, MC, VI.

**DAYS INN**　　Rates Subject to Change　　**Phone:** 412/225-8500
All Year [CP]　　1P: $44- 64　2P/1B: $54- 74　2P/2B: $54- 80　XP: $6　F18
**Location:** On US 40; e of I-70, exit 4. 1370 W Chestnut St 15301. Fax: 412/222-7671. **Terms:** Sr. discount;
reserv deposit; no pets. **Facility:** 104 rooms. 2 stories; interior/exterior corridors; meeting rooms; pool; exer-
Motel　cise room. **Dining:** Restaurant nearby. **Services:** childcare. Fee: coin laundry. **All Rooms:** free movies,
cable TV. **Cards:** AE, CB, DI, DS, MC, VI.

**HOLIDAY INN-MEADOW LANDS**　　AAA Special Value Rates　　**Phone:** 412/222-6200
All Year　　1P: $79- 89　2P/1B: $99　2P/2B: $99　XP: $5　F18
**Location:** Northbound I-79, exit 8B (Race Track Rd), 1/2 mi e; southbound I-79, exit 8 (Meadow Lands), 1
Motor Inn　1/2 mi e. 340 Race Track Rd 15301. Fax: 412/228-1977. **Terms:** Package plans; pets. **Facility:** 138 rooms.
Attractive public areas. 2-bedroom suite, $250; 7 stories; interior corridors; conference facilities; pool, sauna,
steamroom, whirlpool; exercise room. **Dining & Entertainment:** Dining room; 6:30 am-10 pm, Fri-11 pm, Sat
7 am-11 pm & Sun 7 am-10 pm; $10-$20; cocktails/lounge; entertainment, nightclub. **Services:** data ports, secretarial
services. Fee: childcare; coin laundry, airport transportation. **All Rooms:** free & pay movies, cable TV.
**Some Rooms:** coffeemakers, kitchen, microwaves, refrigerators. **Cards:** AE, CB, DI, DS, JCB, MC, VI.

**KNIGHTS INN**　　Rates Subject to Change　　**Phone:** 412/223-8040
All Year　　1P: $41　2P/1B: $47　2P/2B: $47　XP: $6　F18
**Location:** Off US 19; 1/2 mi s of I-70, exit 7A. 25 Knights Inn Dr 15301. Fax: 412/228-6445. **Terms:** Credit
card guarantee; weekly rates; small pets only. **Facility:** 101 rooms. 12 efficiencies, $43.95-$52; 1 story; exterior
Motel　corridors; meeting rooms; small pool. **All Rooms:** free movies, cable TV. **Some Rooms:** coffeemakers,
microwaves, refrigerators. Fee: VCP's. **Cards:** AE, CB, DI, DS, MC, VI.

**RAMADA INN**　　AAA Special Value Rates　　**Phone:** 412/225-9750
All Year　　1P: $50- 64　2P/2B: $56- 70　XP: $6　F18
**Location:** On US 40, 1/2 mi e of I-70, exit 4. 1170 W Chestnut St 15301 (PO Box 293). Fax: 412/223-2912.
**Terms:** Package plans; no pets. **Facility:** 93 rooms. Hilltop location. 2 stories; interior/exterior corridors;
Motor Inn　meeting rooms; pool. **Dining & Entertainment:** Dining room; 7 am-10 pm; $7-$16; cocktails/lounge.
**All Rooms:** cable TV. **Cards:** AE, CB, DI, MC, VI.

**RED ROOF INN**　　Rates Subject to Change　　**Phone:** 412/228-5750
5/1-11/30　　1P: $36　2P/1B: $45　2P/2B: $50　XP: $7　F18
Motel　　12/1-4/30　　1P: $34　2P/1B: $41　2P/2B: $46　XP: $7　F18
**Location:** On US 40; e of I-70, exit 4. 1399 W Chestnut St 15301. Fax: 412/228-5865. **Terms:** Credit card
guarantee; small pets only. **Facility:** 110 rooms. 2 stories; interior/exterior corridors. **Dining:** Restaurant nearby.
**All Rooms:** free movies, combo & shower baths, cable TV. **Cards:** AE, CB, DI, DS, MC, VI.　Roll in showers.

### RESTAURANTS

**ANGELO'S RISTORANTE**　　Dinner: $11-$20　　**Phone:** 412/222-7120
**Location:** On US 40, 3/4 mi e of I-70, exit 4. 955 W Chestnut St 15301. **Hours:** 11 am-11 pm, Fri &
Sat-midnight. Closed: Sun, 11/23 & 12/25. **Reservations:** suggested. **Features:** casual dress; children's
Italian　menu; health conscious menu items; carryout; cocktails & lounge; a la carte. Good wine selection & cruvinet
on premises. Diverse Italian & nouvelle cuisine. Family-owned since 1939. Smoke free premises. **Cards:** AE,
CB, DI, MC, VI.

**BOB EVANS FARMS RESTAURANT**　　Dinner: up to $10　　**Phone:** 412/228-8899
**Location:** S off US 19 from jct I-70 exit 7A. 490 Oaksprings Rd 15301. **Hours:** 6 am-10 pm, Fri & Sat-11:30
American　pm. Closed: 11/23 & 12/25. **Features:** casual dress; children's menu; senior's menu; health conscious menu
items; carryout; a la carte. Budget traveler & family oriented. **Cards:** MC, VI.

**CURINGA'S INN**　　Dinner: $11-$20　　**Phone:** 412/225-7747
**Location:** 2 mi n of I-70 on US19. 1050 Washington Rd 15301. **Hours:** 11 am-10 pm, Fri-11 pm, Sat 4
American　pm-11 pm, Sun noon-8:30 pm. Closed major holidays. **Features:** casual dress; children's menu; carryout;
salad bar; cocktails & lounge. Old English atmosphere. **Cards:** AE, DI, DS, MC, VI.

## WASHINGTON CROSSING

### LODGING

**INN TO THE WOODS BED & BREAKFAST**　　Rates Subject to Change　　**Phone:** 215/493-1974
Fri & Sat 6/15-11/15 [BP]　2P/1B: $120- 155　XP: $35
Sun-Thurs 6/15-11/15 [CP]　2P/1B: $90- 110　XP: $35
Sun-Thurs 5/1-6/14 &
Bed &　11/16-4/30 [CP]　2P/1B: $70- 100　XP: $35
Breakfast　Fri & Sat 5/1-6/14 &
11/16-4/30 [BP]　2P/1B: $110- 135　XP: $35
**Location:** I-95, New Hope exits 31 & 31B, 1 mi n on Taylorsville Rd, 1/2 mi w on Mount Eyre Rd, 1/2 mi n on Walker Rd,
1/2 mi e on Glenwood Rd. 150 Glenwood Rd 18977. Fax: 215/493-3774. **Terms:** Age restrictions may apply; reserv deposit;
7 day notice, cancellation fee imposed; monthly rates; package plans; 2 night min stay, on weekends; no pets. **Facility:** 6
rooms. Old world Bavarian ambience on 10 secluded acres. Indoor atrium with fish pond. Raised stone hearth fireplace in
common area. 3 stories, no elevator; interior corridors; smoke free premises; meeting rooms; volleyball. **Recreation:** hiking
trails. **All Rooms:** combo & shower baths, cable TV. **Some Rooms:** phones. **Cards:** MC, VI.

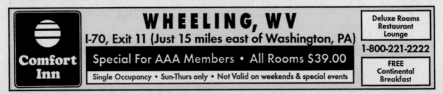

## WAYNE—900

### LODGINGS

**COURTYARD BY MARRIOTT**  AAA Special Value Rates  **Phone:** 610/687-6633
◆◆◆  All Year  1P:  $80  2P/1B:  $80  2P/2B:  $80
Motor Inn  **Location:** Center, on US 30 in Devon Square Business Center. 762 W Lancaster Ave 19087.
Fax: 610/687-1150. **Terms:** Credit card guarantee, 3 day notice; CP, MAP available; no pets. **Facility:** 149 rooms. Attractively furnished guest rooms. 3 stories; interior corridors; meeting rooms; heated indoor/outdoor pool, indoor whirlpool; exercise room. **Dining & Entertainment:** Coffee shop; 6:30 am-10 am, Sat & Sun 7 am-noon; cocktails/lounge. **Services:** data ports; valet laundry. **All Rooms:** free & pay movies, cable TV. **Some Rooms:** refrigerators. **Cards:** AE, CB, DI, DS, MC, VI. *(See color ad p A198)*  🎟 Ⓓ Ⓢ ⊗

**COURTYARD BY MARRIOTT-VALLEY FORGE**  Rates Subject to Change  **Phone:** 610/687-6700
◆◆◆  Sun-Thurs  1P:  $92  2P/1B:  $102  2P/2B:  $102  XP:  $10  F13
Motor Inn  Fri & Sat  1P:  $69  2P/1B:  $79  2P/2B:  $79  XP:  $10  F13
**Location:** From US 202, Warner Rd exit then 1/2 mi s on Swedesford Rd. 1100 Drummers Ln 19087.
Fax: 610/687-1149. **Terms:** Sr. discount; reserv deposit, 3 day notice; weekly rates; BP available; no pets. **Facility:** 150 rooms. 3 stories; interior corridors; meeting rooms; heated indoor pool, whirlpool; exercise room. **Dining:** Restaurant; 6:30 am-2 & 5-10 pm, Sat & Sun 7 am-noon & 5-10 pm; $6-$14; cocktails. **Services:** data ports. Fee: coin laundry. **All Rooms:** free & pay movies, cable TV. **Some Rooms:** refrigerators. **Cards:** AE, DI, DS, MC, VI. *(See color ad p A198)*  🎟 Ⓓ Ⓢ ⊗

**GUEST QUARTERS SUITE HOTEL/VALLEY FORGE**  Rates Subject to Change  **Phone:** 610/647-6700
◆◆◆  Mon-Fri [CP]  1P:  $145  2P/1B:  $165  2P/2B:  $165  XP:  $20  F16
Suite Hotel  Sat & Sun [EP]  1P:  $89  2P/1B:  $89  2P/2B:  $89  XP:  $20  F16
**Location:** In Chesterbrook Complex; 3 mi w on US 202 at Chesterbrook Blvd exit. 888 Chesterbrook Blvd 19087. Fax: 610/889-9420. **Terms:** Sr. discount; reserv deposit; package plans; no pets. **Facility:** 229 rooms. 1-bedroom suites with living room & wet bar. Atrium style lobby. 5 stories; interior corridors; business center, conference facilities; heated indoor pool, sauna, whirlpool; exercise room. **Dining & Entertainment:** Restaurant; 6:30-10 am, 11-2:30 & 5-10 pm, Sat-11 pm, Sun brunch 11 am-3 & 5-10 pm; $8-$19; cocktails/lounge; entertainment. **Services:** data ports, secretarial services; valet laundry; area transportation, within 5 mi. Fee: PC, airport transportation. **All Rooms:** coffeemakers, free & pay movies, refrigerators, cable TV. **Some Rooms:** microwaves. Fee: VCP's, whirlpools. **Cards:** AE, CB, DI, DS, JCB, MC, VI. *(See ad p A199)*  🎟 Ⓓ Ⓢ ⊗

### RESTAURANTS

**A. T. SAMUELS**  Dinner: $21-$30  **Phone:** 610/687-2840
◆◆◆  **Location:** Located in Spread Eagle Village at Lancaster Ave, (US 30) & Eagle Rd. 503 W Lancaster Ave
American  19087. **Hours:** 11:30 am-2:30 & 5-10 pm, Sun-9 pm. Closed major holidays. **Reservations:** suggested. **Features:** casual dress; Sunday brunch; health conscious menu; cocktails & lounge; a la carte. A menu changing with the seasons featuring very well prepared entrees in a Contemporary American cuisine. **Cards:** AE, CB, DI, DS, MC, VI.  ⊗

**LA FOURCHETTE**  Dinner: $21-$30  **Phone:** 610/687-8333
◆◆◆  **Location:** Downtown, on US 30, 1/2 blk n on Wayne Ave. 110 N Wayne Ave 19087. **Hours:** 6 pm-10 pm,
French  Sun 11 am-2:30 & 6-9 pm. Closed major holidays. **Reservations:** suggested. **Features:** semi-formal attire; Sunday brunch; health conscious menu; cocktails & lounge; street parking; a la carte. Warm country French Provincial atmosphere. Gracious service. Creative freshly prepared cuisine. Extensive wine list. **Cards:** AE, CB, DI, MC, VI.  ⊗

**VILLA STRAFFORD**  Dinner: $21-$30  **Phone:** 610/964-1116
◆◆◆  **Location:** From SR 30, right on Strafford Ave. 115 Strafford Ave 19087. **Hours:** 11:30 am-2:30 & 5:30-10
Continental  pm, Sat from 5:30 pm. Closed: Sun, 1/1, 7/4 & 12/25. **Reservations:** suggested. **Features:** semi-formal attire; cocktails; a la carte. Live jazz on Wed, Fri & Sat evenings. Formal dining in elegant setting. **Cards:** AE, CB, DI, MC, VI.  ⊗

## WAYNESBORO—10,000

### LODGING

**BEST WESTERN WAYNESBORO**  Rates Subject to Change  **Phone:** 717/762-9113
◆◆  All Year [BP]  1P:  $49  2P/1B:  $54  2P/2B:  $58  XP:  $5  F2
Motel  **Location:** I-81 exit 3, 7 1/2 mi e on SR 16. 239 W Main St 17268. Fax: 717/762-9113. **Terms:** Reserv deposit, 3 day notice; pets, $5. **Facility:** 52 rooms. 2 rooms with whirlpool, $75 Mon-Thurs, $95 Fri-Sun; 2 stories; exterior corridors; meeting rooms. **Services:** data ports. **All Rooms:** cable TV. **Some Rooms:** Fee: VCP's. **Cards:** AE, CB, DI, DS, MC, VI.  Ⓓ ⊗

## WAYNESBURG—4,300

### LODGINGS

**ECONO LODGE**  Guaranteed Rates  **Phone:** 412/627-5544
⊕  All Year  1P:  $40- 49  2P/1B:  $44- 53  2P/2B:  $53  XP:  $5  F18
◆◆  **Location:** Jct I-79, exit 3 & SR 21. 350 Miller Ln 15370. Fax: 412/627-5544. **Terms:** Sr. discount; reserv
Motel  deposit, 3 day notice; pets. **Facility:** 60 rooms. Hearing impaired smoke detectors avail. 2 stories; exterior corridors. **All Rooms:** free movies, cable TV. **Cards:** AE, CB, DI, DS, JCB, MC, VI.  Ⓓ ⊗

**SUPER 8 MOTEL**  Rates Subject to Change  **Phone:** 412/627-8880
◆◆  All Year [CP]  1P:  $38- 43  2P/1B:  $43- 49  2P/2B:  $45- 49  XP:  $5  F12
Motel  **Location:** Jct I-79, exit 3 & SR 21. 80 Miller Ln 15370. Fax: 412/627-8880. **Terms:** Sr. discount; reserv deposit; pets, upon approval. **Facility:** 56 rooms. 3 stories; interior corridors. **Dining:** Restaurant nearby. **Services:** winter plug-ins. **All Rooms:** free movies, cable TV. **Some Rooms:** Fee: VCP's. **Cards:** AE, CB, DI, DS, MC, VI.  Ⓓ Ⓢ ⊗

# WELLSBORO—3,400

## LODGINGS

**CANYON MOTEL**
Rates Subject to Change — Phone: 717/724-1681
5/1-12/15 [CP]   1P: $28- 35   2P/1B: $35- 46   2P/2B: $38- 49   XP: $5   F12
12/16-4/30 [CP]   1P: $25- 35   2P/1B: $32- 46   2P/2B: $34- 49   XP: $5   F12
**Location:** 2 blks e on US 6 & SR 660. 18 East Ave 16901. Fax: 717/724-5202. **Terms:** Reserv deposit; package plans; pets, smoking rooms only. **Facility:** 28 rooms. 1 two-bedroom unit. 1 story; exterior corridors; heated pool; playground. **Dining:** Restaurant nearby. **Services:** data ports. **All Rooms:** microwaves, free movies, refrigerators, cable TV. **Cards:** AE, CB, DI, DS, MC, VI. *(See ad p A233)*

**COLTON POINT MOTEL**
AAA Special Value Rates — Phone: 717/724-2155
All Year   2P/1B: $40   2P/2B: $45   XP: $5   D
**Location:** 13 mi w on US 6. 16901 (RD 4, Box 138). **Terms:** Reserv deposit, 3 day notice; weekly rates; MAP available; package plans; no pets. **Facility:** 14 rooms. Quiet, rural location. 1 story; exterior corridors. **Dining:** Restaurant, coffee shop; 8 am-10 am. **Recreation:** nature trails; fishing; downhill skiing, snowmobiling. **All Rooms:** shower baths, cable TV, no phones. **Cards:** DS, MC, VI.

**FOXFIRE BED & BREAKFAST**
Rates Subject to Change — Phone: 717/724-5175
All Year [BP]   1P: $32   2P/1B: $65
**Location:** 4 mi w on SR 6/SR 666 to Hills Creek St Park Rd (left) 1 mi follow St Park sign staying left. RD 2, Box 439 16901. **Terms:** Check-in 4 pm; reserv deposit, 7 day notice; weekly rates; pets, $5. **Facility:** 3 rooms. Rustic country farmhouse, views of rolling countryside. Ideal for outdoor activities. Advance reservation required 11/15-4/3. Extra persons not allowed in rooms; 2 stories; interior corridors; smoke free premises. **Dining:** Afternoon tea. **Recreation:** fishing; cross country skiing; hiking trails. **All Rooms:** no phones, no TVs. **Some Rooms:** radios. **Cards:** MC, VI.

**PENN WELLS LODGE**
Rates Subject to Change — Phone: 717/724-3463
Fri & Sat 5/1-1/1   1P: $51- 57   2P/2B: $55- 65   XP: $5
Sun-Thurs 5/1-1/1   1P: $46- 52   2P/2B: $50- 60   XP: $5
1/2-4/30   1P: $30- 52   2P/2B: $39- 60   XP: $5
**Location:** 1 blk n on US 6 & SR 287. 4 Main St 16901. **Terms:** Credit card guarantee, 3 day notice; package plans; no pets. **Facility:** 55 rooms. Closed 12/25. 2 stories; interior/exterior corridors; heated indoor pool, saunas, whirlpool; exercise room, health club, playground. **Dining:** Restaurant nearby. **Services:** data ports. **All Rooms:** free movies, cable TV. **Some Rooms:** coffeemakers, microwaves, refrigerators. **Cards:** AE, CB, DI, DS, MC, VI. *(See ad below)*

**SHERWOOD MOTEL**
Rates Subject to Change — Phone: 717/724-3424
5/1-12/15 [CP]   1P: $28- 35   2P/1B: $35- 46   2P/2B: $38- 49   XP: $5
12/16-4/30 [CP]   1P: $25- 35   2P/1B: $32- 46   2P/2B: $34- 49   XP: $5
**Location:** 1 blk n on US 6 & SR 287. 2 Main St 16901. Fax: 717/724-5658. **Terms:** Reserv deposit; package plans; pets, $5. **Facility:** 32 rooms. Very well maintained. 2 two-bedroom units. 2 stories; exterior corridors; heated pool; playground. **Dining:** Restaurant nearby. **All Rooms:** microwaves, free movies, refrigerators, combo & shower baths, cable TV. **Cards:** AE, CB, DI, DS, MC, VI. *(See ad p A233)*

**TERRACE MOTEL**
Rates Subject to Change — Phone: 717/724-4711
All Year   1P: $26- 30   2P/1B: $30- 38   2P/2B: $34- 40   XP: $5
**Location:** 1/2 mi w on US 6. Rt 6, Box 467 16901. **Terms:** Reserv deposit; weekly rates; no pets. **Facility:** 15 rooms. Several cabins. 2 two-bedroom units. 1 story; exterior corridors. **Dining:** Restaurant nearby. **All Rooms:** free movies, refrigerators, combo & shower baths, cable TV. **Some Rooms:** coffeemakers, 3 efficiencies, no utensils. **Cards:** AE, DS, MC, VI.

## RESTAURANTS

**COACH STOP INN**
Dinner: up to $10 — Phone: 717/724-5361
**Location:** 12 mi w on US 6. Rt 6 16901. **Hours:** 11 am-9 pm, Fri & Sat-10 pm, Sun-8 pm. Closed: 12/24-12/26. **Reservations:** suggested. **Features:** Sunday brunch; children's menu; carryout; salad bar; cocktails. Rural location, casual atmosphere. **Cards:** DS, MC, VI.

**HARLAND'S FAMILY STYLE RESTAURANT**
Dinner: up to $10 — Phone: 717/724-3311
**Location:** 1 blk e. 17 Pearl St 16901. **Hours:** 6 am-10 pm, Fri & Sat to midnight, Sun-10 pm. Closed: 1/1, 11/23 & 12/25. **Features:** children's menu; carryout; salad bar. Fresh fish & special menu on Fri. Homemade soups & pies. **Cards:** MC, VI.

**THE LOG CABIN**
Dinner: $11-$20 — Phone: 814/435-8808
**Location:** 13 mi e on US 6. 16921. **Hours:** 4:30 pm-9 pm, Fri & Sat 11 am-10 pm, Sun 11:30 am-9 pm. Closed: 12/24 & 12/25. **Reservations:** suggested; Fri & Sat. **Features:** children's menu; salad bar; cocktails & lounge. Casual dining in an older log cabin decorated with hunting trophies. Steak & seafood dishes. Fresh trout is a specialty. Soup & salad bar. Sunday menu-all specials $5.95-$6.95. **Cards:** DS, MC, VI.

**PENN WELLS DINING ROOM**
Dinner: $11-$20 — Phone: 717/724-2111
**Location:** On SR 660 s of US 6. 62 Main St 16901. **Hours:** 7-11 am, 11:30-1:30 & 5-10 pm, Sun 7 am-9 pm. Closed: 12/25. **Reservations:** suggested; wknds & summer. **Features:** Sunday brunch; children's menu; carryout; salad bar; cocktails & lounge. Inviting dining room with traditional decor. Varied dinner menu. Smorgasbord Sat for dinner. **Cards:** AE, CB, DI, DS, MC, VI.

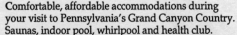
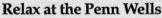

**THE STEAK HOUSE**
**Dinner:** $11-$20
**Phone:** 717/724-9092
**Location:** Center. 29 Main St 16901. **Hours:** 5 pm-9 pm. Closed: Sun, 11/23 & 12/25.
**Reservations:** suggested. **Features:** children's menu; carryout; cocktails & lounge; a la carte. Well-prepared dishes in casual family restaurant. Generous portions, plain presentation. Country inn decor. Homemade pies
Steakhouse & soups, fresh roast turkey dinners. **Cards:** AE, CB, DI, DS, MC, VI.

# WEST CHESTER—18,000

## LODGINGS

**ABBEY GREEN MOTOR LODGE**
Guaranteed Rates
**Phone:** 610/692-3310
All Year
2P/1B: $39- 49 2P/2B: $47- 57 XP: $5 D12
**Location:** 2 mi s on US 202 & 322. 1036 Wilmington Pike 19382. **Terms:** Sr. discount; reserv deposit, 3 day
Motel notice; weekly/monthly rates; 7 night min stay, for 3 efficiencies; pets. **Facility:** 18 rooms. 6 rooms with fireplace; 1 story; exterior corridors; basketball court. **All Rooms:** free movies, combo & shower baths, cable TV. **Some Rooms:** radios, refrigerators. **Cards:** AE, CB, DI, DS, MC, VI.
(D) ⊗

**BEECHWOOD MOTEL**
Rates Subject to Change
**Phone:** 610/399-0970
All Year
2P/1B: $42- 46 2P/2B: $49- 55 XP: $6
**Location:** 3 mi s on US 202 & 322. 1310 Wilmington Pike 19382. **Terms:** Sr. discount; credit card
Motel guarantee; weekly/monthly rates; no pets. **Facility:** 22 rooms. 1 story; exterior corridors. **Dining:** Restaurant nearby. **All Rooms:** free movies, cable TV. **Some Rooms:** 3 efficiencies, no utensils, radios. **Cards:** AE, CB, DI, DS, MC, VI.
(D) ⊗

**WEST CHESTER INN & CONFERENCE CENTER**
Rates Subject to Change
**Phone:** 610/692-1900
All Year
1P: $72 2P/1B: $82- 110 2P/2B: $82- 109 XP: $10 F18
**Location:** 1 1/2 mi s on US 202 & 322 at jct US 322 business route. 943 S High St 19382.
Motor Inn Fax: 610/436-0159. **Terms:** Sr. discount; reserv deposit; weekly/monthly rates; no pets. **Facility:** 141 rooms. Offers a mix of standard rooms & spacious 1-room suites. 3 stories; interior corridors; conference facilities; small pool; exercise room. **Dining & Entertainment:** Restaurant; 6:30 am-3 & 5:30-10 pm, Sat from 8 am, Sun 7:30 am-2 & 4-9 pm, entertainment Thurs-Sat; $11-$17; cocktails/lounge. **Services:** data ports. Fee: coin laundry; airport transportation. **All Rooms:** free movies, cable TV. **Some Rooms:** coffeemakers, 3 efficiencies, microwaves, refrigerators. Fee: VCP's. **Cards:** AE, CB, DI, DS, MC, VI.
(D) ⊗

## RESTAURANT

**DILWORTHTOWN INN** Country Inn
**Dinner:** $11-$20
**Phone:** 610/399-1390
**Location:** 4 mi s on US 202 & 322, 1/4 mi w on Old Wilmington Pike, in Dilworth Village. 1390 Old
Wilmington Pike 19382. **Hours:** 5:30 pm-10 pm, Sat-10:30 pm, Sun 3 pm-9 pm. Closed major holidays.
Continental **Reservations:** required. **Features:** semi-formal attire; cocktails & lounge; a la carte. Candlelight dining in restored historic inn. French influence. Very extensive wine list. **Cards:** AE, CB, DI, DS, MC, VI.

# WEST MIDDLESEX—1,000

## LODGINGS

**RADISSON HOTEL SHARON**
Guaranteed Rates
**Phone:** 412/528-2501
All Year
1P: $72- 92 2P/1B: $82- 92 2P/2B: $82- 92 XP: $8 F18
**Location:** On SR 18, s of I-80 exit 1N. Rt 18 & I-80 16159 (PO Box 596). Fax: 412/528-2306. **Terms:** Sr.
Motor Inn discount; credit card guarantee, 3 day notice; weekly rates; small pets only. **Facility:** 153 rooms. Domed courtyard. 3 stories; interior corridors; conference facilities; heated indoor pool, saunas, whirlpool; exercise room, 25 whirlpools/steambaths. **Dining:** Dining room; 6:30 am-2 & 5-10 pm; $12-$20; cocktails. **Services:** data ports. Fee: coin laundry. **All Rooms:** free & pay movies, cable TV. **Some Rooms:** coffeemakers, refrigerators. **Cards:** AE, CB, DI, DS, JCB, MC, VI.
(D) (S) ⊗

**SHENANGO VALLEY COMFORT INN**
Rates Subject to Change
**Phone:** 412/342-7200
5/1-9/30 [CP]
1P: $50 2P/1B: $55 2P/2B: $55 XP: $5 F16
10/1-4/30 [CP]
1P: $45 2P/1B: $50 2P/2B: $50 XP: $5 F16
Motel **Location:** N on SR 18 at jct I-80, exit 1N. Rt 18 & Wilson Rd 16159. Fax: 412/342-7213. **Terms:** Reserv deposit; weekly rates; pets, $10 dep req, $5 daily. **Facility:** 61 rooms. Good room variety. 2 stories; interior corridors; meeting rooms; heated indoor pool, sauna, whirlpool; exercise room. **Services:** valet laundry.
**Some Rooms:** refrigerators. Fee: VCP's. **Cards:** AE, CB, DI, DS, JCB, MC, VI.

# WEXFORD (See PITTSBURGH ACCOMMODATIONS spotting map page A207; see index starting on page A206)

## LODGING

**ECONO LODGE-PITTSBURGH NORTH**
Rates Subject to Change
**Phone:** 412/935-1000 **87**
Motel All Year
1P: $46- 55 2P/2B: $51- 60 XP: $5 F17
**Location:** 9 mi n, jct I-79, exit 22 & SR 910. 107 VIP Dr 15090. Fax: 412/935-6288. **Terms:** Sr. discount; small pets only. **Facility:** 50 rooms. Nicely furnished rooms. 1 two-bedroom unit. 2 stories; interior corridors.
**Dining:** Restaurant nearby. **Services:** Fee: coin laundry. **All Rooms:** free movies, cable TV. **Some Rooms:** kitchen. Fee: VCP's. **Cards:** AE, CB, DI, DS, JCB, MC, VI.
(D) ⊗

# WHITE HAVEN—1,100 (See POCONO MOUNTAINS & VICINITY ACCOMMODATIONS spotting map pages A212 & A213; see index starting on page A210)

## LODGING

**POCONO DAYS INN**
AAA Special Value Rates
**Phone:** 717/443-0391 **31**
All Year [CP]
1P: $55- 140 2P/1B: $65- 150 2P/2B: $65- 150 XP: $10 F12
**Location:** I-80 exit 42, 2 3/4 mi e on SR 940. 18661 (Rt 940, HCR 1, Box 35). Fax: 717/443-7542.
Motel **Terms:** Credit card guarantee, 3 day notice; weekend rates available; small pets only. **Facility:** 40 rooms. Spacious accommodations. 2 stories; exterior corridors. **All Rooms:** coffeemakers, efficiencies, free movies, cable TV, whirlpools. **Some Rooms:** Fee: VCP's. **Cards:** AE, CB, DI, DS, JCB, MC, VI.
(See color ad p A236)
(D) ⊗

---

**Our bold type listings have a special interest in serving you!**

(See **POCONO MOUNTAINS & VICINITY ACCOMMODATIONS** spotting map pages A212 & A213)

## RESTAURANT

A TOUCH OF VANILLA                          **Dinner:** $21-$30                                    **Phone:** 717/443-8411   ㉖
◆◆◆          **Location:** On SR 940, at jct I-80 exit 42 & tpk exit 35, in Mountain Laurel Resort. 18661. **Hours:** 6 pm-9 pm,
American     Fri & Sat-10 pm. Closed: Sun. **Reservations:** required. **Features:** casual dress; cocktails & lounge; a la
carte. Intimate, artful atmosphere. **Cards:** AE, DI, DS, MC, VI.                                               ⊗

# WILKES-BARRE—47,500     (See POCONO MOUNTAINS & VICINITY ACCOM-
MODATIONS spotting map pages A212 & A213; see index starting on page A210)

## LODGINGS

BEST WESTERN EAST MOUNTAIN INN            Guaranteed Rates              **Phone:** 717/822-1011   ⑮
◆◆◆    All Year                1P: $74-  94  2P/1B:  $74-  99  2P/2B:  $74-  99  XP: $5  F12
Motor Inn    **Location:** From I-81 exit 47A, 1/2 mi se on SR 115. 2400 East End Blvd 18702. Fax: 717/822-6072.
**Terms:** Sr. discount; credit card guarantee; no pets. **Facility:** 156 rooms. On mountain top with view of the
valley & city. Attractive public areas. 7 stories; interior corridors; conference facilities, meeting rooms; heated indoor pool,
sauna, whirlpool; exercise room. **Dining & Entertainment:** 2 restaurants;  6 am-11 pm; $8-$20; cocktails/lounge.
**Services:** data ports; area transportation, downtown, airport transportation. Fee: coin laundry. **All Rooms:** free & pay
movies, cable TV, VCP's. **Some Rooms:** coffeemakers, microwaves, refrigerators. **Cards:** AE, CB, DI, DS, MC, VI.
*(See ad below)*                                                                      Ⓩ Ⓓ Ⓢ ⊗

BEST WESTERN GENETTI HOTEL & CONVENTION CENTER  Rates Subject to Change  **Phone:** 717/823-6152  ⑯
ⓐⓐⓐ    All Year              1P: $49-  69  2P/1B:  $59-  79  2P/2B:  $59-  79  XP: $5  F18
◆◆◆    **Location:** At Market & Washington sts. 77 E Market St 18701. Fax: 717/824-7166. **Terms:** Credit card
Hotel    guarantee; weekly/monthly rates; pets, $25 dep req. **Facility:** 72 rooms. Tasteful, carefully kept rooms. Down-
town 1/2 blk from Public Square. 4 stories; interior corridors; conference facilities; pool. **Dining &
Entertainment:** Restaurant; 7-9 am, 11-2 & 5-9 pm; $7-$15; cocktails/lounge; Sun brunch 9 am-2 pm.
**Services:** data ports. Fee: coin laundry, airport transportation. **All Rooms:** free movies, cable TV.
**Some Rooms:** microwaves, refrigerators. Fee: VCP's. **Cards:** AE, CB, DI, DS, MC, VI. *(See color ad below)*    Ⓓ ⊗

ECONO LODGE                       Rates Subject to Change              **Phone:** 717/823-0600  ⑱
ⓐⓐ    All Year [CP]          1P: $43        2P/1B:  $49        2P/2B:  $53        XP: $6  F18
◆◆    **Location:** On SR 309 at I-81, exit 45 southbound, exit 45B northbound. 1075 Wilkes-Barre Township Blvd
Motel    18702. Fax: 717/823-3294. **Terms:** Sr. discount; reserv deposit; 7 day notice; weekly/monthly rates; no pets.
**Facility:** 104 rooms. Immaculate, attractive rooms. 3 stories; interior corridors; meeting rooms.
**Dining:** Restaurant nearby. **Services:** Fee: coin laundry. **All Rooms:** free movies, cable TV.
**Some Rooms:** refrigerators. **Cards:** AE, CB, DI, DS, MC, VI.                           Ⓩ Ⓓ Ⓢ ⊗

HAMPTON INN WILKES-BARRE AT CROSS CREEK POINTE  Rates Subject to Change  **Phone:** 717/825-3838  ⑲
◆◆◆    All Year [CP]          1P: $58-  71  2P/1B:  $58-  71  2P/2B:  $58-  71
Motel    **Location:** On SR 315, 1/4 mi n of jct I-81, exit 47B. 1063 Hwy 315 18702. Fax: 717/825-8775. **Terms:** Sr.
discount; reserv deposit; small pets only. **Facility:** 123 rooms. Attractive well maintained property on hilltop.
Immaculate housekeeping. 5 stories; interior corridors; meeting rooms. **Services:** data ports; valet laundry. **All Rooms:** free
movies, cable TV. **Cards:** AE, CB, DI, DS, MC, VI.                                       Ⓓ Ⓢ ⊗

HOWARD JOHNSON HOTEL                Guaranteed Rates              **Phone:** 717/824-2411  ㉒
ⓐⓐ    All Year [CP]          1P: $40-  58  2P/1B:  $45-  63  2P/2B:  $52-  70  XP: $10  F18
◆◆    **Location:** I-81, exit 47B to exit 1, 1 mi s on SR 309 (business). 500 Kidder St 18702. Fax: 717/829-9756.
Motor Inn    **Terms:** Sr. discount; monthly rates; AP available; pets. **Facility:** 162 rooms. Pleasing appearance. 2 stories;
interior/exterior corridors; meeting rooms; 2 pools (1 heated, 1 indoor), wading pool, sauna, whirlpool.
**Dining & Entertainment:** Restaurant;  6 am-10 pm; $4-$11; cocktails/lounge; entertainment, nightclub.
**Services:** area transportation, within 15 mi, airport transportation. Fee: coin laundry. **All Rooms:** cable TV. **Some Rooms:**
Fee: refrigerators, VCP's. **Cards:** AE, CB, DI, DS, MC, VI. *(See ad p A237)*                    Ⓓ ⊗

**(See POCONO MOUNTAINS & VICINITY ACCOMMODATIONS spotting map pages A212 & A213)**

**HOWARD JOHNSON MOTOR LODGE**          Rates Subject to Change          Phone: 717/654-3301  🔢
⊕           6/1-9/30                    1P:  $45       2P/1B:  $55       2P/2B:  $50- 60   XP:  $6   F18
◆◆         5/1-5/31 & 10/1-4/30         1P:  $42       2P/1B:  $47       2P/2B:  $55       XP:  $6   F18
Motor Inn  **Location:** 1/4 mi s on SR 315 from I-81 northbound, exit 48, & southbound exit 48A & PA Tpk ne extension,
           exit 37. 307 Rt 315 18640. Fax: 717/883-0288. **Terms:** Sr. discount; package plans; small pets only.
           **Facility:** 120 rooms. Well kept rooms with contemporary furnishings. 2 stories; interior corridors; meeting
rooms; pool. **Dining & Entertainment:** Restaurant; 6 am-midnight, Fri & Sat 24 hrs; $5-$9; cocktail lounge. **Services:**
Fee: coin laundry. **All Rooms:** free movies, cable TV. **Cards:** AE, CB, DI, DS, MC, VI.                    Ⓓ⊗

**KNIGHTS INN**                          Rates Subject to Change          Phone: 717/654-6020  🔢
⊕           All Year                    1P:  $33- 36   2P/1B:  $36- 41   2P/2B:  $41- 43   XP:  $5   F18
◆◆         **Location:** 1/8 mi s on SR 315 from I-81 northbound, exit 48, & southbound exit 48A & PA Tpk NE
Motel      Extension, exit 37. (310 SR 315, PITTSTON). Fax: 717/655-3767. **Terms:** Sr. discount; weekly rates; pets.
           **Facility:** 64 rooms. 6 efficiencies, $10 extra for up to 2 persons; 1 story; exterior corridors.
           **Dining:** Restaurant nearby. **Services:** data ports. **All Rooms:** free movies, cable TV.
**Some Rooms:** microwaves, refrigerators, whirlpools. Fee: VCP's. **Cards:** AE, DI, DS, JCB, MC, VI.
*(See color ad p A220)*                                                                     🔲Ⓓ⊗

**RAMADA HOTEL ON-THE-SQUARE**           Rates Subject to Change          Phone: 717/824-7100  🔢
◆◆◆        All Year                    1P:  $60- 65   2P/1B:  $65- 70   2P/2B:  $65- 70   XP:  $5
Hotel      **Location:** From SR 309, exit 2, s to city center, right 2 blks to Public Square. 20 Public Square 18701.
           Fax: 717/823-5599. **Terms:** Reserv deposit; monthly rates; no pets. **Facility:** 177 rooms. Attractive public
areas. Irish pub. Downtown. 8 stories; interior corridors; conference facilities; exercise room. **Dining & Entertainment:**
Dining room, restaurant; 6:30 am-11 pm; $9-$25; cocktails/lounge. **Services:** secretarial services; valet laundry; area
transportation, within 5 mi; airport transportation. **All Rooms:** free movies, cable TV. **Some Rooms:** microwaves,
refrigerators, whirlpools. **Cards:** AE, DI, DS, MC, VI.                                    Ⓓ⑤⊗

**RED ROOF INN**                         Rates Subject to Change          Phone: 717/829-6422  🔢
◆          5/1-10/31                    1P:  $40- 44   2P/1B:  $48- 52   2P/2B:  $57- 61   XP:  $8   F18
Motel      11/1-4/30                    1P:  $34- 38   2P/1B:  $42- 46   2P/2B:  $48- 52   XP:  $8   F18
           **Location:** On SR 315, at jct SR 315 & SR 315, 3/4 mi w of I-81, exit 1 on to SR 315. 1035 Hwy
315 18702. Fax: 717/829-6422. **Terms:** Credit card guarantee; small pets only. **Facility:** 115 rooms. Many rooms with valley
view. 3 stories; exterior corridors. **Services:** data ports. **All Rooms:** free movies, cable TV. **Cards:** AE, CB, DI, DS, MC, VI.
                                                                                            Ⓓ⊗

**VICTORIA INNS**                        Rates Subject to Change          Phone: 717/655-1234  🔢
⊕           All Year                    1P:  $49       2P/1B:  $55       2P/2B:  $63       XP:  $6   F16
◆◆◆        **Location:** On SR 315 at I-81 (southbound) exit 48 (northbound); exit 47B, exit PA Tpk NE Extension. 400 SR
Motel      315 18641. Fax: 717/655-2267. **Terms:** Sr. discount; credit card guarantee; no pets. **Facility:** 103 rooms.
           Rooms are a mixture of contemporary & art deco styling. 5 stories; interior corridors; meeting rooms; exercise
           room. **Dining & Entertainment:** Restaurant, coffee shop; 6 am-1 am; $5-$24; cocktails/lounge.
**Services:** valet laundry; airport transportation. **All Rooms:** free movies, cable TV. **Some Rooms:** whirlpools. **Cards:** AE,
CB, DI, DS, MC, VI.                                                                          Ⓓ⊗

**THE WOODLANDS INN & RESORT**           Rates Subject to Change          Phone: 717/824-9831  🔢
◆◆◆        All Year                    1P:  $80       2P/1B:  $80- 125  2P/2B:  $80       XP:  $10  F12
Motor Inn  **Location:** I-81 exit 47B onto SR 309 to exit 1, 1/4 mi n on SR 315. 1073 Hwy 315 18702.
           Fax: 717/824-8865. **Terms:** Reserv deposit; weekly/monthly rates; package plans; no pets. **Facility:** 200
rooms. Contemporary rooms. Both high energy & relaxing public areas in wooded area along creek. 2-9 stories; interior corri-
dors; conference facilities; 2 pools (1 heated, 1 indoor), saunas, steamroom, whirlpool; exercise room. Fee: tanning bed.
**Dining & Entertainment:** Restaurant; 7 am-11 pm, Sun 8 am-9 pm; $10-$20; cocktails/lounge; entertainment.
**Services:** data ports; valet laundry. Fee: massage. **All Rooms:** free movies, cable TV. **Some Rooms:** 25 kitchens,
microwaves, refrigerators, whirlpools. **Cards:** AE, CB, DI, DS, MC, VI.                    🔲Ⓓ⊗

**(See POCONO MOUNTAINS & VICINITY ACCOMMODATIONS spotting map pages A212 & A213)**

## RESTAURANTS

**PASTA LOVERS**      **Dinner: $11-$20**      **Phone: 717/821-0800**   21
◆◆      **Location:** I-81 exit 47A, 1 1/4 mi s on SR 309 business route. 410 Wilkes-Barre Township Blvd 18702.
Italian      **Hours:** 11:30 am-9:30 pm, Fri & Sat-10:30 pm, Sun-9 pm. Closed major holidays. **Features:** casual dress;
     carryout; cocktails & lounge; a la carte. Fine pasta, casual Italian garden atmosphere. **Cards:** AE, DI, MC,
VI.          ⊗

**PEKING CHEF**      **Dinner: $11-$20**      **Phone: 717/825-0977**   20
AAA      **Location:** Center. 15 Public Square 18701. **Hours:** 11:30 am-9:30 pm, Fri & Sat-10:30 pm, Sun noon-9 pm.
     Closed: 11/23 & 12/25. **Reservations:** suggested; weekends. **Features:** casual dress; children's menu;
◆◆      health conscious menu; carryout; cocktails & lounge. Specializing in lemon chicken, sweet & sour pork,
Chinese      Mongolian beef. Generous portions. Authentic Chinese cooks from the Orient. On-street parking directly in
     front of restaurant is permissable after 6 pm. **Cards:** AE, DI, MC, VI.      ⊗

# WILLIAMSPORT—31,900

## LODGINGS

**CITY VIEW INN**      Guaranteed Rates      **Phone: 717/326-2601**
AAA      All Year    1P:   $42    2P/1B:   $46    2P/2B:   $46- 48   XP:   $5   F12
     **Location:** 1 1/2 mi s on US 15. 17701 (RD 4, Box 550). **Terms:** Sr. discount; credit card guarantee;
◆◆      weekly/monthly rates; package plans; pets, $5. **Facility:** 36 rooms. Fine view of valley. 1 two-bedroom unit. 2
Motor Inn      stories; exterior corridors; playground. **Dining:** Also, Country House Restaurant, see separate listing.
     **All Rooms:** free movies, cable TV. **Some Rooms:** kitchen, microwaves, refrigerators. **Cards:** AE, CB, DI,
DS, MC, VI. *(See color ad p A237)*      Ⓓ ⊗

**ECONO LODGE**      Guaranteed Rates      **Phone: 717/326-1501**
AAA      5/1-11/4    1P:   $45    2P/1B:   $50    2P/2B:   $50    XP:   $5   F18
     11/5-4/30    1P:   $40    2P/1B:   $45    2P/2B:   $45    XP:   $5   F18
◆◆      **Location:** From Faxon St exit of US 220 & I-180, to Third St, e 3/4 mi. 2401 E 3rd St 17701.
Motor Inn      Fax: 717/326-9776. **Terms:** Sr. discount; package plans; pets. **Facility:** 98 rooms. 2 stories; exterior corridors;
     meeting rooms. **Dining:** Restaurant; $5-$13; cocktails/lounge. **Services:** data ports.
**All Rooms:** free movies, cable TV. **Cards:** AE, DI, DS, JCB, MC, VI. *(See color ad p A237)*      Ⓓ ⊗

**GENETTI HOTEL & CONVENTION CENTER**      Guaranteed Rates      **Phone: 717/326-6600**
AAA      All Year    1P:   $30- 70    2P/1B:   $36- 80    2P/2B:   $36- 80   XP:   $6   F11
     **Location:** Downtown. 200 W Fourth St 17701. Fax: 717/326-5006. **Terms:** Sr. discount; reserv deposit, 3
◆◆      day notice; weekly/monthly rates; AP available; small pets only. **Facility:** 200 rooms. Excellent public areas.
Hotel      Some motel rooms. 3 two-bedroom units. 10 stories; interior/exterior corridors; conference facilities; pool; ex-
     ercise room. **Dining:** Restaurant; 7-10 am, 11-2 & 5-10 pm, Sun 7 am-2 pm, also 5 pm-9 pm during high
season; $8-$13; cocktails; Sun brunch. **Services:** data ports, secretarial services; airport transportation. Fee: coin laundry.
**All Rooms:** free movies, combo & shower baths, cable TV. **Some Rooms:** 5 kitchens, VCP's. Fee: microwaves,
refrigerators. **Cards:** AE, DI, DS, MC, VI. *(See color ad below)*      Ⓓ ⊗

**KINGS INN**
Phone: 717/322-4707
Guaranteed Rates
5/1-12/1 & 4/1-4/30 [CP]    1P: $34- 45  2P/1B: $39- 49  2P/2B: $45- 52  XP: $5  F12
12/2-3/31 [CP]    1P: $29- 39  2P/1B: $34- 39  2P/2B: $36- 42  XP: $5  F12
**Location:** 1/2 mi s on US 15. (590 Montgomery Pike, SOUTH WILLIAMSPORT). Fax: 717/322-0946.
Motor Inn    **Terms:** Reserv deposit; weekly/monthly rates; no pets. **Facility:** 48 rooms. 2 buildings located on hillside with pleasant view of city. 2 suites avail; 2 stories; interior/exterior corridors; meeting rooms. **Dining:** Also, Kings Inn-St. Regis Room, see separate listing. **All Rooms:** free movies, combo & shower baths, cable TV. **Some Rooms:** refrigerators. **Cards:** AE, DI, DS, MC, VI. *(See color ad p A238)*    (D) ⊗

**QUALITY INN WILLIAMSPORT**
Phone: 717/323-9801
Rates Subject to Change
All Year    1P: $50- 55  2P/1B: $56- 61  2P/2B: $56- 61
**Location:** 1 1/4 mi s on US 15. 234 Rt 15 17701. Fax: 717/322-5231. **Terms:** Sr. discount; reserv deposit, 3 day notice; weekly/monthly rates; no pets. **Facility:** 117 rooms. Close to Little League Baseball Museum. 3 stories, no elevator; interior corridors; meeting rooms; pool. **Dining:** Restaurant; 6:30 am-10:30 & 5-9 pm; $7-$14; cocktails. **Services:** Fee: coin laundry. **All Rooms:** free movies, cable TV. **Some Rooms:** microwaves, refrigerators. **Cards:** AE, CB, DI, DS, JCB, MC, VI.    (D) ⊗

**THE REIGHARD HOUSE**
Phone: 717/326-3593
Rates Subject to Change
All Year [BP]    1P: $48- 68  2P/1B: $58- 78  2P/2B: $58- 78  XP: $10
**Location:** Just e of I-180 & US 220N, from Faxon Rd exit, (Shiffler Ave) left on E Third St, 1/4 mi n. 1323 E Third St 17701. Fax: 717/323-4734. **Terms:** Reserv deposit, 3 day notice; no pets. **Facility:** 6 rooms. Restored 1905 Queen Ann home with nicely decorated rooms. Closed 12/20-1/1. 2 stories; interior corridors; designated smoking area. **Dining:** Restaurant nearby. **Services:** data ports; complimentary evening beverages; health club privileges. **All Rooms:** coffeemakers, free movies, combo & shower baths, cable TV. **Cards:** AE, DI, MC, VI.    (D) ⊗

**RIDGEMONT MOTEL**
Phone: 717/321-5300
Guaranteed Rates
All Year    2P/1B: $33    2P/2B: $37    XP: $1-2
**Location:** 2 mi s on US 15. RD 4, Box 536 17701-9590. **Terms:** Small pets only. **Facility:** 8 rooms. 1 story; exterior corridors. **Dining:** Restaurant nearby. **All Rooms:** microwaves, free movies, refrigerators, cable TV. Motel    **Cards:** DS, MC, VI. *(See ad below)*    (D) ⊗

**SHERATON WILLIAMSPORT**
Phone: 717/327-8231
Rates Subject to Change
All Year    1P: $74- 78  2P/1B: $83- 86  2P/2B: $83- 86  XP: $8  F18
**Location:** Downtown, at jct US 220 & SR 15. 100 Pine St 17701. Fax: 717/322-2957. **Terms:** Package plans; small pets only. **Facility:** 148 rooms. Convenient location. 8 suites, 2 with whirlpool avail; 5 stories; interior corridors; conference facilities; heated indoor pool; nintendo games. **Dining:** Dining room; 6:30 am-2 & 5-10 pm; $8-$15; cocktails. **Services:** data ports; health club privileges; valet laundry; area transportation, to hospitals & bus center, airport transportation. **All Rooms:** coffeemakers, free & pay movies, cable TV. **Some Rooms:** microwaves, refrigerators. Fee: VCP's, whirlpools. **Cards:** AE, CB, DI, DS, MC, VI.    ⌷ (D) ⊗

## RESTAURANTS

**THE BAGELRY**
Phone: 717/323-9690
Dinner: up to $10
Ethnic    **Location:** On US Rt 15, in town. 452 Market St 17701. **Hours:** 7 am-6 pm. Closed: Sun, 1/1 & 12/25. **Features:** carryout; cafeteria. Very limited seating. Jewish deli items & pastries. Long-established downtown restaurant.

**COUNTRY HOUSE RESTAURANT**
Phone: 717/326-2601
Dinner: $11-$20
American    **Location:** In City View Inn. 17701. **Hours:** 6:30 am-9 pm. Closed: 1/1, 12/24 & 12/25. **Features:** children's menu; cocktails. Family restaurant. Decor features memorabilia of the 19th-century Pennsylvania logging boom. **Cards:** AE, DI, DS, MC, VI.    ⊗

**KINGS INN-ST. REGIS ROOM**
Phone: 717/322-4707
Dinner: $11-$20
Continental    **Location:** In Kings Inn. 590 Montgomery Pike 17701. **Hours:** 4:30 pm-10 pm, Sat-11 pm. Closed major holidays. **Reservations:** suggested. **Features:** children's menu; carryout; cocktails & lounge. Relaxed casual atmosphere with American cuisine. Many Italian dishes. **Cards:** AE, CB, DI, DS, MC, VI.    ⊗

**THE PETER HERDIC HOUSE**  Historical
Phone: 717/322-0165
Dinner: $11-$20
Continental    **Location:** 4 blks w of Market St, between Elmira & Center. 407 W Fourth St 17701. **Hours:** 11 am-2 & 5-10 pm, Sat from 5 pm, Sun 10 am-2 pm. Closed major holidays. **Features:** Sunday brunch; cocktails & lounge; valet parking. Continental dining in restored 1854 Heritage Victorian mansion. Intimate dining rooms with fine table appointments. **Cards:** AE, MC, VI.    ⊗

**THOMAS LIGHTFOOTE INN**
Phone: 717/326-6396
Dinner: $11-$20
American    **Location:** 5 mi w on I-180, Reach Rd exit, 1 mi s on S Reach Rd. 2887 S Reach Rd 17701. **Hours:** 11 am-2 & 5-9 pm, Fri & Sat 5 pm-10 pm. Closed: Sun, 1/1 & 12/24-12/26. **Reservations:** suggested. **Features:** children's menu; carryout; cocktails. 18th-century tavern. Imaginative variations on traditional American cuisine. Working stone fireplace in dining rooms. Pub downstairs. Some continental entrees. **Cards:** AE, MC, VI.    ⊗

**TRIANGLE TAVERN**
Phone: 717/322-9945
Dinner: up to $10
Italian    **Location:** SR 220E, Faxon St exit, then 1 blk w on E Third St. 308 Shiffler Ave 17701. **Hours:** 11 am-10 pm, Fri & Sat-11 pm. Closed: 4/16 & 12/25. **Features:** casual dress; children's menu; carryout; cocktails. Informal dining with ample portions of southern Italian food. Some American dishes & pizza. Limited off-street parking.    ⊗

## WILLOW GROVE (See PHILADELPHIA & VICINITY ACCOMMODATIONS spotting map pages A196 & A197; see index starting on page A193)

### LODGINGS

**COURTYARD BY MARRIOTT-WILLOW GROVE**   Rates Subject to Change   **Phone:** 215/830-0550  ◆◆◆
Motor Inn
| | Sun-Thurs | 1P: | $94 | 2P/1B: | $104 | 2P/2B: | $104 | XP: $10 | F12 |
| | Fri & Sat | 1P: | $85 | 2P/1B: | $85 | 2P/2B: | $85 | XP: $10 | F12 |

**Location:** 1/10 mi n on SR 611 from jct PA Tpk, exit 27. 2350 Easton Rd, Rt 611 19090. Fax: 215/830-0572.
**Terms:** Check-in 4 pm; weekly rates; no pets. **Facility:** 149 rooms. Many rooms with balcony overlooking central courtyard with gazebo. Weekend rates for up to 4 persons; 3 stories; interior corridors; meeting rooms; heated indoor pool, whirlpool; exercise room. **Dining & Entertainment:** Restaurant; 6:30 am-1 pm, Sat & Sun 7 am-noon; cocktails/lounge.
**Services:** data ports. Fee: coin laundry, airport transportation. **All Rooms:** free & pay movies, cable TV.
**Some Rooms:** refrigerators. **Cards:** AE, DI, DS, MC, VI. *(See color ad p A198)*

**HAMPTON INN-WILLOW GROVE**   Guaranteed Rates   **Phone:** 215/659-3535
| | All Year [CP] | 1P: $79- | 89 | 2P/1B: $85- | 95 | 2P/2B: | $85- | 95 | XP: $6 | F18 |

◆◆◆
Motel
**Location:** 1/4 mi s on SR 611 from jct PA Tpk, exit 27. 1500 Easton Rd 19090 (Rt 611). Fax: 215/659-4040.
**Terms:** No pets. **Facility:** 150 rooms. Modern rooms. Comfortably decorated rooms & lobby area. Sunken seating & breakfast area off lobby. 2 person/2 bed rates for up to 4 persons; 5 stories; interior corridors; meeting rooms; sauna; exercise room, health club privileges (18 & over). **Dining:** Restaurant nearby.
**Services:** data ports; valet laundry; area transportation, by reservation. Fee: airport transportation. **All Rooms:** free & pay movies, cable TV. **Some Rooms:** microwaves, refrigerators. Fee: VCP's. **Cards:** AE, CB, DI, DS, MC, VI.

## WINDBER—4,800

### RESTAURANT

**RIZZO'S RESTAURANT**   Dinner: $11-$20   **Phone:** 814/467-7908
◆◆◆
Italian
**Location:** 3 blks n from jct SR 56 & 160, 2 blks right from light. 2200 Graham Ave 15963. **Hours:** 3 pm-midnight, Sun 11 am-7 pm (last seating). Closed major holidays & Mon. **Reservations:** suggested; weekends. **Features:** casual dress; children's menu; carryout; cocktails & lounge; a la carte, buffet. All soups, pastries & pasta homemade. Very popular; hearty portions. **Cards:** MC, VI.

## WIND GAP—2,700

### LODGING

**TRAVEL INN OF WIND GAP**   Rates Subject to Change   **Phone:** 610/863-4146
| | All Year | | | 2P/1B: | $42- | 48 | 2P/2B: | $52- | 62 | XP: $5 |

◆◆
Motel
**Location:** On SR 512, e of jct SR 33, Bath exit. 499 E Morrestown Rd 18091. Fax: 610/863-4146.
**Terms:** Reserv deposit, 3 day notice; weekly rates; pets, $5. **Facility:** 35 rooms. 1 story; exterior corridors.
**Dining:** Restaurant nearby. **All Rooms:** free movies, combo & shower baths, cable TV.
**Some Rooms:** refrigerators. **Cards:** AE, CB, DI, DS, MC, VI.

## WOMELSDORF—2,300

### RESTAURANT

**THE STOUCH TAVERN 1785**   Historical   Dinner: $11-$20   **Phone:** 610/589-4577
◆◆◆
American
**Location:** Center. 138 W High St 19567. **Hours:** 11:30 am-2 & 5-9 pm, Fri-9:30 pm, Sat 5 pm-9:30 pm, Sun noon-6:30 pm. Closed: Tues, 5/30, 9/4, 1/1-1/6 & 7/4-7/9. **Reservations:** suggested; weekends.
**Features:** casual dress; children's menu; early bird specials; cocktails & lounge; buffet. Pleasant colonial atmosphere. Hearty portions. Smoke free premises. **Cards:** AE, CB, DI, DS, MC, VI.

## WRIGHTSVILLE—2,400

### RESTAURANT

**ACCOMAC INN**   Historical   Dinner: $21-$30   **Phone:** 717/252-1521
◆◆◆
French
**Location:** 1 1/2 mi n of Wrightsville exit off US 30, follow signs. S River Dr 17368. **Hours:** 5:30 pm-9:30 pm, Sun 11 am-2:30 & 4-8:30 pm. Closed: 12/25. **Reservations:** suggested. **Features:** semi-formal attire; children's menu; health conscious menu; carryout; cocktails & lounge; a la carte. A renowned converted 18th-century inn & ferry crossing on the Susquehanna River. Champagne Sun brunch. Sat night & holidays, smoking not permitted. Smoke free premises. **Cards:** AE, DI, DS, MC, VI.

## WYOMISSING—7,300

### LODGINGS

**ECONO LODGE**   Rates Subject to Change   **Phone:** 610/378-5105
◆◆
Motel
| | 10/1-12/15 [CP] | 1P: | $55 | 2P/1B: | $60 | 2P/2B: | $60 | XP: $5 | F18 |
| | 5/1-9/30 [CP] | 1P: | $45 | 2P/1B: | $50 | 2P/2B: | $50 | XP: $5 | F18 |
| | 12/16-4/30 [CP] | 1P: | $35 | 2P/1B: | $40 | 2P/2B: | $40 | XP: $5 | F18 |

**Location:** 1 1/2 mi w, just off US 422 between Park & Papermill rds exits, from US 422E Papermill Rd exit, from US 422W Park Rd exit. 635 Spring St 19610. Fax: 610/373-3181. **Terms:** Sr. discount; credit card guarantee; monthly rates; small pets only, $5. **Facility:** 84 rooms. 4 stories; interior corridors. **Dining:** Restaurant nearby. **Services:** data ports. Fee: coin laundry.
**All Rooms:** combo & shower baths, cable TV. **Some Rooms:** microwaves, refrigerators. **Cards:** AE, CB, DI, DS, MC, VI.
*(See color ad p A217)*

**HAMPTON INN**   AAA Special Value Rates   **Phone:** 610/374-8100
| | All Year [CP] | 1P: $60- | 85 | 2P/1B: $66- | 86 | 2P/2B: | $67- | 87 |

◆◆
Motel
**Location:** Papermill Rd exit off US 422, opposite Berkshire Mall. 1800 Papermill Rd 19610. Fax: 610/374-2076. **Terms:** Reserv deposit, 14 day notice; no pets. **Facility:** 126 rooms. 5 stories; interior corridors; business center, meeting rooms. **Dining:** Restaurant nearby. **Services:** PC; valet laundry; area transportation, to bus terminal, airport transportation. **All Rooms:** free & pay movies, cable TV. **Some Rooms:** microwaves, refrigerators.
**Cards:** AE, CB, DI, DS, MC, VI. *(See color ad p A217)*

**THE INN AT READING**

◆◆◆  
Motor Inn

Rates Subject to Change

Phone: 610/372-7811

Sun-Thurs 5/1-7/31 &  
8/1-11/30       1P: $76- 96   2P/1B: $86- 106   2P/2B: $86- 106   XP: $7   F18  
Fri & Sat 5/1-7/31 &  
12/1-4/30       1P: $52- 68   2P/1B: $52- 68   2P/2B: $52- 68   XP: $7   F18

**Location:** 1 1/2 mi w on US 422, Park Rd exit. 1040 Park Rd 19610. **Fax:** 610/372-4545. **Terms:** Pets. **Facility:** 249 rooms. Large rooms with colonial decor. Weekend rates for up to 4 persons. 5 rooms with exercycle, $5 extra charge; 2 stories; interior corridors; conference facilities; pool, wading pool; exercise room, playground. **Dining & Entertainment:** Dining room; 6:30 am-10 pm, Fri & Sat 7:30 am-11 pm, Sun 7:30 am-9 pm; $10-$21; cocktails/lounge; entertainment. **Services:** valet laundry; airport transportation. **All Rooms:** free movies, cable TV. **Some Rooms:** radios. Fee: refrigerators, VCP's. **Cards:** AE, CB, DI, DS, MC, VI. *(See color ad p A217)*  〔□〕 〔D〕 〔S〕 ⊗

**SHERATON BERKSHIRE HOTEL**

◆◆◆  
Hotel

Rates Subject to Change

Phone: 610/376-3811

All Year       1P: $79- 105   2P/1B: $89- 115   2P/2B: $89- 115   XP: $10   F18  
**Location:** From US 422, exit Papermill Rd, opposite Berkshire Mall. 422 W Papermill Rd 19610. **Fax:** 610/375-7562. **Terms:** Sr. discount; reserv deposit; monthly rates; pets. **Facility:** 256 rooms. Very nice public areas, nicely appointed rooms. 2-4 stories; interior corridors; conference facilities; heated indoor pool, saunas; exercise room. **Dining & Entertainment:** Dining room, restaurant; 6:30 am-10 pm; $9-$20; cocktails/lounge; entertainment, nightclub. **Services:** data ports, PC; valet laundry. **All Rooms:** coffeemakers, free & pay movies, cable TV. **Some Rooms:** refrigerators. **Cards:** AE, CB, DI, DS, MC, VI. *(See color ad p A217)*  〔□〕 〔D〕 〔S〕 ⊗

**WELLESLEY INN**

◆◆  
Motel

Guaranteed Rates

Phone: 610/374-1500

5/1-11/30 & 4/1-4/30 [CP]   1P: $49- 69   2P/1B: $49- 69   2P/2B: $65- 75   XP: $5   F18  
12/1-3/31 [CP]       1P: $36- 69   2P/1B: $36- 69   2P/2B: $50- 69   XP: $5   F18  
**Location:** US 422W, Papermill Rd exit, right at first stop light, then 2 blks to inn. 910 Woodland Ave 19610. **Fax:** 610/374-2554. **Terms:** Sr. discount; reserv deposit; weekly/monthly rates; small pets only, $3. **Facility:** 105 rooms. 4 stories; interior corridors. **Dining:** Restaurant nearby. **Services:** data ports; valet laundry. **All Rooms:** coffeemakers, cable TV. Fee: movies. **Some Rooms:** Fee: microwaves, refrigerators. **Cards:** AE, DI, DS, MC, VI. *(See color ad p A217)*  〔D〕 ⊗

## RESTAURANT

**FINLEY'S AMERICAN RESTAURANT**

◆  
Steak and Seafood

Dinner: $11-$20

Phone: 610/372-8213

**Location:** Penn Ave W, Reading exit off US 222, then 1 mi nw on Business Rt US 422. **Hours:** 11 am-10 pm, Fri & Sat-11 pm. Closed: 11/23 & 12/25. **Features:** casual dress; children's menu; senior's menu; carryout; a la carte. Casual family dining. Seasonally updated specialties. **Cards:** AE, DI, DS, MC, VI. ⊗

# YORK—42,200

## LODGINGS

**BARNHART'S MOTEL**

Ⓐ  
◆◆  
Motel

Guaranteed Rates

Phone: 717/755-2806

All Year [CP]       1P: $28- 42   2P/1B: $34- 42   2P/2B: $36- 42   XP: $5   F12  
**Location:** From I-83 at exit 8E, 1 mi e on Rt 462 (Market St). 3021 E Market St 17402. **Terms:** Weekly rates; no pets. **Facility:** 22 rooms. 1 story; exterior corridors. **Dining:** Restaurant nearby. **Services:** winter plug-ins. **All Rooms:** free movies, refrigerators, combo & shower baths, cable TV. **Some Rooms:** efficiency, microwaves. **Cards:** AE, DI, DS, MC, VI.  〔D〕 ⊗

**BEST WESTERN-WESTGATE**

◆◆  
Motel

Rates Subject to Change

Phone: 717/767-6931

All Year       1P: $56   2P/1B: $66   2P/2B: $66   XP: $5   F18  
**Location:** 2 mi w on US 30 from I-83 exit 9, 1 blk n on Kenneth Rd. 1415 Kenneth Rd 17404. **Fax:** 717/767-6938. **Terms:** Credit card guarantee; small pets only, $25 dep req. **Facility:** 105 rooms. Busy commercial location. 3 stories; interior corridors; conference facilities. **Dining:** Restaurant nearby. **Services:** data ports; valet laundry. **All Rooms:** free movies, cable TV. **Some Rooms:** microwaves, refrigerators. Fee: VCP's. **Cards:** AE, CB, DI, DS, MC, VI.  〔D〕 〔S〕 ⊗

**BUDGET HOST INN SPIRIT OF 76**

Ⓐ  
◆◆  
Motel

Guaranteed Rates

Phone: 717/755-1068

All Year       1P: $30- 35   2P/1B: $35- 40   2P/2B: $35- 45   XP: $4   F12  
**Location:** At I-83, exit 7. 1162 Haines Rd 17402. **Terms:** Reserv deposit, 3 day notice; weekly rates; small pets only. **Facility:** 40 rooms. Many rooms nicely decorated & furnished. 2 stories; exterior corridors. **Dining:** Restaurant nearby. **All Rooms:** combo & shower baths, cable TV. **Some Rooms:** refrigerators. Fee: VCP's. **Cards:** AE, DI, DS, MC, VI. *(See color ad p A83)*  〔D〕 ⊗

**THE CHATEAU MOTEL**

Ⓐ  
◆◆  
Motel

Guaranteed Rates

Phone: 717/757-1714

All Year       1P: $28- 32   2P/1B: $32- 36   2P/2B: $36- 40   XP: $4   F12  
**Location:** From I-83 at exit 8E, 3 mi e on Rt 462 (Market St). 3951 E Market St 17402. **Terms:** Sr. discount; credit card guarantee; no pets. **Facility:** 12 rooms. 1 two-bedroom unit. 1 story; exterior corridors. **All Rooms:** free movies, combo & shower baths, cable TV. **Some Rooms:** refrigerators. **Cards:** DS, MC, VI.  〔D〕 ⊗

**COMFORT INN & SUITES** — AAA Special Value Rates — Phone: 717/741-1000

| | | 1P: | | 2P/1B: | | 2P/2B: | | XP: | |
|---|---|---|---|---|---|---|---|---|---|
| ◆◆◆ | 5/27-10/31 [CP] | $55- | 74 | $66- | 82 | $66- | 82 | $8 | F18 |
| Motel | 5/1-5/26 & 11/1-4/30 [CP] | $53- | 72 | $61- | 80 | $61- | 80 | $8 | F18 |

Location: From I-83 at exit 4, 1 blk w. 140 Leader Heights Rd 17403. Fax: 717/741-5923. Terms: No pets. Facility: 136 rooms. 5 stories; interior corridors; meeting rooms; exercise room. Dining: Restaurant nearby. Services: data ports; guest laundry. All Rooms: free movies, combo & shower baths, cable TV. Some Rooms: microwaves, refrigerators, VCP's, whirlpools. Cards: AE, CB, DI, DS, JCB, MC, VI. Roll in showers. 🛎 Ⓓ Ⓢ ⊗

**DAYS INN HOTEL & CONFERENCE CENTER** — AAA Special Value Rates — Phone: 717/843-9971

| | | 1P: | | 2P/1B: | | 2P/2B: | | XP: | |
|---|---|---|---|---|---|---|---|---|---|
| ◆◆ | 5/1-10/31 & 4/1-4/30 | $55- | 78 | $61- | 84 | $68- | 88 | $6 | F16 |
| Motel | 11/1-3/31 | $49- | 92 | $55- | 78 | $62- | 82 | $6 | F16 |

Location: On US 30; at jct I-83 & US 30, I-83 exit 9E. 222 Arsenal Rd 17402. Fax: 717/843-1806. Terms: Reserv deposit, 3 day notice; weekly/monthly rates; package plans; small pets only. Facility: 124 rooms. Located in busy commercial district. 2 stories; interior corridors; conference facilities; heated pool. Dining & Entertainment: Cocktail lounge; restaurant nearby. Services: data ports; valet laundry. All Rooms: coffeemakers, free & pay movies, cable TV. Some Rooms: 2 efficiencies, microwaves. Cards: AE, DI, DS, MC, VI. Ⓓ Ⓢ

**HAMPTON INN** — Rates Subject to Change — Phone: 717/840-1500

| | | 1P: | | 2P/1B: | | 2P/2B: | | XP: | |
|---|---|---|---|---|---|---|---|---|---|
| ◆◆◆ | 3/2-4/30 [CP] | $68- | 79 | $80- | 87 | $76 | | $10 | F18 |
| Motel | 5/1-5/1 [CP] | $65- | 79 | $77- | 85 | $73 | | $10 | F18 |

Location: Mt Zion Rd at US 30E; at Galleria Mall. 1550 Mt Zion Rd 17402. Fax: 717/840-1567. Terms: Reserv deposit; small pets only. Facility: 144 rooms. Very attractive public areas. 5 stories; interior corridors; meeting rooms; heated pool, whirlpool; exercise room. Dining: Restaurant nearby. Services: data ports. Fee: coin laundry. All Rooms: free movies, cable TV. Some Rooms: refrigerators. Fee: microwaves. Cards: AE, CB, DI, DS, MC, VI. Ⓓ Ⓢ ⊗

**HOLIDAY INN** — AAA Special Value Rates — Phone: 717/755-1966

Ⓐ

| | | 1P: | | 2P/1B: | | 2P/2B: | | XP: | |
|---|---|---|---|---|---|---|---|---|---|
| | All Year | $69- | 79 | $69- | 79 | $69- | 79 | $10 | F19 |

◆◆◆ Motor Inn — Location: 2 3/4 mi e on SR 462, 1 mi e of jct I-83, exit 8E southbound; exit 8 northbound. 2600 E Market St 17402. Fax: 717/755-6936. Terms: Small pets only. Facility: 120 rooms. Located in busy commercial district. 2 stories; exterior corridors; meeting rooms; pool, wading pool. Dining & Entertainment: Restaurant; 6 am-2 & 5:30-10 pm; $9-$15; cocktails/lounge; 24-hour room service. Services: data ports; airport transportation. Fee: coin laundry. All Rooms: coffeemakers, free & pay movies, cable TV. Some Rooms: Fee: microwaves, refrigerators. Cards: AE, CB, DI, DS, JCB, MC, VI. Ⓓ ⊗

**HOLIDAY INN HOLIDOME CONFERENCE CENTER** — Rates Subject to Change — Phone: 717/846-9500

Ⓐ

| | | 1P: | | 2P/1B: | | 2P/2B: | |
|---|---|---|---|---|---|---|---|
| | All Year | $75- | 92 | $75- | 92 | $75- | 92 |

◆◆ Motor Inn — Location: Off SR 74, just n of jct US 30 & Rt 74 at West Manchester Mall. 2000 Loucks Rd 17404. Fax: 717/846-9500. Terms: Sr. discount; reserv deposit, 3 day notice; weekly rates; pets. Facility: 181 rooms. Spacious attractive areas. Located in busy commercial district. 2 stories; interior corridors; conference facilities; miniature golf; 2 pools (1 heated, 1 indoor), sauna, whirlpool; exercise room, playground. Services: data ports. All Rooms: free movies, cable TV. Cards: AE, CB, DI, DS, JCB, MC, VI. Dining & Entertainment: Dining room; 6:30 am-10 pm; $10-$20; cocktails/lounge. Ⓓ Ⓢ ⊗

**HOLIDAY INN-RT 30E** — AAA Special Value Rates — Phone: 717/845-5671

Ⓐ

| | | 1P: | | 2P/1B: | | 2P/2B: | | XP: | |
|---|---|---|---|---|---|---|---|---|---|
| | All Year | $69- | 81 | $69- | 81 | $69- | 81 | $10 | F19 |

◆◆◆ Motor Inn — Location: On US 30; e of I-83, exit 9E. 334 Arsenal Rd 17402. Fax: 717/845-1898. Terms: Credit card guarantee; no pets. Facility: 100 rooms. Located in busy commercial district. 2 stories; exterior corridors; meeting rooms; pool, wading pool. Dining & Entertainment: Restaurant; 6:30 am-1:30 & 5-10 pm; Sat 7 am-1 & 5-10 pm; $8-$13; cocktails/lounge. Services: guest laundry. All Rooms: free & pay movies, cable TV. Cards: AE, CB, DI, DS, JCB, MC, VI. (See color ad p A136) Ⓓ ⊗

**RED ROOF INN** — Rates Subject to Change — Phone: 717/843-8181

| | | 1P: | | 2P/1B: | | 2P/2B: | | XP: | |
|---|---|---|---|---|---|---|---|---|---|
| ◆◆ | All Year | $32- | 45 | $38- | 50 | $44- | 61 | $7 | F18 |
| Motel | | | | | | | | | |

Location: On US 30; e of I-83, exit 9E. 323 Arsenal Rd 17402. Fax: 717/843-8175. Terms: Credit card guarantee; small pets only. Facility: 103 rooms. Located near York Fairgrounds. 3 stories; exterior corridors. Dining: Restaurant nearby. Services: data ports. All Rooms: free movies, cable TV. Cards: AE, CB, DI, DS, MC, VI. Ⓓ ⊗

**SUPER 8 MOTEL** — AAA Special Value Rates — Phone: 717/852-8686

| | | 1P: | | 2P/1B: | | 2P/2B: | | XP: | |
|---|---|---|---|---|---|---|---|---|---|
| ◆◆ | 5/1-10/31 | $45- | 49 | $51 | | $55 | | $5 | F12 |
| Motel | 11/1-4/30 | $42- | 46 | $48 | | $52 | | $5 | F12 |

Location: I-83S exit 10, SR 181 1/2 mi to US 30, I-83N, exit 9W, US 30 1/4 mi w. 40 Arsenal Rd 17404. Fax: 717/852-8686. Terms: Weekly rates; small pets only, $25 dep req. Facility: 94 rooms. Located near York Fairgrounds. 3 stories; interior corridors. Dining: Restaurant nearby. All Rooms: free movies, cable TV. Some Rooms: Fee: VCP's. Cards: AE, DI, DS, MC, VI. Ⓓ ⊗

**YORKTOWNE HOTEL**
All Year                           1P: $52- 82  2P/1B: $59- 96  2P/2B: $78- 96  XP: $7  F18
Rates Subject to Change                                              **Phone:** 717/848-1111
**Location:** On SR 462 eastbound & I-83 business route, 1 blk e of square. 48 E Market St at Duke St 17401.
**Fax:** 717/854-7678. **Terms:** Sr. discount; credit card guarantee; monthly rates; no pets. **Facility:** 150 rooms.
Historic Hotel  National Historic Landmark Hotel located downtown. 8 stories; interior corridors; meeting rooms; exercise room. **Dining:** Dining room, coffee shop; 6:30 am-10 pm, Sun-noon; also, The Commonwealth Room, see separate listing. **Services:** valet parking. **All Rooms:** combo & shower baths, cable TV. **Some Rooms:** 8 efficiencies, refrigerators. **Cards:** AE, DI, DS, MC, VI.

## RESTAURANTS

**BOB EVANS**                                                         **Phone:** 717/845-4856
American
**Dinner:** up to $10
**Location:** On US 30; just e of jct I-83. 303 Arsenal Rd 17402. **Hours:** 6 am-10 pm, Fri & Sat-11:30 pm. Closed: 11/23 & 12/25. **Features:** casual dress; children's menu; senior's menu; carryout; buffet. Mostly short order, also counter seating. **Cards:** MC, VI.

**THE COMMONWEALTH ROOM**                                            **Phone:** 717/848-1111
Continental
**Dinner:** $21-$30
**Location:** In Yorktowne Hotel. 48 E Market St 17401. **Hours:** 5:30 pm-9:30 pm. Closed major holidays. **Reservations:** suggested. **Features:** semi-formal attire; Sunday brunch; cocktails & lounge; valet parking. Warm & comfortably elegant dining room in restored historical downtown hotel. **Cards:** AE, DI, DS, MC, VI.

**FAMILY TIME RESTAURANT**                                           **Phone:** 717/764-0562
American
**Dinner:** up to $10
**Location:** 2 mi w on US 30 from I-83, exit 9, then 1/2 mi n on Kenneth Rd. 1411 Kenneth Rd 17404. **Hours:** 11 am-8 pm, Fri-9 pm, Sat 7 am-9 pm, Sun 7 am-8 pm. Closed: 12/25. **Reservations:** suggested; weekends. **Features:** casual dress; children's menu; senior's menu; carryout; buffet. Pennsylvania Dutch cooking in a relaxed atmosphere. Menu selections for lunch & dinner. **Cards:** DS, MC, VI.

**FINLEY'S AMERICAN RESTAURANT**                                     **Phone:** 717/755-1027
American
**Dinner:** up to $10
**Location:** 3/4 mi e on Market St from I-83, exit 8, 1 blk s on Haines Rd, then 1/2 mi e on Eastern Blvd. 2650 Eastern Blvd 17402. **Hours:** 11 am-10 pm, Fri & Sat-11 pm. Closed: 11/23 & 12/25. **Features:** casual dress; children's menu; senior's menu. Casual family dining. Seasonally updated specialties. Also chicken & rib entrees. **Cards:** AE, DI, DS, MC, VI.

**HORN & HORN SMORGASBORD**                                          **Phone:** 717/843-3706
American
**Dinner:** up to $10
**Location:** On US 30, 1/2 mi w of I-83; in North Mall. 351 Loucks Rd 17404. **Hours:** 11 am-2:30 & 4-8 pm, Thurs & Fri-9 pm, Sat 11 am-9 pm, Sun 10:30 am-7 pm. Closed: Mon & 12/25. **Features:** casual dress; children's menu; senior's menu; buffet. A wide variety of entrees & side dishes. **Cards:** MC, VI.

**ISAAC'S RESTAURANT & DELI**                                        **Phone:** 717/751-0515
American
**Dinner:** up to $10
**Location:** At jct Rt 30 & Mt Zion Rd in Village at Meadowbrook. 2960 Whiteford Rd 17402. **Hours:** 10 am-9 pm, Fri & Sat-10 pm, Sun 11 am-9 pm. Closed: 1/1, 11/23 & 12/25. **Features:** casual dress; children's menu; senior's menu; carryout. Grilled sandwiches, named after birds, plants & flowers. Each sandwich has a unique personality. **Cards:** AE, DS, MC, VI.

**MACKLEY'S MILL**                                                   **Phone:** 717/757-6778
Nouvelle American
**Dinner:** $11-$20
**Location:** 7 1/2 mi e in Hallam, 1/2 mi s. 305 S Broad St 17406. **Hours:** 11 am-3 & 5-9 pm. Closed: Sun & Mon. **Reservations:** suggested; weekends. **Features:** casual dress; cocktails & lounge. Nicely prepared entrees served in a restored 1736 mill. Homemade breads, desserts & soups. **Cards:** MC, VI.

**ROOSEVELT TAVERN**                                                 **Phone:** 717/854-7725
American
**Dinner:** $11-$20
**Location:** 1/2 mi w. 400 W Philadelphia St 17404. **Hours:** 11:30 am-9 pm, Fri & Sat-9:30 pm, Sun 11 am-8 pm. Closed: 12/25 & 1/1. **Reservations:** suggested. **Features:** casual dress; Sunday brunch; children's menu; carryout; cocktails & lounge. Fine dining in casual atmosphere. **Cards:** AE, DI, DS, MC, VI.

**RUTTER'S FAMILY RESTAURANTS**                                      **Phone:** 717/755-6616
American
**Dinner:** up to $10
**Location:** Mt. Zion Rd at US 30E; near Galleria Mall. 1440 Mt. Zion Rd 17402. **Hours:** 5 am-10 pm, Fri & Sat-11 pm, Sun 7 am-10 pm. Closed: 12/25. **Features:** casual dress; children's menu; health conscious menu; carryout; salad bar. Free baby food for infants. Low calorie-low fat menu with printed quantity. Bakery buffet 11 am-2 pm; family style. **Cards:** DS, MC, VI.

## ZELIENOPLE—4,200

## RESTAURANT

**THE KAUFMAN HOUSE**  Historical                                    **Phone:** 412/452-8900
American
**Dinner:** $11-$20
**Location:** Rt 19N. 105 S Main St 16063. **Hours:** 7 am-9 pm, Fri & Sat-10 pm. Closed major holidays. **Reservations:** suggested; weekends. **Features:** casual dress; children's menu; carryout; cocktails & lounge; a la carte. In 1903 landmark building. Breakfast served in older diner-style coffee shop. **Cards:** AE, CB, DI, MC, VI.

# FOR YOUR INFORMATION

*Three handy sections
to help make your
vacation planning easier.*

### AAA Clubs and Branch Offices

Need a sheet map or Triptik map? Run out of travelers checks? Want the latest update on local road conditions? All this information and more awaits you at more than 1,000 AAA and CAA clubs and offices across the United States and Canada—a boon for travelers in an unfamiliar state, province or city. Each listing provides the office address, phone number and hours of service.

### Temperature Chart

Knowing what clothes to pack for a trip can make the difference between pleasant vacationing and unpleasant surprises. Use the temperature chart to help determine your on-the-road wardrobe. The chart, found in each TourBook, lists average monthly maximum and minimum temperatures for representative cities.

### Driving Distances Map

For safety's sake, it makes sense to take regular breaks while driving on the open road. The driving distances map is a quick and useful reference for trip planning—from a 1-day excursion to a cross-country jaunt. It provides both the mileage and the average driving time (excluding stops) between towns and cities located throughout a state or province.

# Extra Attention. No Extra Charge.

The AAA Travel Agency pays attention to detail for all your travel plans—and you don't pay extra. Our travel counselors are trained professionals who can handle any travel need you can think of. And your plans don't have to be high-priced to get high-quality service. We can save you money because we take the time to make special arrangements. So don't go to strangers. Come to AAA for that extra measure of personal service that just can't be bought.

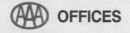 OFFICES

Cities with main offices are listed in bold type with ALL CAPITAL letters. Toll-free member service number in italics. All are closed Saturdays, Sundays and holidays unless otherwise indicated.

The type of service provided is designated below the name of the city where the office is located:

Auto travel services, including books/maps, marked maps and on-demand Triptik maps ✛
Auto travel services, including books/maps, marked maps, but no on-demand Triptik maps ●
Provides books/maps only. No marked maps or on-demand Triptik maps available ■
Travel agency services ▲

## NEW JERSEY

**BRIDGEWATER**—AAA Central-West Jersey, 500 Commons Way, 08807. M-F 9-5, Sa. 9-2. (908) 722-2202. *(800) 374-9806.*✛▲

**CAPE MAY COURT HOUSE**—AAA Mid-Atlantic, 1200 US Rt. 9, S., 08210; *Mailing Address: POB 129, 08210.* M-F 8:45-5. (609) 465-3033.✛

**CHERRY HILL**—AAA SOUTH JERSEY, 201 Kings Hwy., S., 08034-0473. M-F 8:45-5, Th. 8:45-8, Sa. 8:45-1. (609) 428-9000.✛▲

**EDISON**—AAA Central-West Jersey, 561 U.S. Rt. 1, 08817. M-F 9-5, Sa. 9-2. (908) 985-9000.✛▲

**FAIR LAWN**—AAA North Jersey, 23-16 Broadway, 07410. M-F 8:30-5, Sa. 9-3. (201) 703-2000.✛▲

**FLEMINGTON**—AAA Central-West Jersey, 245 Rt. 202, S., 08822. M-F 9-5, Sa. 9-2. (908) 782-3500.✛▲

**FLORHAM PARK**—**NEW JERSEY AUTO. CLUB**, 1 Hanover Rd., 07932-1888. M-F 9-5, W 9-7, Sa. 9-1. (201) 377-7200.✛▲

**MARLBORO**—AAA Central-West Jersey, 318 Rt. 9 At Union Hill Rd., 07746; *Mailing Address: 318 Rt. 9 At Union Hill, Englishtown,m 07726.* M-F 9-5, Sa. 9-2. (908) 972-3100.✛▲

**MILLVILLE**—AAA South Jersey, Cumberland Crossing, Rt. 47 & 55, 08332. M-F 8:45-5, W 8:45-8, Sa. 9-1. (609) 825-1212.✛▲

**MOUNT LAUREL**—AAA Central-West Jersey, 127 Ark Rd., 08054. M-F 9-5, Sa. 9-2. (609) 778-8800.✛▲

**NEWTON**—AAA Central-West Jersey, 65 Newton Sparta Rd., 07860. M-F 9-5, Tu. 9-8, Sa. 9-2. (201) 383-5400.✛▲

**NORTHFIELD**—AAA Mid-Atlantic, 901 Tilton Rd., 08225; *Mailing Address: POB AF, 08225.* M-F 8:45-5, W 8:45-8, Sa. 8:45-1. (609) 646-6000.✛▲

**OCEAN**—AAA Central-West Jersey, Rt. 35 & Sunset Ave., 07712. M-F 9-5, Sa. 9-2. (908) 918-0550.✛▲

**ORADELL**—AAA North Jersey, 505 Kinderkamack Rd., 07649. M-F 8:30-5, Th. 8:30-8, Sa. 9-3. (201) 261-7900.✛▲

**PHILLIPSBURG**—AAA Central-West Jersey, Memorial Pky. & Firth St., 08865; *Mailing Address: POB 110, 08865.* M-F 8:30-5, Tu. 8:30-8, Sa. 9-2. (908) 859-2177.✛▲

**RANDOLPH**—New Jersey Auto. Club, 711 Rt. 10, E., 07869. M-F 9-5, Tu. 9-7, Sa. 9-1. (201) 361-0900.✛▲

**ROBBINSVILLE**—AAA CENTRAL-WEST JERSEY, 3 AAA Dr., 08691. M-F 8:30-5, W 8:30-7:30, Sa. 9-2. (609) 890-2220.✛▲

**SALEM**—AAA South Jersey, 1 Fenwick Plaza, Suite 105, 08079; *POB 103, 08079.* M-F 8:45-5. (609) 935-8525.●▲

**SECAUCUS**—AAA North Jersey, 40C Meadowland Pky., 07094. M-F 8:30-5, W 8:30-8, Sa. 9-3. (201) 902-1393.✛▲

**SEWELL**—AAA South Jersey, Hurffville-Cross Keys/Egg Harbor Rds., 08080. M-F 8:45-5, W 8:45-8, Sa. 8:45-1. (609) 589-6900.✛▲

**SKILLMAN**—AAA Central-West Jersey, 1378 Rt. 206, 08558. M-F 9-5, Sa. 9-2. (609) 683-4400.✛▲

**SPRINGFIELD**—New Jersey Auto. Club, 191 Mountain Ave., 07081. M-F 9-5, Th. 9-7, Sa. 9-1. (201) 467-2651.✛▲

**TOMS RIVER**—AAA Central-West Jersey, 864 Rt. 37, W., 08755. M-F 9-5, Sa. 9-2. (908) 244-6800.✛▲

**VERONA**—New Jersey Auto. Club, 155 Pompton Ave., 07044. M-F 9-5, Th. 9-7, Sa. 9-1. (201) 857-5900.✛▲

**WAYNE**—AAA NORTH JERSEY, 418 Hamburg Tpke., 07470; *Mailing Address: POB 983, 07474-0983.* M-F 8:30-5, Tu. 8:30-8, Sa. 9-3. (201) 956-2200.✛▲

## PENNSYLVANIA

**ALLENTOWN**—AAA LEHIGH VALLEY, 1020 Hamilton St., 18101-1085; *Mailing Address: POB 1910, 18105-1910.* M-F 8:30-5, Th. 11-8, Sa. 9-12. (610) 434-5141.✛▲

**ALLENTOWN**—AAA Lehigh Valley, 1251 S. Cedar Crest, #101A, 18103-6205. M-F 8:30-5, Th. 8:30-6. (610) 820-9620.▲

**ALTOONA**—AAA BLAIR COUNTY, 1634 Valley View Blvd., 16602; *Mailing Address: POB 2690, 16603.* M-F 9-5. (814) 946-1277.✛▲

**AMBRIDGE**—AAA West Penn/West Virginia, 1236 Merchant St., 15003. M-F 9-5, M 9-8. (412) 266-5944.✛▲

**BEDFORD**—AAA Southern Pennsylvania, 317 S. Richard St., 15522; *Mailing Address: POB 678, 15522.* M-F 8:30-5, F 8:30-8, Sa. 8:30-12. (814) 623-5196 *(800) 346-1131.*●▲

**BELLE VERNON**—AAA West Penn/West Virginia, R.D. 2, Rt. 201, 15012-0627; *Mailing Address: POB 627, 15012-0627.* M-F 9-5, Sa. 9-1. (412) 929-3310.✛▲

**BETHLEHEM**—AAA Lehigh Valley, 1520 Stefko Blvd., 18017-6296. M-F 8:30-5, Th. 11-8. (610) 867-7502.✛▲

**BLOOMSBURG**—Valley Auto. Club, 460 Central Rd., 17815. M-F 8-5. (717) 784-3380.✛▲

**BRADFORD**—**MCKEAN COUNTY MOTOR CLUB**, 587 South Ave., 16701; *Mailing Address: POB 371, 16701.* M-F 8:30-5, F 8:30-7. (814) 368-3113.✛

**BROOKVILLE**—AAA West Penn/West Virginia, 195 Main St., 15825. M-F 8:30-5, Sa. 8:30-12. (814) 849-5381.✛▲

**BUTLER**—AAA West Penn/West Virginia, 138 Clearview Cir., 16001; *Mailing Address: POB 1948, 16003-1948.* M-F 9-5:30, Sa. 9-12:30. (412) 287-2713. *(800) 837-8810.*✛▲

**CAMP HILL**—AAA Central Penn Auto. Club, 3433 Trindle Rd., 17011; *Mailing Address: POB 6, 17011.* M-F 9-5, Sa. 9-12. (717) 761-6811.✛▲

**CARBONDALE**—AAA Northeast Penn, 18 S. Main St., 18407. M-F 9-5, Sa. 9-12. (717) 282-1390. *(800) 982-4306.*✛▲

**CARLISLE**—AAA Central Penn Auto. Club, 701C South West St., 17013-4117. M-F 9-5, Sa. 9-12. (717) 243-1844.✛▲

**CHAMBERSBURG**—AAA Southern Pennsylvania, 230 Lincoln Way, E., 17201; *Mailing Address: POB 340, 17201.* M-F 8:30-5, F 8:30-8, Sa. 8:30-12. (717) 264-4191 *(800) 346-1131.*●▲

**CHARLEROI**—AAA West Penn/West Virginia, 149 Pennsylvania Ave., Rt. 8, 15022. M-F 8:30-5, Sa. 8:30-12. (412) 483-8013.✛▲

**CONNELLSVILLE**—AAA West Penn/West Virginia, 131 S. Arch St., 15425. M-F 9-5, Sa. 9-12. (412) 628-1420.✛

**CORRY**—AAA Erie County, 637 N. Center St., 16407. M-F 9-5, M 9-7. (814) 665-3955.✛▲

**COUDERSPORT**—AAA North Central PA, 107 S. Main St., 16915. M-F 8:30-5. (814) 274-8470.✛▲

**CRANBERRY TOWNSHIP**—AAA West Penn/West Virginia, 20399 Landmark, N. #230, 16066. M-F 10-6:30, Sa. 10-2. (412) 772-1122.✛▲

**DALLAS**—Valley Auto. Club, 309/415 Dallas Plaza, Bldg. 4, 18612. M-F 8-5. (717) 675-8282.✛▲

DANVILLE—Valley Auto. Club, 246 Walnut St., Rt. 11, 17821. M-F 8-5. (717) 275-1142.✛▲

DELMONT—AAA West Penn/West Virginia, Salem 22 Plaza, 15626. M-F 9-5. (412) 468-6360.✛▲

DUBOIS—AAA Southern Pennsylvania, Shaffer Rd., DuBois Mall, 15801. M-F 9:30-5, F 9:30-8, Sa. 9:30-12. (814) 371-7001 (800) 346-1131.●▲

EASTON—AAA NORTHAMPTON COUNTY, 3914 Hecktown Rd., 18045; Mailing Address: POB 3080, 18043-3080. M-F 8:30-5, Tu. 11-8. (610) 258-2371.✛▲

EBENSBURG—AAA Southern Pennsylvania, 125 W. High St., 15931. M-F 9-5, F 9-8, Sa. 9-12. (814) 472-7400 (800) 346-1131.●▲

ELLWOOD CITY—AAA West Penn/West Virginia, 506 Lawrence Ave., 16117. M-F 9-5, M 9-8. (412) 758-4549.✛▲

ERIE—AAA ERIE COUNTY, 420 W. 6th St., 16507. M-F 9-5, M 9-7. (814) 454-0123.✛▲

GETTYSBURG—AAA Central Penn Auto. Club, 19 Lincoln Sq., 17325. M-F 9-5, Sa. 9-12. (717) 334-1155.✛▲

GIRARD—AAA Erie County, 511 E. Main St., 16417. M-F 9-5, M 9-7. (814) 774-9695.✛

GREENSBURG—AAA West Penn/West Virginia, 100 Maple Ave., 15601-0458; Mailing Address: POB 458, 15601-0458. M-F 9-5, Sa. 9-1. (412) 834-8300.✛▲

GREENVILLE—AAA West Penn/West Virginia, 311 Main St., 16125; Mailing Address: POB 614, 16125. M-F 8:30-5. (412) 588-4300.✛▲

GROVE CITY—AAA West Penn/West Virginia, 112 Blair St., 16127. M-F 8:30-5. (412) 458-8930.●

HANOVER—AAA Southern Pennsylvania, Carlisle St., 17331. M-F 9-5, W. & F 9-8, Sa. 9-5. (717) 637-2400 (800) 346-1131.●▲

HARRISBURG—AAA CENTRAL PENN AUTO. CLUB, 2023 Market St., 17103; Mailing Address: POB 3261, 17105. M-F 9-5, Sa. 9-12. (717) 236-4021.✛▲

HARRISBURG—AAA Central Penn Auto. Club, 2301 Paxton Church Rd., 17110. M-F 9-5, Sa. 9-12. (717) 657-2244.✛▲

HAVERFORD—AAA Mid-Atlantic, 394 W. Lancaster Ave., 19041. M-F 8:45-5, W 8:45-8, Sa. 8:45-1. (610) 649-9000.✛▲

HAZLETON—AAA Mid-Atlantic, 2 W. Broad St., 18201-6408. M-F 8:30-5, W 8:30-7. (717) 454-6658.✛▲

HERMITAGE—AAA West Penn/West Virginia, 1749 E. State St., 16148. M-F 8:30-5. (412) 981-9141.✛▲

HERSHEY—AAA Central Penn Auto. Club, 11 Briarcrest Sq., 17033; Mailing Address: POB 378, 17033. M-F 9-5, Sa. 9-12. (717) 533-3381.✛▲

HONESDALE—AAA Northeast Penn, 602 Church St., 18431. M-F 9-5. (717) 253-0160.✛▲

HUNTINGDON—AAA Central Penn Auto. Club, 212 4th St., 16652; Mailing Address: POB 397, 16652. M-F 8:30-5, F 8:30-7:30, Sa. 8:30-12:30. (814) 643-1030.✛

INDIANA—AUTOMOBILE CLUB OF INDIANA COUNTY, 1169 Wayne Ave., 15701; Mailing Address: POB 1018, 15701. M-F 8:30-5, Th. 8:30-7. (412) 349-4193.✛▲

JOHNSTOWN—AAA Southern Pennsylvania, Richland Mall, 15904; Mailing Address: POB 3900, 15904. M-F 9-5, W-F 9-8, Sa. 9-3. (814) 269-3641 (800) 346-1131.●▲

JOHNSTOWN—AAA Southern Pennsylvania, 319 Washington St., 15907; Mailing Address: POB 186, 15907. M-F 8:30-5. (814) 535-8585.✛▲

KITTANNING—AAA West Penn/West Virginia, 250 S. Jefferson St., 16201. M-F 8:30-5, Sa. 8:30-12. (412) 543-1924.✛▲

LANCASTER—AAA LANCASTER COUNTY, 804 Estelle Dr., 17601-2121; Mailing Address: POB 1507, 17608-1507. M-F 8-5, W. 10-7, Sa. 8-12. (717) 898-6900.●▲

LANCASTER—AAA Lancaster County, Mailing Address: 34 N. Prince St., 17603-3866. M-F 8-5. (717) 397-4444.▲

LANGHORNE—AAA Mid-Atlantic, 584 Middletown Blvd., #A100, 19047. M-F 8:45-5, W 8:45-8, Sa. 8:45-1. (215) 702-0700.✛▲

LANSDALE—AAA East Penn, 310 W. Main St., 19446-2036. M-F 9-5:30, W 9-6:30. (215) 855-8600. (800) 564-0300.✛▲

LEBANON—AAA Central Penn Auto. Club, 984 Isabel Dr., 17042; Mailing Address: POB 72, 17042. M-F 9-5, Sa. 9-12. (717) 273-8533.✛▲

LEWISBURG—AAA Susquehanna Valley, 530 1/2 N. Derr Dr., 17837. M-F 9-5, Closed 12-1. (717) 524-7455.●

LEWISTOWN—AAA LEWISTOWN, 33 N. Brown St., 17044; Mailing Address: POB 906, 17044-0906. M-F 8:30-5. (717) 242-2221.✛▲

LITITZ—AAA Lancaster County, 118 W. Airport Rd., #B, 17543-9259. M-F 8-5. (717) 560-8706.●

LOCK HAVEN—AAA Southern Pennsylvania, 12 Oriole Rd., 17745. M-T 9-5, F. 9-8, Sa. 9-12. (717) 748-2405 (800)346-1131.●▲

MEADVILLE—AAA West Penn/West Virginia, 246 Park Ave. Plaza, 16335; Mailing Address: POB 830, 16335-0708. M-F 8:30-5. (814) 724-2247.✛▲

MONTROSE—AAA Northeast Penn, 61 Church St., #102, 18801. M-F 9-5. (717) 278-1552.●▲

NEW CASTLE—AAA West Penn/West Virginia, 40 E. St., 16101; Mailing Address: POB 429, 16103. M-F 9-5, M 9-8. (412) 658-8551.✛▲

NEW KENSINGTON—AAA West Penn/West Virginia, 100 Tarentum Bridge Rd., 15068. M-F 9-5. (412) 339-4440.✛▲

NORTH EAST—AAA Erie County, 61 W. Main St., 16428. M-F 9-5, M 9-7. (814) 725-3503.✛

PHILADELPHIA—AAA MID-ATLANTIC, 2040 Market St., 19103. M-F 8-6. (215) 864-5000.✛▲

PHILADELPHIA—AAA Mid-Atlantic, Bustleton Ave. & Levick St., 19149; Mailing Address: 6400 Bustleton Ave., 19149. M-F 8:45-5, W 8:45-8, Sa. 8:45-1. (215) 289-6100.✛▲

PITTSBURGH—AAA WEST PENN/WEST VIRGINIA, 5900 Baum Blvd., 15206. M-F 8:30-5, Sa. 8:30-12. (412) 362-3300.✛▲

PITTSBURGH—AAA West Penn/West Virginia, Penn Ave. & Stanwix St. & Ft. Duquesne Blvd. 15222. M-F 10-7. (412) 391-7704.▲

PITTSBURGH—AAA West Penn/West Virginia, 4790 Mcknight Rd., 15237. M-F 8:30-8, Sa. 8:30-5. (412) 367-7600.▲

PITTSBURGH—AAA West Penn/West Virginia, 201 Penn Center Blvd., 15235. M-F 8:30-8, Sa. 8:30-5. (412) 824-9990.✛▲

PITTSBURGH—AAA West Penn/West Virginia, 538 Smithfield St., 15222. M-F 8:30-5. (412) 338-4300.✛▲

PITTSBURGH—AAA West Penn/West Virginia, 160 Ft. Couch Rd., 15241. M-F 10-8, Sa. 10-5. (412) 363-5100.✛▲

PLYMOUTH MEETNG—AAA Mid-Atlantic, 505 W. Germantown Pike, 19462. M-F 8:45-5, W 8:45-8, Sa. 8:45-1. (610) 825-4001.✛▲

POTTSTOWN—AAA EAST PENN, 95 S. Hanover St., 19464-5447; Mailing Address: POB 559, 19464-0559. M-F 9-5:30, W 9-6:30. (610) 323-6300. (800) 564-0300.✛▲

POTTSVILLE—AAA SCHUYLKILL COUNTY, 340 S. Center St., 17901. M-F 8:30-5, Sa. 9-12. (717) 622-4991. (800) 666-7262.✛▲

PUNXSUTAWNEY—AAA West Penn/West Virginia, 124 W. Mahoning St., 15767. M-F 9-5. (814) 938-6450.■▲

RENO—AAA West Penn/West Virginia, Allegheny Ave., 16343; Mailing Address: POB 72, 16343. M-F 8:30-5. (814) 676-6551.✛▲

ROCHESTER—AAA West Penn/West Virginia, 300 Adams St., 15074. M-F 9-5, M 9-8. (412) 775-8000.✛▲

ST. MARYS—AAA West Penn/West Virginia, 50 S. St. Marys St., 15857; Mailing Address: POB 226, 15857. M-F 8:30-5. (814) 834-7838.✛

SCRANTON—AAA NORTHEAST PENN, 1035 N. Washington Ave., 18509. M-F 8-5, Sa. 8-5. (717) 348-2511. (800) 982-4306.✛▲

SHIPPENSBURG—AAA Southern Pennsylvania, Walnut Bottom Rd., 17257; Mailing Address: POB I, 17257-0697. M-F 9-5, F 9-8, Sa. 9-12. (717) 532-6500.●▲

SOMERSET—AAA West Penn/West Virginia, 110 N. Center Ave., 15501. M-F 9-5, F 9-8. (814) 443-6526.✛▲

SOUTH WILLIAMSPORT—AAA NORTH CENTRAL PA, 1 E. 6th Ave., 17701; Mailing Address: POB 5100, 17701. M-F 8:30-5, M 8:30-9. (717) 323-8431.✛▲

SPRINGFIELD—AAA Mid-Atlantic, 943 W. Sproul Rd., 19064. M-F 8:45-5, W 8:45-8, Sa. 8:45-1. (610) 544-3000.✛▲

STATE COLLEGE—AAA Southern Pennsylvania, 200 Shiloh Rd., 16801. M-F 9-5, W 9-12, Sa. 9-12. (814) 237-0305 (800) 346-1131.●▲

STROUDSBURG—AAA Northeast Penn, International Plaza, Rt. 611, 18360; Mailing Address: Rt. 611, R.D. 7, Box 7495, 18360. M-F 9-5, Sa. 9-12. (717) 421-2500.✛▲

SUNBURY—AAA SUSQUEHANNA VALLEY, 1001 Market St., 17801; Mailing Address: POB 788, 17801-0788. M-F 9-5. (717) 286-4507.✛▲

TAMAQUA—AAA Schuylkill County, 202 E. Broad St., 18252. M-F 8:30-5, Sa. 9-12. (717) 668-1003. (800) 666-7262.●▲

TITUSVILLE—AAA West Penn/West Virginia, 116 W. Central Ave., 16354. M-F 9-5, July & Aug W 9-12. (814) 827-6930.●

TOWANDA—AAA Northeast Penn, 515 Main St., 18848. M-F 9-5, Sa. 9-12. (717) 265-6122.✛

TUNKHANNOCK—AAA Northeast Penn, 25 E. Tioga St., 18657. M-F 9-5, Sa. 9-12. (717) 836-5104.●▲

UNIONTOWN—AAA West Penn/West Virginia, 111 W. Main St., 15401. M-F 9-5, F 9-8. (412) 438-8575.✛▲

WARREN—AAA West Penn/West Virginia, 1419 Market St., Ext., 16365; Mailing Address: POB 925, 16365. M-F 9-5. (814) 723-6660.✛▲

WARRINGTON—AAA Mid-Atlantic, 1635 Easton Rd., 18976. M-F 8:45-5, W 8:45-8. (215) 343-2660.✛▲

WASHINGTON—AAA West Penn/West Virginia, 196 Murtland Ave., 15301. M-F 8:30-5, Sa. 8:30-12. (412) 222-3800.✛▲

WAYNESBORO—AAA Southern Pennsylvania, 20 E. Main St., 17268; Mailing Address: POB 592, 17268. M-F 8:30-5, F 8:30-8, Sa. 8:30-12. (717) 762-9101 (800) 346-1131.✛▲

WAYNESBURG—AAA West Penn/West Virginia, 89 S. Washington St., 15370. M-F 8:30-5, Sa. 8:30-12. (412) 627-3434.✛▲

WELLSBORO—AAA North Central PA, Queen St. & Water St., 16901; Mailing Address: POB 638, 16901. M-F 8:30-5. (717) 724-4134.✛▲

WEST CHESTER—AAA Mid-Atlantic, 844 Paoli Pike, 19380. M-F 8:45-5, W 8:45-8, Sa. 8:45-1. (610) 696-8100.✛▲

WEST MIFFLIN—AAA West Penn/West Virginia, 2070 Lebanon Church Rd., 15122; Mailing Address: 2070 Lebanon Church Rd., Pittsburgh, 15122-2432. M-F 10-6, M & Th. 10-8, Sa. 10-5. (412) 655-6100.✛▲

WEST PITTSTON—Valley Auto. Club, 200 Wyoming Ave., 18643. M-F 9-5:30. (717) 883-2582.✛▲

WHITE OAK—AAA West Penn/West Virginia, 2201 Lincoln Way, 15131. M-F 8-5. (412) 675-3400.✛▲

WILKES-BARRE—VALLEY AUTO. CLUB, —100 Hazle St., 18702; Mailing Address: POB AAA, 18703-0009. M-F 8-5. (717) 824-2444.✛▲

WYOMISSING—AAA READING-BERKS, 920 Van Reed Rd., 19610; Mailing Address: POB 7049, 19610-6049. M-F 9-5, Sa. 9-12. (610) 374-4531.✛▲

YORK—AAA SOUTHERN PENNSYLVANIA, 118 E. Market St., 17401; Mailing Address: POB 2387, 17405. M-F 8:30-5. (717) 845-7676. (800) 346-1131.✛▲

YORK—AAA Southern Pennsylvania, 2512 Eastern Blvd., 17402. M-F 9:30-5, M, W & F 9:30-9, Sa. 9:30-5. (717) 751-0514. (800) 346-1131.✛▲

ZELIENOPLE—AAA West Penn/West Virginia, 200 S. Main St., 16063; Mailing Address: POB 39, 16063. M-F 9-5, Sa. 9-12:30. (412) 452-5504. (800) 860-5504.✛▲

## Temperature Averages - Maximum/Minimum
### From the records of the National Weather Service

| | JAN. | FEB. | MAR. | APR. | MAY | JUNE | JULY | AUG. | SEPT. | OCT. | NOV. | DEC. |
|---|---|---|---|---|---|---|---|---|---|---|---|---|
| **NEW JERSEY** | | | | | | | | | | | | |
| Atlantic City | 43 | 43 | 50 | 60 | 71 | 79 | 84 | 82 | 76 | 67 | 56 | 45 |
| | 27 | 26 | 32 | 42 | 52 | 61 | 66 | 65 | 58 | 48 | 38 | 28 |
| Newark | 40 | 41 | 49 | 61 | 72 | 81 | 86 | 84 | 77 | 66 | 54 | 42 |
| | 25 | 25 | 32 | 42 | 52 | 61 | 67 | 65 | 58 | 47 | 37 | 27 |
| **PENNSYLVANIA** | | | | | | | | | | | | |
| Allentown | 37 | 38 | 47 | 61 | 72 | 81 | 85 | 83 | 76 | 65 | 51 | 39 |
| | 21 | 20 | 28 | 38 | 49 | 58 | 63 | 61 | 54 | 43 | 33 | 23 |
| Erie | 34 | 34 | 42 | 55 | 66 | 76 | 80 | 79 | 72 | 61 | 48 | 37 |
| | 21 | 19 | 26 | 36 | 47 | 57 | 62 | 61 | 55 | 44 | 34 | 25 |
| Harrisburg | 39 | 40 | 49 | 62 | 73 | 82 | 86 | 84 | 77 | 66 | 52 | 41 |
| | 25 | 25 | 32 | 42 | 52 | 61 | 66 | 64 | 56 | 46 | 36 | 26 |
| Philadelphia | 40 | 42 | 50 | 63 | 73 | 82 | 86 | 84 | 77 | 67 | 54 | 42 |
| | 24 | 25 | 32 | 41 | 52 | 60 | 65 | 64 | 56 | 45 | 35 | 26 |
| Pittsburgh | 37 | 38 | 46 | 60 | 71 | 80 | 83 | 82 | 76 | 64 | 50 | 43 |
| | 21 | 21 | 27 | 38 | 48 | 57 | 61 | 60 | 53 | 42 | 32 | 27 |
| Reading | 39 | 41 | 49 | 62 | 73 | 82 | 86 | 84 | 77 | 67 | 53 | 41 |
| | 26 | 26 | 33 | 43 | 53 | 63 | 67 | 66 | 58 | 48 | 38 | 28 |
| Scranton | 33 | 34 | 43 | 56 | 68 | 76 | 81 | 78 | 70 | 60 | 46 | 35 |
| | 21 | 20 | 28 | 38 | 49 | 58 | 62 | 60 | 53 | 42 | 33 | 23 |

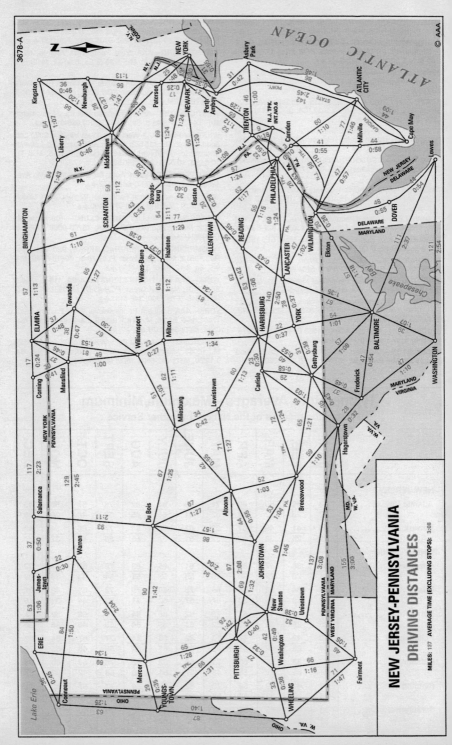

NEW JERSEY-PENNSYLVANIA

DRIVING DISTANCES

MILES: 137    AVERAGE TIME (EXCLUDING STOPS): 3:08

# INDEXES

*The following indexes are designed
to make your travel planning easier and
your travel experience more enjoyable.*

## Points of Interest Index

The Points of Interest Index lists attractions and events described in more detail in the Attractions section of the TourBook. The categories of the index make it possible to discover potential vacation destinations or routes with concentrations of attractions, events or activities of a specific type—making it easier to tailor a trip to your interests. To read about a particular index entry, simply note its page number and turn to the corresponding location in the descriptive text.

AAA uses nearly 200 specific points of interest categories, ranging from Amusement & Theme Parks to Zoological Parks & Exhibits. Also categorized are 15 types of events, 13 types of exhibits and collections and 10 types of sports events.

Index entries appear in the TourBook as an attraction listing, as a town or place listing, or in the general text of a referenced town or place. A ★ denotes a point of interest of unusually high quality. Standard U.S. postal abbreviations have been used for the names of states and Canadian provinces. See the Index Abbreviations box for other abbreviations used.

## Attraction Admission Discount Index

Your AAA membership card can be a key to reduced admission prices at the attractions listed in this index. See the individual attraction listing under the town heading for details.

## Bed and Breakfast Lodgings Index

Some bed and breakfasts listed might have historical significance. Those properties also are referenced in the Historical Lodgings and Restaurants Index.

## Country Inns Index

Some of the country inns listed might have historical significance. Those properties also are referenced in the Historical Lodgings and Restaurants Index.

## Historical Lodgings & Restaurants Index

The indication that Continental [CP] or full breakfast [BP] is included in the room rate reflects whether a property is a bed-and-breakfast facility. See the individual accommodation listing under the town heading for details.

## Resorts Index

Many establishments are located in resort areas; however, the resorts in this index have extensive on-premises recreational facilities. See the individual accommodation listing under the town heading for details.

# POINTS OF INTEREST INDEX

---

# INDEX ABBREVIATIONS

| | | | |
|---|---|---|---|
| NB............................ national battlefield | | NR............................national river | |
| NBP...................national battlefield park | | NS............................. national seashore | |
| NC............................. national cemetery | | NWR.............national wildlife refuge | |
| NF...............................national forest | | PHP................ provincial historic(al) park | |
| NHM.......... national historic(al) monument | | PHS.............. provincial historic(al) site | |
| NHP..................national historic(al) park | | PP................................ provincial park | |
| NHS....................national historic(al) site | | SF................................. state forest | |
| NL............................ national lakeshore | | SHM.............state historic(al) monument | |
| NME............................ national memorial | | SHP................. state historic(al) park | |
| NMO...........................national monument | | SHS................. state historic(al) site | |
| NMP...................... national military park | | SME................................state memorial | |
| NP................................national park | | SP................................. state park | |
| NRA................. national recreation area | | SRA.................. state recreation area | |

# ATTRACTION ADMISSION DISCOUNT INDEX

See individual attraction listings for details. Present your valid AAA or CAA card when purchasing tickets, whether or not a listing shows a discount; some attractions not formally enrolled in the program may still give members a discount.

# BED & BREAKFAST LODGINGS INDEX

Some bed and breakfasts listed below might have historical significance. Those properties are also referenced in the Historical index. The indication that continental [CP] or full breakfast [BP] is included in the room rate reflects whether a property is a Bed-and-Breakfast facility.

## BED & BREAKFAST LODGINGS (cont'd)

# COUNTRY INNS INDEX

Some of the following country inns can also be considered as bed-and-breakfast operations. The indication that continental [CP] or full breakfast [BP] is included in the room rate reflects whether a property is a Bed-and-Breakfast facility.

## NEW JERSEY

### Accommodations

### Restaurants

## PENNSYLVANIA

### Accommodations

### Restaurants

# HISTORICAL LODGINGS & RESTAURANTS INDEX

Some of the following historical lodgings can also be considered as bed-and-breakfast operations. The indication that continental [CP] or full breakfast [BP] is included in the room rate reflects whether a property is a Bed-and-Breakfast facility.

## NEW JERSEY

### Accommodations

# RESORTS INDEX

Many establishments are located in resort areas; however, the following places have extensive on-premises recreational facilities:

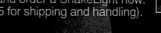

# Travel Information System

**AAA TRAVEL COUNSELORS** are a unique and vital element of AAA's travel information system. They offer what no other auto club can: personalized, top-quality service. Our trained professionals are especially knowledgeable about geography and popular vacation destinations. They can tell you the fastest or most scenic way to get where you're going and update you on highway construction projects and local weather conditions.

**TOURBOOKS** are annually revised catalogs of selected travel information. Listings include AAA-approved attractions, lodgings and restaurants, plus details on sightseeing and valuable AAA discounts.

**TRIPTIK MAPS** show your driving route mile-by-mile. Conveniently spiral-bound, the maps indicate exit numbers and stops for food and gas as well as capsule summaries of places along the way.

**SHEET MAPS** are large-scale regional and state maps, completely researched, revised and reprinted regularly. Our network of AAA clubs and our Road Reporters make AAA maps the most detailed and accurate road maps available.

**CAMPBOOKS** contain comprehensive regional listings of AAA-approved public and private campgrounds across the continent.

**CITIBOOKS** provide complete information about major travel destinations like San Francisco and New York City. Not all clubs carry these booklets, which are extractions from the TourBooks.

# Discounts to go

**F**or sightseeing, staying overnight or going from here to there, **there's more than one way to save money** when you travel with AAA.

## AT ATTRACTIONS

Over 1,500 attractions discount their admission fees to AAA members. Look for the word **"discount"** in the TourBook® listings.

## AT ACCOMMODATIONS

**Special Value**—Lodgings whose listings contain **"Special Value Rates"** give you at least 10 percent off.

**Senior Discount**—If you're 60 or older, you can save at least 10 percent where **"Senior Discount"** appears in a listing.

**Special Discounts**—By separate arrangement with AAA, several large hotel chains offer special discounts or rates to AAA members. Call your AAA office for details.

## ON THE ROAD

AAA has approved a very special and exclusive package with **Hertz Rent-A-Car.** You don't have to worry about hidden charges; you know you'll get a high-quality, dependable vehicle and first-class service. As a AAA member you're entitled to special rates and discounts and a whole package of benefits. Call your AAA office for details and a discount card.

\* Only one of the lodging discounts may be used at a time. The discounts cannot be combined.

 MEMBER DISCOUNT PROGRAM

*Glen Campbell*

# "One phone call is all it takes to find a great room in any town worth singing about."

Whether you're traveling to Phoenix or Wichita or any other great American town, you'll find the right hotel at the right price at Quality, Comfort, Clarion and Sleep hotels, and Econo Lodge, Rodeway and Friendship inns. These hotels have many ways for AAA members to save, including a 10% AAA discount (more at some locations), and a family plan in which kids 18 and under stay free in their parent's or grandparent's room.

Plus they offer AT&T In-Room Long Distance Service for your AT&T Calling Card, AT&T Universal Card and operator-assisted calls (at most locations). For reservations at more than 2,200 North American locations, call 1-800-228-1AAA or your local AAA club. And get a deal that's worth singing about, too.

## Call 1-800-228-1AAA

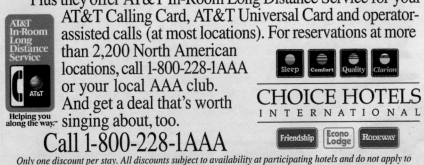

**AT&T In-Room Long Distance Service**

**AT&T**

Helping you along the way.™

Sleep  Comfort  Quality  Clarion

## CHOICE HOTELS
### INTERNATIONAL

Friendship  Econo Lodge  RODEWAY

*Only one discount per stay. All discounts subject to availability at participating hotels and do not apply to AAA Special Value Rates. Certain other restrictions apply.*